NEW

ANNUAL 2006-2007

Published by Invincible Press, an imprint of HarperCollins*Publishers*, 77-85 Fulham Palace Rd, London W6 8JB

First published in 1887

Copyright © Invincible Press 2006

10 9 8 7 6 5 4 3 2 1

A CIP catalogue record for this book is available from the British Library

The HarperCollins website address is: www.harpercollins.co.uk

Editorial compilation by Hayters-Teamwork, Image House, Station Rd, London, N17 9LR

Typesetting by Letterpart Limited, Reigate, Surrey

Printed and bound in Great Britain by Clays Ltd, St Ives plc

ISBN-10 0 00 723423 6

ISBN-13 978 0 00 723423 3

Cover pictures of record-breaking goalscorers Alan Shearer (Copyright © Ian Hodgson/Reuters/Corbis) and Thierry Henry (Copyright © Action Images/Paul Harding).

CONTENTS

A NEW CHAPTER – OR THE SAME OLD STORY?

BY STUART BARNES

Will a new season and a new coach deliver a new sense of optimism about England's international future? Or will it be the same old story of false hopes, under-achievement and major disappointment? The question is being posed by every supporter, every commentator and certainly everyone at the Football Association as Steve McClaren takes over the reins from Sven-Goran Eriksson in the wake of another poor World Cup for Eriksson's side. Some will argue that McClaren can bring much needed passion and purpose to the job. Others insist that the former Middlesbrough manager was, at best, second choice, and lacks the credentials to be a success at the highest level of the game.

The majority may reserve judgement until they see how McClaren settles in during the forthcoming European Championship qualifying campaign – or even until the Championship Finals in Austria and Switzerland in 2008 – before giving their verdict. For when it came to qualifying for the major tournaments, Eriksson's record was a good one. It was when the serious business started that his teams failed to fulfil their potential. The new man certainly has immediate, important decisions to make. Should he retain David Beckham as the former captain moves towards a century of caps, or give Aaron Lennon the opportunity to make the right-wing position his own? Should he install Owen Hargreaves as the permanent midfield anchor after the much-maligned Bayern Munich player proved one of England's rare successes of Germany 2006 and liberate Steven Gerrard to the free role he enjoys and is so successful in for Liverpool? With Michael Owen out for up to a year, will Darren Bent, Jermain Defoe or Dean Ashton be given every opportunity to stake a claim for a regular place? Germany 2006 suggested that McClaren must introduce new blood, along with a new attitude, to a team that flattered to deceive from their opening game against Paraguay to the quarter-final exit against Portugal.

Certainly they were unlucky that neither Owen nor Wayne Rooney went into the tournament fully fit. When Owen sustained a serious knee injury less than five minutes into the group game against Sweden, their predicament reached crisis proportions. It was at that moment that Eriksson's decision to include 17-year-old Theo Walcott in his squad rather than a recognised back-up striker looked even more ridiculous. Peter Crouch strove manfully when called upon. But scoring a hat-trick against Jamaica in a warm-up game is a rather different proposition to facing no-nonsense defenders in the heat of a World Cup. Eriksson eventually opted to play Rooney on his own up front and the Manchester United player's frustration eventually got the better of him against Portugal – with a predictable outcome. England's spirited showing could easily have taken them through before the inevitable result of a penalty shoot-out. Whether they deserved to do so in the light of their overall level of performance against five modest opponents is debatable. It is tempting to say that their finest moment came when Gary Neville lucidly combined inspiration, honesty and realism at a press conference before the Portugal game. 'We have good players and those players have to deliver,' Neville maintained. 'How we do in the tournament will be the measure of this team. Moments like this will decide if this is the golden generation.' What followed suggested the moment has passed.

The tournament was like the curate's egg. On the plus side there were some marvellous matches. Argentina against Mexico in the second round, France's victory over Brazil in the quarter-finals and the classic between Italy and Germany for a place in the final. Goals of the highest calibre were headed by the 24-pass move rounded off by Argentina's Esteban Cambiasso in the rout of Serbia and Montenegro, the stunning volley by team-mate Maxi Rodriguez which settled the duel with Mexico and Joe Cole's strike against Sweden, another model of technique and timing. Ghana delighted many with an irresistible mixture of flair and naivety, while the hosts under Jurgen Klinsmann did everything possible to live up to the marvellous support received from every corner of the country.

But there were too many negatives to make it a great tournament. For all FIFA's insistence on clamping down on foul play, a record number of red and yellow cards was more indicative of a lack of common sense shown by some referees than by their obeying the governing body's edict to the letter. Others were consumed by pressure of the occasion. Even Graham Poll, as hard-nosed an official as there is, got carried away, showing three yellow cards to Josip Simunic before dismissing the Croatia defender, then being shown the door himself when he might have expected to remain for the later stages of the tournament.

To be fair, the men in the middle had far more to worry about than the cynical trip, the sly shirt-pulling or the over-the-top lunges. Diving has become part of the make-up of too many players too interested in winning decisions by deception than by their own ability. 'Cheating has become endemic at this World Cup,' wrote the *Daily Mail* columnist Paul Hayward. 'Where violent tackling was once the principal threat to football's integrity, amateur dramatics have taken over.' England, while far from being the worst offenders, have not been averse to such behaviour in some situations.

We see it in the Premiership and it must be stamped out. On his first day as chief executive of the F.A., Brian Barwick commented: 'It is technically termed "simulation." Let's get real, this is diving.' One hopes this stain on the game is stamped out one way or another and that we can lead the way.

When the minnows departed, along with the flawed giants of Brazil and Argentina, the tournament was rich in irony. Against a background of corruption enveloping four of Serie A's top clubs, Italy might have been expected to falter and fail. Instead their temperament held. They improved with every game and the negativity which had characterised so many Italy teams in the past was nowhere to be seen as Marcello Lippi sent on three attacking substitutes against Germany in the semi-final and was rewarded with a stunning two-goal finish to extra-time. Lippi's team prevailed against France on penalties in the Final, the crucial miss coming from David Trezeguet, whose 'golden goal' winner gave France victory when the teams met in the European Championship Final of 2000. But the biggest irony of all accompanied the dismissal of Zinedine Zidane for butting Marco Materazzi. The France captain's renaissance could have been crowned by victory in the final match of his career. At half-time in Berlin's Olympiastadion, he had been voted the best player of the tournament. Instead, a moment of madness in response to Materazzi's crude provocation signalled a sad end to a distinguished career and defeat for his team.

WORLD CUP QUOTE UNQUOTE

'I was convinced this year was the right time. I was wrong. I'm sorry for the players, for the fans. They deserve something better.' – **Sven-Goran Eriksson**, England coach.

'Don't kill him, I beg you, because for the next few years England needs Wayne Rooney' – **Sven-Goran Eriksson** after Rooney's red card against Portugal.

'He was bang out of order. Winking at the bench and his team-mates sums him up as a person' – **Steven Gerrard**, England midfielder, on Cristiano Ronaldo's part in Rooney's dismissal.

'I walked into Sainsbury's with my girl friend and people were coming up to me and saying "well done." All I could think of was "well done for what?" We hadn't done anything' – **Rio Ferdinand**, England defender.

'Look at the Germans, they are masters at it. There was only one winner. We have to develop that side of the game' – **Gary Neville**, England defender, on another penalty shoot-out failure.

'I have lived the dream' – **David Beckham** after stepping down as England captain.

'I do apologise but I don't regret my behaviour because regretting it would mean he was right to say what he said. I heard them once, then twice, and the third time couldn't control myself' – **Zinedine Zidane**, France captain, on his sending-off after provocative comments by Italy's Marco Materazzi.

'After the conclusion of an extraordinary professional and human experience guiding these players, I believe my role is over' – **Marcello Lippi** on resigning as Italy coach.

'I feel worn out after using up so much energy. I'm going on holiday for six months' – **Jurgen Klinsmann** on stepping down as Germany coach.'

QUALIFYING FOR 2006 WORLD CUP FINALS

EUROPE

GROUP 1

	P	W	D	L	F	A	Pts
HOLLAND	12	10	2	0	27	3	32
CZECH REPUBLIC	12	9	0	3	35	12	27
Romania	12	8	1	3	20	10	25
Finland	12	5	1	6	21	19	16
Macedonia	12	2	3	7	11	24	9
Armenia	12	2	1	9	9	25	7
Andorra	12	1	2	9	4	34	5

Results: Macedonia 3, Armenia 0; Romania 2, Finland 1; Finland 3, Andorra 0; Romania 2, Macedonia 1; Andorra 1, Romania 5; Holland 2, Czech Republic 0; Armenia 0, Finland 2; Czech Republic 1, Romania 0; Finland 3, Armenia 1; Macedonia 2, Holland 2; Andorra 1, Macedonia 0; Armenia 0, Czech Republic 3; Holland 3, Finland 1; Macedonia 0, Czech Republic 2; Armenia 1, Romania 1; Andorra 0, Holland 3; Macedonia 0, Andorra 0; Romania 0, Holland 2; Czech Republic 4, Finland 3; Armenia 2, Andorra 1; Holland 2, Armenia 0; Andorra 0, Czech Republic 4; Macedonia 1, Romania 2; Holland 2, Romania 0; Armenia 1, Macedonia 3; Czech Republic 8, Andorra 1; Finland 0, Holland 4; Romania 3, Armenia 0; Czech Republic 6, Macedonia 1; Macedonia 0, Finland 3; Romania 2, Andorra 0; Andorra 0, Finland 0; Armenia 0, Holland 1; Romania 2, Czech Republic 0; Czech Republic 4, Armenia 1; Finland 5, Macedonia 1; Andorra 0, Holland 2; Finland 0, Romania 1; Andorra 0, Armenia 3; Finland 0, Czech Republic 3; Holland 0, Macedonia 0.

GROUP 2

	P	W	D	L	F	A	Pts
UKRAINE	12	7	4	1	18	7	25
Turkey	12	6	5	1	23	9	23
Denmark	12	6	4	2	24	12	22
Greece	12	6	3	3	15	9	21
Albania	12	4	1	7	11	20	13
Georgia	12	2	4	6	14	25	10
Kazakhstan	12	0	1	11	6	29	1

Results: Denmark 1, Ukraine 1; Turkey 1, Georgia 1; Albania 2, Greece 1; Georgia 2, Albania 0; Kazakhstan 1, Ukraine 2; Greece 0, Turkey 0; Ukraine 1, Greece 1; Turkey 4, Kazakhstan 0; Albania 0, Denmark 2; Ukraine 2, Georgia 0; Kazakhstan 0, Albania 1; Denmark 1, Turkey 1; Greece 3, Kazakhstan 1; Georgia 2, Denmark 2; Turkey 0, Ukraine 3; Greece 2, Denmark 1; Albania 0, Ukraine 2; Denmark 3, Kazakhstan 0; Georgia 1, Greece 3; Turkey 2, Albania 0; Ukraine 1, Denmark 0; Georgia 2, Turkey 5; Greece 2, Albania 0; Ukraine 2, Kazakhstan 0; Albania 3, Georgia 2; Turkey 0, Greece 0; Kazakhstan 0, Turkey 6; Denmark 3, Albania 1; Greece 0, Ukraine 1; Kazakhstan 1, Georgia 2; Albania 2, Kazakhstan 1; Georgia 1, Ukraine 1; Turkey 2, Denmark 2; Denmark 6, Georgia 1; Albania 1, Greece 2; Ukraine 0, Turkey 1; Denmark 1, Greece 0; Georgia 0, Kazakhstan 0; Ukraine 0, Albania 2; Albania 0, Turkey 1; Greece 1, Georgia 0; Kazakhstan 1, Denmark 2.

GROUP 3

	P	W	D	L	F	A	Pts
PORTUGAL	12	9	3	0	35	5	30
Slovakia	12	6	5	1	24	8	23
Russia	12	6	5	1	23	12	23
Estonia	12	5	2	5	16	17	17
Latvia	12	4	3	5	18	21	15
Liechtenstein	12	2	2	8	13	23	8
Luxembourg	12	0	0	12	5	48	0

Results: Liechtenstein 1, Estonia 2; Slovakia 3, Luxembourg 1; Estonia 4, Luxembourg 0; Russia 1, Slovakia 1; Latvia 0, Portugal 2; Luxembourg 3, Latvia 4; Slovakia 7, Liechtenstein 0; Portugal 4, Estonia 0; Luxembourg 0, Russia 4; Slovakia 4, Latvia 1; Liechtenstein 2, Portugal 2; Latvia 2, Estonia 2; Luxembourg 0, Liechtenstein 4; Portugal 7, Russia 1; Russia 4, Estonia 0; Liechtenstein 1, Latvia 3; Luxembourg 0, Portugal 5; Liechtenstein 1, Russia 2; Estonia 1, Slovakia 1; Portugal 1; Estonia 1, Russia 1; Latvia 4, Luxembourg 0; Russia 2, Latvia 0; Portugal 2, Slovakia 0; Estonia 2, Liechtenstein 0; Estonia 0, Portugal 1; Latvia 1, Liechtenstein 0; Luxembourg 0, Slovakia 4; Latvia 1, Russia 1; Liechtenstein 0, Slovakia 0; Estonia 2, Latvia 1; Portugal 6, Luxembourg 0; Russia 2, Liechtenstein 0; Latvia 1, Slovakia 1; Liechtenstein 3, Luxembourg 0; Russia 0, Portugal 0; Portugal 2, Liechtenstein 1; Russia 5, Luxembourg 1; Slovakia 1, Estonia 0; Luxembourg 0, Estonia 2; Portugal 3, Latvia 0; Slovakia 0, Russia 0.

GROUP 4

	P	W	D	L	F	A	Pts
FRANCE	10	5	5	0	14	2	20
SWITZERLAND	10	4	6	0	18	7	18
Israel	10	4	6	0	15	10	18
Republic of Ireland	10	4	5	1	12	5	17
Cyprus	10	1	1	8	8	20	4
Faroe Islands	10	0	1	9	4	27	1

Results: Republic of Ireland 3, Cyprus 0; Switzerland 6, Faroe Islands 0; France 0, Israel 0; Faroe Islands 0, France 2; Switzerland 1, Republic of Ireland 1; Israel 2, Cyprus 1; Cyprus 2, Faroe Islands 2; Israel 2, Switzerland 2; France 0, Republic of Ireland 0; Republic of Ireland 2, Faroe Islands 0; Cyprus 0, France 2; Cyprus 1, Israel 2; France 0, Switzerland 0; Israel 1, Republic of Ireland 1; Israel 1, France 1; Switzerland 1, Cyprus 0; Faroe Islands 1, Switzerland 3; Republic of Ireland 2, Israel 2; Faroe Islands 0, Republic of Ireland 2; Faroe Islands 0, Cyprus 3; France 3, Faroe Islands 0; Switzerland 1, Israel 0; Cyprus 1, Switzerland 3; Faroe Islands 0, Israel 2; Republic of Ireland 0, France 1; Cyprus 0, Republic of Ireland 1; Israel 2, Faroe Islands 1; Switzerland 1, France 1; France 4, Cyprus 0; Republic of Ireland 0, Switzerland 0.

GROUP 5

	P	W	D	L	F	A	Pts
ITALY	10	7	2	1	17	8	23
Norway	10	5	3	2	12	7	18
Scotland	10	3	4	3	9	7	13
Slovenia	10	3	3	4	10	13	12
Belarus	10	2	4	4	12	14	10
Moldova	10	1	2	7	5	16	5

Results: Slovenia 3, Moldova 0; Italy 2, Norway 1; Scotland 0, Slovenia 0; Norway 1, Belarus 1; Moldova 0, Italy 1; Scotland 0, Norway 1; Belarus 4, Moldova 0; Slovenia 1, Italy 0; Norway 3, Slovenia 0; Italy 4, Belarus 3; Moldova 1, Scotland 1; Italy 2, Scotland 0; Moldova 0, Norway 0; Slovenia 1, Belarus 1; Norway 0, Italy 0; Belarus 1, Slovenia 1; Scotland 2, Moldova 0; Belarus 0, Scotland 0; Moldova 2, Belarus 0; Scotland 1, Italy 1; Slovenia 2, Norway 3; Belarus 1, Italy 4; Moldova 1, Slovenia 2; Norway 1, Scotland 2; Italy 1, Slovenia 0; Norway 1, Moldova 0; Scotland 0, Belarus 1; Belarus 0, Norway 1; Italy 2, Moldova 1; Slovenia 0, Scotland 3

GROUP 6

	P	W	D	L	F	A	Pts
ENGLAND	10	8	1	1	17	5	25
POLAND	10	8	0	2	27	9	24
Austria	10	4	3	3	15	12	15
Northern Ireland	10	2	3	5	10	18	9
Wales	10	2	2	6	10	15	8
Azerbaijan	10	1	0	3	7	1	21	3

Results: Northern Ireland 0, Poland 3; Austria 2, England 2; Azerbaijan 1, Wales 1; Wales 2, Northern Ireland 2; Poland 1, England 2; Austria 2, Azerbaijan 0; England 2, Wales 0; Austria 1, Poland 3; Azerbaijan 0, Northern Ireland 0; Northern Ireland 3, Austria 3; Wales 2, Azerbaijan 0; Poland 3; Azerbaijan 0, England 4, Northern Ireland 0; Wales 0, Austria 2; Poland 8, Azerbaijan 0; Poland 1, Northern Ireland 0; Austria 1, Wales 0; England 2, Azerbaijan 0; Azerbaijan 0, Poland 3; Northern Ireland 2, Azerbaijan 0; Poland 3, Austria 2; Wales 0, England 1; Azerbaijan 0, Austria 0; Northern Ireland 1, England 0; Poland 1, Wales 0; England 1, Austria 0; Northern Ireland 2, Wales 3; Austria 2, Northern Ireland 0; England 2, Poland 1; Wales 2, Azerbaijan 0.

GROUP 7

	P	W	D	L	F	A	Pts
SERBIA & MONT.	10	6	4	0	16	1	22
SPAIN	10	5	5	0	19	3	20
Bosnia-Herz.	10	4	4	2	12	9	16
Belgium	10	3	3	4	16	11	12
Lithuania	10	2	4	4	8	9	10
San Marino	10	0	0	10	2	40	0

Results: Belgium 1, Lithuania 1; San Marino 0, Serbia & Montenegro 3; Lithuania 4, San Marino 0; Bosnia-Herzegovina 1, Spain 1; Bosnia-Herzegovina 0, Serbia & Montenegro 0; Spain 2, Belgium 0; Serbia & Montenegro 5, San Marino 0; Lithuania 0, Spain 0; Belgium 0, Serbia & Montenegro 0; San Marino 0, Lithuania 1; Spain 5, San Marino 0; Belgium 4, Bosnia-Herzegovina 1; Serbia & Montenegro 0, Spain 0; Bosnia-Herzegovina 1, Lithuania 1; San Marino 1, Belgium 2; Serbia & Montenegro 0, Belgium 0; Spain 1, Lithuania 0; San Marino 1, Bosnia-Herzegovina 3; Spain 1, Bosnia-Herzegovina 1; Bosnia-Herzegovina 1, Belgium 0; Serbia & Montenegro 2, Lithuania 0; Belgium 8, San Marino 0; Lithuania 0, Bosnia-Herzegovina 1; Spain 1, Serbia & Montenegro 1; Belgium 0, Spain 2; Bosnia-Herzegovina 3, San Marino 0; Lithuania 0, Serbia & Montenegro 2; Lithuania 1, Belgium 1; San Marino 0, Spain 6; Serbia & Montenegro 1, Bosnia-Herzegovina 0.

GROUP 8

	P	W	D	L	F	A	Pts
CROATIA	10	7	3	0	21	5	24
SWEDEN	10	8	0	2	30	4	24
Bulgaria	10	4	3	3	17	17	15
Hungary	10	4	2	4	13	14	14
Iceland	10	1	1	8	14	27	4
Malta	10	0	3	7	4	32	3

Results: Iceland 1, Bulgaria 3; Croatia 3, Hungary 0; Malta 0, Sweden 7; Sweden 0, Croatia 1; Hungary 3, Iceland 2; Sweden 3, Hungary 0; Malta 0, Iceland 0; Croatia 2, Bulgaria 2; Bulgaria 4, Malta 1; Iceland 1, Sweden 4; Malta 0, Hungary 2; Bulgaria 0, Sweden 3; Croatia 4, Iceland 0; Croatia 3, Malta 0; Hungary 1, Bulgaria 1; Bulgaria 1, Croatia 3; Iceland 2, Hungary 3; Sweden 6, Malta 0; Iceland 4, Malta 1; Hungary 4,

Malta 0; Iceland 1, Croatia 3; Sweden 3, Bulgaria 0; Bulgaria 3, Iceland 2; Hungary 0,
Sweden 1; Malta 1, Croatia 1; Bulgaria 2, Hungary 0; Croatia 1, Sweden 0; Hungary 0,
Croatia 0; Malta 1, Bulgaria 1; Sweden 3, Iceland 1.

SOUTH AMERICA

	P	W	D	L	F	A	Pts
BRAZIL	18	9	7	2	35	17	34
ARGENTINA	18	10	4	4	29	17	34
ECUADOR	18	8	4	6	23	19	28
PARAGUAY	18	8	4	6	23	23	28
Uruguay	18	6	7	5	23	28	25
Colombia	18	6	6	6	24	16	24
Chile	18	5	7	6	18	22	22
Venezuela	18	5	3	10	20	28	18
Peru	18	4	6	8	20	28	18
Bolivia	18	4	2	12	20	37	14

Results: Ecuador 2, Venezuela 0; Argentina 2, Chile 2; Peru 4, Paraguay 1; Uruguay 5,
Bolivia 0; Colombia 1, Brazil 2; Venezuela 0, Argentina 3; Chile 2, Peru 1; Bolivia 4,
Colombia 0; Paraguay 4, Uruguay 1; Brazil 1, Ecuador 0; Uruguay 2, Chile 1; Colombia
0, Venezuela 1; Paraguay 2, Ecuador 1; Argentina 3, Bolivia 0; Peru 1, Brazil 1;
Venezuela 2, Bolivia 1; Chile 0, Paraguay 1; Ecuador 0, Peru 0; Colombia 1, Argentina
1; Brazil 3, Uruguay 3; Bolivia 0, Chile 2; Argentina 1, Ecuador 0; Uruguay 0,
Venezuela 3; Paraguay 0, Brazil 0; Peru 0, Colombia 2; Bolivia 2, Paraguay 1;
Venezuela 0, Chile 1; Uruguay 1, Peru 3; Ecuador 2, Colombia 1; Brazil 3, Argentina 1;
Ecuador 3, Bolivia 2; Argentina 0, Paraguay 0; Peru 0, Venezuela 0; Colombia 5,
Uruguay 0; Chile 1, Brazil 1; Peru 1, Argentina 3; Uruguay 1, Ecuador 0; Brazil 3,
Bolivia 1; Paraguay 1, Venezuela 0; Chile 0, Colombia 0; Argentina 4, Uruguay 2;
Bolivia 1, Peru 0; Colombia 1, Paraguay 1; Venezuala 2, Brazil 5; Ecuador 2, Chile 0;
Bolivia 0, Uruguay 0; Paraguay 1, Peru 1; Chile 0, Argentina 0; Brazil 0, Colombia 0;
Venezuela 3, Ecuador 1; Colombia 1, Bolivia 0; Peru 2, Chile 1; Ecuador 1, Brazil 0;
Uruguay 1, Paraguay 0; Argentina 3, Venezuela 2; Venezuela 0, Colombia 0; Chile 1,
Uruguay 1; Brazil 1, Peru 0; Ecuador 5, Paraguay 2; Bolivia 1, Argentina 2; Paraguay 2,
Chile 1; Bolivia 3, Venezuela 1; Argentina 1, Colombia 0; Peru 2, Ecuador 2; Uruguay
1, Brazil 1; Chile 3, Bolivia 1; Ecuador 2, Argentina 0; Brazil 4, Paraguay 1;Venezuela
1, Uruguay 1; Colombia 5, Peru 0; Peru 0, Uruguay 0; Paraguay 4, Bolivia 1; Chile 2,
Venezuela 1; Argentina 3, Brazil 1; Colombia 3, Ecuador 0; Bolivia 1, Ecuador 2; Brazil
5, Chile 0; Paraguay 1, Argentina 0; Uruguay 3, Colombia 2; Venezuela 4, Peru 1;
Argentina 2, Peru 0; Bolivia 1, Brazil 1; Colombia 1, Chile 1; Ecuador 0, Uruguay 0;
Venezuela 0, Paraguay 1; Brazil 3, Venezuela 0; Chile 0, Ecuador 0; Paraguay 0,
Colombia 1; Peru 4, Bolivia 1; Uruguay 1, Argentina 0.

AFRICA

GROUP 1

	P	W	D	L	F	A	Pts
TOGO	10	7	2	1	20	8	23
Senegal	10	6	3	1	21	8	21
Zambia	10	6	1	3	16	10	19
Congo	10	3	1	6	10	14	10
Mali	10	2	2	6	11	14	8
Liberia	10	1	1	8	3	27	4

Results: Congo 2, Togo 3; Senegal 3, Mali 0; Liberia 0, Zambia 5; Togo 3, Liberia 0;
Mali 2, Congo 0; Zambia 0, Senegal 1; Liberia 0, Congo 2; Senegal 2, Togo 2; Zambia
2, Mali 1; Mali 4, Liberia 1; Togo 4, Zambia 1; Congo 0, Senegal 0; Mali 1, Togo 2;
Senegal 6, Liberia 1; Zambia 2, Congo 0; Togo 1, Mali 0; Liberia 0, Senegal 3; Congo

8

2, Zambia 3; Mali 2, Senegal 2; Togo 2, Congo 0; Zambia 1, Liberia 0; Liberia 0, Togo 0; Congo 1, Mali 0; Senegal 1, Zambia 0; Togo 3, Senegal 1; Congo 3, Liberia 0; Mali 1, Zambia 1; Liberia 1, Mali 0; Senegal 2, Congo 0; Zambia 1, Togo 0.

GROUP 2

	P	W	D	L	F	A	Pts
GHANA	10	6	3	1	17	4	21
DR Congo	10	4	4	2	14	10	16
South Africa	10	5	1	4	12	14	16
Burkina Faso	10	4	1	5	14	13	13
Cape Verde Islands	10	3	1	6	8	15	10
Uganda	10	2	2	6	6	15	8

Results: Uganda 2, Burkina Faso 2; South Africa 2, DR Congo 2; Cape Verde Islands 0, Ghana 4; Ghana 2, Uganda 0; DR Congo 2, Cape Verde Islands 1; Burkina Faso 3, South Africa 1; Burkina Faso 2, DR Congo 0; Uganda 1, Cape Verde Islands 0; South Africa 0, Ghana 2; DR Congo 4, Uganda 0; Ghana 1, Burkina Faso 1; Cape Verde Islands 1, South Africa 2; DR Congo 1, Ghana 1; Burkina Faso 1, Cape Verde Islands 2; South Africa 2, Uganda 1; Uganda 0, South Africa 1; Ghana 0, DR Congo 0; Cape Verde Islands 1, Burkina Faso 0; DR Congo 1, South Africa 0; Ghana 2, Cape Verde Islands 0; Burkina Faso 2, Uganda 0; Uganda 1, Ghana 1; Cape Verde Islands 1, DR Congo 1; South Africa 2, Burkina Faso 0; DR Congo 3, Burkina Faso 2; Ghana 3, South Africa 0; Cape Verde Islands 1, Uganda 0; Uganda 1, DR Congo 0; Burkina Faso 1, Ghana 0; South Africa 2 Cape Verde Islands 1.

GROUP 3

	P	W	D	L	F	A	Pts
IVORY COAST	10	7	1	2	20	7	22
Cameroon	10	6	3	1	18	10	21
Egypt	10	5	2	3	26	15	17
Libya	10	3	3	4	8	10	12
Sudan	10	1	3	6	6	22	6
Benin	10	1	2	7	9	23	5

Results: Benin 1, Libya 0; Sudan 1, Ivory Coast 3; Cameroon 1, Egypt 1; Egypt 4, Benin 1; Ivory Coast 2, Cameroon 3; Libya 0, Sudan 0; Sudan 1, Benin 0; Ivory Coast 2, Egypt 0; Cameroon 1, Libya 0; Egypt 6, Sudan 1; Benin 1, Cameroon 4; Libya 0, Ivory Coast 0; Egypt 4, Libya 1; Ivory Coast 3, Benin 0; Cameroon 2, Sudan 1; Benin 0, Ivory Coast 1; Sudan 1, Cameroon 1; Libya 2, Egypt 2; Egypt 3, Cameroon 2; Ivory Coast 5, Sudan 0; Libya 4, Benin 1; Benin 3, Egypt 3; Cameroon 2, Ivory Coast; Sudan 0, Libya 1; Egypt 1, Ivory Coast 2; Benin 1, Sudan 1; Libya 0, Cameroon 0; Sudan 0, Egypt 3; Ivory Coast 2, Libya 0; Cameroon 2, Benin 1.

GROUP 4

	P	W	D	L	F	A	Pts
ANGOLA	10	6	3	1	12	6	21
Nigeria	10	6	3	1	21	7	21
Zimbabwe	10	4	3	3	13	14	15
Gabon	10	2	4	4	11	13	10
Algeria	10	1	5	4	8	15	8
Rwanda	10	1	2	7	6	16	5

Results: Rwanda 0, Angola 1; Gabon 0, Algeria 0; Nigeria 5, Zimbabwe 1; Algeria 2, Nigeria 5; Angola 3, Gabon 0; Zimbabwe 3, Rwanda 1; Algeria 2, Zimbabwe 2; Gabon 3, Rwanda 0; Nigeria 1, Angola 1; Rwanda 1, Nigeria 1; Angola 2, Algeria 1; Zimbabwe 1, Gabon 0; Algeria 1, Rwanda 0; Zimbabwe 2, Angola 0; Nigeria 2, Gabon 0; Angola 1, Zimbabwe 0; Gabon 1, Nigeria 1; Rwanda 1, Algeria 1; Algeria 0, Gabon 3; Angola 1,

Rwanda 0; Zimbabwe 0, Nigeria 3; Nigeria 1, Algeria 0; Gabon 2, Angola 2; Rwanda 0, Zimbabwe 2; Angola 1, Nigeria 0; Zimbabwe 1, Algeria 1; Rwanda 3, Gabon 1; Algeria 0, Angola 0; Nigeria 2, Rwanda 0; Gabon 1, Zimbabwe 1.

GROUP 5

	P	W	D	L	F	A	Pts
TUNISIA	10	6	3	1	25	9	21
Morocco	10	5	5	0	17	7	20
Guinea	10	5	2	3	15	10	17
Kenya	10	3	1	6	8	17	10
Botswana	10	3	0	7	10	18	9
Malawi	10	1	3	6	12	26	6

Results: Tunisia 2, Morocco 2; Botswana 1, Guinea 2; Malawi 3, Kenya 0; Guinea 3, Malawi 1; Morocco 1, Botswana 0; Kenya 0, Tunisia 2; Tunisia 1, Kenya 0; Kenya 0, Morocco 0; Malawi 1, Botswana 3; Tunisia 2, Guinea 0; Guinea 1, Kenya 0; Morocco 4, Malawi 1; Botswana 1, Tunisia 3; Morocco 1, Guinea 0; Tunisia 7, Malawi 0; Kenya 1, Botswana 0; Morocco 5, Kenya 1; Kenya 2, Guinea 1; Guinea 1, Morocco 1; Botswana 2, Kenya 1; Malawi 2, Tunisia 2; Guinea 4, Botswana 0; Morocco 0, Tunisia 1; Kenya 3, Malawai 2; Malawi 1, Guinea 1; Botswana 0, Morocco 0; Guinea 2, Tunisia 1; Botswana 2, Malawi 0; Tunisia 4, Botswana 1; Malawi 1, Morocco 1.

ASIA

FINAL GROUP 1

	P	W	D	L	F	A	Pts
SAUDI ARABIA	6	4	2	0	10	1	14
SOUTH KOREA	6	3	1	2	9	5	10
Uzbekistan	6	1	2	3	7	11	5
Kuwait	6	1	1	4	4	13	4

Results: South Korea 0, Saudi Arabia 1; Uzbekistan 3, Kuwait 0; Saudi Arabia 3, Uzbekistan 0; Kuwait 0, South Korea 4; Saudi Arabia 3, Kuwait 0; Uzbekistan 1, South Korea 1; South Korea 2, Uzbekistan 1; Kuwait 0, Saudi Arabia 0; Saudi Arabia 2, South Korea 0; Kuwait 2, Uzbekistan 1; South Korea 2, Kuwait 0; Uzbekistan 1, Saudi Arabia 1.

FINAL GROUP 2

	P	W	D	L	F	A	Pts
JAPAN	6	5	0	1	9	4	15
IRAN	6	4	1	1	7	3	13
Bahrain	6	1	1	4	4	7	4
North Korea	6	1	0	5	5	11	1

Results: Bahrain 2, North Korea 3; Japan 2, Iran 1; Iran 1, Bahrain 0; North Korea 0, Japan 2; Bahrain 0, Japan 1; Iran 1, North Korea 0; Japan 1, Bahrain 0; North Korea 0. Iran 2; Iran 2, Japan 1; North Korea 1, Bahrain 2; Japan 2, North Korea 1; Bahrain 0, Iran 0.

Group Play-off: First leg – Uzbekistan 1, Bahrain 1. Second leg – Bahrain 0, Uzbekistan 0 (Bahrain won on away goal).

NORTH/CENTRAL AMERICA/CARIBBEAN

FINAL GROUP

	P	W	D	L	F	A	Pts
USA	10	7	1	2	16	6	22
MEXICO	10	7	1	2	22	9	22
COSTA RICA	10	5	1	4	15	14	16
TRIN & TOBAGO	10	4	1	5	10	15	13
Guatemala	10	3	2	5	16	18	11
Panama	10	0	2	8	4	21	2

Results: Trinidad & Tobago 1, USA 2; Panama 0, Guatemala 0; Costa Rica 1, Mexico 2; Costa Rica 2, Panama 1; Guatemala 5, Trinidad & Tobago 1; Mexico 2, USA 1; Trinidad & Tobago 0, Costa Rica 0; USA 2, Guatemala 0; Panama 1, Mexico 1; USA 3, Costa Rica 0; Trinidad & Tobago 2, Panama 0; Guatemala 0, Mexico 2; Mexico 2, Trinidad & Tobago 0; Costa Rica 3, Guatemala 2; Panama 0, USA 3; USA 1, Trinidad & Tobago 0; Guatemala 2, Panama 1; Mexico 2, Costa Rica 0; Trinidad & Tobago 3, Guatemala 2; USA 2, Mexico 0; Panama 1, Costa Rica 3; Costa Rica 2, Trinidad & Tobago 0; Guatemala 0, USA 0; Mexico 5, Panama 0; Costa Rica 3, USA 0; Mexico 5, Guatemala 2; Panama 0, Trinidad & Tobago 1; Guatemala 3, Costa Rica 1; Trinidad & Tobago 2, Mexico 1; USA 2, Panama 0.

OCEANIA

FINAL GROUP

	P	W	D	L	F	A	Pts
AUSTRALIA	5	4	1	0	21	3	13
Solomon Islands	5	3	1	1	9	6	10
New Zealand	5	3	0	2	17	5	9
Fiji	5	1	1	3	3	10	4
Tahiti	5	1	1	3	2	24	4
Vanuatu	5	1	0	4	5	9	3

Results: Vanuatu 0, Solomon Islands 1; Tahiti 0, Fiji 0; Australia 1, New Zealand 0; New Zealand 3, Solomon Islands 0; Australia 9, Tahiti 0; Fiji 1, Vanuatu 0; Australia 6, Fiji 1; Tahiti 0, Solomon Islands 4; New Zealand 2, Vanuatu 4; New Zealand 10, Tahiti 0; Fiji 1, Solomon Islands 2; Vanuatu 0, Australia 3; Tahiti 2, Vanuatu 1; Fiji 0, New Zealand 2; Solomon Islands 2, Australia 2.

Group Play-off: First leg: Australia 7, Solomon Islands 0. Second leg: Solomon Islands 1, Australia 2 (Australia won 9-1 on agg).

QUALIFYING PLAY-OFFS

Europe: First leg – Norway 0, Czech Republic 1; Spain 5, Slovakia 1; Switzerland 2, Turkey 0. Second leg – Czech Republic 1, Norway 0 (Czech Republic won 2-0 on agg); Slovakia 1, Spain 1 (Spain won 6-2 on agg); Turkey 4, Switzerland 2 (agg 4-4, Switzerland won on away goals).

South America/Oceania: First leg – Uruguay 1, Australia 0. Second leg – Australia 1, Uruguay 0 (aet, Australia won 4-2 on pens).

Asia/Concacaf: First leg – Trinidad & Tobago 1, Bahrain 1. Second leg – Bahrain 0, Trinidad & Tobago 1 (Trinidad & Tobago won 2-1 on agg).

WORLD CUP FINALS – 2006

GROUP A

GERMANY 4, COSTA RICA 2
Munich (66,000), Friday, June 9, 2006

Germany (4-4-2): Lehmann, Friedrich, Mertesacker, Metzelder, Lahm, Borowski (Kehl 72), Frings, Schneider (Odonkor 90), Schweinsteiger, Klose (Neuville 79), Podolski. **Scorers:** Lahm (6), Klose (17, 61), Frings (87).

Costa Rica (3-5-1-1): Porras, Umana, Sequeira, Marin, Martinez (Drummond 66), Solis (Bolanos 78), Fonseca, Gonzalez, Centeno, Gomez (Azofeifa 90), Wanchope. **Scorer:** Wanchope (12, 73). **Booked:** Fonseca.

Referee: H. Elizondo (Argentina). **Half-time:** 2-1.

POLAND 0, ECUADOR 2
Gelsenkirchen (52,000), Friday, June 9, 2006

Poland (4-2-3-1): Boruc, Baszczynski, Jop, Bak, Zewlakow, Radomski, Sobolewski (Jelen 67), Smolarek, Szymkowiak, Krzynowek (Kosowski 78), Zurawski (Brozek 83). **Booked:** Smolarek.

Ecuador (4-4-2): Mora, De la Cruz, Hurtado (Guagua 69), Espinoza, Reasco, Valencia, Castillo, E. Tenorio, Mendez, Delgado (Urrutia 83), C. Tenorio (Kaviedes 65). **Scorers:** C. Tenorio (24), Delgado (80). **Booked:** Hurtado, Mendez.

Referee: T. Kamikawa (Japan). **Half-time:** 0-1.

GERMANY 1, POLAND 0
Dortmund (65,000), Wednesday, June 14, 2006

Germany (4-4-2): Lehmann, Friedrich (Odonkor 64), Mertesacker, Metzelder, Lahm, Schneider, Ballack, Frings, Schweinsteiger (Borowski 77), Podolski (Neuville 71), Klose. **Scorer:** Neuville (90). **Booked:** Ballack, Odonkor, Metzelder.

Poland (4-4-1-1): Boruc, Baszczynski, Bosacki, Bak, Zewlakow (Dudka 83), Jelen (Brozek 90), Sobolewski, Radomski, Krzynowek (Lewandowski 77), Zurawski, Smolarek. **Booked:** Kryznowek, Sobolewski, Boruc. **Sent-off:** Sobolewski (75).

Referee: L. Medina Cantalejo (Spain). **Half-time:** 0-0.

ECUADOR 3, COSTA RICA 0
Hamburg (50,000), Thursday, June 15, 2006

Ecuador (4-4-2): Mora, De la Cruz, Hurtado, Espinoza (Guagua 69), Reasco, Valencia (Urrutia 73), Castillo, E. Tenorio, Mendez, C Tenorio (Kaviedes 46), Delgado. **Scorers:** C. Tenorio (8), Delgado (54), Kaviedes (90). **Booked:** Castillo, De la Cruz, Mora.

Costa Rica (3-5-2): Porras, Sequeira, Marin, Umana, Wallace, Solis, Fonseca (Saborio 29), Centeno (Bernard 84), Gonzalez (Hernandez 56), Gomez, Wanchope. **Booked:** Marin, Solis.

Referee: C. Codjia (Benin). **Half-time:** 1-0.

ECUADOR 0, GERMANY 3

Berlin (72,000), Tuesday, June 20, 2006

Ecuador (4-4-2): Mora, De la Cruz, Guagua, Espinoza, Ambrosi, Mendez, Ayovi (Urrutia 68), E. Tenorio, Valencia, (Lara 63), Borja (Benitez 46), Kaviedes. **Booked:** Valencia.

Germany (4-4-2): Lehmann, Friedrich, Huth, Mertesacker, Lahm, Schneider (Asamoah 72), Ballack, Frings (Borowski 66), Schweinsteiger, Klose (Neuville 66), Podolski. **Scorers:** Klose (4, 44), Podolski (57). **Booked:** Borowski.

Referee: V. Ivanov (Russia). **Half-time:** 0-2.

COSTA RICA 1, POLAND 2

Hanover (43,000), Tuesday, June 20, 2006

Costa Rica (3-4-2-1): Porras, Umana, Marin, Badilla, Drummond (Wallace 70), Solis, Centeno, Gonzalez, Bolanos (Saborio 78), Gomez (Hernandez 82), Wanchope. **Scorer:** Gomez (25). **Booked:** Umana, Marin, Gomez, Badilla, Gonzalez.

Poland (4-3-3): Boruc, Baszczynski, Bosacki, Bak, Zewlakow, Szymkowiak, Radomski (Lewandowski 64), Krzynowek, Smolarek (Rasiak 85), Zurawski (Brozek 46), Jelen. **Scorers:** Bosacki (33, 66). **Booked:** Radomski, Bak, Zewlakow, Baszczynski, Boruc.

Referee: S. Maidin (Singapore). **Half-time:** 1-1.

FINAL TABLE

	P	W	D	L	F	A	Pts
GERMANY	3	3	0	0	8	2	9
ECUADOR	3	2	0	1	5	3	6
Poland	3	1	0	2	2	4	3
Costa Rica	3	0	0	3	3	9	0

GROUP B

ENGLAND 1, PARAGUAY 0

Frankfurt (48,000), Saturday, June 10, 2006

England (4-4-2): Robinson (Tottenham), Neville (Manchester Utd.), Ferdinand (Manchester Utd.), Terry (Chelsea), A. Cole (Arsenal), Beckham (Real Madrid), Lampard (Chelsea), Gerrard (Liverpool), J. Cole (Chelsea) (Hargreaves, Bayern Munich, 83), Crouch (Liverpool), Owen (Newcastle Utd.) (Downing, Middlesbrough, 56). **Scorer:** Gamarra (3 og). **Booked:** Gerrard, Crouch.

Paraguay (4-4-2): Villar (Bobadilla 8), Caniza, Caceres, Gamarra, Toledo (Nunez 82), Bonet (Cuevas 68), Paredes, Acuna, Riveros, Santa Cruz, Valdez. **Booked:** Valdez.

Referee: M. Rodriguez (Mexico). **Half-time:** 1-0.

TRINIDAD AND TOBAGO 0 SWEDEN 0

Dortmund (62,959), Saturday, June 10, 2006

Trinidad and Tobago (4-1-4-1): Hislop, Gray, Sancho, Lawrence, A. John, Yorke, Edwards, Birchall, Theobald (Whitley 66), Samuel (Glen 52), S. John. **Booked:** A. John, Yorke. **Sent-off:** A. John (46).

Sweden (4-1-3-2): Shaaban, Alexandersson, Mellberg, Lucic, Edman, Linderoth (Kallstrom 78), Wilhelmsson (Jonson 78), Svensson (Allback 62), Ljungberg, Ibrahimovic, Larsson. **Booked:** Larsson.

Referee: S. Maidin (Singapore). **Half-time:** 0-0.

ENGLAND 2, TRINIDAD AND TOBAGO 0

Nuremberg (41,000), Thursday, June 15, 2006

England (4-4-2): Robinson (Tottenham), Carragher (Liverpool) (Lennon, Tottenham, 58), Ferdinand (Manchester Utd.), Terry (Chelsea), A. Cole (Arsenal), Beckham (Real Madrid), Lampard (Chelsea), Gerrard (Liverpool), J. Cole (Chelsea) (Downing, Middlesbrough 75), Crouch (Liverpool), Owen (Newcastle Utd.) (Rooney, Manchester Utd., 58). **Scorers:** Crouch (83), Gerrard (90). **Booked:** Lampard.

Trinidad and Tobago (4-4-2): Hislop, Edwards, Sancho, Lawrence, Gray, Whitley, Birchall, Yorke, Theobald (Wise 84), Jones (Glen 70), S. John. **Booked:** Theobald, Whitley, Jones, Hislop, Gray.

Referee: T. Kamikawa (Japan). **Half-time:** 0-0.

SWEDEN 1, PARAGUAY 0

Berlin (72,000), Thursday, June 15, 2006

Sweden (4-4-2): Isaksson, Alexandersson, Mellberg, Lucic, Edman, Wilhelmsson (Jonson 68), Linderoth, Kallstrom (Elmander 86), Ljungberg, Larsson, Ibrahimovic (Allback 46). **Scorer:** Ljungberg (89). **Booked:** Linderoth, Lucic, Allback.

Paraguay (4-4-2): Bobadilla, Caniza, Gamarra, Caceres, Nunez, Bonet (Barreto 81), Acuna, Paredes, Riveros (Dos Santos 62), Santa Cruz (Lopez 63),Valdez. **Booked:** Caniza, Nunez, Acuna, Paredes, Baretto.

Referee: L. Michel (Slovakia). **Half-time:** 0-0.

SWEDEN 2, ENGLAND 2

Cologne (45,000), Tuesday, June 20, 2006

Sweden (4-4-2): Isaksson, Alexandersson, Mellberg, Lucic, Edman, Jonson (Wilhelmsson 54), Linderoth (Andersson 90), Kallstrom, Ljungberg, Larsson, Allback (Elmander 75). **Scorers:** Allback (51), Larsson (90). **Booked:** Alexandersson, Ljungberg.

England (4-4-2): Robinson (Tottenham), Carragher (Liverpool), Ferdinand (Manchester Utd.) (Campbell, Arsenal, 56), Terry (Chelsea), A. Cole (Arsenal), Beckham (Real Madrid), Lampard (Chelsea), Hargreaves (Bayern Munich), J. Cole (Chelsea), Owen (Newcastle Utd.) (Crouch, Liverpool, 4), Rooney (Manchester Utd.) (Gerrard, Liverpool, 69). **Scorers:** J. Cole (34), Gerrard (85). **Booked:** Hargreaves.

Referee: M. Busacca (Switzerland). **Half-time:** 0-1.

PARAGUAY 2, TRINIDAD AND TOBAGO 0

Kaiserslautern (46,000), Tuesday, June 20, 2006

Paraguay (4-4-2): Bobadilla, Caniza (Da Silva 89), Caceres (Manzur 77), Gamarra, Nunez, Barreto, Acuna, Paredes, Dos Santos, Santa Cruz, Valdez (Cuevas 66). **Scorers:** Sancho (25 og), Cuevas (86). **Booked:** Paredes, Dos Santos.

Trinidad and Tobago (4-4-2): Jack, Edwards, Lawrence, Sancho, A. John (Jones 31), Birchall, Whitley, (Latapy 66), Yorke, Theobald, Glen (Wise 41), S. John **Booked:** Sancho, Whitley.

Referee: R. Rosetti (Italy). **Half-time:** 1-0.

FINAL TABLE

	P	W	D	L	F	A	Pts
ENGLAND	3	2	1	0	5	2	7
SWEDEN	3	1	2	0	3	2	5

Paraguay	3	1	0	2	2	2	3
Trinidad and Tobago	3	0	1	2	0	4	1

GROUP C

ARGENTINA 2, IVORY COAST 1
Hamburg (49,480), Saturday, June 10, 2006

Argentina (4-1-3-2): Abbondanzieri, Burdisso, Ayala, Heinze, Sorin, Mascherano, Rodriguez, Cambiasso, Riquelme (Aimar 90), Saviola (Gonzalez 75), Crespo (Palacio 64). **Scorers:** Crespo (24), Saviola (38). **Booked:** Saviola, Heinze, Gonzalez.

Ivory Coast (4-4-1-1): Tizie, Eboue, K. Toure, Meite, Boka, Keita (A. Kone 77), Zokora, Y. Toure, Akale (B. Kone 62), Kalou (Dindane (55), Drogba. **Scorer:** Drogba (82). **Booked:** Eboue, Drogba.

Referee: F. De Bleeckere (Belgium). **Half-time:** 2-0.

SERBIA AND MONTENEGRO 0, HOLLAND 1
Leipzig (37,216), Sunday, June 11, 2006

Serbia and Montenegro (4-4-2): Jevric, Dragutinovic, Gavrancic, N. Djordjevic (Koroman 43), Krstajic, Duljaj, Stankovic, P. Djordjevic, Nadj, Kezman (Ljuboja 67), Milosevic (Zigic 46). **Booked:** Stankovic, Koroman, Dragutinovic, Gavrancic.

Holland (4-3-3): Van der Sar, Heitinga, Ooijer, Mathijsen (Boulahrouz 86), Van Bronckhorst, Cocu, Sneijder, Van Bommel (Landzaat 60), Van Persie, Van Nistelrooy (Kuyt 69), Robben. **Scorer:** Robben (18). **Booked:** Van Bronkhorst, Heitinga.

Referee: M. Merk (Germany). **Half-time:** 0-1.

ARGENTINA 6, SERBIA AND MONTENEGRO 0
Gelsenkirchen (52,000), Friday, June 16, 2006

Argentina (4-1-3-2): Abbondanzieri, Burdisso, Ayala, Heinze, Sorin, Mascherano, Gonzalez (Cambiasso 17), Rodriguez (Messi 75), Riquelme, Saviola (Tevez 59), Crespo. **Scorers:** Rodriguez (6, 41), Cambiasso (31), Crespo (78), Tevez (84), Messi (88). **Booked:** Crespo.

Serbia and Montenegro (4-4-2): Jevric, Duljaj, Gavrancic, Dudic, Krstajic, Koroman (Ljuboja 50), Nadj (Ergic 46), P. Djordjevic, Stankovic, Kezman, Milosevic (Vukic 70). **Booked:** Koroman, Nadj, Krstajic. **Sent-off:** Kezman (65).

Referee: R. Rosetti (Italy). **Half-time:** 3-0.

HOLLAND 2, IVORY COAST 1
Stuttgart (52,000), Friday, June 16, 2006

Holland (4-3-3): Van der Sar, Heitinga (Boulahrouz 46), Ooijer, Mathijsen, Van Bronckhorst, Cocu, Sneijder (Van der Vaart 50), Van Bommel, Van Persie, Van Nistelrooy (Landzaat 73), Robben. **Scorers:** Van Persie (23), Van Nistelrooy (27). **Booked:** Robben, Mathijsen, Van Bommel, Boulahrouz.

Ivory Coast (4-4-2): Tizie, Eboue, K. Toure, Meite, B. Kone (Dindane 62), Y. Toure, Boka, Zokora, Romaric (Yapo 62), A. Kone (Akale 73), Drogba, **Scorer:** B. Kone (38). **Booked:** Zokora, Drogba, Boka.

Referee: O. Ruiz (Colombia). **Half-time:** 2-1.

HOLLAND 0, ARGENTINA 0
Frankfurt (48,000), Wednesday, June 21, 2006

Holland (4-3-3): Van der Sar, Jaliens, Boulahrouz, Ooijer, De Cler, Cocu, Sneijder, (Maduro 86), Van der Vaart, Van Persie (Landzaat 67), Van Nistelrooy (Babel 56), Kuyt. **Booked:** Kuyt, Ooijer, De Cler.

Argentina (4-3-3): Abbondanzieri, Burdisso (Coloccini 24), Ayala, Milito, Cufre, Rodriguez, Mascherano, Cambiasso, Messi (Cruz 70), Riquelme (Aimar 80), Tevez. **Booked:** Cambiasso, Mascherano.

Referee: L. Medina Cantalejo (Spain). **Half-time:** 0-0.

IVORY COAST 3, SERBIA AND MONTENEGRO 2
Munich (66,000), Wednesday, June 21, 2006

Ivory Coast (4-4-2): Barry, Eboue, Kouassi, Domoraud, Boka, Akale (B. Kone 60), Zokora, Keita (Kalou 72), Y. Toure, A. Kone, Dindane. **Scorers:** Dindane (37 pen, 67), Kalou (86 pen). **Booked:** Keita, Domoraud, Dindane. **Sent-off:** Domoraud (90).

Serbia and Montenegro (4-4-2): Jevric, N. Djordjevic, Krstajic (Nadj 16), Gavrancic, Dudic, Duljaj, P. Djordjevic, Ilic, Stankovic, Ergic, Zigic (Milosevic 67). **Scorers:** Zigic (10), Ilic (20). **Booked:** Nadj, Dudic, Duljaj, Gavrancic. **Sent-off:** Nadj (67).

Referee: M. Rodriguez (Mexico). **Half-time:** 1-2.

FINAL TABLE

	P	W	D	L	F	A	Pts
ARGENTINA	3	2	1	0	8	1	7
HOLLAND	3	2	1	0	3	1	7
Ivory Coast	3	1	0	2	5	6	3
Serbia & Montenegro	3	0	0	3	2	10	0

GROUP D

MEXICO 3, IRAN 1
Nuremberg (41,000), Sunday, June 11, 2006

Mexico (3-5-2): Sanchez, Marquez, Osorio, Salcido, Mendez, Bravo, Pardo, Torrado (Perez 46), Pineda, Franco (Zinha, 46), Borgetti (Fonseca 52). **Scorers:** Bravo (28, 76), Zinha (79). **Booked:** Torrado, Salcido.

Iran (4-4-2): Mirzapour, Kaabi, Golmohammadi, Rezaei, Nosrati (Borhani 81), Mahdavikia, Teymourian, Nekounam, Karimi (Madanchi 63), Hashemian, Daei. **Scorer:** Golmohammadi (36). **Booked:** Nekounam.

Referee: R. Rosetti (Italy). **Half-time:** 1-1.

ANGOLA 0, PORTUGAL 1
Cologne (45,000), Sunday, June 11, 2006

Angola (3-5-2): Joao Ricardo, Jamba, Kali, Delgado, Loco, Mendonca, Figueiredo (Miloy 80), Andre, Mateus, Ze Kalanga (Edson 70), Akwa (Mantorras 60). **Booked:** Jamba, Loco, Andre.

Portugal (4-3-2-1): Ricardo, Miguel, Fernando Meira, Ricardo Carvalho, Nuno Valente, Figo, Tiago (Viana 83), Petit (Maniche 72), Ronaldo (Costinha 60), Simao Sabrosa, Pauleta. **Scorer:** Pauleta (4). **Booked:** Ronaldo, Nuno Valente.

Referee: J. Larrionda (Uruguay). **Half-time:** 0-1.

MEXICO 0, ANGOLA 0
Hanover (43,000), Friday, June 16, 2006

Mexico (3-5-2): Sanchez, Marquez, Osorio, Salcido, Mendez, Zinha (Arellano 52), Pardo, Torrado, Pineda (Morales 78), Franco (Fonseca 74), Bravo. **Booked:** Pineda.

Angola (4-4-1-1): Joao Ricardo, Loco, Kali, Jamba, Delgado, Ze Kalanga (Miloy 83), Andre, Figueiredo (Rui Marques 73), Mendonca, Mateus (Mantoras 68), Akwa. **Booked:** Delgado, Andre, Ze Kalanga, Joao Ricardo. **Sent-off:** Andre (79).

Referee: S. Maidin (Singapore). **Half-time:** 0-0.

PORTUGAL 2, IRAN 0
Frankfurt (48,000), Saturday, June 17, 2006

Portugal (4-4-1-1): Ricardo, Miguel, Fernando Meira, Ricardo Carvalho, Nuno Valente, Figo (Simao Sabrosa 88), Costinha, Maniche (Petit 67), Deco (Tiago 80), Ronaldo, Pauleta. **Scorers:** Deco (63), Ronaldo (80 pen). **Booked:** Pauleta, Deco, Costinha.

Iran (4-4-2): Mirzapour, Kaabi, Golmohammadi (Bakhtiarizadeh 88), Rezaei, Nosrati, Mahdavikia, Nekounam, Teymourian, Madanchi (Khatibi 66), Karimi (Zandi 65), Hashemian, **Booked:** Nekounam, Madanchi, Kaabi, Golmohammadi.

Referee: E. Poulat (France). **Half-time:** 0-0.

PORTUGAL 2, MEXICO 1
Gelsenkirchen (52,000), Wednesday, June 21, 2006

Portugal (4-5-1): Ricardo, Miguel (Paulo Ferreira 61), Fernando Meira, Ricardo Carvalho, Caneira, Figo (Boa Morte 80), Tiago, Petit, Maniche, Simao Sabrosa, Helder Postiga (Nuno Gomes 69). **Scorers:** Maniche (6), Simao Sabrosa (24 pen). **Booked:** Miguel, Maniche, Boa Morte, Nuno Gomes.

Mexico (3-5-2): Sanchez, Marquez, Rodriguez (Zinha 46), Osorio, Salcido, Mendez (Franco 80), Pardo, Perez, Pineda (Castro 69), Bravo, Fonseca. **Scorer:** Fonseca (29). **Booked:** Rodriguez, Perez, Marquez, Zinha. **Sent-off:** Perez (61).

Referee: L. Michel (Slovakia). **Half-time:** 2-1.

IRAN 1, ANGOLA 1
Leipzig (38,000), Wednesday, June 21, 2006

Iran (4-4-2): Mirzapour, Bakhtiarizadeh, Rezaei, Kaabi (Borhani 67), Nosrati (Shojaei 13), Mahdavikia, Zandi, Teymourian, Madanchi, Hashemian (Khatibi 39), Daei. **Scorer:** Bakhtiarizadeh (75). **Booked:** Madanchi, Teymourian, Zandi.

Angola (4-5-1): Joao Ricardo, Jamba, Kali, Loco, Delgado, Miloy, Figueiredo (Rui Marques 73), Mateus (Love 23), Mendonca, Ze Kalanga, Akwa (Flavio 51). **Scorer:** Flavio (60). **Booked:** Loco, Mendonca, Ze Kalanga.

Referee: M. Shield (Australia). **Half-time:** 0-0.

FINAL TABLE

	P	W	D	L	F	A	Pts
PORTUGAL	3	3	0	0	5	1	9
MEXICO	3	1	1	1	4	3	4
Angola	3	0	2	1	1	2	2
Iran	3	0	1	2	2	6	1

GROUP E

UNITED STATES 0, CZECH REPUBLIC 3
Gelsenkirchen (52,000), Monday, June 12, 2006

United States (4-4-2): Keller, Cherundolo (Johnson 46), Pope, Onyewu, Lewis, Beasley, Mastroeni (O'Brien 46), Reyna, Convey, Donovan, McBride (Wolff 77). **Booked:** Onyewu, Reyna.

Czech Republic (4-1-4-1): Cech, Grygera, Ujfalusi, Rozehnal, Jankulovski, Galasek, Poborsky (Polak 82), Rosicky (Stajner 86), Nedved, Plasil, Koller (Lokvenc 45). **Scorers:** Koller (5), Rosicky (36, 76). **Booked:** Rozehnal, Lokvenc, Rosicky, Grygera.

Referee: C. Amarilla (Paraguay). **Half-time:** 0-2.

ITALY 2, GHANA 0
Hanover (43,000), Monday, June 12, 2006

Italy (4-3-1-2): Buffon, Zaccardo, Nesta, Cannavaro, Grosso, Perrotta, Pirlo, De Rossi, Totti (Camoranesi 56), Gilardino (Iaquinta 64), Toni (Del Piero 82). **Scorers:** Pirlo (40), Iaquinta (83). **Booked:** De Rossi, Camoranesi, Iaquinta.

Ghana (2-1-4-1-2): Kingston, Kuffour, Mensah, E. Addo, Pantsil, Appiah, Muntari, Pappoe (Shilla 46), Essien, Amoah (Pimpong 68), Gyan (Tachie-Mensah 89). **Booked:** Muntari, Gyan.

Referee: C. Simon (Brazil). **Half-time:** 1-0.

CZECH REPUBLIC 0, GHANA 2
Cologne (45,000), Saturday, June 17, 2006

Czech Republic (4-1-4-1): Cech, Grygera, Rozehnal, Ujfalusi, Jankulovski, Galasek (Polak 46), Poborsky (Stajner 56), Rosicky, Nedved, Plasil (Sionkjo 68), Lokvenc. **Booked:** Lokvenc. **Sent-off:** Ujfalusi (65).

Ghana (4-4-2): Kingson, Pantsil, Mensah, Shilla, Mohamed, O. Addo (Boateng 46), Essien, Appiah, Muntari, Amoah (E. Addo 80), Gyan (Pimpong 85). **Scorers:** Gyan (2), Muntari (82). **Booked:** O. Addo, Essien, Gyan, Boateng, Muntari.

Referee: H. Elizondo (Argentina). **Half-time:** 0-1.

ITALY 1, UNITED STATES 1
Kaiserslautern (46,000), Saturday, June 17, 2006

Italy (4-3-1-2): Buffon, Zaccardo (Del Piero 54), Nesta, Cannavaro, Zambrotta, Perrotta, Pirlo, De Rossi, Totti (Gattuso 35), Gilardino, Toni (Iaquinta 61). **Scorer:** Gilardino (22). **Booked:** Totti, Zambrotta. **Sent-off:** De Rossi (28).

United States (4-1-4-1): Keller, Cherundolo, Pope, Onyewu, Bocanegra, Mastroeni, Dempsey (Beasley 62), Reyna, Donovan, Convey (Conrad 52), McBride. **Scorer:** Zaccardo (27 og). **Booked:** Pope. **Sent-off:** Mastroeni (45), Pope (47).

Referee: J. Larrionda (Uruguay). **Half-time:** 1-1.

CZECH REPUBLIC 0, ITALY 2
Hamburg (50,000), Thursday, June 22, 2006

Czech Republic (4-4-1-1): Cech, Grygera, Kovac (Heinz 78), Rozehnal, Jankulovski, Poborskry (Stajner 46), Polak, Nedved, Plasil, Rosicky, Baros (Jarolim 64). **Booked:** Polak. **Sent-off:** Polak (47).

Italy (4-1-3-2): Buffon, Zambrotta, Nesta (Materazzi 17), Cannavaro, Grosso, Pirlo, Camoranesi (Barone 74), Gattuso, Perrotta, Totti, Gilardino (Inzaghi 60). **Scorers:** Materazzi (26), Inzaghi (87). **Booked:** Gattuso.

Referee: B. Archundia (Mexico). **Half-time:** 0-1.

GHANA 2, UNITED STATES 1
Nuremberg (41,000), Thursday, June 22, 2006

Ghana (4-4-2): Kingson, Pantsil, Mensah, Mohamed, Shilla, Boateng (O. Addo 46), Essien, Appiah, Draman (Tachie-Mensah 80), Amoah (E. Addo 59), Pimpong. **Scorers:** Draman (22), Appiah (47 pen). **Booked:** Essien, Shilla, Mensah, Appiah.

United States (4-1-4-1): Keller, Cherundolo (Johnson 61), Onyewu, Conrad, Bocanegra, Reyna (Olsen 40), Dempsey, Donovan, Beasley, Lewis (Convey 74), McBride. **Scorer:** Dempsey (43). **Booked:** Lewis.

Referee: M. Merk (Germany). **Half-time:** 2-1.

FINAL TABLE

	P	W	D	L	F	A	Pts
ITALY	3	2	1	0	5	1	7
GHANA	3	2	0	1	4	3	6
Czech Republic	3	1	0	2	3	4	3
United States	3	0	1	2	2	6	1

GROUP F

AUSTRALIA 3, JAPAN 1
Kaiserslautern (46,000), Monday, June 12, 2006

Australia (3-5-2): Schwarzer, Neill, Moore (Kennedy 61), Chipperfield, Wilkshire (Aloisi 75), Emerton, Grella, Bresciano (Cahill 53), Culina, Viduka, Kewell. **Scorers:** Cahill (84, 89), Aloisi (90). **Booked:** Grella, Moore, Cahill, Aloisi.

Japan (3-5-2): Kawaguchi, Nakazawa, Miyamoto, Tsuboi (Moniwa 56, Oguro 90), Komano, H. Nakata, Fukunishi, Nakamura, Santos, Takahara, Yanagisawa (Ono 70). **Scorer:** Nakamura (26). **Booked:** Miyamoto, Takahara, Moniwa.

Referee: E. Abd El Fatah (Egypt). **Half-time:** 0-1.

BRAZIL 1, CROATIA 0
Berlin (72,000), Tuesday, June 13, 2006

Brazil (4-2-2-2): Dida, Cafu, Lucio, Juan, Roberto Carlos, Emerson, Ze Roberto, Kaka, Ronaldinho, Adriano, Ronaldo (Robinho 69). **Scorer:** Kaka (44). **Booked:** Emerson.

Croatia (4-4-2): Pletikosa, Simic, Simunic, R. Kovac, Babic, Srna, N. Kovac (Leko 40), Tudor, Kranjcar, Klasnic (Olic 56), Prso. **Booked:** N. Kovac, R. Kovac, Tudor.

Referee: B. Archundia (Mexico). **Half-time:** 1-0.

JAPAN 0, CROATIA 0
Nuremberg (41,000), Sunday, June 18, 2006

Japan (4-4-2): Kawaguchi, Kaji, Nakazawa, Miyamoto, Santos, Nakamura, H. Nakata, Fukunishi (Inamoto 46), Ogasawara, Yanagisawa (Tamada 61), Takahara (Oguro 85). **Booked:** Miyamoto, Kawaguchi, Santos.

Croatia (4-4-2): Pletikosa, Simic, R. Kovac, Simunic, Babic, Srna (Bosnjak 87), Kranjcar (Modric 78), Tudor (Olic 70), N. Kovac, Prso, Klasnic. **Booked:** R. Kovac, Srna.

Referee: F. De Bleeckere (Belgium). **Half-time:** 0-0.

BRAZIL 2, AUSTRALIA 0
Munich (66,000), Sunday, June 18, 2006

Brazil (4-2-2-2): Dida, Cafu, Lucio, Juan, Roberto Carlos, Emerson (Gilberto Silva 72), Ze Roberto, Kaka, Ronaldinho, Adriano (Fred 88), Ronaldo (Robinho 72). **Scorers:** Adriano (49), Fred (90). **Booked:** Cafu, Ronaldo.

Australia (4-5-1): Schwarzer, Neill, Moore (Aloisi 69), Popovic (Bresciano 41), Culina, Emerton, Chipperfield, Grella, Cahill (Kewell 56), Sterjovski, Viduka. **Booked:** Emerton, Culina.

Referee: M. Merk (Germany). **Half-time:** 0-0.

CROATIA 2, AUSTRALIA 2
Stuttgart (52,000), Thursday, June 22, 2006

Croatia (4-4-2): Pletikosa, Simic, Tomas (Klasnic 84), Simunic, Babic, Srna, Tudor, N. Kovac, Kranjcar (Leko 65), Olic (Modric 74), Prso. **Scorers:** Srna (2), N. Kovac (56). **Booked:** Simic, Tudor, Simunic, Pletikosa. **Sent-off:** Simic (85), Simunic (90).

Australia (3-5-2): Kalac, Moore, Neill, Chipperfield (Kennedy 75), Emerton, Cahill, Grella (Aloisi 63), Culina, Sterjovski (Bresciano 71), Kewell, Viduka. **Scorers:** Moore (38 pen), Kewell (79). **Booked:** Emerton. **Sent-off:** Emerton (87).

Referee: G. Poll (England). **Half-time:** 1-1.

JAPAN 1, BRAZIL 4
Dortmund (65,000), Thursday, June 22, 2006

Japan (4-1-3-2): Kawaguchi, Kaji, Tsuboi, Nakazawa, Santos, Inamoto, Nakamura, Ogasawara (K. Nakata 56), H. Nakata, Maki (Takahara 60, Oguro 66), Tamada. **Scorer:** Tamada (34). **Booked:** Kaji.

Brazil (4-4-2): Dida (Rogerio Ceni 81), Cicinho, Lucio, Juan, Gilberto, Kaka (Ze Roberto 71), Juninho Pernambucano, Gilberto Silva, Ronaldinho (Ricardinho 71), Ronaldo, Robinho. **Scorers:** Ronaldo (46, 81), Juninho Pernambucano (53), Gilberto (59). **Booked:** Gilberto.

Referee: E. Poulat (France). **Half-time:** 1-1.

FINAL TABLE

	P	W	D	L	F	A	Pts
BRAZIL	3	3	0	0	7	1	9
AUSTRALIA	3	1	1	1	5	5	4
Croatia	3	0	2	1	2	3	2
Japan	3	0	1	2	2	7	1

GROUP G

SOUTH KOREA 2, TOGO 1
Frankfurt (48,000), Tuesday, June 13, 2006

South Korea (3-4-2-1): Lee Woon-jae, Choi Jin-cheul, Kim Young-chul, Kim Jin-kyu (Ahn Jung-hwan 46), Song Chong-gug, Lee Ho, Lee Eul-yong (Kim Nam-il 68), Lee Young-pyo, Park Ji-sung, Lee Chun-soo, Cho Jae-jin (Kim Sang-sik 84). **Scorers:** Lee Chun-soo (54), Ahn Jung-hwan (72). **Booked:** Kim Young-chul, Lee Chun-soo.

Togo (4-4-2): Agassa, Tchangai, Abalo, Nibombe, Assemoassa (Forson 62), Senaya (Toure 55), Mamam, Romao, Salifou (Aziawonou 86), Mohamed Kader. **Scorer:** Mohamed Kader (31). **Booked:** Abalo, Romao, Tchangai. **Sent-off:** Abalo (53).

Referee: G. Poll (England). **Half-time:** 0-1.

FRANCE 0, SWITZERLAND 0
Stuttgart (52,000), Tuesday, June 13, 2006

France (4-2-3-1): Barthez, Sagnol, Thuram, Gallas, Abidal, Makelele, Vieira, Wiltord (Dhorasoo 84), Ribery (Saha 70), Zidane, Henry. **Booked:** Abidal, Zidane, Sagnol.

Switzerland (4-4-2): Zuberbuehler, Magnin, Senderos, Mueller (Djourou 75), Degen, Cabanas, Vogel, Wicky (Margairaz 82), Barnetta, Frei, Streller (Gygax 56). **Booked:** Magnin, Streller, Degen, Cabanas, Frei.

Referee: V. Ivanov. (Russia). **Half-time:** 0-0.

FRANCE 1, SOUTH KOREA 1
Leipzig (43,000), Sunday, June 18, 2006

France (4-2-3-1): Barthez, Sagnol, Thuram, Gallas, Abidal, Makelele, Vieira, Wiltord (Ribery 60), Zidane (Trezeguet 90), Malouda (Dhorassoo 88), Henry. **Scorer:** Henry (9). **Booked:** Abidal, Zidane.

South Korea (4-4-2): Lee Woon-jae, Kim Dong-jin, Kim Yung-chul, Choi Jin-cheul, Lee Young-pyo, Kim Nam-il, Park Ji-sung, Lee Eul-yong (Seol Ki-hyeon 46), Lee Ho (Kim Sang-sik 69), Lee Chun-soo (Ahn Jung-hwan 72), Cho Jae-jin. **Scorer:** Park Ji-sung (81). **Booked:** Kim Dong-jin, Lee Ho.

Referee: B. Archundia (Mexico). **Half-time:** 1-0.

TOGO 0, SWITZERLAND 2
Dortmund (65,000), Monday, June 19, 2006

Togo (4-4-2): Agassa, Toure, Tchangai, Nibombe, Forson, Dossevi (Senaya 69), Romao, Agboh (Salifou 25), Mamam (Malm 87), Adebayor, Mohamed Kader. **Booked:** Salifou, Adebayor, Romao.

Switzerland (4-4-2): Zuberbuehler, Magnin, Mueller, Senderos, Degen, Cabanas (Streller 77), Vogel, Barnetta, Wicky, Gygax (Yakin 46), Frei (Lustrinelli 87). **Scorers:** Frei (16), Barnetta (88).

Referee: C. Amarilla (Paraguay). **Half-time:** 0-1.

SWITZERLAND 2, SOUTH KOREA 0
Hanover (43,000), Friday, June 23, 2006

Switzerland (4-4-2): Zuberbuehler, Degen, Muller, Senderos (Djourou 53), Spycher, Vogel, Barnetta, Cabanas, Yakin (Margairaz 71), Wicky (Behrami 88), Frei. **Scorers:** Senderos (23), Frei (77). **Booked:** Senderos, Yakin, Wicky, Spycher, Djourou.

South Korea (4-1-4-1): Lee Woon-jae, Lee Young-pyo (Ahn Jung-hwan 63), Choi Jin-cheul, Kim Jin-kyu, Kim Dong-jin, Kim Nam-il, Park Ji-sung, Lee Chun-soo, Lee Ho, Park Chu-young (Seol Ki-hyeon 66), Cho Jae-jin. **Booked:** Park Chu-young, Kim Jin-kyu, Lee Chun-soo, Choi Jin-cheul, Ahn Jung-hwan.

Referee: H. Elizondo (Argentina). **Half-time:** 1-0.

TOGO 0, FRANCE 2
Cologne (45,000), Friday, June 23, 2006

Togo (4-4-2): Agassa, Tchangai, Abalo, Nibombe, Forson, Senaya, Salifou, Aziawonou, Mamam (Ulufade 59), Mohamed Kader, Adebayor (Dossevi 75). **Booked:** Aziawonou, Mamam, Salifou.

France (4-4-2): Barthez, Sagnol, Thuram, Gallas, Silvestre, Ribery (Govou 77), Vieira (Diarra 81), Makelele, Malouda (Wiltord 74), Trezeguet, Henry. **Scorers:** Vieira (55), Henry (61). **Booked:** Makelele.

Referee: J. Larrionda (Uruguay). **Half-time:** 0-0.

FINAL TABLE

	P	W	D	L	F	A	Pts
SWITZERLAND	3	2	1	0	4	0	7
FRANCE	3	1	2	0	3	1	5
South Korea	3	1	1	1	3	4	4
Togo	3	0	0	3	1	6	0

GROUP H

SPAIN 4, UKRAINE 0
Leipzig (43,000), Wednesday, June 14, 2006

Spain (4-1-3-2): Casillas, Ramos, Pablo, Puyol, Pernia, Marcos Senna, Xabi Alonso (Albelda 55), Xavi, Luis Garcia (Fabregas 77), Villa (Raul 55), Torres. **Scorers:** Xabi Alonso (13), Villa (17, 48 pen), Torres (81).

Ukraine (4-4-2): Shovkovskyi, Nesmachnyi, Rusol, Vashchuk, Yezerskyi, Gusev (Vorobey 46), Gusin (Shelayev 46), Tymoschuk, Rotan (Rebrov 64), Shevchenko, Voronin. **Booked:** Rusol, Yezerskyi. **Sent-off:** Vashchuk (47).

Referee: M. Busacca (Switzerland). **Half-time:** 2-0.

TUNISIA 2, SAUDI ARABIA 2
Munich (66,000), Wednesday, June 14, 2006

Tunisia (4-4-2): Boumnijel, Trabelski, Jaidi, Haggui, Jemmali, Bouazizi (Nafti 55), Namouchi, Mnari, Chedli (Ghodhbane 69), Jaziri, Chikhaoui (Essediri 82). **Scorers:** Jaziri (23), Jaidi (90). **Booked:** Haggui, Bouazizi, Chedli, Chikhaoui.

Saudi Arabia (3-5-2): Zaid, Dokhi, Tukar, Al-Montashari, Al-Ghamdi, Aziz, Kariri, Al-Temyat (Al-Hawsawi 67), Sulimani, Noor (Ameen 75), Al-Kahtani (Al-Jaber 82). **Scorers:** Al-Kahtani (57), Al-Jaber (84).

Referee: M. Shield (Australia). **Half-time:** 1-0.

SAUDI ARABIA 0, UKRAINE 4
Hamburg (50,000), Monday, June 19, 2006

Saudi Arabia (4-5-1): Zaid, Dokhi (Khathran 55), Tukar, Al-Montashari, Sulimani, Al-Ghamdi, Ameen (Al-Hawsawi 55), Noor (Al-Jaber 76), Kariri, Aziz, Al Kahatani. **Booked:** Dokhi, Al-Ghamdi, Kariri.

Ukraine (4-4-2): Shovkovskyi, Nesmachnyi, Rusol, Sviderskyi, Rebrov (Rotan 71), Gusev, Shelayev, Tymoschuk, Kalinichenko, Voronin (Gusin 78), Shevchenko (Milevskiy 86). **Scorers:** Rusol (4), Rebrov (36), Shevchenko (46), Kalinichenko (84). **Booked:** Nesmachnyi, Kalinichenko, Sviderskyi.

Referee: G. Poll (England). **Half-time:** 0-2.

SPAIN 3, TUNISIA 1
Stuttgart (47,000), Monday, June 19, 2006

Spain (4-1-3-2): Casillas, Ramos, Pablo, Puyol, Pernia, Marcos Senna (Fabregas 46), Xabi Alonso, Xavi, Luis Garcia (Raul 46), Villa (Joaquin 56), Torres. **Scorers:** Raul (71), Torres (76, 90 pen). **Booked:** Puyol, Fabregas.

Tunisia (4-3-2-1): Boumnijel, Trabelsi, Jaidi, Haggui, Ayari (Yahia 57), Bouazizi (Ghodhbane 57), Nafti, Mnari, Namouchi, Chedli (Guemamdia 79), Jaziri. **Scorer:** Mnari (8). **Booked:** Ayari, Trabelsi, Jaidi, Guemandia, Jaziri, Mnari.

Referee: C. Simon (Brazil). **Half-time:** 0-1.

SAUDI ARABIA 0, SPAIN 1
Kaiserslautern (46,000), Friday, June 23, 2006

Saudi Arabia (4-4-2): Zaid, Dokhi, Aziz (Al-Temyat 13), Tukar, Khathran, Noor, Kariri, Sulimani (Massad 81), Al-Montashari, Al-Harthi, Al-Jaber (Al-Hawsawi 68). **Booked:** Al-Jaber, Al-Temyat.

Spain (4-1-4-1): Canizares, Salgado, Juanito, Marchena, Lopez, Albelda, Joaquin, Fabregas (Xavi 66), Iniesta, Reyes (Torres 70), Raul (Villa 46). **Scorer:** Juanito (36). **Booked:** Albelda, Reyes, Marchena.

Referee: C. Codjia (Benin). **Half-time:** 0-1.

UKRAINE 1, TUNISIA 0
Berlin (72,000), Friday, June 23, 2006

Ukraine (4-4-2): Shovkovskyi, Rusol, Nesmachnyi, Sviderskyi, Gusev, Tymoschuk, Shelayev, Kalinichenko (Gusin 75), Rebrov (Vorobey 55), Shevchenko (Milevskiy 88), Voronin. **Scorer:** Shevchenko (70 pen). **Booked:** Sviderskyi, Shelayev, Tymoschuk, Rusol.

Tunisia (4-3-2-1): Boumnijel, Trabelsi, Jaidi, Haggui, Ayari, Bouazizi (Santos 79), Nafti (Ghodhbane 90), Mnari, Namouchi, Chedli (Ben Saada 79), Jaziri. **Booked:** Jaziri, Bouazizi, Jaidi. **Sent-off:** Jaziri (45).

Referee: C. Amarilla (Paraguay). **Half-time:** 0-0.

FINAL TABLE

	P	W	D	L	F	A	Pts
SPAIN	3	3	0	0	8	1	9
UKRAINE	3	2	0	1	5	4	6
Tunisia	3	0	1	2	3	6	1
Saudi Arabia	3	0	1	2	2	7	1

SECOND ROUND

GERMANY 2, SWEDEN 0
Munich (66,000), Saturday, June 24, 2006

Germany (4-4-2): Lehmann, Friedrich, Mertesacker, Metzelder, Lahm, Schneider, Ballack, Frings (Kehl 85), Schweinsteiger (Borowski 72), Podolski (Neuville 74), Klose. **Scorer:** Podolski (4, 12). **Booked:** Frings.

Sweden (4-4-2): Isaksson, Alexandersson, Mellberg, Lucic, Edman, Jonson (Wilhelmsson 52), Linderoth, Kallstrom (Hansson 39), Ljungberg, Ibrahimovic (Allback 72), Larsson. **Booked:** Lucic, Jonson, Allback. **Sent-off:** Lucic (35).

Referee: C. Simon (Brazil). **Half-time:** 2-0.

ARGENTINA 2, MEXICO 1 (aet)
Leipzig (43,000), Saturday, June 24, 2006

Argentina (4-1-3-2): Abbondanzieri, Scaloni, Ayala, Heinze, Sorin, Mascherano, Rodriguez, Cambiasso (Aimar 76), Riquelme, Crespo (Tevez 76), Saviola (Messi 84). **Scorers:** Crespo (10), Rodriguez (98). **Booked:** Heinze, Sorin.

Mexico (3-5-2): Sanchez, Marquez, Osorio, Salcido, Castro, Mendez, Guardado (Pineda 65), Pardo (Torrado 38), Morales (Zinha 74), Borgetti, Fonseca. **Scorer:** Marquez (6). **Booked:** Marquez, Castro, Torrado, Fonseca.

Referee: M. Busacca (Switzerland). **Half-time:** 1-1.

ENGLAND 1, ECUADOR 0
Stuttgart (52,000), Sunday, June 25, 2006

England (4-1-4-1): Robinson (Tottenham), Hargreaves (Bayern Munich), Ferdinand (Manchester Utd.), Terry (Chelsea), A. Cole (Arsenal), Carrick (Tottenham), Beckham (Real Madrid) (Lennon, Tottenham, 87), Gerrard (Liverpool) (Downing, Middlesbrough, 90), Lampard (Chelsea), J. Cole (Chelsea) (Carragher, Liverpool, 77), Rooney (Manchester Utd.). **Scorer:** Beckham (60). **Booked:** Terry, Robinson, Carragher.

Ecuador (4-4-2): Mora, De la Cruz, Hurtado, Espinoza, Reasco, Valencia, Castillo, E. Tenorio (Lara 69), Mendez, C. Tenorio (Kaviedes 72), Delgado. **Booked:** Valencia, C. Tenorio, De la Cruz.

Referee: F. De Bleeckere (Belgium). **Half-time:** 0-0

PORTUGAL 1, HOLLAND 0
Nuremberg (41,000), Sunday, June 25, 2006

Portugal (4-5-1): Ricardo, Miguel, Fernando Meira, Ricardo Carvalho, Nuno Valente, Maniche, Deco, Costinha, Figo (Tiago 84), Ronaldo (Simao Sabrosa 34), Pauleta (Petit 46). **Scorer:** Maniche (23). **Booked:** Maniche, Costinha, Petit, Figo, Deco, Ricardo, Nuno Valente. **Sent-off:** Costinha (46), Deco (78).

Holland (4-3-3): Van der Sar, Boulahrouz, Mathijsen (Van der Vaart 56), Ooijer, Van Bronckhorst, Cocu (Vennegoor of Hesselink 84), Sneijder, Van Bommel (Heitinga 67), Van Persie, Kuyt, Robben. **Booked:** Van Bommel, Boulahrouz, Van Bronckhorst, Sneijder, Van der Vaart. **Sent-off:** Boulahrouz (63), Van Bronckhorst (90).

Referee: V. Ivanov (Russia). **Half-time:** 1-0.

ITALY 1, AUSTRALIA 0
Kaiserslautern (46,000), Monday, June 26, 2006

Italy (4-4-2): Buffon, Zambrotta, Cannavaro, Materazzi, Grosso, Perrotta, Pirlo, Gattuso, Del Piero (Totti 75), Gilardino (Iaquinta 46), Toni (Barzagli 56). **Scorer:** Totti (90 pen). **Booked:** Grosso, Gattuso, Zambrotta. **Sent-off:** Materazzi (50).

Australia (3-5-1-1): Schwarzer, Moore, Neill, Chipperfield, Sterjovski (Aloisi 81), Culina, Grella, Wilkshire, Bresciano, Cahill, Viduka. **Booked:** Grella, Cahill, Wilkshire.

Referee: L. Medina Cantalejo (Spain). **Half-time:** 0-0.

SWITZERLAND 0, UKRAINE 0

(aet, Ukraine won 3-0 on pens)

Cologne (45,000), Monday, June 26, 2006

Switzerland (4-4-2): Zuberbuehler, Degen, Djourou (Grichting 34), Mueller, Magnin, Vogel, Barnetta, Cabanas, Yakin (Streller 64), Wicky, Frei (Lustrinelli 117). **Booked:** Barnetta.

Ukraine (4-4-2): Shovkovskyi, Gusin, Vashchuk, Nesmachnyi, Gusev, Tymoschuk, Shelayev, Vorobey (Rebrov 94), Kalinichenko (Rotan, 75), Shevchenko, Voronin (Milevskiy 111).

Referee: B. Archundia (Mexico). **Half-time:** 0-0.

BRAZIL 3, GHANA 0

Dortmund (65,000), Tuesday, June 27, 2006

Brazil (4-2-2-2): Dida, Cafu, Lucio, Juan, Roberto Carlos, Emerson (Gilberto Silva 46), Ze Roberto, Kaka (Ricardinho 83), Ronaldinho, Ronaldo, Adriano (Juninho Pernambucano 61). **Scorers:** Ronaldo (5), Adriano (46), Ze Roberto (84). **Booked:** Adriano, Juan.

Ghana (4-4-2): Kingson, Pantsil, Mensah, Shilla, Pappoe, Draman, Appiah, E. Addo (Boateng 60), Muntari, Amoah (Tachie-Mensah 70), Gyan. **Booked:** Appiah, Muntari, Pantsil, E. Addo, Gyan. **Sent-off:** Gyan (81).

Referee: L. Michel (Slovakia). **Half-time:** 2-0.

SPAIN 1, FRANCE 3

Hanover (43,000), Tuesday, June 27, 2006

Spain (4-3-1-2): Casillas, Ramos, Pablo, Puyol, Pernia, Fabregas, Xabi Alonso, Xavi (Macos Senna 72), Raul (Luis Garcia 54), Villa (Joaquin 54), Torres. **Scorer:** Villa (28 pen). **Booked:** Puyol.

France (4-2-3-1): Barthez, Sagnol, Thuram, Gallas, Abidal, Makelele, Ribery, Malouda (Govou 74), Zidane, Henry. **Scorers:** Ribery (41), Vieira (83), Zidane (90). **Booked:** Vieira, Ribery, Zidane.

Referee: R. Rosetti (Italy). **Half-time:** 1-1.

QUARTER-FINALS

GERMANY 1, ARGENTINA 1

(aet, Germany won 4-2 on pens)

Berlin (72,000), Friday, June 30, 2006

Germany (4-4-2): Lehmann, Friedrich, Mertesacker, Metzelder, Lahm, Schneider (Odonkor 62), Ballack, Frings, Schweinsteiger (Bowowski 74), Podolski, Klose (Neuville 86). **Scorer:** Klose (80). **Booked:** Podolski, Odonkor, Friedrich.

Argentina (4-4-2): Abbondanzieri (Franco 71), Coloccini, Ayala, Heinze, Sorin, Gonzalez, Mascherano, Riquelme (Cambiasso 72), Rodriguez, Tevez, Crespo (Cruz 78). **Scorer:** Ayala (49). **Booked:** Sorin, Mascherano, Rodriguez, Cruz. **Sent-off:** Cufre.

Referee: L. Michel (Slovakia). **Half-time:** 0-0.

ITALY 3, UKRAINE 0

Hamburg (50,000), Friday, June 30, 2006

Italy (4-4-1-1): Buffon, Zambrotta, Cannavaro, Barzagli, Grosso, Camoranesi (Oddo 68), Pirlo (Barone 68), Gattuso (Zaccardo 77), Perrotta, Totti, Toni. **Scorers:** Zambrotta (6), Toni (59, 69).

Ukraine (4-4-2): Shovkovskyi, Gusev, Sviderskyi (Vorobey 20), Rusol (Vashchuk 47), Nesmachnyi, Shelayev, Tymoschuk, Gusin, Kalinichenko, Milevskiy (Belik 72), Shevchenko. **Booked:** Sviderskyi, Kalinichenko, Milevskiy.

Referee: F. De Bleeckere (Belgium). **Half-time:** 1-0.

ENGLAND 0, PORTUGAL 0

(aet, Portugal won 3-1 on pens)

Gelsenkirchen (52,000), Saturday, July 1, 2006

England (4-5-1): Robinson (Tottenham), Neville (Manchester Utd.), Ferdinand (Manchester Utd.), Terry (Chelsea), A. Cole (Arsenal), Beckham (Real Madrid) (Lennon, Tottenham, 52) (Carragher, Liverpool 119), Gerrard (Liverpool), Hargreaves (Bayern Munich), Lampard (Chelsea), J. Cole (Chelsea) (Crouch, Liverpool 65), Rooney (Manchester Utd.). **Booked:** Terry, Hargreaves. **Sent-off:** Rooney (62). Sven-Goran Eriksson's last game as England coach.

Portugal (4-5-1): Ricardo, Miguel, Fernando Meira, Ricardo Carvalho, Nuno Valente, Figo (Helder Postiga 86), Tiago (Hugo Viana 74), Petit, Maniche, Ronaldo, Pauleta (Simao Sabrosa 63). **Booked:** Petit, Ricardo Carvalho.

Referee: H. Elizondo (Argentina). **Half-time:** 0-0.

BRAZIL 0, FRANCE 1

Frankfurt (48,000), Saturday, July 1, 2006

Brazil (4-1-2-2-1): Dida, Cafu (Cicinho 76), Lucio, Juan, Roberto Carlos, Gilberto Silva, Junior Pernambucano, (Adriano 63), Ze Roberto, Kaka (Robinho 79), Ronaldinho, Ronaldo. **Booked:** Cafu, Juan, Ronaldo, Lucio.

France (4-2-3-1): Barthez, Sagnol, Thuram, Gallas, Abidal, Makelele, Vieira, Ribery (Govou 76), Malouda, Zidane, Henry (Saha 86). **Scorer:** Henry (57). **Booked:** Sagnol, Saha, Thuram.

Referee: L. Medina Cantalejo (Spain). **Half-time:** 0-0.

SEMI-FINALS

GERMANY 0, ITALY 2 (aet)

Dortmund (65,000), Tuesday, July 4, 2006

Germany (4-4-2): Lehmann, Friedrich, Mertesacker, Metzelder, Lahm, Schneider (Odonkor 83), Ballack, Kehl, Borowski (Schweinsteiger 73), Podolski, Klose (Neuville 111). **Booked:** Borowski, Metzelder.

Italy (4-4-1-1): Buffon, Zambrotta, Cannavaro, Materazzi, Grosso, Perrotta (Del Piero 104), Pirlo, Gattuso, Camoranesi (Iaquinta 91), Totti, Toni (Gilardino 74). **Scorers:** Grosso (119), Del Piero (120). **Booked:** Camorensi.

Referee: B. Archundia (Mexico). **Half-time:** 0-0.

PORTUGAL 0, FRANCE 1

Munich (66,000), Wednesday, July 5, 2006

Portugal (4-2-3-1): Ricardo, Miguel (Paulo Ferreira 62), Fernando Meira, Ricardo Carvalho, Nuno Valente, Costinha (Helder Postiga 75), Maniche, Figo, Deco, Ronaldo, Pauleta (Simao Sabrosa 68). **Booked:** Ricardo Carvalho.

France (4-2-3-1): Barthez, Sagnol, Thuram, Gallas, Abidal, Makelele, Vieira, Ribery (Govou 72), Malouda, Zidane, Henry (Saha 85). **Scorer:** Zidane (33 pen). **Booked:** Saha.

Referee: J. Larrionda (Uruguay). **Half-time:** 0-1.

THIRD PLACE PLAY-OFF

GERMANY 3, PORTUGAL 1
Stuttgart (52,000), Saturday, July 8, 2006

Germany (4-4-2): Kahn, Jansen, Nowotny, Metzelder, Lahm, Schneider, Frings, Kehl, Schweinsteiger (Hitzlsperger 79), Podolski (Hanke 71), Klose (Neuville 65). **Scorers:** Schweinsteiger (56, 78), Petit (60 og). **Booked:** Frings, Schweinsteiger.

Portugal (4-2-3-1): Ricardo, Paulo Ferreira, Ricardo Costa, Fernando Meira, Nuno Valente (Nuno Gomes 69), Costinha (Petit 46), Maniche, Ronaldo, Deco, Simao Sabrosa, Pauleta (Figo 77). **Scorer:** Gomes (88). **Booked:** Ricardo Costa, Costinha, Paulo Ferreira.

Referee: T. Kamikawa (Japan). **Half-time:** 0-0.

FINAL

ITALY 1, FRANCE 1
(aet, Italy won 5-3 on pens)
Berlin (69,000), Sunday, July 9, 2006

Italy (4-4-1-1): Buffon, Zambrotta, Cannavaro (capt), Materazzi, Grosso, Perrotta (De Rossi 61), Pirlo, Gattuso, Camoranesi (Del Piero 86), Totti (Iaquinta 61), Toni. **Scorer:** Materazzi (19). **Booked:** Zambrotta. **Coach:** Marcello Lippi.

France (4-2-3-1): Barthez, Sagnol, Thuram, Gallas, Abidal, Makelele, Vieira (Diarra 56), Ribery (Trezeguet 100), Malouda, Zidane (capt), Henry (Wiltord 107). **Scorer:** Zidane (7 pen). **Booked:** Sagnol, Makelele, Malouda. **Sent-off:** Zidane (110). **Coach:** Raymond Domenech.

Penalty shoot-out: Pirlo 1-0, Wiltord 1-1, Materazzi 2-1, Trezeguet missed, De Rossi 3-1, Abidal 3-2, Del Piero 4-2, Sagnol 4-3, Grosso 5-3.

Referee: H. Elizondo (Argentina). **Half-time:** 1-1.

WORLD CUP FACTS AND FIGURES

Match venues: Berlin (72,000), Cologne (45,000), Dortmund (65,000), Frankfurt (48,000), Gelsenkirchen (52,000), Hamburg (50,000), Hanover (43,000), Kaiserslautern (46,000), Leipzig (43,000), Munich (66,000), Nuremberg (41,000), Stuttgart (52,000).

Glory for Italy: Italy became the most successful European team in the World Cup with their fourth triumph – one behind Brazil – after victories in 1934, 1938 and 1982. Captain Fabio Cannavaro lifted the trophy on his 100th international appearance.

Sharing it out: Italy's 12 goals were shared by ten players, matching the number of marksmen for France in their 16-goal total in 1982. Marco Materazzi and Luca Toni were the two Italy players to net twice.

Golden Ball: Zinedine Zidane was named the best player of the tournament, topping a poll of journalists carried out at half-time of the Final against Italy – before he was sent off for head-butting Materazzi.

Red card shame: The France captain was the fourth player to be dismissed in a World Cup Final. Argentina's Pedro Monzon and Gustavo Dezotti saw red against West Germany in 1990 and Marcel Desailly (France) walked against Brazil in 1998.

Record number of cards: Zidane's sending-off was the 28th of the tournament. There was also a record number, 345, of yellow cards handed out.

Golden Shoe: Germany's Miroslav Klose collected the award for the tournament's top scorer with five goals, lowest winning total since the Finals in Chile in 1962. The silver shoe show went to Argentina's Hernan Crespo who netted three times, the same as Brazil's Ronaldo but from a shorter time spent on the pitch.

Ronaldo's record: The striker overtook Gerd Muller as the highest aggregate scorer in World Cup Finals during their 3-0 win over Ghana in the first knock-out round. Ronaldo's goal took his total to 15 in three tournaments, one more than Muller's tally for West Germany in two in the 1970s.

Lev Yashin Award: Italy's Gianluigi Buffon was named the tournament's best goalkeeper. He was beaten only by an own goal by Cristian Zaccardo against the U.S.A. and by Zinedine Zidane's penalty in the Final.

Sportsmanship: Brazil and Spain shared FIFA's Fair Play award for the best record of fair play and sportsmanship.

Entertainment: Portugal were named the most entertaining team of the tournament, despite receiving the most cards – 24 yellow and two red.

Rising star: Lukas Podolski, Germany's 20-year-old striker, won FIFA's Young Player award, beating Portugal's Cristiano Ronaldo who lost the chance of winning by his behaviour against England in the quarter-finals.

Shooting star: Marcus Allback's header for Sweden in the 2-2 group match draw with England was the 2000th goal in the history of the tournament. The first, by Lucien Laurent for France against Mexico in Montevideo, was in 1930.

Terry's world: John Terry was the one England player named in FIFA's All-Star squad from the tournament. Goalkeepers – Buffon (Italy), Lehmann (Germany), Ricardo (Portugal). Defenders – Ayala (Argentina), Cannavaro (Italy), Lahm (Germany), Terry (England), Ricardo Carvalho (Portugal), Thuram (France), Zambrotta (Italy). Midfielders – Ballack (Germany), Figo (Portugal), Gattuso (Italy), Maniche (Portugal), Pirlo (Italy), Vieira (Arsenal), Ze Roberto (Brazil), Zidane (France). Strikers – Crespo (Argentina), Henry (France), Klose (Germany), Toni (Italy), Totti (Italy).

England squad: 1 Robinson (Tottenham), 2 Neville (Manchester Utd.), 3 Ashley Cole (Arsenal), 4 Gerrard (Liverpool), 5 Ferdinand (Manchester Utd.), 6 Terry (Chelsea), 7 Beckham (Real Madrid), 8 Lampard (Chelsea), 9 Rooney (Manchester Utd.), 10 Owen (Newcastle Utd.), 11 Joe Cole (Chelsea), 12 Campbell (Arsenal), 13 James (Manchester City), 14 Bridge (Chelsea), 15 Carragher (Liverpool), 16 Hargreaves (Bayern Munich), 17 Jenas (Tottenham), 18 Carrick (Tottenham), 19 Lennon (Tottenham), 20 Downing (Middlesbrough), 21 Crouch (Liverpool), 22 Carson (Liverpool), 23 Walcott (Arsenal).

Penalty woe: England's defeat by Portugal in the quarter-finals was their fifth on penalties in major tournaments. They lost previous World Cup shoot-outs to West Germany (semi-finals, 1990) and Argentina (second round, 1998) and suffered European Championship heartache against Germany (semi-finals, 1996) and Portugal (quarter-finals, 2004).

First for Beckham: A match-winning free-kick against Ecuador enabled David Beckham to become the first England player to score in three tournaments. He had previously netted against Colombia in 1998 and from the penalty spot against Argentina four years later.

Rooney's red card: Wayne Rooney became the third England player sent off in the World Cup Finals. Ray Wilkins was dismissed against Morocco in 1986 and David Beckham saw red against Argentina in 1998.

Poll axed: Premiership referee Graham Poll had an unhappy tournament – just as he did in 2002. After taking charge of South Korea-Togo and Saudi Arabia-Ukraine, Poll showed three yellow cards to Josip Simunic before sending off the Croatia defender against Australia and was not retained for the later stages of the tournament. Four years earlier, he disallowed two Italy goals against Croatia on his Danish linesman's flag, was criticised by the Italians and did not take charge of another game.

Motty's milestone: John Motson commentated on a record sixth World Cup Final for the BBC, overtaking the total he shared with the late Kenneth Wolstenholme.

WORLD CUP SUMMARIES 1930-2002

1930 IN URUGUAY

WINNERS: Uruguay. RUNNERS-UP: Argentina. THIRD: U.S.A. FOURTH: Yugoslavia.
Other countries taking part: Belgium, Bolivia, Brazil, Chile, France, Mexico, Paraguay, Peru, Rumania, Yugoslavia. **Total entries**: 13.
Venue: All matches played in Montevideo.
Top scorer: Stabile (Argentina) 8 goals.
Final (30.7.30): **Uruguay 4** (Dorado 12, Cea 55, Iriarte 64, Castro 89), **Argentina 2** (Peucelle 29, Stabile 35). **Att**: 90,000.
Uruguay: Ballesteros; Nasazzi (Capt.), Mascheroni, Andrade, Fernandez, Gestido, Dorado, Scarone, Castro, Cea, Iriarte.
Argentina: Botasso; Della Torre, Paternoster, Evaristo (J.), Monti, Suarez, Peucelle, Varallo, Stabile, Ferreira (Capt.), Evaristo (M.).
Referee: Langenus (Belgium). **Half-time**: 1-2.

1934 IN ITALY

WINNERS: Italy. RUNNERS-UP: Czechoslovakia. THIRD: Germany. FOURTH: Austria.
Other countries in finals: Argentina, Austria, Belgium, Brazil, Egypt, France, Holland, Hungary, Rumania, Spain, Sweden, Switzerland, U.S.A. **Total entries**: 29 (16 qualifiers).
Venues: Bologna, Florence, Genoa, Milan, Naples, Rome, Trieste, Turin.
Top scorers: Conen (Germany), Nejedly (Czechoslovakia), Schiavio (Italy), each 4 goals.
Final (Rome, 10.6.34): **Italy 2** (Orsi 82, Schiavio 97), **Czechoslovakia 1** (Puc 70), **after extra time. Att**: 50,000.
Italy: Combi (Capt.); Monzeglio, Allemandi, Ferraris, Monti, Bertolini, Guaita, Meazza, Schiavio, Ferrari, Orsi.
Czechoslovakia: Planicka (Capt.); Zenisek, Ctyroky, Kostalek, Cambal, Krcil, Junek, Svoboda, Sobotka, Nejedly, Puc.
Referee: Eklind (Sweden). **Half-time**: 0-0. **90 mins**: 1-1.

1938 IN FRANCE

WINNERS: Italy. RUNNERS-UP: Hungary. THIRD: Brazil. FOURTH: Sweden.
Other countries in finals: Belgium, Cuba, Czechoslovakia, Dutch East Indies, France, Germany, Holland, Norway, Poland, Rumania, Sweden, Switzerland. **Total entries**: 25 (15 qualifiers).
Venues: Antibes, Bordeaux, Le Havre, Lille, Marseilles, Paris, Reims, Strasbourg, Toulouse.
Top scorer: Leonidas (Brazil) 8 goals.
Final (Paris, 19.6.38): **Italy 4** (Colaussi 6, 36, Piola 15, 81), **Hungary 2** (Titkos 7, Sarosi 65). **Att**: 45,000.
Italy: Olivieri; Foni, Rava, Serantoni, Andreolo, Locatelli, Biavati, Meazza (Capt.), Piola, Ferrari, Colaussi.
Hungary: Szabo; Polgar, Biro, Szalay, Szucs, Lazar, Sas, Vincze, Sarosi (Capt.), Szengeller, Titkos.
Referee: Capdeville (France). **Half-time**: 3-1.

1950 IN BRAZIL

WINNERS: Uruguay. RUNNERS-UP: Brazil. THIRD: Sweden. FOURTH: Spain.
Other countries in finals: Bolivia, Chile, England, Italy, Mexico, Paraguay, Spain, Switzerland, U.S.A., Yugoslavia. **Total entries**: 29 (13 qualifiers).
Venues: Belo Horizonte, Curitiba, Porto Alegre, Recife, Rio de Janeiro, Sao Paulo.
Top scorer: Ademir (Brazil) 9 goals.
Deciding Match (Rio de Janeiro, 16.7.50): **Uruguay 2** (Schiaffino 64, Ghiggia 79), **Brazil 1** (Friaca 47). **Att**: 199,850.

(For the only time, the World Cup was decided on a final pool system, in which the winners of the four qualifying groups met in a six-match series. So, unlike previous and subsequent tournaments, there was no official Final as such, but Uruguay v Brazil was the deciding final match in the final pool).
Uruguay: Maspoli; Gonzales, Tejera, Gambetta, Varela (Capt.), Andrade, Ghiggia, Perez, Miguez, Schiaffino, Moran.
Brazil: Barbosa; Augusto (Capt.), Juvenal, Bauer, Danilo, Bigode, Friaca, Zizinho, Ademir, Jair, Chico.
Referee: Reader (England). **Half-time:** 0-0.

1954 IN SWITZERLAND

WINNERS: West Germany. RUNNERS-UP: Hungary. THIRD: Austria. FOURTH: Uruguay.
Other countries in finals: Belgium, Brazil, Czechoslovakia, England, France, Italy, Korea, Mexico, Scotland, Switzerland, Turkey, Uruguay, Yugoslavia. **Total entries:** 35 (16 qualifiers).
Venues: Basle, Berne, Geneva, Lausanne, Lugano, Zurich.
Top scorer: Kocsis (Hungary) 11 goals.
Final (Berne, 4.7.54): **West Germany 3** (Morlock 12, Rahn 17, 84), **Hungary 2** (Puskas 4, Czibor 9). **Att:** 60,000.
West Germany: Turek; Posipal, Kohlmeyer, Eckel, Liebrich, Mai, Rahn, Morlock, Walter (O.), Walter (F.) (Capt.), Schaefer.
Hungary: Grosics; Buzansky, Lantos, Bozsik, Lorant, Zakarias, Czibor, Kocsis, Hidegkuti, Puskas (Capt.), Toth (J.).
Referee: Ling (England). **Half-time:** 2-2.

1958 IN SWEDEN

WINNERS: Brazil. RUNNERS-UP: Sweden. THIRD: France. FOURTH: West Germany.
Other countries in finals: Argentina, Austria, Czechoslovakia, England, Hungary, Mexico, Northern Ireland, Paraguay, Scotland, Soviet Union, Wales, West Germany, Yugoslavia. **Total entries:** 47 (16 qualifiers).
Venues: Boras, Eskilstuna, Gothenburg, Halmstad, Helsingborg, Malmo, Norrkoping, Orebro, Sandviken, Stockholm, Vasteras.
Top scorer: Fontaine (France) 13 goals.
Final (Stockholm, 29.6.58): **Brazil 5** (Vava 10, 32, Pele 55, 88, Zagalo 76), **Sweden 2** (Liedholm 4, Simonsson 83). **Att:** 49,737.
Brazil: Gilmar; Santos (D.), Santos (N.), Zito, Bellini (Capt.), Orlando, Garrincha, Didi, Vava, Pele, Zagalo.
Sweden: Svensson; Bergmark, Axbom, Boerjesson, Gustavsson, Parling, Hamrin, Gren, Simonsson, Liedholm (Capt.), Skoglund.
Referee: Guigue (France). **Half-time:** 2-1.

1962 IN CHILE

WINNERS: Brazil. RUNNERS-UP: Czechoslovakia. THIRD: Chile. FOURTH: Yugoslavia.
Other countries in finals: Argentina, Bulgaria, Colombia, England, Hungary, Italy, Mexico, Soviet Union, Spain, Switzerland, Uruguay, West Germany, Yugoslavia. **Total entries:** 53 (16 qualifiers).
Venues: Arica, Rancagua, Santiago, Vina del Mar.
Top scorer: Jerkovic (Yugoslavia), 5 goals.
Final (Santiago, 17.6.62): **Brazil 3** (Amarildo 17, Zito 69, Vava 77), **Czechoslovakia 1** (Masopust 16). **Att:** 68,679.
Brazil: Gilmar; Santos (D.), Mauro (Capt.), Zozimo, Santos (N.), Zito, Didi, Garrincha, Vava, Amarildo, Zagalo.
Czechoslovakia: Schroiff; Tichy, Novak, Pluskal, Popluhar, Masopust (Capt.), Pospichal, Scherer, Kvasnak, Kadraba, Jelinek.
Referee: Latychev (Soviet Union). **Half-time:** 1-1.

1966 IN ENGLAND

WINNERS: England. RUNNERS-UP: West Germany. THIRD: Portugal. FOURTH: USSR.
Other countries in finals: Argentina, Brazil, Bulgaria, Chile, France, Hungary, Italy, Mexico, North Korea, Soviet Union, Spain, Switzerland, Uruguay. **Total entries**: 53 (16 qualifiers).
Venues: Birmingham (Villa Park), Liverpool (Goodison Park), London (Wembley and White City), Manchester (Old Trafford), Middlesbrough, Sheffield (Hillsborough), Sunderland.
Top scorer: Eusebio (Portugal) 9 goals.
Final (Wembley, 30.7.66): **England 4** (Hurst 19, 100, 120, Peters 78), **West Germany 2** (Haller 13, Weber 89), **after extra time. Att**: 93,802.
England: Banks; Cohen, Wilson, Stiles, Charlton (J.), Moore (Capt.), Ball, Hurst, Hunt, Charlton (R.), Peters.
West Germany: Tilkowski; Hottges, Schnellinger, Beckenbauer, Schulz, Weber, Haller, Held, Seeler (Capt.), Overath, Emmerich.
Referee: Dienst (Switzerland). **Half-time**: 1-1. **90 mins**: 2-2.

1970 IN MEXICO

WINNERS: Brazil. RUNNERS-UP: Italy. THIRD: West Germany. FOURTH: Uruguay.
Other countries in finals: Belgium, Bulgaria, Czechoslovakia, El Salvador, England, Israel, Mexico, Morocco, Peru, Romania, Soviet Union, Sweden, Uruguay. **Total entries**: 68 (16 qualifiers).
Venues: Guadalajara, Leon, Mexico City, Puebla, Toluca.
Top scorer: Muller (West Germany) 10 goals.
Final (Mexico City, 21.6.70): **Brazil 4** (Pele 18, Gerson 66, Jairzinho 71, Carlos Alberto 87), **Italy 1** (Boninsegna 38). **Att**: 107,412.
Brazil: Felix; Carlos Alberto (Capt.), Brito, Piazza, Everaldo, Clodoaldo, Gerson, Jairzinho, Tostao, Pele, Rivelino.
Italy: Albertosi; Burgnich, Facchetti (Capt.), Cera, Rosato, Bertini (Juliano 72), Domenghini, De Sisti, Mazzola, Boninsegna (Rivera 84), Riva.
Referee: Glockner (East Germany). **Half-time**: 1-1.

1974 IN WEST GERMANY

WINNERS: West Germany. RUNNERS-UP: Holland. THIRD: Poland. FOURTH: Brazil.
Other countries in finals: Argentina, Australia, Brazil, Bulgaria, Chile, East Germany, Haiti, Italy, Scotland, Sweden, Uruguay, Yugoslavia, Zaire. **Total entries**: 98 (16 qualifiers).
Venues: Berlin, Dortmund, Dusseldorf, Frankfurt, Gelsenkirchen, Hamburg, Hanover, Munich, Stuttgart.
Top scorer: Lato (Poland) 7 goals
Final (Munich, 7.7.74): **West Germany 2** (Breitner 25 pen., Muller 43), **Holland 1** (Neeskens 2 pen.). **Att**: 77,833.
West Germany: Maier; Vogts, Schwarzenbeck, Beckenbauer (Capt.), Breitner, Bonhof, Hoeness, Overath, Grabowski, Muller, Holzenbein.
Holland: Jongbloed; Suurbier, Rijsbergen (De Jong 69), Haan, Krol, Jansen, Van Hanegem, Neeskens, Rep, Cruyff (Capt.), Rensenbrink (Van der Kerkhof (R.) 46).
Referee: Taylor (England). **Half-time**: 2-1.

1978 IN ARGENTINA

WINNERS: Argentina. RUNNERS-UP: Holland. THIRD: Brazil. FOURTH: Italy.
Other countries in finals: Austria, France, Hungary, Iran, Italy, Mexico, Peru, Poland, Scotland, Spain, Sweden, Tunisia, West Germany. **Total entries**: 102 (16 qualifiers).
Venues: Buenos Aires, Cordoba, Mar del Plata, Mendoza, Rosario.
Top scorer: Kempes (Argentina) 6 goals.

Final (Buenos Aires, 25.6.78): **Argentina 3** (Kempes 38, 104, Bertoni 115), **Holland 1** (Nanninga 82), **after extra time. Att:** 77,000.
Argentina: Fillol; Passarella (Capt.), Olguin, Galvan, Tarantini, Ardiles (Larrosa 66), Gallego, Ortiz (Houseman 74), Bertoni, Luque, Kempes.
Holland: Jongbloed; Krol (Capt.), Poortvliet, Brandts, Jansen (Suurbier 73), Haan, Neeskens, Van der Kerkhof (W.), Rep (Nanninga 58), Van der Kerkhof (R.), Rensenbrink.
Referee: Gonella (Italy). **Half-time:** 1-0. **90 mins:** 1-1.

1982 IN SPAIN

WINNERS: Italy. RUNNERS-UP: West Germany. THIRD: Poland. FOURTH: France.
Other countries in finals: Algeria, Argentina, Austria, Belgium, Brazil, Cameroon, Chile, Czechoslovakia, El Salvador, England, France, Honduras, Hungary, Kuwait, New Zealand, Northern Ireland, Peru, Scotland, Soviet Union, Spain, Yugoslavia. **Total entries:** 109 (24 qualifiers).
Venues: Alicante, Barcelona, Bilbao, Coruna, Elche, Gijon, Madrid, Malaga, Oviedo, Seville, Valencia, Valladolid, Vigo, Zaragoza.
Top scorer: Rossi (Italy) 6 goals.
Final (Madrid, 11.7.82): **Italy 3** (Rossi 57, Tardelli 69, Altobelli 81), **West Germany 1** (Breitner 84). **Att:** 90,089.
Italy: Zoff (Capt.); Bergomi, Scirea, Collovati, Cabrini, Oriali, Gentile, Tardelli, Conti, Rossi, Graziani (Altobelli 18 – Causio 88).
West Germany: Schumacher; Kaltz, Stielike, Forster (K-H.), Forster (B.), Dremmler (Hrubesch 63), Breitner, Briegel, Rummenigge (Capt.) (Muller 70), Fischer, Littbarski.
Referee: Coelho (Brazil). **Half-time:** 0-0.

1986 IN MEXICO

WINNERS: Argentina. RUNNERS-UP: West Germany. THIRD: France. FOURTH: Belgium.
Other countries in finals: Algeria, Belgium, Brazil, Bulgaria, Canada, Denmark, England, Hungary, Iraq, Italy, Mexico, Morocco, Northern Ireland, Paraguay, Poland, Portugal, Scotland, South Korea, Soviet Union, Spain, Uruguay. **Total entries:** 118 (24 qualifiers).
Venues: Guadalajara, Irapuato, Leon, Mexico City, Monterrey, Nezahualcoyotl, Puebla, Queretaro, Toluca.
Top scorer: Lineker (England) 6 goals.
Final (Mexico City, 29.6.86): **Argentina 3** (Brown 23, Valdano 56, Burruchaga 85), **West Germany 2** (Rummenigge 74, Voller 82). **Att:** 115,026.
Argentina: Pumpido; Cuciuffo, Brown, Ruggeri, Olarticoechea, Batista, Giusti, Maradona (Capt.), Burruchaga (Trobbiani 89), Enrique, Valdano.
West Germany: Schumacher; Berthold, K-H.Forster, Jakobs, Brehme, Briegel, Eder, Matthaus, Magath (Hoeness 62), Allofs (Voller 45), Rummenigge (Capt.).
Referee: Filho (Brazil). **Half-time:** 1-0.

1990 IN ITALY

WINNERS: West Germany. RUNNERS-UP: Argentina. THIRD: Italy. FOURTH: England.
Other countries in finals: Austria, Belgium, Brazil, Cameroon, Colombia, Costa Rica, Czechoslovakia, Egypt, England, Holland, Rep. of Ireland, Romania, Scotland, Spain, South Korea, Soviet Union, Sweden, United Arab Emirates, U.S.A., Uruguay, Yugoslavia. **Total entries:** 103 (24 qualifiers).
Venues: Bari, Bologna, Cagliari, Florence, Genoa, Milan, Naples, Palermo, Rome, Turin, Udine, Verona.
Top scorer: Schillaci (Italy) 6 goals.
Final (Rome, 8.7.90): **Argentina 0, West Germany 1** (Brehme 85 pen.). **Att:** 73,603.
Argentina: Goycochea; Ruggeri (Monzon 45), Simon, Serrizuela, Lorenzo, Basualdo, Troglio, Burruchaga (Calderon 53), Sensini, Maradona (Capt.), Dezotti. **Sent-off:** Monzon (65), Dezotti (86) – first players ever to be sent off in World Cup Final.

West Germany: Illgner; Berthold (Reuter 75), Buchwald, Augenthaler, Kohler, Brehme, Matthaus (Capt.), Littbarski, Hassler, Klinsmann, Voller.
Referee: Codesal (Mexico). **Half-time**: 0-0.

1994 IN U.S.A.

WINNERS: Brazil. RUNNERS-UP: Italy. THIRD: Sweden. FOURTH: Bulgaria.
Other countries in finals: Argentina, Belgium, Bolivia, Bulgaria, Cameroon, Colombia, Germany, Greece, Holland, Mexico, Morocco, Nigeria, Norway, Rep. of Ireland, Romania, Russia, Saudi Arabia, South Korea, Spain, Switzerland, U.S.A. **Total entries**: 144 (24 qualifiers).
Venues: Boston, Chicago, Dallas, Detroit, Los Angeles, New York City, Orlando, San Francisco, Washington.
Top scorers: Salenko (Russia), Stoichkov (Bulgaria), each 6 goals.
Final (Los Angeles, 17.7.94): **Brazil 0, Italy 0**, after extra time; **Brazil** won 3-2 on pens. **Att**: 94,194.
Brazil: Taffarel; Jorginho (Cafu 21), Aldair, Marcio Santos, Branco, Mazinho, Mauro Silva, Dunga (Capt.), Zinho (Viola 105), Romario, Bebeto.
Italy: Pagliuca; Mussi (Apolloni 35), Baresi (Capt.), Maldini, Benarrivo, Berti, Albertini, D. Baggio (Evani 95), Donadoni, R. Baggio, Massaro.
Referee: Puhl (Hungary).
Shoot-out: Baresi over, Marco Santos saved, Albertini 1-0, Romario 1-1, Evani 2-1, Branco 2-2, Massaro saved, Dunga 2-3, R Baggio over.

1998 IN FRANCE

WINNERS: France. RUNNERS-UP: Brazil. THIRD: Croatia. FOURTH: Holland.
Other countries in finals: Argentina, Austria, Belgium, Bulgaria, Cameroon, Chile, Colombia, Denmark, England, Germany, Holland, Iran, Italy, Jamaica, Japan, Mexico, Morocco, Nigeria, Norway, Paraguay, Romania, Saudi Arabia, Scotland, South Africa, South Korea, Spain, Tunisia, U.S.A., Yugoslavia. **Total entries**: 172 (32 qualifiers).
Venues: Bordeaux, Lens, Lyon, Marseille, Montpellier, Nantes, Paris (St Denis, Parc des Princes), Saint-Etienne, Toulouse.
Top scorer: Davor Suker (Croatia) 6 goals.
Final (Paris St Denis, 12.7.98): **Brazil 0, France 3** (Zidane 27, 45, Petit 90). **Att**: 75,000.
Brazil: Traffarel; Cafu, Junior Baiano, Aldair, Roberto Carlos; Dunga (Capt.), Leonardo (Denilson 46), Cesar Sampaio (Edmundo 74), Rivaldo; Bebeto, Ronaldo.
France: Barthez; Thuram, Leboeuf, Desailly, Lizarazu; Karembeu (Boghossian 56), Deschamps (Capt.), Petit, Zidane, Djorkaeff (Viera 75); Guivarc'h (Dugarry 66). **Sent-off**: Desailly (68).
Referee: Belqola (Morocco). **Half-time**: 0-2.

2002 IN JAPAN/SOUTH KOREA

WINNERS: Brazil. RUNNERS-UP: Germany. THIRD: Turkey. FOURTH: South Korea.
Other countries in finals: Argentina, Belgium, Cameroon, China, Costa Rica, Croatia, Denmark, Ecuador, England, France, Italy, Japan, Mexico, Nigeria, Paraguay, Poland, Portugal, Republic of Ireland, Russia, Saudi Arabia, Senegal, Slovenia, South Africa, Spain, Sweden, Tunisia, United States, Uruguay.
Venues: Japan – Ibaraki, Kobe, Miyagi, Niigata, Oita, Osaka, Saitama, Sapporo, Shizuoka, Yokohama. **South Korea** – Daegu, Daejeon, Gwangju, Incheon, Jeonju, Busan, Seogwipo, Seoul, Suwon. Ulsan.
Top scorer: Ronaldo (Brazil) 8 goals.
Final (Yokohama, 30.6.02): **Germany 0, Brazil 2** (Ronaldo 67, 79). **Att**: 69,029.
Germany: Kahn (Capt.), Linke, Ramelow, Metzelder, Frings, Jeremies (Asamoah 77), Hamann, Schneider, Bode (Zeige 84), Klose (Bierhoff 74), Neuville.
Brazil: Marcos, Lucio, Edmilson, Roque Junior, Cafu (Capt.) Kleberson, Gilberto Silva, Roberto Carlos, Ronaldinho (Juninho 85), Rivaldo, Ronaldo (Denilson 90).
Referee: Collina (Italy). **Half-time**: 0-0.

SOCCER DIARY 2005-06

JULY 2005

13 Steven Gerrard scores a hat-trick as Liverpool open their defence of the Champions League title with a 3-0 win over Welsh side TNS in the first qualifying round first leg.

14 Chelsea are fined £9,000 by UEFA for incidents involving players, officials and fans at last season's Champions League game against Barcelona at Stamford Bridge. The Spanish club are fined £2,000.

15 Ashley Cole, who seemed to be on his way out of Arsenal after the 'tapping-up' row involving Chelsea, signs a one-year extension to his contract.

16 Chelsea sign the France Under-21 international midfield player Lassana Diarra from Le Havre for £3m.

17 Yossi Benayoun, an Israel international midfielder, joins West Ham from Racing Santander for £2.5m.

18 Manchester City receive a club-record £21m. from Chelsea for Shaun Wright-Phillips. Sir Alex Ferguson is warned about his future conduct by the F.A. for suggesting there were 'sinister' reasons for referee Neale Barry not awarding Manchester United a penalty against Newcastle last season.

19 Peter Crouch becomes Liverpool's sixth, and biggest, summer signing in a £7m. move from Southampton. Steven Gerrard follows up his hat-trick in the first leg with two goals as Liverpool repeat their 3-0 win over TNS in the Champions League first qualifying round second leg.

20 Manchester United sign Stoke's third-choice goalkeeper Ben Foster, 22, for a fee rising to £3m. Wigan are given the all-clear to make their Premiership debut against Chelsea at the JJB Stadium after settling a police bill of £273,000.

21 The Football League reveal that £2.3m. was paid by clubs to agents between January and June 2005, up from £1.4m. in the corresponding period the previous year.

22 Joey Barton is sent home from Manchester City's tour of Thailand following an incident in a Bangkok hotel bar involving team-mate Richard Dunne and an Everton supporter.

23 Inter Milan decide to go ahead with matches against Leicester, Crystal Palace, Norwich and Portsmouth after first cancelling their pre-season tour of England because of the London bombings.

25 Sir John Hall, Newcastle's life president, confirms an approach for the sale of his stake in the club, sparking speculation about a takeover.

26 Manchester City pay £2.5m. for Aston Villa's Darius Vassell. Millwall's friendly against the Iran national team is called off on police advice.

27 Steve Claridge is sacked after 36 days as Millwall manager and replaced by Colin Lee, formerly in charge at Wolves and Walsall. Joey Barton is fined eight weeks' wages, about £100,000, after being sent home from Manchester City's tour of Thailand. Celtic suffer their worst-ever European defeat when going down 5-0 to Artmedia Bratislava in a Champions League qualifier – Gordon Strachan's first competitive match as manager.

28 Freddie Ljungberg signs a new contract keeping him at Arsenal until 2009. Celtic pay Reggina £2.5m. for the Japan international midfielder Shunsuke Nakamura.

29 England lose a first half lead in the European Under-19 Championship Final at Windsor Park and go down 3-1 to France

31 Rangers open their defence of the Scottish Premier League title with a 3-0 victory over Livingston.

AUGUST 2005

2 Andy Johnson ends summer-long speculation about his future by signing a new five-year contract with Crystal Palace. Celtic win the second leg of their Champions League qualifier against Artmedia Bratislava 4-0, but go out 5-4 on aggregate.

3 Alan Shearer's career in European football comes to an end as Newcastle are knocked out of the Intertoto Cup 4-2 on aggregate in the semi-finals by Deportivo La Coruna. Edgar Davids, one of Europe's most influential players for the past decade, joins Tottenham on a free transfer from Inter Milan.

4 After 11 years at the club, Phil Neville leaves Manchester United for Everton for a £3.5m. fee. Burnley manager Steve Cotterill is fined £1,500 and censured for improper conduct towards doping control officers at the club's training ground.

5 Birmingham sign Walter Pandiani, the Deportivo La Coruna striker who was on loan last season, for £3m. Abusive players will be sent off and managers personalising criticism of referees face disciplinary action under measures announced by the game's governing bodies.

6 Crowds of just over 400,000 for the opening weekend of the Football League season are the highest since 1963. Promoted Luton take pride of place, beating Crystal Palace 2-1 away from home. Hull's first game in the Championship against Queens Park Rangers is marred by fans taunting Rangers' supporters over the London bombings. Swansea mark their first match at a new ground by beating Tranmere 1-0 in front of a crowd of nearly 17,000.

7 Two goals by Didier Drogba give Chelsea a 2-1 victory over Arsenal in the Community Shield.

8 After summer-long negotiations, Rio Ferdinand agrees a new four-year contract with Manchester United worth a reported £100,000 a week. Kleberson leaves Old Trafford for the Turkish club Besiktas in a £2.5m. deal. Hull chairman Adam Pearson closes sections of the KC Stadium until the club investigates the London bombings taunts.

9 Leicester's David Connolly scores the first hat-trick of the season in a 4-2 win over Stoke. The F.A. fine seven clubs for poor disciplinary records – Leicester (£25,000), Leeds (£15,000), Millwall (£10,000), Boston (£7,500), Nottingham Forest (£5,000), Bradford (£3,000) and Chester (£2,000).

10 Chelsea manager Jose Mourinho and Arsenal's Ashley Cole appeal unsuccessfully against guilty verdicts in last season's 'tapping-up' affair. But both have their fines reduced, Mourinho from £200,000 to £75,000 and Cole from £100,000 to £75,000. Djibril Cisse is subjected to racist chants during Liverpool's Champions League qualifier against CSKA Sofia.

11 West Bromwich Albion pay £3m. for Wigan's Nathan Ellington. Arsenal midfielder Francesc Fabregas signs a new six-year contract.

12 Lord Burns, in his report of an inquiry into the structure of the game, confirms the F.A. as its governing body and recommends a dilution of Premier League power.

14 Alan Smith, short of match practice, declines a late call-up to England's squad for a friendly in Denmark and plays instead for Manchester United reserves.

15 The F.A. indicate that England will bid for the 2018 World Cup Finals. Marlon Harewood signs a new five-year contract with West Ham.

16 Chelsea's summer-long pursuit of Michael Essien finally pays off when the Lyon and Ghana midfielder signs for a club-record £24.4m. fee.

17 England are beaten 4-1 by Denmark, their heaviest defeat since losing by the same scoreline to Wales in 1980. In other friendly internationals, Garry O'Connor scores his first goal for Scotland who draw 2-2 with Austria. Wales and Slovenia finish goalless. Northern Ireland have Keith Gillespie sent off in a 1-1 draw with Malta and the Republic of Ireland go down 2-1 to Italy. Tottenham sell Fredi Kanoute to Sevilla for £4.4m. Blackburn are fined £10,000 by the F.A., with a further £50,000 suspended, for a poor disciplinary record.

19 Chelsea's Ricardo Carvalho is fined two weeks' wages by the club after criticising manager Jose Mourinho for leaving him out of the opening game of the season against Wigan. Bell's announce the end of their £700,000-a-year sponsorship of the Scottish League next summer.

20 Alan Thompson and Neil Lennon are sent off as Celtic lose the first Old Firm game of the campaign 3-1 to Rangers. Coventry mark their first appearance in the new £113m. Ricoh Arena with a 3-0 win over Queens Park Rangers.

23 Milan Baros joins Aston Villa from Liverpool for £6.5m. and the Chelsea midfielder Tiago moves to Lyon for the same fee. Despite losing 1-0 to CSKA Sofia in the return leg at Anfield, Liverpool reach the group stage of the Champions League with a 3-2 aggregate win. The F.A. confirm a three-match ban for Southend's Freddy Eastwood and impose a further one game for a 'frivolous' appeal against his sending-off against Huddersfield. Seven Championship teams lose to lower-division opposition in round one of the Carling

Cup. They include Crewe, beaten 5-1 by Lincoln, Ipswich, who go down 2-0 at home to Yeovil, and Queens Park Rangers, knocked out 3-0 at Northampton.

24 Manchester United and Rangers reach the Champions League group stage, but Everton lose their third qualifying round tie to Villarreal. Another Championship side are knocked out in round one of the Carling Cup, Derby losing 1-0 at home to Grimsby.

25 Martin Jol, the Tottenham manager, signs a new three-year-contract. Clinton Morrison rejoins Crystal Palace from Birmingham for £2m.

26 Djibril Cisse comes off the bench to score twice as Champions League winners Liverpool beat UEFA Cup holders CSKA Moscow 3-1 in extra-time to claim the European Super Cup in Monte Carlo. Newcastle pay £9.5m. for the Deportivo La Coruna striker Albert Luque.

27 Bury become the first club to score 1,000 goals in each of the four divisions when Brian Barry-Murphy is on the mark in their League Two match against Wrexham.

30 Newcastle bring Michael Owen back to the Premiership in a club-record £16m. deal with Real Madrid. Aston Villa pay £3.5m. for the PSV Eindhoven defender Wilfred Bouma.

31 Tottenham are involved in four deals as the transfer window closes. They sign Jermaine Jenas from Newcastle for £7m., Grzegorz Rasiak from Derby for £2m. and South Korea full-back Lee Young-pyo from PSV Eindhoven for £1.3m., and sell Erik Edman to Rennes for £2.1m. Other moves include Curtis Davies from Luton to West Bromwich Albion for £3m. and Nolberto Solano's return to Newcastle from Aston Villa for £1.5m.

SEPTEMBER 2005

1 Two Northern Ireland players, Phil Mulryne and Jeff Whitley, are sent home for breaking a squad curfew ahead of World Cup qualifiers against Azerbaijan and England.

2 England make sure of a place in the Play-offs for the European Under-21 Championship Finals with a 4-0 group victory over Wales.

3 England beat Wales 1-0 in their World Cup qualifier with a deflected shot by Joe Cole. Warren Feeney converts a penalty for his first goal for Northern Ireland, who win their first competitive game for nearly four years, 2-0 against Azerbaijan. Scotland hold Italy 1-1 with a goal by Kenny Miller.

5 Glen Johnson is sent home ahead of England's European Under-21 Championship qualifier against Germany because of a poor attitude. Millwall, originally fined £32,500 by the F.A., are cleared on appeal of racist chanting by fans at last season's Carling Cup tie against Liverpool.

6 Bobby Williamson becomes the first managerial casualty of the season, sacked by Plymouth after four successive Championship defeats.

7 David Healy's goal for Northern Ireland inflicts a shock 1-0 World Cup qualifying defeat on England, who suffer their first defeat in the province since 1927. Two by Kenny Miller keep Scotland's hopes alive with a 2-1 away win over Norway, but the Republic of Ireland's chances take a blow in a 1-0 defeat by France and Wales go down by the same scoreline to Poland.

8 Tottenham appoint Damien Comolli, formerly with St Etienne, as their new sporting director to replace Frank Arnesen.

9 Luis Boa Morte ends speculation about his future by signing a new five-year contract with Fulham.

10 Brian Tinnion resigns as manager of Bristol City after a 7-1 defeat by Swansea.

14 Manchester United's Wayne Rooney and Arsenal's Robin van Persie are sent off in opening Champions League group matches against Villarreal and the Swiss side Thun respectively.

15 Aston Villa defender Martin Laursen, who missed seven months of last season, is ruled out for the rest of this campaign with a knee injury.

17 Carlton Palmer resigns as Mansfield manager minutes after a 2-0 defeat at Rochdale, blaming continued abuse from supporters.

19 Manchester United's Wayne Rooney is acclaimed as the game's outstanding youngster in a poll by FIFPro, a worldwide representative organisation for players. Bury sack manager Graham Barrow after a poor start to the season.

20 Grimsby take pride of place in round two of the Carling Cup, beating Tottenham 1-0 with an 89th minute goal by Jean-Paul Kalala. Wycombe look to be on course for another upset when leading Aston Villa 3-1, but the Premiership side score seven times in the second half for an 8-3 win. Tottenham striker Mido is cleared by the F.A. of improper conduct after being sent off against Chelsea.

21 Manchester City lose to Doncaster on penalties in the Carling Cup second round. Arsenal's Gilberto Silva signs a new contract stretching to 2009. Changing kick-off times represent the biggest worry for Premiership fans, according to Professor Derek Fraser, chairman of the Independent Football Commission. Wayne Rooney, sent off against Villarreal, receives a two-match Champions League ban from UEFA, the extra game for 'applauding' referee Kim Milton Nielsen.

22 Bristol Rovers dismiss manager Ian Atkins after one win in their first nine matches of the season.

23 Tony Pulis, sacked by Stoke in June for not signing enough foreign players, is appointed Plymouth's new manager. Gary Johnson leaves Yeovil to become Bristol City manager after the two clubs agree on compensation.

24 Lincoln have three players sent off, Lee Beevers, Paul Morgan and goalkeeper Andy Marriott, in the League Two match against Torquay.

26 Swindon manager Andy King is sacked after a fifth successive defeat. Preston are fined £1,000 and given a suspended two-year transfer ban by the F.A. for dealing with a non-licensed players' agent. Alain Perrin, under-pressure Portsmouth manager, is given a vote of confidence by chairman Milan Mandaric.

27 Amid speculation about the new Wembley, the F.A. insist it will be ready for the F.A. Cup Final on May 13. Portsmouth's Lomana LuaLua is confined to a hospital isolation unit with malaria after collapsing during training.

28 Rangers are beaten 1-0 by Inter Milan in a Champions League match played in an empty San Siro Stadium, the Italian club having been punished by UEFA for previous crowd trouble.

29 Roy Keane announces his intention to leave Manchester United at the end of the season. Everton are knocked out of the UEFA Cup in the first round, losing 5-2 on aggregate to Dinamo Bucharest after a 5-1 defeat in the first leg. Hibernian and Cork also go out. Bolton and Middlesbrough reach the group stage. Millwall's Jody Morris is fined £2,000 and given a further one-match ban by the F.A. for abusive language towards referee Andy D'Urso. In an attempt to dispel rumours about major differences between them, Southampton manager Harry Redknapp and performance director Sir Clive Woodward appear side-by-side at a press conference.

30 The F.A. decide on a scaled-down version of the proposed National Football Centre at Burton upon Trent.

OCTOBER 2005

2 After winning eight successive matches, Hearts drop their first points of the season in a 2-2 draw against Falkirk in the Scottish Premier League.

3 Real Madrid claim to have overtaken Manchester United as the world's biggest football club.

4 Birmingham's Nicky Butt, banned for three matches after being sent off against Portsmouth, is given an extra one-game suspension and fined £8,500 by the F.A. for abusive language.

6 England coach Sven-Goran Eriksson drops Rio Ferdinand for the World Cup qualifier against Austria.

7 Caretaker Steve Thompson is appointed Yeovil manager after a successful spell in charge following the departure of Gary Johnson to Bristol City. Ian Holloway, the Queens Park Rangers manager, is fined £1,500 by the F.A. for abusive language during the Carling Cup defeat by Northampton.

8 David Beckham becomes the first England captain to be sent off and the first England player to be dismissed twice when he receives two yellow cards against Austria. His team hold out for a 1-0 win and a few hours later are guaranteed a place in the World Cup Finals when Czechoslovakia lose 2-0 to Holland. The Republic of Ireland keep alive their chances of qualifying by beating Cyprus 1-0 with Stephen Elliott's first international goal. But Scotland are out of the reckoning after a 1-0 home defeat by Belarus. Carl Robinson's first international goal helps Wales to their first competitive win since March 2003, a 3-2 success over Northern Ireland.

10 Velimir Zajec, whose appointment as Portsmouth's director of football precipitated the departure of manager Harry Redknapp, resigns for 'personal reasons.'

11 England complete their European Under-21 Championship qualifying group on a high note by beating Poland 4-1 in front of a 23,000 crowd at Hillsborough.

12 Four days after scoring the only goal against Austria from the penalty spot, Frank Lampard volleys the winner against Poland, a result which enables England to finish top of their World Cup qualifying group. The Republic of Ireland fail to make it after a goalless draw with Switzerland. Paul Hartley scores his first goal for Scotland in a 3-0 victory over Slovenia, while Wales defeat Azerbaijan 2-0 with two from Ryan Giggs. Northern Ireland's Damien Johnson is sent off in a 2-0 defeat in Vienna, along with Austria's Middlesbrough defender Emanuel Pogatetz.

13 Birmingham's Kenny Cunningham announces his retirement from international football after winning 72 caps for the Republic of Ireland.

14 Manchester United's Roy Keane calls time on his career with the Republic of Ireland after winning 67 caps. FIFA president Sepp Blatter comes under fire from managers and officials for wide-ranging comments about the English game, including Manchester United's 'handling' of Wayne Rooney, 'greedy' players and the number of foreigners in the Premiership.

15 Former Manchester United defender Chris Casper, 30, becomes the League's youngest manager after a successful spell as caretaker at Bury.

16 Newcastle's Stephen Carr, with 41 caps, becomes the third player to announce his international retirement after the Republic of Ireland's failure to reach the World Cup Finals.

17 Swansea announce a £500,000 sponsorship deal with a property company which involves naming their new 20,000-seater ground the Liberty Stadium.

18 Brian Kerr loses his job after failing to take the Republic of Ireland to the World Cup Finals. Thierry Henry, out for eight weeks with a groin injury, becomes Arsenal's record marksman when scoring twice in a 2-0 Champions League win over Sparta Prague to overtake Ian Wright's total of 185. The F.A. decide to take no action over an ugly tackle by Michael Essien on Tal Ben Haim in the Chelsea-Bolton game, despite referee Rob Styles admitting there would have been a red card had he seen it from another angle.

19 Swindon stave off a winding-up order brought by the Inland Revenue by settling an outstanding tax bill.

20 The possibility of Tottenham moving to London's 2012 Olympic Stadium is ended when officials earmark it for a post-Games athletics venue.

22 George Burley, who guided Hearts to the top of the Scottish Premier League, leaves after differences with majority shareholder Vladimir Romanov. Burley claims he was sacked, the club say he went by mutual agreement.

24 The F.A. uphold a claim for mistaken identity and transfer a booking for Newcastle's Scott Parker against Sunderland to team-mate Stephen Carr, who receives a one-match ban.

25 A bitter-sweet day for Crystal Palace manager Iain Dowie, who is banned from the touchline for one match and fined £3,000 by the F.A. for abusive language at Reading, then sees his team dismiss last season's beaten finalists Liverpool from the Carling Cup in the third round.

26 Holders Chelsea are knocked out of the Carling Cup by Charlton on penalties in a third round tie. Southampton chairman Rupert Lowe wins £250,000 libel damages from *The Times* over an article about former manager David Jones.

27 Former England midfielder Paul Gascoigne becomes manager of Conference North club Kettering. Barnet goalkeeper Ross Flitney, sent off after 90 seconds of the Carling Cup tie against Manchester United, has the red card rescinded by the F.A.

28 After a four-year battle and two public inquiries, Brighton are given the go-ahead by Deputy Prime Minister John Prescott for a new 23,000-capacity stadium at Falmer. Chesterfield manager Roy McFarland is given a three-match touchline ban and fined £500 for abusive language at the match against Walsall. The F.A. also fine Burnley's Graham Branch £1,000 and impose a two-match ban for abusive behaviour against Derby.

30 Laurent Robert is fined by Portsmouth for refusing to sit on the substitutes' bench against Sunderland, claiming he had a groin injury.

31 Senior Manchester United officials order the club's TV station not to broadcast an interview in which injured captain Roy Keane criticises team-mates following the 4-1 defeat by Middlesbrough. Mathieu Flamini's move to Arsenal in 2004 is upheld by the Court of Arbitration for Sport, which rejects an appeal by Marseille that they have a prior claim on the player. Stoke defender Marlon Broomes has a ban increased from three to four matches for what the F.A. rules is a 'frivolous' appeal.

NOVEMBER 2005

1 Millwall have three players sent off in separate incidents at Turf Moor – Ben May, Jody Morris and Andy Marshall. Burnley's James O'Connor is also dismissed, but later has an appeal upheld by the F.A. Former Sheffield Wednesday stalwart Peter Shirtliff is appointed Mansfield manager after a spell as caretaker. The referees' body confirm that Premiership official Graham Poll served a two-match suspension last month for an incident at a pre-season training camp.

2 Arsenal qualify for the knock-out stage of the Champions League with two group matches remaining.

3 Manager Alan Pardew is rewarded with a new five-year contract after winning promotion and establishing West Ham in the Premiership. Mike Newell, the Luton manager, receives an F.A. warning for abusive language at half-time of the match against Wolves, but is cleared of a second charge. Carling's sponsorship of the League Cup is extended by a further three years to 2009.

4 Arsenal's Arsene Wenger refuses the offer of a mutual apology from Chelsea's Jose Mourinho after more bitter exchanges between the two managers.

6 Real Madrid's Jonathan Woodgate, out for more than a year with a thigh injury, is denied a return to the England squad after tearing a hamstring.

7 Lennie Lawrence, who has managed six clubs, is appointed director of football at Bristol Rovers, with Paul Trollope continuing as first-team coach. Stoke suspend director of football John Rudge and assistant manager Jan De Koning following complaints from manager Johan Boskamp.

8 The F.A. admit for the first time that plans to open the new Wembley Stadium with the F.A. Cup Final on May 13, 2006, are in doubt. Former Portsmouth and Oxford manager Graham Rix is appointed first-team coach at Hearts.

9 Geoff Thompson, chairman of the F.A., claims England will be in a 'very strong position' to challenge for the 2018 World Cup Finals. Chelsea are ordered to pay up to £2.5m. for three teenagers from lower league clubs – Scott Sinclair (Bristol Rovers), Ryan Bertrand (Gillingham) and Harry Worley (Stockport). Holders Rangers are knocked out of the CIS Insurance Cup, losing 2-0 to Celtic in the quarter-finals.

10 The Scottish F.A. opt out of plans for a Great Britain team at the 2012 Olympics in London. Blackpool dismiss manager Colin Hendry. French full-back Pascal Chimbonda is rewarded with a four-year contract for a major impact made in the Premiership with Wigan.

11 A record crowd for an England Under-21 international, 34,494, watch Peter Taylor's team draw 1-1 with France in the first leg of a European Championship Play-off tie at White Hart Lane.

12 Two goals by Michael Owen in the final five minutes give England a 3-2 win over Argentina in Geneva in a match rated one of their finest-ever friendlies. Andy Webster scores his first for Scotland, who draw 1-1 with the USA. Liverpool's Luis Garcia hits a hat-trick on his full international debut as Spain beat Slovakia 5-1 in a World Cup qualifying Play-off first leg.

14 Neale Cooper resigns after less than six months as manager of struggling Gillingham and is replaced by his assistant, Ronnie Jepson.

15 A controversial penalty four minutes from time costs England a 2-1 defeat by France in their Play-off second leg – and a place in the European Under-21 Championship Finals. Northern Ireland hold Portugal to a 1-1 draw in a senior friendly international.

16 A goal by Wrexham defender Dennis Lawrence gives Trinidad and Tobago victory over Bahrain in World Cup qualifying Play-off second leg – and a place in the Finals. Wales suffer an embarrassing 1-0 defeat by Cyprus in a friendly. Bolton's El-Hadji Diouf is fined £500 by magistrates over a spitting incident involving a young Middlesbrough fan.

17 Sky's monopoly of live Premiership coverage ends after the European Commission opens the way for rival bids for the next TV deal starting in 2007. The League Managers' Association disclose that of 74 managers who underwent a health-screening programme, 47 were diagnosed with heart problems.

18 Roy Keane leaves Manchester United after 12 success-filled years, his rift with Sir Alex Ferguson having become too big to heal. Boston manager Steve Evans receives a £1,000 fine, suspended for 12 months, from the F.A. for abusive language at the match against Peterborough.

19 Mansfield's game at Shrewsbury is postponed after their goalkeeping coach Peter Wilson collapses and dies during the warm up. Leeds pull off the recovery of the season, winning 4-3 at Southampton after trailing 3-0 with 20 minutes remaining. Rotherham have Deon Burton, Lee Williamson and Colin Murdock red carded and manager Mick Harford sent to the stands at Barnsley.

21 Sir Alex Ferguson effectively admits that Roy Keane was forced out of Old Trafford and that his departure was not by mutual consent.

22 Neil Warnock, the Sheffield United manager, is fined £750 by the F.A. for abusive language towards referee Grant Hegley at Reading.

23 Abel Xavier, Middlesbrough's Portuguese defender, is banned for 18 months by UEFA after testing positive for an anabolic steroid at a UEFA Cup match – the first Premiership player found to have taken a performance-enhancing drug. Vodafone end a £36m. shirt sponsorship with Manchester United two years early for 'strategic' reasons. Chelsea and Liverpool qualify for the knock-out stage of the Champions League.

24 Alain Perrin becomes the first Premiership manager of the season to lose his job, sacked by struggling Portsmouth after 21 games in charge. Middlesbrough reach the knock-out stage of the UEFA Cup.

25 George Best dies aged 59 and tributes are paid world-wide to one of the finest players Britain has produced. Sir Alex Ferguson rules out an approach for Bayern Munich's Michael Ballack as Manchester United's replacement for Roy Keane.

26 Frank Lampard makes his 160th successive Premiership appearance for Chelsea, overtaking the record established by David James when he was at Liverpool.

27 Frank Lampard and Steven Gerrard finish second and third to Barcelona's Ronaldinho in the poll for European Footballer of the Year.

28 Chelsea are fined £30,000 by the F.A. for failing to control their supporters in a Carling Cup tie against West Ham last season. West Ham receive a warning. Aston Villa manager David O'Leary is fined £5,000 for remarks about referee Graham Poll at Birmingham. David Beckham opens the first of what he hopes will be a world-wide chain of soccer schools in east London.

29 Referees' chief Keith Hackett apologises to manager Sam Allardyce for not giving advance warning that referee Graham Poll would be testing a new listening device in Bolton's match at Fulham. Doncaster beat Aston Villa 3-0 to reach the quarter-finals of the Carling Cup. Nationwide end a six-year sponsorship deal with the F.A. worth £5m. a year. Millionaire businessman Peter de Savary becomes chairman of Millwall.

30 Leicester are fined £20,000 and Q.P.R. £14,000 by the F.A. for a players' brawl at the Walkers Stadium.

DECEMBER 2005

1 Tim Cahill and Celestine Babayaro are suspended for three matches by the F.A. for swopping blows in the Everton-Newcastle game, an incident missed by referee Howard Webb but caught on video.

2 As speculation mounts about a return to Portsmouth, manager Harry Redknapp walks out on Southampton claiming his position has become untenable.

4 Wales follow Scotland in refusing to be part of any unified British team for the 2012 London Olympics.

5 Paul Gascoigne is sacked after 39 days as Kettering manager amid allegations about his drinking.

6 England are ranked second behind Brazil in the seedings for the World Cup draw. Rangers become the first Scottish side to reach the knock-out stage of the Champions League.

7 Manchester United lose 2-1 to Benfica and for the first time in a decade fail to qualify from the group stage of the Champions League. Harry Redknapp returns to Portsmouth as manager, signing a contract until the end of the season. Crystal Palace chairman Simon Jordan is given a suspended £10,000 fine by the F.A. for criticising referee Brian Curson in a newspaper article.

8 The Football League launch their biggest-ever consultation exercise by inviting fans for their views on issues like refereeing standards, sin-bins, goal-line technology and agents.

9 England receive a favourable World Cup draw, being paired with Sweden, Paraguay and Trinidad and Tobago in their group.

10 Rangers halt their worst run of results for more than a century, ten games without a win, by beating Kilmarnock 3-2. Rotherham sack manager Mick Harford after 17 League and Cup matches without a victory.

11 Charlton sign a £6.6m., four-and-a-half-year sponsorship deal with Spanish property company Llanera, the biggest in the club's history.

13 Relations between Manchester United and the media hit a new low as Sir Alex Ferguson walks out of a press conference after 74 seconds.

14 Bolton join Middlesbrough in the knock-out stage of the UEFA Cup. Bournemouth, with debts of around £7m., sell their Dean Court stadium to a property company for £3.5m. and lease it back for £300,000 a year.

15 Roy Keane chooses Celtic as his new club after leaving Manchester United Michael Essien is banned for two matches by UEFA for a knee-high lunge on Dietmar Hamann which went un-noticed by referee Herbert Fandel in Chelsea's Champions League match against Liverpool.

17 Wycombe lose the last unbeaten record in the four divisions, going down 2-1 at Bury to two goals in the final four minutes of their 22nd match.

18 After establishing a club record of ten matches without conceding a goal, Liverpool are beaten 1-0 by Sao Paulo in the Club World Championship Final in Yokohama.

19 Frank Lampard is named runner-up to Ronaldinho in the World Player of the Year poll, just as he was for the European award. Macclesfield are fined £62,000 by the F.A. and ordered to repay £195,000 to the Football Foundation after an inquiry into the funding of a stand at the League Two club's ground.

20 Colin Lee is appointed director of football at Millwall and replaced as manager, initially on a caretaker basis, by his assistant, 33-year-old former Tottenham player David Tuttle.

21 Doncaster are denied a semi-final place in the Carling Cup by Gilberto Silva's equaliser in stoppage-time of extra-time for Arsenal, who go on to win a penalty shoot-out

22 George Burley, who parted company with Hearts two months ago, is appointed Southampton's head coach, with the club's performance director, Sir Clive Woodward, becoming director of football.

27 Manager Chris Turner leaves bottom-of-the-table Stockport by mutual consent after a 6-0 defeat by Macclesfield.

28 Ron Atkinson, who lost his job as a television pundit in April 2004 for a racist remark, joins Swindon to make a documentary series about the League One club and to offer advice to fledgling manager Iffy Onuora.

29 Sports Minister Richard Caborn urges the F.A. and Premier League to review rules about fixture cancellations after several games are called off at short notice.

30 With the help of the club's most famous supporter, Chancellor Gordon Brown, supporters complete a buy-out of Raith.

31 On the eve of World Cup year, England's Michael Owen is ruled out for more than three months after breaking a bone in his right foot during Newcastle's match at Tottenham.

JANUARY 2006

2 Lincoln manager Keith Alexander is temporarily relieved of his duties only hours before the match against Mansfield.

3 Another Russian revolution hits the Premiership, with multi-millionaire businessman Alexandre Gaydamak paying £15m. for a half-share in Portsmouth.

4 Manchester United make the first big signing of the transfer window by paying Spartak Moscow £7m. for central defender Nemanja Vidic. Liverpool swop full-back Josemi for Villarreal's Jan Kromkamp.

5 Keith Alexander thrashes out his differences with Lincoln and returns to the manager's chair.

6 Portsmouth begin spending their new windfall with a club-record £4.1m. fee for the Auxerre striker Benjani Mwaruwari. Wigan sign central defender Paul Scharner from Brann Bergen for £2m.

7 Thierry Henry calms speculation about his future by insisting he wants to stay at Arsenal.

8 Roy Keane's debut for Celtic ends in a shock 2-1 defeat by Division One side Clyde in round three of the Scottish Cup.

9 After a second spell as caretaker, Alan Knill is appointed Rotherham manager until the end of the season when his position will be reviewed.

10 Manchester United further strengthen their defensive ranks with the £5m. acquisition of Monaco's Patrice Evra. Manchester City defender David Sommeil is banned for three games by the F.A. for a studs-up challenge, missed by referee Alan Wiley, on Tottenham's Lee Young-Pyo. Gordon Chisholm is sacked by Dundee United after ten months as manager.

11 Portsmouth sign three players from Tottenham for a combined £7.5m. – Noe Pamarot, Pedro Mendes and Sean Davis.

12 Steve Staunton, the Republic of Ireland's most-capped player with 102 appearances, is appointed manager, with former England manager Sir Bobby Robson as consultant. Liverpool sign the Brondby defender Daniel Agger for £5.8m. Caretaker Simon Grayson is appointed manager of Blackpool, initially until the end of the season.

13 Arsenal sign two players – striker Emmanuel Adebayor from Monaco for £6m. and the Auxerre midfielder Vasiriki Abou Diaby for £2.5m. Martin Foyle, the Port Vale manager, receives a three-match touchline ban and £500 fine from the F.A. for remarks to a match official at Gillingham.

14 Former Dundee United striker Craig Brewster returns to Tannadice as manager after leaving Inverness.

15 The F.A. declare continued support for England coach Sven-Goran Eriksson after he comes under fire for comments made to an undercover reporter from the *News of the World*.

17 Marcus Bent makes Charlton his ninth club in a ten-year career in a £2m. move from Everton.

18 Jim Gannon, who played for Stockport between 1990 and 2000, is appointed manager until the end of the season after a spell as caretaker.

19 Luton manager Mike Newell is summoned to F.A. headquarters to explain his allegations about financial irregularities in the game. Greg Dyke, former director-general of the BBC, becomes chairman of Brentford after a supporters' trust takeover of the club

20 Southampton's Theo Walcott, the country's most coveted young player, moves to Arsenal for a fee rising to £12m – a world record for a 16-year-old.

21 Dean Ashton joins West Ham from Norwich for £7.25m. – a record for both clubs.

22 Sven-Goran Eriksson is ordered to a meeting with the F.A. after making allegations, in the *News of the World*, of corruption in the English game.

23 Under-pressure Sven-Goran Eriksson agrees a settlement with the F.A. to step down as England coach after the World Cup.

24 The Premier League announce an independent inquiry 'to get to the bottom' of allegations of corruption. A goal by Jason Roberts in the last minute of extra-time sends Wigan into the Carling Cup Final at Arsenal's expense.

25 Manchester United beat Blackburn in the other semi-final. Craig Levein is sacked as Leicester manager after one win in 16 League games. Leroy Rosenior, manager of struggling Torquay, has his contract terminated by mutual consent. Peterborough boss Mark Wright is suspended pending an inquiry by the club.

26 Middlesbrough manager Steve McClaren, linked with the England job, signs a new contract keeping him at the club until 2009. Shefield United pay £1.75m. for Burnley's Ade Akinbiyi – a record for both clubs.

27 Chelsea report an annual loss of £140m. – a record for English football. Robbie Fowler makes a surprise return to Liverpool on a short-term free transfer from Manchester City.

28 Greek striker Georgios Samaras joins Manchester City from the Dutch club Heerenveen for £6m. David Tuttle is confirmed as Millwall manager, at least until the end of the season, with recently-appointed director of football Colin Lee leaving the club.

30 Derby, struggling in the Championship and knocked out of the F.A. Cup by Colchester, sack manager Phil Brown after seven months in the job.

31 Mark Wright, manager of Peterborough for eight months, is dismissed for alleged gross misconduct. Caretaker John Cornforth is confirmed as Torquay manager until the end of the season. Brentford's Dudley Campbell, who a year ago was playing non-league football, joins Birmingham for £500,000.

FEBRUARY 2006

1 Hartlepool manager Martin Scott is suspended by the club over a dressing room incident after the 3-0 home defeat by Blackpool.

2 Graeme Souness is sacked by Newcastle after six matches yield a single point. Glenn Roeder takes over as caretaker, assisted by Alan Shearer. The F.A. sign a four-year sponsorship for the F.A. Cup, at £8m. a year, with energy company E.ON. Crewe are put up for sale for £8m.

3 Bradford's Dean Windass is banned for five games by the F.A. for comments to referee Darren Drysdale after the home game against Brentford.

5 Ian Holloway, linked with the vacant manager's job at Leicester, is suspended by Queens Park Rangers, with the club's former midfielder Gary Waddock appointed caretaker. Charlton's Matt Holland calls time on his international career after 49 Republic of Ireland caps.

6 Arsenal's Sol Campbell returns to training after walking out of Highbury when substituted at half-time of the 3-2 midweek defeat by West Ham Walsall manager Paul Merson is sacked after a 5-0 defeat by Brentford. Celtic's John Hartson retires from international football after winning 51 caps and scoring 14 goals for Wales.

7 Tottenham striker Mido is thrown out of the Egypt squad for protesting about being substituted during the 2-1 semi-final victory over Senegal in the African Cup of Nations. Swindon pull the plug on a TV documentary fronted by Ron Atkinson, with manager Iffy Onoura unhappy about the demands on his players.

8 Amid further speculation that the new Wembley will not be ready for this season's F.A. Cup Final, the F.A. insist no decision has been taken.

9 Former England and West Ham manager Ron Greenwood dies aged 84. Rotherham say they will have to drop out of the League unless they can raise £2m. Rangers announce that Alex McLeish will stand down as manager at the end of the season. Martin Scott, suspended over a dressing room incident, is sacked as Hartlepool manager after an investigation by the club.

10 Everton's Duncan Ferguson is banned for seven matches and fined £5,000 by the F.A. – three games for punching Wigan's Paul Scharner in the midriff and four for an incident immediately afterwards with Pascal Chimbonda. Birmingham's Emile Heskey receives an extra one-match ban and £5,000 fine for failing to leave the field promptly and approaching referee Mike Riley aggressively after being sent off against Arsenal. Chelsea's Didier Drogba has a penalty saved in a shoot-out as the Ivory Coast lose the African Cup of Nations Final to Egypt after a scoreless 120 minutes.

11 Paul Lambert resigns as manager of the Scottish Premier League's bottom club, Livingston.

13 Caretaker Rob Kelly is confirmed as manager after leading Leicester away from the relegation zone with three successive wins. Burnley defender Wayne Thomas is given an 18-month conditional discharge for pushing a police office in the tunnel after his previous club Stoke's game at Millwall last season.

14 Nicky Butt issues a public apology for walking out on Birmingham after being omitted from the squad to face West Ham.

15 Manchester United are overtaken by Real Madrid as the richest football club in the world, according to business advisers Deloitte. John Robertson, formerly in charge of Hearts and Inverness, becomes Livingston's sixth manager in two years.

16 Nottingham Forest manager Gary Megson leaves the club by mutual agreement.

17 After an unbeaten Championship run of 33 matches, Reading go down 3-2 at Luton.

18 Manager Keith Curle parts company with Chester after his team's 11th League defeat in 12 matches.

19 Celtic's 8-1 win at Dunfermline is the biggest since the SPL broke away from the Scottish League in 1998.

20 Mark Wright, sacked by Peterborough last month, returns to his previous club Chester as manager until the end of the season. Former manager Chris Turner returns to Hartlepool as director of sport, with Paul Stephenson in charge of first-team affairs until the end of the season.

21 The F.A. admit that the new Wembley will not be ready for this season's F.A. Cup Final, which goes to Cardiff's Millennium Stadium for the sixth season. Gary Neville is fined £5,000 by the F.A. for over-zealous celebrations of Manchester United's Premiership winner against Liverpool.

22 Two more caretaker-managers are confirmed in the job until the end of the season – Terry Westley at Derby and Walsall's Kevan Broadhurst.

23 Middlesbrough reach the second knock-out round of the UEFA Cup, beating Stuttgart on the away goals rule. Bolton lose 2-1 on aggregate to Marseille. The Premier League decide to take no action against Portsmouth over the appointment of Harry Redknapp as manager after he quit Southampton.

26 Sir Alex Ferguson's decision to play Louis Saha instead of Ruud van Nistelrooy pays off as Manchester United lift the League Cup for the second time. United beat Wigan 4-0 – the Final's biggest margin of victory since Norwich defeated Rochdale 4-0 in 1962 when it was played over two legs.

27 Singer Robbie Williams, who grew up in Stoke-on-Trent, becomes a major shareholder in Port Vale with an estimated £260,000 investment.

28 Former Manchester United striker Dwight Yorke scores both goals as World Cup-bound Trindad & Tobago beat Iceland 2-0 in a friendly watched by a 10,000 crowd at Loftus Road.

MARCH 2006

1 Peter Crouch scores his first international goal and Joe Cole fires a last-minute winner as England come from behind to beat Uruguay 2-1. Steve Staunton makes a successful start as Republic of Ireland manager, Liam Miller opening his account for his country in a 3-0 success. Ivan Sproule also celebrates his first goal for Northern Ireland, netting the winner 78 seconds into his first start against Estonia. Derby's Lewin Nyatanga, at 17 years and 195 days, becomes the youngest international for Wales, who draw 0-0 with Paraguay. Scotland lose 3-1 at home to Switzerland.

2 Tributes are paid to Peter Osgood, an F.A. Cup winner with Chelsea and Southampton, who dies of a heart attack aged 59.

3 Robbie Keane extends his contract at Tottenham until 2010 and 39-year-old Teddy Sheringham signs a new one-year deal with West Ham. Lord Stevens, former Metropolitan Police Commissioner, is appointed head of the Premier League inquiry into alleged irregular payments. Aston Villa's Lee Hendrie is warned by the club about his conduct after being given 60 hours' community service by magistrates for common assault.

6 Mick McCarthy is sacked as Sunderland manager after his team's 22nd defeat in 28 Premiership matches –2-1 by Manchester City. Rangers sign a £48m., ten-year sponsorship deal with JJB Sports.

7 Chelsea go out of the Champions League in the first knock-out round, beaten 3-2 on aggregate by Barcelona. Rangers lose to Villarreal on away goals after a 3-3 scoreline. Nigel Quashie, banned for four matches after being sent off in West Bromwich Albion's home defeat by Middlesbrough, receives an extra one-game suspension and £5,000 fine from the F.A. for abusive language before leaving the pitch. Scotland striker Garry O'Connor becomes the first British player in the Russian Premier League when he joins Lokomotiv Moscow from Hibernian for £1.6m.

8 Holders Liverpool are dismissed from the Champions League by Benfica, who win 3-0 on aggregate, leaving Arsenal as Britain's only survivors after their 1-0 victory over Real Madrid. Morrisons announce the end of a £5m., four-year sponsorship deal with the Scottish F.A. in July.

9 Brighton are forced into another year's delay over a new stadium at Falmer because of a legal challenge from the local council. Queens Park Rangers are fined £5,000 for their players' part in a post-match brawl at Stoke.

10 Arsene Wenger defends his Arsenal side after criticism that there was not a single home-grown player in the victory over Real Madrid.

11 Paul Le Guen, who led Lyon to three French titles before leaving the club last summer, is named as Alex McLeish's successor as Rangers manager at the end of the season.

13 Lord Ashcroft, deputy chairman of the Conservative Party, takes control of Watford following a £6.2m. share issue.

14 Struggling Oxford part company with manager Brian Talbot and replace him, temporarily, with youth team manager Darren Patterson.

15 Middlesbrough reach the quarter-finals of the UEFA Cup, beating Roma on the away goals rule.

16 FIFA president Sepp Blatter warns fans that racism at the World Cup Finals in Germany could lead to their team being expelled from the competition.

18 Gordon Strachan wins his first trophy as manager of Celtic, who beat Dunfermline 3-0 in the CIS Insurance Cup Final.

20 The day before players from the England-West Germany World Cup Final of 1966 visit the site, there is a safety scare at the troubled new Wembley project as a 50-ton roofing rafter falls out of place.

21 During the visit, former West Germany captain Franz Beckenbauer says the new stadium can be the best in the world.

22 Graham Rix, appointed in November, is sacked as coach of Hearts, despite his team's second place in the Scottish Premier League. Rotherham's short-term future is secured when a takeover of the club by a group of local businessmen is completed.

23 Jim Smith begins a second spell as Oxford manager – 21 years after his first ended – as part of businessman Nick Merry's £2m. buy-out of owner Firoz Kassam. Lomana LuaLua is warned about his future conduct by the F.A. for comments made to the media about referee Uriah Rennie after Portsmouth's defeat at Tottenham.

24 Scottish football loses a third sponsor with the Bank of Scotland's announcement of the end of their backing of the S.P.L. when a £17m., nine-year deal ends in 2007.

25 Reading clinch promotion to the Premiership and will play top-flight football for the first time in their 135-year history. The first honours in Scotland go to Second Division Gretna, promoted for the second successive season.

27 Two Tottenham players agree long-term contract extensions, Michael Dawson until 2011 and Aaron Lennon until 2010.

28 Amid growing concern over players diving in matches, Sir Alex Ferguson says the surest way of stamping it out is for referees to show the red card.

30 Three England matches, the Community Shield and planned pop concerts have to find alternative venues after the announcement that the new Wembley will not be ready until 2007 because work is so far behind schedule.

31 Ole Gunnar Solskjaer, whose future seemed to be in doubt after two serious knee injuries followed by a fractured cheekbone, signs a new two-year contract with Manchester United.

APRIL 2006

1 Reading score five second half goals to beat Derby 5-0 and clinch the Championship title. A week after winning promotion, Gretna become the first team from the third tier to reach the Scottish Cup Final by beating Dundee 3-0.

2 In the other semi-final, Hearts are 4-0 winners over Hibernian, who have Ivan Sproule and Gary Smith sent off. Swansea beat Carlisle 2-1 to win the Football League Trophy, the competition re-named after sponsor LDV Vans went into liquidation.

5 Arsenal reach the Champions League semi-finals for the first time with a 2-0 aggregate win over Juventus. John Hartson scores on his 31st birthday against second-place Hearts to give Celtic the Scottish Premier League title with six games remaining.

6 Manchester United sign a four-year sponsorship worth £56.5m. with American insurance company AIG. Middlesbrough, 3-0 down on aggregate to Basle after 23 minutes of their UEFA Cup quarter-final second leg, stage a tremendous recovery to win 4-3 in a 90th minute goal by Massimo Maccarone. A crowd of nearly 15,000 at Selhurst Park watch former Crystal Palace player Geoff Thomas's testimonial, a re-run of the Manchester United–Crystal Palace F.A. Cup Final of 1990, which raises about £150,000 for leukaemia research. Bolton manager Sam Allardyce is fined £2,000 by the F.A. for criticising Mike Riley's refereeing of the goalless draw with Blackburn.

7 Brighton's new stadium project hits another snag when John Prescott admits he made a fundamental factual error when giving the go-ahead, necessitating a new decision by the Deputy Prime Minister. Fulham's Papa Bouba Diop signs a contract extension keeping him at the club until 2009.

9 The F.A. say Sven-Goran Eriksson will speak to Wayne Rooney and Michael Owen following allegations that Rooney ran up £700,000 in gambling debts with a business partner of Owen.

11 A survey by the Professional Footballers' Association shows that the average Premiership player earns £676,000 a year, an increase of 65% since 2000.

13 John Cornforth, manager of Torquay for less than three months, is replaced by the club's football adviser, Ian Atkins. Portsmouth manager Harry Redknapp is fined £1,500 for verbally abusing a match official at Derby while in charge of Southampton.

14 Football agents are paid between £125m. and £150m. a year, according to a survey by *The Independent*. Rob Kelly, appointed manager until the end of the season, is given the job on a permanent basis after steering Leicester away from the threat of relegation.

15 Sheffield United are promoted to the Premiership. Leicester's Matty Fryatt scores the season's quickest goal after 11 seconds against Preston. Forty-four years after resigning from the Football League for financial reasons, Accrington return by winning the Conference title.

18 A supporters' survey conducted by the Football League urges the introduction of sin-bins and goal-line technology.

19 Hermann Hreidarsson is suspended for the final three games of the season for elbowing Luis Boa Morte, an incident which went unpunished in Charlton's game at Fulham.

20 David Tuttle departs as manager of relegated Millwall after three months in charge. Wycombe manager John Gorman, whose wife died of cancer in February, is given compassionate leave for the remainder of the season. Swansea's Lee Trundle and Alan Tate receive police cautions for public order offences relating to their conduct after the Football League Trophy Final win over Carlisle.

22 Liverpool reach the F.A. Cup Final by beating Chelsea 2-1. Steve Bleasdale resigns as Peterborough's caretaker-manager just over an hour before the home match against Macclesfield, claiming interference from TV programme-makers at the club. Two months after becoming Walsall manager, Kevan Broadhurst is sacked after his team are relegated.

23 In the other F.A. Cup semi-final, West Ham overcome Middlesbrough 1-0. Liverpool captain Steven Gerrard is named Footballer of the Year by the P.F.A.

24 Mike Dean is replaced by Alan Wiley as referee for the F.A. Cup Final because his home on the Wirral is deemed too close to Liverpool.

25 Jens Lehmann saves a penalty from Villarreal's Juan Riquelme two minutes from time to preserve a 1-0 aggregate lead and put Arsenal in the Champions League Final for the first time.

26 Barcelona overcome AC Milan by the same scoreline in the other semi-final. Jimmy Bullard, a key midfield figure in Wigan's rise, agrees to join Fulham for £2.5m.

27 For the second time in three weeks, Middlesbrough stage a magnificent UEFA Cup comeback, with Massimo Maccarone again their match-winner. Trailing Steaua Bucharest 3-0 on aggregate midway through the first half, they reach a European final for the first time when Maccarone's 89th minute goal provides a 4-3 win. Arsenal's Thierry Henry becomes the first player to win the Football Writers' Association Footballer of the Year award for the third time. Chelsea are fined £10,000 by the F.A. after their players surround referee Mark Halsey during the game against West Bromwich Albion.

28 Portugal coach Luiz Felipe Scolari turns down the chance to succeed Sven-Goran Eriksson, blaming media intrusion. Liverpool's Luis Garcia and West Ham's Hayden Mullins are ruled out of the F.A. Cup Final after their appeals against red cards at Upton Park are rejected by the F.A.

29 Delight for Chelsea, who complete back-to-back Premiership title wins, but despair for Manchester's Wayne Rooney who breaks a bone in his right foot at Stamford Bridge. Birmingham and West Bromwich Albion are relegated along with Sunderland, while Rushden and Diamonds return to Conference after five years of league football. Alan Curbishley announces the end of 15 years in charge of Charlton. A consortium headed by the club's former vice-chairman Peter Gadsby takes control of Derby.

30 Celtic striker Shaun Maloney becomes the first to be chosen Player of the Year and Young Player of the Year by the Scottish P.F.A. Hearts goalkeeper Craig Gordon is the Scottish Football Writers' Association Player of the Year.

MAY 2006

1 A crowd of more than 13,000 at Millwall see Arsenal beat Leeds 5-0 in the Women's F.A. Cup Final to complete a third league and cup double in six seasons.

2 Tottenham's Ledley King signs a new four-year contract. Richard Money, a European Cup winner with Liverpool in 1981, is appointed Walsall manager. Irish broadcaster Setanta pay £54.5m. to show Scottish Premier League matches until 2010.

3 Hearts become the first Scottish team, apart from Celtic and Rangers, to qualify for the Champions League by clinching the runners-up spot.

4 Middlesbrough's Steve McClaren is named the new England coach. Blackburn manager Mark Hughes signs a new contract stretching to 2009.

5 The Premier League announce a new three-year TV deal worth £1.7 billion – an increase of £682m. – in which Sky lose their monopoly of coverage to Setanta. Manager Brian Little leaves Tranmere by mutual agreement. Relegated Rushden and Diamonds part company with their manager Barry Hunter. Former Bolton and Scunthorpe midfield player Peter Morrison is awarded more than £400,000 compensation for the tackle in a match against Grimsby which ended his career.

6 In a twist of fate, Oxford are relegated to the Conference three weeks after Accrington, the side they replaced in the Football League 44 years ago, are promoted.

8 Sven-Goran Eriksson includes 17-year-old Theo Walcott, who has yet to play a first team game for Arsenal, in England's squad for the World Cup Finals. Harry Redknapp's reward for steering Portsmouth clear of relegation is a new three-year contract.

9 Roy Keane's testimonial match between Manchester United and Celtic at Old Trafford is watched by a record crowd for such an event of 69,591 and raises more than £2m. for various charities.

10 Tottenham's call for their final game of the season against West Ham – a 2-1 defeat which cost the club fourth place – to be replayed because of several players falling ill is rejected by the Premier League. Steve Coppell, named Manager of the Year by the League Managers' Association, signs a new one-year contract with promoted Reading. Danny Wilson is sacked as manager of relegated MK Dons.

11 Manager Joe Royle parts company with Ipswich. A crowd of 52,275 at St James' Park watch Alan Shearer's testimonial match against Celtic, raising more than £1m. for various charities. Rangers pair Kris Boyd and Chris Burke mark their debuts for Scotland with two goals each in a 5-1 win over Bulgaria in the Kirin Cup international in Kobe.

12 Rotherham are deducted ten points from the start of next season for going into administration. Newcastle goalkeeper Shay Given signs a new five-year contract.

13 Liverpool beat West Ham on penalties after a 3-3 draw in the F.A. Cup Final, rated one of the finest in the competition's history. The Scottish Cup Final also goes to a shoot-out, Hearts beating Greta after the team finish 1-1. Scotland draw 0-0 with Japan in Saitama to win the Kirin Cup competition.

14 The Football League Trophy gains a new sponsor, Johnstone's Paint, in an undisclosed seven-figure, three-year deal. Grays retain the F.A. Trophy with a 2-0 victory over Woking at Upton Park.

15 Germany captain Michael Ballack, out-of-contract at Bayern Munich, joins Chelsea in a deal worth a reported £130,000 a week. Tottenham sign a club-record £34m., four-year sponsorship with on-line gaming company Mansion.

16 Glenn Roeder is rewarded for restoring Newcastle's fortunes with the manager's job on a permanent basis, despite not having the required UEFA coaching qualifications. Tests clear a London hotel of causing Tottenham players' sickness before their final game of the season against West Ham. Steve Thompson steps down as Yeovil manager to return to coaching duties.

17 Goalkeeper Jens Lehmann is sent off as Arsenal lose 2-1 to Barcelona in the Champions League Final. Tottenham sign the Bayer Leverkusen striker Dimitar Berbatov for £10.9m. Motherwell manager Terry Butcher joins Australian champions Sydney as coach and is replaced by his assistant, Maurice Malpas.

18 Neil Warnock is banned from the touchline for Sheffield United's first two Premiership matches of the new season over incidents with Leeds manager Kevin Blackwell and Norwich's Nigel Worthington. The F.A. ban Warnock for six games, four of them suspended, and fine him £1,000. Relegated Swindon sack manager Iffy Onuora.

19 Thierry Henry ends all the speculation about his future by signing a new four-year contract with Arsenal.

20 Hereford return to the Football League after a nine-year absence by beating Halifax 3-2 in the Conference Play-off Final.

21 Watford are back in the Premiership after a 3-0 victory over Leeds in the Championship Play-off Final. Aston Villa's Steven Davis, 21, becomes Northern Ireland's youngest captain for their first match of a tour of the U.S.A., a 1-0 defeat by Uruguay in New Jersey.

22 Dennis Wise becomes Swindon's new manager, with former Chelsea team-mate Gus Poyet as his assistant. Stoke's Icelandic owners sell the club back to former chairman Peter Coates for £1.7m.

23 Arsenal sign midfielder Tomas Rosicky from Borussia Dortmund for £6.8m. Nigel Spackman, formerly in charge of Barnsley and Sheffield United, is appointed Millwall manager. Former Nottingham Forest manager Paul Hart takes over at relegated Rushden and Diamonds.

24 Steve Staunton suffers his first defeat as Republic of Ireland manager – 1-0 against Chile at Lansdowne Road. Rangers are fined £13,400 by UEFA for crowd disorder in their Champions League game against Villarreal, but fans are cleared of sectarian chanting. Keith Alexander resigns as Lincoln manager after four successive appearances in the play-offs.

25 Michael Owen comes through his first start of the year after a foot injury in England's 2-1 defeat by Belarus in a B international at Reading. But Robert Green is carried off with a damaged groin, ruled out of the World Cup squad and replaced by Liverpool's Scott Carson. Crystal Palace are fined £42,500 and Watford £35,000 by the F.A. for a players' brawl in the play-off semi-final at Vicarage Road. Bury are deducted one point for fielding an unregistered player against Lincoln and given a suspended £5,000 fine.

26 Terry Venables turns down the chance of a return to Middlesbrough as manager. Johan Boskamp, manager of Stoke for 11 months, leaves to become coach of Standard Liege in Belgium. Wycombe manager John Gorman, who has been on compassionate leave following the death of his wife, is relieved of his duties. Manager Gudjon Thordarson leaves Notts County by mutual agreement.

27 Southampton defender Gareth Bale, at 16 years and 315 days, becomes the youngest Wales international in their 2-1 win over Trinidad and Tobago, taking the record off Derby's Lewin Nyatanga. Northern Ireland have James Quinn sent off in a 2-0 defeat by Romania in Chicago. Barnsley beat Swansea on penalties in the League One Play-off Final.

28 Cheltenham are 1-0 winners over Grimsby in the League Two Play-off Final.

29 Andy Johnson agrees an £8.6m. move from Crystal Palace to Everton – a record for both clubs.

30 Arsenal's Theo Walcott, at 17 years and 75 days, becomes England's youngest international during a 3-1 win over Hungary in which John Terry scores their first international goal. After being unveiled as Charlton's new manager, Iain Dowie is served with a writ issued by Crystal Palace chairman Simon Jordan claiming 'fraudulent misrepresentation' over his departure from Selhurst Park. On the day they sign Feyenoord striker Salomon Kalou for a fee of around £3.5m. Chelsea are fined £10,000 by the F.A. for failing to control their players during last season's defeat at Fulham. Colin Calderwood leaves promoted Northampton to become Nottingham Forest manager. Keith Alexander is named Peterborough manager a week after leaving Lincoln.

31 Chelsea smash the British transfer record with the £30.8m signing of AC Milan's 29-year-old Ukraine striker Andriy Shevchenko.

JUNE 2006

1 Marlon King is ruled out of the Jamaica squad to face England at Old Trafford for an alleged breach of discipline. Oldham part company with manager Ronnie Moore for financial reasons and appoint former midfielder John Sheridan in his place.

2 Manchester United accept a £12m. settlement for 19-year-old John Obi Mikel, enabling the Nigerian midfield player to join Chelsea, who will also pay his Norwegian club Lyn Oslo £4m. Liverpool manager Rafael Benitez signs a new four-year contract. Billy Davies leaves Preston to become Derby manager. Arsenal vice-chairman David Dein is voted off the F.A. executive board, his place going to Manchester United's David Gill.

3 Peter Crouch scores a hat-trick as England complete their competitive World Cup build-up with a 6-0 win over Jamaica, the biggest in Sven-Goran Eriksson's five years as coach.

5 After a seven-year playing career with the club, Jim Magilton is appointed Ipswich manager. Ten days after being relieved of his duties at Wycombe, John Gorman becomes Northampton's new manager. Graham Rodger steps up from assistant manager to take charge at Grimsby.

6 Gareth Southgate is promoted from Middlesbrough captain to manager, despite not having the required UEFA coaching qualifications.

7 A scan on his injured foot offers Wayne Rooney hope of playing in the World Cup. FIFA order fines of £2,205 for players guilty of diving during the finals. Russell Slade is appointed manager of Yeovil, a week after leaving Grimsby.

8 The Premier League voice strong opposition to plans by FIFA for all top divisions in Europe to have no more than 18 teams from the 2007-08 season. The BBC win the rights to continue showing Premiership highlights on *Match of the Day* until at least 2010 with a bid of £171.6m.

9 Germany launch the World Cup Finals with a 4-2 win over Costa Rica. Former Tranmere striker Ronnie Moore returns to the club as manager.

10 England make a winning, if none too impressive, start to their World Cup campaign with a 1-0 victory over Paraguay.

12 Roy Keane calls time on a glittering career, on the advice of his surgeon and the Celtic club doctor, because of a long-standing hip injury. Joe Cole agrees a new four-year contract with Chelsea. Steve Thompson, assistant manager of Notts County in the mid-90s, returns to the club as manager.

13 Manager Tony Pulis resigns as Plymouth manager to return to Stoke, a year after the club sacked him for not buying enough foreign players. Peter Taylor leaves Hull to become Crystal Palace's tenth manager in ten years.

14 The managerial merry-go-round continues. Danny Wilson, sacked by MK Dons, takes over at Hartlepool, while Leroy Rosenior, dismissed by Torquay, moves in at Brentford. Chelsea's Eidur Gudjohnsen joins Barcelona for £8m. and Joleon Lescott leaves Wolves for Everton in a deal rising to £5m.

15 Goals in the final ten minutes by Peter Crouch and Steven Gerrard give England a 2-0 win over Trinidad and Tobago and a place in round two of the World Cup. Lincoln announce a new management team of head coach John Schofield and former Norwich manager John Deehan as director of football.

16 Premier League chairman Dave Richards is knighted in the Queen's Birthday Honours. Barry Ferguson, Rangers and Scotland captain, receives an MBE. So does former Millwall and Queens Park Rangers manager Gordon Jago, for promoting international youth football.

19 Paul Simpson, who led Carlisle from the Conference to League One in successive seasons, becomes Preston's new manager.

20 Michael Owen ruptures ligaments in his right knee after two minutes of the 2-2 draw with Sweden as England top their World Cup group.

21 Michael Owen flies home facing at least six months out of football. Martin Allen, who resigned as Brentford manager, takes over at MK Dons.

22 Liverpool pay £6m. for Blackburn's Craig Bellamy.

23 The Football League lose a claim for £150m. damages against former legal advisers over the collapsed television deal with ITV Digital, a judge awarding just £4 for two 'breaches of duty.' Promoted Colchester secure a temporary High Court injunction preventing manager Phil Parkinson from walking out of the club.

25 A goal from a free-kick by David Beckham gives England victory over Ecuador and a place in the quarter-finals of the World Cup.

26 Swansea's Lee Trundle and Alan Tate are each banned for one match and fined a week's wages by the F.A. of Wales for misconduct after the League Trophy Final at the Millennium Stadium. Their club receive a £2,000 fine.

27 Ian Holloway, who was suspended by Queens Park Rangers in February and settled with the club earlier this month, is appointed manager of Plymouth. Rangers confirm caretaker Gary Waddock as Holloway's successor.

28 Former Arsenal and England stalwart Tony Adams is appointed assistant to Harry Redknapp at Portsmouth.

29 Premiership referee Graham Poll announces his retirement from international football after showing Croatian defender Josip Simunic three yellow cards before sending him off in the World Cup game against Australia. Phil Parkinson leaves Colchester to become Hull's new manager after the clubs agree a £400,000 compensation fee.

30 Bob Murray steps down as Sunderland chairman after 20 years, opening the way for a takeover of the club by a consortium headed by former striker Niall Quinn. Former Celtic and Scotland captain Paul Lambert is appointed Wycombe manager. Neil McDonald, former Newcastle and Everton defender, takes over at Carlisle.

JULY 2006

1 Wayne Rooney is sent off and England lose their World Cup quarter-final against Portugal on penalties after a goalless 120 minutes. Tottenham sign the Ivory Coast midfield player Didier Zakora from St Etienne for £8.2m.

2 David Beckham steps down as England captain after leading the side in 58 of his 94 international appearances. Glenn Hoddle resigns as Wolves manager.

3 The consortium headed by Niall Quinn has a takeover bid of £10m. for Sunderland accepted.

4 Italy score twice through Fabio Grosso and Alessandro Del Piero at the end of extra-time to beat Germany in the first World Cup semi-final.

5 France beat Portugal with a Zinedine Zidane penalty in the other semi-final. More than 15 months after throwing punches at Newcastle team-mate Kieron Dyer during a home match against Aston Villa, Lee Bowyer appears in court and is fined £600 by magistrates.

6 Michael Owen has an operation on his injured knee in Colorado and could be out of action for up to a year. Wigan agree a club-record £5.5m. for Birmingham's Emile Heskey.

7 Sir Bobby Robson, who managed Ipswich to the F.A. Cup, UEFA Cup and to two League Championship runners-up spots, is made club president.

9 France captain Zinedine Zidane scores but is then sent off for head-butting Marco Materazzi as Italy win the World Cup Final on penalties after a 1-1 scoreline.

10 Rangers defender Fernando Ricksen is sent home from the pre-season tour of South Africa after an incident with a stewardess on the flight to Johannesburg.

11 World Cup winner Marcello Lippi steps down as Italy coach. So does Germany's Jurgen Klinsmann.

12 Zinedine Zidane apologises for being sent off in the World Cup Final but insists he has no regrets for his assault on Marco Materazzi, blaming severe provocation. Twenty four hours after Liverpool announce the transfer of Dietmar Hamann to Bolton, the player has a change of heart and joins Manchester City.

13 Robert Huth's £5m. move from Chelsea to Middlesbrough falls through when he fails a medical.

17 Alexandre Gaydamak takes full control of Portsmouth in a deal for chairman Milan Mandaric's remaining shares.

18 Millwall are fined £30,000 by the F.A. with a further £40,000 suspended for 90 yellow cards and 12 reds last season.

19 David O'Leary's contract as Aston Villa manager is terminated in the wake of a dressing room statement critical of chairman Doug Ellis. West Ham's Shaun Newton is banned for seven months by the F.A. after testing positive for cocaine.

NO RED CARDS FOR CHAMPIONS

Reading, who won the Championship, and League Two Macclesfield Town were the only English teams not to have a player sent off in League matches during the 2005-06 season. Champions Celtic, Kilmarnock and Livingston shared the best record in the Scottish Premier League, with one dismissal each.

HIGHLIGHTS OF THE PREMIERSHIP SEASON 2005-06

AUGUST 2005

13 Wayne Rooney scores against his former club as Manchester United launch the new campaign with a 2-0 lunch-time win at Everton. Kevin Phillips, on his debut for Aston Villa, nets the first of four goals in the first nine minutes, the 2-2 scoreline against Bolton remaining to the final whistle. Darren Bent hits two on his debut for Charlton, who, despite having another new signing Darren Ambrose sent off, win 3-1 at promoted Sunderland. West Ham, also back in the top flight, deliver the same scoreline against Blackburn, who have Paul Dickov dismissed. Another red card is shown to Middlesbrough's Ugo Ehiogu in a goalless draw with Liverpool.
14 A last-minute goal by Hernan Crespo enables Chelsea to open their defence of the title with victory against new boys Wigan in front of a record crowd of 23,575 at the JJB Stadium. Jermaine Jenas becomes the fourth player sent off as Newcastle lose 2-0 to two Arsenal goals in the final ten minutes, but the F.A. later agree to referee Steve Bennett's request to downgrade the card to yellow.
20 Two more controversial dismissals are rescinded by the F.A. West Ham's Paul Konchesky is sent off against Newcastle, who fail to take advantage in a goalless draw, and Andy Welsh sees red in Sunderland's 1-0 defeat at Liverpool. Andy Cole opens his account for Manchester City, who win 2-1 at Birmingham, while spectacular volleys by Morten Gamst Pedersen and Tugay earn Blackburn victory by the same scoreline against Fulham.
21 Arsene Wenger's 500th game in charge of Arsenal is spoiled when a fortuitous strike by substitute Didier Drogba enables Chelsea to end a run of 19 matches without a League win over their London rivals.
23 Two goals by Mark Viduka, his first since December, point Middlesbrough to a 3-0 victory at Birmingham. Trevor Sinclair, another player dogged by injury, scores his first for nearly a year and Darius Vassell gets his first for the club as Manchester City go top of the table for 24 hours with a 2-1 success at Sunderland. Nolberto Solano is sent off at Portsmouth, but Aston Villa rescue a 1-1 draw.
24 Frank Lampard celebrates the birth of his daughter with two goals in Chelsea's 4-0 win over West Bromwich Albion. Thierry Henry finds an unlikely scoring partner in Pascal Cygan, both scoring twice as Arsenal come from behind to beat Fulham 4-1. Blackburn's Lucas Neill is sent off in a goalless draw with Tottenham.
27 Asier Del Horno scores his first goal for Chelsea in a 2-0 over Tottenham, who have Mido sent off. Phil Neville is also dismissed in Everton's 1-0 defeat at Fulham. Wigan are off the mark with a Jason Roberts penalty against Sunderland, awarded after just 12 seconds, while Milan Baros, on his Aston Villa debut, nets the only goal against Blackburn. Emile Heskey and Geoff Horsfield both score twice at the Hawthorns, but Heskey's Birmingham prevail 3-2 in the season's first midlands derby against West Bromwich Albion.
28 More gloom for the north east as Middlesbrough go down 3-0 at home to revitalised Charlton and Manchester United win 2-0 at Newcastle. Chelsea end the month two points ahead of Manchester City.

SEPTEMBER 2005

10 Michael Owen, on his debut, wins the free-kick from which Charles N'Zogbia earns Newcastle a point against Fulham after they have Scott Parker red-carded. Joey Barton gives City a point in the Manchester derby after Ruud van Nistelrooy puts United ahead. David Connolly scores on his first appearance for Wigan, who beat West Bromwich Albion 2-1 away from home. Everton's early-season problems continue when Duncan Ferguson's own goal gives Portsmouth victory at Goodison Park.

12 Marlon Harewood registers the season's first Premiership hat-trick in West Ham's 4-0 victory over Aston Villa.

17 Alan Curbishley is presented with an engraved clock by Jose Mourinho to mark 600 games in charge of Charlton, but his team get nothing from Chelsea, whose 2-0 win maintains a 100% record in six games – the best-ever start to a Premiership season. Sunderland are within seconds of ending a run of 20 successive Premiership defeats, spread over two seasons, with a victory when Zoltan Gera heads an equaliser for West Bromwich Albion. Marlon Harewood follows up his hat-trick by scoring once and having a shot against the post ricochet into the net off goalkeeper Tony Warner as West Ham beat Fulham 2-1. James Milner scores his first goal for Aston Villa in a 1-1 draw with Tottenham, while Birmingham hold on for the same result at Portsmouth after having Nicky Butt sent off.

18 Michael Owen opens his account for Newcastle and Alan Shearer claims his first League goal since February as Newcastle win for the first time, 3-0 at Blackburn, despite having Steven Taylor sent off. Manchester City are left cursing their luck after hitting the woodwork five times against Bolton, who pinch victory with Gary Speed's stoppage-time penalty. Henri Camara's first goal for Wigan brings a 1-1 draw against Middlesbrough, but Liverpool and Manchester United are goalless in a dour game at Anfield.

19 Sol Campbell marks his return after a lengthy spell of injury with two headed goals to give Arsenal a 2-0 victory over Everton.

24 Aston Villa's Luke Moore becomes the first player to score against Chelsea, but Frank Lampard nets twice for the champions. They lead by six points from Charlton, who defeat West Bromwich Albion 2-1 with two from Danny Murphy. Manchester United, beaten 2-1 at home by a Morten Gamst Pedersen double for Blackburn, fall ten points behind, while Arsenal trail by 11 after a goalless draw with West Ham. Neil Kilkenny, 19, is sent off on his Premiership debut for Birmingham, who share a 2-2 draw with Liverpool. Portsmouth manager Alain Perrin is sent to the stands for touchline protests during the 1-0 defeat by Bolton.

25 Goals by Tommy Miller and Julio Arca give Sunderland their first Premiership victory in 27 attempts, 2-0 at Middlesbrough.

OCTOBER 2005

1 Trailing to two goals by Charlton's in-form Darren Bent, Tottenham hit back to win 3-2. Manchester United also come from behind to beat Fulham by the same scoreline, Ruud van Nistelrooy scoring twice. Shefki Kuqi comes off the bench to open his account for Blackburn with two in the final ten minutes to set up victory against West Bromwich Albion.

2 Four days after a goalless draw in the Champions League, Chelsea return to Anfield and beat Liverpool 4-1. Birmingham captain Kenny Cunningham is sent off in the 1-0 defeat by Arsenal.

15 Frank Lampard, whose goals against Austria and Poland eased England into the World Cup Finals, claims two more as Chelsea come from behind to beat Bolton 5-1. All five come in the second half when Bolton have Ricardo Gardner sent off. Paul Jewell celebrates his Manager of the Month award as Wigan edge out Newcastle 1-0, although there is controversy as Alan Shearer's header which looks to have crossed the line is disallowed. Wigan have Lee McCulloch dismissed and there is a third red card for Blackburn's Zurab Khizanishvili in the 1-0 defeat at Liverpool. This one is later overturned on appeal. Giuseppe Rossi, 18, comes off the bench for his Premiership debut and is on the mark for Manchester United in their 3-1 victory at Sunderland, while Jermaine Jenas heads his first for Tottenham, who beat struggling Everton 2-0. Surprise of the day is West Bromwich Albion's 2-1 victory over Arsenal, with Kanu scoring against his former club.

16 Aston Villa's Kevin Phillips returns after injury to net the only goal of the local derby against Birmingham. Two by Andy Cole bring Manchester City a 2-1 win over West Ham.

22 A cheeky penalty plot turns into a French farce at Highbury as Robert Pires shapes to pass his spot-kick for Thierry Henry to score, but scuffs his lay-off and Manchester City clear the ball. Arsenal still manage to win with an authentic Pires penalty earlier. Craig Bellamy claims his first Premiership goal for Blackburn, who beat Birmingham 2-0. So does Darren Ambrose for Charlton, who win 2-1 at Portsmouth.

23 Chelsea's 100% record ends in their tenth match, a 1-1 draw against bottom team Everton. Calls for the introduction of goal-line technology are renewed after West Ham's second goal in a 2-1 victory over Middlesbrough is allowed to stand, Mark Schwarzer having fumbled Chris Riggott's touch. Japan's Hidetoshi Nakata scores his first goal for Bolton, who beat West Bromwich Albion 2-0, while Turkey midfielder Emre's first for Newcastle gives them a 3-2 victory over Sunderland and relieves the pressure on manager Graeme Souness.

29 Wigan move up to second with a fifth successive victory, earned by Pascal Chimbonda's stoppage-time strike against Fulham, his first for the club. Two by Craig Bellamy enable Blackburn to cancel out a 2-0 lead established by Chelsea, but the leaders pull away in the second half to win 4-2 and end the month nine points clear. Cristiano Ronaldo scores Manchester United's 1,000th Premiership goal, but his team are hammered 4-1 by Middlesbrough, for whom Gaizka Mendieta nets twice. Two by Matthew Taylor, one a spectacular strike from 40 yards, help Portsmouth come from behind and win 4-1 at Sunderland, while Boudewijn Zenden opens his account for Liverpool, who overcome West Ham 2-0.

30 Darius Vassell makes life difficult for his former team Aston Villa by scoring twice in Manchester City's 3-1 success.

NOVEMBER 2005

5 Steed Malbranque's first goals of the season earn Fulham a 2-1 victory over Manchester City, the club that tried to buy him last summer. Thierry Henry also gets two and Robin van Persie one as Arsenal's new strike partnership continues to blossom in the 3-1 win over Sunderland. Charlton's 100% away record comes to an end in a 4-1 defeat by Blackburn.

6 Darren Fletcher's first of the season for Manchester United, a header from Cristiano Ronaldo's cross, inflicts Chelsea's first defeat.

19 Portsmouth's 3-0 defeat at Liverpool spells the end for manager Alain Perrin. Wigan's run of six successive wins is ended by Arsenal, for whom Thierry Henry scores twice and Robin van Persie once in a 3-2 scoreline. Ruud van Nistelrooy gets two for Manchester United, who make light of the sudden departure of Roy Keane with a 3-1 victory at Charlton. Nathan Ellington's first goals in the top-flight set up West Bromwich Albion for their biggest Premiership success – 4-0 against Everton.

20 Anton Ferdinand's stoppage-time equaliser for West Ham against Tottenham is his first in the Premiership. So too is James Morrison's effort for Middlesbrough in a 3-2 win over Fulham.

26 Frank Lampard marks a record-breaking 160th successive Premiership appearance with his 11th goal of the season, from the penalty spot, as Chelsea win 2-0 at Portsmouth to end the month ten points clear of Manchester United. Edgar Davids scores his first for Tottenham in a 2-1 victory at Wigan. Julian Gray's first of the season enables Birmingham to end a run of five successive defeats with a win at Sunderland and John Arne Riise's first of the campaign for Liverpool is enough to account for Manchester City.

27 Wayne Rooney pays his own tribute to George Best with a superb performance in Manchester United's 2-1 success at West Ham. John O'Shea scores the winner, his first of the season. Bolton have a bad day at Fulham, losing 2-1 to Brian McBride's double, having El-Hadji Diouf sent off for comments to referee Graham Poll in the tunnel afterwards and incurring an automatic Premier League fine of £25,000 for six bookings. Joseph Yobo's first goal since April 2004 gives Everton a 1-0 win over Newcastle.

DECEMBER 2005

3 Peter Crouch breaks his duck for Liverpool with a double strike in a 3-0 win over Wigan. Arsenal's chances of catching Chelsea are almost over as another summer signing, Abdoulaye Faye, heads his first goal for Bolton in a 2-0 victory. Michael Carrick also opens his account after almost a season and a half with Tottenham, who beat Sunderland 3-2. Andy Todd is sent off in Blackburn's 2-0 defeat by Everton and Luis Boa Morte sees red in Fulham's goalless draw against West Bromwich Albion.

4 Charlton's demise after a bright start to the season continues with a 5-2 reversal at home to Manchester City, for whom Andy Cole scores twice.

10 For the second successive week, John Terry heads the only goal of the game for Chelsea, who follow up victory over Middlesbrough by beating Wigan. Charlton end a run of five successive defeats by overcoming Sunderland 2-0 and Birmingham win at home for the first time this season, 1-0 against Fulham. Nolberto Solano's first goal since returning to Newcastle from Aston Villa is enough to beat Arsenal, who have Gilberto Silva sent off. Also dismissed are Chris Riggott in Middlesbrough's 2-0 defeat by Liverpool and Andy Cole as Manchester City lose by the same scoreline to West Bromwich Albion, for whom Diomansy Kamara gets his first Premiership goal. West Ham, defeated 3-2 by Blackburn, have six players booked, triggering a £25,000 fine.

12 Portsmouth are six minutes away from gaining a point in Harry Redknapp's first match back in charge when a controversial penalty is converted by Mido and Tottenham go on to win 3-1.

14 Rio Ferdinand, on his 140th appearance for Manchester United, scores for the first time in a 4-0 victory over Wigan.

17 Michael Owen fires a hat-trick in Newcastle's 4-2 success at West Ham and Henri Camara gets all three for Wigan, who beat Charlton 3-0. David Sommeil sets Manchester City on the way to a 4-1 victory over Birmingham with the quickest goal of the season so far after 42 seconds. Bolton also hit four, without replay, at Everton, who suffer their biggest home defeat for 12 years. Portsmouth's injury-dogged Bulgarian striker, Svetoslav Todorov, is on the mark for the first time since May 2003 to give Harry Redknapp his first success back in charge at Fratton Park, 1-0 against West Bromwich Albion.

18 Arsene Wenger concedes the title after Arsenal lose 2-0 to goals from Arjen Robben and Joe Cole for Chelsea at Highbury.

26 Fulham retrieve a two-goal deficit at Stamford Bridge before Hernan Crespo reasserts Chelsea's authority with the winner. Mark Delaney's first goal for Aston Villa since August 1999 comes in a 4-0 success against Everton. Michael Owen draws a blank on his return to Anfield, where Lee Bowyer is sent off for the second successive season as Newcastle go down 2-0. Also dismissed are Danny Murphy in Charlton's 1-0 defeat by Arsenal, Birmingham's Muzzy Izzet in the 2-0 loss to Tottenham and Portsmouth's Laurent Robert in a 1-1 draw with West Ham. Rio Ferdinand scores for the second time in three League games as Manchester United beat West Bromwich Albion 3-0.

28 Freezing conditions force the postponement of three matches, but there is no stopping Liverpool's march to a ninth successive victory, 3-1 against Everton, who have Phil Neville and Mikel Arteta sent off. Neither are Chelsea disturbed by the absence of Frank Lampard, whose record run of 164 successive Premiership appearances is ended by a virus. The champions beat Manchester City 1-0. Liam Ridgewell doubles his career goals tally for Aston Villa with two in the 3-3 draw at Fulham.

31 Chelsea end the year 11 points clear of Manchester United at the top after a 2-0 victory over Birmingham. Teemu Tainio's first goal in a Tottenham shirt sets up a 2-0 win over Newcastle. Three players open their Premiership account for the season, Louis Saha as United beat Bolton 4-1, Shaun Bartlett as Charlton defeat West Ham 2-0 and Everton's Tim Cahill with the only goal at Sunderland.

JANUARY 2006

2 Liverpool's run of ten successive wins comes to an end in a 2-2 draw at Bolton. Jermaine Pennant scores his first League goal for Birmingham and sets up a second for Mario Melchiot, his first of the season, in the 2-0 success against Wigan. Lee Clark gets his first since rejoining Newcastle in the summer, a last-minute equaliser for 2-2 against Middlesbrough. Steve Watson puts West Bromwich Albion on level terms against Aston Villa, but then concedes the penalty which Milan Baros converts for the winner.

3 Chelsea's grip on the title becomes even stronger as Arsenal and Manchester United share a goalless draw.

14 Thierry Henry bags a hat-trick and Alexander Hleb scores his first goal in English football as Arsenal register the biggest win of the season, 7-0 against Middlesbrough, who have Doriva sent off. Harry Kewell's first for 13 months for Liverpool, a spectacular volley, earns victory over Tottenham, for whom Paul Stalteri sees red. Robbie Fowler's first of the season in the Premiership completes City's 3-1 success against United in the Manchester derby. United's Cristiano Ronaldo is dismissed and so too is Bolton's Hidetoshi Nakata in the goalless draw with Blackburn. Portsmouth field five new players against Everton, but show the same old failings and lose 1-0.

15 Arjen Robben receives a second yellow for celebrating his winner for Chelsea, who come from behind to beat bottom-of-the-table Sunderland 2-1, and Darren Moore is the weekend's sixth dismissal, in West Bromwich Albion's single goal victory at Wigan.

21 Sunderland celebrate their second win of the season, thanks to an own goal from West Bromwich Albion's Steve Watson. Matthew Upson, Mikael Forssell and David Dunn each score their first Premiership goal of the season as Birmingham overwhelm Portsmouth 5-0. Jared Borgetti claims his first for Bolton, who defeat Manchester City 2-0. There are two dismissals, Francesc Fabregas in Arsenal's 1-0 defeat at Everton and Gareth Barry as Aston Villa share a goalless draw at Tottenham.

22 Rio Ferdinand's last-minute header earns Manchester United victory over Liverpool. Marcus Bent comes off the bench to score on his debut and earn Charlton a point at Chelsea.

31 Everton's Duncan Ferguson and Wigan's Jason Roberts are sent off in separate incidents during a 1-1 draw. Emanuel Pogatetz and Stuart Parnaby score for the first time for Middlesbrough, who win 3-0 at Sunderland, and another defender, Fulham's Carlos Bocanegra, gets his first of the season to inflict a 1-0 defeat on Tottenham with a last-minute header. Chelsea's lead over Manchester United is 14 points.

FEBRUARY 2006

1 Sol Campbell walks out of Highbury after being substituted at half-time of Arsenal's 3-2 defeat by West Ham in which Thierry Henry surpasses Cliff Bastin's club record of 150 League goals. The day after a permanent move from Arsenal, David Bentley hits a hat-tick in Blackburn's 4-3 thriller against Manchester United, who have Rio Ferdinand sent off. Also dismissed is Birmingham's Damien Johnson, but they secure a late point at Liverpool with Xabi Alonso's own goal. Portsmouth and Bolton draw 1-1, with Azar Karadas and Khalilou Fadiga on the mark for the first time for their respective club, and Albert Riera claims his first for Manchester City, whose 3-0 victory over Newcastle is followed by the sacking of Graeme Souness.

4 Alan Shearer, assisting caretaker-manager Glenn Roeder following the dismissal of Souness, scores his 201st goal for Newcastle in the 2-0 win over Portsmouth to break Jackie Milburn's club record tally. Luke Moore, 19, nets a hat-trick in Aston Villa's 4-0 victory at Middlesbrough. New-signing Dean Ashton and Dean Koncheský open their account for West Ham, who beat Sunderland 2-0. So too does Emmanuel Adebayor for Arsenal who win by the same scoreline at Birmingham and Wigan's Andreas Johansson against Bolton (1-1). Kevin Campbell puts West Bromwich Albion on the way to a 2-0 success over Blackburn on his 36th birthday. Sunderland's Stephen Wright and Birmingham's Emile Heskey are sent off, along with Stephen Jordan in Manchester City's 1-0 defeat by Everton.

5 Goalkeeper Jose Reina sees red for pushing Arjen Robben in the face as Liverpool go down 2-0 at Chelsea.

8 Jerzy Dudek's first start since Liverpool's Champions League triumph last season is an uncomfortable one. He brings down Darren Bent, who converts the resulting penalty, and Luke Young seals Charlton's 2-0 win with his first goal since September 2004.

11 Middlesbrough spring a surprise, a second minute goal by the Brazilian Fabio Rochembaq paving the way for a 3-0 win over Chelsea. Everton's Iain Turner is sent off nine minutes into his Premiership debut against Blackburn for handling outside the area. He is replaced by another debutant, John Ruddy, who keeps a clean sheet as

Everton hold on 1-0. Newcastle also win with ten men, 2-1 at Aston Villa after Celestine Babayaro sees red. Heidar Helguson and substitute Collins John both score twice as Fulham thrash West Bromwich Albion 6-1. Cristiano Ronaldo gets two as Manchester United win 3-1 at Portsmouth, while Sami Hyypia's first of the season earns Liverpool the points at Wigan.

12 Daryl Murphy's first goal for Sunderland, after 89 minutes, earns a point against Tottenham. Georgios Samaras also comes off the bench to get his first for Manchester City, who beat Charlton 3-2.

13 Two goals by Marlon Harewood point West Ham towards their seventh successive League and FA Cup victory – 3-0 against Birmingham.

14 Arsenal goalkeeper Jens Lehmann keeps Liverpool at bay until Luis Garcia's 87th minute winner at Anfield.

25 Emile Heskey's first goal since early December gives relegation-threatened Birmingham victory over sinking Sunderland. Portsmouth, skating on thin ice, hold out for 65 minutes at Stamford Bridge before Chelsea take control to win 2-0 and go 15 points clear of Manchester United. Nolberto Solano scores twice against Everton to continue Glenn Roeder's successful run as Newcastle caretaker-manager.

26 West Bromwich Albion's problems increase with a 2-0 home defeat by Middlesbrough – Jimmy Floyd Hasselbaink scoring both goals – and the dismissal of Nigel Quashie. Joey Barton is also sent off as Manchester City lose 1-0 at Liverpool.

MARCH 2006

4 Arjen Robben is sent off for the second time in two months, but Chelsea win a bad-tempered match 2-1 against West Bromwich Albion. Fulham manager Chris Coleman hails two-goal Thierry Henry's performance in Arsenal's 4-0 romp at Craven Cottage as one of the finest he has seen. After a blank three months, Middlesbrough's Mark Viduka scores the only goal against Birmingham.

5 Mick McCarthy's three years as Sunderland manager come to an end after a 2-1 defeat by Manchester City, for whom Georgios Samaras scores twice in the first nine minutes. Sunderland have Gary Breen dismissed. Robbie Keane also hits a double in Tottenham's 3-2 win over Blackburn to round off one of the most satisfying weeks of his career in which he signs a new contract and captains the Republic of Ireland.

11 Michael Essien opens his account for Chelsea, then William Gallas strikes a spectacular last-minute winner after Jermaine Jenas equalises for Tottenham. On a day of eye-catching goals, Pedro Mendes hits two from distance, the second at the death, to give Portsmouth their first Premiership win of 2006 – 2-1 against Manchester City. Other two-goal marksmen are Stelios Giannakopoulos, in Bolton's 4-1 victory over West Ham, and James Beattie as Everton overcome Fulham 3-1.

12 Three more players double-up – Thierry Henry in Arsenal's 2-1 win over Liverpool, who have Xabi Alonso sent off, Darren Bent as Charlton beat Middlesbrough by the same scoreline and Wayne Rooney with two in the first 11 minutes for Manchester United against Newcastle (2-0).

15 Liverpool's 5-1 win over Fulham matches their goals tally from the previous eight Premiership games. Stephen Warnock gets his first for the club and Robbie Fowler his first since returning to Anfield.

18 Portsmouth provide Harry Redknapp with a happy return to Upton Park, punishing changes made by West Ham manager Alan Pardew ahead of his side's F.A. Cup sixth round tie against Manchester City with a 4-2 success. Portsmouth close the gap at the bottom on Birmingham, beaten 2-0 by Tottenham for whom Aaron Lennon claims his first Premiership goal, and West Bromwich Albion, defeated 2-1 by Manchester United. Gabriel Agbonlahor marks his debut for Aston Villa with a goal in the 4-1 reversal at Everton. Robbie Savage is dismissed for the first time in club football, but Blackburn prevail 3-2 against Middlesbrough.

19 Fulham end a run of four successive defeats by beating Chelsea for the first time in 27 years, Luis Boa Morte's strike upsetting the leaders, who have William Gallas sent off. Jean Alain Boumsong also sees red as Newcastle go down 3-1 at home to Liverpool.

25 Liverpool's Steven Gerrard is sent off for two yellow cards in the space of a minute in a tempestuous Merseyside derby which his side win 3-1 at Anfield. Everton's Andy Van der Meyde later receives a straight red and there are a further nine yellows, seven of them for Everton, who incur a £25,000 F.A. fine. In another eventful match, Didier Drogba scores both goals in Chelsea's 2-0 victory over Manchester City. A hand-ball for the second is not spotted and City's captain Sylvain Distin receives a second yellow at half-time for refusing to give Rob Styles the match ball when confronting the referee about the incident.

26 Gary Neville, on his 500th appearance for the club, leads Manchester United to a 3-0 win over Birmingham. United finish the month 12 points behind Chelsea, with a match in hand. Bolton retrieve a 3-1 deficit against Middlesbrough, but lose to a last-minute Stuart Parnaby goal.

APRIL 2006

1 Manchester United follow up a 1-0 midweek victory over West Ham by winning 2-1 at Bolton to reduce the deficit to seven points after Chelsea are held to a goalless draw by Birmingham. At the bottom, two goals by Gary O'Neil point revitalised Portsmouth to a 3-1 success at Fulham, who have Michael Brown sent off. Also dismissed is Michael Dawson in Tottenham's 3-1 defeat at Newcastle. Jon Stead finally breaks his duck for Sunderland, who hold Everton 2-2 at Goodison Park, and Vassiriki Diaby gets his first for Arsenal in their 5-0 thumping of Aston Villa.

2 Lee Cattermole scores his first for Middlesbrough to give them victory over fading Manchester City. At the other end of the scale, West Ham's Teddy Sheringham almost breaks the deadlock against Charlton on his 40th birthday, goalkeeper Thomas Myhre denying him.

8 Paul Stalteri's first Premiership goal for Tottenham launches a 2-1 win over Manchester City that boosts their chances of Champions League football next season. Portsmouth twice come from behind to earn a point after two spectacular strikes by Craig Bellamy for Blackburn. A blizzard and waterlogged pitch force Mike Riley to abandon the Sunderland-Fulham match after 22 minutes.

9 Chelsea fall behind to a James Collins goal for West Ham, then have midfielder Maniche sent off. But the defending champions win 4-1, ahead of Manchester United's 2-0 victory over Arsenal in front of the Premiership's first 70,000 crowd at the enlarged Old Trafford. Middlesbrough's George Boateng scores at both ends in the 2-1 defeat by Newcastle.

12 Sol Campbell, back for Arsenal after an absence of more than two months, suffers a broken nose in the 1-1 draw with Portsmouth.

14 Sunderland are relegated, ironically after giving one of their best performances of the season in a goalless draw at Old Trafford with Manchester United, whose chances of catching Chelsea are all but ended.

15 Chelsea win 2-0 at Bolton, who have Tal Ben Haim sent off. Arsenal designate their match against West Bromwich Albion 'Dennis Bergkamp Day' and the Dutchman comes off the bench to score one goal and set up another for Robert Pires in a 3-1 victory. Shaun Newton's first for West Ham brings victory over Manchester City, but Jason Euell's first for nearly 18 months is not enough for Charlton, who lose to two by Fulham's Luis Boa Morte. A brace by Alan Shearer gives Newcastle a 3-1 win over Wigan in an injury-dogged match, with five players having to be substituted in the first half – Wigan's Matt Jackson, Arjan De Zeeuw and Lee McCulloch and the home side's Lee Bowyer and Shola Ameobi.

16 Aston Villa pile more pressure on neighbours Birmingham, Milan Baros netting twice and Gary Cahill opening his account for the club with a spectacular scissors-kick for a 3-1 success.

17 Chelsea close to within a point of a second successive title by beating Everton 3-0 – hours after Manchester United win 2-1 at Tottenham with two goals from Wayne Rooney. Alan Shearer's distinguished career ends prematurely when he sustains a knee injury during Newcastle's 4-1 success at Sunderland in which Michael Chopra and Albert Luque score their first Premiership goals. A first for Andres D'Alessandro puts Portsmouth within reach of potential safety, but then they falter and lose 2-1 at Charlton.

19 An 87th minute winner by Mikael Forssell against Blackburn offers Birmingham hope of beating the drop.

22 Matthew Taylor's 88th minute penalty proves priceless for Portsmouth, delivering a 2-1 win over Sunderland. It puts them almost out of reach of West Bromwich Albion, beaten 3-0 at Newcastle, and two points clear of Birmingham, who share a goalless draw at Everton. Tottenham boost their chances of securing fourth place by holding Arsenal 1-1 at Highbury, while Bolton end a lean run of one point from six matches with a 4-1 victory over Charlton, Ricardo Vaz Te scoring his first Premiership goal.

25 Darius Vassell nets the only goal of the game against Aston Villa – his fourth of the season against his former club in league and F.A. Cup matches – to end Manchester City's run of six successive defeats.

26 Liverpool's Luis Garcia and West Ham's Hayden Mullins are ruled out of the F.A. Cup Final after being sent off in Liverpool's 2-1 victory at Upton Park.

29 Chelsea clinch the title by beating Manchester United 3-0. A fifth minute header from William Gallas calms nerves and Joe Cole and Ricardo Carvalho, with his first of the season in the Premiership, seal victory in a match overshadowed somewhat by a foot injury sustained by Wayne Rooney. Portsmouth complete the great escape as Benjani breaks his scoring duck and Matthew Taylor converts another winner from the penalty spot at Wigan. Their win sends Birmingham and West Bromwich Albion down. Fulham, the only team in the four divisions without an away win, shed this unwanted record thanks to Steed Malbranque's injury-time strike against Manchester City.

MAY 2006

1 Ashley Cole, out since mid-January with a foot injury, returns in Arsenal's 3-0 win at Sunderland.

2 Blackburn secure a UEFA Cup place thanks to Steven Reid's goal against Chelsea, who make eight changes from the side that clinched the title.

4 Sunderland avoid the embarrassment of becoming the first team to go a full season without a home win by beating Fulham 2-1. Arsenal close to within a point of fourth-place Tottenham with a 3-1 victory over Manchester City.

7 A hat-trick by Thierry Henry crowns an emotional – and ultimately successful – day for Arsenal. In Highbury's final match, they beat Wigan 4-2 and make sure of a Champions League place next season at Tottenham's expense. Tottenham, with several players hit by illness, lose 2-1 at West Ham, for whom Carl Fletcher stakes a claim for an F.A. Cup Final place with his first Premiership goal. Four other players achieve that distinction, Blackburn's Zurab Khizanishvili (2-0 v Manchester City), Everton's Victor Anichebe and West Bromwich Albion's Williams Martinez in a 2-2 draw, and Ognjen Koroman in Portsmouth's 3-1 defeat by Liverpool. Alan Curbishley's final match in charge of Charlton is a 4-0 beating by Manchester United. Steve McClaren's last league game with Middlesbrough, a 1-0 defeat by Fulham, is notable for the new England coach fielding ten graduates from the club's Academy. Three players are sent off, including Wigan's Andreas Johansson, who comes off the bench, pulls back Freddie Ljungberg to concede a penalty and departs without touching the ball. The others are Blackburn's Tugay and Newcastle's Stephen Carr in the 1-0 victory over Chelsea. Carr's red card is later rescinded.

CHAMPIONSHIP DOUBLE FOR DOYLE

Which player won league titles with two clubs in the 2005-06 season? The question is likely to be posed in many a sporting quiz after Kevin Doyle's rare double for Reading and Cork City. The 22-year-old striker collected a Coca-Cola Championship medal after scoring 18 goals for runaway leaders Reading. Then, before lining up for the Republic of Ireland in a friendly international against Chile at Lansdowne Road, Doyle was presented with his Eircom League medal, having played sufficient early-season matches for Cork before an £80,000 move to England.

BARCLAYS PREMIERSHIP RESULTS 2005-06

	Arsenal	Aston Villa	Birmingham City	Blackburn Rov.	Bolton Wand.	Charlton Athletic	Chelsea	Everton	Fulham	Liverpool	Manchester City	Manchester Utd.	Middlesbrough	Newcastle Utd.	Portsmouth	Sunderland	Tottenham	W.B.A	West Ham Utd.	Wigan Athletic
Arsenal	-	5-0	1-0	3-0	2-0	3-0	0-2	2-0	4-1	2-0	1-0	0-0	7-0	0-0	4-0	3-1	1-1	3-1	2-3	4-2
Aston Villa	0-0	-	3-1	1-0	2-2	2-0	0-2	4-0	0-1	1-2	1-1	0-2	2-3	1-2	1-0	3-1	1-1	0-0	1-2	0-2
Birmingham City	0-2	0-1	-	2-1	1-0	0-1	0-1	0-2	1-0	2-2	2-1	2-2	0-3	5-0	5-0	2-0	0-2	2-0	2-3	1-1
Blackburn Rov.	1-0	2-0	2-1	-	0-0	4-1	1-0	1-0	1-2	1-0	0-0	4-3	0-4	3-0	2-1	2-0	0-1	2-0	3-2	1-0
Bolton Wand.	2-0	1-0	1-0	0-0	-	4-1	0-2	4-0	1-1	2-2	0-1	1-2	0-1	2-0	1-0	2-0	1-0	1-0	4-1	2-1
Charlton Athletic	1-0	2-0	1-0	4-1	4-1	-	0-2	3-0	2-1	2-0	3-2	1-3	0-3	0-0	1-2	1-3	0-2	1-1	0-0	3-0
Chelsea	1-0	1-1	2-0	4-2	5-1	1-1	-	1-0	3-2	1-3	2-0	1-3	1-0	3-0	2-0	2-0	2-1	4-0	1-1	1-0
Everton	1-0	1-0	0-0	1-0	4-0	3-1	1-1	-	1-0	3-1	2-5	1-1	1-0	2-0	1-0	2-2	0-1	4-0	2-2	1-1
Fulham	1-4	3-1	1-0	2-1	2-0	2-1	1-0	1-0	-	2-0	2-1	3-2	1-0	1-0	3-1	2-1	0-1	2-1	1-0	1-0
Liverpool	1-0	3-1	2-0	1-0	2-0	2-0	1-4	3-1	5-1	-	1-0	0-1	2-0	3-0	3-0	2-0	0-0	0-0	2-1	3-0
Manchester City	1-3	4-1	4-1	0-0	3-2	2-0	0-1	2-0	4-2	0-1	-	1-3	0-1	3-0	3-0	2-1	2-1	0-2	2-1	3-1
Manchester Utd.	2-0	1-0	3-0	1-2	4-1	4-0	0-0	1-1	4-2	1-0	1-1	-	1-0	2-0	3-0	4-0	1-2	4-0	1-0	4-0
Middlesbrough	2-1	0-4	3-0	0-2	4-3	0-3	3-0	2-1	3-2	0-3	1-2	4-1	-	2-2	2-0	0-2	2-3	4-0	2-0	4-0
Newcastle Utd.	1-0	1-1	1-0	0-1	3-1	0-0	0-1	2-0	1-0	1-3	1-0	0-2	2-2	-	0-0	3-1	1-3	3-0	0-0	3-1
Portsmouth	1-1	1-2	1-1	2-2	3-1	1-2	0-2	1-0	1-1	1-3	2-1	1-3	1-0	0-0	-	1-4	1-2	1-0	1-1	2-0
Sunderland	0-3	1-3	0-0	0-1	0-2	1-3	1-2	0-1	1-1	0-0	1-2	1-3	2-0	1-4	1-4	-	1-1	0-0	1-1	0-1
Tottenham	1-1	0-0	2-0	3-2	1-0	3-1	1-2	0-2	1-0	0-0	2-0	1-2	0-2	2-0	3-1	3-2	-	2-0	2-1	2-2
W.B.A	2-1	2-3	2-3	2-0	1-2	1-2	1-2	4-0	0-0	0-2	2-0	1-2	0-2	0-3	2-1	3-0	1-1	-	0-1	1-2
West Ham Utd.	0-0	0-0	3-0	1-2	2-1	0-0	4-1	2-2	2-1	2-1	1-1	1-2	2-0	2-4	2-4	2-0	1-2	1-0	-	1-2
Wigan Athletic	2-3	3-2	1-1	0-3	2-1	3-0	0-1	1-1	1-0	0-1	4-3	1-2	1-1	1-0	2-0	1-0	1-2	0-1	1-2	-

Read across for home results, down for away.

COCA-COLA CHAMPIONSHIP RESULTS 2005–06

Home \ Away	Brighton & H.A.	Burnley	Cardiff City	Coventry City	Crewe Alexandra	Crystal Palace	Derby Co.	Hull	Ipswich Town	Leeds Utd.	Leicester City	Luton Town	Millwall	Norwich	Plymouth Argyle	Preston N.E.	Q.P.R.	Reading	Sheffield Utd.	Sheffield Wed.	Southampton	Stoke City	Watford	Wolves
Brighton & H.A.	–	1-1	1-2	2-2	2-2	2-3	0-0	2-0	1-1	2-1	1-2	1-1	1-2	1-3	2-0	0-0	1-0	0-2	0-1	0-2	0-2	1-5	0-1	1-1
Burnley	3-3	–	3-1	0-0	3-0	1-4	4-0	3-0	3-0	2-1	1-0	3-0	2-1	2-1	1-0	2-1	1-0	0-3	2-1	1-0	3-1	0-0	4-1	1-2
Cardiff City	2-0	0-0	–	1-0	6-1	2-2	6-1	1-1	2-1	2-1	1-1	1-0	2-1	0-1	0-2	0-2	0-0	2-5	2-1	1-0	2-1	1-0	1-3	2-0
Coventry City	2-1	0-0	3-1	–	1-1	1-0	1-1	1-1	1-2	2-1	2-2	2-1	1-0	1-0	3-1	2-2	3-4	1-1	2-0	1-1	1-1	0-1	1-2	2-0
Crewe Alexandra	2-1	3-0	6-1	2-1	–	1-2	5-1	3-3	5-1	0-0	1-0	3-1	4-2	2-2	1-2	0-2	1-2	3-4	1-3	2-0	2-2	1-2	2-1	0-4
Crystal Palace	1-1	1-4	2-2	1-2	5-1	–	0-2	1-1	1-2	0-1	0-1	1-2	1-0	4-1	0-2	2-0	0-0	1-3	2-3	0-2	2-0	2-0	1-1	2-0
Derby Co.	2-0	4-0	0-2	2-2	0-2	2-0	–	2-0	2-0	0-0	2-0	0-0	1-1	1-0	1-2	1-1	2-0	2-1	1-1	1-1	2-2	0-1	3-1	0-3
Hull	2-0	3-0	1-1	2-1	1-2	1-2	2-0	–	2-2	1-1	0-1	1-1	2-1	0-1	3-1	1-1	2-0	1-1	1-3	2-1	2-1	2-1	0-0	2-3
Ipswich Town	1-2	3-0	2-1	3-1	2-2	2-0	3-1	2-3	–	0-0	2-0	2-0	1-1	4-2	0-0	0-4	2-1	0-3	3-1	3-0	3-2	2-1	1-1	1-1
Leeds Utd.	3-3	2-1	1-0	0-1	3-1	1-1	1-0	0-0	0-0	–	1-1	1-0	1-1	1-1	1-2	0-0	2-0	1-1	4-2	2-2	2-1	1-4	1-2	0-3
Leicester City	0-0	1-0	1-1	1-2	3-1	1-1	2-0	0-2	1-2	0-1	–	1-0	0-1	1-1	2-1	3-0	1-3	3-2	2-1	2-0	0-0	2-1	2-2	1-1
Luton Town	3-0	3-0	1-0	0-1	1-2	1-3	2-0	2-0	2-0	0-3	2-1	–	2-1	1-1	2-0	1-0	3-1	1-1	0-4	1-1	3-2	2-1	2-1	1-1
Millwall	0-2	2-1	2-1	0-0	1-1	3-2	2-0	2-1	3-1	1-1	2-1	2-1	–	3-0	0-2	0-3	3-1	0-3	2-0	2-2	0-1	1-0	0-3	0-0
Norwich	3-0	2-1	0-1	1-1	1-1	0-1	1-0	3-1	0-0	1-1	2-1	3-0	1-1	–	0-1	0-0	2-3	0-1	1-1	1-0	4-2	1-2	3-3	1-1
Plymouth Argyle	1-0	1-0	0-2	3-1	0-0	2-0	0-2	0-1	3-1	2-0	4-1	5-1	5-0	1-0	–	3-0	2-1	0-2	1-0	0-3	3-0	1-1	1-2	2-0
Preston N.E.	1-1	2-1	2-1	2-1	3-1	1-1	2-2	1-3	0-0	1-1	4-0	4-0	1-0	3-1	1-1	–	1-2	0-3	1-2	0-0	1-0	1-2	1-1	2-0
Q.P.R.	5-1	1-0	0-0	0-0	1-1	1-1	2-0	1-2	1-1	1-1	3-2	0-2	1-0	2-0	2-0	0-0	–	0-1	0-1	1-1	1-2	3-1	1-4	1-1
Reading	2-1	0-3	2-5	3-0	1-1	1-3	0-3	2-0	2-2	1-1	3-1	0-2	0-0	4-0	0-1	1-2	2-1	–	1-2	0-0	2-1	2-1	1-1	0-2
Sheffield Utd.	1-1	2-1	2-1	2-1	1-3	0-4	1-2	1-1	2-2	3-4	2-1	1-1	0-1	3-1	1-2	2-1	0-4	0-0	–	1-0	0-0	3-1	1-1	1-1
Sheffield Wed.	3-0	1-0	1-0	2-2	2-0	1-1	0-0	2-1	1-0	2-0	1-2	3-2	2-2	3-0	0-0	2-1	2-0	1-1	1-0	–	1-0	1-0	1-3	0-2
Southampton	1-1	3-1	2-1	3-2	2-2	0-1	2-2	1-1	1-0	4-1	0-0	2-1	2-2	2-0	1-2	0-0	1-1	1-1	1-1	3-0	–	1-2	0-0	0-2
Stoke City	1-0	0-0	1-0	0-1	1-2	1-1	1-2	2-1	2-1	0-3	3-1	2-1	1-1	1-2	2-0	1-1	1-3	1-2	3-1	2-1	3-0	–	1-0	1-3
Watford	1-1	4-1	1-3	2-0	2-1	1-2	1-1	3-1	1-1	1-0	1-2	2-1	1-2	3-3	1-2	0-0	2-3	1-1	0-1	1-3	1-2	1-0	–	3-1
Wolves	1-0	1-2	2-0	2-1	0-4	1-0	2-3	0-3	1-1	1-0	1-1	0-0	0-0	1-1	2-0	1-1	1-1	0-2	2-0	1-1	0-2	0-0	1-1	–

Read across for home results, down for away.

COCA-COLA LEAGUE ONE RESULTS 2005–06

Home \ Away	Barnsley	Blackpool	Bournemouth	Bradford City	Brentford	Bristol City	Chesterfield	Colchester Utd.	Doncaster Rov.	Gillingham	Hartlepool Utd.	Huddersfield Town	MK Dons	Nottm. Forest	Oldham Athletic	Port Vale	Rotherham Utd.	Scunthorpe Utd.	Southend Utd.	Swansea City	Swindon Town	Tranmere Rov.	Walsall	Yeovil Town
Barnsley	–	2-2	0-0	0-0	3-1	3-0	1-0	1-0	0-3	1-1	1-0	0-2	3-2	2-2	4-0	1-0	1-1	5-2	2-2	2-2	2-0	1-1	2-1	1-0
Blackpool	1-1	–	1-3	0-2	3-1	1-1	2-4	3-0	0-1	0-3	2-1	0-1	2-3	2-2	0-0	1-0	2-0	5-2	1-2	1-0	2-0	1-1	2-0	1-1
Bournemouth	1-1	1-2	–	2-2	1-2	3-1	0-0	1-2	4-2	1-0	0-3	0-1	2-0	1-1	1-4	1-0	0-0	4-2	1-2	0-4	2-1	0-2	0-0	1-0
Bradford City	0-0	1-0	1-2	–	3-3	2-3	1-1	2-0	2-1	2-1	2-0	0-0	2-0	1-1	1-4	1-2	0-0	4-2	0-2	1-1	2-1	2-2	2-0	1-0
Brentford	3-1	1-1	3-1	2-2	–	2-1	2-4	0-2	0-0	6-0	2-0	2-0	3-1	1-1	3-3	4-2	2-0	2-0	0-3	1-0	7-1	2-0	0-0	3-2
Bristol City	3-0	1-1	3-0	3-3	2-3	–	1-1	2-2	0-1	2-1	2-0	4-3	1-1	1-3	2-1	2-1	3-1	1-1	3-4	0-4	1-1	2-0	5-0	2-1
Chesterfield	0-0	2-4	2-2	1-1	–	1-1	–	0-0	3-2	1-0	1-0	1-2	2-1	3-1	1-1	0-3	1-0	1-0	2-0	1-0	1-2	1-1	1-1	0-3
Colchester Utd.	1-0	3-0	0-1	3-2	1-3	3-0	1-2	–	0-1	5-0	0-0	4-3	2-0	3-1	0-1	2-1	3-4	1-0	3-4	0-4	2-1	3-1	2-2	0-1
Doncaster Rov.	1-0	0-1	4-2	2-2	0-0	0-0	1-2	2-2	–	2-0	3-1	1-2	2-1	3-1	3-2	1-0	3-0	1-0	2-0	0-1	1-2	3-1	2-2	3-2
Gillingham	0-3	2-0	1-0	3-2	3-2	1-0	1-0	2-1	1-0	–	1-0	3-1	5-0	3-2	0-1	0-3	4-1	1-4	1-2	2-2	2-1	0-0	2-2	0-1
Hartlepool Utd.	1-1	0-3	1-1	1-2	1-0	1-2	0-0	2-0	1-1	1-1	–	2-2	2-1	1-2	1-4	2-0	0-0	2-4	2-1	1-1	2-0	0-2	0-2	0-0
Huddersfield Town	1-0	2-2	0-1	0-1	1-2	2-0	4-3	1-2	3-1	2-0	3-1	–	2-2	2-1	0-3	2-1	1-1	0-0	0-0	1-0	7-1	1-3	2-1	0-1
MK Dons	0-2	3-2	2-0	2-0	1-2	2-2	2-0	2-1	2-0	3-1	5-0	3-0	–	0-2	3-1	2-0	2-0	0-1	2-1	1-1	1-1	3-2	1-3	1-1
Nottm. Forest	3-2	2-2	1-1	1-1	1-1	1-3	3-1	3-1	1-0	1-3	1-3	3-1	1-0	–	2-0	3-0	2-0	4-2	3-1	2-1	1-1	2-1	0-2	1-2
Oldham Athletic	3-1	4-0	1-0	0-1	1-4	3-3	2-1	1-1	0-1	3-2	1-1	0-1	3-0	3-2	–	1-0	1-4	2-0	1-2	2-3	4-0	0-1	0-2	2-1
Port Vale	2-2	1-0	1-0	1-2	4-2	2-1	1-1	2-0	1-1	3-0	0-3	1-0	2-1	2-2	0-3	–	0-0	1-3	1-0	2-2	1-2	3-0	2-0	2-0
Rotherham Utd.	0-2	2-0	0-0	1-1	1-1	3-1	3-1	0-0	4-1	1-0	4-1	1-1	1-2	0-0	1-3	2-0	–	2-1	0-2	2-2	1-2	2-3	2-1	1-1
Scunthorpe Utd.	0-3	5-2	4-2	1-0	0-2	2-2	0-0	1-2	1-0	2-2	2-0	0-0	2-0	0-1	4-2	2-3	1-1	–	2-1	2-2	1-2	1-1	1-3	1-1
Southend Utd.	0-1	1-2	1-2	0-2	3-1	3-4	5-1	0-0	2-0	3-1	2-0	0-0	0-1	1-1	2-3	4-0	0-2	2-4	–	1-2	2-2	3-1	1-0	4-2
Swansea City	3-2	1-0	4-2	1-3	1-0	3-2	2-0	7-1	1-3	1-0	2-2	2-2	3-1	1-1	4-0	3-1	2-2	2-2	1-2	–	0-0	2-2	1-0	1-0
Swindon Town	0-3	2-0	0-1	0-3	1-2	1-1	2-0	1-4	2-2	1-0	3-0	2-3	2-0	2-1	2-3	3-0	1-1	1-2	2-1	1-2	–	1-2	1-3	4-1
Tranmere Rov.	0-1	2-0	1-1	4-1	2-0	0-3	4-1	0-3	2-2	0-2	2-2	0-2	1-1	3-2	4-0	1-0	0-2	2-2	2-2	2-5	2-0	–	1-0	0-2
Walsall	2-5	2-0	1-1	2-0	0-0	2-3	2-3	0-2	2-1	2-2	3-1	2-1	1-1	0-1	0-1	3-0	3-1	0-0	2-2	2-5	0-0	0-0	–	2-1
Yeovil Town	2-1	1-1	1-1	1-2	3-2	2-1	1-3	0-1	3-0	1-1	2-0	0-1	1-1	3-0	0-2	1-0	0-0	1-1	0-2	1-0	4-1	0-2	2-1	–

Read across for home results, down for away.

COCA-COLA LEAGUE TWO RESULTS 2005–06

	Barnet	Boston Utd.	Bristol Rov.	Bury	Carlisle Utd.	Cheltenham Town	Chester City	Darlington	Grimsby Town	Leyton Orient	Lincoln City	Macclesfield Town	Mansfield Town	Northampton Town	Notts Co.	Oxford Utd.	Peterborough Utd.	Rochdale	Rushden & D's	Shrewsbury Town	Stockport Co.	Torquay Utd.	Wrexham	Wycombe Wand.
Barnet	–	0-1	1-1	1-1	1-2	1-1	1-3	1-0	1-0	2-3	2-3	1-0	0-1	1-1	2-1	0-0	2-2	1-1	2-1	1-1	0-5	1-0	2-2	0-0
Boston Utd.	2-1	–	3-1	1-0	4-2	3-0	0-0	0-0	2-3	0-1	2-0	2-3	5-2	0-1	3-2	0-1	0-1	1-0	2-1	2-0	2-2	2-0	2-1	1-2
Bristol Rov.	1-1	3-1	–	1-0	1-3	2-3	4-0	0-1	2-3	2-3	1-0	1-1	0-3	4-0	1-0	2-0	1-2	2-0	1-2	2-3	0-1	2-3	1-0	1-3
Bury	0-0	3-1	1-0	–	2-3	2-1	1-3	2-3	0-1	2-1	0-0	2-1	0-3	1-1	0-2	2-0	4-1	0-0	1-0	0-1	0-0	0-0	1-0	4-0
Carlisle Utd.	1-3	4-2	2-3	4-0	–	2-3	0-5	1-1	3-1	0-2	3-1	0-0	1-2	2-1	2-1	1-2	2-1	1-0	5-0	0-0	6-0	0-1	2-1	0-1
Cheltenham Town	0-0	3-0	4-0	2-1	1-1	–	1-0	0-1	0-2	0-2	4-1	2-2	0-0	3-1	0-2	2-1	2-1	2-3	1-2	0-1	3-3	0-1	2-1	0-1
Chester City	2-1	1-0	0-1	2-3	0-1	3-1	–	3-1	0-0	4-2	2-2	2-1	3-1	0-1	0-2	1-1	3-1	4-1	0-2	0-1	1-2	3-2	2-1	1-0
Darlington	3-0	0-0	0-1	1-1	1-1	4-4	1-0	–	0-0	0-2	2-2	3-1	4-0	3-1	0-2	1-2	0-4	1-4	1-3	3-0	1-3	3-2	1-0	1-0
Grimsby Town	0-0	2-3	2-3	0-1	0-0	3-1	3-1	2-2	–	5-0	4-2	4-0	3-1	1-4	4-0	1-2	3-1	2-2	5-1	1-1	1-2	3-0	2-0	1-0
Leyton Orient	4-1	0-1	2-3	2-1	0-3	0-2	3-1	0-1	2-2	–	0-0	3-1	1-2	2-2	0-3	2-1	0-4	4-1	3-1	1-1	6-0	2-1	3-2	1-2
Lincoln City	1-1	2-0	1-0	0-0	3-1	0-1	3-1	2-2	0-0	1-1	–	5-0	1-0	1-3	0-2	0-0	1-0	1-3	5-1	1-1	2-0	3-0	1-0	2-3
Macclesfield Town	4-0	5-2	1-1	2-1	0-0	2-2	2-1	3-1	4-0	2-1	5-0	–	1-1	1-4	0-0	0-1	0-4	4-1	2-0	3-2	0-0	2-0	3-2	4-5
Mansfield Town	1-0	3-2	0-3	0-3	1-2	0-0	3-1	4-0	3-1	1-2	1-0	1-0	–	2-2	0-3	2-0	2-1	1-3	2-0	0-1	0-2	4-1	0-1	2-2
Northampton Town	1-0	4-0	4-0	1-1	2-1	3-1	0-1	3-1	1-4	2-2	1-3	1-4	1-1	–	2-3	0-2	0-4	1-1	1-3	4-2	3-3	0-1	1-1	1-1
Notts Co.	2-0	0-0	1-0	0-2	2-1	0-2	0-2	0-2	4-0	0-3	2-1	0-0	0-3	2-0	–	3-0	3-0	3-0	4-1	0-0	1-1	2-1	2-0	1-1
Oxford Utd.	2-0	0-0	2-0	2-0	1-2	2-1	1-1	1-2	1-2	2-1	0-0	0-1	2-0	0-1	0-3	–	0-0	3-3	2-1	0-0	3-2	2-1	2-1	2-1
Peterborough Utd.	2-2	1-1	1-2	4-1	2-1	2-1	3-1	0-4	0-1	0-1	1-2	1-0	0-2	2-1	0-1	1-0	–	2-1	0-4	2-1	2-1	1-0	0-2	1-1
Rochdale	2-2	0-1	2-0	0-0	1-0	2-3	4-1	1-4	2-2	0-1	1-3	1-3	0-2	1-1	0-3	0-1	1-0	–	2-1	3-0	1-3	3-0	0-3	3-0
Rushden & D's	1-2	2-0	1-2	1-0	0-2	1-1	0-2	1-3	5-1	3-1	5-1	2-0	2-0	1-3	4-1	2-1	0-4	2-1	–	4-1	3-0	0-1	2-1	0-0
Shrewsbury Town	1-1	1-2	2-3	0-1	0-0	0-1	0-1	3-0	1-1	1-1	1-1	3-2	0-1	4-2	0-0	0-0	2-1	3-0	4-1	–	3-1	1-0	1-2	2-0
Stockport Co.	1-1	2-0	0-1	0-0	6-0	3-3	1-2	1-3	1-2	6-0	2-0	0-0	0-2	2-3	0-0	0-1	2-1	1-0	3-2	4-0	–	4-0	1-1	1-1
Torquay Utd.	0-0	2-0	2-3	0-0	0-1	0-1	3-2	3-2	3-0	2-1	3-0	2-0	0-2	1-0	4-1	4-1	1-0	1-0	1-0	1-1	4-2	–	4-2	0-1
Wrexham	3-1	2-1	1-0	1-0	2-1	2-1	2-1	1-0	2-0	1-0	3-2	0-0	0-3	0-3	0-1	2-1	0-2	3-0	2-1	1-1	2-1	1-1	–	4-1
Wycombe Wand.	1-0	1-1	1-3	4-0	0-1	0-0	1-0	1-0	2-2	4-2	0-3	4-5	2-2	1-1	2-0	2-1	1-1	3-0	0-0	2-0	1-1	2-0	2-0	–

Read across for home results, down for away.

ENGLISH FINAL TABLES 2005–06

BARCLAYS PREMIERSHIP

			HOME					AWAY						
		P	W	D	L	F	A	W	D	L	F	A	Pts	GD
1	Chelsea	38	18	1	0	47	9	11	3	5	25	13	91	50
2	Manchester Utd.	38	13	5	1	37	8	12	3	4	35	26	83	38
3	Liverpool	38	15	3	1	32	8	10	4	5	25	17	82	32
4	Arsenal	38	14	3	2	48	13	6	4	9	20	18	67	37
5	Tottenham	38	12	5	2	31	16	6	6	7	22	22	65	15
6	Blackburn Rov.	38	13	3	3	31	17	6	3	10	20	25	63	9
7	Newcastle Utd.	38	11	5	3	28	15	6	2	11	19	27	58	5
8	Bolton Wand.	38	11	5	3	29	13	4	6	9	20	28	56	8
9	West Ham Utd.	38	9	3	7	30	25	7	4	8	22	30	55	-3
10	Wigan Athletic	38	11	3	5	24	26	4	3	12	21	26	51	-7
11	Everton	38	8	4	7	22	22	6	4	9	12	27	50	-15
12	Fulham	38	13	2	4	31	21	1	4	14	17	37	48	-10
13	Charlton Athletic	38	8	4	7	22	21	5	4	10	19	34	47	-14
14	Middlesbrough	38	7	5	7	28	30	5	4	10	20	28	45	-10
15	Manchester City	38	9	2	8	26	20	4	2	13	17	28	43	-5
16	Aston Villa	38	6	6	7	20	20	4	6	9	22	35	42	-13
17	Portsmouth	38	5	7	7	17	24	5	1	13	20	38	38	-25
18	Birmingham City	38	6	5	8	19	20	2	5	12	9	30	34	-22
19	W.B.A.	38	6	2	11	21	24	1	7	11	10	34	30	-27
20	Sunderland	38	1	4	14	12	37	2	2	15	14	32	15	-43

Chelsea and Manchester Utd. go into Champions League group stage; Liverpool and Arsenal into third qualifying round; Blackburn Rov., Tottenham and West Ham Utd. into UEFA Cup.

Prize-money: 1 £9.6m, 2 £9.2m, 3 £8.7m, 4 £8.2m, 5 £7.7m, 6 £7.2m, 7 £6.7m, 8 £6.3m, 9 £5.8m, 10 £5.3m, 11 £4.8m, 12 £4.3m, 13 £3.8m, 14 £3.3m, 15 £2.9m, 16 £2.4m, 17 £1.9m, 18 £1.4m, 19 £970,000, 20 £485,000.

Biggest win: Arsenal 7, Middlesbrough 0.

Highest attendance: 73,006 (Manchester Utd. v Charlton Athletic).

Lowest attendance: 16,550 (Fulham v Birmingham City).

Manager of Year: Jose Mourinho (Chelsea).

Player of Year: Thierry Henry (Arsenal).

Golden Boot: 27 Thierry Henry.

Golden Glove: Jose Reina (Liverpool).

Football Writers' Association Player of Year: Thierry Henry.

P.F.A. Player of Year: Steven Gerrard (Liverpool).

P.F.A. Young Player of Year: Wayne Rooney (Manchester Utd.).

P.F.A. Divisional Team of Year: Given (Newcastle Utd.), Chimbonda (Wigan Athletic), Carragher (Liverpool), Terry (Chelsea), Gallas (Chelsea), Gerrard (Liverpool), Lampard (Chelsea), Joe Cole (Chelsea), Ronaldo (Manchester Utd.), Rooney (Manchester Utd.), Henry (Arsenal).

Leading scorers (all club competitions): 33 Henry (Arsenal); 24 Van Nistelrooy (Manchester Utd.); 23 Gerrard (Liverpool); 22 Darren Bent (Charlton Athletic); 20 Lampard (Chelsea); 19 Rooney (Manchester Utd.), Yakubu (Middlesbrough), Cisse (Liverpool); 17 Bellamy (Blackburn Rov.), Hasselbaink (Middlesbrough); 16 Drogba (Chelsea), Harewood (West Ham Utd.), Keane (Tottenham), Viduka (Middlesbrough); 15 Saha (Manchester Utd.); 14 Roberts (Wigan Athletic), Shearer (Newcastle Utd.); 13 Crespo (Chelsea). **Other:** 17 Ashton (West Ham Utd.) – 11 for Norwich City.

COCA-COLA CHAMPIONSHIP

			HOME				AWAY						
		P	W	D	L	F	A	W	D	L	F	A	Pts	GD
1	Reading	46	19	3	1	58	14	12	10	1	41	18	106	67
2	Sheffield Utd.	46	15	5	3	43	22	11	7	5	33	24	90	30
3	Watford†	46	11	7	5	39	24	11	8	4	38	29	81	24
4	Preston N.E.	46	11	10	2	31	12	9	10	4	28	18	80	29
5	Leeds Utd.	46	13	7	3	35	18	8	8	7	22	20	78	19
6	Crystal Palace	46	13	6	4	39	20	8	6	9	28	28	75	19
7	Wolves	46	9	10	4	24	18	7	9	7	26	24	67	8
8	Coventry City	46	12	7	4	39	22	4	8	11	23	43	63	−3
9	Norwich City	46	12	4	7	34	25	6	4	13	22	40	62	−9
10	Luton Town	46	11	6	6	45	31	6	4	13	21	36	61	−1
11	Cardiff City	46	10	7	6	32	24	6	5	12	26	35	60	−1
12	Southampton	46	9	10	4	26	17	4	9	10	23	33	58	−1
13	Stoke City	46	7	5	11	24	32	10	2	11	30	31	58	−9
14	Plymouth Argyle	46	10	7	6	26	22	3	10	10	13	24	56	−7
15	Ipswich Town	46	8	8	7	28	32	6	6	11	25	34	56	−13
16	Leicester City	46	8	9	6	30	25	5	6	12	21	34	54	−8
17	Burnley	46	11	6	6	34	22	3	6	14	12	32	54	−8
18	Hull City	46	8	8	7	24	21	4	8	11	25	34	52	−6
19	Sheffield Wed.	46	7	8	8	22	24	6	5	12	17	28	52	−13
20	Derby Co.	46	8	10	5	33	27	2	10	11	20	40	50	−14
21	Q.P.R.	46	7	7	9	24	26	5	7	11	26	39	50	−15
22	Crewe Alexandra	46	7	7	9	38	40	2	8	13	19	46	42	−29
23	Millwall	46	4	8	11	13	27	4	8	11	22	35	40	−27
24	Brighton & H.A.	46	4	8	11	21	34	3	9	11	18	37	38	−32

(† Also promoted)

Biggest win: Cardiff City 6, Crewe Alexandra 1; Coventry City 6, Derby Co. 1; Reading 5, Derby Co. 0; Reading 5, Millwall 0.
Highest attendance: 33,439 (Sheffield Wed. v Sheffield Utd.).
Lowest attendance: 5,687 (Crewe Alexandra v Ipswich Town).
Manager of Year: Steve Coppell (Reading).
Player of Year: Phil Jagielka (Sheffield Utd.).
Top League scorer: 21 Marlon King (Watford).
P.F.A. Divisional Team of Year: Hahnemann (Reading), Kelly (Leeds Utd.), Sonko (Reading), Lescott (Wolves), Shorey (Reading), Sidwell (Reading), Jagielka (Sheffield Utd.), Koumas (Cardiff City), Young (Watford), King (Watford), Doyle (Reading).
Leading scorers (all club competitions): 22 King (Watford), Kitson (Reading); 20 Jerome (Cardiff City); 19 Doyle (Reading); 17 Akinbiyi (Sheffield Utd.) − 14 for Burnley, Johnson (Crystal Palace), McSheffrey (Coventry City); 15 Henderson (Watford), Howard (Luton Town), Lita (Reading), Young (Watford); 14 Healy (Leeds Utd.), Hulse (Leeds Utd.); 13 Koumas (Cardiff City), Morrison (Crystal Palace); 12 Adebola (Coventry City), Gallagher (Stoke City), Miller (Wolves). **Others:** 20 Fryatt (Leicester City) − 14 for Walsall; 17 Burton (Sheffield Wed.) − 14 for Rotherham Utd.

COCA-COLA LEAGUE ONE

		P	HOME					AWAY					Pts	GD
			W	D	L	F	A	W	D	L	F	A		
1	Southend Utd.	46	13	6	4	37	16	10	7	6	35	27	82	29
2	Colchester Utd.	46	15	4	4	39	21	7	9	7	19	19	79	18
3	Brentford	46	10	8	5	35	23	10	8	5	37	29	76	20
4	Huddersfield Town	46	13	6	4	40	25	6	10	7	32	34	73	13
5	Barnsley†	46	11	11	1	37	19	7	7	9	25	25	72	18
6	Swansea City	46	11	9	3	42	23	7	8	8	36	32	71	23
7	Nott'm. Forest	46	14	5	4	40	15	5	7	11	27	37	69	15
8	Doncaster Rov.	46	11	6	6	30	19	9	3	11	25	32	69	4
9	Bristol City	46	11	7	5	38	22	7	4	12	28	40	65	4
10	Oldham Athletic	46	12	4	7	32	24	6	7	10	26	36	65	-2
11	Bradford City	46	8	9	6	28	25	6	10	7	23	24	61	2
12	Scunthorpe Utd.	46	8	8	7	36	33	7	7	9	32	40	60	-5
13	Port Vale	46	10	5	8	30	26	6	7	10	19	28	60	-5
14	Gillingham	46	13	4	6	31	21	3	8	12	19	43	60	-14
15	Yeovil Town	46	8	8	7	27	24	7	3	13	27	38	56	-8
16	Chesterfield	46	6	7	10	31	37	8	7	8	32	36	56	-10
17	Bournemouth	46	7	11	5	25	20	5	8	10	24	33	55	-4
18	Tranmere Rov.	46	7	8	8	32	30	6	7	10	18	22	54	-2
19	Blackpool	46	9	8	6	33	27	3	9	11	23	37	53	-8
20	Rotherham Utd.	46	7	9	7	31	26	5	7	11	21	36	52	-10
21	Hartlepool Utd.	46	6	10	7	28	30	5	7	11	16	29	50	-15
22	Milton Keynes Dons	46	8	8	7	28	25	4	6	13	17	41	50	-21
23	Swindon Town	46	9	5	9	31	31	2	10	11	15	34	48	-19
24	Walsall	46	7	7	9	27	34	4	7	12	20	36	47	-23

(† Also promoted)

Biggest win: Bristol City 6, Gillingham 0; Nott'm. Forest 7, Swindon Town 1; Swansea City 7, Bristol City 1.
Highest attendance: 28,193 (Nott'm. Forest v Yeovil Town).
Lowest attendance: 2,721 (Colchester Utd.v Barnsley).
Manager of Year: Steve Tilson (Southend Utd.).
Player of Year: Lee Trundle (Swansea City).
Top League scorer: 23 Eastwood (Southend Utd.), Sharp (Scunthorpe Utd.).
P.F.A. Divisional Team of Year: Flahavan (Southend Utd.), Halford (Colchester Utd.), Sodje (Brentford), Barrett (Southend Utd.), Roberts (Tranmere Rov.), Danns (Colchester Utd.), Robinson (Swansea City), Maher (Southend Utd.), McIndoe (Doncaster Rov.), Sharp (Scunthorpe Utd.), Trundle (Swansea City).
Leading scorers (all club competitions): 25 Eastwood (Southend Utd.); 24 Sharp (Scunthorpe Utd.); 21 Trundle (Swansea City); 20 Hayter (Bournemouth), Windass (Bradford City); 19 Fallon (Swansea City) – 14 for Swindon Town, Iwelumo (Colchester Utd.); 18 Beckett (Oldham Athletic), Greenacre (Tranmere Rov.), McLeod (MK Dons); 17 Robinson (Swansea City); 16 Brooker (Bristol City), Danns (Colchester Utd.), Jevons (Yeovil Town); 15 Akinfenwa (Swansea City), Booth (Huddersfield Town), Hall (Chesterfield), Keogh (Scunthorpe Utd.), Taylor-Fletcher (Huddersfield Town). **Others:** 23 – Tyson (Nott'm. Forest) – 13 for Wycombe Wand.); 19 Grant Holt (Nott'm. Forest) – 15 for Rochdale.

COCA-COLA LEAGUE TWO

			HOME				AWAY						
		P	W	D	L	F	A	W	D	L	F	A	Pts	GD
1	Carlisle Utd.	46	14	3	6	47	23	11	8	4	37	19	86	42
2	Northampton Town	46	11	8	4	30	15	11	9	3	33	22	83	26
3	Leyton Orient	46	11	6	6	29	21	11	9	3	38	30	81	16
4	Grimsby Town	46	13	3	7	37	18	9	5	27	26	78	20	
5	Cheltenham Town†	46	10	7	6	39	31	9	8	6	26	22	72	12
6	Wycombe Wand.	46	9	9	5	41	29	9	8	6	31	27	71	16
7	Lincoln City	46	9	11	3	37	21	6	10	7	28	32	66	12
8	Darlington	46	10	7	6	32	26	6	8	9	26	26	63	6
9	Peterborough Utd.	46	9	7	7	28	21	8	4	11	29	28	62	8
10	Shrewsbury Town	46	10	9	4	33	20	6	4	13	22	35	61	–
11	Boston Utd.	46	11	7	5	34	28	4	9	10	16	32	61	–10
12	Bristol Rov.	46	8	6	9	30	29	9	3	11	29	38	60	–8
13	Wrexham	46	12	6	5	36	19	3	8	12	25	35	59	7
14	Rochdale	46	8	7	8	34	30	6	7	10	32	39	56	–3
15	Chester City	46	7	6	10	30	29	7	6	10	23	30	54	–6
16	Mansfield Town	46	9	7	7	37	29	4	8	11	22	37	54	–7
17	Macclesfield Town	46	10	9	4	35	27	2	9	12	25	44	54	–11
18	Barnet	46	9	8	6	24	22	3	10	10	20	35	54	–13
19	Bury*	46	6	9	8	22	25	6	8	9	23	32	52	–12
20	Torquay Utd.	46	7	9	7	33	31	6	4	13	20	36	52	–13
21	Notts Co.	46	7	11	5	30	26	5	5	13	18	37	52	–15
22	Stockport Co.	46	7	11	5	34	29	4	8	11	23	49	52	–21
23	Oxford Utd.	46	7	7	9	25	30	4	9	10	18	27	49	–14
24	Rushden & Diamonds	46	8	5	10	25	31	3	7	13	19	45	45	–32

(† Also promoted)
(* One point deducted for unregistered player)

Biggest win: Carlisle Utd. 6, Stockport Co. 0; Macclesfield Town 6, Stockport Co. 0.
Highest attendance: 13,467 (Carlisle Utd. v Torquay Utd.).
Lowest attendance: 1,366 (Barnet v Cheltenham Town).
Manager of Year: Paul Simpson (Carlisle Utd.).
Player of Year: Karl Hawley (Carlisle Utd.).
Top League scorer: 22 – Karl Hawley.
P.F.A. Divisional Team of Year: Hart (Shrewsbury Town), Senda (Wycombe Wand.), Johnson (Wycombe Wand.), McAuley (Lincoln City), Lockwood (Leyton Orient), Betsy (Wycombe Wand.), Low (Northampton Town), Jones (Wrexham), Taylor (Northampton Town), Hawley (Carlisle Utd.), Reddy (Grimsby Town).
Leading scorers (all club competitions): 26 Hawley (Carlisle Utd.); 24 McGleish (Northampton Town); 23 Barker (Mansfield Town); 22 Lambert (Rochdale); 21 Walker (Bristol Rov.); 18 Agogo (Bristol Rov.), Mooney (Wycombe Wand.); 17 Crow (Peterborough Utd.), Jones (Grimsby Town); 16 Joachim (Boston Utd.), Bridges (Carlisle Utd.) – 1 for Bristol City; 15 Alexander (Leyton Orient), Mark Jones (Wrexham); 14 Reddy (Grimsby Town); 13 Basham (Oxford Utd.), Easter (Wycombe Wand.) – 11 for Stockport Co., Lowe (Chester City), Odejayi (Cheltenham Town), Wijnhard (Macclesfield Town) – 1 for Darlington.

LEAGUE AND CONFERENCE PLAY-OFFS 2006

From the moment Marlon King scored his 22nd goal of the season to set up a crushing 3-0 win over Crystal Palace in the semi-final first leg at Selhurst Park, Watford had the air of a team going places. Sure enough, they went on to beat Leeds just as convincingly at the Millennium Stadium to climax a remarkable first full season in charge for Adrian Boothroyd, no longer a managerial 'unknown'.

American defender Jay DeMerit, who was playing non-league football 18 months before, headed them in front from Ashley Young's corner. Malky Mackay, promoted in the two previous seasons with Norwich and West Ham but still to play in the Premiership, headed on Gavin Mahon's throw for James Chambers to score with a shot that hit the post and went in off goalkeeper Neil Sullivan.

Then, with Leeds having made little impression, King was brought down by Shaun Derry – the player whose tackle had ended Boothroyd's playing career at the age of 26 when he was with Peterborough – and Darius Henderson put away the penalty.

Barnsley goalkeeper Nick Colgan had a bitter-sweet time in the League One Final. Colgan fumbled Andy Robinson's shot over the line for Swansea's second goal, but Danny Nardiello levelled at 2-2 and in the penalty shoot-out Colgan made a vital save from Alan Tate.

Grimsby, who missed out on automatic promotion on the final day of the regular season, were again cursing their luck when Steve Guinan's curling cross evaded everyone and finished up in the net for Cheltenham's 63rd minute winner in the League Two Final. Steve Mildenhall prevented a second by saving Grant McCann's penalty.

Graham Turner, Hereford's manager, chairman and major shareholder, celebrated a return to the Football League after a nine-year absence when his team twice came from behind to win the Conference Final. Hereford, losing semi-finalists in the two previous seasons, beat Halifax 3-2 with Ryan Green's extra-time goal.

SEMI FINALS, FIRST LEG

COCA-COLA CHAMPIONSHIP

Leeds Utd. 1 (Lewis 74), **Preston N.E.** 1 (Nugent 48). Att: 35,239. **Crystal Palace** 0, **Watford** 3 (King 46, Young 67, Spring 85). Att: 22,880.

LEAGUE ONE

Barnsley 0, **Huddersfield Town** 1 (Taylor-Fletcher 85). Att: 16,127. **Swansea City** 1 (Ricketts 87), **Brentford** 1 (Tabb 29). Att: 19,060.

LEAGUE TWO

Lincoln City 0, **Grimsby Town** 1 (G. Jones 22). Att: 8,037. **Wycombe Wand.** 1 (Mooney 90), **Cheltenham Town** 2 (Finnigan 43, Guinan 75). Att: 5,936.

NATIONWIDE CONFERENCE

Halifax Town 3 (Bushell 17, Sugden 30, Killeen 32), **Grays Athletic** 2 (Oli 65, 77). Att: 3,848. **Morecambe** 1 (Bentley 22), **Hereford Utd.** 1 (Purdie 54 pen). Att: 5,208.

SEMI-FINALS, SECOND LEG

COCA-COLA CHAMPIONSHIP

Preston N.E. 0, **Leeds Utd.** 2 (Hulse 56, Richardson 61). Att: 20,383 (**Leeds Utd.** won 3-1 on agg). **Watford** 0, **Crystal Palace** 0. Att: 19,041 (**Watford** won 3-0 on agg).

LEAGUE ONE

Brentford 0, **Swansea City** 2 (Knight 8, 15). Att: 10,652 (**Swansea City** won 3-1 on agg).
Huddersfield Town 1 (Worthington 65), **Barnsley** 3 (Hayes 58 pen, Reid 71, Nardiello 78). Att: 19,223 (**Barnsley** won 3-2 on agg).

LEAGUE TWO

Cheltenham Town 0, **Wycombe Wand.** 0. Att: 6,813 (**Cheltenham Town** won 2-1 on agg).
Grimsby Town 2 (Futcher 60, G. Jones 82), **Lincoln City** 1 (Robinson 27). Att: 8,062 (**Grimsby Town** won 3-1 on agg).

NATIONWIDE CONFERENCE

Grays Athletic 2 (Kightly 56, Nutter 57), **Halifax Town** 2 (Foster 6, 63 pen). Att: 2,886 (**Halifax Town** won 5-4 on agg). **Hereford Utd.** 3 (Mkandawire 6, Williams 13, Ipoua 107), **Morecambe** 2 (Curtis 8 pen, Twiss 53). Att: 6,278 (aet, **Hereford Utd.** won 4-3 on agg).

FINALS – MILLENNIUM STADIUM

COCA-COLA CHAMPIONSHIP – MAY 21, 2006

Leeds Utd. 0, **Watford** 3 (DeMerit 25, Sullivan 57 og, Henderson 84 pen). Att: 64,736.
Leeds Utd. (4-5-1): Sullivan, Kelly, Butler, Gregan (Bakke 84), Kilgallon, Richardson (Blake 46), Douglas, Derry, Miller (Healy 62), Lewis, Hulse. **Subs not used:** Bennett, Stone. **Booked:** Gregan, Miller, Derry. **Manager:** Kevin Blackwell.
Watford (4-4-2): Foster, Doyley, DeMerit, Mackay, Stewart, Chambers (Bangura 73), Spring, Mahon, Young, Henderson, King. **Subs not used:** Chamberlain, Eagles, Bouazza, Mariappa. **Booked:** Spring, Doyley, Mahon. **Manager:** Adrian Boothroyd.
Referee: M. Dean (Wirral). **Half-time:** 0-1.

LEAGUE ONE – MAY 27, 2006

Swansea City 2 (Fallon 28, Robinson 40), **Barnsley** 2 (Hayes 19, Nardiello 62). Att: 55,419 (aet, **Barnsley** won 4-3 on pens).
Swansea City (4-4-2): Gueret, Tate, Monk, Austin, Ricketts, Britton, Tudur-Jones, O'Leary, Robinson (McLeod 106), Fallon (Akinfenwa 93), Knight (Trundle 68). **Subs not used:** Murphy, Williams. **Manager:** Kenny Jackett.
Barnsley (4-4-2): Colgan, Hassell, Reid, Kay, Heckingbottom, Devaney, McPhail, Howard (Tonge 72), Hayes, Richards (Wright 70), Nardiello (Shuker 100). **Subs not used:** Flinders, Austin. **Booked:** Howard, Reid, Tonge. **Manager:** Andy Ritchie.
Referee: L. Mason (Lancs). **Half-time:** 2-1.

LEAGUE TWO – MAY 28, 2006

Grimsby Town 0, **Cheltenham Town** 1 (Guinan 63). Att: 29,196.
Grimsby Town (4-4-2): Mildenhall, Croft (Futcher 75), Whittle, R. Jones, Newey, Mendes (Goodfellow 84), Bolland, Woodhouse, Parkinson, Reddy (Cohen 27), G. Jones. **Subs not used:** Kamudimba, Toner. **Booked:** Woodhouse. **Manager:** Russell Slade.
Cheltenham Town (4-4-2): Higgs, Gill, Duff, Caines, Armstrong (Bell 27), Vincent (Spencer 78), Finnigan, McCann, Wilson, Gillespie (Odejayi 62), Guinan. **Subs not used:** Brown, Bird. **Booked:** Spencer. **Manager:** John Ward.
Referee: P. Taylor (Herts). **Half-time:** 0-0.

FINAL – WALKERS STADIUM

NATIONWIDE CONFERENCE – MAY 20, 2006

Halifax Town 2 (Killeen 27, Grant 73), **Hereford Utd.** 3 (Williams 34, Ipoua 80, Green 108). Att: 15,499 (aet, **Hereford Utd.** won 3-2 on agg).
Halifax Town (4-3-3): Kennedy, Haslam, Atherton, Quinn, Young (Bushell 61), Thompson, Foster, Doughty (Senior 76), Forrest, Sugden (Grant 65), Killeen. **Subs not used:** Butler, Smikle. **Booked:** Senior. **Manager:** Chris Wilder.
Hereford Utd. (4-4-2): Brown, Green, Mkandawire, Beckwith, Jeannin, Travis, Ferrell, Stanley (Pitman 90), Purdie, Stansfield (Fleetwood 93), Williams (Ipoua 75). **Subs not used:** Mawson, Carey-Bertram. **Booked:** Green, Ipoua, Jeannin, Mkandawire. **Manager:** Graham Turner.
Referee: D. Whitestone (Northants). **Half-time:** 1-1.

PLAY-OFF FINALS – HOME & AWAY

1987 Divs. 1/2: Charlton Athletic beat Leeds Utd. 2-1 in replay (Birmingham City) after 1-1 agg (1-0h, 0-1a). Charlton Athletic remained in Div. 1. Losing semi-finalists: Ipswich Town and Oldham Athletic. **Divs. 2/3: Swindon Town** beat Gillingham 2-0 in replay (Crystal Palace) after 2-2 agg (0-1a, 2-1h). Swindon Town promoted to Div. 2. Losing semi-finalists: Sunderland and Wigan Athletic; Sunderland relegated to Div. 3. **Divs. 3/4: Aldershot** beat Wolves 3-0 on agg (2-0h, 1-0a) and promoted to Div. 3. Losing semi-finalists: Bolton Wand. and Colchester Utd.; Bolton Wand. relegated to Div.4.

1988 Divs. 1/2: Middlesbrough beat Chelsea 2-1 on agg (2-0h, 0-1a) and promoted to Div. 1; Chelsea relegated to Div. 2. Losing semi-finalists: Blackburn Rov. and Bradford City. **Divs. 2/3: Walsall** beat Bristol City 4-0 in replay (h) after 3-3 agg (3-1a, 0-2h) and promoted to Div. 2. Losing semi-finalists: Sheffield Utd. and Notts Co; Sheffield Utd. relegated to Div. 3. **Divs. 3/4: Swansea City** beat Torquay Utd. 5-4 on agg (2-1h, 3-3a) and promoted to Div. 3. Losing semi-finalists: Rotherham Utd. and Scunthorpe Utd.; Rotherham Utd. relegated to Div.4.

1989 Div. 2: Crystal Palace beat Blackburn Rov. 4-3 on agg (1-3a, 3-0h). Losing semi-finalists: Watford and Swindon Town. **Div. 3: Port Vale** beat Bristol Rov. 2-1 on agg (1-1a, 1-0h). Losing semi-finalists: Fulham and Preston N.E. **Div.4: Leyton Orient** beat Wrexham 2-1 on agg (0-0a, 2-1h). Losing semi-finalists: Scarborough and Scunthorpe Utd.

PLAY-OFF FINALS AT WEMBLEY

1990 Div. 2: Swindon Town 1, Sunderland 0 (att: 72,873). Swindon Town promoted, then demoted for financial irregularities; Sunderland promoted. Losing semi-finalists: Blackburn Rov. and Newcastle Utd. **Div. 3: Notts Co.** 2, Tranmere Rov. 0 (att: 29,252). Losing semi-finalists: Bolton Wand. and Bury. **Div. 4: Cambridge Utd.** 1, Chesterfield 0 (att: 26,404). Losing semi-finalists: Maidstone and Stockport Co.

1991 Div. 2: Notts Co. 3, Brighton & H.A. 1 (att: 59,940). Losing semi-finalists: Middlesbrough and Millwall. **Div. 3: Tranmere Rov.** 1, Bolton Wand. 0 (att: 30,217). Losing semi-finalists: Brentford and Bury. **Div. 4: Torquay Utd.** 2, Blackpool 2 – Torquay Utd. won 5-4 on pens (att: 21,615). Losing semi-finalists: Burnley and Scunthorpe Utd.

1992 Div. 2: Blackburn Rov. 1, Leicester City 0 (att: 68,147). Losing semi-finalists: Derby Co. and Cambridge Utd. **Div. 3: Peterborough Utd.** 2, Stockport Co. 1 (att: 35,087). Losing semi-finalists: Huddersfield Town and Stoke City. **Div. 4: Blackpool** 1, Scunthorpe Utd. 1, aet, Blackpool won 4-3 on pens (att: 22,741). Losing semi-finalists: Barnet and Crewe Alexandra.

1993 Div. 1: Swindon Town 4, Leicester City 3 (att: 73,802). Losing semi-finalists: Portsmouth and Tranmere Rov. **Div. 2: W.B.A.** 3, Port Vale 0 (att: 53,471). Losing semi-finalists: Stockport Co. and Swansea City. **Div. 3: York City** 1, Crewe Alexandra 1, aet, York City won 5-3 on pens (att: 22,416). Losing semi-finalists: Bury and Walsall.

1994 Div. 1: Leicester City 2, Derby Co. 1 (att: 73,671). Losing semi-finalists: Millwall and Tranmere Rov. **Div. 2: Burnley** 2, Stockport Co. 1 (att: 44,806). Losing semi-finalists: Plymouth Argyle and York City. **Div. 3: Wycombe Wand.** 4, Preston N.E. 2 (att: 40,109). Losing semi-finalists: Carlisle Utd. and Torquay Utd.

1995 Div. 1: Bolton Wand. 4, Reading 3 (att: 64,107). Losing semi-finalists: Tranmere Rov. and Wolves. **Div. 2: Huddersfield Town** 2, Bristol Rov. 1 (att: 59,175). Losing semi-finalists: Brentford and Crewe Alexandra. **Div. 3: Chesterfield** 2, Bury 0 (att: 22,814). Losing semi-finalists: Mansfield Town and Preston N.E.

1996 Div. 1: Leicester City 2, Crystal Palace 1, aet (att: 73,573). Losing semi-finalists: Charlton Athletic and Stoke City. **Div. 2: Bradford City** 2, Notts Co. 0 (att: 39,972). Losing semi-finalists: Blackpool and Crewe Alexandra. **Div. 3: Plymouth Argyle** 1, Darlington 0 (att: 43,431). Losing semi-finalists: Colchester Utd. and Hereford.

1997 Div. 1: Crystal Palace 1, Sheffield Utd. 0, (att: 64,383). Losing semi-finalists: Ipswich Town and Wolves. **Div. 2: Crewe Alexandra** 1, Brentford 0 (att: 34,149). Losing semi-finalists: Bristol City and Luton Town. **Div. 3: Northampton Town** 1, Swansea City 0 (att: 46,804). Losing semi-finalists: Cardiff City and Chester City.

1998 Div. 1: Charlton Athletic 4, Sunderland 4, aet, Charlton Athletic won 7-6 on pens (att: 77, 739). Losing semi-finalists: Ipswich Town and Sheffield Utd. **Div. 2: Grimsby Town** 1, Northampton Town 0 (att: 62,988). Losing semi-finalists: Bristol Rov. and Fulham. **Div. 3: Colchester Utd.** 1, Torquay Utd. 0 (att: 19,486). Losing semi-finalists: Barnet and Scarborough.

1999 Div. 1: Watford 2, Bolton Wand. 0, (att: 70,343). Losing semi-finalists: Ipswich Town and Birmingham City. **Div. 2: Manchester City** 2, Gillingham 2, aet, Manchester City won 3-1 on pens (att: 76,935). Losing semi-finalists: Preston N.E. and Wigan Athletic. **Div. 3: Scunthorpe Utd.** 1, Leyton Orient 0, (att: 36,985). Losing semi-finalists: Rotherham Utd. and Swansea City.

2000 Div. 1: Ipswich Town 4, Barnsley 2 (att: 73,427). Losing semi-finalists: Birmingham City and Bolton Wand. **Div. 2: Gillingham** 3, Wigan Athletic 2, aet (att: 53,764). Losing semi-finalists: Millwall and Stoke City. **Div. 3: Peterborough Utd.** 1, Darlington 0 (att: 33,383). Losing semi-finalists: Barnet and Hartlepool Utd.

PLAY-OFF FINALS AT MILLENNIUM STADIUM

2001 Div. 1: Bolton Wand. 3, Preston N.E. 0 (att: 54,328). Losing semi-finalists: Birmingham City and W.B.A. **Div. 2: Walsall** 3, Reading 2, aet (att: 50,496). Losing semi-finalists: Stoke City and Wigan Athletic. **Div. 3: Blackpool** 4, Leyton Orient 2 (att: 23,600). Losing semi-finalists: Hartlepool Utd. and Hull City.

2002 Div. 1: Birmingham City 1, Norwich City 1, aet, Birmingham City won 4-2 on pens. (att: 71,597). Losing semi-finalists: Millwall and Wolves. **Div. 2: Stoke City** 2, Brentford 0 (att: 42,523). Losing semi-finalists: Cardiff City and Huddersfield Town. **Div. 3: Cheltenham Town** 3, Rushden & Diamonds 1 (att: 24,368). Losing semi-finalists: Hartlepool Utd. and Rochdale.

2003 Div. 1: Wolves 3, Sheffield Utd. 0 (att: 69,473). Losing semi-finalists: Nott'm. Forest and Reading. **Div. 2: Cardiff City** 1, Q.P.R. 0, aet (att: 66,096). Losing semi-finalists: Bristol City and Oldham Athletic. **Div. 3: Bournemouth** 5, Lincoln City 2 (att: 32,148). Losing semi-finalists: Bury and Scunthorpe Utd.

2004: Div. 1: Crystal Palace 1, West Ham Utd. 0 (att: 72,523). Losing semi-finalists: Ipswich Town and Sunderland. **Div. 2: Brighton & H.A.** 1, Bristol City 0 (att: 65,167).

Losing semi-finalists: Hartlepool Utd. and Swindon Town. **Div. 3: Huddersfield Town** 0, Mansfield Town 0, aet, **Huddersfield Town** won 4-1 on pens (att: 37,298). Losing semi-finalists: Lincoln City and Northampton Town.

2005: Championship: West Ham Utd. 1 Preston N.E. 0 (att: 70,275). Losing semi-finalists: Derby Co. and Ipswich Town. **League 1: Sheffield Wed.** 4, Hartlepool Utd. 2, aet (att: 59,808). Losing semi-finalists: Brentford and Tranmere Rov. **League 2: Southend Utd.** 2, Lincoln City 0, aet (att: 19532). Losing semi-finalists: Macclesfield Town and Northampton Town.

HISTORY OF THE PLAY-OFFS

Play-off matches were introduced by the Football League to decide final promotion and relegation issues at the end of season 1986-87.

A similar series styled "Test Matches" had operated between Divisions One and Two for six seasons from 1893-98, and was abolished when both divisions were increased from 16 to 18 clubs.

Eighty-eight years later, the play-offs were back in vogue. In the first three seasons (1987-88-89), the Finals were played home-and-away, and since they were made one-off matches in 1990, they have featured regularly in Wembley's spring calendar, until the old stadium closed its doors in the Millennium Stadium in Cardiff in 2001.

Through the years, these have been the ups and downs of the play-offs:

1987 Initially, the 12 clubs involved comprised the one that finished directly above those relegated in Divisions One, Two and Three and the three who followed the sides automatically promoted in each section. Two of the home-and-away Finals went to neutral-ground replays, in which **Charlton Athletic** clung to First Division status by denying Leeds Utd. promotion while **Swindon Town** beat Gillingham to complete their climb from Fourth Division to Second in successive seasons, via the play-offs, Sunderland fell into the Third and Bolton Wand. into Division Four, both for the first time. **Aldershot** went up after finishing only sixth in Division Four; in their Final, they beat Wolves, who had finished nine points higher and missed automatic promotion by one point.

1988 Chelsea were relegated from the First Division after losing on aggregate to **Middlesbrough**, who had finished third in Division Two. So Middlesbrough, managed by Bruce Rioch, completed the rise from Third Division to First in successive seasons, only two years after their very existence had been threatened by the bailiffs. Also promoted via the play-offs: **Walsall** from Division Three and **Swansea City** from the Fourth. Relegated, besides Chelsea: Sheffield Utd. (to Division Three) and Rotherham Utd. (to Division Four).

1989 After two seasons of promotion-relegation play-offs, the system was changed to involve the four clubs who had just missed automatic promotion. That format has remained. Steve Coppell's **Crystal Palace**, third in Division Two, returned to the top flight after eight years, beating Blackburn Rov. 4-3 on aggregate after extra time. Similarly, **Port Vale** confirmed third place in Division Three with promotion via the play-offs. For **Leyton Orient**, promotion seemed out of the question in Division Four when they stood 15th. on March 1. But eight wins and a draw in the last nine home games swept them to sixth in the final table, and two more home victories in the play-offs completed their season in triumph.

1990 The play-off Finals now moved to Wembley over three days of the Spring Holiday week-end. On successive afternoons, **Cambridge Utd.** won promotion from Division Four and **Notts Co.** from the Third. Then, on Bank Holiday Monday, the biggest crowd for years at a Football League fixture (72,873) saw Ossie Ardiles' **Swindon Town** beat Sunderland 1-0 to reach the First Division for the first time. A few weeks later, however, Wembley losers **Sunderland** were promoted instead, by default; Swindon were found guilty of "financial irregularities" and stayed in Division Two.

1991 Again, the season's biggest League crowd (59,940) gathered at Wembley for the First Division Final in which **Notts Co.** (having missed promotion by one point) still fulfilled their ambition, beating Brighton & H.A. 3-1. In successive years, County had climbed from Third Division to First via the play-offs – the first club to achieve double promotion by this route. Bolton Wand. were denied automatic promotion in Division Three on goal difference, and lost at Wembley to an extra-time goal by **Tranmere Rov.** The Fourth Division Final made history, with Blackpool beaten 5-4 on penalties by **Torquay Utd.** – first instance of promotion being decided by a shoot-out. In the table, Blackpool had finished seven points ahead of Torquay.

1992 Wembley that Spring Bank Holiday was the turning point in the history of **Blackburn Rov.** Bolstered by Kenny Dalglish's return to management and owner Jack Walker's millions, they beat Leicester City 1-0 by Mike Newell's 45th-minute penalty to achieve their objective – a place in the new Premier League. Newell, who also missed a second-half penalty, had recovered from a broken leg just in time for the play-offs. In the Fourth Division Final **Blackpool** (denied by penalties the previous year) this time won a shoot-out 4-3 against Scunthorpe Utd., who were unlucky in the play-offs for the fourth time in five years. **Peterborough Utd.** climbed out of the Third Division for the first time, beating Stockport Co. 2-1 at Wembley.

1993 The crowd of 73,802 at Wembley to see **Swindon Town** beat Leicester City 4-3 in the First Division Final was 11,000 bigger than that for the F.A. Cup Final replay between Arsenal and Sheffield Wed. Leicester rallied from three down to 3-3 before Paul Bodin's late penalty wiped away Swindon Town's bitter memories of three years earlier, when they were denied promotion after winning at Wembley. In the Third Division Final, **York City** beat Crewe Alexandra 5-3 in a shoot-out after a 1-1 draw, and in the Second Division decider, **W.B.A.** beat Port Vale 3-0. That was tough on Vale, who had finished third in the table with 89 points – the highest total never to earn promotion in any division. They had beaten Albion twice in the League, too.

1994 Wembley's record turn-out of 158,586 spectators at the three Finals started with a crowd of 40,109 to see Martin O'Neill's **Wycombe Wand.** beat Preston N.E. 4-2. They thus climbed from Conference to Second Division with successive promotions. **Burnley's** 2-1 victory in the Second Division Final was marred by the sending-off of two Stockport Co. players, and in the First Division decider **Leicester City** came from behind to beat Derby Co. and end the worst Wembley record of any club. They had lost on all six previous appearances there – four times in the F.A. Cup Final and in the play-offs of 1992 and 1993.

1995 Two months after losing the Coca-Cola Cup Final to Liverpool, Bruce Rioch's **Bolton Wand.** were back at Wembley for the First Division play-off Final. From two goals down to Reading in front of a crowd of 64,107, they returned to the top company after 15 years, winning 4-3 with two extra-time goals. **Huddersfield Town** ended the first season at their new £15m. home with promotion to the First Division via a 2-1 victory against Bristol Rov. – manager Neil Warnock's third play-off success (after two with Notts Co.). Of the three clubs who missed automatic promotion by one place, only **Chesterfield** achieved it in the play-offs, comfortably beating Bury 2-0.

1996 Under new manager **Martin O'Neill** (a Wembley play-off winner with Wycombe Wand. in 1994), **Leicester City** returned to the Premiership a year after leaving it. They had finished fifth in the table, but in the Final came from behind to beat third-placed Crystal Palace by Steve Claridge's shot in the last seconds of extra time. In the Second Division **Bradford City** came sixth, nine points behind Blackpool (3rd), but beat them (from two down in the semi-final first leg) and then clinched promotion by 2-0 v Notts Co. at Wembley. It was City's greatest day since they won the Cup in 1911. **Plymouth Argyle** beat Darlington in the Third Division Final to earn promotion a year after being relegated. It was manager Neil Warnock's fourth play-off triumph in seven seasons after two with Notts Co. (1990 and 1991) and a third with Huddersfield Town in 1995.

1997 High drama at Wembley as **Crystal Palace** left it late against Sheffield Utd. in the First Division play-off final. The match was scoreless until the last 10 seconds when David

Hopkin lobbed Blades' keeper Simon Tracey from 25 yards to send the Eagles back to the Premiership after two seasons of Nationwide action. In the Second Division play-off final, **Crewe Alexandra** beat Brentford 1-0 courtesy of a Shaun Smith goal. **Northampton Town** celebrated their first Wembley appearance with a 1-0 victory over Swansea City thanks to John Frain's injury-time free-kick in the Third Division play-off final.

1998 In one of the finest games ever seen at Wembley, **Charlton Athletic** eventually triumphed 7-6 on penalties over Sunderland. For Charlton Athletic, Wearside-born Clive Mendonca scored a hat-trick and Richard Rufus his first career goal in a match that lurched between joy and despair for both sides as it ended 4-4. Sunderland defender Michael Gray's superb performance ill deserved to end with his weakly struck spot kick being saved by Sasa Ilic. In the Third Division, the penalty spot also had a role to play, as **Colchester Utd.**'s David Gregory scored the only goal to defeat Torquay Utd., while in the Second Division a Kevin Donovan goal gave **Grimsby Town** victory over Northampton Town.

1999: Elton John, watching via a personal satellite link in Seattle, saw his **Watford** side overcome Bolton Wand. 2-0 to reach the Premiership. Against technically superior opponents, Watford prevailed with application and teamwork. They also gave Bolton a lesson in finishing through match-winners Nick Wright and Allan Smart. **Manchester City** staged a remarkable comeback to win the Second Division Final after trailing 2 goals by Carl Asaba and Robert Taylor for Gillingham. Kevin Horlock and Paul Dickov scored in stoppage time and City went on to win on penalties. A goal by Spaniard Alex Calvo-Garcia earned **Scunthorpe Utd.** a 1-0 success against Leyton Orient in the Third Division Final.

2000: After three successive play-off failures, **Ipswich Town** finally secured a place in the Premiership. They overcame the injury loss of leading scorer David Johnson to beat Barnsley 4-2 with goals by 36-year-old Tony Mowbray, Marcus Stewart and substitutes Richard Naylor and Martijn Reuser. With six minutes left of extra-time in the Second Division Final, **Gillingham** trailed Wigan Athletic 2-1. But headers by 38-year-old player-coach Steve Butler and fellow substitute Andy Thomson gave them a 3-2 victory. Andy Clarke, approaching his 33rd birthday, scored the only goal of the Third Division decider for **Peterborough Utd.** against Darlington.

2001: **Bolton Wand.**, unsuccessful play-off contenders in the two previous seasons, made no mistake at the third attempt. They flourished in the new surroundings of the Millennium Stadium to beat Preston N.E. 3-0 with goals by Gareth Farrelly, Michael Ricketts – his 24th of the season – and Ricardo Gardner to reach the Premiership. **Walsall**, relegated 12 months earlier, scored twice in a three-minute spell of extra time to win 3-2 against Reading in the Second Division Final, while **Blackpool** capped a marked improvement in the second half of the season by overcoming Leyton Orient 4-2 in the Third Division Final.

2002: Holding their nerve to win a penalty shoot-out 4-2, **Birmingham City** wiped away the memory of three successive defeats in the semi-finals of the play-offs to return to the top division after an absence of 16 years. Substitute Darren Carter completed a fairy-tale first season as a professional by scoring the fourth spot-kick against Norwich City. **Stoke City** became the first successful team to come from the south dressing room in 12 finals since football was adopted by the home of Welsh rugby, beating Brentford 2-0 in the Second Division Final with Deon Burton's strike and a Ben Burgess own goal. Julian Alsop's 26th goal of the season helped **Cheltenham Town** defeat League newcomers Rushden & Diamonds 3-1 in the Third Division decider.

2003: **Wolves** benefactor Sir Jack Hayward finally saw his £60m. investment pay dividends when the club first supported as a boy returned to the top flight after an absence of 19 years by beating Sheffield Utd. 3-0. It was also a moment to savour for manager Dave Jones, who was forced to leave his previous club Southampton because of child abuse allegations, which were later found to be groundless. **Cardiff City**, away from the game's second tier for 18 years, returned with an extra-time winner from substitute Andy Campbell against Q.P.R after a goalless 90 minutes in the Division Two

Final. **Bournemouth**, relegated 12 months earlier, became the first team to score five in the end-of-season deciders, beating Lincoln City 5-2 in the Division Three Final.

2004: Three tight, tense Finals produced only two goals, the lowest number since the Play-offs were introduced. One of them, scored by Neil Shipperley, gave **Crystal Palace** victory over West Ham Utd., the much-travelled striker tapping in a rebound after Stephen Bywater parried Andy Johnson's shot. It completed a remarkable transformation for Crystal Palace, who were 19th in the table when Iain Dowie left Oldham Athletic to become their manager. **Brighton & H.A.** made an immediate return to Division One in a poor game against Bristol City which looked set for extra-time until Leon Knight netted his 27th goal of the campaign from the penalty spot after 84 minutes. **Huddersfield Town** also went back up at the first attempt, winning the Division Three Final in a penalty shoot-out after a goalless 120 minutes against Mansfield Town.

2005: Goals were few and far between for Bobby Zamora during West Ham Utd.'s Championship season – but what a difference in the Play-offs. The former Brighton & H.A. and Tottenham striker scored three times in the 4-2 aggregate win over Ipswich Town in the semi-finals and was on the mark again with the only goal against Preston N.E. at the Millennium Stadium. Sheffield Wed. were eight minute away from defeat against Hartlepool Utd. in the League One decider when Steven MacLean made it 2-2 from the penalty spot and they went on to win 4-2 in extra-time. Southend Utd., edged out of an automatic promotion place, won the League Two Final 2-0 against Lincoln City, Freddy Eastwood scoring their first in extra-time and making the second for Duncan Jupp. Carlisle Utd. beat Stevenage 1-0 with a goal by Peter Murphy in the Conference Final to regain their League place 12 months after being relegated.

LEAGUE PLAY-OFF CROWDS YEAR BY YEAR

YEAR	MATCHES	AGG. ATT.
1987	20	310,000
1988	19	305,817
1989	18	234,393
1990	15	291,428
1991	15	266,442
1992	15	277,684
1993	15	319,907
1994	15	314,817
1995	15	295,317
1996	15	308,515
1997	15	309,085
1998	15	320,795
1999	15	372,969
2000	15	333,999
2001	15	317,745
2002	15	327,894
2003	15	374,461
2004	15	388,675 (record)
2005	15	353,330
2006	15	340,804

PENALTY SHOOT-OUT MARATHON

An F.A. Cup record for the number of spot-kicks taken in a penalty shoot-out was set in the preliminary round replay between Tunbridge Wells and Littlehampton Town last season. Kent League side Tunbridge won it 16-15 after 40 kicks, the tie lasting for three hours, ten minutes and finishing at 10.55pm. The previous record was 24, with Macclesfield Town beating Forest Green 11-10 after 24 penalties in a first round replay in November 2001.

ENGLISH HONOURS LIST

F.A. PREMIER LEAGUE

	First	Pts.	Second	Pts.	Third	Pts.
1992-3*a*	Manchester Utd.	84	Aston Villa	74	Norwich City	72
1993-4*a*	Manchester Utd.	92	Blackburn Rov.	84	Newcastle Utd.	77
1994-5*a*	Blackburn Rov.	89	Manchester Utd.	88	Nott'm. Forest	77
1995-6*b*	Manchester Utd.	82	Newcastle Utd.	78	Liverpool	71
1996-7*b*	Manchester Utd.	75	Newcastle Utd.	68	Arsenal	68
1997-8*b*	Arsenal	78	Manchester Utd.	77	Liverpool	65
1998-9*b*	Manchester Utd.	79	Arsenal	78	Chelsea	75
1999-00*b*	Manchester Utd.	91	Arsenal	73	Leeds Utd.	69
2000-01*b*	Manchester Utd.	80	Arsenal	70	Liverpool	69
2001-02*b*	Arsenal	87	Liverpool	80	Manchester Utd.	77
2002-03*b*	Manchester Utd.	83	Arsenal	78	Newcastle Utd.	69
2003-04*b*	Arsenal	90	Chelsea	79	Manchester Utd.	75
2004-05*b*	Chelsea	95	Arsenal	83	Manchester Utd.	77
2005-06*b*	Chelsea	91	Manchester Utd.	83	Liverpool	82

Maximum points: *a*, 126; *b*, 114.

FOOTBALL LEAGUE

FIRST DIVISION

1992-3	Newcastle Utd.	96	West Ham Utd.	88	††Portsmouth	88
1993-4	Crystal Palace	90	Nott'm. Forest	83	††Millwall	74
1994-5	Middlesbrough	82	††Reading	79	Bolton Wand.	77
1995-6	Sunderland	83	Derby Co.	79	††Crystal Palace	75
1996-7	Bolton Wand.	98	Barnsley	80	††Wolves	76
1997-8	Nott'm. Forest	94	Middlesbrough	91	††Sunderland	90
1998-9	Sunderland	105	Bradford City	87	††Ipswich Town	86
1999-00	Charlton Athletic	91	Manchester City	89	Ipswich Town	87
2000-01	Fulham	101	Blackburn Rov.	91	Bolton Wand.	87
2001-02	Manchester City	99	W.B.A.	89	††Wolves	86
2002-03	Portsmouth	98	Leicester City	92	††Sheffield Utd.	80
2003-04	Norwich City	94	W.B.A.	86	††Sunderland	79

CHAMPIONSHIP

2004-05	Sunderland	94	Wigan Athletic	87	††Ipswich Town	85
2005-06	Reading	106	Sheffield Utd.	90	Watford	81

Maximum points: 138. ††Not promoted after play-offs.

SECOND DIVISION

1992-3	Stoke City	93	Bolton Wand.	90	††Port Vale	89
1993-4	Reading	89	Port Vale	88	††Plymouth Argyle	85
1994-5	Birmingham City	89	††Brentford	85	††Crewe Alexandra	83
1995-6	Swindon Town	92	Oxford Utd.	83	††Blackpool	82
1996-7	Bury	84	Stockport Co.	82	††Luton Town	78
1997-8	Watford	88	Bristol City	85	Grimsby Town	72
1998-9	Fulham	101	Walsall	87	Manchester City	82
1999-00	Preston N.E.	95	Burnley	88	Gillingham	85
2000-01	Milwall	93	Rotherham Utd.	91	††Reading	86
2001-02	Brighton & H.A.	90	Reading	84	††Brentford	83
2002-03	Wigan Athletic	100	Crewe Alexandra	86	††Bristol City	83
2003-04	Plymouth Argyle	90	Q.P.R.	83	††Bristol City	82

LEAGUE ONE

2004-05	Luton Town 98	Hull City 86	††Tranmere Rov. 79
2005-06	Southend Utd. 82	Colchester Utd. 79	††Brentford 76

Maximum points: 138. †† Not promoted after play-offs.

THIRD DIVISION

1992-3a	Cardiff City 83	Wrexham 80	Barnet 79
1993-4a	Shrewsbury Town 79	Chester City 74	Crewe Alexandra 73
1994-5a	Carlisle Utd. 91	Walsall 83	Chesterfield 81
1995-6b	Preston N.E. 86	Gillingham 83	Bury 79
1996-7b	Wigan Athletic 87	Fulham 87	Carlisle Utd. 84
1997-8b	Notts Co. 99	Macclesfield Town .. 82	Lincoln City 75
1998-9b	Brentford 85	Cambridge Utd. 81	Cardiff City 80
1999-00b	Swansea City 85	Rotherham Utd. 84	Northampton Town . 82
2000-01b	Brighton & H.A. 92	Cardiff City 82	*Chesterfield 80
2001-02b	Plymouth Argyle ... 102	Luton Town 97	Mansfield Town 79
2002-03b	Rushden & Diamonds .. 87	Hartlepool Utd. 85	Wrexham 84
2003-04b	Doncaster Rov. 92	Hull City 88	Torquay Utd. 81

LEAGUE TWO

2004-05b	Yeovil Town 83	Scunthorpe Utd. 80	Swansea City 80
2005-06b	Carlisle Utd. 86	Northampton Town . 83	Leyton Orient 81

Maximum points: a, 126; b, 138; * Deducted 9 points for financial irregularities.

FOOTBALL LEAGUE 1888-1992

	First	Pts.	Second	Pts.	Third	Pts.
1888-89a	Preston N.E. 40	Aston Villa 29	Wolves 28
1889-90a	Preston N.E. 33	Everton 31	Blackburn Rov. 27
1890-1a	Everton 29	Preston N.E. 27	Notts Co. 26
1891-2b	Sunderland 42	Preston N.E. 37	Bolton Wand. 36

OLD FIRST DIVISION

	First	Pts.	Second	Pts.	Third	Pts.
1892-3c	Sunderland 48	Preston N.E. 37	Everton 36
1893-4c	Aston Villa 44	Sunderland 38	Derby Co. 36
1894-5c	Sunderland 47	Everton 42	Aston Villa 39
1895-6c	Aston Villa 45	Derby Co. 41	Everton 39
1896-7c	Aston Villa 47	Sheffield Utd. 36	Derby Co. 36
1897-8c	Sheffield Utd. 42	Sunderland 39	Wolves 35
1898-9d	Aston Villa 45	Liverpool 43	Burnley 39
1899-1900d	Aston Villa 50	Sheffield Utd. 48	Sunderland 41
1900-1d	Liverpool 45	Sunderland 43	Notts Co. 40
1901-2d	Sunderland 44	Everton 41	Newcastle Utd. 37
1902-3d	The Wednesday 42	Aston Villa 41	Sunderland 41
1903-4d	The Wednesday 47	Manchester City 44	Everton 43
1904-5d	Newcastle Utd. 48	Everton 47	Manchester City 46
1905-6e	Liverpool 51	Preston N.E. 47	The Wednesday 44
1906-7e	Newcastle Utd. 51	Bristol City 48	Everton 45
1907-8e	Manchester Utd. 52	Aston Villa 43	Manchester City 43
1908-9e	Newcastle Utd. 53	Everton 46	Sunderland 44
1909-10e	Aston Villa 53	Liverpool 48	Blackburn Rov. 45
1910-11e	Manchester Utd. 52	Aston Villa 51	Sunderland 45
1911-12e	Blackburn Rov. 49	Everton 46	Newcastle Utd. 44
1912-13e	Sunderland 54	Aston Villa 50	Sheffield Wed. 49
1913-14e	Blackburn Rov. 51	Aston Villa 44	Middlesbrough 43
1914-15e	Everton 46	Oldham Athletic 45	Blackburn Rov. 43

1919-20f	W.B.A.	60	Burnley	51	Chelsea	49
1920-1f	Burnley	59	Manchester City	54	Bolton Wand.	52
1921-2f	Liverpool	57	Tottenham	51	Burnley	49
1922-3f	Liverpool	60	Sunderland	54	Huddersfield Town	53
1923-4f	*Huddersfield Town	57	Cardiff City	57	Sunderland	53
1924-5f	Huddersfield Town	58	W.B.A.	56	Bolton Wand.	55
1925-6f	Huddersfield Town	57	Arsenal	52	Sunderland	48
1926-7f	Newcastle Utd.	56	Huddersfield Town	51	Sunderland	49
1927-8f	Everton	53	Huddersfield Town	51	Leicester City	48
1928-9f	Sheffield Wed.	52	Leicester City	51	Aston Villa	50
1929-30f	Sheffield Wed.	60	Derby Co.	50	Manchester City	47
1930-1f	Arsenal	66	Aston Villa	59	Sheffield Wed.	52
1931-2f	Everton	56	Arsenal	54	Sheffield Wed.	50
1932-3f	Arsenal	58	Aston Villa	54	Sheffield Wed.	51
1933-4f	Arsenal	59	Huddersfield Town	56	Tottenham	49
1934-5f	Arsenal	58	Sunderland	54	Sheffield Wed.	49
1935-6f	Sunderland	56	Derby Co.	48	Huddersfield Town	48
1936-7f	Manchester City	57	Charlton Athletic	54	Arsenal	52
1937-8f	Arsenal	52	Wolves	51	Preston N.E.	49
1938-9f	Everton	59	Wolves	55	Charlton Athletic	50
1946-7f	Liverpool	57	Manchester Utd.	56	Wolves	56
1947-8f	Arsenal	59	Manchester Utd.	52	Burnley	52
1948-9f	Portsmouth	58	Manchester Utd.	53	Derby Co.	53
1949-50f	*Portsmouth	53	Wolves	53	Sunderland	52
1950-1f	Tottenham	60	Manchester Utd.	56	Blackpool	50
1951-2f	Manchester Utd.	57	Tottenham	53	Arsenal	53
1952-3f	*Arsenal	54	Preston N.E.	54	Wolves	51
1953-4f	Wolves	57	W.B.A.	53	Huddersfield Town	51
1954-5f	Chelsea	52	Wolves	48	Portsmouth	48
1955-6f	Manchester Utd.	60	Blackpool	49	Wolves	49
1956-7f	Manchester Utd.	64	Tottenham	56	Preston N.E.	56
1957-8f	Wolves	64	Preston N.E.	59	Tottenham	51
1958-9f	Wolves	61	Manchester Utd.	55	Arsenal	50
1959-60f	Burnley	55	Wolves	54	Tottenham	53
1960-1f	Tottenham	66	Sheffield Wed.	58	Wolves	57
1961-2f	Ipswich Town	56	Burnley	53	Tottenham	52
1962-3f	Everton	61	Tottenham	55	Burnley	54
1963-4f	Liverpool	57	Manchester Utd.	53	Everton	52
1964-5f	*Manchester Utd.	61	Leeds Utd.	61	Chelsea	56
1965-6f	Liverpool	61	Leeds Utd.	55	Burnley	55
1966-7f	Manchester Utd.	60	Nott'm. Forest	56	Tottenham	56
1967-8f	Manchester City	58	Manchester Utd.	56	Liverpool	55
1968-9f	Leeds Utd.	67	Liverpool	61	Everton	57
1969-70f	Everton	66	Leeds Utd.	57	Chelsea	55
1970-1f	Arsenal	65	Leeds Utd.	64	Tottenham	52
1971-2f	Derby Co.	58	Leeds Utd.	57	Liverpool	57
1972-3f	Liverpool	60	Arsenal	57	Leeds Utd.	53
1973-4f	Leeds Utd.	62	Liverpool	57	Derby Co.	48
1974-5f	Derby Co.	53	Liverpool	51	Ipswich Town	51
1975-6f	Liverpool	60	Q.P.R.	59	Manchester Utd.	56
1976-7f	Liverpool	57	Manchester City	56	Ipswich Town	52
1977-8f	Nott'm. Forest	64	Liverpool	57	Everton	55
1978-9f	Liverpool	68	Nott'm Forest	60	W.B.A.	59
1979-80f	Liverpool	60	Manchester Utd.	58	Ipswich Town	53
1980-1f	Aston Villa	60	Ipswich Town	56	Arsenal	53
1981-2g	Liverpool	87	Ipswich Town	83	Manchester Utd.	78
1982-3g	Liverpool	82	Watford	71	Manchester Utd.	70
1983-4g	Liverpool	80	Southampton	77	Nott'm. Forest	74

1984-5g	Everton	90	Liverpool	77	Tottenham	77
1985-6g	Liverpool	88	Everton	86	West Ham Utd.	84
1986-7g	Everton	86	Liverpool	77	Tottenham	71
1987-8h	Liverpool	90	Manchester Utd.	81	Nott'm. Forest	73
1988-9j	††Arsenal	76	Liverpool	76	Nott'm. Forest	64
1989-90j	Liverpool	79	Aston Villa	70	Tottenham	63
1990-1j	Arsenal	83	Liverpool	76	Crystal Palace	69
1991-2g	Leeds Utd.	82	Manchester Utd.	78	Sheffield Wed.	75

Maximum points: *a*, 44; *b*, 52; *c*, 60; *d*, 68; *e*, 76; *f*, 84; *g*, 126; *h*, 120; *j*, 114.
*Won on goal average. †Won on goal diff. ††Won on goals scored. No comp. 1915-19 – 1939-46

OLD SECOND DIVISION 1892-1992

	First	Pts.	Second	Pts.	Third	Pts.
1892-3a	Small Heath	36	Sheffield Utd.	35	Darwen	30
1893-4b	Liverpool	50	Small Heath	42	Notts Co.	39
1894-5c	Bury	48	Notts Co.	39	Newton Heath	38
1895-6c	*Liverpool	46	Manchester City	46	Grimsby Town	42
1896-7c	Notts Co.	42	Newton Heath	39	Grimsby Town	38
1897-8c	Burnley	48	Newcastle Utd.	45	Manchester City	39
1898-9d	Manchester City	52	Glossop	46	Leicester Fosse	45
1899-1900d	The Wednesday	54	Bolton Wand.	52	Small Heath	46
1900-1d	Grimsby Town	49	Small Heath	48	Burnley	44
1901-2d	W.B.A.	55	Middlesbrough	51	Preston N.E.	42
1902-3d	Manchester City	54	Small Heath	51	Woolwich Arsenal	48
1903-4d	Preston N.E.	50	Woolwich Arsenal	49	Manchester Utd.	48
1904-5d	Liverpool	58	Bolton Wand.	56	Manchester Utd.	53
1905-6e	Bristol City	66	Manchester Utd.	62	Chelsea	53
1906-7e	Nott'm. Forest	60	Chelsea	57	Leicester Fosse	48
1907-8e	Bradford City	54	Leicester Fosse	52	Oldham Athletic	50
1908-9e	Bolton Wand.	52	Tottenham	51	W.B.A.	51
1909-10e	Manchester City	54	Oldham Athletic	53	Hull City	53
1910-11e	W.B.A.	53	Bolton Wand.	51	Chelsea	49
1911-12e	*Derby Co.	54	Chelsea	54	Burnley	52
1912-13e	Preston N.E.	53	Burnley	50	Birmingham City	46
1913-14e	Notts Co.	53	Bradford P.A.	49	Woolwich Arsenal	49
1914-15e	Derby Co.	53	Preston N.E.	50	Barnsley	47
1919-20f	Tottenham	70	Huddersfield Town	64	Birmingham City	56
1920-1f	*Birmingham City	58	Cardiff City	58	Bristol City	51
1921-2f	Nott'm. Forest	56	Stoke City	52	Barnsley	52
1922-3f	Notts Co.	53	West Ham Utd.	51	Leicester City	51
1923-4f	Leeds Utd.	54	Bury	51	Derby Co.	51
1924-5f	Leicester City	59	Manchester Utd.	57	Derby Co.	55
1925-6f	Sheffield Wed.	60	Derby Co.	57	Chelsea	52
1926-7f	Middlesbrough	62	Portsmouth	54	Manchester City	54
1927-8f	Manchester City	59	Leeds Utd.	57	Chelsea	54
1928-9f	Middlesbrough	55	Grimsby Town	53	Bradford City	48
1929-30f	Blackpool	58	Chelsea	55	Oldham Athletic	53
1930-1f	Everton	61	W.B.A.	54	Tottenham	51
1931-2f	Wolves	56	Leeds Utd.	54	Stoke City	52
1932-3f	Stoke City	56	Tottenham	55	Fulham	50
1933-4f	Grimsby Town	59	Preston N.E.	52	Bolton Wand.	51
1934-5f	Brentford	61	Bolton Wand.	56	West Ham Utd.	56
1935-6f	Manchester Utd.	56	Charlton Athletic	55	Sheffield Utd.	52
1936-7f	Leicester City	56	Blackpool	55	Bury	52
1937-8f	Aston Villa	57	Manchester Utd.	53	Sheffield Utd.	53
1938-9f	Blackburn Rov.	55	Sheffield Utd.	54	Sheffield Wed.	53
1946-7f	Manchester City	62	Burnley	58	Birmingham City	55

Season	First	Pts.	Second	Pts.	Third	Pts.
1947-8f	Birmingham City	59	Newcastle Utd.	56	Southampton	52
1948-9f	Fulham	57	W.B.A.	56	Southampton	55
1949-50f	Tottenham	61	Sheffield Wed.	52	Sheffield Utd.	52
1950-1f	Preston N.E.	57	Manchester City	52	Cardiff City	50
1951-2f	Sheffield Wed.	53	Cardiff City	51	Birmingham City	51
1952-3f	Sheffield Utd.	60	Huddersfield Town	58	Luton Town	52
1953-4f	*Leicester City	56	Everton	56	Blackburn Rov.	55
1954-5f	*Birmingham City	54	Luton Town	54	Rotherham Utd.	54
1955-6f	Sheffield Wed.	55	Leeds Utd.	52	Liverpool	48
1956-7f	Leicester City	61	Nott'm. Forest	54	Liverpool	53
1957-8f	West Ham Utd.	57	Blackburn Rov.	56	Charlton Athletic	55
1958-9f	Sheffield Wed.	62	Fulham	60	Sheffield Utd.	53
1959-60f	Aston Villa	59	Cardiff City	58	Liverpool	50
1960-1f	Ipswich Town	59	Sheffield Utd.	58	Liverpool	52
1961-2f	Liverpool	62	Leyton Orient	54	Sunderland	53
1962-3f	Stoke City	53	Chelsea	52	Sunderland	52
1963-4f	Leeds Utd.	63	Sunderland	61	Preston N.E.	56
1964-5f	Newcastle Utd.	57	Northampton Town	56	Bolton Wand.	50
1965-6f	Manchester City	59	Southampton	54	Coventry City	53
1966-7f	Coventry City	59	Wolves	58	Carlisle Utd.	52
1967-8f	Ipswich Town	59	Q.P.R.	58	Blackpool	58
1968-9f	Derby Co.	63	Crystal Palace	56	Charlton Athletic	50
1969-70f	Huddersfield Town	60	Blackpool	53	Leicester City	51
1970-1f	Leicester City	59	Sheffield Utd.	56	Cardiff City	53
1971-2f	Norwich City	57	Birmingham City	56	Millwall	55
1972-3f	Burnley	62	Q.P.R.	61	Aston Villa	50
1973-4f	Middlesbrough	65	Luton Town	50	Carlisle Utd.	49
1974-5f	Manchester Utd.	61	Aston Villa	58	Norwich City	53
1975-6f	Sunderland	56	Bristol City	53	W.B.A.	53
1976-7f	Wolves	57	Chelsea	55	Nott'm. Forest	52
1977-8f	Bolton Wand.	58	Southampton	57	Tottenham	56
1978-9f	Crystal Palace	57	Brighton & H.A.	56	Stoke City	56
1979-80f	Leicester City	55	Sunderland	54	Birmingham City	53
1980-1f	West Ham Utd.	66	Notts Co.	53	Swansea City	50
1981-2g	Luton Town	88	Watford	80	Norwich City	71
1982-3g	Q.P.R.	85	Wolves	75	Leicester City	70
1983-4g	†Chelsea	88	Sheffield Wed.	88	Newcastle Utd.	80
1984-5g	Oxford Utd.	84	Birmingham City	82	Manchester City	74
1985-6g	Norwich City	84	Charlton Athletic	77	Wimbledon	76
1986-7g	Derby Co.	84	Portsmouth	78	††Oldham Athletic	75
1987-8h	Millwall	82	Aston Villa	78	Middlesbrough	78
1988-9j	Chelsea	99	Manchester City	82	Crystal Palace	81
1989-90j	†Leeds Utd.	85	Sheffield Utd.	85	†† Newcastle Utd.	80
1990-1j	Oldham Athletic	88	West Ham Utd.	87	Sheffield Wed.	82
1991-2j	Ipswich Town	84	Middlesbrough	80	†† Derby Co.	78

Maximum points: *a*, 44; *b*, 56; *c*, 60; *d*, 68; *e*, 76; *f*, 84; *g*, 126; *h*, 132; *j*, 138. * Won on goal average. † Won on goal difference. †† Not promoted after play-offs.

THIRD DIVISION 1958-92

Season	First	Pts.	Second	Pts.	Third	Pts.
1958-9	Plymouth Argyle	62	Hull City	61	Brentford	57
1959-60	Southampton	61	Norwich City	59	Shrewsbury Town	52
1960-1	Bury	68	Walsall	62	Q.P.R.	60
1961-2	Portsmouth	65	Grimsby Town	62	Bournemouth	59
1962-3	Northampton Town	62	Swindon Town	58	Port Vale	54
1963-4	*Coventry City	60	Crystal Palace	60	Watford	58
1964-5	Carlisle Utd.	60	Bristol City	59	Mansfield Town	59
1965-6	Hull City	69	Millwall	65	Q.P.R.	57

1966-7	Q.P.R.	67	Middlesbrough	55	Watford	54
1967-8	Oxford Utd.	57	Bury	56	Shrewsbury Town	55
1968-9	*Watford	64	Swindon Town	64	Luton Town	61
1969-70	Orient	62	Luton Town	60	Bristol Rov.	56
1970-1	Preston N.E.	61	Fulham	60	Halifax Town	56
1971-2	Aston Villa	70	Brighton & H.A.	65	Bournemouth	62
1972-3	Bolton Wand.	61	Notts Co.	57	Blackburn Rov.	55
1973-4	Oldham Athletic	62	Bristol Rov.	61	York City	61
1974-5	Blackburn Rov.	60	Plymouth Argyle	59	Charlton Athletic	55
1975-6	Hereford	63	Cardiff City	57	Millwall	56
1976-7	Mansfield Town	64	Brighton & H.A.	61	Crystal Palace	59
1977-8	Wrexham	61	Cambridge Utd.	58	Preston N.E.	56
1978-9	Shrewsbury Town	61	Watford	60	Swansea City	60
1979-80	Grimsby Town	62	Blackburn Rov.	59	Sheffield Wed.	58
1980-1	Rotherham Utd.	61	Barnsley	59	Charlton Athletic	59
†1981-2	**Burnley	80	Carlisle Utd.	80	Fulham	78
†1982-3	Portsmouth	91	Cardiff City	86	Huddersfield Town	82
†1983-4	Oxford Utd.	95	Wimbledon	87	Sheffield Utd.	83
†1984-5	Bradford City	94	Millwall	90	Hull City	87
†1985-6	Reading	94	Plymouth Argyle	87	Derby Co.	84
†1986-7	Bournemouth	97	Middlesbrough	94	Swindon Town	87
†1987-8	Sunderland	93	Brighton & H.A.	84	Walsall	82
†1988-9	Wolves	92	Sheffield Utd.	84	Port Vale	84
†1989-90	Bristol Rov.	93	Bristol City	91	Notts Co.	87
†1990-1	Cambridge Utd.	86	Southend Utd.	85	Grimsby Town	83
†1991-2	Brentford	82	Birmingham City	81	††Huddersfield T	78

* Won on goal average. ** Won on goal difference. † Maximum points 138 (previously 92). †† Not promoted after play-offs.

FOURTH DIVISION 1958-92

	First	Pts.	Second	Pts.	Third	Pts.	Fourth	Pts.
1958-9	Port Vale	64	Coventry City	60	York City	60	Shrewsbury Town	58
1959-60	Walsall	65	Notts Co.	60	Torquay Utd.	60	Watford	57
1960-1	Peterborough Utd.	66	Crystal Palace	64	Northampton Town	60	Bradford P.A.	60
1961-2	Millwall	56	Colchester Utd.	55	Wrexham	53	Carlisle Utd.	52
1962-3	Brentford	62	Oldham Athletic	59	Crewe Alexandra	59	Mansfield Town	57
1963-4	*Gillingham	60	Carlisle Utd.	60	Workington	59	Exeter City	58
1964-5	Brighton & H.A.	63	Millwall	62	York City	62	Oxford Utd.	61
1965-6	*Doncaster Rov.	59	Darlington	59	Torquay Utd.	58	Colchester Utd.	56
1966-7	Stockport Co.	64	Southport	59	Barrow	59	Tranmere Rov.	58
1967-8	Luton Town	66	Barnsley	61	Hartlepool Utd.	60	Crewe Alexandra	58
1968-9	Doncaster Rov.	59	Halifax Town	57	Rochdale	56	Bradford City	56
1969-70	Chesterfield	64	Wrexham	61	Swansea City	60	Port Vale	59
1970-1	Notts Co.	69	Bournemouth	60	Oldham Athletic	59	York City	56
1971-2	Grimsby Town	63	Southend Utd.	60	Brentford	59	Scunthorpe Utd.	57
1972-3	Southport	62	Hereford	58	Cambridge Utd.	57	Aldershot	56
1973-4	Peterborough Utd.	65	Gillingham	62	Colchester Utd.	60	Bury	59
1974-5	Mansfield Town	68	Shrewsbury Town	62	Rotherham Utd.	58	Chester City	57
1975-6	Lincoln City	74	Northampton Town	68	Reading	60	Tranmere Rov.	58
1976-7	Cambridge Utd.	65	Exeter City	62	Colchester Utd.	59	Bradford City	59
1977-8	Watford	71	Southend Utd.	60	Swansea City	56	Brentford	59
1978-9	Reading	65	Grimsby Town	61	Wimbledon	61	Barnsley	61
1979-80	Huddersfield Town	66	Walsall	64	Newport	61	Portsmouth	60
1980-1	Southend Utd.	67	Lincoln City	65	Doncaster Rov.	56	Wimbledon	55
†1981-2	Sheffield Utd.	96	Bradford City	91	Wigan Athletic	91	Bournemouth	88
†1982-3	Wimbledon	98	Hull City	90	Port Vale	88	Scunthorpe Utd.	83
†1983-4	York City	101	Doncaster Rov.	85	Reading	82	Bristol City	82
†1984-5	Chesterfield	91	Blackpool	86	Darlington	85	Bury	84

80

	First	Pts.	Second	Pts.	Third	Pts.
†1985-6	Swindon Town	102	Chester City	84	Mansfield Town	81
†1986-7	Northampton Town	99	Preston N.E.	90	Southend Utd.	80
†1987-8	Wolves	90	Cardiff City	85	Bolton Wand.	78
†1988-9	Rotherham Utd.	82	Tranmere Rov.	80	Crewe Alexandra	78
†1989-90	Exeter City	89	Grimsby Town	79	Southend Utd.	75
†1990-1	Darlington	83	Stockport Co.	82	Hartlepool Utd.	82
1991-2a	Burnley	83	Rotherham Utd.	77	Mansfield Town	77

	Port Vale	79
	††Wolves	79
	††Scunthorpe Utd.	77
	††Scunthorpe Utd.	77
	††Stockport Co.	74
	Peterborough Utd.	80
	Blackpool	76

* Won on goal average. Maximum points: †, 138; a, 126; previously 92. †† Not promoted after play-offs.

THIRD DIVISION – SOUTH 1920-58

	First	Pts.	Second	Pts.	Third	Pts.
1920-1a	Crystal Palace	59	Southampton	54	Q.P.R.	53
1921-2a	*Southampton	61	Plymouth Argyle	61	Portsmouth	53
1922-3a	Bristol City	59	Plymouth Argyle	53	Swansea City	53
1923-4a	Portsmouth	59	Plymouth Argyle	55	Millwall	54
1924-5a	Swansea City	57	Plymouth Argyle	56	Bristol City	53
1925-6a	Reading	57	Plymouth Argyle	56	Millwall	53
1926-7a	Bristol City	62	Plymouth Argyle	60	Millwall	56
1927-8a	Millwall	65	Northampton Town	55	Plymouth Argyle	53
1928-9a	*Charlton Athletic	54	Crystal Palace	54	Northampton Town	52
1929-30a	Plymouth Argyle	68	Brentford	61	Q.P.R.	51
1930-31a	Notts Co.	59	Crystal Palace	51	Brentford	50
1931-2a	Fulham	57	Reading	55	Southend Utd.	53
1932-3a	Brentford	62	Exeter City	58	Norwich City	57
1933-4a	Norwich City	61	Coventry City	54	Reading	54
1934-5a	Charlton Athletic	61	Reading	53	Coventry City	51
1935-6a	Coventry City	57	Luton Town	56	Reading	54
1936-7a	Luton Town	58	Notts Co.	56	Brighton & H.A.	53
1937-8a	Millwall	56	Bristol City	55	Q.P.R.	53
1938-9a	Newport	55	Crystal Palace	52	Brighton & H.A.	49
1946-7a	Cardiff City	66	Q.P.R.	57	Bristol City	51
1947-8a	Q.P.R.	61	Bournemouth	57	Walsall	51
1948-9a	Swansea City	62	Reading	55	Bournemouth	52
1949-50a	Notts Co.	58	Northampton Town	51	Southend Utd.	51
1950-1d	Nott'm. Forest	70	Norwich City	64	Reading	57
1951-2d	Plymouth Argyle	66	Reading	61	Norwich City	61
1952-3d	Bristol Rov.	64	Millwall	62	Northampton Town	62
1953-4d	Ipswich Town	64	Brighton & H.A.	61	Bristol City	56
1954-5d	Bristol City	70	Leyton Orient	61	Southampton	59
1955-6d	Leyton Orient	66	Brighton & H.A.	65	Ipswich Town	64
1956-7d	*Ipswich Town	59	Torquay Utd.	59	Colchester Utd.	58
1957-8d	Brighton & H.A.	60	Brentford	58	Plymouth Argyle	58

THIRD DIVISION – NORTH 1921-58

	First	Pts.	Second	Pts.	Third	Pts.
1921-2b	Stockport Co.	56	Darlington	50	Grimsby Town	50
1922-3b	Nelson	51	Bradford P.A.	47	Walsall	46
1923-4a	Wolves	63	Rochdale	62	Chesterfield	54
1924-5a	Darlington	58	Nelson	53	New Brighton	53
1925-6a	Grimsby Town	61	Bradford P.A.	60	Rochdale	59
1926-7a	Stoke City	63	Rochdale	58	Bradford P.A.	57
1927-8a	Bradford P.A.	63	Lincoln City	55	Stockport Co.	54
1928-9a	Bradford City	63	Stockport Co.	62	Wrexham	52
1929-30a	Port Vale	67	Stockport Co.	63	Darlington	50
1930-1a	Chesterfield	58	Lincoln City	57	Wrexham	54
1931-2c	*Lincoln City	57	Gateshead	57	Chester City	50
1932-3a	Hull City	59	Wrexham	57	Stockport Co.	54

81

1933-4a	Barnsley	62	Chesterfield	61	Stockport Co.	59
1934-5a	Doncaster Rov.	57	Halifax Town	55	Chester City	54
1935-6a	Chesterfield	60	Chester City	55	Tranmere Rov.	54
1936-7a	Stockport Co.	60	Lincoln City	57	Chester City	53
1937-8a	Tranmere Rov.	56	Doncaster Rov.	54	Hull City	53
1938-9a	Barnsley	67	Doncaster Rov.	56	Bradford City	52
1946-7a	Doncaster Rov.	72	Rotherham Utd.	64	Chester City	56
1947-8a	Lincoln City	60	Rotherham Utd.	59	Wrexham	50
1948-9a	Hull City	65	Rotherham Utd.	62	Doncaster Rov.	50
1949-50a	Doncaster Rov.	55	Gateshead	53	Rochdale	51
1950-1d	Rotherham Utd.	71	Mansfield Town	64	Carlisle Utd.	62
1951-2d	Lincoln City	69	Grimsby Town	66	Stockport Co.	59
1952-3d	Oldham Athletic	59	Port Vale	58	Wrexham	56
1953-4d	Port Vale	69	Barnsley	58	Scunthorpe Utd.	57
1954-5d	Barnsley	65	Accrington	61	Scunthorpe Utd.	58
1955-6d	Grimsby Town	68	Derby Co.	63	Accrington	59
1956-7d	Derby Co.	63	Hartlepool Utd.	59	Accrington	58
1957-8d	Scunthorpe Utd.	66	Accrington	59	Bradford City	57

Maximum points: a, 84; b, 76; c, 80; d, 92. * Won on goal average.

TITLE WINNERS

F.A. PREMIER LEAGUE
Manchester Utd.	8
Arsenal	3
Chelsea	2
Blackburn Rov.	1

FOOTBALL LEAGUE CHAMPIONSHIP
Reading	1
Sunderland	1

DIV.1 (NEW)
Sunderland	2
Bolton Wand.	1
Charlton Athletic	1
Crystal Palace	1
Fulham	1
Manchester City	1
Middlesbrough	1
Newcastle Utd.	1
Norwich City	1
Nott'm. Forest	1
Portsmouth	1

DIV.1 (ORIGINAL)
Liverpool	18
Arsenal	10
Everton	9
Aston Villa	7
Manchester Utd.	7
Sunderland	6
Newcastle Utd.	4
Sheffield Wed.	4
Huddersfield Town	3
Leeds Utd.	3
Wolves	3

Blackburn Rov.	2
Burnley	2
Derby Co.	2
Manchester City	2
Portsmouth	2
Preston N.E.	2
Tottenham	2
Chelsea	1
Ipswich Town	1
Nott'm. Forest	1
Sheffield Utd.	1
W.B.A.	1

LEAGUE ONE
Luton Town	1
Southend Utd.	1

DIV.2 (NEW)
Birmingham City	1
Brighton & H.A.	1
Bury	1
Fulham	1
Millwall	1
Plymouth Argyle	1
Preston N.E.	1
Reading	1
Stoke City	1
Swindon Town	1
Watford	1
Wigan Athletic	1

DIV.2 (ORIGINAL)
Leicester City	6
Manchester City	6
Sheffield Wed.	5
Birmingham City	4

Derby Co.	4
Liverpool	4
Ipswich Town	3
Leeds Utd.	3
Middlesbrough	3
Notts County	3
Preston N.E.	3
Aston Villa	2
Bolton Wand.	2
Burnley	2
Chelsea	2
Grimsby Town	2
Manchester Utd.	2
Norwich City	2
Nott'm Forest	2
Stoke City	2
Tottenham	2
W.B.A.	2
West Ham Utd.	2
Wolves	2
Blackburn Rov.	1
Blackpool	1
Bradford City	1
Brentford	1
Bristol City	1
Bury	1
Coventry City	1
Crystal Palace	1
Everton	1
Fulham	1
Huddersfield Town	1
Luton Town	1
Millwall	1
Newcastle Utd.	1
Oldham Athletic	1
Oxford Utd.	1

Q.P.R.	1	**LEAGUE TWO**	
Sheffield Utd.	1	Carlisle Utd.	1
Sunderland	1	Yeovil Town	1

APPLICATIONS FOR RE-ELECTION

(System discontinued 1987)

14	Hartlepool Utd.	4	Norwich City	2	Oldham Athletic
12	Halifax Town	3	Aldershot	2	Q.P.R.
11	Barrow	3	Bradford City	2	Rotherham Utd.
11	Southport	3	Crystal Palace	2	Scunthorpe Utd.
10	Crewe Alexandra	3	Doncaster Rov.	2	Southend Utd.
10	Newport	3	Hereford	2	Watford
10	Rochdale	3	Merthyr Tyd.	1	Blackpool
8	Darlington	3	Swindon Town	1	Brighton & H.A.
8	Exeter City	3	Torquay Utd.	1	Bristol Rov.
7	Chester City	3	Tranmere Rov.	1	Cambridge Utd.
7	Walsall	2	Aberdare	1	Cardiff City
7	Workington	2	Ashington	1	Carlisle Utd.
7	York City	2	Bournemouth	1	Charlton Athletic
6	Stockport Co.	2	Brentford	1	Mansfield Town
5	Accrington	2	Colchester Utd.	1	Port Vale
5	Gillingham	2	Durham C.	1	Preston N.E.
5	Lincoln City	2	Gateshead	1	Shrewsbury Town
5	New Brighton	2	Grimsby Town	1	Swansea City
4	Bradford P.A.	2	Millwall	1	Thames
4	Northampton Town	2	Nelson	1	Wrexham

RELEGATED CLUBS (TO 1992)

1892-3	In Test matches, Darwen and Sheffield Utd. won promotion in place of Accrington and Notts Co.
1893-4	Tests, Liverpool and Small Heath won promotion. Darwen and Newton Heath relegated.
1894-5	After Tests, Bury promoted, Liverpool relegated.
1895-6	After Tests, Liverpool promoted, Small Heath relegated.
1896-7	After Tests, Notts Co. promoted, Burnley relegated.
1897-8	Test system abolished after success of Burnley and Stoke City, League extended. Blackburn Rov. and Newcastle Utd. elected to First Division. Automatic promotion and relegation introduced.

FIRST DIVISION TO SECOND DIVISION

1898-9	Bolton Wand., Sheffield Wed.
1899-00	Burnley, Glossop
1900-1	Preston N.E., W.B.A.
1901-2	Small Heath, Manchester City
1902-3	Grimsby Town, Bolton Wand.
1903-4	Liverpool, W.B.A.
1904-5	League extended. Bury and Notts Co., two bottom clubs in First Division, re-elected.
1905-6	Nott'm. Forest, Wolves
1906-7	Derby Co., Stoke City
1907-8	Bolton Wand., Birmingham City
1908-9	Manchester City, Leicester Fosse
1909-10	Bolton Wand., Chelsea
1910-11	Bristol City, Nott'm. Forest
1911-12	Preston N.E., Bury

1912-13	Notts Co., Woolwich Arsenal
1913-14	Preston N.E., Derby Co.
1914-15	Tottenham, *Chelsea
1919-20	Notts Co., Sheffield Wed.
1920-1	Derby Co., Bradford P.A.
1921-2	Bradford City, Manchester Utd.
1922-3	Stoke City, Oldham Athletic
1923-4	Chelsea, Middlesbrough
1924-5	Preston N.E., Nott'm. Forest
1925-6	Manchester City, Notts Co.
1926-7	Leeds Utd., W.B.A.
1927-8	Tottenham, Middlesbrough
1928-9	Bury, Cardiff City
1929-30	Burnley, Everton
1930-1	Leeds Utd., Manchester Utd.
1931-2	Grimsby Town, West Ham Utd.
1932-3	Bolton Wand., Blackpool
1933-4	Newcastle Utd., Sheffield Utd.
1934-5	Leicester City, Tottenham
1935-6	Aston Villa, Blackburn Rov.
1936-7	Manchester Utd., Sheffield Wed.
1937-8	Manchester City, W.B.A.
1938-9	Birmingham City, Leicester City
1946-7	Brentford, Leeds Utd.
1947-8	Blackburn Rov., Grimsby Town
1948-9	Preston N.E., Sheffield Utd.
1949-50	Manchester City, Birmingham City
1950-1	Sheffield Wed., Everton
1951-2	Huddersfield Town, Fulham
1952-3	Stoke City, Derby Co.
1953-4	Middlesbrough, Liverpool
1954-5	Leicester City, Sheffield Wed.
1955-6	Huddersfield Town, Sheffield Utd.
1956-7	Charlton Athletic, Cardiff City
1957-8	Sheffield Wed., Sunderland
1958-9	Portsmouth, Aston Villa
1959-60	Luton Town, Leeds Utd.
1960-61	Preston N.E., Newcastle Utd.
1961-2	Chelsea, Cardiff City
1962-3	Manchester City, Leyton Orient
1963-4	Bolton Wand., Ipswich Town
1964-5	Wolves, Birmingham City
1965-6	Northampton Town, Blackburn Rov.
1966-7	Aston Villa, Blackpool
1967-8	Fulham, Sheffield Utd.
1968-9	Leicester City, Q.P.R.
1969-70	Sheffield Wed., Sunderland
1970-1	Burnley, Blackpool
1971-2	Nott'm. Forest, Huddersfield Town
1972-3	W.B.A., Crystal Palace
1973-4	Norwich City, Manchester Utd., Southampton
1974-5	Chelsea, Luton Town, Carlisle Utd.
1975-6	Sheffield Utd., Burnley, Wolves
1976-7	Tottenham, Stoke City, Sunderland
1977-8	Leicester City, West Ham Utd., Newcastle Utd.
1978-9	Q.P.R., Birmingham City, Chelsea
1979-80	Bristol City, Derby Co., Bolton Wand.
1980-1	Norwich City, Leicester City, Crystal Palace

1981-2	Leeds Utd., Wolves, Middlesbrough
1982-3	Manchester City, Swansea City, Brighton & H.A.
1983-4	Birmingham City, Notts Co., Wolves
1984-5	Norwich City, Sunderland, Stoke City
1985-6	Ipswich Town, Birmingham City, W.B.A.
1986-7	Leicester City, Manchester City, Aston Villa
1987-8	Chelsea**, Portsmouth, Watford, Oxford Utd.
1988-9	Middlesbrough, West Ham Utd., Newcastle Utd.
1989-90	Sheffield Wed., Charlton Athletic, Millwall
1990-1	Sunderland, Derby Co.
1991-2	Luton Town, Notts Co., West Ham Utd.

* Subsequently re-elected to First Division when League extended after the war.
** Relegated after play-offs.

SECOND DIVISION TO THIRD DIVISION

1920-1	Stockport Co.
1921-2	Bradford City, Bristol City
1922-3	Rotherham Utd., Bristol City
1923-4	Nelson, Bristol City
1924-5	Crystal Palace, Coventry City
1925-6	Stoke City, Stockport Co.
1926-7	Darlington, Bradford City
1927-8	Fulham, South Shields
1928-9	Port Vale, Clapton Orient
1929-30	Hull City, Notts County
1930-1	Reading, Cardiff City
1931-2	Barnsley, Bristol City
1932-3	Chesterfield, Charlton Athletic
1933-4	Millwall, Lincoln City
1934-5	Oldham Athletic, Notts Co.
1935-6	Port Vale, Hull City
1936-7	Doncaster Rov., Bradford City
1937-8	Barnsley, Stockport Co.
1938-9	Norwich City, Tranmere Rov.
1946-7	Swansea City, Newport
1947-8	Doncaster Rov., Millwall
1948-9	Nott'm. Forest, Lincoln City
1949-50	Plymouth Argyle, Bradford P.A.
1950-1	Grimsby Town, Chesterfield
1951-2	Coventry City, Q.P.R.
1952-3	Southampton, Barnsley
1953-4	Brentford, Oldham Athletic
1954-5	Ipswich Town, Derby Co.
1955-6	Plymouth Argyle, Hull City
1956-7	Port Vale, Bury
1957-8	Doncaster Rov., Notts Co.
1958-9	Barnsley, Grimsby Town
1959-60	Bristol City, Hull City
1960-1	Lincoln City, Portsmouth
1961-2	Brighton & H.A., Bristol Rov.
1962-3	Walsall, Luton Town
1963-4	Grimsby Town, Scunthorpe Utd.
1964-5	Swindon Town, Swansea City
1965-6	Middlesbrough, Leyton Orient
1966-7	Northampton Town, Bury
1967-8	Plymouth Argyle, Rotherham Utd.
1968-9	Fulham, Bury

1969-70	Preston N.E., Aston Villa
1970-1	Blackburn Rov., Bolton Wand.
1971-2	Charlton Athletic, Watford
1972-3	Huddersfield Town, Brighton & H.A.
1973-4	Crystal Palace, Preston N.E., Swindon Town
1974-5	Millwall, Cardiff City, Sheffield Wed.
1975-6	Portsmouth, Oxford Utd., York City
1976-7	Carlisle Utd., Plymouth Argyle, Hereford Utd.
1977-8	Hull City, Mansfield Town, Blackpool
1978-9	Sheffield Utd., Millwall, Blackburn Rov.
1979-80	Fulham, Burnley, Charlton Athletic
1980-1	Preston N.E., Bristol City, Bristol Rov.
1981-2	Cardiff City, Wrexham, Orient
1982-3	Rotherham Utd., Burnley, Bolton Wand.
1983-4	Derby Co., Swansea City, Cambridge Utd.
1984-5	Notts Co., Cardiff City, Wolves
1985-6	Carlisle Utd., Middlesbrough, Fulham
1986-7	Sunderland**, Grimsby Town, Brighton & H.A.
1987-8	Sheffield Utd.**, Reading, Huddersfield Town
1988-9	Shrewsbury Town, Birmingham City, Walsall
1989-90	Bournemouth, Bradford City, Stoke City
1990-1	W.B.A., Hull City
1991-2	Plymouth Argyle, Brighton & H.A., Port Vale

** Relegated after play-offs.

THIRD DIVISION TO FOURTH DIVISION

1958-9	Rochdale, Notts Co., Doncaster Rov., Stockport Co.
1959-60	Accrington, Wrexham, Mansfield Town, York City
1960-1	Chesterfield, Colchester Utd., Bradford City, Tranmere Rov.
1961-2	Newport, Brentford, Lincoln City, Torquay Utd.
1962-3	Bradford P.A., Brighton & H.A., Carlisle Utd., Halifax Town
1963-4	Millwall, Crewe Alexandra, Wrexham, Notts Co.
1964-5	Luton Town, Port Vale, Colchester Utd., Barnsley
1965-6	Southend Utd., Exeter City, Brentford, York City
1966-7	Doncaster Rov., Workington, Darlington, Swansea City
1967-8	Scunthorpe Utd., Colchester Utd., Grimsby Town, Peterborough Utd. (demoted)
1968-9	Oldham Athletic, Crewe Alexandra, Hartlepool Utd., Northampton Town
1969-70	Bournemouth, Southport, Barrow, Stockport Co.
1970-1	Gillingham, Doncaster Rov., Bury, Reading
1971-2	Mansfield Town, Barnsley, Torquay Utd., Bradford City
1972-3	Scunthorpe Utd., Swansea City, Brentford, Rotherham Utd.
1973-4	Cambridge Utd., Shrewsbury Town, Rochdale, Southport
1974-5	Bournemouth, Watford, Tranmere Rov., Huddersfield Town
1975-6	Aldershot, Colchester Utd., Southend Utd., Halifax Town
1976-7	Reading, Northampton Town, Grimsby Town, York City
1977-8	Port Vale, Bradford City, Hereford, Portsmouth
1978-9	Peterborough Utd., Walsall, Tranmere Rov., Lincoln City
1979-80	Bury, Southend Utd., Mansfield Town, Wimbledon
1980-1	Sheffield Utd., Colchester Utd., Blackpool, Hull City
1981-2	Wimbledon, Swindon Town, Bristol City, Chester City
1982-3	Reading, Wrexham, Doncaster Rov., Chesterfield
1983-4	Scunthorpe Utd., Southend Utd., Port Vale, Exeter City
1984-5	Burnley, Orient, Preston N.E., Cambridge Utd.
1985-6	Lincoln City, Cardiff City, Wolves, Swansea City
1986-7	Bolton Wand.**, Carlisle Utd., Darlington, Newport
1987-8	Doncaster Rov., York City, Grimsby Town, Rotherham Utd.**
1988-9	Southend Utd., Chesterfield, Gillingham, Aldershot

1989-90	Cardiff City, Northampton Town, Blackpool, Walsall
1990-1	Crewe Alexandra, Rotherham Utd., Mansfield Town
1991-2	Bury, Shrewsbury Town, Torquay Utd., Darlington

** Relegated after plays-offs.

DEMOTED FROM FOURTH DIVISION TO CONFERENCE

1987	Lincoln City
1988	Newport
1989	Darlington
1990	Colchester Utd.
1991	No demotion
1992	No demotion

DEMOTED FROM THIRD DIVISION TO CONFERENCE

1993	Halifax Town
1994-6	No demotion
1997	Hereford
1998	Doncaster Rov.
1999	Scarborough
2000	Chester City
2001	Barnet
2002	Halifax Town
2003	Exeter City, Shrewsbury Town
2004	Carlisle Utd., York City

DEMOTED FROM LEAGUE TWO TO CONFERENCE

| 2005 | Kidderminster Harr., Cambridge Utd. |
| 2006 | Oxford Utd., Rushden & Diamonds |

RELEGATED CLUBS (SINCE 1993)

1993

Premier League to Div. 1: Crystal Palace, Middlesbrough, Nott'm. Forest
Div. 1 to Div. 2: Brentford, Cambridge Utd., Bristol Rov.
Div. 2 to Div. 3: Preston N.E., Mansfield Town, Wigan Athletic, Chester City

1994

Premier League to Div. 1: Sheffield Utd., Oldham Athletic, Swindon Town
Div. 1 to Div. 2: Birmingham City, Oxford Utd., Peterborough Utd.
Div. 2 to Div. 3: Fulham, Exeter City, Hartlepool Utd., Barnet

1995

Premier League to Div. 1: Crystal Palace, Norwich City, Leicester City, Ipswich Town
Div. 1 to Div. 2: Swindon Town, Burnley, Bristol City, Notts Co.
Div. 2 to Div. 3: Cambridge Utd., Plymouth Argyle, Cardiff City, Chester City, Leyton Orient

1996

Premier League to Div. 1: Manchester City, Q.P.R., Bolton Wand.
Div. 1 to Div. 2: Millwall, Watford, Luton Town
Div. 2 to Div. 3: Carlisle Utd., Swansea City, Brighton & H.A., Hull City

1997

Premier League to Div. 1: Sunderland, Middlesbrough, Nott'm. Forest
Div. 1 to Div. 2: Grimsby Town, Oldham Athletic, Southend Utd.
Div. 2 to Div. 3: Peterborough Utd., Shrewsbury Town, Rotherham Utd., Notts Co.

1998

Premier League to Div. 1: Bolton Wand., Barnsley, Crystal Palace
Div. 1 to Div. 2: Manchester City, Stoke City, Reading
Div. 2 to Div. 3: Brentford, Plymouth Argyle, Carlisle Utd., Southend Utd.

1999

Premier League to Div. 1: Charlton Athletic, Blackburn Rov., Nott'm. Forest
Div. 1 to Div. 2: Bury, Oxford Utd., Bristol City
Div. 2 to Div. 3: York City, Northampton Town, Lincoln City, Macclesfield Town

2000

Premier League to Div. 1: Wimbledon, Sheffield Wed., Watford
Div. 1 to Div. 2: Walsall, Port Vale, Swindon Town
Div. 2 to Div. 3: Cardiff City, Blackpool, Scunthorpe Utd., Chesterfield

2001

Premier League to Div. 1: Manchester City, Coventry City, Bradford City
Div. 1 to Div. 2: Huddersfield Town, Q.P.R., Tranmere Rov.
Div. 2 to Div. 3: Bristol Rov., Luton Town, Swansea City, Oxford Utd.

2002

Premier League to Div. 1: Ipswich Town, Derby Co., Leicester City
Div. 1 to Div. 2: Crewe Alexandra, Barnsley, Stockport Co.
Div. 2 to Div. 3: Bournemouth, Bury, Wrexham, Cambridge Utd.

2003

Premier League to Div. 1: West Ham Utd., W.B.A., Sunderland
Div. 1 to Div. 2: Sheffield Wed., Brighton & H.A., Grimsby Town
Div. 2 to Div. 3: Cheltenham Town, Huddersfield Town, Mansfield Town, Northampton Town

2004

Premier League to Div. 1: Leicester City, Leeds Utd., Wolves
Div. 1 to Div. 2: Walsall, Bradford City, Wimbledon
Div. 2 to Div. 3: Grimsby Town, Rushden & Diamonds, Notts Co., Wycombe Wand.

2005

Premier League to Championship: Crystal Palace, Norwich City, Southampton
Championship to League 1: Gillingham, Nott'm. Forest, Rotherham Utd.
League 1 to League 2: Torquay Utd., Wrexham, Peterborough Utd., Stockport Co.

2006

Premier League to Championship: Birmingham City, W.B.A., Sunderland
Championship to League 1: Crewe Alexandra, Millwall, Brighton & H.A.
League 1 to League 2: Hartlepool Utd., MK Dons, Swindon Town, Walsall

ANNUAL AWARDS

FOOTBALL WRITERS' ASSOCIATION

Footballer of the Year: 1948 Stanley Matthews (Blackpool); **1949** Johnny Carey (Manchester Utd.); **1950** Joe Mercer (Arsenal); **1951** Harry Johnston (Blackpool); **1952** Billy Wright (Wolves); **1953** Nat Lofthouse (Bolton Wand.); **1954** Tom Finney (Preston N.E.); **1955** Don Revie (Manchester Utd.); **1956** Bert Trautmann (Manchester City); **1957** Tom Finney (Preston N.E.); **1958** Danny Blanchflower (Tottenham); **1959** Syd Owen (Luton Town); **1960** Bill Slater (Wolves); **1961** Danny Blanchflower (Tottenham); **1962** Jimmy Adamson (Burnley); **1963** Stanley Matthews (Stoke City); **1964** Bobby Moore (West Ham Utd.); **1965** Bobby Collins (Leeds Utd.); **1966** Bobby Charlton (Manchester Utd.); **1967** Jack Charlton (Leeds Utd.); **1968** George Best (Manchester Utd.); **1969** Tony Book (Manchester City) & Dave Mackay (Derby Co.) – shared; **1970** Billy Bremner (Leeds Utd.); **1971** Frank McLintock (Arsenal); **1972** Gordon Banks (Stoke City); **1973** Pat Jennings (Tottenham); **1974** Ian Callaghan (Liverpool); **1975** Alan Mullery (Fulham); **1976** Kevin Keegan (Liverpool); **1977** Emlyn Hughes (Liverpool); **1978** Kenny Burns (Nott'm Forest); **1979** Kenny Dalglish (Liverpool); **1980** Terry McDermott (Liverpool); **1981** Frans Thijssen (Ipswich Town); **1982** Steve Perryman (Tottenham); **1983** Kenny Dalglish (Liverpool); **1984** Ian Rush (Liverpool); **1985** Neville Southall (Everton); **1986** Gary Lineker (Everton); **1987** Clive Allen (Tottenham); **1988** John Barnes (Liverpool); **1989** Steve Nicol (Liverpool); Special award to the Liverpool players for the compassion shown to bereaved families after the Hillsborough Disaster; **1990** John Barnes (Liverpool); **1991** Gordon Strachan (Leeds Utd.); **1992** Gary Lineker (Tottenham); **1993** Chris Waddle (Sheffield Wed.); **1994** Alan Shearer (Blackburn Rov.); **1995** Jurgen Klinsmann (Tottenham); **1996** Eric Cantona (Manchester Utd.); **1997** Gianfranco Zola (Chelsea); **1998** Dennis Bergkamp (Arsenal); **1999** David Ginola (Tottenham); **2000** Roy Keane (Manchester Utd.); **2001** Teddy Sheringham (Manchester Utd.); **2002** Robert Pires (Arsenal); **2003** Thierry Henry (Arsenal); **2004** Thierry Henry (Arsenal); **2005** Frank Lampard (Chelsea); **2006** Thierry Henry (Arsenal).

PROFESSIONAL FOOTBALLERS' ASSOCIATION

Player of the Year: 1974 Norman Hunter (Leeds Utd.); **1975** Colin Todd (Derby Co.); **1976** Pat Jennings (Tottenham); **1977** Andy Gray (Aston Villa); **1978** Peter Shilton (Nott'm Forest); **1979** Liam Brady (Arsenal); **1980** Terry McDermott (Liverpool); **1981** John Wark (Ipswich Town); **1982** Kevin Keegan (Southampton); **1983** Kenny Dalglish (Liverpool); **1984** Ian Rush (Liverpool); **1985** Peter Reid (Everton); **1986** Gary Lineker (Everton); **1987** Clive Allen (Tottenham); **1988** John Barnes (Liverpool); **1989** Mark Hughes (Manchester Utd.); **1990** David Platt (Aston Villa); **1991** Mark Hughes (Manchester Utd.); **1992** Gary Pallister (Manchester Utd.); **1993** Paul McGrath (Aston Villa); **1994** Eric Cantona (Manchester Utd.); **1995** Alan Shearer (Blackburn Rov.); **1996** Les Ferdinand (Newcastle Utd.); **1997** Alan Shearer (Newcastle Utd.); **1998** Dennis Bergkamp (Arsenal); **1999** David Ginola (Tottenham); **2000** Roy Keane (Manchester Utd.); **2001** Teddy Sheringham (Manchester Utd.); **2002** Ruud van Nistelrooy (Manchester Utd.); **2003** Thierry Henry (Arsenal); **2004** Thierry Henry (Arsenal); **2005** John Terry (Chelsea); **2006** Steven Gerrard (Liverpool).

Young Player of the Year: 1974 Kevin Beattie (Ipswich Town); **1975** Mervyn Day (West Ham Utd.); **1976** Peter Barnes (Manchester City); **1977** Andy Gray (Aston Villa); **1978** Tony Woodcock (Nott'm Forest); **1979** Cyrille Regis (W.B.A.); **1980** Glenn Hoddle (Tottenham); **1981** Gary Shaw (Aston Villa); **1982** Steve Moran (Southampton); **1983** Ian Rush (Liverpool); **1984** Paul Walsh (Luton Town); **1985** Mark Hughes (Manchester Utd.); **1986** Tony Cottee (West Ham Utd.); **1987** Tony Adams (Arsenal); **1988** Paul Gascoigne (Newcastle Utd.); **1989** Paul Merson (Arsenal); **1990** Matthew Le Tissier (Southampton); **1991** Lee Sharpe (Manchester Utd.); **1992** Ryan Giggs (Manchester Utd.); **1993** Ryan

Giggs (Manchester Utd.); **1994** Andy Cole (Newcastle Utd.); **1995** Robbie Fowler (Liverpool); **1996** Robbie Fowler (Liverpool); **1997** David Beckham (Manchester Utd.); **1998** Michael Owen (Liverpool); **1999** Nicolas Anelka (Arsenal); **2000** Harry Kewell (Leeds Utd.); **2001** Steven Gerrard (Liverpool); **2002** Craig Ballamy (Newcastle Utd.); **2003** Jermaine Jenas (Newcastle Utd.); **2004** Scott Parker (Chelsea); **2005** Wayne Rooney (Manchester Utd.); **2006** Wayne Rooney (Manchester Utd.).

Merit Awards: 1974 Bobby Charlton & Cliff Lloyd; **1975** Denis Law; **1976** George Eastham; **1977** Jack Taylor; **1978** Bill Shankly; **1979** Tom Finney; **1980** Sir Matt Busby; **1981** John Trollope; **1982** Joe Mercer; **1983** Bob Paisley; **1984** Bill Nicholson; **1985** Ron Greenwood; **1986** England 1966 World Cup-winning team; **1987** Sir Stanley Matthews; **1988** Billy Bonds; **1989** Nat Lofthouse; **1990** Peter Shilton; **1991** Tommy Hutchison; **1992** Brian Clough; **1993** Manchester Utd., 1968 European Champions; Eusebio; **1994** Billy Bingham; **1995** Gordon Strachan; **1996** Pele; **1997** Peter Beardsley; **1998** Steve Ogrizovic; **1999** Tony Ford; **2000** Gary Mabbutt; **2001** Jimmy Hill; **2002** Niall Quinn; **2003** Sir Bobby Robson; **2004** Dario Gradi; **2005** Shaka Hislop; **2006** George Best.

MANAGER OF THE YEAR (1)

(Chosen by a panel from the governing bodies, media and fans.)

1966 Jock Stein (Celtic); **1967** Jock Stein (Celtic); **1968** Matt Busby (Manchester Utd.); **1969** Don Revie (Leeds Utd.); **1970** Don Revie (Leeds Utd.); **1971** Bertie Mee (Arsenal); **1972** Don Revie (Leeds Utd.); **1973** Bill Shankly (Liverpool); **1974** Jack Charlton (Middlesbrough); **1975** Ron Saunders (Aston Villa); **1976** Bob Paisley (Liverpool); **1977** Bob Paisley (Liverpool); **1978** Brian Clough (Nott'm Forest); **1979** Bob Paisley (Liverpool); **1980** Bob Paisley (Liverpool); **1981** Ron Saunders (Aston Villa); **1982** Bob Paisley (Liverpool); **1983** Bob Paisley (Liverpool); **1984** Joe Fagan (Liverpool); **1985** Howard Kendall (Everton); **1986** Kenny Dalglish (Liverpool); **1987** Howard Kendall (Everton); **1988** Kenny Dalglish (Liverpool); **1989** George Graham (Arsenal); **1990** Kenny Dalglish (Liverpool); **1991** George Graham (Arsenal); **1992** Howard Wilkinson (Leeds Utd.); **1993** Alex Ferguson (Manchester Utd.); **1994** Alex Ferguson (Manchester Utd.); **1995** Kenny Dalglish (Blackburn Rov.); **1996** Alex Ferguson (Manchester Utd.); **1997** Alex Ferguson (Manchester Utd.); **1998** Arsene Wenger (Arsenal); **1999** Alex Ferguson (Manchester Utd.); **2000** Sir Alex Ferguson (Manchester Utd.); **2001** George Burley (Ipswich Town); **2002** Arsene Wenger (Arsenal); **2003** Sir Alex Ferguson (Manchester Utd.); **2004** Arsene Wenger (Arsenal); **2005** Jose Mourinho (Chelsea); **2006** Jose Mourinho (Chelsea).

MANAGER OF THE YEAR (2)

(As chosen by the League Managers' Association and awarded to 'the manager who has made best use of the resources available to him'.)

1993 Dave Bassett (Sheffield Utd.); **1994** Joe Kinnear (Wimbledon); **1995** Frank Clark (Nott'm Forest); **1996** Peter Reid (Sunderland); **1997** Danny Wilson (Barnsley); **1998** David Jones (Southampton); **1999** Alex Ferguson (Manchester Utd.); **2000** Alan Curbishley (Charlton Athletic); **2001** George Burley (Ipswich Town); **2002** Arsene Wenger (Arsenal); **2003** David Moyes (Everton); **2004** Arsene Wenger (Arsenal); **2005** David Moyes (Everton); **2006** Steve Coppell (Reading).

SCOTTISH FOOTBALL WRITERS' ASSOCIATION

Player of the Year: 1965 Billy McNeill (Celtic); **1966** John Greig (Rangers); **1967** Ronnie Simpson (Celtic); **1968** Gordon Wallace (Raith); **1969** Bobby Murdoch (Celtic); **1970** Pat Stanton (Hibernian); **1971** Martin Buchan (Aberdeen); **1972** David Smith (Rangers); **1973** George Connelly (Celtic); **1974** World Cup Squad; **1975** Sandy Jardine (Rangers);

1976 John Greig (Rangers); 1977 Danny McGrain (Celtic); 1978 Derek Johnstone (Rangers); 1979 Andy Ritchie (Morton); 1980 Gordon Strachan (Aberdeen); 1981 Alan Rough (Partick Thistle); 1982 Paul Sturrock (Dundee Utd.); 1983 Charlie Nicholas (Celtic); 1984 Willie Miller (Aberdeen); 1985 Hamish McAlpine (Dundee Utd.); 1986 Sandy Jardine (Hearts); 1987 Brian McClair (Celtic); 1988 Paul McStay (Celtic); 1989 Richard Gough (Rangers); 1990 Alex McLeish (Aberdeen); 1991 Maurice Malpas (Dundee Utd.); 1992 Ally McCoist (Rangers); 1993 Andy Goram (Rangers); 1994 Mark Hateley (Rangers); 1995 Brian Laudrup (Rangers); 1996 Paul Gascoigne (Rangers); 1997 Brian Laudrup (Rangers); 1998 Craig Burley (Celtic); 1999 Henrik Larsson (Celtic); 2000 Barry Ferguson (Rangers); 2001 Henrik Larsson (Celtic); 2002 Paul Lambert (Celtic); 2003 Barry Ferguson (Rangers); 2004 Jackie McNamara (Celtic); 2005 John Hartson (Celtic); 2006 Craig Gordon (Hearts).

SCOTTISH PROFESSIONAL FOOTBALLERS' ASSOCIATION

Player of the Year: 1978 Derek Johnstone (Rangers); 1979 Paul Hegarty (Dundee Utd.); 1980 Davie Provan (Celtic); 1981 Mark McGhee (Aberdeen); 1982 Sandy Clarke (Airdrieonians); 1983 Charlie Nicholas (Celtic); 1984 Willie Miller (Aberdeen); 1985 Jim Duffy (Morton); 1986 Richard Gough (Dundee Utd.); 1987 Brian McClair (Celtic); 1988 Paul McStay (Celtic); 1989 Theo Snelders (Aberdeen); 1990 Jim Bett (Aberdeen); 1991 Paul Elliott (Celtic); 1992 Ally McCoist (Rangers); 1993 Andy Goram (Rangers); 1994 Mark Hateley (Rangers); 1995 Brian Laudrup (Rangers); 1996 Paul Gascoigne (Rangers); 1997 Paolo Di Canio (Celtic) 1998 Jackie McNamara (Celtic); 1999 Henrik Larsson (Celtic); 2000 Mark Viduka (Celtic); 2001 Henrik Larsson (Celtic); 2002 Lorenzo Amoruso (Rangers); 2003 Barry Ferguson (Rangers); 2004 Chris Sutton (Celtic); 2005 John Hartson (Celtic) and Fernando Ricksen (Rangers); 2006 Shaun Maloney (Celtic).

Young Player of Year: 1978 Graeme Payne (Dundee Utd.); 1979 Ray Stewart (Dundee Utd.); 1980 John McDonald (Rangers); 1981 Charlie Nicholas (Celtic); 1982 Frank McAvennie (St. Mirren); 1983 Paul McStay (Celtic); 1984 John Robertson (Hearts); 1985 Craig Levein (Hearts); 1986 Craig Levein (Hearts); 1987 Robert Fleck (Rangers); 1988 John Collins (Hibernian); 1989 Billy McKinlay (Dundee Utd.); 1990 Scott Crabbe (Hearts); 1991 Eoin Jess (Aberdeen); 1992 Phil O'Donnell (Motherwell); 1993 Eoin Jess (Aberdeen); 1994 Phil O'Donnell (Motherwell); 1995 Charlie Miller (Rangers); 1996 Jackie McNamara (Celtic); 1997 Robbie Winters (Dundee Utd.); 1998 Gary Naysmith (Hearts); 1999 Barry Ferguson (Rangers) ; 2000 Kenny Miller (Hibernian); 2001 Stilian Petrov (Celtic); 2002 Kevin McNaughton (Aberdeen); 2003 James McFadden (Motherwell); 2004 Stephen Pearson (Celtic); 2005 Derek Riordan (Hibernian); 2006 Shaun Maloney (Celtic).

SCOTTISH MANAGER OF THE YEAR

1987 Jim McLean (Dundee Utd.); 1988 Billy McNeill (Celtic); 1989 Graeme Souness (Rangers); 1990 Andy Roxburgh (Scotland); 1991 Alex Totten (St. Johnstone); 1992 Walter Smith (Rangers); 1993 Walter Smith (Rangers); 1994 Walter Smith (Rangers); 1995 Jimmy Nicholl (Raith); 1996 Walter Smith (Rangers); 1997 Walter Smith (Rangers); 1998 Wim Jansen (Celtic); 1999 Dick Advocaat (Rangers); 2000 Dick Advocaat (Rangers); 2001 Martin O'Neill (Celtic); 2002 John Lambie (Partick Thistle); 2003 Alex McLeish (Rangers); 2004 Martin O'Neill (Celtic); 2005 Alex McLeish (Rangers); 2006 Gordon Strachan (Celtic).

EUROPEAN FOOTBALLER OF THE YEAR

(Poll conducted by *France Football*) 1956 Stanley Matthews (Blackpool); 1957 Alfredo di Stefano (Real Madrid); 1958 Raymond Kopa (Real Madrid); 1959 Alfredo di Stefano (Real Madrid); 1960 Luis Suarez (Barcelona); 1961 Omar Sivori (Juventus); 1962 Josef Masopust (Dukla Prague); 1963 Lev Yashin (Moscow Dynamo); 1964 Denis Law

(Manchester Utd.); **1965** Eusebio (Benfica) **1966** Bobby Charlton (Manchester Utd.); **1967** Florian Albert (Ferencvaros); **1968** George Best (Manchester Utd.); **1969** Gianni Rivera (AC Milan); **1970** Gerd Muller (Bayern Munich); **1971** Johan Cruyff (Ajax); **1972** Franz Beckenbauer (Bayern Munich); **1973** Johan Cruyff (Barcelona); **1974** Johan Cruyff (Barcelona); **1975** Oleg Blokhin (Dynamo Kiev); **1976** Franz Beckenbauer (Bayern Munich); **1977** Allan Simonsen (Borussia Moenchengladbach); **1978** Kevin Keegan (SV Hamburg); **1979** Kevin Keegan (SV Hamburg); **1980** Karl-Heinz Rummenigge (Bayern Munich); **1981** Karl-Heinz Rummenigge (Bayern Munich); **1982** Paolo Rossi (Juventus); **1983** Michel Platini (Juventus); **1984** Michel Platini (Juventus); **1985** Michel Platini (Juventus); **1986** Igor Belanov (Dynamo Kiev); **1987** Ruud Gullit (AC Milan); **1988** Marco van Basten (AC Milan); **1989** Marco van Basten (AC Milan); **1990** Lothar Matthaus (Inter Milan); **1991** Jean-Pierre Papin (Marseille); **1992** Marco van Basten (AC Milan); **1993** Roberto Baggio (Juventus); **1994** Hristo Stoichkov (Barcelona); **1995** George Weah (AC Milan); **1996** Matthias Sammer (Borussia Dortmund); **1997** Ronaldo (Inter Milan); **1998** Zinedine Zidane (Juventus); **1999** Rivaldo (Barcelona); **2000** Luis Figo (Real Madrid); **2001** Michael Owen (Liverpool); **2002** Ronaldo (Real Madrid); **2003** Pavel Nedved (Juventus); **2004** Andriy Shevchenko (AC Milan); **2005** Ronaldinho (Barcelona).

FIFA WORLD FOOTBALLER OF YEAR

(Voted by national coaches): 1991 Lothar Matthaus (Inter Milan and Germany); **1992** Marco van Basten (AC Milan and Holland); **1993** Roberto Baggio (Juventus and Italy); **1994** Romario (Barcelona and Brazil); **1995** George Weah (AC Milan and Liberia); **1996** Ronaldo (Barcelona and Brazil); **1997** Ronaldo (Inter Milan and Brazil); **1998** Zinedine Zidane (Juventus and France); **1999** Rivaldo (Barcelona and Brazil); **2000** Zinedine Zidane (Juventus and France); **2001** Luis Figo (Real Madrid and Portugal); **2002** Ronaldo (Real Madrid and Brazil); **2003** Zinedine Zidane (Real Madrid and France); **2004** Ronaldinho (Barcelona and Brazil); **2005** Ronaldinho (Barcelona and Brazil).

QUOTE-UNQUOTE

'We are in a transfer market where you first have to let Chelsea make decisions and then come in when they have made that decision. It is frustrating, but it is a fact' – **Arsene Wenger**, Arsenal manager, on Chelsea's spending power.

'Some are treated as devils and some are treated as angels. I don't think we are so ugly to be treated like devils and I don't think Mr Wenger and David Dein and so on are so beautiful to be treated like angels' – **Jose Mourinho**, Chelsea manager, adds to the simmering feud between his club and Arsenal.

'We pay the players Hollywood money and they have a responsibility to perform like a Rolls-Royce' – **Freddy Shepherd**, Newcastle chairman.

'I have been a manager for eight years and a player for 25 years and this is the worst football night I have ever had' – **Gordon Strachan**, Celtic manager, after a 5-0 defeat by Artmedia Bratislava in the first leg of a Champions League qualifier.

'The winner of the Premier League will come from a bunch of one' – **Peter Kenyon**, Chelsea chief executive, whose prediction comes true.

'If we carry on this rhythm we will practically be champions by January' – **William Gallas**, Chelsea defender, whose September boast after seven straight win proves wide of the mark.

'I will be opening all my toys tomorrow' – **David Moyes**, Everton manager, on the eve of his team's first match in the Champions League.

ENGLISH LEAGUE ROLL-CALL

REVIEWS, APPEARANCES, SCORERS 2005-06

(Figures in brackets = appearances as substitute)

F.A. BARCLAYS PREMIERSHIP

ARSENAL

Like Liverpool the previous season, Arsenal were strangley erratic in the Premiership yet so effective in Europe. Real Madrid and Juventus were among those seen off on the way to the Champions League Final, where Barcelona were pushed all the way before the ten men succumbed. But it was the inability to match the likes of West Bromwich Albion, Bolton and Middlesbrough on their own grounds that led to Arsene Wenger conceding the title with barely half the season gone. Thierry Henry's goals, which earned him the Golden Boot award for the third successive season, and the impressive way Cesc Fabregas filled Patrick Vieira's midfield role, were not enough, and Arsenal had to rely on Tottenham's last-day defeat at West Ham to finish fourth. Henry, whose second hat-trick of the campaign came against Wigan in the final, emotional match at Highbury, later pledged his future to the club.

Adebayor, E .... 12(1)	Fabregas, F .... 30(5)	Ljungberg, F .... 21(4)
Bergkamp, D .... 8(16)	Flamini, M .... 19(12)	Lupoli, A .... –(1)
Campbell, S 20	Gilberto Silva 33	Owusu, Q .... –(4)
Clichy, G .... 5(2)	Gilbert, K 2	Pires, R .... 23(10)
Cole, A .... 9(2)	Henry, T .... 30(2)	Reyes, J .... 22(4)
Cygan, P .... 11(1)	Hleb, A .... 17(8)	Senderos, P .... 19(1)
Diaby, V .... 9(3)	Larsson, S .... 2(1)	Song, A .... 3(2)
Djourou, J .... 6(1)	Lauren, B 22	Toure, K 33
Eboue, E .... 11(7)	Lehmann, J 38	Van Persie, R .... 13(11)

League goals (68): Henry 27, Pires 7, Reyes 5, Van Persie 5, Adebayor 4, Fabregas 3, Hleb 3, Bergkamp 2, Campbell 2, Cygan 2, Gilberto Silva 2, Senderos 2, Diaby 1, Ljungberg 1, Opponents 2.
F.A. Cup goals (2): Pires 2. **Carling Cup goals (10):** Van Persie 4, Eboue 1, Gilberto Silva 1, Henry 1, Lupoli 1, Owusu 1, Reyes 1. **Community Shield goals (1):** Fabregas 1.
Champions League goals (15): Henry 5, Fabregas 2, Pires 2, Van Persie 2, Campbell 1, Gilberto Silva 1, Ljungberg 1, Toure 1.
Average home League attendance: 38,184. **Player of Year:** Thierry Henry.

ASTON VILLA

Relegation for Birmingham and West Bromwich Albion left Aston Villa as the only Midlands club in the Premiership, but while supporters derived some satisfaction from that outcome, they had little to enthuse about in their own team's performance. The fact that back-to-back victories were achieved only once – against Sunderland and Charlton in November – summed up a poor campaign which ended with Villa two places above the drop zone. Yet such were the failings of their neighbours, along with Sunderland, that they were never seriously threatened with going down. Amid speculation about the intentions of chairman Doug Ellis and the future of manager David O'Leary, there was a rare chance to celebrate when a 3-1 win against Birmingham completed a double over their biggest rivals.

Agbonlahor, G .... 3(6)	Berger, P .... 3(5)	Delaney, M 12
Angel, J P .... 12(19)	Bouma, W 20	Djemba-Djemba, E .... –(4)
Bakke, E .... 8(6)	Cahill, G .... 6(1)	Gardner, C .... 3(5)
Baros, M .... 24(1)	Davis, S .... 34(1)	Hendrie, L .... 7(9)
Barry, G 36	De la Cruz, U .... 4(3)	Hughes, A 35

93

Laursen, M .... 1 | Moore, L .... 16(11) | Solano, N .... 2(1)
McCann, G .... 32 | Phillips, K .... 20(3) | Sorensen, T 36
Mellberg, O .... 27 | Ridgewell, L .... 30(2) | Taylor, S 2
Milner, J .... 27 | Samuel, J .... 14(5) | Whittingham, P 4

League goals (42): Baros 8, Moore 8, Ridgewell 5, Davis 4, Phillips 4, Angel 3, Barry 3, Agbonlahor 1, Cahill 1, Delaney 1, Hendrie 1, McCann 1, Milner 1, Opponents 1.
F.A. Cup goals (6): Baros 3, Davis 2, Barry 1. **Carling Cup goals (9):** Barry 2, Davis 2, Milner 2, Baros 1, Phillips 1, Opponents 1.
Average home League attendance: 34,111. **Player of Year:** Steven Davis.

BIRMINGHAM CITY

The writing was on the wall for Birmingham when their first seven home matches of the season yielded a single point. A chronic shortage of goals, which continued to the end, was compounded by a catalogue of injuries. Those handicaps proved too much for a team rich in experience but increasingly brittle when it came to the battle for survival. Emile Heskey's tally of four, two of them in one match, summed up the dilemma for Steve Bruce. The manager tried to confront it by bringing in Chris Sutton, while a 5-0 win over Portsmouth hinted at better times. But neither proved the answer, with a 7-0 defeat by Liverpool at St Andrews in the F.A. Cup further undermining confidence. Even so, Birmingham would probably have beaten the drop had it not been for Portsmouth's remarkable late charge.

Birley, M .... –(1) | Heskey, E .... 34 | Painter, M .... 2(2)
Bruce, A .... 3(3) | Izzet, M .... 10(6) | Pandiani, W .... 7(10)
Butt, N .... 22(2) | Jarosik, J .... 19(5) | Pennant, J .... 35(3)
Campbell, D .... 4(7) | Johnson, D .... 31 | Sadler, M 8
Clapham, J .... 13(3) | Kilkenny, N .... 6(12) | Sutton, C 10
Clemence, S .... 13(2) | Latka, M .... 6 | Taylor, Maik 34
Cunningham, K .... 31 | Lazaridis, S .... 11(6) | Taylor, Martin .... 20(1)
Dunn, D .... 8(7) | Melchiot, M .... 22(1) | Tebily, O .... 12(4)
Forssell, M .... 10(17) | Morrison, C .... –(1) | Upson, M 24
Gray, J .... 18(3) | Nafti, M .... 1 | Vaesen, N 4

League goals (28): Jarosik 5, Heskey 4, Butt 3, Forssell 3, Dunn 2, Pandiani 2, Pennant 2, Clapham 1, Gray 1, Melchiot 1, Sutton 1, Upson 1, Opponents 2.
F.A. Cup goals (6): Forssell 3, Dunn 1, Gray 1, Jarosik 1. **Carling Cup goals (7):** Forssell 2, Jarosik 2, Gray 1, Heskey 1, Pennant 1.
Average home League attendance: 27,392. **Player of Year:** Damien Johnson.

BLACKBURN ROVERS

Mark Hughes brought European football back to Ewood Park, while enhancing his own managerial credentials. Blackburn were regarded in some quarters as an over-physical side, not least by Hughes's old boss Sir Alex Ferguson. But there was also plenty to admire in the quality of their attacking play. Craig Bellamy scored some eye-catching goals, none better than two sweetly-struck volleys against Portsmouth. And David Bentley, in his first game since completing a permanent move from Arsenal, hit a hat-trick in one of the games of the season – a 4-3 win over Ferguson's Manchester United a week after United came out on top in the teams' Carling Cup semi-final. Rovers went on to make sure of sixth position, and a place in the UEFA Cup, with Steven Reid's goal against Chelsea.

Bellamy, C .... 22(5) | Gray, M .... 30 | Mokoena, A .... 4(18)
Bentley, D .... 23(6) | Gresko, V .... 1(2) | Neill, L 35
Dickov, P .... 17(4) | Jansen, M .... 1(3) | Nelsen, R 31
Emerton, B .... 17(13) | Johnson, J .... –(3) | Pedersen, M 34
Flitcroft, G .... 1(1) | Khizanishvili, Z ...... 24(2) | Peter, S .... 1(7)
Friedel, B .... 38 | Kuqi, S .... 15(18) | Reid, S .... 31(3)
Gallagher, P .... –(1) | Matteo, D .... 6 | Savage, R 34

Sinama Pongolle, F .. 8(2)   Todd, A .... 20(2)   Tugay, K .... 23(4)
Thompson, D .... 2(4)

League goals (51): Bellamy 13, Pedersen 9, Kuqi 7, Dickov 5, Reid 4, Bentley 3, Todd 2, Emerton 1, Khizanishvili 1, Neill 1, Savage 1, Sinama Pongolle 1, Tugay 1, Opponents 2.
F.A. Cup goals (5): Bellamy 2, Bentley 1, Neill 1, Todd 1. **Carling Cup goals (12):** Bellamy 2, Dickov 2, Bentley 1, Emerton 1, Khizanishvili 1, Kuqi 1, Neill 1, Pedersen 1, Reid 1, Thompson 1.
Average home League attendance: 21,015. **Player of Year:** Craig Bellamy.

BOLTON WANDERERS

Sam Allardyce experienced double disappointment with Bolton's failure to return to Europe and his own unsuccessful bid to become England coach. After losing to Marseille in the UEFA Cup's first knock-out round after qualifying from their group, Bolton looked a good bet for another top six finish. Games in hand meant that even Champions League qualification was not out of the question. Instead, a sequence of six games yielding a single point, pushed them down to eighth. Allardyce, whose side also failed to capitalise on a home draw against West Ham in the F.A. Cup fifth round, was said to have impressed in his interviews with the F.A. but lost out to Steve McClaren as their choice of successor to Sven-Goran Eriksson.

Ben Haim, T .... 32(3)   Fernandes, F .... –(1)   N'Gotty, B .... 27(2)
Borgetti, J .... 5(14)   Fojut, J .... –(1)   Nakata, H .... 14(7)
Campo, I .... 8(7)   Gardner, R .... 27(3)   Nolan, K .... 35(1)
Davies, K 37   Giannakopoulos, S .. 29(5)   O'Brien, J .... 22(1)
Diouf, E-H .... 17(3)   Hunt, N .... 12(8)   Okocha, J-J .... 18(9)
Djetou, M .... 1(2)   Jaaskelainen, J 38   Pedersen, H .... 15(6)
Fadiga, K .... 5(3)   Jaidi, R .... 15(1)   Speed, G .... 29(2)
Faye, A .... 23(4)   Jansen, M 3   Vaz Te, R .... 6(16)

League goals (49): Giannakopoulos 9, Nolan 9, Davies 7, Speed 4, Diouf 3, Jaidi 3, Vaz Te 3, Borgetti 2, Campo 2, Fadiga 1, Faye 1, Nakata 1, Okocha 1, Pedersen 1, Opponents 1.
F.A. Cup goals (5): Giannakopoulos 2, Borgetti 1, Davies 1, Vaz Te 1. **Carling Cup goals (3):** Borgetti 2, Va Te 1. **UEFA Cup goals (8):** Borgetti 2, Nolan 2, Diouf 1, Giannakopoulos 1, N'Gotty 1, Vaz Te 1.
Average home League attendance: 25,265. **Player of Year:** Ricardo Gardner.

CHARLTON ATHLETIC

Alan Curbishley, the Premiership's second longest-serving manager after Sir Alex Ferguson, signalled the end of an era by stepping down after 15 years in charge. His announcement about needing a break came at the final home game of the season – a 2-0 defeat by Blackburn. Curbishley, who played a huge part in establishing the club in the Premiership, deserved a better send-off, although the result may have been in keeping with the view of some that he had taken Charlton as far as he could and needed a new challenge. His final campaign started with four successive wins, but although Darren Bent continued to score regularly, performances predictably fell away, bringing a fifth successive finish below half-way. Curbishley was replaced by Crystal Palace's Iain Dowie.

Ambrose, D .... 19(9)   Fortune, J .... 7(4)   Murphy, D .... 17(1)
Andersen, S 15   Holland, M .... 20(3)   Myhre, T 20
Bartlett, S .... 6(10)   Hreidarsson, H 34   Perry, C .... 27(1)
Bent, D 36   Hughes, B .... 22(11)   Powell, C .... 25(2)
Bent, M .... 12(1)   Johansson, J .... 1(3)   Rommedahl, D .... 19(2)
Bothroyd, J .... 3(15)   Kiely, D 3   Sam, L .... –(2)
El Karkouri, T .... 4(6)   Kishishev, R .... 33(4)   Sankofa, O .... 3(1)
Euell, J .... 5(5)   Lisbie, K .... –(6)   Smertin, A 18

95

Sorondo, G 7   Thomas, J .... 16(9)   Young, L 32
Spector, J .... 13(7)

League goals (41): Bent, D 18, Murphy 4, Ambrose 3, Hughes 3, Bent, M 2, Bothroyd 2, Rommedahl 2, Bartlett 1, Euell 1, Holland 1, Perry 1, Thomas 1, Young 1, Opponents 1.
F.A. Cup goals (11): Bent, D 2, Bothroyd 2, Hughes 2, Rommedahl 2, Fortune 1, Holland 1, Opponents 1. **Carling Cup goals (6):** Bent, D 2, Ambrose 1, Bothroyd 1, Johansson 1, Murphy 1.
Average home League attendance: 26,195. **Player of Year:** Darren Bent.

CHELSEA

Chelsea picked up the baton from the previous season to claim a second successive title just as impressively as the first. They effectively put slow-starting Arsenal and Liverpool out of the running by opening with nine straight victories and went on to dismiss Manchester United's late surge with a 3-0 victory at Stamford Bridge which made sure of top spot. Jose Mourinho spent £53m. bringing in Michael Essien, Shaun Wright-Phillips and Asier Del Horno, but once again it was Frank Lampard's commanding midfield play and John Terry's dominance at the back that stood out. Lampard went one better this time with 20 goals in all competitions, although Chelsea did stumble in the knock-out competitions, losing to Barcelona in the Champions League, Liverpool in the F.A. Cup and Charlton in their defence of the Carling Cup.

Cech, P 34	Essien, M .... 27(4)	Maniche, N .... 3(5)
Cole, C .... –(9)	Gallas, W .... 33(1)	Paulo Ferreira .... 18(3)
Cole, J .... 26(8)	Geremi, N .... 8(7)	Pidgeley, L 1
Crespo, H .... 20(10)	Gudjohnsen, E ..... 16(10)	Ricardo Carvalho .... 22(2)
Cudicini, C .... 3(1)	Huth, R .... 7(6)	Robben, A .... 21(7)
Del Horno, A 25	Johnson, G 4	Smith, J .... –(1)
Diarra, L .... 2(1)	Lampard, F 35	Terry, J 36
Drogba, D .... 20(9)	Makelele, C .... 29(2)	Wright-Phillips, S . 10(17)
Duff, D .... 18(10)		

League goals (72): Lampard 16, Drogba 12, Crespo 10, Cole, J 7, Robben 6, Gallas 5, Terry 4, Duff 3, Essien 2, Geremi 2, Gudjohnsen 2, Del Horno 1, Ricardo Carvalho 1, Opponents 1.
F.A. Cup goals (12): Cole, J 2, Lampard 2, Terry 2, Cole, C 1, Crespo 1, Drogba 1, Gudjohnsen 1, Paulo Ferreira 1, Robben 1. **Carling Cup goals (1):** Terry 1. **Community Shield goals (2):** Drogba 2. **Champions League goals (9):** Lampard 2, Crespo 2, Ricardo Carvalho 2, Cole, J 1, Drogba 1, Opponents 1.
Average home League attendance: 41,901. **Player of Year:** John Terry.

EVERTON

David Moyes and his team picked up the pieces after a stormy first two months of the season to steer a course towards the calm waters of mid-table. Not only did Everton lose seven of the first eight League matches, but their European adventure was over almost as soon as it started. They lost to Villarreal in a Champions League qualifier and went out in the first round of the UEFA Cup to Dinamo Bucharest. After grinding out some wins to move away from the foot of the table, Everton ran into further turbulence in the shape of successive 4-0 defeats by Bolton and Aston Villa and 3-1 reversal against Liverpool in which Phil Neville and Mikel Arteta were sent off. Then came the turning point – a run of 19 points from the next seven fixtures and some much-needed breathing space.

Anichebe, V .... –(2)	Carsley, L .... 3(2)	Kilbane, K .... 21(13)
Arteta, M .... 27(2)	Davies, S .... 22(8)	Kroldrup, P 1
Beattie, J .... 29(3)	Ferguson, D .... 7(20)	Martyn, N 20
Bent, M .... 7(11)	Ferrari, M .... 6(2)	McFadden, J .... 24(8)
Cahill, T 32	Hibbert, T 29	Naysmith, G 7

Neville, P 34	Stubbs, A .... 13(1)	Weir, D .... 32(1)
Nuno Valente 20	Turner, I .... 2(1)	Westerveld, S 2
Osman, L .... 28(7)	Van der Meyde, A ..... 7(3)	Wright, R .... 14(1)
Pistone, A 2	Vaughan, J .... –(1)	Yobo, J 29
Ruddy, J .... –(1)		

League goals (34): Beattie 10, Cahill 6, McFadden 6, Osman 3, Anichebe 1, Arteta 1, Bent 1, Davies 1, Ferguson 1, Weir 1, Yobo 1, Opponents 2.
F.A. Cup goals (4): Arteta 1, Cahill 1, McFadden 1, Osman 1. **Carling Cup goals:** None.
Champions League goals (2): Arteta 1, Beattie 1. **UEFA Cup goals (2):** Cahill 1, Yobo 1.
Average home League attendance: 36,860. **Player of Year:** Mikel Arteta.

FULHAM

Fulham made Craven Cottage a difficult place to visit and so claimed their customary position of just below mid-table. Only Chelsea, Liverpool and Arsenal scored more wins at home. Chris Coleman went up even further in Jose Mourinho's estimation after a 1-0 win over the champions-elect, Liverpool were beaten 2-0 and West Bromwich Albion crushed 6-1. Ironically, what looked to be a comfortable F.A. passage against Leyton Orient turned into one of the shocks of the third round when the League Two side prevailed 2-1. On their travels it was a different story. Fulham were the only team in the four divisions without an away victory until Steed Malbranque's stoppage-time goal against Manchester City. They then provided Sunderland with their only home success.

Boa Morte, L 35	Goma, A 13	McBride, B .... 34(4)
Bocanegra, C .... 20(1)	Helguson, H .... 15(12)	Niemi, A 9
Bridge, W 12	Jensen, C 11	Pearce, I 10
Brown, M .... 6(1)	Jensen, N .... 14(2)	Pembridge, M 5
Christanval, P .... 7(8)	John, C .... 16(19)	Radzinksi, T .... 23(10)
Crossley, M 13	Knight, Z .... 29(1)	Rehman, Z 3
Diop, P .... 21(1)	Leacock, D 5	Rosenior, L .... 22(2)
Elliott, S 12	Legwinski, S .... 10(3)	Volz, M 23
Elrich, A .... 2(4)	Malbranque, S .... 32(2)	Warner, T .... 16(2)

League goals (48): John 11, McBride 9, Helguson 8, Boa Morte 6, Malbranque 6, Diop 2, Jensen, C 2, Radzinski 2, Bocanegra 1, Opponents 1.
F.A. Cup goals (1): John 1. **Carling Cup goals (7):** Helguson 2, Boa Morte 1, McBride 1, Radzinski 1, Rehman 1, Rosenior 1.
Average home League attendance: 20,654. **Player of Year:** Brian McBride.

LIVERPOOL

Steven Gerrard launched Liverpool's marathon season with a hat-trick against Welsh minnows TNS in a Champions League qualifier. The captain ended it in his team's 62nd match by lifting the F.A. Cup after a marvellous final against West Ham. In between, Gerrard was their midfield motivator and, more often than not, their chief source of goals, qualities which earned him the P.F.A. Player of the Year award. Even so, Liverpool were never in a position to challenge Chelsea's dominance in the League after an indifferent start produced only seven points from six matches. The runners-up spot was the best they could hope for and that too finished out of reach, despite victory in their last nine games. Disappointment also in the Champions League when their title defence ended with defeat by Benfica in the first knock-out round.

Agger, D 4	Gerrard, S 32	Reina, J 33
Baros, M .... –(2)	Hamann, D .... 13(4)	Riise, J A .... 24(8)
Carragher, J 36	Hyypia, S .... 35(1)	Sinama Pongolle, F .. 3(4)
Cisse, D .... 19(14)	Josemi, G .... 3(3)	Sissoko, M .... 21(5)
Crouch, P .... 27(5)	Kewell, H .... 22(5)	Traore, D .... 9(6)
Dudek, J .... 5(1)	Kromkamp, J .... 6(7)	Warnock, S .... 15(5)
Finnan, S 33	Luis Garcia .... 15(16)	Xabi Alonso .... 29(6)
Fowler, R .... 9(5)	Morientes, F .... 20(8)	Zenden, B .... 5(2)

League goals (57): Gerrard 10, Cisse 9, Crouch 8, Luis Garcia 7, Fowler 5, Morientes 5, Xabi Alonso 3, Kewell 3, Zenden 2, Hyypia 1. Riise 1, Warnock 1, Opponents 2.
F.A. Cup goals (20): Gerrard 4, Crouch 3, Riise 3, Cisse 2, Sinama Pongolle 2, Xabi Alonso 2, Hyypia 1, Luis Garcia 1, Morientes 1, Opponents 1. **Carling Cup goals (1):** Gerrard 1. **Champions League goals (20):** Gerrard 7, Cisse 6, Morientes 3, Luis Garcia 2, Carragher 1, Sinama Pongolle 1. **Club World Championship goals (3):** Crouch 2, Gerrard 1. **European Super Cup goals (3):** Cisse 2, Luis Garcia 1.
Average home League attendance: 44,344.

MANCHESTER CITY

Stuart Pearce's first full season in charge brimmed with promise until the final two months when his team went to pieces. A 3-1 success against Manchester United was the pick of some impressive wins which had a European place beckoning and put Pearce, himself, in the frame for the England job. Then it all turned sour. City lost nine of their last ten matches to slip to 15th in the table. In addition, genuine F.A. Cup hopes were dashed by a home defeat by West Ham in the sixth round. Injuries were a contributing factor, with the loss of leading scorer Andy Cole particularly significant. But Pearce, as honest a manager as there is in the game, accepted his share of the blame and promised action to put things right.

Barton, J 31	Jordan, S 18	Samaras, G .... 10(4)
Cole, A .... 20(2)	Miller, I .... –(1)	Sibierski, A .... 12(12)
Croft, L .... 4(17)	Mills, D 18	Sinclair, T .... 29(2)
Distin, S 31	Mills, M .... –(1)	Sommeil, D .... 14(2)
Dunne, R .... 31(1)	Musampa, K .... 24(3)	Sun Jihai .... 16(13)
Flood, W .... 1(4)	Onuoha, N .... 8(2)	Thatcher, B 18
Fowler, R .... 0(4)	Reyna, C 22	Vassell, D 36
Ireland, S .... 13(11)	Richards, M .... 11(2)	Wright-Phillips, B ... 1(17)
James, D 38	Riera, A .... 12(3)	

League goals (43): Cole 9, Vassell 8, Barton 6, Samaras 4, Dunne 3, Sinclair 3, Sibierski 2, Sommeil 2, Croft 1, Fowler 1, Mills, D 1, Reyna 1, Riera 1, Wright-Phillips 1.
F.A. Cup goals (8): Fowler 3, Cole 1, Musampa 1, Richards 1, Samaras 1, Vassell 1.
Carling Cup goals (1): Vassell 1.
Average home League attendance: 42,856. **Player of Year:** Richard Dunne.

MANCHESTER UNITED

For most clubs, the runners-up spot together with victory in the Carling Cup would represent major success. By United's high standards, however, there were mixed feelings about a season in which they were again outpaced by Chelsea and failed, for the first time in a decade, to progress beyond the group stage of the Champions League. Defeat by Liverpool in the fifth round of the F.A. Cup also hurt. With a month of the campaign remaining, United had halved Chelsea's lead to seven points after nine successive victories, but then a goalless draw against Sunderland at Old Trafford ended hopes of a stirring climax. So they had to fall back on the lesser of the trophies for some silverware, for once fielding full-strength teams in the competition and brushing aside Wigan 4-0 in the final with a Wayne Rooney-inspired performance.

Bardsley, P .... 3(5)	Keane, R .... 4(1)	Saha, L .... 12(7)
Brown, W .... 17(2)	Miller, L .... –(1)	Scholes, P .... 18(2)
Evra, P .... 7(4)	Neville, G .... 24(1)	Silvestre, M .... 30(3)
Ferdinand, R 37	O'Shea, J 34	Smith, A .... 15(6)
Fletcher, D .... 23(4)	Pique, G .... 1(2)	Solskjaer, O .... –(3)
Giggs, R .... 22(5)	Richardson, K ...... 12(10)	Van der Sar, E 38
Heinze, G .... 2(2)	Ronaldo, C .... 24(9)	Vidic, N .... 9(2)
Howard, T .... –(1)	Rooney, W .... 34(2)	Van Nistelrooy, R .... 28(7)
Ji-Sung Park .... 23(10)	Rossi, G .... 1(4)	

League goals (72): Van Nistelrooy 21, Rooney 16, Ronaldo 9, Saha 7, Ferdinand 3, Giggs 2, Scholes 2, Fletcher 1, O'Shea 1, Park 1 Richardson 1, Rossi 1, Silvestre 1, Smith 1, Opponents 5.
F.A. Cup goals (8): Richardson 3, Rossi 2, Saha 2, Giggs 1. **Carling Cup goals (17):** Saha 6, Ronaldo 2, Rooney 2, Ebanks-Blake, G 1, Miller 1, O'Shea 1, Park 1, Richardson 1, Rossi 1, Van Nistelrooy 1. **Champions League goals (9):** Heinze 2, Van Nistelrooy 2, Giggs 1, Richardson 1, Ronaldo 1, Rooney 1, Scholes 1.
Average home League attendance: 68,764. **Player of Year:** Wayne Rooney.

MIDDLESBROUGH

A bitter-sweet season ended with Steve McClaren departing after the UEFA Cup Final to succeed Sven-Goran Eriksson as England coach. His team lost it 4-0 to Sevilla, but won high praise for thrilling comebacks which turned 3-0 aggregate deficits into 4-3 victories against Basle in the quarter-finals and Steaua Bucharest in the semi-finals. McClaren also experienced ups-and-downs in the Premiership. A 7-0 rout at Arsenal was followed not long after by a 4-0 home defeat by Aston Villa which had some fans calling for his head. A week later, they were all smiles after Chelsea were seen off 3-0 at the Riverside. Despite a disappointing 14th place, there is no doubt the manager left a strong legacy, with ten graduates from the club's Academy playing in the last game against Fulham. Gareth Southgate stepped up from team captain to manager.

Abel Xavier	4	Job, J-D	–(1)	Queudrue, F	26(3)
Bates, M	12(4)	Johnson, A	8(5)	Reiziger, M	4
Boateng, G	25(1)	Jones, B	9	Riggott, C	22
Cattermole, L	10(4)	Kennedy, J	1(2)	Rochemback, F	22
Christie, M	3(3)	Maccarone, M	6(11)	Schwarzer, M	27
Cooper, C	–(1)	McMahon, A	3	Southgate, G	24
Craddock, T	–(1)	Mendieta, G	15(2)	Taylor, A	7(6)
Davies, A	4(8)	Morrison, J	21(3)	Turnbull, R	2
Doriva	19(8)	Nemeth, S	1(4)	Viduka, M	19(8)
Downing, S	11(1)	Parlour, R	11(2)	Walker, J	–(1)
Ehiogu, U	16(2)	Parnaby, S	19(1)	Wheater, D	4(2)
Graham, D	1(2)	Pogatetz, E	21(3)	Yakubu, A	29(5)
Hasselbaink, J	12(10)				

League goals (48): Yakubu 13, Hasselbaink 9, Viduka 7, Queudrue 3, Boateng 2, Maccarone 2, Mendieta 2, Parnaby 2, Rochemback 2, Cattermole 1, Downing 1, Johnson 1, Morrison 1, Pogatetz 1, Opponents 1.
F.A. Cup goals (14): Yakubu 4, Hasselbaink 3, Viduka 2, Mendieta 1, Morrison 1, Parnaby 1, Riggott 1, Rochemback 1. **Carling Cup goals (3):** Hasselbaink 1, Nemeth 1, Vikduka 1. **UEFA Cup goals (18):** Viduka 6, Hasselbaink 4, Maccarone 3, Yakubu 2, Boateng 1, Parnaby 1, Riggott 1.
Average home League attendance: 28,463. **Player of Year:** Aiyegbeni Yakubu.

NEWCASTLE UNITED

Glenn Roeder restored the club's faltering fortunes and was rewarded with the manager's job at the end of the season, despite not having the required UEFA coaching qualifications. The club's Academy chief, installed as caretaker after Graeme Souness was sacked when a run of one point from six games left Newcastle in danger of being sucked into relegation trouble, first insisted he was not interested in a permanent position. But the former West Ham manager grew into the job to such an extent that they climbed to seventh on the back of 32 points accumulated from his 15 matches in charge. Roeder did it without Michael Owen, who was struck by a foot injury ten starts after a £16m. move from Real Madrid, and at the end without Alan Shearer, whose career was ended prematurely by a damaged knee, sustained after his 206th goal for the club.

Ameobi, S	25(5)	Boumsong, J-A	30(3)	Bramble, T	21(3)
Babayaro, C	26(2)	Bowyer, L	18(10)	Carr, S	19

Chopra, M	Jenas, J	Parker, S
6(7)	3(1)	26
Clark, L	Luque, A	Pattison, M
8(14)	6(8)	2(1)
Dyer, K	Milner, J	Ramage, P
4(7)	1(2)	23
Elliott, R	Moore, C	Shearer, A
14(3)	8	31(1)
Emre, B	N'Zogbia, C	Solano, N
19(1)	27(5)	27(2)
Faye, A	O'Brien, A	Taylor, S
14(8)	–(3)	12
Given, S	Owen, M	
38	10(1)	

League goals (47): Shearer 10, Ameobi 9, Owen 7, Solano 6, N'Zogbia 5, Bramble 2, Emre 2, Bowyer 1, Chopra 1, Clark 1, Luque 1, Parker 1, Opponents 1.
F.A. Cup goals (4): Chopra 1, Dyer 1, Parker 1, Shearer 1. **Carling Cup goals (1):** Shearer 1. **Intertoto Cup goals (7):** Milner 2, Shearer 2, Bowyer 1, Chopra 1, N'Zogbia 1.
Average home League attendance: 52,032.

PORTSMOUTH

Harry Redknapp described it as his greatest achievement in 23 years of management – and no wonder. Redknapp's return to Fratton Park after an ill-fated spell at Southampton was greeted with scepticism, if not downright hostility, by many supporters. By the time he had delivered, against all the odds, Premiership safety, he was being hailed as something of a Saint. With ten games remaining, Redknapp's re-shaped side – he brought in eight new players during the January transfer window – were eight points from safety. The tide turned when one of them, Pedro Mendes, scored a spectacular last-minute winner against Manchester City. It was the start of a remarkable run which netted 20 points out of 27, culminating in a 2-1 win at Wigan which sent Birmingham and West Bromwich Albion down alongside Sunderland.

Ashdown, J	Mornar, I	Routledge, W
17	1(1)	3(10)
Cisse, A	Mwaruwari, B	Silva, D
2(1)	16	13
D'Alessandro, A	O'Brien, A	Skopelitis, G
13	29	–(5)
Davis, S	O'Neil, G	Songo'o, F
16(1)	36	–(2)
Diao, S	Olisadebe, E	Stefanovic, D
7(4)	–(2)	27(1)
Griffin, A	Pamarot, N	Taylor, M
20(2)	4(4)	32(2)
Hughes, R	Pericard, V	Todorov, S
21(5)	3(3)	6(18)
Karadas, A	Primus, L	Viafara, J
4(13)	20	10(4)
Kiely, D	Priske, B	Vignal, G
15	26(4)	13(1)
Koroman, O	Robert, L	Vukic, Z
1(2)	13(4)	6(3)
LuaLua, L		Westerveld, S
24(1)		6
Mbesuma, C		
–(4)		

League goals (37): LuaLua 7, O'Neil 6, Taylor 6, Todorov 4, Mendes 3, Silva 2, D'Alessandro 1, Davis 1, Karadas 1, Koroman 1, Mwaruwari 1, Robert 1, Viafara 1, Vukic 1, Opponents 1.
F.A. Cup goals (2): Davis 1, Silva 1. **Carling Cup goals (2):** O'Neil 1, Taylor 1.
Average home League attendance: 19,839. **Player of Year:** Gary O'Neil.

SUNDERLAND

When Sunderland lost their first five games, it was clear that another grim season in the top flight was about to unfold. Few expected, however, that it would be quite as bad as the one which culminated in relegation in 2003. In the event, it proved even worse. They finished bottom with 15 points, four fewer than the record low three years previously, and failed by one to match the four victories in that campaign. At least caretaker Kevin Ball and his players avoided the embarrassment of becoming the first at any senior level to go a full season without a home win when goals by Anthony Le Tallec and Chris Brown accounted for Fulham. Perhaps it was not surprising. By Premiership standards, Mick McCarthy had little more than loose change to spend on new players. What did grate for many, though, was the dismissal of the manager in early March when their fate was virtually sealed.

Alnwick, B	Arca, J	Bassila, C
5	22(2)	12(1)

Breen, G .... 33(2)	Kyle, K .... 9(4)	Robinson, C .... 3(2)
Brown, C .... 10(3)	Lawrence, L .... 19(10)	Smith, D .... 1(2)
Caldwell, S .... 23(1)	Le Tallec, A .... 12(15)	Stead, J .... 21(9)
Collins, D .... 22(1)	Leadbitter, G .... 8(4)	Stubbs, A .... 8(2)
Davis, K 33	McCartney, G 13	Welsh, A .... 12(2)
Delap, R .... 5(1)	Miller, T .... 27(2)	Whitehead, D 37
Elliott, S .... 11(4)	Murphy, D .... 5(13)	Woods, M .... 1(6)
Gray, A .... 13(8)	Nosworthy, N .... 24(6)	Wright, S 2
Hoyte, J 27		

League goals (26): Lawrence 3, Le Tallec 3, Miller 3, Whitehead 3, Elliott 2, Arca 1, Breen 1, Brown 1, Collins 1, Delap 1, Gray 1, Hoyte 1, Kyle 1, Murphy 1, Stead 1, Stubbs 1, Opponents 1.
F.A. Cup goals (4): Arca 1, Le Tallec 1, Collins, N 1, Whitehead 1. **Carling Cup goals (1):** Le Tallec 1.
Average home League attendance: 33,904. **Player of Year:** Dean Whitehead.

TOTTENHAM HOTSPUR

Martin Jol guided Tottenham to a best-ever Premiership finish – and for a long time their return to European football looked as if it would be in the Champions League rather than the UEFA Cup. That Arsenal came up on the rails to claim fourth place on the final day of the season, when Tottenham were hit by a virus on the eve of their game against West Ham, took nothing away from the continued improvement under Jol, which suggests the good times could be returning to White Hart Lane. If something had to give, it was in the knock-out competitions which for so long have been the club's strong point. They were dismissed, embarrassingly, from the Carling Cup at Grimsby and surrendered a two-goal lead to lose to Leicester at the first hurdle in the F.A. Cup.

Barnard, L .... –(3)	Jackson, J .... –(1)	Pamarot, N .... –(2)
Brown, M .... 2(7)	Jenas, J 30	Mendes, P .... 3(3)
Carrick, M 35	Kanoute, F .... –(1)	Rasiak, G .... 4(4)
Davenport, C .... 1(3)	Keane, R .... 25(11)	Reid, A .... 7(6)
Davids, E .... 28(3)	Kelly, S 9	Robinson, P 38
Dawson, M .... 31(1)	King, L 26	Routledge, W .... 2(1)
Defoe, J .... 23(13)	Lennon, A .... 21(6)	Stalteri,P 33
Edman, E 3	Mido .... 24(3)	Tainio, T .... 22(2)
Gardner, A .... 16(1)	Murphy, D .... 2(8)	Young-Pyo Lee 31
Huddlestone, T .... –(4)	Naybet, N .... 2(1)	

League goals (53): Keane 16, Mido 11, Defoe 9, Jenas 6, King 3, Carrick 2, Lennon 2, Davids 1, Stalteri 1, Tainio 1, Opponents 1.
F.A. Cup goals (2): Jenas 1, Stalteri 1. **Carling Cup goals:** None.
Average home League attendance: 36,073. **Player of Year:** Robbie Keane.

WEST BROMWICH ALBION:

Albion looked a decent bet to survive after a solid 2-0 win over Blackburn in early February accompanied the acquisition in the transfer window of Nigel Quashie to stiffen their midfield. Instead, they were hammered 6-1 by Fulham next time out, Quashie then picked up a five-match ban and by the time he returned, his new team were sinking like a stone. Albion, in fact, failed to win any of their final 13 matches and there was to be no repeat of the great escape achieved 12 months earlier. A team that in the first half of the campaign had battled to beat Arsenal and Tottenham at the Hawthorns, as well as thumping Everton 4-0, seemed to run out of heart and spirit when the going started to get really tough.

Albrechtsen, M ...... 26(5)	Clement, N .... 29(2)	Gaardsoe, T 7
Campbell, K .... 19(10)	Davies, C 33	Gera, Z .... 12(3)
Carter, D .... 11(9)	Earnshaw, R .... 4(8)	Greening, J .... 37(1)
Chaplow, R .... 4(3)	Ellington, N .... 15(16)	Hodgkiss, J .... –(1)

Horsfield, G .... 10(8)	Kirkland, C 10	Quashie, N 9
Hoult, R .... –(1)	Kozak, J .... 4(2)	Robinson, P 33
Inamoto, J .... 16(6)	Kuszczak, T 28	Scimeca, R 2
Johnson, A 8	Martinez, W .... 1(1)	Wallwork, R 31
Kamara, D .... 21(5)	Moore, D .... 3(2)	Watson, S .... 28(2)
Kanu, N .... 17(8)	Nicholson, S .... –(4)	

League goals (31): Ellington 5, Kanu 5, Horsfield 4, Campbell 3, Davies 2, Gera 2, Greening 2, Albrechtsen 1, Carter 1, Clement 1, Earnshaw 1, Kamara 1, Martinez 1, Quashie 1, Watson 1.
F.A. Cup goals (3): Chaplow 2, Gera 1. **Carling Cup goals (8):** Ellington 3, Earnshaw 2, Inamoto 1, Kamara 1, Kanu 1.
Average home League attendance: 25,403. **Player of Year:** Jonathan Greening.

WEST HAM UNITED

The disappointment of losing one of the great F.A. Cup Finals of all time to Liverpool on penalties in no way clouded West Ham's season. Alan Pardew finally won over the last of the Upton Park sceptics by building and developing a side that played in the truest traditions of the club. The manager strengthened his squad wisely after promotion and made an important addition in mid-season by paying a club-record £7.25m. to link Dean Ashton with Marlon Harewood up front. With Nigel Reo-Coker a maturing captain, Pardew's side may finally have come of age in a 3-2 victory over Arsenal at Highbury, while an equally satisfying 2-1 win over Tottenham six days before the Cup Final confirmed a place in the top half of the table.

Aliadiere, J .... 1(6)	Ferdinand, A .... 32(1)	Noble, M .... 4(1)
Ashton, D .... 9(2)	Fletcher, C .... 6(6)	Reid, K .... 1(1)
Bellion, D .... 2(6)	Gabbidon, D .... 31(1)	Reo-Coker, N 31
Benayoun, Y .... 30(4)	Harewood, M .... 31(6)	Repka, T 19
Bywater, S .... –(1)	Hislop, S 16	Scaloni, L 13
Carroll, R 19	Katan, Y .... 2(4)	Sheringham, T ..... 15(11)
Clarke, C 2	Konchesky, P .... 36(1)	Walker, J 3
Collins, J .... 13(1)	Mullins, H 35	Ward, E .... 3(1)
Dailly, C .... 6(16)	Newton, S .... 8(18)	Zamora, R .... 17(17)
Etherington, M 33		

League goals (52): Harewood 14, Sheringham 6, Zamora 6, Benayoun 5, Reo-Coker 5, Ashton 3, Collins 2, Etherington 2, Ferdinand 2, Fletcher 1, Konchesky 1, Newton 1, Opponents 4.
F.A. Cup goals (11): Ashton 2, Harewood 2, Zamora 2, Etherington 1, Mullins 1, Sheringham 1, Opponents 2. **Carling Cup goals (4):** Zamora 2, Bellion 1, Dailly 1.
Average home League attendance: 33,742. **Player of Year:** Danny Gabbidon.

WIGAN ATHLETIC

They were everyone's favourites to go straight back down after a fleeting taste of the big time. Instead, Wigan needed just 90 minutes to take to Premiership football like a duck to water. Paul Jewell's energetic and effervescent side were unlucky to lose to Hernan Crespo's last-minute winner for Chelsea on the opening day of the season, but it wasn't long before the new boys had launched an impressive run of eight wins in nine matches and were breathing down the necks of the defending champions. It couldn't last, of course, with home form becoming increasingly erratic. By then however, Wigan had accumulated sufficient points to guard against any prospect of a relegation struggle. Their mid-table finish was complemented by a place in the Carling Cup Final, where even a 4-0 defeat by Manchester United was unable to mask another considerable achievement.

Baines, L .... 35(2)	Chimbonda, P 37	Filan, J 15
Bullard, J .... 35(1)	Connolly, D .... 4(13)	Francis, D .... 16(4)
Camara, H .... 25(4)	De Zeeuw, A 31	Henchoz, S 26

Jackson, M .... 11(5)	Mellor, N 3	Taylor, R .... 3(8)
Johansson, A .... 6(10)	Pollitt, M .... 23(1)	Teale, G .... 20(4)
Kavanagh, G .... 32(3)	Roberts, J 34	Thompson, D .... 7(3)
Mahon, A .... 5(1)	Scharner, P .... 14(2)	Wright, D .... 1(1)
McCulloch, L .... 27(3)	Skoko, J .... 3(2)	Ziegler, R .... 5(5)
McMillan, S .... –(2)		

League goals (45): Camara 12, Roberts 8, McCulloch 5, Bullard 4, Johansson 4, Scharner 3, Chimbonda 2, Thompson 2, Connolly 1, Francis 1, Mahon 1, Mellor 1, Opponents 1.
F.A. Cup goals (4): Roberts 2, Connolly 1, Johansson 1. **Carling Cup goals (9):** Roberts 4, Johansson 2, Connolly 1, Scharner 1, Taylor 1.
Average home League attendance: 20,609. **Player of Year:** Arjan De Zeeuw.

COCA-COLA CHAMPIONSHIP

BRIGHTON & HOVE ALBION

Brighton had scrapped their way to survival at the end of the previous season, but there was no escape this time for a club continuing to operate without a proper ground, a decent crowd and as a consequence a lack of resources. Manager Mark McGhee admitted that until a new stadium was built, the struggle will continue. A lack of goals that McGhee was unable to cure meant his team were always up against it. Late on, Gifton Noel-Williams came in to form a useful partnership alongside Colin Kazim-Richards, with both players prominent in a 2-0 win over fellow-strugglers Millwall which raised a glimmer of hope. But that was immediately crushed by a home defeat by Southampton and Brighton finished bottom 12 points adrift.

Blayney, A 8	Gatting, J .... 5(7)	Lynch, J 16
Butters, G .... 43(2)	Hammond, D .... 40(1)	Mayo, K .... 14(4)
Carole, S .... 34(6)	Hart, G .... 31(4)	McCammon, M ...... 3(4)
Carpenter, R .... 31(1)	Henderson, W 32	McPhee, C .... 2(5)
Chaigneau, F 1	Hinshelwood, A ...... 10(1)	McShane, P 38
Cox, D .... –(1)	Jarrett, A .... 9(2)	Nicolas, A .... 4(7)
Dodd, J .... 6(1)	Kazim-Richards,	Noel-Williams, G 7
El-Abd, A .... 23(6)	C .... 25(17)	Oatway, C .... 17(1)
Elphick, G .... 1(1)	Knight, L .... 22(3)	Reid, P .... 36(2)
Elphick, T .... –(1)	Kuipers, M 5	Robinson, J .... 15(12)
Frutos, A .... 27(9)	Loft, D .... –(3)	Turienzo, F .... 1(3)

League goals (39): Kazim-Richards 6, Knight 5, Hammond 4, McShane 4, Frutos 3, Butters 2, Carole 2, Noel-Williams 2, Reid 2, Carpenter 1, Hart 1, Loft 1, Lynch 1, Mayo 1, Oatway 1, Robinson 1, Opponents 1.
F.A. Cup goals: None. **Carling Cup goals (2):** McCammon 1, Robinson 1.
Average home League attendance: 6,802. **Player of Year:** Paul McShane.

BURNLEY

A season of the proverbial two halves for Burnley, who entertained hopes of sustaining a challenge for the play-offs after climbing to fifth with Ade Akinbiyi's 12th Championship goal in the Boxing Day defeat of Stoke. But that was as good as it got. Akinbiyi, whose tally included a hat-trick against Luton, failed to add to it in the next four matches, then joined Sheffield United for a club-record £1.75m. His old team struggled to fill to gap, so much so that the remaining 17 matches produced only seven goals and three victories. Two of those wins came after Andy Gray was brought in on loan from Sunderland to halt the slide, which eventually left Burnley in 17th position.

Akinbiyi, A 29	Courtney, D .... 1(6)	Elliott, W .... 23(13)
Bardsley, P 6	Coyne, D .... 7(1)	Grant, L 1
Bermingham, K .... 1(3)	Duff, M .... 39(2)	Gray, A 9
Branch, G .... 29(8)	Dyer, N .... 4(1)	Harley, J 41

Hyde, M .... 39(2)	Mahon, A .... 7(1)	O'Connor, J 46
Jensen, B .... 38(1)	McCann, C .... 15(8)	Ricketts, M .... 12(1)
Karbassiyoon, D .... -(5)	McGreal, J .... 33(2)	Sinclair, F .... 36(1)
Lafferty, K .... 3(8)	Noel-Williams, G .. 17(12)	Spicer, J .... 22(12)
Lowe, K .... 10(6)	O'Connor, G .... 26(3)	Thomas, W .... 12(4)

League goals (46): Akinbiyi 12, O'Connor, G 7, Elliott 3, Gray 3, O'Connor, J 3, Spicer 3, Branch 2, Dyer 2, Harley 2, McCann 2, Noel-Williams 2, Ricketts 2, Lafferty 1, Thomas 1, Opponents 1.
F.A. Cup goals (1): O'Connor, G 1. **Carling Cup goals (5):** Akinbiyi 2, Duff 1, Lowe 1, Spicer 1.
Average home League attendance: 12,461. **Player of Year:** Jon Harley.

CARDIFF CITY

Cardiff faltered and fell away just as an improved season's work was promising something tangible. With seven games remaining, a team reshaped by Dave Jones and given a cutting edge by 20-year-old striker Cameron Jerome, were two points away from a play-off place. But only two more points were forthcoming and they slipped out of contention. Jones was only unhappy that the opportunity had not been seized, although a place in the top half still contrasted sharply with the previous campaign when safety was not ensured until the penultimate match. Jerome scored 20 goals in all competitions and broke into the England Under 21 team.

Alexander, N 46	Jacobson, J .... -(1)	Ndumbu-Nsungu, G .. 4(7)
Ardley, N .... 22(8)	Jerome, C 44	Parry, N .... 11(16)
Barker, C 41	Koumas, J .... 42(2)	Purse, D 39
Blake, D .... -(1)	Ledley, J 42	Ricketts, M 17
Boland, W .... 11(4)	Lee, A .... 6(19)	Scimeca, R .... 17(1)
Cooper, K .... 31(5)	Loovens, G .... 32(1)	Thompson, S 14
Cox, N .... 21(6)	McDonald, C .... -(1)	Weston, R .... 26(4)
Darlington, J .... 7(2)	Mulryne, P .... 1(3)	Whitley, J .... 32(2)
Ferretti, A .... -(4)		

League goals (58): Jerome 18, Koumas 12, Purse 5, Ricketts 5, Thompson 4, Ledley 3, Cooper 2, Cox 2, Lee 2, Loovens 2, Parry 1, Scimeca 1, Whitley 1.
F.A. Cup goals (1): Jerome 1. **Carling Cup goals (4):** Jerome 1, Koumas 1, Ledley 1, Purse 1.
Average home League attendance: 11,720.

COVENTRY CITY

Coventry marked the start of a new era in the £113m. Ricoh Arena by achieving their best finish since relegation from the Premiership in 2001. Crowds rose by an average of 5,000, offering further evidence that, on and off the field, the club could be back in business after some lean times. Last-minute work on the stadium meant the first game had to be delayed for a fortnight. Micky Adams was also forced to wait for some time before his team became established as a consistent force at home. A 6-1 victory over Derby helped them do that and although the play-offs were never a realistic proposition, eighth place represented considerable progress.

Adebola, D .... 39(5)	Hughes, S .... 18(1)	Page, R 32
Bywater, S 14	Hutchison, D .... 10(14)	Scowcroft, J .... 37(4)
Davis, L .... -(2)	Impey, A .... 4(12)	Shaw, R .... 24(1)
Doyle, M 44	Ince, C .... -(1)	Sofiane, Y .... -(1)
Duffy, R .... 30(2)	John, S .... 21(4)	Thornton, K .... 4(12)
Flood, W .... 7(1)	Jorgensen, C .... 15(12)	Turner, B .... -(1)
Fulop, M 31	McSheffrey, G 43	Watson, P .... 1(2)
Giddings, S .... 1(1)	Morrell, A .... 10(24)	Whing, A .... 24(8)
Hall, M .... 38(1)	Nalis, L .... 5(1)	Williams, A .... 12(2)
Heath, M .... 23(2)	Osbourne, I .... 7(3)	Wise, D .... 11(2)

Wood, N .... −(4)

League goals (62): McSheffrey 15, Adebola 12, John 10, Wise 6, Hutchison 4, Jorgensen 3, Scowcroft 3, Morrell 2, Nalis 2, Flood 1, Heath 1, Page 1, Opponents 2.
F.A. Cup goals (2): John 1, McSheffrey 1. **Carling Cup goals (3):** Heath 1, McSheffrey 1, Morrell 1.
Average home League attendance: 21,136. **Player of Year:** Gary McSheffrey.

CREWE ALEXANDRA

Dario Gradi had made something of a habit of keeping Crewe at a level above and beyond their status, but this time the task was beyond the manager, in his 23rd year at the club. They were relegated in a season which started brightly enough with success against Burnley followed by three draws, but which did not take off again until it was too late. Crewe showed considerable spirit to win half of their final eight games, in addition to coming from two goals down against Crystal Palace for a point at Selhurst Park. That rally, however, was not enough to compensate for what had gone before – a total of just five victories. The most damaging spell ran from mid-November to late February when 16 games delivered only four points.

Bell, L .... 14(3)	Maynard, N .... −(1)	Suhaj, P .... 1(5)
Bignot, P .... 4(1)	McCready, C .... 19(6)	Taylor, G 15
Bougherra, M 11	Moses, A .... 12(3)	Tomlinson, S .... 1(1)
Cochrane, J .... 2(2)	Moss, D .... 30(1)	Tonkin, A 27
Foster, S .... 36(3)	O'Connor, M .... −(2)	Turnbull, R 29
Grant, A 10	Otsemobor, J 16	Ugarte, J .... −(2)
Higdon, M .... 15(11)	Rivers,M .... 9(8)	Varney, L .... 15(12)
Johnson, E .... 16(6)	Rix, B .... 1(1)	Vaughan, D .... 28(6)
Jones, B .... 43(1)	Roberts, G .... 27(6)	Walker, R .... 17(1)
Jones, S .... 36(5)	Rodgers, L .... 13(13)	Williams, B .... 16(1)
Lunt, K 43		

League goals (57): Jones, B 6, Rodgers 6, Johnson 5, Jones, S 5, Varney 5, Vaughan 5, Lunt 4, Taylor 4, Foster 3, Higdon 3, Rivers 3, Bell 2, Roberts 2, Bougherra 1, Maynard 1, Walker 1, Opponents 1.
F.A. Cup goals (1): Jones, B 1. **Carling Cup goals (1):** Walker 1.
Average home League attendance: 6,731. **Player of Year:** Billy Jones.

CRYSTAL PALACE

A season which started with high hopes of an immediate return to the Premiership ended in crushing disappointment and the departure of manager Iain Dowie. Palace were always playing catch-up for the automatic promotion places after a sluggish start contrasted sharply with the way Reading and Sheffield United came flying out of the blocks. Dowie continued to back his team's chances in the play-offs, banking on Andy Johnson's goals to make the difference, but hadn't bargained for a nightmare semi-final against Watford at Selhurst Park. Missed chances in the first half were punished by a 3-0 drubbing and there was no way back in the second leg. Dowie was succeeded by Hull's Peter Taylor.

Andrews, W .... 5(19)	Hughes, M .... 30(10)	Popovic, T 10
Black, T .... −(1)	Johnson, A .... 30(3)	Reich, M .... 14(7)
Borrowdale, G .... 26(4)	Kiraly, G 43	Riihilahti, A .... 9(6)
Boyce, E 42	Kolkka, J .... 1(2)	Soares, T .... 38(6)
Butterfield, D .... 9(4)	Leigertwood, M ...... 18(9)	Speroni, J .... 3(1)
Freedman, D .... 19(15)	Macken, J .... 13(11)	Ward, D .... 42(1)
Hall, F 39	McAnuff, J .... 35(6)	Watson, B .... 40(2)
Hudson, M .... 8(7)	Morrison, C .... 32(8)	

Play-offs – appearances: Boyce 2, Hall 2, Hughes 2, Johnson 2, Kiraly 2, McAnuff 2, Popovic 2, Soares 2, Freedman 1(1), Watson 1(1), Borrowdale 1, Leigertwood 1, Morrison 1, Ward 1, Butterfield −(1), Macken −(1), Reich −(1).

League goals (67): Johnson 15, Morrison 13, McAnuff 7, Freedman 6, Ward 5, Watson 4, Hughes 2, Macken 2, Reich 2, Riihilahti 2, Andrews 1, Boyce 1, Hall 1, Soares 1, Opponents 5. **Play-offs – goals:** None.
F.A. Cup goals (6): Johnson 2, Freedman 1, Hughes 1, McAnuff 1, Ward 1. **Carling Cup goals (7):** Reich 2, Freedman 1, Granville 1, Hughes 1, Popovic 1, Opponents 1.
Average home League attendance: 19,457. **Player of Year:** Emmerson Boyce.

DERBY COUNTY

No team in the division fell further than debt-ridden Derby, who finished fifth from bottom a year after reaching the play-offs. Phil Brown, appointed as manager in the summer after George Burley's resignation, was sacked in January in the wake of a 6-1 beating at Coventry and an F. A. Cup fourth round defeat at Colchester. Caretaker Terry Westley managed to avoid the bottom three, but was ruled out of the job on a permanent basis after a six-man consortium took control of the club, aiming to restore fortunes on and off the field. Preston's Billy Davies was the new appointment.

Addison, M 2	Hajto, T 5	Mills, P .... –(1)
Ainsworth, L .... –(2)	Holdsworth, D .... –(3)	Moore, D 14
Barnes, G .... 15(4)	Holmes, L .... 9(9)	Nyatanga, L .... 23(1)
Bisgaard, M .... 25(8)	Idiakez, I .... 41(1)	Peschisolido, P ... 14(20)
Blackstock, D .... 8(1)	Jackson, J .... 3(3)	Poole, K 6
Bolder, A .... 25(10)	Jackson, R .... 20(6)	Rasiak, G 6
Camp, L 40	John, S .... 6(1)	Smith, T 43
Davies, A .... 22(1)	Johnson, M .... 30(1)	Thirlwell, P .... 15(6)
Doyle, N .... –(4)	Johnson, S .... 26(4)	Thome, E .... 3(1)
Edworthy, M 30	Kenna, J .... 15(1)	Tudgay, M .... 11(10)
El Hamdaoui, M ...... 5(4)	Lisbie, K 7	Whittingham, P 11
Fadiga, K .... 2(2)	McIndoe, M .... 6(2)	Wright, A 7
Graham, D .... 11(3)		

League goals (53): Idiakez 11, Smith 8, Peschisolido 5, Bisgaard 4, Blackstock 3, Davies 3, El Hamdaoui 3, Johnson, S 3, Bolder 2, Rasiak 2, Tudgay 2, Barnes 1, Lisbie 1, Johnson, M 1, Moore 1, Nyatanga 1, Opponents 2.
F.A. Cup goals (3): Peschisolido 2, Smith 1. **Carling Cup goals:** None.
Average home League attendance: 24,166. **Player of Year:** Tommy Smith.

HULL CITY

A period of consolidation had to be the target after back-to-back promotions and Peter Taylor's side achieved it in a tough division. Hull won enough matches against teams outside the leading group to stay clear of any trouble. And while it was much harder against top-six opposition, only rarely were they completely outplayed. The one victory at this level was particularly satisfying, Jon Parkin continuing to impress after his mid-season move from Macclesfield with the winner against Leeds in front of a 23,000 crowd at the KC Stadium. Taylor was later interviewed for the vacant Charlton job, but chose, initially, to stay on Humberside, while continuing his work with the England Under 21 side. But he then left to take over at Crystal Palace and was succeeded by Colchester's Phil Parkinson.

Andrews, K .... 24(2)	Duke, M .... 1(1)	Myhill, B 45
Ashbee, I 6	Edge, R 8	Noble, M .... 4(1)
Barmby, N .... 21(5)	Elliott, S .... 26(14)	Parkin, J 18
Brown, C 13	Ellison, K .... 15(8)	Paynter, B .... 11(11)
Burgess, B .... 3(11)	Fagan, C .... 29(12)	Price, J .... 10(5)
Coles, D 9	France, R .... 30(5)	Rogers, A 9
Collins, S 17	Fry, R .... –(1)	Rui Marques, R 1
Cort, L 42	Green, S .... 20(18)	Thelwell, A .... 7(2)
Dawson, A .... 17(1)	Joseph, M .... 2(3)	Welsh, J .... 29(3)
Delaney, M .... 45(1)	Lynch, S .... 15(1)	Wiseman, S .... 8(3)
Duffy, D .... 5(10)	McPhee, S .... 2(2)	Woodhouse, C ...... 14(4)

League goals (49): Elliott 7, Barmby 5, Fagan 5, Parkin 5, Cort 4, Green 4, Duffy 3, Paynter 3, Burgess 2, France 2, Price 2, Welsh 2, Brown 1, Ellison 1, Opponents 3.
F.A. Cup goals: None. **Carling Cup goals (1):** Price 1.
Average home League attendance: 19,841. **Player of Year:** Bo Myhill.

IPSWICH TOWN

Joe Royle's fourth season in charge at Portman Road proved his poorest – and his last. He left by mutual agreement with Ipswich having a rare finish in the bottom half of the table. It was uphill from the start. Leading lights Darren Bent, Shefki Kuqi and Tommy Miller had moved on to Premiership clubs, while replacement strikers Nicky Forster and Sam Parkin were dogged by injuries. Although results picked up in the New Year – a 2-1 win at Norwich proving the pick – the improvement was not sustained for long enough to close the gap on the play-off places. For Forster, at least, there was a degree of satisfaction when he returned for the final four matches and scored in each. Royle was replaced by long-serving midfield player Jim Magilton.

Barron, S	14(1)	Garvan, O	29(2)	Peters, J	4(9)
Bowditch, D	14(7)	Haynes, D	6(13)	Price, L	25
Brekke-Skard, V	2(1)	Horlock, K	13(4)	Proudlock, A	3(6)
Casement, C	2(3)	Juan, J	24(10)	Richards, M	31(7)
Clarke, B	1(1)	Lee, A	14	Sito, C	31(7)
Collins, A	2(1)	Magilton, J	25(9)	Supple, S	21(1)
Currie, D	39(7)	McDonald, D	4(10)	Trotter, L	–(1)
De Vos, J	41	McEveley, J	17(2)	Westlake, I	19(7)
Fish, M	1	Naylor, R	42	Williams, G	12
Forster, N	17(3)	Parkin, S	17(3)	Wilnis, F	33(2)
Fuller, R	3				

League goals (53): Forster 7, Currie 5, Juan 5, Parkin 5, Lee 4, Richards 4, De Vos 3, Garvan 3, Haynes 3, Naylor 3, Fuller 2, Westlake 2, Magilton 1, McDonald 1, McEveley 1, Williams 1, Wilnis 1, Opponents 1.
F.A. Cup goals: None. **Carling Cup goals:** None.
Average home League attendance: 24,252. **Player of Year:** Fabian Wilnis.

LEEDS UNITED

Kevin Blackwell took Leeds a step nearer a return to the top-flight after the financial nightmare that almost destroyed the club. They qualified comfortably for the play-offs, helped along the way by one of the best performances of the season by any team – a 3-0 deficit at Southampton transformed into a 4-3 win in the final 20 minutes. Form in the run-in, however, was poor, with one win in ten and a worrying shortage of goals. Red cards for Richard Cresswell and Stephen Crainey then took the edge off a solid success against Preston in the semi-finals. Both were ruled out of the final, although Blackwell offered no excuses for a poor display, Watford controlling the game from start to finish to win 3-0.

Bakke, E	7(3)	Graham, D	1(2)	Miller, L	26(2)
Beckford, J	–(5)	Gregan, S	28	Moore, I	2(18)
Bennett, I	4	Griffiths, J	–(2)	Pugh, D	1(11)
Blake, R	31(10)	Harding, D	20	Richardson, F	13(10)
Butler, P	44	Healy, D	24(18)	Ricketts, M	1(3)
Crainey, S	24	Hulse, R	32(7)	Stone, S	1(1)
Cresswell, R	12(4)	Kelly, G	44	Sullivan, N	42
Derry, S	41	Kilgallon, M	22(3)	Walton, S	3(1)
Douglas, J	32(8)	Lewis, E	42(1)	Wright, J	3
Einarsson, G	6(4)				

Play-offs – appearances: Derry 3, Gregan 3, Hulse 3, Kelly 3, Kilgallon 3, Lewis 3, Miller 3, Sullivan 3, Crainey 2, Douglas 2, Richardson 2, Bakke 1(1), Healy 1(1), Butler 1, Blake –(2), Cresswell –(2), Stone –(2).

League goals (57): Healy 12, Hulse 12, Blake 11, Cresswell 5, Douglas 5, Lewis 5, Butler 3, Kilgallon 1, Miller 1, Richardson 1, Opponents 1. **Play-offs – goals (3):** Hulse 1, Lewis 1, Richardson 1.
F.A. Cup goals (4): Healy 2, Hulse 1, Kelly 1. **Carling Cup goals (4):** Cresswell 2, Richardson 1, Ricketts 1.
Average home League attendance: 22,354.

LEICESTER CITY

A stirring F.A. Cup third round comeback against Tottenham, which turned a 2-0 deficit into a 3-2 victory, did not disguise Leicester's failings in the Championship. They came to a head when defeat by Plymouth left Craig Levein's side third from bottom after one win in 16 games. Levein paid the price and his assistant Rob Kelly was installed as caretaker. The transformation in results was immediate. Kelly's stay was extended until the end of the season. Then, with survival ensured, the manager's job on a permanent basis. By the end of the season, Leicester had netted 28 points from his 16 games in charge and moved up six places in the table.

Brevett, R ....–(1)	Henderson, P ....14(1)	Smith, R ....10(7)
Connolly, D 5	Hughes, S ....28(6)	Stearman, R ....31(3)
Douglas, R 32	Hume, I ....28(9)	Sylla, M ....24(4)
Dublin, D ....15(6)	Johansson, N 39	Tiatto, D ....11(7)
Fryatt, M ....18(1)	Kisnorbo, P ....36(1)	Welsh, A ....4(6)
Gerrbrand, P ....14(3)	Maybury, A 40	Wesolowski, J ....3(2)
Gilbert, P ....4(1)	McCarthy, P ....37(1)	Wilcox, J ....3(3)
Gudjonsson, J ....40(2)	O'Grady, C ....–(13)	Williams, G ....26(5)
Hamill, J ....7(5)	Sheehan, A 2	De Vries, M ....20(9)
Hammond, E ....15(18)		

League goals (51): Hume 9, Gudjonsson 8, Fryatt 6, De Vries 6, Connolly 4, Hammond 3, Hughes 3, Stearman 3, McCarthy 2, Kisnorbo 2, Maybury 1, O'Grady 1, Smith 1, Tiatto 1, Welsh 1, Williams 1.
F.A. Cup goals (3): Hammond 1, Hughes 1, De Vries 1. **Carling Cup goals (7):** De Vries 2, Gudjonsson 1, Hamill I, Johansson 1, Stearman 1, Williams 1.
Average home League attendance: 22,233. **Player of Year:** Joey Gudjonsson.

LUTON TOWN

Mike Newell, one of the game's brightest young managers, took his promoted side into the upper reaches of the table against all the odds. A 2-1 away win over Crystal Palace on the opening day was followed by victory over Southampton, immediately dispelling any worries of an inferiority complex. Indeed, for much of the first half of the season, Luton's free-flowing football was rewarded by a place in the top six. They were unable to maintain that momentum, although a 3-2 win over Reading – the first defeat for the champions-elect in 34 matches – reminded everyone of their ability. Steve Howard was the club's leading scorer for the fifth successive year.

Andrew, C ....–(1)	Davis, J ....17(4)	Morgan, D ....25(11)
Barnett, L ....12(8)	Edwards, C ....38(4)	Nicholls, K ....31(1)
Bell, D ....2(7)	Feeney, W ....29(13)	Perrett, R ....9(2)
Beresford, M 41	Foley, K ....35(3)	Robinson, S 26
Brill, D 5	Heikkinen, M ....38(1)	Showunmi, E ....15(26)
Brkovic, A ....39(3)	Holmes, P ....16(7)	Stevens, D ....–(1)
Coyne, C ....28(2)	Howard, S ....40(3)	Underwood, P ....28(1)
Davies, C 6	Keane, K ....5(5)	Vine, R ....21(10)

League goals (66): Howard 14, Vine 10, Brkovic 8, Feeney 6, Morgan 6, Nicholls 5, Coyne 2, Edwards 2, Heikkinen 2, Holmes 2, Robinson 2, Andrew 1, Davies 1, Keane 1, Showunmi 1, Opponents 3.
F.A. Cup goals (3): Howard 1, Nicholls 1, Robinson 1. **Carling Cup goals (3):** Coyne 1, Feeney 1, Opponents 1.

Average home League attendance: 9,139. **Player of Year:** Marcus Heikkinen.

MILLWALL

From the moment Steve Claridge was sacked before the start of the campaign after 36 days, there seemed an inevitability about the outcome of Millwall's season. Two more managers, Colin Lee and David Tuttle, came and went, leaving a fourth in caretaker Alan McLeary to preside over the last rites. With 12 red cards – three of them in one match at Burnley for Andy Marshall, Jody Morris and Ben May – accompanying relegation, it was a wretched time in every respect. An unlikely 2-0 win at Watford, offered a glimmer of hope, but it was immediately extinguished by a home defeat by Brighton. Nigel Spackman, formerly manager of Barnsley and Sheffield United, has the job of picking up the pieces.

Asaba, C	17(4)	Healy, J	–(1)	Phillips, M	19(3)
Braniff, K	9(6)	Hendry, W	2(1)	Pooley, D	–(1)
Cameron, C	5	Hutchison, D	7(4)	Powel, B	8(4)
Cogan, B	6(8)	Ifil, P	16	Robinson, P	29(3)
Craig, T	26(2)	Igoe, S	3(2)	Robinson, T	–(1)
Doyle, C	14	Jones, P	3	Serioux, A	2(3)
Dunne, A	40	Lawrence, M	30(1)	Simpson, J	8(5)
Dyer, B	9(1)	Livermore, D	41	Vincent, J	18(1)
Dyer, L	2(4)	Marshall, A	29	Whitbread, Z	25
Elliott, M	33(6)	May, B	24(15)	Williams, A	12
Fangueiro, C	1(8)	Morris, J	24	Williams, M	8(14)
Hayles, B	21(2)	Peeters, B	–(2)	Wright, J	15

League goals (35): May 10, Hayles 4, Williams 4, Asaba 3, Dyer, B 2, Elliott 2, Hutchison 2, Livermore 2, Wright 2, Powel 1, Simpson 1, Williams, A 1, Opponents 1.
F.A. Cup goals (1): Williams, M 1. **Carling Cup goals (9):** Dunne 2, Asaba 1, Elliott 1, Fangueiro 1, Hayles 1, Livermore 1, May 1, Robinson 1.
Average home League attendance: 9,529. **Player of Year:** David Livermore.

NORWICH CITY

Relegated Norwich were offered the chance of a flying start to the season by three successive home games, the fixture at Coventry being reversed because of unfinished work on the new Ricoh Arena. Instead, all three were drawn, there was no victory until the seventh time of asking and however much Nigel Worthington chopped and changed his side, they fell short of the quality required for an immediate return to the Premiership. Five successive victories at the end of 2005 provided some impetus, ahead of the sale of Dean Ashton to West Ham for a club record £7.25m. But then defeats in quick succession by Preston, Watford, Reading and, most painfully, Ipswich at Carrow Road, exposed Norwich's limitations.

Ashton, D	28	Green, R	42	Marney, D	12(1)
Brennan, J	12(6)	Henderson, I	8(16)	McKenzie, L	11(9)
Charlton, S	17(4)	Huckerby, D	39(4)	McVeigh, P	22(14)
Colin, J	24(1)	Hughes, A	35(1)	Rehman, Z	5
Davenport, C	14(1)	Jarrett, J	6(5)	Robinson, C	18(4)
Doherty, G	39(3)	Jarvis, Rossi	–(3)	Safri, Y	25(5)
Drury, A	39	Jarvis, Ryan	1(3)	Shackell, J	16(1)
Earnshaw, R	13(2)	Johansson, J	6(6)	Spillane, M	2
Etuhu, D	15(4)	Lisbie, K	4(2)	Thorne, P	11(10)
Fleming, C	31(5)	Louis-Jean, M	2	Wright, D	5
Gallacher, P	4				

League goals (56): Ashton 10, Earnshaw 8, Huckerby 8, McVeigh 7, McKenzie 4, Johansson 3, Hughes 2, Charlton 1, Davenport 1, Doherty 1, Fleming 1, Henderson 1, Lisbie 1, Jarvis, Ryan 1, Safri 1, Thorne 1, Opponents 5.

F.A. Cup goals (1): McVeigh 1. **Carling Cup goals (4):** Ashton 1, Huckerby 1, McKenzie 1, Opponents 1.
Average home League attendance: 24,952. **Player of Year:** Gary Doherty.

PLYMOUTH ARGYLE

Bobby Williamson became the season's first managerial casualty when four successive defeats followed a bright start in which four points were gained against two teams who would go on to promotion – Reading and Watford. He was replaced by Tony Pulis, sacked by Stoke during the summer. Despite a lack of goals, Plymouth failed to score in 21 matches, Pulis secured an improvement of three places on the previous campaign's 17th place finish. That came after a 2-1 victory over Ipswich on the final day, with the winner from veteran Micky Evans on his last appearance at Home Park. When Pulis returned to Stoke, the club replaced him with the former Queens Park Rangers manager Ian Holloway.

Aljofree, H .... 36(1)	Doumbe, M 43	Norris, D .... 44(1)
Barness, A .... 33(3)	Evans, M .... 36(9)	Pericard, V .... 14(1)
Brevett, R .... 12(1)	Gudjonsson, B .... 6(4)	Pulis, A .... –(5)
Buzsaky, A .... 16(18)	Hodges, L .... 12(1)	Reid, R .... –(1)
Capaldi, T .... 38(3)	Jarrett, J 7	Taylor, S .... 8(10)
Chadwick, N .... 26(11)	Larrieu, R 45	Ward, E .... 15(1)
Clarke, L 5	Lasley, K .... –(5)	West, T 4
Connolly, P .... 27(4)	McCormick, L 1	Wotton, P 45
Derbyshire, M .... 2(10)	Mendes, N 2	Zebroski, C .... –(4)
Djordjic, B .... 9(13)	Nalis, L 20	

League goals (39): Wotton 8, Chadwick 5, Buzsaky 4, Evans 4, Pericard 4, Capaldi 3, Norris 2, Aljofree 1, Djordjic 1, Doumbe 1, Nalis 1, Taylor 1, Ward 1, Opponents 3.
F.A. Cup goals: None. **Carling Cup goals (3):** Buzsaky 1, Taylor 1, Wotton 1.
Average home League attendance: 13,776. **Player of Year:** David Norris.

PRESTON NORTH END

The lights went out on Preston's chances of promotion – in more ways than one. Deepdale was hit by a power failure at half-time of the play-off semi-final against Leeds and there was more gloom for the home side after a delay of 25 minutes. They lost 2-0, having gone into the game in a good position on the back of a 1-1 draw in the first leg at Elland Road. Following defeat by West Ham in the 2005 final, it was another disappointing end to the season, particularly as they entered the knock-out phase as the form team. Preston overcame injury problems to win six of their last seven matches, including a 2-0 success against Leeds on the last day of the regular campaign. The departure of Billy Davies for Derby dealt the club another blow, the manager being replaced by Carlisle's Paul Simpson.

Agyemang, P .... 19(23)	Jarrett, J .... 8(2)	Nowland, A .... 9(4)
Alexander, G .... 39(1)	Johnson, J .... 2(1)	Nugent, D .... 27(5)
Anyinsah, J .... –(3)	Jones, D .... 21(3)	O'Neil, B .... 22(3)
Cresswell, R 3	Lucketti, C .... 23(5)	Ormerod, B .... 13(2)
Davidson, C .... 26(1)	Mawene, Y .... 26(4)	Sedgwick, C .... 39(7)
Davis, C .... 37(3)	McKenna, P .... 40(1)	Stewart, M 4
Dichio, D .... 18(15)	Mears, T .... 27(5)	Stock, B .... 4(2)
Etuhu, D .... 6(7)	Nash, C 46	Whaley, S .... 7(9)
Hibbert, D .... –(10)	Neal, L .... 13(11)	Wilson, K .... 3(3)
Hill, M .... 24(2)		

Play-offs – appearances: Alexander 2, Davis 2, Dichio 2, Mawene 2, McKenna 2, Mears 2, Nash 2, Nugent 2, O'Neil 2, Ormerod 2, Jarrett 1, Stewart 1, Agyemang–(2), Whaley –(2), Sedgwick –(1).

League goals (59): Nugent 10, Agyemang 6, Davidson 4, Ormerod 4, Sedgwick 4, Alexander 3, Davis 3, Jones 3, Nowland 3, Whaley 3, Etuhu 2, McKenna 2, Mears 2, Neal 2, Jarrett 1, Johnson 1, Lucketti 1, Mawene 1, O'Neil 1, Stock 1, Opponents 2.
Play-offs – goals (1): Nugent 1.
F.A. Cup goals (5): Dichio 2, Alexander 1, O'Neil 1, Sedgwick 1. **Carling Cup goals (2):** Alexander 1, Dichio 1.
Average home League attendance: 14,619. **Player of Year:** Claude Davis.

QUEENS PARK RANGERS

Troubled times at Loftus Road, with Ian Holloway 's five years as manager coming to an end and Rangers finishing one place above the relegation zone. Holloway was suspended by the club in early February after speculation linking him with the vacant job at Leicester. He eventually settled with the club in the summer and caretaker Gary Waddock was confirmad as his sucessor. Waddock had started with two wins out of three and his team in mid-table. But Rangers failed to win any of their final 11 matches and although not in danger of going down, were glad to see the back of the season.

Ainsworth, G .... 33(10)	Dyer, L 15	Moore, S .... 11(14)
Baidoo, S .... 6(9)	Evatt, I .... 21(6)	Nygaard, M .... 20(7)
Bailey, S 5	Furlong, P .... 31(6)	Rose, M 15
Barnes, P 1	Gallen, K 18	Rowlands, M .... 12(2)
Bean, M .... 4(5)	Hislop, M 1	Royce, S 30
Bignot, M 44	Jones, P 14	Santos, G .... 25(6)
Bircham, M .... 24(2)	Jones, R .... –(2)	Shimmin, D .... 1(1)
Brown, A .... 1(1)	Kus, M 3	Shittu, D 45
Clarke, L 1	Langley, R .... 22(11)	Sturridge, D .... 6(3)
Cole, J .... 1(2)	Lomas, S .... 18(3)	Taylor, A .... 1(2)
Cook, L .... 34(6)	Lowe, K 1	Ukah, U .... –(1)
Doherty, T .... 14(1)	Milanese, M .... 22(4)	Youssouf, S .... 2(4)
Donnelly, S .... 3(5)	Miller, A 1	

League goals (50): Ainsworth 9, Nygaard 9, Furlong 7, Cook 4, Gallen 4, Shittu 4, Langley 3, Baidoo 2, Bircham 2, Moore 2, Rowlands 2, Santos 1, Opponents 1.
F.A. Cup goals: None. **Carling Cup goals:** None.
Average home League attendance: 13,440. **Player of Year:** Danny Shittu.

READING

Reading romped into the Premiership as champions with a record-breaking points total which also brought Steve Coppell the League Managers' Association Manager of the Year award. His team lost at home to Plymouth on the opening day, but did not taste defeat again for another six months, winning 25 Championship games and drawing eight in that period before falling to Luton. They went on to accumulate 106 points, one more than Sunderland's total in 1999, and score 99 goals with a prolific strike force of Dave Kitson, Leroy Lita and Republic of Ireland international Kevin Doyle, at £80,000 one of the bargain buys of the season. Coppell, fortunate with injuries, was able to field a settled side for much of the time – eight players making 40 or more appearances – and no team came close to matching their consistency.

Baradji, S .... –(1)	Halls, J 1	Makin, C .... 11(1)
Convey, B 45	Harper, J .... 44(1)	Murty, G 40
Cox, S .... –(2)	Hunt, S 3 (35)	Obinna, E .... –(6)
Dobson, M .... –(1)	Ingimarsson, I 46	Oster, J .... 11(22)
Doyle, K .... 41(4)	Kitson, D .... 27(7)	Shorey, N 40
Golbourne, S .... –(1)	Lita, L .... 22(4)	Sidwell, S .... 29(4)
Gunnarsson, B ..... 19(10)	Little, G .... 34(1)	Sonko, I 46
Hahnemann, M 45	Long, S .... 1(10)	Stack, G 1

League goals (99): Doyle 18, Kitson 18, Lita 11, Sidwell 10, Convey 7, Harper 7, Little 5, Gunnarsson 4, Long 3, Sonko 3, Hunt 2, Ingimarsson 2, Shorey 2, Halls 1, Murty 1, Oster 1, Opponents 4.
F.A. Cup goals (6): Lita 3, Doyle 1, Hunt 1, Long 1. Carling Cup goals (6): Kitson 4, Lita 1, Oster 1.
Average home League attendance: 20,207. Player of Year: Kevin Doyle.

SHEFFIELD UNITED

Neil Warnock dreamed of taking United into the Premiership and after some near misses the Sheffield-born manager finally achieved his goal. Ten wins in the opening 11 matches even suggested they might eventually go up as champions. After that, Reading displayed the greater consistency to move clear at the top. But United, strong, organised and disciplined, continued to do enough to withstand a lean run in February/March when only one win in eight enabled Leeds to close to within four points. Warnock, who along the way had turned down an offer to take charge of Portsmouth before Harry Redknapp's return to Fratton Park, supervised a revival in fortunes which eventually doubled that advantage.

Akinbiyi, A .... 10(5)	Gray, A 1	Nalis, L .... 3(1)
Armstrong, C .... 21(3)	Harley, J 4	Pericard, V .... 3(8)
Bromby, L 35	Horsfield, G .... 1(2)	Quinn, A .... 23(4)
Collins, N 2	Ifill, P .... 28(11)	Shaw, P .... –(1)
Deane, B .... –(2)	Jagielka, P 46	Shipperley, N .... 34(5)
Dyer, B .... 3(2)	Kabba, S .... 21(13)	Short, C .... 20(3)
Flitcroft, G .... 3(3)	Kenny, P 46	Tonge, M .... 23(7)
Forte, J .... –(1)	Kozluk, R .... 21(6)	Unsworth, D .... 33(1)
Francis, S .... –(1)	Lucketti, C .... 2(1)	Webber, D .... 24(11)
Geary, D .... 17(3)	Montgomery, N ...... 34(5)	Wright, A .... 3(3)
Gillespie, K .... 8(22)	Morgan, C .... 37(2)	

League goals (76): Shipperley 11, Webber 10, Ifill 9, Kabba 9, Jagielka 8, Morgan 4, Quinn 4, Unsworth 3, Akinbiyi 3, Tonge 3, Armstrong 2, Pericard 2, Bromby 1, Dyer 1, Gray 1, Montgomery 1, Opponents 3.
F.A. Cup goals (1): Kabba 1. Carling Cup goals (1): Ross 1.
Average home League attendance: 23,650. Player of Year: Phil Jagielka.

SHEFFIELD WEDNESDAY

Manager Paul Sturrock kept his promise to celebrate in a kilt if Wednesday beat the drop, an achievement delivered by a strong finish to the season in difficult circumstances. The Scot's promoted side were in the bottom three at Christmas after failing to score in seven successive matches and were only two points clear of Millwall with eight games remaining. Then, Deon Burton and Marcus Tudgay started contributing vital goals. Back-to-back wins over Preston and Wolves eased the pressure and a 2-0 success at Brighton finally settled the nerves. Wednesday wrapped things up by beating Derby to finish ten points clear of the drop zone.

Adams, S 8	Eagles, C .... 21(4)	O'Brien, B .... 34(10)
Adamson, C 5	Folly, Y 14	Partridge, R .... 6(12)
Agbonlahor, G .... 4(4)	Gilbert, P 17	Peacock, L .... 19(3)
Best, L .... 5(8)	Graham, D .... 19(5)	Proudlock, A .... –(6)
Bischoff, M 4	Heckingbottom, P 4	Rocastle, C .... 14(3)
Brunt, C .... 35(9)	Hills, J .... 26(1)	Ross, M 1
Bullen, L .... 12(16)	Lee, G .... 14(1)	Simek, F .... 42(1)
Burton, D .... 15(2)	Lucas, D 18	Spurr, T 2
Carson, S 9	MacLean, S .... 4(2)	Tudgay, M .... 14(4)
Collins, P 3	McAllister, S .... 1(1)	Weaver, N 14
Corr, B .... 7(9)	McGovern, J-P .... 3(4)	Whelan, G .... 40(3)
Coughlan, G 33	Murphy, D 4	Wood, R .... 27(3)
Diallo, D .... 8(3)		

League goals (39): Brunt 7, Tudgay 5, Coughlan 4, Burton 3, Eagles 3, Best 2, Graham 2, MacLean 2, O'Brien 2, Peacock 2, Lee 1, Simek 1, Whelan 1, Wood 1, Opponents 3.
F.A. Cup goals (2): Heckingbottom 2. **Carling Cup goals (6):** Proudlock 2, Coughlan 1, Graham 1, Partridge 1, Peacock 1.
Average home League attendance: 24,853. **Player of Year:** Graham Couglan.

SOUTHAMPTON

George Burley returned to management after an acrimonious departure from Hearts to restore some stability and deliver a small measure of success to a club facing a second traumatic season after relegation. Burley, who came in when Harry Redknapp returned to Portsmouth, needed a couple of months – and a major change of personnel – to start turning things around. During that time, a run of one goal in seven games, set alarm bells ringing before a 3-0 win over Sheffield Wednesday offered some breathing space. The lack of goals was eventually eased by Ricardo Fuller's return from a loan spell at Ipswich. Fuller scored six times in the final six matches, five of which were won, to lift Southampton to mid-table.

Baird, C .... 16(1)	Higginbotham, D 37	Ostlund, A .... 10(2)
Bale, G 2	Jones, K .... 17(17)	Pahars, M .... 5(3)
Belmadi, D .... 21(1)	Kenton, D .... 12(1)	Potter, D .... 8(2)
Best, L .... 1(2)	Kosowski, K .... 12(6)	Powell, D .... 24(1)
Bialkowski, B 5	Lundekvam, C 34	Prutton, D .... 14(3)
Blackstock, D .... 7(12)	Madsen, P .... 8(1)	Quashie, N 24
Brennan, J .... 13(1)	McCann, N .... 7(4)	Rasiak, G .... 12(1)
Chaplow, R 11	McGoldrick, D 1	Smith, P .... 9(1)
Cranie, M .... 7(4)	Mills, M .... 3(1)	Surman, A .... 11(1)
Delap, R .... 12(4)	Miller, K 7	Svensson, M 7
Dyer, N .... 10(7)	Niemi, A 25	Walcott, T .... 13(8)
Folly, Y 2	Oakley, M 29	Wise, D .... 8(3)
Fuller, R .... 21(9)	Ormerod, B .... 13(5)	Wright, J 13
Hajto, T .... 15(5)		

League goals (49): Fuller 9, Jones 4, Quashie 4, Rasiak 4, Walcott 4, Belmadi 3, Blackstock 3, Higginbotham 3, Madsen 2, Oakley 2, Surman 2, Chaplow 1, Kosowski 1, Lundekvam 1, Ormerod 1, Pahars 1, Powell 1, Wise 1, Opponents 2.
F.A. Cup goals (5): Kenton 1, Jones 1, Prutton 1, Quashie 1, Walcott 1. **Carling Cup goals (3):** Blackstock 1, Dyer 1, Ormerod 1.
Average home League attendance: 23,613. **Player of Year:** Claus Lundekvam.

STOKE CITY

A case of déjà vu at the Britannia Stadium, where a mid-table finish was followed by the departure of the manager. This time it was Johan Boskamp on the way out, leaving to join Standard Liege in Belgium shortly after Stoke's Icelandic owners sold the club back to former chairman Peter Coates. Boskamp bowed out on a high note, a 5-1 win at Brighton highlighted by 19-year-old Adam Rooney's hat-trick. It was the team's tenth away win, a record bettered only by the three promoted clubs, Reading, Sheffield United and Watford. At home it was a different story with 11 defeats, the worst in the division. Tony Pulis returned as manager, a year after being sacked for not signing enough foreign players.

Bangoura, S .... 23(1)	Garret, R .... –(2)	Kopteff, P .... 3(3)
Brammer, D .... 38(2)	Halls, J 13	Paterson, M .... 2(1)
Broomes, M .... 36(1)	Harper, K .... 5(9)	Rooney, A .... 2(3)
Buxton, J .... 25(7)	Hazley, M .... –(1)	Russell, D .... 35(2)
Chadwick, L .... 33(3)	Henry, K .... 11(13)	Sidibe, M .... 37(5)
Dickinson, C .... 4(1)	Hill, C .... 12(1)	Sigurdsson, H ...... 10(13)
Duberry, M 41	Hoefkens, C 44	Simonsen, S 45
Dyer, B .... 2(9)	Junior .... 16(6)	Skoko, J 9
Gallagher, P .... 32(5)	Kolar, M .... 12(2)	Sweeney, P .... 8(9)

113

Taggart, G 3   Wilkinson, A .... 4(2)   De Goey, E .... 1(1)

League goals (54): Gallagher 11, Bangoura 9, Sidibe 6, Rooney 4, Hoefkens 3, Russell 3, Broomes 2, Chadwick 2, Halls 2, Skoko 2, Brammer 1, Buxton 1, Duberry 1, Harper 1, Kolar 1, Sigurdsson 1, Sweeney 1, Taggart 1, Opponents 1.
F.A. Cup goals (3): Chadwick 1, Gallagher 1, Sidibe 1. **Carling Cup goals (1):** Brammer 1.
Average home League attendance: 14,432. **Player of Year:** Carl Hoefkens.

WATFORD

Adrian Boothroyd led Watford into the Premiership, just as he had promised the club's board of directors, with one of the great managerial achievements of the season. His team were among the favourites to go down after a close call a few months earlier, but proved a model of consistency to reach the play-offs. A 3-0 win at Crystal Palace set them up perfectly for the final, where that scoreline was repeated with a nerveless performance against Leeds. Boothroyd's tactical acumen and man-management skills in his first full season in charge brought the best out of a blend of youth and experience. No-one benefited more than Marlon King, transformed from a striker whose career was going nowhere into the Championship's leading marksman.

Agbonlahor, G .... 1(1)	Diagouraga, T 1	Mackay, M .... 35(3)
Bangura, A .... 11(24)	Doyley, L .... 40(4)	Mahon, G .... 35(3)
Benjamin, T 2	Eagles, C .... 16(1)	Mariappa, A .... 1(2)
Blizzard, D .... 9(1)	Fletcher, C 3	McNamee, A .... 26(12)
Bouazza, H .... 3(11)	Foster, B 44	Osborne, J 1
Carlisle, C .... 30(2)	Francis, F .... –(1)	Robinson, T .... –(1)
Chamberlain, A .... 2(1)	Grant, J .... 2(5)	Spring, M .... 36(3)
Chambers, J .... 26(12)	Henderson, D .... 27(3)	Stewart, J .... 29(6)
DeMerit, J .... 27(5)	King, M .... 40(1)	Young, A .... 38(1)
Devlin, P .... 21(2)		

Play-offs – appearances: Chambers 3, DeMerit 3, Foster 3, Doyley 3, King 3, Mackay 3, Mahon 3, Spring 3, Stewart 3, Young 3, Henderson 2(1), Bangura 1(2), Eagles –(1).
League goals (77): King 21, Henderson 14, Young 13, Spring 8, Carlisle 3, Eagles 3, Mackay 3, Mahon 3, DeMerit 2, Devlin 2, Bangura 1, Bouazza 1, McNamee 1, Opponents 2. **Play-offs – goals (6):** DeMerit 1, Henderson 1, King 1, Spring 1, Young 1, Opponents 1.
F.A. Cup goals: None. **Carling Cup goals (5):** Carlisle 2, Blizzard 1, Bouazza 1, Young 1.
Average home League attendance: 15,415. **Player of Year:** Marlon King.

WOLVERHAMPTON WANDERERS

It was a case of back to the drawing board for Glenn Hoddle and further frustration for supporters demanding a return to the Premiership. Once again Wolves came up short because of too many drawn matches, particularly at Molineux where ten teams came away with a point, together with four who claimed all three. Even so, with eight games remaining, they occupied a play-off position after former manager Dave Jones's Cardiff were beaten 2-0. But with everything to play for, Wolves failed to maintain the momentum. They did not win any of the next six, a 3-1 home defeat by Sheffield Wednesday exposing their weaknesses, and finished eight points adrift of a top six spot. Hoddle later resigned after 18 months in the job.

Aliadiere, J .... 12(2)	Gobern, L .... –(1)	Murray, M 1
Anderton, D .... 20(4)	Gyepes, G .... 19(1)	Naylor, L .... 38(2)
Cameron, C .... 20(7)	Huddlestone, T .... 12(1)	Ndah, G .... 6(8)
Clarke, L .... 10(14)	Ince, P .... 15(3)	Oakes, M .... 16(1)
Cort, C .... 24(7)	Jones, D 1	Olofinjana, S .... 6(7)
Craddock, J .... 17(1)	Kennedy, M .... 37(3)	Postma, S 29
Davies, M .... 12(8)	Lescott, J 46	Ricketts, R .... 17(8)
Edwards, R .... 39(3)	Lowe, K 3	Rosa, D .... 6(3)
Frankowski, T .... 12(4)	McNamara, J .... 9(1)	Ross, M .... 13(5)
Ganea, I .... 11(7)	Miller, K .... 33(2)	Seol, K .... 22(10)

League goals (50): Cort 11, Miller 10, Cameron 4, Ganea 4, Seol 4, Ince 3, Aliadiere 2, Kennedy 2, Rosa 2, Anderton 1, Clarke 1, Davies 1, Huddlestone 1, Lescott 1, Naylor 1, Ndah 1, Opponents 1.
F.A. Cup goals (1): Clarke 1. **Carling Cup goals (6):** Cameron 2, Miller 2, Anderton 1, Ganea 1.
Average home League attendance: 23,624. **Player of Year:** Kenny Miller

COCA-COLA LEAGUE ONE

BARNSLEY

Andy Ritchie, one-time Manchester United and Leeds United striker, took Barnsley into the Championship in his first full season as manager. His team held their nerve in a tense battle for the play-off places, winning at Walsall on the last day of the season to confirm fifth place. A 1-0 home defeat by Huddersfield in the semi-finals was reversed by goals from Paul Hayes (pen), Paul Reid and Danny Nardiello in the return game. Then, after Hayes and Nardiello were again on the mark against Swansea in the final, Nicky Colgan gave them victory in a penalty shoot-out by saving from Alan Tate.

Austin, N 38	Heckingbottom, P ... 17(1)	Reid, P .... 31(2)
Burns, J .... 32(1)	Howard, B .... 25(6)	Richards, M .... 29(9)
Carbon, M .... 21(3)	Jarman, N .... –(9)	Shuker, C .... 45(1)
Colgan, N 43	Kay, A .... 33(3)	Tonge, D .... 14(10)
Conlon, B .... 8(3)	Kell, R .... –(2)	Vaughan, A .... –(1)
Devaney, M .... 34(4)	Laight, R .... –(1)	Watt, S 3
Flinders, S 30	McParland, A .... –(8)	Williams, R .... 13(9)
Hassell, B .... 25(3)	McPhail, S .... 30(4)	Wright, T .... 7(10)
Hayes, P .... 38(7)	Nardiello, D .... 11(23)	Wroe, N .... 6(6)

Play-offs – appearances: Colgan 3, Devaney 3, Hassell 3, Heckingbottom 3, Howard 3, Kay 3, McPhail 3, Nardiello 3, Reid 3, Richards 3, Hayes 2, Shuker 1(2), Wright –(2), Tonge –(1).
League goals (62): Richards 12, Shuker 10, Devaney 6, Hayes 6, Howard 5, Nardiello 5, Burns 3, Hassell 2, McPhail 2, Williams 2, Carbon 1, Conlon 1, Heckingbottom 1, Kay 1, Watt 1, Wright 1, Opponents 3. **Play-offs – goals (5):** Hayes 2 Nardiello 2, Reid 1.
F.A. Cup goals (8): Hayes 5, Devaney 2, Kell 1. **Carling Cup goals (2):** Burns 2.
League Trophy goals (2): Nardiello 1, Opponents 1.
Average home League attendance: 9,045. **Player of Year:** Nick Colgan.

BLACKPOOL

Simon Grayson made a flying start as manager when Colin Hendry was sacked in mid-November after one victory in nine, along with a 4-1 F.A. Cup defeat by Doncaster. Blackpool beat Scunthorpe 5-2 and it was their home form at the end of the season that proved decisive when they were one of several teams caught up in the struggle to beat the drop. A run of seven unbeaten matches at Bloomfield Road was rounded off with the point needed for survival, leading scorer Keigan Parker scoring two fine goals against Gillingham.

Armstrong, C 5	Fox, D .... 4(3)	Morris, I .... 21(9)
Bean, M 17	Gobern, L .... 4(4)	Murphy, J .... 28(6)
Blinkhorn, M .... 4(12)	Gordon, D 1	Parker, K .... 36(4)
Burns, J .... 4(2)	Grayson, S .... 8(4)	Pogliacomi, L 15
Butler, T .... 19(5)	Harkins, G 4	Prendergast, R .... 19(5)
Clarke, P 46	Jones, L 31	Taylor, A 3
Coid, D 13	Joseph, M .... 15(1)	Taylor, S .... 3(1)
Donnelly, C .... 17(7)	Kay, M .... –(1)	Southern, K .... 36(6)
Doolan, J .... 15(4)	Kuqi, N .... 1(3)	Stockley, S .... 3(4)
Edge, L .... –(1)	Lasley, K .... 4(4)	Vernon, S .... 10(7)
Edwards, R .... 28(4)	McGregor, M .... 16(5)	Warrender, D .... 13(2)

Wilcox, J 26   Williams, G .... 6(3)   Wright, T .... 10(3)
Wiles, S .... 14(13)   Wood, N 7

League goals (56): Parker 12, Murphy 8, Clarke 6, Wright 6, Morris 3, Wiles 3, Williams 3, Blinkhorn 2, Donnelly 2, Southern 2, Bean 1, Burns 1, Butler 1, Fox 1, Gobern 1, Harkins 1, Vernon 1, Opponents 2.
F.A. Cup goals (1): Clarke 1. **Carling Cup goals (3):** Clarke 1, Grayson 1, Parker 1.
League Trophy goals (5): Blinkhorn 1, Harkins 1, McGregor 1, Southern 1, Vernon 1.
Average home League attendance: 5,819. **Player of Year:** Peter Clarke.

BOURNEMOUTH

James Hayter went one better than his 19 league goals in the previous season, but for his team there was a drop of nine places to 17th. Another disappointment was a home defeat by Tamworth in the F.A. Cup. There was an improvement, however, in the club's financial situation with the sale and lease back of the Fitness First Stadium. Hayter's hat-trick against Blackpool lifted Bournemouth to the fringes of a play-off place at the mid-way point. After that, only three more victories were forthcoming, leading to a nervy final few weeks in which they were among several teams looking over their shoulder.

Broadhurst, K .... 3(4)   Griffiths, A .... 6(1)   Purches, S .... 22(4)
Brown, A .... 3(1)   Hart, C .... 32(7)   Rix, B .... 7(4)
Browning, M .... 41(1)   Hayter, J 46   Rodrigues, D .... 13(16)
Cooke, S .... 18(13)   Howe, E .... 16(4)   Rowe, J .... –(2)
Cooper, S .... 33(2)   Hudson, K .... –(1)   Spicer, J 4
Coutts, J .... –(11)   Keene, J .... 6(5)   Stewart, G 42
Fletcher, S .... 21(6)   Maher, S .... 4(2)   Stock, B 26
Foley, S .... 33(2)   Moss, N 4   Surman, A 24
Fordyce, D 3   O'Connor, J .... 37(2)   Tindall, J .... 5(6)
Gowling, J .... 11(2)   Pitman, B .... 4(15)   Young, N 42

League goals (49): Hayter 20, Surman 6, Foley 5, Fletcher 4, Rodrigues 3, Stock 3, Cooke 2, Keene 2, Griffiths 1, O'Connor 1, Pitman 1, Opponents 1.
F.A. Cup goals (1): Stock 1. **Carling Cup goals:** None. **League Trophy goals (4):** Keene 2, Cooke 1, Pitman 1.
Average home League attendance: 6,459. **Player of Year:** James Hayter.

BRADFORD CITY

Dean Windass continued to defy advancing years for another 20-goal season, highlighted by hat-tricks against Scunthorpe and, in the Carling Cup, against Rochdale. The league treble came on his 37th birthday when he returned from a five-match ban imposed by the F.A. for comments made to referee Darren Drysdale after the home game against Brentford. Too many home defeats held Bradford back in the previous campaign. This time an identical 11th place finish was largely the result of 19 drawn matches, nine of them at home.

Bentham, C .... 6(1)   Emanuel, L .... 23(14)   Schumacher, S ..... 24(6)
Bower, M 45   Holloway, D .... 21(3)   Stewart, D .... 20(3)
Bridge-Wilkinson, M 36   Howarth, R .... 10(1)   Swift, J .... 4(1)
Brown, J .... 2(11)   Kearney, J .... 11(4)   Symes, M .... 1(2)
Cadamarteri, D ..... 25(14)   Morrison, O .... 7(3)   Taylor, A 24
Claridge, S .... 14(12)   Muirhead, B .... 26(6)   Wetherall, D 46
Colbeck, J .... 5(6)   Penford, T .... 9(1)   Wilbraham, A 5
Cooke, A .... 10(7)   Petta, B .... 23(4)   Windass, D 40
Crooks, L .... 14(1)   Ricketts, D 36   Wright, J .... –(1)
Edghill, R 19

League goals (51): Windass 16, Bridge-Wilkinson 5, Claridge 5, Wetherall 5, Petta 4, Bower 2, Cadamarteri 2, Emanuel 2, Brown 1, Cooke 1, Edghill 1, Kearney 1, Muirhead 1, Schumacher 1, Stewart 1, Symes 1, Wilbraham 1, Opponents 1.
F.A. Cup goals (6): Bower 1, Cooke 1, Crooks 1, Edghill 1, Wetherall 1, Windass 1.

Carling Cup goals (6): Windass 3, Bridge-Wilkinson 1, Cadamarteri 1, Schumacher 1.
League Trophy goals (2): Brown 2.
Average home League attendance: 8,264. **Player of Year:** David Wetherall.

BRENTFORD

Martin Allen's side came unstuck after looking promotion material for much of the season. They were edged out of the second automatic place by Colchester, whose form during the run-in proved more productive. Despite the loss of leading scorer Lloyd Owusu, Brentford took a 1-1 scoreline to Griffin Park for the second leg of the play-off semi-final against Swansea. But they conceded two goals in the opening 15 minutes to Leon Knight and a failure to reply led to speculation about Allen's future. That outcome left a 2-1 F.A. Cup win over Sunderland as the season's high point, Dudley Campbell scoring both goals to earn himself a £500,000 move to Birmingham. Allen resigned and was replaced by former Torquay manager Leroy Rosenior.

Bankole, A 2	Lewis, J .... 11(3)	Rankin, I .... 31(6)
Brooker, P .... 32(4)	Mousinho, J .... 3(4)	Rhodes, A .... 5(12)
Campbell, D .... 13(10)	Nelson, S .... 44(1)	Skulason, O 2
Charles, D .... –(2)	Newman, R .... 29(1)	Smith, J 7
Dobson, M .... 3(3)	O'Connor, K 30	Sodje, S 43
Fitzgerald, S .... 3(8)	Osborne, K 1	Tabb, J 42
Frampton, A 36	Owusu, L .... 39(3)	Tillen, S .... 20(13)
Gayle, M .... 16(8)	Peters, R .... 1(9)	Turner, M 46
Hutchinson, E ...... 17(10)	Pratley, D .... 25(7)	Willock, C .... 5(8)
Keenan, J .... –(3)		

Play-offs – appearances: Frampton 2, Nelson 2, Newman 2, O'Connor 2, Pratley 2, Rankin 2, Smith 2, Tabb 2, Turner 2, Tillen 1(1), Gayle 1, Rankin 1, Sodje 1, Brooker –(2), Willock –(1).
League goals (72): Owusu 12, Campbell 9, O'Connor 7, Rankin 7, Tabb 6, Sodje 5, Brooker 4, Pratley 4, Frampton 3, Newman 3, Gayle 3, Hutchinson 2, Turner 2, Fitzgerald 1, Peters 1, Rhodes 1, Willock 1, Opponents 2. **Play-offs – goals (1):** Tabb 1.
F.A. Cup goals (9): Campbell 3, Owusu 2, Rankin 2, O'Connor 1, Sodje 1. **Carling Cup goals:** None. **League Trophy goals (1):** Fitzgerald 1.
Average home League attendance: 6,774. **Player of Year:** Jay Tabb.

BRISTOL CITY

Gary Johnson must have wondered what he had let himself when City's sliding fortunes, which had forced Brian Tinnion's resignation after a 7-1 defeat by Swansea, showed no sign of being arrested. The former Yeovil manager, attracted by the greater potential of the Ashton Gate club, saw them hit rock bottom in early December after seven straight losses. Then, with the fans beginning to lose faith, he engineered a complete transformation. It netted 42 points in the second half of the season, an achievement matched only by Southend on their way to the title, and left City as one of the few teams regretting the end of the season.

Abbey, N .... –(1)	Green, A .... 1(1)	Russell, A .... 21(6)
Andrew, C .... 1(2)	Heywood, M .... 22(2)	Sankofa, O 8
Basso, A 29	Joseph, M 3	Savage, B .... 15(8)
Bridges, M .... 4(7)	Keogh, R .... 4(6)	Skuse, C .... 29(9)
Brooker, S .... 34(3)	Madjo, G .... 1(4)	Smith, G .... 4(7)
Brown, S .... 23(6)	McCammon, M .... 8(3)	Smith, J .... 4(2)
Carey, L 38	Murray, S .... 31(6)	Stewart, M .... 16(11)
Cotterill, D .... 37(8)	Noble, D .... 23(1)	Wilkshire, L ...... 20(16)
Fontaine, L .... 14(1)	Orr, B .... 35(3)	Williams, J .... –(1)
Fortune, C .... 4(2)	Partridge, D 11	Woodman, C .... 36(1)
Gillespie, S .... 3(1)	Phillips, L .... 17(2)	Youga, K 4
Golbourne, S .... 4(1)	Quinn, J .... 2(1)	

League goals (66): Brooker 16, Murray 10, Cotterill 7, Stewart 5, Wilkshire 5, McCammon 4, Russell 4, Carey 3, Heywood 2, Skuse 2, Brown 1, Gillespie 1, Keogh 1, Noble 1, Orr 1, Quinn 1, Savage 1, Woodman 1. **F.A. Cup goals:** None. **Carling Cup goals (2):** Bridges 1, Golbourne 1. **League Trophy goals (2):** Madjo 1, Murray 1.
Average home League attendance: 11,725. **Player of Year:** Steve Brooker.

CHESTERFIELD

Chesterfield were grateful to have stored up enough points to offset a slump in the final third of the season. Otherwise, a return of eight points from 15 matches would have had serious consequences. The slide, culminating in a 4-0 home defeat by Swansea, pushed them down to 16th, along with a share of the worst goals against record – 73 – in the division. Paul Hall's 15 goals at the other end included a hat-trick against Bristol City which helped lift the team to within one point of a play-off place at the turn of the year.

Allison, W .... 26(6)	Foyle, A .... –(1)	Muggleton, C 3
Allott, M 43	Hall, P .... 44(1)	N'Toya, T .... 1(3)
Bailey, A .... 17(1)	Hazell, R .... 30(3)	Nicholson, S .... 24(1)
Beckwith, R 2	Heath, C .... 1(3)	Niven, D 42
Blatherwick, S .... 29(1)	Hurst, K .... 30(7)	O'Hara, C 19
Clingan, S .... 14(7)	Jackson, ... –(2)	O'Hare, A .... 15(7)
Davies, G .... 13(7)	Kovacs, J 9	Picken, P 32
De Bolla, M .... 2(2)	Lancaster, S .... –(1)	Roche, B 41
Downes, A .... 20(2)	Larkin, C .... 31(10)	Smith, A .... 10(16)
Folan, C .... 8(19)		

League goals (63): Hall 15, Allison 11, Larkin 7, Nicholson 5, Niven 5, O'Hara 5, Hurst 4, Allott 3, Smith 3, Blatherwick 2, Clingan 1, De Bolla 1, Picken 1.
F.A. Cup goals (1): Hurst 1. **Carling Cup goals (2):** Hurst 1, Niven 1. **League Trophy goals:** None.
Average home League attendance: 4,772. **Player of Year:** Mark Allott.

COLCHESTER UNITED

Phil Parkinson's unfancied side made light of a stuttering start to the season to reach English football's second tier for the first time in the club's 69-year history. They also savoured a memorable F.A. Cup run, knocking out Sheffield United and Derby and then taking the lead in a fifth round tie at Stamford Bridge before Joe Cole scored two late goals to see Chelsea through. Colchester, who had soared with a run of 40 points in 15 matches, lost some of their focus before and after that glamour tie. But Parkinson eventually put them back on track for a Essex promotion double with champions Southend which, inevitably, brought him to the attention of some bigger clubs and led to his departure for Hull.

Baldwin, P .... 20(5)	Elokobi, G .... 10(2)	King, R .... –(3)
Brown, W 38	Garcia, R .... 9(13)	Richards, G .... 12(3)
Campbell-Ryce, J ..... 1(3)	Gerken, D .... 5(2)	Stockley, S .... 21(5)
Chilvers, L .... 33(1)	Guy, J .... –(2)	Thorpe, T .... 5(9)
Clarke, B .... 2(4)	Halford, G 45	Vernon, S .... 4(3)
Cureton, J .... 7(1)	Howell, D .... 1(3)	Watson, K .... 43(1)
Danns, N .... 38(3)	Hunt, S .... –(2)	White, J .... 32(3)
Davison, A 41	Iwelumo, C 46	Williams, G .... 6(11)
Duguid, K .... 26(9)	Izzet, K .... 19(14)	Yeates, M .... 42(2)

League goals (58): Iwelumo 17, Danns 8, Halford 7, Garcia 5, Yeates 5, Cureton 4, Brown 2, Chilvers 2, Elokobi 2, Stockley 1, Vernon 1, Williams 1, Opponents 4.
F.A. Cup goals (17): Danns 5, Cureton 3, Iwelumo 2, Brown 1, Garcia 1, Halford 1, Watson 1, Williams 1, Yeates 1, Opponents 1. **Carling Cup goals:** None. **League Trophy goals (7):** Danns 3, Garcia 2, Duguid 1, Elokobi 1.
Average home League attendance: 3,969. **Player of Year:** Wayne Brown.

DONCASTER ROVERS

A sparkling Carling Cup run and healthy league position enabled Doncaster to look back on a good season. They knocked out Manchester City and Aston Villa on the way to a fifth round tie against Arsenal, who needed Gilberto Silva's equaliser in stoppage-time of injury-time, then victory in a penalty shoot-out to go through. Slow-starting Rovers were bottom after eight league matches, but drew confidence from a narrow defeat at Colchester to begin a steady climb. They finished strongly to reach eighth, while putting pressure on Swansea for the final play-off place, which the Welsh side confirmed with victory in their last game.

Albrighton, M 16	Horlock, K 13	Oji, S .... 1(3)
Armstrong, A .... 1(5)	Hughes, A .... 4(2)	Predic, U .... 3(3)
Blayney, A 16	Lee, G 20	Price, J 11
Budtz, J 20	Marples, S .... 12(3)	Ravenhill, R .... 23(4)
Coppinger, J .... 32(4)	McCormack, R ...... 12(7)	Roberts, N .... 17(13)
Fenton, N .... 21(4)	McDaid, S 35	Roberts, S .... 23(4)
Forte, J .... 9(4)	McGuire, P 11	Ryan, T 7
Fortune-West, L ... 16(11)	McIndoe, M .... 29(4)	Seremet, D 1
Foster, S 17	McSporran, J 2	Thornton, S .... 23(6)
Green, P .... 23(11)	Mulligan, D .... 22(10)	Timlin, M 3
Griffiths, A 4	Nelthorpe, C 1	Warrington, A 9
Guy, L .... 18(13)	Offiong, R .... 2(3)	Wheater, D 7
Heffernan, P .... 22(4)		

League goals (55): McIndoe 8, Heffernan 7, Coppinger 5, McCormack 5, Forte 4, Price 4, Green 3, Guy 3, Ravenhill 3, Fenton 2, Fortune-West 2, Green 2, Mulligan 2, Roberts, N 2, Thornton 2, Lee 1, Roberts, S 1, Wheater 1.
F.A. Cup goals (7): Heffernan 3, McIndoe 2, Mulligan 2. **Carling Cup goals (9):** Heffernan 3, McIndoe 3, Green 1, Hughes 1,Thornton 1. **League Trophy goals (7):** Fortune-West 2, Guy 2, Offiong 1, Opponents 2.
Average home League attendance: 6,139. **Player of Year:** Sean McDaid.

GILLINGHAM

Ronnie Jepson offered his Gillingham players a choice after they slipped into the bottom four after a 6-0 defeat by Bristol City – feel sorry for yourselves or come out fighting. They chose the latter course of action and won the next six matches to remove the fear of a second successive relegation. What also pleased the manager, who took over when Neale Cooper resigned in mid-November, was that four of those victories came against teams aiming for promotion – Brentford, Swansea, Huddersfield and Southend. With a better finish to the season, they would have finished in the top half instead of just below.

Ashikodi, M .... –(4)	Crofts, A 45	Mulligan, G .... 10(3)
Black, T 17	Flynn, M .... 30(6)	Pouton, A .... 19(4)
Brown, J 39	Fobi-Edusei, A ...... 5(1)	Rose, R .... 13(1)
Bullock, T 6	Grant, G .... 1(9)	Sancho, B .... 16(3)
Byfield, D .... 27(2)	Harris, N .... 28(8)	Saunders, M .... 3(1)
Claridge, S 1	Hessenthaler, A ...... 14(2)	Shields, P .... 6(11)
Clohessy, S .... 18(2)	Hislop, S .... 2(6)	Smith, P 3
Cochrane, J 5	Hope, C .... 20(4)	Spiller, D .... 21(11)
Collin, F .... 1(5)	Jackman, D .... 35(7)	Stone, C .... –(3)
Corneille, M .... –(2)	Jarvis, M .... 25(3)	Wallis, J .... 16(1)
Cox, I 36	Johnson, L .... 30(5)	Williams, T 13
Crichton, P 1		

League goals (50): Byfield 13, Flynn 6, Harris 6, Black 5, Jarvis 3, Crofts 2, Pouton 2, Sancho 2, Clohessy 1, Cochrane 1, Collin 1, Grant 1, Hessenthaler 1, Hope 1, Johnson 1, Mulligan 1, Shields 1, Opponents 2.
F.A. Cup goals (2): Jarvis 1, Saunders 1. **Carling Cup goals (4):** Byfield 1, Crofts 1, Jarvis 1, Opponents 1. **League Trophy goals (4):** Jarvis 2, Collin 1, Jackman 1.

HARTLEPOOL UNITED

Another last-game cliff-hanger for Hartlepool, who 12 months earlier reached the play-offs with a point gained at Bournemouth. This time, a late equaliser by James Brown against Port Vale proved not enough to stave off relegation. It was not a happy return to the club for former manager Chris Turner, who took up a position as director of sport with Paul Stephenson, temporarily, in charge of first team affairs following the sacking of Martin Scott. There was no significant improvement in results after these changes in mid-February, although four points gained against promotion-chasing Nottingham Forest and Brentford in successive matches had offered some hope of survival. Danny Wilson came in as the new manager, a month after leaving MK Dons.

Barron, M .... 13(2)	Foley, D .... 1(10)	Porter, J .... 6(2)
Boyd, A .... 12(9)	Humphreys, R 46	Proctor, M .... 22(4)
Brackstone, J 2	Istead, S .... 4(6)	Robertson, H 2
Brown, J .... –(4)	Jones, C 1	Robson, M .... 13(6)
Bullock, L .... 22(9)	Konstantopoulos, D 46	Strachan, G .... 6(3)
Butler, T .... 26(2)	Llewellyn, C .... 24(5)	Sweeney, A .... 34(1)
Clark, B .... 28(4)	Maidens, M .... 11(9)	Tinkler, M .... 11(4)
Clarke, D .... 6(6)	McDonald, D .... 4(1)	Turnbull, S .... 16(5)
Collins, N 22	Nash, G 3	Walker, J .... 1(3)
Craddock, D 4	Nelson, M 43	Williams, D .... 33(6)
Daly, J .... 18(12)	Pittman, J .... 2(1)	Williams, E .... 24(12)

League goals (44): Williams, E 7, Proctor 5, Sweeney 5, Boyd 4, Bullock 4, Porter 3, Daly 2, Humphreys 2, Istead 2, Nelson 2, Brown 1, Butler 1, Maidens 1, McDonald 1, Robson 1, Strachan 1, Tinkler 1, Opponents 1.
F.A. Cup goals (3): Butler 1, Llewellyn 1, Nelson 1. **Carling Cup goals (4):** Daly 2, Proctor 2. **League Trophy goals:** None.
Average home League attendance: 4,811. **Player of Year:** Ritchie Humphreys.

HUDDERSFIELD TOWN

For the second successive season, Peter Jackson and his team were left wondering what might have been. They missed out on a play-off place in 2005 when eight victories in the last nine matches just failed to make up for previous inconsistency. This time, automatic promotion was on the cards until the last month when five points from six games were not enough to take that final step. After winning the first leg of their play-off semi-final at Barnsley with a goal from Gary Taylor-Fletcher, they faltered again to lose the second 3-1.

Abbott, P .... 27(9)	Collins, M .... 9(8)	Mirfin, D .... 27(4)
Adams, D 40	Graham, D .... 15(1)	Rachubka, P 34
Ahmed, A .... 4(9)	Holdsworth, A .... 37(5)	Schofield, D .... 37(4)
Booth, A .... 32(4)	Hudson, M .... 25(4)	Senior, P .... 12(1)
Brandon, C .... 36(4)	McAliskey, J .... –(9)	Smith, D .... 7(1)
Carss, A .... 10(7)	McCombe, J 1	Taylor-Fletcher, G . 30(13)
Clarke, N 46	McIntosh, M .... 20(2)	Worthington, J 41
Clarke, T .... 16(1)	Mendes, J .... –(5)	Young, M .... –(2)

Play-offs – appearances: Adams 2, Booth 2, Clarke, N 2, Graham 2, Holdsworth 2, Hudson 2, McIntosh 2, Rachubka 2, Schofield 2, Taylor-Fletcher 2, Worthington 2, Abbott –(1), Brandon –(1).
League goals (72): Booth 13, Abbott 12, Taylor-Fletcher 10, Graham 9, Schofield 9, McIntosh 4, Worthington 4, Brandon 3, Hudson 3, Clarke, T 1, Collins 1, Holdsworth 1, Mirfin 1, Opponents 1. **Play-offs – goals (2):** Taylor-Fletcher 1, Worthington 1.
F.A. Cup goals (6): Booth 2, Brandon 1, Holdsworth 1, Schofield 1, Taylor-Fletcher 1.
Carling Cup goals (5): Taylor-Fletcher 3, Abbott 2. **League Trophy goals (1):** Mirfin 1.
Average home League attendance: 13,058. **Player of Year:** Andy Booth.

MILTON KEYNES DONS

Just when a second successive great escape was on the cards after four victories had closed the gap on the teams above them, Dons slipped back and went down. One route was blocked when fellow strugglers Tranmere beat them in stoppage time. Then, on the final day of the season when they had somehow survived 12 months earlier, a goalless draw at Rotherham meant that it was the Yorkshire side staying up. Danny Wilson, whose team were always playing catch-up after failing to win any of their opening ten games, lost his job as a result. In came the former Brentford manager Martin Allen.

Baker, M 37	McClenahan, T .... 24(5)	Platt, C .... 34(6)
Batista, R 9	McKoy, N .... 5(11)	Puncheon, J 1
Carrilho, M .... 1(2)	McLeod, I .... 33(6)	Quinn, S .... 13(2)
Chorley, B .... 25(1)	Mills, P 16	Ricketts, M .... 4(1)
Crooks, L .... 22(1)	Mitchell, P 39	Rizzo, N .... 15(14)
Edds, G .... 32(9)	Morgan, C .... 38(2)	Small, W .... 24(4)
Filipe Morais, F ...... 11(2)	Oyedele, S .... 2(1)	Smith, G .... 18(7)
Harding, B .... 8(2)	Palmer, S .... 1(1)	Taylor, S .... 10(7)
Kamara, M .... 6(17)	Partridge, D 18	Wilbraham, A .... 16(15)
Lewington, D 44		

League goals (45): McLeod 17, Platt 6, Wilbraham 4, Edds 3, Smith 3, Taylor 3, Harding 2, Kamara 2, Rizzo 2, Lewington 1, Mills 1, Small 1.
F.A. Cup goals (8): Edds 2, Platt 2, McLeod 1, Rizzo 1, Smith 1, Opponents 1. **Carling Cup goals:** None. **League Trophy goals (7):** Smith 3, Wilbraham 2, Mills 1, Small 1.
Average home League attendance: 5,776. **Player of Year:** Dean Lewington.

NOTTINGHAM FOREST

Gary Megson's uneasy relationship with Forest and their fans came to an end when he stepped down in mid-February after little more than 12 months as manager. His relegated side were a dozen points off a play-off place and had gone out of the F.A. Cup and Carling Cup to lower division opposition. In as caretakers came Ian McParland and Frank Barlow with a joint initiative which turned around the club's season. It started with a 7-1 rout of Swindon, in which Nicky Southall scored a hat-trick, and was sustained until a top six place was beckoning. Had Forest not faltered, dropping seven points in their final three matches, they would have claimed an unlikely top six spot instead of missing out by one place. Colin Calderwood came from Northampton to be the new manager.

Bastians, F .... 2(9)	Fernandez, V .... –(1)	Morgan, W .... 41(2)
Bennett, J 18	Friio, D .... 11(6)	Padula, G 3
Bopp, E .... 2(10)	Gardner, R .... 6(6)	Pedersen, R .... 17(1)
Breckin, I 46	Gerrard, P .... 21(1)	Perch, J .... 34(4)
Clingan, S .... 14(1)	Harris, N .... –(1)	Southall, N .... 37(3)
Commons, K .... 36(1)	Holt, Gary .... 23(3)	Taylor, G .... 17(3)
Cullip, D .... 10(1)	Holt, Grant .... 18(1)	Thompson, J .... 28(7)
Curtis, J 27	Hoult, R 8	Tyson, N 28
Dadi, E .... –(5)	Johnson, R .... 12(5)	Vickerton, M .... –(1)
Dobie, S .... 6(2)	Lester, J .... 15(23)	Weir-Daley, S .... –(6)
Eaden, N .... 26(2)		

League goals (67): Tyson 10, Breckin 8, Commons 8, Southall 8, Lester 5, Holt, Grant 4, Taylor 4, Johnson 3, Perch 3, Thompson 3, Bennett 2, Dobie 2, Morgan 2, Bopp 1, Friio 1, Weir-Daley 1, Opponents 2.
F.A. Cup goals (3): Taylor 2, Holt, Gary 1. **Carling Cup goals (2):** Breckin 2. **League Trophy goals (2):** Bopp 1, Weir-Daley 1.
Average home League attendance: 20,257. **Player of Year:** Ian Breckin.

OLDHAM ATHLETIC

A fairly anonymous season was suddenly transformed by a burst of six wins in seven games. It started with a 3-0 success against Nottingham Forest and ended when Luke Beckett scored a hat-trick against Blackpool. Oldham closed a sizeable gap on the play-off pack as a result, leaving Ronnie Moore full of optimism about the run-in. But the bubble burst with a home defeat by struggling MK Dons and Moore and his team were left deflated by a complete loss of momentum which left them six points adrift of the top six and Moore making way for John Sheridan to take charge. All Beckett's 18 goals came in league matches.

Beckett, L .... 27(7)	Grant, A 2	Porter, C .... 18(13)
Bonner, M .... 5(2)	Grant, L 16	Scott, R .... 19(2)
Branston, G 38	Haining, W .... 13(2)	Stam, S .... 9(4)
Butcher, R .... 32(4)	Hall, C .... 3(14)	Swailes, C .... 14(1)
Day, C 30	Hall, D .... 9(1)	Taylor, C .... 11(3)
Eardley, N 1	Hughes, M .... 30(3)	Tierney, M .... 13(6)
Edwards, P .... 29(5)	Killen, C .... 10(2)	Warne, P .... 38(2)
Eyres, D .... 15(6)	Liddell, A 29	Wellens, R 45
Facey, D .... –(3)	Owen, G 17	Wolfenden, M .... –(1)
Forbes, T .... 33(6)		

League goals (58): Beckett 18, Liddell 9, Warne 9, Porter 7, Butcher 4, Wellens 4, Killen 2, Branston 1, Eyres 1, Hughes 1, Scott 1.
F.A. Cup goals (6): Porter 2, Hall, C 1, Eyres 1, Liddell 1, Warne 1. **Carling Cup goals:** None. **League Trophy goals (1):** Liddell 1.
Average home League attendance: 5,796. **Player of Year:** Richie Wellens.

PORT VALE

A climb of five places to 13th and a good F.A. Cup run represented a solid season's work for Port Vale. Michael Cummins contributed ten goals from midfield to their league effort which included two wins over Southend – only one other team completed the double over the eventual champions. Vale beat Wrexham, Bristol Rovers and Doncaster to reach the fourth round of the Cup for the first time in a decade, then held Aston Villa for more than an hour at Villa Park before two goals by Milan Baros opened the way for the Premiership side's 3-1 win.

Abbey, G .... 19(1)	Doherty, S .... 3(3)	Paynter, B 16
Bell, M .... 14(1)	Fortune, C .... 20(5)	Pilkington, G 46
Birchall, C .... 23(8)	Goodlad, M 46	Porter, A 2
Briscoe, L .... –(4)	Hulbert, R .... –(1)	Rowland, S .... 13(5)
Cardle, J .... 1(5)	Husbands, M .... 6(18)	Sam, N .... –(4)
Clarke, D .... –(1)	Innes, M .... 17(6)	Smith, J .... 18(9)
Collins, S 15	James, C .... 30(5)	Sonner, D .... 25(4)
Constantine, L 30	Lowndes, N .... 30(5)	Talbot, J .... 4(1)
Cornes, C .... 7(3)	Matthews, L .... –(3)	Togwell, S .... 26(1)
Cummins, M .... 36(3)	McGregor, M 14	Walsh, M 4
Dinning, T .... 33(2)	Mulligan, G .... 8(2)	

League goals (49): Constantine 10, Cummins 10, Lowndes 5, Cornes 4, Husbands 4, Bell 2, Dinning 2, Fortune 2, Paynter 2, Pilkington 2, Togwell 2, Birchall 1, Mulligan 1, Smith 1, Sonner 1.
F.A. Cup goals (7): Constantine 2, Togwell 2, Birchall 1, Husbands 1, Lowndes 1. **Carling Cup goals (1):** Cummins 1. **League Trophy goals (1):** Smith 1.
Average home League attendance: 4,665. **Player of Year:** George Pilkington.

ROTHERHAM UNITED

Rotherham did just enough top avoid a second successive relegation when a goalless draw in the final game against MK Dons sent their opponents down instead. Now they must do it all again after having ten points deducted for going into administration. Alan

Knill has the task of beating the odds, having been rewarded for staying up amid all the club's financial problems. Knill, who stepped up from first-team coach when Mick Harford was sacked as manager in mid-December after 17 league and cup matches without a victory, received a two-year contract.

Barker, S .... 42(1)	Gilchrist, P .... 9(2)	Murdock, C 39
Brogan, S .... –(3)	Hoskins, W .... 7(16)	Newsham, M .... –(3)
Burton, D 24	Hurst, P .... 28(3)	Otsemobor, J .... 4(6)
Butler, M .... 33(6)	Keane, M .... 26(2)	Quinn, S 16
Campbell-Ryce, J ..... 4(3)	Leadbitter, G .... 3(2)	Robertson, G .... 30(5)
Conlon, B 3	McLaren, P .... 35(4)	Shaw, P .... 15(2)
Cutler, N 22	Minto, S .... 5(1)	Taylor, R .... –(1)
Duncum, S 1	Monkhouse, A .... 7(5)	Williamson, L 37
Evans, P 4	Montgomery, G 24	Worrell, D .... 40(1)
Forte, J .... 8(3)	Mullin, J .... 40(3)	

League goals (52): Burton 12, Butler 7, Forte 4, Hoskins 4, Shaw 4, Williamson 4, Barker 3, McLaren 3, Mullin 2, Murdock 2, Conlon 1, Leadbitter 1, Monkhouse 1, Robertson 1, Opponents 3.
F.A. Cup goals (3): McLaren 2, Burton 1. **Carling Cup goals (3):** Burton 1, Otsemobor 1, Opponents 1. **League Trophy goals (4):** Butler 1, Evans 1, Hoskins 1, Newsham 1.
Average home League attendance: 5,323. **Player of Year:** Lee Williamson.

SCUNTHORPE UNITED

Billy Sharp and Andy Keogh, a pair of promising young strikers, were instrumental in promoted Scunthorpe achieving their highest league finish since 1966. Sharp was the division's joint top scorer in league games on 23 with Southend's Freddy Eastwood, while Keogh's performances earned him a place in the Republic of Ireland Under 21 side. Scunthorpe also leaked plenty of goals, undermining their chances of holding on to an early-season play-off place and at one point later in the season threatening to drive them into trouble. But successive away wins over Gillingham and Port Vale in the space of four days took the pressure off and paved the way for a mid-table spot.

Allanson, A .... –(1)	Goodwin, J .... 10(3)	Ryan, R .... 7(6)
Baraclough, I .... 37(1)	Hinds, R 42	Sharp, B .... 35(2)
Beagrie, P .... 21(9)	Johnson, T .... 3(11)	Sparrow, M .... 30(9)
Butler, A .... 15(1)	Keogh, A .... 40(5)	Stanton, N .... 21(1)
Byrne, C .... 25(7)	MacKenzie, N .... 12(2)	Taylor, C .... 31(14)
Corden, W .... 5(4)	Musselwhite, P 28	Till, P .... 6(2)
Crosby, A .... 38(4)	Parton, A .... 3(3)	Timlin, M .... –(1)
Ehui, I .... –(3)	Ridley, L .... 2(1)	Torpey, S .... 16(10)
Evans, T 18	Rose, M 15	Williams, M .... 28(1)
Foster, S 18		

League goals (68): Sharp 23, Keogh 11, Hinds 6, Beagrie 5, Sparrow 5, Baraclough 3, Crosby 3, Taylor 3, Goodwin 2, MacKenzie 2, Butler 1, Byrne 1, Johnson 1, Ridley 1, Torpey 1.
F.A. Cup goals (5): Keogh 3, Baraclough 1, Johnson 1. **Carling Cup goals (2):** Hinds 1, Ryan 1. **League Trophy goals (4):** Crosby 1, Johnson 1, Keogh 1, Sharp 1.
Average home League attendance: 5,171. **Player of Year:** Richard Hinds.

SOUTHEND UNITED

Six days after running the London Marathon, Steve Tilson saw his team complete a marathon success of their own. Southend, joint favourites to go straight back down, upset all the odds by topping the table and sharing an even more unlikely promotion double with runners-up Colchester. Tilson, now one of the most sought-after young managers in the game, made the most of a settled squad, largely free of injuries, and another productive season for Freddy Eastwood. League One's leading scorer included hat-tricks against Bristol City and Chesterfield in his total of 25 in all competitions – one better than the previous season – this time in tandem up front with the veteran Shaun Goater.

Ademeno, C .... –(1)	Flahavan, D 43	Lawson, J .... 7(16)
Barrett, A 45	Goater, S .... 28(6)	Maher, K 44
Bentley, M .... 20(13)	Gower, M .... 34(6)	Moussa, F .... –(1)
Bradbury, L .... 11(4)	Gray, W .... 23(16)	Pettefer, G .... 5(6)
Campbell-Ryce, J ... 7(6)	Griemink, B 3	Prior, S .... 15(2)
Cole, M .... 19(10)	Guttridge, L 41	Smith, J .... 3(10)
Eastwood, F .... 34(6)	Hunt, L .... 23(7)	Sodje, E .... 12(1)
Edwards, A .... 19(1)	Jupp, D 29	Wilson, C .... 41(3)

League goals (72): Eastwood 23, Goater 11, Gray 9, Gower 6, Bentley 5, Guttridge 5, Barrett 3, Lawson 2, Wilson 2, Bradbury 1, Cole 1, Maher 1, Smith 1, Sodje 1, Opponents 1.
F.A. Cup goals (2): Eastwood 2. **Carling Cup goals:** None. **League Trophy goals:** None.
Average home League attendance: 8,053. **Player of Year:** Freddy Eastwood.

SWANSEA CITY

Their first visit to the Millennium Stadium was successful, a 2-1 win over Carlisle in the Football League Trophy Final achieved by goals from Lee Trundle and Adebayor Akinfenwa. The return, with a place in the Championship at stake, ended in heartbreak. Swansea came from behind against Barnsley in the Play-off Final to lead through Rory Fallon and Andy Robinson, but conceded an equaliser and lost a penalty shoot-out when Alan Tate's spot-kick was saved by Nicky Colgan. They had been top going into the New Year, then began to fall away and needed to win the last game at Chesterfield to make sure of holding on to sixth place.

Akinfenwa, A .... 29(5)	Gueret, W 46	Ricketts, S .... 43(1)
Anderson, I .... –(5)	Iriekpen, E 28	Robinson, A .... 29(10)
Austin, K .... 23(3)	Knight, L .... 10(7)	Tate, A .... 42(1)
Bean, M 9	Lowe, K 4	Thorpe, L .... –(3)
Britton, L .... 36(2)	MacDonald, S .... 2(5)	Trundle, L .... 34(2)
Connor, P .... 5(8)	Martinez, R .... 34(5)	Tudur-Jones, O .... 17(4)
Edwards, C .... 1(1)	McLeod, K .... 23(6)	Watt, S 2
Fallon, R .... 12(5)	Monk, G 33	Way, D .... 2(3)
Forbes, L .... 12(17)	Nugent, K .... –(1)	Williams,T .... 13(4)
Goodfellow, M .... 5(6)	O'Leary, K .... 12(3)	

Play-offs – appearances: Austin 3, Britton 3, Fallon 3, Gueret 3, Knight 3, Monk 3, Ricketts 3, Robinson 3, Tate 3, Tudur-Jones 3, O'Leary 2, MacDonald 1, Trundle –(3), Akinfenwa –(2), Forbes –(2), McLeod –(1), Williams –(1).
League goals (78): Trundle 20, Robinson 12, Akinfenwa 9, Knight 8, McLeod 7, Britton 4, Fallon 4, Forbes 4, Tudur-Jones 4, Martinez 2, Bean 1, Connor 1, Monk 1, O'Leary 1, Ricketts 1. **Play-offs – goals (5):** Knight 2, Fallon 1, Ricketts 1, Robinson 1.
F.A. Cup goals: None. **Carling Cup goals (1):** Akinfenwa 1. **League Trophy goals (17):** Akinfenwa 5, Robinson 5, Knight 2, Britton 1, Connor 1, Forbes 1, Monk 1, Trundle 1.
Average home League attendance: 14,111. **Player of Year:** Leon Britton.

SWINDON TOWN

Dennis Wise fought and won plenty of battles during his playing career and now faces the challenge of restoring the fortunes of a club in the bottom division for the first time for 20 years. The former Chelsea midfielder was appointed manager after a season in which Andy King paid the price for an indifferent start and his successor Iffy Onuora was ousted with the team finishing second from bottom. Swindon showed improved form in mid-season, but were back in trouble with a 7-1 defeat by Nottingham Forest and fell away again after victory at Scunthorpe had offered some hope.

Brown, A .... 23(4)	Benjamin, T .... 5(3)	Bouazza, H .... 11(2)

Collins, P 13	Jarrett, A .... 2(4)	Pook, M .... 26(4)
Comyn-Platt, C ...... 13(9)	Jenkins, S .... 17(7)	Reeves, A .... –(1)
Cureton, J .... 22(8)	Jutkiewicz, L .... 3(2)	Roberts, C .... 4(17)
Diagouraga, T .... 5(3)	McDermott, N .... 9(4)	Shakes, R .... 26(11)
Evans, R 32	McPhee, C .... 6(2)	Smith, J 38
Fallon, R 25	Miglioranzi, S .... 22(5)	Smith, P .... 5(4)
Gurney, A .... 24(4)	Mikolanda, P .... 1(4)	Stroud, D .... 1(1)
Heath, C .... 8(3)	Nicholas, A .... 31(2)	Summerbee, N 1
Heaton, T 14	Nicolau, N .... 3(2)	Thorpe, T .... 6(1)
Holgate, A .... 2(4)	O'Hanlon, S 40	Wells, B .... –(4)
Ifil, J .... 34(2)	Peacock, L .... 11(4)	Whalley, G .... 23(1)

League goals (46): Fallon 12, Cureton 7, O'Hanlon 4, Roberts 3, Shakes 3, Brown 2, Benjamin 2, Bouazza 2, McDermott 2, Peacock 2, Comyn-Platt 1, Gurney 1, Heath 1, Jenkins 1, Miglioranzi 1, Thorpe 1, Opponents 1.
F.A. Cup goals (3): Comyn-Platt 1, Fallon 1, Gurney 1. **Carling Cup goals (1):** Pook 1.
League Trophy goals (3): Bouazza 1, Fallon 1, Roberts 1.
Average home League attendance: 5,950. **Player of Year:** Rhys Evans.

TRANMERE ROVERS

Four successive defeats forced fading Tranmere into a relegation dogfight against MK Dons in their penultimate match. They won with a stoppage-time goal by Delroy Facey to stay up, but it was a sharp contrast to the previous year's third-place finish and manager Brian Little left by mutual agreement the day before the final fixture after three seasons at the club. Although his side scored four-goal victories against Oldham, Chesterfield and Yeovil – in which Chris Greenacre got a hat-trick on the way to 18 for the campaign – a total of 21 goalless games was too many for any real progress to be made. Former Rovers striker Ronnie Moore is the new manager.

Achterberg, J 19	Hume, I .... 5(1)	Raven, D 11
Aiston, S .... 23(13)	Jackson, M 41	Roberts, G 44
Bruce, A .... 10(1)	James, O .... –(1)	Seremet, D 13
Dagnall, C .... –(6)	Jennins, A .... 24(14)	Sharps, I 39
Davies, S .... 6(16)	Jones, M 1	Summerbee, N .... 4(2)
Facey, D .... 30(7)	Linwood, P .... 12(2)	Tremarco, C .... 14(4)
Francis, S .... 16(1)	McAteer, J .... 23(6)	Whitmore, T .... –(4)
Goodison, I .... 32(6)	Murray, M 2	Wilson, S 12
Greenacre, C 45	O'Leary, S .... 19(2)	Zola, C .... 15(7)
Harrison, D .... 26(9)	Rankine, M .... 20(4)	

League goals (50): Greenacre 16, Facey 8, Zola 4, Aiston 3, Jackson 3, O'Leary 3, Davies 2, Harrison 2, Roberts 2, Francis 1, Goodison 1, Hume 1, Jennings 1, Sharps 1, Tremarco 1, Opponents 1.
F.A. Cup goals (1): Greenacre 1. **Carling Cup goals (1):** Sharps 1. **League Trophy goals (5):** Facey 1, Greenacre 1, Harrison 1, Jennings 1, Rankine 1.
Average home League attendance: 7,211. **Player of Year:** Chris Greenacre.

WALSALL

Paul Merson looked to be heading in the right direction as Walsall entered 2005 in a healthy mid-table position within striking distance of the top six. A few weeks later Merson lost his job after a 5-0 defeat at Brentford, the team's fortunes having taken a sudden turn for the worse. Caretaker Kevan Broadhurst was confirmed in the job until the end of the season, but he too was sacked when a second relegation in three seasons was confirmed at the end of a run of two points from eight games. Richard Money, a European Cup winner in his days with Liverpool, was the board's latest choice as manager.

Atieno, T .... 1(1)	Bennett, J .... 17(2)	Broad, J 2
Barrowman, A .... 10(3)	Bradley, M .... –(3)	Claridge, S 7

Constable, J .... 7(10)	Larrosa, R .... 2(5)	Skora, S 4
Demontagnac, I .... 14(10)	Leary, M .... 12(3)	Smith, G 13
Devlin, P 8	Leitao, J .... 20(3)	Smith, P 8
Fitzgerald, S .... 1(4)	McDermott, D .... –(1)	Standing, M .... 10(10)
Fox, D 33	Merson, P .... 6(1)	Staunton, S .... 5(2)
Fryatt, M 23	Mills, P 14	Sztybel, J 1
Gerrard, A .... 32(2)	Murphy, J 14	Taylor, D .... 4(7)
Gillett, S 2	Nicholls, A .... 4(4)	Taylor, K .... 15(6)
Gilmartin, R 2	Oakes, A 25	Tilt, L .... –(1)
Harkness, J 1	Osborn, S .... 27(5)	Timm, M .... 6(3)
Husbands, M .... 1(3)	Pead, C .... 38(1)	Westwood, C .... 26(3)
James, K .... 12(3)	Roper, I .... 24(1)	Wrack, D 7
Keates, D 14	Ruddy, J 5	Wright, M .... 23(7)
Kinsella, M .... 6(4)		

League goals (47): Fryatt 11, Leitao 5, Constable 3, Smith, G 3, Westwood 3, Demontagnac 2, Keates 2, Taylor, K 2, Osborn 2, Skora 2, Wright 2, Barrowman 1, Bennett 1, Claridge 1, Devlin 1, James 1, Leary 1, Smith, P 1, Timm 1, Opponents 2. **F.A. Cup goals (8):** James 3, Fryatt 2, Kinsella 1, Leary 1, Leitao 1. **Carling Cup goals:** None. **League Trophy goals (6):** Constable 2, Bennett 1, Fryatt 1, Leitao 1, Nicholls 1. **Average home League attendance:** 5,392. **Player of Year:** Anthony Gerrard.

YEOVIL TOWN

Yeovil lost Gary Johnson, architect of the club's rise from non-league football, to Bristol City six weeks into the season – and there were times when the team he left behind lost their way. Most worrying was a two-month spell beginning in the New Year which brought only one victory from ten matches – a 3-0 success against Chesterfield in which Arron Davies scored all three goals. It left them one place above the drop zone. But Steve Thompson, who had replaced Johnson, managed to restore enough of the winning habit to secure a 15th place finish before reverting to coaching duties. In came former Grimsby manager Russell Slade.

Alvarez, L 4	Harrold, M .... 28(14)	Rocastle, C .... 5(3)
Amankwaah, K 38	Jevons, P .... 35(3)	Rose, M .... –(1)
Barry, A 4	Johnson, L 26	Skiverton, T 36
Bastianini, P .... 15(5)	Jones, N .... 37(6)	Sodje, E .... 17(2)
Cohen, C .... 29(1)	Lindegaard, A .... 14(9)	Terry, P .... 34(8)
Collis, S .... 21(2)	Lockwood, A .... 18(2)	Way, D 15
Davies, A .... 27(12)	Melono, G 1	Weale, C 25
Doherty, T 1	Miles, C .... 18(12)	Webb, D .... –(4)
Fontaine, L 10	Oliver, L .... –(3)	Williams, D .... –(1)
Gall, K .... 11(26)	Poole, D .... 20(5)	Wilson, M .... 1(1)
Guyett, S .... 16(5)		

League goals (54): Jevons 15, Harrold 9, Davies 8, Skiverton 6, Bastianini 3, Gall 2, Johnson 2, Poole 2, Alvarez 1, Amankwaah 1, Cohen 1, Sodje 1, Terry 1, Way 1, Opponents 1. **F.A. Cup goals (5):** Davies 2, Jevons 1, Johnson 1, Terry 1, Way 1. **Carling Cup goals (3):** Davies 1, Gall 1, Way 1. **League Trophy goals:** None. **Average home League attendance:** 6,511. **Player of Year:** Chris Cohen.

COCA-COLA LEAGUE TWO

BARNET

Paul Fairclough's first season of league football after wide-ranging managerial experience in the Conference got off to an encouraging start with ten points from four matches. After that it was a struggle, Barnet failing to win again until the end of October. They were among a host of teams drawn into a relegation struggle which stretched to the final match when a 2-1 win over Rushden and Diamonds ensured safety. High spot of the campaign was a Carling Cup third round tie against Manchester United at Old Trafford. Goalkeeper Ross Flitney was sent off 90 seconds into a 4-1 defeat for deliberate handling, but later had the red card rescinded by the F.A.

Bailey, N 45	Gross, A .... 18(2)	Roache, L .... 2(6)
Batt, D .... 12(10)	Hatch, L .... 21(14)	Sinclair, D .... 39(5)
Bowditch, B .... 3(3)	Hendon, I .... 34(1)	Soares, L .... 14(6)
Charles, A .... 39(1)	Hessenthaler, A 16	Strevens, B .... 31(4)
Clist, S .... 12(2)	Kandol, T 13	Tynan, S 7
Flitney, R 35	King, S .... 31(1)	Varney, A .... -(1)
Fuller, B 15	Lee, D .... 24(3)	Vernazza, P .... 11(6)
Graham, R .... 13(2)	Norville, J .... 7(15)	Warhurst, P .... 7(2)
Grazioli, G .... 27(2)	Reed, M 4	Yakubu, I 26

League goals (44): Bailey 7, Grazioli 7, Strevens 5, Hendon 4, Kandol 4, Lee 4, Hatch 2, Norville 2, Sinclair 2, Fuller 1, Graham 1, Hesenthaler 1, Roache 1, Soares 1, Yakubu 1, Opponents 1.
F.A. Cup goals: None. **Carling Cup goals (7):** Lee 2, Bailey 1, Grazioli 1, King 1, Roache 1, Sinclair 1. **League Trophy goals (3):** Bailey 1, Norville 1, Sinclair 1. **Average home League attendance:** 2,577. **Player of Year:** Nicky Bailey.

BOSTON UNITED

Boston matched their highest league position, 11th, and accumulated their best points total, 61, since moving up from the Conference in 2002. High spot was a run of 13 points from five matches which brought Steve Evans the Manager of the Month award for October. Low points were 5-0 defeats by Carlisle and Mansfield. Most annoying for chairman Jon Sotnik was a report of an unusually high level of betting for one of their matches, an allegation he instructed the club's lawyers to investigate.

Abbey, N 17	Holland, C .... 29(5)	Noble, D .... 10(1)
Canoville, L .... 42(1)	Joachim, J .... 41(2)	Norris, R .... -(1)
Clare, D .... -(1)	Johnson, G .... 3(1)	Ross, I .... 13(1)
Clarke, J .... 12(3)	Keene, J 6	Rusk, S .... 24(10)
Dudfield, L .... 21(15)	Kuipers, M 15	Silk, G .... 11(3)
Edkins, A .... -(1)	Lee, J .... 11(6)	Talbot, S .... 28(2)
Ellender, P 25	Logan, C 13	Thomas, D .... 15(20)
Futcher, B .... 13(1)	Maylett, B .... 23(15)	Till, P .... 10(6)
Galbraith, D .... 6(6)	McCann, A .... 31(4)	Whelan, N .... 8(7)
Greaves, M .... 31(3)	McSporran, J .... -(2)	White, A 37
Green, F .... 5(1)	Melton, S .... -(3)	Wright, C 1
Hall, A .... 5(7)		

League goals (50): Joachim 14, Dudfield 5, Ross 4, Whelan 4, White 4, Rusk 3, Lee 2, Talbot 2, Thomas 2, Canoville 1, Clarke 1, Ellender 1, Greaves 1, Green 1, Keene 1, Maylett 1, Till 1, Opponents 2.
F.A. Cup goals (5): Joachim 2, Futcher 1, Lee 1, Maylett 1, Rusk 1, Talbot 1. **Carling Cup goals:** None. **League Trophy goals (2):** Maylett 1, White 1.
Average home League attendance: 2,519. **Player of Year:** Alan White.

BRISTOL ROVERS

Nine home defeats undermined Rovers' chances of making a real impact on the promotion race. The weakness was obvious from the start of the season, contributed heavily to manager Ian Atkins losing his job and continued to hinder efforts to close the gap on the leading teams. Productive away form under Paul Trollope kept them in with an outside chance of a place in the play-offs. But losing during the run-in to struggling Rushden and Diamonds at the Memorial Ground proved particularly damaging and Rovers came up six points short after another defeat there, this time by Macclesfield, in their final fixture.

Agogo, J .... 41(1)	Forrester, J .... 3(14)	Lines, C .... 1(3)
Anderson, J .... 10(2)	Gibb, A .... 21(12)	Louis, J .... 2(6)
Bass, J .... 7(2)	Haldane, L .... 19(11)	Mullings, D .... –(4)
Book, S 1	Hinton, C .... 34(2)	Ryan, R 14
Campbell, S .... 31(7)	Hunt, J 40	Shearer, S 45
Carruthers, C .... 39(1)	Igoe, S .... 10(1)	Somner, M 1
Disley, C .... 37(5)	Leary, M .... 12(1)	Walker, R .... 44(2)
Edwards, C .... 12(3)	Lescott, A .... 35(2)	Williams, R .... 2(5)
Elliott, S 45		

League goals (59): Walker 20, Agogo 16, Disley 8, Haldane 3, Elliott 2, Forrester 2, Anderson 1, Campbell 1, Carruthers 1, Edwards 1, Hunt 1, Igoe 1, Opponents 2.
F.A. Cup goals (3): Agogo 2, Gibb 1. **Carling Cup goals:** None. **League Trophy goals (1):** Walker 1.
Average home League attendance: 5,989. **Player of Year:** Richard Walker.

BURY

Bury's season had a sting in the tail – a one point deduction for fielding an unregistered player against Lincoln. With so little separating so many teams at the bottom, it could have had dire consequences. But Chris Casper's side had picked up sufficient points during the run-in to survive the punishment. Former Manchester United defender Casper had become, at 30, the league's youngest manager after impressing during a spell as caretaker in the wake of Graham Barrow's dismissal with only one win on the board from the opening nine matches.

Adams, N .... 9(6)	Gobern, L 7	Ross, I .... 6(1)
Anyinsah, J 3	Grundy, A .... –(1)	Saunders, B 1
Barlow, S .... 2(11)	Hannah, D .... 1(1)	Schmeichel, K 15
Barry-Murphy, B ..... 35(5)	Hardiker, J 11	Scott, P .... 40(1)
Brass, C .... 6(1)	Jarman, N .... 1(1)	Sedgemore, J .... 3(6)
Buchanan, D .... 22(1)	Kennedy, T .... 28(5)	Smart, A .... 11(2)
Burke, S .... –(1)	Marrison, C .... 8(8)	Speight, J .... 7(10)
Burns, J 1	Mattis, D .... 32(4)	Tipton, M .... 15(9)
Challinor, D 46	Newby, J .... 4(6)	Unsworth, L .... –(3)
Daly, J 11	Parrish, A .... 6(2)	Whaley, S 23
Dootson, C .... 4(1)	Pugh, M .... 3(3)	Williams, T 3
Edwards, N 24	Quigley, L .... –(1)	Woodthorpe, C ...... 31(2)
Fitzgerald, J .... 22(5)	Reet, D 6	Youngs, T .... 16(14)
Flitcroft, D 43		

League goals (45): Whaley 7, Mattis 5, Kennedy 4, Reet 4, Barry-Murphy 3, Tipton 3, Youngs 3, Daly 2, Scott 2, Speight 2, Adams 1, Challinor 1, Flitcroft 1, Gobern 1, Newby 1, Pugh 1, Smart 1, Opponents 3.
F.A. Cup goals (2): Kennedy 1, Scott 1. **Carling Cup goals:** None. **League Trophy goals (1):** Sedgemore 1.
Average home League attendance: 2,593. **Player of Year:** Dave Flitcroft

CARLISLE UNITED

Carlisle swept to their second successive promotion, Karl Hawley topped the division's scoring list and Paul Simpson was named Manager of the Year. For good measure, they had the biggest crowds, completing a season to remember for a club in crisis 18 months earlier with their ground flooded and re-arranged Conference fixtures piling up. Hawley's stoppage-time equaliser at Mansfield, his 26th in all competitions, made sure they went up and a goalless draw at Stockport on the final day confirmed his side as champions. Carlisle also reached the League Trophy Final, losing 2-1 to Swansea at the Millennium Stadium. Success, however, came at a price, with Simpson moving to Preston. Neil McDonald, former Newcastle and Everton player, took over.

Andrews, L 1	Aranalde, Z .... 38(1)	Arnison, P .... 39(2)

Beharall, D 6	Holmes, D .... 30(10)	Murray, G .... 3(23)
Billy, C 45	Livesey, D .... 34(2)	Nade, R .... 10(12)
Bridges, M .... 23(2)	Lumsdon, C .... 37(1)	O'Brien, A .... 2(3)
Grand, S .... 2(6)	McClen, J .... –(2)	Rivers, M .... 2(2)
Gray, K 44	McGill, B .... 18(8)	Simpson, P .... 4(5)
Hackney, S .... 9(21)	Murphy, P .... 38(6)	Westwood, K 35
Hawley, K 46	Murray, A .... 29(8)	Williams, T 11

League goals (84): Hawley 22, Bridges 15, Holmes 7, Lumsdon 7, Hackney 6, Aranalde 5, Livesey 4, Murray, G 3, Gray 3, McGill 3, Grand 2, Murphy 2, Nade 2, Murray, A 1, O'Brien 1, Opponents 1.
F.A. Cup goals: None. **Carling Cup goals (1):** Murray, A 1. **League Trophy goals (9):** Hawley 4, Grand 1, Holmes 1, Murphy 1, Murray, A 1, Murray, G 1.
Average home League attendance: 7,218. **Player of Year:** Karl Hawley

CHELTENHAM TOWN

Manager John Ward drew inspiration from the success of his former club Watford to lead Cheltenham to an equally unexpected promotion. They went into the play-offs on a high, having confirmed their place with wins over Notts County (2-0) and Mansfield (5-0). Wycombe were overcome 2-1 on aggregate in the semi-finals thanks to goals from John Finnigan and Steve Guinan. Then, Guinan's 63rd minute goal settled the final against Grimsby, the team they had twice lost to in the league. An F.A. Cup tie at home against Newcastle added spice to the season, with Cheltenham giving a good account before losing the fourth round tie 2-0.

Armstrong, C .... 28(6)	Finnigan, J .... 38(1)	Rose, M 3
Bell, M .... 7(2)	Gallinagh, A 1	Spencer, D .... 17(29)
Bird, D .... 18(18)	Gill, J .... 41(1)	Taylor, M .... 9(1)
Bradshaw, G .... –(3)	Gillespie, S .... 4(10)	Townsend, M .... 30(1)
Brown, A 3	Guinan, S .... 27(3)	Victory, J .... 19(3)
Brown, S 1	Higgs, S 45	Vincent, A .... 1(12)
Caines, G .... 35(4)	McCann, G .... 38(1)	Wilson, B .... 41(2)
Connolly, A .... 4(1)	Melligan, J .... 40(2)	Wylde, M .... –(1)
Duff, S .... 18(2)	Odejayi, K .... 38(3)	Yao, S .... –(3)

Play-offs – appearances: Armstrong 3, Caines 3, Duff 3, Finnigan 3, Gill 3, Guinan 3, Higgs 3, McCann 3, Vincent 3, Wilson 3, Odejayi 2(1), Gillespie 1(1), Spencer –(3), Bell –(2), Bird –(1).
League goals (65): Odejayi 11, Wilson 9, McCann 8, Guinan 7, Melligan 6, Gillespie 5, Finnigan 4, Spencer 3, Armstrong 2, Victory 2, Vincent 2, Bird 1, Connolly 1, Caines 2, Opponents 2. **Play-offs – goals (3):** Guinan 2, Finnigan 1.
F.A. Cup goals (7): Odejayi 2, Finnigan 1, Guinan 1, McCann 1, Melligan 1, Wilson 1.
Carling Cup goals (5): McCann 2, Caines 1, Melligan 1, Victory 1. **League Trophy goals (9):** Gillespie 2, Wilson 2, Armstrong 1, Connolly 1, Duff 1, Spencer 1, Victory 1.
Average home League attendance: 3,453. **Player of Year:** Brian Wilson.

CHESTER CITY

Three weeks after being fired by Peterborough, Mark Wright returned to Chester for a second spell as manager and turned around a season that had relegation written all over it. Wright took over when 11 defeats in 12 matches had cost Keith Curle his job. There was no instant cure, with the next five matches producing a single point. But he eventually got things right, starting with Derek Asamoah's hat-trick against Boston. Four more victories followed, along with four more goals for the player on loan from Lincoln. That meant Chester were able to compensate for failing to score in their final four matches, finishing in 15th place.

Albrighton, M 9	Bertos, L .... 2(3)	Branch, M .... 23(4)
Artell, D .... 34(3)	Blundell, G .... 23(7)	Brookfield, R .... –(1)
Asamoah, D .... 14(3)	Bolland, P .... 12(4)	Corden, W 2

Curle, T .... –(2)	Gillet, S 8	Richardson, M ...... 22(12)
Curtis,T .... 34(5)	Harrison, P 4	Roberts, M 1
Davies, B .... 42(3)	Hessey, S .... 17(2)	Robertson, C .... –(1)
Dimech, L .... 27(3)	Horwood, E 1	Ruddy, J 4
Dove, C .... 2(3)	Lowe, R .... 28(4)	Rutherford, P .... 1(5)
Drummond, S .... 41(1)	MacKenzie, C 30	Tait, P .... 3(6)
Edwards, J 10	McNiven, S 41	Vaughan, S .... 7(11)
El-Kholti, A .... 7(15)	Regan, C .... 39(2)	Walker, J .... 13(8)
Ellender, P 5		

League goals (53): Lowe 10, Asamoah 8, Blundell 7, Davies 7, Drummond 6, Branch 5, Richardson 4, Artell 2, Bolland 1, Curtis 1, Edwards 1, McNiven 1.
F.A. Cup goals (7): Lowe 3, Richardson 2, Branch 1, Drummond 1. **Carling Cup goals (1):** Davies 1. **League Trophy goals:** None.
Average home League attendance: 2,964. **Player of Year:** Stewart Drummond.

DARLINGTON

The difference was not as small as the previous season's when everything boiled down to goal difference. But it was still another frustrating finish, one place off the play-offs, for Darlington. With their chances drifting away through a lack of goals, David Hodgson's side briefly came good by putting four past Lincoln and scoring twice against Rochdale and Torquay for three wins in eight days at the beginning of April. After that, lapses in home form proved costly. Defeats by Northampton and Bury – the latter after leading 2-1 – and a draw against Wrexham on the final day of the season left them three points short of Lincoln in seventh position.

Appleby, M .... 18(8)	Johnson, J 9	Ndumbu-Nsungu,
Atieno, T .... –(3)	Johnson, S .... 35(7)	G .... 11(10)
Bates, G .... 6(3)	Kandol, T .... 6(1)	Peacock, A .... 17(10)
Beaumont, J .... –(1)	Keltie, C .... 23(1)	Russell, S 30
Bossu, B 9	Kendrick, J 21	Schmeichel, K 4
Clarke, M .... 42(1)	Knight, D 3	Sodje, A .... 17(19)
Close, B .... 4(2)	Lafferty, K 9	Stamp,P .... 5(3)
Cooke, A .... 11(3)	Logan, C .... 27(6)	Stockdale, R 3
Dickman, J .... 35(3)	Maddison, N .... –(1)	Thomas, S .... –(6)
Duke, D .... 17(3)	Martis, S .... 39(1)	Valentine, R 43
Hopkins, P .... 3(2)	McDermott, N .... 1(2)	Wainwright, N ...... 23(16)
Hutchinson, J 19	McGurk, D .... 2(1)	Webster, A .... 6(7)
Jameson, N .... 1(4)	McLeod, M .... 2(2)	Wijnhard, C .... 5(3)

League goals (58): Ndumbu-Nsungu 10, Sodje 8, Johnson, S 7, Logan 4, Clarke 3, Cooke 3, Johnson, J 3, Lafferty 3, Wainwright 3, Dickman 2, Kandol 2, Martis 2, Bates 1, Duke 1, Hopkins 1, Stamp 1, Webster 1, Wijnhard 1, Opponents 2.
F.A. Cup goals: None. **Carling Cup goals (1):** Logan 1. **League Trophy goals (1):** Ndumbu-Nsungu 1.
Average home League attendance: 4,198. **Player of Year:** Shelton Martis.

GRIMSBY TOWN

So near, yet so far. Grimsby were a matter of moments away from regaining their League One status on the final day of the season when Ryan Gilligan's equaliser for Northampton at Blundell Park and Lee Steele's winner for Leyton Orient at Oxford cost them third place. The play-offs offered no salvation, despite victory in the semi-finals against a Lincoln side who had trounced them 5-0 a few weeks earlier. Russell Slade's team went down to a fortuitous goal by Steve Guinan for underdogs Cheltenham and Slade left the club three days later after failing to agree a new contract. His assistant, Graham Rodger, took over.

Andrew, C .... 3(5)	Bloomer, M 3	Cohen, G .... 32(8)
Barwick, T .... 2(6)	Bolland, P 44	Crane, T .... 3(2)

Croft, G .... 26(7)	Kamudimba, J-P .... 14(7)	North, D .... –(1)
Downey, G .... –(1)	Jones, G .... 34(6)	Parkinson, A ...... 32(8)
Francis, S 5	Jones, R .... 38(2)	Ramsden, S .... 8(4)
Futcher, B .... 12(3)	McDermott, J 32	Reddy, M .... 42(2)
Goodfellow, M ...... 8(2)	Mendes, J .... 8(7)	Toner, C .... 24(7)
Gritton, M .... 7(19)	Mildenhall, S 46	Whittle, J 32
Hegarty, N .... –(2)	Newey, T .... 35(3)	Woodhouse, C 16

Play-offs – appearances: Bolland 3, Jones, G 3, Mendes 3, Mildenhall 3, Newey 3, Parkinson 3, Whittle 3, Woodhouse 3, Cohen 2(1), Croft 2(1), Jones, R 2, Futcher 1(2), Reddy 1(2), McDermott 1, Toner –(2), Goodfellow –(1).
League goals (64): Reddy 14, Jones, G 13, Cohen 6, Kamudimba 5, Bolland 4, Jones, R 4, Parkinson 4, Toner 3, Futcher 2, Gritton 2, Andrew 1, Crane 1, Downey 1, Goodfellow 1, McDermott 1, Newey 1, Woodhouse 1. **Play-offs – goals (3):** Jones, G 2, Futcher 1.
F.A. Cup goals: Jones, G 1. **Carling Cup goals (2):** Jones, G 1, Kamudimba 1.
League Trophy goals (1): Ashton P, 1.
Average home League attendance: 5,151. **Player of Year:** Rob Jones.

LEYTON ORIENT

Barry Hearn was dancing with delight at the Kassam Stadium as Orient secured their first automatic promotion since 1970 in a nail-biting final game which also sent Oxford into the Conference. With both teams needing to win, former Oxford striker Lee Steele scored in stoppage-time for a 3-2 result which rewarded his team for a strong finish to the season. It came after an indifferent run, which threatened their chances of a top three place, and produced 18 points from eight matches. Orient's away form was the key to success, no team in the division winning more games or scoring more goals on their travels.

Alexander, G .... 42(4)	Echanomi, E .... –(16)	Morris, G .... 3(1)
Barnard, D .... 14(13)	Garner, G 43	Palmer, A 3
Carlisle, W .... 3(9)	Hanson, C .... –(2)	Saah, B .... 2(1)
Connor, P .... 15(1)	Ibehre, J .... 22(11)	Simpson, M 45
Corden, W 8	Keith, J .... 41(1)	Steele, L .... 14(13)
Demetriou, J .... 1(2)	Lockwood, M 42	Tann, A .... 8(2)
Dolan, J 1	Mackie, J 40	Tudor, S .... 29(4)
Duncan, D .... –(1)	McMahon, D .... 17(16)	Zakuani, G 43
Easton, C .... 36(5)	Miller, J .... 34(2)	

League goals (67): Alexander 14, Ibehre 8, Lockwood 8, Mackie 6, Connor 5, Easton 4, Steele 4, Tudor 4, Echanomi 3, Corden 2, Keith 2, McMahon 2, Miller 1, Simpson 1, Tann 1, Zakuani 1, Opponents 1.
F.A. Cup goals (6): Steele 2, Easton 1, Keith 1, Mackie 1, Tudor 1. **Carling Cup goals (1):** McMahon 1. **League Trophy goals (2):** Alexander 1, Hanson 1.
Average home League attendance: 4,699. **Player of Year:** Matthew Lockwood.

LINCOLN CITY

Keith Alexander took Lincoln into the play-offs for the fourth successive season – and once again he and his team had nothing to show for it. They had every reason to be confident of a semi-final meeting with Grimsby, having beaten their Lincolnshire rivals 5-0 a few weeks earlier and going on to claim seventh place in the table. This time, however, Grimsby won 1-0 at Sincil Bank and completed a 3-1 aggregate win in the second leg. Alexander resigned, but was back in a job a week later when taking over at Peterborough. John Schofield (head coach) and John Deeham (director of football) are the club's new management team.

Asamoah, D .... 19(6)	Birch, G .... 23(14)	Butcher, R 4
Bacon, D .... –(1)	Bloomer, M .... 7(5)	Cryan, C 37
Beevers, L .... 28(5)	Brown, N .... 37(2)	Forrester, J 9

Foster, L .... 14(2)	Marriott, A 43	Rayner, S 3
Frecklington, L ...... 3(15)	Mayo, P .... 25(3)	Robinson, M .... 20(12)
Green, F .... 23(5)	McAuley, G .... 33(2)	Robinson, S .... 11(1)
Gritton, M .... 4(6)	McCombe, J 38	Ryan, O .... 4(6)
Hughes, J .... 18(4)	Mettam, L .... –(1)	Stirling, J .... –(6)
Keates, D .... 19(2)	Molango, M .... 5(5)	Wilkinson, T .... –(1)
Kerr, S 41	Morgan, P .... 19(1)	Yeo, S .... 11(1)
Logan, R 8		

Play-offs – appearances: Beevers 2, Brown 2, Forrester 2, Hughes 2, Kerr 2, Marriott 2, McAuley 2, McCombe 2, Morgan 2, Robinson 2, Green 1(1), Yeo 1(1), Frecklington –(2), Birch –(1), Mayo –(1).
League goals (65): Birch 8, Brown 7, Robinson, M 7, Forrester 5, McAuley 5, Yeo 5, Keates 4, McCombe 4, Green 3, Mayo 3, Asamoah 2, Frecklington 2, Hughes 2, Kerr 2, Logan 2, Beevers 1, Butcher 1, Foster 1, Gritton 1. **Play-offs – goals (1):** Robinson 1.
F.A. Cup goals (2): Mayo 1, Robinson, M 1. **Carling Cup goals (9):** Birch 2, Robinson, M 2, Beevers 1, Green 1, Kerr 1, Molango 1, Opponents 1. **League Trophy goals (1):** Brown 1.
Average home League attendance: 4,739. **Player of Year:** Jamie McCombe.

MACCLESFIELD TOWN

The return of Jon Parkin after missing the first three months of the season helped lift Macclesfield out of the bottom two. Parkin, with 22 to his credit in the previous campaign, scored seven goals in 11 appearances, including a brace in the 6-0 win over Stockport and a 5-4 thriller at Wycombe. But his departure to Hull in a £150,000 transfer and a return by his old team to their wayward away form meant they were always in danger. Macclesfield had the worst record in the division on their travels although, ironically, it was a 3-2 victory at Bristol Rovers on the final day, secured by Marcus Richardson's late goal, that made sure of safety.

Bailey, M 6	Lee, T 11	Russell, A .... 12(1)
Barras, A 7	MacKenzie, N .... 4(2)	Sandwith, K .... 34(1)
Beresford, D .... 9(7)	McIntyre, K 44	Smart, A .... 7(2)
Brightwell, I .... 10(1)	McNeil, M 12	Swailes, D 39
Briscoe, M .... 11(2)	Miles, J .... 8(16)	Teague, A .... 23(2)
Bullock, M .... 38(2)	Morley, D 45	Townson, K .... 3(15)
Deasy, T .... 2(1)	Navarro, A 27	Whitaker, D .... 40(1)
Fettis, A 33	Parkin, J .... 9(2)	Wijnhard, C .... 19(1)
Harsley, P 45	Richardson, M 8	

League goals (60): Wijnhard 8, Bullock 7, Parkin 7, Harsley 6, McIntyre 5, Miles 4, Whitaker 4, Richardson 3, Sandwith 3, Russell 2, Swailes 2, Townson 2, Briscoe 1, MacKenzie 1, McNeil 1, Morley 1, Teague 1, Opponents 2.
F.A. Cup goals (1): Wijnhard 1. **Carling Cup goals (4):** Bullock 1, MacKenzie 1, Townson 1, Whitaker 1. **League Trophy goals (14):** Wijnhard 3, Parkin 2, Sandwith 2, Beresford 1, Harsley 1, McNeil 1, Smart 1, Teague 1, Townson 1, Whitaker 1.
Average home League attendance: 2,274. **Player of Year:** Danny Whitaker.

MANSFIELD TOWN

Carlton Palmer's resignation, blamed on abuse from supporters after one win in nine at the start of the season, led to a first job in management for Peter Shirtliff. The former Sheffield Wednesday stalwart, appointed after a spell as caretaker, led his team into the top half of the table, with Richie Barker scoring regularly, and they would have stayed there but for a poor finish which brought only three points from six games, the last one a 5-0 home defeat by Cheltenham. Barker was the division's third leading striker in all competitions, behind Karl Hawley and Scott McGleish, with 23 to his credit.

Arnold, N .... 5(3)	Barker, R .... 41(2)	Birchall, A .... 15(16)
Baptiste, A .... 40(1)	Beardsley, C .... 2(1)	Brown, S .... 15(14)

Buxton, J .... 36(3)	Littlejohn, A .... –(7)	Rundle, A .... 27(8)
Coke, G .... 33(7)	Lloyd, C .... 3(9)	Russell, A .... 7(11)
D'Laryea, J 29	McLachlan, F .... 7(1)	Talbot, J 6
Dawson, S .... 31(9)	Palmer, C 1	Tipton, M 4
Day, R 21	Peers, G .... 12(1)	Uhlenbeek, G .... 28(12)
Hjelde, J-O .... 30(1)	Pressman, K 41	White, J 5
Jacobs, K .... 4(1)	Reet, D .... 16(2)	Wilson, L .... 14(1)
Jelleyman, G .... 33(1)		

League goals (59): Barker 18, Brown 10, Reet 5, Rundle 5, Coke 4, Birchall 2, Day 2, Peers 2, Russell 2, Uhlenbeek 2, Arnold 1, Baptiste 1, Dawson 1, Hjelde 1, Jelleyman 1, Wilson 1, Opponents 1.
F.A. Cup goals (7): Barker 4, Birchall 1, Brown 1, Coke 1. **Carling Cup goals (4):** Barker 1, Brown 1, Coke 1, Jelleyman 1. **League Trophy goals:** None.
Average home League attendance: 3,560. **Player of Year:** Richie Barker.

NORTHAMPTON TOWN

Northampton won promotion but lost the man who steered them to the runners-up spot behind Carlisle. Former Tottenham defender Colin Calderwood left to become Nottingham Forest's manager after his team had wiped away the disappointment of losing play-off semi-finals in the two previous seasons. They overcame a patchy start to lay strong foundations for a perfectly-timed finish which netted 23 points out of 27.
Scott McLeish made sure his team went up with the winner against Chester in the penultimate game, his 24th in all competitions. It ranked him second to Carlisle's Karl Hawley. Calderwood was replaced by former Wycombe mangager John Gorman.

Bojic, P .... 18(18)	Hand, J .... 8(3)	Low, J .... 29(6)
Chambers, L .... 42(1)	Harper, L 46	McGleish, S .... 39(3)
Cross, S .... –(4)	Hunt, D .... 35(5)	Mendes, J .... 9(3)
Crowe, J 41	Jess, E .... 35(3)	Mikolanda, P 2
Doig, C .... 36(2)	Johnson, Bradley ... 1(2)	Rowson, D .... 13(16)
Dudfield, L .... 2(4)	Johnson, Brett .... 2(4)	Sabin, E .... 4(2)
Dyche, S .... 34(1)	Johnson, G .... 22(2)	Smith, M .... 22(4)
Galbraith, D .... 1(3)	Kirk, A .... 20(9)	Taylor, I 33
Gilligan,R .... 4(19)	Lee, J .... 8(3)	Westwood, A .... –(3)

League goals (63): McGleish 17, Kirk 8, Taylor 7, Low 5, Bojic 4, Gilligan 4, Hunt 3, Smith 3, Crowe 2, Doig 2, Mendes 2, Dudfield 1, Johnson, G 1, Jess 1, Lee 1, Opponents 2.
F.A. Cup goals (8): McGleish 4, Bojic 1, Doig 1, Low 1, Smith 1. **Carling Cup goals (3):** Kirk 1, McGleish 1, Sabin 1. **League Trophy goals (7):** Cross 2, McGleish 2, Bojic 1, Kirk 1, Mendes 1.
Average home League attendance: 5,935. **Player of Year:** Scott McGleish.

NOTTS COUNTY

No team fell away as much as Notts County, who were separated from a play-off place only by goal difference with a third of season left and looked a good bet to go one step further. Manager Gudjon Thordarson promised changes in personnel after winning just one of the last 16 matches and being sucked into a relegation struggle. The league's oldest club were kept guessing about their fate until the final day of the season when two goals in the last four minutes by Dan Martin and Julien Baudet from the penalty spot rescued a point against Bury and kept them two places away from the drop. Thordarson later left by mutual agreement to be replaced by a former Meadow Lane favourite, Steve Thompson.

Baudet, J 42	Dadi, E .... 9(2)	Friars, E 5
Berry, T .... 4(1)	De Bolla, M .... 8(6)	Frost, S .... –(4)
Chillingworth, D .... 8(5)	Doyle, N 12	Gill, M .... 7(7)
Crooks, L 18	Edwards, M .... 45(1)	Gordon, G .... 4(2)

Hurst, G .... 15(3)	O'Callaghan, B .... 30(3)	Tann, A .... 4(1)
Long, S .... 7(12)	Palmer, C .... 25(4)	Ullathorne, R .... 31(2)
Marshall, S 1	Pilkington, K 45	White, A .... 10(16)
Martin, D .... 16(6)	Pipe, D 43	Williams, M .... –(1)
McGoldrick, D .... 4(2)	Scoffham, S .... 22(8)	Wilson, A .... 33(1)
McMahon, L .... 23(6)	Sheridan, J .... 13(14)	Zadkovich, R .... –(1)
Needham, L .... 21(1)	Sissoko, N .... 1(2)	

League goals (48): Hurst 9, Edwards 7, Baudet 6, Scoffham 5, Martin 4, Chillingworth 2, Dadi 2, Pipe 2, White 2, Crooks 1, De Bolla 1, Friars 1, Long 1, O'Callaghan 1, Palmer 1, Sheridan 1, Wilson 1, Opponents 1.
F.A. Cup goals (3): Baudet 1, McMahon 1, Tann 1. **Carling Cup goals (1):** Palmer 1.
League Trophy goals (2): Long 1, McMahon 1.
Average home League attendance: 5,466. **Player of Year:** David Pipe.

OXFORD UNITED

Jim Smith's return as manager to the club he left 21 years earlier offered Oxford hope of avoiding Conference football after a struggling season under Brian Talbot. It was not to be. Needing to win the last of the eight games under Smith in front of a record crowd of 12,243 at the Kassam Stadium, they were beaten 3-2 in stoppage-time by Leyton Orient. The winner was scored by former Oxford striker Lee Steele and there was another bitter irony as they went down three weeks after Accrington, the side they had replaced in the Football League in 1962, were promoted as Conference champions.

Ashton, J .... 32(1)	Goodhind, W .... 4(2)	Quinn, J 44
Basham, S .... 30(10)	Gray, S 10	Roach, N .... 1(6)
Beechers, B .... –(1)	Griffin, A .... 8(1)	Robinson, M 44
Bradbury, J .... 18(4)	Guatelli, A 4	Roget, L .... 32(1)
Brooks, J .... 4(5)	Hackett, C .... 19(2)	Sabin, E .... 28(1)
Burgess, A .... 12(4)	Hargreaves, C .... 34(1)	Sills, T .... 9(4)
Campbell, A .... 3(2)	Horsted, L .... 1(3)	Smith, J .... 5(1)
Davies, C .... 10(10)	Hughes, R .... –(3)	Stirling, J .... 6(4)
Dempster, J 6	Mansell, L 44	Tardif, C .... 10(1)
E'Beyer, M .... 3(3)	Morgan, D .... 1(2)	Turley, W .... 32(1)
Fitzgerald, S .... 2(1)	N'Toya, T .... 7(1)	Weedon, D .... 1(1)
Gemmill, S .... –(1)	Odubade, Y .... 4(4)	Willmott, C .... 38(3)

League goals (43): Basham 8, Sabin 7, Bradbury 5, N'Toya 4, Davies 2, Hackett 2, Quinn 2, Roget 2, Willmott 2, Ashton 1, Burgess 1, E'Beyer 1, Fitzgerald 1, Hargreaves 1, Mansell 1,Morgan 1, Odubade 1, Wills 1.
F.A. Cup goals (6): Basham 5, Sabin 1. **Carling Cup goals:** None. **League Trophy goals (3):** Mansell 1, Roget 1, Sabin 1.
Average home League attendance: 5,442. **Player of Year:** Lee Mansell.

PETERBOROUGH UNITED

There was rarely a dull moment during Barry Fry's time in management and little changed in his first season as club owner. Fry sacked Mark Wright at the end of January for alleged misconduct and received caretaker Steve Bleasdale's resignation – citing interference over team selection from TV programme-makers at the club – just before the penultimate home match of the season against Macclesfield. Then, he appointed Keith Alexander a week after Alexander resigned as Lincoln manager. Peterborough were in a play-off position with five games left, but missed out after losing four of them.

Arber, M 46	Crow, D .... 34(4)	Holden, D .... 34(1)
Benjamin, T .... 5(15)	Day, J .... 19(6)	Huke, S 3
Bolland, P 17	Farrell, D .... 19(10)	Kennedy, P .... 10(4)
Boucard, A .... 2(1)	Gain, P 37	Kuqi, N 1
Burton, S .... 17(2)	Hand, J 9	Logan, R .... 13(15)
Carden, P 42	Harrison, L 6	Miller, A 2

Newton, A .... 36(4)	Ryan, T .... 6(1)	Thorpe, L 6
Opara, L .... 2(6)	Semple, R .... 11(17)	Tyler, M 40
Plummer, C .... 16(6)	St Ledger, S 43	Willock, C .... 9(6)
Quinn, J .... 21(3)		

League goals (57): Crow 15, Quinn 7, Farrell 6, Logan 4, Gain 3, Holden 3, Newton 3, Semple 3, Willock 3, Arber 2, Burton 2, Benjamin 1, Day 1, Opara 1, Plummer 1, St Ledger 1, Opponents 1.
F.A. Cup goals: None. **Carling Cup goals (1):** Plummer 1. **League Trophy goals (5):** Crow 2, Benjamin 1, Hand 1, Logan 1.
Average home League attendance: 4,363. **Player of Year:** Danny Crow.

ROCHDALE

Rickie Lambert and Grant Holt had Rochdale riding high in the first half of the season with 26 goals between them. Two each in a 4-3 win over Shrewsbury lifted the team to fourth in the table. But after being sent off against Wycombe, Holt played only one more game for the club before a £300,000 move to Nottingham Forest and they were not the same force again. While Lambert took his total for the campaign to 22 and finished joint top league scorer with Carlisle's Karl Hawley, Rochdale fell away to settle just below midway, a drop of five places on 2004-05.

Bayliss, D 4	Doolan, J .... 16(2)	Kitchen, B .... 3(5)
Boardman, J .... 17(4)	Gallimore, A .... 32(2)	Lambert, R .... 43(3)
Brisco, N .... 14(2)	Gilks, M 46	McArdle, R .... 16(3)
Brown, G .... 6(10)	Goodall, A .... 37(3)	Moyo-Modise, C .... 1(8)
Cartwright, L .... 21(6)	Goodhind, W 10	Ramsden, S 15
Christie, I .... 10(4)	Holt, G 21	Sturrock, B .... 15(16)
Clarke, J .... 21(1)	Griffiths, G 29	Tait, P .... 4(7)
Coleman, T 1	Jackson, M 12	Thompson, J .... –(1)
Cooksey, E .... 27(7)	Jaszczun, T .... 12(5)	Warner, S .... 16(8)
Dagnall, C .... 15(6)	Jones, G 42	

League goals (66): Lambert 22, Holt 14, Sturrock 6, Jones 4, Cooksey 3, Dagnall 3, Goodall 3, Christie 2, Griffiths 2, Boardman 1, Cartwright 1, McArdle 1, Ramsden 1, Tait 1, Warner 1, Opponents 1.
F.A. Cup goals: None. **Carling Cup goals:** None. **League Trophy goals (5):** Tait 2, Holt 1, Opponents 2.
Average home League attendance: 2,807. **Player of Year:** Rickie Lambert.

RUSHDEN AND DIAMONDS

Paul Hart was entrusted with the task of trying to bring back the good times to Nene Park after five years of league football came to an end with a return to the Conference. The club's former defender Barry Hunter had been unable to prevent a second relegation in three seasons and was replaced by former Nottingham Forest manager Hart. With four matches left, Rushden had shown signs of coming good at the right time, moving on to the shoulder of teams above them thanks to an improved run of form. But they lost all four to finish seven points adrift in bottom spot.

Allen, G 5	Dempster, J .... 13(1)	Mikolanda, P .... 7(2)
Armstrong, A .... 6(3)	Gier, R .... 34(1)	Mills, G .... 7(4)
Bell, D .... 13(1)	Grainger, D .... 2(12)	Nicholls, A .... 26(4)
Berry, T .... 13(7)	Gulliver, P 40	O'Grady, C .... 20(2)
Broughton, D .... 32(5)	Hatswell, W 17	Okuonghae, M .... 15(6)
Bull, R 19	Hawkins, P .... 20(1)	Pearson, G .... 16(6)
Burgess, A .... 7(2)	Hunter, B .... –(5)	Ruddy, J 3
Caskey, D .... 17(1)	Jackson, S .... 8(6)	Savage, D .... 30(2)
Castle, P 1	Joseph, M 1	Shaw, T .... –(1)
Chillingworth, D .... 3(3)	Kelly, M .... 39(2)	Stokes, T .... 18(1)
Crane, D 8	McCafferty, N .... 19(4)	Taylor, J .... 4(8)

Tomlin, L .... 4(17)   Tynan, S .... 13(1)   Young, J .... 19(1)
Turner, J .... 4(7)   Woodman, A 3

League goals (44): Broughton 6, Jackson 5, Gulliver 4, O'Grady 4, Bell 3, Dempster 3, Kelly 3, Savage 2, Allen 1, Caskey 1, Grainger 1, Hatswell 1, Mikolanda 1, Okuonghae 1, Pearson 1, Taylor 1, Turner 1, Opponents 1.
F.A. Cup goals (1): Armstrong 1. **Carling Cup goals:** None. **League Trophy goals (1):** Pearson 1.
Average home League attendance: 3,162. **Player of Year:** Phil Gulliver.

SHREWSBURY TOWN

A season of steady progress for Shrewsbury ended with a dream move for 19-year-old Joe Hart. The 6ft 3in goalkeeper, who did not made his league debut until April 2005, played in all 46 matches, watched closely by Manchester City, who were impressed enough to pay £600,000 for his services, a fee that could eventually reach £1.5m. Hart's team were five points adrift of a play-off position. But a rise of 11 places, helped by four points gained against the eventual champions Carlisle, was a satisfactory one after the fourth-from-bottom finish in 2004-05.

Adaggio, M .... –(5)   Hart, J 46   McClen, J 4
Ashton, N .... 39(5)   Herd, B .... 45(1)   McMenamin, C .... 40(3)
Burton, S .... 15(1)   Hogg, S .... 7(5)   Sharp, K .... 27(3)
Cadwallader, G .... –(2)   Hope, R 42   Smith, B .... 9(3)
Cowan, G .... 9(6)   Hurst, G .... 15(1)   Sorvel, N .... 44(1)
Darby, D .... 7(4)   Jackson, M .... 2(3)   Stallard, M ...... 25(12)
Denny, J .... 7(7)   Langmead, K .... 29(13)   Tolley, J .... 30(3)
Edwards, D .... 27(3)   Leslie, S .... –(1)   Walton, D .... 15(1)
Evans, R .... 2(4)   Lyng, C .... –(1)   Whitehead, S .... 20(3)

League goals (55): McMenamin 10, Langmead 9, Stallard 6, Burton 4, Sorvel 4, Tolley 4, Hurst 3, Darby 2, Edwards 2, Herd 2, Hope 2, Walton 2, Ashton 1, Cowan 1, Sharp 1, Smith 1, Opponents 1.
F.A. Cup goals (5): Edwards 2, Hope 1, McMenamin 1, Tolley 1. **Carling Cup goals (3):** Denny 2, Stallard 1. **League Trophy goals:** None.
Average home League attendance: 3,996. **Player of year:** Dave Edwards.

STOCKPORT COUNTY

Jim Gannon gave Stockport a decade's service as a player and now aims to restore their fortunes as manager. His first task, saving the club from a second successive relegation, was achieved after he succeeded Chris Turner in the wake of a 6-0 Boxing Day defeat at Macclesfield which had cast them adrift at the bottom of the table. Any two from ten teams could have gone down in a tense climax to the season. But Gannon's side survived, despite failing to score in four of the last five matches, a draw at home to champions Carlisle in the final fixture making sure they avoided dropping into the Conference.

Allen, D .... 13(9)   Easter, J .... 18(1)   Robertson, M 2
Beharall, D .... 10(2)   Ellis, D .... –(3)   Robinson, M 44
Boshell, D .... 28(5)   Foster, L .... –(1)   Singh, H .... 19(5)
Bramble, T .... 33(4)   Greenwood, R .... 17(5)   Smylie, D .... 1(2)
Briggs, K .... 39(2)   Griffin, A .... 20(1)   Spencer, J 34
Clare, R .... 31(3)   Griffin, D 4   Strachan, G 4
Collins, A .... 2(1)   Hamshaw, M .... 35(4)   Symes, M .... –(1)
Crowe, D .... 1(5)   Hughes, M 3   Taylor, J 9
Crowther, R .... –(1)   Ikeme, C 9   Tunnicliffe, J .... –(1)
Dickinson, L .... 12(9)   Le Fondre, A ...... 4(18)   Vaughan, A 10
Dje, L .... 5(2)   Malcolm, M .... 10(13)   Ward, J .... 7(2)
Dolan, J 2   O'Connor, K .... 6(1)   Williams, A .... 33(3)
Duke, M 3   Raynes, M .... 23(2)   Williams, C .... 1(2)

Wolski, M .... 14(6)

League goals (57): Easter 8, Dickinson 7, Le Fondre 7, Bramble 5, Hamshaw 5, Briggs 4, Malcolm 3, Clare 2, Griffin 2, Robinson 2, Boshell 1, O'Connor 1, Raynes 1, Singh 1, Vaughan 1, Ward 1, Williams, A 1, Wolski 1, Opponents 1.
F.A. Cup goals (6): Easter 3, Briggs 2, Wolski 1. **Carling Cup goals (2):** Boshell 1, Le Fondre 1. **League Trophy goals (1):** Opponents 1.
Average home League attendance: 4,772. **Player of Year:** Ashley Williams.

TORQUAY UNITED

Chairman Mike Bateson's gamble in putting Torquay's fate in the hands of Ian Atkins with six matches remaining paid off handsomely. From a seemingly hopeless position, the club's football adviser delivered 13 points – including a 2-1 success at promoted Carlisle – to avoid the drop into the Conference. It was a remarkable change in fortunes for a side that had struggled from the start under Leroy Rosenior and continued to do so when Rosenior was replaced by John Cornforth in late January. Atkins, who began the season in charge at Bristol Rovers, was rewarded with the manager's job on a permanent basis.

Afful, L .... –(5)	Hockley, M .... 25(11)	Reed, S 11
Andrews, L .... 6(1)	Hollands, D 10	Robinson, P .... 12(9)
Bedeau, A .... 26(5)	Kuffour, J .... 34(9)	Sako, M .... 10(15)
Coleman, L .... 7(7)	Lawless, A .... 11(3)	Sharp, J .... 30(2)
Connell, A .... 12(10)	Lloyd, A .... 19(1)	Sow, M .... 9(2)
Constantine, L .... 10(5)	Lockwood, A 9	Stonebridge, I 3
Flynn, P 1	Marriott, A 46	Taylor, C .... 27(4)
Garner, D .... 40(3)	McAliskey, J 3	Thorpe, L 10
Hancox, R .... –(1)	McGlinchey, B .... 4(1)	Villis, M .... 11(1)
Hewlett, M .... 18(6)	Phillips, M .... 23(3)	Woodman, C 2
Hill, K .... 41(1)	Priso, C .... 1(2)	Woods, S .... 35(3)

League goals (53): Bedeau 9, Hill 9, Kuffour 8, Connell 7, Lockwood 3, Phillips 3, Robinson 3, Sako 3, Thorpe 3, Garner 2, Constantine 1, Hewlett 1, Hollands 1.
F.A. Cup goals (3): Bedeau 2, Stonebridge 1. **Carling Cup goals:** None. **League Trophy goals (1):** Kuffour 1.
Average home League attendance: 2,851. **Player of Year:** Kevin Hill.

WREXHAM

Wrexham faltered after eight goals in eight games by Matt Derbyshire, on loan from Blackburn, raised hopes of a challenge for an immediate return to League One. They moved to within two points of a play-off place with a month of the season remaining, but were unable to maintain the momentum, four successive defeats leaving them with too much ground to recover. There was a better outcome in the summer when this financially troubled club received permission from the Football League for a 28-day extension in which to complete a £3.25m. takeover by a consortium headed by local businessman Neville Dickens.

Bayliss, D .... 21(1)	Jones, Michael .... 6(1)	Spender, S .... 15(4)
Bennett, D .... 20(13)	Lawrence, D .... 38(1)	Ugarte, J 2
Crowell, M .... 26(3)	Linwood, P .... 8(1)	Walters, J .... 33(5)
Derbyshire, M 16	Mackin, L .... 3(14)	Warhurst, P .... 6(5)
Done, M .... 1(5)	McEvilly, L .... 15(8)	Whitley, J 10
Ferguson, D .... 36(3)	Pejic, S 26	Williams, D 45
Foy, R .... 7(10)	Reed, J .... –(3)	Williams, Marc .... 2(2)
Holt, A .... 35(1)	Roche, L 17	Williams, Mike .... 7(5)
Ingham, M 40	Smith, A .... 15(5)	Williams, S .... 14(1)
Jones, Mark 42		

League goals (61): Jones, Mark 13, Derbyshire 10, McEvilly 7, Walters 5, Williams, D 4, Crowell 3, Foy 3, Holt 3, Bennett 2, Ferguson 2, Lawrence 2, Williams, S 2, Spender 2, Roche 1, Warhurst 1, Opponents 1.
F.A. Cup goals (1): McEvilly 1. **Carling Cup goals:** None. **League Trophy goals (3):** Jones, Mark 2, Ferguson 1.
Average home League attendance: 4,477. **Player of Year:** Danny Williams.

WYCOMBE WANDERERS

Tragedy accompanied Wycombe's failure to win promotion after an unbeaten start to the season spanning 21 matches. Players were badly affected by the death in a car accident of 21-year-old midfield player Mark Philo. The following month manager John Gorman's wife.Myra died of cancer and he was later placed on compassionate leave from the club. His team, with assistant Steve Brown in temporary charge, slipped from the top of the table and were beaten 2-1 on aggregate by Cheltenham in the play-off semi-finals. Then, the club 'reluctantly' decided to relieve Gorman of his duties, maintaining that he needed more time to deal with his loss. The new manager is Paul Lambert, former Celtic and Scotland captain.

Antwi, W 5	Easton, C .... 40(4)	Oakes, S .... 31(6)
Anya, I .... –(2)	Gregory, S .... –(1)	Senda, D 44
Betsy, K .... 41(1)	Griffin, C .... 13(8)	Stonebridge, I .... 8(19)
Bloomfield, M .... 35(4)	Johnson, R 45	Talia, F 35
Bowditch, D .... 9(2)	Keogh, R .... 2(1)	Torres, S .... 13(11)
Burnell, J .... 27(6)	Lee, R .... 28(3)	Turner, I 3
Collins, A .... 3(2)	Lonergan, A 2	Tyson, N 15
Dixon, J .... –(17)	Martin, R .... 11(12)	Williams, S 1
Duke, M 5	Mooney, T .... 44(1)	Williamson, M .... 38(2)
Easter, J .... 8(7)		

Play-offs – appearances: Antwi 2, Betsy 2, Bloomfield 2, Easton 2, Johnson 2, Lee 2, Martin 2, Mooney 2, Senda 2, Williams 2, Easter 1(1), Stonebridge 1, Burnell –(1), Griffin –(1), Oakes –(1), Williamson –(1).
League goals (72): Mooney 17, Tyson 11, Betsy 8, Johnson 7, Bloomfield 5, Williamson 5, Griffin 3, Martin 3, Easter 2, Oakes 2, Stonebridge 2, Bowditch 1, Collins 1, Easton 1, Torres 1, Opponents 3. **Play-offs – goals (1):** Mooney 1.
F.A. Cup goals (1): Burnell 1. **Carling Cup goals (6):** Tyson 2, Dixon 1, Johnson 1, Mooney 1, Stonebridge 1. **League Trophy goals (6):** Griffin 4, Easton 2.
Average home League attendance: 5,444. **Player of Year:** Roger Johnson.

QUOTE-UNQUOTE

'I'm proud of my name. Shaun Wright-Phillips doesn't just sign Wright, does he?' – **Jan Vennegoor of Hesselink**, PSV Eindhoven striker.

'I'm not a big cricket man, but I found myself watching how tense it was, down to the last ball' – **David Beckham**, England captain, on the nail-biting finish to the England-Australia third Test.

'I wasn't properly prepared' – **David James**, England goalkeeper, after coming off the bench for the second half of the friendly against Denmark and letting in four goals.

'We're top of the table, it's my 50th goal and my girlfriend has given birth to our first daughter. It's the best week of my life' – **Frank Lampard**, Chelsea midfielder, after scoring twice against West Bromwich Albion.

'He's fat, he's round, he's given us a ground' – **Brighton** fans' chant after Deputy Prime Minister John Prescott grants the club permission for a new stadium.

LEAGUE CLUB MANAGERS

Figure in brackets = number of managerial changes at club since the War.

BARCLAYS PREMIERSHIP

Club	Manager	Date
Arsenal (11)	Arsene Wenger	October 1996
Aston Villa		
Blackburn Rov. (22)	Mark Hughes	September 2004
Bolton Wand. (17)	Sam Allardyce	October 1999
Charlton Athletic (13)	Iain Dowie	May 2006
Chelsea (19)	Jose Mourinho	June 2004
Everton (16)	David Moyes	March 2002
Fulham (23)	Chris Coleman	May 2003
Liverpool (10)	Rafael Benitez	June 2004
Manchester City (25)	Stuart Pearce	May 2005
Manchester Utd. (8)	Sir Alex Ferguson	November 1986
Middlesbrough (17)	Gareth Southgate	June 2006
Newcastle Utd. (19)	Glenn Roeder	May 2006
Portsmouth (24)	Harry Redknapp+	December 2005
Reading (16)	Steve Coppell	October 2003
Sheffield Utd. (29)	Neil Warnock	December 1999
Tottenham (18)	Martin Jol	November 2004
Watford (24)	Adrian Boothroyd	March 2005
West Ham Utd. (9)	Alan Pardew	September 2003
Wigan Athletic (15)	Paul Jewell	June 2001

+ Second spell at club. Number of changes since elected to Football League: Wigan Athletic 1978.

COCA-COLA LEAGUE – CHAMPIONSHIP

Club	Manager	Date
Barnsley (18)	Andy Ritchie	May 2005
Birmingham City (21)	Steve Bruce	December 2001
Burnley (20)	Steve Cotterill	June 2004
Cardiff City (26)	Dave Jones	May 2005
Colchester Utd.		
Coventry City (26)	Micky Adams	January 2005
Crystal Palace (32)	Peter Taylor	June 2006
Derby Co. (19)	Billy Davies	June 2006
Hull City (22)	Phil Parkinson	June 2006
Ipswich Town (10)	Jim Magilton	June 2006
Leeds Utd. (20)	Kevin Blackwell	May 2004
Leicester City (20)	Rob Kelly	February 2006
Luton Town (19)	Mike Newell	June 2003
Norwich City (21)	Nigel Worthington	January 2001
Plymouth Argyle (28)	Ian Holloway	June 2006
Preston N.E. (23)	Paul Simpson	June 2006
Q.P.R. (22)	Gary Waddock	June 2006
Sheffield Wed. (23)	Paul Sturrock	September 2004
Southampton (18)	George Burley	December 2005
Stoke City (22)	Tony Pulis+	June 2006
Southend Utd. (26)	Steve Tilson	March 2004
Sunderland		
W.B.A. (25)	Bryan Robson	November 2004
Wolves		

+ Second spell at club.

LEAGUE ONE

Club	Manager	Date
Blackpool (23)	Simon Grayson	January 2006
Bournemouth (18)	Sean O'Driscoll	August 2000
Bradford City (28)	Colin Todd	June 2004
Brentford (26)	Leroy Rosenior	June 2006
Brighton & H.A. (26)	Mark McGhee	October 2003
Bristol City (20)	Gary Johnson	September 2005
Carlisle Utd. (1)	Neil McDonald	June 2006
Cheltenham Town (3)	John Ward	November 2003
Chesterfield (16)	Roy McFarland	May 2003
Crewe Alexandra (17)	Dario Gradi	June 1983
Doncaster Rov. (-)	Dave Penney	January 2002
Gillingham (19)	Ronnie Jepson	November 2005
Huddersfield Town (21)	Peter Jackson	June 2003
Leyton Orient (20)	Martin Ling	October 2003
Millwall (26)	Nigel Spackman	May 2006
Northampton Town (26)	John Gorman	June 2006
Nott'm. Forest (15)	Colin Calderwood	May 2006
Oldham Athletic (22)	John Sheridan	June 2006
Port Vale (18)	Martin Foyle	February 2004
Rotherham Utd. (20)	Alan Knill	January 2006
Scunthorpe Utd. (21)	Brian Laws ++	February 1997
Swansea City (27)	Kenny Jackett	April 2004
Tranmere Rov. (17)	Ronnie Moore	June 2006
Yeovil Town (2)	Russell Slade	June 2006

++ Reinstated three weeks after leaving club in 2004. Number of changes since elected to Football League: Cheltenham Town 1999; Yeovil Town 2003. Since returning: Doncaster Rov. 2003, Carlisle Utd. 2005.

LEAGUE TWO

Club	Manager	Date
Accrington Stanley (-)	John Coleman	July 1999
Barnet (-)	Paul Fairclough	May 2004
Boston Utd. (2)	Steve Evans+	February 2004
Bristol Rov. (22)	Paul Trollope	November 2005
Bury (21)	Chris Casper	October 2005
Chester City (3)	Mark Wright+	February 2006
Darlington (30)	David Hodgson	November 2003
Grimsby Town (28)	Graham Rodger	June 2006
Hartlepool Utd. (29)	Danny Wilson	June 2006
Hereford Utd. (-)	Graham Turner	August 1995
Lincoln City (24)	John Schofield	June 2006
Macclesfield Town (5)	Brian Horton	April 2004
Mansfield Town (24)	Peter Shirtliff	November 2005
Milton Keynes Dons (12)	Martin Allen	June 2006
Notts Co. (29)	Steve Thompson	June 2006
Peterborough Utd. (22)	Keith Alexander	May 2006
Rochdale (28)	Steve Parkin+	December 2003
Shrewsbury Town (1)	Gary Peters	November 2004
Stockport Co. (32)	Jim Gannon	January 2006
Swindon Town (22)	Dennis Wise	May 2006
Torquay Utd. (30)	Ian Atkins	April 2006
Walsall (30)	Richard Money	May 2006
Wrexham (17)	Denis Smith	October 2001
Wycombe Wand. (7)	Paul Lambert	June 2006

+ Second spell at club. Number of changes since elected to Football League: Peterborough Utd. 1960; Wycombe Wand. 1993; Macclesfield Town 1997; Boston Utd. 2002. Since returning: Chester City, Shrewsbury Town 2004; Barnet 2005; Accrington Stanley, Hereford Utd. 2006.

ATTENDANCES 2005-06

Premiership crowds fell for a third successive season, but this time by less than 0.5%. Biggest winners were the three promoted clubs – Wigan whose average attendance rose by 78% to 20,609, West Ham with a 23% increase to 33,742 and Sunderland whose average of 33,904 was up nearly 18%. Eight other clubs reported increases, the majority marginal ones. There were significant falls at Middlesbrough (11%), Aston Villa (8.6%) and Manchester City (5%).

Gates in the Championship continued to rise, with 247 matches topping 20,000. Overall, the Football League figures for the three divisions were beaten, for the modern era, only by the previous season's total. Scottish Premier League crowds soared to 3.7m., highest for top-flight football there since the 1960s.

LEAGUE CROWDS SINCE 1980

	Total	Div. One	Div. Two	Div. Three	Div. Four
1979-80	24,623,975	12,163,002	6,112,025	3,999,328	2,349,620
1980-81	21,907,569	11,392,894	5,175,442	3,637,854	1,701,379
1981-82	20,006,961	10,420,793	4,750,463	2,836,915	1,998,790
1982-83	18,766,158	9,295,613	4,974,937	2,943,568	1,552,040
1983-84	18,358,631	8,711,448	5,359,757	2,729,942	1,557,484
1984-85	17,849,835	9,761,404	4,030,823	2,667,008	1,390,600
1985-86	16,498,868	9,037,854	3,555,343	2,495,991	1,409,680
1986-87	17,383,032	9,144,676	4,168,131	2,354,784	1,715,441
1987-88	17,968,887	8,094,571	5,350,754	2,751,275	1,772,287
1988-89	18,477,565	7,809,993	5,827,805	3,048,700	1,791,067
1989-90	19,466,826	7,887,658	6,884,439	2,803,551	1,891,178
1990-91	19,541,341	8,618,709	6,297,733	2,847,813	1,777,086
1991-92	20,487,273	9,989,160	5,809,787	2,993,352	1,694,974

New format	Total	Premier	Div. One	Div. Two	Div. Three
1992-93	20,657,327	9,759,809	5,874,017	3,483,073	1,540,428
1993-94	21,693,889	10,655,059	6,487,104	2,972,702	1,579,024
1994-95	21,856,223	11,213,371	6,044,293	3,037,752	1,560,807
1995-96	21,844,416	10,469,107	6,566,349	2,843,652	1,965,308
1996-97	22,791,527	10,804,762	6,804,606	3,332,451	1,849,708
1997-98	24,679,527	11,091,773	8,330,018	3,503,264	1,767,220
1998-99	25,435,981	11,620,765	7,543,369	4,169,697	2,102,150
1999-2000	25,342,478	11,668,222	7,811,420	3,700,433	2,162,403
2000-01	26,067,729	12,503,732	7,912,046	3,490,250	2,161,701
2001-02	27,835,107	13,043,118	8,402,142	3,981,252	2,408,595
2002-03	28,340,946	13,468,965	8,519,866	3,892,400	2,459,715
2003-04	29,196,787	13,307,037	8,771,259	4,143,691	2,974,800

New format	Total	Premier	Championship	League One	League Two
2004-05	29,244,481	12,880,062	9,610,170	4,270,604	2,483,645
2005-06	29,046,992	12,830,320	9,719,264	4,182,320	2,315,088

All-time record Football League attendance aggregate: 41,271,414 in season 1948-49 (88 clubs). The average was 22,333.

NATIONAL REFEREES 2006-07

SELECT GROUP

Bennett, Steve (Kent)
Clattenburg Mark (Tyne and Wear)
Dean, Mike (Wirral)
Dowd, Phil (Staffs)
D'Urso, Andy (Essex)
Foy, Chris (Merseyside)
Gallagher, Dermot (Oxon)
Halsey, Mark (Lancs)

Knight, Barry (Kent)
Poll, Graham (Herts)
Rennie, Uriah (Yorks)
Riley, Mike (Yorks)
Styles, Rob (Hants)
Walton, Peter (Northants)
Webb, Howard (Yorks)
Wiley, Alan (Staffs)

NATIONAL GROUP

Armstrong, Paul (Berks)
Atkinson, Martin (Yorks)
Bates, Tony (Staffs)
Beeby, Richard (Northants)
Booth, Russell (Notts)
Boyeson, Carl (Yorks)
*Bratt, Steve (West Midlands)
Cowburn, Mark (Lancs)
Crossley, Phil (Kent)
Curson, Brian (Leics)
Deadman, Darren (Cambs)
*Desmond, Bob (Wilts)
Dorr, Steve (Worcs)
Drysdale, Darren (Lincs)
Friend, Kevin (Leics)
*Graham, Fred (Essex)
Hall, Andy (West Midlands)
*Haywood, Mark (Yorks)
Hegley, Grant (Herts)
Hill, Keith (Herts)
Ilderton, Eddie (Tyne & Wear)
Jones, Michael (Cheshire)
Joslin, Phil (Notts)
Kettle, Trevor (Rutland)
Laws, Graham (Tyne & Wear)
*Lee, Ray (Essex)
*Lewis, Rob (Shrops)
Marriner, Andre (West Midlands)
Mason, Lee (Lancs)
Mathieson, Scott (Cheshire)
*McDermid, Danny (London)

Melin, Paul (Surrey)
Miller, Nigel (Co Durham)
Miller, Pat (Beds)
Moss, Jon (Yorks)
Oliver, Clive (Northumberland)
Olivier, Ray (West Midlands)
Parkes, Trevor (West Midlands)
Penn, Andy (West Midlands)
Penton, Clive (Sussex)
Pike, Mike (Cumbria)
Probert, Lee (Gloucs)
Prosser, Phil (Yorks)
Robinson, Paul (Yorks)
Russell, Mike (Herts)
Salisbury, Graham (Lancs)
*Shoebridge, Rob (Derbys)
Singh, Jarnail (Middx)
Stroud, Keith (Hants)
Sutton, Gary (Lincs)
Swarbrick, Neil (Lancs)
Tanner, Steve (Somerset)
*Taylor, Anthony (Cheshire)
Taylor, Paul (Herts)
Thorpe, Mike (Norfolk)
Webster, Colin (Tyne & Wear)
*Whitestone, Dean (Northants)
Williamson, Iain (Berks)
Woolmer, Andy (Northants)
Wright, Kevin (Cambs)

(* New appointments)

MANAGERIAL MERRY-GO-ROUND

Nearly half the 92 league clubs kicked off the new season with a different manager from the one in charge at the start of the 2005-06 campaign. League Two had the biggest turnover, involving 15 clubs. There were 13 changes in the Championship, 12 in League One and five in the Premiership. In addition, the two clubs who were relegated to the Conference, Oxford and Rushden and Diamonds, also brought in new managers.

F.A. CUP 2005-06

FIRST ROUND

Barnet 0, Southend Utd. 1
Barnsley 1, Darlington 0
Bournemouth 1, Tamworth 2
Bradford City 2, Tranmere Rov. 1
Bristol City 0, Notts Co. 2
Burnham 1, Aldershot 3
Burscough 3, Gillingham 2
Bury 2, Scunthorpe Utd. 2
Cambridge City 0, Hereford 1
Chasetown 1, Oldham Athletic 1
Cheltenham Town 1, Carlisle Utd. 0
Chester City 2, Folkestone 1
Chippenham 1, Worcester 1
Colchester Utd. 9, Leamington 1
Doncaster Rov. 4, Blackpool 1
Eastbourne 1, Oxford Utd. 1
Grimsby Town 1, Bristol Rov. 2
Halifax Town 1, Rushden & Diamonds 1
Hartlepool Utd. 2, Dag. & Redbridge 1
Histon 0, Hednesford 0
Huddersfield Town 4, Welling 1
Kettering 1, Stevenage 3
Leyton Orient 0, Chesterfield 0
Lincoln City 1, MK Dons 1
Macclesfield Town 1, Yeovil Town 1
Merthyr 1, Walsall 2
Morecambe 1, Northwich 3
Nott'm. Forest 1, Weymouth 1
Nuneaton 2, Ramsgate 1
Peterborough Utd. 0, Burton 0
Port Vale 2, Wrexham 1
Rochdale 0, Brentford 1
Rotherham Utd. 3, Mansfield Town 4
Shrewsbury Town 4, Braintree 1
Southport 1, Woking 1
Stockport Co. 2, Swansea City 0
Swindon Town 2, Boston Utd. 2
Torquay Utd. 1, Harrogate 0
Wycombe Wand. 1, Northampton Town 3
York City 0, Grays 3

FIRST ROUND REPLAYS

Boston Utd. 4, Swindon Town 1
Burton 1, Peterborough Utd. 0

Chesterfield 1, Leyton Orient 2
Harrogate 0, Torquay Utd. 0
(aet, Torquay Utd. won 6-5 on pens)
MK Dons 2, Lincoln City 1
Oldham Athletic 4, Chasetown 0
Oxford Utd. 3, Eastbourne 0
Rushden & Diamonds 0, Halifax Town 0
(aet, Rushden & Diamonds won 5-4 on
pens)
Scunthorpe Utd. 1, Bury 0 (aet)
Weymouth 0, Nott'm. Forest 2
Woking 1, Southport 0 (aet)
Worcester 1, Chippenham 0
Yeovil Town 4, Macclesfield Town 0

SECOND ROUND

Aldershot 0, Scunthorpe Utd. 1
Barnsley 1, Bradford City 1
Boston Utd. 1, Doncaster Rov. 2
Burton 4, Burscough 1
Cheltenham Town 1, Oxford Utd. 1
Chester City 3, Nott'm. Forest 0
Hartlepool Utd. 1, Tamworth 2
Hereford 2, Stockport Co. 2
Mansfield Town 3, Grays 0
Nuneaton 2, Histon 2
Oldham Athletic 1, Brentford 1
Port Vale 1, Bristol Rov. 1
Rushden & Diamonds 0, Leyton Orient 1
Shrewsbury Town 1, Colchester Utd. 2
Southend Utd. 1, MK Dons 2
Stevenage 2, Northampton Town 2
Torquay Utd. 2, Notts Co. 1
Walsall 2, Yeovil Town 0
Woking 0, Northwich 0
Worcester 0, Huddersfield Town 1

SECOND ROUND REPLAYS

Bradford City 3, Barnsley 5 (aet)
Brentford 1, Oldham Athletic 0
Bristol Rov. 0, Port Vale 1
Histon 1, Nuneaton 2
Northampton Town 2, Stevenage 0
Northwich 2, Woking 1
Oxford Utd. 1, Cheltenham Town 2

LIVERPOOL FIGHT BACK TO WIN DRAMATIC F.A. CUP FINAL

THIRD ROUND	FOURTH ROUND	FIFTH ROUND	SIXTH ROUND	SEMI-FINALS	FINAL
Liverpool ... 5	Liverpool ... 3				
*Luton Town ... 3	*Portsmouth ... 1	*Liverpool ... 1			
Portsmouth ... 0			Liverpool ... 7		
*Wolves ... 1	*Wolves ... 0				
Plymouth Argyle ... 0	Manchester Utd. ... 3	Manchester Utd. ... 0			
*Burton ... 0:0				Liverpool ... 2	
Manchester Utd. ... 0:5					
Stoke City ... 0:+A1	*Stoke City ... 2				
Tamworth ... 0:1	Walsall ... 1	*Stoke City ... 0			
*Barnsley ... 1:0			*Birmingham City ... 0		
Walsall ... 1:2	*Reading ... 1:1				
*W.B.A. ... 1:2	Birmingham City ... 1:2	Birmingham City ... 1			
*Torquay Utd. ... 1+3					Liverpool ... +C3
Birmingham City ... 0:2					
*Millwall ... 1:0	*Everton ... 1:1				
Everton ... 1:1	Chelsea ... 1:4	*Chelsea ... 3			
*Chelsea ... 2			*Chelsea ... 1		
Huddersfield Town ... 1	*Colchester Utd. ... 3				
*Sheffield Utd. ... 1	Derby Co. ... 1	Colchester Utd. ... 1			
Colchester Utd. ... 2				Chelsea ... 1	
*Derby Co. ... 1					
Burnley ... 1	*Cheltenham Town ... 0				
*Cheltenham Town ... 2:1	Newcastle Utd. ... 1	*Newcastle Utd. ... 1			
Chester City ... 2:0			Newcastle Utd. ... 0		
*Newcastle Utd. ... 1	*Leicester City ... 0				
Mansfield Town ... 0	Southampton ... 1	Southampton ... 0			
*Leicester City ... 2					
Tottenham ... 4					
*Southampton ... 3					
MK Dons ... 1					

144

Knock-out competition chart (reading left → right to the Final):

- *Sheffield Wed. ...... 2 / Charlton Athletic 4
  - *Charlton Athletic ...... 2 / Leyton Orient 1
- *Fulham ...... 2 / Leyton Orient 1
    - *Charlton Athletic ...... 0:2 / Brentford 1
- *Stockport Co. ...... 3 / Brentford 0
  - *Brentford ...... 2 / Sunderland 1
- *Sunderland ...... 1 / Norwich 0
      - Charlton Athletic 3
- *Preston N.E. ...... 1 / Crewe Alexandra 1
  - *Preston N.E. ...... 1:2 / Crystal Palace 1:1
- *Crystal Palace ...... 4 / Northampton Town 1
    - *Preston N.E. ...... 0 / Middlesbrough 0:4
- *Brighton & H.A. ...... 0 / Coventry City 1
  - *Coventry City ...... 1:0 / Middlesbrough 1:1
- Middlesbrough ...... 1:5 / *Hull City 1
        - Middlesbrough 2
          - Middlesbrough 0
- Aston Villa ...... 1 / *Port Vale 1
  - *Aston Villa ...... 3 / Port Vale 1
- Doncaster ...... 2 / *Manchester City 3
    - *Aston Villa ...... 1:1 / Manchester City 1:2
- Scunthorpe Utd. ...... 1 / *Wigan Athletic ... 1:+B3
  - *Manchester City ...... 1 / Wigan Athletic 0
- Leeds Utd. ...... 1:3 / *Watford 1
      - *Manchester City 1
- Bolton Wand. ...... 2 / *Arsenal 0
  - *Bolton Wand. ...... 1 / Arsenal 0
            - West Ham Utd. 1
- Cardiff City ...... 2 / *Blackburn Rov. 3
    - *Bolton Wand. ...... 0:1 / West Ham Utd. 2
- Q.P.R. ...... 0 / *Norwich City 1
  - Blackburn Rov. ...... 0:2 / *West Ham Utd. 4
- *Norwich City ...... 1 / West Ham Utd. 2
        - **West Ham Utd. 2**
          - **West Ham Utd. 2**
              - **West Ham Utd. 3**

*Drawn at home. +After extra-time. A – Stoke City won 5-4 on pens. B – Wigan Athletic won 4-2 on pens. C – Liverpool won 3-1 on pens.
Semi-finals: Liverpool v Chelsea at Old Trafford; West Ham Utd. v Middlesbrough at Villa Park.

145

ROUND BY ROUND HIGHLIGHTS

FIRST ROUND

Burscough's part-timers took pride of place, coming from behind to beat Gillingham 3-2 with two goals in the final two minutes, an own goal by Ian Cox and the winner from David Rowan. Two lowly Conference sides accounted for League opposition, Tamworth winning 2-1 at Bournemouth and Burton beating Peterborough 1-0 in a replay. Colchester set a club record in the competition with a 9-1 victory over Leamington. Hat-tricks were scored by Steve Basham for Oxford, who saw off Eastbourne 3-0 in a replay, and Paul Brayson in a 3-1 success for Northwich against Morecambe.

SECOND ROUND

Tamworth, one of the few part-time teams left in the Conference, produced another notable performance, a 2-1 victory at Hartlepool which proved particularly sweet for their manager Mark Cooper, who used to play for the north-east club. Burton set up a dream tie against Manchester United by beating Burscough 4-1, while another goal for Paul Brayson enabled Northwich to edge out Woking 2-1 in a replay.

THIRD ROUND

The two Conference teams continued to distinguish themselves. Tamworth took Stoke to a replay and succumbed only in a penalty shoot-out. Burton also gained a goalless draw, against Manchester United, before losing 5-0 at Old Trafford. A last-minute spot-kick by Gez Murphy earned Nuneaton a second chance against Middlesbrough and he scored two more as the Premiership side prevailed 5-2 in the replay. Biggest scalp of the round was taken by Leyton Orient, who knocked out Fulham 2-1 at Craven Cottage. In the most exciting tie, Liverpool came from 3-1 down to win 5-3 at Luton, Xabi Alonso scoring from 60 yards with Luton goalkeeper Marlon Beresford stranded upfield. Mark de Vries hit a 90th minute winner for Leicester, who retrieved a 2-0 deficit to beat Tottenham 3-2, and Reading did the same in a replay against West Bromwich Albion with a hat-trick by Leroy Lita. Robbie Fowler also got three in Manchester City's 3-1 win over Scunthorpe. An eventful third round was also notable for a complete absence of red cards.

FOURTH ROUND

Dudley Campbell earned himself a £500,000 move to Birmingham by scoring both goals for Brentford in a 2-1 win over Sunderland. Two by Colchester's Neil Danns against Derby (3-1) were also rewarded – by a money-spinning fifth round tie against Chelsea. Leyton Orient were denied a replay against Charlton by substitute Jay Bothroyd's last-minute winner (2-1), while Cheltenham gave Newcastle a run for their money before going down 2-0. Four days after losing to Wigan in the semi-finals of the Carling Cup, holders Arsenal went out to a Stelios Giannakopoulos goal for Bolton.

FIFTH ROUND

Colchester took the lead at Stamford Bridge with an own goal by Ricardo Carvalho and Chelsea needed a double from Joe Cole in the final 11 minutes to go through 3-1. Brentford's run also came to an end by the same scoreline at Charlton. Micah Richards, 17, turned the airwaves blue in a post-match interview after heading a stoppage-time equaliser for Manchester City, who won the replay against Aston Villa 2-1. In the big match of the round, a Peter Crouch header for Liverpool accounted for Manchester United.

SIXTH ROUND

Two goals by Dean Ashton gave West Ham a 2-1 win at Manchester City in the first of the quarter-finals played on four successive midweek days to help give England players a month's break before the World Cup Finals. The following night, Liverpool ran riot at St Andrews, adding to Birmingham's Premiership problems with a 7-0 victory launched by Sami Hyypia's first minute goal. Chelsea captain John Terry netted the only goal of the tie with Newcastle, and after Charlton and Middlesbrough finished goalless, Steve McClaren's side went through 4-2 in the replay.

SEMI-FINALS

Rafael Benitez won the tactical battle with Jose Mourinho as John Arne Riise fired a free-kick through Chelsea's defensive wall and Luis Garcia volleyed a sumptuous second for Liverpool. Didier Drogba pulled one back, but Joe Cole lifted a late chance over and his team had to settle for retaining the Premiership title. Marlon Harewood's 78th minute winner against Middlesbrough put West Ham into the final for the first time for 26 years.

FINAL

John Motson described it as arguably the finest F.A. Cup Final in modern times – and there can't have been many among the millions watching on television, or those fortunate enough to be in the Millennium Stadium, prepared to challenge that assertion by the BBC commentator. The honours went to Liverpool, the sympathy to West Ham. Yet, in one sense, everyone was a winner, from the inspirational Steven Gerrard, to his villain-turned-hero goalkeeper Jose Reina, to the hobbling Marlon Harewood, who wearily scuffed wide the chance of a winner 90 seconds from the end of extra-time. They all contributed to a match brimming with goals of every description, dramatic comebacks, a West Ham performance in the best traditions of that club and finally a penalty lottery. What a contrast to the previous season when the first-ever shoot-out had followed a sterile, goalless draw between Manchester United and Arsenal.

Liverpool started out on the Cup trail by coming from 3-1 down to win 5-3 at Luton and it was this never-say-die spirit which proved the biggest single factor in their seventh victory in the competition. When Jamie Carragher turned Lionel Scaloni's cross into his own net and Reina spilled Matthew Etherington's shot into the path of Dean Ashton, they were staring at a surprise defeat by the underdogs. But Djibril Cisse's measured finish at the far post from Gerrard's diagonal cross was followed by a sweet volley of his own by the captain from Peter Crouch's knock-down for 2-2.

Then, with West Ham on the brink of a famous victory after Paul Konchesky's cross sailed over the head of Reina, Gerrard came up with one of the great F.A. Cup Final goals – a 35-yard volley into the bottom corner. Reina went some way to making amends for his blunders by somehow touching Nigel Reo-Coker's deflection onto the post and his rehabilitation was completed by penalty saves from Bobby Zamora, Konchesky and Anton Ferdinand. The occasion was also too much for Hyypia, but Dietmar Hamann, Gerrard and John Arne Riise held their nerve to fire spot-kicks past Shaka Hislop, their experience of this kind of pressure situation proving crucial.

LIVERPOOL 3, WEST HAM UNITED 3

(aet, Liverpool won 3-1 on pens)

Millennium Stadium (74,000), Saturday, May 13, 2006

Liverpool (4-4-2): Reina, Finnan, Carragher, Hyypia, Riise, Gerrard, Xabi Alonso (Kromkamp 67), Sissoko, Kewell (Morientes 48), Cisse, Crouch (Hamann 71). **Subs not used:** Dudek, Traore. **Scorers:** Cisse (32), Gerrard (54, 90). **Booked:** Carragher, Hamann. **Manager:** Rafael Benitez.

West Ham Utd. (4-4-2): Hislop, Scaloni, Ferdinand, Gabbidon, Konchesky, Benayoun, Fletcher (Dailly 77), Reo-Coker, Etherington (Sheringham 85), Ashton (Zamora 71), Harewood. **Subs not used:** Walker, Collins. **Scorers:** Carragher (21 og), Ashton (28), Konchesky (64). **Booked:** Ashton. **Manager:** Alan Pardew.

Penalty shoot-out: Hamann 1-0, Zamora saved, Hyypia saved, Sheringham 1-1, Gerrard 2-1, Konchesky saved, Riise 3-1, Ferdinand saved.

Referee: A. Wiley (Staffs). **Half-time:** 1-2.

HOW THEY REACHED THE FINAL

LIVERPOOL

Round 3: 5-3 away to Luton Town (Sinama Pongolle 2, Xabi Alonso 2, Gerrard)
Round 4: 2-1 away to Portsmouth (Gerrard pen, Riise)
Round 5: 1-0 home to Manchester Utd. (Crouch)
Round 6: 7-0 away to Birmingham City (Crouch 2, Hyypia, Morientes, Riise, Ciise, Tebily og)
Semi-final (Old Trafford): 2-1 v Chelsea (Riise, Luis Garcia)

WEST HAM UNITED

Round 3: 2-1 away to Norwich City (Mullins, Zamora)
Round 4: 4-2 home to Blackburn Rov. (Sheringham pen, Etherington, Zamora, Khizanishvili og)
Round 5: 0-0 away to Bolton Wand.; replay: 2-1 (Harewood, Jaaskelainen og)
Round 6: 2-1 away to Manchester City (Ashton 2)
Semi-final (Villa Park): 1-0 v Middlesbrough (Harewood).

FINAL FACTS AND FIGURES

• Liverpool's victory was their seventh in the competition after successes in 1965, 1974, 1986, 1989, 1992 and 2001.

• Survivors from the 2001 team against Arsenal were Steven Gerrard, Jamie Carragher, Sami Hyypia and Dietmar Hamann.

• It was Liverpool's 62nd game of the season which started on July 13 with a Champions League qualifier against the Welsh team TNS.

• West Ham were in the final for the first time since 1980 when Trevor Brooking's headed goal defeated Arsenal.

• It was the biggest aggregate scoreline since Blackpool's 4-3 win over Bolton in the 'Matthews Final' of 1953.

• The last time the winners scored more than Liverpool's 20 in six ties without a replay was in the 1947-48 season when Manchester United started out with a 6-4 away win over Aston Villa and went on to beat Blackpool 4-2 in the final for a total of 22.

• Jamie Carragher's own goal was the first since the one conceded by Nottingham Forest's Des Walker against Tottenham in 1991.

• Mike Dean, the original choice as referee, was dropped by the F.A. because his home on the Wirral was deemed to be too close to Liverpool. He was replaced by Alan Wiley, from Staffordshire, who also took charge of last season's Carling Cup Final between Manchester United and Wigan.

• One of the assistant referees, Peter Kirkup, woke up on the morning of the match with a stye in his eye, couldn't see properly and was replaced by Ceri Richards.

F.A. CUP FINAL TEAMS 1900-2006

1900 BURY – Thompson; Darroch, Davidson, Pray, Leeming, Ross, Richards, Wood, McLuckie, Sagar, Plant. **SOUTHAMPTON** – Robinson; Meehan, Durber, Meston, Chadwick, Petrie, Turner, Yates, Farrell, Wood, Milward. **Scorers:** Bury – McLuckie 2, Wood, Plant.

1901 TOTTENHAM – Clawley; Erentz, Tait, Norris, Hughes, Jones, Smith, Cameron, Brown, Copeland, Kirwan. **SHEFFIELD UTD.** – Foulke; Thickett, Boyle, Johnson, Morren, Needham, Bennett, Field, Hedley, Priest, Lipsham. **Scorers:** (first match) Tottenham – Brown 2, Sheff. Utd. – Bennett, Priest. **Scorers:** (second match) Tottenham – Cameron, Smith, Brown, Sheff. Utd. – Priest.

1902 SHEFFIELD UTD. – Foulke; Thickett, Boyle, Needham, Wilkinson, Johnson, Barnes, Common, Hedley, Priest, Lipsham. (Bennett injured in first match and Barnes took his place in the replay). **SOUTHAMPTON** – Robinson; C. B. Fry, Molyneux, Bowman, Lee, A. Turner, Wood, Brown, Chadwick, J. Turner, Metson. **Scorers:** (first match) Sheff. Utd. – Common, Southampton – Wood. **Scorers:** (second match) Sheff. Utd. – Hedley, Barnes, Southampton – Brown.

1903 BURY – Monteith; Lindsey, McEwan, Johnson, Thorpe, Ross, Richards, Wood, Sagar, Leeming, Plant. **DERBY CO.** – Fryer; Methven, Morris, Warren, Goodall (A.), May, Warrington, York, Boag, Richards, Davis. **Scorers:** Bury – Ross, Sagar, Leeming 2, Wood, Plant.

1904 MANCHESTER CITY – Hillman; McMahon, Burgess, Frost, Hynde, S. B. Ashworth, Meredith, Livingstone, Gillespie, Turnbull (A.), Booth. **BOLTON WAND.** – D. Davies; Brown, Struthers, Clifford, Greenhalgh, Freebairn, Stokes, Marsh, Yenson, White, Taylor. **Scorer:** Manchester City – Meredith.

1905 ASTON VILLA – George; Spencer, Miles, Pearson, Leake, Windmill, Brawn, Garratty, Hampton, Bache, Hall. **NEWCASTLE UTD.** – Lawrence; McCombie, Carr, Gardner, Aitken, McWilliam, Rutherford, Howie, Appleyard, Veitch, Gosnell. **Scorer:** Aston Villa – Hampton 2.

1906 EVERTON – Scott; Balmer (W.), Crelly, Makepeace, Taylor, Abbott, Sharp, Bolton, Young, Settle, H. P. Hardman. **NEWCASTLE UTD.** – Lawrence; McCombie, Carr, Gardner, Aitken, McWilliam, Rutherford, Howie, Veitch, Orr, Gosnell. **Scorer:** Everton – Young.

1907 SHEFFIELD WED. – Lyall; Layton, Burton, Brittleton, Crawshaw, Bartlett, Chapman, Bradshaw, Wilson, Stewart, Simpson. **EVERTON** – Scott; Balmer (W.), Balmer (R.), Makepeace, Taylor, Abbott, Sharp, Bolton, Young, Settle, H. P. Hardman. **Scorers:** Sheff. Wed. – Stewart, Simpson, Everton – Sharp.

1908 WOLVES – Lunn; Jones, Collins, Rev. K. R. G. Hunt, Wooldridge, Bishop, Harrison, Shelton, Hedley, Radford, Pedley. **NEWCASTLE UTD.** – Lawrence; McCracken, Pudan, Gardner, Veitch, McWilliam, Rutherford, Howie, Appleyard, Speedle, Wilson. **Scorers:** Wolves – Hunt, Hedley, Harrison, Newcastle Utd. – Howie.

1909 MANCHESTER UTD. – Moger; Stacey, Hayes, Duckworth, Roberts, Bell, Meredith, Halse, Turnbull (J.), Turnbull (A.), Wall. **BRISTOL CITY** – Clay; Annan, Cottle, Hanlin, Wedlock, Spear, Staniforth, Hardy, Gilligan, Burton, Hilton. **Scorer:** Manchester Utd. – Turnbull (A.).

1910 NEWCASTLE UTD. – Lawrence; McCracken, Carr, Veitch, Low, McWilliam, Rutherford, Howie, Shepherd, Higgins, Wilson. (Whitson was injured in first match and Carr took his place in the replay). **BARNSLEY** – Mearns; Downs, Ness, Glendinning, Boyle, Utley, Bartrop, Gadsby, Lillycrop, Tufnell, Forman. **Scorers:** (first match) Newcastle Utd. – Rutherford, Barnsley – Tufnell. **Scorer:** (second match) Newcastle Utd. – Shepherd 2 (1 pen.).

1911 BRADFORD CITY – Mellors; Campbell, Taylor, Robinson, Torrance, McDonald, Logan, Spiers, O'Rourke, Devine, Thompson. (Gildea played centre half in the first match). **NEWCASTLE UTD.** – Lawrence; McCracken, Whitson, Veitch, Low, Willis, Rutherford, Jobey, Stewart, Higgins, Wilson. **Scorer:** Bradford City – Spiers.

1912 BARNSLEY – Cooper; Downs, Taylor, Glendinning, Bratley, Utley, Bartrop, Tufnell, Lillycrop, Travers, Moore. **W.B.A.** – Pearson; Cook, Pennington, Baddeley, Buck, McNeal, Jephcott, Wright, Pailor, Bower, Shearman. **Scorer:** Barnsley – Tufnell.

1913 ASTON VILLA – Hardy; Lyons, Weston, Barber, Harrop, Leach, Wallace, Halse, Hampton, Stephenson (C.), Bache. **SUNDERLAND** – Butler; Gladwin, Ness, Cuggy, Thompson, Low, Mordue, Buchan, Richardson, Holley, Martin. **Scorer:** Aston Villa – Barber.

1914 BURNLEY – Sewell; Bamford, Taylor, Halley, Boyle, Watson, Nesbit, Lindley, Freeman, Hodgson, Mosscrop. **LIVERPOOL** – Campbell; Longworth, Pursell, Fairfoul, Ferguson, McKinlay, Sheldon, Metcalfe, Miller, Lacey, Nicholl. **Scorer:** Burnley – Freeman.

1915 SHEFFIELD UTD. – Gough; Cook, English, Sturgess, Brelsford, Utley, Simmons, Fazackerley, Kitchen, Masterman, Evans. **CHELSEA** – Molyneux; Bettridge, Harrow, Taylor, Logan, Walker, Ford, Halse, Thompson, Croal, McNeil. **Scorers:** Sheff. Utd. – Simmons, Fazackerley, Kitchen.

1920 ASTON VILLA – Hardy; Smart, Weston, Ducat, Barson, Moss, Wallace, Kirton, Walker, Stephenson (C.), Dorrell. **HUDDERSFIELD TOWN** – Mutch; Wood, Bullock, Slade, Wilson, Watson, Richardson, Mann, Taylor, Swan, Islip. **Scorer:** Aston VIlla – Kirton.

1921 TOTTENHAM – Hunter; Clay, McDonald, Smith, Walters, Grimsdell; Banks, Seed, Cantrell, Bliss, Dimmock. **WOLVES** – George; Woodward, Marshall, Gregory, Hodnett, Riley, Lea, Burrill, Edmonds, Potts, Brooks. **Scorer:** Tottenham – Dimmock.

1922 HUDDERSFIELD TOWN – Mutch; Wood, Wadsworth, Slade, Wilson, Watson, Richardson, Mann, Islip, Stephenson, Smith (W.H.). **PRESTON N.E.** – J. F. Mitchell; Hamilton, Doolan, Duxbury, McCall, Williamson, Rawlings, Jefferis, Roberts, Woodhouse, Quinn. **Scorer:** Huddersfield Town – Smith (pen.).

1923 BOLTON WAND. – Pym; Haworth, Finney, Nuttall, Seddon, Jennings, Butler, Jack, Smith (J. R.), Smith (J.), Vizard. **WEST HAM UTD.** – Hufton; Henderson, Young, Bishop, Kay, Tresadern, Richards, Brown, Watson (V.), Moore, Ruffell. **Scorers:** Bolton Wand. – Jack, Smith (J. R.).

1924 NEWCASTLE UTD. – Bradley; Hampson, Hudspeth, Mooney, Spencer, Gibson, Low, Cowan, Harris, McDonald, Seymour. **ASTON VILLA** – Jackson; Smart, Mort, Moss, Dr. V. E. Milne, Blackburn, York, Kirton, Capewell, Walker, Dorrell. **Scorers:** Newcastle Utd. – Harris, Seymour.

1925 SHEFFIELD UTD. – Sutcliffe; Cook, Milton, Pantling, King, Green, Mercer, Boyle, Johnson, Gillespie, Tunstall. **CARDIFF CITY** – Farquharson; Nelson, Blair, Wake, Keenor, Hardy, Davies (W.), Gill, Nicholson, Beadles, Evans (J.). **Scorer:** Sheff. Utd. – Tunstall.

1926 BOLTON WAND. – Pym; Haworth, Greenhalgh, Nuttall, Seddon, Jennings, Butler, Jack, Smith (J. R.), Smith (J.), Vizard. **MANCHESTER CITY** – Goodchild; Cookson, McCloy, Pringle, Cowan, McMullan, Austin, Browell, Roberts, Johnson, Hicks. **Scorer:** Bolton Wand. – Jack.

1927 CARDIFF CITY – Farquharson; Nelson, Watson, Keenor, Sloan, Hardy, Curtis, Irving, Ferguson, Davies (L.), McLachlan. **ARSENAL** – Lewis; Parker, Kennedy, Baker, Butler, John, Hulme, Buchan, Brain, Blyth, Hoar. **Scorer:** Cardiff City – Ferguson.

1928 BLACKBURN ROV. – Crawford; Hutton, Jones, Healless, Rankin, Campbell, Thornewell, Puddefoot, Roscamp, McLean, Rigby. **HUDDERSFIELD TOWN** – Mercer; Goodall, Barkas, Redfern, Wilson, Steele, Jackson (A.), Kelly, Brown, Stephenson, Smith (W.H.). **Scorers:** Blackburn Rov. – Roscamp 2, McLean, Huddersfield Town – Jackson.

1929 BOLTON WAND. – Pym; Haworth, Finney, Kean, Seddon, Nuttall, Butler, McClelland, Blackmore, Gibson, Cook (W.). **PORTSMOUTH** – Gilfillan; Mackie, Bell, Nichol, McIlwaine, Thackeray, Forward, Smith (J.), Weddle, Watson, Cook (F.). **Scorers:** Bolton Wand. – Butler, Blackmore.

1930 ARSENAL – Preedy; Parker, Hapgood, Baker, Seddon, John, Hulme, Jack, Lambert, James, Bastin. **HUDDERSFIELD TOWN** – Turner; Goodall, Spence, Naylor, Wilson, Campbell, Jackson (A.), Kelly, Davies, Raw, Smith (W. H.). **Scorers:** Arsenal – James, Lambert.

1931 W.B.A. – Pearson; Shaw, Trentham, Magee, Richardson (W.), Edwards, Glidden, Carter, Richardson (W. G.), Sandford, Wood. **BIRMINGHAM CITY** – Hibbs; Liddell, Barkas, Cringan, Morrall, Leslie, Briggs, Crosbie, Bradford, Gregg, Curtis. **Scorers:** W.B.A. – Richardson (W. G.) 2, Birmingham City – Bradford.

1932 NEWCASTLE UTD. – McInroy; Nelson, Fairhurst, McKenzie, Davidson, Weaver, Boyd, Richardson, Allen, McMenemy, Lang. **ARSENAL** – Moss; Parker, Hapgood, Jones

150

(C.), Roberts, Male, Hulme, Jack, Lambert, Bastin, John. **Scorers:** Newcastle Utd. – Allen 2, Arsenal – John.

1933 EVERTON – Sagar; Cook, Cresswell, Britton, White, Thomson, Geldard, Dunn, Dean, Johnson, Stein. **MANCHESTER CITY** – Langford; Cann, Dale, Busby, Cowan, Bray, Toseland, Marshall, Herd, McMullan, Brook. **Scorers:** Everton – Stein, Dean, Dunn.

1934 MANCHESTER CITY – Swift; Barnett, Dale, Busby, Cowan, Bray, Toseland, Marshall, Tilson, Herd, Brook. **PORTSMOUTH** – Gilfillan; Mackie, Smith (W.), Nichol, Allen, Thackeray, Worrall, Smith (J.), Weddle, Easson, Rutherford. **Scorers:** Manchester City – Tilson 2, Portsmouth – Rutherford.

1935 SHEFFIELD WED. – Brown; Nibloe, Catlin, Sharp, Millership, Burrows, Hooper, Surtees, Palethorpe, Starling, Rimmer. **W.B.A.** – Pearson; Shaw, Trentham, Murphy, Richardson (W.), Edwards, Glidden, Carter, Richardson (W. G.), Sandford, Boyes. **Scorers:** Sheff. Wed. – Rimmer 2, Palethorpe, Hooper, W.B.A. – Boyes, Sandford.

1936 ARSENAL – Wilson; Male, Hapgood, Crayston, Roberts, Copping, Hulme, Bowden, Drake, James, Bastin. **SHEFFIELD UTD.** – Smith; Hooper, Wilkinson, Jackson, Johnson, McPherson, Barton, Barclay, Dodds, Pickering, Williams. **Scorer:** Arsenal – Drake.

1937 SUNDERLAND – Mapson; Gorman, Hall, Thomson, Johnston, McNab, Duns, Carter, Gurney, Gallacher, Burbanks. **PRESTON N.E.** – Burns; Gallimore, Beattie (A.), Shankly, Tremelling, Milne, Dougal, Beresford, O'Donnell (F.), Fagan, O'Donnell (H.). **Scorers:** Sunderland – Gurney, Carter, Burbanks, Preston N.E. – O'Donnell (F.).

1938 PRESTON N.E. – Holdcroft; Gallimore, Beattie (A.), Shankly, Smith, Batey, Watmough, Mutch, Maxwell, Beattie (R.), O'Donnell (H.). **HUDDERSFIELD TOWN** – Hesford; Craig, Mountford, Willingham, Young, Boot, Hulme, Isaac, McFadyen, Barclay, Beasley. **Scorer:** Preston N.E. – Mutch (pen.).

1939 PORTSMOUTH – Walker; Morgan, Rochford, Guthrie, Rowe, Wharton, Worrall, McAlinden, Anderson, Barlow, Parker. **WOLVES** – Scott; Morris, Taylor, Galley, Cullis, Gardiner, Burton, McIntosh, Westcott, Dorsett, Maguire. **Scorers:** Portsmouth – Barlow, Anderson, Parker 2, Wolves – Dorsett.

1946 DERBY CO. – Woodley; Nicholas, Howe, Bullions, Leuty, Musson, Harrison, Carter, Stamps, Doherty, Duncan. **CHARLTON ATHLETIC** – Bartram; Phipps, Shreeve, Turner (H.), Oakes, Johnson, Fell, Brown, A. A. Turner, Welsh, Duffy. **Scorers:** Derby Co. – Turner (H.) (o.g.), Doherty, Stamps 2, Charlton Athletic – Turner (H.).

1947 CHARLTON ATHLETIC – Bartram; Croker (P.), Shreeve, Johnson, Phipps, Whittaker, Hurst, Dawson, Robinson (W.), Welsh, Duffy. **BURNLEY** – Strong; Woodruff, Mather, Attwell, Brown, Bray, Chew, Morris, Harrison, Potts, F. P. Kippax. **Scorer:** Charlton Athletic – Duffy.

1948 MANCHESTER UTD. – Crompton; Carey, Aston, Anderson, Chilton, Cockburn, Delaney, Morris, Rowley, Pearson, Mitten. **BLACKPOOL** – Robinson; Shimwell, Crosland, Johnston, Hayward, Kelly, Matthews, Munro, Mortensen, Dick, Rickett. **Scorers:** Manchester Utd. – Rowley 2, Pearson, Anderson, Blackpool – Shimwell (pen.), Mortensen.

1949 WOLVES – Williams; Pritchard, Springthorpe, Crook (W.), Shorthouse, Wright, Hancocks, Smyth, Pye, Dunn, Mullen. **LEICESTER CITY** – Bradley; Jelly, Scott, Harrison (W.), Plummer, King, Griffiths, Lee, Harrison (J.), Chisholm, Adam. **Scorers:** Wolves – Pye 2, Smyth, Leicester City – Griffiths.

1950 ARSENAL – Swindin; Scott, Barnes, Forbes, Compton (L.), Mercer, Cox, Logie, Goring, Lewis, Compton (D.). **LIVERPOOL** – Sidlow; Lambert, Spicer, Taylor, Hughes, Jones, Payne, Baron, Stubbins, Fagan, Liddell. **Scorer:** Arsenal – Lewis 2.

1951 NEWCASTLE UTD. – Fairbrother; Cowell, Corbett, Harvey, Brennan, Crowe, Walker, Taylor, Milburn, Robledo (G.), Mitchell. **BLACKPOOL** – Farm; Shimwell, Garrett, Johnston, Hayward, Kelly, Matthews, Mudie, Mortensen, W. J. Slater, Perry. **Scorer:** Newcastle Utd. – Milburn 2.

1952 NEWCASTLE UTD. – Simpson; Cowell, McMichael, Harvey, Brennan, Robledo (E.), Walker, Foulkes, Milburn, Robledo (G.), Mitchell. **ARSENAL** – Swindin; Barnes, Smith (L.), Forbes, Daniel, Mercer, Cox, Logie, Holton, Lishman, Roper. **Scorer:** Newcastle Utd. – Robledo (G.).

1953 BLACKPOOL – Farm; Shimwell, Garrett, Fenton, Johnston, Robinson, Matthews, Taylor, Mortensen, Mudie, Perry. **BOLTON WAND.** – Hanson; Ball, Banks (R.), Wheeler,

Barrass, Bell, Holden, Moir, Lofthouse, Hassall, Langton. **Scorers:** Blackpool – Mortensen 3, Perry, Bolton Wand. – Lofthouse, Moir, Bell.

1954 W.B.A. – Sanders; Kennedy, Millard, Dudley, Dugdale, Barlow, Griffin, Ryan, Allen, Nicholls, Lee. **PRESTON N.E.** – Thompson; Cunningham, Walton, Docherty, Marston, Forbes, Finney, Foster, Wayman, Baxter, Morrison. **Scorers:** W.B.A. – Allen 2 (1 pen.), Griffin, Preston N.E. – Morrison, Wayman.

1955 NEWCASTLE UTD. – Simpson; Cowell, Batty, Scoular, Stokoe, Casey, White, Milburn, Keeble, Hannah, Mitchell. **MANCHESTER CITY** – Trautmann; Meadows, Little, Barnes, Ewing, Paul, Spurdle, Hayes, Revie, Johnstone, Fagan. **Scorers:** Newcastle Utd. – Milburn, Mitchell, Hannah, Manchester City – Johnstone.

1956 MANCHESTER CITY – Trautmann; Leivers, Little, Barnes, Ewing, Paul, Johnstone, Hayes, Revie, Dyson, Clarke. **BIRMINGHAM CITY** – Merrick; Hall, Green, Newman, Smith, Boyd, Astall, Kinsey, Brown, Murphy, Govan. **Scorers:** Manchester City – Hayes, Dyson, Johnstone, Birmingham City – Kinsey.

1957 ASTON VILLA – Sims; Lynn, Aldis, Crowther, Dugdale, Saward, Smith, Sewell, Myerscough, Dixon, McParland. **MANCHESTER UTD.** – Wood; Foulkes, Byrne, Colman, Blanchflower, Edwards, Berry, Whelan, Taylor (T.), Charlton, Pegg. **Scorers:** Aston Villa – McParland 2, Manchester Utd. – Taylor.

1958 BOLTON WANDERERS – Hopkinson; Hartle, Banks (T.), Hennin, Higgins, Edwards, Birch, Stevens, Lofthouse, Parry, Holden. **MANCHESTER UTD.** – Gregg; Foulkes, Greaves, Goodwin, Cope, Crowther, Dawson, Taylor (E.), Charlton, Viollet, Webster. **Scorer:** Bolton Wand. – Lofthouse 2.

1959 NOTT'M FOREST – Thomson; Whare, McDonald, Whitefoot, McKinlay, Burkitt, Dwight, Quigley, Wilson, Gray, Imlach. **LUTON TOWN** – Baynham; McNally, Hawkes, Groves, Owen, Pacey, Bingham, Brown, Morton, Cummins, Gregory. **Scorers:** Nott'm. Forest – Dwight, Wilson, Luton Town – Pacey.

1960 WOLVES – Finlayson; Showell, Harris, Clamp, Slater, Flowers, Deeley, Stobart, Murray, Broadbent, Horne. **BLACKBURN ROV.** – Leyland; Bray, Whelan, Clayton, Woods, McGrath, Bimpson, Dobing, Dougan, Douglas, MacLeod. **Scorers:** Wolves – McGrath (o.g.), Deeley 2.

1961 TOTTENHAM – Brown; Baker, Henry, Blanchflower, Norman, Mackay, Jones, White, Smith, Allen, Dyson. **LEICESTER CITY** – Banks; Chalmers, Norman, McLintock, King, Appleton, Riley, Walsh, McIlmoyle, Keyworth, Cheesebrough. **Scorers:** Tottenham – Smith, Dyson.

1962 TOTTENHAM – Brown; Baker, Henry, Blanchflower, Norman, Mackay, Medwin, White, Smith, Greaves, Jones. **BURNLEY** – Blacklaw; Angus, Elder, Adamson, Cummings, Miller, Connelly, McIlroy, Pointer, Robson, Harris. **Scorers:** Tottenham – Greaves, Smith, Blanchflower (pen.), Burnley – Robson.

1963 MANCHESTER UTD. – Gaskell; Dunne, Cantwell, Crerand, Foulkes, Setters, Giles, Quixall, Herd, Law, Charlton. **LEICESTER CITY** – Banks; Sjoberg, Norman, McLintock, King, Appleton, Riley, Cross, Keyworth, Gibson, Stringfellow. **Scorers:** Manchester Utd. – Law, Herd 2, Leicester City – Keyworth.

1964 WEST HAM UTD. – Standen; Bond, Burkett, Bovington, Brown, Moore, Brabrook, Boyce, Byrne, Hurst, Sissons. **PRESTON N.E.** – Kelly; Ross, Smith, Lawton, Singleton, Kendall, Wilson, Ashworth, Dawson, Spavin, Holden. **Scorers:** West Ham Utd. – Sissons, Hurst, Boyce, Preston N.E. – Holden, Dawson.

1965 LIVERPOOL – Lawrence; Lawler, Byrne, Strong, Yeats, Stevenson, Callaghan, Hunt, St. John, Smith, Thompson. **LEEDS UTD.** – Sprake; Reaney, Bell, Bremner, Charlton, Hunter, Giles, Storrie, Peacock, Collins, Johanneson. **Scorers:** Liverpool – Hunt, St. John, Leeds Utd. – Bremner.

1966 EVERTON – West; Wright, Wilson, Gabriel, Labone, Harris, Scott, Trebilcock, Young, Harvey, Temple. **SHEFFIELD WED.** – Springett; Smith, Megson, Eustace, Ellis, Young, Pugh, Fantham, McCalliog, Ford, Quinn. **Scorers:** Everton – Trebilcock 2, Temple, Sheff. Wed. – McCalliog, Ford.

1967 TOTTENHAM – Jennings; Kinnear, Knowles, Mullery, England, Mackay, Robertson, Greaves, Gilzean, Venables, Saul. **CHELSEA** – Bonetti; Harris (A.), McCreadie, Hollins, Hinton, Harris (R.), Cooke, Baldwin, Hateley, Tambling, Boyle. **Scorers:** Tottenham – Robertson, Saul, Chelsea – Tambling.

1968 W.B.A. – Osborne; Fraser, Williams, Brown, Talbut, Kaye (Clarke), Lovett, Collard, Astle, Hope, Clark. **EVERTON** – West; Wright, Wilson, Kendall, Labone, Harvey, Husband, Ball, Royle, Hurst, Morrissey. **Scorer:** W.B.A. – Astle.

1969 MANCHESTER CITY – Dowd; Book, Pardoe, Doyle, Booth, Oakes, Summerbee, Bell, Lee, Young, Coleman. **LEICESTER CITY** – Shilton; Rodrigues, Nish, Roberts, Woollett, Cross, Fern, Gibson, Lochhead, Clarke, Glover (Manley). **Scorer:** Manchester City – Young.

1970 CHELSEA – Bonetti; Webb, McCreadie, Hollins, Dempsey, Harris (R.) (Hinton), Baldwin, Houseman, Osgood, Hutchinson, Cooke. **LEEDS UTD.** – Sprake; Madeley, Cooper, Bremner, Charlton, Hunter, Lorimer, Clarke, Jones, Giles, Gray. **Scorers:** Chelsea – Houseman, Hutchinson, Leeds Utd. – Charlton, Jones. **Replay: CHELSEA** – Bonetti; Harris (R.), McCreadie, Hollins, Dempsey, Webb, Baldwin, Cooke, Osgood (Hinton), Hutchinson, Houseman. **LEEDS UTD.** – Harvey; Madeley, Cooper, Bremner, Charlton, Hunter, Lorimer, Clarke, Jones, Giles, Gray. **Scorers:** Chelsea – Osgood, Webb, Leeds Utd. – Jones.

1971 ARSENAL – Wilson; Rice, McNab, Storey (Kelly), McLintock, Simpson, Armstrong, Graham, Radford, Kennedy, George. **LIVERPOOL** – Clemence; Lawler, Lindsay, Smith, Lloyd, Hughes, Callaghan, Evans (Thompson), Heighway, Toshack, Hall. **Scorers:** Arsenal – Kelly, George, Liverpool – Heighway.

1972 LEEDS UTD. – Harvey; Reaney, Madeley, Bremner, Charlton, Hunter, Lorimer, Clarke, Jones, Giles, Gray. **ARSENAL** – Barnett; Rice, McNab, Storey, McLintock, Simpson, Armstrong, Ball, Radford (Kennedy), George, Graham. **Scorer:** Leeds Utd. – Clarke.

1973 SUNDERLAND – Montgomery; Malone, Guthrie, Horswill, Watson, Pitt, Kerr, Hughes, Halom, Porterfield, Tueart. **LEEDS UTD.** – Harvey; Reaney, Cherry, Bremner, Madeley, Hunter, Lorimer, Clarke, Jones, Giles, Gray (Yorath). **Scorer:** Sunderland – Porterfield.

1974 LIVERPOOL – Clemence; Smith, Lindsay, Thompson, Cormack, Hughes, Keegan, Hall, Heighway, Toshack, Callaghan. **NEWCASTLE UTD.** – McFaul; Clark, Kennedy, McDermott, Howard, Moncur, Smith (Gibb), Cassidy, Macdonald, Tudor, Hibbitt. **Scorers:** Liverpool – Keegan (2), Heighway.

1975 WEST HAM UTD. – Day; McDowell, Lampard, Bonds, Taylor (T.), Lock, Jennings, Paddon, Taylor (A.), Brooking, Holland. **FULHAM** – Mellor; Cutbush, Fraser, Mullery, Lacy, Moore, Mitchell, Conway, Busby, Slough, Barrett. **Scorer:** West Ham Utd. – Taylor (A.) 2.

1976 SOUTHAMPTON – Turner; Rodrigues, Peach, Holmes, Blyth, Steele, Gilchrist, Channon, Osgood, McCalliog, Stokes. **MANCHESTER UTD.** – Stepney; Forsyth, Houston, Daly, Greenhoff (B.), Buchan, Coppell, McIlroy, Pearson, Macari, Hill (McCreery). **Scorer:** Southampton – Stokes.

1977 MANCHESTER UTD. – Stepney; Nicholl, Albiston, McIlroy, Greenhoff (B.), Buchan, Coppell, Greenhoff (J.), Pearson, Macari, Hill (McCreery). **LIVERPOOL** – Clemence; Neal, Jones, Smith, Kennedy, Hughes, Keegan, Case, Heighway, McDermott, Johnson (Callaghan). **Scorers:** Manchester Utd. – Pearson, Greenhoff (J.), Liverpool – Case.

1978 IPSWICH TOWN – Cooper; Burley, Mills, Talbot, Hunter, Beattie, Osborne (Lambert), Wark, Mariner, Geddis, Woods. **ARSENAL** – Jennings; Rice, Nelson, Price, O'Leary, Young, Brady (Rix), Sunderland, Macdonald, Stapleton, Hudson. **Scorer:** Ipswich Town – Osborne.

1979 ARSENAL – Jennings; Rice, Nelson, Talbot, O'Leary, Young, Brady, Sunderland, Stapleton, Price (Walford), Rix. **MANCHESTER UTD.** – Bailey; Nicholl, Albiston, McIlroy, McQueen, Buchan, Coppell, Greenhoff (J.), Jordan, Macari, Thomas. **Scorers:** Arsenal – Talbot, Stapleton, Sunderland, Manchester Utd. – McQueen, McIlroy.

1980 WEST HAM UTD. – Parkes; Stewart, Lampard, Bonds, Martin, Devonshire, Allen, Pearson, Cross, Brooking, Pike. **ARSENAL** – Jennings; Rice, Devine (Nelson), Talbot, O'Leary, Young, Brady, Sunderland, Stapleton, Price, Rix. **Scorer:** West Ham Utd. – Brooking.

1981 TOTTENHAM – Aleksic; Hughton, Miller, Roberts, Perryman, Villa (Brooke), Ardiles, Archibald, Galvin, Hoddle, Crooks. **MANCHESTER CITY** – Corrigan; Ranson, McDonald, Reid, Power, Caton, Bennett, Gow, Mackenzie, Hutchison (Henry), Reeves. **Scorer:** Tottenham – Hutchison (o.g.), Manchester City – Hutchison. **Replay: TOTTENHAM** – Aleksic; Hughton, Miller, Roberts, Perryman, Villa, Ardiles, Archibald, Galvin, Hoddle,

Crooks. **MANCHESTER CITY** – Corrigan; Ranson, McDonald (Tueart), Reid, Power, Caton, Bennett, Gow, Mackenzie, Hutchison, Reeves. **Scorers:** Tottenham – Villa 2, Crooks, Manchester City – Mackenzie, Reeves (pen.).

1982 TOTTENHAM – Clemence; Hughton, Miller, Price, Hazard (Brooke), Perryman, Roberts, Archibald, Galvin, Hoddle, Crooks. **Q.P.R.** – Hucker; Fenwick, Gillard, Waddock, Hazell, Roeder, Currie, Flanagan, Allen (Micklewhite), Stainrod, Gregory. **Scorers:** Tottenham – Hoddle, Q.P.R. – Fenwick. **Replay: TOTTENHAM** – Clemence; Hughton, Miller, Price, Hazard (Brooke), Perryman, Roberts, Archibald, Galvin, Hoddle, Crooks. **Q.P.R.** – Hucker; Fenwick, Gillard, Waddock, Hazell, Neill, Currie, Flanagan, Micklewhite (Burke), Stainrod, Gregory. **Scorer:** Tottenham – Hoddle (pen.).

1983 MANCHESTER UTD. – Bailey; Duxbury, Albiston, Wilkins, Moran, McQueen, Robson, Muhren, Stapleton, Whiteside, Davies. **BRIGHTON & H.A.** – Moseley; Ramsey (Ryan), Pearce, Grealish, Gatting, Stevens, Case, Howlett, Robinson, Smith, Smillie. **Scorers:** Manchester Utd. – Stapleton, Wilkins, Brighton & H.A. – Smith, Stevens. **Replay: MANCHESTER UTD.** – Bailey; Duxbury, Albiston, Wilkins, Moran, McQueen, Robson, Muhren, Stapleton, Whiteside, Davies. **BRIGHTON & H.A.** – Moseley; Gatting, Pearce, Grealish, Foster, Stevens, Case, Howlett (Ryan), Robinson, Smith, Smillie. **Scorers:** Manchester Utd. – Robson 2, Whiteside, Muhren (pen.).

1984 EVERTON – Southall; Stevens, Bailey, Ratcliffe, Mountfield, Reid, Steven, Heath, Sharp, Gray, Richardson. **WATFORD** – Sherwood; Bardsley, Price (Atkinson), Taylor, Terry, Sinnott, Callaghan, Johnston, Reilly, Jackett, Barnes. **Scorers:** Everton – Sharp, Gray.

1985 MANCHESTER UTD. – Bailey; Gidman, Albiston (Duxbury), Whiteside, McGrath, Moran, Robson, Strachan, Hughes, Stapleton, Olsen. **EVERTON** – Southall; Stevens, Van den Hauwe, Ratcliffe, Mountfield, Reid, Steven, Sharp, Gray, Bracewell, Sheedy. **Scorer:** Manchester Utd. – Whiteside. **Sent-off:** Moran.

1986 LIVERPOOL – Grobbelaar; Lawrenson, Beglin, Nicol, Whelan, Hansen, Dalglish, Johnston, Rush, Molby, MacDonald. **EVERTON** – Mimms; Stevens (Heath), Van den Hauwe, Ratcliffe, Mountfield, Reid, Steven, Lineker, Sharp, Bracewell, Sheedy. **Scorers:** Liverpool – Rush 2, Johnston, Everton – Lineker.

1987 COVENTRY CITY – Ogrizovic; Phillips, Downs, McGrath, Kilcline (Rodger), Peake, Bennett, Gynn, Regis, Houchen, Pickering. **TOTTENHAM** – Clemence; Hughton (Claesen), Thomas (M.), Hodge, Gough, Mabbutt, Allen (C.), Allen (P.), Waddle, Hoddle, Ardiles (Stevens). **Scorers:** Coventry City – Bennett, Houchen, Mabbutt (o.g.), Tottenham – Allen (C.), Mabbutt.

1988 WIMBLEDON – Beasant; Goodyear, Phelan, Jones, Young, Thorn, Gibson (Scales), Cork (Cunningham), Fashanu, Sanchez, Wise. **LIVERPOOL** – Grobbelaar; Gillespie, Ablett, Nicol, Spackman (Molby), Hansen, Beardsley, Aldridge (Johnston), Houghton, Barnes, McMahon. **Scorer:** Wimbledon – Sanchez.

1989 LIVERPOOL – Grobbelaar; Ablett, Staunton (Venison), Nicol, Whelan, Hansen, Beardsley, Aldridge (Rush), Houghton, Barnes, McMahon. **EVERTON** – Southall; McDonald, Van den Hauwe, Ratcliffe, Watson, Bracewell (McCall), Nevin, Steven, Sharp, Cottee, Sheedy (Wilson). **Scorers:** Liverpool – Aldridge, Rush 2, Everton – McCall 2.

1990 MANCHESTER UTD. – Leighton; Ince, Martin (Blackmore), Bruce, Phelan, Pallister (Robins), Robson, Webb, McClair, Hughes, Wallace. **CRYSTAL PALACE** – Martyn; Pemberton, Shaw, Gray (Madden), O'Reilly, Thorn, Barber (Wright), Thomas, Bright, Salako, Pardew. **Scorers:** Manchester Utd. – Robson, Hughes 2, Crystal Palace – O'Reilly, Wright 2. **Replay: MANCHESTER UTD.** – Sealey; Ince, Martin, Bruce, Phelan, Pallister, Robson, Webb, McClair, · Hughes, Wallace. **CRYSTAL PALACE** – Martyn; Pemberton, Shaw, Gray, O'Reilly, Thorn, Barber (Wright), Thomas, Bright, Salako (Madden), Pardew. **Scorer:** Manchester Utd. – Martin.

1991 TOTTENHAM – Thorstvedt; Edinburgh, Van den Hauwe, Sedgley, Howells, Mabbutt, Stewart, Gascoigne (Nayim), Samways (Walsh), Lineker, Allen. **NOTT'M FOREST** – Crossley; Charles, Pearce, Walker, Chettle, Keane, Crosby, Parker, Clough, Glover (Laws), Woan (Hodge). **Scorers:** Tottenham – Stewart, Walker (o.g.), Nott'm Forest – Pearce.

1992 LIVERPOOL – Grobbelaar; Jones (R.), Burrows, Nicol, Molby, Wright, Saunders, Houghton, Rush (I.), McManaman, Thomas. **SUNDERLAND** – Norman; Owers, Ball,

Bennett, Rogan, Rush (D.) (Hardyman), Bracewell, Davenport, Armstrong (Hawke), Byrne, Atkinson. **Scorers:** Liverpool – Thomas, Rush (I.).

1993 ARSENAL – Seaman; Dixon, Winterburn, Linighan, Adams, Parlour (Smith), Davis, Merson, Jensen, Wright (O'Leary), Campbell. **SHEFFIELD WED.** – Woods; Nilsson, Worthington, Palmer, Hirst, Anderson (Hyde), Waddle (Bart-Williams), Warhurst, Bright, Sheridan, Harkes. **Scorers:** Arsenal – Wright, Sheff. Wed. – Hirst. **Replay: ARSENAL** – Seaman; Dixon, Winterburn, Linighan, Adams, Davis, Jensen, Merson, Smith, Wright (O'Leary), Campbell. **SHEFFIELD WED.** – Woods; Nilsson (Bart-Williams), Worthington, Palmer, Hirst, Wilson (Hyde), Waddle, Warhurst, Bright, Sheridan, Harkes. **Scorers:** Arsenal – Wright, Linighan, Sheff. Wed. – Waddle.

1994 MANCHESTER UTD. – Schmeichel; Parker, Bruce, Pallister, Irwin (Sharpe), Kanchelskis (McClair), Keane, Ince, Giggs, Cantona, Hughes. **CHELSEA** – Kharine; Clarke, Johnsen, Kjeldbjerg, Sinclair, Burley (Hoddle), Newton, Wise, Peacock, Stein (Cascarino), Spencer. **Scorers:** Manchester Utd. – Cantona 2 (2 pens.), Hughes, McClair.

1995 EVERTON – Southall; Jackson, Watson, Unsworth, Ablett, Horne, Parkinson, Hinchcliffe, Stuart, Limpar (Amokachi), Rideout (Ferguson). **MANCHESTER UTD.** – Schmeichel; Neville (G.), Bruce (Giggs), Pallister, Irwin, Butt, Keane, Ince, Sharpe (Scholes), McClair, Hughes. **Scorer:** Everton – Rideout.

1996 MANCHESTER UTD. – Schmeichel; Irwin, May, Pallister, Neville (P.), Beckham (Neville, G.), Keane, Butt, Giggs, Cantona, Cole (Scholes). **LIVERPOOL** – James; McAteer, Scales, Wright, Babb, Jones (Thomas), McManaman, Redknapp, Barnes, Collymore (Rush), Fowler. **Scorer:** Manchester Utd. – Cantona.

1997 CHELSEA – Grodas; Sinclair, Lebouef, Clarke, Minto, Petrescu, Di Matteo, Newton, Wise, Zola (Vialli), Hughes (M.). **MIDDLESBROUGH** – Roberts; Blackmore, Pearson, Festa, Fleming, Stamp, Emerson, Mustoe (Vickers), Hignett (Kinder), Juninho, Ravanelli, (Beck). **Scorers:** Chelsea – Di Matteo, Newton.

1998 ARSENAL – Seaman; Dixon, Adams, Keown, Winterburn, Parlour, Petit, Vieira, Overmars, Wreh (Platt), Anelka. **NEWCASTLE** – Given; Barton (Watson), Dabizas, Howey, Pearce (Andersson), Pistone, Batty, Lee, Speed, Shearer, Ketsbaia (Barnes). **Scorers:** Arsenal – Overmars, Anelka.

1999 MANCHESTER UTD. – Schmeichel; Neville (G.), Johnsen, May, Neville (P.); Beckham, Scholes (Stam), Keane (Sheringham), Giggs; Cole (Yorke), Solskjaer. **NEWCASTLE UTD.** – Harper; Griffin, Charvet, Dabizas, Domi; Lee, Hamann (Ferguson), Speed, Solano (Maric); Ketsbaia (Glass), Shearer. **Scorers:** Manchester Utd. – Sheringham, Scholes.

2000 CHELSEA – De Goey; Melchiot, Desailly, Leboeuf, Babayaro, Di Matteo, Wise, Deschamps, Poyet, Weah (Flo), Zola (Morris). **ASTON VILLA** – James; Ehiogu, Southgate, Barry, Delaney. Taylor (Stone), Boateng, Merson, Wright (Hendrie), Dublin, Carbone (Joachim). **Scorer:** Chelsea – Di Matteo.

2001 LIVERPOOL – Westerveld; Babbel, Henchoz, Hyypia, Carragher, Murphy (Berger), Hamann (McAllister), Gerrard, Smicer (Fowler), Heskey, Owen. **ARSENAL** – Seaman; Dixon (Bergkamp), Keown, Adams, Cole, Ljungberg, Grimandi, Vieira, Pires, Henry, Wiltord (Parlour). **Scorers:** Liverpool – Owen 2, Arsenal – Ljungberg.

2002 ARSENAL – Seaman; Lauren, Campbell, Adams, Cole, Wiltord (Keown), Parlour, Vieira, Ljungberg, Bergkamp (Edu), Henry (Kanu). **CHELSEA** – Cudicini; Melchiot, Desailly, Gallas, Babayaro (Terry), Gronkjaer, Lampard, Petit, Le Saux, Hasselbaink (Zola), Gudjohnsen. **Scorers:** Arsenal – Parlour, Ljungberg.

2003 ARSENAL – Seaman; Lauren, Keown, Luzhny, Cole, Ljungberg, Parlour, Gilberto Silva, Pires, Bergkamp (Wiltord), Henry. **SOUTHAMPTON** – Niemi (Jones); Baird (Fernandes), Lundekvam, Svensson (M.), Bridge, Telfer, Oakley, Svensson (A.) (Tessem), Marsden, Beattie, Ormerod. **Scorer:** Arsenal – Pires.

2004 MANCHESTER UTD. – Howard (Carroll); G. Neville, Brown, Silvestre, O'Shea, Fletcher (Butt), Keane, Ronaldo (Solskjaer), Scholes, Giggs, Van Nistelrooy. **MILLWALL:** Marshall; Elliott, Lawrence, Ward, Ryan (Cogan), Wise (Weston), Ifill, Cahill, Livermore, Sweeney, Harris (McCammon). **Scorers:** Manchester Utd. – Van Nistelrooy (2), Ronaldo.

2005 ARSENAL – Lehmann; Lauren, Toure, Senderos, Cole, Fabregas (Van Persie), Gilberto Silva, Vieira, Pires (Edu), Reyes, Bergkamp (Ljungberg). **MANCHESTER UTD.** – Carroll; Brown, Ferdinand, Silvestre, O'Shea (Fortune), Fletcher (Giggs), Keane, Scholes, Rooney, Van Nistelrooy, Ronaldo.

2006 LIVERPOOL – Reina; Finnan, Carragher, Hyypia, Riise, Gerrard, Xabi Alonso (Kronkamp), Sissoko, Kewell (Morientes), Cisse, Crouch (Hamann). **WEST HAM UTD.** – Hislop; Scaloni, Ferdinand, Gabbidon, Konchesky, Benayoun, Fletcher (Dailly), Reo-Coker, Etherington (Sheringham), Ashton (Zamora), Harewood. **Scorers:** Liverpool – Gerrard 2, Cisse, West Ham Utd. – Ashton, Konchesky, Carragher (o.g.).

F.A. CUP FINALS – COMPLETE RESULTS

AT KENNINGTON OVAL

1872	The Wanderers beat Royal Engineers (1-0)

AT LILLIE BRIDGE, LONDON

1873	The Wanderers beat Oxford University (2-1)

AT KENNINGTON OVAL

1874	Oxford University beat Royal Engineers (2-0)
1875	Royal Engineers beat Old Etonians (2-0 after a 1-1 draw)
1876	The Wanderers beat Old Etonians (3-0 after a 0-0 draw)
1877††	The Wanderers beat Oxford University (2-1)
1878*	The Wanderers beat Royal Engineers (3-1)
1879	Old Etonians beat Clapham Rov. (1-0)
1880	Clapham Rov. beat Oxford University (1-0)
1881	Old Carthusians beat Old Etonians (3-0)
1882	Old Etonians beat Blackburn Rov. (1-0)
1883††	Blackburn Olympic beat Old Etonians (2-1)
1884	Blackburn Rov. beat Queen's Park (Glasgow) (2-1)
1885	Blackburn Rov. beat Queen's Park (Glasgow) (2-0)
1886†a	Blackburn Rov. beat W.B.A. (2-0 after a 0-0 draw)
1887	Aston Villa beat W.B.A. (2-0)
1888	W.B.A. beat Preston N.E. (2-1)
1889	Preston N.E. beat Wolves (3-0)
1890	Blackburn Rov. beat Sheffield Wed. (6-1)
1891	Blackburn Rov. beat Notts Co. (3-1)
1892	W.B.A. beat Aston Villa (3-0)

AT FALLOWFIELD, MANCHESTER

1893	Wolves beat Everton (1-0)

AT GOODISON PARK

1894	Notts Co. beat Bolton Wand. (4-1)

AT CRYSTAL PALACE

1895	Aston Villa beat W.B.A. (1-0)
1896	Sheffield Wed. beat Wolves (2-1)
1897	Aston Villa beat Everton (3-2)
1898	Nott'm. Forest beat Derby Co. (3-1)
1899	Sheffield Utd. beat Derby Co. (4-1)
1900	Bury beat Southampton (4-0)
1901†††	Tottenham beat Sheffield Utd. (3-1 after a 2-2 draw)
1902	Sheffield Utd. beat Southampton (2-1 after a 1-1 draw)
1903	Bury beat Derby Co. (6-0)

1904	Manchester City beat Bolton Wand. (1-0)
1905	Aston Villa beat Newcastle Utd. (2-0)
1906	Everton beat Newcastle Utd. (1-0)
1907	Sheffield Wed. beat Everton (2-1)
1908	Wolves beat Newcastle Utd. (3-1)
1909	Manchester Utd. beat Bristol City (1-0)
1910**	Newcastle Utd. beat Barnsley (2-0 after a 1-1 draw)
1911*b*	Bradford City beat Newcastle Utd. (1-0 after a 0-0 draw)
1912*c*	Barnsley beat W.B.A. (1-0 after a 0-0 draw)
1913	Aston Villa beat Sunderland (1-0)
1914	Burnley beat Liverpool (1-0)

AT OLD TRAFFORD
| 1915 | Sheffield Utd. beat Chelsea (3-0) |

AT STAMFORD BRIDGE
1920††	Aston Villa beat Huddersfield Town (1-0)
1921	Tottenham beat Wolves (1-0)
1922	Huddersfield Town beat Preston N.E. (1-0)

AT WEMBLEY
1923	Bolton Wand. beat West Ham Utd. (2-0)
1924	Newcastle Utd. beat Aston Villa (2-0)
1925	Sheffield Utd. beat Cardiff City (1-0)
1926	Bolton Wand. beat Manchester City (1-0)
1927	Cardiff City beat Arsenal (1-0)
1928	Blackburn Rov. beat Huddersfield Town (3-1)
1929	Bolton Wand. beat Portsmouth (2-0)
1930	Arsenal beat Huddersfield Town (2-0)
1931	W.B.A. beat Birmingham City (2-1)
1932	Newcastle Utd. beat Arsenal (2-1)
1933	Everton beat Manchester City (3-0)
1934	Manchester City beat Portsmouth (2-1)
1935	Sheffield Wed. beat W.B.A. (4-2)
1936	Arsenal beat Sheffield Utd. (1-0)
1937	Sunderland beat Preston N.E. (3-1)
1938††	Preston N.E. beat Huddersfield Town (1-0)
1939	Portsmouth beat Wolves (4-1)
1946††	Derby Co. beat Charlton Athletic (4-1)
1947††	Charlton Athletic beat Burnley (1-0)
1948	Manchester Utd. beat Blackpool (4-2)
1949	Wolves beat Leicester City (3-1)
1950	Arsenal beat Liverpool (2-0)
1951	Newcastle Utd. beat Blackpool (2-0)
1952	Newcastle Utd. beat Arsenal (1-0)
1953	Blackpool beat Bolton Wand. (4-3)
1954	W.B.A. beat Preston N.E. (3-2)
1955	Newcastle Utd. beat Manchester City (3-1)
1956	Manchester City beat Birmingham City (3-1)
1957	Aston Villa beat Manchester Utd. (2-1)
1958	Bolton Wand. beat Manchester Utd. (2-0)
1959	Nott'm. Forest beat Luton Town (2-1)
1960	Wolves beat Blackburn Rov. (3-0)
1961	Tottenham beat Leicester City (2-0)
1962	Tottenham beat Burnley (3-1)
1963	Manchester Utd. beat Leicester City (3-1)
1964	West Ham Utd. beat Preston N.E. (3-2)
1965††	Liverpool beat Leeds Utd. (2-1)

1966	Everton beat Sheffield Wed. (3-2)
1967	Tottenham beat Chelsea (2-1)
1968††	W.B.A. beat Everton (1-0)
1969	Manchester City beat Leicester City (1-0)
1970††•	Chelsea beat Leeds Utd. (2-1 after a 2-2 draw)
1971††	Arsenal beat Liverpool (2-1)
1972	Leeds Utd. beat Arsenal (1-0)
1973	Sunderland beat Leeds Utd. (1-0)
1974	Liverpool beat Newcastle Utd. (3-0)
1975	West Ham Utd. beat Fulham (2-0)
1976	Southampton beat Manchester Utd. (1-0)
1977	Manchester Utd. beat Liverpool (2-1)
1978	Ipswich Town beat Arsenal (1-0)
1979	Arsenal beat Manchester Utd. (3-2)
1980	West Ham Utd. beat Arsenal (1-0)
1981	Tottenham beat Manchester City (3-2 after a 1-1 draw)
1982	Tottenham beat Q.P.R. (1-0 after a 1-1 draw)
1983	Manchester Utd. beat Brighton & H.A. (4-0 after a 2-2 draw)
1984	Everton beat Watford (2-0)
1985††	Manchester Utd. beat Everton (1-0)
1986	Liverpool beat Everton (3-1)
1987††	Coventry City beat Tottenham (3-2)
1988	Wimbledon beat Liverpool (1-0)
1989††	Liverpool beat Everton (3-2)
1990	Manchester Utd. beat Crystal Palace (1-0 after a 3-3 draw)
1991††	Tottenham beat Nott'm. Forest (2-1)
1992	Liverpool beat Sunderland (2-0)
1993††	Arsenal beat Sheffield Wed. (2-1 after a 1-1 draw)
1994	Manchester Utd. beat Chelsea (4-0)
1995	Everton beat Manchester Utd. (1-0)
1996	Manchester Utd. beat Liverpool (1-0)
1997	Chelsea beat Middlesbrough (2-0)
1998	Arsenal beat Newcastle Utd. (2-0)
1999	Manchester Utd. beat Newcastle Utd. (2-0)
2000	Chelsea beat Aston Villa (1-0)

AT MILLENNIUM STADIUM

2001	Liverpool beat Arsenal (2-1)
2002	Arsenal beat Chelsea (2-0)
2003	Arsenal beat Southampton (1-0)
2004	Manchester Utd. beat Millwall (3-0)
2005***	Arsenal 0, Manchester Utd. 0
2006****	Liverpool 3, West Ham Utd. 3

†† After extra time. * Won outright but restored to the Association. *a* Replayed at Baseball Ground. † A special trophy was awarded for the third consecutive win. ††† Replayed at Burnden Park. ** Replayed at Goodison Park. *b* Replayed at Old Trafford. new trophy provided. *c* Replayed at Bramall Lane. • Replayed at Old Trafford. *** aet, Arsenal won 5-4 on pens. **** aet, Liverpool won 3-1 on pens.
(All replays since 1981 played at Wembley.)

SUMMARY OF F.A. CUP WINS

Manchester Utd.	11	Newcastle Utd.	6	Sheffield Utd.	4
Arsenal	10	Everton	5	Wolves	4
Tottenham	8	The Wanderers	5	Chelsea	3
Aston Villa	7	W.B.A.	5	Sheffield Wed.	3
Liverpool	7	Bolton Wand.	4	West Ham Utd.	3
Blackburn Rov.	6	Manchester City	4	Bury	2

Nott'm. Forest 2	Burnley 1	Leeds Utd. 1
Old Etonians 2	Cardiff City 1	Notts Co. 1
Preston N.E. 2	Charlton Athletic 1	Old Carthusians 1
Sunderland 2	Clapham Rov. 1	Oxford University 1
Barnsley 1	Coventry City 1	Portsmouth 1
Blackburn Olympic 1	Derby Co. 1	Royal Engineers 1
Blackpool 1	Huddersfield Town 1	Southampton 1
Bradford City 1	Ipswich Town 1	Wimbledon 1

APPEARANCES IN FINALS
(Figures do not include replays)

Arsenal 17	West Ham Utd. 5	Notts Co. 2
Manchester Utd. 17	Derby Co. 4	Queen's Park (Glas.) 2
Liverpool 13	Leeds Utd. 4	Blackburn Olympic* 1
Newcastle Utd. 13	Leicester City 4	Bradford City* 1
Everton 12	Oxford University 4	Brighton & H.A. 1
Aston Villa 10	Royal Engineers 4	Bristol City 1
W.B.A. 10	Southampton 4	Coventry City* 1
Tottenham 9	Sunderland 4	Crystal Palace 1
Blackburn Rov. 8	Blackpool 3	Fulham 1
Manchester City 8	Burnley 3	Ipswich Town* 1
Wolves 8	Nott'm. Forest 3	Luton Town 1
Bolton Wand. 7	Portsmouth 3	Middlesbrough 1
Chelsea 7	Barnsley 2	Millwall 1
Preston N.E. 7	Birmingham City 2	Old Carthusians* 1
Old Etonians 6	Bury* 2	Q.P.R. 1
Sheffield Utd. 6	Cardiff City 2	Watford 1
Sheffield Wed. 6	Charlton Athletic 2	Wimbledon* 1
Huddersfield Town 5	Clapham Rov. 2	(* Denotes undefeated)
The Wanderers* 5		

APPEARANCES IN SEMI-FINALS
(Figures do not include replays)

Arsenal 25, Manchester Utd. 24, Everton 23, Liverpool 22, Aston Villa 19, W.B.A. 19, Blackburn Rov. 17, Newcastle Utd. 17, Tottenham 17, Chelsea 16, Sheffield Wed. 16, Wolves 14, Bolton Wand. 13, Derby Co. 13, Sheffield Utd. 13, Nott'm. Forest 12, Sunderland 12, Southampton 11, Manchester City 10, Preston N.E. 10, Birmingham City 9, Burnley 8, Leeds Utd. 8, Huddersfield Town 7, Leicester City 7, West Ham Utd. 7, Fulham 6, Old Etonians 6, Oxford University 6, Notts Co. 5, Portsmouth 5, The Wanderers 5, Luton Town 4, Millwall 4, Queen's Park (Glasgow) 4, Royal Engineers 4, Watford 4, Blackpool 3, Cardiff City 3, Clapham Rov. 3, *Crystal Palace 3, Ipswich Town 3, Middlesbrough 3, Norwich City 3, Old Carthusians 3, Oldham Athletic 3, Stoke City 3, The Swifts 3, Barnsley 2, Blackburn Olympic 2, Bristol City 2, Bury 2, Charlton Athletic 2, Grimsby Town 2, Swansea City Town 2, Swindon Town 2, Wimbledon 2, Bradford City 1, Brighton & H.A. 1, Cambridge University 1, Chesterfield 1, Coventry City 1, Crewe Alexandra 1, Darwen 1, Derby Co. Junction 1, Hull City 1, Marlow 1, Old Harrovians 1, Orient 1, Plymouth Argyle 1, Port Vale 1, Q.P.R. 1, Rangers (Glasgow) 1, Reading 1, Shropshire Wand. 1, Wycombe Wand. 1, York City 1.
(*A previous and different Crystal Palace club also reached the semi-final in season 1871-72)

RECORD LEAGUE CUP WIN FOR MANCHESTER UNITED

THIRD ROUND	FOURTH ROUND	FIFTH ROUND	SEMI-FINALS	FINAL
*Manchester Utd. 4				
Barnet 1	*Manchester Utd. 3			
*Fulham 2	W.B.A. 1	Manchester Utd. 3		
W.B.A. .... †3				
*Mansfield Town 2	*Millwall 2		Manchester Utd. 1:2	
Millwall 3	Birmingham City .... †B2	*Birmingham City 1		
*Birmingham City 2				
Norwich City 1				Manchester Utd. 4
*Everton 0	*Middlesbrough 2			
Middlesbrough 1	Crystal Palace 1	*Middlesbrough 0		
*Crystal Palace 2				
Liverpool 1			*Blackburn Rov. 1:1	
Chelsea 1	*Charlton Athletic 2	Blackburn Rov. 1		
Charlton Athletic .... †A1	Blackburn Rov. 3			
*Blackburn Rov. 3				
Leeds Utd. 0				
*Doncaster Rov. 2	*Doncaster Rov. 3	*Doncaster Rov. 2		
Gillingham 0	Aston Villa 0			
*Aston Villa 1			Arsenal .... 0:†2	
Burnley 0				
*Sunderland 0	*Arsenal 3	Arsenal .... †C2		
Arsenal 3	Reading 0			
*Reading 2				
Sheffield Utd. 0				

160

*Bolton Wand. 1
West Ham Utd. 0

*Cardiff City 1
Leicester City 1

*Grimsby Town 0
Newcastle Utd. 0

Watford 0
*Wigan Athletic .... †3

*Bolton Wand. .... †2

Leicester City 1

Newcastle Utd. 0

*Wigan Athletic 1

Bolton Wand. 0

*Wigan Athletic 1:1

*Wigan Athletic 2

Wigan Athletic 0

*Drawn at home; in semi-finals, first leg. † After extra-time. A – Charlton Athletic won 5-4 on pens. B – Birmingham City won 4-3 on pens. C – Arsenal won 3-1 on pens.

FIRST ROUND: Blackpool 2, Hull City 1; Bristol City 2, Barnet 4; Burnley 2, Carlisle Utd. 1; Bury 0, Leicester City 3; Cheltenham Town 5, Brentford 3; Crystal Palace 3, Walsall 0; Gillingham 1, Oxford Utd. 0; Hartlepool Utd. 3, Darlington 1; Ipswich Town 0, Yeovil Town 2; Leeds Utd. 2, Oldham Athletic 0; Leyton Orient 1, Luton Town 3; Lincoln City 5, Crewe Alexandra 1; Mansfield Town 1, Stoke City 1 (aet; Mansfield Town won 3-0 on pens); Millwall 2, Bristol Rov. 0; MK Dons 0, Norwich City 1 (aet); Northampton Town 3, Q.P.R. 0; Nott'm. Forest 2, Macclesfield Town 3; Plymouth Argyle 4, Peterborough Utd. 1; Preston N.E. 2, Barnsley 2 (aet, Barnsley won 5-4 on pens); Reading 3, Swansea City 1 (aet); Rochdale 0, Bradford City 5; Rotherham Utd. 3, Port Vale 1; Scunthorpe Utd. 2, Tranmere Rov.1; Sheffield Utd. 1, Boston Utd. 0; Southend Utd. 0, Southampton 3; Shrewsbury Town 3, Brighton & H.A. 2 (aet); Stockport Co. 2, Sheffield Wed. 4 (aet); Swindon Town 1, Wycombe Wand. 3; Watford 3, Notts Co. 1; Wolves 5, Chester City 1; Wrexham 0, Doncaster Row. 1; Chesterfield 2, Huddersfield Town 4; Colchester Utd. 0, Cardiff City 2; Derby Co. 0, Grimsby Town 1; Rushden & Diamonds 0, Coventry City 3; Torquay Utd. 0, Bournemouth 0 (aet, Bournemouth won 4-3 on pens).

SECOND ROUND: Barnet 2, Plymouth Argyle 1; Burnley 3, Barnsley 0; Cardiff City 2, Macclesfield Town 1; Charlton Athletic 3, Hartlepool Utd.1; Crystal Palace 1, Coventry City 0; Gillingham 3, Portsmouth 2 (aet); Grimsby Town 1, Tottenham 0; Leicester City 2, Blackpool 1; Mansfield Town 1, Southampton 0; Norwich City 2, Northampton Town 0; Reading 1, Luton Town 0; Rotherham Utd. 0, Leeds Utd. 2; Scunthorpe 0, Birmingham City 2; Sheffield Wed. 2, West Ham Utd. 4; Shrewsbury Town 0, Sheffield Utd. 0 (aet, Sheffield Utd. won 4-3 on pens); Sunderland 1, Cheltenham Town 0; Watford 2, Wolves 1 (aet); W.B.A. 4, Bradford City 1; Wigan Athletic 1, Bournemouth 0; Wycombe Wand. 3, Aston Villa 8; Yeovil Town 1, Millwall 2; Blackburn Row. 3, Huddersfield Town 1; Doncaster Row. 1, Manchester City 1 (aet, Doncaster Row. won 3-0 on pens); Fulham 5, Lincoln City 4 (aet).

CARLING CUP FINAL

MANCHESTER UNITED 4, WIGAN ATHLETIC 0

Millennium Stadium (66,866), Sunday, February 26, 2006

Manchester Utd. (4-4-2): Van der Sar, Neville (capt), Ferdinand, Brown (Vidic 82), Silvestre (Evra 82), Ronaldo (Richardson 73), O'Shea, Giggs, Park, Rooney, Saha. **Subs not used:** Howard, Van Nistelrooy. **Scorers:** Rooney (33, 61), Saha (55), Ronaldo (60). **Booked:** Ronaldo. **Manager:** Sir Alex Ferguson.

Wigan Athletic (4-4-2): Pollitt (Filan 14), Chimbonda, Henchoz (McCulloch 62), De Zeeuw (capt), Baines, Teale, Kavanagh (Ziegler 72), Scharner, Bullard, Roberts, Camara. **Subs not used:** Jackson, Johansson. **Manager:** Paul Jewell.

Referee: A. Wiley (Staffs). **Half-time:** 1-0.

Sir Alex Ferguson admitted he was taking a gamble by leaving out leading marksman Ruud van Nistelrooy. Not only could it have cost Manchester United their last chance of some silverware, but the manager's decision to play Louis Saha instead ran the risk of undermining his own position. In the event, Ferguson was fully vindicated as his side lifted the League Cup for the second time, even though he still ran into some flak by declining to bring Van Nistelrooy off the bench with the trophy safe. Saha had played a major role in United reaching the Final by scoring in earlier rounds against West Bromwich Albion, Birmingham and Blackburn. Here, he struck the decisive second goal, had a hand in three others and overall made sure than Van Nistelrooy was never missed.

Wigan deserved every bit of credit for getting so far, on top of making an excellent impression in their first season of Premiership football. But this was not to be the day of the underdog. It started badly when goalkeeper Mike Pollitt pulled a hamstring after three minutes and eventually had to be replaced by John Filan. The substitute was beaten first by Rooney, who ended a run of 12 appearances without a goal after Saha flicked on Edwin Van der Sar's clearance.

The goalkeeper denied Henri Camara, who had turned Rio Ferdinand early in the second half, and United responded with three goals in six minutes. First, Ryan Giggs and Cristiano Ronaldo combined to release Gary Neville, whose cross was converted at the second attempt by Saha after Filan kept out his first shot. Next, Saha punished a Stephane Henchoz error to set up Ronaldo. Then, Saha and Ferdinand helped on a Giggs free-kick for Rooney to apply the finishing touch.

Wigan were being outplayed in every department, although there was no excuse for Ronaldo rubbing it in with a spot of ball-juggling. Camara and his strike partner Jason Roberts were incensed. So, too, was Giggs who also had a go at the Portuguese winger. At the end, United celebrated a record victory in a competition they had been forced to take seriously for once. It was the competition's biggest margin in a single Final. Only Norwich's 4-0 success against Rochdale in the two-leg 1962 Final matches it.

HOW THEY REACHED THE FINAL

MANCHESTER UNITED

Round 3: 4-1 home to Barnet (Miller, Richardson, Rossi, Ebanks-Blake)
Round 4: 3-1 home to W.B.A. (Ronaldo pen, Saha, O'Shea)
Round 5: 3-1 away to Birmingham City (Saha 2, Park)
Semi-finals: v Blackburn Rov. – first leg, 1-1 away (Saha); second leg 2-1 home (Van Nistelrooy, Saha); won 3-2 on agg.

WIGAN ATHLETIC

Round 2: 1-0 home to Bournemouth (Roberts)
Round 3: 3-0 home to Watford (Taylor pen, Johansson 2) – aet
Round 4: 1-0 home to Newcastle Utd. (Connolly pen)
Round 5: 2-0 home to Bolton Wand. (Roberts 2)
Semi-finals: v Arsenal – first leg, 1-0 home (Scharner); second leg, 1-2 away (Roberts) –
aet; won on away goal.

LEAGUE CUP – COMPLETE RESULTS

LEAGUE CUP FINALS

1961*	Aston Villa beat Rotherham Utd. 3-2 on agg. (0-2a, 3-0h)
1962	Norwich City beat Rochdale 4-0 on agg. (3-0a, 1-0h)
1963	Birmingham City beat Aston Villa 3-1 on agg. (3-1h, 0-0a)
1964	Leicester City beat Stoke City 4-3 on agg. (1-1a, 3-2h)
1965	Chelsea beat Leicester City 3-2 on agg. (3-2h, 0-0a)
1966	W.B.A. beat West Ham Utd. 5-3 on agg. (1-2a, 4-1h)

AT WEMBLEY

1967	Q.P.R. beat W.B.A. (3-2)
1968	Leeds Utd. beat Arsenal (1-0)
1969*	Swindon Town beat Arsenal (3-1)
1970*	Manchester City beat W.B.A. (2-1)
1971	Tottenham beat Aston Villa (2-0)
1972	Stoke City beat Chelsea (2-1)
1973	Tottenham beat Norwich City (1-0)
1974	Wolves beat Manchester City (2-1)
1975	Aston Villa beat Norwich City (1-0)
1976	Manchester City beat Newcastle Utd. (2-1)
1977†*	Aston Villa beat Everton (3-2 after 0-0 and 1-1 draws)
1978††	Nott'm. Forest beat Liverpool (1-0 after 0-0 draw)
1979	Nott'm. Forest beat Southampton (3-2)
1980	Wolves beat Nott'm. Forest (1-0)
1981†††	Liverpool beat West Ham Utd. (2-1 after 1-1 draw)

MILK CUP

1982*	Liverpool beat Tottenham (3-1)
1983*	Liverpool beat Manchester Utd. (2-1)
1984**	Liverpool beat Everton (1-0 after *0-0 draw)
1985	Norwich City beat Sunderland (1-0)
1986	Oxford Utd. beat Q.P.R. (3-0)

LITTLEWOODS CUP

1987	Arsenal beat Liverpool (2-1)
1988	Luton Town beat Arsenal (3-2)
1989	Nott'm. Forest beat Luton Town (3-1)
1990	Nott'm. Forest beat Oldham Athletic (1-0)

RUMBELOWS CUP

1991	Sheffield Wed. beat Manchester Utd. (1-0)
1992	Manchester Utd. beat Nott'm. Forest (1-0)

COCA-COLA CUP

1993	Arsenal beat Sheffield Wed. (2-1)
1994	Aston Villa beat Manchester Utd. (3-1)
1995	Liverpool beat Bolton Wand. (2-1)
1996	Aston Villa beat Leeds Utd. (3-0)
1997	Leicester City beat Middlesbrough (*1-0 after *1-1 draw) ★
1998	Chelsea beat Middlesbrough (2-0)

WORTHINGTON CUP (AT MILLENNIUM STADIUM FROM 2001)

1999	Tottenham beat Leicester City (1-0)
2000	Leicester City beat Tranmere Rov. (2-1)
2001	Liverpool beat Birmingham City (5-4 on pens after *1-1 draw)
2002	Blackburn Rov. beat Tottenham (2-1)
2003	Liverpool beat Manchester Utd. (2-0)

CARLING CUP

2004	Middlesbrough beat Bolton Wand. (2-1)
2005*	Chelsea beat Liverpool (3-2)
2006	Manchester Utd. beat Wigan Athletic (4-0)

* After extra time. † First replay at Hillsborough, second replay at Old Trafford. †† Replayed at Old Trafford. ††† Replayed at Aston Villa Park. ** Replayed at Maine Road. ★ Replayed at Hillsborough

SUMMARY OF LEAGUE CUP WINNERS

Liverpool	7	Manchester Utd.	2	Middlesbrough	1
Aston Villa	5	Norwich City	2	Oxford Utd.	1
Nott'm Forest	4	Wolves	2	Q.P.R.	1
Chelsea	3	Blackburn Rov.	1	Sheffield Wed.	1
Leicester City	3	Birmingham City	1	Stoke City	1
Tottenham	3	Leeds Utd.	1	Swindon Town	1
Arsenal	2	Luton Town	1	W.B.A.	1
Manchester City	2				

LEAGUE CUP FINAL APPEARANCES

10 Liverpool; **7** Aston Villa; **6** Manchester Utd., Nott'm. Forest; **5** Arsenal, Leicester City, Tottenham; **4** Chelsea, Norwich City; **3** Manchester City, Middlesbrough, W.B.A.; **2** Birmingham City, Bolton Wand., Everton, Leeds Utd., Luton Town, Q.P.R., Sheffield Wed., Stoke City, West Ham Utd., Wolves; **1** Blackburn Rov., Newcastle Utd., Oldham Athletic, Oxford Utd., Rochdale, Rotherham Utd., Southampton, Sunderland, Swindon Town, Tranmere Rov., Wigan Athletic. **(Figures do not include replays).**

LEAGUE CUP SEMI-FINAL APPEARANCES

13 Liverpool; **12** Aston Villa; **11** Arsenal; **10** Manchester Utd., Tottenham; **8** Chelsea; **7** West Ham Utd.; **6** Nott'm Forest; **5** Blackburn Rov., Leeds Utd., Leicester City, Manchester City, Middlesbrough, Norwich City; **4** Birmingham City, Bolton Wand., Sheffield Wed., W.B.A.; **3** Burnley, Crystal Palace, Everton, Ipswich Town, Q.P.R., Sunderland, Swindon Town, Wolves; **2** Bristol City, Coventry City, Luton Town, Oxford Utd., Plymouth Argyle, Southampton, Stoke City, Tranmere Rov., Watford, Wimbledon; **1** Blackpool, Bury, Cardiff City, Carlisle Utd., Chester City, Derby Co., Huddersfield Town, Newcastle Utd., Oldham Athletic, Peterborough, Rochdale, Rotherham Utd., Sheffield Utd., Shrewsbury Town, Stockport Co., Walsall, Wigan Athletic. **(Figures do not include replays).**

OTHER COMPETITIONS 2005-06

FOOTBALL LEAGUE TROPHY

FIRST ROUND

Northern: Barnsley 2, Doncaster Rov. 5; Blackpool 4, Wrexham 3 (aet); Boston Utd. 2, Huddersfield Town 1, Cambridge Utd. 3, Chester City 0; Grimsby Town 1, Morecambe 1 (aet, Morecambe won 4-3 on pens); Halifax 6, Bury 1; Kidderminster 2, Darlington 1; Macclesfield Town 2, Chesterfield 0; Mansfield Town 0, Hereford 1; Oldham Athletic 1, Carlisle 1 (aet, Carlisle Utd. won 6-5 on pens); Rochdale 3, Stockport Co. 1; Rotherham Utd. 3, Accrington 3 (aet, Rotherham Utd. won 3-2 on pens); Scunthorpe Utd. 1, Hartlepool Utd. 0; Tranmere Rov. 2, Lincoln City 1.
Southern: Barnet 3, Bristol City 2; Bournemouth 4, Aldershot 1; Brentford 1, Oxford Utd. 1 (aet, Oxford Utd. won 4-3 on pens); Gillingham 2, Crawley 0; Leyton Orient 2, Yeovil Town 0; MK Dons 3, Exeter 2; Northampton Town 5, Notts Co. 2; Peterborough Utd. 2, Bristol Rov. 1 (aet); Rushden & Diamonds 1, Southend Utd. 0; Shrewsbury Town 0, Cheltenham Town 2; Swindon Town 2, Stevenage 0; Torquay Utd. 1, Swansea City 3; Woking 3, Nott'm. Forest 2; Wycombe Wand. 2, Dagenham & Redbridge 1 (aet).

SECOND ROUND

Northern: Boston Utd. 0, Kidderminster 3; Cambridge Utd. 3, Doncaster Rov. 2; Carlisle Utd. 2, Blackpool 1; Halifax 1, Scunthorpe Utd. 3; Hereford 2, Port Vale 1 (aet); Morecambe 0, Bradford City 1; Rotherham Utd. 1, Macclesfield Town 2; Tranmere Rov. 3, Rochdale 2.
Southern: Barnet 0, MK Dons 3; Colchester Utd. 3, Northampton Town 2 (aet); Gillingham 2, Wycombe Wand. 2 (aet, Wycombe Wand. won 3-1 on pens); Oxford Utd. 1, Leyton Orient 0; Peterborough Utd. 2, Swindon Town 1; Swansea City 4, Rushden & Diamonds 0; Walsall 1, Bournemouth 0; Woking 1, Cheltenham Town 5 (aet).

QUARTER-FINALS

Northern: Hereford 2, Scunthorpe Utd. 0; Kidderminster 2, Bradford City 1; Macclesfield Town 4, Cambridge Utd. 2; Tranmere Rov. 0, Carlisle Utd. 0 (aet, Carlisle Utd. won 11-10 on pens).
Southern: Cheltenham Town 2, Oxford Utd. 1; MK Dons 1, Colchester Utd. 2; Swansea City 3, Peterborough Utd. 1 (aet); Walsall 3, Wycombe Wand. 2.

SEMI-FINALS

Northern: Carlisle Utd. 1, Kidderminster 0; Macclesfield Town 2, Hereford 0.
Southern: Cheltenham Town 0, Colchester Utd. 1; Swansea City 2, Walsall 2 (aet, Swansea City won 6-5 on pens).

AREA FINALS

Northern first leg: Carlisle Utd. 2 (Hawley 20, Murphy 90), Macclesfield Town 1 (Smart 9). Att: 5,706. **Second leg:** Macclesfield Town 3 (Teague 4, McNeil 28, Townson 120), Carlisle Utd. 2 (Hawley 42, Grand 109). Att: 3,598 (aet, agg 4-4, Carlisle Utd. won on away goals).
Southern first leg: Swansea City 1 (Akinfenwa 40), Colchester Utd. 0. Att: 7,285. **Second leg:** Colchester Utd. 1 (Danns 46), Swansea City 2 (Britton 52, Knight 56). Att: 3,236 (Swansea City won 3-1 on agg).

FINAL

CARLISLE UNITED 1, SWANSEA CITY 2
Millennium Stadium (42,028), Sunday, April 2, 2006

Carlisle Utd. (4-4-2): Westwood, Livesey, Gray, Arnison (Grand 89), Aranalde, Murphy, Billy, Lumsdon, A. Murray (Hackney 79), Holmes (G. Murray 71), Hawley. **Subs not used:** Williams, McGill. **Scorer:** A. Murray (40). **Booked:** A. Murray, Arnison. **Manager:** Paul Simpson.

Swansea City (4-4-2): Gueret, Ricketts, Monk, Lowe, Tate, O'Leary (Knight 63), Britton, Robinson (Martinez 83), Tudur-Jones, Akinfenwa, Trundle. **Subs not used:** Murphy, Austin, Forbes. **Scorers:** Trundle (3), Akinfenwa (81). **Manager:** Kenny Jackett.

Referee: A. Leake (Lancs). **Half-time:** 1-1

FINALS – RESULTS

Associated Members' Cup
1984   (Hull City) Bournemouth 2, Hull City 1
Freight Rover Trophy
1985   (Wembley) Wigan Athletic 3, Brentford 1
1986   (Wembley) Bristol City 3, Bolton Wand. 0
1987   (Wembley) Mansfield Town 1, Bristol City 1 (aet; Mansfield Town won 5-4 on pens.)
Sherpa Van Trophy
1988   (Wembley) Wolves 2, Burnley 0
1989   (Wembley) Bolton Wand. 4, Torquay Utd. 1
Leyland Daf Cup
1990   (Wembley) Tranmere Rov. 2, Bristol Rov. 1
1991   (Wembley) Birmingham City 3, Tranmere Rov. 2
Autoglass Trophy
1992   (Wembley) Stoke City 1, Stockport Co. 0
1993   (Wembley) Port Vale 2, Stockport Co. 1
1994   (Wembley) Huddersfield Town 1, Swansea City 1 (aet; Swansea City won 3-1 on pens.)
Auto Windscreens Shield
1995   (Wembley) Birmingham City 1, Carlisle Utd. 0 (Birmingham City won in sudden-death overtime)
1996   (Wembley) Rotherham Utd. 2, Shrewsbury Town 1
1997   (Wembley) Carlisle Utd. 0, Colchester Utd. 0 (aet; Carlisle Utd. won 4-3 on pens.)
1998   (Wembley) Grimsby Town 2, Bournemouth 1 (Grimsby Town won with golden goal in extra time)
1999   (Wembley) Wigan Athletic 1, Millwall 0
2000   (Wembley) Stoke City 2, Bristol City 1
LDV Vans Trophy
2001   (Millennium Stadium) Port Vale 2, Brentford 1
2002   (Millennium Stadium) Blackpool 4, Cambridge Utd. 1
2003   (Millennium Stadium) Bristol City 2, Carlisle Utd. 0
2004   (Millennium Stadium) Blackpool 2, Southend Utd. 0
2005   (Millennium Stadium) Wrexham 2, Southend Utd. 0
Football League Trophy
2006   (Millennium Stadium) Swansea City 2, Carlisle Utd. 1

OTHER LEAGUE CLUBS' CUP COMPETITIONS

FINALS – AT WEMBLEY

Full Members' Cup (Discontinued after 1992)
1985-86   Chelsea 5, Manchester City 4
1986-87   Blackburn Rov. 1, Charlton Athletic 0

Simod Cup
1987-88   Reading 4, Luton Town 1
1988-89   Nott'm. Forest 4, Everton 3
Zenith Data Systems Cup
1989-90   Chelsea 1, Middlesbrough 0
1990-91   Crystal Palace 4, Everton 1
1991-92   Nott'm Forest 3, Southampton 2

ANGLO-ITALIAN CUP (Discontinued after 1996: * Home club)

1970   *Napoli 0, Swindon Town 3
1971   *Bologna 1, Blackpool 2 (aet)
1972   *AS Roma 3, Blackpool 1
1973   *Fiorentina 1, Newcastle Utd. 2
1993   Derby Co. 1, Cremonese 3 (at Wembley)
1994   Notts Co. 0, Brescia 1 (at Wembley)
1995   Ascoli 1, Notts Co. 2 (at Wembley)
1996   Port Vale 2, Genoa 5 (at Wembley)

F.A. VASE FINALS

At Wembley (until 2001)
1975   Hoddesdon Town 2, Epsom & Ewell 1
1976   Billericay Town 1, Stamford 0*
1977   Billericay Town 2, Sheffield 1 (replay Nottingham, after a 1-1 draw at Wembley)
1978   Blue Star 2, Barton Rov. 1
1979   Billericay Town 4, Almondsbury Greenway 1
1980   Stamford 2, Guisborough Town 0
1981   Whickham 3, Willenhall Town 2*
1982   Forest Green Rov. 3, Rainworth Miners' Welfare 0
1983   V.S. Rugby 1, Halesowen Town 0
1984   Stansted 3, Stamford 2
1985   Halesowen Town 3, Fleetwood Town 1
1986   Halesowen Town 3, Southall 0
1987   St. Helens Town 3, Warrington Town 2
1988   Colne Dynamoes 1, Emley 0*
1989   Tamworth 3, Sudbury Town 0 (replay Peterborough Utd., after a 1-1 draw at Wembley)
1990   Yeading 1, Bridlington 0 (replay Leeds Utd., after 0-0 draw at Wembley)
1991   Guiseley 3, Gresley Rov. 1 (replay Bramall Lane, Sheffield, after a 4-4 draw at Wembley)
1992   Wimborne Town 5, Guiseley 3
1993   Bridlington Town 1, Tiverton Town 0
1994   Diss Town 2, Taunton Town 1*
1995   Arlesey Town 2, Oxford City 1
1996   Brigg Town 3, Clitheroe 0
1997   Whitby Town 3, North Ferriby Utd. 0
1998   Tiverton Town 1, Tow Law Town 0
1999   Tiverton Town 1, Bedlington Terriers 0
2000   Deal Town 1, Chippenham Town 0

2001   Taunton Town 2, Berkhamsted 1 (Villa Park)
2002   Whitley Bay 1, Tiptree Utd. 0* (Villa Park)
2003   Brigg Town 2, AFC Sudbury 1 (Upton Park)
2004   Winchester City 2, AFC Sudbury 0 (St Andrews)
2005   Didcot Town 3, AFC Sudbury 2 (White Hart Lane)
2006   Nantwich Town 3, Hillingdon Borough 1 (St Andrews)

* After extra time

F.A. TROPHY

FIRST ROUND

Accrington 2, Altrincham 0; Aldershot 1, Grays 1; Alfreton 1, Histon 1; Barrow 2, Clitheroe 1; Bognor 1, Hereford 7; Boreham Wood 1, Leighton 0; Burton 0, Worksop 1; Canvey Island 4, Kingstonian 1; Dagenham 2, Thurrock 0; Dorchester 3, Cambridge Utd. 2; East Thurrock 0, Gravesend 2; Exeter 2, Bishop's Stortford 1; Farnborough 0, Cambridge City 2; Halesowen 1, Tamworth 2; Halifax 0, Southport 0; Kettering 2, Farsley 1; Kidderminster 4, Scarborough 0; Salisbury 1, Harlow 0; Solihull 2, Hednesford 1; Stafford 4, Lancaster 2; Stalybridge 1, Droylsden 0; Stevenage 0, Crawley 2; York 1, Northwich 2; Uxbridge 1, Woking 2; Vauxhall 0, Morecambe 4; Warrington 1, Blyth 2; Welling 4, Redbridge 1. Weston Super Mare 3, Barking 2; Weymouth 0, Forest Green 1; Wimbledon 2 St Albans 3; Worcester 1, Hayes 0; Yeading 1, Carshalton 2. **Replays:** Grays 1, Aldershot 0; Histon 2, Alfreton 1; Southport 0, Halifax 1.

SECOND ROUND

Barrow 1, Cambridge City 2; Blyth 1, Welling 3; Boreham Wood 3, Gravesend 1; Canvey Island 0, Salisbury 1; Carshalton 2, Accrington 2; Crawley 3, Worcester 1; Dagenham 2, Kettering 1; Forest Green 3, Dorchester 1; Exeter 3, Histon 2; Halifax 0, Hereford 1; Kidderminster 0, Grays 1; Stafford 1, Morecambe 0; Stalybridge 1, Solihull 0; Tamworth 1, St Albans 0; Weston Super Mare 1, Worksop 1; Woking 1, Northwich 1. **Replays:** Accrington 2, Carshalton 0; Northwich 1, Woking 2 (aet); Worksop 2, West Super Mare 1.

THIRD ROUND

Accrington 1, Worksop 1; Crawley 0, Boreham Wood 2; Exeter 1, Cambridge City 0; Hereford 0, Grays 1; Salisbury 0, Stalybridge 0; Stafford 2, Forest Green 1; Tamworth 0, Dagenham 0; Woking 3, Welling 2. **Replays:** Dagenham 3, Tamworth 0; Worksop 1, Accrington 1 (aet, Worksop won 4-2 on pens); Stalybridge 0, Salisbury 1.

FOURTH ROUND

Exeter 3, Salisbury 1; Grays 1, Dagenham 1; Woking 1, Stafford 1; Worksop 0, Boreham Wood 1. **Replays:** Dagenham 2, Grays 4. Stafford 2, Woking 4.

SEMI-FINALS

First leg: Boreham Wood 0, Woking 1; Exeter 2, Grays 1. **Second leg:** Grays 2, Exeter 0 (Grays won 3-2 on agg); Woking 2, Boreham Wood 0 (Woking won 3-0 on agg).

168

GRAYS 2, WOKING 0
Upton Park (13,800), Sunday, May 14, 2006

Grays (4-4-2): Bayes, Sambrook, Nutter, Stuart, Thurgood, Oli, Martin, McLean, Kightly (Williamson 90), Poole, Hanson. **Subs not used:** Eyre, Hooper, Olayinka, Mawer, Edwards. **Scorers:** Oli (41), Poole (45). **Booked:** Sambrook. **Manager:** Mark Stimson.

Woking (4-4-2): Jalal, Hutchinson, Jackson, Nethercott (Liam Cockerill 60), MacDonald, Murray, Smith (Watson 60), Evans (Blackman 83), Ferguson, Richards, McAllister. **Subs not used:** Davies, El-Salahi. **Booked:** Watson. **Manager:** Glenn Cockerill.

Referee: H. Webb (South Yorks). **Half-time:** 2-0

F.A. TROPHY FINALS

At Wembley
1970   Macclesfield Town 2, Telford Utd. 0
1971   Telford Utd. 3, Hillingdon Borough 2
1972   Stafford Rangers 3, Barnet 0
1973   Scarborough 2, Wigan Athletic 1*
1974   Morecambe 2, Dartford 1
1975   Matlock Town 4, Scarborough 0
1976   Scarborough 3, Stafford Rangers 2*
1977   Scarborough 2, Dagenham 1
1978   Altrincham 3, Leatherhead 1
1979   Stafford Rangers 2, Kettering Town 0
1980   Dagenham 2, Mossley 1
1981   Bishop's Stortford 1, Sutton Utd. 0
1982   Enfield 1, Altrincham 0*
1983   Telford Utd. 2, Northwich Victoria 1
1984   Northwich Victoria 2, Bangor City 1 (replay Stoke City, after a 1-1 draw at Wembley)
1985   Wealdstone 2, Boston Utd. 1
1986   Altrincham 1, Runcorn 0
1987   Kidderminster Harriers 2, Burton Albion 1 (replay W.B.A., after a 0-0 draw at Wembley)
1988   Enfield 3, Telford Utd. 2 (replay W.B.A., after a 0-0 draw at Wembley)
1989   Telford Utd. 1, Macclesfield Town 0*
1990   Barrow 3, Leek Town 0
1991   Wycombe Wand. 2, Kidderminster Harriers 1
1992   Colchester Utd. 3, Witton Albion 1
1993   Wycombe Wand. 4, Runcorn 1
1994   Woking 2, Runcorn 1
1995   Woking 2, Kidderminster 1
1996   Macclesfield Town 3, Northwich Victoria 1
1997   Woking 1, Dagenham & Redbridge 0*
1998   Cheltenham Town 1, Southport 0
1999   Kingstonian 1, Forest Green Rov. 0
2000   Kingstonian 3, Kettering Town 2

At Villa Park
2001   Canvey Island 1, Forest Green Rov. 0
2002   Yeovil Town 2, Stevenage Borough 0
2003   Burscough 2, Tamworth 1
2004   Hednesford Town 3, Canvey Island 2
2005   Grays Athletic 1, Hucknall Town 1* (Grays Athletic won 6-5 on pens)

F.A. YOUTH CUP WINNERS

Year	Winners	Runners-up	Aggregate
1953	Manchester Utd.	Wolves	9-3
1954	Manchester Utd.	Wolves	5-4
1955	Manchester Utd.	W.B.A.	7-1
1956	Manchester Utd.	Chesterfield	4-3
1957	Manchester Utd.	West Ham Utd.	8-2
1958	Wolves	Chelsea	7-6
1959	Blackburn Rov.	West Ham Utd.	2-1
1960	Chelsea	Preston N.E.	5-2
1961	Chelsea	Everton	5-3
1962	Newcastle Utd.	Wolves	2-1
1963	West Ham Utd.	Liverpool	6-5
1964	Manchester Utd.	Swindon Town	5-2
1965	Everton	Arsenal	3-2
1966	Arsenal	Sunderland	5-3
1967	Sunderland	Birmingham City	2-0
1968	Burnley	Coventry City	3-2
1969	Sunderland	W.B.A.	6-3
1970	Tottenham	Coventry City	4-3
1971	Arsenal	Cardiff City	2-0
1972	Aston Villa	Liverpool	5-2
1973	Ipswich Town	Bristol City	4-1
1974	Tottenham	Huddersfield Town	2-1
1975	Ipswich Town	West Ham Utd.	5-1
1976	W.B.A.	Wolves	5-0
1977	Crystal Palace	Everton	1-0
1978	Crystal Palace	Aston Villa	*1-0
1979	Millwall	Manchester City	2-0
1980	Aston Villa	Manchester City	3-2
1981	West Ham Utd.	Tottenham	2-1
1982	Watford	Manchester Utd.	7-6
1983	Norwich City	Everton	6-5
1984	Everton	Stoke City	4-2
1985	Newcastle Utd.	Watford	4-1
1986	Manchester City	Manchester Utd.	3-1
1987	Coventry City	Charlton Athletic	2-1
1988	Arsenal	Doncaster Rov.	6-1
1989	Watford	Manchester City	2-1
1990	Tottenham	Middlesbrough	3-2
1991	Millwall	Sheffield Wed.	3-0
1992	Manchester Utd.	Crystal Palace	6-3
1993	Leeds Utd.	Manchester Utd.	4-1
1994	Arsenal	Millwall	5-3
1995	Manchester Utd.	Tottenham	†2-2
1996	Liverpool	West Ham Utd.	4-1
1997	Leeds Utd.	Crystal Palace	3-1
1998	Everton	Blackburn Rov.	5-3
1999	West Ham Utd.	Coventry City	9-0
2000	Arsenal	Coventry City	5-1
2001	Arsenal	Blackburn Rov.	6-3
2002	Aston Villa	Everton	4-2

2003	Manchester Utd.	Middlesbrough	3-1
2004	Middlesbrough	Aston Villa	4-0
2005	Ipswich Town	Southampton	3-2
2006	Liverpool	Manchester City	3-2

(* One match only; † Manchester Utd. won 4-3 on pens.)

WELSH CUP FINAL

Rhyl 2, Bangor City 0 (at Racecourse Ground).

WOMEN'S F.A. CUP FINAL

Arsenal 5, Leeds Utd. 0 (at The Den).

WOMEN'S PREMIER LEAGUE CUP FINAL

Charlton Athletic 2, Arsenal 1 (at Causeway Stadium).

F.A. SUNDAY CUP FINAL

Helton Lyons CC (Durham) 5, St Josephs (Luton) 3 (at Anfield).

F.A. COMMUNITY SHIELD

ARSENAL 1, CHELSEA 2

Millennium Stadium (58,014), Sunday, August 7, 2005

Arsenal (4-4-2): Lehmann, Lauren (Hoyte 77), Toure, Senderos (Cygan 71), Cole, Ljungberg (Reyes 71), Flamini (Gilberto Silva 46), Fabregas, Pires (Hleb 46), Bergkamp (Van Persie, 46), Henry. **Sub not used:** Howard. **Scorer:** Fabregas (65). **Booked:** Fabregas.

Chelsea (4-3-3): Cech, Paulo Ferreira, Gallas, Terry, Del Horno, Makelele, Lampard (Geremi 89), Gudjohnsen (Tiago 58), Duff (J. Cole 74), Drogba (Crespo 59), Robben (Wright-Phillips 69). **Subs not used:** Cudicini, Ricardo Carvalho. **Scorer:** Drogba (8, 57). **Booked:** Lampard, Makelele.

Referee: H. Webb (South Yorks). **Half-time:** 1-0.

CHARITY SHIELD RESULTS (POST WAR)

Year	Winners	Runners-up	Score
1948	Arsenal	Manchester Utd.	4-3
1949	Portsmouth	Wolves	*1-1
1950	England World Cup XI	F.A. Canadian Tour Team	4-2
1951	Tottenham	Newcastle Utd.	2-1
1952	Manchester Utd.	Newcastle Utd.	4-2
1953	Arsenal	Blackpool	3-1
1954	Wolves	W.B.A.	*4-4
1955	Chelsea	Newcastle Utd.	3-0
1956	Manchester Utd.	Manchester City	1-0
1957	Manchester Utd.	Aston Villa	4-0
1958	Bolton Wand.	Wolves	4-1
1959	Wolves	Nott'm. Forest	3-1
1960	Burnley	Wolves	*2-2
1961	Tottenham	F.A. XI	3-2
1962	Tottenham	Ipswich Town	5-1

1963	Everton	Manchester Utd.	4-0
1964	Liverpool	West Ham Utd.	*2-2
1965	Manchester Utd.	Liverpool	*2-2
1966	Liverpool	Everton	1-0
1967	Manchester Utd.	Tottenham	*3-3
1968	Manchester City	W.B.A.	6-1
1969	Leeds Utd.	Manchester City	2-1
1970	Everton	Chelsea	2-1
1971	Leicester City	Liverpool	1-0
1972	Manchester City	Aston Villa	1-0
1973	Burnley	Manchester City	1-0
1974	Liverpool	Leeds Utd.	1-1
	(Liverpool won 6-5 on penalties)		
1975	Derby Co.	West Ham Utd.	2-0
1976	Liverpool	Southampton	1-0
1977	Liverpool	Manchester Utd.	*0-0
1978	Nott'm. Forest	Ipswich Town	5-0
1979	Liverpool	Arsenal	3-1
1980	Liverpool	West Ham Utd.	1-0
1981	Aston Villa	Tottenham	*2-2
1982	Liverpool	Tottenham	1-0
1983	Manchester Utd.	Liverpool	2-0
1984	Everton	Liverpool	1-0
1985	Everton	Manchester Utd.	2-0
1986	Everton	Liverpool	*1-1
1987	Everton	Coventry City	1-0
1988	Liverpool	Wimbledon	2-1
1989	Liverpool	Arsenal	1-0
1990	Liverpool	Manchester Utd.	*1-1
1991	Arsenal	Tottenham	*0-0
1992	Leeds Utd.	Liverpool	4-3
1993	Manchester Utd.	Arsenal	1-1
	(Manchester Utd. won 5-4 on penalties)		
1994	Manchester Utd.	Blackburn Rov.	2-0
1995	Everton	Blackburn Rov.	1-0
1996	Manchester Utd.	Newcastle Utd.	4-0
1997	Manchester Utd.	Chelsea	1-1
	(Manchester Utd. won 4-2 on penalties)		
1998	Arsenal	Manchester Utd.	3-0
1999	Arsenal	Manchester Utd.	2-1
2000	Chelsea	Manchester Utd.	2-0
2001	Liverpool	Manchester Utd.	2-1

COMMUNITY SHIELD RESULTS

Year	Winners	Runners-up	Score
2002	Arsenal	Liverpool	1-0
2003	Manchester Utd.	Arsenal	1-1
	(Manchester Utd. won 4-3 on penalties)		
2004	Arsenal	Manchester Utd.	3-1
2005	Chelsea	Arsenal	2-1

(Fixture played at Wembley since 1974. Millennium Stadium since 2001.
*Trophy shared)

SCOTTISH LEAGUE RESULTS 2005-06

BANK OF SCOTLAND PREMIER LEAGUE

	Aberdeen	Celtic	Dundee Utd.	Dunfermline	Falkirk	Hearts	Hibernian	Inverness CT	Kilmarnock	Livingston	Motherwell	Rangers
Aberdeen	–	1-3	2-0	0-0	3-0	1-1	0-1	0-0	1-2	0-0	2-2	3-2
	–	2-2	–	–	1-0	–	1-0	–	2-2	3-0	2-2	2-0
	–	–	–	–	–	–	4-0	–	0-0	–	–	–
Celtic	2-0	–	2-0	0-1	3-1	1-1	3-2	2-1	4-2	2-1	5-0	3-0
	3-0	–	3-3	–	2-1	1-0	1-1	2-1	2-0	–	–	0-0
Dundee Utd.	1-1	2-4	–	2-1	2-1	0-3	1-0	1-1	0-0	2-0	1-1	0-0
	1-1	–	–	0-1	0-2	1-1	–	2-4	2-2	3-1	–	1-4
Dunfermline	0-2	0-4	2-1	–	0-1	1-4	1-2	0-1	0-1	0-1	0-3	3-3
	1-0	1-8	1-1	–	1-1	–	–	2-2	–	3-2	1-1	–
	–	–	–	–	–	–	–	0-1	–	–	–	–
Falkirk	1-2	0-3	1-3	1-2	–	2-2	0-2	0-2	1-2	1-1	0-1	1-1
	–	–	1-0	0-0	–	1-2	0-0	1-4	–	1-0	1-1	1-2
Hearts	2-0	2-3	3-0	2-0	5-0	–	4-0	0-0	1-0	2-1	2-1	1-0
	1-2	3-0	–	4-0	–	–	4-1	–	2-0	–	3-0	1-1
	1-0	–	–	–	–	–	–	–	–	–	–	–
Hibernian	1-2	0-1	2-1	1-1	2-3	2-0	–	1-2	4-2	3-0	2-1	2-1
	–	1-2	3-1	3-1	–	2-1	–	0-2	2-1	7-0	–	1-2
Inverness CT	1-1	1-1	1-1	2-1	0-3	0-1	2-0	–	2-2	3-0	1-2	0-1
	0-1	–	1-0	–	2-0	0-0	–	–	3-3	–	0-1	2-3
Kilmarnock	4-2	0-1	2-1	3-2	1-1	2-4	3-1	2-2	–	3-0	4-1	2-3
	–	1-4	–	1-0	2-1	1-0	2-2	–	–	3-1	2-0	1-3
Livingston	0-0	0-5	1-0	1-1	0-2	1-4	1-2	1-1	0-3	–	1-2	2-2
	–	0-2	3-1	0-1	0-1	2-3	–	2-1	–	–	0-1	–
	–	–	–	–	–	–	–	0-1	–	–	–	–
Motherwell	3-1	4-4	4-5	1-0	5-0	1-1	1-3	0-2	2-2	1-0	–	0-1
	–	1-3	2-0	2-3	3-1	–	2-2	0-1	–	2-1	–	–
	–	–	1-1	–	–	–	–	–	–	–	–	–
Rangers	0-0	3-1	3-0	5-1	2-2	1-0	0-3	1-1	3-0	3-0	2-0	–
	1-1	0-1	–	1-0	–	2-0	2-0	–	4-0	4-1	1-0	–

Read across for home results, down for away

BELL'S FIRST DIVISION

	Airdrie Utd.	Brechin City	Clyde	Dundee	Hamilton Acad.	Queen of South	Ross Co.	St Johnstone	St Mirren	Stranraer
Airdrie Utd.	–	6-0	1-3	4-0	2-2	4-0	0-1	3-1	0-1	1-0
	–	3-3	1-1	7-0	0-0	1-1	2-3	2-1	1-4	3-0
Brechin City	1-1	–	1-1	1-3	1-2	1-1	1-4	1-4	2-3	2-3
	0-0	–	3-1	0-3	0-1	1-1	3-3	0-2	0-3	0-0
Clyde	1-0	2-1	–	1-1	1-1	1-0	1-0	0-1	1-2	1-0
	3-1	5-1	–	3-3	2-2	3-0	2-0	2-3	0-1	1-1
Dundee	0-2	1-0	3-3	–	1-1	3-1	0-0	2-1	3-2	1-1
	2-3	0-1	0-1	–	2-4	2-3	0-0	0-1	4-0	2-1
Hamilton Acad.	1-1	3-0	1-1	1-1	–	5-2	2-1	0-1	3-1	2-0
	1-0	2-0	2-0	0-0	–	0-2	0-0	1-2	0-0	1-0
Queen of South	1-0	0-0	1-2	0-0	1-2	–	2-3	1-3	0-1	1-1
	2-0	0-0	2-1	1-3	1-1	–	0-0	3-2	0-0	1-0
Ross Co.	2-2	1-0	3-1	3-0	0-0	1-1	–	2-1	0-4	2-1
	0-1	2-0	0-1	0-0	2-1	3-1	–	2-2	0-2	2-1
St Johnstone	1-0	3-1	0-0	1-1	5-1	4-0	1-1	–	1-2	1-1
	2-2	3-0	1-0	0-0	1-1	2-1	1-1	–	0-0	3-2
St Mirren	2-1	1-0	2-0	0-0	2-1	2-0	2-0	0-0	–	0-0
	1-1	3-2	2-1	2-1	0-2	1-0	0-1	0-1	–	3-1
Stranraer	1-0	1-1	1-2	0-0	1-2	0-0	2-3	1-1	1-2	–
	1-1	2-0	0-5	1-1	5-4	1-0	2-2	0-2	0-1	–

Read across for home results, down for away

BELL'S SECOND DIVISION

	Alloa Athletic	Ayr Utd.	Dumbarton	Forfar Athletic	Gretna	Morton	Partick Thistle	Peterhead	Raith Rov.	Stirling Albion
Alloa Athletic	–	0–4	1–4	1–1	0–3	0–3	1–6	4–1	1–2	2–4
	–	1–1	1–0	0–1	0–3	0–0	2–1	0–2	1–1	0–0
Ayr Utd.	1–1	–	2–0	2–1	1–3	0–1	2–2	1–1	2–1	2–5
	0–1	–	2–0	0–1	2–4	1–1	1–2	1–2	0–0	3–0
Dumbarton	1–1	6–0	–	2–0	0–1	1–1	1–2	1–0	1–2	2–0
	0–1	4–5	–	0–0	0–2	0–2	2–3	2–3	0–1	3–2
Forfar Athletic	3–1	1–2	2–0	–	1–3	0–1	2–3	3–2	5–2	3–0
	3–0	1–0	2–3	–	2–1	0–2	0–0	0–1	0–2	1–2
Gretna	4–0	2–2	1–0	5–1	–	3–1	2–2	3–0	5–1	1–0
	2–1	3–0	3–0	1–2	–	1–2	6–1	3–1	2–1	6–0
Morton	5–2	2–1	4–0	1–0	0–2	–	2–1	2–1	2–0	1–2
	4–1	0–4	4–0	3–0	2–2	–	1–0	0–0	2–0	1–0
Partick Thistle	4–2	1–0	3–2	1–0	3–3	2–0	–	1–3	1–3	0–0
	2–3	2–2	2–1	1–0	0–2	1–1	–	0–1	1–0	0–3
Peterhead	3–1	3–3	1–0	4–2	0–2	1–0	1–1	–	0–1	1–3
	3–2	1–2	3–1	1–1	1–3	2–1	2–1	–	0–0	2–0
Raith Rov.	4–2	3–3	3–2	0–2	1–3	1–2	1–1	0–2	–	5–2
	0–1	1–1	0–0	1–0	0–1	1–1	1–2	1–0	–	2–3
Stirling Albion	1–2	3–3	0–0	4–2	0–5	0–2	1–2	1–3	1–0	–
	0–0	1–0	3–1	3–1	2–1	3–1	1–2	2–1	2–2	–

Read across for home results, down for away

BELL'S THIRD DIVISION

	Albion Rov.	Arbroath	Berwick Rangers	Cowdenbeath	East Fife	East Stirling	Elgin City	Montrose	Queens Park	Stenhousemuir
Albion Rov.	–	2-2	0-2	0-3	2-4	4-2	0-2	1-1	1-1	0-2
	–	0-2	0-1	1-3	3-1	2-0	1-2	1-1	1-0	1-2
Arbroath	1-2	–	4-0	0-3	1-0	7-2	2-0	2-1	1-1	1-1
	1-0	–	0-2	4-1	2-1	2-1	0-1	3-0	1-0	3-2
Berwick Rangers	0-1	3-0	–	1-0	3-0	3-2	3-1	1-1	1-2	0-2
	2-1	2-1	–	1-0	1-1	1-0	1-1	1-1	1-0	3-0
Cowdenbeath	2-1	3-2	0-1	–	3-1	5-1	5-2	2-0	0-2	4-1
	2-1	4-2	1-1	–	4-1	5-0	2-1	2-0	6-0	1-1
East Fife	1-1	1-1	0-4	1-0	–	3-1	1-2	3-2	1-0	2-3
	1-0	0-3	1-1	2-1	–	1-2	0-2	4-0	0-1	2-1
East Stirling	3-1	3-1	1-2	0-1	1-2	–	0-2	1-1	0-4	0-0
	1-0	0-4	0-1	1-1	2-1	–	0-2	1-0	0-0	0-7
Elgin City	2-2	2-0	2-2	0-3	1-2	1-1	–	0-0	2-2	1-2
	2-1	4-1	1-3	0-4	5-3	3-0	–	1-1	1-2	0-2
Montrose	0-2	1-0	0-0	0-1	3-1	3-0	2-0	–	0-1	0-3
	2-2	0-1	1-2	0-3	0-2	2-0	1-3	–	0-0	0-2
Queens Park	3-1	2-2	1-3	0-2	2-0	3-0	3-0	0-3	–	1-2
	1-1	0-0	0-1	2-2	1-1	3-1	3-3	2-2	–	2-0
Stenhousemuir	1-0	2-0	0-1	2-0	2-1	6-1	3-1	6-2	1-0	–
	1-0	0-0	1-0	1-2	4-2	5-0	1-2	5-1	1-2	–

Read across for home results, down for away

SCOTTISH FINAL TABLES 2005-06

BANK OF SCOTLAND PREMIER LEAGUE

		P	HOME W	D	L	F	A	AWAY W	D	L	F	A	Pts	GD
1	Celtic	38	14	4	1	41	15	14	3	2	52	22	91	56
2	Hearts	38	15	2	2	43	9	7	6	6	28	22	74	40
3	Rangers	38	13	4	2	38	11	8	6	5	29	26	73	30
4	Hibernian	38	11	1	7	39	24	6	4	9	22	32	56	5
5	Kilmarnock	38	11	3	5	39	29	4	4	8	24	35	55	−1
6	Aberdeen	38	8	9	3	30	17	5	6	7	16	23	54	6
7	Inverness CT	38	5	6	7	21	21	10	7	3	30	17	58	13
8	Motherwell	38	7	5	7	35	31	6	8	5	20	30	49	−6
9	Dundee Utd.	38	5	8	6	22	28	2	4	13	19	38	33	−25
10	Falkirk	38	2	6	11	14	30	6	3	10	21	34	33	−29
11	Dunfermline	38	3	5	11	17	39	5	4	10	16	29	33	−35
12	Livingston	38	3	4	12	15	33	1	2	16	10	46	18	−54

(After 33 matches, League split into top six and bottom six teams, each playing five further games.)

Leading scorers (all competitions): 37 Boyd (Rangers) – 17 for Kilmarnock; 20 Dargo (Inverness CT), Hartson (Celtic), Riordan (Hibernian), Zurawski (Celtic); 18 Lovenkrands (Rangers); 17 Hartley (Hearts), Skacel (Hearts); 16 Maloney (Celtic); 15 Burchill (Dunfermline); 14 O'Connor (Hibernian); 13 Naismith (Kilmarnock); 12 Foran (Motherwell), Jankauskas (Hearts), McDonald, Scott (Motherwell); Prso (Rangers).
Manager of Year: Gordon Strachan (Celtic).

BELL'S FIRST DIVISION

		P	HOME W	D	L	F	A	AWAY W	D	L	F	A	Pts	GD
1	St Mirren	36	11	4	3	23	12	12	3	3	29	16	76	24
2	St Johnstone	36	8	9	1	30	14	10	3	5	29	20	66	25
3	Hamilton	36	9	6	3	25	12	6	8	4	28	27	59	14
4	Ross Co.	36	8	6	4	24	19	6	8	4	23	21	56	7
5	Clyde	36	9	5	4	30	18	6	5	7	24	25	55	12
6	Airdrie Utd.	36	8	5	5	41	21	3	7	8	16	22	45	14
7	Dundee	36	6	5	7	26	25	3	11	4	17	25	43	−7
8	Queen of South	36	5	7	6	17	19	2	5	11	14	35	33	−23
9	Stranraer†	36	4	7	7	20	27	1	7	10	13	26	29	−20
10	Brechin	36	1	7	10	18	36	1	4	13	10	38	17	−46

† Also relegated

Play-offs (on agg) – Semi-finals: Partick Thistle 4, Stranraer 3; Peterhead 1, Morton 0.
Final: Partick Thistle 3, Peterhead 3 (aet, Partick Thistle won 4-2 on pens).

Leading scorers (all competitions): 18 Lynch (Dundee); 17 Sutton (St Mirren); 16 Scotland (St Johnstone); 15 Prunty (Airdrie Utd.); 14 Williams (Clyde); 13 Hamilton (Stranraer), Milne (St Johnstone), Rankin (Ross Co.); 12 Kean (St Mirren), O'Donnell (Clyde); 11 McLaren (Airdrie Utd.), Higgins (Ross Co.).
Manager of Year: Gus MacPherson (St Mirren).
Player of Year (overall award): John Rankin (Ross Co.).

BELL'S SECOND DIVISION

			HOME				AWAY						
		P	W	D	L	F	A	W	D	L	F	A	Pts	GD
1	Gretna	36	14	2	2	53	15	14	2	2	44	15	88	67
2	Morton	36	13	2	3	36	16	8	5	5	22	17	70	25
3	Peterhead	36	9	4	5	29	22	8	2	8	24	25	57	5
4	Partick Thistle†	36	8	4	6	25	27	8	5	5	32	29	57	1
5	Stirling Alb.	36	8	4	6	28	28	7	2	9	26	35	51	−9
6	Ayr Utd.	36	5	5	8	23	26	5	7	6	33	35	42	−5
7	Raith Rov.	36	5	5	8	25	28	6	4	8	19	26	42	−10
8	Forfar Athletic	36	8	1	9	29	25	4	3	11	15	30	40	−11
9	Alloa Athletic	36	3	5	10	15	37	5	3	10	21	40	32	−41
10	Dumbarton	36	5	3	10	26	26	2	2	14	14	37	26	−23

† Also promoted.

Play-offs (on agg) – Semi-finals: Alloa Athletic 2, Arbroath 1; Berwick Rangers 1, Stenhousemuir 0. **Final:** Alloa Athletic 5, Berwick Rangers 2.

Leading scorers (all competitions): 25 Deuchar (Gretna), Grady (Gretna); 22 Roberts (Partick Thistle); 19 McManus (Raith Rov); 18 Lilley (Morton); 16 McGuffie (Gretna), Rodgers (Dumbarton); 15 Connolly (Stirling Alb.), 14 Linn (Peterhead), Vareille (Ayr Utd.), Wardlaw (Ayr Utd.).

Manager of Year: Rowan Alexander (Gretna).

BELL'S THIRD DIVISION

			HOME				AWAY						
		P	W	D	L	F	A	W	D	L	F	A	Pts	GD
1	Cowdenbeath	36	14	2	2	51	18	10	2	6	30	16	76	47
2	Berwick Rangers	36	11	4	3	28	14	12	3	3	26	13	76	27
3	Stenhousemuir	36	13	1	4	45	17	10	3	5	33	21	73	40
4	Arbroath	36	12	2	4	35	18	4	5	9	22	29	55	10
5	Elgin City	36	6	5	7	28	30	9	2	7	27	28	52	−3
6	Queens Park	36	6	7	5	29	24	7	5	6	18	18	51	5
7	East Fife	36	9	2	7	24	24	4	2	12	24	40	43	−16
8	Albion Rov.	36	4	4	10	20	31	3	4	11	19	29	29	−21
9	Montrose	36	5	3	10	15	23	1	7	10	16	36	28	−28
10	East Stirling	36	5	4	9	14	30	1	1	16	14	59	23	−61

Leading scorers: 20 Johnston (Elgin City); 19 Cramb (Stenhousemuir); 17 Buchanan (Cowdenbeath), McGrillen (Stenhousemuir); 13 Haynes (Berwick Rangers), Hutchison (Berwick Rangers); 10 Brazil (Arbroath), Booth (Elgin City), Henslee (Montrose), McLeish (Berwick Rangers), Mercer (Stenhousemuir).

Manager of Year: Mixu Paatelainen (Cowdenbeath).

SCOTTISH HONOURS LIST

PREMIER DIVISION

	First	Pts.	Second	Pts.	Third	Pts.
1975-6	Rangers	54	Celtic	48	Hibernian	43
1976-7	Celtic	55	Rangers	46	Aberdeen	43
1977-8	Rangers	55	Aberdeen	53	Dundee Utd.	40
1978-9	Celtic	48	Aberdeen	45	Dundee Utd.	44
1979-80	Aberdeen	48	Celtic	47	St Mirren	42
1980-81	Celtic	56	Aberdeen	49	Rangers	44
1981-2	Celtic	55	Aberdeen	53	Rangers	43
1982-3	Dundee Utd.	56	Celtic	55	Aberdeen	55
1983-4	Aberdeen	57	Celtic	50	Dundee Utd.	47
1984-5	Aberdeen	59	Celtic	52	Dundee Utd.	47
1985-6	*Celtic	50	Hearts	50	Dundee Utd.	47
1986-7	Rangers	69	Celtic	63	Dundee Utd.	60
1987-8	Celtic	72	Hearts	62	Rangers	60
1988-9	Rangers	56	Aberdeen	50	Celtic	46
1989-90	Rangers	51	Aberdeen	44	Hearts	44
1990-1	Rangers	55	Aberdeen	53	Celtic	41
1991-2	Rangers	72	Hearts	63	Celtic	62
1992-3	Rangers	73	Aberdeen	64	Celtic	60
1993-4	Rangers	58	Aberdeen	55	Motherwell	54
1994-5	Rangers	69	Motherwell	54	Hibernian	53
1995-6	Rangers	87	Celtic	83	Aberdeen	55
1996-7	Rangers	80	Celtic	75	Dundee Utd.	60
1997-8	Celtic	74	Rangers	72	Hearts	67

PREMIER LEAGUE

	First	Pts.	Second	Pts.	Third	Pts.
1998-99	Rangers	77	Celtic	71	St Johnstone	57
1999-2000	Rangers	90	Celtic	69	Hearts	54
2000-01	Celtic	97	Rangers	82	Hibernian	66
2001-02	Celtic	103	Rangers	85	Livingston	58
2002-03	*Rangers	97	Celtic	97	Hearts	63
2003-04	Celtic	98	Rangers	81	Hearts	68
2004-05	Rangers	93	Celtic	92	Hibernian	61
2005-06	Celtic	91	Hearts	74	Rangers	73

Maximum points: 72 except 1986-8, 1991-4 (88), 1994-2000 (108), 2001-06 (114).
* Won on goal difference.

FIRST DIVISION (Scottish Championship until 1975-76)

	First	Pts.	Second	Pts.	Third	Pts.
1890-1a	††Dumbarton	29	Rangers	29	Celtic	24
1891-2b	Dumbarton	37	Celtic	35	Hearts	30
1892-3a	Celtic	29	Rangers	28	St Mirren	23
1893-4a	Celtic	29	Hearts	26	St Bernard's	22
1894-5a	Hearts	31	Celtic	26	Rangers	21
1895-6a	Celtic	30	Rangers	26	Hibernian	24
1896-7a	Hearts	28	Hibernian	26	Rangers	25
1897-8a	Celtic	33	Rangers	29	Hibernian	22
1898-9a	Rangers	36	Hearts	26	Celtic	24
1899-1900a	Rangers	32	Celtic	25	Hibernian	24
1900-1c	Rangers	35	Celtic	29	Hibernian	25

Season	First	Pts	Second	Pts	Third	Pts
1901-2a	Rangers	28	Celtic	26	Hearts	22
1902-3b	Hibernian	37	Dundee	31	Rangers	29
1903-4d	Third Lanark	43	Hearts	39	Rangers	38
1904-5a	†Celtic	41	Rangers	41	Third Lanark	35
1905-6a	Celtic	46	Hearts	39	Rangers	38
1906-7f	Celtic	55	Dundee	48	Rangers	45
1907-8f	Celtic	55	Falkirk	51	Rangers	50
1908-9f	Celtic	51	Dundee	50	Clyde	48
1909-10f	Celtic	54	Falkirk	52	Rangers	49
1910-11f	Rangers	52	Aberdeen	48	Falkirk	44
1911-12f	Rangers	51	Celtic	45	Clyde	42
1912-13f	Rangers	53	Celtic	49	Hearts	41
1913-14g	Celtic	65	Rangers	59	Hearts	54
1914-15g	Celtic	65	Hearts	61	Rangers	50
1915-16g	Celtic	67	Rangers	56	Morton	51
1916-17g	Celtic	64	Morton	54	Rangers	53
1917-18f	Rangers	56	Celtic	55	Kilmarnock	43
1918-19f	Celtic	58	Rangers	57	Morton	47
1919-20h	Rangers	71	Celtic	68	Motherwell	57
1920-1h	Rangers	76	Celtic	66	Hearts	56
1921-2h	Celtic	67	Rangers	66	Raith	56
1922-3g	Rangers	55	Airdrieonians	50	Celtic	40
1923-4g	Rangers	59	Airdrieonians	50	Celtic	41
1924-5g	Rangers	60	Airdrieonians	57	Hibernian	52
1925-6g	Celtic	58	Airdrieonians	50	Hearts	50
1926-7g	Rangers	56	Motherwell	51	Celtic	49
1927-8g	Rangers	60	Celtic	55	Motherwell	55
1928-9g	Rangers	67	Celtic	51	Motherwell	50
1929-30g	Rangers	60	Motherwell	55	Aberdeen	53
1930-1g	Rangers	60	Celtic	58	Motherwell	56
1931-2g	Motherwell	66	Rangers	61	Celtic	48
1932-3g	Rangers	62	Motherwell	59	Hearts	50
1933-4g	Rangers	66	Motherwell	62	Celtic	47
1934-5g	Rangers	55	Celtic	52	Hearts	50
1935-6g	Celtic	68	Rangers	61	Aberdeen	61
1936-7g	Rangers	61	Aberdeen	54	Celtic	52
1937-8g	Celtic	61	Hearts	58	Rangers	49
1938-9f	Rangers	59	Celtic	48	Aberdeen	46
1946-7f	Rangers	46	Hibernian	44	Aberdeen	39
1947-8g	Hibernian	48	Rangers	46	Partick	46
1948-9i	Rangers	46	Dundee	45	Hibernian	39
1949-50i	Rangers	50	Hibernian	49	Hearts	43
1950-1i	Hibernian	48	Rangers	38	Dundee	38
1951-2i	Hibernian	45	Rangers	41	East Fife	37
1952-3i	*Rangers	43	Hibernian	43	East Fife	39
1953-4i	Celtic	43	Hearts	38	Partick	35
1954-5f	Aberdeen	49	Celtic	46	Rangers	41
1955-6f	Rangers	52	Aberdeen	46	Hearts	45
1956-7f	Rangers	55	Hearts	53	Kilmarnock	42
1957-8f	Hearts	62	Rangers	49	Celtic	46
1958-9f	Rangers	50	Hearts	48	Motherwell	44
1959-60f	Hearts	54	Kilmarnock	50	Rangers	42
1960-1f	Rangers	51	Kilmarnock	50	Third Lanark	42
1961-2f	Dundee	54	Rangers	51	Celtic	46
1962-3f	Rangers	57	Kilmarnock	48	Partick	46
1963-4f	Rangers	55	Kilmarnock	49	Celtic	47
1964-5f	*Kilmarnock	50	Hearts	50	Dunfermline	49
1965-6f	Celtic	57	Rangers	55	Kilmarnock	45

1966-7f	Celtic	58	Rangers	55	Clyde	46
1967-8f	Celtic	63	Rangers	61	Hibernian	45
1968-9f	Celtic	54	Rangers	49	Dunfermline	45
1969-70f	Celtic	57	Rangers	45	Hibernian	44
1970-1f	Celtic	56	Aberdeen	54	St Johnstone	44
1971-2f	Celtic	60	Aberdeen	50	Rangers	44
1972-3f	Celtic	57	Rangers	56	Hibernian	45
1973-4f	Celtic	53	Hibernian	49	Rangers	48
1974-5f	Rangers	56	Hibernian	49	Celtic	45

* Won on goal average. †Won on deciding match. ††Title shared.
Competition suspended 1940-46 (Second World War).

SCOTTISH CHAMPIONSHIP WINS

Rangers	*51	Hibernian	4	Kilmarnock	1
Celtic	40	Dumbarton	*2	Motherwell	1
Aberdeen	4	Dundee	1	Third Lanark	1
Hearts	4	Dundee Utd.	1	(* Incl. 1 shared)

FIRST DIVISION

(Since formation of Premier Division)

	First	Pts.	Second	Pts.	Third	Pts.
1975-6d	Partick	41	Kilmarnock	35	Montrose	30
1976-7j	St Mirren	62	Clydebank	58	Dundee	51
1977-8j	*Morton	58	Hearts	58	Dundee	57
1978-9j	Dundee	55	Kilmarnock	54	Clydebank	54
1979-80j	Hearts	53	Airdrieonians	51	Ayr	44
1980-1j	Hibernian	57	Dundee	52	St Johnstone	51
1981-2j	Motherwell	61	Kilmarnock	51	Hearts	50
1982-3j	St Johnstone	55	Hearts	54	Clydebank	50
1983-4j	Morton	54	Dumbarton	51	Partick	46
1984-5j	Motherwell	50	Clydebank	48	Falkirk	45
1985-6j	Hamilton	56	Falkirk	45	Kilmarnock	44
1986-7k	Morton	57	Dunfermline	56	Dumbarton	53
1987-8k	Hamilton	56	Meadowbank	52	Clydebank	49
1988-9j	Dunfermline	54	Falkirk	52	Clydebank	48
1989-90j	St Johnstone	58	Airdrieonians	54	Clydebank	44
1990-1j	Falkirk	54	Airdrieonians	53	Dundee	52
1991-2k	Dundee	58	Partick	57	Hamilton	57
1992-3k	Raith	65	Kilmarnock	54	Dunfermline	52
1993-4k	Falkirk	66	Dunfermline	65	Airdrieonians	54
1994-5l	Raith	69	Dunfermline	68	Dundee	68
1995-6l	Dunfermline	71	Dundee Utd.	67	Greenock Morton	67
1996-7l	St Johnstone	80	Airdrieonians	60	Dundee	58
1997-8l	Dundee	70	Falkirk	65	Raith	60
1998-9l	Hibernian	89	Falkirk	66	Ayr	62
1999-2000l	St Mirren	76	Dunfermline	71	Falkirk	68
2000-01l	Livingston	76	Ayr Utd.	69	Falkirk	56
2001-02l	Partick Thistle	66	Airdrie	56	Ayr Utd.	52
2002-03l	Falkirk	81	Clyde	72	St Johnstone	67
2003-04l	Inverness CT	70	Clyde	69	St Johnstone	57
2004-05l	Falkirk	75	St Mirren	60	Clyde	60
2005-06l	St Mirren	76	St Johnstone	66	Hamilton Acad.	59

Maximum points: a, 36; b, 44; c, 40; d, 52; e, 60; f, 68; g, 76; h, 84; i, 60; j, 78;
k, 88; l, 108. * Won on goal difference.

SECOND DIVISION

	First	Pts.	Second	Pts.	Third	Pts.
1921-2a	Alloa	60	Cowdenbeath	47	Armadale	45
1922-3a	Queen's Park	57	Clydebank	52	St Johnstone	50
1923-4a	St Johnstone	56	Cowdenbeath	55	Bathgate	44
1924-5a	Dundee Utd.	50	Clydebank	48	Clyde	47
1925-6a	Dunfermline	59	Clyde	53	Ayr	52
1926-7a	Bo'ness	56	Raith	49	Clydebank	45
1927-8a	Ayr	54	Third Lanark	45	King's Park	44
1928-9b	Dundee Utd.	51	Morton	50	Arbroath	47
1929-30a	*Leith Athletic	57	East Fife	57	Albion	54
1930-1a	Third Lanark	61	Dundee Utd.	50	Dunfermline	47
1931-2a	*East Stirling	55	St Johnstone	55	Stenhousemuir	46
1932-3c	Hibernian	55	Queen of South	49	Dunfermline	47
1933-4c	Albion	45	Dunfermline	44	Arbroath	44
1934-5c	Third Lanark	52	Arbroath	50	St Bernard's	47
1935-6c	Falkirk	59	St Mirren	52	Morton	48
1936-7c	Ayr	54	Morton	51	St Bernard's	48
1937-8c	Raith	59	Albion	48	Airdrieonians	47
1938-9c	Cowdenbeath	60	Alloa	48	East Fife	48
1946-7d	Dundee Utd.	45	Airdrieonians	42	East Fife	31
1947-8e	East Fife	53	Albion	42	Hamilton	40
1948-9e	*Raith	42	Stirling	42	Airdrieonians	41
1949-50e	Morton	47	Airdrieonians	44	St Johnstone	36
1950-1e	*Queen of South	45	Stirling	45	Ayr	36
1951-2e	Clyde	44	Falkirk	43	Ayr	39
1952-3e	Stirling	44	Hamilton	43	Queen's Park	37
1953-4e	Motherwell	45	Kilmarnock	42	Third Lanark	36
1954-5e	Airdrieonians	46	Dunfermline	42	Hamilton	39
1955-6b	Queen's Park	54	Ayr	51	St Johnstone	49
1956-7b	Clyde	64	Third Lanark	51	Cowdenbeath	45
1957-8b	Stirling	55	Dunfermline	53	Arbroath	47
1958-9b	Ayr	60	Arbroath	51	Stenhousemuir	46
1959-60b	St Johnstone	53	Dundee Utd.	50	Queen of South	49
1960-1b	Stirling	55	Falkirk	54	Stenhousemuir	50
1961-2b	Clyde	54	Queen of South	53	Morton	44
1962-3b	St Johnstone	55	East Stirling	49	Morton	48
1963-4b	Morton	67	Clyde	53	Arbroath	46
1964-5b	Stirling	59	Hamilton	50	Queen of South	45
1965-6b	Ayr	53	Airdrieonians	50	Queen of South	47
1966-7b	Morton	69	Raith	58	Arbroath	57
1967-8b	St Mirren	62	Arbroath	53	East Fife	49
1968-9b	Motherwell	64	Ayr	53	East Fife	48
1969-70b	Falkirk	56	Cowdenbeath	55	Queen of South	50
1970-1b	Partick	56	East Fife	51	Arbroath	46
1971-2b	*Dumbarton	52	Arbroath	52	Stirling	50
1972-3b	Clyde	56	Dunfermline	52	Raith	47
1973-4b	Airdrieonians	60	Kilmarnock	58	Hamilton	55
1974-5b	Falkirk	54	Queen of South	53	Montrose	53

SECOND DIVISION (MODERN)

	First	Pts.	Second	Pts.	Third	Pts.
1975-6d	*Clydebank	40	Raith	40	Alloa	35
1976-7f	Stirling	55	Alloa	51	Dunfermline	50
1977-8f	*Clyde	53	Raith	53	Dunfermline	50
1978-9f	Berwick Rangers	54	Dunfermline	52	Falkirk	50
1979-80f	Falkirk	50	East Stirling	49	Forfar	46

1980-1f	Queen's Park	50	Queen of South	46	Cowdenbeath	45
1981-2f	Clyde	59	Alloa	50	Arbroath	50
1982-3f	Brechin	55	Meadowbank	54	Arbroath	49
1983-4f	Forfar	63	East Fife	47	Berwick Rangers	43
1984-5f	Montrose	53	Alloa	50	Dunfermline	49
1985-6f	Dunfermline	57	Queen of South	55	Meadowbank	49
1986-7f	Meadowbank	55	Raith	52	Stirling	52
1987-8f	Ayr	61	St Johnstone	59	Queen's Park	51
1988-9f	Albion	50	Alloa	45	Brechin	43
1989-90f	Brechin	49	Kilmarnock	48	Stirling	47
1990-1f	Stirling	54	Montrose	46	Cowdenbeath	45
1991-2f	Dumbarton	52	Cowdenbeath	51	Alloa	50
1992-3f	Clyde	54	Brechin	53	Stranraer	53
1993-4f	Stranraer	56	Berwick Rangers	48	Stenhousemuir	47
1994-5g	Greenock Morton	64	Dumbarton	60	Stirling	58
1995-6g	Stirling	81	East Fife	67	Berwick Rangers	60
1996-7g	Ayr	77	Hamilton	74	Livingston	64
1997-8g	Stranraer	61	Clydebank	60	Livingston	59
1998-9g	Livingston	77	Inverness Cal.	72	Clyde	53
1999-2000g	Clyde	65	Alloa	64	Ross County	62
2000-01g	Partick Thistle	75	Arbroath	66	Berwick Rangers	54
2001-02g	Queen of South	67	Alloa Athletic	59	Forfar Athletic	53
2002-03g	Raith Rov.	59	Brechin City	55	Airdrie Utd.	54
2003-04g	Airdrie Utd.	70	Hamilton	62	Dumbarton	60
2004-05g	Brechin City	72	Stranraer	62	Morton	62
2005-06g	Gretna	88	Morton	70	Peterhead	57

Maximum points: a, 76; b, 72; c, 68; d, 52; e, 60; f, 78; g, 108. * Won on goal average.

THIRD DIVISION (MODERN)

	First	Pts.	Second	Pts.	Third	Pts.
1994-5	Forfar	80	Montrose	67	Ross County	60
1995-6	Livingston	72	Brechin	63	Caledonian Th.	57
1996-7	Inverness Cal.T.	76	Forfar	67	Ross County	77
1997-8	Alloa	76	Arbroath	68	Ross County	67
1998-9	Ross County	77	Stenhousemuir	64	Brechin	59
1999-2000	Queen's Park	69	Berwick Rangers	66	Forfar	61
2000-01	*Hamilton	76	Cowdenbeath	76	Brechin	72
2001-02	Brechin City	73	Dumbarton	61	Albion Rov.	59
2002-03	Morton	72	East Fife	71	Albion Rov.	70
2003-04	Stranraer	79	Stirling	77	Gretna	68
2004-05	Gretna	98	Peterhead	78	Cowdenbeath	51
2005-06	*Cowdenbeath	76	Berwick Rangers	76	Stenhousemuir	73

Maximum points: 108. * Won on goal difference.

RELEGATED FROM PREMIER DIVISION

1975-6	Dundee, St Johnstone	1983-4	St Johnstone, Motherwell
1976-7	Kilmarnock, Hearts	1984-5	Dumbarton, Morton
1977-8	Ayr, Clydebank	1985-6	No relegation
1978-9	Hearts, Motherwell	1986-7	Clydebank, Hamilton
1979-80	Dundee, Hibernian	1987-8	Falkirk, Dunfermline, Morton
1980-1	Kilmarnock, Hearts	1988-9	Hamilton
1981-2	Partick, Airdrieonians	1989-90	Dundee
1982-3	Morton, Kilmarnock	1990-1	No relegation

1991-2	St Mirren, Dunfermline	1999-2000	No relegation
1992-3	Falkirk, Airdrieonians	2000-01	St Mirren
1993-4	St J'stone, Raith, Dundee	2001-02	St Johnstone
1994-5	Dundee Utd.	2002-03	No relegation
1995-6	Falkirk, Partick Thistle	2003-04	Partick Thistle
1996-7	Raith	2004-05	Dundee
1997-8	Hibernian	2005-06	Livingston
1998-9	Dunfermline		

RELEGATED FROM FIRST DIVISION

1975-6	Dunfermline, Clyde	1991-2	Montrose, Forfar
1976-7	Raith, Falkirk	1992-3	Meadowbank, Cowdenbeath
1977-8	Alloa, East Fife	1993-4	Dumbarton, Stirling Alb.,
1978-9	Montrose, Queen of South		Clyde, Morton, Brechin
1979-80	Arbroath, Clyde	1994-5	Ayr, Stranraer
1980-1	Stirling, Berwick Rangers	1995-6	Hamilton, Dumbarton
1981-2	East Stirling, Queen of South	1996-7	Clydebank, East Fife
1982-3	Dunfermline, Queen's Park	1997-8	Partick, Stirling Alb.
1983-4	Raith, Alloa	1998-9	Hamilton, Stranraer
1984-5	Meadowbank, St Johnstone	1999-2000	Clydebank
1985-6	Ayr, Alloa	2000-01	Morton, Alloa
1986-7	Brechin, Montrose	2001-02	Raith Rov.
1987-8	East Fife, Dumbarton	2002-03	Alloa Athletic, Arbroath
1988-9	Kilmarnock, Queen of South	2003-04	Ayr, Brechin
1989-90	Albion, Alloa	2004-05	Partick Thistle, Raith Rov.
1990-1	Clyde, Brechin	2005-06	Brechin, Stranraer

RELEGATED FROM SECOND DIVISION

1993-4	Alloa, Forfar, E. Stirling,	1998-9	East Fife, Forfar
	Montrose, Queen's Park,	1999-2000	Hamilton
	Arbroath, Albion,	2000-01	Queen's Park, Stirling Alb.
	Cowdenbeath	2001-02	Morton
1994-5	Meadowbank, Brechin	2002-03	Stranraer, Cowdenbeath
1995-6	Forfar, Montrose	2003-04	East Fife, Stenhousemuir
1996-7	Dumbarton, Berwick Rangers	2004-05	Arbroath, Berwick Rangers
1997-8	Stenhousemuir, Brechin	2005-06	Dumbarton

QUOTE-UNQUOTE

'I think the biggest pressure in our game is to have no pressure' – **Arsene Wenger**, Arsenal manager.

'I can't believe what I've just seen. If somebody had written this script you wouldn't believe it' – **Steve Gibson**, Middlesbrough chairman, after his team, for the second successive UEFA Cup tie, overturn a three-goal deficit against Steaua Bucharest to reach their first European final.

'Most managers get booted out of the back door . . . I was clapped out of the front door' – **Alan Curbishley** on his decision to leave Charlton after 15 years in charge.

'He's got great credentials, but my granny could probably have managed Brazil to World Cup success' – **Gary Lineker**, former England striker, before Luiz Felipe Scolari ruled himself out of the England manager's job.

'I think with my heart and it told me to stay' – **Thierry Henry** on his decision to stay with Arsenal.

'I assume I have some very happy chairmen' – **Richard Scudamore**, Premier League chief executive, announcing a new TV deal worth £1.7 billion, an increase of 66%.

BANK OF SCOTLAND PREMIER LEAGUE ROLL CALL

APPEARANCES AND SCORERS 2005-06

(Figures in brackets = appearances as substitute)

ABERDEEN

Ground: Pittodrie Stadium, Pittodrie Street, Aberdeen, AB24, 5QH. **Capacity:** 22,199. **Telephone:** 01224 650400. **Colours:** Red and white. **Nickname:** Dons.

Anderson, R 36	Esson, R 18	Maguire, C .... –(1)
Byrne, R .... 18(1)	Foster, R .... 8(17)	McNaughton, K 34
Clark, C .... 30(1)	Griffin, D .... 9(1)	Muirhead, S .... 10(8)
Considine, A .... 8(4)	Hart, M 4	Nicholson, B .... 32(1)
Craig, S .... –(3)	Langfield, J 20	Severin, S 28
Crawford, S .... 27(3)	Lovell, S .... 22(5)	Smith, J 35
Dempsey, G .... 17(7)	MacFarlane, N .... 2(4)	Snoyl, F .... 9(3)
Diamond, A .... 31(2)	Macauley, K .... 3(2)	Stewart, J .... 2(15)
Donald, D .... –(1)	Mackie, D .... 11(17)	Winter, J .... 4(3)

League goals (46): Lovell 8, Smith 8, Anderson 6, Crawford 5, Mackie 4, Severin 3, Stewart 3, Clark 2, Nicholson 2, Foster 1, Snoyl 1, Winter 1, Opponents 2. **Tennents Cup goals (3):** Crawford 2, Nicholson 1. **CIS Cup goals (5):** Lovell 2, Nicholson 1, Smith 1, Winter 1. **Average home League attendance:** 12,728.

CELTIC

Ground: Celtic Park, Glasgow, G40 3RE. **Capacity:** 60,832. **Telephone:** 0845 671 1888. **Colours:** Green and white. **Nickname:** Bhoys.

Agathe, D .... –(4)	Lennon, N 32	Sutton, C .... 7(1)
Balde, B 28	Maloney, S .... 27(9)	Telfer, P 36
Beattie, C .... 7(6)	Marshall, D 4	Thompson, A .... 11(5)
Boruc, A 34	McGeady, A .... 11(9)	Varga, S .... 9(1)
Camara, M 18	McGlinchey, M .... –(1)	Virgo, A .... 3(7)
Dublin, D .... 3(8)	McManus, S 36	Wallace, R .... 8(3)
Hartson, J .... 29(6)	Nakamura, S .... 30(3)	Wilson, M .... 14(1)
Keane, K 10	Pearson, S .... 2(16)	Zurawski, M .... 22(2)
Lawson, P .... 1(2)	Petrov, S .... 36(1)	

League goals (93): Hartson 18, Zurawski 16, Maloney 13, Petrov 10, McManus 7, Beattie 6, Nakamura 6, McGeady 4, Pearson 2, Sutton 2, Thompson 2, Balde 1, Dublin 1, Keane 1, Lennon 1, Telfer 1, Varga 1, Opponents 1. **Tennents Cup goals (1):** Zurawski 1. **CIS Cup goals (9):** Maloney 3, Zurawski 3, Dublin 1, Hartson 1, Opponents 1. **Champions League goals (4):** Beattie 1, Hartson 1, McManus 1, Thompson 1. **Average home League attendance:** 58,150.

DUNDEE UNITED

Ground: Tannadice Park, Tannadice Street, Dundee, DD3 7JW. **Capacity:** 14,223. **Telephone:** 01382 833166. **Colours:** Tangerine and white. **Nickname:** Terrors.

Abbot, S .... 2(1)	Brewster, C .... –(1)	Crawford, S 4
Archibald, A 33	Cameron, G .... 2(2)	Duff, S .... 24(5)
Brebner, G 26	Canero, P .... 9(2)	Easton, W .... –(1)

Fernandez, D .... 29(1) McCracken, D .... 34 Robertson, D .... 6(5)
Gardiner, R .... 4 McInnes, D .... 9(3) Robson, B .... 30(1)
Goodwillie, D .... –(10) McIntyre, J .... 18(7) Samson, C 8
Kenneth, G .... 12(4) Miller, L .... 22(12) Samuel, C .... 23(12)
Kerr, M .... 35 Mulgrew, C .... 13 Stillie, D 30
Mair, L .... 5(1) Ritchie, P .... 20(1) Wilson, M .... 20(1)

League goals (41): Miller 8, Samuel 7, Fernandez 5, Brebner 4, Canero 2, McCracken 2, McInnes 2, Mulgrew 2, Archibald 1, Goodwillie 1, Kenneth 1, Kerr 1, McIntyre 1, Robertson 1, Robson 1, Opponents 2.
Tennents Cup goals (2): Fernandez 2. **CIS Cup goals:** None.
Average home League attendance: 8,198.

DUNFERMLINE ATHLETIC

Ground: East End Park, Halbeath Road, Dunfermline, KY12 7RB. **Capacity:** 12,558. **Telephone:** 01383 724295. **Colours:** Black and white. **Nickname:** Pars.

Burchill, M .... 24(7) Labonte, A .... 19(3) Simmons, S .... 3(3)
Campbell, A .... 1(4) Makel, L .... 20 Skerla, A .... 1(1)
Campbell, I .... 14(3) Mason, G .... 29 Tarachulski, B ...... 12(15)
Daquin, F .... 2(7) McCunnie, J .... 18(4) Thomson, S .... 23(2)
Donnelly, S .... 8(5) McGregor, A .... 26 Tod, A .... 26(4)
Dunn, J .... –(1) Morrison, S .... 3 Wilson, C .... 6(8)
Gunnlaugsson, G ...... –(1) Muirhead, S .... 11(1) Wilson, S 31
Halliwell, B .... 12 Phinn, N .... 1(2) Young, Darren .... 20(1)
Horsted, L .... 6(5) Ross, G .... 21(2) Young, Derek .... 13(5)
Hunt, N .... 22(10) Shields, G .... 33 Zambernardi, Y ...... 13(2)

League goals (33): Burchill 12, Hunt 4, Tod 3, Makel 2, Mason 2, Ross 2, Young, Darren 2, Campbell, I 1, Daquin 1, Donnelly 1, Shields 1, Wilson 1, Young, Derek 1.
Tennents Cup goals (3): Hunt 1, Mason 1, Young, Derek 1. **CIS Cup goals (9):** Burchill 3, Young, Derek 3, Mason 1, McCunnie 1, Young, Darren 1.
Average home League attendance: 6,206.

FALKIRK

Ground: Falkirk Stadium, Westfield, Falkirk, FK2 9DX. **Capacity:** 6,200. **Telephone:** 01324 624121. **Colours:** Navy blue and white. **Nickname:** Bairns.

Barr, D .... –(1) Ireland, C .... 23 Moutinho, P .... 8(20)
Churchill, G .... –(1) Latapy, R .... 24(6) O'Donnell, S .... 21(6)
Craig, L .... 10(6) Lawrie, A .... 27(2) O'Neil, J .... 3(5)
Cregg, P .... 14(2) Lescinel, J-F .... 8 Rodrigues, T .... 31(1)
Dodds, K .... 8(1) Lima, V .... 18(7) Ross, J .... 16(1)
Duffy, D .... 19(2) Manuel Santos, V .... 3 Scally, N .... 13(5)
Ferguson, A .... 9 McBreen, D .... 21(11) Scobie, T .... 2(1)
Glennon, M .... 21 McPherson, C .... 12(6) Thomson, A .... –(4)
Gow, A .... 30(4) McStay, R .... 1(4) Thomson, S .... 30(2)
Howard, M .... 8 McSween, I .... –(1) Twaddle, M .... 5(1)
Hughes, J .... 1 Milne, K .... 32(1)

League goals (35): Duffy 9, Gow 6, McBreen 6, Latapy 2, Milne 2, Moutinho 2, Ross 2, Cregg 1, Ireland 1, O'Donnell 1, Thomson, S 1, Opponents 2.
Tennents Cup goals (5): Gow 3, McBreen 2. **CIS Cup goals (3):** O'Donnell 2, Gow 1.
Average home League attendance: 5, 516.

HEART OF MIDLOTHIAN

Ground: Tynecastle Stadium, Gorgie Road, Edinburgh, EH11 2NL. **Capacity:** 18,000. **Telephone:** 0131 200 7200. **Colours:** Maroon and white. **Nickname:** Jam Tarts.

Aguiar, B .... 10 Banks, S .... 2(1) Barasa, N .... 1(3)

Bednar, R .... 19(3)	Hackett, C .... 1(1)	Petras, M .... 4(1)
Berra, C .... 10(2)	Hartley, P 34	Pospisil, M .... 13(11)
Beslija, M .... 2(2)	Jankauskas, E ..... 24(1)	Pressley, S .... 29(10)
Brellier, J .... 28(2)	Johnson, L .... 1(3)	Simmons, S .... 1(10)
Camazzola, S .... 5(3)	MacFarlane, N .... 1(2)	Skacel, R .... 33(2)
Cesnauskis, D ..... 15(10)	Makela, J .... –(2)	Straceny, L .... 1(1)
Elliot, C .... 17(11)	McAllister, J .... 8(9)	Tall, I .... 3(1)
Fyssas, T 32	McCann, N 1	Thorarinsson, H .... –(1)
Goncalves, J .... 3(1)	Mikoliunas, S ...... 16(7)	Wallace, L .... 2(11)
Gordon, C 36	Neilson, R .... 36(1)	Webster, A 30

League goals (71): Skacel 16, Hartley 14, Jankauskas 8, Bednar 7, Pospisil 7, Elliot 5, Pressley 5, Mikoliunas 3, Aguiar 1, Berra 1, Makela 1, Simmons 1, Webster 1, Opponents 1.
Tennents Cup goals (12): Hartley 3, Jankauskas 2, Pressley 2, Cesnauskis 1, Elliot 1, McAllister 1, Pospisil 1, Skacel 1. **CIS Cup goals (2):** Jankauskas 2.
Average home League attendance: 16,776.

HIBERNIAN

Ground: Easter Road Stadium, Albion Place, Edinburgh EH7 5QG. **Capacity:** 17,462. **Telephone:** 0131 661 2159. **Colours:** Green and white. **Nickname:** Hibees.

Benjelloun, A .... 2(3)	Killeen, C .... 6(1)	O'Connor, G .... 24(2)
Beuzelin, G 21	Konde, O .... 7(4)	Riordan, D .... 32(4)
Brown, Scott .... 16(3)	Konte, A .... 1(12)	Rudge, N .... 4(2)
Brown, Simon .... 7(1)	Lynch, S .... –(2)	Shields, J 7
Caldwell, G 34	Malkowski, Z .... 31(1)	Shiels, D .... 8(8)
Campbell, R .... –(1)	McCluskey, J .... –(3)	Smith, G .... 19(1)
Dalglish, P .... 4(7)	McDonald, K .... –(2)	Sproule, I .... 18(14)
Fletcher, S .... 16(18)	Morrow, S .... –(8)	Stewart, M .... 24(1)
Glass, S .... 23(5)	Murphy, D 30	Thomson, K .... 28(3)
Hogg, C .... 21(2)	Murray, A 1	Whittaker, S 34

League goals (61): Riordan 16, O'Connor 11, Fletcher 8, Beuzelin 5, Sproule 4, Killen 3, Shiels 2, Benjelloun 1, Brown, Scott 1, Caldwell 1, Dalglish 1, Glass 1, Hogg 1, Murphy 1, Stewart 1, Whittaker 1, Opponents 3.
Tennents Cup goals (14): O'Connor 3, Sproule 3, Fletcher 2, Brown, Scott 2, Caldwell 1, Killen 1, Riordan 1, Stewart 1. **CIS Cup goals (2):** Riordan 2. **UEFA Cup goals (1):** Riordan 1.
Average home League attendance: 13,565.

INVERNESS CALEDONIAN THISTLE

Ground: Caledonian Stadium, East Longman, Inverness, IV1 1FF. **Capacity:** 7,512. **Telephone:** 01463 222880. **Colours:** Royal blue. **Nickname:** Caley Thistle.

Bayne, G .... 8(9)	Golabek, S .... 14(3)	Morgan, A .... 14(8)
Black, I .... 24(2)	Hart, R .... 11(20)	Munro, G 32
Brewster, C .... 17(1)	Hastings, R .... 26(1)	Proctor, D .... 12(5)
Brown, M 37	Hislop, S .... –(3)	Soane, S .... –(1)
Dargo, C .... 30(2)	Juanjo, C .... –(2)	Sutherland, A 1
Dods, D 37	Keogh, L .... 5(3)	Tokely, R 34
Duncan, A .... 29(2)	McAllister, R .... 2(11)	Wilson, B .... 33(1)
Fox, L .... 9(8)	McBain, R .... 17(1)	Wyness, D .... 18(9)
Fraser, M 1	McCaffrey, S .... 7(1)	

League goals (51): Dargo 16, Wyness 8, Brewster 6, Wilson 4, Morgan 3, Proctor 3, Tokely 3, Bayne 2, Dods 2, Black 1, Duncan 1, Fox 1, Hart 1.
Tennents Cup goals (6): Dargo 2, Wyness 2, McAllister 1, McBain 1. **CIS Cup goals (9):** Wilson 2, Dargo 1, Duncan 1, Fox 1, Hart 1, McBain 1, Munro 1, Wyness 1.
Average home League attendance: 5,061.

KILMARNOCK

Ground: Rugby Park, Kilmarnock, KA1 2DP. **Capacity:** 18,128. **Telephone:** 01563 545300. **Colours:** White and blue. **Nickname:** Killie.

Boyd, K	18(1)	Hay, G	35	Murray, S	1(14)
Campbell, R	–(2)	Invincible, D	34(3)	Naismith, S	32(4)
Combe, A	32	Johnston, A	36(1)	Nish, C	25(9)
Di Giacomo, P	2(10)	Leven, P	4(2)	Smith, G	6(1)
Dodds, R	6(5)	Lilley, D	8(3)	Wales, G	18(12)
Ford, S	32	Locke, G	10(5)	Wilson, L	11(2)
Fowler, J	38	McDonald, G	16(11)	Wright, F	27
Greer, G	27				

League goals (63): Boyd 15, Naismith 13, Wales 8, Invincible 7, Nish 7, McDonald 3, Ford 2, Fowler 2, Greer 2, Johnston 2, Dodds 1, Lilley 1.
Tennents Cup goals (1): Nish 1. **CIS Cup goals (7):** Boyd 2, Di Giacomo 1, Dodds 1, Invincible 1, Wales 1, Opponents 1.
Average home League attendance: 7,071.

LIVINGSTON

Ground: Almondvale Stadium, Livingston, EH54 7DN. **Capacity:** 10,016. **Telephone:** 01506 417000. **Colours:** Gold and black. **Nickname:** Livvy's Lions.

Adam, S	–(2)	Hislop, S	7(7)	Pinxten, H	26
Adams, D	21(4)	Hoolahan, W	14(2)	Roy, L	6
Barrett, G	6	Lambert, P	7	Scott, M	8(11)
Barrett , N	6(3)	Mackay, D	38	Snodgrass, R	12(14)
Boyd, S	2(2)	McKenzie, R	32	Strong, G	28(2)
Brittain, R	33(2)	McLaughlin, S	1(2)	Tesevic, D	2(2)
Dair, J	21(1)	McNamee, D	13(1)	Tierney, P	25(6)
Dalglish, P	15(2)	McPake, J	5(10)	Vincze, G	12(6)
Dorado, E	17(4)	Miller, G	2(2)	Walker, A	28(5)
Dorrans, G	4(4)	Morrow, S	11	Weir, S	–(1)
Healy, C	6(3)	Pereira, R	5(6)	Whelan, N	5(3)

League goals (25): Brittain 4, Snodgrass 4, Dalglish 3, Pinxten 3, Healy 2, Morrow 2, Hislop 1, Mackay 1, Pereira 1, Strong 1, Vincze 1, Walker 1, Whelan 1.
Tennents Cup goals (2): Brittain 1, Dalglish 1. **CIS Cup goals (5):** Dalglish 2, Dair 1, Mackay 1, Pereira 1.
Average home League attendance: 4,964.

MOTHERWELL

Ground: Fir Park, Firpark Street, Motherwell ML1 2QN. **Capacity:** 13,742. **Telephone:** 01698 333333. **Colours:** Claret and amber. **Nickname:** Well.

Clarkson, D	12(18)	Kerr, B	32(4)	McLean, B	27(3)
Coakley, A	–(1)	Kinniburgh, W	17(4)	Meldrum, C	7(1)
Corrigan, M	27(2)	Lee Smith, D	–(1)	O'Donnell, P	23(6)
Craigan, S	36	Leitch, S	1	Paterson, J	10(9)
Donnelly, R	1(1)	Marshall, G	1	Quinn, P	15(3)
Fagan, S	11(5)	McBride, K	15(6)	Reynolds, M	1
Fitzpatrick, M	1(8)	McCormack, A	24	Smith, A	3(4)
Foran, R	29(3)	McDonald, Scott	30(4)	Smith, G	30
Hamilton, J	30(4)	McDonald, Steve	1(1)	Thermeus, A	–(1)
Hammell, S	32(1)	McGarry, S	2(7)	Wright, K	–(1)
Keogh, D	–(1)				

League goals (55): Foran 11, McDonald, Scott 11, Hamilton 10, Clarkson 4, Kerr 3, McLean 3, Craigan 2, Kinniburgh 2, McCormack 2, O'Donnell 2, Corrigan 1, Fagan 1, Fitzpatrick 1, McBride 1, Paterson 1.

Tennents Cup goals: None. **CIS Cup goals (6):** Clarkson 1, Foran 1, Hamilton 1, Kerr 1, Lee Smith 1, McDonald, Scott 1.
Average home League attendance: 6,250.

RANGERS

Ground: Ibrox Park, Edmison Drive, Glasgow, G51 2XD. **Capacity:** 50,444. **Telephone:** 0870 600 1972. **Colours:** Royal blue and white. **Nickname:** Gers.

Adam, C .... –(1)	Jeffers, F .... 4(4)	Pierre-Fanfan, J 7
Andrews, M .... 21(2)	Klos, S 2	Prso, D .... 29(3)
Ashikodi, M .... –(1)	Kyrgiakos, S 28	Rae, G .... 4(4)
Ball, M 2	Lovenkrands, P .... 23(10)	Rae, A .... 5(4)
Bernard, O 9	Lowing, A .... 1(1)	Ricksen, F .... 20(1)
Boyd, K .... 15(2)	Malcolm, R .... 11(2)	Robinson, L .... –(1)
Buffel, T .... 25(4)	McCormack, R ...... 2(6)	Rodriguez, J .... 20(1)
Burke, C .... 25(2)	Murray, I .... 26(4)	Ross, M .... –(1)
Ferguson, B 32	Namouchi, H .... 6(1)	Smith, S .... 16(2)
Hemdani, B .... 18(1)	Nieto, F .... –(3)	Thompson, S .... 4(10)
Hutton, A .... 17(2)	Novo, N .... 10(14)	Waterreus, R 36

League goals (67): Boyd 17, Lovenkrands 14, Prso 9, Ferguson 5, Buffel 4, Andrews 3, Burke 3, Novo 2, Thompson 2, Kyrgiakos 1, McCormack 1, Nieto 1, Pierre-Fanfan 1, Rodriguez 1, Opponents 3.
Tennents Cup goals (5): Boyd 3, Kyrgiakos 1, McCormack 1. **CIS Cup goals (5):** Buffel 2, Bieto 2, Andrews 1. **Champions League goals (13):** Lovenkrands 4, Prso 3, Buffel 1, Kyrgiakos 1, McCormack 1, Novo 1, Ricksen 1, Thompson 1.
Average home League attendance: 49,245.

QUOTE-UNQUOTE

'I saw a headline saying Arsenal are flying the flag for Britain in the Champions League, but I had to wonder where the British involvement was when I saw the team' – **Alan Pardew**, West Ham manager, on Arsenal's reliance on foreign players.

'Racism starts there. It's a regressive way of thinking' – **Arsene Wenger** replies to Pardew's comments in caustic fashion.

'They've labelled me arrogant, vain, despotic and just about every adjective in the dictionary. They can continue to do so, but I will never change' – **Jose Mourinho**, Chelsea manager.

'What's the point in sacking the manager with ten games to go? Whoever comes in is not going to save us' – **Kevin Kyle**, Sunderland striker, after the dismissal of Mick McCarthy.

'Football is about fairness, opportunity, excitement and variety. It is not a closed shop where only the richest and most powerful are invited to the table' – **UEFA**, European football's governing body, warning top clubs about forming a breakaway Champions League.

'I've got to a point now where I don't like footballers. It's so one-sided with them and it does hurt' – **David Sullivan**, Birmingham's co-owner, after a 7-0 home defeat by Liverpool in the quarter-finals of the F.A. Cup.

'I can't believe I just danced for a future King ... surreal' – **Peter Crouch**, England striker, after giving Prince William a repeat of his bizarre goal celebration.

'Better managers and coaches than me will tell you that when he's on that form and in that mood you just hope and pray' – **Chris Coleman**, Fulham manager, hailing two-goal Thierry Henry's performance in Arsenal's 4-0 win at Craven Cottage

STRACHAN'S FIRST TROPHY WITH CELTIC

SECOND ROUND	THIRD ROUND	FOURTH ROUND	SEMI-FINALS	FINAL
● **Bye**	*Celtic .... †2	*Celtic 2	Celtic 2	Celtic 3
*Falkirk 2	Falkirk 1			
Partick Thistle 1				
● **Bye**	*Rangers .... †5	Rangers 0		
*Peterhead 2	Clyde 2			
Clyde 3				
*St Johnstone 0	*St Mirren 0	*Motherwell 1	Motherwell 1	
St Mirren 1	Motherwell 1			
*Motherwell 2	*Stranraer 0	Aberdeen 0		
Hamilton Acad. 1	Aberdeen 2			
*Stranraer 3				
Dundee 1				
*Aberdeen 3	*Livingston 1	*Livingstone .... †2	Livingston 0	
Berwick Rangers 0	Hearts 0			
*Raith Row. 1	*Inverness CT 2	Inverness CT 1		
Livingston 2	Dundee Utd. 0			
*Queen's Park 0				
Hearts 2				
*Inverness CT 6				
Alloa Athletic 1				
● **Bye**				

190

*Ross Co. 1
Ayr Utd. 2

*Ayr Utd. 1

Dunfermline Ath. 0

● Bye

Hibernian 0

Hibernian 2

Hibernian 1

*Kilmarnock 4
Stirling Albion 1

*Kilmarnock 3

*Dunfermline Ath. 3

*Gretna 0
Dunfermline Ath. 1

Dunfermline Ath. 4

FIRST ROUND: Albion Row. 1, Gretna 2; Alloa Athletic 2, Arbroath 1; Berwick Rangers 4, Elgin City 2; Brechin City 0, Partick Thistle +A0; Cowdenbeath 2, St Johnstone 3; East Fife 0, Stranraer 1; East Stirling 1, Queen's Park 3; Forfar Athletic 1, Ross Co. 4; Hamilton Acad. 2, Dumbarton 1; Montrose 0, Clyde 1; Morton 1, Ayr Utd. 2; Raith Row. 2, Airdrie Utd. 0; Stenhousemuir 0, Peterhead 1; Stirling Albion 2, Queen of the South 1.

\+Drawn at home. +After extra-time. A – Partick Thistle won 3-1 on pens. Semi-finals: Celtic v Motherwell at Hampden Park. Dunfermline Ath. v Livingston at Easter Road.

CIS INSURANCE CUP FINAL

CELTIC 3, DUNFERMLINE ATHLETIC 0

Hampden Park (50,090), Sunday, March 19, 2006.

Celtic (4-4-2): Boruc, Telfer, Balde, McManus, Wallace, Nakamura, Keane (Dublin 61), Lennon (capt), Maloney, Zurawski, Petrov. **Subs not used:** Marshall, Thompson, Pearson, Varga. **Scorers:** Zurawski (43), Maloney (76), Dublin (90). **Manager:** Gordon Strachan.

Dunfermline Athletic (4-4-2): McGregor, Shields, Wilson, Ross (Donnelly 77), Campbell (Young 62), Mason, Thomson (capt), Daquin (Tarachulski 84), Labonte, Makel, Burchill. **Subs not used:** Halliwell, Tod. **Booked:** Mason, Daquin, Makel. **Manager:** Jim Leishman.

Referee: S. Dougal (Scotland). **Half-time:** 0-1.

SCOTTISH LEAGUE CUP FINALS

1946	Aberdeen beat Rangers (3-2)
1947	Rangers beat Aberdeen (4-0)
1948	East Fife beat Falkirk (4-1 after 0-0 draw)
1949	Rangers beat Raith Rov. (2-0)
1950	East Fife beat Dunfermline Athletic (3-0)
1951	Motherwell beat Hibernian (3-0)
1952	Dundee beat Rangers (3-2)
1953	Dundee beat Kilmarnock (2-0)
1954	East Fife beat Partick Thistle (3-2)
1955	Hearts beat Motherwell (4-2)
1956	Aberdeen beat St Mirren (2-1)
1957	Celtic beat Partick Thistle (3-0 after 0-0 draw)
1958	Celtic beat Rangers (7-1)
1959	Hearts beat Partick Thistle (5-1)
1960	Hearts beat Third Lanark (2-1)
1961	Rangers beat Kilmarnock (2-0)
1962	Rangers beat Hearts (3-1 after 1-1 draw)
1963	Hearts beat Kilmarnock (1-0)
1964	Rangers beat Morton (5-0)
1965	Rangers beat Celtic (2-1)
1966	Celtic beat Rangers (2-1)
1967	Celtic beat Rangers (1-0)
1968	Celtic beat Dundee (5-3)
1969	Celtic beat Hibernian (6-2)
1970	Celtic beat St Johnstone (1-0)
1971	Rangers beat Celtic (1-0)
1972	Partick Thistle beat Celtic (4-1)
1973	Hibernian beat Celtic (2-1)
1974	Dundee beat Celtic (1-0)
1975	Celtic beat Hibernian (6-3)
1976	Rangers beat Celtic (1-0)
1977†	Aberdeen beat Celtic (2-1)
1978†	Rangers beat Celtic (2-1)
1979	Rangers beat Aberdeen (2-1)
1980	Dundee Utd. beat Aberdeen (3-0 after 0-0 draw)
1981	Dundee Utd. beat Dundee (3-0)
1982	Rangers beat Dundee Utd. (2-1)
1983	Celtic beat Rangers (2-1)
1984†	Rangers beat Celtic (3-2)
1985	Rangers beat Dundee Utd. (1-0)
1986	Aberdeen beat Hibernian (3-0)
1987	Rangers beat Celtic (2-1)
1988†	Rangers beat Aberdeen (5-3 on pens. after 3-3 draw)
1989	Rangers beat Aberdeen (3-2)
1990†	Aberdeen beat Rangers (2-1)
1991†	Rangers beat Celtic (2-1)
1992	Hibernian beat Dunfermline Athletic (2-0)
1993†	Rangers beat Aberdeen (2-1)
1994	Rangers beat Hibernian (2-1)
1995	Raith Rov. beat Celtic (6-5 on pens. after 2-2 draw)
1996	Aberdeen beat Dundee (2-0)
1997	Rangers beat Hearts (4-3)
1998	Celtic beat Dundee Utd. (3-0)
1999	Rangers beat St Johnstone (2-1)

2000	Celtic beat Aberdeen (2-0)
2001	Celtic beat Kilmarnock (3-0)
2002	Rangers beat Ayr Utd. (4-0)
2003	Rangers beat Celtic (2-1)
2004	Livingston beat Hibernian (2-0)
2005	Rangers beat Motherwell (5-1)
2006	Celtic beat Dunfermline Athletic (3-0)

(† After extra time; Skol Cup 1985-93, Coca-Cola Cup 1995-97, CIS Insurance Cup 1999)

SUMMARY OF SCOTTISH LEAGUE CUP WINNERS

Rangers	24	Dundee	3	Livingston	1
Celtic	13	East Fife	3	Motherwell	1
Aberdeen	6	Dundee Utd.	2	Partick Thistle	1
Hearts	4	Hibernian	2	Raith Rov.	1

BELL'S SCOTTISH CHALLENGE CUP 2005-06

First round: Arbroath 1, Stranraer 3; Ayr Utd. 0, Stirling Albion 1 (aet); Brechin City 3, Clyde 2 (aet); East Fife 0, Stenhousemuir 4; Dundee 2, East Stirling 0; Morton 3, Gretna 2 (aet); Partick Thistle 2, Cowdenbeath 0; Peterhead 1, Berwick Rangers 2 (aet); Queen of the South 4, Albion Rov. 0; Queen's Park 0, Hamilton Acad. 3; Raith Rov. 3, Elgin City 1 (aet); Ross Co. 2, Montrose 1; St Johnstone 2, Alloa Athletic 0; St Mirren 1, Forfar Athletic 0 (aet).

Second round: Brechin City 0, Morton 2; Dundee 1, Airdrie Utd. 1 (aet, Dundee won 3-2 on pens); Partick Thistle 4, St Johnstone 4 (aet, St Johnstone won 8-7 on pens); Raith Rov. 2, Dumbarton 1 (aet); Ross Co. 0, Hamilton Acad. 1; Queen of the South 1, St Mirren 2; Stirling Albion 2, Berwick Rangers 1; Stranraer 1, Strenhousemuir 2.

Third round: Hamilton Acad. 2, Dundee 0; St Johnstone 5, Raith Rov. 1; St Mirren 3, Stenhousemuir 2; Stirling Albion 1, Morton 2.

Semi-finals: St Johnstone 1, Hamilton Acad. 2; St Mirren 0, Morton 0 (aet, St Mirren won 4-2 on pens).

FINAL

ST MIRREN 2, HAMILTON ACADEMICAL 1

Excelsior Stadium, Airdrie (9,612), Sunday, November 6, 2005

St Mirren (4-4-2): Smith, Van Zanten, Millen (Reilly 76), Potter, Broadfoot, Murray, Adam (Mehmet 69), McGowne, Lappin, Kean, Sutton. **Subs not used:** Reid, Corcoran, Hinchcliffe. **Scorers:** Lappin (22), Sutton (80). **Booked:** Broadfoot, Murray. **Manager:** Gus MacPherson.

Hamilton Acad. (4-4-2): McEwan, Thomson, Balmer (Robertson 81), McLaughlin, Tunbridge, Wilson, Neil, MacKenzie, Fleming, Jones (Carrigan 38), Keogh (Gilhaney 77). **Subs not used:** Ferguson. Jellema. **Scorer:** Tunbridge (47). **Booked:** Thomson, Tunbridge. **Manager:** Billy Reid.

Referee: S. Dougal (Scotland). **Half-time:** 1-0.

GALLANT GRETNA BEATEN IN PENALTY SHOOT-OUT

THIRD ROUND	FOURTH ROUND	FIFTH ROUND	SEMI-FINALS	FINAL
Gretna 1	Gretna 0:4	*Gretna 1	Gretna 3	Gretna 1
*St Johnstone .. 0				
*Clyde 2	*Clyde 0:0			
Celtic 1				
*Spartans 3	*Spartans 0:0	St Mirren 0		
Queens Park 2				
*St Mirren 3	St Mirren 0:3			
Motherwell 0				
*Queen of the South .. 1:0	*Hamilton Acad. 0:3	*Hamilton Acad. 0:2	Dundee 0	
Hamilton Acad. .... 1+1				
*Alloa Athletic 1:2	Alloa Athletic 0:0			
Livingston 1:1				
*Dunfermline 3	*Airdrie Utd. 1:0	Dundee .... 0+3		
Airdrie Utd. 4				
*Dundee 1:2	Dundee 1:2			
Stranraer 0				
*Falkirk 2	*Falkirk 1:1	*Falkirk 1	Hibernian 0	
Brechin City 1				
*Ross Co. 5	Ross Co. 1:0			
Forfar Athletic 0				
*Rangers 5	*Rangers 0	Hibernian 5		
Peterhead 0				
*Hibernian 6	Hibernian 0			
Arbroath 3				

*Inverness CT ... 1:2			
Ayr Utd. ... 1:0	*Inverness CT ... 2:1		
*Stirling Alb. ... 0		Patrick Thistle ... 1	
Patrick Thistle ... 1	Patrick Thistle ... 2:+A1		Hearts ... +B1
*Dundee Utd. ... 2			
Aberdeen ... 3	Aberdeen ... 0	Hearts ... 4	
Kilmarnock ... 2			
*Hearts ... 3	*Hearts ... 3	*Hearts ... 2	

FIRST ROUND: Alloa Athletic 9, Selkirk 0; Cowdenbeath 0, Morton 3; Dumbarton 4, Forres Mechs 1; Spartans 1, Berwick Rangers 0; Stenhousemuir 3, East Stirling 2; Stirling Alb. 2, Elgin City 1; Partick Thistle 1, Albion Rov. 1; Preston Athletic 2, Gretna 6. **Replay:** Albion Rov. 1, Partick Thistle 3.

SECOND ROUND: Alloa Athletic 1, Montrose 0; Arbroath 1, Dumbarton 0; Ayr Utd. 3, Morton 2; East Fife 0, Peterhead 3; Gretna 6, Cove Rangers 1; Lossiemouth 0, Spartans 5; Queens Park 2, Raith Rov. 0; Stenhousemuir 1, Partick Thistle 4; Stirling Alb. 1, Inverurie Locos 0; Threave Rov. 0, Forfar Athletic 4.

*Drawn at home. +After extra-time. Semi-finals at Hampden Park. A – Partick Thistle won 4-2 on pens. B – Hearts won 4-2 on pens.

TENNENTS SCOTTISH CUP FINAL

GRETNA 1, HEARTS 1

(aet, Hearts won 4-2 on pens)
Hampden Park (51,232), Saturday, May 13, 2006

Gretna (3-5-2): Main, Birch, Innes, Townsley, McGuffie, Tosh, Nicholls (Graham 55), O'Neil, Skelton, Deuchar (McQuilken 102), Grady. **Subs not used:** Mathieson, Berkeley, Henderson. **Scorer:** McGuffie (76). **Booked:** Birch, Tosh. **Manager:** Rowan Alexander.

Hearts (4-4-2): Gordon, Neilson, Pressley, Tall, Fyssas, Cesnauskis (Mikoliunas 86), Hartley, Aguiar (Brellier 72), Skacel, Bednar (Pospisil 69), Jankauskas. **Subs not used:** Banks, Berra. **Scorer:** Skacel (39). **Booked:** Skacel, Fyssas, Hartley. **Sent-off:** Hartley. **Coach:** Valdas Ivanauskas.

Penalty shoot-out: Pressley 0-1, Grady 1-1, Neilson 1-2, Birch 2-2, Skacel 2-3, Townsley saved, Pospisil 2-4, Skelton missed.

Referee: D. McDonald. **Half-time:** 0-1.

195

SCOTTISH F.A. CUP FINALS

1874	Queen's Park beat Clydesdale (2-0)
1875	Queen's Park beat Renton (3-0)
1876	Queen's Park beat Third Lanark (2-0 after 1-1 draw)
1877	Vale of Leven beat Rangers (3-2 after 0-0, 1-1 draws)
1878	Vale of Leven beat Third Lanark (1-0)
1879	Vale of Leven awarded Cup (Rangers withdrew after 1-1 draw)
1880	Queen's Park beat Thornlibank (3-0)
1881	Queen's Park beat Dumbarton (3-1)
1882	Queen's Park beat Dumbarton (4-1 after 2-2 draw)
1883	Dumbarton beat Vale of Leven (2-1 after 2-2 draw)
1884	Queen's Park awarded Cup (Vale of Leven withdrew from Final)
1885	Renton beat Vale of Leven (3-1 after 0-0 draw)
1886	Queen's Park beat Renton (3-1)
1887	Hibernian beat Dumbarton (2-1)
1888	Renton beat Cambuslang (6-1)
1889	Third Lanark beat Celtic (2-1)
1890	Queen's Park beat Vale of Leven (2-1 after 1-1 draw)
1891	Hearts beat Dumbarton (1-0)
1892	Celtic beat Queen's Park (5-1)
1893	Queen's Park beat Celtic (2-1)
1894	Rangers beat Celtic (3-1)
1895	St. Bernard's beat Renton (2-1)
1896	Hearts beat Hibernian (3-1)
1897	Rangers beat Dumbarton (5-1)
1898	Rangers beat Kilmarnock (2-0)
1899	Celtic beat Rangers (2-0)
1900	Celtic beat Queen's Park (4-3)
1901	Hearts beat Celtic (4-3)
1902	Hibernian beat Celtic (1-0)
1903	Rangers beat Hearts (2-0 after 0-0, 1-1 draws)
1904	Celtic beat Rangers (3-2)
1905	Third Lanark beat Rangers (3-1 after 0-0 draw)
1906	Hearts beat Third Lanark (1-0)
1907	Celtic beat Hearts (3-0)
1908	Celtic beat St. Mirren (5-1)
1909	Cup withheld because of riot after two drawn games in Final between Celtic and Rangers (2-2, 1-1)
1910	Dundee beat Clyde (2-1 after 2-2, 0-0 draws)
1911	Celtic beat Hamilton Academical (2-0 after 0-0 draw)
1912	Celtic beat Clyde (2-0)
1913	Falkirk beat Raith Rov. (2-0)
1914	Celtic beat Hibernian (4-1 after 0-0 draw)
1915-19	No competition (World War 1)
1920	Kilmarnock beat Albion Rov. (3-2)
1921	Partick Thistle beat Rangers (1-0)
1922	Morton beat Rangers (1-0)
1923	Celtic beat Hibernian (1-0)
1924	Airdrieonians beat Hibernian (2-0)
1925	Celtic beat Dundee (2-1)
1926	St. Mirren beat Celtic (2-0)
1927	Celtic beat East Fife (3-1)
1928	Rangers beat Celtic (4-0)
1929	Kilmarnock beat Rangers (2-0)
1930	Rangers beat Partick Thistle (2-1 after 0-0 draw)
1931	Celtic beat Motherwell (4-2 after 2-2 draw)
1932	Rangers beat Kilmarnock (3-0 after 1-1 draw)

1933	Celtic beat Motherwell (1-0)
1934	Rangers beat St. Mirren (5-0)
1935	Rangers beat Hamilton Academical (2-1)
1936	Rangers beat Third Lanark (1-0)
1937	Celtic beat Aberdeen (2-1)
1938	East Fife beat Kilmarnock (4-2 after 1-1 draw)
1939	Clyde beat Motherwell (4-0)
1940-6	No competition (World War 2)
1947	Aberdeen beat Hibernian (2-1)
1948†	Rangers beat Morton (1-0 after 1-1 draw)
1949	Rangers beat Clyde (4-1)
1950	Rangers beat East Fife (3-0)
1951	Celtic beat Motherwell (1-0)
1952	Motherwell beat Dundee (4-0)
1953	Rangers beat Aberdeen (1-0 after 1-1 draw)
1954	Celtic beat Aberdeen (2-1)
1955	Clyde beat Celtic (1-0 after 1-1 draw)
1956	Hearts beat Celtic (3-1)
1957†	Falkirk beat Kilmarnock (2-1 after 1-1 draw)
1958	Clyde beat Hibernian (1-0)
1959	St. Mirren beat Aberdeen (3-1)
1960	Rangers beat Kilmarnock (2-0)
1961	Dunfermline Athletic beat Celtic (2-0 after 0-0 draw)
1962	Rangers beat St. Mirren (2-0)
1963	Rangers beat Celtic (3-0 after 1-1 draw)
1964	Rangers beat Dundee (3-1)
1965	Celtic beat Dunfermline Athletic (3-2)
1966	Rangers beat Celtic (1-0 after 0-0 draw)
1967	Celtic beat Aberdeen (2-0)
1968	Dunfermline Athletic beat Hearts (3-1)
1969	Celtic beat Rangers (4-0)
1970	Aberdeen beat Celtic (3-1)
1971	Celtic beat Rangers (2-1 after 1-1 draw)
1972	Celtic beat Hibernian (6-1)
1973	Rangers beat Celtic (3-2)
1974	Celtic beat Dundee Utd. (3-0)
1975	Celtic beat Airdrieonians (3-1)
1976	Rangers beat Hearts (3-1)
1977	Celtic beat Rangers (1-0)
1978	Rangers beat Aberdeen (2-1)
1979†	Rangers beat Hibernian (3-2 after two 0-0 draws)
1980†	Celtic beat Rangers (1-0)
1981	Rangers beat Dundee Utd. (4-1 after 0-0 draw)
1982†	Aberdeen beat Rangers (4-1)
1983†	Aberdeen beat Rangers (1-0)
1984†	Aberdeen beat Celtic (2-1)
1985	Celtic beat Dundee Utd. (2-1)
1986	Aberdeen beat Hearts (3-0)
1987†	St. Mirren beat Dundee Utd. (1-0)
1988	Celtic beat Dundee Utd. (2-1)
1989	Celtic beat Rangers (1-0)
1990†	Aberdeen beat Celtic (9-8 on pens. after 0-0 draw)
1991†	Motherwell beat Dundee Utd. (4-3)
1992	Rangers beat Airdrieonians (2-1)
1993	Rangers beat Aberdeen (2-1)
1994	Dundee Utd. beat Rangers (1-0)
1995	Celtic beat Airdrieonians (1-0)
1996	Rangers beat Hearts (5-1)

1997	Kilmarnock beat Falkirk (1-0)
1998	Hearts beat Rangers (2-1)
1999	Rangers beat Celtic (1-0)
2000	Rangers beat Aberdeen (4-0)
2001	Celtic beat Hibernian (3-0)
2002	Rangers beat Celtic (3-2)
2003	Rangers beat Dundee (1-0)
2004	Celtic beat Dunfermline Athletic (3-1)
2005	Celtic beat Dundee Utd. (1-0)
2006†	Hearts beat Gretna (4-2 on pens after 1-1 draw)

(† After extra time; Cup sponsored by Tennents since season 1989-90)

SUMMARY OF SCOTTISH CUP WINNERS

Celtic 33, Rangers 31, Queen's Park 10, Aberdeen 7, Hearts 7, Clyde 3, Kilmarnock 3, St. Mirren 3, Vale of Leven 3, Dunfermline Ath. 2, Falkirk 2, Hibernian 2, Motherwell 2, Renton 2, Third Lanark 2, Airdrieonians 1, Dumbarton 1, Dundee 1, Dundee Utd. 1, East Fife 1, Morton 1, Partick Thistle 1, St. Bernard's 1.

FOOTBALL'S CHANGING HOMES

Arsenal moved into their impressive new Emirates Stadium in July 2006 – while just five miles away in north London the Wembley redevelopment continued to flounder. The club spent £220m. on constructing the 60,000-seater arena which sits just a long goal-kick from Highbury, their home for 93 years. The project did not commence until February 2004, but was finished well in time for the 2006-07 season.

In stark contrast, the new Wembley was still unfinished at the start of the domestic campaign, nearly four full years since the bulldozers knocked down the famous old twin towers. The 90,000-seater stadium was scheduled to be ready by August 2005, but continued construction problems blighted the redevelopment and eventually forced the F.A. to abandon their plans to take the 2006 F.A. Cup Final back to its spiritual home. Instead, the showpiece match was again played at Cardiff's Millennium Stadium and there were fears that construction firm Multiplex would not meet their new deadline of September 2006 because of further wrangling. There is no doubt the new Wembley will be a fantastic venue, but it has cost a massive £757m. to complete and caused major embarrassment for the F.A. who will take control of the venue when it is finally finished.

Arsenal, meanwhile, are set to enjoy an increase in turnover of £55m. a season now they have expanded their capacity which will put them closer to **Manchester United** in the financial battle off the pitch. United, however, are anxious to keep one step ahead and developing corner stands at Old Trafford will increase the capacity to 76,000. **Sheffield United** return to the Premiership with an increased capacity of 32,500, while **Liverpool** and **Everton** both continue to press ahead with moves for new grounds. Liverpool have had plans for a 60,000-seater stadium in Stanley Park re-confirmed by the city's planning committee, although local protesters say they will fight it. Everton, whose previous scheme to relocate to a waterfront site at King's Dock was abandoned, are looking at a 55,000-capacity arena in the Kirkby area of the city.

Doncaster Rovers expect to be the next club to move into a new home, with a £32m. stadium seating nearly 16,000 scheduled to be ready by the end of 2006. Work on a new ground for **Cardiff City** could begin by the end of the year. The £100m. development opposite crumbling Ninian Park will incorporate a replacement for Cardiff Athletics Stadium. It will have a capacity of 30,000, with the capability of doubling that figure. **Oldham Athletic** continue to pursue their aim of building a futuristic 16,000-seater sports, leisure and corporate facility, although the key is support from local investors.

Gillingham are considering a number of new sites, while **Milton Keynes Dons**, who play at the National Hockey Stadium in front of crowds of 4,000, want a home of their own. Football's longest-running project, a new stadium for **Brighton and Hove Albion** at Falmer, goes on. The club are still aiming for a move around 2009, but a High Court action by Lewes District Council is the latest obstacle.

CONFERENCE FINAL TABLES 2005-2006

NATIONWIDE CONFERENCE

			HOME				AWAY						
		P	W	D	L	F	A	W	D	L	F	A	Pts	GD
1	Accrington	42	16	3	2	38	17	12	4	5	38	28	91	31
2	Hereford†	42	11	7	3	30	14	11	7	3	29	19	80	26
3	Grays	42	7	9	5	46	32	14	4	3	48	23	76	39
4	Halifax	42	14	6	1	31	11	7	6	8	24	29	75	15
5	Morecambe	42	15	4	2	44	17	7	4	10	24	74	74	27
6	Stevenage	42	15	3	3	38	15	4	9	8	24	32	69	15
7	Exeter	42	11	3	7	41	22	7	6	8	24	26	63	17
8	York	42	10	5	6	36	26	7	7	7	27	22	63	15
9	Burton	42	8	7	6	23	21	8	5	8	27	31	60	−2
10	Dag. & Redbridge	42	8	4	9	31	32	8	6	7	32	27	58	4
11	Woking	42	8	7	6	30	20	6	7	8	28	27	56	11
12	Cambridge	42	11	6	4	35	25	4	4	13	16	32	55	−6
13	Aldershot	42	10	4	7	30	30	6	2	13	31	44	54	−13
14	Canvey	42	6	8	7	23	27	4	10	24	31	51	51	−11
15	Kidderminster	42	8	5	8	21	27	5	6	10	18	28	50	16
16	Gravesend	42	8	4	9	25	25	5	6	10	20	32	49	−12
17	Crawley***	42	9	4	8	27	22	3	7	11	21	33	44	−7
18	Southport	42	7	3	11	24	38	3	7	11	12	30	40	−32
19	Forest Green	42	7	7	7	31	27	1	7	13	18	35	38	−13
20	Tamworth	42	7	4	10	17	23	4	4	13	15	40	38	−31
21	Altrincham**	42	7	5	9	25	30	3	6	12	15	41	23	−31
22	Scarborough*	42	4	7	10	24	30	5	3	13	16	36	37	−26

† Also promoted, * Relegated for breach of Creditors' rules, ** Deducted 18 pts for ineligible player, *** Deducted 3 pts for exceeding player budget.

Manager of Year: John Coleman (Accrington). **Goalscorer of Year:** Andy Bishop (York). **Player of Year:** Ian Craney (Accrington). **Fair Play award:** Burton. **Leading scorers:** 23 Bishop (York); 21 Richards (Woking); 17 Carlton (Morecambe), Little (Altrincham); 16 Donaldson (York), Mullin (Accrington); 15 Moore (Dagenham); 14 Kightly (Grays), Roberts (Accrington); 13 Clare (Burton), Craney (Accrington), Grant (Halifax), Phillips (Exeter), Poole (Grays).

CONFERENCE CHAMPIONS

1979-80	Altrincham	1993-94	Kidderminster Harriers
1980-81	Altrincham	1994-95	Macclesfield Town
1981-82	Runcorn	1995-96	Stevenage Borough
1982-83	Enfield	1996-97*	Macclesfield Town
1983-84	Maidstone Utd.	1997-98*	Halifax Town
1984-85	Wealdstone	1998-99*	Cheltenham Town
1985-86	Enfield	1999-2000*	Kidderminster Harriers
1986-87*	Scarborough	2000-01*	Rushden & Diamonds
1987-88*	Lincoln City	2001-02*	Boston Utd.
1988-89*	Maidstone Utd.	2002-03*	Yeovil Town
1989-90*	Darlington	2003-04*	Chester City
1990-91*	Barnet	2004-05*	Barnet
1991-92*	Colchester Utd.	2005-06*	Accrington
1992-93*	Wycombe Wand.		

(* Promoted to Football League)

Conference – Record Attendance: 9,432, Lincoln City v Wycombe Wand., May 2, 1988.

NATIONWIDE CONFERENCE RESULTS 2004-05

Results grid — home teams listed down the left (rows), away teams across the top (columns). Diagonal (team vs itself) is blank.

Home \ Away	Accrington	Aldershot	Altrincham	Burton	Cambridge	Canvey	Crawley	Dag. & Red.	Exeter	Forest Green	Gravesend	Grays	Halifax	Hereford	Kidderminster	Morecambe	Scarborough	Southport	Stevenage	Tamworth	Woking	York
Accrington		3-2	1-0	0-2	1-0	1-0	4-2	1-0	1-2	2-0	1-1	2-3	2-2	2-1	2-0	2-0	1-0	4-0	1-1	2-1	2-1	2-1
Aldershot	1-4		0-2	2-1	0-2	2-1	3-2	3-1	1-2	4-2	0-3	2-3	3-1	2-1	2-0	1-4	2-1	0-1	1-1	2-0	1-1	1-1
Altrincham	0-1	5-1		1-0	4-0	1-0	2-2	0-5	1-1	5-0	1-1	0-2	3-1	0-1	3-0	0-4	1-1	0-0	2-0	2-0	0-4	0-3
Burton	0-2	1-2	1-2		2-0	1-2	3-1	0-5	2-0	1-0	0-0	0-3	3-1	2-1	3-0	0-4	2-1	0-0	3-1	2-0	1-1	0-0
Cambridge	0-2	0-2	4-0	2-0		3-1	1-0	2-2	2-1	2-2	0-0	1-1	3-1	0-2	0-2	2-2	2-1	2-1	3-1	1-2	1-1	2-0
Canvey	0-2	2-1	1-0	2-0	3-1		1-0	1-2	2-1	2-0	0-0	2-1	2-0	2-1	2-1	2-2	2-1	2-1	1-1	0-1	0-2	2-0
Crawley	0-1	2-0	3-1	1-0	3-1	3-1		0-0	1-0	1-0	1-2	1-3	1-0	0-2	3-0	1-3	0-2	3-1	1-1	2-1	2-3	1-1
Dag. & Red.	0-1	2-0	4-1	1-0	4-0	3-1			0-2	1-0	1-2	1-2	2-2	0-2	3-0	1-3	0-2	3-1	2-2	2-1	2-2	1-1
Exeter	1-3	4-0	1-2	1-2	1-0	2-0	3-1	3-1		0-0	1-2	1-2	1-0	1-2	3-0	2-0	1-1	5-0	2-2	3-0	2-3	1-2
Forest Green	1-1	4-2	5-0	4-0	0-0	2-0	2-2	0-3	0-0		0-0	1-2	4-2	1-2	3-0	3-1	5-1	1-2	0-2	1-3	0-3	1-2
Gravesend	1-3	0-3	1-1	0-0	5-3	2-0	2-0	1-3	3-0	2-2		1-3	4-0	2-2	1-2	1-2	5-0	1-1	0-2	1-3	2-2	0-0
Grays	1-2	2-1	2-0	0-1	1-0	0-1	2-0	0-4	0-0	2-2	6-1		1-1	2-2	2-2	0-0	5-0	1-1	2-2	5-0	2-2	1-1
Halifax Town	2-2	1-1	1-1	2-3	1-0	2-0	2-2	3-1	0-0	1-0	2-0	1-3		2-1	1-2	1-2	5-0	1-1	2-2	4-0	2-2	1-0
Hereford	2-0	1-1	2-0	1-1	3-0	1-1	2-0	3-1	3-0	1-0	0-2	2-1	1-1		0-1	1-0	2-1	1-1	0-0	0-1	3-1	1-0
Kidderminster	2-0	5-2	2-0	0-1	0-1	3-2	1-0	1-2	2-2	1-2	3-0	4-0	1-0	1-1		1-0	0-1	1-1	4-1	0-1	3-1	0-0
Morecambe	3-2	2-2	2-0	3-0	2-2	2-0	1-2	3-1	2-2	2-2	3-0	2-0	2-0	1-0	0-1		2-1	0-0	0-0	0-0	3-1	2-0
Scarborough	2-0	0-1	1-2	0-1	2-0	2-0	0-2	0-3	0-3	3-1	0-2	1-4	2-0	1-4	1-4	0-3		0-1	1-3	0-1	1-0	0-2
Southport	3-1	2-0	3-0	3-2	3-1	2-1	2-1	2-0	0-3	3-1	2-0	0-1	2-0	0-3	0-0	0-1	3-1		3-2	0-0	1-0	1-0
Stevenage	3-1	2-1	3-0	1-1	3-1	3-0	2-1	1-1	1-1	3-1	2-0	0-1	1-2	0-0	1-4	0-3	2-1	0-1		3-1	1-0	1-0
Tamworth	1-2	2-1	1-1	1-1	1-1	2-1	2-2	0-0	1-1	2-1	1-3	1-2	1-2	1-1	0-1	0-3	0-2	0-1	2-0		1-1	0-3
Woking	0-1	1-2	3-1	2-2	1-1	1-1	0-0	0-0	2-1	1-3	1-3	2-2	2-2	1-1	0-1	0-1	4-0	0-1	3-2	5-0		2-0
York	2-4	3-2	5-0	0-1	1-0	2-1	0-0	1-1	4-2	5-1	1-0	0-2	0-2	1-3	2-2	1-1	3-1	0-0	0-1	2-1	2-1	

Read across for home results, down for away

200

NATIONWIDE NORTH

		P	W	D	L	F	A	Pts	GD
1	Northwich	42	29	5	8	97	49	92	48
2	Stafford†	42	25	10	7	68	34	85	34
3	Nuneaton	42	22	11	9	68	43	77	25
4	Droylsden	42	20	12	10	80	56	72	24
5	Harrogate	42	22	5	15	66	56	71	10
6	Kettering	42	19	10	13	63	49	67	14
7	Stalybridge	42	19	9	14	74	54	66	20
8	Worcester	42	16	14	12	58	46	62	12
9	Moor Green	42	15	16	11	67	64	61	3
10	Hinckley	42	14	16	12	60	55	58	5
11	Hyde	42	15	11	16	68	61	56	7
12	Hucknall	42	14	13	15	56	55	55	1
13	Workington	42	14	13	15	60	62	55	-2
14	Barrow	42	12	11	19	62	67	47	-5
15	Lancaster	42	12	11	19	52	66	47	-14
16	Gainsborough	42	11	13	18	45	65	46	-20
17	Alfreton	42	10	15	17	46	58	45	-12
18	Vauxhall	42	12	7	23	50	71	43	-21
19	Worksop	42	10	11	21	46	71	41	-25
20	Redditch	42	9	12	21	53	78	39	-25
21	Leigh*	42	9	13	20	45	79	39	-34
22	Hednesford	42	7	14	21	42	87	35	-45

† Also promoted * Deducted 1 pt

NATIONWIDE SOUTH

		P	W	D	L	F	A	Pts	GD
1	Weymouth*	42	30	4	8	80	34	90	46
2	St Albans†	42	27	5	10	94	47	86	47
3	Farnborough	42	23	9	10	65	41	78	24
4	Lewes	42	21	10	11	78	57	73	21
5	Histon	42	21	8	13	70	56	71	14
6	Havant**	42	21	10	11	64	48	70	16
7	Cambridge**	42	20	10	12	78	46	67	32
8	Eastleigh	42	21	3	18	65	58	66	7
9	Welling	42	16	17	9	58	44	65	14
10	Thurrock	42	16	10	16	60	60	58	–
11	Dorchester	42	16	7	19	60	72	55	-12
12	Bognor	42	12	13	17	54	55	49	-1
13	Sutton	42	13	10	19	48	61	49	-13
14	Weston-S-Mare	42	14	7	21	57	88	49	-31
15	Bishop's Stortford	42	11	15	16	55	63	48	-8
16	Yeading	42	13	8	21	47	62	47	-15
17	Eastbourne	42	10	16	16	51	61	46	-10
18	Newport	42	12	8	22	50	67	44	-17
19	Basingstoke	42	12	8	22	47	72	44	-25
20	Hayes	42	11	9	22	47	60	42	-13
21	Carshalton	42	8	16	18	42	68	40	-26
22	Maidenhead***	42	8	9	25	49	99	32	-50

† Also promoted * Deducted 4 pts ** Deducted 3 pts *** Deducted 1pt

OTHER LEAGUES 2005-06

UNIBOND PREMIER DIVISION

		P	W	D	L	F	A	Pts	GD
1	Blyth	42	26	11	5	79	32	89	47
2	Frickley	42	26	8	8	72	36	86	36
3	Marine	42	23	12	7	61	25	81	36
4	Farsley†	42	23	10	9	84	34	79	50
5	North Ferriby	42	21	10	11	77	54	73	23
6	Whitby	42	18	10	14	60	59	64	1
7	Burscough	42	19	6	17	64	64	63	–
8	Witton	42	17	9	16	68	55	60	13
9	Matlock	42	16	11	15	60	55	59	5
10	Telford	42	14	17	11	54	52	59	2
11	Ossett	42	17	7	18	57	61	58	–4
12	Leek	42	14	14	14	50	53	56	–3
13	Prescot	42	15	8	19	49	60	53	–11
14	Guiseley	42	14	9	19	45	58	51	–13
15	Ashton	42	13	10	19	62	63	49	–1
16	Ilkeston	42	12	13	17	48	51	49	–3
17	Gateshead	42	12	10	20	52	77	46	–25
18	Radcliffe	42	12	8	22	54	62	44	–8
19	Lincoln	42	10	14	18	44	64	44	–20
20	Wakefield	42	11	9	22	38	69	42	–31
21	Bradford	42	10	9	23	64	86	39	–22
22	Runcorn	42	6	11	25	36	108	29	–72

†Also promoted

SOUTHERN PREMIER DIVISION

		P	W	D	L	F	A	Pts	GD
1	Salisbury	42	30	5	7	83	27	95	56
2	Bath City	42	28	8	9	66	33	83	33
3	King's Lynn	42	25	7	10	73	41	82	32
4	Chippenham	42	22	11	9	69	45	77	24
5	Bedford†	42	22	10	10	69	53	76	16
6	Yate	42	21	5	16	78	74	68	4
7	Banbury	42	17	11	14	66	61	62	5
8	Halesowen	42	15	15	12	54	45	60	9
9	Merthyr	42	17	9	16	62	58	60	4
10	Mangotsfield	42	15	13	14	67	67	58	–
11	Grantham	42	15	11	16	49	49	56	–
12	Tiverton	42	14	10	18	69	65	52	4
13	Gloucester	42	14	10	18	57	60	52	–3
14	Hitchin	42	13	12	17	59	76	51	–17
15	Rugby	42	13	11	18	58	66	50	–8
16	Cheshunt	42	13	9	20	57	70	48	–13
17	Team Bath	42	14	6	22	55	68	48	–13
18	Cirencester	42	14	4	24	49	68	46	–19
19	Northwood	42	12	6	24	53	88	42	–35

		P	W	D	L	F	A	Pts	GD
20	Evesham	42	9	14	19	46	58	41	−12
21	Aylesbury	42	9	12	21	43	69	39	−26
22	Chesham	42	9	9	24	43	84	36	−41

†Also promoted

RYMAN PREMIER DIVISION

		P	W	D	L	F	A	Pts	GD
1	Braintree	42	28	10	4	74	32	94	42
2	Heybridge	42	28	3	11	70	46	87	24
3	Fisher†	42	26	7	9	84	46	85	38
4	Wimbledon	42	22	11	9	67	36	77	31
5	Hampton	42	24	3	15	73	54	75	19
6	Staines	42	20	10	12	74	56	70	18
7	Billericay	42	19	12	11	69	45	69	24
8	Worthing	42	19	10	13	71	60	67	11
9	Walton	42	19	7	16	55	50	64	5
10	Chelmsford	42	18	10	14	57	62	64	−5
11	Bromley	42	16	14	12	57	49	62	8
12	East Thurrock	42	18	5	19	60	60	59	−
13	Folkestone	42	16	10	16	47	51	58	−4
14	Margate	42	11	17	14	49	55	50	−6
15	Leyton	42	13	9	20	58	61	48	−3
16	Harrow	42	13	9	20	56	73	48	−17
17	Slough	42	13	8	21	63	75	47	−12
18	Wealdstone	42	13	5	24	68	82	44	−14
19	Hendon	42	9	12	21	44	64	39	−20
20	Maldon	42	8	11	23	41	73	35	−32
21	Windsor	42	8	8	26	37	75	32	−38
22	Redbridge	42	3	5	34	28	97	14	−69

†Also promoted

WELSH PREMIER LEAGUE

		P	W	D	L	F	A	Pts	GD
1	TNS	34	27	5	2	87	17	86	70
2	Llanelli	34	21	5	8	64	28	68	36
3	Rhyl	34	18	10	6	65	30	64	35
4	Carmarthen	34	17	6	11	62	42	57	20
5	Port Talbot	34	15	11	8	47	30	56	17
6	Welshpool	34	15	9	10	59	48	54	11
7	Aberystwyth	34	14	10	10	59	48	52	11
8	Haverfordwest	34	12	14	8	49	36	50	13
9	Bangor	34	14	3	17	51	54	45	−3
10	Caersws	34	11	12	11	44	56	45	−12
11	Porthmadog	34	12	8	14	57	59	44	−2
12	Connah's Quay	34	10	8	16	36	46	38	−10
13	Caernarfon	34	9	10	15	47	55	37	−8
14	Newtown	34	10	6	18	42	61	36	−19
15	Cefn Druids	34	7	11	16	42	58	32	−16
16	Airbus UK	34	8	8	18	35	60	32	−25
17	Cwmbran*	34	8	8	18	42	73	19	−31
18	Cardiff Grange**	34	4	4	26	23	110	15	−87

*Deducted 13 points. **Deducted 1 point

SCOT-ADS HIGHLAND LEAGUE

		P	W	D	L	F	A	Pts	GD
1	Deveronvale	28	20	4	4	77	29	64	48
2	Inverurie	28	19	3	6	72	26	60	46
3	Buckie	28	16	8	4	48	23	56	25
4	Forres	28	17	3	8	76	37	54	39
5	Keith	28	16	4	8	63	41	52	22
6	Huntly	28	15	6	7	66	41	51	25
7	Fraserburgh	28	13	6	9	68	45	45	23
8	Cove	28	12	6	10	55	46	42	9
9	Clachnacuddin	28	12	5	11	56	57	41	−1
10	Nairn	28	12	4	12	57	46	40	11
11	Rothes	28	9	1	18	48	75	28	−27
12	Wick	28	7	4	17	41	67	25	−26
13	Lossiemouth	28	7	4	17	40	97	25	−57
14	Brora	28	4	1	23	31	82	13	−51
15	Fort William	28	1	1	26	18	104	4	−86

BARCLAYS PREMIERSHIP RESERVE LEAGUE

NORTH

		P	W	D	L	F	A	Pts	GD
1	Manchester Utd.	28	19	2	7	68	32	59	36
2	Aston Villa	28	16	8	4	59	26	56	33
3	Manchester City	28	15	8	5	47	37	53	10
4	Middlesbrough	28	15	7	6	50	27	52	23
5	Newcastle Utd.	28	12	8	8	45	40	44	5
6	Liverpool	28	13	5	10	31	31	44	−
7	Sunderland	28	11	7	10	40	41	40	−1
8	Everton	28	10	8	10	31	35	38	−4
9	Leeds Utd.	28	9	11	8	27	31	38	−4
10	Blackburn Rov.	28	8	7	13	38	46	31	−8
11	Birmingham City	28	7	9	12	32	36	30	−4
12	Wolves	28	6	8	14	28	37	26	−9
13	Bolton Wand.	28	6	6	16	25	46	24	−21
14	W.B.A	28	6	6	16	26	55	24	−29
15	Wigan Athletic	28	5	4	19	24	51	19	−27

SOUTH

		P	W	D	L	F	A	Pts	GD
1	Tottenham	26	20	3	3	57	13	63	44
2	Southampton	26	16	3	7	50	26	51	24
3	Arsenal	26	14	7	5	60	34	49	26
4	Charlton Athletic	26	14	4	8	38	29	46	9
5	Coventry City	26	13	1	12	30	36	40	−6
6	Chelsea	26	10	9	7	34	24	39	10
7	Fulham	26	11	3	12	26	32	36	−6
8	Crystal Palace	26	10	5	11	43	42	35	1
9	Ipswich	26	10	1	15	44	54	31	−10
10	West Ham Utd.	26	7	8	11	37	38	29	−1
11	Leicester City	26	7	7	12	38	57	28	−19
12	Watford	26	8	3	15	25	51	27	−26
13	Portsmouth	26	6	4	16	35	54	22	−19
14	Norwich City	26	4	6	16	19	46	18	−27

PONTIN'S HOLIDAY'S LEAGUE

DIVISION ONE CENTRAL

		P	W	D	L	F	A	Pts	GD
1	Sheffield Wed.	18	10	5	3	26	13	35	13
2	Huddersfield Town	18	10	4	4	24	16	34	8
3	Oldham Athletic	18	9	5	4	29	17	32	12
4	Sheffield Utd.	18	9	3	6	42	28	30	14
5	Nottm. Forest	18	6	5	7	34	27	23	7
6	Stoke City	18	7	2	9	22	30	23	−8
7	Barnsley	18	6	4	8	26	33	22	−7
8	Walsall	18	6	3	9	29	41	21	−12
9	Rotherham	18	3	8	7	26	30	17	−4
10	Bradford City	18	3	3	12	19	42	12	−23

DIVISION ONE WEST

		P	W	D	L	F	A	Pts	GD
1	Carlisle Utd.	18	11	4	3	39	16	37	23
2	Bury	18	9	4	5	31	25	31	6
3	Preston N.E.	18	7	8	3	32	22	29	10
4	Tranmere Rov.	18	7	7	4	30	26	28	4
5	Blackpool	18	8	1	9	31	31	25	0
6	Shrewsbury Town	18	6	6	6	23	25	24	−2
7	Rochdale	18	7	1	10	23	35	22	−12
8	Chester City	18	4	6	8	21	30	18	−9
9	Burnley	18	5	5	8	26	31	17	−5
10	Wrexham	18	3	4	11	22	37	13	−15

DIVISION ONE EAST

		P	W	D	L	F	A	Pts	GD
1	Doncaster Rov.	18	11	3	4	34	16	36	18
2	Sheffield Utd.	18	10	1	7	39	27	31	12
3	Hull City	18	8	7	3	28	24	31	4
4	Lincoln City	18	7	6	5	29	28	27	1
5	Darlington	18	8	3	7	24	38	27	−14
6	Scarborough	18	7	5	6	31	26	26	5
7	York City	18	8	2	8	26	23	26	3
8	Hartlepool Utd.	18	7	4	7	33	24	25	9
9	Scunthorpe Utd.	18	4	4	10	16	26	16	−10
10	Grimsby Town	18	0	5	13	17	45	5	−28

PONTINS HOLIDAY'S COMBINATION

CENTRAL DIVISION

		P	W	D	L	F	A	Pts	GD
1	Reading	16	12	2	2	48	10	38	38
2	Millwall	16	10	2	4	37	21	32	16
3	Brighton & H.A.	16	9	2	5	40	21	29	19
4	Gillingham	16	8	3	5	25	25	27	−
5	Q.P.R.	16	5	6	5	30	26	21	4
6	Wycombe Wand.	16	6	1	9	27	26	19	1
7	Aldershot	16	5	1	10	24	42	16	−18
8	Crawley	16	4	0	12	23	39	12	−16
9	Woking	16	3	3	10	12	56	12	−44

WALES AND WEST DIVISION

		P	W	D	L	F	A	Pts	GD
1	Cheltenham Town	16	13	2	1	33	17	41	16
2	Cardiff City	16	9	4	3	28	14	31	14
3	Swindon Town	16	7	4	5	36	25	25	11
4	Bristol City	16	7	4	5	27	20	25	7
5	Yeovil Town	16	5	4	7	33	26	19	7
6	Bristol Rov.	16	5	3	8	29	26	18	3
7	Plymouth Argyle	16	4	6	6	23	24	18	–1
8	Bournemouth	16	5	2	9	30	37	17	–7
9	Swansea City	16	2	1	13	20	70	7	–50

EAST DIVISION

		P	W	D	L	F	A	Pts	GD
1	Luton Town	16	12	2	2	44	19	38	25
2	Northampton Town	16	10	3	3	34	13	33	21
3	Colchester Utd.	16	10	3	3	33	21	33	12
4	MK Dons	16	7	5	4	27	18	26	9
5	Southend Utd.	16	6	2	8	20	25	20	–5
6	Leyton Orient	16	5	1	10	20	31	16	–11
7	Barnet	16	5	1	10	25	40	16	–15
8	Stevenage	16	5	1	10	15	30	16	–15
9	Oxford Utd.	16	1	5	10	13	33	8	–20

F.A. WOMEN'S PREMIER LEAGUE

		P	W	D	L	F	A	Pts	GD
1	Arsenal	18	16	2	0	83	20	50	63
2	Everton	18	14	2	2	46	20	44	26
3	Charlton Athletic	18	12	3	3	41	13	39	28
4	Doncaster Rov.	18	7	2	9	32	34	23	–2
5	Bristol Academy	18	4	8	6	19	29	20	–10
6	Birmingham City	18	6	2	10	24	40	20	–16
7	Leeds Utd.	18	4	6	8	27	36	18	–9
8	Fulham	18	4	2	12	24	45	14	–21
9	Sunderland	18	3	4	11	22	57	13	–35
10	Chelsea	18	3	3	12	22	46	12	–24

QUOTE-UNQUOTE

'This is for the benefit of everyone connected with English football, especially the fans' – **Brian Barwick**, chief executive of the F.A. on Sven-Goran Eriksson stepping down after the World Cup.

'In simple terms, we have taken some pain now for long-term gain' – **Peter Kenyon**, Chelsea chief executive, after the club posted a record annual loss of £140m.

'My wife will be glad about Mourinho coming to Bramall Lane because he's a good-looking swine, isn't he?' – **Neil Warnock**, Sheffield United manager, after promotion to the Premiership.

'If we were a book in a bookshop we wouldn't be filed under fact, it would have to be fiction' – **Paul Jewell**, Wigan manager, on the club's remarkable rise.

'He has a big smile on his face because he knows what it's like to get up and six in the morning and work in a warehouse' – **Steve Bruce**, Birmingham manager, on Dudley Campbell's rise from Ryman League football to the Premiership.

IRISH FOOTBALL 2005-06

EIRCOM LEAGUE

PREMIER DIVISION

		P	W	D	L	F	A	Pts
1	Cork City	33	22	8	3	53	18	74
2	Derry City	33	22	6	5	56	25	72
3	Shelbourne	33	20	7	6	62	25	67
4	Drogheda Utd.	33	12	12	9	40	33	48
5	Longford Town	33	12	9	12	29	32	45
6	Bohemians	33	13	6	14	42	47	45
7	Bray Wand.	33	11	6	16	40	57	39
8	Waterford Utd.	33	9	7	17	30	49	34
9	U.C.D.	33	7	12	14	28	44	33
10	St Patrick's Ath.	33	7	11	15	26	36	32
11	Shamrock Rov.*	33	9	8	16	33	52	27
12	Finn Harps	33	5	6	22	30	51	21

(* Deducted 8 points)

Leading Scorer: 22 Jason Byrne (Shelbourne). **Player of Year:** Mark Farren (Derry City). **Young Player of Year:** Pat McCourt (Derry City). **Personality of Year:** Damien Richardson (Cork City). **Goalkeeper of Year:** Michael Devine (Cork City).

FIRST DIVISION

		P	W	D	L	F	A	Pts
1	Sligo Rov.	36	15	16	5	45	27	61
2	Dublin City	36	15	14	7	57	34	59
3	Cobh Ramblers	36	15	11	10	49	40	56
4	Kilkenny City	36	15	8	12	46	33	53
5	Galway Utd.	36	14	11	11	46	43	53
6	Dundalk	36	12	13	11	44	40	49
7	Limerick F.C.	36	13	9	14	44	49	48
8	Kildare County	36	10	11	15	33	42	41
9	Monaghan Utd.	36	9	9	18	36	66	36
10	Athlone Town	36	6	10	20	28	52	28

Leading Scorer: 17 Kieran O'Reilly (Cobh Ramblers). **Player of Year:** Kieran O'Reilly.

FAI CARLSBERG CUP FINAL

Cork City 0, **Drogheda Utd.** 2 (Whelan, O'Brien) – Lansdowne Road, December 4, 2005.

Cork City: Devine, Horgan, Bennett, Murray, Woods, Gamble, O'Halloran (O'Brien), O'Callaghan, Kearney, Fenn (Behan), O'Flynn.

Drogheda Utd: Connor, Lynch, Gartland, Gray, Webb, Robinson, Whelan, Bradley (Keegan), Sandvliet, Ristilla (Rooney), O'Brien (Bernard).

Referee: I. Stokes (Dublin).

EIRCOM LEAGUE CUP FINAL

Derry City 2 (Murphy, McWalter og), **UCD** 1 (Byrne) – Belfield Park, September 20, 2005.

SETANTA SPORTS CUP FINAL

Drogheda Utd. 1 (Leech), **Cork City** 0 (aet) – Tolka Park, Dublin, April 22, 2006.

CARNEGIE IRISH LEAGUE

PREMIER DIVISION

		P	W	D	L	F	A	Pts
1	Linfield	30	23	6	1	88	23	75
2	Glentoran	30	19	6	5	60	27	63
3	Portadown	30	16	6	8	56	36	54
4	Dungannon Swifts	30	13	10	7	60	41	49
5	Cliftonville	30	13	8	9	45	35	47
6	Newry City	30	12	9	9	45	35	45
7	Ballymena Utd.	30	13	6	11	42	48	45
8	Lisburn Distillery	30	12	8	10	44	38	44
9	Coleraine	30	11	4	15	40	57	37
10	Limavady	30	9	9	12	42	49	36
11	Loughall	30	9	7	14	33	38	34
12	Larne	30	7	9	14	42	63	30
13	Glenavon	30	7	9	14	35	59	30
14	Armagh City	30	9	3	18	38	69	30
15	Institute	30	6	8	16	37	58	26
16	Ards	30	6	2	22	31	62	20

Leading Scorer: 26 Peter Thompson (Linfield). **Player of Year:** Glenn Ferguson (Linfield). **Young Player of Year:** Philip Simpson (Glentoran). **Manager of Year:** David Jeffrey (Linfield)

FIRST DIVISION

		P	W	D	L	F	A	Pts
1	Crusaders	22	20	1	1	51	13	61
2	Donegal Celtic	22	13	5	4	41	25	44
3	Dundela	22	10	5	7	32	28	35
4	Bangor	22	10	3	9	42	32	33
5	Banbridge Town	22	8	6	8	29	29	30
6	Tobermore Utd.	22	8	5	9	33	37	29
7	Carrick Rangers	22	8	4	10	25	29	28
8	Coagh Utd.	22	8	3	11	25	26	27
9	Harland&Wolff	22	7	4	11	21	31	25
10	Moyola Park	22	7	3	12	32	50	24
11	Ballyclare Coms.	22	6	5	11	32	37	23
12	Ballymoney Utd.	22	3	4	15	18	44	13

Leading Scorer: 13 David Rainey (Crusaders).

NATIONWIDE IRISH CUP FINAL

Linfield 2 (Thompson 2), **Glentoran** 1 (Halliday) – Windsor Park, May 6, 2006

Linfield: Mannus, McShane, Murphy, Mouncey, Kearney (McCann), Ervin, Gault, McAreavy (Hunter), Ferguson, Thompson, Bailie.

Glentoran: Morris, Melaugh, Simpson, Glendinning, Lockhart, Berry (Tolan), McDonagh, Nixon, Ward, Halliday, Browne (Morgan),

Referee: M. Ross (Carrickfergus).

CIS LEAGUE CUP FINAL

Linfield 3 (Ferguson 3), **Glentoran** 0 – Windsor Park, December 10, 2005.

COUNTY ANTRIM SHIELD FINAL

Linfield 2 (Kearney, Ferguson), **Ballymena Utd.** 1 (Kelbie) – Seaview, February 7, 2006.

QUOTE-UNQUOTE

'I've walked into restaurants with my wife to the roar of 'Psycho! Psycho! and they expect me to respond with a two-fisted salute. I just put my head down in embarrassment and walk past' – **Stuart Pearce**, Manchester City manager.

'I should be the happiest manager in the world and I am not. This is the worst club in the world to be a manager. You can win, you can achieve, but it is never enough. I thought a couple of times about closing the door and saying goodbye at the end of the season' – **Jose Mourinho** puts something of a damper on Chelsea's second successive Premiership title.

'The person who got the medal will have a fantastic memory, or he goes to eBay and makes a fortune' – **Jose Mounrinho**, in lighter vein, on the lucky fan who caught the championship medal he threw into the crowd at Stamford Bridge.

'It's clearly in an offside position' – **Graham Taylor**, Five Live match summariser, as a squirrel on the pitch interrupts the Arsenal-Villarreal Champions League semi-final at Highbury.

'It wasn't a monkey off our backs, it was the whole Planet of the Apes' – **Mick McCarthy**, former Sunderland manager, after a run of 26 Premiership matches without a win ends with a 2-0 success against Middlesbrough.

'I would like to be here winning trophies for 20 years, for sure' – **Rafael Benitez**, Liverpool manager.

'I've seen the money they are making at our level and I can only imagine the money they are making at the Premiership level!' – **Mike Newell**, Luton manager, claiming bungs are still rife in the game.

'I am not an expert on football, but then I wasn't an expert on shipyards, refineries or entertainment' – **Peter de Savary**, multi-millionaire entrepreneur, after taking over as Millwall chairman.

'What are you meant to do? Smile sweetly and jog back to the half-way line' – **Gary Neville**, Manchester United captain, defending his over-the-top celebrations in front of Liverpool fans after Rio Ferdinand's last-minute winner at Old Trafford.

'Being a robot, devoid of passion and spirit, is obviously the way forward for the modern-day footballer and I ask the authorities where is football being taken?' – **Gary Neville** after being fined £5,000 by the F.A.

UEFA CHAMPIONS LEAGUE 2005-06

FIRST QUALIFYING ROUND, FIRST LEG

Glentoran 1 (Ward 78), **Shelbourne** 2 (Byrne 55, 65 pen). Att: 2,500. **Liverpool** 3 (Gerrard 8, 21, 89), **Total Network Solutions** 0. Att: 44,760.

FIRST QUALIFYING ROUND, SECOND LEG

Shelbourne 4 (Heary 14, Byrne 32 pen, 71, Crowe 58), **Glentoran** 1 (McCann 21). Att: 6,000 (**Shelbourne** won 6-2 on agg). **Total Network Solutions** 0, **Liverpool** 3 (Cisse 26, Gerrard 85, 86). Att: 8,009 – played at Wrexham (**Liverpool** won 6-0 on agg).

FIRST QUALIFYING ROUND (ON AGGREGATE)

Anorthosis Famagusta 2, Dinamo Minsk 1; Artmedia Bratislava 4, Kairat Almaty 3 (aet); Dinamo Tbilisi 2, Levadia Tallinn 1; Dudelange 4, Zrinjski Mostar 1 (aet); FBK Kaunas 8, Torshavn 2; Haka 3, Pyunik Yerevan 2; Neftchi Baku 4, Hafnarfjordur 1; Rabotnicki Skopje 6, Skonto Riga 1; Sheriff Tiraspol 6, Sliema Wdrs 1; SK Tirana 3, Gorica 2.

SECOND QUALIFYING ROUND, FIRST LEG

Artmedia Bratislava 5 (Helledrand 43, 75, 90, Vascak 57, Mikulic 78), **Celtic** 0. Att: 17,262. FBK Kaunas 1 (Barevicius 21), **Liverpool** 3 (Cisse 27, Carragher 30, Gerrard 54 pen). Att: 8,300. **Shelbourne** 0, Steaua Bucharest 0. Att: 8,000.

SECOND QUALIFYING ROUND, SECOND LEG

Celtic 4 (Thompson 22 pen, Hartson 45, McManus 54, Beattie 82), Artmedia Bratislava 0. Att: 50,063 (Artmedia Bratislava won 5-4 on agg). **Liverpool** 2 (Gerrard 77, Cisse 86), FBK Kaunas 0. Att: 43,717 (**Liverpool** won 5-1 on agg). Steaua Bucharest 4 (Nicolita 20, Iacob 26, Dinita 62, Oprita 90 pen), **Shelbourne** 1 (Byrne 39). Att: 10,000 (Steaua Bucharest won 4-1 on agg).

SECOND QUALIFYING ROUND (ON AGGREGATE)

Anderlecht 5, Neftchi Baku 1; Anorthosis Famagusta 3, Trabzonspor 2; Brondby 5, Dinamo Tbilisi 1; CSKA Sofia 4, SK Tirana 0; Debrecen 8, Hajduk Split 0; FC Thun 3, Dynamo Kiev 2; Lokomotiv Moskow 3, Rabotnicki Skopje 1; Malmo 5, Maccabi Haifa 4; Partizan Belgrade 2, Sheriff Tiraspol 0; Rapid Vienna 9, Dudelange 3; Valerenga 5, Haka 1.

THIRD QUALIFYING ROUND, FIRST LEG

Anorthosis Famagusta 1 (Frousos 72), **Rangers** 2 (Novo 64, Ricksen 71). Att: 16,900. CSKA Sofia 1 (Dimitrov 45), **Liverpool** 0 (Morientes 31, 58, Cisse 25). Att: 16,512. **Everton** 1 (Beattie 42), Villarreal 2 (Figueroa 27, Josico 45). Att: 37,685. **Manchester Utd.** 3 (Rooney 7, Van Nistelrooy 49, Ronaldo 63), Debrecen 0. Att: 51,701.

THIRD QUALIFYING ROUND, SECOND LEG

Debrecen 0, **Manchester Utd.** 3 (Heinze 20, 61, Richardson 65). Att: 27,000 (**Manchester Utd.** won 6-0 on agg). **Liverpool** 0, CSKA Sofia 1 (Iliev 16). Att: 42,175 (**Liverpool** won 3-2 on agg). **Rangers** 2 (Buffel 39, Prso 58), Anorthosis Famagusta 0.

Att: 48,500 (**Rangers** won 4-1 on agg). Villarreal 2 (Soron 21, Forlan 90), **Everton** 1 (Arteta 69). Att: 22, 000 (Villarreal won 4-2 on agg).

THIRD QUALIFYING ROUND (ON AGGREGATE)

Ajax 5, Brondby 3; Anderlect 4, Slavia Prague 1; Artmedia Bratislava O Partizan Belgrade O (aet, Artmedia Bratislava won 4-3 on pens); FC Bruges 1, Valerenga 1 (aet, FC Bruges won 4-3 on pens); FC Thun 4, Malmo 4; Inter Milan 3, Shakhtar Donetsk 1; Panathinaikos 5, Wisla Krakow 4 (aet); Rapid Vienna 2, Lokomotiv Moscow 1; Real Betis 3, Monaco 2; Rosenborg 4, Steaua Bucharest 3; Werder Bremen 4, Basle 2; Udinese 4, Sporting Lisbon 2.

GROUP STAGE

GROUP A

September 14, 2005
FC Bruges 1 (Matondo 85), **Juventus** 2 (Nedved 66, Trezeguet 75). Att: 29,975.
Rapid Vienna O, **Bayern Munich** 1 (Guerrero 60). Att: 49,000.

September 27, 2005
Bayern Munich 1 (Demichelis 32), **FC Bruges** O. Att: 65,527.
Juventus 3 (Trezeguet 27, Mutu 82, Ibrahimovic 85), **Rapid Vienna** O. Att: 49,521.

October 18, 2005
Bayern Munich 2 (Deisler 32, Demichelis 39), **Juventus** 1 (Ibrahimovic 90). Att: 60,000.
Rapid Vienna O, **FC Bruges** 1 (Balaban 75). Att: 45,000.

November 2, 2005
FC Bruges 3 (Portillo 8, Balaban 25, Verheyen 63), **Rapid Vienna** 2 (Kincl 1, Adamski 81). Att: 26,000.
Juventus 2 (Trezeguet 61, 85), **Bayern Munich** 1 (Deisler 66). Att: 19,000.

November 22, 2005
Bayern Munich 4 (Deisler 21, Karimi 54, Makaay 72, 76), **Rapid Vienna** O. Att: 66,000.
Juventus 1 (Del Piero 80), **FC Bruges** O. Att: 35,000.

December 7, 2005
FC Bruges 1 (Portillo 32), **Bayern Munich** 1 (Pizarro 21). Att: 27,860.
Rapid Vienna 1 (Kincl 52), **Juventus** 3 (Del Piero 35, 45, Ibrahimovic 41). Att: 46,500.

FINAL TABLE

	P	W	D	L	F	A	Pts
JUVENTUS	6	5	0	1	12	5	15
BAYERN MUNICH	6	4	1	1	10	4	13
FC Bruges	6	2	1	3	6	7	7
Rapid Vienna	6	0	0	6	3	15	0

GROUP B

September 14, 2005
Arsenal 2 (Gilberto Silva 51, Bergkamp 90), **FC Thun** 1 (Ferreira 53). Att: 34,498.
Arsenal (4-4-2): Alumunia, Lauren, Toure, Campbell, Cole, Ljungberg (Hleb 81), Fabregas (Bergkamp 72), Gilberto Silva, Pires, Van Persie, Reyes (Owusu 81). **Sent-off:** Van Persie.

Sparta Prague 1 (Matusovic 66), **Ajax** 1 (Sneijder 90). Att: 19,500.

September 27, 2005
Ajax 1 (Rosenberg 71), **Arsenal** 2 (Ljungberg 2, Pires 69 pen). Att: 50,000.
Arsenal (4-4-2): Almunia, Lauren, Toure, Campbell, Cole, Hleb (Cygan 90), Fabregas, Flamini, Pires (Clichy 88), Ljungberg, Reyes (Owusu 81).
FC Thun 1 (Hodzic 89), **Sparta Prague** 0. Att: 10,300.

October 18, 2005
Ajax 2 (Anastasiou 36, 55), **FC Thun** 0. Att: 50,000.
Sparta Prague 0, **Arsenal** 2 (Henry 21, 74). Att: 12,528.
Arsenal (4-4-2): Lehmann, Lauren, Toure, Cygan, Clichy, Fabregas (Owusu 87), Flamini, Gilberto Silva, Pires, Reyes (Henry 15), Van Persie (Eboue 73).

November 2, 2005
Arsenal 3 (Henry 23, Van Persie 81, 86), **Sparta Prague** 0. Att: 35,155.
Arsenal (4-4-2): Almunia, Lauren, Toure, Campbell, Clichy, Pires (Fabregas 73), Flamini, Gilberto Silva, Reyes (Eboue 82), Bergkamp, Henry (Van Persie 67).
FC Thun 2 (Lustrinelli 56, Spadoto 74), **Ajax** 4 (Sneijder 26, Anastasiou 63, De Jong 90, Boukhari 90). Att: 31,340.

November 22, 2005
Ajax 2 (De Jong 68, 89), **Sparta Prague** 1 (Petras 90). Att: 42,000.
FC Thun 0, **Arsenal** 1 (Pires 88 pen). Att: 32,000.
Arsenal (4-4-2): Almunia, Eboue, Senderos, Campbell, Cygan (Lauren 87), Ljungberg, Song (Fabregas 57), Flamini, Reyes, Van Persie, Henry (Pires 71).

December 7, 2005
Arsenal 0, **Ajax** 0. Att: 35,376.
Arsenal (4-4-2): Almunia, Eboue, Toure, Senderos, Lauren (Gilbert 75), Owusu, Larsson, Flamini, Hleb (Fabregas 62), Reyes (Van Persie 65),Henry.
Sparta Prague 0, **FC Thun** 0. Att: 9,233.

FINAL TABLE

	P	W	D	L	F	A	Pts
ARSENAL	6	5	1	0	10	2	16
AJAX	6	3	2	1	10	6	11
FC Thun	6	1	1	4	4	9	4
Sparta Prague	6	0	2	4	2	9	2

GROUP C

September 14, 2005
Udinese 3 (Iaquinta 28, 73, 76), **Panathinaikos** 0. Att: 41,652.
Werder Bremen 0, **Barcelona** 2 (Deco 13, Ronaldinho 77 pen). Att: 42,466.

September 27, 2005
Barcelona 4 (Ronaldinho 13, 32, 90 pen, Deco 41), **Udinese** 1 (Felipe 24). Att: 70,000.
Panathinaikos 2 (Gonzalez 6 pen, Mantzios 8), **Werder Bremen** 1 (Klose 41). Att: 50,000.

October 18, 2005
Panathinaikos 0, **Barcelona** 0. Att: 65,000.
Udinese 1 (Di Natale 86), **Werder Bremen** 1 (Felipe 64 og). Att: 43,952

November 2, 2005
Barcelona 5 (Van Bommel 1, Eto'o 14, 40, 65, Messi 34), **Panathinaikos** 0. Att: 75,000.
Werder Bremen 4 (Klose 15, Baumann 24, Micoud 51, 67), **Udinese** 3 (Di Natale 54, 57, Schulz 60 og). Att: 35,211.

November 22, 2005
Barcelona 3 (Gabri 14, Ronaldinho 26, Larsson 71), **Werder Bremen** 1 (Borowski 22 pen). Att: 85,000.
Panathinaikos 1 (Charalambidis 45), **Udinese** 2 (Iaquinto 80, Candela 83). Att: 35,000.

December 7, 2005
Udinese 0, **Barcelona** 2 (Ezquerro 86, Iniesta 90). Att: 28,000.
Werder Bremen 5 (Micoud 2 pen, Valdez 28, 32, Klose 51, Frings 90), **Panathinaikos** 1 (Morris 53). Att: 38,000.

FINAL TABLE

	P	W	D	L	F	A	Pts
BARCELONA	6	5	1	0	16	2	16
WERDER BREMEN	6	2	1	3	12	12	7
Udinese	6	2	1	3	10	12	7
Panathinaikos	6	1	1	4	4	16	4

GROUP D

September 14, 2005
Benfica 1 (Miccoli 90), **Lille** 0. Att: 38,000.
Villarreal 0, **Manchester Utd.** 0. Att: 22,000.
Manchester Utd. (4-4-1-1): Van der Sar, O'Shea, Ferdinand, Silvestre, Heinze (Richardson 33), Fletcher, Smith, Scholes, Ronaldo (Giggs 80), Rooney, Van Nistelrooy (Ji-Sung Park 80). **Sent-off:** Rooney.

September 27, 2005
Lille 0, **Villarreal** 0. Att: 50,000.
Manchester Utd. 2 (Giggs 39, Van Nistelrooy 85), **Benfica** 1 (Simao 59). Att: 66,112.
Manchester Utd. (4-2-3-1): Van der Sar, Bardsley, Ferdinand, O'Shea, Richardson, Fletcher, Smith, Ronaldo, Scholes, Giggs, Van Nistelrooy.

October 18, 2005
Manchester Utd. 0, **Lille** 0. Att: 60,626.
Manchester Utd. (4-4-1-1): Van der Sar, Bardsley, Ferdinand, Silvestre, O'Shea, Ronaldo, Fletcher, Smith, Giggs (Ji-Sung Park 83), Scholes, Van Nistelrooy. **Sent-off:** Scholes.
Villarreal 1 (Riquelme 73 pen), **Benfica** 1 (Manuel 77). Att: 24,500.

November 2, 2005
Benfica 0, **Villarreal** 1 (Senna 82). Att: 30,000.
Lille 1 (Acimovic 38), **Manchester Utd.** 0. Att: 65,000.
Manchester Utd. (4-3-3): Van der Sar, O'Shea, Ferdinand, Brown, Silvestre, Fletcher, Smith, Richardson (Ji-Sung Park 65), Ronaldo (Rossi 90), Van Nistelrooy, Rooney.

November 22, 2005
Lille 0, **Benfica** 0. Att: 60,000.
Manchester Utd. 0, **Villarreal** 0. Att: 67,471.
Manchester Utd. (4-4-2): Van der Sar, Brown (Neville 73), Ferdinand, Silvestre, O'Shea, Fletcher (Ji-Sung Park 53), Smith (Saha 81), Scholes, Ronaldo, Rooney, Van Nistelrooy.

December 7, 2005
Benfica 2 (Geovanni 16, Beto 34), **Manchester Utd.** 1 (Scholes 6). Att: 61,000.
Manchester Utd. (4-4-2): Van der Sar, Neville, Ferdinand, Silvestre, O'Shea, Ronaldo (Ji-Sung Park 53), Smith, Scholes, Giggs (Saha 60), Rooney, Van Nistelrooy.
Villarreal 1 (Guayre 67), **Lille** 0. Att: 22,500.

FINAL TABLE

	P	W	D	L	F	A	Pts
VILLARREAL	6	2	4	0	3	1	10
BENFICA	6	2	2	2	5	5	8
Lille	6	1	3	2	1	2	6
Manchester Utd.	6	1	3	2	3	4	6

GROUP E

September 13, 2005
AC Milan 3 (Kaka 18, 86, Shevchenko 89), **Fenerbahce** 1 (Alex 63 pen). Att: 75,000.
PSV Eindhoven 1 (Vennegoor of Hesselink 33), **Schalke** 0. Att: 33,500.

September 28, 2005
Fenerbahce 3 (Alex 41 pen, 68, Appiah 90), **PSV Eindhoven** 0. Att: 21,895.
Schalke 2 (Larsen 3, Altintop 70), **AC Milan** 2 (Seedorf 1, Shevchenko 59). Att: 60,000.

October 19, 2005
AC Milan 0, **PSV Eindhoven** 0. Att: 69,763.
Fenerbahce 3 (Luciano 14, Marcio Nobre 73, Appiah 79), **Schalke** 3 (Lincoln 59, 62, Kuranyi 77). Att: 50,000.

November 1, 2005
PSV Eindhoven 1 (Farfan 12), **AC Milan** 0. Att: 35,500.
Schalke 2 (Kuranyi 32, Sand 90), **Fenerbahce** 0. Att: 59,000.

November 23, 2005
Fenerbahce 0, **AC Milan** 4 (Shevchenko 16, 52, 70, 76). Att: 50,000.
Schalke 3 (Kobiashvili 18 pen, 73, 79 pen), **PSV Eindhoven** 0. Att: 30,000.

December 6, 2005
AC Milan 3 (Pirlo 42, Kaka 52, 60), **Schalke** 2 (Poulsen 44, Lincoln 66). Att: 82,000.
PSV Eindhoven 2 (Cocu 14, Farfan 85), **Fenerbahce** 0. Att: 30,000.

FINAL TABLE

	P	W	D	L	F	A	Pts
AC MILAN	6	3	2	1	12	6	11
PSV EINDHOVEN	6	3	1	2	4	8	10
Schalke	6	2	2	2	12	9	8
Fenerbahce	6	1	1	4	7	14	4

GROUP F

September 13, 2005
Lyon 3 (Carew 21, Juninho 26, Wiltord 31), **Real Madrid** 0. Att: 39,500.
Olympiakos 1 (Lago 19 og), **Rosenborg** 3 (Skjelbred 43, Mavrogenidis 47 og, Storflor 90). Att: 30,000

September 28, 2005
Real Madrid 2 (Raul 9, Soldado 87), **Olympiakos** 1 (Kafes 47). Att: 52,000.
Rosenborg 0, **Lyon** 1 (Cris 45). Att: 20,620.

October 19, 2005
Lyon 2 (Juninho 4, Govou 89), **Olympiakos** 1 (Kafes 84). Att: 40,000.
Real Madrid 4 (Woodgate 48, Raul 52, Helguera 68, Beckham 82), **Rosenborg** 1 (Strand 40). Att: 69,053.

November 1, 2005
Olympiakos 1 (Babangida 3), **Lyon** 4 (Juninho 41, Carew 43, 57, Diarra 55). Att: 29,555.
Rosenborg 0, **Real Madrid** 2 (Dorsin 26 og, Guti 41). Att: 20,122.

November 23, 2005
Real Madrid 1 (Guti 41), **Lyon** 1 (Carew 72). Att: 59,000.
Rosenborg 1 (Helstad 88), **Olympiakos** 1 (Rivaldo 25). Att: 17,450.

December 6, 2005
Lyon 2 (Benzema 33, Fred 90), **Rosenborg** 1 (Braaten 68). Att: 40,000.
Olympiakos 2 (Bulut 50, Rivaldo 87), **Real Madrid** 1 (Sergio 7). Att: 31,456.

FINAL TABLE

	P	W	D	L	F	A	Pts
LYON	6	5	1	0	13	4	16
REAL MADRID	6	3	1	2	10	8	10
Rosenborg	6	1	1	4	6	11	4
Olympiakos	6	1	1	4	7	13	4

GROUP G

September 13, 2005
Chelsea 1 (Lampard 19), **Anderlecht** 0. Att: 29,575.
Chelsea (4-3-3): Cech, Paulo Ferreira, Ricardo Carvalho, Terry, Gallas, Makelele, Lampard, Essien (Huth 90), Duff (J. Cole 76), Drogba, Robben (Wright-Phillips 66).
Real Betis 1 (Arzu 51), **Liverpool** 2 (Sinama-Pongolle 2, Luis Garcia 14). Att: 45,000.
Liverpool (4-4-1-1): Reina, Josemi, Carragher, Hyypia, Traore, Sinama-Pongolle (Gerrard 74), Sissoko, Xabi Alonso, Zenden (Riise 66), Luis Garcia, Crouch (Cisse 59).

September 28, 2005
Anderlecht 0, **Real Betis** 1 (Oliveira 69). Att: 27,500.
Liverpool 0, **Chelsea** 0. Att: 42,743.
Liverpool (4-2-3-1): Reina, Finnan, Carragher, Hyypia, Traore, Hamann, Xabi Alonso, Cisse (Sinama-Pongolle 77), Gerrard, Luis Garcia, Crouch.
Chelsea (4-3-3): Cech, Paulo Ferreira, Ricardo Carvalho, Terry, Gallas, Makelele, Lampard, Essien, Duff (Crespo 74), Drogba (Huth 90), Robben (Wright-Phillips 64).

October 19, 2005
Anderlecht 0, **Liverpool** 1 (Cisse 20). Att: 25,000.
Liverpool (4-4-1-1): Reina, Josemi, Carragher, Hyypia, Traore, Sissoko (Zenden 82), Xabi Alonso, Hamann, Riise (Warnock 88), Luis Garcia, Cisse (Kewell 74).
Chelsea 4 (Drogba 24, Ricardo Carvalho 44, Cole 59, Crespo 64), **Real Betis** 0. Att: 36,457.
Chelsea (4-3-3): Cudicini, Gallas, Ricardo Carvalho, Terry, Del Horno, Essien, Makelele (Diarra 76), Lampard, Wright-Phillips (Gudjohnsen 67), Drogba (Crespo 46), J. Cole.

November 1, 2005
Liverpool 3 (Morientes 34, Luis Garcia 61, Cisse 89), **Anderlecht** 0. Att: 42,607.
Liverpool (4-4-2): Reina, Finnan, Carragher, Hyypia, Riise, Gerrard (Kewell 79), Sissoko,
Xabi Alonso, Luis Garcia, Morientes (Zenden 52), Crouch (Cisse 72).
Real Betis 1 (Dani 28), **Chelsea** 0. Att: 55,000.
Chelsea (4-3-3): Cech, Paulo Ferreira, Ricardo Carvalho, Terry, Gallas, Essien, Makelele,
Lampard, J. Cole (Wright-Phillips 46), Gudjohnsen (Drogba 46), Robben (Duff 65).

November 23, 2005
Anderlecht 0, **Chelsea** 2 (Crespo 8, Ricardo Carvalho 15). Att: 21,070
Chelsea (4-3-3): Cech, Gallas, Ricardo Carvalho, Terry, Del Horno, Essien
Lampard, Gudjohnsen (Geremi 78), J. Cole (Diarra 63), Crespo (C. Cole 86), Duff.
Liverpool 0, **Real Betis** 0. Att: 42,077.
Liverpool (4-4-2): Reina, Finnan, Carragher, Hyypia, Riise, Gerrard (Potter 90), Sissoko,
Hamann, Zenden, Crouch (Kewell 83), Morientes (Cisse 67).

December 6, 2005
Chelsea 0, **Liverpool** 0. Att: 41,598.
Chelsea (4-3-3): Cech, Paulo Ferreira (Del Horno 46), Ricardo Carvalho, Terry, Gallas,
Gudjohnsen, Essien, Lampard, Duff (Wright-Phillips 73), Drogba, Robben (C. Cole 73).
Liverpool (4-4-2): Reina, Finnan, Carragher, Hyypia, Traore, Gerrard, Sissoko, Hamann,
Riise (Kewell 61), Luis Garcia (Sinama-Pongolle 80), Crouch (Morientes 68).
Real Betis 0, **Anderlecht** 1 (Kompany 44). Att: 55,259.

FINAL TABLE

	P	W	D	L	F	A	Pts
LIVERPOOL	6	3	3	0	6	1	12
CHELSEA	6	3	2	1	7	1	11
Real Betis	6	2	1	3	3	7	7
Anderlecht	6	1	0	5	1	8	3

GROUP H

September 13, 2005
Artmedia Bratislava 0, **Inter Milan** 1 (Cruz 17). Att: 27,000.
Rangers 3 (Lovenkrands 35, Prso 59, Kyrgiakos 85), **FC Porto** 2 (Pepe 47, 71).
Att: 48,599.
Rangers (4-4-2): Waterreus, Ricksen, Kyrgiakos, Rodriguez, Bernard, Namouchi (Novo
72), Murray, Ferguson, Lovenkrands (Buffel 55), Jeffers (Thompson 84), Prso.

September 28, 2005
FC Porto 2 (Gonzalez 32, Diego 39), **Artmedia Bratislava** 3 (Petras 45, Kozak 54, Borbely
74). Att: 48,000.
Inter Milan 1 (Pizarro 49), **Rangers** 0 – played behind close doors.
Rangers (4-4-1-1): Waterreus, Ricksen, Kyrgiakos, Rodriguez, Bernard, Namouchi
(Thomson 89), Murray (Nieto 84), Ferguson, Lovenkrands, Buffel (Jeffers 77), Prso.

October 19, 2005
FC Porto 2 (Materazzi 22 og, McCarthy 35), **Inter Milan** 0. Att: 25,000.
Rangers 0, **Artmedia Bratislava** 0. Att: 49,018.
Rangers (4-4-2): Waterreus, Ricksen, Rodriguez, Kyrgiakos (Andrews 57), Bernard,
Namouchi (Burke 74), Ferguson, Hemdani, Lovenkrands, Nieto (Thompson 38), Prso.

November 1, 2005
Artmedia Bratislava 2 (Borbely 8, Kozak 59), **Rangers** 2 (Prso 3, Thompson 44).
Att: 6,527.

Rangers (4-4-2): Waterreus, Hutton, Rodriguez, Kyrgiakos, Bernard (Murray 90), Ricksen, Ferguson, Hemdami, Lovenkrands, Thompson (Jeffers 70), Prso.
Inter Milan 2 (Julio Cruz 75 pen, 82), **FC Porto** 1 (Hugo Almeida 16) – played behind closed doors.

November 23, 2005
FC Porto 1 (Lopez 60), **Rangers** 1 (McCormack 83). Att: 48,000.
Rangers (4-1-4-1): Waterreus, Ricksen, Andrews, Kyrgiakos, Murray, Hemdani, Namouchi, Ferguson, Rae (Thompson 60), Lovenkrands (Burke 77), Jeffers (McCormack 74).
Inter Milan 4 (Figo 28, Adriano 41, 59, 74), **Artmedia Bratislava** 0 – played behind closed doors.

December 6, 2005
Artmedia Bratislava 0, **FC Porto** 0. Att: 7,000.
Rangers 1 (Lovenkrands 38), **Inter Milan** 1 (Adriano 30). Att: 49,170.
Rangers (4-4-1-1): Waterreus., Ricksen, Andrews, Kyriakos, Murray, Burke, Ferguson, Malcolm, Namouchi, Buffel, Lovenkrands.

FINAL TABLE

	P	W	D	L	F	A	Pts
INTER MILAN	6	4	1	1	9	4	13
RANGERS	6	1	4	1	7	7	7
Artmedia Bratislava	6	1	3	2	5	9	6
FC Porto	6	1	2	3	8	9	5

FIRST KNOCK-OUT ROUND, FIRST LEG

February 21, 2006
Bayern Munich 1 (Ballack 23), **AC Milan** 1 (Shevchenko 57 pen). Att: 66,000.
Benfica 1 (Luisao 84), **Liverpool** 0. Att: 65,000.
Liverpool (4-4-2): Reina, Finnan, Carragher, Hyypia, Riise, Luis Garcia, Sissoko (Hamann 35), Xabi Alonso, Kewell, Fowler (Cisse 66), Morientes (Gerrard 78).
PSV Eindhoven 0, **Lyon** 1 (Juninho 65). Att: 35,000.
Real Madrid 0, **Arsenal** 1 (Henry 47). Att: 80,000.
Arsenal (4-5-1): Lehmann, Eboue, Toure, Senderos, Flamini, Hleb (Pires 75), Fabregas (Song 90), Gilberto Silva, Ljungberg, Reyes (Diaby 80), Henry.

February 22, 2006
Ajax 2 (Huntelaar 16, Rosales 20), **Inter Milan** 2 (Stankovic 49, Cruz 89). Att: 51,000.
Chelsea 1 (Motta 59 og), **Barcelona** 2 (Terry 71 og, Eto'o 80). Att: 39,521.
Chelsea (4-3-3): Cech, Paulo Ferreira, Ricardo Carvalho, Terry, Del Horno, Makelele, Gudjohnsen, Lampard, J. Cole (Geremi 38), Crespo (Drogba 46), Robben (Wright-Phillips 77). **Sent-off:** Del Horno
Rangers 2 (Lovenkrands 22, Pena 82 og), **Villarreal** 2 (Riquelme 8 pen, Forlan 35). Att: 49,372.
Rangers (4-4-2): Waterreus, Hutton, Kyrgiakos, Rodriguez, Smith, Burke, Hemdani, Ferguson, Namouchi (Buffel 68), Lovenkrands (Novo 74), Prso (Boyd 88).
Werder Bremen 3 (Schulz 39, Borowski 87, Micoud 90), **Juventus** 2 (Nedved 74, Trezeguet 82). Att: 42,000.

FIRST KNOCK-OUT ROUND, SECOND LEG

March 7, 2006
Barcelona 1 (Ronaldinho 78), **Chelsea** 1 (Lampard 90 pen). Att: 98,000 (**Barcelona** won 3-2 on agg).

Chelsea (4-3-3): Cech, Paulo Ferreira, Ricardo Carvalho, Terry, Gallas, J. Cole (Huth 82), Makelele, Lampard, Duff (Gudjohnsen 58), Drogba (Crespo 58), Robben.
Juventus 2 (Trezeguet 65, Emerson 88), **Werder Bremen** 1 (Micoud 13). Att: 40,000 (agg 4-4, **Juventus** won on away goals).
Villarreal 1 (Arruabarrena 49), **Rangers** 1 (Lovenkrands 12). Att: 23,000 (agg 3-3, **Villarreal** won on away goals).
Rangers (4-4-2): Waterreus, Hutton, Kyrgiakos, Rodriguez, Murray, Burke (Novo 86), Ferguson, Hemdani, Namouchi, Buffel (Boyd 63), Lovenkrands.

March 8, 2006
AC Milan 4 (Inzaghi 8, 47, Shevchenko 25, Kaka 59), **Bayern Munich** 1 (Ismael 36). Att: 71,032 (**AC Milan** won 5-2 on agg).
Arsenal 0, **Real Madrid** 0. Att: 35,487 (**Arsenal** won 1-0 on agg).
Arsenal (4-5-1): Lehmann, Eboue, Toure, Senderos, Flamini, Hleb (Bergkamp 87), Fabregas, Gilberto Silva, Ljungberg, Reyes (Pires 67), Henry.
Liverpool 0, **Benfica** 2 (Simao 36, Miccoli 89). Att: 42,745 (**Benfica** won 3-0 on agg).
Liverpool (4-4-2): Reina, Finnan, Carragher, Traore, Warnock (Hamann 70), Luis Garcia, Gerrard, Xabi Alonso, Kewell (Cisse 63), Morientes (Fowler 70), Crouch.
Lyon 4 (Tiago 26, 45, Wiltord 71, Fred 90), **PSV Eindhoven** 0. Att: 41,000 (**Lyon** won 5-0 on agg).

March 14, 2006
Inter Milan 1 (Stankovic 57), **Ajax** 0. Att: 60,000 (**Inter Milan** won 3-2 on agg).

QUARTER-FINALS, FIRST LEG

March 28, 2006
Arsenal 2 (Fabregas 40, Henry 69), **Juventus** 0. Att: 35,472.
Arsenal (4-4-1-1): Lehmann, Eboue, Toure, Senderos, Flamini, Hleb, Gilberto Silva, Fabregas, Reyes (Van Persie 81), Pires, Henry.
Benfica 0, **Barcelona** 0. Att: 65,000.

March 29, 2006
Inter Milan 2 (Adriano 7, Martins 54), **Villarreal** 1 (Forlan 1). Att: 80,000.
Lyon 0, **AC Milan** 0. Att: 39,016.

QUARTER-FINALS, SECOND LEG

April 4, 2006
AC Milan 3 (Inzaghi 25, 88, Shevchenko 90), **Lyon** 1 (Diarra 31). Att: 80,000 (AC Milan won 3-1 on agg).
Villarreal 1 (Arruabarrena 58), **Inter Milan** 0. Att: 22,500 (agg 2-2, **Villarreal** won on away goal).

April 5, 2006
Barcelona 2 (Ronaldinho 19, Eto'o 88), **Benfica** 0. Att: 90,000 (**Barcelona** won 2-0 on agg).
Juventus 0, **Arsenal** 0. Att: 50,000 (**Arsenal** won 2-0 on agg).
Arsenal (4-1-4-1): Lehmann, Eboue, Toure, Senderos, Flamini, Gilberto Silva, Hleb (Diaby 85), Ljungberg, Fabregas, Reyes (Pires 63), Henry.

SEMI-FINALS, FIRST LEG

April 18, 2006
AC Milan 0, **Barcelona** 1 (Giuly 57). Att: 85,000.

April 19, 2006
Arsenal 1 (Toure 41), **Villarreal** 0. Att: 35,438.
Arsenal (4-5-1): Lehmann, Eboue, Toure, Senderos, Flamini, Hleb (Bergkamp 79), Fabregas, Gilberto Silva, Pires. Ljungberg (Van Persie 79), Henry.

SEMI-FINALS, SECOND LEG

April 25, 2006
Villarreal 0, **Arsenal** 0. Att: 23,000 (**Arsenal** won 1-0 on agg).
Arsenal (4-1-4-1): Lehmann, Eboue, Toure, Campbell, Flamini (Clichy 8), Gilberto Silva, Hleb, Fabregas, Ljungberg, Reyes (Pires 69), Henry.

April 26, 2006
Barcelona 0, **AC Milan** 0. Att: 90,000 (**Barcelona** won 1-0 on agg).

EUROPEAN CUP FINAL

BARCELONA 2, ARSENAL 1

Paris (79,500), Wednesday, May 17, 2006

Barcelona (4-2-1-3): Valdes, Oleguer (Belletti 70), Marquez, Puyol, Van Bronckhorst, Van Bommel (Larsson 60), Edmilson (Iniesta 46), Deco, Giuly, Ronaldinho, Eto'o. **Subs not used:** Jorquera, Motta, Xavi, Sylvinho. **Scorers:** Eto'o (76), Belletti (80). **Booked:** Oleguer, Larsson. **Coach:** Frank Rijkaard.

Arsenal (4-1-4-1): Lehmann, Eboue, Toure, Campbell, Cole, Gilberto Silva, Hleb (Reyes 84), Pires (Almunia 19), Fabregas (Flamini 74), Ljungberg, Henry. **Subs not used:** Bergkamp, Van Persie, Senderos, Clichy. **Scorer:** Campbell (37). **Booked:** Eboue, Henry. **Sent-off:** Lehmann. **Manager:** Arsene Wenger.

Referee: T. Hauge (Norway). **Half-time:** 0-1.

All the talk beforehand was about Ronaldinho and Henry; of Eto'o and Fabregas; of which one would have the biggest influence on the game. No-one mentioned Henrik Larsson, once Scotland's most prolific scorer, now marking time on the Barcelona bench before returning to his native Sweden to join Helsingborgs. Yet it was the player who accumulated 242 goals in 315 appearances for Celtic who would ultimately break Arsenal hearts, just when it was beginning to look as if their first European Cup Final would be blessed with success.

Ironically, it wasn't the razor-sharp finishing that has characterised Larsson's illustrious career, but two delicately-directed passes opening the way for Eto'o to cancel out Sol Campbell's header in the 76th minute and for fellow-substitute Juliano Belletti to guide the winner past Manuel Almunia four minutes later. Both were difficult chances from awkward angles. Both raised question marks about the positioning and reactions of the substitute goalkeeper.

He had earlier excelled when deflecting the ball against the post after Eto'o twisted past Campbell to make space for a shot. But in the final reckoning, it was a bad night for both Almunia and Jens Lehmann, sent off in the 18th minute for tripping Eto'o after the Cameroon striker ran clear on to Ronaldinho's pass. Would Arsenal have been better served by the Norwegian referee Terje Hauge allowing Ludovic Giuly's subsequent tap-in to have counted and showing Lehmann a yellow and not a red card?

When Campbell connected firmly with Thierry Henry's free-kick after 37 minutes and his team then closed ranks to frustrate all Barcelona's attempts to make their numerical advantage count, the answer would have been a resounding 'no.' And certainly had

Henry later done justice to Freddie Ljungberg's defence-splitting pass, the question would never have been asked. Instead, the captain's weak effort was smothered by Victor Valdes, inviting Barcelona to step up their game and 34-year-old Larsson to punish some tired legs and weary minds.

FINAL FACTS AND FIGURES

* Barcelona's victory was their second in the competition, 14 years after a 1-0 defeat of Sampdoria at Wembley.

* Frank Rijkaard, who was in the successful AC Milan side of 1989 and 1990 and the victorious 1995 Ajax team, joined an elite list to have won the trophy as player and coach.

* Jens Lehmann became the first player in 51 European Cup Finals to be sent off.

* Samuel Eto'o's equaliser was the first goal Arsenal had conceded in ten matches in the competition, since Markus Rosenberg's for Ajax in the second game of their qualifying group.

* UEFA replaced assistant referee Ole Hermann Borgan with fellow Norwegian Arild Sundet for the final because he had posed for a photograph wearing a Barcelona shirt.

Leading scorers (from group games onwards): 9 Shevchenko (AC Milan); 7 Ronaldinho (Barcelona); 6 Eto'o (Barcelona), Trezeguet (Juventus); 5 Adriano (Inter Milan), Henry (Arsenal), Kaka (AC Milan), Micoud (Werder Bremen).

EUROPEAN CUP FINALS

1956	Real Madrid 4, Reims 3 (Paris)
1957	Real Madrid 2, Fiorentina 0 (Madrid)
1958†	Real Madrid 3, AC Milan 2 (Brussels)
1959	Real Madrid 2, Reims 0 (Stuttgart)
1960	Real Madrid 7, Eintracht Frankfurt 3 (Glasgow)
1961	Benfica 3, Barcelona 2 (Berne)
1962	Benfica 5, Real Madrid 3 (Amsterdam)
1963	AC Milan 2, Benfica 1 (Wembley)
1964	Inter Milan 3, Real Madrid 1 (Vienna)
1965	Inter Milan 1, Benfica 0 (Milan)
1966	Real Madrid 2, Partizan Belgrade 1 (Brussels)
1967	Celtic 2, Inter Milan 1 (Lisbon)
1968†	Manchester Utd. 4, Benfica 1 (Wembley)
1969	AC Milan 4, Ajax 1 (Madrid)
1970†	Feyenoord 2, Celtic 1 (Milan)
1971	Ajax 2, Panathinaikos 0 (Wembley)
1972	Ajax 2, Inter Milan 0 (Rotterdam)
1973	Ajax 1, Juventus 0 (Belgrade)
1974	Bayern Munich 4, Atletico Madrid 0 (replay Brussels, after a 1-1 draw, Brussels)
1975	Bayern Munich 2, Leeds Utd. 0 (Paris)
1976	Bayern Munich 1, St. Etienne 0 (Glasgow)
1977	Liverpool 3, Borussia Moenchengladbach 1 (Rome)
1978	Liverpool 1, Brugge 0 (Wembley)
1979	Nott'm. Forest 1, Malmo 0 (Munich)

1980	Nott'm. Forest 1, Hamburg 0 (Madrid)
1981	Liverpool 1, Real Madrid 0 (Paris)
1982	Aston Villa 1, Bayern Munich 0 (Rotterdam)
1983	SV Hamburg 1, Juventus 0 (Athens)
1984†	Liverpool 1, AS Roma 1 (Liverpool won 4-2 on penalties) (Rome)
1985	Juventus 1, Liverpool 0 (Brussels)
1986†	Steaua Bucharest 0, Barcelona 0 (Steaua won 2-0 on penalties) (Seville)
1987	Porto 2, Bayern Munich 1 (Vienna)
1988†	PSV Eindhoven 0, Benfica 0 (PSV won 6-5 on penalties) (Stuttgart)
1989	AC Milan 4, Steaua Bucharest 0 (Barcelona)
1990	AC Milan 1, Benfica 0 (Vienna)
1991†	Red Star Belgrade 0, Marseille 0 (Red Star won 5-3 on penalties) (Bari)
1992	Barcelona 1, Sampdoria 0 (Wembley)
1993	Marseille 1, AC Milan 0 (Munich)
1994	AC Milan 4, Barcelona 0 (Athens)
1995	Ajax 1, AC Milan 0 (Vienna)
1996†	Juventus 1, Ajax 1 (Juventus won 4-2 on penalties) (Rome)
1997	Borussia Dortmund 3, Juventus 1 (Munich)
1998	Real Madrid 1, Juventus 0 (Amsterdam)
1999	Manchester Utd. 2, Bayern Munich 1 (Barcelona)
2000	Real Madrid 3, Valencia 0 (Paris)
2001	Bayern Munich 1, Valencia 1 (Bayern Munich won 5-4 on penalties) (Milan)
2002	Real Madrid 2, Bayer Leverkusen 1 (Glasgow)
2003†	AC Milan 0, Juventus 0 (AC Milan won 3-2 on penalties) (Manchester)
2004	FC Porto 3, Monaco 0 (Gelsenkirchen)
2005†	Liverpool 3, AC Milan 3 (Liverpool won 3-2 on penalties) (Istanbul)
2006	Barcelona 2, Arsenal 1 (Paris)

(† After extra time)

QUOTE-UNQUOTE

'Georgie Best was everywhere, with Elvis hips and Beatles hair, a real wizard on the ball, he was the greatest of them all' – poem on a floral tribute to the Manchester United legend.

'He carried us for years, it was an honour to carry him' – **Derek Dougan**, a Northern Ireland team-mate of Best who was one of the pall-bearers at his funeral.

'I'm looking forward to pitting my wits against (Jose) Mourinho, but I'll need a new coat and a new suit' – **Peter Jackson**, Huddersfield manager, on being paired with Chelsea in the F.A. Cup third round.

'I had a double brandy before the game. Before it used to be four bottles of whisky' – **Paul Gascoigne** after his return to football as Kettering manager ends in tears amid accusations of heavy drinking.

'We need to get back to the Birmingham team that was hard to beat and rather ugly, just like their manager' – **Steve Bruce** on hard times for his team at St Andrews.

'I would say 'grow up.' People in football are role models and have to act accordingly' – **Richard Caborn**, Sports Minister, on the continuing spat between Jose Mourinho and Arsene Wenger.

'How do you tell your wife you are just popping out to play a match and then not come back for five days?' – **Rafael Benitez**, Liverpool manager, reflecting on Test cricket.

UEFA CUP 2005-06

PRE-TOURNAMENT INTERTOTO CUP (SELECTED RESULTS)

FIRST ROUND

Dinaburg 4, **Bangor City** 1 (2-0h, 2-1a); Zalgiris Vilnius 2, **Lisburn Distillery** 0 (1-0h, 1-0a).

THIRD ROUND

First leg: ZTS Dubnica 1 (Tesak 42), **Newcastle Utd.** 3 (Chopra 4, N'Zogbia 6, Milner 70. Att: 6,000. **Second leg: Newcastle Utd.** 2 (Shearer 72, 90), ZTS Dubnica 0. Att: 25,135 (**Newcastle Utd.** won 5-1 on agg).

SEMI-FINALS

First leg: Deporivo La Coruna 2 (Castro 11, Andrade 58), **Newcastle Utd.** 1 (Bowyer 47). Att: 16,000. **Second leg: Newcastle Utd.** 1 (Milner 39), Deportivo La Coruna 2 (Andrade 45, Munitis 48). Att: 35,200 (Deportivo La Coruna won 4-2 on agg).

FINALS

Hamburg 1, Valencia 0 (1-0h, 0-0a); Lens 4, Cluj 2 (3-1h, 1-1a); Marseille 5, Deportivo La Coruna 3 (5-1h, 0-2a).

FIRST QUALIFYING ROUND, FIRST LEG

Ekranas 0, **Cork City** 2 (O'Donovan 25, O'Callaghan 90). Att: 4,100. **Linfield** 1 (Mouncey 6), Ventspils 0. Att: 2,000. **Longford Town** 2 (Paisley 35, Ferguson 54), **Carmarthen** 0. Att: 2,000. **Portadown** 1 (Arkins 90 pen), Viking 2 (Ostenstad 53 pen, Kopteff 79). Att: 800. **Rhyl** 2 (Hunt 11, 70), Atlantas 1 (Zvingilas 77). Att: 1,570.

FIRST QUALIFYING ROUND, SECOND LEG

Atlantas 3 (Laurisas 14 pen, 68, Petreikis 78), **Rhyl** 2 (Stones 33, G. Powell 62). Att: 2,500 (agg 4-4, **Rhyl** won on away goals). **Carmarthen** 5 (Thomas 16, 75, Lloyd 49, 54 pen, Cotterrall 80), **Longford Town** 1 (Myler 20 pen). Att: 850 (**Carmarthen** won 5-3 on agg). **Cork City** 0, Ekranas 1 (Klimavicius 60). Att: 6,000 (**Cork City** won 2-1 on agg). Ventspils 2 (Rekhviashvili 39, Rimkus 90), **Linfield** 1 (Thompson 8). Att: 800 (agg 2-2, **Linfield** won on away goal). Viking 1 (Nhleko 56), **Portadown** 0. Att: 4,300 (Viking won 3-1 on agg).

FIRST QUALIFYING ROUND, ON AGGREGATE

Allianssi 4, Petange 1; Apoel Nicosia 6, Birkirkara 0; Banants Yerevan 4, Lokomotiv Tbilisi 3; Baskimi 4, Zepce Limorad 1; BATE 6, Torpedo Kutaisi 0; Domzale 8, Domagnano 0; Efb 7, Flora 2; Keflavik 6, Etzella 0; Mainz 4, Mika Ashtarak 0; Metalurgs 6, Runavik 0; Mtz-Ripo 3, Ferencvaros 2; MyPa 2, MK Tallinn 1; Nistru Otaci 5, Khazar Lenkoran 2; Omonia Nicosia 6, Hibernians 0; Rapid Bucharest 10, Sant Julia 0; Siroki Brijeg 4, Teuta 3; Torshavn 3, Vestmannaeyjar 2; Vaduz 2, Dacia 1; Vardar 1, Elbasan 1 (Vardar won on away goal); Zilina 3, Karat Baku 2.

SECOND QUALIFYING ROUND, FIRST LEG

Djurgarden 1 (Amoah 80), **Cork City** 1 (Fenn). Att: 4,854. FC Copenhagen 2 (Dos Santos 48, Gravgaard 54), **Carmarthen** 0. Att: 11,314. Halmstad 1 (Johansson 31), **Linfield** 1 (Kearney 72). Att: 1,197. Mypa 0, **Dundee Utd.** 0. Att: 1,820. **Rhyl** 0, Viking 1 (Kopteff 19). Att: 1,540.

SECOND QUALIFYING ROUND, SECOND LEG

Carmarthen 0, FC Copenhagen 2 (Moller 37, 39). Att: 882 (FC Copenhagen won 4-0 on agg). **Cork City** 0, Djurgarden 0. Att: 7,000 (agg 1-1, **Cork City** won on away goal). **Dundee Utd.** 2 (Kerr 15, Samuel 29), MyPa 2 (Adriano 74 pen, 81). Att: 9,600 (Agg 2-2, MyPa won on away goals). **Linfield** 2 (Mouncey 54, Ferguson 82), Halmstad 4 (Thorvaldsson 10, Jonsson 33, Preko 45, Djuric 74). Att: 4,000 (Halmstad won 5-3 on agg). Viking 2 (Nhleko 7, 25), **Rhyl** 1 (Adamson 36). Att: 3,500 (Viking won 3-1 on agg).

SECOND QUALIFYING ROUND, ON AGGREGATE

Apoel Nicosia 3, Maccabi Tel-Aviv 2; Austria Vienna 4, Zilina 3; Besiktas 6, Vaduz 1; Brann Bergen 2, Allianssi 0; Dinamo Bucharest 4, Omonia Nicosia 3; Dnipro 8, Banants Yerevan 2; Donzale 3, Ashdod 3 (Donzale won on away goals); FC Zurich 5, Legia Warsaw 1; GAK 3, Nistru Otaci 0; Genk 6, Metalurgs 2; Grasshoppers 3, Plock 3 (Grasshoppers won on away goals); Groclin 4, Banska Bystrica 1; Krylya Sovetov 4, BATE 0; Levski Sofia 3, Publikum 1; Liteks Lovetch 2, Rijeka 2 (Liteks Lovetch won on away goals); Lokomotiv Plovdiv 2, OFK 2 (Lokomotiv Plovdiv won on away goal); Maccabi Petah-Tikva 11, Baskimi 0; Mainz 4, Keflavik 0; Metalurh 5, Sopron 1; Midtjylland 4, Torshavn 3; Siroki Brijeg 5, Zeta 2; Rapid Vienna 4, Vardar 1; Red Star Belgrade 7, Inter Zapresic 1; Teplice 3, Mtz-Ripo 2; Tromso 1 Efb 1 (Tromso won 3-2 on pens); Zenit St Petersburg 3, Pasching 3 (Zenit St Petersburg won on away goals).

FIRST ROUND, FIRST LEG

Bolton Wand. 2 (Diouf 72, Borgetti 90), Lokomotiv Plovdiv 1 (Jancevski 28). Att: 19,723. Dinamo Bucharest 5 (Niculescu 27, Zicu 55, Petre 71, Bratu 75, 90), **Everton** 1 (Yobo 30). Att: 11,500. **Hibernian** 0, Dnipro 0. Att: 16,861. Slavia Prague 2 (Hrdlicka 61, Pitak 79), **Cork City** 0. Att: 4,694. **Middlesbrough** 2 (Boateng 28, Viduka 83), FC Xanthi 0. Att: 14,191.

FIRST ROUND, SECOND LEG

Cork City 1 (O'Callaghan 66 pen), Slavia Prague 2 (Pitak 27, Vicek 63). Att: 7,000. (Slavia Prague won 4-1 on agg). Dnipro 5 (Nazarenko 1, Shershun 26, Shelaev 39 pen, Melaschenko 86, 90), **Hibernian** 1 (Riordan 24). Att: 4,000 (Dnipro won 5-1 on agg). **Everton** 1 (Cahill 28), Dinamo Bucharest 0. Att: 21,843 (Dinamo Bucharest won 5-2 on agg). FC Xanthi 0, **Middlesbrough** 0. Att: 5,013 (**Middlesbrough** won 2-0 on agg). Lokomotiv Plovdiv 1 (Iliev 51), **Bolton Wand.** 2 (Tunchev 79 og, Nolan 86). Att: 14,000 (**Bolton Wand.** won 4-2 on agg).

FIRST ROUND, ON AGGREGATE

AZ Alkmaar 6, Krylya Sovetov 6 (AZ Alkmaar won on away goals); Basle 6, Siroki Brijeg 0; Besiktas 4, Malmo 2; Brondby 3, FC Zurich 2; CSKA Moscow 6, Midtjylland 2; CSKA Sofia 2, Bayer Leverkusen 0; Espanyol 3, Teplice 1; Grasshoppers 4, MyPa 1; Guimaraes 4, Wisla Krakow 0; Halmstad 4, Sporting Lisbon 4 (Halmstad won on away goals); Hamburg 2, FC Copenhagen 1; Heerenveen 5, Banik Ostrava 2; Hertha Berlin 4, Apoel Nicosia 1; Lens 5, Groclin 3; Levski Sofia 2, Auxerre 2 (Levski Sofia won on away goals);

Liteks Lovetch 3, Genk 2; Lokomotiv Moscow 5, Brann Bergen 3; Maccabi Petah-Tikva 5, Partizan Belgrade 4; Marseille 0, Germinal Beerschot 0 (aet, Marseille won 4-1 on pens); Monaco 5, Willem II 1; Palermo 6, Anorthosis Famagusta 1; PAOK Salonika 3, Metalurh 3 (PAOK Salonika won on away goals); Rapid Vienna 2, Feyenoord 1; Red Star Belgrade 1, Braga 1 (Red Star Belgrade won on away goal); Rennes 3, Osasuna 1; Roma 5, Aris Salonika 1; Sampdoria 2, Vitoria Setubal 1; Sevilla 2, Mainz 0; Shakhtar Donetsk 6, Debrecen 1; Steaua Bucharest 6, Valerenga 1; Strasbourg 7, Graz 0; Stuttgart 2, Domzale 1; Tromso 2, Galatasaray 1; Zenit St Petersburg 1, AEK Athens 0.

GROUP STAGE

GROUP A

Match-day 1: CSKA Sofia 0, Hamburg 1 (Beinlich 57). Att: 22,000. Viking 1 (Nhleko 18), Monaco 0. Att: 9,684.
   Match-day 2: Hamburg 2 (Van der Vaart 21, Lauth 66), Viking 0. Att: 37,521. Slavia Prague 4 (Fort 5, 75, Vlcek 36, Pitak 56), CSKA Sofia 2 (Gargorov 10, Sakaliev 58). Att: 7,171.
   Match-day 3: Monaco 2 (Adebayor 44, Veigneau 90), Hamburg 0. Att: 18,000. Viking 2 (Nhleko 26, Gaarde 55), Slavia Prague 2 (Vlcek 51, Pitak 83). Att: 7,941.
   Match-day 4: CSKA Sofia 2 (Yanev 35 pen, Dah Zadi 47), Viking 0. Att: 7,000. Slavia Prague 0, Monaco 2 (Maoulida 11, 71). Att: 12,540.
   Match-day 5: Hamburg 2 (Barbarez 9, Mpenza 57), Slavia Prague 0. Att: 46,253. Monaco 2 (Kapo 50, Squillaci 75), CSKA Sofia 1 (Dimitrov 84). Att: 9,279.

FINAL TABLE

	P	W	D	L	F	A	Pts
MONACO	4	3	0	1	6	2	9
HAMBURG	4	3	0	1	5	2	9
SLAVIA PRAGUE	4	1	1	2	6	8	4
Viking	4	1	1	2	3	6	4
CSKA Sofia	4	1	0	3	5	7	3

GROUP B

Match-day 1: Maccabi Petah-Tikva 1 (Golan 45), Palermo 2 (Brienza 11, Terlizzi 77). Att: 3,964. Lokomotiv Moscow 0, Espanyol 1 (Tamudo 53). Att: 13,718.
   Match-day 2: Brondy 2 (Lantz 67, Absalonsen 83), Maccabi Petah-Tikva 0. Att: 14,188. Palermo 0, Lokomotiv Moscow 0. Att: 15,823.
   Match-day 3: Lokomotiv Moscow 4 (Loskov 60, 65, 84, Lebedenko 63), Brondby 2 (Retov 11, Skouba 28). Espanyol 1 (Luis Garcia 90), Palermo 1 (Gonzalez 45). Att: 9,114.
   Match-day 4: Brondby 1 (Skoubo 66), Espanyol 1 (Tamudo 42). Att: 21,399. Maccabi Petah-Tikva 0, Lokomotiv Moscow 4 (Loskov 27, Lebedenko 47, 48, Ruopolo 52). Att: 4,000.
   Match-day 5: Espanyol 1 (Pochettino 83), Maccabi Petah-Tikva 0. Att: 5,000. Palermo 3 (Makinwa 24, Rinaudo 44, 88), Brondby 0. Att: 4,521.

FINAL TABLE

	P	W	D	L	F	A	Pts
PALERMO	4	2	2	0	6	2	8
ESPANYOL	4	2	2	0	4	2	8
LOKOMOTIV MOSCOW	4	2	1	1	8	3	7
Brondby	4	1	1	2	5	8	4
Maccabi Petah-Tikva	4	0	0	4	1	9	0

GROUP C

Match-day 1: Halmstad 0, Hertha Berlin 1 (Neuendorf 67). Att: 2,136. Steaua Bucharest 4 (Iacob 13, Goian 16, Dica 43, 63). Lens 0. Att: 20,000.

Match-day 2: Lens 5 (Cousin 16, 23, 47, Jomaa 73, Lachor 90), Halmstad 0. Att: 20,000. Sampdoria 0, Steaua Bucharest 0. Att: 17,194.

Match-day 3: Halmstad 1 (Djuric 18), Sampdoria 3 (Volpi 31, Diana 67, 86). Att: 3,126. Hertha Berlin 0, Lens 0. Att: 18,510.

Match-day 4: Sampdoria 0, Hertha Berlin 0. Att: 16,507. Steaua Bucharest 3 (Radoi 11, Goian 63, Iacob 71), Halmstad 0. Att: 25,000.

Match-day 5: Hertha Berlin 0, Steaua Bucarest 0. Att: 15,603. Lens 2 (Thomert 10, Jomaa 90), Sampdoria 1 (Flachi 23). Att: 31,473.

FINAL TABLE

	P	W	D	L	F	A	Pts
STEAUA BUCHAREST	4	2	2	0	7	0	8
LENS	4	2	1	1	7	5	7
HERTHA BERLIN	4	1	3	0	1	0	6
Sampdoria	4	1	2	1	4	3	5
Halmstad	4	0	0	4	1	12	0

GROUP D

Match-day 1: Dnipro 1 (Matyukhin 69), AZ Alkmaar 2 (Arveladze 13, Sektioui 52). Att: 12,000. Grasshoppers 0, **Middlesbrough** 1 (Hasselbaink 10). Att: 8,500.

Match-day 2: Liteks Lovetch 2 (Novakovic 13, Sandrinho 81), Grasshoppers 1 (Dos Santos 90). Att: 4,500. **Middlesbrough** 3 (Yakubu 36, Viduka 50, 56), Dnipro 0. Att: 12,953.

Match-day 3: AZ Alkmaar 0, **Middlesbrough** 0. Att: 8,461. Dnipro 0, Liteks Lovetch 2 (Novakovic 72, Nazarenko 90 og). Att: 11,000.

Match-day 4: Grasshoppers 2 (Toure 85, Renggli 90), Dnipro 3 (Nazarenko 39, Kravchenko 62, Milhailenko 83). Att: 1,808. Liteks Lovetch 0, AZ Alkmaar 2 (Van Galen 10, Sektioui 82). Att: 4,000.

Match-day 5: AZ Alkmaar 1 (Koevermans 70), Grasshoppers 0. Att: 8,153. **Middlesbrough** 2 (Maccarone 80, 86), Liteks Lovetch 0. Att: 9,436.

FINAL TABLE

	P	W	D	L	F	A	Pts
MIDDLESBROUGH	4	3	1	0	6	0	10
AZ ALKMAAR	4	3	1	0	5	1	10
LITEKS LOVETCH	4	2	0	2	4	5	6
Dnipro	4	1	0	3	4	9	3
Grasshoppers	4	0	0	4	3	7	0

GROUP E

Match-day 1: Basle 0, Strasbourg 2 (Diane 15, Boka 25). Att: 16,623. Tromso 1 (Aarst 42), Roma 2 (Kuffour 35, Cufre 84). Att: 5,982.

Match-day 2: Red Star Belgrade 1 (Purovic 25), Basle 2 (Delgado 30 pen, Rossi 88) – played behind closed doors. Strasbourg 2 (Pagis 38, Arrache 66), Tromso 0. Att: 8,516.

Match-day 3: Roma 1 (Cassano 73), Strasbourg 1 (Bellaid 52). Att: 8,500. Tromso 3 (Kibebe 22, Aarst 37, 74 pen), Red Star Belgrade 1 (Zigic 24). Att: 4,289.

Match-day 4: Basle 4 (Petric 17, Delgado 61, Chipperfield 67, Degen 75), Tromso 3 (Strand 2, 29, Aarst 19). Att: 14,718. Red Star Belgrade 3 (Zigic 37, 86, Purovic 77), Roma 1 (Nonda 23). Att: 35,186.

Match-day 5: Roma 3 (Taddei 14, Totti 45, Nonda 49), Basle 1 (Petric 78). Att: 15,000. Strasbourg 2 (Gameiro 79, 90), Red Star Belghrade 2 (Basta 34, Djokaj 64). Att: 13,416.

FINAL TABLE

	P	W	D	L	F	A	Pts
STRASBOURG	4	2	2	0	7	3	8
ROMA	4	2	1	1	7	6	7
BASLE	4	2	0	2	7	9	6
Red Star Belgrade	4	1	1	2	7	8	4
Tromso	4	1	0	3	7	9	3

GROUP F

Match-day 1: CSKA Moscow 1 (Vagner Love 80), Marseille 2 (Lamouchi 23, Niang 38). Att: 12,000. Dinamo Bucharest 0, Heerenveen 0. Att: 10,000.

Match-day 2: Heerenveen 0, CSKA Moscow 0. Att: 20,200. Levski Sofia 1 (Angelov 90), Dinamo Bucharest 0. Att: 15,000.

Match-day 3: CSKA Moscow 2 (Vagner Love 49, 73), Levski Sofia 1 (Domovchiyski 90). Att: 6,000. Marseille 1 (Taiwo 90 pen), Heerenveen 0. Att: 14,777.

Match-day 4: Dinamo Bucharest 1 (Munteanu 72), CSKA Moscow 0. Att: 13,000. Levski Sofia 1 (Yovov 56), Marseille 0. Att: 12,000.

Match-day 5: Heerenveen 2 (Samaras 54, Hanssen 90), Levski Sofia 1 (Ivanov 52). Att: 20,025. Marseille 2 (Cesar 39, Delfim 45), Dinamo Bucharest 1 (Niculescu 52). Att: 15,909.

FINAL TABLE

	P	W	D	L	F	A	Pts
MARSEILLE	4	3	0	1	5	3	9
LEVSKI SOFIA	4	2	0	2	4	4	6
HEERENVEEN	4	1	2	1	2	2	5
CSKA Moscow	4	1	1	2	3	4	4
Dinamo Bucharest	4	1	1	2	2	3	4

GROUP G

Match-day 1: Rennes 0, Stuttgart 2 (Tomasson 87, Ljuboja 90 pen). Att: 22,847. Shakhtar Donetsk 1 (Brandao 68 pen), PAOK Salonika 0. Att: 24,650.

Match-day 2: Rapid Bucharest 2 (Niculae 42, Buga 67), Rennes 0. Att: 7,120. Stuttgart 0, Shakhtar Donetsk 2 (Ferdinandinho 31, Marica 88). Att: 15,200.

Match-day 3: PAOK Salonika 1 (Karipidis 48), Stuttgart 2 (Ljuboja 85, 90 pen). Att: 35,000. Shakhtar Donetsk 0, Rapid Bucharest 1 (Maldarasanu 87). Att: 25,000.

Match-day 4: Rapid Bucharest 1 (Maldarasanu 45), PAOK Salonika 0. Att: 12,100. Rennes 0, Shakhtar Donetsk 1 (Elano 38 pen). Att: 18,727.

Match-day 5: PAOK Salonika 5 (Rochat 4 og, Christodoulopoulos 38, Yiasoumi 79, 89, Salpigidis 83 pen), Rennes 1 (Briand 70). Att: 3,000. Stuttgart 2 (Gomex 20, 37), Rapid Bucharest 1 (Burdujan 80). Att: 14,000.

FINAL TABLE

	P	W	D	L	F	A	Pts
RAPID BUCHAREST	4	3	0	1	5	2	9
SHAKHTAR DONETSK	4	3	0	1	4	1	9
STUTTGART	4	3	0	1	6	4	9
PAOK Salonika	4	1	0	3	6	5	3
Rennes	4	0	0	4	1	10	0

GROUP H

Match-day 1: Besiktas 1 (Ailton 7), **Bolton Wand.** 1 (Borgetti 29). Att: 17,027. Zenit St Petersburg 2 (Spivak 39 pen, Arshavin 54), Guimaraes 1 (Neca 59). Att: 20,500.
  Match-day 2: Bolton Wand. 1 (Nolan 24), Zenit St Petersburg 0. Att: 15,905. Sevilla 3 (Saviola 64, Kanoute 65, 89), Besiktas 0. Att: 38,500.
  Match-day 3: Guimaraes 1 (Saganowski 86), **Bolton Wand.** 1 (Vaz Te 88). Att: 6,000. Zenit St Petersburg 2 (Kerzhakov 11, 89), Sevilla 1 (Puerta 90). Att: 20,000.
  Match-day 4: Besiktas 1 (Akin 25), Zenit St Petersburg 1 (Gorshkov 30). Att: 16,440. Sevilla 3 (Saviola 10, 27, Correia 39), Guimaraes 1 (Benachour 44). Att: 35,000.
  Match-day 5: Bolton Wand. 1 (N'Gotty 65), Sevilla 1 (Correia 74). Att: 15,623. Guimaraes 1 (Saganowski 12), Besiktas 3 (Toraman 9, 60, Youla 18). Att: 5,000.

FINAL TABLE

	P	W	D	L	F	A	Pts
SEVILLA	4	2	1	1	8	4	7
ZENIT ST PETERSBURG	4	2	1	1	5	4	7
BOLTON WAND.	4	1	3	0	4	3	6
Besiktas	4	1	2	1	5	6	5
Guimaraes	4	0	1	3	4	9	1

ROUND OF 32

FIRST LEG

Artmedia Bratislava 0, Levski Sofia 1 (Angelov 9). Att: 5,720. Basle 1 (Degen 78), Monaco 0. Att: 14,143. **Bolton Wand.** 0, Marseille 0. Att: 19,288. FC Bruges 1 (Portillo 61), Roma 2 (Vanaudenaerde 44 og, Perrotta 74). Att: 27,138. FC Thun 1 (Adriano 30), Hamburg 0. Att: 18,500. Heerenveen 1 (Bruggink 24), Steaua Bucharest 3 (Dica 29, Goian 76, Paraschiv 78). Att: 21,000. Hertha Berlin 0, Rapid Bucharest 1 (Negru 68 pen). Att: 13,430. Lille 3 (Fauvergue 19, Dernis 57, Odemwingie 77), Shakhtar Donetsk 2 (Brandao 89, Marica 90). Att: 19,880.
  Liteks Lovetch 0, Strasbourg 2 (Le Pen 2, Diane 82). Att: 3,000. Lokomotiv Moscow 0, Sevilla 1 (Jordi 75). Att: 10,223. Real Betis 2 (Tardelli 70, Robert 79), AZ Alkmaar 0. Att: 12,000. Rosenborg 0, Zenit St Petersburg 2 (Arshavin 22, Kerzhakov 32). Att: 11,082. Schalke 2 (Bordon 67, Ernst 88), Espanyol 1 (Luis Garcia 34). Att: 53,642. Slavia Prague 2 (Jarolim 28, Barzagli 49 og), Palermo 1 (Conteh 40). Att: 6,500. Stuttgart 1 (Ljuboja 88), **Middlesbrough** 2 (Hasselbaink 20, Parnaby 49). Udinese 3 (Di Natale 35, Barreto 61, 82), Lens 0. Att: 8,000. Udinese 3 (Di Natale 35, Barreto 61, 82), Lens 0. Att: 8,000.

SECOND LEG

AZ Alkmaar 2 (Arveladze 26, Jaliens 35), Real Betis 1 (Melli 94). Att: 11,000 (aet, Real Betis won 3-2 on agg). Espanyol 0, Schalke 3 (Kuranyi 54, Sand 70, Lincoln 73). Att: 18,100 (Schalke won 5-1 on agg). Hamburg 2 (Van Buyten 2, 33), FC Thun 0. Att:

227

40,254 (Hamburg won 2-1 on agg). Lens 1 (Frau 55), Udinese 0. Att: 26,292 (Udinese won 3-1 on agg). Levski Sofia 2 (Angelov 14, 27), Artmedia Bratislava 0. Att: 23,441 (Levski Sofia won 3-0 on agg). Marseille 2 (Ribery 45, Ben Haim 68 og), **Bolton Wand.** 1 (Giannakopolous 25). Att: 38,351 (Marseille won 2-1 on agg). **Middlesbrough** 0, Stuttgart 1 (Tiffert 13). Att: 24,018 (agg 2-2, **Middlesbrough** won on away goals). Monaco 1 (Vieri 21 pen), Basle 1 (Majstorovic 56). Att: 11,955 (Basle won 2-1 on agg).
   Palermo 1 (Godeas 51), Slavia Prague 0. Att: 8,063 (agg 2-2, Palermo won on away goals). Rapid Bucharest 2 (Niculae 50, Buga 79), Hertha Berlin 0. Att: 15,000 (Rapid Bucharest won 3-0 on agg). Roma 2 (Amantino 55, Bovo 71), FC Bruges 1 (Verheyen 60). Att: 15,209 (Roma won 4-2 on agg). Sevilla 2 (Maresca 34, Puerta 90), Lokomotiv Moscow 0. Att: 22,000 (Sevilla won 3-0 on agg). Shakhtar Donetsk 0, Lille 0. Att: 23,250 (Lille won 3-2 on agg). Steaua Bucharest 0, Heerenveen 1 (Bruggink 85). Att: 50,000 (Steaua Bucharest won 3-2 on agg). Strasbourg 0, Liteks Lovetch 0. Att: 9,610 (Strasbourg won 2-0 on agg). Zenit St Petersburg 2 (Kerzhakov 55, Denisov 86), Rosenborg 1 (Riseth 45). Att: 21,500 (Zenit St Petersburg won 4-1 on agg.).

ROUND OF 16

FIRST LEG

Basle 2 (Delgado 8, Kuzmanovic 89), Strasbourg 0. Att: 45,023. Lille 1 (Dernis 24), Sevilla 0. Att: 11,009. Marseille 0, Zenit St Petersburg 1 (Arshavin 51). Att: 38,000. **Middlesbrough** 1 (Yakubu 12 pen), Roma 0. Att: 25,354. Palermo 1 (Breinza 15), Schalke 0. Att: 10,581. Rapid Bucharest 2 (Niculae 45, Buga 88), Hamburg 0. Att: 15,000. Steaua Bucharest 0, Real Betis 0. Att: 45,023. Udinese 0, Levski Sofia 0. Att: 9,000.

SECOND LEG

Hamburg 3 (Lauth 24, Barbarez 36, Van der Vaart 62), Rapid Bucharest 1 (Buga 51). Att: 37,866 (agg 3-3, Rapid Bucharest won on away goals). Levski Sofia 2 (Borimirov 51, Tomasic 63), Udinese 1 (Tissone 22). Att: 37,136 (Levski Sofia won 2-1 on agg). Real Betis 0, Steaua Bucharest 3 (Nicolita 54, 82, Iacob 78). Att: 20,000 (Steaua Bucharest won 3-1 on agg). Roma 2 (Mancini 43, 66 pen), **Middlesbrough** 1 (Hasselbaink 32). Att: 32,642 (agg 2-2, **Middlesbrough** won on away goals). Schalke 3 (Kobiashvili 44 pen, Larsen 72, Azaouagh 80), Palermo 1. Att: 52,151 (Schalke won 3-1 on agg). Sevilla 2 (Kanoute 29, Luis Fabiano 45). Lille 0. Att: 41,000 (Sevilla won 2-1 on agg). Strasbourg 2 (Carlier 11, Kante 78), Basle 2 (Da Silva 3, 26). Att: 8,115 (Basle won 4-2 on agg). Zenit St Petersburg 1 (Kerzhakov 69), Marseille 1 (Dehu 74). Att: 21,000 (Zenit St Petersburg won 2-1 on agg).

QUARTER FINALS, FIRST LEG

Basle 2 (Delgado 43, Degen 45), **Middlesbrough** 0. Att: 23,639. Levski Sofia 1 (Borimirov 6), Schalke 3 (Varela 48, Lincoln 69, Asamoah 79). Att: 40,000. Rapid Bucharest 1 (Moldovan 50), Steaua Bucharest 1 (Nicolita 5). Att: 15,000. Sevilla 4 (Saviola 15, 80, Marti 56 pen, Adriano 90), Zenit St Petersburg 1 (Kerzhakov 45). Att: 28,633.

QUARTER-FINALS, SECOND LEG

Middlesbrough 4 (Viduka 33, 57, Hasselbaink 79, Maccarone 90), Basle 1 (Da Silva 23). Att: 24,521 (**Middlesbrough** won 4-3 on agg). Schalke 1 (Lincoln 58), Levski Sofia 1 (Angelov 24). Att: 52,973 (Schalke won 4-2 on agg). Steaua Bucharest 0, Rapid Bucharest 0. Att: 45,000 (agg 1-1, Steaua Bucharest won on away goal).

Zenit St Petersburg 1 (Hyun 50), Sevilla 1 (Kepa 66). Att: 18,500 (Sevilla won 5-2 on agg).

SEMI-FINALS, FIRST LEG

Schalke 0, Sevilla 0. Att: 53,551. Steaua Bucharest 1 (Dica 30), **Middlesbrough** 0. Att: 41,000.

SEMI-FINALS, SECOND LEG

Middlesbrough 4 (Maccarone 33, 89, Viduka 64, Riggott 73), Steaua Bucharest 2 (Dica 16, Golan 24). Att: 34,622 (**Middlesbrough** won 4-3 on agg). Sevilla 1 (Puerta 101), Schalke 0. Att: 45,000 (aet, Sevilla won 1-0 on agg).

FINAL

MIDDLESBROUGH 0, SEVILLA 4
Eindhoven (36,500), Wednesday, May 10, 2006

Middlesbrough (4-4-2): Schwarzer, Parnaby, Riggott, Southgate (capt), Queudrue (Yakubu 70), Morrison (Maccarone 46), Boateng, Rochemback, Downing, Viduka (Cattermole 85), Hasselbaink. **Subs not used:** Jones, Ehiogu, Parlour, Bates. **Booked:** Rochemback. **Manager:** Steve McClaren.

Sevilla (4-4-2): Palop, Alves, Javi Navarro (capt), Escude, David, Jesus Navas, Maresca, Marti, Adriano (Puerta 85), Luis Fabiano (Renato 72), Saviola (Kanoute 46). **Subs not used:** Notario, Aitor Ocio, Fernando Sales, Kepa. **Scorers:** Luis Fabiano (26), Maresca (78, 84), Kanoute (89). **Booked:** Alves, Maresca. **Coach:** Juande Ramos.

Referee: H. Fandel (Germany). **Half-time:** 0-1.

Rarely can a team have reached a European final with sheer bravado and never-say-die spirit. Rarely can a team have then suffered crushing disappointment on the big night. Such was the roller-coaster ridden by Steve McClaren and his Middlesbrough players in the space of a few weeks at the end of last season.

Twice they were on the brink of going out of the competition when falling 3-0 behind on aggregate in second leg matches at the Riverside – first against Basle in the quarter-finals, then against Steaua Bucharest with a place in the final at stake. Each time McClaren threw caution to the wind, played with four strikers and was rewarded with 4-3 victories.

But in his final game in charge before succeeding Sven-Goran Eriksson as England coach, McClaren had no answer to the style and subtleties of Sevilla who went ahead midway through the first half, defied Middlesbrough's charge after the break and then picked them off on the counter with three goals in the final 12 minutes.

The outcome might have been different if Mark Viduka had put away his side's best chance instead of having his shot saved by Andres Palop after Chris Riggott's knock-down, or if strong appeals for a penalty when Javi Navarro piled into the back of Viduka had not been rejected by the German referee Herbert Fandel.

Instead, Sevilla retained the lead established when Luis Fabiano leapt like a salmon above Riggott to head in a diagonal Daniel Alves cross, stayed firm at the back when coming under considerable pressure, then fully exploited the gaps when their opponents were committed to all-out attack.

The damage was done by two former English League players – Enzo Maresca, once of West Bromwich Albion, and the former West Ham and Tottenham striker Fredi Kanoute. Mark Schwarzer, playing with a protective mask after sustaining a fractured cheekbone in the F.A. Cup semi-final defeat by West Ham, parried Kanoute's shot into the path of Maresca, who followed that tap-in by beating the goalkeeper from the edge of the penalty box. Finally, the Italian's shot was spilled by Schwarzer, leaving Kanoute with another simple follow-up.

It was the biggest winning margin since the UEFA Cup Final switched from being decided over two legs in 1998 and meant that McClaren began and ended his Middlesbrough career with a 4-0 defeat, Arsenal having inflicted that scoreline at the start of the 2001-02 Premiership season.

UEFA CUP FINALS

1972	Tottenham beat Wolves 3-2 on agg. (2-1a, 1-1h)
1973	Liverpool beat Borussia Moenchengladbach 3-2 on agg. (3-0h, 0-2a)
1974	Feyenoord beat Tottenham 4-2 on agg. (2-2a, 2-0h)
1975	Borussia Moenchengladbach beat Twente Enschede 5-1 on agg. (0-0h, 5-1a)
1976	Liverpool beat Brugge 4-3 on agg. (3-2h, 1-1a)
1977	Juventus beat Atletico Bilbao on away goals after 2-2 agg. (1-0h, 1-2a)
1978	PSV Eindhoven beat Bastia 3-0 on agg. (0-0a, 3-0h)
1979	Borussia Moenchengladbach beat Red Star Belgrade 2-1 on agg. (1-1a, 1-0h)
1980	Eintracht Frankfurt beat Borussia Moenchengladbach on away goals after 3-3 agg. (2-3a, 1-0h)
1981	Ipswich Town beat AZ 67 Alkmaar 5-4 on agg. (3-0h, 2-4a)
1982	IFK Gothenburg beat SV Hamburg 4-0 on agg. (1-0h, 3-0a)
1983	Anderlecht beat Benfica 2-1 on agg. (1-0h, 1-1a)
1984	Tottenham beat Anderlecht 4-3 on penalties after 2-2 agg. (1-1a, 1-1h)
1985	Real Madrid beat Videoton 3-1 on agg. (3-0a, 0-1h)
1986	Real Madrid beat Cologne 5-3 on agg. (5-1h, 0-2a)
1987	IFK Gothenburg beat Dundee Utd. 2-1 on agg. (1-0h, 1-1a)
1988	Bayer Leverkusen beat Espanol 3-2 on penalties after 3-3 agg. (0-3a, 3-0h)
1989	Napoli beat VfB Stuttgart 5-4 on agg. (2-1h, 3-3a)
1990	Juventus beat Fiorentina 3-1 on agg. (3-1h, 0-0a)
1991	Inter Milan beat AS Roma 2-1 on agg. (2-0h, 0-1a)
1992	Ajax beat Torino on away goals after 2-2 agg. (2-2a, 0-0h)
1993	Juventus beat Borussia Dortmund 6-1 on agg. (3-1a, 3-0h)
1994	Inter Milan beat Salzburg 2-0 on agg. (1-0a, 1-0h)
1995	Parma beat Juventus 2-1 on agg. (1-0h, 1-1a)
1996	Bayern Munich beat Bordeaux 5-1 on agg. (2-0h, 3-1a)
1997	FC Schalke beat Inter Milan 4-1 on penalties after 1-1 agg. (1-0h, 0-1a)
1998	Inter Milan beat Lazio 3-0 (one match) – Paris
1999	Parma beat Marseille 3-0 (one match) – Moscow
2000	Galatasaray beat Arsenal 4-1 on penalties after 0-0 (one match) – Copenhagen
2001	Liverpool beat Alaves 5-4 on golden goal (one match) – Dortmund
2002	Feyenoord beat Borussia Dortmund 3-2 (one match) – Rotterdam
2003	FC Porto beat Celtic 3-2 on silver goal (one match) – Seville
2004	Valencia beat Marseille 2-0 (one match) – Gothenburg
2005	CSKA Moscow beat Sporting Lisbon 3-1 (one match) – Lisbon
2006	Sevilla beat Middlesbrough 4-0 (one match) – Eindhoven

FAIRS CUP FINALS

(As UEFA Cup previously known)

1958	Barcelona beat London 8-2 on agg. (2-2a, 6-0h)
1960	Barcelona beat Birmingham 4-1 on agg. (0-0a, 4-1h)
1961	AS Roma beat Birmingham City 4-2 on agg. (2-2a, 2-0h)
1962	Valencia beat Barcelona 7-3 on agg. (6-2h, 1-1a)
1963	Valencia beat Dynamo Zagreb 4-1 on agg. (2-1a, 2-0h)
1964	Real Zaragoza beat Valencia 2-1 (Barcelona)
1965	Ferencvaros beat Juventus 1-0 (Turin)
1966	Barcelona beat Real Zaragoza 4-3 on agg. (0-1h, 4-2a)
1967	Dynamo Zagreb beat Leeds Utd. 2-0 on agg. (2-0h, 0-0a)
1968	Leeds Utd. beat Ferencvaros 1-0 on agg. (1-0h, 0-0a)
1969	Newcastle Utd. beat Ujpest Dozsa 6-2 on agg. (3-0h, 3-2a)
1970	Arsenal beat Anderlecht 4-3 on agg. (1-3a, 3-0h)
1971	Leeds Utd. beat Juventus on away goals after 3-3 agg. (2-2a, 1-1h)

CUP-WINNERS' CUP FINALS

1961	Fiorentina beat Rangers 4-1 on agg. (2-0 Glasgow first leg, 2-1 Florence second leg)
1962	Atletico Madrid beat Fiorentina 3-0 (replay Stuttgart, after a 1-1 draw, Glasgow)
1963	Tottenham beat Atletico Madrid 5-1 (Rotterdam)
1964	Sporting Lisbon beat MTK Budapest 1-0 (replay Antwerp, after a 3-3 draw, Brussels)
1965	West Ham Utd. beat Munich 1860 2-0 (Wembley)
1966†	Borussia Dortmund beat Liverpool 2-1 (Glasgow)
1967†	Bayern Munich beat Rangers 1-0 (Nuremberg)
1968	AC Milan beat SV Hamburg 2-0 (Rotterdam)
1969	Slovan Bratislava beat Barcelona 3-2 (Basle)
1970	Manchester City beat Gornik Zabrze 2-1 (Vienna)
1971†	Chelsea beat Real Madrid 2-1 (replay Athens, after a 1-1 draw, Athens)
1972	Rangers beat Moscow Dynamo 3-2 (Barcelona)
1973	AC Milan beat Leeds Utd. 1-0 (Salonika)
1974	Magdeburg beat AC Milan 2-0 (Rotterdam)
1975	Dynamo Kiev beat Ferencvaros 3-0 (Basle)
1976	Anderlecht beat West Ham Utd. 4-2 (Brussels)
1977	SV Hamburg beat Anderlecht 2-0 (Amsterdam)
1978	Anderlecht beat Austria WAC 4-0 (Paris)
1979†	Barcelona beat Fortuna Dusseldorf 4-3 (Basle)
1980†	Valencia beat Arsenal 5-4 on penalties after a 0-0 draw (Brussels)
1981	Dynamo Tbilisi beat Carl Zeiss Jena 2-1 (Dusseldorf)
1982	Barcelona beat Standard Liege 2-1 (Barcelona)
1983†	Aberdeen beat Real Madrid 2-1 (Gothenburg)
1984	Juventus beat Porto 2-1 (Basle)
1985	Everton beat Rapid Vienna 3-1 (Rotterdam)
1986	Dynamo Kiev beat Atletico Madrid 3-0 (Lyon)
1987	Ajax beat Lokomotiv Leipzig 1-0 (Athens)
1988	Mechelen beat Ajax 1-0 (Strasbourg)
1989	Barcelona beat Sampdoria 2-0 (Berne)
1990	Sampdoria beat Anderlecht 2-0 (Gothenburg)
1991	Manchester Utd. beat Barcelona 2-1 (Rotterdam)
1992	Werder Bremen beat Monaco 2-0 (Lisbon)
1993	Parma beat Royal Antwerp 3-1 (Wembley)

1994	Arsenal beat Parma 1-0 (Copenhagen)
1995†	Real Zaragoza beat Arsenal 2-1 (Paris)
1996	Paris St. Germain beat Rapid Vienna 1-0 (Brussels)
1997	Barcelona beat Paris St. Germain 1-0 (Rotterdam)
1998	Chelsea beat VfB Stuttgart 1-0 (Stockholm)
1999	Lazio beat Real Mallorca 2-1 (Villa Park, Birmingham)

(† After extra time)

INTER-CONTINENTAL CUP

Year	Winners	Runners-up	Score		
1960	Real Madrid (Spa.)	Penarol (Uru.)	0-0	5-1	
1961	Penarol (Uru.)	Benfica (Por.)	0-1	2-1	5-0
1962	Santos (Bra.)	Benfica (Por.)	3-2	5-2	
1963	Santos (Bra.)	AC Milan (Ita.)	2-4	4-2	1-0
1964	Inter Milan (Ita.)	Independiente (Arg.)	0-1	2-0	1-0
1965	Inter Milan (Ita.)	Independiente (Arg.)	3-0	0-0	
1966	Penarol (Uru.)	Real Madrid (Spa.)	2-0	2-0	
1967	Racing (Arg.)	Celtic (Sco.)	0-1	2-1	1-0
1968	Estudiantes (Arg.)	Manchester Utd. (Eng.)	1-0	1-1	
1969	AC Milan (Ita.)	Estudiantes (Arg.)	3-0	1-2	
1970	Feyenoord (Hol.)	Estudiantes (Arg.)	2-2	1-0	
1971	Nacional (Uru.)	Panathanaikos (Gre.)*	1-1	2-1	
1972	Ajax (Hol.)	Independiente (Arg.)	1-1	3-0	
1973	Independiente (Arg.)	Juventus (Ita.)*	1-0	#	
1974	Atletico Madrid (Spa.)*	Independiente (Arg.)	0-1	2-0	
1975	Not played				
1976	Bayern Munich (W.Ger.)	Cruzeiro (Bra.)	2-0	0-0	
1977	Boca Juniors (Arg.)	Borussia Mönchengladbach (W.Ger.)*	2-2	3-0	
1978	Not played				
1979	Olimpia Asuncion (Par.)	Malmö (Swe.)*	1-0	2-1	
1980	Nacional (Arg.)	Nott'm. Forest (Eng.)	1-0		
1981	Flamengo (Bra.)	Liverpool (Eng.)	3-0		
1982	Penarol (Uru.)	Aston Villa (Eng.)	2-0		
1983	Porto Alegre (Bra.)	SV Hamburg (W.Ger.)	2-1		
1984	Independiente (Arg.)	Liverpool (Eng.)	1-0		
1985	Juventus (Ita.)	Argentinos Juniors (Arg.)	2-2 (aet)		
	(Juventus won 4-2 on penalties)				
1986	River Plate (Arg.)	Steaua Bucharest (Rum.)	1-0		
1987	Porto (Por.)	Penarol (Arg.)	2-1 (aet)		
1988	Nacional (Uru.)	PSV Eindhoven (Hol.)	1-1 (aet)		
	(Nacional won 7-6 on penalties)				
1989	AC Milan (Ita.)	Nacional (Col.)	1-0 (aet)		
1990	AC Milan (Ita.)	Olimpia Asuncion (Par.)	3-0		
1991	Red Star (Yug.)	Colo Colo (Chi.)	3-0		
1992	Sao Paulo (Bra.)	Barcelona (Spa.)	2-1		
1993	Sao Paulo (Bra.)	AC Milan (Ita.)	3-2		
1994	Velez Sarsfield (Arg.)	AC Milan (Ita.)	2-0		
1995	Ajax (Hol.)	Gremio (Bra.)	0-0 (aet)		
	(Ajax won 4-3 on penalties)				
1996	Juventus (Ita.)	River Plate (Arg.)	1-0		
1997	Borussia Dortmund (Ger.)	Cruzeiro (Arg.)	2-0		
1998	Real Madrid (Spa.)	Vasco da Gama (Bra.)	2-1		
1999	Manchester Utd. (Eng.)	Palmeiras (Bra.)	1-0		

2000	Boca Juniors (Arg.)	Real Madrid (Spa.)	2-1
2001	Bayern Munich (Ger.)	Boca Juniuors (Arg.)	1-0
2002	Real Madrid (Spa.)	Olimpia Ascuncion (Par.)	2-0
2003	Boca Juniors (Arg.)	AC Milan (Ita.)	1-1

(Boca Juniors won 3-1 on penalties)

| 2004 | FC Porto (Por.) | Caldas (Col.) | 0-0 |

(FC Porto won 8-7 on penalties)

Played as a single match in Japan since 1980
* European Cup runners-up. # One match only.
Summary: 43 contests; South America 22 wins, Europe 23 wins.

WORLD CLUB CHAMPIONSHIP FINAL

SAO PAULO 1, LIVERPOOL 0

Yokohama (66,821), Sunday, December 18, 2005

Sao Paulo (4-4-2): Rogerio Ceni, Fabao, Diego Lugano, EdCarlos, Cicinho, Junior, Josue, Danilo, Mineiro, Amoroso, Aloisio (Grafite 75). **Scorer:** Mineiro (26). **Booked:** Lugano, Rogerio Ceni.

Liverpool (4-4-1-1): Reina, Finnan, Carragher, Hyypia, Warnock (Riise 77), Gerrard, Xabi Alonso, Sissoko (Sinama Pongolle 77), Kewell, Luis Garcia, Morientes (Crouch 85).

Referee: B. Archundia (Mexcico). **Half-time:** 1-0.

EUROPEAN SUPERCUP

LIVERPOOL 3, CSKA MOSCOW 1 (aet)

Monaco (10,000), Friday, August 26, 2005

Liverpool (4-5-1): Reina, Josemi, (Sinama Pongolle 55), Hyypia, Carragher, Riise (Cisse 79), Finnan, Luis Garcia, Xabi Alonso (Sissoko 71), Hamann, Zenden, Morientes. **Scorers:** Cisse (82, 102), Luis Garcia (109). **Booked:** Hyypia, Luis Garcia, Sinama Pongolle, Zenden.

CSKA Moskow (4-4-2): Akinfev, Ignashvich, A. Berezutsky, V. Berezutsky, Ordia (Gusev 90), Daniel Carvalho, Vagner Love, Krasic (Dudu 85), Zhirkov (Semberas 66), Aldonin, Rahimic. **Scorer:** Daniel Carvalho (28). **Booked:** Rahimic.

Referee: R. Temmink (Holland). **Half-time:** 0-1.

QUOTE-UNQUOTE

'If I said I'd go back now I'd be crucified – that's all I need' – **Harry Redknapp**, Southampton manager, on speculation of a move back to Portsmouth.

'I just wanted to come back. It took me less than a minute to sign the contract, which didn't even have any figures on it' – **Harry Redknapp** on his return to Fratton Park.

'The saga had got to the stage of being an embarrassment to football as a whole' – **Rupert Lowe**, Southampton chairman, on the Redknapp affair.

EUROPEAN TABLES 2005-06

FRANCE

		P	W	D	L	F	A	Pts	GD
1	Lyon	38	25	9	4	73	31	84	42
2	Bordeaux	38	18	15	5	43	25	69	18
3	Lille	38	16	14	8	56	31	62	25
4	Lens	38	14	18	6	48	34	60	14
5	Marseille	38	16	12	10	44	35	60	9
6	Auxerre	38	17	8	13	50	39	59	11
7	Rennes	38	18	5	15	48	49	59	−1
8	Nice	38	16	10	12	36	31	58	5
9	Paris SG	38	13	13	12	44	38	52	6
10	Monaco	38	13	13	12	42	36	52	6
11	Le Mans	38	13	13	12	33	36	52	−3
12	Nancy	38	12	12	14	35	37	48	−2
13	St Etienne	38	11	14	13	29	39	47	−10
14	Nantes	38	11	12	15	37	41	45	−4
15	Sochaux	38	11	11	16	34	47	44	−13
16	Toulouse	38	10	11	17	36	47	41	−11
17	Troyes	38	9	12	17	37	47	39	−10
18	Ajaccio	38	8	9	21	27	53	33	−26
19	Strasbourg	38	5	14	19	33	56	29	−23
20	Metz	38	6	11	21	26	59	29	−33

Leading scorers: 21 Pauleta (Paris SG); 14 Fred (Lyon), Odemwingie (Lille); 13 Cousin (Lens); 12 Pieroni (Auxerre), Wiltord (Lyon); 11 Ilan (Sochaux), Utaka (Rennes); 10 Chevanton (Monaco), Diallo (Nantes), Luyindula (Auxerre), Moreira (Toulouse), Niang (Marseille), Pagis (Marseille).
Cup Final: Paris SG 2, Marseille 1.

GERMANY

		P	W	D	L	F	A	Pts	GD
1	Bayern Munich	34	22	9	3	67	32	75	35
2	Werder Bremen	34	21	7	6	79	37	70	42
3	Hamburg	34	21	5	8	53	30	68	23
4	Schalke	34	16	13	5	47	31	61	16
5	Bayer Leverkusen	34	14	10	10	64	49	52	15
6	Hertha Berlin	34	12	12	10	52	48	48	4
7	Borussia Dortmund	34	11	13	10	45	42	46	3
8	Nuremberg	34	12	8	14	49	51	44	−2
9	Stuttgart	34	9	16	9	37	39	43	−2
10	Borussia M'Gladbach	34	10	12	12	42	50	42	−8
11	Mainz	34	9	11	14	46	47	38	−1
12	Hannover	34	7	17	10	43	47	38	−4
13	Arminia Bielefeld	34	10	7	17	32	47	37	−15
14	Eintracht Frankfurt	34	9	9	16	42	51	36	−9
15	Wolfsburg	34	7	13	14	33	55	34	−22
16	Kaiserslautern	34	8	9	17	47	71	33	−24
17	Cologne	34	7	9	18	49	71	30	−22
18	Duisburg	34	5	12	17	34	63	27	−29

Leading scorers: 25 Klose (Werder Bremen); 21 Berbatov (Bayer Leverkusen); 20 Altintop (Kaiserslautern); 17 Makaay (Bayern Munich), Vittek (Nuremberg); 15 Klasnic (Werder Bremen); 14 Ballack (Bayern Munich); 13 Smolarek (Borussia Dortmund); 12 Amanatidis (Eintracht Frankfurt), Klimowicz (Wolfsburg), Marcelinho (Hertha Berlin), Podolski (Cologne), Thurk (Mainz).
Cup Final: Bayern Munich 1, Eintracht Frankfurt 0.

HOLLAND

		P	W	D	L	F	A	Pts	GD
1	PSV Eindhoven	34	26	6	2	71	23	84	48
2	AZ Alkmaar	34	23	5	6	78	32	74	46
3	Feyenoord	34	21	8	5	79	34	71	45
4	Ajax	34	18	6	10	66	41	60	25
5	Groningen	34	16	8	10	46	43	56	3
6	Utrecht	34	16	7	11	48	44	55	4
7	Heerenveen	34	14	8	12	63	58	50	5
8	Roda JC	34	15	5	14	57	54	50	3
9	FC Twente	34	13	8	13	44	36	47	8
10	NEC	34	13	8	13	43	43	47	–
11	Vitesse	34	13	5	16	52	54	44	–2
12	RKC	34	11	6	17	48	58	39	–10
13	Heracles	34	11	6	17	35	58	39	–23
14	Sparta	34	10	7	17	34	50	37	–16
15	Den Haag	34	10	5	19	36	62	35	–26
16	NAC	34	8	9	17	45	66	33	–21
17	Willem II	34	7	7	20	45	66	28	–21
18	Roosendaal	34	1	6	27	22	90	9	–68

Leading scorers: 32 Huntelaar (Ajax); 22 Arveladze (AZ Alkmaar), Kuijt (Feyenoord); 20 Farfan (PSV Eindhoven); 15 Kalou (Feyenoord); 13 Kone (PSV Eindhoven); 12 Hoogendorp (Waalwijk), Nkufo (FC Twente); 11 Vennegoor of Hesselink (PSV Eindhoven), Rosenberg (Ajax).
Cup Final: Ajax 2, PSV Eindhoven 1.

ITALY

		P	W	D	L	F	A	Pts	GD
1	Juventus*	38	27	10	1	71	24	91	47
2	AC Milan	38	28	4	6	85	31	88	54
3	Inter Milan	38	23	7	8	68	30	76	38
4	Fiorentina**	38	22	8	8	66	41	74	25
5	Roma	38	19	12	7	70	42	69	28
6	Lazio**	38	16	14	8	57	47	62	10
7	Chievo	38	13	15	10	54	49	54	5
8	Palermo	38	13	13	12	50	52	52	–2
9	Livorno	38	12	13	13	37	44	49	–7
10	Parma	38	12	9	17	46	60	45	–14
11	Empoli	38	13	6	19	47	61	45	–14
12	Ascoli	38	9	16	13	43	53	43	–10
13	Udinese	38	11	10	17	40	54	43	–14
14	Sampdoria	38	10	11	17	47	51	41	–4
15	Reggina	38	11	8	19	39	65	41	–26
16	Cagliari	38	8	15	15	42	55	39	–13
17	Siena	38	9	12	17	42	60	39	–18
18	Messina	38	6	13	19	33	59	31	–26
19	Lecce	38	7	8	23	30	57	29	–27
20	Treviso	38	3	12	23	24	56	21	–32

* Juventus relegated to Serie B and stripped of this and previous season's title for corruption offences. ** Fiorentina and Lazio also found guilty and relegated.

Leading scorers: 31 Toni (Fiorentina); 23 Trezeguet (Juventus); 22 Suazo (Cagliari); 20 Lucarelli (Livorno); 19 Shevchenko (AC Milan), Tavano (Empoli); 17 Gilardino (AC Milan); 16 Rocchi (Lazio); 15 Cruz (Inter Milan), Totti (Roma); 14 Kaka (AC Milan); 13 Adriano (Inter Milan), Di Napoli (Messina), Pellissier (Chievo).
Cup Final: Inter Milan 4, Roma 2 (on agg).

PORTUGAL

		P	W	D	L	F	A	Pts	GD
1	FC Porto	34	24	7	3	54	16	79	38
2	Sporting Lisbon	34	22	6	6	50	24	72	26
3	Benfica	34	20	7	7	51	29	67	22
4	Sporting Braga	34	17	7	10	38	22	58	16
5	Nacional	34	14	10	10	40	32	52	8
6	Boavista	34	12	14	8	37	29	50	8
7	Uniao Leiria	34	13	8	13	44	42	47	2
8	Vitoria Setubal	34	14	4	16	28	33	46	−5
9	Amadora	34	12	9	13	31	33	45	−2
10	Maritimo	34	10	14	10	38	37	44	1
11	Pacos Ferreira	34	11	9	14	38	49	42	−11
12	Gil Vicente	34	11	7	16	37	42	40	−5
13	Academica	34	10	9	15	37	48	39	−11
14	Naval	34	11	6	17	35	48	39	−13
15	Belenenses	34	11	6	17	40	42	39	−2
16	Rio Ave	34	8	10	16	34	53	34	−19
17	Guimaraes	34	8	10	16	28	41	34	−13
18	Penafiel	34	2	9	23	20	61	15	−41

Leading scorers: 17 Meyong (Belenenses); 15 Liedson (Sporting Lisbon), Nuno Gomes (Benfica), Tomas (Sporting Braga); 14 Pinto (Nacional); 13 Joeano (Academica); 12 Saganowski (Guimaraes); 11 Goulart (Nacional); 10 Cesar (Uniao Leiria), Gaucho (Rio Ave).
Cup Final: FC Porto 1, Vitoria Setubal 0.

SPAIN

		P	W	D	L	F	A	Pts	GD
1	Barcelona	38	25	7	6	80	35	82	45
2	Real Madrid	38	20	10	8	70	40	70	30
3	Valencia	38	19	12	7	58	33	69	25
4	Osasuna	38	21	5	12	49	43	68	6
5	Sevilla	38	20	8	10	54	39	68	15
6	Celta Vigo	38	20	4	14	45	33	64	12
7	Villarreal	38	14	15	9	50	39	57	11
8	Deportivo La Coruna	38	15	10	13	47	45	55	2
9	Getafe	38	15	9	14	54	49	54	5
10	Atletico Madrid	38	13	13	12	45	37	52	8
11	Real Zaragoza	38	10	16	12	46	51	46	−5
12	Athletic Bilbao	38	11	12	15	40	46	45	−6
13	Mallorca	38	10	13	15	37	51	43	−14
14	Real Betis	30	10	12	16	34	51	42	−17
15	Espanyol	38	10	11	17	36	56	41	−20
16	Real Sociedad	38	11	7	20	48	65	40	−17
17	Racing Santander	38	9	13	16	36	49	40	−13
18	Alaves	38	9	12	17	35	54	39	−19
19	Cadiz	38	8	12	18	36	52	36	−16
20	Malaga	38	5	9	24	36	68	24	−32

Leading scorers: 25 Eto'o (Barcelona), Villa (Valencia); 18 Ronaldinho (Barcelona); 15 Milito (Zaragoza); 14 Ronaldo (Real Madrid); 13 Baiano (Celta Vigo), Torres (Atletico Madrid); 12 Ewerthon (Real Zaragoza), Riquelme (Villarreal), Tristan (Deportivo La Coruna); 11 Aloisi (Alaves), Arango (Mallorca), Milosevic (Osasuna).
Cup Final: Espanyol 4, Real Zaragoza 1.

EUROPEAN CHAMPIONSHIP 2008

Italy and France, who contested the World Cup Final, will resume rivalry in Paris on September 6 at the start of qualifying for the 2008 European Championship. They have been drawn in the same group, along with Scotland, who were also in Italy's qualifying section for Germany 2006. When the big two met in the 2000 European Final in Rotterdam, France won 2-1 with a 'golden goal' in extra-time by David Trezeguet, the player whose penalty miss proved crucial in July's World Cup decider.

England, under new coach Steve McClaren, break new ground with qualifying games against Andorra and Estonia. Their main opposition in a comfortable-looking group is likely to come from Croatia and Russia. In Euro 2004 they beat Croatia 4-2, Wayne Rooney scoring twice, when reaching the quarter-finals. England have not played Russia since the break-up of the USSR. Wales and the Republic of Ireland meet in a group headed by Germany and the Czech Republic, while Northern Ireland are up against Spain and Sweden.

UEFA have made changes to the qualifying format. There will be no play-offs. The seven group winners and runners-up go through to the Finals, along with the joint host countries, Austria and Switzerland. Championship venues in Austria are Innsbruck, Klagenfurt, Salzburg and Vienna. In Switzerland, there will be matches in Basle, Berne, Geneva and Zurich. The opening game is in Basle on June 7, 2008 and the Final in the Ernst Happel Stadium (Capacity 50,000) in Vienna on June 29. Draw for the Finals is provisionally scheduled for December 2007. The first qualifying matches, including Championship newcomers Kazakhstan against Belgium in Brussels, are on August 16.

QUALIFYING GROUPS

Group A: Armenia, Azerbaijan, Belgium, Finland, Kazakhstan, Poland, Portugal, Serbia & Montenegro.
Group B: Faroe Islands, France, Georgia, Italy, Lithuania, **Scotland**, Ukraine.
Group C: Bosnia-Herzegovina, Greece, Hungary, Malta, Moldova, Norway, Turkey.
Group D: Cyprus, Germany, Czech Republic, **Republic of Ireland**, San Marino, Slovakia, **Wales**.
Group E: Andorra, **England**, Croatia, Estonia, Israel, Macedonia, Russia.
Group F: Denmark, Iceland, Latvia, Liechtenstein, **Northern Ireland**, Spain, Sweden.
Group G: Albania, Belarus, Bulgaria, Holland, Luxembourg, Romania, Slovenia.

PREVIOUS FINALS

1960	*USSR	2	Yugoslavia	1	(Paris)
1964	Spain	2	USSR	1	(Madrid)
1968	**Italy	2	Yugoslavia	0	(Rome)
1972	West Germany	3	USSR	0	(Brussels)
1976	***Czechoslovakia	2	West Germany	2	(Belgrade)
1980	West Germany	2	Belgium	1	(Rome)
1984	France	2	Spain	0	(Paris)
1988	Holland	2	USSR	0	(Munich)
1992	Denmark	2	Germany	0	(Gothenburg)
1996	+Germany	2	Czech Republic	1	(Wembley)
2000	+France	2	Italy	1	(Rotterdam)
2004	Greece	1	Portugal	0	(Lisbon)

* After extra-time. ** Replay after 1-1. *** Czechoslovakia won 5-3 on pens. + Golden goal winner.

BRITISH AND IRISH INTERNATIONALS
2005-06

(*Denotes new cap)

WORLD CUP 2006 – QUALIFYING

WALES 0, ENGLAND 1
Group 6, Millennium Stadium (70,715), Saturday, September 3, 2005

Wales (5-3-1-1): Coyne (Burnley), Duffy (Portsmouth), Page (Coventry City) (Collins, West Ham Utd., 64), Gabbidon (West Ham Utd.), Partridge (Bristol City), Ricketts (Swansea City), Davies (Everton) (Earnshaw, W.B.A., 69), Fletcher (West Ham Utd.), Robinson (Sunderland) (Koumas, Cardiff City, 54), Giggs (Manchester Utd.), Hartson (Celtic). **Booked:** Hartson.

England (4-5-1): Robinson (Tottenham), Young (Charlton Athletic), Ferdinand (Manchester Utd.), Carragher (Liverpool), A. Cole (Arsenal), Wright-Phillips (Chelsea) (Defoe, Tottenham, 68), Gerrard (Liverpool) (Richardson, Manchester Utd., 84), Beckham (Real Madrid), Lampard (Chelsea), J. Cole (Chelsea) (Hargreaves, Bayern Munich, 77), Rooney (Manchester Utd.). **Scorer:** J. Cole (54).

Referee: V. Ivanov (Russia). **Half-time:** 0-0.

SCOTLAND 1, ITALY 1
Group 5, Hampden Park (50,185), Saturday, September 3, 2005

Scotland (4-1-4-1): Gordon (Hearts), Alexander (Preston N.E.), Weir (Everton), Webster (Hearts), McNamara (Wolves), Dailly (West Ham Utd.), Hartley (Hearts), Fletcher (Manchester Utd.), Ferguson (Rangers), Quashie (Southampton) (McCann, Southampton, 67), Miller (Wolves) (*Beattie, Celtic, 77). **Scorer:** Miller (13). **Booked:** Dailly, Ferguson, Beattie.

Italy (4-3-1-2): Peruzzi, Zaccardo (Grosso 46), Nesta, Cannavaro, Zambrotta, Gattuso, Pirlo, De Rossi (Camoranesi 66), Totti, Iaquinta (Toni 71), Vieri. **Scorer:** Grosso (76). **Booked:** Zambrotta, Totti, De Rossi.

Referee: L. Michel (Slovakia). **Half-time:** 1-0.

NORTHERN IRELAND 2, AZERBAIJAN 0
Group 6, Windsor Park (11,909), Saturday, September 3, 2005

Northern Ireland (4-4-2): Taylor (Birmingham City), Baird (Southampton), Hughes (Aston Villa), Craigan (Motherwell), Capaldi (Plymouth Argyle), Gillespie (Sheffield Utd.), Johnson (Birmingham City), Davis (Aston Villa), Elliott (Hull City) (Robinson, Luton Town, 89), Healy (Leeds Utd.) (Jones, Crewe Alexandra, 79), Quinn (Peterborough Utd.) (Feeney, Luton Town, 72). **Scorers:** Elliott (60), Feeney (85 pen).

Azerbaijan (3-4-2-1): Kramarenko, Amirbekov, Tagizade (Nabiev 84), Muzika, Imamaliyev, M. Gurbanov (Ponomaryov 65) Sadygov, Guliyev, Hajiyev, Kerimov, Aliyev (Shukurov 74). **Booked:** Guliyev, Aliyev, Amirbekov, Sadygov.

Referee: D. Stanisic (Serbia & Montenegro). **Half-time:** 0-0.

NORTHERN IRELAND 1, ENGLAND 0
Group 6, Windsor Park (14,000), Wednesday, September 7, 2005

Northern Ireland (4-4-2): Taylor (Birmingham City), Baird (Southampton), Hughes (Aston Villa), Craigan (Motherwell), Capaldi (Plymouth Argyle), Gillespie (Sheffield Utd.), Johnson (Birmingham City), Davis (Aston Villa), Elliott (Hull City), Healy (Leeds Utd.), Quinn (Peterborough Utd.) (Feeney, Luton Town, 79). **Scorer:** Healy (74). **Booked:** Johnson, Capaldi, Baird.

England (4-3-2-1): Robinson (Tottenham), Young (Charlton Athletic), Ferdinand (Manchester Utd.), Carragher (Liverpool), A. Cole (Arsenal), Lampard (Chelsea) (Hargreaves, Bayern Munich, 84), Beckham (Real Madrid), Gerrard (Liverpool) (Defoe, Tottenham, 75), Wright-Phillips (Chelsea) (J. Cole, Chelsea, 52) Rooney (Manchester Utd.), Owen (Newcastle Utd.). **Booked:** Rooney.

Referee: M. Busacca (Switzerland). **Half-time:** 0-0.

NORWAY 1, SCOTLAND 2
Group 5, Oslo (24,904), Wednesday, September 7, 2005

Norway (4-4-2): Myhre, Solli (Haested 46), Riseth, Lundekvam, Bergdolmo, Valencia (Braaten 46), Grindheim, Andresen, Riise, Ostenstad (Aarst 46), Carew. **Scorer:** Aarst (89). **Booked:** Carew.

Scotland (3-5-1-1): Gordon (Hearts), Pressley (Hearts), Weir (Everton), Webster (Hearts), Alexander (Preston N.E.), Hartley (Hearts), Ferguson (Rangers), McNamara (Wolves), Fletcher (Manchester Utd.), McFadden (Everton) (Beattie, Celtic, 71), Miller (Wolves) (McCann, Southampton, 45). **Scorer:** Miller (21, 31). **Booked:** McFadden.

Referee: A.Hamer (Luxembourg). **Half-time:** 0-2.

POLAND 1, WALES 0
Group 6, Warsaw (14,000), Wednesday, September 7, 2005

Poland (4-4-2): Boruc, Rzasa, Jop, Bak, Baszczynski, Smolarek (Zewlakow 88), Sobolewski, Szymkowiak, Kosowski (Radomski 80), Zurawski, Rasiak (Frankowski 65). **Scorer:** Zurawski (53 pen). **Booked:** Szymkowiak.

Wales (3-5-2): Coyne (Burnley), Collins (West Ham Utd.), Gabbidon (West Ham Utd.), Partridge (Bristol City), Edwards (Wolves) (Duffy, Portsmouth, 46), S. Davies (Everton), Fletcher (West Ham Utd.), Koumas (Cardiff City) (C. Davies, Oxford Utd., 69), Ricketts (Swansea City), Earnshaw (W.B.A.), (*Ledley, Cardiff City, 82), Giggs (Manchester Utd.). **Booked:** Gabbidon.

Referee: C. Laursen (Denmark). **Half-time:** 0-0.

REPUBLIC OF IRELAND 0, FRANCE 1
Group 4, Lansdowne Road (35,000), Wednesday, September 7, 2005

Republic of Ireland (4-4-2): Given (Newcastle Utd.), Carr (Newcastle Utd.), Cunningham (Birmingham City), Dunne (Manchester City), O'Shea (Manchester Utd.), Reid (Tottenham), Roy Keane (Manchester Utd.), Kilbane (Everton) (Doherty, Norwich City, 78), Duff (Chelsea), Robbie Keane (Tottenham), Morrison (Crystal Palace) (Harte, Levante, 78). **Booked:** Morrison, Roy Keane, Carr, Reid.

France (4-1-3-1-1): Coupet, Sagnol (Givet 90), Thuram, Boumsong, Gallas, Makelele, Wiltord, Vieira (Cisse 76), Dhorasoo, Zidane (Malouda 70), Henry. **Scorer:** Henry (68). **Booked:** Sagnol, Zidane.

Referee: H. Fandel (Germany). **Half-time:** 0-0.

ENGLAND 1, AUSTRIA 0
Group 6, Old Trafford (64,882), Saturday, October 8, 2005

England (4-4-2): Robinson (Tottenham), Young (Charlton Athletic), Terry (Chelsea), Campbell (Arsenal) (Ferdinand, Manchester Utd., 64), Carragher (Liverpool), Beckham (Real Madrid), Lampard (Chelsea), Cole (Chelsea) (King, Tottenham 61), Crouch (Liverpool), Owen (Newcastle Utd.) (Richardson, Manchester Utd., 80). **Scorer:** Lampard (25 pen). **Booked:** Beckham, Cole. **Sent-off:** Beckham.

Austria (4-4-1-1): Macho, Dober, Scharner, Stranzl, Ibertsberger (Lasnik 79), Schopp (Kuljic 64), Aufhauser, Kiesenebner, Ivanschitz, Weissenberger (Sariyar 46), Linz. **Booked:** Scharner, Schopp, Ivanschitz.

Referee: L. Medina Cantalejo (Spain). **Half-time:** 1-0.

SCOTLAND 0, BELARUS 1
Group 5, Hampden Park (51,105), Saturday, October 8, 2005

Scotland (4-1-4-1): Gordon (Hearts), Alexander (Preston N.E.), Pressley (Hearts), Weir (Everton), Murray (Rangers) (*Maloney, Celtic, 46), Dailly (West Ham Utd.), Hartley (Hearts), Fletcher (Manchester Utd.), Ferguson (Rangers), McCulloch (Wigan Athletic), Miller (Wolves). **Booked:** McCulloch, Ferguson.

Belarus (4-4-1-1): Khomutovsky, Korytko, Tarlovsky, Ostrovsky, Lavrik, Kalachev, Kovba, Kulchy, Bulyga (Sascheka 88), Hleb, Kutuzov. **Scorer:** Kutuzov (6). **Booked:** Korytko, Lavrik.

Referee: Z. Szabo (Hungary). **Half-time:** 0-1.

NORTHERN IRELAND 2, WALES 3
Group 6, Windsor Park (14,000), Saturday, October 8, 2005

Northern Ireland (4-4-2): Taylor (Birmingham City), Duff (Burnley) (Jones, Crewe Alexandra, 73), Craigan (Motherwell), Murdoch (Rotherham Utd.), Capaldi (Plymouth Argyle), Gillespie (Sheffield Utd.), Johnson (Birmingham City), Davis (Aston Villa), Elliott (Hull City) (Brunt, Sheffield Wed., 65), Healy (Leeds Utd.), Quinn (Peterborough Utd.). **Scorers:** Gillespie (46), Davis (50). **Booked:** Elliott, Capaldi.

Wales (4-4-2): Jones (Wolves), Delaney (Aston Villa), J. Collins (West Ham Utd.) (Duffy, Portsmouth, 51), Partridge (Bristol City), Ricketts (Swansea City) (D. Collins, Sunderland, 87), Davies (Everton), Fletcher (West Ham Utd.), Robinson (Sunderland), Giggs (Manchester Utd.), Hartson (Celtic), Earnshaw (W.B.A.) (Vaughan, Crewe Alexandra, 76). **Scorers:** Davies (27), Robinson (38), Giggs (61). **Booked:** Delaney, Partridge.

Referee: R. Bossen (Holland). **Half-time:** 0-2.

CYPRUS 0, REPUBLIC OF IRELAND 1
Group 4, Nicosia (13,546), Saturday, October 8, 2005

Cyprus (4-4-2): Panayiotou, Ilia (Maragkos 74), Lambou, Louka, Garpozis, Charalampidis, Michail, Makridis, Aloneftis, Okkas (Yasoumi 69), Constantinou (Krassas 31). **Booked:** Okkas, Lambrou.

Republic of Ireland (4-4-2): Given (Newcastle Utd.), Carr (Newcastle Utd.), Cunningham (Birmingham City), Dunne (Manchester Utd.), O'Shea (Manchester Utd.), Finnan (Liverpool) (Holland, Charlton Athletic, 46), Kavanagh (Wigan Athletic), Kilbane (Everton), Duff (Chelsea) (Reid, Blackburn Rov., 61), Keane (Tottenham) (Connolly, Wigan Athletic, 80), Elliott (Sunderland). **Scorer:** Elliott (6). **Booked:** Kavanagh.

Referee: V. Kassai (Hungary). **Half-time:** 0-1.

ENGLAND 2, POLAND 1
Group 6, Old Trafford (65,467), Wednesday, October 12, 2005

England (4-1-3-1-1): Robinson (Tottenham), Young (Charlton Athletic), Ferdinand (Manchester Utd.), Terry (Chelsea), Carragher (Liverpool), King (Tottenham), Wright-Phillips (Chelsea) (Crouch, Liverpool, 67), Cole (Chelsea) (Smith, Manchester Utd., 86), Rooney (Manchester Utd.), Owen (Newcastle Utd.) (Jenas, Tottenham, 83). **Scorers:** Owen (44), Lampard (80).

Poland (4-1-3-2): Boruc, Baszczynski, Jop, Bak, Zewlakow, Lewandowski, Smolarek (Krzynowek 46), Sobolewski (Radomski 79), Kosowski, Zurawski (Frankowski 38), Rasiak. **Scorer:** Frankowski(45). **Booked:** Baszczynski, Sobolewski.

Referee: K. Milton Nielsen (Denmark). **Half-time:** 1-1.

SLOVENIA 0, SCOTLAND 3
Group 5, Celje (10,000), Wednesday, October 12, 2005

Slovenia (4-4-2): Samir, Mavric (Pecnik 24) (Ilic 55), Bostjan, Zlogar, Knavs, Ceh, Koren, Cimirotic, Komac, Acimovic, Rodic (Siljak 55). **Booked:** Ceh, Rodic.

Scotland (3-5-2): Gordon (Hearts), Webster (Hearts), Pressley (Hearts) (G. Caldwell, Hibernian, 46), Weir (Everton), Dailly (West Ham Utd.), Fletcher (Manchester Utd.), Hartley (Hearts), Quashie (Southampton) (S. Caldwell, Sunderland, 74), Alexander (Preston N.E.), Miller (Wolves) (O'Connor, Hibernian, 46), McFadden (Everton). **Scorers:** Fletcher (4), McFadden (47), Hartley (84). **Booked:** Gordon, G. Caldwell.

Referee: R Temmink (Holland). **Half-time:** 0-1.

WALES 2, AZERBAIJAN 0
Group 6, Millennium Stadium (50,000), Wednesday, October 12, 2005

Wales (4-2-3-1): Jones (Millwall), Duffy (Portsmouth), J. Collins (West Ham Utd.), Gabbidon (West Ham Utd.), D. Collins (Sunderland) (Ricketts, Swansea City, 53), Robinson (Sunderland), Fletcher (West Ham Utd.) (*Crofts, Gillingham, 69), Davies (Everton), Vaughan (Crewe Alexandra), Giggs (Manchester Utd.) (*Cotterill, Bristol City, 73), Hartson (Celtic). **Scorer:** Giggs (3, 51). **Booked:** Duffy, Fletcher.

Azerbaijan (4-5-1): Kramarenko, Shukurov, Sadygov, Agayev (Bakhshiev 80), Amirbekov, Tagizade, Muzika, Guliyev, Kerimov, Imamaliyev (Poladov 89), Ismaylov.

Referee: M. Hansson (Sweden). **Half-time:** 1-0.

AUSTRIA 2, NORTHERN IRELAND 0
Group 6, Vienna (13,000), Wednesday, October 12, 2005

Austria (4-4-2): Macho, Dober (Ibertsberger 46), Scharner, Stranzl, Pogatetz, Schopp (Standfest 54), Aufhauser, Kiesenebner, Ivanschitz, Linz, Wallner (Gercaliu 77). **Scorer:** Aufhauser (44, 90). **Booked:** Aufhauser, Wallner. **Sent-off:** Pogatetz.

Northern Ireland: Taylor (Birmingham City), Baird (Southampton), Craigan (Motherwell), Duff (Burnley), Murdock (Rotherham Utd.), Gillespie (Sheffield Utd.), Johnson (Birmingham City), Davis (Aston Villa), Brunt (Sheffield Wed.) (Elliott, Hull City, 76), Quinn (Peterborough Utd.) (Feeney, Luton Town, 57), Healy (Leeds Utd.) (Jones, Crewe Alexandra, 69). **Booked:** Gillespie, Brunt, Quinn, Baird, Craigan. **Sent-off:** Johnson.

Referee: A. Briakos (Greece). **Half-time:** 1-0.

REPUBLIC OF IRELAND 0, SWITZERLAND 0
Group 4, Lansdowne Road (35,000), Wednesday, October 12, 2005

Republic of Ireland (4-4-2): Given (Newcastle Utd.), Carr (Newcastle Utd.), Dunne (Manchester City), Cunningham (Birmingham City), Harte (Levante), A. Reid (Tottenham) (S. Reid, Blackburn Rov., 80), O'Shea (Manchester Utd.), Holland (Charlton Athletic (Athletic), Kilbane (Everton), Morrison (Crystal Palace) (Doherty, Norwich City, 86), Keane (Tottenham) (Elliott, Sunderland, 68). **Booked:** Dunne, A. Reid. (Brian Kerr's last game as manager).

Switzerland (4-1-4-1): Zuberbuhler, Degen, Muller, Senderos, Magnin, Vogel, Barnetta (Gygax 89), Volanthen (Streller 53), Cabanas, Wicky, Frei. **Booked:** Wicky, Cabanas.

Referee: M. Merk (Germany). **Half-time:** 0-0.

FRIENDLY INTERNATIONALS

DENMARK 4, ENGLAND 1
Copenhagen (41,438), Wednesday, August 17, 2005

Denmark (4-2-3-1): Sorensen, Priske, Nielsen (Gravgaard 46), Agger, N. Jensen, Gravesen, Poulsen (D. Jensen 86), Gronkjaer (Rommedahl 46), C. Jensen (Perez 72), Jorgensen, Tomasson (Larsen 64). **Scorers:** Rommedahl (60), Tomasson (63), Gravgaard (67), Larsen (90).

England (4-4-2): Robinson (Tottenham) (James, Manchester City, 46), Neville (Manchester Utd.) (Johnson, Chelsea, 46), Ferdinand (Manchester Utd.), Terry (Chelsea) (Carragher, Liverpool, 46), A. Cole (Arsenal), Beckham (Real Madrid), Gerrard (Liverpool) (Jenas, Newcastle Utd., 82), Lampard (Chelsea) (Hargreaves, Bayern Munich, 64), J. Cole (Chelsea); Rooney (Manchester Utd.), Defoe (Tottenham) (Owen, Real Madrid, 46). **Scorer:** Rooney (87). **Booked:** Johnson, A. Cole.

Referee: T. Henning Ovrebo (Norway). **Half-time:** 0-0.

AUSTRIA 2, SCOTLAND 2
Graz (13,800), Wednesday, August 17, 2005

Austria (4-4-2): Payer (Schranz 46), Dospel (Standfest 54), Ehman, Pogatetz, Gercaliu, Schopp (Ibertsberger 68), Kuhbauer (Saumel 78), Aufhauser, Ivanschitz, Mayrieb (Akagunduz 63), Vastic (Kuljic 63). **Scorers:** Ibertsberger (83), Standfest (87).

Scotland (3-5-2): Gordon (Hearts) Douglas, Leicester City, 46), Caldwell (Sunderland), Pressley (Hearts) (Anderson, Aberdeen, 46), Webster (Hearts), McNamara (Wolves), Dailly (West Ham Utd.), O'Neil (Preston N.E.) (Severin, Aberdeen, 46), Quashie (Southampton) (Hughes, Portsmouth, 73), Alexander (Preston N.E.), Miller (Wolves) (*Riordan, Hibernian, 46) O'Connor (Hibernian). **Scorers:** Miller (3), O'Connor (39).

Referee: S. Dereli (Turkey). **Half-time:** 0-2.

WALES 0, SLOVENIA 0
Swansea (10,016), Wednesday, August 17, 2005

Wales (3-5-2): Coyne (Burnley), *Duffy (Portsmouth) (Edwards, Wolves, 73), Page (Coventry City), Gabbidon (West Ham Utd.), Partridge (Bristol City) (Roberts, Tranmere Rov., 89), Ricketts (Swansea City), Robinson (Sunderland) (*Davies, Oxford Utd., 85), Fletcher (West Ham Utd.), Vaughan (Crewe Alexandra) (Parry, Cardiff City, 68), Earnshaw (W.B.A.) (*Williams, West Ham Utd., 61), Hartson (Celtic). **Booked:** Hartson.

Slovenia (4-3-1-2): B. Mavric (Handanovic 62), M. Mavric (Sukalo 46), Knavs, Cesar, Filekovic, Kornac (Pecnik 87), Zlogar, Pokorn (Ilic 56), Ceh, Lavric (Rodic 46), Acimovic (Cimirotic 46). **Booked:** Mavric.

Referee: I. Stokes (Republic of Ireland). **Half-time:** 0-0.

MALTA 1, NORTHERN IRELAND 1
Valletta (1,850), Wednesday, August 17, 2005

Malta (4-4-2): Haber, Pullicino (Chantar 62), Dimech (Scicluna 62), Said, Wellman, Briffa, Agius (Mallia 74), Anonam, Woods, Mattocks (Zahra 79), Cohen (Sammut 86). **Scorer:** Woods (35). **Sent-off:** Woods.

Northern Ireland (3-5-2): Taylor (Birmingham City), Craigan (Motherwell), Hughes (Aston Villa), Murdock (Rotherham Utd.), Gillespie (Sheffield Utd.), Johnson (Birmingham City), Whitley (Cardiff City) (Jones, Crewe Alexandra, 59), Davis (Aston Villa) (Mulryne, Cardiff City, 89), Elliott (Hull City) (Brunt, Sheffield Wed., 59), Healy (Leeds Utd.), Quinn (Peterborough Utd.) (Feeney, Luton Town, 69). **Scorer:** Healy (9). **Sent-off:** Gillespie.

Referee: M. Riley (England). **Half-time:** 1-1.

REPUBLIC OF IRELAND 1, ITALY 2
Lansdowne Road (44,000), Wednesday, August 17, 2005

Republic of Ireland (4-3-3): Given (Newcastle Utd.), Finnan (Liverpool) (Carr, Newcastle Utd., 57), Cunningham (Birmingham City), Dunne (Manchester City) (O'Brien, Portsmouth, 46), O'Shea (Manchester Utd.) (Miller, Manchester Utd., 78), S. Reid (Blackburn Rov.), Holland (Charlton Athletic) (Harte, Levante, 40), Kilbane (Everton), A. Reid (Tottenham) (Elliott, Sunderland, 73), Morrison (Birmingham City), Duff (Chelsea). **Scorer:** A. Reid (32). **Booked:** Cunningham.

Italy (4-3-1-2): Roma, Zaccardo, Cannavaro (Barzagli 63), Nesta (Materazzi 46), Zambrotta, Gattuso, Pirlo (Barone 76), De Rossi (Grosso 46), Del Piero (Diana 46), Vieri, Gilardino (Iaquinta 46). **Scorers:** Pirlo (10), Gilardino (31). **Booked:** Gattuso.

Referee: P. Costa (Portugal). **Half-time:** 1-2.

ENGLAND 3, ARGENTINA 2
Geneva (29,000), Saturday, November 12, 2005

England (4-1-3-2): Robinson (Tottenham), Young (Charlton Athletic) (Crouch, Liverpool, 81), Ferdinand (Manchester Utd.), Terry (Chelsea), Bridge (Chelsea) (Konchesky, West Ham Utd., 46), King (Tottenham) (Cole, Chelsea, 57), Beckham (Real Madrid), Lampard (Chelsea), Gerrard (Liverpool), Rooney (Manchester Utd.), Owen (Newcastle Utd.). **Scorers:** Rooney (39), Owen (86, 90). **Booked:** Lampard, Young, Cole.

Argentina (4-1-3-2): Abbondanzieri, Zanetti, Ayala (Coloccini 74), Samuel, Sorin, Demichelis, Rodriguez, Riquelme (Gonzalez 84), Cambiasso, Tevez (Cruz 86), Crespo (Saviola 70). **Scorers:** Crespo (34), Samuel (53). **Booked:** Rodriguez, Samuel.

Referee: P. Leuba (Switzerland). **Half-time:** 1-1.

SCOTLAND 1, UNITED STATES 1
Hampden Park (26,708), Saturday, November 12, 2005

Scotland (3-4-2-1): Gordon (Hearts), Weir (Everton) (G. Caldwell, Hibernian, 46), Pressley (Hearts) (S. Caldwell, Sunderland, 46), Webster (Hearts), Dailly (West Ham Utd.), Hartley (Hearts), Quashie (Southampton) (*Brown, Hibernian, 73) Alexander (Preston N.E.), Fletcher (Manchester Utd.), McCann (Southampton) (McFadden, Everton, 63), O'Connor (Hibernian) (Maloney, Celtic, 74). **Scorer:** Webster. **Booked:** Dailly.

United States (4-4-2): Keller, Cherundolo, Berhalter, Bocanegra (Conrad 79), Spector, Gaven (Olsen 46), Zavagnin (Quaranta 46), Carroll, Beasley (Pearce 76), Ching, Wolff. (Rolfe 57). **Scorer:** Wolff (9 pen).

Referee: A. Undiano (Spain). **Half-time:** 1-1.

NORTHERN IRELAND 1, PORTUGAL 1
Windsor Park (20,000), Tuesday, November 15, 2005

Northern Ireland (4-4-2): Taylor (Birmingham City), Gillespie (Sheffield Utd.) (*Shiels, Hibernian, 87), Craigan (Motherwell), Murdock (Rotherham Utd.), Capaldi (Plymouth Argyle), Jones (Crewe Alexandra) (McAuley, Lincoln City, 46), Davis (Aston Villa), Brunt (Sheffield Wed.), Elliott (Hull City) (McCann, Cheltenham Town, 46), Feeney (Luton Town) (*Sproule, Hibernian, 87), Quinn (Peterborough Utd.) (*Thompson, Linfield, 76). **Scorer:** Feeney (54). **Booked:** Quinn, Gillespie, Capaldi.

Portugal (4-2-3-1): Santos, Paulo Ferreira, Ricardo Carvalho, Meira, Ribeiro, Costinho, Petit, Ronaldo (Postiga 69), Tiago (Frechaut 77), Boa Morte (Caneira 63), Pauleta (Nuno Gomes 46). **Scorer:** Craigan (41 og).

Referee: H. Webb (England). **Half-time:** 0-1.

CYPRUS 1, WALES 0
Limassol (1,000), Wednesday, November 16, 2005

Cyprus (4-4-2): Morfis (Georgallides 71), Okkarides, Lambrou (Louka 79), Michael, Charalambidis, Elia (Theofilou 70), Garpozis, Krassas, Makrides, Okkas, Yiasoumi (Alecou 76). **Scorer:** Micahel (42 pern).

Wales (4-4-2): *Price (Ipswich Town), Duffy (Portsmouth) (Edwards, Wolves, 76), Gabbidon (West Ham Utd., Page (Coventry City), Collins (Sunderland) (Williams, West Ham Utd., 46), Ricketts (Swansea City), Fletcher (West Ham Utd.), Robinson (Sunderland), Vaughan (Crewe Alexandra) (Earnshaw, W.B.A., 66), Bellamy (Blackburn Rov.), Hartson (Celtic). **Booked:** Fletcher.

Referee: H. Jacov (Israel). **Half-time:** 1-0.

ENGLAND 2, URUGUAY 1
Anfield (40,013), Wednesday, March 1, 2006

England (4-4-2): Robinson (Tottenham), Neville (Manchester Utd.), Ferdinand (Manchester Utd.), Terry (Chelsea) (King, Tottenham, 46), Bridge (Chelsea) (Carragher, Liverpool, 28), Beckham (Real Madrid) (Wright-Phillips, Chelsea, 63), Gerrard (Liverpool) (Jenas, Tottenham, 46), Carrick (Tottenham), Cole (Chelsea), Rooney (Manchester Utd.) (Crouch, Liverpool, 63), *D. Bent (Charlton Athletic). **Scorers:** Crouch (75), Cole (90). **Booked:** Beckham, Carragher.

Uruguay (4-1-2-2-1): Carini (Viera 46), Diogo, Lugano, Godin, Lima, Pouso, Varela, Perez (Gonzalez 88), Vargas (Pereira 76), Regueiro (Martinez 83), Forlan (Medina 86). **Scorer:** Pouso (26). **Booked:** Lugano, Diogo, Forlan.

Referee: S. Farina (Italy). **Half-time:** 0-1.

SCOTLAND 1, SWITZERLAND 3
Hampden Park (20,952), Wednesday, March 1, 2006

Scotland (3-5-2): Gordon (Hearts) (*N. Alexander, Cardiff City, 46), G. Caldwell (Hibernian), Weir (Everton) (S. Caldwell, Sunderland, 46), Webster (Hearts), Dailly (West Ham Utd.), Fletcher (Manchester Utd.), Ferguson (Rangers) (*Teale, Wigan Athletic, 50), Quashie (W.B.A.), G. Alexander (Preston N.E.), McFadden (Everton), Miller (Wolves). **Scorer:** Miller (55).

Switzerland (4-2-3-1): Zuberbuhler (Coltori 46), Degen, Grichting, Senderos (Smiljanic 73), Behrami (Djourou 46), Vogel (Czemaili 81), Wicky (Vonlanthen 46), Gygax, Cabanas, Barnetta, Streller (Lustrinelli 73). **Scorers:** Barnetta (21), Gygax (41), Cabanas (69).

Referee: B. Coue (France). **Half-time:** 0-2.

WALES 0, PARAGUAY 0
Millennium Stadium (12,324), Wednesday, March 1, 2006

Wales (3-5-1-1): Jones (Q.P.R.) (Price, Ipswich Town, 66), Collins (West Ham Utd.), Gabbidon (West Ham Utd.), *Nyatanga (Derby Co.), Edwards (Wolves), Davies (Everton) (Crofts, Gillingham, 76), Fletcher (West Ham Utd.) (Robinson, Norwich City, 75), Koumas (Cardiff City) (Ledley, Cardiff City, 69), Ricketts (Swansea City), Giggs (Manchester Utd.) (Cotterill, Bristol City, 85), Bellamy (Blackburn Rov.) (Earnshaw, Norwich City, 78).

Paraguay (4-4-2): Villar, Caniza, Da Silva, Caceres, Toledo, Barreto (Gavilan 58) Acuna, Humberto Paredes, Dos Santos (Riveros 67), Haedo Valdez (Cardozo 70), Ramirez (Cabanas 76).

Referee: D. McDonald (Scotland). **Half-time:** 0-0.

NORTHERN IRELAND 1, ESTONIA 0
Windsor Park (14,000), Wednesday, March 1, 2006

Northern Ireland (4-4-2): Taylor (Birmingham City), McAuley (Lincoln City), Craigan (Motherwell) (*McLean, Motherwell, 46), Duff (Burnley), Capaldi (Plymouth Argyle), Sproule (Hibernian) (Jones, Crewe Alexandra, 46), Baird (Southampton), Davis (Aston Villa) (Elliott, Hull City, 68), Brunt (Sheffield Wed.) (McCann, Cheltenham Town, 68), Quinn (Peterborough Utd.) (Thompson, Linfield, 59), Healy (Leeds Utd.) (Feeney, Luton Town, 59). **Scorer:** Sproule (2).

Estonia (4-5-1): Poom, Jaager, Stepanov, Piijroja, Rooba, Teever (Kuresoo 73), Rahn (Reim 78), Lindpere (Oper 54), Dmitrijev, Sidorenkov (Ahjupera 83), Neemelo. **Booked:** Rahn, Dmitrijev.

Referee: P. Vink (Holland). **Half-time:** 1-0.

REPUBLIC OF IRELAND 3, SWEDEN 0
Lansdowne Road (34,000), Wednesday, March 1, 2006

Republic of Ireland (4-3-1-2): Given (Newcastle Utd.) (*Henderson, Brighton & H.A., 48), *J. O'Brien (Bolton Wand.) (Kilbane, Everton, 60), A. O'Brien (Portsmouth), Dunne (Manchester City), Harte (Levante) (Miller, Leeds Utd.), Reid (Blackburn Rov.), O'Shea (Manchester Utd.) (Kavanagh, Wigan Athletic, 48), Duff (Chelsea), Keane (Tottenham), Elliott (Sunderland) (*Ireland, Manchester City, 48) *Doyle (Reading) (Morrison, Crystal Palace, 69). **Scorers:** Duff (35), Keane (47), Miller (70). **Booked:** Reid. (Steve Staunton's first game as manager).

Sweden (4-1-3-2): Isaksson, Ostlund (C. Andersson, 74), Mellberg, Hansson, Edman, Linderoth (D. Andersson 70), Elmander (Jonson 60), Kallstrom (Svensson 60), Wilhelmsson, Larsson (Allback 80), Ibrahimovic (Rosenberg 35). **Booked:** Ostlund, C. Andersson.

Referee: D. Ledentu (France). **Half-time:** 1-0.

BULGARIA 1, SCOTLAND 5
Kirin Cup, Kobe (5,780), Thursday, May 11, 2006

Bulgaria (4-4-2): Kolev (Mihaylov 71), Kirilov, Topuzavov, Karaslavov (Yanev 55), Wagner, Todarov, Telkiyski, Angelov, Domovchisky (Iliev 71), Petrov, Todorov (Genkov 71). **Scorer:** Todarov (26). **Booked:** Petrov, Angelov, Wagner.

Scotland (5-3-2): Alexander (Cardiff City), Murty (Reading) (McNamee, Livingston, 82), Anderson (Aberdeen), Weir (Everton), Caldwell (Hibernian), Naysmith (Everton), Teale (Wigan Athletic) (*Burke, Rangers, 74), Fletcher (Manchester Utd.), Severin (Aberdeen) (Rae, Rangers, 70), McCulloch (Wigan Athletic) (Murray, Rangers, 79), *Boyd (Rangers) (McFadden, Everton, 52). **Scorers:** Boyd (12, 43), McFadden (69), Burke (76, 88). **Booked:** Caldwell, McFadden.

Referee: T. Kamikawa (Japan). **Half-time:** 1-2.

JAPAN 0, SCOTLAND 0
Kirin Cup, Saitama (58,648), Saturday, May 13, 2006

Japan (4-4-2):Kawaguchi, Miyamoto, Santos, Nakazawa (Tsuboi 50), Kaji, Fukunishi, Ogasawara, Ono, Endo (Sato 72), Kubo (Maki 62), Tamada. **Booked:** Miyamoto, Santos.

Scotland (5-3-2): Alexander (Cardiff City), Murty (Reading) (McNamee, Livingston, 79), Anderson (Aberdeen), Weir (Everton), Caldwell (Hibernian), Naysmith (Everton) (Murray, Rangers, 46), Teale (Wigan Athletic) (Burke, Rangers, 59), Fletcher (Manchester Utd.), Severin (Aberdeen) (Rae, Rangers, 46), McCulloch (Wigan Athletic) (*Miller, Dundee Utd., 69), McFadden (Everton) (Boyd, Rangers, 59). **Booked:** Caldwell, McFadden, McCulloch, Fletcher, Boyd.

Referee: E. Gonzalez (Spain). **Half-time:** 0-0.

NORTHERN IRELAND 0, URUGUAY 1
New Jersey (10,000), Sunday, May 21, 2006

Northern Ireland (4-4-2): Ingham (Wrexham), Duff (Burnley) (*Webb, Ross Co. 83), Murdock (Rotherham Utd.) (McAuley, Lincoln City, 83), Craigan (Motherwell), Capaldi (Plymouth Argyle), Jones (Burnley) (Thompson, Linfield, 60), Davis (Aston Villa), *Clingan (Nott'm. Forest), *Hughes (Lincoln City) (Shiels, Hibernian, 75), Sproule (Hibernian), Quinn (Peterborough Utd.) (*Lafferty, Burnley, 75). **Booked:** Hughes, Sproule.

Uruguay (4-4-2): Carini, Scotti, Estoyanoff (Surraco 83), Valdez, Godin, Lopez, Perez Ruso, Giacomazzi, Garcia, Abreu, Vargas. **Scorer:** Estoyanoff (33). **Booked:** Scotti, Perez Ruso, Giacomazzi,

Referee: A. Bruce (U.S.A.). **Half-time:** 0-1.

REPUBLIC OF IRELAND 0, CHILE 1
Lansdowne Road (41,200), Wednesday, May 24, 2006

Republic of Ireland (3-4-3): Given (Newcastle Utd.) (Henderson, Brighton & H.A., 54), *Kelly (Tottenham) (A. Reid, Tottenham, 84), Dunne (Manchester City), Breen (unatt) (Harte, Levante, 53), Kilbane (Everton), Miller (Manchester Utd.) (Kavanagh, Wigan Athletic, 54), S. Reid (Blackburn Rov.), O'Shea (Manchester Utd.) (McGeady, Celtic, 54), Doyle (Reading) (Byrne, Shelbourne, 72), Keane (Tottenham), Duff (Chelsea). **Booked:** S. Reid, Kavanagh.

Chile (4-4-2): Bravo, Jara, Vargas, Contreras, Olarra, Jimenez, Acuna, Iturra, Gonzalez (Zenteno 90), Navia (Sanchez 76), Suazo (Galaz 81). **Scorer:** Iturra (49). **Booked:** Contreras, Iturra, Acuna, Jimenez.

Referee: M. Ingvarsson (Sweden). **Half-time:** 0-0.

WALES 2, TRINIDAD & TOBAGO 1
Graz, Austria (8,000), Saturday, May 27, 2006

Wales (3-5-2): *Brown (Gillingham) (*Garner, Leyton Orient, 46), Collins (West Ham Utd.), Gabbidon (West Ham Utd.), Partridge (Bristol City) (Nyatanga, Derby Co., 46), Robinson (Norwich City), S. Davies (Everton) (*A. Davies, Yeovil Town, 77), Fletcher (West Ham Utd.) (Crofts, Gillingham, 46), Vaughan (Crewe Alexandra) (*Bale, Southampton, 54), Ledley (Cardiff City), Cotterill (Bristol City) (C. Davies, Verona, 46), Earnshaw (Norwich City). **Scorer:** Earnshaw (38, 87).

Trinidad & Tobago (3-5-2): Jack, Gray, Andrews (Samuel 34), Lawrence, A. John, Edwards, Birchall, Yorke, Theobald (Whitley 78), Jones (Latapy 61), S. John. **Scorer:** S. John (32).

Referee: S. Messner (Austria). **Half-time:** 1-1.

NORTHERN IRELAND 0, ROMANIA 2
Chicago (6,000), Saturday, May 27, 2006

Northern Ireland (4-4-2): *Blayney (Doncaster Rov.), Duff (Burnley), McAuley (Lincoln City) (Murdock, Rotherham Utd., 80), Craigan (Motherwell), Capaldi (Plymouth Argyle) (J. Hughes, Lincoln City, 64), Davis (Aston Villa), Clingan (Nott'm. Forest), Sproule (Hibernian) (*M. Hughes, Oldham Athletic, 64), Shiels (Hibernian), Thompson (Linfield), Quinn (Peterborough Utd.). **Booked:** Thompson, M. Hughes. **Sent-off:** Quinn.

Romania (4-4-2): Coman, Badoi, Goian (Iencsi 64), Maftei, Pulhac, Bostina, Nicolita, Radoi (Fzorih 64), Niculae (Mutu 64), Balan (Rat 64), Ruga. **Scorers:** Balan (7), Nicolae (13).

Referee: M. Kennedy (U.S.A.). **Half-time:** 0-2.

ENGLAND 3, HUNGARY 1
Old Trafford (56,323), Tuesday, May 30, 2006

England (4-1-3-1-1): Robinson (Tottenham), Neville (Manchester Utd.) (Hargreaves, Bayern Munich, 46), Ferdinand (Manchester Utd.), Terry (Chelsea) (Campbell, Arsenal, 76), A. Cole (Arsenal), Carragher (Liverpool), Beckham (Real Madrid), Lampard (Chelsea), Gerrard (Liverpool) (Crouch, Liverpool, 65), J. Cole (Chelsea), Owen (Newcastle Utd.) (*Walcott, Arsenal, 65). **Scorers:** Gerrard (47), Terry (51), Crouch (84). **Booked:** Campbell, Beckham.

Hungary (4-3-2-1): Kiraly, Feher, Eger, Komlosi (Vanczak 9), Halmosi, Molnar (Vadocz 83), Dardai, Toth (Torghelle 61), Gera, Huszti, Szabics (Polonkai 73). **Scorer:** Dardai (55). **Booked:** Feher.

Referee: P. Vink (Holland). **Half-time:** 0-0.

ENGLAND 6, JAMAICA 0

Old Trafford (70,373), Saturday, June 3, 2006

England (4-4-2): Robinson (Tottenham) (James, Manchester City, 46) Carragher (Liverpool), Ferdinand (Manchester Utd.), Terry (Chelsea) (Campbell, Arsenal, 31), A. Cole (Arsenal) (Bridge, Chelsea, 35), Beckham (Real Madrid) (*Lennon, Tottenham, 68), Lampard (Chelsea) (Carrick, Tottenham, 68), Gerrard (Liverpool) (Downing, Middlesbrough, 78), J. Cole (Chelsea), Crouch (Liverpool), Owen (Newcastle Utd.). **Scorers:** Lampard (11), Taylor (17 og), Crouch (29, 67, 89), Owen (32).

Jamaica (4-4-2): Ricketts, Daley, Stewart, Davis, Reid, Campbell-Ryce, Taylor (Crawford 46), Euell (Stephenson 78), Hue (Johnson 84), Fuller (Bennett 75), Shelton (Burton 47). **Booked:** Taylor.

Referee: K. Plautz (Austria). **Half-time:** 4-0.

BRITISH AND IRISH UNDER-21 INTERNATIONALS 2005-06

EUROPEAN UNDER-21 CHAMPIONSHIP – 2006

WALES 0, ENGLAND 4

Group 6, Racecourse Ground (4,109), Friday, September 2, 2005

Wales: Hennessey (Wolves), Beevers (Lincoln City), Gilbert (Leicester City), Tudur-Jones (Swansea City), Anthony (Cardiff City), Nyatanga (Derby Co.) (Adam Davies, Cambridge Utd., 55), Birchall (Mansfield Town), Crofts (Gillingham), C. Davies (Oxford Utd.) (Fleetwood, Cardiff City, 72), Cotterill (Bristol City), Arron Davies (Yeovil Town).

England: Carson (Liverpool), Johnson (Chelsea), Ridgewell (Aston Villa) (Hunt, Bolton Wand., 57), Ferdinand (West Ham Utd.), Dawson (Tottenham), Reo-Coker (West Ham Utd.), Milner (Newcastle Utd.), Ambrose (Charlton Athletic), C. Cole (Chelsea) (Welsh, Hull City, 60), Stead (Sunderland) (Nugent, Preston N.E., 61), Whittingham (Aston Villa).

Scorers – England: Stead (5), Whittingham (27, 89), Dawson (68). **Half-time:** 0-2.

SCOTLAND 2, ITALY 2

Group 5, Fir Park (5,913), Friday, September 2, 2005

(Italy awarded match 3-0 – Scotland included suspended player)

Scotland: Marshall (Celtic), Berra (Hearts), Robertson (Rotherham Utd.), Diamond (Aberdeen), Collins (Sunderland), Brown (Hibernian), Whittaker (Hibernian), Thomson (Hibernian) (Lawson, Celtic, 64), Duffy (Falkirk) (Turner, Everton, 76), Wilson (Dundee Utd.), Gallagher (Blackburn Rov.). **Sent-off:** Marshall.

Scorers – Scotland: Diamond (45), Gallagher (74). **Italy:** Lazzari (53), Pepe (76). **Half-time:** 1-0.

GERMANY 1, ENGLAND 1

Group 6, Mainz (10,000), Tuesday, September 6, 2005

England: Carson (Liverpool), Hunt (Bolton Wand.) (Baines, Wigan Athletic, 46), Taylor (Newcastle Utd.), Dawson (Tottenham), Ferdinand (West Ham Utd.), Welsh (Hull City) (Nugent, Preston N.E., 78), O'Neil (Portsmouth), Reo-Coker (West Ham Utd.), Whittingham (Aston Villa) (Soares, Crystal Palace, 46), Milner (Newcastle Utd.), C. Cole (Chelsea).

Scorers – Germany: Kiessling (17). **England:** Taylor (42). **Half-time:** 1-1.

NORWAY 0, SCOTLAND 1
Group 5, Drammen (2,207), Tuesday, September 6, 2005

Scotland: Turner (Everton), Berra (Hearts), Robertson (Rotherham Utd.), Watt (Chelsea), Collins (Sunderland), Brown (Hibernian), Wilson (Dundee Utd.), Thomson (Hibernian), Clarkson (Motherwell) (Brighton, Clyde, 46), Lawson (Celtic), Gallagher (Blackburn Rov.).

Scorer – Scotland: Gallagher (7). **Half-time:** 0-1.

POLAND 3, WALES 2
Group 6, Mazowiecki (2,000), Tuesday, September 6, 2005

Wales: Hennessey (Wolves), Beevers (Lincoln City), Gilbert (Leicester City), Tudur-(Swansea City) (Pulis, Stoke City, 60), Anthony (Cardiff City) (Adam Davies, Cambridge Utd., 57), Nyatanga (Derby Co.), Arron Davies (Yeovil Town), Crofts (Gillingham), Calliste (Liverpool), Cotterill (Bristol City), Vaughan (Crewe Alexandra).

Scorers – Poland: Brozek (18, 53), Gregorek (83). **Wales:** Cotterill (13), Vaughan (38). **Half-time:** 1-2.

REPUBLIC OF IRELAND 1, FRANCE 2
Group 4, Cork (6,500), Tuesday, September 6, 2005

Republic of Ireland: Henderson (Brighton & H.A.), Kelly (Tottenham), Fitzgerald (Bury), Paisley (Longford Town), Sheehan (Leicester City) (Kearney, Cork City, 84), Flood (Manchester City), O'Brien (Bolton Wand.), Dawson (Mansfield Town) (O'Donovan, Cork, City, 46), McGeady (Celtic), Murphy (Sunderland), Doyle (Reading).

Scorers – Republic of Ireland: (Murphy 33). **France:** Le Tallec (39 pen), Bergougnoux (71). **Half-time:** 1-1.

ENGLAND 1, AUSTRIA 2
Group 6, Elland Road (28,030), Friday, October 7, 2005

England: Carson (Liverpool), S. Taylor (Newcastle Utd.), Dawson (Tottenham), Ferdinand (West Ham Utd.) (R. Taylor, Wigan Athletic, 71), Baines (Wigan Athletic), Milner (Newcastle Utd.), Soares (Crystal Palace) (Moore, Aston Villa, 61), Huddlestone (Tottenham), Lennon (Tottenham), C. Cole (Chelsea) (Jerome, Cardiff City, 87) Thomas (Charlton Athletic).

Scorers – England: Cole (18). **Austria:** Janko (56, 76). **Half-time:** 1-0.

SCOTLAND 2, BELARUS 3
Group 5, Broadwood Stadium (3,192), Friday, October 7, 2005

Scotland: Turner (Everton), Berra (Hearts), Robertson (Rotherham Utd.), Watt (Chelsea), Collins (Sunderland), Wilson (Dundee Utd.), Whittaker (Hibernian), McCunnie (Dunfermline) (Diamond, Aberdeen, 67), Duffy (Falkirk) (Brighton, Clyde, 80), Lawson (Celtic), Gallagher (Blackburn Rov.). **Sent-off:** Berra, Gallagher.

Scorers – Scotland: Duffy (2), Robertson (45). **Belarus:** McCunnie (58 og), Kovel (66), Afanasyev (78). **Half-time:** 2-0.

GERMANY 4, WALES 0
Group 6, Hamburg (3,000), Friday, October 7, 2005

Wales: Worgan (unatt), Spender (Wrexham), Nyatanga (Derby Co.) (Wiggins, Crystal Palace, 86) Anthony (Cardiff City), Adam Davies (Cambridge Utd.), Gilbert (Leicester City), Jones (Wrexham) (Birchall, Mansfield Town, 68) Arron Davies (Yeovil Town), Pulis (Stoke City), Ledley (Cardiff City), Calliste (Liverpool).

Scorers – Germany: Rafael (3, 51), Fathi (54), Masmanidis (79). **Half-time:** 1-0.

CYPRUS 1, REPUBLIC OF IRELAND 1
Group 4, Larnaca (2,000), Friday, October 7, 2005

Republic of Ireland: Henderson (Brighton & H.A.), Keane (Luton Town) (McStay, Portadown, 43), McShane (Brighton & H.A.), Fitzgerald (Bury), Painter (Birmingham City), Flood (Manchester City), O'Brien, (Bolton Wand.) (Whelan, Sheffield Wed., 46), Potter (Liverpool), McGeady (Celtic), Tabb (Brentford), Ward (Bohemians) (Bermingham, Burnley, 74).

Scorers – Cyprus: Panayi (30). **Republic of Ireland:** Flood (76). **Half-time:** 1-0.

ENGLAND 4, POLAND 1
Group 6, Hillsborough (23,110), Tuesday, October 11, 2005

England: Carson (Liverpool), R. Taylor (Wigan Athletic) (Onuoha, Manchester City, 85), S. Taylor (Newcastle Utd.), Ferdinand (West Ham Utd.), Whittingham (Aston Villa), Reo-Coker (West Ham Utd.), Huddlestone (Tottenham), O'Neil (Portsmouth), Lennon (Tottenham), C. Cole (Chelsea) (Stead, Sunderland, 87), Thomas (Charlton Athletic) (Milner, Newcastle Utd.,65).

Scorers – England: Cole (18), Thomas (21), S. Taylor (37, 88). **Poland:** Kikut (39). **Half-time:** 3-1.

SLOVENIA 3, SCOTLAND 0
Group 5, Velenje (800), Tuesday, October 11, 2005

Scotland: Smith (Motherwell), Diamond (Aberdeen), Robertson (Rotherham Utd.), Watt (Chelsea) (Mulgrew, Celtic, 46), Collins (Sunderland), McCormack (Rangers), Whittaker (Hibernian), McCunnie (Dunfermline), Duffy (Falkirk) (Naismith, Kilmarnock, 68), Lawson (Celtic) (Lappin, St Mirren, 46), Clarkson (Motherwell).

Scorers – Slovenia: Collins (35 og), Stevanovic (61, 90). **Half-time:** 1-0.

WALES 3, AZERBAIJAN 0
Group 6, Newport (3,227), Tuesday, October 11, 2005

Wales: Worgan (unatt), Beevers (Lincoln City), Gilbert (Leicester City), Morgan (MK Dons), Nyatanga (Derby Co.), Davies (Yeovil Town), Pulis (Stoke City) (MacDonald, Swansea City, 79), Jones (Wrexham), McDonald (Cardiff City) (Pritchard, Swansea City, 60), Birchall (Mansfield Town), Calliste (Liverpool).

Scorers – Wales: Pritchard (65), Birchall (70), Gilbert (87). **Half-time:** 0-0.

REPUBLIC OF IRELAND 0, SWITZERLAND 1
Group 4, Tolka Park (2,500), Tuesday, October 11, 2005

Republic of Ireland: Henderson (Brighton & H.A.), Deery (Derry City), McShane (Brighton & H.A.), Fitzgerald (Bury), Painter (Birmingham City), Flood (Manchester City), Whelan (Sheffield Wed.), O'Brien (Bolton Wand.) (O'Donovan, Cork City, 81), McGeady (Celtic), Ward (Bohemians), Tabb (Brentford.).

Scorer – Switzerland: Degen (13). **Half-time:** 0-1.

ENGLAND 1, FRANCE 1
Play-off first leg, White Hart Lane (34,494), Friday, November 11, 2005

England: Carson (Liverpool), Taylor (Wigan Athletic), Dawson (Tottenham), Ferdinand (West Ham Utd.), Whittingham (Aston Villa), Milner (Newcastle Utd.) (Ashton, Norwich City, 79), Huddlestone (Tottenham), Richardson (Manchester Utd.), Ambrose (Charlton Athletic), D. Bent (Charlton Athletic), C. Cole (Chelsea).

Scorers – England: Ambrose (88). **France:** Le Tallec (47). **Half-time:** 0-0.

FRANCE 2, ENGLAND 1
Play-off second leg, Nancy (15,000), Tuesday, November 15, 2005

England: Carson (Liverpool), Taylor (Wigan Athletic), Dawson (Tottenham), Ferdinand (West Ham Utd.), Onuoha (Manchester City) (Whittingham, Aston Villa, 79), Ambrose (Charlton Athletic) (Ashton, Norwich City, 66), Huddlestone (Tottenham), O'Neil (Portsmouth), Richardson (Manchester Utd.), D. Bent (Charlton Athletic), C. Cole (Chelsea) (Jerome, Cardiff City, 89).

Scorers – France: Ribery (59), Briand (86 pen). **England:** D. Bent (55). **Half-time:** 0-0.

LIECHTENSTEIN 1, NORTHERN IRELAND 4
2008 Preliminary round, Vaduz (600), Wednesday, April 12, 2006

Northern Ireland: McGovern (Celtic), S. Ward (Glentoran), Hughes (Lincoln City), Clingan (Nott'm. Forest), McChrystal (Derry), McArdle (Rochdale), Gilfillan (Gretna) (J. Ward, Aston Villa), Clarke (Newry) (McVey, Coleraine), Morrow (Livingston), Stewart (Wolves) (Smylie, Newcastle Utd.), Scullion (Dungannon).

Scorers – Liechtenstein: Hughes (7 og). **Northern Ireland:** Morrow (33, 61), Gilfillan (58), Scullion (84). **Half-time:** 1-1.

ESTONIA 0, WALES 2
2008 Preliminary round, Tallinn (750), Wednesday, May 10, 2006

Wales: Price (Ipswich Town), Duffy (Portsmouth), Wiggins (Crystal Palace), Ledley (Cardiff City), James, Souhampton, 65), Morgan (MK Dons), Nyatanga (Derby Co.), A. Davies (Yeovil Town), Crofts (Gillingham), C. Davies (Verona) (Calliste (Liverpool, 86), Cotterill (Bristol City), McDonald (Cardiff City).

Scorers: Cotterill (28 pen), A. Davies (75). **Half-time:** 0-1.

NORTHERN IRELAND 4, LIECHTENSTEIN 0
2008 Preliminary round, Drumahoe (1,000), Wednesday, May 10, 2006

Northern Ireland: McGovern (Celtic), S. Ward (Glentoran), Hughes (Lincoln City) (Friars, Notts Co., 46), McArdle (Rochdale), McChrystal (Derry), Clarke (Newry) (Lafferty, Burnley 60), Gilfillan (Gretna) (J. Ward, Aston Villa 67), Clingan (Nott'm. Forest), Thompson (Linfield), Shiels (Hibernian), Scullion (Dungannon).

Scorers – Northern Ireland: Thompson (9), Clarke (41), Shiels (42), McArdle (78). **Half-time:** 3-0.

AZERBAIJAN 1, REPUBLIC OF IRELAND 2
2008 Preliminary round, Baku (1,500), Thursday, May 11, 2006

Republic of Ireland: Quigley (UCD), Foley (Luton Town). R. Keogh (Bristol City), Bruce (Birmingham City), Painter (Birmingham City), Keegan (Drogheda), Flood (Manchester City), Timlin (Fulham), O'Donovan (Cork City) (Long, Reading, 62), A. Keogh (Scunthorpe Utd.), McGeady (Celtic). **Sent-off:** Quigley.

Scorers – Azerbaijan: Aghakishiyev (20). **Republic of Ireland:** A. Keogh (58, 88). **Half-time:** 1-0.

REPUBLIC OF IRELAND 3, AZERBAIJAN 0
2008 Preliminary round, Kilkenny (1,600), Thursday, May 18, 2006

Republic of Ireland: Gilmartin (Walsall), Foley (Luton Town), R. Keogh (Bristol City), Bruce (Birmingham City), Painter (Birmingham City), Keegan (Drogheda) (Dicker, UCD, 85), Flood (Manchester City) (Tabb, Brentford, 74), Timlin (Fulham), O'Donovan (Cork City), A. Keogh (Scunthorpe Utd.) (Behan, Cork City, 84), McGeady (Celtic).

Scorers – Republic of Ireland: O'Donovan (37), Foley (69), A. Keogh (75). **Half-time:** 1-0.

WALES 5, ESTONIA 1

2008 Preliminary round, Racecourse Ground (1,575), Wednesday, May 24, 2006

Wales: Price (Ipswich Town), Spender (Wrexham), Wiggins (Crystal Palace) (Bale, Southampton, 67), Crofts (Gillingham) (R. Davies, W.B.A., 74), Morgan (MK Dons), Mike Williams (Wrexham), MacDonald (Swansea City), Edwards (Shrewsbury Town), C. Davies (Verona) (D. Williams, Yeovil Town, 52), Calliste (Liverpool), A. Davies (Yeovil Town).

Scorers – Wales: C. Davies (3, 27, 44), A. Davies (43, 73). **Estonia:** Gossev (60). **Half-time:** 4-0.

FRIENDLY INTERNATIONALS

DENMARK 0, ENGLAND 1

Herning (4,012), Tuesday, August 16, 2005

England: Carson (Liverpool) (Camp, Derby Co., 46), Hunt (Bolton Wand.), Davenport (Tottenham), Dawson (Tottenham) (Ferdinand, West Ham Utd., 46), Ridgewell (Aston Villa) (Whittingham, Aston Villa, 46), Milner (Newcastle Utd.), Reo-Coker (West Ham Utd.), (Soares, Crystal Palace, 46), Richardson (Manchester Utd.), Downing (Middlesbrough) (Ambrose, Charlton Athletic, 46), C. Cole (Chelsea), Ashton (Norwich City) (Stead, Sunderland, 46).

Scorer – England: Ambrose (90). **Half-time:** 0-0.

AUSTRIA 1, SCOTLAND 3

Koflach (1,200), Tuesday, August 16, 2005

Scotland: Marshall (Celtic), Berra (Hearts), Morrison (Dunfermline) (Kinniburgh, Motherwell, 30), Diamond (Aberdeen) (Collins, Sunderland, 46), Robertson (Rotherham Utd.), Brown (Hibernian), Whittaker (Hibernian), Thomson (Hibernian) (Lawson, Celtic, 80), Maloney (Celtic), Beattie (Celtic) (Clarkson, Motherwell, 74), Gallagher (Blackburn Rov.) (Duffy, Falkirk, 69).

Scorers – Austria: Thonhofer (51). **Scotland:** Robertson (23), Beattie (30 pen, 65). **Half-time:** 0-2.

WALES 3, MALTA 1

Llanelli (1,157), Tuesday, August 16, 2005

Wales: Hennessey (Wolves) (Worgan, unatt., 46), Beevers (Lincoln City) (Martin, Derby Co., 46) Gilbert (Leicester City) (Adam Davies, Cambridge Utd., 46), Anthony (Cardiff City) (Jacobson, Cardiff City, 65), Pulis (Stoke City), Nyatanga (Derby Co.), Crofts (Gillingham), Arron Davies (Yeovil Town), Cotterill (Bristol City), Pritchard (Swansea City) (Fleetwood, Cardiff City, 56), Birchall (Mansfield Town) (Tudur-Jones, Swansea City, 60).

Scorers – Wales: Crofts (10), Pritchard (48), Arron Davies (70). **Malta:** Bajada (76). **Half-time:** 1-0.

NORTHERN IRELAND 2, REPUBLIC OF IRELAND 2

Lurgan (1,200), Tuesday, August 16, 2005

Northern Ireland: McGovern (Celtic), Hughes (Oldham Athletic), McChrystal (Derry), McLean (Rangers), Webb (Ross Co.), Gault (Linfield) (Smylie, Newcastle Utd., 73), Gilfillan (Gretna) (Ward, Glentoran, 54), Higgins (Derry), Braniff (Millwall) (Shiels, Hibernian, 76), Morrow (Hibernian) (Thompson, Linfield, 76), McCourt (Derry) (Friars, Notts Co., 70).

Republic of Ireland: Henderson (Brighton & H.A.), Foley (Luton Town), Kelly (Tottenham), Fitzgerald (Bury), Sheehan (Leicester City), Cregg (Arsenal) (O'Donovan, Cork City, 59) O'Brien (Bolton Wand.), Whelan (Sheffield Wed.) (Dawson, Mansfield Town), Tabb (Brentford), Murphy (Sunderland), Doyle (Reading).

Scorers – Northern Ireland: Sheehan (36 og), Webb (51). **Republic of Ireland:** Doyle (64, 72 pen). **Half-time:** 1-0.

CYPRUS 3, WALES 3
Paphos (1,200), Tuesday, November 15, 2005

Wales: Pearce (Bristol City) (Letheren, Swansea City, 77), Powell (Bolton Wand.) (Anthony, Cardiff City, 55), Jacobson (Cardiff City) (James, Southampton, 77), Spender (Wrexham), A. Davies (Cambridge Utd.) (Crowell, Wrexham, 55), Nyatanga (Derby Co.) Crofts (Gillingham), Pulis (Stoke City) (Wiggins, Crystal Palace, 55), Calliste (Liverpool) (Pritchard, Swansea City, 66), Cotterill (Bristol City), Jones (Wrexham). **Sent-off:** Crowell.

Scorers – Cyprus: Pavlou (16, 36), Eleftheriou (90). **Wales:** Jones (31), Cotterill (40), Efthimiou (90, og). **Half-time:** 2-2.

MADEIRA 1, REPUBLIC OF IRELAND 1
Madeira Tournament (2,000), Tuesday, February 14, 2006

Republic of Ireland: Quigley (UCD), Keane (Luton Town), R. Keogh (Bristol City), Deans (Waterford Utd.) (Tyrrell, Drogheda, 61), Hand (Huddersfield Town), O'Donovan (Cork City) (Hayes, Reading, 46), Dicker (UCD) (O'Connor, Wolves, 61), Timlin (Fulham), O'Brien (Newcastle Utd.) (Stokes, Arsenal, 74), Ward (Bohemians) (O'Carroll, Celtic, 46), A. Keogh (Scunthorpe Utd.).

Scorers – Madeira: Patricio (59). **Republic of Ireland:** Hayes (78). **Half-time:** 0-0.

REPUBLIC OF IRELAND 2, FINLAND 1
Madeira Tournament (1,500), Wednesday, February 15, 2006

Republic of Ireland: Randolph (Charlton Athletic), Keane (Luton Town), R. Keogh (Bristol City), Deans (Waterford Utd.), Hand (Huddersfield Town), O'Donovan (Cork City) (O'Carroll, Celtic, 72), Dicker (UCD), Grant (Waterford Utd.), (O'Connor, Wolves, 72), Stokes (Arsenal), Ward (Bohemians) (Tyrrell, Drogheda Utd., 90), A. Keogh (Scunthorpe Utd.) (O'Brien (Newcastle Utd., 46).

Scorers – **Republic of Ireland:** Ward (49), Dicker (90). **Finland:** Hetemaj (67 pen). **Half-time:** 1-0.

REPUBLIC OF IRELAND 2, PORTUGAL 1
Madeira Tournament (2,000), Friday, February 17, 2006

Republic of Ireland: Quigley (UCD), Keane (Luton Town), R. Keogh (Bristol City), O'Dea (Celtic), Hand (Huddersfield Town), Grant (Waterford Utd.) (Deans, Waterford Utd., 84), Dicker (UCD), Timlin (Fulham), O'Brien (Newcastle Utd.) (O'Donovan, Cork City, 90), Stokes (Arsenal), Ward (Bohemians).

Scorers – Republic of Ireland: Grant (3), Ward (43). **Portugal:** Veloso (89). **Half-time:** 2-0.

ENGLAND 3, NORWAY 1
Madejski Stadium (15,022), Tuesday, February 28, 2006

England: Carson (Liverpool) (Camp, Derby Co., 46), Johnson (Chelsea) (Hoyte, Arsenal, 65), Ferdinand (West Ham Utd.), Ridgewell (Aston Villa) (Davies (W.B.A., 46), Whittingham (Aston Villa) (Taylor, Middlesbrough, 64), Reo-Coker (West Ham Utd.) (Soares, Crystal Palace, 46), Huddlestone (Tottenham), Bentley (Blackburn Rov.) (Welsh, Hull City, 72), Routledge (Tottenham) (McLeod, MK Dons, 73), Nugent (Preston N.E.) (Jerome (Cardiff City, 46), Milner (Newcastle Utd.) (Lita, Reading, 46).

Scorers – England: Whittingham (24), Bentley (54, 60). **Norway:** Steenslid (52).

SCOTLAND 4, ICELAND 0
Firhill Stadium (1,024), Tuesday, February 28, 2006

Scotland: Marshall (Celtic) (Turner, Everton, 46), Irvine (Celtic), Diamond (Aberdeen) (Brighton, Clyde, 69), Kinniburgh (Motherwell), Berra (Hearts), Lawson (Celtic), Scott (Livingston) (Foster, Aberdeen, 44), Naismith (Kilmarnock) (Bryson, Clyde, 83), Elliot (Hearts) (Clarkson, Motherwell, 69), Woods (Sunderland) (Quinn, Celtic, 37), Adam (Rangers).

Scorers – Scotland: Naismith (1), Scott (19), Elliot (29, 57). **Half-time:** 3-0.

WALES 0, NORTHERN IRELAND 1
Llanelli (400), Tuesday, February 28, 2006

Wales: Pearce (Bristol City), Lawless (Torquay Utd.) (Marc Williams, Wrexham, 83), Wiggins (Crystal Palace) (Jacobson, Cardiff City, 87), Mackin (Wrexham) (R. Davies, W.B.A., 56), Adam Davies (Cambridge Utd.), Mike Williams (Wrexham), Arron Davies (Yeovil Town), Hughes (Regensburg) (Easter, Cardiff City, 46), MacDonald (Swansea City) (James, Southampton, 56), C. Davies (Verona) (Pritchard, Swansea City, 73), Calliste (Liverpool).

Northern Ireland: McGovern (Celtic), Ward (Glentoran), Hughes (Lincoln City), Clarke (Newry) (McVey, Coleraine, 66), McChrystal (Derry), McArdle (Rochdale), Gilfillan (Gretna) (Ervin, Linfield, 46), Clingan (Nott'm. Forest), Scullion (Dungannon) (Friars, Notts Co., 71), Lafferty (Burnley) (Smylie, Newcastle Utd., 84), Morrow (Hibernian) (Stewart, Wolves, 87).

Scorer – Northern Ireland: Morrow (24). **Half-time:** 0-1.

REPUBLIC OF IRELAND 1, SWEDEN 0
Drogheda (2,500), Tuesday, February 28, 2006

Republic of Ireland: Quigley (UCD) (Doyle, Millwall, 46), Foley (Luton Town), McShane (Brighton & H.A.), Bruce (Birmingham City), Painter (Birmingham City) (Hand, Huddersfield Town, 90), Whelan (Sheffield Wed.) (Dicker, UCD, 68), Potter (Liverpool), Timlin (Fulham), Flood (Manchester City), Ward (Bohemians) (Leech, Drogheda, 79), Yeates (Colchester Utd.) (Behan, Cork City, 90).

Scorer – Republic of Ireland: Ward (77). **Half-time:** 0-0.

WALES 1, CYPRUS 0
Port Talbot (1,200), Tuesday, May 16, 2006

Wales: Pearce (Bristol City), Gunter (Cardiff City) (Critchell, Southampton, 50), Wiggins (Crystal Palace) (Calliste, Liverpool, 46), Crowell (Wrexham) (James, Southampton, 55), Morgan (MK Dons), Mike Williams (Wrexham), Spender (Wrexham) (McDonald, Cardiff City, 51), Edwards (Shrewsbury Town) (R. Davies, W.B.A., 64), C. Davies (Verona) (D. Williams, Yeovil Town), 77), A Davies (Yeovil Town), Bale (Southampton).

Scorer – Wales: Mike Williams (45). **Half-time:** 1-0.

NORTHERN IRELAND 1, SCOTLAND 0
Drumahoe (350), Tuesday, May 16, 2006

Northern Ireland: McGovern (Celtic), S. Ward (Glentoran), Friars (Notts Co.) (McCaffrey, Hibernian, 58), McVey (Coleraine) (Callaghan, Limavady, 53), McChrystal (Derry), Evans, McGowan (Clyde), Gilfillan (Gretna), Stewart (Wolves), Ramsey (Lisburn) (J. Ward, Aston Villa, 46), Scullion (Dungannon) (Buchanan, 71).

Scotland: Marshall (Celtic), Whittaker (Hibernian), Wilson (Celtic), Lawson (Celtic), P. Quinn (Motherwell), Broadfoot (St Mirren), Foster (Aberdeen), Naismith (Kilmarnock), Duffy (Hull City) (McCormack, Rangers, 77), Adam (Rangers), Woods (Sunderland) (Mulgrew, Celtic, 65).

Scorer – Northern Ireland: Stewart (62). **Half-time:** 0-0.

Scotland: Marshall (Celtic), Irvine (Celtic), P. Quinn (Motherwell), Broadfoot (St Mirren), Mulgrew (Celtic), Wilson (Celtic), Whittaker (Hibernian), R. Quinn (Celtic) (McCormack, Rangers, 74), Clarkson (Motherwell) (Duffy, Hull City, 68), Adam (Rangers), Naismith, (Kilmarnock).

Scorers – Scotland: Naismith (46). **Turkey:** Gulec (55 pen). **Sent-off:** Adam. **Half-time:** 0-0.

EUROPEAN UNDER-21 CHAMPIONSHIP QUALIFYING TABLES

GROUP 1

	P	W	D	L	F	A	Pts
Holland	10	7	2	1	21	7	23
Czech Republic	10	6	3	1	26	8	21
Romania	10	6	1	3	17	8	19
Macedonia	10	2	3	5	9	18	9
Finland	10	2	1	7	9	16	7
Armenia	10	1	2	7	2	25	5

GROUP 2

	P	W	D	L	F	A	Pts
Denmark	12	9	2	1	30	12	29
Ukraine	12	7	2	3	22	7	23
Greece	12	6	2	4	18	9	20
Turkey	12	5	4	3	15	9	19
Georgia	12	3	2	7	22	11	11
Albania	12	2	3	7	9	27	9
Kazakhstan	12	2	1	9	8	23	7

GROUP 3

	P	W	D	L	F	A	Pts
Portugal	10	10	0	0	29	3	30
Russia	10	6	1	3	24	6	19
Slovakia	10	6	1	3	12	9	19
Latvia	10	3	3	4	10	16	12
Estonia	10	0	3	7	4	24	3
Luxembourg	10	0	2	8	4	25	2

GROUP 4

	P	W	D	L	F	A	Pts
France	8	6	1	1	13	5	19
Switzerland	8	4	3	1	15	8	15
Israel	8	4	3	1	11	7	15
Republic of Ireland	8	1	2	5	10	14	5
Cyprus	8	0	1	7	2	17	1

GROUP 5

	P	W	D	L	F	A	Pts
Italy	10	8	1	1	16	3	25
Slovenia	10	4	3	3	13	13	15
Norway	10	4	2	4	14	13	14
Belarus	10	4	1	5	20	19	13
Moldova	10	3	2	5	8	12	11
Scotland	10	1	3	6	6	17	6

GROUP 6

	P	W	D	L	F	A	Ps
Germany	10	7	3	0	24	5	24
England	10	6	3	1	21	7	21
Poland	10	3	4	3	18	18	13
Austria	10	3	2	5	9	14	11
Wales	10	3	1	6	9	21	10
Azerbaijan	10	0	3	7	1	17	3

GROUP 7

	P	W	D	L	F	A	Pts
Belgium	10	7	3	0	25	6	24
Serbia & Mont.	10	7	1	2	29	11	22
Spain	10	6	2	2	37	8	20
Bosnia-Herz.	10	3	1	6	17	20	10
Lithuania	10	3	1	6	9	16	10
San Marino	10	0	0	10	4	60	0

GROUP 8

	P	W	D	L	F	A	Pts
Croatia	10	8	1	1	14	6	25
Hungary	10	6	1	3	12	7	19
Sweden	10	6	0	4	16	12	18
Iceland	10	4	1	5	15	11	13
Bulgaria	10	2	1	7	9	17	7
Malta	1-	1	2	7	3	16	5

Play-offs to decide Championship finalists (on agg): Denmark 4, Russia 1; France 3, England 2; Germany 3, Czech Republic 0; Holland 2, Slovenia 0; Italy 2, Hungary 1; Portugal 3, Switzerland 2; Serbia & Montenegro 5, Croatia 2; Ukraine 5, Belgium 4.

FINALS – PORTUGAL (MAY 23-JUNE 4, 2006)

GROUP A

	P	W	D	L	F	A	Pts
FRANCE	3	3	0	0	6	0	9
SERBIA & MONT.	3	1	0	2	2	3	3
Portugal	3	1	0	2	1	3	3
Germany	3	1	0	2	1	4	3

Results: Serbia & Montenegro 0, Germany 1; Portugal 0, France 1; France 3, Germany 0; Portugal 0, Serbia & Montenegro 2; Germany 0, Portugal 1; France 2, Serbia & Montenegro 0.

GROUP B

	P	W	D	L	F	A	Pts
UKRAINE	3	2	0	1	4	3	6
HOLLAND	3	1	1	1	3	3	4
Italy	3	1	1	1	4	4	4
Denmark	3	0	2	1	5	6	2

Results: Ukraine 2, Holland 1; Italy 3, Denmark 3; Denmark 1, Holland 1; Italy 1, Ukraine 0; Holland 1, Italy; Denmark 1, Ukraine 2.

Semi-finals: France 2, Holland 3 (aet); Ukraine 0, Serbia & Montenegro 0 (aet, Ukraine won 5-4 on pens). **Final** (Oporto): Holland 3, Ukraine 0.

QUOTE-UNQUOTE

'I think he is one of those . . . voyeurs. He likes to watch other people. There are some guys who have a big telescope to see what happens in other families' – **Jose Mourinho**, Chelsea manager, on Arsenal's Arsene Wenger.

'His remarks are out of order, disconnected from reality and disrespectful. When you give success to stupid people, it sometimes makes them more stupid' – **Arsene Wenger** in response.

'He is the best in the world' – **Jose Mourinho**, Chelsea manager, on midfielder Frank Lampard.

'You see your great players getting older and you have to make changes. That is the horrible part when you are manager of this club' – **Sir Alex Ferguson** on Roy Keane's departure from Old Trafford.

'People are talking about me more than they talk about Eastenders' – **Thierry Henry**, Arsenal striker, on transfer speculation.

'It was nice to get some monetary reward from the Brighton fans' – **Iain Dowie**, Crystal Palace manager, on being pelted with coins after his side scored a late winner.

'He is the complete footballer and he is still only 20' – **Sven-Goran Eriksson** on Wayne Rooney after his impressive performance in the 3-2 win over Argentina.

'They had better take away his bootlaces, his belt and his tie after that' – **Mark Lawrenson**, BBC pundit, after former Sunderland manager Mick McCarthy digests another home defeat.

OTHER BRITISH & IRISH INTERNATIONAL RESULTS
ENGLAND

v. ALBANIA

		E	A
1989	Tirana (W.C.)	2	0
1989	Wembley (W.C.)	5	0
2001	Tirana (W.C.)	3	1
2001	Newcastle (W.C.)	2	0

v. ARGENTINA

		E	A
1951	Wembley	2	1
1953*	Buenos Aires	0	0
1962	Rancagua (W.C.)	3	1
1964	Rio de Janeiro	0	1
1966	Wembley (W.C.)	1	0
1974	Wembley	2	2
1977	Buenos Aires	1	1
1980	Wembley	3	1
1986	Mexico City (W.C.)	1	2
1991	Wembley	2	2
1998†	St Etienne (W.C.)	2	2
2000	Wembley	0	0
2002	Sapporo (W.C.)	1	0
2005	Geneva	3	2

(* Abandoned after 21 mins. – rain)
(† England lost 3-4 on pens.)

v. AUSTRALIA

		E	A
1980	Sydney	2	1
1983	Sydney	0	0
1983	Brisbane	1	0
1983	Melbourne	1	1
1991	Sydney	1	0
2003	West Ham	1	3

v. AUSTRIA

		E	A
1908	Vienna	6	1
1908	Vienna	11	1
1909	Vienna	8	1
1930	Vienna	0	0
1932	Stamford Bridge	4	3
1936	Vienna	1	2
1951	Wembley	2	2
1952	Vienna	3	2
1958	Boras (W.C.)	2	2
1961	Vienna	1	3
1962	Wembley	3	1
1965	Wembley	2	3
1967	Vienna	1	0
1973	Wembley	7	0
1979	Vienna	3	4
2004	Vienna (W.C.)	2	2
2005	Old Trafford (W.C.)	1	0

v. AZERBAIJAN

		E	A
2004	Baku (W.C.)	1	0
2005	Newcastle (W.C.)	2	0

v. BELGIUM

		E	B
1921	Brussels	2	0
1923	Highbury	6	1
1923	Antwerp	2	2
1924	West Bromwich	4	0
1926	Antwerp	5	3
1927	Brussels	9	1
1928	Antwerp	3	1
1929	Brussels	5	1
1931	Brussels	4	1
1936	Brussels	2	3
1947	Brussels	5	2
1950	Brussels	4	1
1952	Wembley	5	0
1954	Basle (W.C.)	4	4
1964	Wembley	2	2
1970	Brussels	3	1
1980	Turin (E.C.)	1	1
1990	Bologna (W.C.)	1	0
1998*	Casablanca	0	0
1999	Sunderland	2	1

(* England lost 3-4 on pens.)

v. BOHEMIA

		E	B
1908	Prague	4	0

v. BRAZIL

		E	B
1956	Wembley	4	2
1958	Gothenburg (W.C.)	0	0
1959	Rio de Janeiro	0	2
1962	Vina del Mar (W.C.)	1	3
1963	Wembley	1	1
1964	Rio de Janeiro	1	5
1969	Rio de Janeiro	1	2
1970	Guadalajara (W.C.)	0	1
1976	Los Angeles	0	1
1977	Rio de Janeiro	0	0
1978	Wembley	1	1
1981	Wembley	0	1
1984	Rio de Janeiro	2	0
1987	Wembley	1	1
1990	Wembley	1	0
1992	Wembley	1	1
1993	Washington	1	1
1995	Wembley	1	3
1997	Paris (T.F.)	0	1
2000	Wembley	1	1
2002	Shizuoka (W.C.)	1	2

v. BULGARIA

		E	B
1962	Rancagua (W.C.)	0	0
1968	Wembley	1	1
1974	Sofia	1	0
1979	Sofia (E.C.)	3	0
1979	Wembley (E.C.)	2	0
1996	Wembley	1	0
1998	Wembley (E.C.)	0	0
1999	Sofia (E.C.)	1	1

v. CAMEROON

		E	C
1990	Naples (W.C.)	3	2
1991	Wembley	2	0
1997	Wembley	2	0
2002	Kobe (Japan)	2	2

v. CANADA

		E	C
1986	Vancouver	1	0

v. CHILE

		E	C
1950	Rio de Janeiro (W.C.)	2	0
1953	Santiago	2	1
1984	Santiago	0	0
1989	Wembley	0	0
1998	Wembley	0	2

v. CHINA

		E	C
1996	Beijing	3	0

v. C.I.S.
(formerly Soviet Union)

		E	C
1992	Moscow	2	2

v. COLOMBIA

		E	C
1970	Bogota	4	0
1988	Wembley	1	1
1995	Wembley	0	0
1998	Lens (W.C.)	2	0
2005	New York	3	2

v. CROATIA

		E	C
1995	Wembley	0	0
2003	Ipswich	3	1
2004	Lisbon (E.C.)	4	2

v. CYPRUS

		E	C
1975	Wembley (E.C.)	5	0
1975	Limassol (E.C.)	1	0

v. CZECH REPUBLIC

		E	C
1998	Wembley	2	0

v. CZECHOSLOVAKIA

		E	C
1934	Prague	1	2
1937	White Hart Lane	5	4
1963	Bratislava	4	2
1966	Wembley	0	0
1970	Guadalajara (W.C.)	1	0
1973	Prague	1	1
1974	Wembley (E.C.)	3	0
1975*	Bratislava (E.C.)	1	2
1978	Wembley (E.C.)	1	0
1982	Bilbao (W.C.)	2	0
1990	Wembley	4	2
1992	Prague	2	2

(* Aband. 0-0, 17 mins. prev. day – fog)

v. DENMARK

		E	D
1948	Copenhagen	0	0
1955	Copenhagen	5	1
1956	W'hampton (W.C.)	5	2
1957	Copenhagen (W.C.)	4	1
1966	Copenhagen	2	0
1978	Copenhagen (E.C.)	4	3
1979	Wembley (E.C.)	1	0
1982	Copenhagen (E.C.)	2	2
1983	Wembley (E.C.)	0	1
1988	Wembley	1	0
1989	Copenhagen	1	1
1990	Wembley	1	0
1992	Malmo (E.C.)	0	0
1994	Wembley	1	0
2002	Niigata (W.C.)	3	0
2003	Old Trafford	2	3
2005	Copenhagen	1	4

v. EAST GERMANY

		E	EG
1963	Leipzig	2	1
1970	Wembley	3	1
1974	Leipzig	1	1
1984	Wembley	1	0

v. ECUADOR

		E	Ec
1970	Quito	2	0
2006	Stuttgart (W.C.)	1	0

v. EGYPT

		E	Eg
1986	Cairo	4	0
1990	Cagliari (W.C.)	1	0

v. F.I.F.A.

		E	F
1938	Highbury	3	0
1953	Wembley	4	4
1963	Wembley	2	1

v. FINLAND

		E	F
1937	Helsinki	8	0
1956	Helsinki	5	1
1966	Helsinki	3	0
1976	Helsinki (W.C.)	4	1
1976	Wembley (W.C.)	2	1
1982	Helsinki	4	1
1984	Wembley (W.C.)	5	0
1985	Helsinki (W.C.)	1	1
1992	Helsinki	2	1
2000	Helsinki (W.C.)	0	0
2001	Liverpool (W.C.)	2	1

v. FRANCE

		E	F
1923	Paris	4	1
1924	Paris	3	1
1925	Paris	3	2
1927	Paris	6	0
1928	Paris	5	1
1929	Paris	4	1
1931	Paris	2	5
1933	White Hart Lane	4	1
1938	Paris	4	2
1947	Highbury	3	0
1949	Paris	3	1
1951	Highbury	2	2
1955	Paris	0	1
1957	Wembley	4	0
1962	Hillsborough (E.C.)	1	1
1963	Paris (E.C.)	2	5
1966	Wembley (W.C.)	2	0
1969	Wembley	5	0
1982	Bilbao (W.C.)	3	1
1984	Paris	0	2
1992	Wembley	2	0
1992	Malmo (E.C.)	0	0
1997	Montpellier (T.F.)	1	0
1999	Wembley	0	2
2000	Paris	1	1
2004	Lisbon (E.C.)	1	2

v. GEORGIA

		E	G
1996	Tbilisi (W.C.)	2	0
1997	Wembley (W.C.)	2	0

v. GERMANY/WEST GERMANY

		E	G
1930	Berlin	3	3
1935	White Hart Lane	3	0
1938	Berlin	6	3
1954	Wembley	3	1
1956	Berlin	3	1
1965	Nuremberg	1	0
1966	Wembley	1	0
1966	Wembley (W.C.F.)	4	2
1968	Hanover	0	1
1970	Leon (W.C.)	2	3

		E	G
1972	Wembley (E.C.)	1	3
1972	Berlin (E.C.)	0	0
1975	Wembley	2	0
1978	Munich	1	2
1982	Madrid (W.C.)	0	0
1982	Wembley	1	2
1985	Mexico City	3	0
1987	Dusseldorf	1	3
1990*	Turin (W.C.)	1	1
1991	Wembley	0	1
1993	Detroit	1	2
1996†	Wembley (E.C.)	1	1
2000	Charleroi (E.C.)	1	0
2000	Wembley (W.C.)	0	1
2001	Munich (W.C.)	5	1

(* England lost 3-4 on pens.)
(† England lost 5-6 on pens.)

v. GREECE

		E	G
1971	Wembley (E.C.)	3	0
1971	Athens (E.C.)	2	0
1982	Salonika (E.C.)	3	0
1983	Wembley (E.C.)	0	0
1989	Athens	2	1
1994	Wembley	5	0
2001	Athens (W.C.)	2	0
2001	Old Trafford (W.C.)	2	2

v. HOLLAND

		E	H
1935	Amsterdam	1	0
1946	Huddersfield	8	2
1964	Amsterdam	1	1
1969	Amsterdam	1	0
1970	Wembley	0	0
1977	Wembley	0	2
1982	Wembley	2	0
1988	Wembley	2	2
1988	Dusseldorf (E.C.)	1	3
1990	Cagliari (W.C.)	0	0
1993	Wembley (W.C.)	2	2
1993	Rotterdam (W.C.)	0	2
1996	Wembley (E.C.)	4	1
2001	White Hart Lane	0	2
2002	Amsterdam	1	1
2005	Villa Park	0	0

v. HUNGARY

		E	H
1908	Budapest	7	0
1909	Budapest	4	2
1909	Budapest	8	2
1934	Budapest	1	2
1936	Highbury	6	2
1953	Wembley	3	6
1954	Budapest	1	7
1960	Budapest	0	2
1962	Rancagua (W.C.)	1	2
1965	Wembley	1	0

		E	H
1978	Wembley	4	1
1981	Budapest (W.C.)	3	1
1981	Wembley (W.C.)	1	0
1983	Wembley (E.C.)	2	0
1983	Budapest (E.C.)	3	0
1988	Budapest	0	0
1990	Wembley	1	0
1992	Budapest	1	0
1996	Wembley	3	0
1999	Budapest	1	1
2006	Old Trafford	3	1

v. ICELAND

		E	I
1982	Reykjavik	1	1
2004	City of Manchester	6	1

v. REPUBLIC OF IRELAND

		E	RI
1946	Dublin	1	0
1950	Goodison Park	0	2
1957	Wembley (W.C.)	5	1
1957	Dublin (W.C.)	1	1
1964	Dublin	3	1
1977	Wembley	1	1
1978	Dublin (E.C.)	1	1
1980	Wembley (E.C.)	2	0
1985	Wembley	2	1
1988	Stuttgart (E.C.)	0	1
1990	Cagliari (W.C.)	1	1
1990	Dublin (E.C.)	1	1
1991	Wembley (E.C.)	1	1
1995*	Dublin	0	1

(* Abandoned 27 mins. – crowd riot)

v. ISRAEL

		E	I
1986	Tel Aviv	2	1
1988	Tel Aviv	0	0

v. ITALY

		E	I
1933	Rome	1	1
1934	Highbury	3	2
1939	Milan	2	2
1948	Turin	4	0
1949	White Hart Lane	2	0
1952	Florence	1	1
1959	Wembley	2	2
1961	Rome	3	2
1973	Turin	0	2
1973	Wembley	0	1
1976	New York	3	2
1976	Rome (W.C.)	0	2
1977	Wembley (W.C.)	2	0
1980	Turin (E.C.)	0	1
1985	Mexico City	1	2
1989	Wembley	0	0
1990	Bari (W.C.)	1	2

		E	I
1996	Wembley (W.C.)	0	1
1997	Nantes (T.F.)	2	0
1997	Rome (W.C.)	0	0
2000	Turin	0	1
2002	Leeds	1	2

v. JAMAICA

		E	J
2006	Old Trafford	6	0

v. JAPAN

		E	J
1995	Wembley	2	1
2004	City of Manchester	1	1

v. KUWAIT

		E	K
1982	Bilbao (W.C.)	1	0

v. LIECHTENSTEIN

		E	L
2003	Vaduz (E.C.)	2	0
2003	Old Trafford (E.C.)	2	0

v. LUXEMBOURG

		E	L
1927	Luxembourg	5	2
1960	Luxembourg (W.C.)	9	0
1961	Highbury (W.C.)	4	1
1977	Wembley (W.C.)	5	0
1977	Luxembourg (W.C.)	2	0
1982	Wembley (E.C.)	9	0
1983	Luxembourg (E.C.)	4	0
1998	Luxembourg (E.C.)	3	0
1999	Wembley (E.C.)	6	0

v. MACEDONIA

		E	M
2002	Southampton (E.C.)	2	2
2003	Skopje (E.C.)	2	1

v. MALAYSIA

		E	M
1991	Kuala Lumpur	4	2

v. MALTA

		E	M
1971	Valletta (E.C.)	1	0
1971	Wembley (E.C.)	5	0
2000	Valletta	2	1

v. MEXICO

		E	M
1959	Mexico City	1	2
1961	Wembley	8	0
1966	Wembley (W.C.)	2	0
1969	Mexico City	0	0
1985	Mexico City	0	1
1986	Los Angeles	3	0
1997	Wembley	2	0
2001	Derby	4	0

v. MOLDOVA

		E	M
1996	Kishinev	3	0
1997	Wembley (W.C.)	4	0

v. MOROCCO

		E	M
1986	Monterrey (W.C.)	0	0
1998	Casablanca	1	0

v. NEW ZEALAND

		E	NZ
1991	Auckland	1	0
1991	Wellington	2	0

v. NIGERIA

		E	N
1994	Wembley	1	0
2002	Osaka (W.C.)	0	0

v. NORWAY

		E	N
1937	Oslo	6	0
1938	Newcastle	4	0
1949	Oslo	4	1
1966	Oslo	6	1
1980	Wembley (W.C.)	4	0
1981	Oslo (W.C.)	1	2
1992	Wembley (W.C.)	1	1
1993	Oslo (W.C.)	0	2
1994	Wembley	0	0
1995	Oslo	0	0

v. PARAGUAY

		E	P
1986	Mexico City (W.C.)	3	0
2002	Anfield	4	0
2006	Frankfurt (W.C.)	1	0

v. PERU

		E	P
1959	Lima	1	4
1961	Lima	4	0

v. POLAND

		E	P
1966	Goodison Park	1	1
1966	Chorzow	1	0
1973	Chorzow (W.C.)	0	2
1973	Wembley (W.C.)	1	1
1986	Monterrey (W.C.)	3	0
1989	Wembley (W.C.)	3	0
1989	Katowice (W.C.)	0	0
1990	Wembley (E.C.)	2	0
1991	Poznan (E.C.)	1	1
1993	Chorzow (W.C.)	1	1
1993	Wembley (W.C.)	3	0
1996	Wembley (W.C.)	2	1
1997	Katowice (W.C.)	2	0
1999	Wembley (E.C.)	3	1
1999	Warsaw (E.C.)	0	0
2004	Katowice (W.C.)	2	1

v. PORTUGAL

		E	P
1947	Lisbon	10	0
1950	Lisbon	5	3
1951	Goodison Park	5	2
1955	Oporto	1	3
1958	Wembley	2	1
1961	Lisbon (W.C.)	1	1
1961	Wembley (W.C.)	2	0
1964	Lisbon	4	3
1964	Sao Paulo	1	1
1966	Wembley (W.C.)	2	1
1969	Wembley	1	0
1974	Lisbon	0	0
1974	Wembley (E.C.)	0	0
1975	Lisbon (E.C.)	1	1
1986	Monterrey (W.C.)	0	1
1995	Wembley	1	1
1998	Wembley	3	0
2000	Eindhoven (E.C.)	2	3
2002	Villa Park	1	1
2004	Faro	1	1
2004*	Lisbon (E.C.)	2	2
2006†	Gelsenkirchen (W.C.) ..	0	0

(† England lost 1–3 on pens)
(*England lost 5–6 on pens)

v. ROMANIA

		E	R
1939	Bucharest	2	0
1968	Bucharest	0	0
1969	Wembley	1	1
1970	Guadalajara (W.C.)	1	0
1980	Bucharest (W.C.)	1	2
1981	Wembley (W.C.)	0	0
1985	Bucharest (W.C.)	0	0
1985	Wembley (W.C.)	1	1
1994	Wembley	1	1
1998	Toulouse (W.C.)	1	2
2000	Charleroi (E.C.)	2	3

v. SAN MARINO

		E	SM
1992	Wembley (W.C.)	6	0
1993	Bologna (W.C.)	7	1

v. SAUDI ARABIA

		E	SA
1988	Riyadh	1	1
1998	Wembley	0	0

v. SERBIA-MONTENEGRO

		E	S-M
2003	Leicester	2	1

v. SLOVAKIA

		E	S
2002	Bratislava (E.C.)	2	1

		E	S
2003	Middlesbrough (E.C.) ..	2	1

v. SOUTH AFRICA

		E	SA
1997	Old Trafford	2	1
2003	Durban	2	1

v. SOUTH KOREA

		E	SK
2002	Seoguipo	1	1

v. SOVIET UNION (see also C.I.S.)

		E	SU
1958	Moscow	1	1
1958	Gothenburg (W.C.)	2	2
1958	Gothenburg (W.C.)	0	1
1958	Wembley	5	0
1967	Wembley	2	2
1968	Rome (E.C.)	2	0
1973	Moscow	2	1
1984	Wembley	0	2
1986	Tbilisi	1	0
1988	Frankfurt (E.C.)	1	3
1991	Wembley	3	1

v. SPAIN

		E	S
1929	Madrid	3	4
1931	Highbury	7	1
1950	Rio de Janeiro (W.C.) ..	0	1
1955	Madrid	1	1
1955	Wembley	4	1
1960	Madrid	0	3
1960	Wembley	4	2
1965	Madrid	2	0
1967	Wembley	2	0
1968	Wembley (E.C.)	1	0
1968	Madrid (E.C.)	2	1
1980	Barcelona	2	0
1980	Naples (E.C.)	2	1
1981	Wembley	1	2
1982	Madrid (W.C.)	0	0
1987	Madrid	4	2
1992	Santander	0	1
1996*	Wembley (E.C.)	0	0
2001	Villa Park	3	0
2004	Madrid	0	1
(* England won 4-2 on pens.)			

v. SWEDEN

		E	S
1923	Stockholm	4	2
1923	Stockholm	3	1
1937	Stockholm	4	0
1948	Highbury	4	2
1949	Stockholm	1	3
1956	Stockholm	0	0
1959	Wembley	2	3
1965	Gothenburg	2	1
1968	Wembley	3	1

		E	S
1979	Stockholm	0	0
1986	Stockholm	0	1
1988	Wembley (W.C.)	0	0
1989	Stockholm (W.C.)	0	0
1992	Stockholm (E.C.)	1	2
1995	Leeds	3	3
1998	Stockholm (E.C.)	1	2
1999	Wembley (E.C.)	0	0
2001	Old Trafford	1	1
2002	Saitama (W.C.)	1	1
2004	Gothenburg	0	1
2006	Cologne (W.C.)	2	2

v. SWITZERLAND

		E	S
1933	Berne	4	0
1938	Zurich	1	2
1947	Zurich	0	1
1949	Highbury	6	0
1952	Zurich	3	0
1954	Berne (W.C.)	2	0
1962	Wembley	3	1
1963	Basle	8	1
1971	Basle (E.C.)	3	2
1971	Wembley (E.C.)	1	1
1975	Basle	2	1
1977	Wembley	0	0
1980	Wembley (W.C.)	2	1
1981	Basle (W.C.)	1	2
1988	Lausanne	1	0
1995	Wembley	3	1
1996	Wembley (E.C.)	1	1
1998	Berne	1	1
2004	Coimbra (E.C.)	3	0

v. TRINIDAD & TOBAGO

		E	T
2006	Nuremberg (W.C.)	2	0

v. TUNISIA

		E	T
1990	Tunis	1	1
1998	Marseille (W.C.)	2	0

v. TURKEY

		E	T
1984	Istanbul (W.C.)	8	0
1985	Wembley (W.C.)	5	0
1987	Izmir (E.C.)	0	0
1987	Wembley (E.C.)	8	0
1991	Izmir (E.C.)	1	0
1991	Wembley (E.C.)	1	0
1992	Wembley (W.C.)	4	0
1993	Izmir (W.C.)	2	0
2003	Sunderland (E.C.)	2	0
2003	Istanbul (E.C.)	0	0

v UKRAINE

		E	U
2000	Wembley	2	0

2004	Newcastle	E 3	U 0

v. URUGUAY

		E	U
1953	Montevideo	1	2
1954	Basle (W.C.)	2	4
1964	Wembley	2	1
1966	Wembley (W.C.)	0	0
1969	Montevideo	2	1
1977	Montevideo	0	0
1984	Montevideo	0	2
1990	Wembley	1	2
1995	Wembley	0	0
2006	Anfield	2	1

v. U.S.A.

		E	USA
1950	Belo Horizonte (W.C.)	0	1
1953	New York	6	3
1959	Los Angeles	8	1
1964	New York	10	0
1985	Los Angeles	5	0
1993	Boston	0	2
1994	Wembley	2	0
2005	Chicago	2	1

v. YUGOSLAVIA

		E	Y
1939	Belgrade	1	2
1950	Highbury	2	2
1954	Belgrade	0	1
1956	Wembley	3	0
1958	Belgrade	0	5
1960	Wembley	3	3
1965	Belgrade	1	1
1966	Wembley	2	0
1968	Florence (E.C.)	0	1
1972	Wembley	1	1
1974	Belgrade	2	2
1986	Wembley (E.C.)	2	0
1987	Belgrade (E.C.)	4	1
1989	Wembley	2	1

ENGLAND'S RECORD

England's first international was a 0-0 draw against Scotland in Glasgow, on the West of Scotland cricket ground, Partick, on November 30, 1872. Their complete record, at the start of 2006-07, is:

P	W	D	L	F	A
840	474	205	161	1875	858

ENGLAND "B" TEAM RESULTS
(England score shown first)

1949	Finland (A)	4	0
1949	Holland (A)	4	0
1950	Italy (A)	0	5
1950	Holland (H)	1	0
1950	Holland (A)	0	3
1950	Luxembourg (A)	2	1
1950	Switzerland (H)	5	0
1952	Holland (A)	1	0
1952	France (A)	1	7
1953	Scotland (A)	2	2
1954	Scotland (H)	1	1
1954	Germany (A)	4	0
1954	Yugoslavia (A)	1	2
1954	Switzerland (A)	0	2
1955	Germany (H)	1	1
1955	Yugoslavia (H)	5	1
1956	Switzerland (H)	4	1
1956	Scotland (A)	2	2
1957	Scotland (H)	4	1
1978	W. Germany (A)	2	1
1978	Czechoslovakia (A)	1	0
1978	Singapore (A)	8	0
1978	Malaysia (A)	1	1
1978	N. Zealand (A)	4	0
1978	N. Zealand (A)	3	1
1978	N. Zealand (A)	4	0
1979	Austria (A)	1	0
1979	N. Zealand (H)	4	1
1980	U.S.A. (H)	1	0
1980	Spain (H)	1	0
1980	Australia (H)	1	0
1981	Spain (A)	2	3
1984	N. Zealand (H)	2	0
1987	Malta (A)	2	0
1989	Switzerland (A)	2	0
1989	Iceland (A)	2	0
1989	Norway (A)	1	0
1989	Italy (H)	1	1
1989	Yugoslavia (H)	2	1
1990	Rep. of Ireland (A)	1	4
1990	Czechoslovakia (H)	2	0
1990	Algeria (A)	0	0
1991	Wales (A)	1	0
1991	Iceland (H)	1	0

1991	Switzerland (H)	2	1
1991	Spanish XI (A)	1	0
1992	France (H)	3	0
1992	Czechoslovakia (A)	1	0
1992	C.I.S. (A)	1	1

1994	N. Ireland (H)	4	2
1995	Rep. of Ireland (H)	2	0
1998	Chile (H)	1	2
1998	Russia (H)	4	1
2006	Belarus (H)	1	2

GREAT BRITAIN V. REST OF EUROPE (F.I.F.A.)

		GB	RofE
1947	Glasgow	6	1

		GB	RofE
1955	Belfast	1	4

SCOTLAND

v. ARGENTINA

		S	A
1977	Buenos Aires	1	1
1979	Glasgow	1	3
1990	Glasgow	1	0

v. AUSTRALIA

		S	A
1985*	Glasgow (W.C.)	2	0
1985*	Melbourne (W.C.)	0	0
1996	Glasgow	1	0
2000	Glasgow	0	2

(* World Cup play-off)

v. AUSTRIA

		S	A
1931	Vienna	0	5
1933	Glasgow	2	2
1937	Vienna	1	1
1950	Glasgow	0	1
1951	Vienna	0	4
1954	Zurich (W.C.)	0	1
1955	Vienna	4	1
1956	Glasgow	1	1
1960	Vienna	1	4
1963*	Glasgow	4	1
1968	Glasgow (W.C.)	2	1
1969	Vienna (W.C.)	0	2
1978	Vienna (E.C.)	2	3
1979	Glasgow (E.C.)	1	1
1994	Vienna	2	1
1996	Vienna (W.C.)	0	0
1997	Glasgow (W.C.)	2	0

(* Abandoned after 79 minutes)

| 2003 | Glasgow | 0 | 2 |
| 2005 | Graz | 2 | 2 |

v. BELARUS

		S	B
1997	Minsk (W.C.)	1	0
1997	Aberdeen (W.C.)	4	1
2005	Minsk (W.C.)	0	0
2005	Glasgow (W.C.)	0	1

v. BELGIUM

		S	B
1947	Brussels	1	2
1948	Glasgow	2	0
1951	Brussels	5	0
1971	Liege (E.C.)	0	3
1971	Aberdeen (E.C.)	1	0
1974	Brugge	1	2
1979	Brussels (E.C.)	0	2
1979	Glasgow (E.C.)	1	3
1982	Brussels (E.C.)	2	3
1983	Glasgow (E.C.)	1	1
1987	Brussels (E.C.)	1	4
1987	Glasgow (E.C.)	2	0
2001	Glasgow (W.C.)	2	2
2001	Brussels (W.C.)	0	2

v. BOSNIA

		S	B
1999	Sarajevo (E.C.)	2	1
1999	Glasgow (E.C.)	1	0

v. BRAZIL

		S	B
1966	Glasgow	1	1
1972	Rio de Janeiro	0	1
1973	Glasgow	0	1
1974	Frankfurt (W.C.)	0	0
1977	Rio de Janeiro	0	2
1982	Seville (W.C.)	1	4
1987	Glasgow	0	2
1990	Turin (W.C.)	0	1
1998	St. Denis (W.C.)	1	2

v. BULGARIA

		S	B
1978	Glasgow	2	1
1986	Glasgow (E.C.)	0	0
1987	Sofia (E.C.)	1	0
1990	Sofia (E.C.)	1	1
1991	Glasgow (E.C.)	1	1
2006	Kobe	5	1

v. CANADA

		S	C
1983	Vancouver	2	0

		S	C
1983	Edmonton	3	0
1983	Toronto	2	0
1992	Toronto	3	1
2002	Edinburgh	3	1

v. CHILE

		S	C
1977	Santiago	4	2
1989	Glasgow	2	0

v. C.I.S. (formerly Soviet Union)

		S	C
1992	Norrkoping (E.C.)	3	0

v. COLOMBIA

		S	C
1988	Glasgow	0	0
1996	Miami	0	1
1998	New York	2	2

v. COSTA RICA

		S	C
1990	Genoa (W.C.)	0	1

v. CROATIA

		S	C
2000	Zagreb (W.C.)	1	1
2001	Glasgow (W.C.)	0	0

v. CYPRUS

		S	C
1968	Nicosia (W.C.)	5	0
1969	Glasgow (W.C.)	8	0
1989	Limassol (W.C.)	3	2
1989	Glasgow (W.C.)	2	1

v. CZECH REPUBLIC

		S	C
1999	Glasgow (E.C.)	1	2
1999	Prague (E.C.)	2	3

v. CZECHOSLOVAKIA

		S	C
1937	Prague	3	1
1937	Glasgow	5	0
1961	Bratislava (W.C.)	0	4
1961	Glasgow (W.C.)	3	2
1961*	Brussels (W.C.)	2	4
1972	Porto Alegre	0	0
1973	Glasgow (W.C.)	2	1
1973	Bratislava (W.C.)	0	1
1976	Prague (W.C.)	0	2
1977	Glasgow (W.C.)	3	1

(* World Cup play-off)

v. DENMARK

		S	D
1951	Glasgow	3	1
1952	Copenhagen	2	1
1968	Copenhagen	1	0
1970	Glasgow (E.C.)	1	0

		S	D
1971	Copenhagen (E.C.)	0	1
1972	Copenhagen (W.C.)	4	1
1972	Glasgow (W.C.)	2	0
1975	Copenhagen (E.C.)	1	0
1975	Glasgow (E.C.)	3	1
1986	Neza (W.C.)	0	1
1996	Copenhagen	0	2
1998	Glasgow	0	1
2002	Glasgow	0	1
2004	Copenhagen	0	1

v. EAST GERMANY

		S	EG
1974	Glasgow	3	0
1977	East Berlin	0	1
1982	Glasgow (E.C.)	2	0
1983	Halle (E.C.)	1	2
1986	Glasgow	0	0
1990	Glasgow	0	1

v. ECUADOR

		S	E
1995	Toyama, Japan	2	1

v. EGYPT

		S	E
1990	Aberdeen	1	3

v. ESTONIA

		S	E
1993	Tallinn (W.C.)	3	0
1993	Aberdeen	3	1
1996	Tallinn (W.C.) *	No result	
1997	Monaco (W.C.)	0	0
1997	Kilmarnock (W.C.)	2	0
1998	Edinburgh (E.C.)	3	2
1999	Tallinn (E.C.)	0	0

(* Estonia absent)

		S	E
2004	Tallinn	1	0

v. FAROE ISLANDS

		S	F
1994	Glasgow (E.C.)	5	1
1995	Toftir (E.C.)	2	0
1998	Aberdeen (E.C.)	2	1
1999	Toftir (E.C.)	1	1
2002	Toftir (E.C.)	2	2
2003	Glasgow (E.C.)	3	1

v. FINLAND

		S	F
1954	Helsinki	2	1
1964	Glasgow (W.C.)	3	1
1965	Helsinki (W.C.)	2	1
1976	Glasgow	6	0
1992	Glasgow	1	1
1994	Helsinki (E.C.)	2	0
1995	Glasgow (E.C.)	1	0
1998	Edinburgh	1	1

v. FRANCE

		S	F
1930	Paris	2	0
1932	Paris	3	1
1948	Paris	0	3
1949	Glasgow	2	0
1950	Paris	1	0
1951	Glasgow	1	0
1958	Orebro (W.C.)	1	2
1984	Marseilles	0	2
1989	Glasgow (W.C.)	2	0
1990	Paris (W.C.)	0	3
1997	St. Etienne	1	2
2000	Glasgow	0	2
2002	Paris	0	5

v. GERMANY/WEST GERMANY

		S	G
1929	Berlin	1	1
1936	Glasgow	2	0
1957	Stuttgart	3	1
1959	Glasgow	3	2
1964	Hanover	2	2
1969	Glasgow (W.C.)	1	1
1969	Hamburg (W.C.)	2	3
1973	Glasgow	1	1
1974	Frankfurt	1	2
1986	Queretaro (W.C.)	1	2
1992	Norrkoping (E.C.)	0	2
1993	Glasgow	0	1
1999	Bremen	1	0
2003	Glasgow (E.C.)	1	1
2003	Dortmund (E.C.)	1	2

v. GREECE

		S	G
1994	Athens (E.C.)	0	1
1995	Glasgow	1	0

v. HOLLAND

		S	H
1929	Amsterdam	2	0
1938	Amsterdam	3	1
1959	Amsterdam	2	1
1966	Glasgow	0	3
1968	Amsterdam	0	0
1971	Amsterdam	1	2
1978	Mendoza (W.C.)	3	2
1982	Glasgow	2	1
1986	Eindhoven	0	0
1992	Gothenburg (E.C.)	0	1
1994	Glasgow	0	1
1994	Utrecht	1	3
1996	Birmingham (E.C.)	0	0
2000	Arnhem	0	0
2003*	Glasgow (E.C.)	1	0
2003*	Amsterdam (E.C.)	0	6

(* Qual. Round play-off)

v. HUNGARY

		S	H
1938	Glasgow	3	1
1955	Glasgow	2	4
1955	Budapest	1	3
1958	Glasgow	1	1
1960	Budapest	3	3
1980	Budapest	1	3
1987	Glasgow	2	0
2004	Glasgow	0	3

v. ICELAND

		S	I
1984	Glasgow (W.C.)	3	0
1985	Reykjavik (WC)	1	0
2002	Reykjavik (E.C.)	2	0
2003	Glasgow (E.C)	2	1

v. IRAN

		S	I
1978	Cordoba (W.C.)	1	1

v. REPUBLIC OF IRELAND

		S	RI
1961	Glasgow (W.C.)	4	1
1961	Dublin (W.C.)	3	0
1963	Dublin	0	1
1969	Dublin	1	1
1986	Dublin (E.C.)	0	0
1987	Glasgow (E.C.)	0	1
2000	Dublin	2	1
2003	Glasgow (E.C.)	0	2

v. ISRAEL

		S	I
1981	Tel Aviv (W.C.)	1	0
1981	Glasgow (W.C.)	3	1
1986	Tel Aviv	1	0

v. ITALY

		S	I
1931	Rome	0	3
1965	Glasgow (W.C.)	1	0
1965	Naples (W.C.)	0	3
1988	Perugia	0	2
1992	Glasgow (W.C.)	0	0
1993	Rome (W.C.)	1	3
2005	Milan (W.C.)	0	2
2005	Glasgow (W.C.)	1	1

v. JAPAN

		S	J
1995	Hiroshima	0	0
2006	Saitama	0	0

v. LATVIA

		S	L
1996	Riga (W.C.)	2	0
1997	Glasgow (W.C.)	2	0
2000	Riga (W.C.)	1	0
2001	Glasgow (W.C.)	2	1

v. LITHUANIA

		S	L
1998	Vilnius (E.C.)	0	0
1999	Glasgow (E.C.)	3	0
2003	Kaunas (E.C.)	0	1
2003	Glasgow (E.C.)	1	0

v. LUXEMBOURG

		S	L
1947	Luxembourg	6	0
1986	Glasgow (E.C.)	3	0
1987	Esch (E.C.)	0	0

v. MALTA

		S	M
1988	Valletta	1	1
1990	Valletta	2	1
1993	Valletta (W.C.)	3	0
1993	Valletta (W.C.)	2	0
1997	Valletta	3	2

v. MOLDOVA

		S	M
2004	Chisinau (W.C.)	1	1
2005	Glasgow (W.C.)	2	0

v. MOROCCO

		S	M
1998	St. Etienne (W.C.)	0	3

v. NEW ZEALAND

		S	NZ
1982	Malaga (W.C.)	5	2
2003	Edinburgh	1	1

v. NIGERIA

		S	N
2002	Aberdeen	1	2

v. NORWAY

		S	N
1929	Bergen	7	3
1954	Glasgow	1	0
1954	Oslo	1	1
1963	Bergen	3	4
1963	Glasgow	6	1
1974	Oslo	2	1
1978	Glasgow (E.C.)	3	2
1979	Oslo (E.C.)	4	0
1988	Oslo (W.C.)	2	1
1989	Glasgow (W.C.)	1	1
1992	Oslo	0	0
1998	Bordeaux (W.C.)	1	1
2003	Oslo	0	0
2004	Glasgow (W.C.)	0	1
2005	Oslo (W.C.)	2	1

v. PARAGUAY

		S	P
1958	Norrkoping (W.C.)	2	3

v. PERU

		S	P
1972	Glasgow	2	0
1978	Cordoba (W.C.)	1	3
1979	Glasgow	1	1

v. POLAND

		S	P
1958	Warsaw	2	1
1960	Glasgow	2	3
1965	Chorzow (W.C.)	1	1
1965	Glasgow (W.C.)	1	2
1980	Poznan	0	1
1990	Glasgow	1	1
2001	Bydgoszcz	1	1

v. PORTUGAL

		S	P
1950	Lisbon	2	2
1955	Glasgow	3	0
1959	Lisbon	0	1
1966	Glasgow	0	1
1971	Lisbon (E.C.)	0	2
1971	Glasgow (E.C.)	2	1
1975	Glasgow	1	0
1978	Lisbon (E.C.)	0	1
1980	Glasgow (E.C.)	4	1
1980	Glasgow (W.C.)	0	0
1981	Lisbon (W.C.)	1	2
1992	Glasgow (W.C.)	0	0
1993	Lisbon (W.C.)	0	5
2002	Braga	0	2

v. ROMANIA

		S	R
1975	Bucharest (E.C.)	1	1
1975	Glasgow (E.C.)	1	1
1986	Glasgow	3	0
1990	Glasgow (E.C.)	2	1
1991	Bucharest (E.C.)	0	1
2004	Glasgow	1	2

v. RUSSIA

		S	R
1994	Glasgow (E.C.)	1	1
1995	Moscow (E.C.)	0	0

v. SAN MARINO

		S	SM
1991	Serravalle (E.C.)	2	0
1991	Glasgow (E.C.)	4	0
1995	Serravalle (E.C.)	2	0
1995	Glasgow (E.C.)	5	0
2000	Serravalle (W.C.)	2	0
2001	Glasgow (W.C.)	4	0

v. SAUDI ARABIA

		S	SA
1988	Riyadh	2	2

v. SLOVENIA

		S	SL
2004	Glasgow (W.C.)	0	0
2005	Celje (W.C.)	3	0

v. SOUTH AFRICA

		S	SA
2002	Hong Kong	0	2

v. SOUTH KOREA

		S	SK
2002	Busan	1	4

v. SOVIET UNION
(see also C.I.S. and RUSSIA)

		S	SU
1967	Glasgow	0	2
1971	Moscow	0	1
1982	Malaga (W.C.)	2	2
1991	Glasgow	0	1

v. SPAIN

		S	Sp
1957	Glasgow (W.C.)	4	2
1957	Madrid (W.C.)	1	4
1963	Madrid	6	2
1965	Glasgow	0	0
1975	Glasgow (E.C.)	1	2
1975	Valencia (E.C.)	1	1
1982	Valencia	0	3
1985	Glasgow (W.C.)	3	1
1985	Seville (W.C.)	0	1
1988	Madrid	0	0
2004*	Valencia	1	1

(*Abandoned after 59 mins. – floodlight failure)

v. SWEDEN

		S	Swe
1952	Stockholm	1	3
1953	Glasgow	1	2
1975	Gothenburg	1	1
1977	Glasgow	3	1
1980	Stockholm (W.C.)	1	0
1981	Glasgow (W.C.)	2	0
1990	Genoa (W.C.)	2	1
1995	Solna	0	2
1996	Glasgow	1	0
1997	Gothenburg (W.C.)	1	2
2004	Edinburgh	1	4

v. SWITZERLAND

		S	Sw
1931	Geneva	3	2

		S	Sw
1948	Berne	1	2
1950	Glasgow	3	1
1957	Basle (W.C.)	2	1
1957	Glasgow (W.C.)	3	2
1973	Berne	0	1
1976	Glasgow	1	0
1982	Berne (E.C.)	0	2
1983	Glasgow (E.C.)	2	2
1990	Glasgow (E.C.)	2	1
1991	Berne (E.C.)	2	2
1992	Berne (W.C.)	1	3
1993	Aberdeen (W.C.)	1	1
1996	Birmingham (E.C.)	1	0
2006	Glasgow	1	3

v. TRINIDAD + TOBAGO

		S	T
2004	Hibernian	4	1

v. TURKEY

		S	T
1960	Ankara	2	4

v. U.S.A.

		S	USA
1952	Glasgow	6	0
1992	Denver	1	0
1996	New Britain, Conn	1	2
1998	Washington	0	0
2005	Glasgow	1	1

v. URUGUAY

		S	U
1954	Basle (W.C.)	0	7
1962	Glasgow	2	3
1983	Glasgow	2	0
1986	Neza (W.C.)	0	0

v. YUGOSLAVIA

		S	Y
1955	Belgrade	2	2
1956	Glasgow	2	0
1958	Vaasteras (W.C.)	1	1
1972	Belo Horizonte	2	2
1974	Frankfurt (W.C.)	1	1
1984	Glasgow	6	1
1988	Glasgow (W.C.)	1	1
1989	Zagreb (W.C.)	1	3

v. ZAIRE

		S	Z
1974	Dortmund (W.C.)	2	0

WALES

v. ALBANIA

		W	A
1994	Cardiff (E.C.)	2	0
1995	Tirana (E.C.)	1	1

v. ARGENTINA

		W	A
1992	Gifu (Japan)	0	1
2002	Cardiff	1	1

v. ARMENIA

		W	A
2001	Yerevan (W.C.)	2	2
2001	Cardiff (W.C.)	0	0

v. AUSTRIA

		W	A
1954	Vienna	0	2
1955	Wrexham	1	2
1975	Vienna (E.C.)	1	2
1975	Wrexham (E.C.)	1	0
1992	Vienna	1	1
2005	Cardiff	0	2
2005	Vienna	0	1

v. AZERBAIJAN

		W	A
2002	Baku (E.C.)	2	0
2003	Cardiff (E.C.)	4	0
2004	Baku (W.C.)	1	1
2005	Cardiff (W.C.)	2	0

v. BELARUS

		W	B
1998	Cardiff (E.C.)	3	2
1999	Minsk (E.C.)	2	1
2000	Minsk (W.C.)	1	2
2001	Cardiff (W.C.)	1	0

v. BELGIUM

		W	B
1949	Liege	1	3
1949	Cardiff	5	1
1990	Cardiff (E.C.)	3	1
1991	Brussels (E.C.)	1	1
1992	Brussels (W.C.)	0	2
1993	Cardiff (W.C.)	2	0
1997	Cardiff (W.C.)	1	2
1997	Brussels (W.C.)	2	3

v. BOSNIA-HERZEGOVINA

		W	B-H
2003	Cardiff	2	2

v. BRAZIL

		W	B
1958	Gothenburg (W.C.)	0	1
1962	Rio de Janeiro	1	3
1962	Sao Paulo	1	3
1966	Rio de Janeiro	1	3
1966	Belo Horizonte	0	1
1983	Cardiff	1	1
1991	Cardiff	1	0
1997	Brasilia	0	3
2000	Cardiff	0	3

v. BULGARIA

		W	B
1983	Wrexham (E.C.)	1	0
1983	Sofia (E.C.)	0	1
1994	Cardiff (E.C.)	0	3
1995	Sofia (E.C.)	1	3

v. CANADA

		W	C
1986	Toronto	0	2
1986	Vancouver	3	0
2004	Wrexham	1	0

v. CHILE

		W	C
1966	Santiago	0	2

v. COSTA RICA

		W	C
1990	Cardiff	1	0

v. CROATIA

		W	C
2002	Varazdin	1	1

v. CYPRUS

		W	C
1992	Limassol (W.C.)	1	0
1993	Cardiff (W.C.)	2	0
2005	Limassol	0	1

v. CZECHOSLOVAKIA (see also R.C.S.)

		W	C
1957	Cardiff (W.C.)	1	0
1957	Prague (W.C.)	0	2
1971	Swansea (E.C.)	1	3
1971	Prague (E.C.)	0	1
1977	Wrexham (W.C.)	3	0
1977	Prague (W.C.)	0	1
1980	Cardiff (W.C.)	1	0
1981	Prague (W.C.)	0	2
1987	Wrexham (E.C.)	1	1
1987	Prague (E.C.)	0	2

v. CZECH REPUBLIC

		S	CR
2002	Cardiff	0	0

v. DENMARK

		W	D
1964	Copenhagen (W.C.)	0	1
1965	Wrexham (W.C.)	4	2
1987	Cardiff (E.C.)	1	0
1987	Copenhagen (E.C.)	0	1
1990	Copenhagen	0	1
1998	Copenhagen (E.C.)	2	1
1999	Anfield (E.C.)	0	2

v. EAST GERMANY

		W	EG
1957	Leipzig (W.C.)	1	2
1957	Cardiff (W.C.)	4	1
1969	Dresden (W.C.)	1	2
1969	Cardiff (W.C.)	1	3

v. ESTONIA

		W	E
1994	Tallinn	2	1

v. FAROE ISLANDS

		W	Fl
1992	Cardiff (W.C.)	6	0
1993	Toftir (W.C.)	3	0

v. FINLAND

		W	F
1971	Helsinki (E.C.)	1	0
1971	Swansea (E.C.)	3	0
1986	Helsinki (E.C.)	1	1
1987	Wrexham (E.C.)	4	0
1988	Swansea (W.C.)	2	2
1989	Helsinki (W.C.)	0	1
2000	Cardiff	1	2
2002	Helsinki (E.C.)	2	0
2003	Cardiff (E.C.)	1	1

v. FRANCE

		W	F
1933	Paris	1	1
1939	Paris	1	2
1953	Paris	1	6
1982	Toulouse	1	0

v. GEORGIA

		W	G
1994	Tbilisi (E.C.)	0	5
1995	Cardiff (E.C.)	0	1

v. GERMANY/WEST GERMANY

		W	G
1968	Cardiff	1	1
1969	Frankfurt	1	1
1977	Cardiff	0	2
1977	Dortmund	1	1
1979	Wrexham (E.C.)	0	2
1979	Cologne (E.C.)	1	5
1989	Cardiff (W.C.)	0	0
1989	Cologne (W.C.)	1	2
1991	Cardiff (E.C.)	1	0
1991	Nuremberg (E.C.)	1	4
1995	Dusseldorf (E.C.)	1	1
1995	Cardiff (E.C.)	1	2
2002	Cardiff	1	0

v. GREECE

		W	G
1964	Athens (W.C.)	0	2
1965	Cardiff (W.C.)	4	1

v. HOLLAND

		W	H
1988	Amsterdam (W.C.)	0	1
1989	Wrexham (W.C.)	1	2
1992	Utrecht	0	4
1996	Cardiff (W.C.)	1	3
1996	Eindhoven (W.C.)	1	7

v. HUNGARY

		W	H
1958	Sanviken (W.C.)	1	1
1958	Stockholm (W.C.)	2	1
1961	Budapest	2	3
1963	Budapest (E.C.)	1	3
1963	Cardiff (E.C.)	1	1
1974	Cardiff (E.C.)	2	0
1975	Budapest (E.C.)	2	1
1986	Cardiff	0	3
2004	Budapest	2	1
2005	Cardiff	2	0

v. ICELAND

		W	I
1980	Reykjavik (W.C.)	4	0
1981	Swansea (W.C.)	2	2
1984	Reykjavik (W.C.)	0	1
1984	Cardiff (W.C.)	2	1
1991	Cardiff	1	0

v. IRAN

		W	I
1978	Tehran	1	0

v. REPUBLIC OF IRELAND

		W	RI
1960	Dublin	3	2
1979	Swansea	2	1
1981	Dublin	3	1
1986	Dublin	1	0
1990	Dublin	0	1
1991	Wrexham	0	3
1992	Dublin	1	0
1993	Dublin	1	2
1997	Cardiff	0	0

v. ISRAEL

		W	I
1958	Tel Aviv (W.C.)	2	0
1958	Cardiff (W.C.)	2	0
1984	Tel Aviv	0	0
1989	Tel Aviv	3	3

v. ITALY

		W	I
1965	Florence	1	4
1968	Cardiff (W.C.)	0	1
1969	Rome (W.C.)	1	4
1988	Brescia	1	0
1996	Terni	0	3
1998	Anfield (E.C.)	0	2
1999	Bologna (E.C.)	0	4
2002	Cardiff (E.C.)	2	1
2003	Milan (E.C.)	0	4

v. JAMAICA

		W	J
1998	Cardiff	0	0

v. JAPAN

		W	J
1992	Matsuyama	1	0

v. KUWAIT

		W	K
1977	Wrexham	0	0
1977	Kuwait City	0	0

v. LATVIA

		W	L
2004	Riga	2	0

v. LUXEMBOURG

		W	L
1974	Swansea (E.C.)	5	0
1975	Luxembourg (E.C.)	3	1
1990	Luxembourg (E.C.)	1	0
1991	Luxembourg (E.C.)	1	0

v. MALTA

		W	M
1978	Wrexham (E.C.)	7	0
1979	Valletta (E.C.)	2	0
1988	Valletta	3	2
1998	Valletta	3	0

v. MEXICO

		W	M
1958	Stockholm (W.C.)	1	1
1962	Mexico City	1	2

v. MOLDOVA

		W	M
1994	Kishinev (E.C.)	2	3
1995	Cardiff (E.C.)	1	0

v. NORWAY

		W	N
1982	Swansea (E.C.)	1	0
1983	Oslo (E.C.)	0	0
1984	Trondheim	0	1
1985	Wrexham	1	1
1985	Bergen	2	4
1994	Cardiff	1	3
2000	Cardiff (W.C.)	1	1
2001	Oslo (W.C.)	2	3
2004	Oslo	0	0

v. PARAGUAY

		W	P
2006	Cardiff	0	0

v. POLAND

		W	P
1973	Cardiff (W.C.)	2	0
1973	Katowice (W.C.)	0	3
1991	Radom	0	0
2000	Warsaw (W.C.)	0	0
2001	Cardiff (W.C.)	1	2
2004	Cardiff (W.C.)	2	3
2005	Warsaw (W.C.)	0	1

v. PORTUGAL

		W	P
1949	Lisbon	2	3

		W	P
1951	Cardiff	2	1
2000	Chaves	0	3

v. QATAR

		W	Q
2000	Doha	1	0

v. R.C.S. (formerly Czechoslovakia)

		W	RCS
1993	Ostrava (W.C.)	1	1
1993	Cardiff (W.C.)	2	2

v. REST OF UNITED KINGDOM

		W	UK
1951	Cardiff	3	2
1969	Cardiff	0	1

v. ROMANIA

		W	R
1970	Cardiff (E.C.)	0	0
1971	Bucharest (E.C.)	0	2
1983	Wrexham	5	0
1992	Bucharest (W.C.)	1	5
1993	Cardiff (W.C.)	1	2

v. RUSSIA (See also Soviet Union)

		W	R
2003*	Moscow (E.C.)	0	0
2003*	Cardiff (E.C.)	0	1
(* Qual. Round play-offs)			

v. SAN MARINO

		W	SM
1996	Serravalle (W.C.)	5	0
1996	Cardiff (W.C.)	6	0

v. SAUDI ARABIA

		W	SA
1986	Dahran	2	1

v. SERBIA + MONTENEGRO

		W	S
2003	Belgrade (E.C.)	0	1
2003	Cardiff (E.C.)	2	3

v. SLOVENIA

		W	S
2005	Swansea	0	0

v. SOVIET UNION (See also Russia)

		W	SU
1965	Moscow (W.C.)	1	2
1965	Cardiff (W.C.)	2	1
1981	Wrexham (W.C.)	0	0
1981	Tbilisi (W.C.)	0	3
1987	Swansea	0	0

v. SPAIN

		W	S
1961	Cardiff (W.C.)	1	2
1961	Madrid (W.C.)	1	1
1982	Valencia	1	1

		W	S
1984	Seville (W.C.)	0	3
1985	Wrexham (W.C.)	3	0

v. SWEDEN

		W	S
1958	Stockholm (W.C.)	0	0
1988	Stockholm	1	4
1989	Wrexham	0	2
1990	Stockholm	2	4
1994	Wrexham	0	2

v. SWITZERLAND

		W	S
1949	Berne	0	4
1951	Wrexham	3	2
1996	Lugano	0	2
1999	Zurich (E.C.)	0	2
1999	Wrexham (E.C.)	0	2

v. TRINIDAD & TOBAGO

		W	T
2006	Graz	2	1

v. TUNISIA

		W	T
1998	Tunis	0	4

v. TURKEY

		W	T
1978	Wrexham (E.C.)	1	0
1979	Izmir (E.C.)	0	1
1980	Cardiff (W.C.)	4	0
1981	Ankara (W.C.)	1	0
1996	Cardiff (W.C.)	0	0
1997	Istanbul (W.C.)	4	6

v. UKRAINE

		W	U
2001	Cardiff (W.C.)	1	1
2001	Kiev (W.C.)	1	1

v. URUGUAY

		W	U
1986	Wrexham	0	0

v. U.S.A.

		W	USA
2003	San Jose	0	2

v. YUGOSLAVIA

		W	Y
1953	Belgrade	2	5
1954	Cardiff	1	3
1976	Zagreb (E.C.)	0	2
1976	Cardiff (E.C.)	1	1
1982	Titograd (E.C.)	4	4
1983	Cardiff (E.C.)	1	1
1988	Swansea	1	2

NORTHERN IRELAND

v. ALBANIA

		NI	A
1965	Belfast (W.C.)	4	1
1965	Tirana (W.C.)	1	1
1983	Tirana (E.C.)	0	0
1983	Belfast (E.C.)	1	0
1992	Belfast (W.C.)	3	0
1993	Tirana (W.C.)	2	1
1996	Belfast (W.C.)	2	0
1997	Zurich (W.C.)	0	1

v. ALGERIA

		NI	A
1986	Guadalajara (W.C.)	1	1

v. ARGENTINA

		NI	A
1958	Halmstad (W.C.)	1	3

v. ARMENIA

		NI	A
1996	Belfast (W.C.)	1	1
1997	Yerevan (W.C.)	0	0
2003	Yerevan (E.C.)	0	1
2003	Belfast (E.C.)	0	1

v. AUSTRALIA

		NI	A
1980	Sydney	2	1
1980	Melbourne	1	1
1980	Adelaide	2	1

v. AUSTRIA

		NI	A
1982	Madrid (W.C.)	2	2
1982	Vienna (E.C.)	0	2
1983	Belfast (E.C.)	3	1
1990	Vienna (E.C.)	0	0
1991	Belfast (E.C.)	2	1
1994	Vienna (E.C.)	2	1
1995	Belfast (E.C.)	5	3
2004	Belfast (W.C.)	3	3
2005	Vienna (W.C.)	0	2

v. AZERBAIJAN

		NI	A
2004	Baku (W.C.)	0	0
2005	Belfast (W.C.)	2	0

v. BARBADOS

		NI	B
2004	Bridgetown	1	1

v. BELGIUM

		NI	B
1976	Liege (W.C.)	0	2
1977	Belfast (W.C.)	3	0

	NI	B
1997 Belfast	3	0

v. BRAZIL

	NI	B
1986 Guadalajara (W.C.)	0	3

v. BULGARIA

	NI	B
1972 Sofia (W.C.)	0	3
1973 Sheffield (W.C.)	0	0
1978 Sofia (E.C.)	2	0
1979 Belfast (E.C.)	2	0
2001 Sofia (W.C.)	3	4
2001 Belfast (W.C.)	0	1

v. CANADA

	NI	C
1995 Edmonton	0	2
1999 Belfast	1	1
2005 Belfast	0	1

v. CHILE

	NI	C
1989 Belfast	0	1
1995 Edmonton, Canada	0	2

v. COLOMBIA

	NI	C
1994 Boston, USA	0	2

v. CYPRUS

	NI	C
1971 Nicosia (E.C.)	3	0
1971 Belfast (E.C.)	5	0
1973 Nicosia (W.C.)	0	1
1973 Fulham (W.C.)	3	0
2002 Belfast	0	0

v. CZECHOSLOVAKIA/CZECH REPUBLIC

	NI	C
1958 Halmstad (W.C.)	1	0
1958 Malmo (W.C.)	2	1
2001 Belfast (W.C.)	0	1
2001 Teplice (W.C.)	1	3

v. DENMARK

	NI	D
1978 Belfast (E.C.)	2	1
1979 Copenhagen (E.C.)	0	4
1986 Belfast	1	1
1990 Belfast (E.C.)	1	1
1991 Odense (E.C.)	1	2
1992 Belfast (W.C.)	0	1
1993 Copenhagen (W.C.)	0	1
2000 Belfast (W.C.)	1	1
2001 Copenhagen (W.C.)	1	1

v. ESTONIA

	NI	E
2004 Tallinn	1	0
2006 Belfast	1	0

v. FAROE ISLANDS

	NI	FI
1991 Belfast (E.C.)	1	1
1991 Landskrona, Sw. (E.C.)	5	0

v. FINLAND

	NI	F
1984 Pori (W.C.)	0	1
1984 Belfast (W.C.)	2	1
1998 Belfast (E.C.)	1	0
1999 Helsinki (E.C.)	1	4
2003 Belfast	0	1

v. FRANCE

	NI	F
1951 Belfast	2	2
1952 Paris	1	3
1958 Norrkoping (W.C.)	0	4
1982 Paris	0	4
1982 Madrid (W.C.)	1	4
1986 Paris	0	0
1988 Belfast	0	0
1999 Belfast	0	1

v. GERMANY/WEST GERMANY

	NI	G
1958 Malmo (W.C.)	2	2
1960 Belfast (W.C.)	3	4
1961 Berlin (W.C.)	1	2
1966 Belfast	0	2
1977 Cologne	0	5
1982 Belfast (E.C.)	1	0
1983 Hamburg (E.C.)	1	0
1992 Bremen	1	1
1996 Belfast	1	1
1997 Nuremberg (W.C.)	1	1
1997 Belfast (W.C.)	1	3
1999 Belfast (E.C.)	0	3
1999 Dortmund (E.C.)	0	4
2005 Belfast	1	4

v. GREECE

	NI	G
1961 Athens (W.C.)	1	2
1961 Belfast (W.C.)	2	0
1988 Athens	2	3
2003 Belfast (E.C.)	0	2
2003 Athens (E.C.)	0	1

v. HOLLAND

	NI	H
1962 Rotterdam	0	4
1965 Belfast (W.C.)	2	1
1965 Rotterdam (W.C.)	0	0
1976 Rotterdam (W.C.)	2	2
1977 Belfast (W.C.)	0	1

v. HONDURAS

	NI	H
1982 Zaragoza (W.C.)	1	1

v. HUNGARY

		NI	H
1988	Budapest (W.C.)	0	1
1989	Belfast (W.C.)	1	2
2000	Belfast	0	1

v. ICELAND

		NI	I
1977	Reykjavik (W.C.)	0	1
1977	Belfast (W.C.)	2	0
2000	Reykjavik (W.C.)	0	1
2001	Belfast (W.C.)	3	0

v. REPUBLIC OF IRELAND

		NI	RI
1978	Dublin (E.C.)	0	0
1979	Belfast (E.C.)	1	0
1988	Belfast (W.C.)	0	0
1989	Dublin (W.C.)	0	3
1993	Dublin (W.C.)	0	3
1993	Belfast (W.C.)	1	1
1994	Belfast (E.C.)	0	4
1995	Dublin (E.C.)	1	1
1999	Dublin	1	0

v. ISRAEL

		NI	I
1968	Jaffa	3	2
1976	Tel Aviv	1	1
1980	Tel Aviv (W.C.)	0	0
1981	Belfast (W.C.)	1	0
1984	Belfast	3	0
1987	Tel Aviv	1	1

v. ITALY

		NI	I
1957	Rome (W.C.)	0	1
1957	Belfast	2	2
1958	Belfast (W.C.)	2	1
1961	Bologna	2	3
1997	Palermo	0	2
2003	Campobasso	0	2

v. LATVIA

		NI	L
1993	Riga (W.C.)	2	1
1993	Belfast (W.C.)	2	0
1995	Riga (E.C.)	1	0
1995	Belfast (E.C.)	1	2

v. LIECHTENSTEIN

		NI	L
1994	Belfast (E.C.)	4	1
1995	Eschen (E.C.)	4	0
2002	Vaduz	0	0

v. LITHUANIA

		NI	L
1992	Belfast (W.C.)	2	2
1993	Vilnius (W.C.)	1	0

v. LUXEMBOURG

		NI	L
2000	Luxembourg	3	1

v. MALTA

		NI	M
1988	Belfast (W.C.)	3	0
1989	Valletta (W.C.)	2	0
2000	Ta'Qali	3	0
2000	Valletta (W.C.)	1	0
2001	Valletta (W.C.)	1	0
2005	Valletta	1	1

v. MEXICO

		NI	M
1966	Belfast	4	1
1994	Miami	0	3

v. MOLDOVA

		NI	M
1998	Belfast (E.C.)	2	2
1999	Kishinev (E.C.)	0	0

v. MOROCCO

		NI	M
1986	Belfast	2	1

v. NORWAY

		NI	N
1974	Oslo (E.C.)	1	2
1975	Belfast (E.C.)	3	0
1990	Belfast	2	3
1996	Belfast	0	2
2001	Belfast	0	4
2004	Belfast	1	4

v. POLAND

		NI	P
1962	Katowice (E.C.)	2	0
1962	Belfast (E.C.)	2	0
1988	Belfast	1	1
1991	Belfast	3	1
2002	Limassol (Cyprus)	1	4
2004	Belfast (W.C.)	0	3
2005	Warsaw (W.C.)	0	1

v. PORTUGAL

		NI	P
1957	Lisbon (W.C.)	1	1
1957	Belfast (W.C.)	3	0
1973	Coventry (W.C.)	1	1
1973	Lisbon (W.C.)	1	1
1980	Lisbon (W.C.)	0	1
1981	Belfast (W.C.)	1	0
1994	Belfast (E.C.)	1	2
1995	Oporto (E.C.)	1	1
1997	Belfast (W.C.)	0	0
1997	Lisbon (W.C.)	0	1
2005	Belfast	1	1

v. ROMANIA

		NI	R
1984	Belfast (W.C.)	3	2
1985	Bucharest (W.C.)	1	0
1994	Belfast	2	0
2006	Chicago	0	2

v. SERBIA + MONTENEGRO

		NI	S
2004	Belfast	1	1

v. SLOVAKIA

		NI	S
1998	Belfast	1	0

v. SOVIET UNION

		NI	SU
1969	Belfast (W.C.)	0	0
1969	Moscow (W.C.)	0	2
1971	Moscow (E.C.)	0	1
1971	Belfast (E.C.)	1	1

v. SPAIN

		NI	S
1958	Madrid	2	6
1963	Bilbao	1	1
1963	Belfast	0	1
1970	Seville (E.C.)	0	3
1972	Hull (E.C.)	1	1
1982	Valencia (W.C.)	1	0
1985	Palma, Majorca	0	0
1986	Guadalajara (W.C.)	1	2
1988	Seville (W.C.)	0	4
1989	Belfast (W.C.)	0	2
1992	Belfast (W.C.)	0	0
1993	Seville (W.C.)	1	3
1998	Santander	1	4
2002	Belfast	0	5
2002	Albacete (E.C.)	0	3
2003	Belfast (E.C.)	0	0

v. ST KITTS + NEVIS

		NI	SK
2004	Basseterre	2	0

v. SWEDEN

		NI	S
1974	Solna (E.C.)	2	0
1975	Belfast (E.C.)	1	2
1980	Belfast (W.C.)	3	0
1981	Stockholm (W.C.)	0	1

		NI	S
1996	Belfast	1	2

v. SWITZERLAND

		NI	S
1964	Belfast (W.C.)	1	0
1964	Lausanne (W.C.)	1	2
1998	Belfast	1	0
2004	Zurich	0	0

v. THAILAND

		NI	T
1997	Bangkok	0	0

v. TRINIDAD + TOBAGO

		NI	T
2004	Port of Spain	3	0

v. TURKEY

		NI	T
1968	Belfast (W.C.)	4	1
1968	Istanbul (W.C.)	3	0
1983	Belfast (E.C.)	2	1
1983	Ankara (E.C.)	0	1
1985	Belfast (W.C.)	2	0
1985	Izmir (W.C.)	0	0
1986	Izmir (E.C.)	0	0
1987	Belfast (E.C.)	1	0
1998	Istanbul (E.C.)	0	3
1999	Belfast (E.C.)	0	3

v. UKRAINE

		NI	U
1996	Belfast (W.C.)	0	1
1997	Kiev (W.C.)	1	2
2002	Belfast (E.C.)	0	0
2003	Donetsk (E.C.)	0	0

v. URUGUAY

		NI	U
1964	Belfast	3	0
1990	Belfast	1	0
2006	New Jersey	0	1

v. YUGOSLAVIA

		NI	Y
1975	Belfast (E.C.)	1	0
1975	Belgrade (E.C.)	0	1
1982	Zaragoza (W.C.)	0	0
1987	Belfast (E.C.)	1	2
1987	Sarajevo (E.C.)	0	3
1990	Belfast (E.C.)	0	2
1991	Belgrade (E.C.)	1	4
2000	Belfast	1	2

REPUBLIC OF IRELAND

v. ALBANIA

		RI	A
1992	Dublin (W.C.)	2	0
1993	Tirana (W.C.)	2	1
2003	Tirana (E.C.)	0	0
2003	Dublin (E.C.)	2	1

v. ALGERIA

		RI	A
1982	Algiers	0	2

v. ANDORRA

		RI	A
2001	Barcelona (W.C.)	3	0

v. [2001]

		RI	A
2001	Dublin (W.C.)	3	1

v. ARGENTINA

		RI	A
1951	Dublin	0	1
1979*	Dublin	0	0
1980	Dublin	0	1
1998	Dublin	0	2

(* Not regarded as full Int.)

v. AUSTRALIA

		RI	A
2003	Dublin	2	1

v. AUSTRIA

		RI	A
1952	Vienna	0	6
1953	Dublin	4	0
1958	Vienna	1	3
1962	Dublin	2	3
1963	Vienna (E.C.)	0	0
1963	Dublin (E.C.)	3	2
1966	Vienna	0	1
1968	Dublin	2	2
1971	Dublin (E.C.)	1	4
1971	Linz (E.C.)	0	6
1995	Dublin (E.C.)	1	3
1995	Vienna (E.C.)	1	3

v. BELGIUM

		RI	B
1928	Liege	4	2
1929	Dublin	4	0
1930	Brussels	3	1
1934	Dublin (W.C.)	4	4
1949	Dublin	0	2
1950	Brussels	1	5
1965	Dublin	0	2
1966	Liege	3	2
1980	Dublin (W.C.)	1	1
1981	Brussels (W.C.)	0	1
1986	Brussels (E.C.)	2	2
1987	Dublin (E.C.)	0	0
1997*	Dublin (W.C.)	1	1
1997*	Brussels (W.C.)	1	2

(* World Cup play-off)

v. BOLIVIA

		RI	B
1994	Dublin	1	0
1996	East Rutherford, N.J.	3	0

v. BRAZIL

		RI	B
1974	Rio de Janeiro	1	2
1982	Uberlandia	0	7
1987	Dublin	1	0
2004	Dublin	0	0

v. BULGARIA

		RI	B
1977	Sofia (W.C.)	1	2
1977	Dublin (W.C.)	0	0
1979	Sofia (E.C.)	0	1
1979	Dublin (E.C.)	3	0
1987	Sofia (E.C.)	1	2
1987	Dublin (E.C.)	2	0
2004	Dublin	1	1

v. CAMEROON

		RI	C
2002	Niigata (W.C.)	1	1

v. CANADA

		RI	C
2003	Dublin	3	0

v. CHILE

		RI	C
1960	Dublin	2	0
1972	Recife	1	2
1974	Santiago	2	1
1982	Santiago	0	1
1991	Dublin	1	1
2006	Dublin	0	1

v. CHINA

		RI	C
1984	Sapporo	1	0
2005	Dublin	1	0

v. CROATIA

		RI	C
1996	Dublin	2	2
1998	Dublin (E.C.)	2	0
1999	Zagreb (E.C.)	0	1
2001	Dublin	2	2
2004	Dublin	1	0

v. CYPRUS

		RI	C
1980	Nicosia (W.C.)	3	2
1980	Dublin (W.C.)	6	0
2001	Nicosia (W.C.)	4	0
2001	Dublin (W.C.)	4	0
2004	Dublin (W.C.)	3	0
2005	Nicosia (W.C.)	1	0

v. CZECHOSLOVAKIA/CZECH REPUBLIC

		RI	C
1938	Prague	2	2
1959	Prague	2	0
1959	Bratislava (E.C.)	0	4
1961	Dublin (W.C.)	1	3
1961	Prague (W.C.)	1	7
1967	Dublin (E.C.)	0	2
1967	Prague (E.C.)	2	1
1969	Dublin (W.C.)	1	2
1969	Prague (W.C.)	0	3
1979	Prague	1	4

		RI	C
1981	Dublin	3	1
1986	Reykjavik	1	0
1994	Dublin	1	3
1996	Prague	0	2
1998	Olomouc	1	2
2000	Dublin	3	2
2004	Dublin	2	1

v. DENMARK

		RI	D
1956	Dublin (W.C.)	2	1
1957	Copenhagen (W.C.)	2	0
1968*	Dublin (W.C.)	1	1
1969	Copenhagen (W.C.)	0	2
1969	Dublin (W.C.)	1	1
1978	Copenhagen (E.C.)	3	3
1979	Dublin (E.C.)	2	0
1984	Copenhagen (W.C.)	0	3
1985	Dublin (W.C.)	1	4
1992	Copenhagen (W.C.)	0	0
1993	Dublin (W.C.)	1	1
2002	Dublin	3	0

(* Abandoned after 51 mins. – fog)

v. ECUADOR

		RI	E
1972	Natal	3	2

v. EGYPT

		RI	E
1990	Palermo (W.C.)	0	0

v. ESTONIA

		RI	E
2000	Dublin (W.C.)	2	0
2001	Tallinn (W.C.)	2	0

v. FAROE ISLANDS

		RI	F
2004	Dublin (W.C.)	2	0
2005	Torshavn (W.C.)	2	0

v. FINLAND

		RI	F
1949	Dublin (W.C.)	3	0
1949	Helsinki (W.C.)	1	1
1990	Dublin	1	1
2000	Dublin	3	0
2002	Helsinki	3	0

v. FRANCE

		RI	F
1937	Paris	2	0
1952	Dublin	1	1
1953	Dublin (W.C.)	3	5
1953	Paris (W.C.)	0	1
1972	Dublin (W.C.)	2	1
1973	Paris (W.C.)	1	1
1976	Paris (W.C.)	0	2
1977	Dublin (W.C.)	1	0

		RI	F
1980	Paris (W.C.)	0	2
1981	Dublin (W.C.)	3	2
1989	Dublin	0	0
2004	Paris (W.C.)	0	0
2005	Dublin (W.C.)	0	1

v. GEORGIA

		RI	G
2002	Tbilisi (E.C.)	2	1
2003	Dublin (E.C.)	2	0

v. GERMANY/WEST GERMANY

		RI	G
1935	Dortmund	1	3
1936	Dublin	5	2
1939	Bremen	1	1
1951	Dublin	3	2
1952	Cologne	0	3
1955	Hamburg	1	2
1956	Dublin	3	0
1960	Dusseldorf	1	0
1966	Dublin	0	4
1970	Berlin	1	2
1979	Dublin	1	3
1981	Bremen	0	3
1989	Dublin	1	1
1994	Hanover	2	0
1995*	Dublin	1	0
2002	Ibaraki (W.C.)	1	1

(*v. W. Germany 'B')

v. GREECE

		RI	G
2000	Dublin	0	1
2002	Athens	0	0

v. HOLLAND

		RI	H
1932	Amsterdam	2	0
1934	Amsterdam	2	5
1935	Dublin	3	5
1955	Dublin	1	0
1956	Rotterdam	4	1
1980	Dublin (W.C.)	2	1
1981	Rotterdam (W.C.)	2	2
1982	Rotterdam (E.C.)	1	2
1983	Dublin (E.C.)	2	3
1988	Gelsenkirchen (E.C.)	0	1
1990	Palermo (W.C.)	1	1
1994	Tilburg	1	0
1994	Orlando (W.C.)	0	2
1995*	Liverpool (E.C.)	0	2
1996	Rotterdam	1	3

(* Qual. Round play-off)

2000	Amsterdam (W.C.)	2	2
2001	Dublin (W.C.)	1	0
2004	Amsterdam	1	0

v. HUNGARY

		RI	H
1934	Dublin	2	4
1936	Budapest	3	3
1936	Dublin	2	3
1939	Cork	2	2
1939	Budapest	2	2
1969	Dublin (W.C.)	1	2
1969	Budapest (W.C.)	0	4
1989	Budapest (W.C.)	0	0
1989	Dublin (W.C.)	2	0
1992	Gyor	2	1

v. ICELAND

		RI	I
1962	Dublin (E.C.)	4	2
1962	Reykjavik (E.C.)	1	1
1982	Dublin (E.C.)	2	0
1983	Reykjavik (E.C.)	3	0
1986	Reykjavik	2	1
1996	Dublin (W.C.)	0	0
1997	Reykjavik (W.C.)	4	2

v. IRAN

		RI	I
1972	Recife	2	1
2001*	Dublin (W.C.)	2	0
2001*	Tehran (W.C.)	0	1
(*Qual. Round play-off)			

v. ISRAEL

		RI	I
1984	Tel Aviv	0	3
1985	Tel Aviv	0	0
1987	Dublin	5	0
2005	Tel Aviv (W.C.)	1	1
2005	Dublin (W.C.)	2	2

v. JAMAICA

		RI	J
2004	Charlton	1	0

v. ITALY

		RI	I
1926	Turin	0	3
1927	Dublin	1	2
1970	Florence (E.C.)	0	3
1971	Dublin (E.C.)	1	2
1985	Dublin	1	2
1990	Rome (W.C.)	0	1
1992	Boston, USA	0	2
1994	New York (W.C.)	1	0
2005	Dublin	1	2

v. LATVIA

		RI	L
1992	Dublin (W.C.)	4	0
1993	Riga (W.C.)	2	0
1994	Riga (E.C.)	3	0
1995	Dublin (E.C.)	2	1

v. LIECHTENSTEIN

		RI	L
1994	Dublin (E.C.)	4	0
1995	Eschen (E.C.)	0	0
1996	Eschen (W.C.)	5	0
1997	Dublin (W.C.)	5	0

v. LITHUANIA

		RI	L
1993	Vilnius (W.C.)	1	0
1993	Dublin (W.C.)	2	0
1997	Dublin (W.C.)	0	0
1997	Zalgiris (W.C.)	2	1

v. LUXEMBOURG

		RI	L
1936	Luxembourg	5	1
1953	Dublin (W.C.)	4	0
1954	Luxembourg (W.C.)	1	0
1987	Luxembourg (E.C.)	2	0
1987	Luxembourg (E.C.)	2	1

v. MACEDONIA

		RI	M
1996	Dublin (W.C.)	3	0
1997	Skopje (W.C.)	2	3
1999	Dublin (E.C.)	1	0
1999	Skopje (E.C.)	1	1

v. MALTA

		RI	M
1983	Valletta (E.C.)	1	0
1983	Dublin (E.C.)	8	0
1989	Dublin (W.C.)	2	0
1989	Valletta (W.C.)	2	0
1990	Valletta	3	0
1998	Dublin (E.C.)	1	0
1999	Valletta (E.C.)	3	2

v. MEXICO

		RI	M
1984	Dublin	0	0
1994	Orlando (W.C.)	1	2
1996	New Jersey	2	2
1998	Dublin	0	0
2000	Chicago	2	2

v. MOROCCO

		RI	M
1990	Dublin	1	0

v. NIGERIA

		RI	N
2002	Dublin	1	2
2004	Charlton	0	3

v. NORWAY

		RI	N
1937	Oslo (W.C.)	2	3
1937	Dublin (W.C.)	3	3
1950	Dublin	2	2
1951	Oslo	3	2

		RI	N
1954	Dublin	2	1
1955	Oslo	3	1
1960	Dublin	3	1
1964	Oslo	4	1
1973	Oslo	1	1
1976	Dublin	3	0
1978	Oslo	0	0
1984	Oslo (W.C.)	0	1
1985	Dublin (W.C.)	0	0
1988	Oslo	0	0
1994	New York (W.C.)	0	0
2003	Dublin	1	0

v. PARAGUAY

		RI	P
1999	Dublin	2	0

v. POLAND

		RI	P
1938	Warsaw	0	6
1938	Dublin	3	2
1958	Katowice	2	2
1958	Dublin	2	2
1964	Cracow	1	3
1964	Dublin	3	2
1968	Dublin	2	2
1968	Katowice	0	1
1970	Dublin	1	2
1970	Poznan	0	2
1973	Wroclaw	0	2
1973	Dublin	1	0
1976	Poznan	2	0
1977	Dublin	0	0
1978	Lodz	0	3
1981	Bydgoszcz	0	3
1984	Dublin	0	0
1986	Warsaw	0	1
1988	Dublin	3	1
1991	Dublin (E.C.)	0	0
1991	Poznan (E.C.)	3	3
2004	Bydgoszcz	0	0

v. PORTUGAL

		RI	P
1946	Lisbon	1	3
1947	Dublin	0	2
1948	Lisbon	0	2
1949	Dublin	1	0
1972	Recife	1	2
1992	Boston, USA	2	0
1995	Dublin (E.C.)	1	0
1995	Lisbon (E.C.)	0	3
1996	Dublin	0	1
2000	Lisbon (W.C.)	1	1
2001	Dublin (W.C.)	1	1
2005	Dublin	1	0

v. ROMANIA

		RI	R
1988	Dublin	2	0
1990*	Genoa	0	0
1997	Bucharest (W.C.)	0	1
1997	Dublin (W.C.)	1	1

(* Rep. won 5-4 on pens.)

v. RUSSIA (See also Soviet Union)

		RI	R
1994	Dublin	0	0
1996	Dublin	0	2
2002	Dublin	2	0
2002	Moscow (E.C.)	2	4
2003	Dublin (E.C.)	1	1

v. SAUDI ARABIA

		RI	SA
2002	Yokohama (W.C.)	3	0

v. SOUTH AFRICA

		RI	SA
2000	New Jersey	2	1

v. SOVIET UNION
(See also Russia)

		RI	SU
1972	Dublin (W.C.)	1	2
1973	Moscow (W.C.)	0	1
1974	Dublin (E.C.)	3	0
1975	Kiev (E.C.)	1	2
1984	Dublin (W.C.)	1	0
1985	Moscow (W.C.)	0	2
1988	Hanover (E.C.)	1	1
1990	Dublin	1	0

v. SPAIN

		RI	S
1931	Barcelona	1	1
1931	Dublin	0	5
1946	Madrid	1	0
1947	Dublin	3	2
1948	Barcelona	1	2
1949	Dublin	1	4
1952	Madrid	0	6
1955	Dublin	2	2
1964	Seville (E.C.)	1	5
1964	Dublin (E.C.)	0	2
1965	Dublin (W.C.)	1	0
1965	Seville (E.C.)	1	4
1965	Paris (W.C.)	0	1
1966	Dublin (E.C.)	0	0
1966	Valencia (E.C.)	0	2
1977	Dublin	0	1
1982	Dublin (E.C.)	3	3
1983	Zaragoza (E.C.)	0	2
1985	Cork	0	0
1988	Seville (W.C.)	0	2
1989	Dublin (W.C.)	1	0
1992	Seville (W.C.)	0	0
1993	Dublin (W.C.)	1	3

	RI	S
2002* Suwon (W.C.)	1	1

(*Rep. lost 3-2 on pens.)

v. SWEDEN

		RI	S
1949	Stockholm (W.C.)	1	3
1949	Dublin (W.C.)	1	3
1959	Dublin	3	2
1960	Malmo	1	4
1970	Dublin (E.C.)	1	1
1970	Malmo (E.C.)	0	1
1999	Dublin	2	0
2006	Dublin	3	0

v. SWITZERLAND

		RI	S
1935	Basle	0	1
1936	Dublin	1	0
1937	Berne	1	0
1938	Dublin	4	0
1948	Dublin	0	1
1975	Dublin (E.C.)	2	1
1975	Berne (E.C.)	0	1
1980	Dublin	2	0
1985	Dublin (W.C.)	3	0
1985	Berne (W.C.)	0	0
1992	Dublin	2	1
2002	Dublin (E.C.)	1	2
2003	Basle (E.C.)	0	2
2004	Basle (W.C.)	1	1
2005	Dublin (W.C.)	0	0

v. TRINIDAD & TOBAGO

		RI	T&T
1982	Port of Spain	1	2

v. TUNISIA

		RI	T
1988	Dublin	4	0

v. TURKEY

		RI	T
1966	Dublin (E.C.)	2	1
1967	Ankara (E.C.)	1	2
1974	Izmir (E.C.)	1	1
1975	Dublin (E.C.)	4	0
1976	Ankara	3	3
1978	Dublin	4	2
1990	Izmir	0	0
1990	Dublin (E.C.)	5	0
1991	Istanbul (E.C.)	3	1
1999	Dublin (E.C.)	1	1
1999	Bursa (E.C.)	0	0
2003	Dublin	2	2

v. URUGUAY

		RI	U
1974	Montevideo	0	2
1986	Dublin	1	1

v. U.S.A.

		RI	USA
1979	Dublin	3	2
1991	Boston	1	1
1992	Boston	4	1
1992	Washington	1	3
1996	Boston	1	2
2000	Foxboro	1	1
2002	Dublin	2	1

v. YUGOSLAVIA

		RI	Y
1955	Dublin	1	4
1988	Dublin	2	0
1998	Belgrade (E.C.)	0	1
1999	Dublin (E.C.)	2	1

BRITISH & IRISH INTERNATIONAL APPEARANCES SINCE THE WAR (1946-2006)

(As at start of season 2006-07. In year shown, 2006 = season 2005-06 etc.
*Also a pre-war International player. Totals include appearances as substitute).

ENGLAND

A'Court, A. (Liverpool, 1958-9) 5
Adams, T. (Arsenal, 1987-2001) 66
Allen, A. (Stoke City, 1960) 3
Allen, C. (Q.P.R., Tottenham, 1984-8) 5
Allen, R. (W.B.A., 1952-5) 5
Anderson, S. (Sunderland, 1962) 2
Anderson, V. (Nott'm. Forest, Arsenal, Manchester Utd., 1979-88) 30
Anderton, D. (Tottenham, 1994-2002) 30
Angus, J. (Burnley, 1961) 1
Armfield, J. (Blackpool, 1959-66) 43
Armstrong, D. (Middlesbrough, Southampton, 1980-4) 3
Armstrong, K. (Chelsea, 1955) 1
Astall, G. (Birmingham City, 1956) 2
Astle, J. (W.B.A., 1969-70) 5

Thompson, T. (Aston Villa, Preston N.E., 1952-7) 2
Thomson, R. (Wolves, 1964-5) 8
Todd, C. (Derby Co., 1972-7) 27
Towers, A. (Sunderland, 1978) 3
Tueart, D. (Manchester City, 1975-7) .. 6

Ufton, D. (Charlton Athletic, 1954) 1
Unsworth, D. (Everton, 1995) 1
Upson, M. (Birmingham City, 2003-5) 7

Vassell, D. (Aston Villa, 2002-4) 22
Venables, T. (Chelsea, 1965) 2
Venison, B. (Newcastle Utd., 1995) ... 2
Viljoen, C. (Ipswich Town, 1975) 2
Viollet, D. (Manchester Utd., 1960) ... 2

Waddle, C. (Newcastle Utd., Tottenham, Marseille, 1985-92) 62
Waiters, A. (Blackpool, 1964-5) 5
Walcott, T. (Arsenal, 2006) 1
Walker, D. (Nott'm. Forest, Sampdoria, Sheffield Wed., 1989-94) 59
Walker, I. (Tottenham, Leicester City, 1996-2004) 4
Wallace, D. (Southampton, 1986) 1
Walsh, P. (Luton Town, 1983-4) 5
Walters, M. (Rangers, 1991) 1
Ward, P. (Brighton & H.A., 1980) 1
Ward, T. (Derby Co., 1948) 2
Watson, D. (Sunderland, Manchester City, Werder Bremen, Southampton, Stoke City, 1974-82) 65
Watson, D. (Norwich City, Everton, 1984-8) 12
Watson, W. (Sunderland, 1950-1) 4
Webb, N. (Nott'm. Forest, Manchester Utd., 1988-92) 26
Weller, K. (Leicester City, 1974) 4
West, G. (Everton, 1969) 3

NORTHERN IRELAND

Aherne, T. (Belfast Celtic, Luton Town, 1947-50) 4
Anderson, T. (Manchester Utd., Swindon Town, Peterborough Utd., 1973-9) 22
Armstrong, G. (Tottenham, Watford, Real Mallorca, W.B.A., 1977-86) 63

Baird, C. (Southampton, 2003-6) 20
Barr, H. (Linfield, Coventry City, 1962-3) 3
Best, G. (Manchester Utd., Fulham, 1964-77) 37
Bingham, W. (Sunderland, Luton Town, Everton, Port Vale, 1951-64) 56
Black, K. (Luton Town, Nott'm. Forest, 1988-94) 30

Wheeler, J. (Bolton Wand., 1955) 1
White, D. (Manchester City, 1993) 1
Whitworth, S. (Leicester City, 1975-6) 7
Whymark, T. (Ipswich Town, 1978) 1
Wignall, F. (Nott'm. Forest, 1965) 2
Wilcox, J. (Blackburn Rov., Leeds Utd., 1996-2000) 3
Wilkins, R. (Chelsea, Manchester Utd., AC Milan, 1976-87) 84
Williams, B. (Wolves, 1949-56) 24
Williams, S. (Southampton, 1983-5) .. 6
Willis, A. (Tottenham, 1952) 1
Wilshaw, D. (Wolves, 1954-7) 12
Wilson, R. (Huddersfield Town, Everton, 1960-8) 63
Winterburn, N. (Arsenal, 1990-3) 2
Wise, D. (Chelsea, 1991-2001) 21
Withe, P. (Aston Villa, 1981-5) 11
Wood, R. (Manchester Utd., 1955-6) .. 3
Woodcock, A. (Nott'm. Forest, Cologne, Arsenal, 1977-86) 42
Woodgate, J. (Leeds Utd., Newcastle Utd., 1999-2004) 5
Woods, C. (Norwich City, Rangers, Sheffield Wed., 1984-93) 43
Worthington, F. (Leicester City, 1974-5) 8
Wright, I. (Crystal Palace, Arsenal, West Ham Utd., 1991-9) 33
Wright, M. (Southampton, Derby Co., Liverpool, 1984-96) 45
Wright, R. (Ipswich Town, Arsenal, 2000-02) 2
Wright, T. (Everton, 1968-70) 11
Wright, W. (Wolves, 1947-59) 105
Wright-Phillips, S. (Manchester City, Chelsea, 2005-6) 8

Young, G. (Sheffield Wed., 1965) 1
Young, L. (Charlton Athletic, 2005) 7

Blair, R. (Oldham Athletic, 1975-6) ... 5
Blanchflower, R.D. (Barnsley, Aston Villa, Tottenham, 1950-63) 56
Blanchflower, J. (Manchester Utd., 1954-8) 12
Blayney, A. (Doncaster Rov., 2006) 1
Bowler, G. (Hull City, 1950) 3
Braithwaite, R. (Linfield, Middlesbrough, 1962-5) 10
Brennan, R. (Luton Town, Birmingham City, Fulham, 1949-51) 5
Briggs, W. (Manchester Utd., Swansea City, 1962-5) 2
Brotherston, N. (Blackburn Rov., 1980-5) 27
Bruce, W. (Glentoran, 1961-7) 2
Brunt, C. (Sheffield Wed., 2005-6) 7

SCOTLAND

290

297

Phelan, T. (Wimbledon, Manchester City, Chelsea, Everton, Fulham, 1992-2000) 42

Quinn, A. (Sheffield Wed., Sheffield Utd., 2003-5) 6
Quinn, B. (Coventry City, 2000) 4
Quinn, N. (Arsenal, Manchester City, Sunderland, 1986-2002) 91

Reid, A. (Nott'm. Forest, Tottenham, 2004-6) 20
Reid, S. (Millwall, Blackburn Rov., 2002-6) 18
Richardson, D. (Shamrock R., Gillingham, 1972-80) 3
Ringstead, A. (Sheffield Utd., 1951-9) 20
Robinson, M. (Brighton & H.A., Liverpool, Q.P.R., 1981-6) 24
Roche, P. (Shelbourne, Manchester Utd., 1972-6) 8
Rogers, E. (Blackburn Rov., Charlton Athletic, 1968-73) 19
Rowlands, M. (Q.P.R, 2004) 3
Ryan, G. (Derby Co., Brighton & H.A., 1978-85) 18
Ryan, R. (W.B.A., Derby Co., 1950-56) 16

Sadlier, R. (Millwall, 2002) 1
Savage, D. (Millwall, 1996) 5
Saward, P. (Millwall, Aston Villa, Huddersfield Town, 1954-63) 18
Scannell, T. (Southend Utd., 1954) 1
Scully, P. (Arsenal, 1989) 1
Sheedy, K. (Everton, Newcastle Utd., 1984-93) 46
Sheridan, J. (Leeds Utd., Sheffield Wed., 1988-96) 34
Slaven, B. (Middlesbrough, 1990-3) ... 7
Sloan, P. (Arsenal, 1946) 2
Smyth, M. (Shamrock R., 1969) 1

Stapleton, F. (Arsenal, Manchester Utd., Ajax, Derby Co., Le Havre, Blackburn Rov., 1977-90) 71
Staunton, S. (Liverpool, Aston Villa, Liverpool, Crystal Palace, Aston Villa, 1989-2002) 102
*Stevenson, A. (Everton, 1947-9) 6
Strahan, F. (Shelbourne, 1964-5) 5
Swan, M. (Drumcondra, 1960) 1
Synnott, N. (Shamrock R., 1978-9) ... 3

Thomas, P. (Waterford, 1974) 2
Thompson, J. (Nott'm. Forest, 2004) .. 1
Townsend, A. (Norwich City, Chelsea, Aston Villa, Middlesbrough, 1989-97) 70
Traynor, T. (Southampton, 1954-64) ... 8
Treacy, R. (W.B.A., Charlton Athletic, Swindon Town, Preston N.E., Shamrock R., 1966-80) 42
Tuohy, L. (Shamrock R., Newcastle Utd., Shamrock R., 1956-65) 8
Turner, A. (Celtic, 1963) 2

Vernon, J. (Belfast Celtic, 1946) 2

Waddock, G. (Q.P.R., Millwall, 1980-90) 21
Walsh, D. (W.B.A., Aston Villa, 1946-54) 20
Walsh, J. (Limerick, 1982) 1
Walsh, M. (Blackpool, Everton, Q.P.R., Porto, 1976-85) 21
Walsh, M. (Everton, Norwich City, 1982-3) 4
Walsh, W. (Manchester City, 1947-50) 9
Waters, J. (Grimsby Town, 1977-80) ... 2
Whelan, R. (St Patrick's Ath., 1964) .. 2
Whelan, R. (Liverpool, Southend Utd., 1981-95) 53
Whelan, L. (Manchester Utd., 1956-7) 4
Whittaker, R. (Chelsea, 1959) 1

INTERNATIONAL GOALSCORERS 1946-2006

(As at start of season 2006-07)

ENGLAND

Charlton, R 49	Channon 21	Smith, R 13
Lineker 48	Keegan 21	Francis, T 12
Greaves 44	Peters 20	Barnes, J 11
Owen 36	Haynes 18	Douglas 11
Finney 30	Hunt, R 18	Lampard, Frank Jnr. .. 11
Lofthouse 30	Beckham 17	Mannion 11
Shearer 30	Lawton 16	Rooney 11
Platt 27	Taylor, T 16	Sheringham 11
Robson, B 26	Woodcock 16	Clarke, A 10
Hurst 24	Scholes 14	Flowers, R 10
Mortensen 23	Chivers 13	Gascoigne 10
	Mariner 13	Lee, F 10

Milburn 10
Wilshaw 10
Beardsley 9
Bell 9
Bentley 9
Gerrard 9
Hateley 9
Wright, I 9
Ball 8
Broadis 8
Byrne, J 8
Hoddle 8
Kevan 8
Anderton 7
Connelly 7
Coppell 7
Fowler 7
Paine 7
Charlton, J 6
Cole, J 6
Crouch 6
Johnson 6
Macdonald 6
Mullen 6
Rowley 6
Vassell 6
Waddle 6
Adams 5
Atyeo 5
Baily 5
Brooking 5
Carter 5
Edwards 5
Ferdinand, L 5
Heskey 5
Hitchens 5
Latchford 5
Neal 5
Pearce 5
Pearson, Stan 5
Pearson, Stuart 5
Pickering, F 5
Barmby 4
Barnes, P 4
Bull 4
Dixon, K 4
Hassall 4
Revie 4
Robson, R 4
Steven 4
Watson, Dave
  (Sunderland) 4
Webb 4
Baker 3
Blissett 3
Butcher 3
Currie 3
Elliott 3
Francis, G 3

Grainger 3
Kennedy, R 3
McDermott 3
McManaman 3
Matthews, S 3
Merson 3
Morris 3
O'Grady 3
Peacock 3
Ramsey 3
Sewell 3
Wilkins 3
Wright, W 3
Allen, R 2
Anderson 2
Bradley 2
Broadbent 2
Brooks 2
Cowans 2
Eastham 2
Froggatt, J 2
Froggatt, R 2
Haines 2
Hancocks 2
Hunter 2
Ince 2
Keown 2
Lee, R 2
Lee, S 2
Moore 2
Perry 2
Pointer 2
Richardson 2
Royle 2
Southgate 2
Stone 2
Taylor, P 2
Tueart 2
Wignall 2
Worthington 2
A'Court 1
Astall 1
Beattie, K 1
Bowles 1
Bradford 1
Bridge 1
Bridges 1
Campbell 1
Chamberlain 1
Cole, Andy 1
Crawford 1
Defoe 1
Dixon, L 1
Ehiogu 1
Ferdinand, R 1
Goddard 1
Hirst 1
Hughes, E 1
Jeffers 1

Kay 1
Kidd 1
King 1
Langton 1
Lawler 1
Lee, J 1
Le Saux 1
Mabbutt 1
Marsh 1
Medley 1
Melia 1
Mullery 1
Murphy 1
Nicholls 1
Nicholson 1
Palmer 1
Parry 1
Redknapp 1
Sansom 1
Shackleton 1
Smith, A (1989-92) 1
Smith, A (2001-5) 1
Stiles 1
Summerbee 1
Tambling 1
Terry 1
Thompson, Phil 1
Viollet 1
Wallace 1
Walsh 1
Weller 1
Wise 1
Withe 1
Wright, M 1
Wright-Phillips, S 1

N. IRELAND

Healy 19
Clarke 13
Armstrong 12
Quinn, J.M. 12
Dowie 11
Bingham 10
Crossan, J 10
McIlroy, J 10
McParland 10
Best 9
Whiteside 9
Dougan 8
Irvine, W 8
O'Neill, M (1972-85) .. 8
McAdams 7
Taggart, G 7
Wilson, S 7
Gray 6
McLaughlin 6
Nicholson, J 6
Wilson, K 6

Cush 5
Hamilton, W 5
Hughes, M 5
Magilton 5
McIlroy, S 5
Simpson 5
Smyth, S 5
Walsh, D 5
Anderson, T 4
Elliott 4
Hamilton, B 4
McGrath 4
McMorran 4
O'Neill, M. (1989-96) . 4
Quinn, S.J. 4
Brotherston 3
Harvey, M 3
Lockhart 3
Lomas 3
McDonald 3
McMordie 3
Morgan, S 3
Mulryne 3
Nicholl, C 3
Spence, D 3
Tully 3
Blanchflower, D 2
Casey 2
Clements 2
Doherty, P 2
Feeney (2002–6) 2
Finney 2
Gillespie 2
Harkin 2
Lennon 2
McMahon 2
Neill, W 2
O'Neill, J 2
Peacock 2
Penney 2
Stewart, I 2
Whitley 2
Barr 1
Black 1
Blanchflower, J 1
Brennan 1
Campbell, W 1
Caskey 1
Cassidy 1
Cochrane, T 1
Crossan, E 1
D'Arcy 1
Davis 1
Doherty, L 1
Elder 1
Ferguson 1
Ferris 1
Griffin 1
Hill, C 1

Humphries 1
Hunter, A 1
Hunter, B 1
Johnston 1
Jones, J 1
Jones,S 1
McCartney 1
McClelland (1961) 1
McCrory 1
McCurdy 1
McGarry 1
McVeigh 1
Moreland 1
Morrow 1
Murdock 1
Nelson 1
Nicholl, J 1
O'Boyle 1
O'Kane 1
Patterson, D 1
Rowland 1
Sproule 1
Stevenson 1
Walker 1
Welsh 1
Williams 1
Wilson, D 1

SCOTLAND

Dalglish 30
Law 30
Reilly 22
McCoist 19
Johnston, M 14
Collins, J 12
Gilzean 12
Steel 12
Jordan 11
Collins, R 10
Johnstone, R 10
Stein 10
Gallacher 9
McFadden 9
McStay 9
Mudie 9
St John 9
Brand 8
Gemmill, A 8
Leggat 8
Robertson, J (1978-84) . 8
Wilson, D 8
Dodds 7
Durie 7
Gray, A 7
Miller, K 7
Wark 7
Booth 6
Brown, A 6

Cooper 6
Gough 6
Liddell 6
Murdoch 6
Rioch 6
Waddell 6
Dailly 5
Henderson, W 5
Hutchison 5
Macari 5
Masson 5
McAllister G. 5
McQueen 5
Nevin 5
Nicholas 5
O'Hare 5
Scott, A 5
Strachan 5
Young, A 5
Archibald 4
Caldow 4
Crawford 4
Hamilton 4
Hartford 4
Herd, D. 4
Jackson, D 4
Johnstone, J 4
Lorimer 4
Mackay, D 4
Mason 4
McGinlay 4
McKinlay, W. 4
McLaren 4
Smith, G 4
Souness 4
Baxter 3
Bremner, W 3
Burley, C 3
Chalmers 3
Fletcher 3
Gibson 3
Graham, G 3
Gray, E 3
Greig 3
Hendry 3
Lennox 3
MacDougall 3
McCann 3
McInally, A 3
McNeill 3
McPhail 3
Morris 3
Robertson, J (1991-5) .. 3
Sturrock 3
Thompson, ... 3
White 3
Baird, S 2
Bauld 2
Boyd, K 2

O'Sullivan 1	Moran 6	Kelly, G 2
Parry 1	Cummins 5	Leech 2
Paul 1	Fagan, F 5	McCarthy 2
Powell, A 1	Giles 5	McLoughlin 2
Powell, D 1	Holland 5	O'Connor 2
Price, P 1	Kilbane 5	O'Farrell 2
Roberts, P 1	Lawrenson 5	O'Reilly, J 2
Robinson, C 1	Rogers 5	Reid, S 2
Smallman 1	Sheridan 5	Ambrose 1
Taylor 1	Treacy 5	Anderson 1
Williams, A 1	Walsh, D 5	Carroll 1
Williams, G.E 1	Byrne, J 4	Dempsey 1
Williams, G.G 1	Doherty 4	Duffy 1
Young 1	Dunne, R 4	Elliott 1
	Irwin 4	Finnan 1
REP. OF IRELAND	McGee 4	Fitzgerald, J 1
Keane, Robbie 26	Martin, M 4	Fullam, J 1
Quinn, N 21	O'Neill, K 4	Galvin 1
Stapleton 20	Robinson 4	Glynn 1
Aldridge 19	Tuohy 4	Grimes 1
Cascarino 19	Carey, J 3	Healy 1
Givens 19	Coad 3	Holmes 1
Cantwell 14	Conway 3	Hughton 1
Daly 13	Farrell 3	Kavanagh 1
Harte 11	Fogarty 3	Kernaghan 1
Brady 9	Haverty 3	Mancini 1
Connolly 9	Kennedy, Mark 3	McCann 1
Keane, Roy 9	Kinsella 3	McPhail 1
Kelly, D 9	McAteer 3	Miller 1
Morrison 9	Reid, A 3	Mooney 1
Sheedy 9	Ryan, R 3	Moroney 1
Curtis 8	Waddock 3	Mulligan 1
Grealish 8	Walsh, M 3	O'Brien 1
McGrath, P 8	Whelan 3	O'Callaghan, K 1
Staunton 8	Barrett 2	O'Keefe 1
Duff 7	Conroy 2	O'Leary 1
Fitzsimons 7	Dennehy 2	O'Neill, F 1
Ringstead 7	Eglington 2	O' Shea 1
Townsend 7	Fallon 2	Ryan, G 1
Breen G 6	Fitzgerald, P 2	Slaven 1
Coyne 6	Foley 2	Sloan 1
Houghton 6	Gavin 2	Strahan 1
McEvoy 6	Hale 2	Waters 1
Martin, C 6	Hand 2	
	Hurley 2	

LAMPARD AT THE DOUBLE

Frank Lampard was runner-up to Barcelona and Brazil star Ronaldinho in polls for the 2005 World and European Player of the Year awards. World: 1 Ronaldinho, 2 Lampard, 3 Samuel Eto'o, 4 Thierry Henry, 5 Adriano, 6 Andriy Shevchenko, 7 Steven Gerrard, 8 Kaka, 9 Paolo Maldini, 10 Didier Drogba. European: 1 Ronaldinho, 2 Lampard, 3 Gerrard, 4 Henry, 5 Shevchenko, 6 Maldini, 7 Adriano, 8 Zlatan Ibrahimovic, 9 Kaka, 10 equal Eto'o and John Terry.

HOME INTERNATIONAL RESULTS

Note: In the results that follow, W.C. = World Cup, E.C. = European Championship. TF = Tournoi de France. For Northern Ireland read Ireland before 1921.

ENGLAND V. SCOTLAND
Played 110; England 45; Scotland 41; drawn 24. Goals: England 192, Scotland 169.

Year	Venue	E	S	Year	Venue	E	S
1872	Glasgow	0	0	1932	Wembley	3	0
1873	The Oval	4	2	1933	Glasgow	1	2
1874	Glasgow	1	2	1934	Wembley	3	0
1875	The Oval	2	2	1935	Glasgow	0	2
1876	Glasgow	0	3	1936	Wembley	1	1
1877	The Oval	1	3	1937	Glasgow	1	3
1878	Glasgow	2	7	1938	Wembley	0	1
1879	The Oval	5	4	1939	Glasgow	2	1
1880	Glasgow	4	5	1947	Wembley	1	1
1881	The Oval	1	6	1948	Glasgow	2	0
1882	Glasgow	1	5	1949	Wembley	1	3
1883	Sheffield	2	3	1950	Glasgow (W.C.)	1	0
1884	Glasgow	0	1	1951	Wembley	2	3
1885	The Oval	1	1	1952	Glasgow	2	1
1886	Glasgow	1	1	1953	Wembley	2	2
1887	Blackburn	2	3	1954	Glasgow (W.C.)	4	2
1888	Glasgow	5	0	1955	Wembley	7	2
1889	The Oval	2	3	1956	Glasgow	1	1
1890	Glasgow	1	1	1957	Wembley	2	1
1891	Blackburn	2	1	1958	Glasgow	4	0
1892	Glasgow	4	1	1959	Wembley	1	0
1893	Richmond	5	2	1960	Glasgow	1	1
1894	Glasgow	2	2	1961	Wembley	9	3
1895	Goodison Park	3	0	1962	Glasgow	0	2
1896	Glasgow	1	2	1963	Wembley	1	2
1897	Crystal Palace	1	2	1964	Glasgow	0	1
1898	Glasgow	3	1	1965	Wembley	2	2
1899	Birmingham	2	1	1966	Glasgow	4	3
1900	Glasgow	1	4	1967	Wembley (E.C.)	2	3
1901	Crystal Palace	2	2	1968	Glasgow (E.C.)	1	1
1902	Birmingham	2	2	1969	Wembley	4	1
1903	Sheffield	1	2	1970	Glasgow	0	0
1904	Glasgow	1	0	1971	Wembley	3	1
1905	Crystal Palace	1	0	1972	Glasgow	1	0
1906	Glasgow	1	2	1973	Wembley	5	0
1907	Newcastle	1	1	1973	Wembley	1	0
1908	Glasgow	1	1	1974	Glasgow	0	2
1909	Crystal Palace	2	0	1975	Wembley	5	1
1910	Glasgow	0	2	1976	Glasgow	1	2
1911	Goodison Park	1	1	1977	Wembley	1	2
1912	Glasgow	1	1	1978	Glasgow	1	0
1913	Stamford Bridge	1	0	1979	Wembley	3	1
1914	Glasgow	1	3	1980	Glasgow	2	0
1920	Sheffield	5	4	1981	Wembley	0	1
1921	Glasgow	0	3	1982	Glasgow	1	0
1922	Birmingham	0	1	1983	Wembley	2	0
1923	Glasgow	2	2	1984	Glasgow	1	1
1924	Wembley	1	1	1985	Glasgow	0	1
1925	Glasgow	0	2	1986	Wembley	2	1
1926	Manchester	0	1	1987	Glasgow	0	0
1927	Wembley	2	1	1988	Wembley	1	0
1928	Wembley	1	5	1989	Glasgow	2	0
1929	Glasgow	0	1	1996	Wembley (E.C.)	2	0
1930	Wembley	5	2	1999	Glasgow (E.C.)	2	0
1931	Glasgow	0	2	1999	Wembley (E.C.)	0	1

ENGLAND V. WALES

Played 99; England won 64; Wales 14; drawn 21. Goals: England 242, Wales 90.

Year	Venue	E	W	Year	Venue	E	W
1879	The Oval	2	1	1933	Newcastle	1	2
1880	Wrexham	3	2	1934	Cardiff	4	0
1881	Blackburn	0	1	1935	Wolverhampton	1	2
1882	Wrexham	3	5	1936	Cardiff	1	2
1883	The Oval	5	0	1937	Middlesbrough	2	1
1884	Wrexham	4	0	1938	Cardiff	2	4
1885	Blackburn	1	1	1946	Maine Road	3	0
1886	Wrexham	3	1	1947	Cardiff	3	0
1887	The Oval	4	0	1948	Villa Park	1	0
1888	Crewe	5	1	1949	Cardiff (W.C.)	4	1
1889	Stoke	4	1	1950	Sunderland	4	2
1890	Wrexham	3	1	1951	Cardiff	1	1
1891	Sunderland	4	1	1952	Wembley	5	2
1892	Wrexham	2	0	1953	Cardiff (W.C.)	4	1
1893	Stoke	6	0	1954	Wembley	3	2
1894	Wrexham	5	1	1955	Cardiff	1	2
1895	Queens Club, London	1	1	1956	Wembley	3	1
1896	Cardiff	9	1	1957	Cardiff	4	0
1897	Bramall Lane	4	0	1958	Villa Park	2	2
1898	Wrexham	3	0	1959	Cardiff	1	1
1899	Bristol	4	0	1960	Wembley	5	1
1900	Cardiff	1	1	1961	Cardiff	1	1
1901	Newcastle	6	0	1962	Wembley	4	0
1902	Wrexham	0	0	1963	Cardiff	4	0
1903	Portsmouth	2	1	1964	Wembley	2	1
1904	Wrexham	2	2	1965	Cardiff	0	0
1905	Anfield	3	1	1966	Wembley (E.C.)	5	1
1906	Cardiff	1	0	1967	Cardiff (E.C.)	3	0
1907	Fulham	1	1	1969	Wembley	2	1
1908	Wrexham	7	1	1970	Cardiff	1	1
1909	Nottingham	2	0	1971	Wembley	0	0
1910	Cardiff	1	0	1972	Cardiff	3	0
1911	Millwall	3	0	1972	Cardiff (W.C.)	1	0
1912	Wrexham	2	0	1973	Wembley (W.C.)	1	1
1913	Bristol	4	3	1973	Wembley	3	0
1914	Cardiff	2	0	1974	Cardiff	2	0
1920	Highbury	1	2	1975	Wembley	2	2
1921	Cardiff	0	0	1976	Wrexham	2	1
1922	Anfield	1	0	1976	Cardiff	1	0
1923	Cardiff	2	2	1977	Wembley	0	1
1924	Blackburn	1	2	1978	Cardiff	3	1
1925	Swansea	2	1	1979	Wembley	0	0
1926	Selhurst Park	1	3	1980	Wrexham	1	4
1927	Wrexham	3	3	1981	Wembley	0	0
1927	Burnley	1	2	1982	Cardiff	1	0
1928	Swansea	3	2	1983	Wembley	2	1
1929	Stamford Bridge	6	0	1984	Wrexham	0	1
1930	Wrexham	4	0	2004	Old Trafford (W.C.)	2	0
1931	Anfield	3	1	2005	Cardiff (W.C.)	1	0
1932	Wrexham	0	0				

ENGLAND V. N. IRELAND

Played 98; England won 75; Ireland 7; drawn 16. Goals: England 323, Ireland 81.

Year	Venue	E	I	Year	Venue	E	I
1882	Belfast	13	0	1936	Stoke	3	1
1883	Aigburth, Liverpool	7	0	1937	Belfast	5	1
1884	Belfast	8	1	1938	Old Trafford	7	0
1885	Whelley Range, Manchester	4	0	1946	Belfast	7	2
1886	Belfast	6	1	1947	Goodison Park	2	2
1887	Bramall Lane	7	0	1948	Belfast	6	2
1888	Belfast	5	1	1949	Maine Road (W.C.)	9	2
1889	Goodison Park	6	1	1950	Belfast	4	1
1890	Belfast	9	1	1951	Villa Park	2	0
1891	Wolverhampton	6	1	1952	Belfast	2	2
1892	Belfast	2	0	1953	Goodison Park (W.C.)	3	1
1893	Perry Barr, Birmingham	6	1	1954	Belfast	2	0
1894	Belfast	2	2	1955	Wembley	3	0
1895	Derby	9	0	1956	Belfast	1	1
1896	Belfast	2	0	1957	Wembley	2	3
1897	Nottingham	6	0	1958	Belfast	3	3
1898	Belfast	3	2	1959	Wembley	2	1
1899	Sunderland	13	2	1960	Belfast	5	2
1900	Dublin	2	0	1961	Wembley	1	1
1901	Southampton	3	0	1962	Belfast	3	1
1902	Belfast	1	0	1963	Wembley	8	3
1903	Wolverhampton	4	0	1964	Belfast	4	3
1904	Belfast	3	1	1965	Wembley	2	1
1905	Middlesbrough	1	1	1966	Belfast (E.C.)	2	0
1906	Belfast	5	0	1967	Wembley (E.C.)	2	0
1907	Goodison Park	1	0	1969	Belfast	3	1
1908	Belfast	3	1	1970	Wembley	3	1
1909	Bradford P.A.	4	0	1971	Belfast	1	0
1910	Belfast	1	1	1972	Wembley	0	1
1911	Derby	2	1	1973	*Goodison Park	2	1
1912	Dublin	6	1	1974	Wembley	1	0
1913	Belfast	1	2	1975	Belfast	0	0
1914	Middlesbrough	0	3	1976	Wembley	4	0
1919	Belfast	1	1	1977	Belfast	2	1
1920	Sunderland	2	0	1978	Wembley	1	0
1921	Belfast	1	1	1979	Wembley (E.C.)	4	0
1922	West Bromwich	2	0	1979	Belfast	2	0
1923	Belfast	1	2	1979	Belfast (E.C.)	5	1
1924	Goodison Park	3	1	1980	Wembley	1	1
1925	Belfast	0	0	1982	Wembley	4	0
1926	Anfield	3	3	1983	Belfast	0	0
1927	Belfast	0	2	1984	Wembley	1	0
1928	Goodison Park	2	1	1985	Belfast (W.C.)	1	0
1929	Belfast	3	0	1985	Wembley (W.C.)	0	0
1930	Bramall Lane	5	1	1986	Wembley (E.C.)	3	0
1931	Belfast	6	2	1987	Belfast (E.C.)	2	0
1932	Blackpool	1	0	2005	Old Trafford (W.C.)	4	0
1933	Belfast	3	0	2005	Belfast (W.C.)	0	1
1935	Goodison Park	2	1				
1935	Belfast	3	1				

(* Switched from Belfast because of political situation in N. Ireland)

SCOTLAND V. WALES

Played 103; Scotland won 60; Wales 20; drawn 23. Goals: Scotland 237, Wales 116.

Year	Venue	S	W		Year	Venue	S	W
1876	Glasgow	4	0		1933	Edinburgh	2	5
1877	Wrexham	2	0		1934	Cardiff	2	3
1878	Glasgow	9	0		1935	Aberdeen	3	2
1879	Wrexham	3	0		1936	Cardiff	1	1
1880	Glasgow	5	1		1937	Dundee	1	2
1881	Wrexham	5	1		1938	Cardiff	1	2
1882	Glasgow	5	0		1939	Edinburgh	3	2
1883	Wrexham	3	0		1946	Wrexham	1	3
1884	Glasgow	4	1		1947	Glasgow	1	2
1885	Wrexham	8	1		1948	Cardiff (W.C.)	3	1
1886	Glasgow	4	1		1949	Glasgow	2	0
1887	Wrexham	2	0		1950	Cardiff	3	1
1888	Edinburgh	5	1		1951	Glasgow	0	1
1889	Wrexham	0	0		1952	Cardiff (W.C.)	2	1
1890	Paisley	5	0		1953	Glasgow	3	3
1891	Wrexham	4	3		1954	Cardiff	1	0
1892	Edinburgh	6	1		1955	Glasgow	2	0
1893	Wrexham	8	0		1956	Cardiff	2	2
1894	Kilmarnock	5	2		1957	Glasgow	1	1
1895	Wrexham	2	2		1958	Cardiff	3	0
1896	Dundee	4	0		1959	Glasgow	1	1
1897	Wrexham	2	0		1960	Cardiff	0	2
1898	Motherwell	5	2		1961	Glasgow	2	0
1899	Wrexham	6	0		1962	Cardiff	3	2
1900	Aberdeen	5	2		1963	Glasgow	2	1
1901	Wrexham	1	1		1964	Cardiff	2	3
1902	Greenock	5	1		1965	Glasgow (E.C.)	4	1
1903	Cardiff	1	0		1966	Cardiff (E.C.)	1	1
1904	Dundee	1	1		1967	Glasgow	3	2
1905	Wrexham	1	3		1969	Wrexham	5	3
1906	Edinburgh	0	2		1970	Glasgow	0	0
1907	Wrexham	0	1		1971	Cardiff	0	0
1908	Dundee	2	1		1972	Glasgow	1	0
1909	Wrexham	2	3		1973	Wrexham	2	0
1910	Kilmarnock	1	0		1974	Glasgow	2	0
1911	Cardiff	2	2		1975	Cardiff	2	2
1912	Tynecastle	1	0		1976	Glasgow	3	1
1913	Wrexham	0	0		1977	Glasgow (W.C.)	1	0
1914	Glasgow	0	0		1977	Wrexham	0	0
1920	Cardiff	1	1		1977	Anfield (W.C.)	2	0
1921	Aberdeen	2	1		1978	Glasgow	1	1
1922	Wrexham	1	2		1979	Cardiff	0	3
1923	Paisley	2	0		1980	Glasgow	1	0
1924	Cardiff	0	2		1981	Swansea	0	2
1925	Tynecastle	3	1		1982	Glasgow	1	0
1926	Cardiff	3	0		1983	Cardiff	2	0
1927	Glasgow	3	0		1984	Glasgow	2	1
1928	Wrexham	2	2		1985	Glasgow (W.C.)	0	1
1929	Glasgow	4	2		1985	Cardiff (W.C.)	1	1
1930	Cardiff	4	2		1997	Kilmarnock	0	1
1931	Glasgow	1	1		2004	Cardiff	0	4
1932	Wrexham	3	2					

311

SCOTLAND V. N. IRELAND

Played 93; Scotland won 62; Ireland 15; drawn 16. Goals: Scotland 257, Ireland 81.

Year	Venue	S	I	Year	Venue	S	I
1884	Belfast	5	0	1934	Glasgow	1	2
1885	Glasgow	8	2	1935	Belfast	1	2
1886	Belfast	7	2	1936	Edinburgh	2	1
1887	Belfast	4	1	1937	Belfast	3	1
1888	Belfast	10	2	1938	Aberdeen	1	1
1889	Glasgow	7	0	1939	Belfast	2	0
1890	Belfast	4	1	1946	Glasgow	0	0
1891	Glasgow	2	1	1947	Belfast	0	2
1892	Belfast	3	2	1948	Glasgow	3	2
1893	Glasgow	6	1	1949	Belfast	8	2
1894	Belfast	2	1	1950	Glasgow	6	1
1895	Glasgow	3	1	1951	Belfast	3	0
1896	Belfast	3	3	1952	Glasgow	1	1
1897	Glasgow	5	1	1953	Belfast	3	1
1898	Belfast	3	0	1954	Glasgow	2	2
1899	Glasgow	9	1	1955	Belfast	1	2
1900	Belfast	3	0	1956	Glasgow	1	0
1901	Glasgow	11	0	1957	Belfast	1	1
1902	Belfast	5	1	1958	Glasgow	2	2
1902	Belfast	3	0	1959	Belfast	4	0
1903	Glasgow	0	2	1960	Glasgow	5	1
1904	Dublin	1	1	1961	Belfast	6	1
1905	Glasgow	4	0	1962	Glasgow	5	1
1906	Dublin	1	0	1963	Belfast	1	2
1907	Glasgow	3	0	1964	Glasgow	3	2
1908	Dublin	5	0	1965	Belfast	2	3
1909	Glasgow	5	0	1966	Glasgow	2	1
1910	Belfast	0	1	1967	Belfast	0	1
1911	Glasgow	2	0	1969	Glasgow	1	1
1912	Belfast	4	1	1970	Belfast	1	0
1913	Dublin	2	1	1971	Glasgow	0	1
1914	Belfast	1	1	1972	Glasgow	2	0
1920	Glasgow	3	0	1973	Glasgow	1	2
1921	Belfast	2	0	1974	Glasgow	0	1
1922	Glasgow	2	1	1975	Glasgow	3	0
1923	Belfast	1	0	1976	Glasgow	3	0
1924	Glasgow	2	0	1977	Glasgow	3	0
1925	Belfast	3	0	1978	Glasgow	1	1
1926	Glasgow	4	0	1979	Glasgow	1	0
1927	Belfast	2	0	1980	Belfast	0	1
1928	Glasgow	0	1	1981	Glasgow (W.C.)	1	1
1929	Belfast	7	3	1981	Glasgow	2	0
1930	Glasgow	3	1	1981	Belfast (W.C.)	0	0
1931	Belfast	0	0	1982	Belfast	1	1
1932	Glasgow	3	1	1983	Glasgow	0	0
1933	Belfast	4	0	1984	Belfast	0	2
				1992	Glasgow	1	0

WALES V. N. IRELAND

Played 92; Wales won 43; Ireland 27; drawn 22. Goals: Wales 187, Ireland 131.

Year	Venue	W	I
1882	Wrexham	7	1
1883	Belfast	1	1
1884	Wrexham	6	0
1885	Belfast	8	2
1886	Wrexham	5	0
1887	Belfast	1	4
1888	Wrexham	11	0
1889	Belfast	3	1
1890	Shrewsbury	5	2
1891	Belfast	2	7
1892	Bangor	1	1
1893	Belfast	3	4
1894	Swansea	4	1
1895	Belfast	2	2
1896	Wrexham	6	1
1897	Belfast	3	4
1898	Llandudno	0	1
1899	Belfast	0	1
1900	Llandudno	2	0
1901	Belfast	1	0
1902	Cardiff	0	3
1903	Belfast	0	2
1904	Bangor	0	1
1905	Belfast	2	2
1906	Wrexham	4	4
1907	Belfast	3	2
1908	Aberdare	0	1
1909	Belfast	3	2
1910	Wrexham	4	1
1911	Belfast	2	1
1912	Cardiff	2	3
1913	Belfast	1	0
1914	Wrexham	1	2
1920	Belfast	2	2
1921	Swansea	2	1
1922	Belfast	1	1
1923	Wrexham	0	3
1924	Belfast	1	0
1925	Wrexham	0	0
1926	Belfast	0	3
1927	Cardiff	2	2
1928	Belfast	2	1
1929	Wrexham	2	2
1930	Belfast	0	7
1931	Wrexham	3	2
1932	Belfast	0	4
1933	Wrexham	4	1
1934	Belfast	1	1
1935	Wrexham	3	1
1936	Belfast	2	3
1937	Wrexham	4	1
1938	Belfast	0	1
1939	Wrexham	3	1
1947	Belfast	1	2
1948	Wrexham	2	0
1949	Belfast	2	0
1950	Wrexham (W.C.)	0	0
1951	Belfast	2	1
1952	Swansea	3	0
1953	Belfast	3	2
1954	Wrexham (W.C.)	1	2
1955	Belfast	3	2
1956	Cardiff	1	1
1957	Belfast	0	0
1958	Cardiff	1	1
1959	Belfast	1	4
1960	Wrexham	3	2
1961	Belfast	5	1
1962	Cardiff	4	0
1963	Belfast	4	1
1964	Swansea	2	3
1965	Belfast	5	0
1966	Cardiff	1	4
1967	Belfast (E.C.)	0	0
1968	Wrexham (E.C.)	2	0
1969	Belfast	0	0
1970	Swansea	1	0
1971	Belfast	0	1
1972	Wrexham	0	0
1973	*Goodison Park	0	1
1974	Wrexham	1	0
1975	Belfast	0	1
1976	Swansea	1	0
1977	Belfast	1	1
1978	Wrexham	1	0
1979	Belfast	1	1
1980	Cardiff	0	1
1982	Wrexham	3	0
1983	Belfast	1	0
1984	Swansea	1	1
2004	Cardiff (W.C.)	2	2
2005	Belfast (W.C.)	3	2

(* Switched from Belfast because of political situation in N. Ireland)

TRANSFER TRAIL

★ = British record fee at that time
A = Record all-British deal
B = British record for goalkeeper
D = Record deal between English and Scottish clubs

E = Record fee paid by Scottish club
F = Record fee to Scottish club
K = Record for teenager
L = Most expensive foreign import
(● Re dates, 1/00 = Jan 2000 etc)

	Player	From	To	Date	£
★L	Andriy Shevchenko	AC Milan	Chelsea	5/06	30,800,000
★AM	Rio Ferdinand	Leeds Utd.	Manchester Utd.	7/02	28,250,000
★	Juan Sebastian Veron	Lazio	Manchester Utd.	7/01	28,100,000
K	Wayne Rooney	Everton	Manchester Utd.	8/04	27,000,000
	Marc Overmars	Arsenal	Barcelona	7/00	25,000,000
	Michael Essien	Lyon	Chelsea	8/05	24,400,000
	David Beckham	Manchester Utd.	Real Madrid	7/03	23,300,000
	Didier Drogba	Marseille	Chelsea	7/04	23,200,000
★	Nicolas Anelka	Arsenal	Real Madrid	8/99	22,500,000
	Shaun Wright-Phillips	Manchester City	Chelsea	7/05	21,000,000
	Ruud van Nistelrooy	PSV Eindhoven	Manchester Utd.	4/01	19,000,000
AC	Rio Ferdinand	West Ham Utd.	Leeds Utd.	11/00	18,000,000
	Jose Reyes	Sevilla	Arsenal	1/04	17,400,000
	Damien Duff	Blackburn Rov.	Chelsea	7/03	17,000,000
	Hernan Crespo	Inter Milan	Chelsea	8/03	16,800,000
	Claude Makelele	Real Madrid	Chelsea	9/03	16,600,000
	Ricardo Carvalho	FC Porto	Chelsea	7/04	16,500,000
	Michael Owen	Real Madrid	Newcastle Utd.	8/05	16,000,000
	Adrian Mutu	Parma	Chelsea	8/03	15,800,000
★	Alan Shearer	Blackburn Rov.	Newcastle Utd.	7/96	15,000,000
	Jimmy F. Hasselbaink	Atl. Madrid	Chelsea	6/00	15,000,000
	Juan Sebastian Veron	Manchester Utd.	Chelsea	8/03	15,000,000
	Djibril Cisse	Auxerre	Liverpool	7/04	14,000,000
	Patrick Vieira	Arsenal	Juventus	7/05	13,700,000
	Paulo Ferreira	Porto	Chelsea	7/04	13,500,000
	Jonathan Woodgate	Newcastle Utd.	Real Madrid	8/04	13,400,000
	Jaap Stam	Manchester Utd.	Lazio	8/01	13,300,000
	Robbie Keane	Coventry City	Inter Milan	7/00	13,000,000
	Sylvain Wiltord	Bordeaux	Arsenal	8/00	13,000,000
	Nicolas Anelka	Paris St. Germain	Manchester City	5/02	13,000,000
	Louis Saha	Fulham	Manchester Utd.	1/04	12,825,000
	Dwight Yorke	Aston Villa	Manchester Utd.	8/98	12,600,000
	Cristiano Ronaldo	Sporting Lisbon	Manchester Utd.	8/03	12,240,000
	Juninho	Middlesbrough	Atl. Madrid	7/97	12,000,000
	Jimmy F. Hasselbaink	Leeds Utd.	Atl. Madrid	8/99	12,000,000
DE	Tore Andre Flo	Chelsea	Rangers	11/00	12,000,000
	Robbie Keane	Inter Milan	Leeds Utd.	12/00	12,000,000
	Arjen Robben	PSV Eindhoven	Chelsea	4/04	12,000,000
	Theo Walcott	Southampton	Arsenal	1/06	12,000,000
	Steve Marlet	Lyon	Fulham	8/01	11,500,000
	Sergei Rebrov	Dynamo Kiev	Tottenham	5/00	11,000,000
	Frank Lampard	West Ham Utd.	Chelsea	6/01	11,000,000
	Robbie Fowler	Liverpool	Leeds Utd.	11/01	11,000,000
	Dimitar Berbatov Bayer	Leverkusen	Tottenham	5/06	10,900,000
	Jaap Stam	PSV Eindhoven	Manchester Utd.	5/98	10,750,000
	Xabi Alonso	Real Sociedad	Liverpool	8/04	10,700,000
	Thierry Henry	Juventus	Arsenal	8/99	10,500,000
	Laurent Robert	Paris St. Germain	Newcastle Utd.	8/01	10,500,000

	Chris Sutton	Blackburn Rov.	Chelsea	7/99	10,000,000
	Emile Heskey	Leicester City	Liverpool	2/00	10,000,000
	El Hadji Diouf	Lens	Liverpool	6/02	10,000,000
	Scott Parker	Charlton Athletic	Chelsea	1/04	10,000,000
	Alexander Hleb	Stuttgart	Arsenal	6/05	10,000,000
	Juan Pablo Angel	River Plate (Arg.)	Aston Villa	1/01	9,500,000
	Albert Luque	Dep. La Coruna	Newcastle Utd.	8/05	9,500,000
	Jonathan Woodgate	Leeds Utd.	Newcastle Utd.	1/03	9,000,000
	Andy Johnson	Crystal Palace	Everton	5/06	8,600,000
F	Giovanni van Bronckhorst	Rangers	Arsenal	6/01	8,500,000
★	Stan Collymore	Nott'm Forest	Liverpool	6/95	8,500,000
	Hugo Viana	Sporting Lisbon	Newcastle Utd.	6/02	8,500,000
	Dean Richards	Southampton	Tottenham	9/01	8,100,000
	Massimo Maccarone	Empoli	Middlesbrough	7/02	8,100,000
	Andrei Kanchelskis	Everton	Fiorentina	1/97	8,000,000
	Dietmar Hamann	Newcastle Utd.	Liverpool	7/99	8,000,000
	Ugo Ehiogu	Aston Villa	Middlesbrough	10/00	8,000,000
	Francis Jeffers	Everton	Arsenal	6/01	8,000,000
	Andy Cole	Manchester Utd.	Blackburn Rov.	12/01	8,000,000
	Tiago	Benfica	Chelsea	7/04	8,000,000
	Michael Owen	Liverpool	Real Madrid	8/04	8,000,000
	Jean-Alain Boumsong	Rangers	Newcastle Utd.	1/05	8,000,000
	Asier del Horno	Athletic Bilbao	Chelsea	6/05	8,000,000
	Eidur Gudjohnsen	Chelsea	Barcelona	6/06	8,000,000
B	Fabien Barthez	Monaco	Manchester Utd.	5/00	7,800,000
	Jesper Gronkjaer	Ajax Amsterdam	Chelsea	10/00	7,800,000
★	Dennis Bergkamp	Inter Milan	Arsenal	6/95	7,500,000
	Kevin Davies	Southampton	Blackburn Rov.	6/98	7,500,000
	John Hartson	West Ham Utd.	Wimbledon	1/99	7,500,000
	Emmanuel Petit	Barcelona	Chelsea	6/01	7,500,000
	Diego Forlan	Independiente (Arg.)	Manchester Utd.	1/02	7,500,000
	Barry Ferguson	Rangers	Blackburn Rov.	8/03	7,500,000
	Aiyegbeni Yakubu	Portsmouth	Middlesbrough	6/05	7,500,000
	Dean Ashton	Norwich City	West Ham Utd.	1/06	7,250,000
	Olivier Dacourt	Lens	Leeds Utd.	5/00	7,200,000
★	Andy Cole	Newcastle Utd.	Manchester Utd.	1/95	7,000,000
	Fabrizio Ravanelli	Juventus	Middlesbrough	7/96	7,000,000
	Stan Collymore	Liverpool	Aston Villa	5/97	7,000,000
	Marc Overmars	Ajax Amsterdam	Arsenal	6/97	7,000,000
	Duncan Ferguson	Everton	Newcastle Utd.	11/98	7,000,000
	Lauren	Real Mallorca	Arsenal	5/00	7,000,000
	Carl Cort	Wimbledon	Newcastle Utd.	7/00	7,000,000
	Edwin Van der Sar	Juventus	Fulham	8/01	7,000,000
	Boudewijn Zenden	Barcelona	Chelsea	8/01	7,000,000
	Seth Johnson	Derby Co.	Leeds Utd.	10/01	7,000,000
	Robbie Keane	Leeds Utd.	Tottenham	8/02	7,000,000
	Wayne Bridge	Southampton	Chelsea	7/03	7,000,000
	Jermain Defoe	West Ham Utd.	Tottenham	2/04	7,000,000
	Alan Smith	Leeds Utd.	Manchester Utd.	5/04	7,000,000
	Jermaine Jenas	Newcastle Utd.	Tottenham	8/05	7,000,000
	Nemanja Vidic	Spartak Moscow	Manchester Utd.	1/06	7,000,000
	Geremi	Real Madrid	Chelsea	7/03	6,900,000
	Petr Cech	Rennes	Chelsea	7/04	6,900,000
	Gabriel Heinze	Paris St. Germain	Manchester Utd.	6/04	6,900,000
	Tomas Rosicky	Borussia Dortmund	Arsenal	5/06	6,800,000
	Paul Merson	Middlesbrough	Aston Villa	8/98	6,750,000

Corrado Grabbi	Ternana (It.)	Blackburn Rov.	6/01	6,750,000
Tore Andre Flo	Rangers	Sunderland	8/02	6,750,000
Faustino Asprilla	Parma	Newcastle Utd.	2/96	6,700,000
David Platt	Bari	Juventus	6/92	6,500,000
Olivier Dacourt	Everton	Lens	6/99	6,500,000
Kieron Dyer	Ipswich Town	Newcastle Utd.	7/99	6,500,000
Craig Bellamy	Coventry City	Newcastle Utd.	6/01	6,500,000
Gareth Southgate	Aston Villa	Middlesbrough	7/01	6,500,000
Michael Ball	Everton	Rangers	8/01	6,500,000
John Hartson	Coventry City	Celtic	8/01	6,500,000
Fernando Morientes	Real Madrid	Liverpool	1/05	6,500,000
Scott Parker	Chelsea	Newcastle Utd.	6/05	6,500,000
Milan Baros	Liverpool	Aston Villa	8/05	6,500,000
Tiago	Chelsea	Lyon	8/05	6,500,000

BRITISH RECORD TRANSFERS FROM FIRST £1,000 DEAL

Player	From	To	Date	£
Alf Common	Sunderland	Middlesbrough	2/1905	1,000
Syd Puddefoot	West Ham Utd.	Falkirk	2/22	5,000
Warney Cresswell	S. Shields	Sunderland	3/22	5,500
Bob Kelly	Burnley	Sunderland	12/25	6,500
David Jack	Bolton Wand.	Arsenal	10/28	10,890
Bryn Jones	Wolves	Arsenal	8/38	14,500
Billy Steel	Morton	Derby Co.	9/47	15,000
Tommy Lawton	Chelsea	Notts Co.	11/47	20,000
Len Shackleton	Newcastle Utd.	Sunderland	2/48	20,500
Johnny Morris	Manchester Utd.	Derby Co.	2/49	24,000
Eddie Quigley	Sheffield Wed.	Preston N.E.	12/49	26,500
Trevor Ford	Aston Villa	Sunderland	10/50	30,000
Jackie Sewell	Notts Co.	Sheffield Wed.	3/51	34,500
Eddie Firmani	Charlton Athletic	Sampdoria	7/55	35,000
John Charles	Leeds Utd.	Juventus	4/57	65,000
Denis Law	Manchester City	Torino	6/61	100,000
Denis Law	Torino	Manchester Utd.	7/62	115,000
Allan Clarke	Fulham	Leicester City	6/68	150,000
Allan Clarke	Leicester City	Leeds Utd.	6/69	165,000
Martin Peters	West Ham Utd.	Tottenham	3/70	200,000
Alan Ball	Everton	Arsenal	12/71	220,000
David Nish	Leicester City	Derby Co.	8/72	250,000
Bob Latchford	Birmingham City	Everton	2/74	350,000
Graeme Souness	Middlesbrough	Liverpool	1/78	352,000
Kevin Keegan	Liverpool	Hamburg	6/77	500,000
David Mills	Middlesbrough	W.B.A.	1/79	516,000
Trevor Francis	Birmingham City	Nott'm. Forest	2/79	1,180,000
Steve Daley	Wolves	Manchester City	9/79	1,450,000
Andy Gray	Aston Villa	Wolves	9/79	1,469,000
Bryan Robson	W.B.A.	Manchester Utd.	10/81	1,500,000
Ray Wilkins	Manchester Utd.	AC Milan	5/84	1,500,000
Mark Hughes	Manchester Utd.	Barcelona	5/86	2,300,000
Ian Rush	Liverpool	Juventus	6/87	3,200,000
Chris Waddle	Tottenham	Marseille	7/89	4,250,000
David Platt	Aston Villa	Bari	7/91	5,500,000
Paul Gascoigne	Tottenham	Lazio	6/92	5,500,000
Andy Cole	Newcastle Utd.	Manchester Utd.	1/95	7,000,000
Dennis Bergkamp	Inter Milan	Arsenal	6/95	7,500,000

Stan Collymore	Nott'm. Forest	Liverpool	6/95	8,500,000
Alan Shearer	Blackburn Rov.	Newcastle Utd.	7/96	15,000,000
Nicolas Anelka	Arsenal	Real Madrid	8/99	22,500,000
Juan Sebastian Veron	Lazio	Manchester Utd.	7/01	28,100,000
Rio Ferdinand	Leeds Utd.	Manchester Utd.	7/02	28,250,000
Andriy Shevchenko	AC Milan	Chelsea	5/06	30,800,000

• **World's first £1m. transfer:** Guiseppe Savoldi, Bologna to Napoli, July 1975.

TOP FOREIGN SIGNINGS

Player	From	To	Date	£
Zinedine Zidane	Juventus	Real Madrid	7/01	47,200,000
Luis Figo	Barcelona	Real Madrid	7/00	37,200,000
Hernan Crespo	Parma	Lazio	7/00	35,000,000
Ronaldo	Inter Milan	Real Madrid	8/02	33,000,000
Gianluigi Buffon	Parma	Juventus	7/01	32,600,000
Christian Vieri	Lazio	Inter Milan	6/99	31,000,000
Alessandro Nesta	Lazio	AC Milan	8/02	30,200,000
Hernan Crespo	Lazio	Inter Milan	8/02	29,000,000
Gaizka Mendieta	Valencia	Lazio	7/01	28,500,000
Pavel Nedved	Lazio	Juventus	7/01	25,000,000
Rui Costa	Fiorentina	AC Milan	7/01	24,500,000
Gabriel Batistuta	Fiorentina	Roma	5/00	22,000,000
Lilian Thuram	Parma	Juventus	6/01	22,000,000
Nicolas Anelka	Real Madrid	Paris St. Germain	7/00	21,700,000
Filippo Inzaghi	Juventus	AC Milan	7/01	21,700,000
Denilson	Sao Paulo	Real Betis	7/97	21,400,000
Marcio Amoroso	Udinese	Parma	6/99	21,000,000
Ronaldinho	Paris St Germain	Barcelona	7/03	21,000,000
Antonio Cassano	Bari	Roma	3/01	20,000,000
Javier Saviola	River Plate	Barcelona	7/01	20,000,000
Juan Sebastian Veron	Parma	Lazio	6/99	19,800,000
Hidetoshi Nakata	Roma	Parma	7/01	19,100,000
Ronaldo	Barcelona	Inter Milan	6/97	18,000,000
Francesco Toldo	Fiorentina	Inter Milan	7/01	18,000,000
Christian Vieri	Atletico Madrid	Lazio	8/98	17,500,000
David Trezeguet	Monaco	Juventus	6/00	17,500,000
Savo Milosevic	Real Zaragoza	Parma	7/00	17,000,000
Andrei Shevchenko	Dynamo Kiev	AC Milan	6/99	15,700,000
Vincenzo Montella	Sampdoria	Roma	6/99	15,300,000
Clarence Seedorf	Real Madrid	Inter Milan	12/99	15,000,000
Walter Samuel	Roma	Real Madrid	5/04	15,000,000

WORLD RECORD FEE FOR TEENAGER
£27m. for **Wayne Rooney**, aged 18, Everton to Manchester Utd., Aug. 2004.

WORLD RECORD FOR 16-YEAR-OLD
£12m. for **Theo Walcott**, Southampton to Arsenal, Jan. 2006.

RECORD CONFERENCE FEE
£250,000: **Andy Clarke**, Barnet to Wimbledon, Feb 1991; **Barry Hayles**, Stevenage Borough to Bristol Rov., Aug. 1997; **Jason Roberts**, Hayes to Wolves, Sept. 1997.

RECORD FEE BETWEEN NON-LEAGUE CLUBS
£180,000 for **Justin Jackson**, Morecambe to Rushden & Diamonds (Conference), June 2000.

MILESTONES OF SOCCER

1848 First code of rules compiled at Cambridge University.
1857 Sheffield F.C., world's oldest football club, formed.
1862 Notts Co. (oldest League club) formed.
1863 Football Association founded – their first rules of game agreed.
1871 F.A. Cup introduced.
1872 First official International: Scotland 0, England 0. Corner-kick introduced.
1873 Scottish F.A. formed; Scottish Cup introduced.
1874 Shinguards introduced.
1875 Crossbar introduced (replacing tape).
1876 F.A. of Wales formed.
1877 Welsh Cup introduced.
1878 Referee's whistle first used.
1880 Irish F.A. founded; Irish Cup introduced.
1883 Two-handed throw-in introduced.
1885 Record first-class score (Arbroath 36, Bon Accord 0 – Scottish Cup). Professionalism legalised.
1886 International Board formed.
1887 Record F.A. Cup score (Preston N.E. 26, Hyde 0).
1888 Football League founded by Wm. McGregor. First matches on Sept. 8.
1889 Preston N.E. win Cup and League (first club to complete Double).
1890 Scottish League and Irish League formed.
1891 Goal-nets introduced. Penalty-kick introduced.
1892 Inter-League games began. Football League Second Division formed.
1893 F.A. Amateur Cup launched.
1894 Southern League formed.
1895 F.A. Cup stolen from Birmingham shop window – never recovered.
1897 First Players' Union formed. Aston Villa win Cup and League.
1898 Promotion and relegation introduced.
1901 Maximum wage rule in force (£4 a week). Tottenham first professional club to take F.A. Cup South. First six-figure attendance (110,802) at F.A. Cup Final.
1902 Ibrox Park disaster (25 killed). Welsh League formed.
1904 F.I.F.A. founded (7 member countries).
1905 First £1,000 transfer (Alf Common, Sunderland to Middlesbrough).
1907 Players' Union revived.
1908 Transfer fee limit (£350) fixed in January and withdrawn in April.
1911 New F.A. Cup trophy – in use to 1991. Transfer deadline introduced.
1914 King George V first reigning monarch to attend F.A. Cup Final.
1916 Entertainment Tax introduced.
1919 League extended to 44 clubs.
1920 Third Division (South) formed.
1921 Third Division (North) formed.
1922 Scottish League (Div. II) introduced.
1923 Beginning of football pools. First Wembley Cup Final.
1924 First International at Wembley (England 1, Scotland 1). Rule change allows goals to be scored direct from corner-kicks.
1925 New offside law.
1926 Huddersfield Town complete first League Championship hat-trick.
1927 First League match broadcast (radio): Arsenal v Sheff. Utd. First radio broadcast of Cup Final (winners Cardiff City). Charles Clegg, president of F.A., becomes first knight of football.
1928 First £10,000 transfer – David Jack (Bolton Wand. to Arsenal). W.R. ('Dixie') Dean (Everton) creates League record – 60 goals in season. Britain withdraws from F.I.F.A.
1930 Uruguay first winners of World Cup.
1931 W.B.A. win Cup and promotion.

318

1933 Players numbered for first time in Cup Final (1-22).

1934 Sir Frederick Wall retires as F.A. secretary; successor Stanley Rous. Death of Herbert Chapman (Arsenal manager).

1935 Arsenal equal Huddersfield Town's Championship hat-trick record. Official two-referee trials.

1936 Joe Payne's 10-goal League record (Luton Town 12, Bristol Rov. 0).

1937 British record attendance: 149,547 at Scotland v England match.

1938 First live TV transmission of F.A. Cup Final. Football League 50th Jubilee. New pitch marking – arc on edge of penalty-area. Laws of Game re-drafted by Stanley Rous. Arsenal pay record £14,500 fee for Bryn Jones (Wolves).

1939 Compulsory numbering of players in Football League. First six-figure attendance for League match (Rangers v Celtic, 118,567). All normal competitions suspended for duration of Second World War.

1945 Scottish League Cup introduced.

1946 British associations rejoin F.I.F.A. Bolton Wand. disaster (33 killed) during F.A. Cup tie with Stoke City. Walter Winterbottom appointed England's first director of coaching.

1947 Great Britain beat Rest of Europe 6-1 at Hampden Park, Glasgow. First £20,000 transfer – Tommy Lawton, Chelsea to Notts Co.

1949 Stanley Rous, secretary F.A., knighted. England's first home defeat outside British Champ. (0-2 v Eire).

1950 Football League extended from 88 to 92 clubs. World record crowd (203,500) at World Cup Final, Brazil v Uruguay, in Rio. Scotland's first home defeat by foreign team (0-1 v Austria).

1951 White ball comes into official use.

1952 Newcastle Utd. first club to win F.A. Cup at Wembley in successive seasons.

1953 England's first Wembley defeat by foreign opponents (3-6 v Hungary).

1954 Hungary beat England 7-1 in Budapest.

1955 First F.A. Cup match under floodlights (prelim. round replay): Kidderminster Harriers v Brierley Hill Alliance.

1956 First F.A. Cup ties under floodlights in competition proper. First League match by floodlight (Portsmouth v Newcastle Utd.). Real Madrid win the first European Cup.

1957 Last full Football League programme on Christmas Day. Entertainment Tax withdrawn.

1958 Manchester Utd. air crash at Munich. League re-structured into four divisions.

1960 Record transfer fee: £55,000 for Denis Law (Huddersfield Town to Manchester City). Wolves win Cup, miss Double and Championship hat-trick by one goal. For fifth time in ten years F.A. Cup Final team reduced to ten men by injury. F.A. recognise Sunday football. Football League Cup launched.

1961 Tottenham complete the first Championship-F.A. Cup double this century. Maximum wage (£20 a week) abolished in High Court challenge by George Eastham. First British £100-a-week wage paid (by Fulham to Johnny Haynes). First £100,000 British transfer – Denis Law, Manchester City to Torino. Sir Stanley Rous elected president of F.I.F.A.

1962 Manchester Utd. raise record British transfer fee to £115,000 for Denis Law.

1963 F.A. Centenary. Season extended to end of May due to severe winter. First pools panel. English "retain and transfer" system ruled illegal in High Court test case.

1964 Rangers' second great hat-trick – Scottish Cup, League Cup and League. Football League and Scottish League guaranteed £500,000 a year in new fixtures copyright agreement with Pools. First televised 'Match of the Day' (BBC2): Liverpool 3, Arsenal 2.

1965 Bribes scandal – ten players jailed (and banned for life by F.A.) for match-fixing 1960-3. Stanley Matthews knighted in farewell season. Arthur Rowley (Shrewsbury Town) retires with record of 434 League goals. Substitutes allowed for injured players in Football League matches (one per team).

1966 England win World Cup (Wembley).

1967 Alf Ramsey, England manager, knighted; O.B.E. for captain Bobby Moore. Celtic become first British team to win European Cup. First substitutes allowed in F.A. Cup Final (Tottenham v Chelsea) but not used. Football League permit loan transfers (two per club).

1968 First F.A. Cup Final televised live in colour (BBC2 – W.B.A. v Everton). Manchester Utd. first English club to win European Cup.
1970 F.I.F.A/U.E.F.A approve penalty shoot-out in deadlocked ties.
1971 Arsenal win League Championship and F.A. Cup.
1973 Football League introduce 3-up, 3-down promotion/relegation between Divisions 1, 2 and 3 and 4-up, 4-down between Divisions 3 and 4.
1974 First F.A. Cup ties played on Sunday. League football played on Sunday for first time. Last F.A. Amateur Cup Final. Joao Havelange (Brazil) succeeds Sir Stanley Rous as F.I.F.A. president.
1975 Scottish Premier Division introduced.
1976 Football League introduce goal difference (replacing goal average) and red/yellow cards.
1977 Liverpool achieve the double of League Championship and European Cup. Don Revie defects to United Arab Emirates when England manager – successor Ron Greenwood.
1978 Freedom of contract for players accepted by Football League. P.F.A. lifts ban on foreign players in English football. Football League introduce Transfer Tribunal. Viv Anderson (Nott'm. Forest) first black player to win a full England cap. Willie Johnston (Scotland) sent home from World Cup Finals in Argentina after failing dope test.
1979 First all-British £500,000 transfer – David Mills, M'bro' to W.B.A. First British million pound transfer (Trevor Francis – B'ham to Nott'm. Forest). Andy Gray moves from Aston Villa to Wolves for a record £1,469,000 fee.
1981 Tottenham win 100th F.A. Cup Final. Liverpool first British side to win European Cup three times. Three points for a win introduced by Football League. Q.P.R. install Football League's first artificial pitch. Death of Bill Shankly, manager-legend of Liverpool 1959-74. Record British transfer – Bryan Robson (W.B.A. to Manchester Utd.), £1,500,000.
1982 Aston Villa become sixth consecutive English winners of European Cup. Tottenham retain F.A. Cup – first club to do so since Tottenham 1961 and 1962. Football League Cup becomes the (sponsored) Milk Cup.
1983 Liverpool complete League Championship-Milk Cup double for second year running. Manager Bob Paisley retires. Aberdeen first club to do Cup-Winners' Cup and domestic Cup double. Football League clubs vote to keep own match receipts. Football League sponsored by Canon, Japanese camera and business equipment manufacturers – 3-year agreement starting 1983-4. Football League agree 2-year contract for live TV coverage of ten matches per season (5 Friday night, BBC, 5 Sunday afternoon, ITV).
1984 One F.A. Cup tie in rounds 3, 4, 5 and 6 shown live on TV (Friday or Sunday). Aberdeen take Scottish Cup for third successive season, win Scottish Championship, too. Tottenham win UEFA Cup on penalty shoot-out. Liverpool win European Cup on penalty shoot-out to complete unique treble with Milk Cup and League title (as well as Championship hat-trick). N. Ireland win the final British Championship. France win European Championship – their first honour. F.A. National Soccer School opens at Lilleshall. Britain's biggest score this century: Stirling Alb. 20, Selkirk 0 (Scottish Cup).
1985 Bradford City fire disaster – 56 killed. First £1m. receipts from match in Britain (F.A. Cup Final). Kevin Moran (Manchester Utd.) first player to be sent off in F.A. Cup Final. Celtic win 100th Scottish F.A. Cup Final. European Cup Final horror (Liverpool v Juventus, riot in Brussels) 39 die. UEFA ban all English clubs indefinitely from European competitions. No TV coverage at start of League season – first time since 1963 (resumption delayed until January 1986). Sept: first ground-sharing in League history – Charlton Athletic move from The Valley to Selhurst Park (Crystal Palace).
1986 Liverpool complete League and Cup double in player-manager Kenny Dalglish's first season in charge. Swindon Town (4th Div. Champions) set League points record (102). League approve reduction of First Division to 20 clubs by 1988. Everton chairman Philip Carter elected president of Football League. Death of Sir Stanley Rous (91). 100th edition of *News of the World* Football Annual. League Cup sponsored for next three years by Littlewoods (£2m.). Football League voting majority (for rule changes) reduced from ¾ to ⅔. Wales move HQ from Wrexham to Cardiff

City after 110 years. Two substitutes in F.A. Cup and League (Littlewoods) Cup. Two-season League/TV deal (£6.2m.):- BBC and ITV each show seven live League matches per season, League Cup semi-finals and Final. Football League sponsored by *Today* newspaper. Luton Town first club to ban all visiting supporters; as sequel are themselves banned from League Cup. Oldham Athletic and Preston N.E. install artificial pitches, making four in F. League (following Q.P.R. and Luton Town).

1987 League introduce play-off matches to decide final promotion/relegation places in all divisions. Re-election abolished – bottom club in Div. 4 replaced by winners of GM Vauxhall Conference. Two substitutes approved for Football League 1987-8. Red and yellow disciplinary cards (scrapped 1981) re-introduced by League and F.A. Football League sponsored by Barclays. First Div. reduced to 21 clubs.

1988 Football League Centenary. First Division reduced to 20 clubs.

1989 Soccer gets £74m. TV deal: £44m. over 4 years, ITV; £30m. over 5 years, BBC/BSB. But it costs Philip Carter the League Presidency. Ted Croker retires as F.A. chief executive; successor Graham Kelly, from Football League. Hillsborough disaster: 95 die at F.A. Cup semi-final (Liverpool v Nott'm. Forest). Arsenal win closest-ever Championship with last kick. Peter Shilton sets England record with 109 caps.

1990 Nott'm. Forest win last Littlewoods Cup Final. Both F.A. Cup semi-finals played on Sunday and televised live. Play-off finals move to Wembley; Swindon Town win place in Div. 1, then relegated back to Div. 2 (breach of financial regulations) – Sunderland promoted instead. England reach World Cup semi-final in Italy and win F.I.F.A. Fair Play Award. Peter Shilton retires as England goalkeeper with 125 caps (world record). Graham Taylor (Aston Villa) succeeds Bobby Robson as England manager. Int. Board amend offside law (player 'level' no longer offside). F.I.F.A. make "pro foul" a sending-off offence. English clubs back in Europe (Manchester Utd. and Aston Villa) after 5-year exile.

1991 First F.A. Cup semi-final at Wembley (Tottenham 3, Arsenal 1). Bert Millichip (F.A. chairman) and Philip Carter (Everton chairman) knighted. End of artificial pitches in Div. 1 (Luton Town, Oldham Athletic). Scottish League reverts to 12-12-14 format (as in 1987-8). Penalty shoot-out introduced to decide F.A. Cup ties level after one replay.

1992 Introduction of fourth F.A. Cup (previous trophy withdrawn). F.A. launch Premier League (22 clubs). Football League reduced to three divisions (71 clubs). Record TV-sport deal: BSkyB/BBC to pay £304m. for 5-year coverage of Premier League. ITV do £40m., 4-year deal with F. League. Channel 4 show Italian football live (Sundays). F.I.F.A. approve new back-pass rule (goalkeeper must not handle ball kicked to him by team-mate). New League of Wales formed. Record all-British transfer, £3.3m.: Alan Shearer (Southampton to Blackburn Rov.). Charlton Athletic return to The Valley after 7-year absence.

1993 Barclays end 6-year sponsorship of F. League. For first time both F.A. Cup semi-finals at Wembley (Sat., Sun.). Arsenal first club to complete League Cup/F.A. Cup double. Rangers pull off Scotland's domestic treble for fifth time. F.A. in record British sports sponsorship deal (£12m. over 4 years) with brewers Bass for F.A. Carling Premiership, from Aug. Brian Clough retires after 18 years as Nott'm. Forest manager; as does Jim McLean (21 years manager of Dundee Utd.). Football League agree 3-year, £3m. sponsorship with Endsleigh Insurance. Premier League introduce squad numbers with players' names on shirts. Record British transfer: Duncan Ferguson, Dundee Utd. to Rangers (£4m.). Record English-club signing: Roy Keane, Nott'm. Forest to Manchester Utd. (£3.75m.). Graham Taylor resigns as England manager after World Cup exit (Nov.). Death in Feb. of Bobby Moore (51), England World-Cup winning captain 1966.

1994 Death of Sir Matt Busby. Terry Venables appointed England coach. Manchester Utd. complete the Double. Last artificial pitch in English football goes – Preston N.E. revert to grass, summer 1994. Bobby Charlton knighted. Scottish League format changes to four divisions of ten clubs. Record British transfer: Chris Sutton, Norwich City to Blackburn Rov. (£5m.). Sept: F.A. announce first sponsorship of F.A. Cup – Littlewoods Pools (4-year, £14m. deal, plus £6m. for Charity Shield). Death of Billy Wright.

1995 New record British transfer: Andy Cole, Newcastle Utd. to Manchester Utd. (£7m.). First England match abandoned through crowd trouble (v Rep. of Ireland, Dublin). Blackburn Rov. Champions for first time since 1914. Premiership reduced to 20 clubs. British transfer record broken again: Stan Collymore, Nott'm. Forest to Liverpool (£8½m.). Starting season 1995-6, teams allowed to use 3 substitutes per match, not necessarily including a goalkeeper. European Court of Justice upholds Bosman ruling, barring transfer fees for players out of contract and removing limit on number of foreign players clubs can field.

1996 Death of Bob Paisley (77), ex-Liverpool, most successful manager in English Football. F.A. appoint Chelsea manager Glenn Hoddle to succeed Terry Venables as England coach after Euro 96. Manchester Utd. first English club to achieve Double twice (and in 3 seasons). Football League completes £125m., 5-year TV deal with BSkyB starting 1996-7. England stage European Championship, reach semi-finals, lose on pens to tournament winners Germany. Keith Wiseman succeeds Sir Bert Millichip as F.A. Chairman. Linesmen become known as "referees' assistants". Coca-Cola Cup experiment with own disciplinary system (red, yellow cards). Alan Shearer football's first £15m. player (Blackburn Rov. to Newcastle Utd.). Nigeria first African country to win Olympic soccer. Nationwide Building Society sponsor Football League in initial 3-year deal worth £5.25m. Peter Shilton first player to make 1000 League apps.

1997 Howard Wilkinson appointed English football's first technical director. England's first home defeat in World Cup (0-1 v Italy). Ruud Gullit (Chelsea) first foreign coach to win F.A. Cup. Rangers equal Celtic's record of 9 successive League titles. Manchester Utd. win Premier League for fourth time in 5 seasons. New record World Cup score: Iran 17, Maldives 0 (qual. round). Season 1997-8 starts Premiership's record £36m., 4-year sponsorship extension with brewers Bass (Carling).

1998 In French manager Arsene Wenger's second season at Highbury, Arsenal become second English club to complete the double twice. Chelsea also win two trophies under new player-manager Gianluca Vialli (Coca-Cola Cup, Cup Winners' Cup). France win 16th World Cup competition. In breakaway from Scottish League, top ten clubs form new Premiership under SFA, starting season 1998-9. Football League celebrates its 100th season, 1998-9. New F.A. Cup sponsors – French insurance giants AXA (25m., 4-year deal). League Cup becomes Worthington Cup in £23m., 5-year contract with brewers Bass. Nationwide Building Society's sponsorship of Football League extended to season 2000-1.

1999 F.A. buy Wembley Stadium (£103m.) for £320m., plan rebuilding (Aug. 2000-March 2003) as new national stadium (Lottery Sports fund contributes £110m.) Scotland's new Premier League takes 3-week mid-season break in January. Sky screen Oxford Utd. v Sunderland (Div. 1) as first pay-per-view match on TV. F.A. sack England coach Glenn Hoddle; Fulham's Kevin Keegan replaces him at £1m. a year until 2003. Sir Alf Ramsey, England's World Cup-winning manager, dies aged 79. With effect 1999, F.A. Cup Final to be decided on day (via penalties, if necessary). Hampden Park re-opens for Scottish Cup Final after £63m. refit. Alex Ferguson knighted after Manchester Utd. complete Premiership, F.A. Cup, European Cup treble. Starting season 1999-2000, UEFA increase Champions League from 24 to 32 clubs. End of Cup-Winners' Cup (merged into 121-club UEFA Cup). F.A. allow holders Manchester Utd. to withdraw from F.A. Cup to participate in FIFA's inaugural World Club Championship in Brazil in January. Chelsea first British club to field an all-foreign line-up at Southampton (Prem). F.A. vote in favour of streamlined 14-man board of directors to replace its 92-member council.

2000 Scot Adam Crozier takes over as F.A. chief executive. Wales move to Cardiff's £125m. Millennium Stadium (v Finland). Brent Council approve plans for new £475m. Wembley Stadium (completion target spring 2003); demolition of old stadium to begin after England v Germany (World Cup qual.). Fulham Ladies become Britain's first female professional team. F.A. Premiership and Nationwide League to introduce (season 2000-01) rule whereby referees advance free-kick by 10 yards and caution player who shows dissent, delays kick or fails to retreat 10 yards. Scottish football increased to 42 League clubs in 2000-01 (12 in Premier League and 3 divisions of ten; Peterhead and Elgin City elected from Highland League). France win European Championship – first time a major Int. tournament has been jointly hosted (Holland/

Belgium). England's £10m. bid to stage 2006 World Cup fails; vote goes to Germany. England manager Kevin Keegan resigns after 1-0 World Cup defeat by Germany in Wembley's last International. Lazio's Swedish coach Sven-Goran Eriksson agrees to become England head coach.

2001 Scottish Premier League experiment with split into two 5-game mini leagues (6 clubs in each) after 33 matches completed. New transfer system agreed by FIFA/UEFA is ratified. Barclaycard begin £48m., 3-year sponsorship of the Premiership, and Nationwide's contract with the Football League is extended by a further 3 years (£12m.). ITV, after winning auction against BBC's Match of the Day, begin £183m., 3-season contract for highlights of Premiership matches; BSkyB's live coverage (66 matches per season) for next 3 years will cost £1.1bn. BBC and BSkyB pay £400m. (3-year contract) for live coverage of F.A. Cup and England home matches. ITV and Ondigital pay £315m. to screen Nationwide League and Worthington Cup matches. In new charter for referees, top men can earn up to £60,000 a season in Premiership. Real Madrid break world transfer record, buying Zinedine Zidane from Juventus for £47.2m. F.A. introduce prize money, round by round, in F.A. Cup.

2002 Scotland appoint their first foreign manager, Germany's former national coach Bertie Vogts replacing Craig Brown. Collapse of ITV Digital deal, with Football League owed £178m., threatens lower-division clubs. Arsenal complete Premiership/F.A. Cup Double for second time in 5 seasons, third time in all. Newcastle Utd. manager Bobby Robson knighted in Queen's Jubilee Honours. Brazil win World Cup for fifth time. New record British transfer and world record for defender, £28.25m. Rio Ferdinand (Leeds Utd. to Manchester Utd.). Transfer window introduced to British football. F.A. Charity Shield renamed F.A. Community Shield. After 2-year delay, demolition of Wembley Stadium begins. October: Adam Crozier, F.A. chief executive, resigns.

2003 F.A. Cup draw (from 4th. Round) reverts to Monday lunchtime. Scottish Premier League decide to end mid-winter shut-down. Mark Palios appointed F.A. chief executive. For first time, two Football League clubs demoted (replaced by two from Conference). Ban lifted on loan transfers between Premiership clubs. July: David Beckham becomes record British export (Man. Utd. to Real Madrid, £23.3m.). Biggest takeover in British football history – Russian oil magnate Roman Abramovich buys control of Chelsea for £150m. Wimbledon leave rented home at Selhurst Park, become England's first franchised club in 68-mile move to Milton Keynes.

2004 Arsenal first club to win Premiership with unbeaten record and only the third in English football history to stay undefeated through League season. Trevor Brooking knighted in Queen's Birthday Honours. Wimbledon change name to Milton Keynes Dons. Greece beat hosts Portugal to win European Championship as biggest outsiders (80-1 at start) ever to succeed in major Int. tournament. New contracts – Premiership in £57m. deal with Barclays, seasons 2004-07. Coca-Cola replace Nationwide as Football League sponsors (£15m. over 3 years), rebranding Div. 1 as Football League Championship, with 2nd. and 3rd. Divs, becoming Leagues 1 and 2. After 3 years, BBC Match of the Day wins back Premiership highlights from ITV with 3-year, £105m. contract (2004-07). All-time League record of 49 unbeaten Premiership matches set by Arsenal. Under new League rule, Wrexham forfeit 10 points for going into administration.

2005 Brian Barwick, controller of ITV Sport, becomes F.A. chief executive. Foreign managers take all major trophies for English clubs: Chelsea, in Centenary year, win Premiership (record 95 points) and League Cup in Jose Mourinho's first season; Arsene Wenger's Arsenal win F.A. Cup in Final's first penalty shoot-out; under new manager Rafael Benitez, Liverpool lift European Cup on penalties after trailing 0-3 in Champions League Final. Wigan Athletic, a League club only since 1978, promoted to Premiership. In new record British-club take-over, American tycoon Malcolm Glazer buys Manchester Utd. for £790m. Bury become the first club to score 1,000 goals in each of the four divisions. Tributes are paid world-wide to George Best, who dies aged 59.

2006 Steve Staunton succeeds Brian Kerr as Republic of Ireland manager. Chelsea post record losses of £140m. Sven-Goran Eriksson agrees a settlement to step down as England coach. Steve McClaren replaces him. The Premier League announce a new 3-year TV deal worth £1.7 billion under which Sky lose their monopoly of coverage. Chelsea smash the British transfer record, paying £30.8m. for Andriy Shevchenko. Italy win the World Cup on penalties.

FINAL WHISTLE – OBITUARIES 2005-06

SEPTEMBER 2005

NOEL CANTWELL, 73, was a strong-tackling full-back who captained Manchester United and the Republic of Ireland. He moved to Old Trafford for a £29,500 fee in 1960 after making nearly 250 appearances for West Ham and winning a Division Two championship medal in 1958. He led United to the 1963 F.A. Cup with a 3-1 victory over Leicester, and four years later they were League champions. Cantwell succeeded Jimmy Hill as manager of Coventry (1967-72) and had two spells in charge of Peterborough from 1972-77 and 1986-88. He also coached New England and Jacksonville in the North American League. Cantwell, who found time to play cricket for Ireland, won 36 caps for the Republic between 1954-67 and captained the side 22 times.

GORDON MCKEAG, 76, was a former chairman of Newcastle and president of the Football League. A solicitor, he took over his family's position in the boardroom at St James' Park in 1972 after the death of his father and became chairman in 1988 following the resignation of Stan Seymour. He stepped down after a power struggle ended with a successful takeover bid headed by Sir John Hall and left the board in 1992. McKeag, an F.A. councillor, was a member of the disciplinary commission that banned Manchester United's Eric Cantona for nine months in 1995 for kicking an abusive fan at Crystal Palace

OCTOBER 2005

JOHNNY HAYNES, 71, had a major influence on English football – on and off the field. He was the David Beckham of his generation, an England captain with an aura of glamour about him and the first player to represent his country at every level from the schools team upwards. He was also the forerunner of today's high-earners, becoming the first in the domestic game to earn £100 a week, following the abolition of the maximum wage in 1961. This cultured inside-forward was a one-club man, resisting all attempts to lure him from Fulham, for whom he made his debut at 17 and totalled nearly 600 League appearances, scoring 145 goals. Tottenham and AC Milan were among the clubs who unsuccessfully sought his services. He never won a major club honour, but was an influential figure at international level, winning 56 caps and leading England 22 times. Haynes scored the first of 18 goals on his debut against Northern Ireland when 19 and gave one of his finest performances in the 9-3 win over Scotland at Wembley in 1961. His last appearance was in the 3-1 defeat by Brazil in the 1962 World Cup Finals in Chile. Later that year, he was seriously injured in a car crash and was never chosen by Sir Alf Ramsey when the man who was to lead England to World Cup glory in 1966 took over from Walter Winterbottom as manager. Haynes, who had a brief spell as Fulham player-manager when Bobby Robson was sacked in 1968, ended his career with Durban City in South Africa. He died from injuries sustained in a car crash. In memory of their greatest player, Fulham decided to rename the Stevenage Road Stand the Johnny Haynes Stand.

VIVIEN FELTON, 76, had a brief career with Crystal Palace after joining the club from Barnet in 1954. He could play centre-half or centre-forward, but made only two senior team appearances in 1955-56 before returning to his non-league roots.

NOVEMBER 2005

GEORGE BEST, 59, was among the finest players Britain has ever produced, an irresistible blend of speed, strength, balance, dribbling skills and scoring power. He was also the first to bring a pop star image to the game. Had his career not run alongside this playboy lifestyle which embraced the 'Swinging Sixties,' it could have reached even greater heights. The Belfast-born son of a shipyard worker was spotted by a Manchester United scout while a schoolboy and signed as a professional under legendary manager Sir Matt Busby when 17. Together with Denis Law and Bobby Charlton he formed a trio that inspired United to the League championship in 1965 and 1967. In the intervening year, Best scored twice in a dazzling performance against Benfica in a European Cup second round tie. Two years later, he scored again against the Portuguese side as United won the European Cup Final 4-1 at Wembley. Alongside that trophy, he collected English and European Footballer of the Year awards. Best scored six goals in an F.A. Cup tie against Northampton in 1970, but his off-field activities began to seriously worry the club and the arrival of hard-line Tommy Docherty as manager was the beginning of the end. Best retired, made a brief return, and finally left Old Trafford in 1974, having made 361 League appearances and scored 137 goals. Over the next nine years he played for several clubs at home, including Stockport, Fulham, Hibernian and Bournemouth, as well as in America for Los Angeles, Fort Lauderdale and San Jose. Best made 37 appearances and scored nine goals for Northern Ireland, but never had the opportunity to display his ability on the biggest stage of all – the World Cup Finals. Belfast City Airport has been renamed George Best Airport as a permanent tribute.

GEORGE SWINDIN, 90, won three League titles in different decades with Arsenal, played in two F.A. Cup Finals and managed the club. The goalkeeper's first title success, under George Allison, came in 1938 when his team finished one point ahead of Wolves. In 1948, with Tom Whittaker in charge, Swindin conceded only 32 goals – then a record – as Arsenal outpaced Manchester United by seven points. The hat-trick was completed in 1953 when Arsenal pipped Preston on goal average. They defeated Liverpool 2-0 to win the F.A. Cup in 1950, but lost 1-0 to Newcastle at Wembley two years later when an injury to full-back Wally Barnes left them a man short for most of the match. After 297 appearances, Swindin began his managerial career at Peterborough, returning to Highbury in 1958 charged with the job of rebuilding the club after some lean years. He signed players like Tommy Docherty and George Eastham and finished third in his first season. But Arsenal then found themselves in the shadow of neighbours Tottenham and he left in 1962. He later managed Norwich and Cardiff and a number of non-league clubs before retiring and settling in Spain.

PETER WILSON, 52, was Mansfield's goalkeeping coach, who suffered a heart attack shortly before the team were due to play a League Two match at Shrewsbury and died later in hospital. He had collapsed after spending ten minutes on the pitch working with goalkeeper Kevin Pressman. The game was postponed. Wilson joined the club only a fortnight before from Leicester.

FRANK MILES, 72, was Hereford's chairman during the most significant years in the club's history. Their 2-1 victory over Newcastle in January 1972 was one of the most famous of all F.A. Cup shocks and paved the way for the club's election to the Football League. Colin Addison, whom businessman Miles had appointed manager following the departure of John Charles, led his team to promotion from Division Four in their first season and his successor, John Sillett, won the Third Division title in 1976. But after successive relegations and an F.A. Cup defeat by Wealdstone, Miles stepped down after nine years in the chair.

DECEMBER 2005

TED DITCHBURN, 84, was an ever-present in goal for Tottenham's renowned 'push and run' team that won the League title in 1951. The previous season they had been Division Two champions. His ability to launch attacks with prodigious kicking and accurate throws was a key part of that success. Team-mate and future Tottenham manager Bill Nicholson described him as a 'colossus.' Ditchburn, who had huge hands and almost followed his father into professional boxing, played 418 League games for the club between 1946-59. During one eight-year spell, he missed only two matches, including a run of 247 successive appearances. He won six England caps and was a member of the squad for the 1950 World Cup in Brazil. After leaving White Hart Lane, he played non-league football for Romford and Braintree.

LAJOS BAROTI, 91, coached Hungary in a record 117 matches, including four World Cups – Sweden (1958), Chile (1962), England (1966) and Argentina (1978). He also led the team to a bronze medal at the 1960 Rome Olympics and was credited with preparing the team that won gold in Tokyo in 1964. Baroti, who played twice for the national team, coached Benfica to three Portuguese titles between 1980-82 and also worked with the Peru national side in the 1970s.

JANUARY 2006

MARK PHILO, 21, died in a car accident only hours before his team, Wycombe, played Notts County in a League Two match. It went ahead at the request of his family and manager John Gorman broke the news to his players after their 2-0 victory. The young midfielder has been earmarked for a place on the substitutes' bench. He joined the club at 15 and made 17 League appearances, having fought back from a broken ankle to impress in a handful of games at the end of 2004-05 season to earn a new contract.

FRANK BUTLER, 89, was one the best-known names in Fleet Street sports journalism and also edited the *News of the World Football Annual* for several years. He was appointed sports editor of the *Sunday Express* at the age of 24, doubling as chief sports writer of the *Daily Express*. In 1949 he moved to the *News of the World* and stayed for 33 years, rising from columnist to sports editor and assistant editor. Butler's passion was boxing. He was a founder member of the Boxing Writers' Club, an administrative steward of the British Boxing Board of Control and wrote a number of books, including a biography of Muhammad Ali.

ALF MCMICHAEL, 78, made 433 appearances for Newcastle and won 40 caps for Northern Ireland, playing in the team that reached the World Cup quarter-finals in Sweden in 1958. The left-back was signed from Irish League club Linfield in 1949 and three years later gained an F.A. Cup winners' medal when Newcastle beat Arsenal 1-0. When his playing career ended, McMichael managed South Shields and his home-town team Bangor in County Down.

FEBRUARY 2006

STUART MASON, 57, was a full-back who won three England youth caps. He began his career at Wrexham, had a spell at Liverpool and then appeared for Doncaster, Wrexham again, Chester, Rochdale and Crewe. Mason later played for Bangor and Oswestry and had a short spell as Oswestry manager. A talented cricketer who reached Minor Counties level, he went back to Wrexham to become assistant commercial manager.

RON GREENWOOD, 84, was hailed as one of the game's great innovators during his time as manager of West Ham and England. He was in charge at Upton Park for more than 600 games from 1961-1974 and had a further three years as general manager. His team beat Preston 3-2 in the 1964 F.A. Cup Final and returned to Wembley a year later when Bobby Moore lifted the Cup Winners' Cup after a 2-0 victory over Munich 1860. Greenwood took over the England job in 1977 after Don Revie walked out to become coach of the United Arab Emirates. His first match in charge was a goalless draw against Switzerland, but he brought stability to a team that had failed to qualify for the 1978 World Cup Finals in Argentina. England were eliminated in the first group of the European Championship in Italy in 1980 and, despite not losing a game, went out at the second group stage of the 1982 World Cup in Spain after Kevin Keegan missed a late headed chance against the host country. Greenwood resigned after 33 wins and 12 draws in 55 games and was replaced by Bobby Robson. Three years later he received the P.F.A. Merit Award and in 2002 was inducted in the the F.A.'s Hall of Fame.

Greenwood, who was also awarded the MBE, played at centre-half for Chelsea, Bradford Park Avenue, Brentford and Fulham and made one appearance for England B.

JOHN PRENTICE, 79, had six months as manager of Scotland in 1966. They drew 1-1 with Brazil before the World Cup Finals, but after defeats by England, Holland and Portugal he returned to club management with Dundee. He had previously been in charge of Arbroath, Falkirk and Clyde. High point of his playing career was lifting the Scottish Cup in 1957 when Falkirk beat Kilmarnock 2-1 in a replay. Prentice, who was also a midfielder with Hearts and Rangers, later moved to Australia and died there.

JIM PAUL, 68, was Aston Villa's kit man for 27 years. Among those attending his funeral were David O'Leary and three of his predecessors as Villa manager, Graham Taylor, John Gregory and Ron Atkinson.

SCOTT CHESHIRE, 78, was Chelsea's historian who saw his first match at Stamford Bridge on Boxing Day 1933. He wrote 'Chelsea, A Complete Record 1905-91', and contributed to the club's programme. He represented Oxford in the first Varsity match played at Wembley in 1953 and was master-in-charge of Repton School football from 1959-67.

MARCH 2006

PETER OSGOOD, 59, epitomised London in the 'Swinging Sixties,' a stylish forward with the showman's touch who won the F.A. Cup with Chelsea and then again with Southampton. Tommy Docherty, building an exciting new team at Stamford Bridge, signed him in 1964 and he scored twice on his debut – a League Cup fifth round tie against Workington. In the 1969-70 season Osgood netted in every round of the F.A. Cup – the last player to do so – completing the run with a diving header as Leeds were beaten 2-1 in a replay. He was also on the mark in Chelsea's 1-1 draw with Real Madrid in the Cup Winners' Cup Final in Athens in 1971 and in the replay which his team won 2-1. Transfer-listed after a training ground row with Docherty's successor, Dave Sexton, he joined Southampton for £275,000 in 1974 and two years later helped them to a shock 1-0 win over Manchester United at Wembley. After a spell on loan with Norwich, Osgood played briefly for Philadelphia before returning to Chelsea for one more season. He made 380 appearances for the club, scoring 150 goals. There were four England caps, including two substitute appearances against Romania and Czechoslovakia during the 1970 World Cup Finals in Mexico. He died after collapsing at a family funeral, having continued his link with Chelsea by working for the club on the hospitality side.

CHARLIE WAYMAN, 84, also played for Southampton and, like Peter Osgood, was one of a select band of players who scored in every round of the F.A. Cup. But whereas Osgood twice lifted the trophy, Wayman's Preston were beaten 3-2 by West Bromwich Albion in the 1954 final. He was a diminutive centre-forward who had a tremendous strike rate at every club he played for in the years immediately after the Second World War. He began at Newcastle, played alongside a young Brian Clough at Middlesbrough and ended his career at Darlington. In 382 League matches for those four clubs, Wayman scored 254 goals, yet never received the international recognition many in the game felt he merited.

JIMMY JOHNSTONE, 61, was one of Celtic's 'Lisbon Lions,' the first British team to win the European Cup. 'Jinking Jimmy' was instrumental in that 1967 triumph when Celtic beat Zurich, Nantes, the Yugoslav side Volvodina, Dukla Prague and then Inter Milan 2-1 in the final held in the Portuguese capital. Johnstone played for Celtic's youth team at 13 and was a ball-boy on senior match-days. He signed in 1961 and became a regular after Jock Stein took over at Parkhead. His fiery temperament often landed him into trouble, but Stein knew how to get the best out of him and he was an integral part of the side that won nine successive Scottish League titles. The little winger made 515 appearances for the club, scoring 129 goals. He shared four Scottish Cup and five League Cup successes and in 2002 was voted Celtic's greatest-ever player by supporters. Johnstone won 23 caps for Scotland and would have gained many more but for a fear of flying. Later, he played for San Jose, Sheffield United, Dundee, Shelbourne and Elgin before retiring. He had suffered from motor neurone disease. As a tribute, Celtic players wore the No 7 on their shorts for the CIS Insurance Cup Final victory over Dunfermline.

ROY CLARKE, 80, was a Manchester City and Wales stalwart who made 369 appearances for the Maine Road club, scored 79 goals and was an F.A. Cup winner. He missed out on the 1955 final when City were beaten 3-1 by Newcastle through injury, but 12 months later helped them to victory over Birmingham by the same scoreline. Clarke, who was inducted into the club's Hall of Fame two years ago, won 22 caps for Wales and netted five goals. He finished his playing career with Stockport, had a brief spell as manager of Northwich Victoria, then returned to manage City's Social Club, a position he held for 25 years.

ARTHUR LEVER, 84, was a solid, dependable full-back with Cardiff in the post-War years, playing every match in their Third Division South title-winning side of the 1946-47 season. That was the start of the club's rise to the top-flight, and although he had moved on when it was achieved, his contribution was valuable. Lever joined Leicester in 1950 for £17,000 – a huge fee in those days – and won his one Wales cap against Scotland at Ninian Park in 1952. An abundance of talented full-backs denied him more. In any other period, he would have been the first-choice. He returned to Wales after four seasons at Filbert Street to play for Newport, before retiring with an achilles injury in 1957.

GEORGE DUNKLEY, 81, was a goalkeeper with Millwall who made his debut against Crystal Palace in 1944. He played 35 times in the War-time Football League South before a broken leg sustained against Arsenal virtually ended his career.

LEN CROWE, 77, had a spell on the books of Crystal Palace and played for a number of Army teams before he was one of the first players to sign for Cambridge United when the club changed their name from Abbey United in 1951. An inside right, he made 131 appearances and scored 29 goals between 1951-55.

APRIL 2006

BILLY KIERNAN, 80, was a goal-scoring left-winger whose tally of 93 in 401 matches for Charlton between 1949-61 ranks him seventh among the club's all-time leading marksmen. He was signed as an amateur by Charlton's legendary manager Jimmy Seed in 1943, but was released two years later. After serving as a captain in the Royal Ulster Rifles, he caught the eye of scouts for a second time when playing in Hong Kong and was recommended to both Charlton and Chelsea by former Derby centre-half Eric Keen, then a coach with the Hong Kong F.A. At first Seed did not recognise him, but was grateful for this second chance as Kiernan became a key player after making his League debut against Stoke in October 1949. He won an England B cap against Germany in 1955 and after leaving Charlton in 1961, played for Guildford.

TELE SANTANA, 74, was one of Brazil's finest coaches, who led the national side into two World Cups. In Spain in 1982 they were involved in one of the most memorable matches in the history of the tournament – a 3-2 second group defeat by Italy, who went on to win the trophy. Four years later in Mexico, Brazil lost a penalty shoot-out to France in the quarter-finals. Santana went on to coach Sao Paulo to the South American Libertadores Cup in successive seasons – and the World Club Cup on each occasion, his team beating first Barcelona, then AC Milan. Previously, he led Atletico Mineiro to the inaugural Brazilian championship in 1971 and was also in charge of Fluminense, Flamengo and Palmeiras. He retired after a stroke in 1996.

JOHN LYALL, 66, was forced to give up playing by injury at the age of 24, but enjoyed a long and successful managerial career with West Ham, continuing and further developing the best footballing traditions of that club. He rose through the coaching ranks at Upton

Park, succeeded Ron Greenwood in 1974 and won the F.A. Cup in his first season with a 2-0 victory over Fulham. The following season, his team reached the Cup Winners' Cup Final, losing 4-2 to Anderlecht. A second F.A. Cup success came in 1980 when Arsenal were defeated by a rare headed goal by Trevor Brooking, the last time a team from outside the top flight won the trophy. A year later, West Ham lost 2-1 to Liverpool in a League Cup Final replay but returned to the old First Division as champions. In 1986, they finished third behind Liverpool and Everton, but were denied a place in Europe by the ban on English clubs following the Heysel disaster. Lyall was sacked after relegation in 1989, returning to management with Ipswich the following summer and enjoying a Second Division title win in 1992 which lifted the club into the newly-formed Premiership. He resigned midway through the 1994-95 season with Ipswich bottom of the table. Less than a fortnight after he died of a heart attack, West Ham reached the F.A. Cup Final for the first time since 1980 by beating Middlesbrough.

BRIAN LABONE, 66, ranked among the finest defenders Everton have ever produced, a player who was involved in two of the most dramatic comebacks in F.A. Cup and World Cup history. After the first, in the F. A. Cup Final of 1966, he lifted the trophy when his side came from 2-0 down to beat Sheffield Wednesday 3-2. Four years later, he was in the England side that lost a two-goal quarter-final lead to West Germany in Mexico. It was Labone's 26th and final cap, his first having come in 1962 against Northern Ireland. He made the first of 534 appearances for Everton in 1958 and was described by his manager Harry Catterick as 'the last of the Corinthians.' He won League championship medals in 1963 when Everton finished six points ahead of Tottenham, and in 1970 when they headed Leeds by nine points. Up to the time of his death, he was working for the club looking after sponsors on match-days.

NORBERT 'NOBBY' LAWTON, 66, captained Preston in their 3-2 defeat by West Ham in the 1964 F.A. Cup Final. The wing-half began his career with Manchester United in 1958, and also played for Brighton and Lincoln, making a total of 311 league appearances for the four clubs.

BRYAN HARVEY, 67, saved six penalties during the 1964-65 season when Northampton were promoted to the First Division, finishing a point behind champions Newcastle. He made 181 appearances in five seasons for the club after a £4,000 move from Blackpool. The goalkeeper started his career at Newcastle.

GERRY BOWLER, 82, was capped three times by Northern Ireland at centre-half while playing for Hull in 1949-50. He was also with Portsmouth and Millwall, making 211 league appearances, after starting out with Distillery.

MAY 2006

LES OLIVE, 78, joined Manchester United straight from school as a 14-year-old office boy and rose to become one of the game's leading administrators after fulfilling a boyhood dream by keeping goal for the first team in two games in 1953. He took over as club secretary when Walter Crickmer was among those who died in the 1958 Munich air crash and held the position for three decades. Olive later became a director and in total served the club for 64 years.

KEN MALCOLM, 79, was part of the Alf Ramsey revolution during which Ipswich rose from obscurity to become champions of England in six seasons. They won the Third Division South in 1957, Division Two in 1961 when Malcolm missed only one game, and Division One 12 months later. The rugged full-back, who joined the club from Arbroath, sustained a slipped disc three matches into that season, but had the distinction of captaining Ipswich in their first European match at Portman Road – a 10-0 win over Maltese side Floriana in the preliminary round of the European Cup. Malcolm retired in 1964 after 293 appearances, then helped new manager Jackie Milburn launch a youth system that would pay handsome dividends in the years to come.

KEVIN O'FLANAGAN, 86, was Ireland's best-known sporting figure in the years immediately before and after the Second World War. He represented his country at football and rugby and was known as the 'Flying Doctor,' winning national sprint and long jump titles. He was a member of the International Olympic Committee from 1976-1995 and played a leading role in the field of sports medicine. O'Flanagan, an inside forward, scored on his international debut in a World Cup qualifier against Norway in 1937, going on to win ten caps. He played club football for Bohemians and had a season as an amateur with Arsenal in 1945-46.

JUNE 2006

BOB FERGUSON, 88, joined York from Middlesbrough in the summer of 1939 and kept goal for the club during the War. He finally made his league debut for them against Chester in a Third Division North match in 1947, before moving on to Peterborough and ending his career with Goole. He also played Bradford League cricket and was a prolific-scoring wicketkeeper.

JIMMY MCNAB, 66, made 539 league appearances, more than half of them for Sunderland, where he was best known for his role at left-half in the 1964 Second Division promotion-winning team alongside the likes of Jim Montgomery, Charlie Hurley and Len Ashurst. He missed out on a testimonial in those days, but in 1999 became the first player to have a match in his honour at the Stadium of Light. McNab, who twice sustained a broken leg, also played more than 200 games for Preston before finishing his career at Stockport.

QUOTE-UNQUOTE

'A few clubs are richer than ever. All too often the source of this wealth are individuals with little or no interest in the game, who happen upon football as a means of serving some hidden agenda. They throw pornographic amounts of money at it, but do not understand that football is more about grass-roots than idols' – **Sepp Blatter**, FIFA president.

'I felt like Bruce Willis' – **Jose Mourinho**, Chelsea manager, taking a break from football to ride the Armageddon roller-coaster at Euro Disney.

'I'd love to tell you how I feel, but I can't. I'm under strict instructions from my wife. I can't keep giving the F.A. the kind of money (in fines) I've given them over the years' – **Graeme Souness**, former Newcastle manager, declining to comment on Alan Shearer's disallowed, over-the-line header against Wigan.

'There is no problem with me and Clive (Woodward) in any shape or form. I haven't got a problem. We have a terrific relationship – we get on ever so well' – **Harry Redknapp** tries to scotch suggestions of a rift between him and Southampton's director of football during his spell at St Mary's.

'People think we don't care about the game, but when I walked out of Windsor Park I felt lower than a snake's belly' – **Rio Ferdinand**, England defender, after the World Cup qualifying defeat by Northern Ireland.

'I would love this place to be my garden' – **Thierry Henry**, Arsenal striker, dreams of adopting the Highbury pitch after the move to a new stadium.

'British players are brought up to go out at 13 and drink alcopops, so you can't expect them to join a club and stop completely. There's a lack of discipline in this country' – **Sam Allardyce**, Bolton manager.

RECORDS SECTION

INDEX

GOALSCORING

(† Football League pre 1992-3. * Home team)

Highest: *Arbroath 36, Bon Accord (Aberdeen) 0, in **Scottish Cup** 1st Round, Sept. 12, 1885. On same day, also in Scottish Cup 1st Round, Dundee Harp beat Aberdeen Rov. 35-0.

Internationals: England 15, *France 0, in Paris, 1906 (Amateur); England 13 *Ireland 0, in Belfast, Feb. 18, 1882 (record in U.K.); *England 9, Scotland 3, at Wembley, Apr. 15, 1961; Biggest England win at Wembley: 9-0 v Luxembourg (E.Champ), Dec. 15, 1982.

Other record wins: Scotland: 11-0 v Ireland (Glasgow, Feb. 23, 1901); **Northern Ireland:** 7-0 v Wales (Belfast, Feb. 1, 1930); **Wales:** 11-0 v Ireland (Wrexham, Mar. 3, 1888); **Rep. of Ireland:** 8-0 v Malta (E. Champ., Dublin, Nov. 16, 1983).

Record International defeats: England: 1-7 v Hungary (Budapest, May 23, 1954); **Scotland:** 3-9 v England (Wembley, April 15, 1961); **Ireland:** 0-13 v England (Belfast, Feb. 18, 1882); **Wales:** 0-9 v Scotland (Glasgow, March 23, 1878); **Rep. of Ireland:** 0-7 v Brazil (Uberlandia, May 27, 1982).

World Cup: Qualifying round – Australia 31, American Samoa 0, world record Int. score (April 11, 2001); Australia 22, Tonga 0 (April 9, 2001); Iran 19, Guam 0 (Nov. 25, 2000); Maldives 0, Iran 17 (June 2, 1997). **Finals – highest scores:** Hungary 10, El Salvador 1 (Spain, June 15, 1982); Hungary 9, S. Korea 0 (Switzerland, June 17, 1954); Yugoslavia 9, Zaire 0 (W. Germany, June 18, 1974).

European Championship: Qualifying round – highest scorers: Spain 12, Malta 1 (Seville, Dec. 21, 1983); – France 10, Azerbaijan 0 (Auxerre, Sept. 6, 1995). **Finals – highest score:** Holland 6, Yugoslavia 1 (Quarter-final, Rotterdam, June 25, 2000).

F.A. Cup: *Preston N.E. 26, Hyde 0, 1st Round, Oct. 15, 1887.

League Cup: *West Ham Utd. 10, Bury 0 (2nd Round, 2nd Leg, Oct 25, 1983); *Liverpool 10, Fulham 0 (2nd Round, 1st Leg, Sept. 23, 1986). **Record Aggregates:** Liverpool 13, Fulham 2 (10-0h, 3-2a), Sept. 23-Oct. 7, 1986; West Ham Utd. 12, Bury 1 (2-1a, 10-0h), Oct. 4-25, 1983; Liverpool 11, Exeter City 0 (5-0h, 6-0a), Oct 7-28, 1981.

F.A. Premier League (beginning 1992-3): *Manchester Utd. 9, Ipswich Town 0, Mar. 4, 1995. **Record away win:** Manchester Utd. 8, *Nott'm. Forest 1, Feb. 6, 1999.

Highest aggregate scores in Premier League – 9: Manchester Utd. 9, Ipswich Town 0, Mar. 4, 1995; Nott'm. Forest 1, Manchester Utd. 8, Feb. 6, 1999; Blackburn Rov. 7, Sheff. Wed. 2, Aug. 25, 1997; Southampton 6, Manchester Utd. 3, Oct. 26, 1996; Tottenham 7, Southampton 2, Mar. 11, 2000; Tottenham 4, Arsenal 5, Nov. 13, 2004.

†Football League (First Division): *Aston Villa 12, Accrington 2, Mar. 12, 1892; *Tottenham 10, Everton 4, Oct. 11, 1958 (highest 1st. Div. aggregate that century); *W.B.A. 12, Darwen 0, Apr. 4, 1892; *Nott'm. Forest 12, Leicester Fosse 0, Apr. 21, 1909. **Record away win:** Sunderland 9, *Newcastle Utd. 1, Dec. 5, 1908; Wolves 9, *Cardiff City 1, Sept. 3, 1955; W.B.A 8, *Wolves 0, Dec. 27, 1893.

New First Division (beginning 1992-3): *Bolton Wand. 7, Swindon Town 0, Mar. 8, 1997; Sunderland 7, Oxford Utd. 0, Sept. 19, 1998. **Record away win:** Birmingham City 7, *Stoke City 0, Jan. 10, 1998; Birmingham City 7, *Oxford Utd. 0, Dec. 12, 1998.

Record aggregates (11 goals): *Grimsby Town 6, Burnley 5, Oct. 29, 2002; *Burnley 4, Watford 7, Apr. 5, 2003.

†**Second Division:** *Manchester City 11, Lincoln City 3, Mar. 23, 1895; *Newcastle Utd. 13, Newport County 0, Oct. 5, 1946; *Small Heath 12, Walsall Town Swifts 0, Dec. 17, 1892; *Darwen 12, Walsall 0, Dec. 26, 1896; *Small Heath 12, Doncaster Rov. 0, Apr. 11, 1903. **Record away win:** Sheffield Utd. 10, *Burslem Port Vale 0, Dec. 10, 1892.

New Second Division (beginning 1992-3): *Hartlepool Utd. 1, Plymouth Argyle 8, May 7, 1994; *Hartlepool Utd. 8, Grimsby Town 1, Sept. 12, 2003.

†**Third Division:** *Gillingham 10, Chesterfield 0, Sept. 5, 1987; *Tranmere Rov. 9, Accrington Stanley 0, Apr. 18, 1959; *Brighton & H.A. 9, Southend Utd. 1, Nov. 22, 1965; *Brentford 9, Wrexham 0, Oct. 15, 1963. **Record away win:** Fulham 8, *Halifax Town 0, Sept. 16, 1969.

New Third Premier Division (beginning 1992-3): *Barnet 1, Peterborough Utd. 9, Sept. 5, 1998.

†**Third Division (North):** *Stockport Co. 13, Halifax Town 0 (still joint biggest win in F. League – see Div. 2) Jan. 6, 1934; *Tranmere Rov. 13, Oldham Athletic 4, Dec. 26, 1935. *(17 is highest Football League aggregate score).* **Record away win:** Barnsley 9, *Accrington Stanley 0, Feb. 3, 1934.

†**Third Division (South):** *Luton Town 12, Bristol Rov. 0, Apr. 13, 1936; *Bristol City 9, Gillingham 4, Jan. 15, 1927; *Gillingham 9, Exeter City 4, Jan. 7, 1951. **Record away win:** Walsall 8, *Northampton Town 0, Apr. 8, 1947.

†**Fourth Division:** *Oldham Athletic 11, Southport 0, Dec. 26, 1962; *Hartlepool Utd. 10, Barrow 1, Apr. 4, 1959; *Wrexham 10, Hartlepool Utd. 1, Mar. 3, 1962. **Record away win:** Rotherham Utd. 8, *Crewe Alexandra 1, Sept. 8, 1973.

Scottish Premier Division – Highest aggregate: 11 goals – Celtic 8, Hamilton 3, Jan. 3, 1987; Motherwell 5, Aberdeen 6, Oct. 20, 1999. **Other highest team scores:** Aberdeen 8, Motherwell 0 (Mar. 26, 1979); Kilmarnock 1, Rangers 8 (Sept. 6, 1980); Hamilton 0, Celtic 8 (Nov. 5, 1988).

Scottish League Div. 1: *Celtic 11, Dundee 0, Oct. 26, 1895. **Record away win:** Hibs 11, *Airdrie 1, Oct. 24, 1959.

Scottish League Div. 2: *Airdrieonians 15, Dundee Wanderers 1, Dec. 1, 1894. (biggest win in history of League football in Britain).

Record modern Scottish League aggregate (12 goals): Brechin City 5, Cowdenbeath 7, Div. 2, Jan. 18, 2003.

Record British score since 1900: Stirling Albion 20, Selkirk 0 (Scottish Cup 1st. Round, Dec. 8, 1984). Winger Davie Thompson (7 goals) was one of 9 Stirling players to score.

LEAGUE GOALS – BEST IN SEASON (Before restructure in 1992)

Div.		Goals	Games
1	W.R. (Dixie) Dean, Everton, 1927-8	60	39
2	George Camsell, Middlesbrough, 1926-7	59	37
3(S)	Joe Payne, Luton Town, 1936-7	55	39
3(N)	Ted Harston, Mansfield Town, 1936-7	55	41
3	Derek Reeves, Southampton, 1959-60	39	46
4	Terry Bly, Peterborough Utd., 1960-1	52	46

(Since restructure in 1992)

Div.		Goals	Games
1	Guy Whittingham, Portsmouth, 1992-3	42	46
2	Jimmy Quinn, Reading, 1993-4	35	46
3	Andy Morrell, Wrexham, 2002-03	34	45

F.A. PREMIER LEAGUE – BEST IN SEASON

Andy Cole **34 goals** (Newcastle Utd. – 40 games, 1993-4); Alan Shearer **34 goals** (Blackburn Rov. – 42 games, 1994-5).

FOOTBALL LEAGUE – BEST MATCH HAULS
(Before restructure in 1992)

Div.		Goals

1	Ted Drake (Arsenal), away to Aston Villa, Dec. 14, 1935	7
	James Ross (Preston N.E.) v Stoke City, Oct 6, 1888	7
2	*Neville (Tim) Coleman (Stoke City) v Lincoln City, Feb. 23, 1957 .	7
	Tommy Briggs (Blackburn Rov.) v Bristol Rov., Feb. 5, 1955	7
3(S)	Joe Payne (Luton Town) v Bristol Rov., April 13, 1936	10
3(N)	Robert ('Bunny') Bell (Tranmere Rov.) v Oldham Athletic, Dec. 26, 1935 – he also missed a penalty	9
3	Barrie Thomas (Scunthorpe Utd.) v Luton Town, April 24, 1965	5
	Keith East (Swindon Town) v Mansfield Town, Nov. 20, 1965	5
	Steve Earle (Fulham) v Halifax Town, Sept. 16, 1969	5
	Alf Wood (Shrewsbury Town) v Blackburn Rov., Oct. 2, 1971	5
	Tony Caldwell (Bolton Wand.) v Walsall, Sept 10, 1983	5
	Andy Jones (Port Vale) v Newport Co., May 4, 1987	5
4	Bert Lister (Oldham Athletic) v Southport, Dec. 26, 1962	6

* Scored from the wing

(SINCE RESTRUCTURE IN 1992)

Div.   *Goals*

1   **4** in match – John Durnin (Oxford Utd. v Luton Town, 1992-3); Guy Whittingham (Portsmouth v Bristol Rov. 1992-3); Craig Russell (Sunderland v Millwall, 1995-6); David Connolly (Wolves at Bristol City 1998-9); Darren Byfield (Rotherham Utd. at Millwall, 2002–03); David Connolly (Wimbledon at Bradford City, 2002–03); Marlon Harewood (Nott'm. F. v Stoke City, 2002–03); Michael Chopra (Watford at Burnley, 2002–03); Robert Earnshaw (Cardiff City v Gillingham, 2003–04).

2   **5** in match – Paul Barnes (Burnley v Stockport Co., 1996-7); Robert Taylor (all 5, Gillingham at Burnley, 1998-9); Lee Jones (all 5, Wrexham v Cambridge Utd., 2001-02).

3   **5** in match – Tony Naylor (Crewe Alexandra v Colchester Utd., 1992-3); Steve Butler (Cambridge Utd. v Exeter City, 1993-4); Guiliano Grazioli (Peterborough Utd. at Barnet, 1998-9).

Lge. 1   **5** in match – Juan Ugarte (Wrexham at Hartlepool Utd., 2004-05).

F.A. PREMIER LEAGUE – BEST MATCH HAUL

5 goals in match: Andy Cole (Manchester Utd. v Ipswich Town, Mar. 4, 1995); Alan Shearer (Newcastle Utd. v Sheffield Wed., Sept. 19, 1999).

SCOTTISH LEAGUE

Div.		*Goals*
	Kris Boyd (Kilmarnock) v Dundee Utd., Sept. 25, 2004	5
Prem.	Kenny Miller (Rangers) v St. Mirren, Nov. 4, 2000	5
	Marco Negri (Rangers) v Dundee Utd., Aug. 23, 1997	5
	Paul Sturrock (Dundee Utd.) v Morton, Nov. 17, 1984	5
1	Jimmy McGrory (Celtic) v Dunfermline Athletic, Jan. 14, 1928 ...	8
1	Owen McNally (Arthurlie) v Armadale, Oct. 1, 1927	8
2	Jim Dyet (King's Park) v Forfar Athletic, Jan. 2, 1930, on his debut for the club	8
2	John Calder (Morton) v Raith Rov., April 18, 1936	8
2	Norman Haywood (Raith Rov.) v Brechin, Aug. 20, 1937	8

SCOTTISH LEAGUE – BEST IN SEASON

Prem.	Brian McClair (Celtic, 1986-7)	35
	Henrik Larsson (Celtic, 2000-01)	35
1	William McFadyen (Motherwell, 1931-2)	53
2	*Jimmy Smith (Ayr, 1927-8 – 38 appearances)	66

(*British record)

CUP FOOTBALL

Scottish Cup: John Petrie (Arbroath) v Bon Accord, at Arbroath, 1st Round, Sept. 12, 1885 .... **13**

F.A. Cup: Ted MacDougall (Bournemouth) v Margate, 1st Round, Nov. 20, 1971 .... **9**

F.A. Cup Final: Billy Townley (Blackburn Rov.) v Sheffield Wed., at Kennington Oval, 1890; Jimmy Logan (Notts Co.) v Bolton Wand., at Everton, 1894; Stan Mortensen (Blackpool) v Bolton Wand., at Wembley, 1953 .... **3**

League Cup: Frank Bunn (Oldham Athletic) v Scarborough (3rd Round), Oct. 25, 1989 .... **6**

Scottish League Cup: Jim Fraser (Ayr) v Dumbarton, Aug. 13, 1952; Jim Forrest (Rangers) v Stirling Albion, Aug. 17, 1966 .... **5**

Scottish Cup: Most goals in match since war: **10** by **Gerry Baker** (St. Mirren) in 15-0 win (1st. Round) v Glasgow Univ., Jan 30, 1960; **9** by his brother **Joe Baker** (Hibernian) in 15-1 win (2nd. Round) v Peebles Rov., Feb. 11, 1961.

AGGREGATE LEAGUE SCORING RECORDS

Goals

* Arthur Rowley (1947-65, WBA, Fulham, Leicester City, Shrewsbury Town) **434**

† Jimmy McGrory (1922-38, Celtic, Clydebank) **410**

Hughie Gallacher (1921-39, Airdrieonians, Newcastle Utd., Chelsea, Derby Co., Notts Co., Grimsby Town, Gateshead) **387**

William ('Dixie') Dean (1923-37, Tranmere Rov., Everton, Notts County) **379**

Hugh Ferguson (1916-30, Motherwell, Cardiff City, Dundee) **362**

■ Jimmy Greaves (1957-71, Chelsea, Tottenham, West Ham Utd.) **357**

Steve Bloomer (1892-1914, Derby Co., Middlesbrough, Derby Co.) **352**

George Camsell (1923-39, Durham City, Middlesbrough) **348**

Dave Halliday (1920-35, St. Mirren, Dundee, Sunderland, Arsenal, Manchester City, Clapton Orient) **338**

John Aldridge (1979-98, Newport, Oxford Utd., Liverpool, Tranmere Rov.) **329**

John Atyeo (1951-66, Bristol City) **315**

Joe Smith (1908-29, Bolton Wand., Stockport Co.) **315**

Victor Watson (1920-36, West Ham Utd., Southampton) **312**

Harry Johnson (1919-36, Sheffield Utd., Mansfield Town) **309**

Bob McPhail (1923–1939, Airdrie, Rangers) **306**

(* **Rowley** scored 4 for WBA, 27 for Fulham, 251 for Leicester City, 152 for Shrewsbury Town. ■ **Greaves's** 357 is record top-division total (he also scored 9 League goals for AC Milan). **Aldridge** also scored 33 League goals for Real Sociedad. † **McGrory** scored 397 for Celtic, 13 for Clydebank.)

Most League goals for one club: 349 – Dixie Dean (Everton 1925-37); **326 – George Camsell** (Middlesbrough 1925-39); **315 – John Atyeo** (Bristol City 1951-66); **306 – Vic Watson** (West Ham Utd. 1920-35); **291 – Steve Bloomer** (Derby Co. 1892-1906, 1910-14); **259 – Arthur Chandler** (Leicester City 1923-35); **255 – Nat Lofthouse** (Bolton Wand. 1946-61); **251 – Arthur Rowley** (Leicester City 1950-58).

Over 500 Goals: Jimmy McGrory (Celtic, Clydebank and Scotland) scored a total of 550 goals in his first-class career (1922-38).

Over 1,000 goals: Brazil's **Pele** is reputedly the game's all-time highest scorer with 1,282 goals in 1,365 matches (1956-77), but many of them were scored in friendlies for his club, Santos. He scored his 1,000th goal, a penalty, against Vasco da Gama in the Maracana Stadium, Rio, on November 19, 1969. Pele (born Oct. 23, 1940) played regularly for Santos from the age of 16. During his career, he was sent off only once. He played 95 'A' Internationals for Brazil and in their World Cup-winning teams in 1958 and 1970. ● Pele (Edson Arantes do Nascimento) was subsequently Brazil's Minister for Sport. He never played at Wembley, apart from being filmed there scoring a goal for a commercial. Aged 57, Pele received an 'honorary knighthood' (Knight Commander of the British Empire) from the Queen at Buckingham Palace on December 3, 1997.

MOST LEAGUE GOALS IN SEASON: DEAN'S 60

W.R. ('Dixie') Dean, Everton centre-forward, created a League scoring record in 1927-8 with an aggregate of 60 in 39 First Division matches. He also scored three goals in F.A. Cup-ties, and 19 in representative games (total for the season 82).

  George Camsell, of Middlesbrough, previously held the record with 59 goals in 37 Second Division matches in 1926-7, his total for the season being 75.

SHEARER'S RECORD 'FIRST'

Alan Shearer (Blackburn Rov.) is the only player to score more than 30 top-division goals in 3 successive seasons since the war: 31 in 1993-4, 34 in 1994-5, 31 in 1995-6. **Thierry Henry** (Arsenal) is the first player to score more than 20 Premiership goals in five consecutive seasons (2002–6). **David Halliday** (Sunderland) topped 30 First Div. goals in 4 consecutive seasons with totals of 38, 36, 36 and 49 from 1925-26 to 1928-29.

MOST GOALS IN A MATCH

September 12, 1885: John Petrie set the all-time British individual record for a first-class match when, in Arbroath's 36-0 win against Bon Accord (Scottish Cup first round), he scored **13**
April 13, 1936: Joe Payne set the still-existing individual record on his debut as a centre-forward, for Luton Town v Bristol Rov. (Div. III South). In a 12-0 win he scored **10**

ROWLEY'S ALL-TIME RECORD

Arthur Rowley is English football's **top club scorer** with a total of 464 goals for WBA, Fulham, Leicester City and Shrewsbury Town (1947-65). They comprised 434 in the League, 26 F.A. Cup, 4 League Cup.

  Jimmy Greaves is second with a total of 420 goals for Chelsea, AC Milan, Tottenham and West Ham Utd., made up of 366 League, 35 F.A. Cup, 10 League Cup and 9 in Europe. He also scored nine goals for Italian club AC Milan.

  John Aldridge retired as a player at the end of the season 1997-98 with a career total of 329 Football League goals for Newport, Oxford Utd., Liverpool and Tranmere Rov. (1979-98). In all competitions for those clubs he scored 410 goals in 737 apps. He also scored 45 goals in 63 games for Spanish club Real Sociedad.

MOST GOALS IN INTERNATIONAL MATCHES

THIRTEEN BY
Archie Thompson for Australia v American Samoa in World Cup (Oceania Group qualifier) at Coff's Harbour, New South Wales, April 11, 2001. Result: 31-0.

SEVEN BY
Stanley Harris for England v France in Amateur International in Paris, November 1, 1906. Result: 15-0.

SIX BY
Nat Lofthouse for Football League v Irish League, at Wolves, September 24, 1952. Result: 7-1.
Joe Bambrick for Ireland against Wales, in Belfast, February 1, 1930. Result: 7-0.
W.C. Jordan in Amateur International for England v France, at Park Royal, March 23, 1908. Result: 12-0.
Vivian Woodward for England v Holland in Amateur International, at Chelsea, December 11, 1909. Result: 9-1.

FIVE BY
Howard Vaughton for England v Ireland (Belfast) February 18, 1882. Result: 13-0.
Steve Bloomer for England v Wales (Cardiff City) March 16, 1896. Result: 9-1.

Hughie Gallacher for Scotland against Ireland (Belfast), February 23, 1929. Result: 7-3.
Willie Hall for England v Northern Ireland, at Old Trafford, November 16, 1938. Five in succession (first three in 3½ mins. – fastest International hat-trick). Result: 7-0.
Malcolm Macdonald for England v Cyprus (Wembley) April 16, 1975. Result: 5-0.
Hughie Gallacher for Scottish League against Irish League (Belfast) November 11, 1925. Result: 7-3.
Barney Battles for Scottish League against Irish League (Firhill Park, Glasgow) October 31, 1928. Result: 8-2.
Bobby Flavell for Scottish League against Irish League (Belfast) April 30, 1947. Result: 7-4.
Joe Bradford for Football League v Irish League (Everton) September 25, 1929. Result: 7-2.
Albert Stubbins for Football League v Irish League (Blackpool) October 18, 1950. Result: 6-3.
Brian Clough for Football League v Irish League (Belfast) September 23, 1959. Result: 5-0.

LAST ENGLAND PLAYER TO SCORE . . .

3 goals: Peter Crouch v Jamaica (6–0), friendly, Old Trafford, Jun. 3, 2006.
4 goals: Ian Wright v San Marino (7-1), World Cup qual., Bologna, Nov. 17, 1993.
5 goals: Malcolm Macdonald v Cyprus (5-0), Eur. Champ. qual., Wembley, Apr. 16, 1975.

INTERNATIONAL TOP SHOTS

		Goals	Games
England	– Bobby Charlton (1958-70)	49	106
N. Ireland	– David Healy (2000-6)	19	49
Scotland	– Denis Law (1958-74)	30	55
	– Kenny Dalglish (1971-86)	30	102
Wales	– Ian Rush (1980-96)	28	73
Rep. of I.	– Robbie Keane (1998-2006)	26	66

ENGLAND'S TOP MARKSMEN

(As at start of season 2006-07)

	Goals	Games
Bobby Charlton (1958-70)	49	106
Gary Lineker (1984-92)	48	80
Jimmy Greaves (1959-67)	44	57
Michael Owen (1998-2006)	36	80
Tom Finney (1946-58)	30	76
Nat Lofthouse (1950-58)	30	33
Alan Shearer (1992-2000)	30	63
Vivian Woodward (1903-11)	29	23
Steve Bloomer (1895-1907)	28	23
David Platt (1989-96)	27	62
Bryan Robson (1979-91)	26	90
Geoff Hurst (1966-72)	24	49
Stan Mortensen (1947-53)	23	25
Tommy Lawton (1938-48)	22	23
Mike Channon (1972-77)	21	46
Kevin Keegan (1972-82)	21	63

CONSECUTIVE GOALS FOR ENGLAND

Steve Bloomer scored in TEN consecutive appearances (19 goals) for **England** between March 1895 and March 1899.

Jimmy Greaves scored 11 goals in five consecutive England matches from the start of season 1960–61.

Paul Mariner scored in five consecutive **England** appearances (7 goals) between November 1981 and June 1982.

ENGLAND'S TOP FINAL SERIES MARKSMAN

Gary Lineker with 6 goals at 1986 World Cup in Mexico.

ENGLAND TOP SCORERS IN COMPETITIVE INTERNATIONALS

Gary Lineker 22 goals in 39 matches; **Michael Owen** 22 in 48; **Alan Shearer** 20 in 31.

MOST ENGLAND HAT-TRICKS

Jimmy Greaves 6; **Gary Lineker** 5.

MOST GOALS FOR ENGLAND U-21S

13 – Alan Shearer (11 apps.) Francis Jeffers (13 apps.)

'GOLDEN GOAL' DECIDERS

The Football League, in an experiment to avoid penalty shoot-outs, introduced a new 'golden goal' system in the 1994-95 **Auto Windscreens Shield** to decide matches in the knock-out stages of the competition in which scores were level after 90 minutes. The first goal scored in overtime ended play.

Iain Dunn (Huddersfield Town) became the first player in British football to settle a match by this sudden-death method. His 107th-minute goal beat Lincoln City 3-2 on Nov. 30, 1994, and to mark his 'moment in history' he was presented with a golden football trophy.

The AWS Final of 1995 was decided when **Paul Tait** headed the only goal for Birmingham City against Carlisle Utd. 13 minutes into overtime – the first time a match at Wembley had been decided by the 'golden goal' formula.

First major International tournament match to be decided by sudden death was the Final of the **1996 European Championship** at Wembley in which Germany beat Czech Rep. 2-1 by **Oliver Bierhoff's** goal in the 95th minute.

In the **1998 World Cup Finals** (2nd Round), host country France beat Paraguay 1-0 on **Laurent Blanc's** Golden Goal (114 mins.).

France won the **2000 European Championship** with Golden Goals in the semi-final, 2-1 v Portugal (Zinedine Zidane pen, 117 mins), and in the Final, 2-1 v Italy (David Trezeguet, 103 mins).

Galatasaray (Turkey) won the **European Super Cup** 2-1 against Real Madrid (Monaco, August 25, 2000) with a 103rd min Golden Goal, a penalty.

Liverpool won the **UEFA Cup** 5-4 against Alaves with a 117th min Golden Goal, an own goal, in the Final in Dortmund (May 19, 2001).

In the **2002 World Cup Finals**, 3 matches were decided by Golden Goals: in the 2nd Round Senegal beat Sweden 2-1 (Henri Camara, 104 mins) and South Korea beat Italy 2-1 (Ahn Jung – hwan, 117 mins); in the Quarter-final, Turkey beat Senegal 1-0 (Ilhan Mansiz, 94 mins).

France won the **2003 FIFA Confederations Cup** Final against Cameroon (Paris, June 29) with a 97th-minute Golden Goal by Thierry Henry.

Doncaster Rov. won promotion to Football League with a 110th-minute Golden Goal winner (3–2) in the Conference Play-off Final against Dagenham & Redbridge at Stoke City (May 10, 2003).

Germany won the **Women's World Cup Final** 2-1 v Sweden (Los Angeles, October 12, 2003) with a 98th-minute Golden Goal.

GOLD TURNS TO SILVER

Starting with the 2003 Finals of the UEFA Cup and Champions' League/European Cup, UEFA introduced a new rule by which a Silver Goal could decide the winners if the scores were 'level' after 90 minutes.

Team leading after 15 minutes' extra time win match. If sides level, a second period of 15 minutes is to be played. If still no winner, result to be decided by penalty shoot-out.

UEFA said the change was made because the Golden Goal put too much pressure on referees and prompted teams to play negative football.

Although both 2003 Euro Finals went to extra time, neither was decided by a Silver Goal. The new rule applied in the 2004 European Championship Finals, and Greece won their Semi-final against the Czech Republic with a 105th-minute Silver Goal.

The **International Board** decided (Feb. 28 2004) that the Golden/Silver Goal rule was 'unfair' and that from July 1 competitive International matches level after extra time would, when necessary, be settled on penalties.

PREMIERSHIP TOP SHOTS (1992-2006)

Alan Shearer	260	Jimmy Floyd Hasselbaink	125
Andy Cole	185	Dwight Yorke	122
Thierry Henry	164	Ian Wright	113
Robbie Fowler	159	Dion Dublin	111
Les Ferdinand	150	Matthew Le Tissier	101
Teddy Sheringham	145	(As at start of season 2006-07)	
Michael Owen	125		

LEAGUE GOAL RECORDS

The highest goal-scoring aggregates in the Football League, Premier and Scottish League are as follows:

FOR

	Goals	Games	Club	Season
Prem.	97	38	Manchester Utd.	1999-2000
Div. 1	128	42	Aston Villa	1930-1
New Div. 1	108	46	Manchester City	2001-02
New Champ.	99	46	Reading	2005-06
Div. 2	122	42	Middlesbrough	1926-7
New Div. 2	89	46	Millwall	2000-01
New Lge. 1	87	46	Luton Town	2004-05
Div. 3(S)	127	42	Millwall	1927-8
Div. 3(N)	128	42	Bradford City	1928-9
Div. 3	111	46	Q.P.R.	1961-2
New Div. 3	96	46	Luton Town	2001-02
New Lge. 2	90	46	Yeovil Town	2004-05
Div. 4	134	46	Peterborough Utd.	1960-1
Scot. Prem.	105	38	Celtic	2003-04
Scot. L. 1	132	34	Hearts	1957-8
Scot. L. 2	142	34	Raith Rov.	1937-8
Scot. L. 3 (Modern)	130	36	Gretna	2004-05

AGAINST

	Goals	Games	Club	Season
Prem.	100	42	Swindon Town	1993-4
Div. 1	125	42	Blackpool	1930-1
New Div. 1	102	46	Stockport Co.	2001-02
New Champ.	86	46	Crewe Alexandra	2004-05
Div. 2	141	34	Darwen	1898-9
New Div. 2	102	46	Chester City	1992-3
New Lge. 1	98	46	Stockport Co.	2004-05
Div. 3(S)	135	42	Merthyr T.	1929-30
Div. 3(N)	136	42	Nelson	1927-8
Div. 3	123	46	Accrington S.	1959-60
New Div. 3	113	46	Doncaster Rov.	1997-8
New Lge. 2	85	46	Kidderminster Harriers	2004-05
Div. 4	109	46	Hartlepool Utd.	1959-60
Scot. Prem.	100	36	Morton	1984-5
Scot. Prem.	100	44	Morton	1987-8

Scot. L. 1	137	38	Leith A.	1931-2
Scot. L. 2	146	38	Edinburgh City	1931-2
Scot. L. 3 (Modern)	118	36	East Stirling	2003-04

BEST DEFENSIVE RECORDS – *Denotes under old offside law

Div.	Goals Agst.	Games	Club	Season
Prem.	15	38	Chelsea	2004-05
1	16	42	Liverpool	1978-9
1	*15	22	Preston N.E.	1888-9
New Div. 1	28	46	Sunderland	1998-9
New Champ.	35	46	Wigan Athletic	2004-05
2	18	28	Liverpool	1893-4
2	*22	34	Sheffield Wed.	1899-1900
2	24	42	Birmingham City	1947-8
2	24	42	Crystal Palace	1978-9
New Div. 2	25	46	Wigan Athletic	2002-03
New Lge. 1	50	46	Colchester Utd.	2004-05
3(S)	*21	42	Southampton	1921-2
3(S)	30	42	Cardiff City	1946-7
3(N)	*21	38	Stockport Co.	1921-2
3(N)	21	46	Port Vale	1953-4
3	30	46	Middlesbrough	1986-7
New Div. 3	20	46	Gillingham	1995-6
New Lge. 2	42	46	Scunthorpe Utd.	2004-05
4	25	46	Lincoln City	1980-1

SCOTTISH LEAGUE

Div.	Goals Agst.	Games	Club	Season
Prem.	18	38	Celtic	2001-02
1	*12	22	Dundee	1902-3
1	*14	38	Celtic	1913-14
2	20	38	Morton	1966-7
2	*29	38	Clydebank	1922-3
2	29	36	East Fife	1995-6
New Div. 3	21	36	Brechin	1995-6

TOP SCORERS (LEAGUE ONLY)

		Goals	Div.
2005–06	Thierry Henry (Arsenal)	27	Prem.
2004-05	Stuart Elliott (Hull City)	27	Lge. 1
	Phil Jevons (Yeovil Town)	27	Lge. 2
	Dean Windass (Bradford City)	27	Lge. 1
2003-04	Thierry Henry (Arsenal)	30	Prem
2002-03	Andy Morrell (Wrexham)	34	3
2001-02	Shaun Goater (Manchester City)	28	1
	Bobby Zamora (Brighton & H.A.)	28	2
2000-01	Bobby Zamora (Brighton & H.A.)	28	3
1999-00	Kevin Phillips (Sunderland)	30	Prem.
1998-9	Lee Hughes (W.B.A.)	31	1
1997-8	Pierre van Hooijdonk (Nott'm Forest)	29	1
	Kevin Phillips (Sunderland)	29	1
1996-7	Graeme Jones (Wigan Athletic)	31	3
1995-6	Alan Shearer (Blackburn Rov.)	31	Prem.

1994-5	Alan Shearer (Blackburn Rov.)	34	Prem.
1993-4	Jimmy Quinn (Reading)	35	2
1992-3	Guy Whittingham (Portsmouth)	42	1
1991-2	Ian Wright (Crystal Palace 5, Arsenal 24)	29	1
1990-1	Teddy Sheringham (Millwall)	33	2
1989-90	Mick Quinn (Newcastle Utd.)	32	2
1988-9	Steve Bull (Wolves)	37	3
1987-8	Steve Bull (Wolves)	34	4
1986-7	Clive Allen (Tottenham)	33	1
1985-6	Gary Lineker (Everton)	30	1
1984-5	Tommy Tynan (Plymouth Argyle)	31	3
	John Clayton (Tranmere Rov.)	31	4
1983-4	Trevor Senior (Reading)	36	4
1982-3	Luther Blissett (Watford)	27	1
1981-2	Keith Edwards (Hull City 1, Sheffield Utd. 35)	36	4
1980-1	Tony Kellow (Exeter City)	25	3
1979-80	Clive Allen (Queens Park Rangers)	28	2
1978-9	Ross Jenkins (Watford)	29	3
1977-8	Steve Phillips (Brentford)	32	4
	Alan Curtis (Swansea City)	32	4
1976-7	Peter Ward (Brighton & H.A.)	32	3
1975-6	Dixie McNeil (Hereford)	35	3
1974-5	Dixie McNeil (Hereford)	31	3
1973-4	Brian Yeo (Gillingham)	31	4
1972-3	Bryan (Pop) Robson (West Ham Utd.)	28	1
1971-2	Ted MacDougall (Bournemouth)	35	3
1970-1	Ted MacDougall (Bournemouth)	42	4
1969-70	Albert Kinsey (Wrexham)	27	4
1968-9	Jimmy Greaves (Tottenham)	27	1
1967-8	George Best (Manchester Utd.)	28	1
	Ron Davies (Southampton)	28	1
1966-7	Ron Davies (Southampton)	37	1
1965-6	Kevin Hector (Bradford P.A.)	44	4
1964-5	Alick Jeffrey (Doncaster Rov.)	36	4
1963-4	Hugh McIlmoyle (Carlisle Utd.)	39	4
1962-3	Jimmy Greaves (Tottenham)	37	1
1961-2	Roger Hunt (Liverpool)	41	2
1960-1	Terry Bly (Peterborough Utd.)	52	4

100 LEAGUE GOALS IN SEASON

Manchester City, First Div. Champions in 2001-02, scored 108 goals.

Bolton Wanderers, First Div. Champions in 1996-7, reached 100 goals, the first side to complete a century in League football since 103 by Northampton Town (Div. 4 Champions) in 1986-7.

Last League Champions to reach **100** League goals: **Tottenham** (115 in 1960-1). Last century of goals in the top division: 111 by runners-up **Tottenham** in 1962-3.

Wolves topped 100 goals in four successive First Division seasons (1957-8, 1958-9, 1959-60, 1960-1).

In 1930-1, the Championship top three all scored a century of League goals: 1 Arsenal (127), 2 Aston Villa (128), 3 Sheffield Wed. (102).

100 GOALS AGAINST

Swindon Town, relegated with 100 goals against in 1993-4, were the first top-division club to concede a century of League goals since **Ipswich Town** (121) went down in 1964. Most goals conceded in the top division: 125 by **Blackpool** in 1930-31, but they avoided relegation.

MOST LEAGUE GOALS ON ONE DAY

A record of 209 goals in the four divisions of the Football League (43 matches) was set on **January 2, 1932**: 56 in Div. 1, 53 in Div. 2, 57 in Div. 3 South and 43 in Div. 3 North. There were two 10-goal aggregates: Bradford City 9, Barnsley 1 in Div. 2 and Coventry City 5, Fulham 5 in Div. 3 South.

That total of 209 League goals on one day was equalled on **February 1, 1936** (44 matches): 46 in Div. 1, 46 in Div. 2, 49 in Div. 3 South and 69 in Div. 3 North. Two matches in the Northern Section produced 23 of the goals: Chester 12, York City 0 and Crewe Alexandra 5, Chesterfield 6.

MOST GOALS IN TOP DIV. ON ONE DAY

This record has stood since December 26, 1963, when **66 goals** were scored in the ten First Division matches played.

MOST F.A. PREMIER LEAGUE GOALS ON ONE DAY

47, in nine matches on May 8, 1993 (last day of season).

FEWEST PREMIERSHIP GOALS IN ONE WEEK-END

10, in 10 matches on November 24/25, 2001

FEWEST FIRST DIV. GOALS ON ONE DAY

For full/near full programme: **Ten goals,** all by home clubs, in ten matches on April 28, 1923 (day of Wembley's first F.A. Cup Final).

SCORERS IN CONSECUTIVE TOP-DIVISION MATCHES

Stan Mortensen scored in 11 consecutive Division One games for Blackpool in season 1950–51. **Ruud van Nistelroy** (Manchester Utd.) scored 13 goals in last 8 games of season 2002-03 and in first 2 of 2003-04. Since the last war, 3 other players scored in 10 successive matches in the old First Division: **Billy McAdams** (Man. City, 1957-58), **Ron Davies** (Southampton, 1966-67) and **John Aldridge** (Liverpool, May-Oct. 1987).

SCORER FOR 6 PREMIERSHIP CLUBS

Les Ferdinand (Q.P.R., Newcastle Utd., Tottenham, West Ham Utd., Leicester City, Bolton Wand.)

SCORERS FOR 5 PREMIERSHIP CLUBS

Stan Collymore (Nott'm. Forest, Liverpool, Aston Villa, Leicester City, Bradford City); **Mark Hughes** (Manchester Utd., Chelsea, Southampton, Everton, Blackburn Rov.); **Nick Barmby** (Tottenham, Middlesbrough, Everton, Liverpool, Leeds Utd.); **Benito Carbone** (Sheff. Wed., Aston Villa, Bradford City, Derby Co., Middlesbrough); **Ashley Ward** (Norwich City, Derby Co., Barnsley, Blackburn Rov. Bradford City); **Teddy Sheringham** (Nottm. Forest, Tottenham, Manchester Utd., Portsmouth, West Ham Utd.).

SCORERS IN MOST CONSECUTIVE LEAGUE MATCHES

Arsenal broke the record by scoring in 55 successive Premiership fixtures: the last match in season 2000-01, then all 38 games in winning the Championship in 2001–02, and the first 16 in season 2002–03. The sequence ended with a 2–0 defeat away to Man. Utd. on December 7, 2002.

Chesterfield previously held the record, having scored in 46 consecutive matches in Div. 3 (North), starting on Christmas Day 1929 and ending on December 27, 1930.

SIX-OUT-OF-SIX HEADERS

When **Oxford Utd.** beat Shrewsbury Town 6-0 (Div. 2) on April 23, 1996, all six goals were headers.

FIVE IN A MATCH

Latest players to score 5 goals in a top-division match: **Tony Woodcock** (for Arsenal in 6-2 win away to Aston Villa) and **Ian Rush** (Liverpool 6, Luton Town 0), both on October 29, 1983; **Andy Cole** (Manchester Utd. 9, Ipswich Town 0) on March 4, 1995; **Alan Shearer** (Newcastle Utd. 8, Sheffield Wed. 0) on September 19, 1999.

ALL-ROUND MARKSMAN

Alan Cork scored in four divisions of the Football League and in the F.A. Premier League in his 18-season career with Wimbledon, Sheffield Utd. and Fulham (1977-95).

MOST CUP GOALS

F.A. Cup – most goals in one season: 20 by Jimmy Ross (Preston N.E., runners-up 1887-8); 15 by Albert (Sandy) Brown (Tottenham, winners 1900-1).

Most F.A. Cup goals in individual careers: 49 by Harry Cursham (Notts Co. 1877-89); this century: 44 by Ian Rush (39 for Liverpool, 4 for Chester City, 1 for Newcastle Utd. 1979-98). Denis Law was the previous highest F.A. Cup scorer in the 20th century with 41 goals for Huddersfield Town, Manchester City and Manchester Utd. (1957-74).

Most F.A. Cup Final goals by individual: 5 by Ian Rush for Liverpool (2 in 1986, 2 in 1989, 1 in 1992).

HOTTEST CUP HOT-SHOT

Geoff Hurst scored 21 cup goals in season 1965-66: 11 League Cup, 4 F.A. Cup and 2 Cup-Winners' Cup for West Ham Utd., and 4 in the World Cup for England.

SCORERS IN EVERY ROUND

Twelve players have scored in **every round** of the F.A. Cup in one season, from opening to Final inclusive: **Archie Hunter** (Aston Villa, winners 1887); **Sandy Brown** (Tottenham, winners 1901); **Harry Hampton** (Aston Villa, winners 1905); **Harold Blackmore** (Bolton Wand., winners 1929); **Ellis Rimmer** (Sheffield Wed., winners 1935); **Frank O'Donnell** (Preston N.E., beaten 1937); **Stan Mortensen** (Blackpool, beaten 1948); **Jackie Milburn** (Newcastle Utd., winners 1951); **Nat Lofthouse** (Bolton Wand., beaten 1953); **Charlie Wayman** (Preston N.E., beaten 1954); **Jeff Astle** (W.B.A., winners 1968); **Peter Osgood** (Chelsea, winners 1970).

Blackmore and the next seven completed their 'set' in the Final at Wembley; Osgood did so in the Final replay at Old Trafford.

Only player to score in every **Football League Cup** round possible in one season: **Tony Brown** for W.B.A., winners 1965-6, with 9 goals in 10 games (after bye in Round 1).

TEN IN A ROW

Dixie McNeill scored for Wrexham in **ten successive** F.A. Cup rounds (18 goals): 11 in Rounds 1-6, 1977-8; 3 in Rounds 3-4, 1978-9; 4 in Rounds 3-4, 1979-80.

Stan Mortensen (Blackpool) scored 25 goals in 16 F.A. Cup rounds out of 17 (1946-51).

TOP MATCH HAULS IN F.A. CUP

Ted MacDougall scored nine goals, a record for the competition proper, in the F.A. Cup first round on November 20, 1971, when Bournemouth beat Margate 11-0. On November 23, 1970 he had scored six in an 8-1 first round replay against Oxford City.

Other six-goal F.A. Cup scorers include **George Hilsdon** (Chelsea v Worksop, 9-1, 1907-8), **Ronnie Rooke** (Fulham v Bury, 6-0, 1938-9), **Harold Atkinson** (Tranmere Rov. v Ashington, 8-1, 1952-3), **George Best** (Manchester Utd. v Northampton Town 1969-70, 8-2 away), and **Duane Darby** (Hull City v Whitby, 8-4, 1996-7).

Denis Law scored all six for Manchester City at Luton Town (6-2) in an F.A. Cup 4th Round tie on January 28, 1961, but none of them counted – the match was abandoned (69 mins.) because of a waterlogged pitch. He also scored City's goal when the match was played again, but they lost 3-1.

Tony Philliskirk scored **five** when Peterborough Utd. beat Kingstonian 9-1 in an F.A. Cup 1st Round replay on November 25, 1992, but had them wiped from the records. With the score at 3-0, the Kingstonian goalkeeper was concussed by a coin thrown from the crowd and unable to play on. The F.A. ordered the match to be replayed at Peterborough behind closed doors, and Kingstonian lost 1-0.

● Two players have scored **ten goals** in F.A. Cup preliminary round matches: **Chris Marron** for South Shields against Radcliffe in September 1947; **Paul Jackson** when Sheffield-based club Stocksbridge Park Steels beat Oldham Town 17–1 on August 31, 2002. He scored 5 in each half and all ten with his feet – goal times 6, 10, 22, 30, 34, 68, 73, 75, 79, 84 mins.

QUICKEST GOALS AND RAPID SCORING

A goal in **4 seconds** was claimed by **Jim Fryatt**, for Bradford P.A. v Tranmere Rov. (Div. 4, April 25, 1965), and by **Gerry Allen** for Whitstable Town v Danson (Kent League, March 3,1989). **Damian Mori** scored in 4 seconds for Adelaide City v Sydney Utd. (Australian National League, December 6, 1995).

Goals after 6 seconds – **Albert Mundy** for Aldershot v Hartlepool Utd., October 25, 1958; **Barrie Jones** for Notts County v Torquay Utd., March 31, 1962; **Keith Smith** for Crystal Palace v Derby Co., December 12, 1964.

9.6 seconds by **John Hewitt** for Aberdeen at Motherwell, 3rd Round, January 23, 1982 (fastest goal in Scottish Cup history).

Colin Cowperthwaite reputedly scored in **3½ seconds** for Barrow v Kettering (Alliance Premier League) on December 8, 1979, but the timing was unofficial.

Phil Starbuck scored for Huddersfield Town only **3 seconds** after entering the field as 54th min. substitute at home to Wigan Athletic (Div. 2) on Easter Monday, April 12, 1993. A corner-kick was delayed, awaiting his arrival, and he scored with a header.

Malcolm Macdonald scored after **5 seconds** (officially timed) in Newcastle Utd.'s 7-3 win in a pre-season friendly at St. Johnstone on July 29, 1972.

Scored first kick: Billy Foulkes (Newcastle Utd.) for Wales v England at Cardiff, October 20, 1951, in his first International match.

Six goals in seven minutes in Preston N.E.'s record 26-0 F.A. Cup 1st Round win v Hyde, October 15, 1887.

Five in 20 minutes: Frank Keetley in Lincoln City's 9-1 win over Halifax Town in Div. 3 (North), January 16, 1932; **Brian Dear** for West Ham Utd. v W.B.A. (6-1, Div.1) April 16, 1965. **Kevin Hector** for Bradford P.A. v Barnsley (7–2, Div. 4) November 20, 1965.

Four in five minutes: by **John McIntyre** for Blackburn Rov. v Everton (Div. 1), September 16, 1922; **W.G. (Billy) Richardson** for W.B.A. v West Ham Utd. (Div. 1), November 7, 1931.

Three in three minutes: Billy Lane for Watford v Clapton Orient (Div.3S), December 20, 1933; **Johnny Hartburn** for Leyton Orient v Shrewsbury Town (Div. 3S), January 22, 1955; **Gary Roberts** for Brentford v Newport, (Freight Rover Trophy, South Final), May 17, 1985; **Gary Shaw** for Shrewsbury Town v Bradford City (Div. 3), December 22, 1990.

Fastest hat-trick in League History: 2 mins. 20 secs. by Bournemouth's 84th-minute substitute **James Hayter** in 6-0 home win v Wrexham (Div. 2) on February 24, 2004 (goal times 86, 87, 88 mins.).

Three in 2½ minutes: Jimmy Scarth for Gillingham v Leyton Orient (Div. 3S), November 1, 1952.

Two in nine seconds: Jamie Bates with last kick of first half, **Jermaine McSporran** 9 seconds into second half when Wycombe Wand. beat Peterborough Utd. 2-0 at home (Div. 2) on September 23, 2000.

Arsenal scored six goals in 18 minutes (71-89 mins.) in 7-1 home win (Div. 1) v Sheffield Wed., February 15, 1992.

Plymouth Argyle scored five goals in first 18 minutes in 7-0 home win v Chesterfield (Div. 2), January 3, 2004.

Sunderland scored eight goals in 28 minutes at Newcastle Utd. (9-1 Div 1), December 5, 1908. Newcastle went on to win the Championship.

Southend Utd. scored all seven goals in 29 minutes in 7-0 win at home to Torquay Utd. (Leyland Daf Cup, Southern quarter-final), February 26, 1991. Score was 0-0 until 55th. minute.

Six goals in first 19 minutes by Tranmere Rov. when they beat Oldham Athletic 13-4 (Div. 3 North) on December 26, 1935.

Notts Co. scored six second-half goals in 12 minutes (Tommy Lawton 3, Jackie Sewell 3) when they beat Exeter City 9-0 (Div. 3 South) at Meadow Lane on October 16, 1948.

World's fastest goal: 2.8 seconds, direct from kick-off, by Argentinian **Ricardo Olivera** for Rio Negro v Soriano (Uruguayan League), December 26, 1998.

Fastest International goal: 8.3 secs. by **Davide Gualtieri** for San Marino v England (World Cup qual., Bologna, November 17, 1993).

Fastest International hat-trick: 3 minutes 15 seconds by **Masashi Nakayami** for Japan in 9-0 win v Brunei in Macao (Asian Cup), February 16, 2000.

Fastest International hat-trick in British matches: 3½ minutes by **Willie Hall** for England v N. Ireland at Old Trafford, Manchester, November 16, 1938. (Hall scored 5 in 7-0 win); 4½ minutes by **Arif Erdem** for Turkey v N. Ireland, European Championship, at Windsor Park, Belfast, on September 4, 1999.

Fastest International goal by substitute: 5 seconds by **John Jensen** for Denmark v Belgium (Eur. Champ.), October 12, 1994.

Fastest England goals: 17 seconds by **Tommy Lawton** v Portugal in Lisbon, May 25, 1947. 27 seconds by **Bryan Robson** v. France in World Cup at Bilbao, Spain on June 16, 1982; 37 seconds by **Gareth Southgate** v South Africa in Durban, May 22, 2003; 30 seconds by **Jack Cock** v Ireland, Belfast, October 25, 1919; 30 seconds by **Bill Nicholson** v Portugal at Goodison Park, May 19, 1951. 38 seconds by **Bryan Robson** v Yugoslavia at Wembley, December 13, 1989; 42 seconds by **Gary Lineker** v Malaysia in Kuala Lumpur, June 12, 1991.

Fastest goal by England substitute: 10 seconds by **Teddy Sheringham** v Greece (World Cup qualifying match) at Old Trafford, October 6, 2001.

Fastest F.A. Cup Final goals: 30 seconds by **John Devey**, for Aston Villa v W.B.A., 1895; at Wembley: 42 seconds by **Roberto di Matteo**, for Chelsea v Middlesbrough, 1997.

Fastest goal by substitute in F.A. Cup Final: 96 seconds by **Teddy Sheringham** for Manchester Utd. v Newcastle Utd. at Wembley, May 22, 1999.

Fastest League Cup Final goal: 45 seconds by **John Arne Riise** for Liverpool v Chelsea, 2005.

Fastest goal on full League debut: 7.7 seconds by **Freddy Eastwood** for Southend Utd. v Swansea City (Lge. 2), October 16, 2004. He went on to score hat-trick in 4-2 win.

Fastest goal in cup final: 4.07 seconds by 14-year-old **Owen Price** for Ernest Bevin College, Tooting, beaten 3-1 by Barking Abbey in Heinz Ketchup Cup Final at Arsenal Stadium on May 18, 2000. Owen, on Tottenham's books, scored from inside his own half when the ball was played back to him from kick-off.

Fastest F.A. Cup hat-tricks: In 3 minutes by **Billy Best** for Southend Utd. v Brentford (2nd. Round, December 7, 1968); 2 minutes 20 seconds by **Andy Locke** for Nantwich v Droylesden (1st. Qual. Round, September 9, 1995).

F.A. Premier League – fastest scoring: Four goals in 4 minutes, 44 seconds by Tottenham at home to Southampton on Sunday, February 7, 1993.

Premiership – fast scoring away: When Aston Villa won 5-0 at Leicester (January 31, 2004), all the goals were scored in 18 second-half minutes (50-68).

Fastest First Division hat-tricks since war: Graham Leggat, 3 goals in 3 minutes (first half) when Fulham beat Ipswich Town 10-1 on Boxing Day, 1963; Nigel Clough, 3 goals in 4 minutes (81, 82, 85 pen) when Nott'm. Forest beat Q.P.R. 4-0 on December 13, 1987.

Fastest goal in Champions League: 20.07 seconds by **Gilbert Silva** for Arsenal away to PSV Eindhoven (Group A), September 26, 2002.

F.A. Premier League – fastest hat-trick: 4½ minutes (26, 29, 31) by **Robbie Fowler** in Liverpool 3, Arsenal 0 on Sunday, August 28, 1994.

Fastest hat-trick of headers: Dixie Dean's 5 goals in Everton's 7–2 win at home to Chelsea (Div. 1) on November 14, 1931 included 3 headers between 5th and 15th-minutes.

Fastest Premier League goals: 10 seconds by **Ledley King** for Tottenham away to Bradford City, December 9, 2000; 10.4 seconds by **Alan Shearer** for Newcastle Utd. V Manchester City, January 18, 2003; 11 seconds by **Mark Viduka** for Leeds Utd. V Charlton Athletic Ath., March 17, 2001; 12.5 seconds by **James Beattie** for Southampton at Chelsea, August 28, 2004; 13 seconds by **Chris Sutton** for Blackburn Rov. at Everton, April 1, 1995; 13 seconds by **Dwight Yorke** for Aston Villa at Coventry City, September 30, 1995.

Fastest top-division goal: 7 seconds by **Bobby Langton** for Preston N.E. v Manchester City (Div. 1), August 25, 1948.

Fastest Premier League goal by substitute: 9 seconds by **Shaun Goater**, Manchester City's equaliser away to Manchester Utd. (1–1), Feb. 9, 2003.

Four in 13 minutes by Premier League substitute: Ole Gunnar Solskjaer for Manchester Utd. away to Nott'm. Forest, Feb. 6, 1999.

Fastest Scottish hat-trick: 2½ mins. by **Ian St. John** for Motherwell away to Hibernian (Scottish League Cup), August 15, 1959.

Fastest all-time hat-trick: Reported at 1 min. 50 secs. by **Eduardo Maglioni** for Independiente against Gimnasia de la Plata in Argentina First Division, March 18, 1973.

Fastest goal in Women's Football: 7 seconds by **Angie Harriott** for Launton Ladies v Thame Utd. (Southern League, Prem. Div.), season 1998-9.

FASTEST GOALS IN WORLD CUP FINAL SERIES

10.8 secs. by **Hakan Sukur** for Turkey against South Korea in 3rd/4th-place match at Taegu, June 29, 2002.

15 secs. by **Vaclav Masek** for Czechoslovakia v Mexico (in Vina, Chile, 1962).

27 secs. by **Bryan Robson** for England v France (in Bilbao, Spain, 1982).

TOP MATCH SCORES SINCE WAR

By English clubs: 13-0 by Newcastle Utd. v Newport (Div. 2, Oct. 1946); **13-2** by Tottenham v Crewe Alexandra (F.A. Cup 4th. Rd. replay, Feb. 1960); **13-0** by Chelsea v Jeunesse Hautcharage, Lux. (Cup-Winners' Cup 1st. Rd., 2nd. Leg, Sept. 1971).

By Scottish club: 20-0 by Stirling Albion v Selkirk (E. of Scotland League) in Scottish Cup 1st. Rd. (Dec. 1984). That is the highest score in British first-class football since Preston N.E. beat Hyde 26-0 in F.A. Cup, Oct. 1887.

GOALS BY WINGERS

	Season	Matches	Goals
Cliff Bastin (Arsenal)	(Div. I) 1932-3	42	33
Bob Ferrier (Motherwell)	(Div. I) 1929-30	27	32
Ken Dawson (Falkirk)	(Div. II) 1935-6	34	39

GOALS BY GOALKEEPERS

Goalkeepers who have scored with long clearances include:

Pat Jennings for Tottenham away to Manchester Utd. (goalkeeper Alex Stepney) on August 12, 1967 (F.A. Charity Shield).

Peter Shilton for Leicester City at Southampton (goalkeeper Campbell Forsyth) on October 14, 1967 (Div. 1).

Ray Cashley for Bristol City at home to Hull City (goalkeeper Jeff Wealands) on September 18, 1973 (Div. 2).

Steve Sherwood for Watford away to Coventry City (goalkeeper Raddy Avramovic) on January 14, 1984 (Div. 1).

Steve Ogrizovic for Coventry City away to Sheffield Wed. (goalkeeper Martin Hodge) on October 25, 1986 (Div. 1).

Andy Goram for Hibernian at home to Morton (goalkeeper David Wylie) on May 7, 1988 (Scottish Premier Div.).

Andy McLean, on Irish League debut, for Cliftonville v Linfield (goalkeeper George Dunlop) on August 20, 1988.

Alan Paterson for Glentoran against Linfield (goalkeeper George Dunlop) on November 30, 1988 (Irish League Cup Final at The Oval, Belfast). His long punt (87 mins) gave Glentoran a 2-1 victory – the only instance of a goalkeeper scoring the winning goal in a senior cup final in the UK.

Ray Charles for East Fife at Stranraer (goalkeeper Bernard Duffy) on February 28, 1990 (Scottish Div. 2).

Iain Hesford scored Maidstone's winner (3-2 v Hereford, Div. 4, November 2, 1991) with long kick-out that went first bounce past Tony Elliott in opposite goal.

Chris Mackenzie for Hereford at home to Barnet (goalkeeper Mark Taylor) in Div. 3, August 12, 1995.

Mark Bosnich (Aston Villa) scored the last goal (a penalty) when Australia beat Solomon Islands 13-0 in World Cup Oceania Zone qualifier in Sydney on June 11, 1997.

Steve Mildenhall (Notts Co.) scored a free-kick from his own half past Mansfield Town's Kevin Pilkington for the winning goal (4-3, away) in the Worthington Cup 1st Round on August 21, 2001.

Mart Poom headed Sunderland's last-seconds equaliser (1-1) away to his former club Derby Co. (goalkeeper Andy Oakes), Div. 1, September 20, 2003.

Brad Friedel (Blackburn Rov.) shot late equaliser against Charlton Athletic 'keeper Dean Kiely at The Valley (Premiership, February 21, 2004) but finished on losing side, 2-3.

Paul Robinson (Leeds Utd.) headed last-minute equaliser (2-2) at home to Swindon Town (Carling Cup, 2nd Round, September 24, 2003). Leeds won 4-3 on penalties.

Andy Lonergan (Preston) scored equaliser (1-1) at Leicester, in Coca-Cola Championship on October 2, 2004 with 95-yard punt past 'keeper Kevin Pressman, who slipped on wet turf.

Most goals by a goalkeeper in a League season: 5 (all penalties) by **Arthur Birch** for Chesterfield (Div. 3 North), 1923-4.

Arthur Wilkie, Reading's goalkeeper at home to Halifax Town (Div. 3) on August 31, 1962, injured a hand, then played as a forward and scored twice in a 4-2 win.

Alex Stepney was Manchester Utd.'s joint top scorer for two months in season 1973-4 with two penalties.

Alan Fettis, N. Ireland goalkeeper, scored twice for Hull City in Div. 2 in season 1994-5: as a substitute in 3-1 home win v Oxford Utd. (Dec. 17) and, when selected outfield, with last-minute winner (2-1) at Blackpool on May 6.

Peter Schmeichel, Manchester Utd.'s goalkeeper, headed an 89th minute equaliser (2-2) from Ryan Giggs' corner in the UEFA Cup 1st. Round, 2nd leg against Rotor Volgograd (Russia) on September 26, 1995, but United lost the tie on away goals.

On October 20, 2001, **Schmeichel** became the first goalkeeper to score in the Premiership when, following a corner, he volleyed Aston Villa's second goal in their 3-2 defeat at Everton.

In League matches for Swansea City, **Roger Freestone** scored with a penalty at Oxford Utd. (Div. 2, April 30, 1995) and, in 1995-6 (Div. 2) with penalties at home to Shrewsbury Town (August 12) and Chesterfield (August 26).

Goalkeeper **Jimmy Glass**, on loan from Swindon Town, scored the winner that kept Carlisle Utd. in the Football League on May 8, 1999. With only ten seconds of injury time left, he went upfield for a corner and shot the goal that beat Plymouth Argyle 2-1 at Brunton Park. It preserved Carlisle Utd.'s League existence since 1928 and sent Scarborough down to the Conference.

Tony Roberts (Dagenham & Redbridge), only known goalkeeper to score from open play in the F.A. Cup, away to Basingstoke in 4th Qual. Round on October 27, 2001. His last-minute equaliser (2-2) forced a replay, which Dagenham won 3-0 and went on to the 3rd Round proper.

Jose Luis Chilavert, Paraguay's Int. goalkeeper, scored a hat-trick of penalties when his club Velez Sarsfield beat Ferro Carril Oeste 6-1 in the Argentine League on November 28, 1999. In all, he scored 8 goals in his 72 Internationals.

OWN GOALS

Most by player in one season: 5 by **Robert Stuart** (Middlesbrough) in 1934-35.

Three in match by one team: Sheffield Wed.'s Vince Kenny, Norman Curtis and Eddie Gannon in 5–4 defeat at home to W.B.A. (Div. 1) on December 26, 1952; Rochdale's George Underwood, Kenny Boyle and Danny Murphy in 7–2 defeat at Carlisle (Div. 3 North), December 25, 1954; Sunderland's Stephen Wright and Michael Proctor (2) in 24, 29, 32 minutes at home to Charlton Athletic (1–3, Premiership), February 1, 2003.

Two in match by one player: Chris Nicholl (Aston Villa) scored all 4 goals in 2-2 draw away to Leicester City (Div. 1), March 20, 1976; Jamie Carragher (Liverpool) in first half at home to Manchester Utd. (2-3) in Premiership, September 11, 1999; Jim Goodwin (Stockport Co.) in 1–4 defeat away to Plymouth Argyle (Div. 2), September 23, 2002; Michael Proctor (Sunderland) in 1–3 defeat at home to Charlton Athletic Ath. (Premiership), February 1, 2003.

Fastest own goals: 8 seconds by Pat Kruse of Torquay Utd., for Cambridge Utd. (Div. 4), January 3, 1977; in First Division, 16 seconds by Steve Bould (Arsenal) away to Sheffield Wed., February 17, 1990.

Late own-goal man: Frank Sinclair (Leicester City) put through his own goal in the 90th minute of Premiership matches away to Arsenal (L1-2) and at home to Chelsea (D2-2) in August 1999.

Half an own goal each: Chelsea's second goal in a 3-1 home win against Leicester City on December 18, 1954 was uniquely recorded as 'shared own goal.' Leicester City defenders Stan Milburn and Jack Froggatt, both lunging at the ball in an attempt to clear, connected simultaneously and sent it rocketing into the net.

Match of 149 own goals: When Adama, Champions of Malagasy (formerly Madagascar) won a League match 149–0 on October 31, 2002, all 149 were own goals scored by opponents Stade Olympique De L'Emryne. They repeatedly put the ball in their own net in protest at a refereeing decision.

MOST SCORERS IN MATCH

Liverpool set a Football League record with EIGHT scorers when they beat Crystal Palace 9-0 (Div.1) on September 12, 1989. Their marksmen were: Steve Nicol (7 and 88 mins), Steve McMahon (16), Ian Rush (45), Gary Gillespie (56), Peter Beardsley (61), John Aldridge pen. (67), John Barnes (79) and Glenn Hysen (82).

Fifteen years earlier, Liverpool had gone one better with NINE different scorers when they achieved their record win, 11-0 at home to Stromsgodset (Norway) in the Cup-Winners' Cup 1st. round, 1st leg on September 17, 1974.

Eight players scored for Swansea City when they beat Sliema, Malta, 12-0 in the Cup-Winners' Cup 1st round, 1st leg on September 15, 1982.

Nine Stirling Albion players scored in the 20-0 win against Selkirk in the Scottish Cup 1st. Round on December 8, 1984.

LONG SCORING RUNS

Tom Phillipson scored in 13 consecutive matches for Wolves (Div. 2) in season 1926-27, which is still an English League record. Bill Prendergast scored in 13 successive League and Cup appearances for Chester City (Div. 3 North) in season 1938-39.

Dixie Dean scored in 12 consecutive games (23 goals) for Everton in Div. 2 in 1930-1.

Danish striker Finn Dossing scored in 15 consecutive matches (Scottish record) for Dundee Utd. (Div. 1) in 1964-5.

Marco Negri (Rangers) scored in all the first 10 Premier games of 1997-8, a total of 12 goals.

Jermain Defoe, 18, on loan from West Ham Utd., equalled a single-season post-war record by scoring for Bournemouth in 10 consecutive matches (Div. 2), October-January 2000-01. Billy McAdams did likewise for Manchester City (1957-8), as did Ron Davies for Southampton (1966-7).

John Aldridge (Liverpool) scored in 10 successive First Division matches – the last game of season 1986-7 and the first nine in 1987-8.

Kevin Russell (Wrexham) scored in nine consecutive matches in Div. 4, March-May, 1988.

Ruud van Nistelrooy (Manchester Utd.) holds the record for scoring in most consecutive Premiership matches in one season – 8 (11 goals) in December-January, 2001-02. He repeated the feat in the last 8 Premiership games (13 goals, including 5 penalties and 2 hat-tricks) of season 2002–03.

Ian Wright scored on 12 successive first-team appearances, including 7 Premiership, for Arsenal (Sept. 15-Nov. 23, 1994).

50-GOAL PLAYERS

With **52** goals for **Wolves** in 1987-8 (34 League, 12 Sherpa Van Trophy, 3 Littlewoods Cup, 3 F.A. Cup), **Steve Bull** became the first player to score 50 in a season for a League club since **Terry Bly** for 4th Division newcomers Peterborough Utd. in 1960-1. Bly's 54 comprised 52 League goals and 2 in the F.A. Cup, and included 7 hat-tricks, still a post-war League record.

Bull was again the country's top scorer with 50 goals in season 1988-9: 37 League, 2 Littlewoods Cup and 11 Sherpa Van Trophy.

Between Bly and Bull, the highest individual scoring total for a season was 49 by two players: Ted MacDougall (Bournemouth 1970-1, 42 League, 7 F.A. Cup) and Clive Allen (Tottenham 1986-7, 33 League, 12 Littlewoods Cup, 4 F.A. Cup).

HOT SHOTS

Jimmy Greaves was First Division top scorer (League goals) six times in 11 seasons: 32 for Chelsea (1958-9), 41 for Chelsea (1960-1) and, for Tottenham, 37 in 1962-3, 35 in 1963-4, 29 in 1964-5 (joint top) and 27 in 1968-9.

Brian Clough (Middlesbrough) was the Second Division's leading scorer in three successive seasons: 40 goals in 1957-8, 42 in 1958-9 and 39 in 1959-60.

John Hickton (Middlesbrough) was top Div. 2 scorer three times in four seasons: 24 goals in 1967-8, 24 in 1969-70 and 25 in 1970-1.

MOST HAT-TRICKS

Nine by **George Camsell** (Middlesbrough) in Div. 2, 1926-7, is the record for one season. Most League hat-tricks in career: 37 by **Dixie Dean** for Tranmere Rov. and Everton (1924-38).

Most **top division** hat-tricks in a season since last war: six by **Jimmy Greaves** for Chelsea (1960-1). **Alan Shearer** scored five hat-tricks for Blackburn Rov. in the Premier League, season 1995-96.

Frank Osborne (Tottenham) scored three consecutive hat-tricks in Div. 1 in October-November 1925, against Liverpool, Leicester City (away) and West Ham Utd.

Tom Jennings (Leeds Utd.) scored hat-tricks in three successive First Div. matches (Sept-Oct, 1926): 3 goals v Arsenal, 4 at Liverpool, 4 v Blackburn Rov. Leeds Utd. were relegated at the end of the season.

Jack Balmer (Liverpool) scored only three hat-tricks in a 17-year career - in successive First Div. matches (Nov. 1946): 3 v Portsmouth, 4 at Derby Co., 3 v Arsenal. No other Liverpool player scored during that 10-goal sequence by Balmer.

Gilbert Alsop scored hat-tricks in three successive matches for Walsall in Div. 3 South in April 1939: 3 at Swindon Town, 3 v Bristol City and 4 v Swindon Town.

Alf Lythgoe scored hat-tricks in three successive games for Stockport Co. (Div. 3 North) in March 1934: 3 v Darlington, 3 at Southport and 4 v Wrexham.

TRIPLE HAT-TRICKS

There have been at least three instances of **3 hat-tricks being scored** for **one team** in a Football League match:-

April 21, 1909: Enoch West, Billy Hooper and Alfred Spouncer scored 3 apiece for Nott'm. Forest (12-0 v Leicester Fosse, Div. 1).

March 3, 1962: Ron Barnes, Wyn Davies and Roy Ambler registered hat-tricks in Wrexham's 10-1 win against Hartlepool Utd. (Div. 4).

November 7, 1987: Tony Adcock, Paul Stewart and David White each scored 3 goals for Manchester City in 10-1 win at home to Huddersfield Town (Div. 2).

For the first time in the Premiership, **three hat-tricks** were completed **on one day** (September 23, 1995): Tony Yeboah for Leeds Utd. at Wimbledon; Alan Shearer for Blackburn Rov. v Coventry City; and Robbie Fowler with 4 goals for Liverpool v Bolton Wand.

In the F.A. Cup, **Jack Carr**, **George Elliott** and **Walter Tinsley** each scored 3 in Middlesbrough's 9-3 first round win against Goole in Jan. 1915. **Les Allen** scored 5, **Bobby Smith** 4 and **Cliff Jones** 3 when Tottenham beat Crewe Alexandra 13-2 in a fourth-round replay in February 1960.

HAT-TRICKS v THREE 'KEEPERS

When West Ham Utd. beat Newcastle Utd. 8-1 (Div.1) at home on April 21, 1986 **Alvin Martin** scored 3 goals against different 'keepers: Martin Thomas injured a shoulder and was replaced, in turn, by outfield players Chris Hedworth and Peter Beardsley.

Jock Dodds of Lincoln City had done the same **against** West Ham Utd. on December 18, 1948, scoring past **Ernie Gregory**, **Tommy Moroney** and **George Dick**. The Hammers lost 3-4.

David Herd (Manchester Utd.) scored against three Sunderland goalkeepers (Jim Montgomery, Charlie Hurley and Johnny Parke) in 5-0 First Division home win on Nov. 26, 1966.

Brian Clark, of Bournemouth, scored against three Rotherham Utd. goalkeepers (Jim McDonagh,, Conal Gilbert and Michael Leng twice) in 7-2 win at Rotherham Utd. (Div. 3) on Oct. 10, 1972.

On Oct. 16, 1993 (Div.3) **Chris Pike** (Hereford) scored a hat-trick against different goalkeepers. Opponents Colchester Utd., beaten 5-0, became the first team in League history to have two 'keepers sent off in the same game.

On Dec. 18, 2004 (League 1), in 6-1 defeat at Hull, Tranmere Rov. used three goalkeepers: **John Achterberg** and **Russell Howarth** both retired injured, and defender **Theo Whitmore** kept goal for the second half.

EIGHT-DAY HAT-TRICK TREBLE

Joe Bradford of Birmingham City scored three hat-tricks in eight days in September 1929-30 v Newcastle Utd. (won 5-1) on the 21st, 5 for the Football League v Irish League (7-2) on the 25th, and 3 in his club's 5-7 defeat away to Blackburn Rov. on the 28th.

PREMIERSHIP DOUBLE HAT-TRICK

Robert Pires and **Jermaine Pennant** each scored 3 goals in Arsenal's 6–1 win at home to Southampton (May 7, 2003).

TON UP – BOTH ENDS

Manchester City are the only club to **score and concede** a century of League goals in the same season. When fifth in the 1957-8 Championship, they scored 104 goals and gave away 100.

TOURNAMENT TOP SHOTS

Most individual goals in a World Cup Final series: 13 by **Just Fontaine** for France, in Sweden 1958. Most in European Championship Finals: 9 by **Michel Platini** for France, in France 1984.

MOST GOALS ON CLUB DEBUT

Jim Dyet scored **eight** in King's Park's 12-2 win against Forfar Athletic (Scottish Div. 2, Jan. 2, 1930).

Len Shackleton scored **six** times in Newcastle Utd.'s 13-0 win v Newport County (Div. 2, Oct. 5, 1946) in the week he joined them from Bradford Park Avenue.

MOST GOALS ON LEAGUE DEBUT

Five by **George Hilsdon**, for Chelsea (9-2) v Glossop, Div. 2 Sept. 1, 1906. **Alan Shearer**, with three goals for Southampton (4-2) v Arsenal, April 9, 1988, became, at 17, the youngest player to score a First Division hat-trick on his full debut.

CLEAN-SHEET RECORDS

On the way to promotion from Div. 3 in season 1995-6, **Gillingham's** ever-present goalkeeper **Jim Stannard** set a clean-sheet record. In 46 matches, he achieved 29 shut-outs (17 at home, 12 away), beating the 28 by Ray Clemence for Liverpool (42 matches in Div. 1, 1978-9) and the previous best in a 46-match programme of 28 by Port Vale (Div. 3 North, 1953-4). In conceding only 20 League goals in 1995-6, Gillingham created a defensive record for the lower divisions.

Chris Woods, Rangers' England goalkeeper, set a British record in season 1986-7 by going 1,196 minutes without conceding a goal. The sequence began in the UEFA Cup match against Borussia Moenchengladbach on Nov. 26, 1986 and ended when Rangers were sensationally beaten 1-0 at home by Hamilton in the Scottish Cup 3rd. Round on Jan. 31, 1987 with a 70th.-minute goal by Adrian Sprott.

The previous British record of 1,156 minutes without a goal conceded was held by Aberdeen goalkeeper **Bobby Clark** (season 1970-1).

Chelsea goalkeeper **Petr Cech** set a Premiership clean-sheet record of 1,024 consecutive minutes (including 10 complete matches) in season 2004-05.

Most clean sheets in season in top English division: 28 by Liverpool (42 matches) in 1978-79; 25 by Chelsea (38 matches) in 2004-05.

There have been three instances of clubs keeping 11 consecutive clean sheets in the Football League: Millwall (Div. 3 South, 1925-6), York City (Div. 3, 1973-4) and Reading (Div. 4, 1978-9). In his sequence, Reading goalkeeper **Steve Death** set the existing League shut-out record of 1,103 minutes.

Mark Leonard (Chesterfield) kept a clean sheet in 8 consecutive Div.3 away games (Jan-April 1994).

Sasa Ilic remained unbeaten for over 14 hours with 9 successive shut-outs (7 in FL Div. 1, 2 in play-offs) to equal a Charlton Athletic club record in Apr./May 1998. He had 12 clean sheets in 17 first team games after winning promotion from the reserves with 6 successive clean sheets.

Sebastiano Rossi kept a clean sheet in 8 successive away matches for AC Milan (Nov. 1993-Apr. 1994).

A world record of 1,275 minutes without conceding a goal was set in 1990-1 by **Abel Resino**, the Atletico Madrid goalkeeper. He was finally beaten by Sporting Gijon's Enrique in Atletico's 3-1 win on March 19, 1991.

In International football, the record is held by **Dino Zoff** with a shut-out for Italy (Sept. 1972 to June 1974) lasting 1,142 minutes.

LOW SCORING

Fewest goals by any club in season in Football League: **24** by **Stoke City** (Div. 1, 42 matches, 1984-5); **24** by **Watford** (Div. 2, 42 matches, 1971-2). In 46-match programme, **27** by **Stockport Co.** (Div. 3, 1969-70).

Arsenal were the lowest Premier League scorers in its opening season (1992-3) with 40 goals in 42 matches, but won both domestic cup competitions. In subsequent seasons the lowest Premier League scorers were **Ipswich Town** (35) in 1993-4, **Crystal Palace** (34) in 1994-5, **Manchester City** (33) in 1995-6 and **Leeds Utd.** (28) in 1996-7 until **Sunderland** set the Premiership's new fewest-goals record with only 21 in 2002-03.

LONG TIME NO SCORE

The world International non-scoring record was set by **Northern Ireland** when they played 13 matches and 1,298 minutes without a goal. The sequence began against Poland on Feb. 13, 2002 and ended 2 years and 5 days later when David Healy scored against Norway (1-4) in Belfast on Feb. 18, 2004.

Longest non-scoring sequences in Football League: 11 matches by **Coventry City** in 1919-20 (Div. 2); 11 matches by **Hartlepool Utd.** in 1992-3 (Div. 2). After beating

Crystal Palace 1-0 in the F.A. Cup 3rd round on Jan. 2, they went 13 games and 2 months without scoring (11 League, 1 F.A. Cup, 1 Autoglass Trophy). The sequence ended after 1,227 blank minutes with a 1-1 draw at Blackpool (League) on March 6.

In the **Premier League** (Oct.-Jan. season 1994-5) Crystal Palace failed to score in nine consecutive matches.

The British non-scoring club record is held by **Stirling Albion**: 14 consecutive matches (13 League, 1 Scottish Cup) and 1,292 minutes play, from Jan. 31, 1981 until Aug. 8, 1981 (when they lost 4-1 to Falkirk in the League Cup).

In season 1971-2, **Mansfield Town** did not score in any of their first nine home games in Div. 3. They were relegated on goal difference of minus two.

F.A. CUP CLEAN SHEETS

Most consecutive F.A. Cup matches without conceding a goal: 11 by **Bradford City**. The sequence spanned 8 rounds, from 3rd. in 1910-11 to 4th. Round replay in 1911-12, and included winning the Cup in 1911.

ATTENDANCES

GREATEST WORLD CROWDS

World Cup, Maracana Stadium, Rio de Janeiro, July 16, 1950. Final match (Brazil v Uruguay) attendance 199,850; receipts £125,000.

Total attendance in three matches (including play-off) between Santos (Brazil) and AC Milan for the Inter-Continental Cup (World Club Championship) 1963, exceeded 375,000.

BRITISH RECORD CROWDS

Most to pay: 149,547, Scotland v England, at Hampden Park, Glasgow, April 17, 1937. This was the first all-ticket match in Scotland (receipts £24,000).

At Scottish F.A. Cup Final: 146,433, Celtic v Aberdeen, at Hampden Park, April 24, 1937. Estimated another 20,000 shut out.

For British club match (apart from a Cup Final): 143,470, Rangers v Hibernian, at Hampden Park, March 27, 1948 (Scottish Cup semi-final).

F.A. Cup Final: 126,047, Bolton Wand. v West Ham Utd., April 28, 1923. Estimated 150,000 in ground at opening of Wembley Stadium.

World Cup Qualifying Ties: 120,000, Cameroon v Morocco, Yaounde, November 29, 1981; 107,580, Scotland v Poland, Hampden Park, October 13, 1965.

European Cup: 135,826, Celtic v Leeds Utd. (semi-final, 2nd. leg) at Hampden Park, Glasgow, April 15, 1970.

European Cup Final: 127,621, Real Madrid v Eintracht Frankfurt, at Hampden Park, Glasgow, May 18, 1960.

European Cup-Winners' Cup Final: 100,000, West Ham Utd. v TSV Munich, at Wembley, May 19, 1965.

Scottish League: 118,567, Rangers v Celtic, January 2, 1939.

Scottish League Cup Final: 107,609, Celtic v Rangers, at Hampden Park, October 23, 1965.

Football League old format: First Div.: 83,260, Manchester Utd. v Arsenal, January 17, 1948 (at Maine Road); **Second Div.:** 70,302 Tottenham v Southampton, February 25, 1950; **Third Div. South:** 51,621, Cardiff City v Bristol City, April 7, 1947; **Third Div. North:** 49,655, Hull City v Rotherham Utd., December 25, 1948; **Third Div.:** 49,309, Sheffield Wed. v Sheffield Utd., December 26, 1979; **Fourth Div.:** 37,774, Crystal Palace v Millwall, March 31, 1961.

Premier League: 73,006, Manchester Utd. v Charlton Athletic, May 7, 2006.

Football League – New Div. 1: 41,214, Sunderland v Stoke City, April 25, 1998; **New Div. 2:** 32,471, Manchester City v York City, May 8, 1999; **New Div. 3:** 22,319 Hull City v Hartlepool Utd., December 26, 2002. **New Champs:** 47,350 Sunderland v Stoke City,

May 8, 2005; **New Lge. 1** 28,798 Sheffield Wed. v Bristol City, May 7, 2005; **New Lge. 2:** 13,467 Carlisle Utd. v Torquay Utd., April 29, 2006.

In English Provinces: 84,569, Manchester City v Stoke City (F.A. Cup 6th Round), March 3, 1934.

Record for Under-21 International: 34,494 England v France, at Tottenham, November 11, 2005.

Record for friendly match: 104,679, Rangers v Eintracht Frankfurt, at Hampden Park, Glasgow, October 17, 1961.

Record Football League aggregate (season): 41,271,414 (1948-9) – 88 clubs.

Record Football League aggregate (single day): 1,269,934, December 27, 1949, previous day, 1,226,098.

Record average home League attendance for season: 68,764 by Manchester Utd. in 2005–06.

Long-ago League attendance aggregates: 10,929,000 in 1906-07 (40 clubs); 28,132,933 in 1937-8 (88 clubs).

Last 1m. crowd aggregate, League (single day): 1,007,200, December 27, 1971.

Record Amateur match attendance: 100,000 for F.A. Amateur Cup Final, Pegasus v Harwich & Parkeston at Wembley, April 11, 1953.

Record Cup-tie aggregate: 265,199, at two matches between Rangers and Morton, in the Scottish Cup Final, 1947-8.

Abandoned match attendance records: In England – 63,480 at Newcastle Utd. v Swansea City F.A. Cup 3rd round, Jan. 10, 1953, abandoned 8 mins (0-0), fog.

In Scotland: 94,596 at Scotland v Austria (4-1), Hampden Park, May 8, 1963. Referee Jim Finney ended play (79 minutes) after Austria had two players sent off and one carried off.

Colchester Utd.'s record crowd (19,072) was for the F.A. Cup 1st round tie v Reading on Nov. 27, 1948, abandoned 35 minutes (0-0), fog.

SMALLEST CROWDS

Smallest League attendances: 13, Stockport Co. v Leicester City (Div. 2, May 7, 1921; played at Old Trafford – Stockport ground closed); 469, Thames v Luton Town (Div. 3 South, December 6, 1930).

Lowest post-war League attendance: 450 Rochdale v Cambridge Utd. (Div. 3, February 5, 1974).

Lowest Premier League crowd: 3,039 for Wimbledon v Everton, Jan. 26, 1993 (smallest top-division attendance since war).

Lowest Saturday post-war top-division crowd: 3,231 for Wimbledon v Luton Town, Sept. 7, 1991 (Div. 1).

Lowest Football League crowds, new format – Div. 1: 849 for Wimbledon v Rotherham Utd., (Div. 1) October 29, 2002 (smallest att. in top two divisions since war); 1,054 Wimbledon v Wigan Athletic (Div. 1), Sept. 13, 2003 in club's last home match when sharing Selhurst Park; **Div. 2:** 1,077, Hartlepool Utd. v Cardiff City, March 22, 1994; **Div. 3:** 739, Doncaster Rov. v Barnet, March 3, 1998.

Lowest top-division crowd at a major ground since the war: 4,554 for Arsenal v Leeds Utd. (May 5, 1966) – fixture clashed with live TV coverage of Cup-Winners' Cup Final (Liverpool v Borussia Dortmund).

Smallest League Cup attendances: 612, Halifax Town v Tranmere Rov. (1st Round, 2nd Leg) September 6, 2000; 664, Wimbledon v Rotherham Utd. (3rd Round), November 5, 2002.

Smallest League Cup attendance at top-division ground: 1,987 for Wimbledon v Bolton Wand. (2nd Round, 2nd Leg) Oct. 6, 1992.

Smallest Wembley crowds for England matches: 15,628 v Chile (Rous Cup, May 23, 1989 – affected by Tube strike); 20,038 v Colombia (Friendly, Sept. 6, 1995); 21,432 v Czech. (Friendly, Apr. 25, 1990); 21,142 v Japan (Umbro Cup, June 3, 1995); 23,600 v Wales (British Championship, Feb. 23, 1983); 23,659 v Greece (Friendly, May 17, 1994); 23,951 v East Germany (Friendly, Sept. 12, 1984); 24,000 v N. Ireland (British Championship, Apr. 4, 1984); 25,756 v Colombia (Rous Cup, May 24, 1988); 25,837 v Denmark (Friendly, Sept. 14, 1988).

Smallest Int. modern crowd: 221 for Poland v N. Ireland (4-1, friendly) at Limassol, Cyprus, on February 13, 2002. Played at neutral venue at Poland's World Cup training base.

Smallest Int. modern crowds at home: N.Ireland: 2,500 v Chile (Belfast, May 26, 1989 – clashed with ITV live screening of Liverpool v Arsenal Championship decider); **Scotland:** 7,843 v N.Ireland (Hampden Park, May 6, 1969); **Wales:** 2,315 v N.Ireland (Wrexham, May 27, 1982).

Smallest attendance for post-war England match: 2,378 v San Marino (World Cup) at Bologna (Nov. 17, 1993). Tie clashed with Italy v Portugal (World Cup) shown live on Italian TV.

Smallest paid attendance for British first-class match: 29 for Clydebank v East Stirling, CIS Scottish League Cup 1st Round, July 31, 1999. Played at Morton's Cappielow Park ground, shared by Clydebank, the match clashed with the Tall Ships Race which attracted 200,000 to the area.

F.A. CUP CROWD RECORD (OUTSIDE FINAL)

The first F.A. Cup-tie shown on closed-circuit TV (5th. Round, Saturday, March 11, 1967, kick-off 7pm) drew a total of 105,000 spectators to Goodison Park and Anfield. This is the biggest attendance for a single F.A. Cup match other than the Final. At Goodison, 64,851 watched the match 'for real', while 40,149 saw the TV version on eight giant screens at Anfield. Everton beat Liverpool 1-0.

LOWEST SEMI-FINAL CROWD

The smallest F.A. Cup semi-final attendance since the war was 17,987 for Manchester Utd. v Crystal Palace replay, at Villa Park on April 12, 1995. Crystal Palace supporters largely boycotted tie after a fan died in car-park clash outside pub in Walsall before first match. Previous lowest: 25,963 for Wimbledon v Luton Town, at Tottenham on April 9, 1988.

Lowest quarter-final crowd since the war: 8,735 for Chesterfield v Wrexham on March 9, 1997.

Smallest F.A. Cup 3rd. Round attendances for matches between League clubs: 1,833 for Chester City v Bournemouth (at Macclesfield Town) Jan. 5, 1991; 1,966 for Aldershot v Oxford Utd., Jan. 10, 1987.

PRE-WEMBLEY CUP FINAL CROWDS

AT CRYSTAL PALACE

1895	42,560	1902	48,036	1908	74,967
1896	48,036	Replay	33,050	1909	67,651
1897	65,891	1903	64,000	1910	76,980
1898	62,017	1904	61,734	1911	69,098
1899	73,833	1905	101,117	1912	54,434
1900	68,945	1906	75,609	1913	120,028
1901	110,802	1907	84,584	1914	72,778

AT OLD TRAFFORD

1915	50,000

AT STAMFORD BRIDGE

1920	50,018	1921	72,805	1922	53,000

RECEIPTS RECORDS

Wembley Stadium underwent its first considerable alteration during 1962-3 in preparation for the World Cup in 1966. Higher admission fees at the 1963 F.A. Cup Final resulted in 100,000 spectators paying a record £89,000.

This is how Wembley's receipts records subsequently rose:

1968 F.A. Cup Final (Everton v W.B.A.)	£110,000
1968 European Cup Final (Manchester Utd. v Benfica)	£120,000
1976 F.A. Cup Final (Southampton v Manchester Utd.)	£420,000
1978 F.A. Cup Final (Ipswich Town v Arsenal)	£500,000

```
1981  England v Hungary (World Cup) ......................................... £671,000
1982  F.A. Cup Final (Tottenham v Q.P.R.) ................................. £886,000
       (plus £605,000 for replay)
1984  F.A. Cup Final (Everton v Watford) ................................. £919,000
*1985 F.A. Cup Final (Manchester Utd. v Everton) .............. £1,100,000
1986  F.A. Cup Final (Liverpool v Everton) .......................... £1,100,000
†1987 League Cup Final (Arsenal v Liverpool) .................. £1,000,000
1987  F.A. Cup Final (Coventry City v Tottenham) ............ £1,286,737
1988  F.A. Cup Final (Wimbledon v Liverpool) ................... £1,422,814
1989  F.A. Cup Final (Liverpool v Everton) .......................... £1,600,000
1990  League Cup Final (Nott'm Forest v Oldham Athletic) .. £1,650,000
1990  F.A. Cup Final (Manchester Utd. v Crystal Palace – first match) .. £2,000,000
1991  League Cup Final (Manchester Utd. v Sheffield Wed.) ......... £2,000,000
1991  F.A. Cup Final (Nott'm F. v Tottenham) .................... £2,016,000
1992  F.A. Cup Final (Liverpool v Sunderland) ................. £2,548,174
1993  F.A. Cup Final (Arsenal v Sheffield W. – first match) .... £2,818,000
       (Replay took receipts for both matches to £4,695,200)
1994  F.A. Cup Final record (Manchester Utd. v Chelsea) ......... £2,962,167
1997  League Cup Final record (Leicester City v Middlesbrough) ..... £2,750,000
1998  League Cup Final record (Chelsea v Middlesbrough) .......... £2,983,000
•2000 F.A. Cup Final record (Chelsea v Aston Villa) .......... £3,100,000
```

EARLY CUP FINAL RECEIPTS

```
1885  Blackburn Rov. v Queens Park ..................................... £442
1913  Aston Villa v Sunderland ...................................... £9,406
1923  Bolton Wand. v West Ham Utd., first Wembley Final ...... £27,776
1939  Portsmouth v Wolves ........................................... £29,000
1946  Derby Co. v Charlton Athletic ............................... £45,000
```

INTERNATIONAL RECORDS

MOST APPEARANCES

Peter Shilton, England goalkeeper, then aged 40, retired from International football after the 1990 World Cup Finals with the European record number of caps – 125. Previous record (119) was set by **Pat Jennings**, Northern Ireland's goalkeeper from 1964-86, who retired on his 41st birthday during the 1986 World Cup in Mexico. Shilton's England career spanned 20 seasons from his debut against East Germany at Wembley on Nov. 25, 1970.

Four players have completed a century of appearances in full International matches for England. **Billy Wright** of Wolves, was the first, retiring in 1959 with a total of 105 caps.

Bobby Charlton, of Manchester Utd., beat Wright's record in the World Cup match against West Germany in Leon, Mexico, in June 1970 and **Bobby Moore,** of West Ham Utd., overtook Charlton's 106 caps against Italy in Turin, in June 1973. Moore played 108 times for England, a record that stood until **Shilton** reached 109 against Denmark in Copenhagen (June 7, 1989).

Kenny Dalglish became Scotland's first 100-cap International v Romania (Hampden Park, March 26, 1986).

World's most-capped player: Mohamed Al-Deayea (Saudi Arabia goalkeeper) 173 caps (1990–2004).

Most-capped European player: Lothar Matthaus 150 Internationals for Germany (1980-2000).

Most-capped European goalkeeper: Thomas Ravelli, 143 Internationals for Sweden (1981-97).

Gillian Coultard, (Doncaster Belles), England Women's captain, received a special presentation from Geoff Hurst to mark 100 caps when England beat Holland 1-0 at Upton Park on October 30, 1997. She made her Int. debut at 18 in May 1981, and retired at the end of season 1999-2000 with a record 119 caps (30 goals).

BRITAIN'S MOST-CAPPED PLAYERS

(As at start of season 2006-07)

England

Peter Shilton	125
Bobby Moore	108
Bobby Charlton	106
Billy Wright	105
Bryan Robson	90

Scotland

Kenny Dalglish	102
Jim Leighton	91
Alex McLeish	77
Paul McStay	76
Tommy Boyd	72

Wales

Neville Southall	92
Gary Speed	85
Dean Saunders	75
Peter Nicholas	73
Ian Rush	73
Mark Hughes	72
Joey Jones	72

Northern Ireland

Pat Jennings	119
Mal Donaghy	91
Sammy McIlroy	88

Republic of Ireland

Steve Staunton	102
Niall Quinn	91
Tony Cascarino	88
Paul McGrath	83
Pat Bonner	80
Ray Houghton	73
Liam Brady	72
Frank Stapleton	71
Kevin Moran	71
Andy Townsend	70

MOST ENGLAND CAPS IN ROW

Most consecutive International appearances: 70 by **Billy Wright**, for England from October 1951 to May 1959. He played 105 of England's first 108 post-war matches.

England captains most times: Billy Wright and **Bobby Moore**, 90 each.
England captains – 4 in match (v Serbia & Montenegro at Leicester June 3, 2003): **Michael Owen** was captain for the first half and after the interval the armband passed to **Emile Heskey** (for 15 minutes), **Philip Neville** (26 minutes) and substitute **Jamie Carragher** (9 minutes, including time added).

ENGLAND'S TALLEST

At 6ft. 7in., Southampton striker **Peter Crouch** became England's tallest-ever International when he made his debut against Colombia in New Jersey, USA on May 31, 2005.

MOST PLAYERS FROM ONE CLUB IN ENGLAND SIDES

Arsenal supplied seven men (a record) to the England team v Italy at Highbury on November 14, 1934. They were: Frank Moss, George Male, Eddie Hapgood, Wilf Copping, Ray Bowden, Ted Drake and Cliff Bastin. In addition, Arsenal's Tom Whittaker was England's trainer.

Since then until 2001, the most players from one club in an England team was six from **Liverpool** against Switzerland at Wembley in September 1977. The side also included a Liverpool old boy, Kevin Keegan (Hamburg).

Seven **Arsenal** men took part in the England – France (0-2) match at Wembley on February 10, 1999. Goalkeeper David Seaman and defenders Lee Dixon, Tony Adams and Martin Keown lined up for England. Nicolas Anelka (2 goals) and Emmanuel Petit started the match for France and Patrick Vieira replaced Anelka.

Manchester Utd. equalled Arsenal's 1934 record by providing England with seven players in the World Cup qualifier away to Albania on March 28, 2001. Five started the match – David Beckham (captain), Gary Neville, Paul Scholes, Nicky Butt and Andy Cole – and two went on as substitutes: Wes Brown and Teddy Sheringham.

INTERNATIONAL SUBS RECORDS

Malta substituted all 11 players in their 1-2 home defeat against England on June 3, 2000. Six substitutes by England took the total replacements in the match to 17, then an International record.

Most substitutions in match by **England**: 11 in second half by Sven-Goran Eriksson against Holland at Tottenham on August 15, 2001; 11 against Italy at Leeds on March 27, 2002; Italy sent on 8 players from the bench – the total of 19 substitutions was then a record for an England match; 11 against Australia at Upton Park on February 12, 2003 (entire England team changed at half-time); 11 against Iceland at City of Manchester Stadium on June 5, 2004.

Forty-three players, a record for an England match, were used in the International against Serbia & Montenegro at Leicester on June 3, 2003. England sent on 10 substitutes in the second half and their opponents changed all 11 players.

The **Republic of Ireland** sent on 12 second-half substitutes, using 23 players in all, when they beat Russia 2-0 in a friendly International in Dublin on February 13, 2002.

First England substitute: Wolves winger **Jimmy Mullen** replaced injured Jackie Milburn (15 mins.) away to Belgium on May 18, 1950. He scored in a 4-1 win.

ENGLAND'S WORLD CUP-WINNERS

At Wembley, July 30, 1966, 4-2 v West Germany (2-2 after 90 mins), scorers Hurst 3, Peters. Team: Banks; Cohen, Wilson, Stiles, Charlton (J.), Moore (Captain), Ball, Hurst, Charlton (R.), Hunt, Peters. Manager **Alf Ramsey** fielded that same eleven in six successive matches (an England record): the World Cup quarter-final, semi-final and Final, and the first three games of the following season. England wore red shirts in the Final and Her Majesty the Queen presented the Cup to Bobby Moore. The players each received a £1,000 bonus, plus £60 World Cup Final appearance money, all less tax, and Ramsey a £6,000 bonus from the F.A. The match was shown live on TV (in black and white).

BRAZIL'S RECORD RUN

Brazil hold the record for the longest unbeaten sequence in International football: 45 matches from 1993-7. The previous record of 31 matches undefeated was held by Hungary between June 1950 and July 1954.

ENGLAND MATCHES ABANDONED

May 17, 1953 v **Argentina** (Friendly, Buenos Aires) after 23 mins. (0–0) – rain.
Oct. 29, 1975 v **Czechoslovakia** (Eur. Champ. Qual., Bratislava) after 17 mins. (0–0) – fog. Played next day.
Feb. 15, 1995 v **Rep. of Ireland** (Friendly, Dublin) after 27 mins. (1–0) – crowd disturbance.

ENGLAND POSTPONEMENT

Nov 21, 1979 v **Bulgaria** (Eur. Champ. qual., Wembley postponed for 24 hours – fog.

ENGLAND UNDER COVER

England played indoors for the first time when they beat Argentina 1-0 in the World Cup at the Sapporo Dome, Japan, on June 7, 2002.

ALL-SEATED INTERNATIONALS

The first **all-seated crowd** (30,000) for a full International in Britain saw **Wales** and **West Germany** draw 0-0 at Cardiff City Arms Park on May 31, 1989. The terraces were closed.

England's first all-seated International at Wembley was against Yugoslavia (2-1) on December 13, 1989 (attendance 34,796). The terracing behind the goals was closed for conversion to seating.

The first **full-house all-seated** International at Wembley was for England v Brazil (1-0) on March 28, 1990, when a capacity 80,000 crowd paid record British receipts of £1,200,000.

ENGLAND 'ON THE ROAD'

Since Wembley Stadium closed in October 2000, England have played home fixtures at 14 club grounds (to end of season 2004-05): Manchester Utd. (10), Aston Villa (3), Liverpool (3), Newcastle (3), Manchester City (2), Derby, Tottenham, Leeds, Southampton, West Ham, Sunderland, Leicester, Middlesbrough and Ipswich.

FIRST BLACK CAPS

First black player for **England** in a senior International was Nott'm. Forest full-back **Viv Anderson** against Czechoslovakia at Wembley on November 29, 1978.

Aston Villa's **Ugo Ehiogu** was **England's** first black captain (U-21 v Holland at Portsmouth, April 27, 1993).

Paul Ince (Manchester Utd.) became the first black player to captain **England** in a **full International** (v U.S.A., Boston, June 9, 1993).

First black British International was **Eddie Parris** (Bradford Park Avenue) for Wales against N. Ireland in Belfast on December 5, 1931.

MOST NEW CAPS IN ENGLAND TEAM

6, by **Sir Alf Ramsey** (v Portugal, April 3, 1974) and **by Sven-Goran Eriksson** (v Australia, February 12, 2003; 5 at half-time when 11 changes made).

PLAYED FOR MORE THAN ONE COUNTRY

Multi-nationals in senior International football include: **Johnny Carey** (1938-53) – caps Rep. of Ireland 29, N. Ireland 7; **Ferenc Puskas** (1945-62) – caps Hungary 84, Spain 4; **Alfredo di Stefano** (1950-6) – caps Argentina 7, Spain 31; **Ladislav Kubala** (1948-58) – caps, Hungary 3, Czechoslovakia 11, Spain 19, only player to win full Int. honours with 3 countries. Kubala also played in a fourth Int. team, scoring twice for FIFA v England at Wembley in 1953.

Eleven players, including Carey, appeared for both N. Ireland and the Republic of Ireland in seasons directly after the last war.

Cecil Moore, capped by N. Ireland in 1949 when with Glentoran, played for USA v England in 1953.

Hawley Edwards played for England v Scotland in 1874 and for Wales v Scotland in 1876.

Jack Reynolds (Distillery and W.B.A.) played for both Ireland (5 times) and England (8) in the 1890s.

Bobby Evans (Sheffield Utd.) had played 10 times for Wales when capped for England, in 1910-11. He was born in Chester of Welsh parents.

In recent years several players have represented USSR and one or other of the breakaway republics. The same applies to Yugoslavia and its component states. **Josip Weber** played for Croatia in 1992 and made a 5-goal debut for Belgium in 1994.

3-GENERATION INTERNATIONAL FAMILY

When Bournemouth striker **Warren Feeney** was capped away to Liechtenstein on March 27, 2002, he became the third generation of his family to play for Northern Ireland. He followed in the footsteps of his grandfather James (capped twice in 1950) and father Warren Snr. (1 in 1976).

FATHERS & SONS CAPPED BY ENGLAND

George Eastham senior (pre-war) and **George Eastham** junior; **Brian Clough** and **Nigel Clough**; **Frank Lampard** senior and **Frank Lampard** junior.

FATHER & SON SAME-DAY CAPS

Iceland made father-and-son Int. history when they beat Estonia 3-0 in Tallin on April 24, 1996. Arnor Gudjohnsen (35) started the match and was replaced (62 mins.) by his 17-year-old son Eidur.

LONGEST UNBEATEN START TO ENGLAND CAREER

Steven Gerrard, 21 matches (W16, D5) 2000–03.

SUCCESSIVE ENGLAND HAT-TRICKS

The last player to score a hat-trick in consecutive England matches was **Dixie Dean** on the summer tour in May 1927, against Belgium (9-1) and Luxembourg (5-2).

POST-WAR HAT-TRICKS v ENGLAND

November 25, 1953, scorer **Nandor Hidegkuti** (England 3, Hungary 6, Wembley); May 11, 1958, scorer **Aleksandar Petakovic** (Yugoslavia 5, England 0, Belgrade); May 17, 1959, scorer **Juan Seminario** (Peru 4, England 1, Lima); June 15, 1988, scorer **Marco Van Basten** (Holland 3, England 1, European Championship, Dusseldorf).

NO-SAVE GOALKEEPERS

Chris Woods did not have one save to make when England beat San Marino 6-0 (World Cup) at Wembley on February 17, 1993. He touched the ball only six times throughout the match.

Gordon Banks had a similar no-save experience when England beat Malta 5-0 (European Championship) at Wembley on May 12, 1971. Malta did not force a goal-kick or corner, and the four times Banks touched the ball were all from back passes.

FOOTBALL'S GOVERNING BODIES

By June 2005, a total of 205 National Associations were members of the Federation Internationale de Football Association (**F.I.F.A.**, founded May, 1904), and the Union of European Football Associations (**U.E.F.A.**, founded June, 1954) embraced 52 countries.

The seven original members of the F.I.F.A. were Belgium, Denmark, France, Holland, Spain, Sweden and Switzerland.

FIFA WORLD YOUTH CHAMPIONSHIP (UNDER-20)

Finals: 1977 (Tunis) Soviet Union 2, Mexico 2 (Soviet won 9-8 on pens.); **1979** (Tokyo) Argentina 3, Soviet Union 1; **1981** (Sydney) W. Germany 4, Qatar 0; **1983** (Mexico City) Brazil 1, Argentina 0; **1985** (Moscow) Brazil 1, Spain 0; **1987** (Santiago) Yugoslavia 1, W. Germany 1 (Yugoslavia won 5-4 on pens.); **1989** (Riyadh) Portugal 2, Nigeria 0; **1991** (Lisbon) Portugal 0, Brazil 0 (Portugal won 4-2 on pens.); **1993** (Sydney) Brazil 2,

Ghana 1; **1995** (Qatar) Argentina 2, Brazil 0; **1997** (Kuala Lumpur) Argentina 2, Uruguay 1; **1999** (Lagos) Spain 4, Japan 0; **2001** (Buenos Aires) Argentina 3, Ghana 0; **2003** (Dubai) Brazil 1, Spain 0; **2005** (Utrecht) Argentina 2, Nigeria 1.

FAMOUS CLUB FEATS

Chelsea were Premiership winners in 2004-05, their centenary season with the highest points total (95) ever recorded by England Champions. They set these other records: Most Premiership wins in season (29); most clean sheets (25) and fewest goals conceded (15) in top-division history. They also won the League Cup in 2005.

Arsenal created an all-time English League record sequence of 49 unbeaten Premiership matches (W36, D13), spanning 3 seasons, from May 7, 2003 until losing 2-0 away to Manchester United on October 24, 2004. It included all 38 games in season 2003-04.

The Double: There have been ten instances of a club winning the Football League/Premiership title and the F.A. Cup in the same season. **Manchester Utd.** and **Arsenal** have each done so three times:-

Preston N.E. 1888-89; **Aston Villa** 1896-97; **Tottenham** 1960-61; **Arsenal** 1970-71, 1997-98, 2001-02; **Liverpool** 1985-86; **Manchester Utd.** 1993-94, 1995-96, 1998-99.

The Treble: Liverpool were the first English club to win three major competitions in one season when in 1983-84, Joe Fagan's first season as manager, they were League Champions, League Cup winners and European Cup winners.

Sir Alex Ferguson's **Manchester Utd.** achieved an even more prestigious treble in 1998-99, completing the domestic double of Premiership and F.A. Cup and then winning the European Cup.

Liverpool completed a unique treble by an English club with three cup successes under Gerard Houllier in season 2000-01: the League Cup, F.A. Cup and UEFA Cup.

Liverpool the first English club to win five major trophies in one calendar year (February-August 2001): League Cup, F.A. Cup, UEFA Cup, Charity Shield, UEFA Super Cup.

As Champions in season 2001-02, **Arsenal** set a Premiership record by winning the last 13 matches. They were the first top-division club since Preston N.E. in the League's inaugural season (1888-9) to maintain an unbeaten away record.

(See Scottish section for treble feats by Rangers and Celtic.)

Home Runs: Sunderland lost only one home Div. 1 game out of 73 in five seasons, 1891 to 1896. **Brentford** won all 21 home games in 1929-30 in the Third Division (South). Others have won all home games in a smaller programme.

Record Home Run: Liverpool went 85 competitive first-team games unbeaten at home between losing 2-3 to Birmingham City on January 21, 1978 and 1-2 to Leicester City on January 31, 1981. They comprised 63 in the League, 9 League Cup, 7 in European competition and 6 F.A. Cup. Leicester were relegated that season.

Millwall were unbeaten at home in the League for 59 consecutive matches from 1964-67.

Third to First: Charlton Athletic, in 1936, became the first club to advance from the Third to First Division in successive seasons. **Queen's Park Rangers** were the second club to achieve the feat in 1968, and **Oxford Utd.** did it in 1984 and 1985 as Champions of each division. Subsequently, **Derby Co.** (1987), **Middlesbrough** (1988), **Sheffield Utd.** (1990) and **Notts Co.** (1991) climbed from Third Division to First in consecutive seasons.

Watford won successive promotions from the modern Second Division to the Premier League in 1997-8, 1998-9. **Manchester City** equalled the feat in 1998-9, 1999-2000.

Fourth to First: Northampton Town, in 1965 became the first club to rise from the Fourth to the First Division. **Swansea City** climbed from the Fourth Division to the First (three promotions in four seasons), 1977-8 to 1980-1. **Wimbledon** repeated the feat, 1982-3 to 1985-6 **Watford** did it in five seasons, 1977-8 to 1981-2. **Carlisle Utd.** climbed from Fourth Division to First, 1964-74.

Non-League to First: When **Wimbledon** finished third in the Second Division in 1986, they completed the phenomenal rise from non-League football (Southern League) to the First Division in nine years. Two years later they won the F.A. Cup.

Tottenham, in 1960-1, not only carried off the First Division Championship and the F.A. Cup for the first time that century but set up other records by opening with 11 successive wins, registering most First Division wins (31), most away wins in the

League's history (16), and equalling Arsenal's First Division records of 66 points and 33 away points. They already held the Second Division record of 70 points (1919-20).

Arsenal, in 1993, became the first club to win both English domestic cup competitions (F.A. Cup and League Cup) in the same season. **Liverpool** repeated the feat in 2000-01.

Preston N.E., in season 1888-9, won the first League Championship without losing a match and the F.A. Cup without having a goal scored against them. Only other English clubs to remain unbeaten through a League season were **Liverpool** (Div. 2 Champions in 1893-4) and **Arsenal** (Premiership Champions 2003-04).

Bury, in 1903, also won the F.A. Cup without conceding a goal.

Everton won Div. 2, Div. 1 and the F.A. Cup in successive seasons, 1930-1, 1931-2, 1932-3.

Liverpool won the League Championship in 1964, the F.A. Cup in 1965 and the Championship again in 1966. In 1978 they became the first British club to win the European Cup in successive seasons. **Nott'm. Forest** repeated the feat in 1979 and 1980.

Liverpool won the League Championship six times in eight seasons (1976-83) under **Bob Paisley's** management.

Sir Alex Ferguson's **Manchester Utd.** have won the F.A. Premier League in eight of its 14 seasons (1993-2006). They were runners-up twice and third three times.

Most Premiership wins in season: 29 by Chelsea in 2004-05, 2005–06.

Biggest points-winning margin by League Champions: 18 by Manchester Utd. (1999-2000).

COVENTRY UNIQUE

Coventry City are the only club to have played in the Premier League, all four previous divisions of the Football League, in both sections (North and South) of the old Third Division and in the Coca-Cola Championship.

FAMOUS UPS & DOWNS

Sunderland: Relegated in 1958 after maintaining First Division status since their election to the Football League in 1890. They dropped into Division 3 for the first time in 1987.

Aston Villa: Relegated with **Preston N.E.** to the Third Division in 1970.

Arsenal up: When the League was extended in 1919, Woolwich Arsenal (sixth in Division Two in 1914-15, last season before the war) were elected to Division One. Arsenal have been in the top division ever since.

Tottenham down: At that same meeting in 1919 Chelsea (due for relegation) retained their place in Division One but the bottom club (Tottenham) had to go down to Division Two.

Preston N.E. and Burnley down: Preston N.E., the first League Champions in season 1888-9, dropped into the Fourth Division in 1985. So did Burnley, also among the League's original members in 1888. In 1986, Preston N.E. had to apply for re-election.

Wolves' fall: Wolves, another of the Football League's original members, completed the fall from First Division to Fourth in successive seasons (1984-5-6).

Lincoln City out: Lincoln City became the first club to suffer automatic demotion from the Football League when they finished bottom of Div. 4, on goal difference, in season 1986-7. They were replaced by Scarborough, champions of the GM Vauxhall Conference. Lincoln City regained their place a year later.

Swindon Town up and down: In the 1990 play-offs, Swindon Town won promotion to the First Division for the first time, but remained in the Second Division because of financial irregularities.

MOST CHAMPIONSHIP WINS

Liverpool, by winning the First Division in 1976-7, established a record of 10 Championship victories. They later increased the total to 18. **Manchester Utd.** are second with 15 League titles (7 Football League, 8 Premier League) and **Arsenal** third with 13 (10 Football League, 3 Premier League).

LONGEST CURRENT MEMBERS OF TOP DIVISION

Arsenal (since 1919), Everton (1954), Liverpool (1962), Manchester Utd. (1975).

CHAMPIONS: FEWEST PLAYERS

Liverpool used only 14 players (five ever-present) when they won the League Championship in season 1965-6. **Aston Villa** also called on no more than 14 players to win the title in 1980-81, with seven ever-present.

UNBEATEN CHAMPIONS

Only two clubs have become Champions of England with an unbeaten record: **Preston N.E.** as the Football League's first winners in 1888-9 (22 matches) and **Arsenal**, Premiership winners in 2003-04 (38 matches).

LEAGUE HAT-TRICKS

Huddersfield Town created a record in 1924-5-6 by winning the League Championship three years in succession.
    Arsenal equalled this League hat-trick in 1933-4-5, **Liverpool** in 1982-3-4 and **Manchester United** in 1999-2000-01.

'SUPER DOUBLE' WINNERS

Since the war, there have been three instances of players appearing in and then managing F.A. Cup and Championship-winning teams:
    Joe Mercer: Player in Arsenal Championship teams 1948, 1953 and in their 1950 F.A. Cup side; manager of Manchester City when they won Championship 1968, F.A. Cup 1969.
    Kenny Dalglish: Player in Liverpool Championship-winning teams 1979, 1980, 1982, 1983, 1984, player-manager 1986, 1988, 1990; player-manager when Liverpool won F.A. Cup (to complete Double) 1986; manager of Blackburn Rov., Champions 1995.
    George Graham: Played in Arsenal's Double-winning team in 1971, and as manager took them to Championship success in 1989 and 1991 and the F.A. Cup – League Cup double in 1993.

ORIGINAL TWELVE

The original 12 members of the Football League (formed in 1888) were: **Accrington, Aston Villa, Blackburn Rov., Bolton Wand., Burnley, Derby Co., Everton, Notts Co., Preston N.E., Stoke City, W.B.A.** and **Wolves.**
    Results on the opening day (September 8, 1888): Bolton Wand. 3, Derby Co. 6; Everton 2, Accrington 1; Preston N.E. 5, Burnley 2; Stoke City 0, W.B.A. 2; Wolves 1, Aston Villa 1. Preston N.E. had the biggest first-day crowd: 6,000. Blackburn Rov. and Notts Co. did not play that day. They kicked off a week later (September 15) – Blackburn Rov. 5, Accrington 5; Everton 2, Notts Co. 1.

FASTEST CLIMBS

Three promotions in four seasons by two clubs – **Swansea City:** 1978 third in Div.4; 1979 third in Div.3; 1981 third in Div.2; **Wimbledon:** 1983 Champions of Div.4; 1984 second in Div.3; 1986 third in Div.2.

MERSEYSIDE RECORD

Liverpool is the only city to have staged top-division football – through Everton and/or Liverpool – in **every season** since League football began in 1888.

EARLIST PROMOTIONS TO TOP DIVISION POST-WAR

March 23, 1974, Middlesbrough; March 25, 2006, Reading.

EARLIEST RELEGATIONS POST-WAR

From top division: **Q.P.R.** went down from the old First Division on March 29, 1969. From modern First Division: **Stockport Co.** on March 16, 2002, with 7 matches still to play; **Wimbledon** on April 6, 2004, with 7 matches to play.

LEAGUE RECORDS

DOUBLE CHAMPIONS

Nine men have played in and managed League Championship-winning teams:
Ted Drake Player – Arsenal 1934, 1935, 1938. Manager – Chelsea 1955.
Bill Nicholson Player – Tottenham 1951. Manager – Tottenham 1961.
Alf Ramsey Player – Tottenham 1951. Manager – Ipswich Town 1962.
Joe Mercer Player – Everton 1939, Arsenal 1948, 1953. Manager – Manchester City 1968.
Dave Mackay Player – Tottenham 1961. Manager – Derby Co. 1975.
Bob Paisley Player – Liverpool 1947. Manager – Liverpool 1976, 1977, 1979, 1980, 1982, 1983.
Howard Kendall Player – Everton 1970. Manager – Everton 1985, 1987.
Kenny Dalglish Player – Liverpool 1979, 1980, 1982, 1983, 1984. Player-manager – Liverpool 1986, 1988, 1990. Manager – Blackburn Rov. 1995.
George Graham Player – Arsenal 1971. Manager – Arsenal 1989, 1991.

MOST LEAGUE CHAMPIONSHIP MEDALS

Kenny Dalglish: 9 – 8 for Liverpool (5 as player, 1979-80-82-83-84; 3 as player-manager, 1986-88-90); 1 for Blackburn Rov. (as manager, 1995). As a player he also won 4 Scottish Championship medals with Celtic (1972-73-74-77). **Phil Neal:** 8 for Liverpool (1976-77-79-80-82-83-84-86); **Alan Hansen:** 8 for Liverpool (1979-80-82-83-84-86-88-90); **Ryan Giggs:** 8 for Manchester Utd. (1993–94–96–97–99–2000–01–03); **Sir Alex Ferguson:** 8 as Manchester Utd. manager (1993-94-96-97-99-2000-01-03).

CANTONA'S FOUR-TIMER

Eric Cantona played in four successive Championship-winning teams: Marseille 1990-1, Leeds Utd. 1991-2, Manchester Utd. 1992-3 and 1993-4.

ARRIVALS AND DEPARTURES

The following are the Football League arrivals and departures since 1923:

Year	In	Out
1923	Doncaster Rov.	Stalybridge Celtic
	New Brighton	
1927	Torquay Athletic	Aberdare Athletic
1928	Carlisle Utd.	Durham City
1929	York City	Ashington
1930	Thames	Merthyr Tydfil
1931	Mansfield Town	Newport County
	Chester City	Nelson
1932	Aldershot	Thames
	Newport County	Wigan Borough
1938	Ipswich Town	Gillingham
1950	Colchester Utd.	
	Gillingham	
	Scunthorpe Utd.	
	Shrewsbury Town	
1951	Workington	New Brighton
1960	Peterborough Utd.	Gateshead
1962	Oxford Utd.	Accrington Stanley (resigned)
1970	Cambridge Utd.	Bradford P.A.
1972	Hereford Utd.	Barrow
1977	Wimbledon	Workington
1978	Wigan Athletic	Southport
1987	Scarborough	Lincoln City
1988	Lincoln City	Newport County
1989	Maidstone Utd.	Darlington

1990	Darlington	Colchester Utd.	
1991	Barnet		
1992	Colchester Utd.	Aldershot, Maidstone (resigned)	
1993	Wycombe Wand.	Halifax Town	
1997	Macclesfield Town	Hereford Utd.	
1998	Halifax Town	Doncaster Rov.	
1999	Cheltenham Town	Scarborough	
2000	Kidderminster Harriers	Chester City	
2001	Rushden & Diamonds	Barnet	
2002	Boston Utd.	Halifax Town	
2003	Yeovil Town, Doncaster Rov.	Exeter City, Shrewsbury Town	
2004	Chester City, Shrewsbury Town	Carlisle Utd., York City	
2005	Barnet, Carlisle Utd.	Kidderminster, Cambridge Utd.	
2006	Accrington Stanley, Hereford Utd.	Oxford Utd., Rushden & Diamonds	

Leeds City were expelled from Div. 2 in October, 1919; Port Vale took over their fixtures.

EXTENSIONS TO FOOTBALL LEAGUE

Clubs	Season	Clubs	Season
12 to 14	1891-2	44 to 66+	1920-1
14 to 28*	1892-3	66 to 86†	1921-2
28 to 31	1893-4	86 to 88	1923-4
31 to 32	1894-5	88 to 92	1950-1
32 to 36	1898-9	92 to 93	1991-2
36 to 40	1905-6	(Reverted to 92 when Aldershot closed,	
40 to 44	1919-20	March 1992)	

* Second Division formed. + Third Division (South) formed from Southern League clubs.
† Third Division (North) formed.
Football League reduced to 70 clubs and three divisions on the formation of the F.A.
Premier League in 1992; increased to 72 season 1994-5, when Premier League
reduced to 20 clubs.

RECORD RUNS

Arsenal hold the record unbeaten sequence in the English League – 49 Premiership matches (36 wins, 13 draws) from May 7, 2003 until October 24, 2004 when beaten 2-0 away to Manchester United.

The record previously belonged to **Nott'm. Forest** – 42 First Division matches (21 wins, 21 draws) from November 19, 1977 until beaten 2-0 at Liverpool on December 9, 1978.

Best debuts: Ipswich Town won the First Division at their first attempt in 1961-2. **Peterborough Utd.** in their first season in the Football League (1960-1) not only won the Fourth Division but set the all-time scoring record for the League of 134 goals. **Hereford Utd.** were promoted from the Fourth Division in their first League season, 1972-3. **Wycombe Wand.** were promoted from the Third Division (via the play-offs) in their first League season, 1993-4.

Record winning sequence in a season: 14 consecutive League victories (all in Second Division): **Manchester Utd.** 1904-5, **Bristol City** 1905-6 and **Preston N.E.** 1950-1.

Best winning start to League season: 13 successive victories in Div. 3 by **Reading**, season 1985-6.

Best starts in 'old' First Division: 11 consecutive victories by **Tottenham** in 1960-1; 10 by **Manchester Utd.** in 1985-6. **Newcastle Utd.** won their first 11 matches in the 'new' First Division in 1992-3.

Longest unbeaten sequence (all competitions): 40 by **Nott'm. Forest**, March-December 1978. It comprised 21 wins, 19 draws (in 29 League matches, 6 League Cup, 4 European Cup, 1 Charity Shield).

Longest unbeaten starts to League season: 38 matches (26 wins, 12 draws) in **Arsenal's** undefeated Premiership season, 2003-4; 29 matches – **Leeds Utd.**, Div. 1 1973-4 (19 wins, 10 draws); **Liverpool**, Div. 1 1987-8 (22 wins, 7 draws).

Most consecutive League matches unbeaten in a season: 38 **Arsenal** Premiership season 2003-4 (see above); 33 **Reading** (25 wins, 8 draws) 2005–6.

Longest winning sequence in Div. 1: 13 matches by **Tottenham** – last two of season 1959-60, first 11 of 1960-1.

Longest winning one-season sequences in Championship: 13 matches by **Preston N.E.** in 1891-2; 13 by **Sunderland**, also in 1891-2.

Longest unbeaten home League sequence in top division: 63 matches (49 wins, 14 draws) by **Liverpool** (February 1978–December 1980).

Premier League – best starts to season: (before **Arsenal** unbeaten through season 2003-4): 12 games unbeaten – **Nott'm. Forest** in 1995-6, **Arsenal** in 1997-8, **Aston Villa** in 1998-9, **Liverpool** 2002-3.

Best winning start to Premiership season: 9 consecutive victories by Chelsea in 2005-06.

Premier League – most consecutive wins (two seasons): 14 by **Arsenal**, February-August, 2002.

Premier League's record unbeaten run: 40 matches (W28, D12) by **Arsenal** (May 7, 2003–May 15, 2004). **In one season**, all 38 matches by Arsenal (W26, D12) in 2003-4.

Premier League – longest unbeaten away run: 23 matches (W16, D7) by **Arsenal** (Aug. 18, 2001–Sept. 28, 2002); and by **Arsenal** again (W13, D10), April 5 2003–May 15, 2004.

Record home-win sequences: Bradford Park Avenue won 25 successive home games in Div. 3 North – the last 18 in 1926-7 and the first 7 the following season. Longest run of home wins in the top division is 21 by **Liverpool** – the last 9 of 1971-2 and the first 12 of 1972-3.

British record for successive League wins: 25 by **Celtic** (Scottish Premier League), 2003-4.

WORST SEQUENCES

Cambridge Utd. experienced the longest run without a win in Football League history in season 1983-4: 31 matches (21 lost, 10 drawn). They finished bottom of the Second Division.

Worst losing start to a League season: 12 consecutive defeats by **Manchester Utd.** (Div. 1), 1930-1.

Worst Premier League start: **Swindon Town** 15 matches without win (6 draws, 9 defeats), 1993-4.

Worst Premier League sequence: **Sunderland** 26 matches without win (3 draws, 23 defeats), December 2002 – September 2005.

Premier League – most consecutive defeats: 20 **Sunderland** last 15 matches, 2002-3, first five matches 2005-06.

Longest non-winning start to League season: 25 matches (4 draws, 21 defeats) by **Newport County**, Div. 4. Worst no-win League starts since then: 16 matches by **Burnley** (9 draws, 7 defeats in Div. 2, 1979-80); 16 by **Hull City** (10 draws, 6 defeats in Div. 2, 1989-90); 16 by **Sheffield Utd.** (4 draws, 12 defeats in Div. 1, 1990-91).

Most League defeats in season: 34 by **Doncaster Rov.** (Div. 3) 1997-8; 33 by **Wimbledon** (Div. 1) 2003-4.

Fewest League wins in season: 1 by **Loughborough Town** (Div. 2, season 1899-1900). They lost 27, drew 6, goals 18-100 and dropped out of the League. (See also Scottish section).

Fewest home League wins in season: 1 by **Loughborough Town** (Div. 2, 1899-1900), **Notts Co.** (Div. 1, 1904-5), **Woolwich Arsenal** (Div. 1, 1912-13), **Blackpool** (Div. 1, 1966-7), **Rochdale** (Div. 3, 1973-4), **Sunderland** (Premiership, 2005-06).

Most home League defeats in season: 18 by **Cambridge Utd.** (Div. 3, 1984-5).

Away League defeats record: 24 in row by **Nelson** (Div. 3 North) – 3 in April 1930 followed by all 21 in season 1930-31. They then dropped out of the League.

Biggest defeat in Champions' season: During **Newcastle Utd.'s** Championship-winning season in 1908-9, they were beaten 9-1 at home by Sunderland on December 5.

WORST START BY EVENTUAL CHAMPIONS

Sunderland took only 2 points from their first 7 matches in season 1912-13 (2 draws, 5 defeats). They won 25 of the remaining 31 games to clinch their fifth League title.

SUNDERLAND'S WOE

Sunderland were relegated in season 2002–03 as the worst-ever team in the Premiership: fewest wins (4), fewest points (19), fewest goals (21) and with the longest run of consecutive defeats (15). They were relegated again in 2005-06 with three wins and 15 points.

UNBEATEN LEAGUE SEASON

Only three clubs have completed an English League season unbeaten: **Preston N.E.** (22 matches in 1888-9, the League's first season), **Liverpool** (28 matches in Div. 2, 1893-4) and **Arsenal** (38 matches in Premiership, 2003-4).

100 PER CENT HOME RECORDS

Five clubs have won every home League match in a season, four of them in the old Second Division: **Liverpool** (14) in 1893-4, **Bury** (15) in 1894-5, **Sheffield Wed.** (17) in 1899-1900 and **Small Heath**, subsequently Birmingham (17) in 1902-3. The last club to do it, **Brentford**, won all 21 home games in Div. 3 South in 1929-30.

    Rotherham Utd. just failed to equal that record in 1946-7. They won their first 20 home matches in Div. 3 North, then drew the last 3-3 v Rochdale.

BEST HOME LEAGUE RECORDS IN TOP FLIGHT

Newcastle Utd., 1906-07 (P19, W18, D1); **Chelsea** 2005-6 (P19, W18, D1).

MOST CONSECUTIVE CLEAN SHEETS

Football League – 11: Millwall (Div. 3 South 1925-26); **York City** (Div. 3 1973-74); **Reading** (Div. 4, 1978-79). **Premiership – 10: Chelsea** (2004-05).

WORST HOME RUNS

Most consecutive home League defeats: 8 by **Rochdale**, who took only 11 points in Div. 3 North in season 1931-2; 8 by **Stockport Co.** (Div.1) in season 2001-02; 8 by **Sunderland** (Premiership), season 2002–03.

    Between November 1958 and October 1959 **Portsmouth** drew 2 and lost 14 out of 16 consecutive home games.

    West Ham Utd. did not win in the Premiership at Upton Park in season 2002–03 until the 13th. home match on January 29.

MOST AWAY WINS IN SEASON

Doncaster Rovers won 18 of their 21 away League fixtures when winning Div. 3 North in 1946-7.

AWAY WINS RECORD

Most consecutive away League wins: 10 by Tottenham (Div. 1) – 8 at start of 1960-1, after ending previous season with 2 away victories.

100 PER CENT HOME WINS ON ONE DAY

Div. 1 – All 11 home teams won on Feb. 13, 1926 and on Dec. 10, 1955. **Div. 2** – All 12 home teams won on Nov. 26, 1988. **Div. 3**, all 12 home teams won in the week-end programme of Oct. 18-19, 1968.

NO HOME WINS IN DIV. ON ONE DAY

Div. 1 – 8 away wins, 3 draws in 11 matches on Sept. 6, 1986. **Div. 2** – 7 away wins, 4 draws in 11 matches on Dec. 26, 1987. **Premier League** – 6 away wins, 5 draws in 11 matches on Dec. 26, 1994.

    The week-end **Premiership** programme on Dec. 7-8-9, 1996 produced no home win in the ten games (4 aways, 6 draws). There was again no home victory (3 away wins, 7 draws) in the week-end **Premiership** fixtures on September 23-24, 2000.

MOST DRAWS IN A SEASON (FOOTBALL LEAGUE)

23 by **Norwich City** (Div. 1, 1978-9), **Exeter City** (Div. 4, 1986-7). **Cardiff City** and **Hartlepool Utd.** (both Div. 3, 1997-8). Norwich City played 42 matches, the others 46.

MOST DRAWS IN ONE DIV. ON ONE DAY

On September 18, 1948 **nine** out of 11 First Division matches were drawn.

MOST DRAWS IN PREMIER DIV. PROGRAMME

Over the week-ends of December 2-3-4, 1995, and September 23-24, 2000, seven out of the ten matches finished level.

FEWEST DRAWS IN SEASON (46 MATCHES)

3 by **Reading** (Div. 3 South, 1951–2); **Bradford City Park Avenue** (Div. 3 North, 1956–7); **Tranmere Rov.** (Div. 4, 1984–5); **Southend Utd.** (Div. 3, 2002–3).

HIGHEST-SCORING DRAWS IN LEAGUE

Leicester City 6, Arsenal 6 (Div. 1 April 21, 1930) and **Charlton Athletic 6, Middlesbrough 6** (Div 2. October 22, 1960)
 Latest 6-6 draw in first-class football was between Tranmere Rov. and Newcastle Utd. in the Zenith Data Systems Cup 1st. Round on October 1, 1991. The score went from 3-3 at 90 minutes to 6-6 after extra time, and Tranmere Rov. won 3-2 on penalties. In Scotland: Queen of the South 6, Falkirk 6 (Div. 1, September 20, 1947).'
 Most recent 5-5 draws in top division: Southampton v Coventry City (Div. 1, May 4, 1982); Q.P.R. v Newcastle Utd. (Div. 1, Sept. 22, 1984).

DRAWS RECORDS

Most consecutive drawn matches in Football League: 8 by **Torquay Utd.** (Div. 3), Oct. 25 – Dec. 13, 1969; Chesterfield (Lge. 1), Nov. 26 – Jan. 2 (2005-6).
 Longest sequence of draws by the same score: six 1-1 results by **Q.P.R.** in season 1957-8.
 Tranmere Rov. became the first club to play **five consecutive 0-0 League draws**, in season 1997-8.

IDENTICAL RECORDS

There is only **one instance** of two clubs in one division finishing a season with identical records. In 1907-8, **Blackburn Rov.** and **Woolwich Arsenal** were bracketed equal 14th. in the First Division with these figures: P38, W12, D12, L14, Goals 51-63, Pts. 36.
 The total of **1195 goals** scored in the Premier League in season 1993-4 was **repeated** in 1994-5.

DEAD LEVEL

Millwall's record in Division Two in season 1973-74 was P42, W14, D14, L14, F51, A51, Pts 42.

CHAMPIONS OF ALL DIVISIONS

Wolves and **Burnley** are the only clubs to have won the Championships of the old Divisions 1, 2, 3 and 4. Wolves were also **Champions** of the **Third Division North**.

POINTS DEDUCTIONS

Season 2000–1: Chesterfield (Div. 3) had 9 points deducted (plus £20,000 fine) for breach of transfer regulations and falsifying gate receipts. They finished in third (promotion) place.
 Season 2002–3: Boston Utd. entered the Football League under a double penalty. On charges of contractual irregularities, they were fined £100,000 by the F.A. and deducted 4 points.

Season 2004-5: Wrexham were deducted 10 points in December 2004 after going into administration. The penalty resulted in their being relegated from League One. **Cambridge United** were deducted 10 points for going into administration in April 2005 after finishing bottom of League Two.

Season 2005-6: Rotherham Utd. were deducted 10 points from the start of next season for going into administration.

Bury were deducted 1 point from 2005-6 season for fielding an unregistered player. Among previous points penalties imposed:

Nov. 1990: **Arsenal** deducted 2 points and **Man. United** 1 point following mass player brawl at Old Trafford.

Dec. 1996: **Brighton** docked 2 points for two pitch invasions by fans.

Jan. 1997: **Middlesbrough** deducted 3 points for refusing to play Premiership match at Blackburn because of injuries and illness.

● June 1994: **Tottenham** deducted 12 points (reduced to 6) and banned from next season's F.A. Cup for making illegal payments to players. On appeal, points deduction annulled and Spurs re-instated in Cup.

NIGHTMARE STARTS

Most goals conceded by a goalkeeper on League debut: 13 by **Steve Milton** when Halifax Town lost 13-0 at Stockport Co. (Div. 3 North) on January 6, 1934.

Post-war: 11 by Crewe Alexandra's new goalkeeper **Dennis Murray** (Div. 3 North) on September 29, 1951, when Lincoln City won 11-1.

RELEGATION ODD SPOTS

None of the Barclays Premiership relegation places in season 2004-5 were decided until the last day (Sunday, May 15). **WBA** (botton at kick-off) survived with a 2-0 home win against Portsmouth, and the three relegated clubs were Southampton (1-2 v Man. United), Norwich City (0-6 at Fulham) and Crystal Palace (2-2 at Charlton).

In season 1937-8, **Manchester City** were the highest-scoring team in the First Division with 80 goals (3 more than Champions Arsenal), but they finished in 21st place and were relegated – a year after winning the Championship. They scored more goals than they conceded (77).

That season produced the **closest relegation battle** in top-division history, with only 4 points spanning the bottom 11 clubs in Div. 1. WBA went down with Manchester City.

Twelve years earlier, in 1925-6, City went down to Division 2 despite totalling 89 goals – still the most scored in any division by a relegated team. Manchester City also scored 31 F.A. Cup goals that season, but lost the Final 1-0 to Bolton Wanderers.

Cardiff City were relegated from Div. 1 in season 1928-9, despite conceding fewest goals in the division (59). They also scored fewest (43).

On their way to relegation from the First Division in season 1984–85, **Stoke City** twice lost ten matches in a row.

RELEGATION TREBLES

Two Football League clubs have been relegated three seasons in succession. **Bristol City** fell from First Division to Fourth in 1980-1-2, and **Wolves** did the same in 1984-5-6.

END OF CHRISTMAS 'CERTAINTY'

In season 2004-5, **W.B.A.** became the first Premiership club to avoid relegation after being bottom of the table at Christmas.

OLDEST CLUBS

Oldest Association Football Club is **Sheffield F.C.** (formed in 1857). The oldest Football League clubs are **Notts Co.**, 1862; **Nott'm. Forest**, 1865; and **Sheffield Wed.**, 1866.

FOUR DIVISIONS

In **May, 1957**, the Football League decided to re-group the two sections of the Third Division into Third and Fourth Divisions in **season 1958-9**.

The Football League was reduced to three divisions on the formation of the F.A. Premier League in **1992**.

In season 2004-5, under new sponsors Coca-Cola, the titles of First, Second and Third Divisions were changed to League Championship, League One and League Two.

THREE UP – THREE DOWN

The Football League Annual General Meeting of June 1973 agreed to adopt the promotion and relegation system of three up and three down.

The **new system** came into effect in **season 1973-4** and applied only to the first three divisions; four clubs were still relegated from the Third and four promoted from the Fourth.

It was the first change in the promotion and relegation system for the top two divisions in 81 years.

PLAY-OFF FINALS
HIGHEST SCORES

Div. 1	1993	(Wembley)	Swindon Town 4, Leicester City 3
	1995	(Wembley)	Bolton Wand. 4, Reading 3
	1998	(Wembley)	Charlton Athletic 4, Sunderland 4 (Charlton Athletic won 7–6 on pens.)
Div. 2	1993	(Wembley)	W.B.A. 3, Port Vale 0
	2000	(Wembley)	Gillingham 3, Wigan Athletic 2
	2001	(Cardiff)	Walsall 3, Reading 2
Div. 3	2003	(Cardiff)	Bournemouth 5, Lincoln City 2

BIGGEST ATTENDANCES

Div. 1	1998	(Wembley)	Charlton Athletic v Sunderland	77,739
Div. 2	1999	(Wembley)	Manchester City v Gillingham	76,935
Div. 3	1997	(Wembley)	Northampton Town v Swansea City	46,804

MOST LEAGUE APPEARANCES

Players with more than 700 English League apps. (as at end of season 2005-06).

1005   **Peter Shilton** 1966-97 (286 Leicester City, 110 Stoke City, 202 Nott'm. Forest, 188 Southampton, 175 Derby Co., 34 Plymouth Argyle, 1 Bolton Wand., 9 Leyton Orient).

931   **Tony Ford** 1975-2002 (423 Grimsby Town, 9 Sunderland, 112 Stoke City, 114 W.B.A., 5 Bradford City, 76 Scunthorpe Utd., 103 Mansfield Town, 89 Rochdale).

824   **Terry Paine** 1956-77 (713 Southampton, 111 Hereford).

795   **Tommy Hutchison** 1968-91 (165 Blackpool, 314 Coventry City, 46 Manchester City, 92 Burnley, 178 Swansea City). In addition, 68 Scottish League apps. for Alloa 1965-68, giving career League app. total of 863.

790   **Neil Redfearn** 1982-2004 (35 Bolton Wand., 100 Lincoln City, 46 Doncaster Rov., 57 Crystal Palace, 24 Watford, 62 Oldham Athletic, 292 Brnsley, 30 Charlton Athletic, 17 Bradford City, 22 Wigan Athletic, 42 Halifax Town, 54 Boston Utd., 9 Rochdale).

782   **Robbie James** 1973-94 (484 Swansea City, 48 Stoke City, 87 Q.P.R., 23 Leicester City, 89 Bradford City, 51 Cardiff City).

777   **Alan Oakes** 1959-84 (565 Manchester City, 211 Chester City, 1 Port Vale).

773   **Dave Beasant** 1980-2003 (340 Wimbledon, 20 Newcastle Utd., 6 Grimsby Town, 4 Wolves, 133 Chelsea, 88 Southampton, 139 Nott'm. F., 27 Portsmouth, 16 Brighton).

770   **John Trollope** 1960-80 (all for Swindon Town, record total for one club).

764   **Jimmy Dickinson** 1946-65 (all for Portsmouth).

761   **Roy Sproson** 1950-72 (all for Port Vale).

760   **Mick Tait** 1974-97 (64 Oxford Utd., 106 Carlisle Utd., 33 Hull City, 240 Portsmouth, 99 Reading, 79 Darlington, 139 Hartlepool Utd.).

758   **Billy Bonds** 1964-88 (95 Charlton Athletic, 663 West Ham Utd.).

758 **Ray Clemence** 1966-88 (48 Scunthorpe Utd., 470 Liverpool, 240 Tottenham).

757 **Pat Jennings** 1963-86 (48 Watford, 472 Tottenham, 237 Arsenal).

757 **Frank Worthington** 1966-88 (171 Huddersfield Town, 210 Leicester City, 84 Bolton Wand., 75 Birmingham City, 32 Leeds Utd., 19 Sunderland, 34 Southampton, 31 Brighton & H.A., 59 Tranmere Rov., 23 Preston N.E., 19 Stockport Co.).

749 **Ernie Moss** 1968-88 (469 Chesterfield, 35 Peterborough Utd., 57 Mansfield Town, 74 Port Vale, 11 Lincoln City, 44 Doncaster Rov., 26 Stockport Co., 23 Scarborough, 10 Rochdale).

746 **Les Chapman** 1966-88 (263 Oldham Athletic, 133 Huddersfield Town, 70 Stockport Co., 139 Bradford City, 48 Rochdale, 53 Preston N.E.).

744 **Asa Hartford** 1967-90 (214 W.B.A., 260 Manchester City, 3 Nott'm. F., 81 Everton, 28 Norwich City, 81 Bolton Wand., 45 Stockport Co., 7 Oldham Athletic, 25 Shrewsbury Town).

743 **Alan Ball** 1963-84 (146 Blackpool, 208 Everton, 177 Arsenal, 195 Southampton, 17 Bristol Rov.).

743 **John Hollins** 1963-84 (465 Chelsea, 151 Q.P.R., 127 Arsenal).

743 **Phil Parkes** 1968-91 (52 Walsall, 344 Q.P.R., 344 West Ham Utd., 3 Ipswich Town).

737 **Steve Bruce** 1979-99 (205 Gillingham, 141 Norwich City, 309 Manchester Utd. 72 Birmingham City, 10 Sheffield Utd.).

732 **Mick Mills** 1966-88 (591 Ipswich Town, 103 Southampton, 38 Stoke City).

731 **Ian Callaghan** 1959-81 (640 Liverpool, 76 Swansea City, 15 Crewe Alexandra).

731 **David Seaman** 1982-2003 (91 Peterborough Utd, 75 Birmingham City, 141 Q.P.R., 405 Arsenal, 19 Manchester City).

725 **Steve Perryman** 1969-90 (655 Tottenham, 17 Oxford Utd., 53 Brentford).

722 **Martin Peters** 1961-81 (302 West Ham Utd., 189 Tottenham, 207 Norwich City, 24 Sheffield Utd.).

718 **Mike Channon** 1966-86 (511 Southampton, 72 Manchester City, 4 Newcastle Utd., 9 Bristol Rov., 88 Norwich City, 34 Portsmouth).

716 **Ron Harris** 1961-83 (655 Chelsea, 61 Brentford).

716 **Mike Summerbee** 1959-79 (218 Swindon Town, 357 Manchester City, 51 Burnley, 3 Blackpool, 87 Stockport Co.).

714 **Glenn Cockerill** 1976-98 (186 Lincoln City, 26 Swindon Town, 62 Sheffield Utd., 387 Southampton, 90 Leyton Orient, 40 Fulham, 23 Brentford).

705 **Keith Curle** 1981-2003 (32 Bristol Rov., 16 Torquay Utd., 121 Bristol City, 40 Reading, 93 Wimbledon, 171 Manchester City, 150 Wolves, 57 Sheffield Utd., 11 Barnsley, 14 Mansfield Town.

705 **Phil Neal** 1968-89 (186 Northampton Town, 455 Liverpool, 64 Bolton Wand.).

705 **John Wile** 1968-86 (205 Peterborough Utd., 500 W.B.A.).

701 **Neville Southall** 1980-2000 (39 Bury, 578 Everton, 9 Port Vale, 9 Southend, 12 Stoke, 53 Torquay, 1 Bradford City).

● **Stanley Matthews** made 701 League apps. 1932-65 (322 Stoke City, 379 Blackpool), incl. 3 for Stoke City at start of 1939-40 before season abandoned (war).

● Goalkeeper **John Burridge** made a total of 771 League appearances in a 28-season career in English and Scottish football (1968-96). He played 691 games for 15 English clubs (Workington, Blackpool, Aston Villa, Southend Utd., Crystal Palace, Q.P.R., Wolves, Derby Co., Sheffield Utd., Southampton, Newcastle Utd., Scarborough, Lincoln City, Manchester City and Darlington) and 80 for 5 Scottish clubs (Hibernian, Aberdeen, Dumbarton, Falkirk and Queen of the South).

LONGEST LEAGUE APPEARANCE SEQUENCE

Harold Bell, centre-half of Tranmere Rov., was ever-present for the first nine post-war seasons (1946-55), achieving a League record of 401 consecutive matches. Counting F.A. Cup and other games, his run of successive appearances totalled 459.

The longest League sequence since Bell's was 394 appearances by goalkeeper **Dave Beasant** for Wimbledon, Newcastle Utd. and Chelsea. His nine-year run began on August 29, 1981 and was ended by a broken finger sustained in Chelsea's League Cup-tie against Portsmouth on October 31, 1990. Beasant's 394 consecutive League games comprised 304 for Wimbledon (1981-8), 20 for Newcastle Utd. (1988-9) and 70 for Chelsea (1989-90).

Phil Neal made 366 consecutive First Division appearances for Liverpool between December 1974 and September 1983, a remarkable sequence for an outfield player in top-division football.

MOST CONSECUTIVE PREMIERSHIP APPEARANCES

164 by **Frank Lampard** (Chelsea) October 2001 – December 2005.

EVER-PRESENT DEFENCE

The **entire defence** of Huddersfield Town played in all 42 Second Division matches in season 1952-3, namely, Bill Wheeler (goal), Ron Staniforth and Laurie Kelly (full-backs), Bill McGarry, Don McEvoy and Len Quested (half-backs). In addition, Vic Metcalfe played in all 42 League matches at outside-left.

FIRST SUBSTITUTE USED IN LEAGUE

Keith Peacock (Charlton Athletic), away to Bolton Wand. (Div. 2) on August 21, 1965.

FROM PROMOTION TO CHAMPIONS

Clubs who have become Champions of England a year after winning promotion: **Liverpool** 1905, 1906; **Everton** 1931, 1932; **Tottenham** 1950, 1951; **Ipswich Town** 1961, 1962; **Nott'm. Forest** 1977, 1978. The first four were placed top in both seasons; Forest finished third and first.

PREMIERSHIP'S FIRST MULTI-NATIONAL LINE-UP

Chelsea made history on December 26, 1999 when starting their Premiership match at Southampton without a single British player in the side.

Fulham's Unique XI: In the Worthington Cup 3rd. Round at home to Bury on November 6, 2002, **Fulham** fielded 11 players of 11 different nationalities. Ten were full Internationals, with Lee Clark an England U–21 cap.

On February 14, 2005 **Arsenal** became the first English club to select an all-foreign match squad when Arsene Wenger named 16 non-British players at home to Crystal Palace (Premiership).

THREE-NATION CHAMPION

Trevor Steven earned eight Championship medals, in three countries: two with Everton (1985, 1987); five with Rangers (1990, 1991, 1993, 1994, 1995) and one with Marseille in 1992.

LEEDS NO-WAY AWAY

Leeds Utd., in 1992-3, provided the first instance of a club failing to win an away League match as reigning Champions.

PIONEERS IN 1888 AND 1992

Three clubs among the twelve who formed the Football League in 1888 were also founder members of the F.A. Premier League: **Aston Villa**, **Blackburn Rov.** and **Everton**.

CHAMPIONS (MODERN) WITH TWO CLUBS – PLAYERS

Francis Lee (Manchester City 1968, Derby Co. 1975); **Ray Kennedy** (Arsenal 1971, Liverpool 1979, 1980, 1982); **Archie Gemmill** (Derby Co. 1972, 1975, Nott'm. F. 1978); **John McGovern** (Derby Co. 1972, Nott'm. F. 1978) **Larry Lloyd** (Liverpool 1973, Nott'm. F. 1978); **Peter Withe** (Nott'm. F. 1978, Aston Villa 1981); **John Lukic** (Arsenal

1989, Leeds Utd. 1992); **Kevin Richardson** (Everton 1985, Arsenal 1989); **Eric Cantona** (Leeds Utd. 1992, Manchester Utd. 1993, 1994, 1996, 1997); **David Batty** (Leeds Utd. 1992, Blackburn Rov. 1995), **Bobby Mimms** (Everton 1987, Blackburn Rov. 1995), **Henning Berg** (Blackburn Rov. 1995, Manchester United 1999, 2001).

TITLE TURNABOUTS

In January 1996, **Newcastle Utd.** led the Premier League by 13 points. They finished runners-up to Manchester Utd.

At Christmas 1997, **Arsenal** were 13 points behind leaders Manchester Utd. and still 11 points behind at the beginning of March 1998. But a run of 10 wins took the title to Highbury.

On March 2, 2003, **Arsenal**, with 9 games left, went 8 points clear of Manchester Utd., who had a match in hand. United won the Championship by 5 points.

● In March 2002, **Wolves** were in second (automatic promotion) place in Nationwide Div. 1, 11 points ahead of W.B.A., who had 2 games in hand. They were overtaken by Albion on the run-in, finished third, then failed in the play-offs. A year later they won promotion to the Premiership via the play-offs.

CLUB CLOSURES

Four clubs have left the Football League in mid-season: **Leeds City** (expelled Oct. 1919); **Wigan Borough** (Oct. 1931, debts of £20,000); **Accrington Stanley** (March 1962, debts £62,000); **Aldershot** (March 1992, debts £1.2m.). **Maidstone Utd.**, with debts of £650,000, closed August 1992, on the eve of the season.

FOUR-DIVISION MEN

In season 1986-7, goalkeeper **Eric Nixon**, became the first player to appear in **all four divisions** of the Football League **in one season**. He served two clubs in Div. 1: Manchester City (5 League games) and Southampton (4); in Div. 2 Bradford City (3); in Div. 3 Carlisle Utd. (16); and in Div. 4 Wolves (16). Total appearances: 44.

Harvey McCreadie, a teenage forward, played in four divisions over two seasons inside a calendar year – from Accrington (Div. 3) to Luton Town (Div. 1) in January 1960, to Div. 2 with Luton Town later that season and to Wrexham (Div. 4) in November.

Tony Cottee played in all four divisions in season 2000-01, for Leicester City (Premiership), Norwich City (Div. 1), Barnet (Div. 3, player-manager) and Millwall (Div. 2).

FATHERS & SONS

When player-manager **Ian Bowyer** (39) and **Gary Bowyer** (18) appeared together in the **Hereford Utd.** side at Scunthorpe Utd. (Div.4, April 21, 1990), they provided the first instance of father and son playing in the same team in a Football League match for 39 years. Ian Bowyer played as substitute, and Gary scored Hereford's injury-time equaliser in a 3-3 draw.

Alec (39) and **David** (17) **Herd** were the previous father-and-son duo in League football – for **Stockport Co.**, 2-0 winners at Hartlepool Utd. (Div.3 North) on May 5, 1951.

When **Preston N.E.** won 2-1 at Bury in Div. 3 on January 13, 1990, the opposing goalkeepers were brothers: **Alan Kelly** (21) for Preston N.E. and **Gary** (23) for Bury. Their father, **Alan Kelly Senior** (who kept goal for Preston N.E. in the 1964 F.A. Cup Final and won 47 Rep. of Ireland caps) flew from America to watch the sons he taught to keep goal line up on opposite sides.

George Eastham Snr. (manager) and son **George Eastham Jnr.** were inside-forward partners for Ards in the Irish League in season 1954-5.

FATHER & SON BOTH CHAMPIONS

John Aston Snr. won a Championship medal with Manchester Utd. in 1952 and **John Aston Jnr.** did so with the club in 1967.

FATHER & SON RIVAL MANAGERS

When **Bill Dodgin senior** took Bristol Rov. to Fulham for an F.A. Cup 1st Round tie in Nov. 1970, the opposing manager was his son, **Bill junior**.

FATHER & SON ON OPPOSITE SIDES

It happened for the first time in F.A. Cup history (1st. Qual. Round on Sept. 14, 1996) when 21-year-old **Nick Scaife** (Bishop Auckland) faced his father **Bobby** (41), who played for Pickering. Both were in midfield. Home side Bishops won 3-1.

THREE BROTHERS IN SAME SIDE

Southampton provided the first instance for 65 years of three brothers appearing together in a First Division side when **Danny Wallace** (24) and his 19-year-old twin brothers **Rodney** and **Ray** played against Sheffield Wed.on October 22, 1988. In all, they made 25 appearances together for Southampton until September 1989.

A previous instance in Div. 1 was provided by the Middlesbrough trio, **William**, **John** and **George Carr** with 24 League appearances together from January 1920 to October 1923.

The **Tonner** brothers, **Sam**, **James** and **Jack**, played together in 13 Second Division matches for Clapton Orient in season 1919-20.

Brothers **David**, **Donald** and **Robert Jack** played together in Plymouth Argyle's League side in 1923.

TWIN TEAM-MATES (see also **Wallace twins** above)

Twin brothers **David** and **Peter Jackson** played together for three League clubs (Wrexham, Bradford City and Tranmere Rov.) from 1954-62.

The **Morgan** twins, **Ian** and **Roger**, played regularly in the Q.P.R. forward line from 1964-68.

W.B.A.'s **Adam** and **James Chambers**, 18, were the first twins to represent England (v Cameroon in World Youth Championship, April 1999). They first played together in Albion's senior team, aged 19, in the League Cup 2nd. Round against Derby Co. in September 2000.

SIR TOM DOES THE HONOURS

Sir Tom Finney, England and Preston N.E. legend, opened the Football League's new headquarters on their return to Preston on Feb. 23, 1999. Preston had been the League's original base for 70 years before the move to Lytham St. Annes in 1959.

SHORTENED MATCHES

The 0-0 score in the Bradford City v Lincoln City Third Division fixture on May 11, 1985, abandoned through fire after 40 minutes, was subsequently confirmed as a result. It is the shortest officially completed League match on record, and was the fourth of only five instances in Football League history of the score of an unfinished match being allowed to stand.

The other occasions: **Middlesbrough 4, Oldham Athletic 1** (Div. 1, April 3, 1915), abandoned after 55 minutes when Oldham Athletic defender Billy Cook refused to leave the field after being sent off; **Barrow 7, Gillingham 0** (Div. 4, Oct. 9, 1961), abandoned after 75 minutes because of bad light, the match having started late because of Gillingham's delayed arrival.

A crucial **Manchester derby** (Div.1) was abandoned after 85 minutes, and the result stood, on April 27, 1974, when a pitch invasion at Old Trafford followed the only goal, scored for City by Denis Law, which relegated Manchester Utd., Law's former club.

Only instance of a first-class match in England being abandoned **'through shortage of players'** occurred in the First Division at Bramall Lane on March 16, 2002. Referee Eddie Wolstenholme halted play after 82 minutes because **Sheffield Utd.** were reduced to 6 players against **W.B.A.** They had had 3 men sent off (goalkeeper and 2 substitutes), and with all 3 substitutes used and 2 players injured, were left with fewer than the required minimum of 7 on the field. Promotion contenders W.B.A. were leading 3-0, and the League ordered the result to stand.

The last 60 seconds of **Birmingham City v Stoke City** (Div. 3, 1-1, on Feb. 29, 1992) were played behind locked doors. The ground had been cleared after a pitch invasion.

A First Division fixture, **Sheffield Wed. v Aston Villa** (Nov. 26, 1898), was abandoned through bad light after 79½ mins. with Wed. leading 3-1. The Football League ruled that the match should be completed, and the remaining 10½ minutes were played **four months later** (Mar. 13, 1899), when Wed. added another goal to make the result 4-1.

F.A. CUP RECORDS

(See also Goalscoring section)

CHIEF WINNERS

Eleven Times: Manchester Utd.
Ten Times: Arsenal.
Eight Times: Tottenham.
Seven Times: Aston Villa, Liverpool.
Three Times in Succession: The Wanderers (1876-7-8) and Blackburn Rov. (1884-5-6).
Trophy Handed Back: The F.A. Cup became the Wanderers' absolute property in 1878, but they handed it back to the Association on condition that it was not to be won outright by any club.
In Successive Years by Professional Clubs: Blackburn Rov. (in 1890 and 1891); Newcastle Utd. (in 1951 and 1952); Tottenham (in 1961 and 1962); Tottenham again (in 1981 and 1982) and Arsenal (in 2002 and 2003).
Record Final-tie score: Bury 6, Derby Co. 0 (1903).
Most F.A. Cup wins at Wembley: Manchester Utd. 9, Arsenal 7, Tottenham 6, Newcastle Utd. 5, Liverpool 5.

SECOND DIVISION WINNERS

Notts Co. (1894), Wolves (1908), Barnsley (1912), West Bromwich Albion (1931), Sunderland (1973), Southampton (1976), West Ham Utd. (1980). When Tottenham won the Cup in 1901 they were a Southern League club.

'OUTSIDE' SEMI-FINALISTS

Wycombe Wand., in 2001, became the eighth team from outside the top two divisions to reach the semi-finals, following Millwall (1937), Port Vale (1954), York City (1955), Norwich City (1959), Crystal Palace (1976), Plymouth Argyle (1984) and Chesterfield (1997). None reached the Final.

FOURTH DIVISION QUARTER-FINALISTS

Oxford Utd. (1964), Colchester Utd. (1971), Bradford City (1976), Cambridge Utd. (1990).

FOUR TROPHIES

The latest F.A. Cup, first presented at Wembley in 1992, is a replica of the one it replaced, which had been in existence since 1911. 'It was falling apart and was not going to last much longer,' said the FA.

The new trophy is the fourth F.A. Cup. These were its predecessors:

1895 First stolen from shop in Birmingham when held by Aston Villa. Never seen again.
1910 Second presented to Lord Kinnaird on completing 21 years as F.A. president. This trophy was bought by Birmingham City chairman David Gold at Christie's (London) for £420,000 in May 2005 and presented to the National Football Museum at Preston.
1992 Third 'gracefully retired' after 80 years' service (1911-91).

There are three F.A. Cups currently in existence. The retired model is still used for promotional work. The present trophy stays with the winners until the following March. A third, identical Cup is secreted in the F.A. vaults as cover against loss of the existing trophy.

FINALISTS RELEGATED

Four clubs have reached the F.A. Cup Final in a season of relegation, and all lost at Wembley: Manchester City 1926, Leicester City 1969, Brighton & H.A. 1983, Middlesbrough 1997.

GIANT-KILLING

(* Home team; R = Replay; Season 2005 = 2004-05)

2006	*Bournemouth 1	Tamworth 2
2006	*Burscough 3	Gillingham 2
2006	*Burton 1	Peterborough 0R
2006	*Hartlepool Utd. ... 1	Tamworth 2
2006	*Fulham 1	Leyton Orient 2
2006	*Colchester Utd. ... 3	Derby Co. 1
2005	*Hinckley 2	Torquay Utd. 0
2005	*Histon 2	Shrewsbury T. 0
2005	*Slough 2	Walsall 1
2005	*Exeter City 1	Grimsby Town 0
2005	*Carlisle Utd. 1	Bristol Rov. 0R
2005	*Exeter City 1	Doncaster Rov. 1
2005	*Oldham Ath. 1	Manchester City .. 0
2005	*Rotherham Utd. .. 0	Yeovil 3
2004	*Hornchurch 2	Darlington 1
2004	*Scarborough 2	Doncaster Rov. 0
2004	*Port Vale 0	Scarborough 1
2004	*Scarborough 1	Southend Utd. 0R
2004	*Accrington 1	Huddersfield T. ... 0
2004	*Accrington 0	Bournemouth 0R
	(Accrington won on pens).	
2004	*Stevenage 2	Stockport Co. 1
2004	*Torquay Utd. 1	Burton Alb. 0
2004	*Telford 3	Brentford 0
2004	*Crewe Alex. 0	Telford 1
2004	*Colchester Utd. ... 3	Coventry City 1R
2004	*Bolton Wand. ... 1	Tranmere Rov. ... 2R
2004	*Gillingham 3	Charlton Ath. 2
2003	*Chesterfield 1	Morecambe 1
2003	*Colchester Utd. .. 0	Chester City 1
2003	*Southport 4	Notts Co. 2
2003	Margate 1	Leyton Orient 0R
	(at Dover)	
2003	*Q.P.R. 1	Vauxhall Mot .... 1 R
	(Vauxhall won on pens.)	
2003	*Shrewsbury T. 2	Everton 1
2003	*Dagenham & R. .. 2	Plymouth .... 0 R
2003	*Darlington 2	Farnborough 3
2003	*Rochdale 2	Coventry City 0
2003	*Liverpool 0	Crystal Palace 2
2003	*Sunderland 0	Watford 1
2002	*Wigan Athletic ... 0	Canvey Island 1
2002	*Canvey Island ... 1	Northampton T. ... 0
2002	*Dagenham & R .. 3	Exeter City 0R
2002	*Cardiff City 2	Leeds Utd. 1
2002	*Derby Co. 1	Bristol Rov. 3

2001	*Wycombe Wand. .. 2	Wolves 1
2001	*Wimbledon 2	Wycombe Wand. .. 2R
	(Wycombe Wand. won on pens).	
2001	*Leicester City 1	Wycombe Wand. .. 2
2001	*Brentford 1	Kingstonian 3
2001	*Yeovil 5	Colchester Utd. ... 1
2001	*Southend Utd. ... 0	Kingstonian 1
2001	*Nuneaton 1	Stoke City 0R
2001	*Hull City 0	Kettering 1R
2001	*Northwich Vic. ... 1	Bury 0R
2001	*Port Vale 1	Canvey Island ... 2R
2001	*Lincoln City 0	Dagenham & R. .. 1
2001	*Morecambe 2	Cambridge Utd. .. 1
2001	*Blackpool 0	Yeovil 1
2001	*Everton 0	Tranmere Rov. ... 3
2001	*Tranmere Rov. ... 4	Southampton 3R
2000	*Rushden & D 2	Scunthorpe Utd. .. 0
2000	*Chesterfield 1	Enfield 2
2000	*Hereford 1	York City 0
2000	*Ilkeston Town ... 2	Carlisle Utd. 1
2000	*Hereford 1	Hartlepool Utd. ... 0
1999	*Bedlington T 4	Colchester Utd. ... 1
1999	*Hednesford 3	Barnet 1
1999	*Mansfield Town .. 1	Southport 2
1999	*Rushden & D 1	Shrewsbury Town . 0
1999	*Southend Utd. ... 0	Doncaster Rov. 1
1999	*Yeovil Town 2	Northampton T 0
1999	*Aston Villa 0	Fulham 2
1998	*Hull City 0	Hednesford 2
1998	Lincoln City 3	Emley 3R
	(at Huddersfield; Emley won on pens).	
1998	*Leyton O 0	Hendon 1R
1998	*Swindon Town ... 1	Stevenage 2
1998	*Stevenage 2	Cambridge Utd. ... 1
1997	*Millwall 1	Woking 1R
1997	*Brighton & H.A. . 1	Sudbury Town ... 1R
	(Sudbury won on pens).	
1997	*Blackpool 0	Hednesford 1
1997	*Cambridge Utd. . 0	Woking 2
1997	*Leyton O. 1	Stevenage 2
1997	*Hednesford 1	York City 0
1997	*Chesterfield 1	Nott'm. Forest ... 0
1996	*Hitchin 2	Bristol Rov. 1
1996	*Woking 2	Barnet 1R
1996	*Bury 0	Blyth Spartans ... 2
1996	*Gravesend 2	Colchester Utd. ... 0

1995	*Kingstonian	2	Brighton & H.A.	1
1995	*Enfield	1	Cardiff City	0
1995	*Marlow	2	Oxford Utd.	0
1995	*Woking	1	Barnet	0R
1995	*Hitchin	4	Hereford	2R
1995	Torquay Utd.	0	Enfield	1R
1995	*Altrincham	1	Wigan Athletic	0
1995	*Wrexham	2	Ipswich Town	1
1995	*Scarborough	2	Port Vale	0
1994	*Colchester Utd.	3	Sutton	4
1994	*Yeovil	1	Fulham	0
1994	*Torquay Utd.	0	Sutton	1
1994	*Halifax Town	1	W.B.A.	1
1994	*Birmingham C.	1	Kidderminster	2
1994	*Stockport Co.	2	Q.P.R.	1
1994	*Liverpool	0	Bristol City	1R
1994	*Arsenal	1	Bolton Wand.	3R
1994	*Leeds Utd.	1	Oxford Utd.	3R
1994	*Luton Town	2	Newcastle Utd.	0R
1994	*Kidderminster	1	Preston N.E.	0
1994	*Cardiff City	1	Manchester City	0
1993	*Hereford	1	Yeovil	2R
1993	*Torquay Utd.	2	Yeovil	5
1993	*Altrincham	2	Chester City	0R
1993	*Cardiff City	2	Bath	3
1993	*Chesterfield	2	Macclesfield	2R
(Macclesfield Town won on pens.)				
1993	*Marine	4	Halifax Town	1
1993	*Stafford	2	Lincoln City	1R
1993	*Hartlepool Utd.	1	Crystal Palace	0
1993	*Liverpool	0	Bolton Wand.	2R
1992	*Fulham	0	Hayes	2
1992	*Crawley	4	Northampton	2
1992	*Telford	2	Stoke City	1R
1992	*Aldershot	0	Enfield	1
1992	*Halifax Town	1	Witton A.	2R
1992	*Maidstone	1	Kettering	2
1992	*Walsall	0	Yeovil	1R
1992	*Farnborough	4	Torquay Utd.	3
1992	*Wrexham	2	Arsenal	1
1991	*Scarborough	0	Leek	2
1991	*Northampton	0	Barnet	1
1991	*Hayes	1	Cardiff City	0R
1991	*Chorley	2	Bury	1
1991	*Shrewsbury T	1	Wimbledon	0
1991	*W.B.A.	0	Woking	4
1990	*Aylesbury	0	Southend Utd.	1
1990	*Scarborough	0	Whitley Bay	1
1990	*Welling	0	Gillingham	0R
1990	*Whitley Bay	2	Preston N.E.	0
1990	*Northampton	1	Coventry City	0
1990	*Cambridge Utd.	1	Millwall	0R
1989	*Sutton	2	Coventry City	1
1989	*Halifax Town	2	Kettering	3R
1989	*Kettering	2	Bristol Rov.	1
1989	*Bognor	2	Exeter City	1
1989	*Leyton Orient	0	Enfield	1R
1989	*Altrincham	3	Lincoln City	2
1989	*Wrexham	2	Runcorn	3R
1988	*Sutton	3	Aldershot	0
1988	*Peterborough	1	Sutton	3
1988	*Carlisle Utd.	2	Macclesfield	4
1988	*Macclesfield	4	Rotherham Utd.	0
1988	*Chester City	0	Runcorn	1
1988	*Cambridge Utd.	0	Yeovil	1
1987	*Caernarfon	1	Stockport Co.	0
1987	Chorley	3	Wolves	0R
(at Bolton)				
1987	*Telford	3	Burnley	0
1987	*York City	1	Caernarfon	0
1987	*Aldershot	3	Oxford Utd.	0
1987	*Wigan Athletic	1	Norwich City	0
1987	*Charlton Ath.	1	Walsall	2
1986	*Stockport Co.	0	Telford	1
1986	*Wycombe W.	2	Colchester Utd.	0
1986	*Dagenham	2	Cambridge Utd.	1
1986	*Blackpool	1	Altrincham	2
1986	*Birmingham C.	1	Altrincham	2
1986	*Peterborough	1	Leeds Utd.	0
1985	*Telford	2	Lincoln City	0
1985	*Preston N.E.	1	Telford	4
1985	*Telford	1	Bradford City	1
1985	*Telford	3	Darlington	0R
1985	*Blackpool	0	Altrincham	1
1985	*Wimbledon	1	Nott'm. Forest	0R
1985	*Orient	2	W.B.A.	1
1985	*Dagenham	1	Peterborough	0
1985	*Swindon Town	1	Dagenham	2R
1985	*York City	1	Arsenal	0
1984	*Halifax Town	1	Whitby	3
1984	*Bournemouth	2	Manchester Utd.	0
1984	*Telford	2	Stockport Co.	0
1984	*Telford	3	Northampton	2R
1984	Telford	4	*Rochdale	1
1983	*Cardiff City	2	Weymouth	3
1981	*Exeter City	3	Leicester City	1R
1981	*Exeter City	4	Newcastle Utd.	0R
1980	*Halifax Town	1	Manchester City	0
1980	*Harlow	1	Leicester City	0R
1980	*Chelsea	0	Wigan Athletic	1
1979	*Newport	2	West Ham Utd.	1
1978	*Wrexham	4	Newcastle	1R
1978	*Stoke City	2	Blyth Spartans	3
1976	*Leeds Utd.	0	Crystal Palace	1
1975	*Brighton & H.A.	0	Leatherhead	1
1975	*Burnley	0	Wimbledon	1
1972	*Hereford	2	Newcastle	1R
1971	*Colchester Utd.	3	Leeds Utd.	2
1969	*Mansfield Town	3	West Ham Utd.	0
1967	*Swindon Town	3	West Ham Utd.	0R
1967	*Manchester U.	1	Norwich City	2
1966	*Ipswich Town	2	Southport	3R
1965	*Peterborough	2	Arsenal	1
1964	*Newcastle Utd.	1	Bedford Town	2
1964	*Aldershot	2	Aston Villa	1R
1961	*Coventry City	1	Kings Lynn	2
1961	*Chelsea	2	Crewe Alex.	1
1960	*Manchester City	1	South'ton	5

1959	*Norwich City	3	Manchester U	0	1955	*Blackpool	0	York City	2
1959	*Worcester	2	Liverpool	1	1954	*Arsenal	1	Norwich City	2
1959	*Tooting	3	Bournemouth	1	1954	*Port Vale	2	Blackpool	0
1959	*Tooting	2	Northampton	1	1952	*Everton	1	Leyton Orient	3
1958	*Newcastle Utd.	1	Scunthorpe Utd.	3	1949	*Yeovil Town	2	Sunderland	1
1957	*Wolves	0	Bournemouth	1	1948	*Colchester Utd.	1	Huddersfield	0
1957	*Bournemouth	3	Tottenham	1	1948	*Arsenal	0	Bradford P.A.	1
1957	*Derby Co.	1	New Brighton	3	1938	*Chelmsford	4	Southampton	1
1956	*Derby Co.	1	Boston United	6	1933	*Walsall	2	Arsenal	0
1955	*York City	2	Tottenham	1	1922	*Everton	0	Crystal Palace	6

YEOVIL TOP GIANT-KILLERS

Yeovil's victories over Colchester Utd. and Blackpool in season 2000-01 gave them a total of 20 F.A. Cup wins against League opponents. They set another non-League record by reaching the third round 13 times.

This was Yeovil's triumphant (non-League) Cup record against League clubs: 1924-5 Bournemouth 3-2; 1934-5 Crystal Palace 3-0, Exeter City 4-1; 1938-9 Brighton & H.A. 2-1; 1948-9 Bury 3-1, Sunderland 2-1; 1958-9 Southend Utd. 1-0; 1960-1 Walsall 1-0; 1963-4 Southend Utd. 1-0, Crystal Palace 3-1; 1970-1 Bournemouth 1-0; 1972-3 Brentford 2-1; 1987-8 Cambridge Utd. 1-0; 1991-2 Walsall 1-0; 1992-3 Torquay Utd. 5-2, Hereford 2-1; 1993-4 Fulham 1-0; 1998-9 Northampton 2-0; 2000-01 Colchester Utd. 5-1, Blackpool 1-0.

NON-LEAGUE BEST

Since League football began in 1888, three non-League clubs have reached the F.A. Cup Final. **Sheffield Wed.** (Football Alliance) were runners-up in 1890, as were **Southampton** (Southern League) in 1900 and 1902. **Tottenham** won the Cup as a Southern League team in 1901.

Otherwise, the **furthest progress** by non-League clubs has been to the **5th. Round** on 5 occasions: Colchester Utd. 1948, Yeovil 1949, Blyth Spartans 1978, Telford 1985 and Kidderminster 1994.

Greatest number of non-League sides to reach the **3rd. Round** is 6 in 1978: Blyth, Enfield, Scarborough, Tilbury, Wealdstone and Wigan Athletic. Since then, 5 in 1988: Bath City, Macclesfield Town, Maidstone, Sutton and Yeovil.

Most to reach **Round 4**: 3 in 1957 (Rhyl, New Brighton, Peterborough Utd.) and 1975 (Leatherhead, Stafford and Wimbledon).

Five non-League clubs reaching **Round 3** in 2001 was a Conference record. They were Chester City, Yeovil, Dagenham & Redbridge, Morecambe and Kingstonian.

In season 2002–3, **Team Bath** became the first University-based side to reach the F.A. Cup 1st. Round since Oxford University (Finalists in 1880).

NON-LEAGUE 'LAST TIMES'

Last time no non-League club reached Round 3: 1951. Last time only one did so: 1969 (Kettering Town). Last time only two: 2005 (Yeading and Exeter City).

TOP-DIVISION SCALPS

Victories in F.A. Cup by non-League clubs over top-division teams since 1900 include:-1900-1 (Final, replay), **Tottenham** 3, Sheffield Utd. 1 (Tottenham then in Southern League); 1919-20 **Cardiff City** 2, Oldham Athletic 0, and Sheffield Wed. 0, **Darlington** 2; 1923-4 **Corinthians** 1, Blackburn Rov. 0; 1947-8 **Colchester Utd.** 1, Huddersfield Town 0; 1948-9 **Yeovil Town** 2, Sunderland 1; 1971-2 **Hereford Utd.** 2, Newcastle Utd. 1; 1974-5 Burnley 0, **Wimbledon** 1; 1985-6 Birmingham City 1, **Altrincham** 2; 1988-9 **Sutton Utd.** 2, Coventry City 1.

FIVE WINNING MEDALS

The Hon. Arthur Kinnaird (The Wanderers and Old Etonians), **Charles Wollaston** (The Wanderers) and **Jimmy Forrest** (Blackburn Rov.) each earned five F.A. Cup winners' medals. Kinnaird, later president of the F.A., played in nine of the first 12 F.A. Cup

Finals, and was on the winning side three times for The Wanderers, in 1873 (captain), 1877, 1878 (captain), and twice as captain of Old Etonians (1879, 1882).

MOST WINNERS' MEDALS AT WEMBLEY

4 – **Mark Hughes** (3 for Manchester Utd., 1 for Chelsea).

3 – **Dick Pym** (3 clean sheets in Finals), **Bob Haworth**, **Jimmy Seddon**, **Harry Nuttall**, **Billy Butler** (all Bolton Wand.); **David Jack** (2 Bolton Wand., 1 Arsenal); **Bob Cowell**, **Jack Milburn**, **Bobby Mitchell** (all Newcastle Utd.); **Dave Mackay** (Tottenham); **Frank Stapleton** (1 Arsenal, 2 Manchester Utd.); **Bryan Robson** (3 times winning captain); **Arthur Albiston**, **Gary Pallister** (all Manchester Utd.); **Bruce Grobbelaar**, **Steve Nicol**, **Ian Rush** (all Liverpool); **Roy Keane**, **Peter Schmeichel**; **Ryan Giggs** (all Manchester Utd.); **Dennis Wise** (1 Wimbledon, 2 Chelsea).

● Arsenal's **David Seaman** and **Ray Parlour** have each earned 4 winners' medals (2 at Wembley, 2 at Cardiff) as have Manchester Utd's **Roy Keane** and **Ryan Giggs** (3 at Wembley, 1 at Cardiff).

MOST WEMBLEY FINALS

Eight players appeared in five F.A. Cup Finals at Wembley, replays excluded:-
● Joe Hulme (Arsenal: 1927, lost; 1930 won; 1932 lost; 1936 won; Huddersfield Town: 1938 lost).
● Johnny Giles (Manchester Utd.: 1963 won; Leeds Utd.: 1965 lost; 1970 drew at Wembley, lost replay at Old Trafford; 1972 won; 1973 lost).
● Pat Rice (all for Arsenal: 1971 won; 1972 lost; 1978 lost; 1979 won; 1980 lost).
● Frank Stapleton (Arsenal: 1978 lost; 1979 won; 1980 lost; Manchester Utd.: 1983 won; 1985 lost).
● Ray Clemence (Liverpool: 1971 lost; 1974 won; 1977 lost; Tottenham: 1982 won; 1987 lost).
● Mark Hughes (Manchester Utd.: 1985 won; 1990 won; 1994 won; 1995 lost; Chelsea: 1997 won).
● John Barnes (Watford: 1984 lost; Liverpool: 1988 lost; 1989 won; 1996 lost; Newcastle Utd.: 1998, sub, lost): he was the first player to lose Wembley F.A. Cup Finals with three different clubs.
● Roy Keane (Nott'm Forest: 1991 lost; Manchester Utd.: 1994 won; 1995 lost; 1996 won; 1999 won).
Stapleton, Clemence and Hughes also played in a replay, making six actual F.A. Cup Final appearances for each of them.
Glenn Hoddle also made six F.A. Cup Final appearances at Wembley: 5 for Tottenham (incl. 2 replays), in 1981, 1982 and 1987, and 1 for Chelsea as sub in 1994.
▲Paul Bracewell played in four F.A. Cup Finals without being on the winning side – for Everton 1985, 1986, 1989, Sunderland 1992.

MOST WEMBLEY/CARDIFF FINAL APPEARANCES

7 by **Roy Keane** (Nott'm F: 1991 lost; Manchester Utd.: 1994 won; 1995 lost; 1996 won; 1999 won; 2004 won; 2005 lost).

6 by **Ryan Giggs** (Manchester Utd.): 1994 won; 1995 lost; 1996 won; 1999 won; 2004 won; 2005 lost.

5 by **David Seaman** and **Ray Parlour** (Arsenal): 1993 lost; 1998 won; 2001 lost; 2002 won; 2003 won; **Dennis Wise** (Wimbledon 1988 won; Chelsea 1994 lost; 1997 won; 2000 won; Millwall 2004 lost).

WINNING GOALKEEPER-CAPTAINS

1988 **Dave Beasant** (Wimbledon); 2003 **David Seaman** (Arsenal).

MOST-WINNING MANAGER

Sir Alex Ferguson (Man. Utd.) 5 times (1990, 1994, 1996, 1999, 2004).

PLAYER-MANAGERS IN FINAL

Kenny Dalglish (Liverpool, 1986); **Glenn Hoddle** (Chelsea, 1994); **Dennis Wise** (Millwall, 2004).

DEBUTS IN FINAL

Alan Davies (Manchester Utd. v Brighton & H.A., 1983); **Chris Baird** (Southampton v Arsenal, 2003); **Curtis Weston** (Millwall substitute v Manchester Utd., 2004).

SEMI-FINALS AT WEMBLEY

1991 Tottenham 3, Arsenal 1; **1993** Sheffield Wed. 2, Sheffield Utd. 1; Arsenal 1, Tottenham 0; **1994** Chelsea 2, Luton 0; Manchester Utd. 1, Oldham 1; **2000** Aston Villa beat Bolton 4-1 on pens. (after 0-0); Chelsea 2, Newcastle Utd 1.

FIRST ENTRANTS (1871-2)

Barnes, Civil Service, Crystal Palace, Clapham Rov., Donnington School (Spalding), Hampstead Heathens, Harrow Chequers, Hitchin, Maidenhead, Marlow, Queen's Park (Glasgow), Reigate Priory, Royal Engineers, Upton Park and Wanderers. Total 15. Three scratched. 2006-7 entry: 687.

F.A. CUP FIRSTS

Out of country: Cardiff City, by defeating Arsenal 1-0 in the 1927 Final at Wembley, became the first and only club to take the F.A. Cup out of England.

All-English Winning XI: First club to win the F.A. Cup with all-English XI: Blackburn Olympic in 1883. Others since: W.B.A. in 1888 and 1931, Bolton Wand. (1958), Manchester City (1969), West Ham Utd. (1964 and 1975).

Non-English Winning XI: Liverpool in 1986 (Mark Lawrenson, born Preston, was a Rep. of Ireland player).

Won both Cups: Old Carthusians won the F.A. Cup in 1881 and the F.A. Amateur Cup in 1894 and 1897. **Wimbledon** won Amateur Cup in 1963, F.A. Cup in 1988.

MOST GAMES NEEDED TO WIN

Barnsley played a record 12 matches (20 hours' football) to win the F.A. Cup in season 1911-12. All six replays (one in Rd. 1, three in Rd. 4 and one in each of semi-final and Final) were brought about by goalless draws.

Arsenal played 11 F.A. Cup games when winning the trophy in 1979. Five of them were in the 3rd. Rd. against Sheffield Wed..

LONGEST TIES

6 matches (11 hours): **Alvechurch v Oxford City** (4th. qual. round, 1971-2). Alvechurch won 1-0.

5 matches (9 hours, 22 mins – record for competition proper): **Stoke City v Bury** (3rd. round, 1954-5). Stoke City won 3-2.

5 matches: Chelsea v Burnley (4th. round, 1955-6). Chelsea won 2-0.

5 matches: Hull City v Darlington (2nd. round, 1960-1). Hull City won 3-0.

5 matches: Arsenal v Sheffield Wed. (3rd. round, 1978-9). Arsenal won 2-0.

Other marathons (qualifying comp., all 5 matches, 9 hours): **Barrow v Gillingham** (last qual. round, 1924-5) – winners Barrow; **Leyton v Ilford** (3rd. qual. round, 1924-5) – winners Leyton; **Falmouth Town v Bideford** (3rd. qual. round, 1973-4) – winners Bideford.

End of Cup Final replays: The F.A. decided that, with effect from 1999, there would be no Cup Final replays. In the event of a draw after extra-time, the match would be decided on penalties. This happened for the first time in 2005, when **Arsenal** beat **Manchester United** 5-4 on penalties after a 0-0 draw.

F.A. Cup marathons ended in season 1991-2, when the penalty shoot-out was introduced to decide ties still level after one replay and extra-time.

- In 1932-3 **Brighton & H.A.** (Div. 3 South) played 11 F.A. Cup games, including replays, and scored 43 goals, without getting past Rd 5. They forgot to claim exemption and had to play from 1st Qual. Round.

LONGEST ROUND

The longest round in F.A. Cup history was the **third round** in season **1962-3**. It took 66 days to complete, lasting from January 5 to March 11, and included 261 postponements because of bad weather.

LONGEST UNBEATEN RUN

23 matches by **Blackburn Rov.** In winning the Cup in three consecutive years (1884-5-6), they won 21 ties (one in a replay), and their first Cup defeat in four seasons was in a first round replay of the next competition.

RE-STAGED TIES

Sixth round, March 9, 1974: Newcastle Utd. 4, Nott'm. Forest 3. Match declared void by F.A. and ordered to be replayed following a pitch invasion after Newcastle had a player sent off. Forest claimed the hold-up caused the game to change its pattern. The tie went to two further matches at Goodison Park (0-0, then 1-0 to Newcastle).

Third round, January 5, 1985: Burton Albion 1, Leicester City 6 (at Derby Co.). Burton goalkeeper Paul Evans was hit on the head by a missile thrown from the crowd, and continued in a daze. The F.A. ordered the tie to be played again, behind closed doors at Coventry City (Leicester won 1- 0).

First round replay, November 25, 1992: Peterborough Utd. 9 (Tony Philliskirk 5), Kingstonian 1. Match expunged from records because, at 3-0 after 57 mins, Kingstonian were reduced to ten men when goalkeeper Adrian Blake was concussed by a 50 pence coin thrown from the crowd. The tie was re-staged on the same ground behind closed doors (Peterborough won 1-0).

Fifth round: Within an hour of holders Arsenal beating Sheffield Utd. 2-1 at Highbury on February 13, 1999, the Football Association took the unprecedented step of declaring the match void because an unwritten rule of sportsmanship had been broken. With United's Lee Morris lying injured, their goalkeeper Alan Kelly kicked the ball into touch. Play resumed when manager Steve Bruce's players, referee Peter Jones confirmed the goal. Both managers absolved Kanu of cheating but Arsenal's Arsene Wenger offered to replay the match. With the F.A. immediately approving, it was re-staged at Highbury ten days later (ticket prices halved) and Arsenal again won 2-1.

PRIZE FUND

The makeover of the F.A. Cup competition took off in 2001-02 with the introduction of round-by-round prize-money.

F.A. CUP FOLLIES 1999-2000

The F.A. broke with tradition by deciding the 3rd. Round be moved from its regular January date and staged before Christmas. Criticism was strong, gates poor and the 3rd. Round in 2000-01 reverted to the New Year.

By allowing the holders Manchester Utd. to withdraw from the 1999-2000 Cup competition in order to play in FIFA's inaugural World Club Championship in Brazil in January, the F.A. were left with an odd number of clubs in the 3rd. Round. Their solution was a **'lucky losers'** draw among clubs knocked out in Round 2. Darlington, beaten at Gillingham, won it to re-enter the competition, then lost 2-1 away to Aston Villa.

HAT-TRICKS IN FINAL

There have been three in the history of the competition: **Billy Townley** (Blackburn Rov., 1890), **Jimmy Logan** (Notts Co., 1894) and **Stan Mortensen** (Blackpool, 1953).

MOST APPEARANCES

88 by **Ian Callaghan** (79 for Liverpool, 7 for Swansea City, 2 for Crewe Alexandra); 87 by **John Barnes** (31 for Watford, 51 for Liverpool, 5 for Newcastle Utd.); 86 by **Stanley Matthews** (37 for Stoke City, 49 for Blackpool); 84 by **Bobby Charlton** (80 for Manchester Utd., 4 for Preston N.E.); 84 by **Pat Jennings** (3 for Watford, 43 for Tottenham, 38 for Arsenal); 84 by **Peter Shilton** for seven clubs (30 for Leicester City, 7 for Stoke City, 18 for Nottm. Forest, 17 for Southampton, 10 for Derby Co., 1 for Plymouth Argyle, 1 for Leyton Orient); 82 by **David Seaman** (5 for Peterborough Utd., 5 for Birmingham City, 17 for Q.P.R., 54 for Arsenal, 1 for Manchester City.

THREE-CLUB FINALISTS

Four players have appeared in the F.A. Final for three clubs: **Harold Halse** for Manchester Utd. (1909), Aston Villa (1913) and Chelsea (1915); **Ernie Taylor** for Newcastle Utd. (1951), Blackpool (1953) and Manchester Utd. (1958); **John Barnes** for Watford (1984), Liverpool (1988, 1989, 1996) and Newcastle Utd. (1998); **Dennis Wise** for Wimbledon (1988), Chelsea (1994, 1997, 2000), Millwall (2004)..

CUP MAN WITH TWO CLUBS IN SAME SEASON

Stan Crowther, who played for Aston Villa against Manchester Utd. in the 1957 F.A. Cup Final, appeared for both Villa and United in the 1957-8 competition. United signed him directly after the Munich air crash and, in the circumstances, he was given special dispensation to play for them in the Cup, including the Final.

CAPTAIN'S CUP DOUBLE

Martin Buchan is the only player to have captained Scottish and English F.A. Cup-winning teams – Aberdeen in 1970 and Manchester Utd. in 1977.

MEDALS BEFORE AND AFTER

Two players appeared in F.A. Cup Final teams before and after the war: **Raich Carter** was twice a winner (Sunderland 1937, Derby Co. 1946) and **Willie Fagan** twice on the losing side (Preston N.E. 1937, Liverpool 1950).

DELANEY'S COLLECTION

Scotland winger **Jimmy Delaney** uniquely earned Scottish, English, Northern Ireland and Republic of Ireland cup medals. He was a winner with Celtic (1937), Manchester Utd. (1948) and Derry City (1954) and a runner-up with Cork City (1956).

STARS WHO MISSED OUT

Internationals who never won an F.A. Cup winner's medal include: **Tommy Lawton, Tom Finney, Johnny Haynes, Gordon Banks, George Best, Terry Butcher, Peter Shilton, Martin Peters, Nobby Stiles, Alan Ball, Malcolm Macdonald, Alan Shearer.**

CUP WINNERS AT NO COST

Not one member of **Bolton's** 1958 F.A. Cup-winning team cost the club a transfer fee. Each joined the club for a £10 signing-on fee.

ALL-INTERNATIONAL CUP WINNERS

In **Manchester Utd.'s** 1985 Cup-winning team v Everton, all 11 players were full Internationals, as was the substitute who played. So were ten of Everton's team.

   Arsenal's Cup-winning line-ups in the 2002 and 2003 Finals were all full Internationals, as were all 14 players who appeared for **Manchester Utd.** in the 2004 final.

NO-CAP CUP WINNERS

Sunderland, in 1973, were the last F.A. Cup-winning team not to include an International player, although some were capped later.

11-NATIONS LINE-UP

Liverpool fielded a team of 11 different nationalities in the F.A. Cup 3rd Round at Yeovil on Jan. 4, 2004.

HIGH-SCORING SEMI-FINALS

The **record team score** in F.A. Cup semi-finals is 6: 1891-2 WBA 6, Nott'm. Forest 2; 1907-8 Newcastle Utd. 6, Fulham 0; 1933-4 Manchester City 6, Aston Villa 1.

Most goals in semi-finals (aggregate): 17 in 1892 (4 matches) and 1899 (5 matches). In modern times: 15 in 1958 (3 matches, including Manchester Utd. 5, Fulham 3 – highest-scoring semi-final since last war); 16 in 1989-90 (Crystal Palace 4, Liverpool 3; Manchester Utd. v Oldham Athletic 3-3, 2-1. **All 16 goals** in those three matches were scored by **different players**.

Last hat-trick in an F.A. Cup semi-final was scored by **Alex Dawson** for Manchester Utd. in 5-3 replay win against Fulham at Highbury in 1958.

SEMI-FINAL VENUES

Villa Park has staged more such matches (54 including replays) than any other ground. Next is Hillsborough (33).

FOUR SPECIAL AWAYS

For the only time in F.A. Cup history, **all four quarter-finals** in season 1986-7 were won by the away team.

DRAWS RECORD

In season 1985-6, **seven** of the eight F.A. Cup 5th. Round ties went to replays – a record for that stage of the competition.

LUCK OF THE DRAW

In the F.A. Cup on Jan. 11, 1947, eight of **London**'s ten Football League clubs involved in the 3rd. Round were drawn at home (including Chelsea v Arsenal). Only Crystal Palace played outside the capital (at Newcastle Utd.).

Contrast: In the 3rd. Round in Jan. 1992, Charlton Athletic were the only London club drawn at home (against Barnet), but the venue of the Farnborough v West Ham Utd. tie was reversed on police instruction. So Upton Park staged Cup-ties on successive days, with West Ham Utd. at home on the Saturday and Charlton Athletic (who shared the ground) on Sunday.

Arsenal were drawn away in every round on the way to reaching the F.A. Cup Finals of 1971 and 1972. **Manchester Utd.** won the Cup in 1990 without playing once at home.

The 1999 F.A. Cup finalists **Manchester Utd.** and **Newcastle Utd.** were both drawn at home every time in Rounds 3-6.

On their way to the semi-finals of both domestic Cup competitions in season 2002–03, **Sheffield Utd.** were drawn at home ten times out of ten and won all ten matches – six in the League's Worthington Cup and four in the F.A. Cup.

ALL TOP-DIVISION VICTIMS

Only instance of an F.A. Cup-winning club meeting top-division opponents in every round was provided by Manchester Utd. in 1947-8. They beat Aston Villa, Liverpool, Charlton Athletic, Preston N.E., then Derby Co. in the semi-final and Blackpool in the Final.

In **contrast**, these clubs have reached the Final without playing top-division opponents on the way: West Ham Utd. (1923), Bolton Wand. (1926), Blackpool (1948), Bolton Wand. (1953), Millwall (2004).

WON CUP WITHOUT CONCEDING GOAL

1873 **The Wanderers** (1 match; as holders, exempt until Final); 1889 **Preston N.E.** (5 matches); 1903 **Bury** (5 matches). In 1966 **Everton** reached Final without conceding a goal (7 matches), then beat Sheffield Wed. 3-2 at Wembley.

HOME ADVANTAGE

For the first time in F.A. Cup history, all eight ties in the 1992-3 5th. Round were won (no replays) by the **clubs drawn at home**. Only other instance of eight home wins at the 'last 16' stage of the F.A. Cup was in 1889-90, in what was then the 2nd. Round.

FEWEST TOP-DIVISION CLUBS IN LAST 16 (5TH. ROUND)

5 in 1958; **6** in 1927, 1970, 1982; **7** in 1994, 2003; **8** in 2002, 2004.

SIXTH-ROUND ELITE

For the first time in F.A. Cup 6th. Round history, dating from 1926, when the format of the competition changed, **all eight quarter-finalists** in 1995-6 were from the top division.

SEMI-FINAL – DOUBLE DERBIES

There have been only two instances of both F.A. Cup semi-finals in the same year being local derbies: **1950** Liverpool beat Everton 2-0 (Maine Road), Arsenal beat Chelsea 1-0 after 2-2 draw (both at Tottenham); **1993** Arsenal beat Tottenham 1-0 (Wembley), Sheffield Wed. beat Sheffield Utd. 2-1 (Wembley).

TOP CLUB DISTINCTION

Since the Football League began in 1888, there has never been an F.A. Cup Final in which **neither club** represented the top division.

SPURS OUT – AND IN

Tottenham were banned, pre-season, from the 1994-5 F.A. Cup competition because of financial irregularities, but were readmitted on appeal and reached the semi-finals.

BROTHERS IN F.A. CUP FINAL TEAMS (Modern Times)

1950 Denis and Leslie Compton (Arsenal); **1952** George and Ted Robledo (Newcastle Utd.); **1967** Ron and Allan Harris (Chelsea); **1977** Jimmy and Brian Greenhoff (Manchester Utd.); **1996** and **1999** Gary and Phil Neville (Manchester Utd.)

FIRST SPONSORS

Littlewoods Pools became the first sponsors of the F.A. Cup in season 1994-5 in a £14m., 4-year deal. French insurance giants **AXA** took over (season 1998-9) in a sponsorship worth £25m. over 4 years. German energy company **E.ON** agreed a 4-year sponsorship (worth £32m.) from season 2006-07.

FIRST GOALKEEPER-SUBSTITUTE IN FINAL

Paul Jones (Southampton), who replaced injured Antti Niemi against Arsenal in 2003.

LEAGUE CUP RECORDS

(See also Goalscoring section)

Highest scores: West Ham Utd. 10-0 v Bury (2nd. Rd., 2nd. Leg 1983-4; agg. 12-1); Liverpool 10-0 v Fulham (2nd. Rd., 1st. Leg 1986-7; agg. 13-2).
Most League Cup goals (career): 49 Geoff Hurst (43 West Ham Utd., 6 Stoke City, 1960-75); 49 Ian Rush (48 Liverpool, 1 Newcastle Utd., 1981-98).
Highest scorer (season): 12 Clive Allen (Tottenham 1986-7 in 9 apps).
Most goals in match: 6 Frank Bunn (Oldham Athletic v Scarborough, 3rd. Rd., 1989-90).
Fewest goals conceded by winners: 3 by Leeds Utd. (1967-8), Tottenham (1970-1), Aston Villa (1995-6).
Most winner's medals: 5 Ian Rush (Liverpool).
Most appearances in Final: 6 Kenny Dalglish (Liverpool 1978-87), Ian Rush (Liverpool 1981-95).

League Cup sponsors: Milk Cup 1981-6, Littlewoods Cup 1987-90, Rumbelows Cup 1991-2, Coca-Cola Cup 1993-8. Worthington Cup 1999-2003, Carling Cup from season 2003-4.

Norwich City unique: In 1985, Norwich City became (and they remain) the only club to win a major domestic cup and be relegated in the same season. They won the League's Milk Cup and went down from the old First Division.

Liverpool's League Cup records: Winners a record 7 times. **Ian Rush** only player to win 5 times. Rush also first to play in 8 winning teams in Cup Finals **at Wembley**, all with Liverpool (F.A. Cup 1986-89-92; League Cup 1981-82-83-84-95).

Britain's first under-cover Cup Final: Worthington Cup Final between Blackburn Rov. and Tottenham at Cardiff's Millennium Stadium on Sunday, February 24, 2002. With rain forecast, the retractable roof was closed on the morning of the match.

DISCIPLINE

SENDINGS-OFF

Season 2003-4 set an **all-time record** of 504 players sent off in English domestic football competitions. There were 58 in the Premiership, 390 Nationwide League, 28 F.A. Cup (excluding non-League dismissals), 22 League Cup, 2 in Nationwide play-offs, 4 in LDV Vans Trophy.

The 58 Premiership red cards was 13 fewer than the record English **top-division** total of 71 in 2002-03. **Bolton Wand.** were the only club in the English divisions without a player sent off in any first-team competition that season.

Worst day for dismissals in English football history was December 13, 2003 with 19 red cards (2 Premiership and the 17 in the Nationwide League setting a **Football League record** for one day).

Previous worst overall total was 18 on November 16, 2002 (1 Premier League, 5 Nationwide League, 12 in F.A. Cup 1st. Round – 7 of those non-League). That equalled the **F.A. Cup's worst disciplinary day** (12 dismissals in 1st. Round on November 20, 1982).

Most players ordered off in **Anglo-Scottish football on one day:** 25, all League, on Oct. 16, 1999 (14 in England, 11 in Scotland).

● In the entire first season of post-war League football (1946-7) only 12 players were sent off, followed by 14 in 1949-50, and the total League dismissals for the first nine seasons after the war was 104.

The worst pre-war total was 28 in each of seasons 1921-2 and 1922-3.

ENGLAND SENDINGS-OFF

Wayne Rooney's red card aginst Portugal in the World Cup quarter-final was England's 11th sending off in their international history. In the qualifying match against Austria, David Beckham became the first England captain to be dismissed and the first England player to be sent off twice.

June 5, 1968 **Alan Mullery**	v Yugoslavia (Florence, Eur. Champ.)
June 6, 1973 **Alan Ball**	v Poland (Chorzow, World Cup qual.)
June 15, 1977 **Trevor Cherry**	v Argentina (Buenos Aires, friendly)
June 6, 1986 **Ray Wilkins**	v Morocco (Monterrey, World Cup Finals)
June 30, 1998 **David Beckham**	v Argentina (St. Etienne, World Cup Finals)
Sept. 5, 1998 **Paul Ince**	v Sweden (Stockholm, Eur. Champ. qual.)
June 5, 1999 **Paul Scholes**	v Sweden (Wembley, Eur. Champ. qual.)
Sept. 8, 1999 **David Batty**	v Poland (Warsaw, Eur. Champ. qual.)
Oct. 16, 2002 **Alan Smith**	v Macedonia (Southampton, Eur. Champ. qual.)
Oct. 8, 2005 **David Beckham**	v Austria (Old Trafford, World Cup qual.)
July 1, 2006 **Wayne Rooney**	v Portugal (Gelsenkirchen, World Cup Finals)

Other countries: Most recent sendings-off of players representing other Home Countries: **N. Ireland** – James Quinn (friendly v Romania, Chicago, May 2006); **Scotland** – James

McFadden (World Cup v Norway, Hampden Park, Oct. 2004); **Wales – Robbie Savage** (World Cup v N. Ireland, Cardiff, Sept. 2004); **Rep. of Ireland – Andy O'Brien** (World Cup v Israel, Dublin, June 2005).

England dismissals at other levels:-

U-23 (4): **Stan Anderson** (v Bulgaria, Sofia, May 19, 1957); **Alan Ball** (v Austria, Vienna, June 2, 1965); **Kevin Keegan** (v E. Germany, Magdeburg, June 1, 1972); **Steve Perryman** (v Portugal, Lisbon, Nov. 19, 1974).

U-21 (12): **Sammy Lee** (v Hungary, Keszthely, June 5, 1981); **Mark Hateley** (v Scotland, Hampden Park, April 19, 1982); **Paul Elliott** (v Denmark, Maine Road, Manchester, March 26, 1986); **Tony Cottee** (v W. Germany, Ludenscheid, September 8, 1987); **Julian Dicks** (v Mexico, Toulon, France, June 12, 1988); **Jason Dodd** (v Mexico, Toulon, May 29, 1991; 3 Mexico players also sent off in that match); **Matthew Jackson** (v France, Toulon, May 28, 1992); **Robbie Fowler** (v Austria, Kafkenberg, October 11, 1994); **Alan Thompson** (v Portugal, Oporto, September 2, 1995); **Terry Cooke** (v Portugal, Toulon, May 30, 1996); **Ben Thatcher** (v Italy, Rieti, October 10, 1997); **John Curtis** (v Greece, Heraklion, November 13, 1997); **Jody Morris** (v Luxembourg, Grevenmacher, October 13, 1998); **Stephen Wright** (v Germany, Derby Co., October 6, 2000); **Alan Smith** (v Finland, Valkeakoski, October 10, 2000); **Luke Young** and **John Terry** (v Greece, Athens, June 5, 2001); **Shola Ameobi** (v Portugal, Rio Maior, March 28, 2003); **Jermaine Pennant** (v Croatia, Upton Park, August 19, 2003); **Glen Johnson** (v Turkey, Istanbul, October 10, 2003); **Nigel Reo-Coker** (v Azerbaijan, Baku, October 12, 2004); **Glen Johnson** (v Spain, Henares, November 16, 2004).

England 'B' (1): **Neil Webb** (v Algeria, Algiers, December 11, 1990).

MOST DISMISSALS IN INTERNATIONAL MATCHES

19 (10 Chile, 9 Uruguay), June 25, 1975; **6** (2 Mexico, 4 Argentina), 1956; **6** (5 Ecuador, 1 Uruguay), Jan. 4, 1977 (4 Ecuadorians sent off in 78th min., match abandoned, 1-1); **5** (Holland 3, Brazil 2), June 6, 1999 in Goianio, Brazil.

INTERNATIONAL STOPPED THROUGH DEPLETED SIDE

Portugal v Angola (5-1), friendly International in Lisbon on November 14, 2001, abandoned (68 mins) because Angola were down to 6 players (4 sent off, 1 carried off, no substitutes left).

MOST 'CARDS' IN WORLD CUP FINALS MATCH

20 in Portugal v Holland quarter-final, Nuremberg, June 25, 2006 (9 yellow, 2 red, Portugal; 7 yellow, 2 red, Holland).

FIVE OFF IN ONE MATCH

For the first time since League football began in 1888, **five** players were sent off in one match (two Chesterfield, three Plymouth Argyle) in Div. 2 at Saltergate on **Feb. 22, 1997.** Four were dismissed (two from each side) in a goalmouth brawl in the last minute.

Second instance of **five** sent off in a League match was on **Dec. 2, 1997:** 4 Bristol Rov. players, 1 Wigan Athletic in Div. 2 match at Wigan. Four of those dismissals came in the 45th minute.

Third instance occurred on **Nov. 23, 2002:** Exeter City 3, Cambridge Utd. 2 – all in the last minute.

Matches with **four** Football League club players being sent off in one match:
Jan. 8, 1955 Crewe Alexandra v Bradford City (Div. 3 North), two players from each side.

Dec. 13, 1986 Sheffield Utd. (1 player) v Portsmouth (3) in Div. 2.

Aug. 18, 1987 Port Vale v Northampton Town (Littlewoods Cup 1st. Round, 1st. Leg), two players from each side.

Dec. 12, 1987 Brentford v Mansfield Town (Div. 3), two players from each side.

Sept. 6, 1992 First instance in British first-class football of **four players from one side** being sent off in one match. Hereford Utd.'s seven survivors, away to Northampton Town (Div. 3), held out for a 1-1 draw.

Mar. 1, 1977 Norwich City v Huddersfield Town (Div. 1), two from each side.

Oct. 4, 1977 Shrewsbury Town (1 player), Rotherham Utd. (3) in Div. 3.

Aug. 22, 1998 Gillingham v Bristol Rov. (Div. 2), two from each side, all after injury-time brawl.

Mar. 16, 2001 Bristol City v Millwall (Div. 2), two from each side.

Aug. 17, 2002 Lincoln City (1 player), Carlisle Utd. (3) in Div. 3.

Aug. 26, 2002 (Wycombe Wand. v Q.P.R. (Div. 2), two from each side.

Nov. 1, 2005 Burnley (1 player) v Millwall (3) in Championship.

Four Stranraer players were sent off away to Airdrie (Scottish Div. 1) on Dec. 3, 1994, and that Scottish record was equalled when **four Hearts men** were ordered off away to Rangers (Prem. Div.) on **Sept. 14, 1996. Albion Rov.** had **four players** sent off (3 in last 8 mins) away to Queen's Park (Scottish Div. 3) on **August 23, 1997.**

In the **Island Games** in Guernsey (July 2003), five players (all from Rhodes) were sent off against Guernsey for violent conduct and the match was abandoned by referee Wendy Toms.

Most dismissals one team, one match: Five players of America Tres Rios in first ten minutes after disputed goal by opponents Itaperuna in Brazilian cup match in Rio de Janeiro on Nov. 23, 1991. Tie then abandoned and awarded to Itaperuna.

Eight dismissals in one match: Four on each side in S. American Super Cup quarter-final (Gremio, Brazil v Penarol, Uruguay) in Oct. 1993.

Five dismissals in one season – Dave Caldwell (2 with Chesterfield, 3 with Torquay Utd.) in 1987-88.

First instance of **four dismissals in Scottish match**: three **Rangers** players (all English – Terry Hurlock, Mark Walters, Mark Hateley) and **Celtic's** Peter Grant in Scottish Cup quarter-final at Parkhead on Mar. 17, 1991 (Celtic won 2-0).

Four players (3 Hamilton, 1 Airdrie) were sent off in Scottish Div. 1 match on Oct. 30, 1993.

Four players (3 Ayr, 1 Stranraer) were sent off in Scottish Div. 1 match on Aug. 27, 1994.

In Scottish Cup first round replays on Dec. 16, 1996, there were two instances of **three players of one side sent off**: Albion Rov. (away to Forfar) and Huntly (away to Clyde).

FASTEST SENDINGS-OFF

World record – 10 secs: Giuseppe Lorenzo (Bologna) for striking opponent in Italian League match v Parma, December 9, 1990.

Domestic – 13 secs: Kevin Pressman (Sheffield Wed. goalkeeper at Wolves, Div. 1, Sunday, Aug. 14, 2000); **15 secs: Simon Rea** (Peterborough Utd. at Cardiff, Div. 2, Nov. 2, 2002). **19 secs: Mark Smith** (Crewe Alexandra goalkeeper at Darlington, Div. 3, Mar. 12, 1994). **Premier League** – 72 secs: **Tim Flowers** (Blackburn Rov. goalkeeper v Leeds Utd., Feb. 1, 1995).

In World Cup – 55 secs: Jose Batista (Uruguay v Scotland at Neza, Mexico, June 13, 1986).

In European competition – 90 secs: Sergei Dirkach (Dynamo Moscow v Ghent UEFA Cup 3rd round, 2nd leg, December 11, 1991).

Fastest F.A. Cup dismissal – 52 secs: **Ian Culverhouse** (Swindon Town defender, deliberate hand-ball on goal-line, away to Everton, 3rd. Round, Sunday Jan. 5, 1997).

Fastest League Cup dismissal – 33 secs: **Jason Crowe** (Arsenal substitute v Birmingham City, 3rd Round, Oct. 14, 1997).

Fastest Sending-off on debut: See **Jason Crowe** (above).

Fastest Sending-off of substitute – 0 secs: **Walter Boyd** (Swansea City) for striking opponent before ball in play after he went on (83 mins) at home to Darlington, Div. 3, Nov. 23, 1999. **90 secs: Andreas Johansson** (Wigan Athletic), without kicking a ball, for shirt-pulling (penalty) away to Arsenal (Premiership), May 7, 2006.

MOST SENDINGS-OFF IN CAREER

21 – **Willie Johnston** (Rangers 7, WBA 6, Vancouver Whitecaps 4, Hearts 3, Scotland 1)

21 – **Roy McDonough** (13 in Football League – Birmingham City, Walsall, Chelsea, Colchester Utd., Southend Utd., Exeter City, Cambridge Utd. + 8 non-league).

  13 – **Steve Walsh** (Wigan Athletic, Leicester City, Norwich City, Coventry City).

  13 – **Martin Keown** (Arsenal, Aston Villa, Everton).

  12 – **Dennis Wise** (Wimbledon, Chelsea, Leicester City, Millwall).

  12 – **Vinnie Jones** (Wimbledon, Leeds Utd., Sheffield Utd., Chelsea, Q.P.R.).

12 – **Mark Dennis** (Birmingham City, Southampton, Q.P.R.).
12 – **Roy Keane** (Manchester Utd., Rep. of Ireland).
12 – **Alan Smith** (Leeds Utd., Manchester Utd., England U–21, England).
10 – **Patrick Vieira** (Arsenal).
Most Premiership Sendings-off: Patrick Vieira 9, Duncan Ferguson 8, Vinnie Jones 7, Roy Keane 7.

● **Carlton Palmer** holds the unique record of having been sent off with each of his five Premiership clubs: Sheffield Wed., Leeds Utd., Southampton, Nott'm. Forest and Coventry City.

F.A. CUP FINAL SENDINGS-OFF

Kevin Moran (Man. United) v Everton, Wembley, 1985; **Jose Antonio Reyes** (Arsenal) v Man. United, Cardiff, 2005.

WEMBLEY SENDINGS-OFF

Manchester Utd.'s **Kevin Moran**, first player to be sent off in the F.A. Cup Final (v Everton, 1985), was one of 22 dismissals in major matches at Wembley:

Aug. 1948 **Branko Stankovic** (Yugoslavia) v Sweden, Olympic Games.
July 1966 **Antonio Rattin** (Argentina captain) v England, World cup q-final.
Aug. 1974 **Billy Bremner** (Leeds Utd.) and **Kevin Keegan** (Liverpool), Charity Shield.
Mar. 1977 **Gilbert Dresch** (Luxembourg) v England, World Cup.
May 1985 **Kevin Moran** (Manchester Utd.) v Everton, F.A. Cup Final.
Apr. 1993 **Lee Dixon** (Arsenal) v Tottenham, F.A. Cup semi-final.
May 1993 **Peter Swan** (Port Vale) v W.B.A., Div. 2 Play-off Final.
Mar. 1994 **Andrei Kanchelskis** (Manchester Utd.) v Aston Villa, League Cup Final.
May 1994 **Mike Wallace**, **Chris Beaumont** (Stockport) v Burnley, Div. 2 Play-off Final.
June 1995 **Tetsuji Hashiratani** (Japan) v England, Umbro Cup.
May 1997 **Brian Statham** (Brentford) v Crewe Alexandra, Div. 2 Play-off Final.
Apr. 1998 **Capucho** (Portugal) v England, friendly.
Nov. 1998 **Ray Parlour** (Arsenal) and Tony Vareilles (Lens), Champions League.
Mar. 1999 **Justin Edinburgh** (Tottenham) v Leicester City, League Cup Final.
June 1999 **Paul Scholes** (England) v Sweden, European Championship qual.
Feb. 2000 **Clint Hill** (Tranmere) v Leicester City, League Cup.
Apr. 2000 **Mark Delaney** (Aston Villa) v Bolton Wand., F.A. Cup semi-final.
May 2000 **Kevin Sharp** (Wigan Athletic) v Gillingham, Div. 2 Play-off Final.
Aug. 2000 **Roy Keane** (Manchester Utd. captain) v Chelsea, Charity Shield.

WEMBLEY'S SUSPENDED CAPTAINS

Suspension prevented four **club captains** playing at Wembley in modern finals, in successive years.

Three were in F.A. Cup Finals – **Glenn Roeder** (Q.P.R., 1982), **Steve Foster** (Brighton & H.A., 1983) and **Wilf Rostron** (Watford, 1984) – and Sunderland's **Shaun Elliott** was barred from the 1985 Milk Cup Final.

Roeder was banned from Q.P.R.'s 1982 Cup Final replay against Tottenham, and Foster was ruled out of the first match in Brighton & H.A.'s 1983 Final against Manchester Utd.

BOOKINGS RECORDS

Most players of one Football League club booked in one match is **TEN** – members of the Mansfield Town team away to Crystal Palace in F.A. Cup third round, January 1963.

Fastest bookings – 3 seconds after kick-off, **Vinnie Jones** (Chelsea, home to Sheffield Utd., F.A. Cup fifth round, February 15, 1992); 5 seconds after kick-off: **Vinnie Jones** (Sheffield Utd., away to Manchester City, Div. 1, January 19, 1991). He was sent-off (54 mins) for second bookable offence.

FIGHTING TEAM-MATES

Charlton Athletic's **Mike Flanagan** and **Derek Hales** were sent off for fighting each other five minutes from end of F.A. Cup 3rd Round tie at home to Southern League Maidstone on Jan. 9, 1979.

Bradford City's **Andy Myers** and **Stuart McCall** had a fight during the 1-6 Premiership defeat at Leeds on Sunday, May 13, 2001.

On Sept. 28, 1994 the Scottish F.A. suspended Hearts players **Graeme Hogg** and **Craig Levein** for ten matches for fighting each other in a pre-season 'friendly' v Raith.

Blackburn Rovers' England Internationals **Graeme Le Saux** and **David Batty** clashed away to Spartak Moscow (Champions League) on Nov. 22, 1995. Neither was sent off.

Newcastle United's England Internationals **Lee Bowyer** and **Kieron Dyer** were sent off for fighting each other at home to Aston Villa (Premiership on Apr. 2, 2005).

FOOTBALL'S FIRST BETTING SCANDAL

A Football League investigation into the First Division match which ended Manchester Utd 2, Liverpool 0 at Old Trafford on Good Friday, April 2, 1915 proved that the result had been 'squared' by certain players betting on the outcome. Four members of each team were suspended for life, but some of the bans were lifted when League football resumed in 1919 in recognition of the players' war service.

PLAYERS JAILED

Ten professional footballers found guilty of conspiracy to fraud by 'fixing' matches for betting purposes were given prison sentences at Nottingham Assizes on Jan. 26, 1965.

Jimmy Gauld (Mansfield Town), described as the central figure, was given four years. Among the others sentenced, Tony Kay (Sheffield Wed., Everton & England), Peter Swan (Sheffield Wed. & England) and David 'Bronco' Layne (Sheffield Wed.) were suspended from football for life by the F.A.

DRUGS BAN

Abel Xavier (Middlesbrough) was the first Premiership player found to have taken a performancing-enchancing drug. He was banned by UEFA for 18 months in November 2005 after testing positive for an anabolic steroid. The ban was reduced to a year in July 2006 by the Court of Arbitration for Sport.

LONG SUSPENSIONS

The longest suspension (8 months) in modern times for a player in British football has been imposed on two Manchester Utd. footballers. First, French international captain **Eric Cantona**, following his attack on a spectator as he left the pitch after being sent off at Crystal Palace (Prem. League) on Jan. 25, 1995.

The club immediately suspended him to the end of the season and fined him 2 weeks' wages (est. £20,000). Then, on a disrepute charge, the F.A. fined him £10,000 (February 1995) and extended the ban to September 30 (which FIFA confirmed as world wide).

A subsequent 2-weeks' jail sentence on Cantona for assault was altered, on appeal, to 120 hours' community service, which took the form of coaching schoolboys in the Manchester area.

On December 19, 2003 an F.A. commission, held at Bolton F.C., suspended **Rio Ferdinand** (Manchester Utd. & England) from football for 8 months (plus £50,000 fine) for failing to take a random drug test at the club's training ground on September 23. The ban operated from January 12, 2004.

October 1998: Paolo Di Canio (Sheff. Wed.) banned for 11 matches and fined £10,000 for pushing referee Paul Alcock after being sent off at home to Arsenal (Prem.), Sept. 26.

March 2005: David Prutton (Southampton) banned for 10 matches (plus 1 for red card) and fined £6,000 by F.A. for shoving referee Alan Wiley when sent off at home to Arsenal (Prem.), Feb. 26.

Seven-month ban: Frank Barson, 37-year-old Watford centre-half, sent off at home to Fulham (Div. 3 South) on September 29, 1928, was suspended by the F.A. for the remainder of the season.

Twelve-month ban: Oldham Athletic full-back **Billy Cook** was given a 12-month suspension for refusing to leave the field when sent off at Middlesbrough (Div. 1), on April 3, 1915. The referee abandoned the match with 35 minutes still to play, and the score (4-1 to Middlesbrough) was ordered to stand.

Long Scottish bans: September 1954: Willie Woodburn, Rangers and Scotland centre-half, suspended for rest of career after fifth sending-off in 6 years.

Billy McLafferty, Stenhousemuir striker, was banned (April 14) for 8½ months, to Jan. 1, 1993, and fined £250 for failing to appear at a disciplinary hearing after being sent off against Arbroath on Feb. 1.

Twelve-match ban: On May 12, 1994 Scottish F.A. suspended Rangers forward **Duncan Ferguson** for 12 matches for violent conduct v Raith on Apr. 16. On Oct. 11, 1995, Ferguson (then with Everton) sent to jail for 3 months for the assault (served 44 days); Feb. 1, 1996 Scottish judge quashed 7 matches that remained of SFA ban on Ferguson.

On September 29, 2001 the SFA imposed a **17-match suspension** on Forfar Athletic's former Scottish International **Dave Bowman** for persistent foul and abusive language when sent off against Stranraer on September 22. As his misconduct continued, he was shown **5 red cards** by the referee.

TOP FINES

Clubs: £1,500,000 (increased from original £600,000) Tottenham: Dec. 1994, financial irregularities.; **£300,000** (reduced to £75,000 on appeal) Chelsea: June 2005, illegal approach to Arsenal's Ashley Cole.; **£175,000** Arsenal: Oct. 2003, players' brawl v Manchester Utd.; **£150,000** Leeds Utd.: Mar. 2000, players' brawl v Tottenham; **£150,000** Tottenham: Mar. 2000, players brawl v Leeds Utd.; **£105,000** Chelsea: Jan 1991, irregular payments.; **£100,000** Boston Utd.: July 2002, contract irregularities.; **£62,000** Macclesfield Town: Dec. 2005, funding of a stand at club's ground.

Players: £150,000 Roy Keane (Manchester Utd.): Oct. 2002, disrepute offence over autobiography.; **£100,000** (reduced to £75,000 on appeal) Ashley Cole (Arsenal): June 2005, illegal approach by Chelsea.; **£45,000** Patrick Vieira (Arsenal): Oct. 1999, tunnel incidents v West Ham Utd.; **£40,000** Lauren (Arsenal): Oct. 2003, players' fracas v Manchester Utd.; **£32,000** Robbie Fowler (Liverpool): Apr. 1999, simulating drug-taking and incident with Graeme Le Saux v Chelsea.; **£30,000** Lee Bowyer (Newcastle Utd.): Apr. 2005, fighting with team-mate Kieron Dyer v Aston Villa.

* In eight seasons with Arsenal (1996-2004) Patrick Vieira was fined a toal of £122,000 by the F.A. for disciplinary offences.

Managers: £200,000 (reduced to £75,000 on appeal) Jose Mourinho (Chelsea): June 2005, illegal approach to Arsenal's Ashley Cole.; **£20,000** Graeme Souness (Newcastle Utd.): June 2005, criticising referee v Everton.; **£15,000** Graeme Souness (Blackburn Rov.): Oct. 2002, sent off v Liverpool.; **£15,000** Arsene Wenger (Arsenal): Dec 2004, comments about Manchester Utd.'s Ruud van Nistelrooy.; **£10,000** Arsene Wenger (Arsenal): Feb. 2001, incident with fourth official v Sunderland.; **£10,000** Graeme Souness (Blackburn Rov.): Apr. 2002, verbal abusing referee v Middlesbrough.; **£10,000** Sir Alex Ferguson (Manchester Utd.): Oct. 2003, verbally abusing match officials v Newcastle Utd.; **£10,000** Graeme Souness (Blackburn Rov.): May 2004, verbally abusing referee v Tottenham.; **£10,000** Graeme Souness (Newcastle Utd.): Dec. 2004, altercation with referee v Fulham.

*£68,000 F.A.: May 2003, pitch invasions and racist chanting by fans during England v Turkey, Stadium of Light.

MANAGERS

INTERNATIONAL RECORDS

(As at start of season 2006-07)

	P	W	D	L	F	A
Lawrie Sanchez	24	6	8	10	23	34
(N. Ireland – appointed Jan. 2004)						

Walter Smith (Scotland – appointed Dec. 2004)	12	4	5	3	17	12
John Toshack (Wales – appointed Nov. 2004)	11	4	2	5	9	9
Steve Staunton (Rep. of Ireland-appointed Jan. 2006)	2	1	0	1	3	1
Final records						
Sven-Goran Eriksson (England, Jan. 2001 – July 2006)	67	40	17	10	128	61
Brian Kerr (Rep. of Ireland, Jan. 2003 – Oct. 2005)	33	18	11	4	39	20

ENGLAND'S MANAGERS

		P	W	D	L
1946-62	**Walter Winterbottom**	139	78	33	28
1963-74	**Sir Alf Ramsey**	113	69	27	17
1974	**Joe Mercer**, caretaker	7	3	3	1
1974-77	**Don Revie**	29	14	8	7
1977-82	**Ron Greenwood**	55	33	12	10
1982-90	**Bobby Robson**	95	47	30	18
1990-93	**Graham Taylor**	38	18	13	7
1994-96	**Terry Venables**, coach	23	11	11	1
1996-99	**Glenn Hoddle**, coach	28	17	6	5
1999	**Howard Wilkinson**, caretaker	1	0	0	1
1999-2000	**Kevin Keegan**, coach	18	7	7	4
2000	**Howard Wilkinson**, caretaker	1	0	1	0
2000	**Peter Taylor**, caretaker	1	0	0	1
2001-2006	**Sven-Goran Eriksson**, coach	67	40	17	10

INTERNATIONAL MANAGER CHANGES

England: Walter Winterbottom 1946-62 (initially coach); **Alf Ramsey** (Feb. 1963-May 1974); **Joe Mercer** (caretaker May 1974); **Don Revie** (July 1974-July 1977); **Ron Greenwood** (Aug. 1977-July 1982); **Bobby Robson** (July 1982-July 1990); **Graham Taylor** (July 1990-Nov. 1993); **Terry Venables**, coach (Jan. 1994-June 1996); **Glenn Hoddle**, coach (June 1996-Feb. 1999); **Howard Wilkinson** (caretaker Feb. 1999); **Kevin Keegan** coach (Feb. 1999-Oct. 2000); **Howard Wilkinson** (caretaker Oct. 2000); **Peter Taylor** (caretaker Nov. 2000); **Sven-Goran Eriksson** (Jan. 2001 – Aug. 2006); **Steve McClaren** (since Aug. 2006).

N. Ireland (modern): Peter Doherty (1951-62); **Bertie Peacock** (1962-67); **Billy Bingham** (1967-Aug. 1971); **Terry Neill** (Aug. 1971-Mar. 1975); **Dave Clements** (player-manager Mar. 1975-1976); **Danny Blanchflower** (June 1976-Nov. 1979); **Billy Bingham** (Feb. 1980-Nov. 1993); **Bryan Hamilton** Feb. 1994-Feb. 1998); **Lawrie McMenemy** (Feb. 1998-Nov. 1999); **Sammy McIlroy** (Jan. 2000-Oct. 2003); **Lawrie Sanchez** (since Jan. 2004).

Scotland (modern): Bobby Brown (Feb. 1967-July 1971); **Tommy Docherty** (Sept. 1971- Dec. 1972); **Willie Ormond** (Jan. 1973-May 1977); **Ally MacLeod** (May 1977-Sept.1978); **Jock Stein** (Oct. 1978-Sept. 1985); **Alex Ferguson** (caretaker Oct. 1985-June 1986); **Andy Roxburgh**, coach (July 1986-Sept. 1993); **Craig Brown** (Sept. 1993-Oct. 2001); **Berti Vogts** (Feb. 2002 – Oct. 2004); **Walter Smith** (since Dec. 2004).

Wales (modern): Mike Smith (July 1974-Dec. 1979); **Mike England** (Mar. 1980-Feb. 1988); **David Williams** (caretaker Mar. 1988); **Terry Yorath** (Apr. 1988-Nov. 1993); **John Toshack** (Mar. 1994, one match); **Mike Smith** (Mar. 1994-June 1995); **Bobby Gould** (Aug. 1995-June 1999); **Mark Hughes** (Aug. 1999 – Oct. 2004); **John Toshack** (since Nov. 2004).

Rep. of Ireland (modern): Liam Tuohy (Sept. 1971-Nov. 1972); **Johnny Giles** (Oct. 1973-Apr. 1980, initially player-manager); **Eoin Hand** (June 1980-Nov. 1985); **Jack**

Charlton (Feb. 1986-Dec. 1995); **Mick McCarthy** (Feb. 1996-Oct. 2002); **Brian Kerr** (Jan. 2003 – Oct. 2005); **Steve Staunton** (since Jan. 2006).

FIRST BLACK ENGLAND MANAGER
Chris Ramsey, 36, in charge of England's U-20 squad for the World Youth Championship in Nigeria, April 1999. He was Brighton & H.A.'s right-back in the 1983 F.A. Cup Final v Manchester Utd.

YOUNGEST LEAGUE MANAGERS
Ivor Broadis, 23, appointed player-manager of Carlisle Utd., August 1946; **Chris Brass**, 27, appointed player-manager of York City, June 2003; **Terry Neill**, 28, appointed player-manager of Hull City, June 1970;
  Graham Taylor, 28, appointed manager of Lincoln City, December 1972.

LONGEST-SERVING LEAGUE MANAGERS – ONE CLUB
Fred Everiss, secretary-manager of W.B.A. for 46 years (1902-48); **George Ramsay**, secretary-manager of Aston Villa for 42 years (1884-1926); **John Addenbrooke**, Wolves, for 37 years (1885-1922). Since last war, **Sir Matt Busby**, in charge of Manchester Utd. for 25 seasons (1945-69, 1970-71); **Jimmy Seed** at Charlton Athletic for 23 years (1933-56); **Dario Gradi** at Crewe Alexandra for 23 years (1983–2006).

LAST ENGLISH MANAGER TO WIN CHAMPIONSHIP
Howard Wilkinson (Leeds Utd.), season 1991–92.

1,000-TIME MANAGERS
Only five have managed in more than 1,000 English League games: **Alec Stock**, **Brian Clough**, **Jim Smith**, **Graham Taylor** and **Dario Gradi**.
  Sir Matt Busby, **Dave Bassett**, **Lennie Lawrence**, **Alan Buckley**, **Denis Smith**, **Joe Royle**, **Sir Alex Ferguson** and **Brian Horton** have each managed more than 1,000 matches in all first class competitions.

SHORT-TERM MANAGERS

		Departed
3 Days	Bill Lambton (Scunthorpe Utd.)	April 1959
7 Days	Tim Ward (Exeter City)	March 1953
7 Days	Kevin Cullis (Swansea City)	February 1996
10 Days	Dave Cowling (Doncaster Rov.)	October 1997
10 Days	Peter Cormack (Cowdenbeath)	December 2000
13 Days	Johnny Cochrane (Reading)	April 1939
13 Days	Micky Adams (Swansea City)	October 1997
16 Days	Jimmy McIlroy (Bolton Wand.)	November 1970
20 Days	Paul Went (Leyton Orient)	October 1981
27 Days	Malcolm Crosby (Oxford Utd.)	January 1998
28 Days	Tommy Docherty (Q.P.R.)	December 1968
32 Days	Steve Coppell (Manchester City)	November 1996
36 Days	Steve Claridge (Millwall)	July 2005
39 Days	Paul Gascoigne (Kettering)	December 2005
41 Days	Steve Wicks (Lincoln City)	October 1995
44 Days	Brian Clough (Leeds Utd.)	September 1974
44 Days	Jock Stein (Leeds Utd.)	October 1978
48 Days	John Toshack (Wales)	March 1994
48 Days	David Platt (Sampdoria coach)	February 1999
49 Days	Brian Little (Wolves)	October 1986
49 Days	Terry Fenwick (Northampton Town)	February 2003
61 Days	Bill McGarry (Wolves)	November 1985

● In May 1984, Crystal Palace named **Dave Bassett** as manager, but he changed his mind four days later, without signing the contract, and returned to Wimbledon.

- **Brian Laws** lost his job at Scunthorpe Utd. on March 25, 2004 and was re-instated three weeks later.
- In an angry outburst after a play-off defeat in May 1992, Barnet chairman Stan Flashman sacked manager **Barry Fry** and re-instated him a day later.

EARLY-SEASON MANAGER SACKINGS

2004 Paul Sturrock (Southampton) 9 days; **2004** Sir Bobby Robson (Newcastle Utd.) 16 days; **2003** Glenn Roeder (West Ham) 15 days; **2000** Alan Buckley (Grimsby Town) 10 days; **1997** Kerry Dixon (Doncaster Rov.) 12 days; **1996** Sammy Chung (Doncaster Rov.) on morning of season's opening League match; **1996** Alan Ball (Manchester City) 12 days; **1994** Kenny Hibbitt (Walsall) and Kenny Swain (Wigan Athletic) 20 days; **1993** Peter Reid (Manchester City) 12 days; **1991** Don Mackay (Blackburn Rov.) 14 days; **1989** Mick Jones (Peterborough Utd.) 12 days; **1980** Bill McGarry (Newcastle Utd.) 13 days; **1979** Dennis Butler (Port Vale) 12 days; **1977** George Petchey (Leyton O.) 13 days; **1977** Willie Bell (Birmingham City) 16 days; **1971** Len Richley (Darlington) 12 days.

FEWEST MANAGERS

West Ham Utd. have had only ten managers in their 105-year history: Syd King, Charlie Paynter, Ted Fenton, Ron Greenwood, John Lyall, Lou Macari, Billy Bonds, Harry Redknapp, Glenn Roeder and Alan Pardew.

RECORD START FOR MANAGER

Arsenal were unbeaten in 17 League matches from the start of season 1947-8 under new manager Tom Whittaker.

MANAGER CHOSEN BY POLL

A month after being sacked by Third Division promotion winners Hartlepool Utd., **Mike Newell** became manager of Luton Town in June 2003. He was appointed via a telephone poll which the club, under a new board, conducted among fans, players, shareholders and season-ticket holders.

MANAGER DOUBLES

Four managers have won the League Championship with different clubs: **Tom Watson**, secy-manager with Sunderland (1892-3-5) and Liverpool (1901); **Herbert Chapman** with Huddersfield Town (1923-4, 1924-5) and Arsenal (1930-1, 1932-3); **Brian Clough** with Derby Co. (1971-2) and Nott'm. Forest (1977-8); **Kenny Dalglish** with Liverpool (1985-6, 1987-8, 1989-90) and Blackburn Rov. (1994-5).

Managers to win the F.A. Cup with different clubs: **Billy Walker** (Sheffield Wed. 1935, Nott'm. Forest 1959); **Herbert Chapman** (Huddersfield Town 1922, Arsenal 1930).

Kenny Dalglish (Liverpool) and **George Graham** (Arsenal) completed the Championship/F.A. Cup double as both player and manager with a single club. **Joe Mercer** won the Championship as a player with Everton, the Championship twice and F.A. Cup as a player with Arsenal and both competitions as manager of Manchester City.

FIRST CHAIRMAN-MANAGER

On December 20, 1988, after two years on the board, Dundee Utd. manager **Jim McLean** was elected chairman, too. McLean, Scotland's longest-serving manager (appointed on November 24, 1971), resigned at end of season 1992-3 (remained chairman).

Ron Noades was chairman-manager of Brentford from July 1998 – March 2001.

TOP DIVISION PLAYER–MANAGERS

Les Allen (Q.P.R. 1968-9); **Johnny Giles** (W.B.A. 1976-7); **Howard Kendall** (Everton 1981-2); **Kenny Dalglish** (Liverpool, 1985-90); **Trevor Francis** (Q.P.R., 1988-9); **Terry Butcher** (Coventry City, 1990-1), **Peter Reid** (Manchester City, 1990-93), **Trevor Francis** (Sheffield Wed., 1991-4), **Glenn Hoddle**, (Chelsea, 1993-5), **Bryan Robson** (Middlesbrough, 1994-7), **Ray Wilkins** (Q.P.R., 1994-6), **Ruud Gullit** (Chelsea, 1996-8), **Gianluca Vialli** (Chelsea, 1998-2000).

FIRST FOREIGN MANAGER IN ENGLISH LEAGUE

Uruguayan **Danny Bergara** (Rochdale 1988-9).

FOREIGN TRIUMPH

Former Dutch star **Ruud Gullit** became the first foreign manager to win a major English competition when Chelsea took the F.A. Cup in 1997.

Arsene Wenger and **Gerard Houllier** became the first foreign managers to receive recognition when they were awarded honorary OBEs in the Queen's Birthday Honours in June 2003 'for their contribution to English football and Franco-British relations.'

MANAGERS OF POST-WAR CHAMPIONS (*Double Winners)

1947 George Kay (Liverpool); **1948** Tom Whittaker (Arsenal); **1949** Bob Jackson (Portsmouth); **1950** Bob Jackson (Portsmouth); **1951** Arthur Rowe (Tottenham); **1952** Matt Busby (Manchester Utd.); **1953** Tom Whittaker (Arsenal).

1954 Stan Cullis (Wolves); **1955** Ted Drake (Chelsea); **1956** Matt Busby (Manchester Utd.); **1957** Matt Busby (Manchester Utd.); **1958** Stan Cullis (Wolves); **1959** Stan Cullis (Wolves); **1960** Harry Potts (Burnley).

1961 *Bill Nicholson (Tottenham); **1962** Alf Ramsey (Ipswich Town); **1963** Harry Catterick (Everton); **1964** Bill Shankly (Liverpool); **1965** Matt Busby (Manchester Utd.); **1966** Bill Shankly (Liverpool); **1967** Matt Busby (Manchester Utd.).

1968 Joe Mercer (Manchester City); **1969** Don Revie (Leeds Utd.); **1970** Harry Catterick (Everton); **1971** *Bertie Mee (Arsenal); **1972** Brian Clough (Derby Co.); **1973** Bill Shankly (Liverpool); **1974** Don Revie (Leeds Utd.).

1975 Dave Mackay (Derby Co.); **1976** Bob Paisley (Liverpool); **1977** Bob Paisley (Liverpool); **1978** Brian Clough (Nott'm. Forest); **1979** Bob Paisley (Liverpool); **1980** Bob Paisley (Liverpool); **1981** Ron Saunders (Aston Villa).

1982 Bob Paisley (Liverpool); **1983** Bob Paisley (Liverpool); **1984** Joe Fagan (Liverpool); **1985** Howard Kendall (Everton); **1986** *Kenny Dalglish (Liverpool – player/manager); **1987** Howard Kendall (Everton).

1988 Kenny Dalglish (Liverpool – player/manager); **1989** George Graham (Arsenal); **1990** Kenny Dalglish (Liverpool); **1991** George Graham (Arsenal); **1992** Howard Wilkinson (Leeds Utd.); **1993** Alex Ferguson (Manchester Utd.).

1994 *Alex Ferguson (Manchester Utd.); **1995** Kenny Dalglish (Blackburn Rov.); **1996** *Alex Ferguson (Manchester Utd.); **1997** Alex Ferguson (Manchester Utd.); **1998** *Arsene Wenger (Arsenal); **1999** *Alex Ferguson (Manchester Utd.); **2000** Sir Alex Ferguson (Manchester Utd.); **2001** Sir Alex Ferguson (Manchester Utd.); **2002** *Arsene Wenger (Arsenal); **2003** Sir Alex Ferguson (Manchester Utd.); **2004** Arsene Wenger (Arsenal); **2005** Jose Mourinho (Chelsea); **2006** Jose Mourinho (Chelsea).

SIR ALEX IS TOPS

With 27 major prizes **Sir Alex Ferguson** has the most successful managerial record with Scottish and English clubs combined. At **Aberdeen** (1978-86) he won ten top prizes: 3 Scottish Championships, 4 Scottish Cups, 1 Scottish League Cup, 1 Cup-Winners' Cup, 1 European Super Cup.

Manchester Utd. winning the Premiership in 2001 made Sir Alex the outright most successful manager in English football, the first to win seven League titles, the first to win three in a row. He achieved an eighth Premiership success in 2003.

His Carling Cup success in 2006 was United's 17th major trophy in 16 seasons: 1990 F.A. Cup, 1991 Cup-Winners' Cup, 1992 League Cup, 1993 League Championship, 1994 League Championship and F.A. Cup, 1996 Championship and F.A. Cup; 1997 Championship; 1999 Championship; F.A. Cup and European Cup; 2000 Championship; 2001 Championship; 2003 Championship; F.A. Cup 2004; Carling Cup 2006.

BOB PAISLEY'S HONOURS

Bob Paisley won 13 major competitions for Liverpool (1974-83): 6 League Championships, 3 European Cups, 3 League Cups, 1 UEFA Cup.

FOUR FOR MOURINHO

Jose Mourinho has led four consecutive title-winning teams – FC Porto (2002-3, 2003-4) and Chelsea (2004-5, 2005-6).

MANAGERS WITH MOST F.A. CUP SUCCESSES

5 Sir Alex Ferguson (Manchester Utd.); **4** Arsene Wenger (Arsenal); **3** Charles Foweraker (Bolton Wand.), John Nicholson (Sheffield Utd.), Bill Nicholson (Tottenham).

HOLE-IN-ONE MANAGER

Three days after appointing **Bobby Williamson** manager, from Hibernian, **Plymouth Argyle** clinched promotion and the Second Division Championship by beating Q.P.R. 2-1 on April 24, 2004.

RELEGATION 'DOUBLES'

Managers associated with two clubs relegated in same season: **John Bond** in 1985-6 (Swansea City and Birmingham City); **Ron Saunders** in 1985-6 (W.B.A. – and their reserve team – and Birmingham City); **Bob Stokoe** in 1986-7 (Carlisle Utd. and Sunderland); **Billy McNeill** in 1986-7 (Manchester City and Aston Villa); **Dave Bassett** in 1987-8 (Watford and Sheffield Utd.); **Mick Mills** in 1989-90 (Stoke City and Colchester Utd.).

WEMBLEY STADIUM

INVASION DAY

Memorable scenes were witnessed at the **first F.A. Cup Final at Wembley, April 28, 1923,** between **Bolton** and **West Ham**. An accurate return of the attendance could not be made owing to thousands breaking in, but there were probably more than 200,000 spectators present. The match was delayed for 40 minutes by the crowd invading the pitch. Official attendance was 126,047.

Gate receipts totalled £27,776. The two clubs and the Football Association each received £6,365 and the F.A. refunded £2,797 to ticket-holders who were unable to get to their seats. Cup Final admission has since been by ticket only.

REDUCED CAPACITY

Capacity of the all-seated **Wembley Stadium** was 78,000. The last 100,000 attendance was for the 1985 F.A. Cup Final between Manchester Utd. and Everton.

WEMBLEY'S FIRST UNDER LIGHTS

November 30, 1955 (England 4, Spain 1), when the floodlights were switched on after 73 minutes (afternoon match played in damp, foggy conditions).
First Wembley International played throughout under lights: England 8, N. Ireland 3 on evening of November 20, 1963 (att: 55,000).

MOST WEMBLEY APPEARANCES BY PLAYER

59 by Tony Adams (24 Arsenal, 35 England).

WEMBLEY HAT-TRICKS

Three players have scored hat-tricks in major cup finals at Wembley: **Stan Mortensen** for Blackpool v Bolton Wand. (F.A. Cup Final, 1953), **Geoff Hurst** for England v West Germany (World Cup Final, 1966) and **David Speedie** for Chelsea v Manchester City (Full Members Cup, 1985).

ENGLAND'S WEMBLEY DEFEATS

England have lost 18 matches to foreign opponents at Wembley:

Nov.	1953	3-6 v Hungary	Sept.	1983	0-1 v Denmark
Oct.	1959	2-3 v Sweden	June	1984	0-2 v Russia
Oct.	1965	2-3 v Austria	May	1990	1-2 v Uruguay
Apr.	1972	1-3 v W. Germany	Sept.	1991	0-1 v Germany
Nov.	1973	0-1 v Italy	June	1995	1-3 v Brazil
Feb.	1977	0-2 v Holland	Feb.	1997	0-1 v Italy
Mar.	1981	1-2 v Spain	Feb.	1998	0-2 v Chile
May	1981	0-1 v Brazil	Feb.	1999	0-2 v France
Oct.	1982	1-2 v W. Germany	Oct.	2000	0-1 v Germany

A further defeat came in **Euro 96**. After drawing the semi-final with Germany 1-1, England went out 6-5 on penalties.

FASTEST GOALS AT WEMBLEY

In first-class matches: **38 seconds** by **Bryan Robson** in England's 2-1 win against Yugoslavia on December 13, 1989; **44 seconds** by **Bryan Robson** for England in 4-0 win v N. Ireland on February 23, 1982; **42 seconds** by **Roberto di Matteo** for Chelsea in the 1997 F.A. Cup Final v Middlesbrough.

Fastest goal in **any** match at Wembley: **20 seconds** by **Maurice Cox** for Cambridge University against Oxford on December 5, 1979.

FOUR WEMBLEY HEADERS

When **Wimbledon** beat Sutton Utd. 4-2 in the F.A. Amateur Cup Final at Wembley on May 4, 1963, Irish centre-forward **Eddie Reynolds** headed all four goals.

WEMBLEY ONE-SEASON DOUBLES

In 1989, **Nott'm. Forest** became the first club to win two Wembley Finals in the same season (Littlewoods Cup and Simod Cup).

In 1993, **Arsenal** made history there as the first club to win the League (Coca-Cola) Cup and the F.A. Cup in the same season. They beat Sheffield Wed. 2-1 in both finals.

SUDDEN-DEATH DECIDERS

First Wembley Final decided on sudden death (first goal scored in overtime): April 23, 1995 – **Birmingham City** beat Carlisle Utd. (1-0, Paul Tait 103 mins.) to win Auto Windscreens Shield.

First instance of a 'golden goal' deciding a major International tournament was at Wembley on June 30, 1996, when **Germany** beat the Czech Republic 2-1 in the European Championship Final with Oliver Bierhoff's goal in the 95th minute.

SHADOWS OVER SOCCER

DAYS OF TRAGEDY – CLUBS

Season 1988-9 brought the worst disaster in the history of British sport, with the death of 96 Liverpool supporters (200 injured) at the **F.A. Cup semi-final** against Nott'm. Forest at **Hillsborough, Sheffield**, on Saturday, April 15. The tragedy built up in the minutes preceding kick-off, when thousands surged into the ground at the Leppings Lane end. Many were crushed in the tunnel between entrance and terracing, but most of the victims were trapped inside the perimeter fencing behind the goal. The match was abandoned without score after six minutes' play. The dead included seven women and girls, two teenage sisters and two teenage brothers. The youngest victim was a boy of ten, the oldest 67-year-old Gerard Baron, whose brother Kevin played for Liverpool in the 1950 Cup Final. (*Total became 96 in March 1993, when Tony Bland died after being in a coma for nearly four years).

The two worst disasters in one season in British soccer history occurred at the end of 1984-5. On May 11, the last Saturday of the League season, 56 people (two of them visiting supporters) were burned to death – and more than 200 taken to hospital – when fire destroyed the main stand at the **Bradford City-Lincoln City** match at Valley Parade.

The wooden, 77-year-old stand was full for City's last fixture before which, amid scenes of celebration, the club had been presented with the Third Division Championship trophy. The fire broke out just before half-time and, within five minutes, the entire stand was engulfed.

Eighteen days later, on May 29, at the European Cup Final between **Liverpool** and **Juventus** at the Heysel Stadium, Brussels, 39 spectators (31 of them Italian) were crushed or trampled to death and 437 injured. The disaster occurred an hour before the scheduled kick-off when Liverpool supporters charged a Juventus section of the crowd at one end of the stadium, and a retaining wall collapsed.

The sequel was a 5-year ban by UEFA on English clubs generally in European competition, with a 6-year ban on Liverpool.

On May 26, 1985 ten people were trampled to death and 29 seriously injured in a crowd panic on the way into the **Olympic Stadium, Mexico City** for the Mexican Cup Final between local clubs National University and America.

More than 100 people died and 300 were injured in a football disaster at **Nepal's national stadium** in Katmandu in March 1988. There was a stampede when a violent hailstorm broke over the capital. Spectators rushed for cover, but the stadium exits were locked, and hundreds were trampled in the crush.

In South Africa, on January 13, 1991 40 black fans were trampled to death (50 injured) as they tried to escape from fighting that broke out at a match in the gold-mining town of Orkney, 80 miles from Johannesburg. The friendly, between top teams **Kaiser Chiefs** and **Orlando Pirates**, attracted a packed crowd of 20,000. Violence erupted after the referee allowed Kaiser Chiefs a disputed second-half goal to lead 1-0.

Disaster struck at the French Cup semi-final (May 5, 1992), with the death of 15 spectators and 1,300 injured when a temporary metal stand collapsed in the Corsican town of Bastia. The tie between Second Division **Bastia** and French Champions **Marseille** was cancelled. **Monaco**, who won the other semi-final, were allowed to compete in the next season's Cup-Winners' Cup.

A total of 318 died and 500 were seriously injured when the crowd rioted over a disallowed goal at the National Stadium in Lima, Peru, on May 24, 1964. **Peru** and **Argentina** were competing to play in the Olympic Games in Tokyo.

That remained sport's heaviest death toll until October 20, 1982, when (it was revealed only in July 1989) 340 Soviet fans were killed in Moscow's Lenin Stadium at the UEFA Cup second round first leg match between **Moscow Spartak** and **Haarlem (Holland)**. They were crushed on an open stairway when a last-minute Spartak goal sent departing spectators surging back into the ground.

Among other crowd disasters abroad: **June 1968** – 74 died in **Argentina**. Panic broke out at the end of a goalless match between River Plate and Boca Juniors at Nunez, Buenos Aires, when Boca supporters threw lighted newspaper torches on to fans in the tiers below.

February 1974 – 49 killed in **Egypt** in crush of fans clamouring to see Zamalek play Dukla Prague.

September 1971 – 44 died in **Turkey**, when fighting among spectators over a disallowed goal (Kayseri v Siwas) led to a platform collapsing.

The then worst disaster in the history of British football, in terms of loss of life, occurred at Glasgow Rangers' ground at **Ibrox Park**, January 2, 1971.

Sixty-six people were trampled to death (100 injured) as they tumbled down Stairway 13 just before the end of the **Rangers v Celtic** New Year's match. That disaster led to the 1975 Safety of Sports Grounds legislation.

The Ibrox tragedy eclipsed even the Bolton disaster in which 33 were killed and about 500 injured when a wall and crowd barriers collapsed near a corner-flag at the **Bolton Wand. v Stoke City** F.A. Cup sixth round tie on March 9, 1946. The match was completed after half an hour's stoppage.

In a previous crowd disaster at **Ibrox** on April 5, 1902, part of the terracing collapsed during the Scotland v England International and 25 people were killed. The match, held up for 20 minutes, ended 1-1, but was never counted as an official International.

Eight leading players and three officials of **Manchester Utd.** and eight newspaper representatives were among the 23 who perished in the air crash at Munich on February 6, 1958, during take-off following a European Cup-tie in Belgrade. The players were Roger Byrne, Geoffrey Bent, Eddie Colman, Duncan Edwards, Mark Jones, David Pegg, Tommy Taylor and Liam Whelan, and the officials were Walter Crickmer (secretary), Tom Curry (trainer) and Herbert Whalley (coach). The newspaper representatives were Alf Clarke, Don Davies, George Follows, Tom Jackson, Archie Ledbrooke, Henry Rose, Eric Thompson and Frank Swift (former England goalkeeper of Manchester City).

On May 14, 1949, the entire team of Italian Champions **Torino,** 8 of them Internationals, were killed when the aircraft taking them home from a match against Benfica in Lisbon crashed at Superga, near Turin. The total death toll of 28 included all the club's reserve players, the manager, trainer and coach.

On February 8, 1981, 24 spectators died and more than 100 were injured at a match **in Greece.** They were trampled as thousands of the 40,000 crowd tried to rush out of the stadium at Piraeus after Olympiakos beat AEK Athens 6-0.

On November 17, 1982, 24 people (12 of them children) were killed and 250 injured when fans stampeded at the end of a match at the Pascual Guerrero stadium in **Cali, Colombia.** Drunken spectators hurled fire crackers and broken bottles from the higher stands on to people below and started a rush to the exits.

On December 9, 1987, the 18-strong team squad of **Alianza Lima,** one of Peru's top clubs, were wiped out, together with 8 officials and several youth players, when a military aircraft taking them home from Puccalpa crashed into the sea off Ventillana, ten miles from Lima. The only survivor among 43 on board was a member of the crew.

On April 28, 1993, 18 members of **Zambia's International** squad and 5 ZFA officials died when the aircraft carrying them to a World Cup qualifying tie against Senegal crashed into the Atlantic soon after take-off from Libreville, Gabon.

On October 16, 1996, 81 fans were crushed to death and 147 seriously injured in the 'Guatemala Disaster' at the World Cup qualifier against Costa Rica in Mateo Flores stadium. The tragedy happened an hour before kick-off, allegedly caused by ticket forgery and overcrowding – 60,000 were reported in the 45,000-capacity ground – and safety problems related to perimeter fencing.

On July 9, 1996, 8 people died, 39 injured in riot after derby match between **Libya's two top clubs** in Tripoli. Al-Ahli had beaten Al-Ittihad 1-0 by a controversial goal.

On April 6, 1997, 5 spectators were crushed to death at **Nigeria's national stadium** in Lagos after the 2-1 World Cup qualifying victory over Guinea. Only two of five gates were reported open as the 40,000 crowd tried to leave the ground.

It was reported from the **Congo** (October 29, 1998) that a bolt of lightning struck a village match, killing all 11 members of the home team Benatshadi, but leaving the opposing players from Basangana unscathed. It was believed the surviving team wore better-insulated boots.

On January 10, 1999 eight fans died and 13 were injured in a stampede at **Egypt's Alexandria Stadium.** Some 25,000 spectators had pushed into the ground. Despite the tragedy, the cup-tie between Al-Ittihad and Al-Koroum was completed.

Three people suffocated and several were seriously injured when thousands of fans forced their way into **Liberia's national stadium** in Monrovia at a goalless World Cup qualifying match against Chad on April 23, 2000. The stadium (capacity 33,000) was reported 'heavily overcrowded'.

On Sunday, July 9, 2000 12 spectators died from crush injuries when police fired tear gas into the 50,000 crowd after South Africa scored their second goal in a World Cup group qualifier against Zimbabwe in **Harare.** A stampede broke out as fans scrambled to leave the national stadium. Players of both teams lay face down on the pitch as fumes swept over them. FIFA launched an investigation and decided that the result would stand, with South Africa leading 2-0 at the time of the 84th-minute abandonment.

On April 11, 2001, at one of the biggest matches of the South African season, 43 died and 155 were injured in a crush at **Ellis Park, Johannesburg.** After tearing down a fence, thousands of fans surged into a stadium already packed to its 60,000 capacity for the Premiership derby between top Soweto teams Kaizer Chiefs and Orlando Pirates. The match was abandoned at 1-1 after 33 minutes. In January 1991, 40 died in a crowd crush at a friendly between the same clubs at Orkney, 80 miles from Johannesburg.

On April 29, 2001, seven people were trampled to death and 51 injured when a riot broke out at a match between two of Congo's biggest clubs, Lupopo and Mazembe at **Lubumbashi**, southern Congo.

On May 6, 2001, two spectators were killed in Iran and hundreds were injured when a glass fibre roof collapsed at the over-crowded Mottaqi Stadium at **Sari** for the match between Pirouzi and Shemshak Noshahr.

On May 9, 2001, in Africa's worst football disaster, 123 died and 93 were injured in a stampede at the national stadium in **Accra, Ghana**. Home team Hearts of Oak were leading 2-1 against Asante Kotoko five minutes from time, when Asanti fans started hurling bottles on to the pitch. Police fired tear gas into the stands, and the crowd panicked in a rush for the exits, which were locked. It took the death toll at three big matches in Africa in April/May to 173.

On August 12, 2001, two players were killed by lightning and ten severely burned at a **Guatemala** Third Division match between Deportivo Culquimulilla and Pueblo Nuevo Vinas.

On November 1, 2002, two players died from injuries after lightning struck Deportivo Cali's training ground in **Colombia**.

On March 12, 2004, five people were killed and more than 100 injured when spectators stampeded shortly before the Syrian Championship fixture between Al-Jihad and Al-Fatwa in **Qameshli**, Northern Syria. The match was cancelled.

On October 10, 2004, three spectators died in a crush at the African Zone World Cup qualifier between **Guinea** and **Morocco** (1-1) at Conakry, Guinea.

On March 25, 2005, five were killed as 100,000 left the Azadi Stadium, **Tehran**, after Iran's World Cup qualifying win (2-1) against Japan.

DAYS OF TRAGEDY – PERSONAL

Sam Wynne, Bury right-back, collapsed five minutes before half-time in the First Division match away to Sheffield Utd. on April 30, 1927, and died in the dressing-room.

John Thomson, Cheltic and Scotland goalkeeper, sustained a fractured skull when diving at an opponent's feet in the Rangers v Celtic League match on September 5, 1931, and died the same evening.

Sim Raleigh (Gillingham), injured in a clash of heads at home to Brighton & H.A. (Div. 3 South) on December 1, 1934, continued to play but collapsed in second half and died in hospital the same night.

James Thorpe, Sunderland goalkeeper, was injured during the First Division match at home to Chelsea on February 1, 1936 and died in a diabetic coma three days later.

Derek Dooley, Sheffield Wed. centre-forward and top scorer in 1951-52 in the Football League with 46 goals in 30 matches, broke a leg in the League match at Preston N.E. on February 14, 1953, and, after complications set in, had to lose the limb by amputation.

John White Tottenham's Scottish International forward, was killed by lightning on a golf course at Enfield, North London in July, 1964.

Tommy Allden Highgate Utd. centre-half was struck by lightning during an Amateur Cup quarter-final with Enfield Town on February 25, 1967. He died the following day. Four other players were also struck but recovered.

Roy Harper died while refereeing the York City–Halifax Town (Div. 4) match on May 5, 1969.

Jim Finn collapsed and died from a heart attack while refereeing Exeter City v Stockport Co. (Div. 4) on September 16, 1972.

Scotland manager **Jock Stein**, 62, collapsed and died at the end of the Wales-Scotland World Cup qualifying match (1-1) at Ninian Park, Cardiff on September 10, 1985.

David Longhurst, York City forward, died after being carried off two minutes before half-time in the Fourth Division fixture at home to Lincoln City on September 8, 1990. The match was abandoned (0-0). The inquest revealed that Longhurst suffered from a rare heart condition.

Mike North collapsed while refereeing Southend Utd. v Mansfield Town (Div. 3) on April 16, 2001 and died shortly afterwards. The match was abandoned and re-staged on May 8, with the receipts donated to his family.

Marc-Vivien Foe, on his 63rd appearance in Cameroon's midfield, collapsed unchallenged in the centre circle after 72 minutes of the FIFA Confederations Cup semi-final against Colombia in Lyon, France, on June 26, 2003, and despite the efforts of the stadium medical staff he could not be revived. He had been on loan to Manchester City from Olympique Lyonnais in season 2002–03, and poignantly scored the club's last goal at Maine Road.

Paul Sykes, Folkestone Invicta (Ryman league) striker, died on the pitch during the Kent Senior Cup semi-final against Margate on April 12, 2005. He collapsed after an innocuous off-the-ball incident.

Craig Gowans, Falkirk apprentice, was killed at the club's training ground on July 8, 2005 when he came into contact with power lines.

Peter Wilson, Mansfield Town goalkeeping coach, died of a heart attack after collapsing during the warm-up of the League Two game away to Shrewsbury on November 19, 2005. The game was postponed.

GREAT SERVICE

'For services to Association Football', **Stanley Matthews** (Stoke City, Blackpool and England), already a C.B.E., became the first professional footballer to receive a knighthood. This was bestowed in 1965, his last season.

Before he retired and five days after his 50th birthday, he played for Stoke City to set a record as the oldest First Division footballer (v. Fulham, February 6, 1965).

Over a brilliant span of 33 years, he played in 886 first-class matches, including 54 full Internationals (plus 31 in war time), 701 League games (including 3 at start of season 1939-40, which was abandoned on the outbreak of war) and 86 F.A. Cup-ties, and scored 95 goals. He was never booked in his career.

Sir Stanley died on February 23 2000, three weeks after his 85th birthday. His ashes were buried under the centre circle of Stoke's Britannia Stadium. After spending a number of years in Toronto, he made his home back in the Potteries in 1989, having previously returned to his home town, Hanley, Stoke-on-Trent in October, 1987 to unveil a life-size bronze statue of himself.

The inscription reads: 'Sir Stanley Matthews, CBE. Born Hanley, 1 February 1915. His name is symbolic of the beauty of the game, his fame timeless and international, his sportsmanship and modesty universally acclaimed. A magical player, of the people, for the people.'

On his home-coming in 1989, Sir Stanley was made President of Stoke City, the club he joined as a boy of 15 and served as a player for 20 years between 1931 and 1965, on either side of his spell with Blackpool.

In July 1992 FIFA honoured him with their 'Gold merit award' for outstanding services to the game.

Former England goalkeeper **Peter Shilton** has made more first-class appearances (1,387) than any other footballer in British history. He played his 1,000th. League game in Leyton Orient's 2-0 home win against Brighton & H.A. on Dec. 22, 1996 and in all played 9 times for Orient in his final season. He retired from International football after the 1990 World Cup in Italy with 125 caps, then a world record.

Shilton's career spanned 32 seasons, 20 of them on the International stage. He made his League debut for Leicester City in May 1966, two months before England won the World Cup.

His 1,387 first-class appearances comprise a record 1,005 in the Football League, 125 Internationals, 102 League Cup, 86 F.A. Cup, 13 for England U-23s, 4 for the Football League and 52 other matches (European Cup, UEFA Cup, World Club Championship, Charity Shield, European Super Cup, Full Members' Cup, Play-offs, Screen Sports Super Cup, Anglo-Italian Cup, Texaco Cup, Simod Cup, Zenith Data Systems Cup and Autoglass Trophy).

Shilton appeared more times at Wembley (57) than any other player: 52 for England, 2 League Cup Finals, 1 F.A. Cup Final, 1 Charity Shield match, and 1 for the Football League. He passed a century of League appearances with each of his first five clubs: Leicester City (286), Stoke City (110), Nott'm. Forest (202), Southampton (188) and Derby Co. (175) and subsequently played for Plymouth Argyle, Bolton Wand. and Leyton Orient.

His club honours, all gained with Nott'm. Forest: League Championship 1978, League Cup 1979, European Cup 1979 and 1980, PFA Player of Year 1978.

Five other British footballers have made more than 1,000 first-class appearances:

Ray Clemence, formerly with Tottenham, Liverpool and England, retired through injury in season 1987-8 after a goalkeeping career of 1,119 matches starting in 1965-6. Clemence played 50 times for his first club, Scunthorpe Utd.; 665 for Liverpool; 337 for Tottenham; his 67 representative games included 61 England caps.

A third great British goalkeeper, **Pat Jennings**, ended his career (1963-86) with a total of 1,098 first-class matches for Watford, Tottenham, Arsenal and N. Ireland. They were made up of 757 in the Football League, 119 full Internationals, 84 F.A. Cup appearances, 72 League/Milk Cup, 55 European club matches, 2 Charity Shield, 3 Other Internationals, 1 Under-23 cap, 2 Texaco Cup, 2 Anglo-Italian Cup and 1 Super Cup. Jennings played his 119th. and final International on his 41st birthday, June 12, 1986, against Brazil in Guadalajara in the Mexico World Cup.

Yet another outstanding 'keeper, **David Seaman**, passed the 1,000 appearances milestone for clubs and country in season 2002–03, reaching 1,004 when aged 39, he captained Arsenal to F.A. Cup triumph against Southampton.

With Arsenal, Seaman won 3 Championship medals, the F.A. Cup 4 times, the Double twice, the League Cup and Cup-Winners' Cup once each. After 13 seasons at Highbury, he joined Manchester City (June 2003) on a free transfer. He played 26 matches for City before a shoulder injury forced his retirement in January 2004, aged 40.

Seaman's 22-season career composed 1,046 first-class matches: 955 club apps. (Peterborough Utd. 106, Birmingham City 84, Q.P.R. 175, Arsenal 564, Manchester City 26); 75 senior caps for England, 6 'B' caps and 10 at U-21 level.

Defender **Graeme Armstrong**, 42-year-old commercial manager for an Edinburgh whisky company and part-time assistant-manager and captain of Scottish Third Division club Stenhousemuir, made the 1000th first team appearance of his career in the Scottish Cup 3rd Round against Rangers at Ibrox on January 23, 1999. He was presented with the Man of the Match award before kick-off.

Against East Stirling on Boxing Day, he had played his 864th League game, breaking the British record for an outfield player set by another Scot, Tommy Hutchison, with Alloa, Blackpool, Coventry City, Manchester City, Burnley and Swansea City.

Armstrong's 24-year career, spent in the lower divisions of the Scottish League, began as a 1-match trialist with Meadowbank Thistle in 1975 and continued via Stirling Albion, Berwick Rangers, Meadowbank and, from 1992, Stenhousemuir.

Tony Ford became the first English outfield player to reach 1000 senior appearances in Rochdale's 1-0 win at Carlisle (Auto Windscreens Shield) on March 7, 2000. Grimsby-born, he began his 26-season midfield career with Grimsby Town and played for 7 other League clubs: Sunderland (loan), Stoke City, W.B.A., Bradford City (loan), Scunthorpe Utd., Mansfield Town and Rochdale. He retired, aged 42, in 2001 with a career record of 1072 matches (121 goals) and his total of 931 League games is exceeded only by Peter Shilton's 1005.

TEN KNIGHTS OF SOCCER

Dave Richards, chairman of the Premier League and of the Football Foundation, became the tenth senior football figure to receive a knighthood when he was honoured in the Queen's Birthday Honours in June, 2006 for services to sport.

The elite list reads: **Stanley Matthews** (1965), **Alf Ramsey** (1967), **Matt Busby** (1968), **Bobby Charlton** (1994), **Tom Finney** (1998), **Geoff Hurst** (1998), **Alex Ferguson** (1999), **Bobby Robson** (2002), **Trevor Brooking** (2004), **Dave Richards** (2006).

PENALTIES

The **penalty-kick** was introduced to the game, following a proposal to the Irish F.A. in 1890 by William McCrum, son of the High Sheriff for Co. Omagh, and approved by the International Football Board on June 2, 1891.

First penalty scored in a first-class match in England was by John Heath, for Wolves v Accrington Stanley (5-0 in Div. 1, September 14, 1891).

The greatest influence of the penalty has come since the 1970s, with the introduction of the shoot-out to settle deadlocked ties in various competitions.

Manchester Utd. were the first club to win a competitive match in British football via a shoot-out (4-3 away to Hull City, Watney Cup semi-final, August 5, 1970); in that penalty contest, George Best was the first player to score, Denis Law the first to miss.

The shoot-out was adopted by FIFA and UEFA the same year (1970).

In season 1991-2, penalty shoot-outs were introduced to decide **F.A. Cup ties** still level after one replay and extra time.

Wembley saw its first penalty contest in the 1974 Charity Shield. Since then many major matches across the world have been settled in this way, including:

1974	**F.A. Charity Shield** (Wembley): Liverpool beat Leeds Utd. 6-5 (after 1-1).
1976	**Eur. Champ. Final** (Belgrade): Czech. beat W. Germany 5-3 (after 2-2).
1980	**Cup-Winners' Cup Final** (Brussels): Valencia beat Arsenal 5-4 (0-0).
1980	**Eur. Champ. 3rd/4th place play-off** (Naples): Czechoslovakia beat Italy 9-8 (after 1-1).
1982	**World Cup s-final** (Seville): West Germany beat France 5-4 (after 3-3).
1984	**European Cup Final** (Rome): Liverpool beat AS Roma 4-2 (after 1-1).
1984	**UEFA Cup Final**: Tottenham (home) beat Anderlecht 4-3 (2-2 agg.).
1984	**Eur. Champ. s-final** (Lyon): Spain beat Denmark 5-4 (after 1-1).
1986	**European Cup Final** (Seville): Steaua Bucharest beat Barcelona 2-0 (0-0). Barcelona's four penalties were all saved.
1987	**Freight Rover Trophy Final** (Wembley): Mansfield Town beat Bristol City 5-4 (after 1-1).
1987	**Scottish League (Skol) Cup Final** (Hampden Park): Rangers beat Aberdeen 5-3 (after 3-3).
1988	**European Cup Final** (Stuttgart): PSV Eindhoven beat Benfica 6-5 (after 0-0).
1988	**UEFA Cup Final**: Bayer Leverkusen (home) beat Espanyol 3-2 after 3-3 (0-3a, 3-0h).
1990	**Scottish F.A. Cup Final** (Hampden Park): Aberdeen beat Celtic 9-8 (0-0).
1990	**World Cup** (in Italy): 2nd. Round: Rep. of Ireland beat Romania 5-4 (after 0-0); q-final: Argentina beat Yugoslavia 3-2 (after 0-0); s-finals: Argentina beat Italy 4-3 (after 1-1); West Germany beat England 4-3 (1-1).
1991	**European Cup Final** (Bari): Red Star Belgrade beat Marseille 5-3 (after 0-0).
1991	**Barclays League Play-off** (4th. Div. Final – Wembley): Torquay Utd. beat Blackpool 5-4 (after 2-2).
1992	**F.A. Cup s-final** replay (Villa Park): Liverpool beat Portsmouth 3-1 (after 0-0).
1992	**Barclays League Play-off** (4th. Div. Final – Wembley): Blackpool beat Scunthorpe Utd. 4-3 (after 1-1).
1992	**Eur. Champ. s-final** (Gothenburg): Denmark beat Holland 5-4 (after 2-2).
1993	**Barclays League Play-off** (3rd Div. Final – Wembley): York City beat Crewe Alexandra 5-3 (after 1-1).
1993	**F.A. Charity Shield** (Wembley): Manchester Utd. beat Arsenal 5-4 (after 1-1).
1994	**League (Coca-Cola) Cup s-final**: Aston Villa beat Tranmere Rov. 5-4 (after 4-4, 1-3a, 3-1h).
1994	**Autoglass Trophy Final** (Wembley): Swansea City beat Huddersfield Town 3-1 (after 1-1).
1994	**World Cup** (Los Angeles): **Final**: Brazil beat Italy 3-2 (after 0-0).
1994	**Scottish League (Coca-Cola) Cup Final** (Ibrox Park): Raith beat Celtic 6-5 (after 2-2).
1995	**Cup-Winners' Cup s-final**: Arsenal beat Sampdoria away 3-2 (5-5 agg.)
1995	**Copa America Final** (Montevideo): Uruguay beat Brazil 5-3 (after 1-1).
1996	**European Cup Final** (Rome): Juventus beat Ajax 4-2 (after 1-1).
1996	**European U-21 Champ. Final** (Barcelona): Italy beat Spain 4-2 (after 1-1).
1996	**Eur. Champ. q-finals**: England beat Spain (Wembley) 4-2 after 0-0, **s-finals**: Germany beat England (Wembley) 6-5 after 1-1; Czech Republic beat France (Old Trafford) 6-5 after 0-0.

1997	**Auto Windscreens Shield Final** (Wembley): Carlisle Utd. beat Colchester Utd. 4-3 (after 0-0)
1997	**UEFA Cup Final:** FC Schalke beat Inter Milan 4-1 (after 1-1 agg.).
1998	**Nationwide League play-off** (1st Div. Final Wembley): Charlton Athletic beat Sunderland 7-6 (after 4-4).
1998	**World Cup Finals:** (St Etienne): Argentina beat England (2nd Round) 4-3 (after 2-2).
1999	**Nationwide League play-offs Div. 1 s-final:** Watford beat Birmingham City 7-6 away (after 1-1); **Div. 2 Final (Wembley):** Manchester City beat Gillingham 3-1 (after 2-2).
1999	**Women's World Cup Final** (Pasedena): U.S.A. beat China 5-4 (after 0-0).
2000	**African Nations Cup Final** (Lagos): Cameroon beat Nigeria 4-3 (after 0-0).
2000	**F.A. Cup s-final** (Wembley): Aston Villa beat Bolton Wand. 4-1 (after 0-0).
2000	**UEFA Cup Final** (Copenhagen): Galatasaray beat Arsenal 4-1 (after 0-0).
2000	**Eur. Champ. s-final** (Amsterdam): Italy beat Holland 3-1 (after 0-0). Holland missed 5 penalties in match – 2 in normal play, 3 in shoot-out. Italy survived with ten men after 33rd minute sending-off.
2000	**Olympic Final** (Sydney): Cameroon beat Spain 5-3 (after 2-2). Spain led 2-0, then had 2 men sent off.
2001	**League (Worthington) Cup Final** (Millennium Stadium, Cardiff): Liverpool beat Birmingham City 5-4 (after 1-1).
2001	**Champions League Final** (Milan): Bayern Munich beat Valencia 5-4 (after 1-1).
2002	**Eur. U-21 Champ. Final** (Basle): Czech Republic beat France 3-1 (after 0-0).
2002	**Nationwide League** play-off (1st Div. Final, Millennium Stadium, Cardiff): Birmingham City beat Norwich City 4-2 (after 1-1).
2002	**World Cup Finals:** (Suwon): Spain beat Rep. of Ireland (2nd Round) 3-2 (after 1-1).
2003	**Champions League Final** (Old Trafford): AC Milan beat Juventus 3–2 (after 0–0).
2003	**F.A. Community Shield** (Millennium Stadium): Manchester Utd. beat Arsenal 4-3 (after 1-1).
2004	**Nationwide League play-off Div. 3 Final** (Millennium Stadium): Huddersfield Town beat Mansfield Town 4-1 (after 0-0).
2004	**Eur. Champ. q-finals:** Portugal beat England (Lisbon) 6-5 after 2-2.
2004	**Copa America Final** (Lima): Brazil beat Argentina 4-2 (after 2-2).
2005	**Coca-Cola League 1 play-off s-final:** Hartlepool Utd. beat Tranmere Rov. 6-5 away (after 2-2 agg.)
2005	**F.A. Cup Final** (Cardiff): Arsenal beat Manchester Utd. 5-4 (after 0-0).
2005	**Champions League Final** (Istanbul): Liverpool beat AC Milan 3-2 (after 3-3).
2005	**World Cup qual.** (Sydney): Australia beat Uruguay 4-2 (after 1-1).
2006	**African Cup of Nations Final** (Cairo): Egypt beat Ivory Coast 4-2 (after 0-0).
2006	**F.A. Cup Final** (Millennium Stadium): Liverpool beat West Ham Utd. 3-1 (after 3-3).
2006	**Scottish Cup Final** (Hampden Park): Hearts beat Gretna 4-2 (after 1-1).
2006	**Coca-Cola League 1 play-off Final** (Millennium Stadium): Barnsley beat Swansea City 4-3 (after 2-2).
2006	**World Cup Finals** (Germany): Ukraine beat Switzerland 3-0 (after 0-0, 2nd rd.); Germany beat Argentina 4-2 (after 1-1, q. final); Portugal beat England 3-1 (after 0-0, q. final); Italy beat France 5-3 (after 1-1, final).

Footnote: Highest-recorded score in a penalty shoot-out between Football League clubs was **Aldershot's 11-10** victory at home to **Fulham** after their 1-1 draw in the Freight Rover Trophy Southern quarter-final on February 10, 1987. Seven spot-kicks were missed or saved in a record 28-penalty shoot-out at senior level.

In South America in 1992, in a 26-shot competition, **Newell's Old Boys** beat America 11-10 in the Copa Libertadores.

Longest-recorded penalty contest in first-class matches was in Argentina in 1988 – from 44 shots, **Argentinos Juniors** beat **Racing Club 20-19**. **Genclerbirligi** beat **Galatasaray** 17-16 in a Turkish Cup-tie in 1996. Only one penalty was missed.

Highest-scoring shoot-outs in **Int. football**: North Korea beat Hong Kong 11-10 (after 3-3 draw) in an Asian Cup match in 1975; and Ivory Coast beat Ghana 11-10 (after 0-0 draw) in African Nations Cup Final, 1992.

Most penalties needed to settle an adult game in Britain: 44 in Norfolk Primary Cup 4th Round replay, December 2000. Aston Village side **Freethorpe** beat Foulsham 20-19 (5 kicks missed). All 22 players took 2 penalties each, watched by a crowd of 20. The sides had drawn 2-2, 4-4 in a tie of 51 goals.

Penalty that took 24 days: That is how long elapsed between the award and the taking of a penalty in an Argentine Second Division match between **Atalanta** and **Defensores** in 2003. A riot ended the original match with 5 minutes left, and the game was resumed on 30 April behind closed doors with the penalty that caused the abandonment. Lucas Ferreiro scored it to give Atalanta a 1–0 win.

INTERNATIONAL PENALTIES, MISSED

Four penalties out of five were missed when **Colombia** beat **Argentina** 3-0 in a Copa America group tie in Paraguay in July 1999. Martin Palmeiro missed three for Argentina and Colombia's Hamilton Ricard had one spot-kick saved.

In the European Championship semi-final against Italy in Amsterdam on June 29, 2000, **Holland** missed five penalties – two in normal time, three in the penalty contest which Italy won 3-1 (after 0-0). Dutch captain Frank de Boer missed twice from the spot.

F.A. CUP SHOOT-OUTS

The **first** penalty contest in the F.A. Cup took place in **1972**. In the days of the play-off for third place, the match was delayed until the eve of the following season when losing semi-finalists Birmingham City and Stoke City met at St Andrews on Aug. 5. The score was 0-0 and Birmingham City won 4-3 on penalties.

Recordd Shoot-out: 40 kicks, Tunbridge Wells beating Littlehampton 16-15 (9 missed) in prelim. round replay (2-2 aet) on August 30, 2005. In competition proper Macclesfield Town beat Forest Green Rov. (away) 11-10 in 1st Round replay (1-1 aet) on November 28, 2001 which stretched to 24 kicks.

Shoot-out abandoned: The F.A. Cup 1st Round replay between Oxford City and Wycombe Wand. at Wycombe on November 9, 1999 was abandoned (1-1) after extra time because, as the penalty shoot-out was about to begin, a fire broke out under a stand. Wycombe won the second replay 1-0 at Oxford Utd.'s ground.

First F.A. Cup Final to be decided by shoot-out was in 2005 (May 21), when Arsenal beat Manchester Utd. 5-4 on penalties at Cardiff's Millennium Stadium (0-0 after extra time). A year later (May 13) Liverpool beat West Ham Utd. 3-1 (3-3 after extra-time).

MISSED CUP FINAL PENALTIES

John Aldridge (Liverpool) became the first player to miss a penalty in the F.A. Cup Final at Wembley – and the second in the competition's history (previously Charlie Wallace, of Aston Villa, in the 1913 Final against Sunderland at Crystal Palace) – when Wimbledon's Dave Beasant saved his shot in May 1988. Seven previous penalties had been scored in this Final at Wembley.

Another crucial penalty miss at Wembley was by Arsenal's **Nigel Winterburn,** Luton Town's Andy Dibble saving his spot-kick in the 1988 Littlewoods Cup Final, when a goal would have put Arsenal 3-1 ahead. Instead, they lost 3-2.

Winterburn was the third player to fail with a League Cup Final penalty at Wembley, following **Ray Graydon** (Aston Villa) against Norwich City in 1975 and **Clive Walker** (Sunderland), who shot wide in the 1985 Milk Cup Final, also against Norwich City (won 1-0). Graydon had his penalty saved by Kevin Keelan, but scored from the rebound and won the cup for Aston Villa (1-0).

Tottenham's **Gary Lineker** saw his penalty saved by Nott'm. Forest goalkeeper Mark Crossley in the 1991 F.A. Cup Final.

Derby Co.'s Martin Taylor saved a penalty from **Eligio Nicolini** in the Anglo-Italian Cup Final at Wembley on March 27, 1993, but Cremonese won 3-1.

LEAGUE PENALTIES RECORD

Most penalties in Football League match: Five – 4 to Crystal Palace (3 missed), 1 to Brighton & H.A. (scored) in Div. 2 match at Selhurst Park on March 27 (Easter Monday), 1989. Crystal Palace won 2-1. Three of the penalties were awarded in a 5-minute spell. The match also produced 5 bookings and a sending-off.

Other teams missing 3 penalties in a match: **Burnley** v Grimsby Town (Div. 2), February 13, 1909; **Manchester City** v Newcastle Utd. (Div. 1), January 17, 1912.

HOTTEST MODERN SPOT-SHOT

Matthew Le Tissier ended his career in season 2001-02 with the distinction of having netted 48 out of 49 first-team penalties for Southampton. He scored the last 27 after his only miss when Nott'm. Forest keeper Mark Crossley saved in a Premier League match at The Dell on March 24, 1993.

SPOT-KICK HAT-TRICKS

Right-back **Joe Willetts** scored three penalties when Hartlepool Utd. beat neighbours Darlington 6–1 (Div. 3N) on Good Friday 1951.

Danish International **Jan Molby**'s only hat-trick in English football, for Liverpool in a 3-1 win at home to Coventry City (Littlewoods Cup, 4th round replay, Nov. 26, 1986) comprised three goals from the penalty spot.

It was the first such hat-trick in a major match for two years – since **Andy Blair** scored three penalties for Sheffield Wed. against Luton Town (Milk Cup 4th. round, Nov. 20 1984).

Portsmouth's **Kevin Dillon** scored a penalty hat-trick in the Full Members Cup (2nd rd.) at home to Millwall (3-2) on Nov. 4, 1986.

Alan Slough scored a hat-trick of penalties in an away game and was on the losing side, when Peterborough Utd. were beaten 4-3 at Chester City (Div. 3, Apr. 29, 1978).

Penalty hat-tricks in **International football**: **Dimitris Saravakos** (in 9 mins.) for Greece v Egypt in 1990. He scored 5 goals in match. **Henrik Larsson**, among his 4 goals in Sweden's 6-0 home win v Moldova in World Cup qualifying match, June 6, 2001.

MOST PENALTY GOALS (LEAGUE) IN SEASON

Thirteen out of 13 by **Francis Lee** for Manchester City (Div. 1) in 1971-2. His goal total for the season was 33. In season 1988-9, **Graham Roberts** scored 12 League penalties for Second Division Champions Chelsea. In season 2004-5, **Andrew Johnson** scored 11 Premiership penalties for Crystal Palace, who were relegated.

PENALTY-SAVE SEQUENCES

Ipswich Town goalkeeper **Paul Cooper** saved eight of the ten penalties he faced in 1979-80. **Roy Brown** (Notts Co.) saved six in a row in season 1972-3.

Andy Lomas, goalkeeper for Chesham Utd. (Diadora League) claimed a record eight **consecutive** penalty saves – three at the end of season 1991-2 and five in 1992-3.

Mark Bosnich (Aston Villa) saved five in two consecutive matches in 1993-4: three in Coca-Cola Cup semi-final penalty shoot-out v Tranmere Rov. (Feb. 26), then two in Premiership at Tottenham (Mar. 2).

MISSED PENALTIES SEQUENCE

Against Wolves in Div. 2 on Sept. 28, 1991, **Southend Utd.** missed their seventh successive penalty (five of them the previous season).

SCOTTISH RECORDS
(See also under 'Goals' & 'Discipline')

RANGERS' MANY RECORDS

Rangers' record-breaking feats include:-
League Champions: 51 times (once joint holders) – world record.

Winning every match in Scottish League (18 games, 1898-9 season).

Major hat-tricks: Rangers have completed the domestic treble (League Championship, League Cup and Scottish F.A. Cup) a record seven times (1948-9, 1963-4, 1975-6, 1977-8, 1992-3, 1998-9, 2002-3).

League & Cup double: 16 times.

Nine successive Championships (1989-97). Four men played in all nine sides: Richard Gough, Ally McCoist, Ian Ferguson and Ian Durrant.

107 major trophies: Championships 51, Scottish Cup 31, League Cup 24, Cup-Winners' Cup 1.

CELTIC'S GRAND SLAM

Celtic's record in 1966-7 was the most successful by a British club in one season. They won the **Scottish League**, the **Scottish Cup**, the **Scottish League Cup** and became the first British club to win the **European Cup**. They also won the **Glasgow Cup**.

Celtic have 3 times achieved the Scottish treble (League Championship, League Cup and F.A. Cup), in 1966-7, 1968-9 and 2000-01 (in Martin O'Neill's first season as their manager). They became Scottish Champions for 2000-01 with a 1-0 home win against St. Mirren on April 7 – the earliest the title had been clinched for 26 years, since Rangers' triumph on March 29, 1975.

They have won the Scottish Cup 32 times, and have completed the League and Cup double 13 times.

Celtic won nine consecutive Scottish League titles (1966-74) under Jock Stein.

They set a **British record** of 25 consecutive League wins in season 2003-04 (Aug. 15 to Mar. 14). They were unbeaten for 77 matches (all competitions) at Celtic Park from August 22, 2001, to April 21, 2004.

UNBEATEN SCOTTISH CHAMPIONS

Celtic and **Rangers** have each won the Scottish Championship with an unbeaten record: Celtic in 1897-98 (P18, W15, D3), Rangers in 1898-99 (P18, W18).

LARSSON SUPREME

After missing most of the previous campaign with a broken leg, Swedish International **Henrik Larsson**, with 53 goals in season 2000-01, set a post-war record for Celtic and equalled the Scottish Premier League record of 35 by Brian McClair (Celtic) in 1986-7. Larsson's 35 earned him Europe's Golden Shoe award.

His 7 seasons as a Celtic player ended, when his contract expired in May 2004, with a personal total of 242 goals in 315 apps. (third-highest scorer in the club's history). He helped Celtic win 4 League titles, and at 32 he moved to Barcelona (free) on a 2-year contract.

SCOTTISH CUP HAT-TRICKS

Aberdeen's feat of winning the Scottish F.A. Cup in 1982-3-4 made them only the third club to achieve that particular hat-trick.

Queen's Park did it twice (1874-5-6 and 1880-1-2), and **Rangers** have won the Scottish Cup three years in succession on three occasions: 1934-5-6, 1948-9-50 and 1962-3-4.

SCOTTISH CUP FINAL DISMISSALS

Four players have been sent off in the Scottish F.A. Cup Final: **Jock Buchanan** (Rangers v. Kilmarnock, 1929), **Roy Aitken** (Celtic v Aberdeen, 1984), **Walter Kidd** (Hearts captain v Aberdeen, 1986), **Paul Hartley** (Hearts v Gretna, 2006).

RECORD SEQUENCES

Celtic hold Britain's League record of 62 matches undefeated, from November 13, 1915 to April 21, 1917, when Kilmarnock won 2-0 at Parkhead. They won 49, drew 13 (111 points) and scored 126 goals to 26.

Greenock Morton in 1963-4 accumulated 67 points out of 72 and scored 135 goals.

Queens Park did not have a goal scored against them during the first seven seasons of their existence (1867-74, before the Scottish League was formed).

EARLIEST PROMOTIONS IN SCOTLAND

Dundee promoted from Div. 2, February 1, 1947; **Greenock Morton** promoted from Div. 2, March 2, 1964; **Gretna** promoted from Div. 3, March 5, 2005.

WORST HOME SEQUENCE

After gaining promotion to Div. 1 in 1992, **Cowdenbeath** went a record 38 consecutive home League matches without a win. They ended the sequence (drew 8, lost 30) when beating Arbroath 1-0 on April 2, 1994, watched by a crowd of 225.

ALLY'S RECORDS

Ally McCoist became the first player to complete 200 goals in the Premier Division when he scored Rangers' winner (2-1) at Falkirk on December 12, 1992. His first was against Celtic in September 1983, and he reached 100 against Dundee on Boxing Day 1987.

When McCoist scored twice at home to Hibernian (4-3) on December 7, 1996, he became Scotland's record post-war League marksman, beating Gordon Wallace's 264.

Originally with St. Johnstone (1978-81), he spent two seasons with Sunderland (1981-3), then joined Rangers for £200,000 in June 1983.

In 15 seasons at Ibrox, he scored 355 goals for Rangers (250 League), and helped them win 10 Championships (9 in succession), 3 Scottish Cups and earned a record 9 League Cup winner's medals. He won the European Golden Boot in consecutive seasons (1991-2, 1992-3).

His 9 Premier League goals in three seasons for Kilmarnock gave him a career total of 281 Scottish League goals when he retired at the end of 2000-01.

FIVE IN A MATCH

Paul Sturrock set an individual scoring record for the Scottish Premier Division with 5 goals in Dundee Utd.'s 7-0 win at home to Morton on November 17, 1984. **Marco Negri** equalled the feat with all 5 when Rangers beat Dundee Utd. 5-1 at Ibrox (Premier Division) on August 23, 1997, and **Kenny Miller** scored 5 in Rangers' 7-1 win at home to St. Mirren on November 4, 2000. **Kris Boyd** scored all Kilmarnock's goals in a 5-2 SPL win at home to Dundee Utd. on September 25, 2004.

NEGRI'S TEN-TIMER

Marco Negri scored in Rangers' first ten League matches (23 goals) in season 1997-8 – a Premier Division record. The previous best sequence was 8 by Ally MacLeod for Hibernian in 1978.

DOUBLE SCOTTISH FINAL

Rangers v Celtic drew **129,643** and **120,073** people to the Scottish Cup Final and replay at Hampden Park, Glasgow, in 1963. Receipts for the two matches totalled £50,500.

MOST SCOTTISH CHAMPIONSHIP MEDALS

13 by **Sandy Archibald** (Rangers, 1918-34). Post-war record: **10** by Bobby Lennox (Celtic, 1966-79).

Alan Morton won **nine** Scottish Championship medals with Rangers in 1921-23-24-25-27-28-29-30-31. **Ally McCoist** played in the Rangers side that won nine successive League titles (1989-97).

Between 1927 and 1939 **Bob McPhail** helped Rangers win nine Championships, finish second twice and third once. He scored 236 League goals but was never top scorer in a single season.

TOP SCOTTISH LEAGUE SCORERS IN SEASON

Raith Rovers (Div. 2) 142 goals in 1937-38; **Morton** (Div. 2) 135 goals in 1963-64; **Hearts** (Div. 1) 132 goals in 1957-58; **Falkirk** (Div. 2) 132 goals in 1935-36; **Gretna** (Div. 3) 130 goals in 2004-05.

SCOTTISH CUP – NO DECISION

The **Scottish F.A.** withheld their Cup and medals in 1908-9 after Rangers and Celtic played two drawn games in the Final. Spectators rioted.

FEWEST LEAGUE WINS IN SEASON

Clydebank won only one of 36 matches in Div. 1, season 1999-2000. It came on March 7 (2-1 at home to Raith).

HAMPDEN'S £63M. REDEVELOPMENT

On completion of redevelopment costing £63m. **Hampden Park**, home of Scottish football and the oldest first-class stadium in the world, was re-opened full scale for the Rangers-Celtic Cup Final on May 29, 1999.

Work on the 'new Hampden' (capacity 52,000) began in 1992. The North and East stands were restructured (£12m.); a new South stand and improved West stand cost £51m. The Millennium Commission contributed £23m. and the Lottery Sports Fund provided a grant of £3.75m.

GRETNA'S RISE

Since joining the Scottish League in 2002, Gretna have won the Bell's Third and Second Division titles and become the first team from the third tier to reach the Scottish Cup Final, having taken Hearts to penalties last season.

DEMISE OF AIRDRIE AND CLYDEBANK

In May 2002, First Division **Airdrieonians**, formed in 1878, went out of business. They had debts of £3m. Their place in the Scottish League was taken by **Gretna**, from the English Unibond League, who were voted into Div. 3. Second Division **Clydebank** folded in July 2002 and were taken over by the new **Airdrie United** club.

GREAT SCOTS

In February 1988, the Scottish F.A. launched a national **Hall of Fame**, initially comprising the first 11 Scots to make 50 International appearances, to be joined by all future players to reach that number of caps. Each member receives a gold medal, invitation for life at all Scotland's home matches, and has his portrait hung at Scottish F.A. headquarters in Glasgow.

MORE CLUBS IN 2000

The **Scottish Premier League** increased from 10 to 12 clubs in season 2000-1.

The **Scottish Football League** admitted two new clubs – Peterhead and Elgin City from the Highland League – to provide three divisions of 10 in 2000-1.

NOTABLE SCOTTISH 'FIRSTS'

- The father of League football was a Scot, **William McGregor**, a draper in Birmingham. The 12-club Football League kicked off in September 1888, and McGregor was its first president.
- **Hibernian** were the first British club to play in the European Cup, by invitation. They reached the semi-final when it began in 1955-6.
- **Celtic** were Britain's first winners of the European Cup, in 1967.
- Scotland's First Division became the **Premier Division** in season 1975-6.
- Football's **first International** was staged at the West of Scotland cricket ground, Partick, on November 30, 1872: Scotland 0, England 0.

- Scotland introduced its **League Cup** in 1945-6, the first season after the war. It was another 15 years before the Football League Cup was launched.
- The Scottish F.A. Cup has been **sponsored** by Tennents for the last 16 seasons.
- Scotland pioneered the use in British football of **two substitutes** per team in League and Cup matches.
- The world's **record football score** belongs to Scotland: Arbroath 36, Bon Accord 0 (Scottish Cup first round) on September 12, 1885.
- The Scottish F.A. introduced the **penalty shoot-out** to their Cup Final in 1990.
- On Jan. 22, 1994 all six matches in the **Scottish Premier Division** ended as draws.
- Scotland's new Premier League introduced a **3-week shut-down** in January 1999 – first instance of British football adopting the winter break system that operates in a number of European countries. The SPL ended its New Year closure after 2003.
- **Rangers** made history at home to St. Johnstone (Premier League, 0-0, March 4, 2000) when fielding a team entirely without Scottish players.

SCOTTISH CUP SHOCK RESULTS

1885-86 (1) Arbroath 36, Bon Accord 0
1921-22 (F) Morton 1, Rangers 0
1937-38 (F) East Fife 4, Kilmarnock 2 (replay, after 1-1)
1960-61 (F) Dunfermline 2, Celtic 0 (replay, after 0-0)
1966-67 (1) Berwick Rangers 1, Rangers 0
1979-80 (3) Hamilton 2, Keith 3
1984-85 (1) Stirling Albion 20, Selkirk 0
1984-85 (3) Inverness Thistle 3, Kilmarnock 0
1986-87 (3) Rangers 0, Hamilton 1
1994-95 (3) Stenhousemuir 2, Aberdeen 0
1998-99 (4) Aberdeen 0, Livingston 1
1999-2000 (3) Celtic 1, Inverness Caledonian Thistle 3
2002-03 (5) Inverness Caledonian Thistle 1, Celtic 0
2005-06 (3) Clyde 2, Celtic 1
Scottish League (Coca-Cola) Cup Final shock
1994-95 Raith 2, Celtic 2 (Raith won 6-5 on pens.)

SCOTTISH DISCIPLINE (MODERN) – MAJOR PUNISHMENTS

1989 (June) fine **Hearts** £93,000, following TV infringement at UEFA Cup q-final.
1994 (August) Scottish League fine **Celtic** record £100,000 for poaching manager Tommy Burns from Kilmarnock.
1996 (November) UEFA fine **Celtic** £42,000 and **Alan Stubbs** £28,000 for using unlicensed agents in summer transfer from Bolton Wanderers.
1999 (August) Scottish Premier League fine **Celtic** £45,000 for their part in disturbances at home match with Rangers, May 2.
2000 (April) Scottish League deduct a record 15 points from **Hamilton Academical**, following their players (in protest over unpaid wages) refusing to turn up for Div. 2 fixture at Stenhousemuir on April 1. As a result, Hamilton relegated at end of season.

MISCELLANEOUS

NATIONAL ASSOCIATIONS FORMED

F.A.	1863
F.A. of Wales	1876
Scottish F.A.	1873
Irish F.A.	1904
Federation of International Football Associations (FIFA)	1904

NATIONAL & INTERNATIONAL COMPETITIONS LAUNCHED

INNOVATIONS

Size of Ball: Fixed in **1872**.

Shinguards: Introduced and registered by Sam Weller Widdowson (Nott'm. Forest & England) in **1874**.

Referee's Whistle: First used on Nott'm. Forest's ground in **1878**.

Professionalism: Legalised in England in the summer of **1885** as a result of agitation by Lancashire clubs.

Goal-nets: Invented and patented in **1890** by Mr. J. A. Brodie of Liverpool. They were first used in the North v South match in January, **1891**.

Referees and Linesmen: Replaced umpires and referees in January, **1891**.

Penalty-kick: Introduced at Irish F.A.'s request in the season **1891-2**. The penalty law ordering the goalkeeper to remain on the goal-line came into force in September, **1905**, and the order to stand on his goal-line until the ball is kicked arrived in **1929-30**.

White ball: First came into official use in **1951**.

Floodlighting: First F.A. Cup-tie (replay), Kidderminster Harriers v Brierley Hill Alliance, **1955**. First Football League match: Portsmouth v Newcastle Utd. (Div. 1), 1956.

Heated pitch to beat frost tried by Everton at Goodison Park in **1958**.

First Soccer Closed-circuit TV: At Coventry City ground in October **1965** (10,000 fans saw their team win at Cardiff City, 120 miles away).

Substitutes (one per team) were first allowed in Football League matches at the start of season **1965-6**. Three substitutes (one a goalkeeper) allowed, two of which could be used, in Premier League matches, **1992-93**. The Football League introduced three substitutes for **1993-94**.

Three points for a win: This was introduced by the Football League in **1981-2**, by FIFA in World Cup games in 1994, and by the Scottish League in the same year.

Offside law amended, player 'level' no longer offside, and 'professional foul' made sending-off offence, **1990**.

Penalty shoot-outs introduced to decide F.A. Cup ties level after one replay and extra time, **1991-2**.

New back-pass rule – goalkeeper must not handle ball kicked to him by team-mate, **1992**.

Linesmen became 'referees' assistants', **1998**.

Goalkeepers not to hold ball longer than 6 seconds, **2000**.

Free-kicks advanced by ten yards against opponents failing to retreat, **2000**.

DERBY DAYS: COMPLETE LEAGUE RESULTS

Arsenal v Tottenham: Played 138 (all top div.); Arsenal 56 wins, Tottenham 45, Drawn 37.

Aston Villa v Birmingham City: Played 104; Aston Villa 41, Birmingham City 36, Drawn 27.

Everton v Liverpool: Played 174 (all top div.); Liverpool 65, Everton 55, Drawn 54.

Ipswich Town v Norwich City: Played 74; Ipswich Town 35, Norwich City 27, Drawn 12.

Manchester City v Manchester Utd.: Played 134; United 51, City 35, Drawn 48.

Middlesbrough v Newcastle Utd.: Played 106; Newcastle Utd. 43, Middlesbrough 33, Drawn 30.

Newcastle Utd. v Sunderland: Played 128; Newcastle Utd. 48, Sunderland 41, Drawn 39 (incl. 1990 play-offs – Sunderland win and draw).

Middlesbrough v Sunderland: Played 124; Sunderland 54, Middlesbrough 39, Drawn 31.

Nott'm. Forest v Notts Co.: Played 86; Forest 35, County 28, Drawn 23.

Sheffield Utd. v Sheffield Wed.: Played 106; United 41, Wednesday 32, Drawn 33.

Portsmouth v Southampton: Played 30; Southampton 14, Portsmouth 8, Drawn 8.

Port Vale v Stoke City: Played 44; Stoke City 16, Port Vale 14, Drawn 14.

Bristol City v Bristol Rovers: Played 86; City 33, Rovers 25, Drawn 28.

Celtic v Rangers: Played 280; Rangers 108, Celtic 91, Drawn 81.

Dundee v Dundee Utd.: Played 123; United 58, Dundee 38, Drawn 27.

Hearts v Hibernian: Played 239; Hearts 97, Hibernian 71, Drawn 71.

YOUNGEST AND OLDEST

Youngest Caps   *Age*

Gareth Bale (Wales v Trinidad & Tobago, May 27, 2006)   **16** years **315** days

Norman Whiteside (N. Ireland v Yugoslavia, June 17, 1982)   **17** years **41** days

Theo Walcott (England v Hungary, May 30, 2006)   **17** years **75** days

Johnny Lambie (Scotland v Ireland, March 20, 1886)   **17** years **92** days

Jimmy Holmes (Rep. of Ireland v Austria, May 30, 1971)   **17** years **200** days

Youngest England scorer: Wayne Rooney (17 years, 317 days) v Macedonia, Skopje, September 6, 2003.

Youngest England captains: Bobby Moore (v Czech., Bratislava, May 29, 1963), 22 years, 47 days; Michael Owen (v Paraguay, Anfield, April 17, 2002), 22 years, 117 days.

Youngest England players to reach 50 caps: Michael Owen (23 years, 6 months) v Slovakia at Middlesbrough, June 11, 2003; Bobby Moore (25 years, 7 months) v Wales at Wembley, November 16, 1966.

Youngest player in World Cup Final: Pele (Brazil) aged 17 years, 237 days v Sweden in Stockholm, June 12, 1958.

Youngest player to appear in World Cup Finals: Norman Whiteside (N. Ireland v Yugoslavia in Spain – June 17, 1982, age 17 years and 42 days.

Youngest First Division player: Derek Forster (Sunderland goalkeeper v Leicester City, August 22, 1964) aged 15 years, 185 days.

Youngest First Division scorer: At 16 years and 57 days, schoolboy Jason Dozzell (substitute after 30 minutes for Ipswich Town at home to Coventry City on February 4, 1984). Ipswich Town won 3-1 and Dozzell scored their third goal.

Youngest F.A. Premier League player: Aaron Lennon (Leeds Utd. sub. v Tottenham, August 23, 2003, 16 years, 129 days.

Youngest F.A. Premier League scorer: James Vaughan (Everton, home to Crystal Palace, April 10, 2005), 16 years, 271 days.

Youngest F.A. Premier League captain: Lee Cattermole (Middlesbrough away to Fulham, May 7, 2006) aged 18 years, 47 days.

Youngest player sent off in Premier League: Wayne Rooney (Everton, away to Birmingham City, December 26, 2002) aged 17 years, 59 days.

Youngest First Division hat-trick scorer: Alan Shearer, aged 17 years, 240 days, in Southampton's 4-2 home win v Arsenal (April 9, 1988) on his full debut. Previously, Jimmy Greaves (17 years, 309 days) with 4 goals for Chelsea at home to Portsmouth (7-4), Christmas Day, 1957.

Youngest to complete 100 Football League goals: Jimmy Greaves (20 years, 261 days) when he did so for Chelsea v Manchester City, November 19, 1960.

Youngest players in Football League: Albert Geldard (Bradford Park Avenue v Millwall, Div. 2, September 16, 1929) aged 15 years, 158 days; Ken Roberts (Wrexham v Bradford Park Avenue, Div. 3 North, September 1, 1951) also 15 years, 158 days.

Youngest Football League scorer: Ronnie Dix (for Bristol Rov. v Norwich City, Div. 3 South, March 3, 1928) aged 15 years, 180 days.

Youngest player in Scottish League: Goalkeeper Ronnie Simpson (Queens Park) aged 15 in 1946.

Youngest player in F.A. Cup: Andy Awford, Worcester City's England Schoolboy defender, aged 15 years, 88 days when he substituted in second half away to Boreham Wood (3rd. qual. round) on October 10, 1987.

Youngest player in F.A. Cup proper: Schoolboy Lee Holmes (15 years, 277 days) for Derby Co. away to Brentford in 3rd. Round on January 4, 2003.

Youngest Wembley Cup Final captain: Barry Venison (Sunderland v Norwich City, Milk Cup Final, March 24, 1985 – replacing suspended captain Shaun Elliott) – aged 20 years, 220 days.

Youngest F.A. Cup-winning captain: Bobby Moore (West Ham Utd., 1964, v Preston N.E.), aged 23 years, 20 days.

Youngest F.A. Cup Final captain: David Nish aged 21 years and 212 days old when he captained Leicester City against Manchester City at Wembley on April 26, 1969.

Youngest F.A. Cup Final player: Curtis Weston (Millwall sub. last 3 mins v Manchester Utd., 2004) aged 17 years, 119 days.

Youngest F.A. Cup Final scorer: Norman Whiteside (Manchester Utd. v Brighton & H.A. in 1983 replay at Wembley), aged 18 years, 19 days.

Youngest F.A. Cup Final managers: Stan Cullis, Wolves (33) v Leicester City, 1949; Steve Coppell, Crystal Palace (34) v Manchester Utd., 1990; Ruud Gullit, Chelsea (34) v Mid'bro', 1997.

Youngest player in Football League Cup: Kevin Davies (Chesterfield sub at West Ham Utd., 2nd Round, 2nd Leg on September 22, 1993) aged 16 years, 183 days.

Youngest Wembley scorer: Norman Whiteside (Manchester Utd. v Liverpool, Milk Cup Final, March 26, 1983) aged 17 years, 324 days.

Youngest Wembley Cup Final goalkeeper: Chris Woods (18 years, 125 days) for Nott'm Forest v Liverpool, League Cup Final on March 18, 1978.

Youngest Wembley F.A. Cup Final goalkeeper: Peter Shilton (19 years, 219 days) for Leicester City v Manchester City, April 26, 1969.

Youngest senior International at Wembley: Salomon Olembe (sub for Cameroon v England, November 15, 1997), aged 16 years, 342 days.

Youngest winning manager at Wembley: Roy McDonough aged 33 years. 6 months, 24 days as player-manager of Colchester Utd., F.A. Trophy winners on May 10, 1992.

Youngest scorer in full International: Mohamed Kallon (Sierra Leone v Congo, African Nations Cup, April 22, 1995), reported as aged 15 years, 192 days.

Youngest player sent off in World Cup Final series: Rigobert Song (Cameroon v Brazil, in USA, June 1994) aged 17 years, 358 days.

Youngest F.A. Cup Final referee: Kevin Howley, of Middlesbrough, aged 35 when in charge of Wolves v Blackburn Rov., 1960.

Youngest player in England U-23 team: Duncan Edwards (v. Italy, Bologna, January 20, 1954), aged 17 years, 112 days.

Youngest player in England U-21 team: Lee Sharpe (v. Greece, away, February 7, 1989), aged 17 years, 254 days.

Youngest player in Scotland U-21 team: Christian Dailly (v Romania, Hampden Park, Sept. 11, 1990), aged 16 years, 330 days.

Youngest player in senior football: Cameron Campbell Buchanan, Scottish-born outside right, aged 14 years, 57 days when he played for Wolves v W.B.A. in War-time League match, September 26, 1942.

Youngest player in peace-time senior match: Eamon Collins (Blackpool v Kilmarnock, Anglo-Scottish Cup quarter-final 1st. leg, September 9, 1980) aged 14 years, 323 days.

World's youngest player in top-division match: Centre-forward Fernando Rafael Garcia, aged 13, played for 23 minutes for Peruvian club Juan Aurich in 3-1 win against Estudiantes on May 19, 2001.

Oldest player to appear in Football League: New Brighton manager Neil McBain (51 years, 120 days) as emergency goalkeeper away to Hartlepool Utd. (Div. 3 North, March 15, 1947).

Other oldest post-war League players: Sir Stanley Matthews (Stoke City, 1965, 50 years, 5 days); Peter Shilton (Leyton Orient 1997, 47 years, 126 days); Dave Beasant

(Brighton & H.A. 2003, 44 years, 46 days); Alf Wood (Coventry City, 1958, 43 years, 199 days); Tommy Hutchison (Swansea City, 1991, 43 years, 172 days).

Oldest Football League debutant: Andy Cunningham, for Newcastle Utd. at Leicester City (Div. 1) on February 2, 1929, aged 38 years, 2 days.

Oldest post-war debut in English League: Defender David Donaldson (35 years, 7 months, 23 days) for Wimbledon on entry to Football League (Div. 4) away to Halifax Town, August 20, 1977.

Oldest player to appear in First Division: Sir Stanley Matthews (Stoke City v Fulham, February 6, 1965), aged 50 years, 5 days – on that his last League appearance, the only 50-year-old ever to play in the top division.

Oldest players in Premier League: Goalkeepers John Burridge (Manchester City v Q.P.R., May 14, 1995), aged 43 years, 5 months, 11 days; Steve Ogrizovic (Coventry City v Sheffield Wed., May 6, 2000), aged 42 years, 7 months, 24 days; Neville Southall (Bradford City v Leeds Utd., March 12, 2000), aged 41 years, 5 months, 26 days. Outfield: Gordon Strachan (Coventry City v Derby Co., May 3, 1997) aged 40 years, 2 months, 24 days.

Oldest player for British professional club: John Ryan (owner-chairman of Conference club Doncaster Rov., played as substitute for last minute in 4–2 win at Hereford on April 26, 2003), aged 52 years, 11 months, 3 weeks.

Oldest F.A. Cup Final player: Walter (Billy) Hampson (Newcastle Utd. v Aston Villa on April 26, 1924), aged 41 years, 257 days.

Oldest F.A. Cup Final scorers: Bert Turner (Charlton Athletic v Derby Co., April 27, 1946) aged 36 years, 312 days. Scored for both sides. Teddy Sherringham (West Ham Utd. v Liverpool, May 13, 2006) aged 40 years, 41 days. Scored in penalty shoot-out.

Oldest F.A. Cup-winning team: Arsenal 1950 (average age 31 years, 2 months). Eight of the players were over 30, with the three oldest centre-half Leslie Compton 37, and skipper Joe Mercer and goalkeeper George Swindin, both 35.

Oldest World Cup-winning captain: Dino Zoff, Italy's goalkeeper v W. Germany in 1982 Final, aged 40 years, 92 days.

Oldest player capped by England: Stanley Matthews (v. Denmark, Copenhagen, May 15, 1957), aged 42 years, 103 days.

Oldest England scorer: Stanley Matthews (v N. Ireland, Belfast, October 6, 1956), aged 41 years, 248 days.

Oldest British International player: Billy Meredith (Wales v England at Highbury, March 15, 1920), aged 45 years, 229 days.

Oldest 'new caps': Goalkeeper Alexander Morten, aged 41 years, 113 days when earning his only England Cap against Scotland on March 8, 1873; Arsenal centre-half Leslie Compton, at 38 years, 64 days when he made his England debut in 4-2 win against Wales at Sunderland on November 15, 1950. **For Scotland:** Goalkeeper Ronnie Simpson (Celtic) at 36 years, 186 days v England at Wembley, April 15, 1967.

Longest Football League career: This spanned 32 years and 10 months, by Stanley Matthews (Stoke City, Blackpool, Stoke City) from March 19, 1932 until February 6, 1965.

Smallest F.A. Cup-winning captain: 5ft. 4in. – Bobby Kerr (Sunderland v Leeds Utd., 1973).

SHIRT NUMBERING

Numbering players in Football League matches was made compulsory in 1939. Players wore numbered shirts (1-22) in the F.A. Cup Final as an experiment in 1933 (Everton 1-11 v Manchester City 12-22).

Squad numbers for players were introduced by the F.A. Premier League at the start of season 1993-4. They were optional in the Football League until made compulsory in 1999-2000.

Names on shirts: For first time, players wore names as well as numbers on shirts in League Cup and F.A. Cup Finals, 1993.

SUBSTITUTES

In **1965**, the Football League, by 39 votes to 10, agreed that **one substitute** be allowed for an injured player at any time during a League match. First substitute used in Football League: Keith Peacock (Charlton Athletic), away to Bolton Wand. in Div. 2, August 21, 1965.

Two substitutes per team were approved for the League (Littlewoods) Cup and F.A. Cup in season 1986-7 and two were permitted in the Football League for the first time in 1987-8.

Three substitutes (one a goalkeeper), two of which could be used, introduced by the Premier League for 1992-3. The Football League followed suit for 1993-4.

Three substitutes (one a goalkeeper) were allowed at the World Cup Finals for the first time at US '94.

Three substitutes (any position) introduced by Premier League and Football League in 1995-6.

First substitute to score in F.A. Cup Final: Eddie Kelly (Arsenal v Liverpool, 1971).

The **first recorded use of a substitute was in 1889** (Wales v Scotland at Wrexham on April 15) when Sam Gillam arrived late – although he was a Wrexham player – and Allen Pugh (Rhostellyn) was allowed to keep goal until he turned up. The match ended 0-0.

When Dickie Roose, the Welsh goalkeeper, was injured against England at Wrexham, March 16, 1908, Dai Davies (Bolton Wand.) was allowed to take his place as substitute. Thus Wales used 12 players. England won 7-1.

END OF WAGE LIMIT

Freedom from the maximum wage system – in force since the formation of the Football League in 1888 – was secured by the Professional Footballers' Association in 1961. About this time Italian clubs renewed overtures for the transfer of British stars and Fulham's **Johnny Haynes** became the first British player to earn £100 a week.

THE BOSMAN RULING

On December 15, 1995 the **European Court of Justice** ruled that clubs had no right to transfer fees for out-of-contract players, and the outcome of the 'Bosman case' irrevocably changed football's player-club relationship. It began in 1990, when the contract of 26-year-old **Jean-Marc Bosman**, a midfield player with FC Liege, Belgium, expired. French club Dunkirk wanted him but were unwilling to pay the £500,000 transfer fee, so Bosman was compelled to remain with Liege. He responded with a lawsuit against his club and UEFA on the grounds of 'restriction of trade', and after five years at various court levels the European Court of Justice ruled not only in favour of Bosman but of all professional footballers.

The end of restrictive labour practices revolutionised the system. It led to a proliferation of transfers, rocketed the salaries of elite players who, backed by an increasing army of agents, found themselves in a vastly improved bargaining position as they moved from team to team, league to league, nation to nation. Removing the limit on the number of foreigners clubs could field brought an increasing ratio of such signings, not least in England and Scotland.

Bosman's one-man stand opened the way for footballers to become millionaires, but ended his own career. All he received for his legal conflict was 16 million Belgian francs (£312,000) in compensation, a testimonial of poor reward and martyrdom as the man who did most to change the face of football.

INTERNATIONAL SHOCK RESULTS

1950 U.S.A. 1, England 0 (World Cup Finals).
1953 England 3, Hungary 6 (International friendly).
1954 Hungary 7, England 1 (International friendly)
1962 Bangor 2, Napoli 0 (Cup-Winners' Cup).
1966 North Korea 1, Italy 0 (World Cup Finals).
1982 Spain 0, Northern Ireland 1; Algeria 2, West Germany 1 (World Cup Finals).
1990 Cameroon 1, Argentina 0; Scotland 0, Costa Rica 1; Sweden 1 Costa Rica 2 (World Cup Finals).
1990 Faroe Islands 1, Austria 0 (European Championship qualifying).
1992 Denmark 2, Germany 0 (European Championship Final).
1993 U.S.A. 2, England 0 (U.S. Cup tournament).
1993 Argentina 0, Colombia 5 (World Cup qualifying).
1993 France 2, Israel 3 (World Cup qualifying).
1994 Bulgaria 2, Germany 1 (World Cup Finals).

1994 Moldova 3, Wales 2; Georgia 5 Wales 0 (European Championship qualifying).
1995 Belarus 1, Holland 0 (European Championship qualifying).
1996 Nigeria 4, Brazil 3 (Olympic Games).
1998 U.S.A. 1, Brazil 0 (Concacaf Gold Cup).
1998 Croatia 3, Germany 0 (World Cup Finals).
2000 Scotland 0, Australia 2 (International friendly).
2001 Australia 1, France 0; Australia 1, Brazil 0 (Confederations Cup).
2001 Honduras 2, Brazil 0 (Copa America).
2001 Germany 1 England 5 (World Cup qualifying).
2002 France 0 Senegal 1; South Korea 2,Italy 1 (World Cup Finals).
2003: England 1, Australia 3 (Friendly international).
2004: Portugal 0, Greece 1 (European Championship Final).
2005: Northern Ireland 1, England 0 (World Cup qualifying).

GREAT RECOVERIES

On December 21, 1957, Charlton Athletic were losing 5-1 against Huddersfield Town (Div. 2) at The Valley with only 28 minutes left, and from the 15th minute, had been reduced to ten men by injury, but they won 7-6, with left-winger Johnny Summers scoring five goals. Huddersfield Town (managed by Bill Shankly) remain the only team to score six times in a League match and lose.

Among other notable comebacks: on November 12, 1904 (Div. 1), Sheffield Wed. were losing 0-5 at home to Everton, but drew 5-5. At Anfield on December 4, 1909 (Div.1), Liverpool trailed 2-5 to Newcastle Utd. at half-time, then won 6-5. On Boxing Day, 1927, in Div. 3 South, Northampton Town won 6-5 at home to Luton Town after being 1-5 down at half-time. On September 22, 1984 (Div. 1), Q.P.R. drew 5-5 at home to Newcastle Utd. after trailing 0-4 at half-time. On April 12, 1993 (Div. 1) Swindon Town were 1-4 down at Birmingham City with 30 minutes left, but won 6-4.

Other astonishing turnabouts in Div.1 include: Grimsby Town (3-5 down) won 6-5 at W.B.A. on Apr. 30, 1932; and Derby Co. beat Manchester Utd. 5-4 (from 1-4) on Sept. 5, 1936.

With 5 minutes to play, Ipswich Town were losing 3-0 at Barnsley (Div. 1, March 9, 1996), but drew 3-3.

On Sunday, Jan. 19, 1997 (Div. 1), Q.P.R. were 0-4 down away to Port Vale at half-time and still trailing 1-4 with 5 minutes left. They drew 4-4.

Tranmere Rov. retrieved a 3-0 half-time deficit to beat Southampton 4-3 in an F.A. Cup fifth round replay at home on Feb. 20, 2001.

Premier League comebacks: Jan. 4, 1994 – Liverpool were 3 down after 24 mins. at home to Manchester Utd., drew 3-3; Nov. 8, 1997 – Derby Co. led 3-0 after 33 mins. at Elland Road, but Leeds Utd. won 4-3 with last-minute goal; Sept. 29, 2001 – Manchester Utd. won 5-3 at Tottenham after trailing 3-0 at half-time.

Season 2003-04 produced some astonishing turn-rounds. **Premiership** (Oct. 25): In bottom-two clash at Molineux, Wolves were 3 down at half-time v Leicester City, but won 4-3. Feb. 22: Leicester City, down to 10 men, rallied from 3-1 down at Tottenham to lead 4-3. Result 4-4.

First Division (Nov. 8): West Ham Utd. led 3-0 after 18 mins at home to WBA, but lost 4-3.

F.A. Cup 4th **Round replay** (Feb. 4): At half-time, Tottenham led 3-0 at home to Manchester City, but City, reduced to 10 men, won 4-3.

In the 1966 World Cup quarter-final (July 23) at Goodison Park, North Korea led Portugal 3-0, but Eusebio scored 4 times to give Portugal a 5-3 win.

Liverpool produced the most extraordinary recovery in the 50-year history of **European Cup Finals**. In the **Champions League Final** against AC Milan in Istanbul on May 25, 2005, they were 0-3 down at half-time, drew 3-3 after extra time and then won the trophy for the fifth time, 3-2 on penalties.

On November 19, 2005 **Leeds Utd.** retrieved a 3-0 deficit against Southampton in the final 20 minutes to win their **Championship** game 4-3.

GOALS THAT WERE WRONGLY GIVEN

Tottenham's last-minute winner at home to Huddersfield (Div. 1) on April 2, 1952: Eddie Baily's corner-kick struck referee W.R. Barnes in the back, and the ball rebounded to Baily, who centred for Len Duquemin to head into the net. Baily had infringed the Laws by playing the ball twice, but the result (1-0) stood. Those two points helped Spurs to finish Championship runners-up; Huddersfield were relegated.

The second goal (66 mins) in **Chelsea's** 2-1 home win v Ipswich Town (Div. 1) on Sept. 26, 1970: Alan Hudson's low shot from just beyond the penalty-area hit the stanchion on the outside of goal and the ball rebounded on to the pitch. But instead of the goal-kick, referee Roy Capey gave a goal, on a linesman's confirmation. TV pictures proved otherwise. But the Football League quoted from the Laws of the Game: 'The referee's decision on all matters is final.' And though it was wrong, the goal stood and sent Chelsea on the way to victory.

MATCHES OFF

Worst day for postponements: Feb. 9, 1963, when 57 League fixtures in England and Scotland were frozen off. Only 7 Football League matches took place, and the entire Scottish programme was wiped out

Worst other weather-hit days:

Jan. 12, 1963 and Feb. 2, 1963 – on both those Saturdays, only 4 out of 44 Football League matches were played.

Jan. 1, 1979 – 43 out of 46 Football League fixtures postponed.

Jan. 17, 1987 – 37 of 45 scheduled Football League fixtures postponed; only 2 Scottish matches survived.

Feb. 8-9, 1991 – only 4 of the week-end's 44 Barclays League matches survived the freeze-up (4 of the postponements were on Friday night). In addition, 11 Scottish League matches were off.

Jan. 27, 1996 – 44 Cup and League matches in England and Scotland were frozen off. The ten fixtures played comprised 3 F.A. Cup (4th. Round), 1 in Div. 1, 5 in Scottish Cup (3rd. Round), 1 in Scottish Div. 2.

Fewest matches left on one day by postponements was during the Second World War – Feb. 3, 1940 when, because of snow, ice and fog only one out of 56 regional league fixtures took place. It resulted Plymouth Argyle 10, Bristol City 3.

The Scottish Cup second round tie between Inverness Thistle and Falkirk in season 1978-9 was **postponed 29 times** because of snow and ice. First put off on Jan. 6, it was eventually played on Feb. 22. Falkirk won 4-0.

Pools Panel's busiest days: Jan. 17, 1987 and Feb. 9, 1991 – on both dates they gave their verdict on 48 postponed coupon matches.

FEWEST 'GAMES OFF'

Season 1947-8 was the best since the war for English League fixtures being played to schedule. Only **six** were postponed.

LONGEST SEASON

The latest that League football has been played in a season was **June 7, 1947** (six weeks after the F.A. Cup Final). The season was extended because of mass postponements caused by bad weather in mid-winter.

The latest the F.A. Cup competition has ever been completed was in season 1981-2, when Tottenham beat Q.P.R. 1-0 in a Final replay at Wembley on May 27.

Worst winter hold-up was in season 1962-3. The Big Freeze began on Boxing Day and lasted until March, with nearly 500 first-class matches postponed. The F.A. Cup 3rd. Round was the longest on record – it began with only three out of 32 ties playable on January 5 and ended 66 days and 261 postponements later on March 11. The Lincoln City-Coventry City tie was put off 15 times. The Pools Panel was launched that winter, on January 26, 1963.

HOTTEST DAYS

The Nationwide League kicked off season 2003-04 on August 9 with pitch temperatures of 102 degrees recorded at Luton Town v Rushden & Diamonds and Bradford City v Norwich City.

On the following day, there was a pitch temperature of 100 degrees for the Community Shield match between Manchester Utd. and Arsenal at Cardiff's Millennium Stadium.

FOOTBALL ASSOCIATION SECRETARIES/ CHIEF EXECUTIVES

Ebenezer Morley (1863-66), **Robert Willis** (1866-68), **R.G. Graham** (1868-70), **Charles Alcock** (1870-95, paid from 1887), 1895-1934 **Sir Frederick Wall**, 1934-62 **Sir Stanley Rous**, 1962-73 **Denis Follows**, 1973-89 **Ted Croker** (latterly chief executive), 1989-99 **Graham Kelly** (chief executive), 2000-02 **Adam Crozier** (chief executive), 2003-04 **Mark Palios** (chief executive). Since January 2005 **Brian Barwick** (chief executive).

FOOTBALL'S SPONSORS

Football League: Canon 1983-6; Today Newspaper 1986-7; Barclays 1987-93; Endsleigh Insurance 1993-6; Nationwide Building Society 1996-2001 then extended to 2004; Coca-Cola 2004-7.

League Cup: Milk Cup 1982-6; Littlewoods 1987-90; Rumbelows 1991-2; Coca-Cola Cup 1993-8; Worthington Cup 1998-2003; Carling Cup 2003-6.

Premier League: Carling 1993-2001; Barclaycard 2001-04; Barclays 2004-07.

F.A. Cup: Littlewoods 1994-8; AXA 1998-2002; EON 2006-10.

SOCCER HEADQUARTERS

Football Association: 25 Soho Square, London W1D 4FA (moved from Lancaster Gate, London W2, September 2000).

F.A. Premier League: 11 Connaught Place, London W1 2ET.

Football League: Edward VII Quay, Navigation Way, Preston PR2 2YF. **London Office:** 11 Connaught Place, London W2 2ET.

Professional Footballers' Association: 2 Oxford Court, Bishopsgate, Manchester M2 3WQ.

Scottish Football Association: Hampden Park, Glasgow G42 9AY.

Scottish Premier League: National Stadium, Hampden Park, Glasgow G42 9EB.

Scottish Football League: Hampden Park, Glasgow G42 9EB.

Irish Football Association: 20 Windsor Avenue, Belfast BT9 6EG.

Irish Football League: 96 University Street, Belfast BT7 1HE.

League of Ireland: 80 Merrion Square, Dublin 2.

Football Association of Ireland: 80 Merrion Square, Dublin 2.

Welsh Football Association: 3 Westgate Street, Cardiff CF1 1DD.

Football Conference: Collingwood House, Schooner Court, Crossways, Dartford, Kent DA2 6QQ.

FIFA: P.O. Box 85, 8030 Zurich, Switzerland.

UEFA: Route de Geneve, CH-1260, Nyon, Geneva, Switzerland.

NEW HOMES OF SOCCER

Newly-constructed League grounds in England since the war: 1946 Hull City (Boothferry Park); 1950 Port Vale (Vale Park); 1955 Southend Utd. (Roots Hall); 1988 Scunthorpe Utd. (Glanford Park); 1990 Walsall (Bescot Stadium); 1990 Wycombe Wand. (Adams Park); 1992 Chester City (Deva Stadium, Bumpers Lane); 1993 Millwall (New Den); 1994 Huddersfield Town (Alfred McAlpine Stadium, Kirklees); 1994 Northampton Town (Sixfields Stadium); 1995 Middlesbrough (Riverside Stadium); 1997 Bolton Wand. (Reebok Stadium); 1997 Derby Co. (Pride Park); 1997 Stoke City (Britannia Stadium); 1997 Sunderland (Stadium of Light); 1998 Reading (Madejski Stadium); 1999 Wigan Athletic (JJB Stadium); 2001 Southampton (St. Mary's Stadium); 2001 Oxford Utd. (Kassam Stadium); 2002 Leicester City (Walkers Stadium); 2002 Hull City (Kingston Communications Stadium); 2003 Manchester City (City of Manchester Stadium); 2003 Darlington (New Stadium); 2005 Coventry City (Ricoh Arena); Swansea City (Stadium of Swansea, Morfa); 2006 Arsenal (Emirates Stadium).

● Wycombe Wand. now Causeway Stadium; Chester City now Saunders Honda Stadium; Huddersfield Town now Galpharm Stadium; Swansea City now Liberty Stadium.

GROUND-SHARING

Crystal Palace and **Charlton Athletic** (Selhurst Park, 1985-91); **Bristol Rov.** and **Bath City** (Twerton Park, Bath, 1986-96); **Partick Thistle** and **Clyde** (Firhill Park, Glasgow, 1986-91;

in seasons 1990-1, 1991-2 **Chester City** shared **Macclesfield Town's** ground (Moss Rose). **Crystal Palace** and **Wimbledon** shared Selhurst Park, from season 1991-2, when **Charlton Athletic** (tenants) moved to rent Upton Park from **West Ham Utd. Clyde** moved to Douglas Park, **Hamilton Academicals'** home, in 1991-2. **Stirling Albion** shared **Stenhousemuir's** ground, Ochilview Park, in 1992-3. In 1993-4, **Clyde** shared **Partick's** home until moving to Cumbernauld. In 1994-5, **Celtic** shared Hampden Park with **Queen's Park** (while Celtic Park was redeveloped); **Hamilton** shared **Partick's** ground. **Airdrie** shared **Clyde's** Broadwood Stadium. **Bristol Rov.** left Bath City's ground at the start of season 1996-7, sharing Bristol Rugby Club's Memorial Ground. **Clydebank** shared **Dumbarton's** Boghead Park from 1996-7 until renting **Greenock Morton's** Cappielow Park in season 1999-2000. **Brighton** shared **Gillingham's** ground in seasons 1997-8, 1998-9. **Fulham** shared Q.P.R.'s home at Loftus Road in seasons 2002-3, 2003-4, returning to Craven Cottage in August 2004.

Inverness Caledonian Thistle moved to share Aberdeen's Pittodrie Stadium in 2004-5 after being promoted to the SPL.

ARTIFICIAL TURF

Q.P.R. were the first British club to install an artificial pitch, in 1981. They were followed by **Luton Town** in 1985, and **Oldham Athletic** and **Preston N.E. in 1986.** Q.P.R. reverted to grass in 1988, as did Luton Town and promoted Oldham Athletic in season 1991-2 (when artificial pitches were banned in Div. 1). **Preston N.E.** were the last Football League club playing 'on plastic' in 1993-4, and their Deepdale ground was restored to grass for the start of 1994-5.

Stirling Albion were the **first Scottish club** to play on plastic, in season 1987-8.

DOUBLE RUNNERS-UP

There have been nine instances of clubs finishing **runner-up in both the League Championship and F.A. Cup in the same season:** 1928 Huddersfield Town; 1932 Arsenal; 1939 Wolves; 1962 Burnley; 1965 and 1970 Leeds Utd.; 1986 Everton; 1995 Manchester Utd; 2001 Arsenal.

CORNER-KICK RECORDS

Not a single corner-kick was recorded when **Newcastle Utd.** drew 0-0 at home to **Portsmouth** (Div.1) on December 5, 1931.

The record for **most corners** in a match for one side is believed to be **Sheffield Utd.'s 28** to West Ham Utd.'s 1 in Div.2 at Bramall Lane on October 14, 1989. For all their pressure, Sheffield Utd. lost 2-0.

Nott'm. Forest led Southampton 22-2 on corners (Premier League, Nov. 28, 1992) but lost the match 1-2.

Tommy Higginson (Brentford, 1960s) once passed back to his own goalkeeper from a corner kick.

When **Wigan Athletic** won 4-0 at home to Cardiff City (Div. 2) on February 16, 2002, all four goals were headed in from corners taken by N. Ireland International **Peter Kennedy.**

Steve Staunton (Rep. of Ireland) is believed to be the only player to score direct from a corner in **two** Internationals.

NO OFFSIDE

Not one offside decision was given in the **Brazil-Turkey** World Cup semi-final at Saitama, Japan, on June 26, 2002.

SACKED AT HALF-TIME

Leyton Orient sacked **Terry Howard** on his 397th. appearance for the club – at half-time in a Second Division home defeat against Blackpool (Feb. 7, 1995) for 'an unacceptable performance'. He was fined two weeks' wages, given a free transfer and moved to Wycombe Wanderers.

Bobby Gould resigned as **Peterborough United's** head coach at half-time in their 1-0 defeat in the LDV Vans Trophy 1st Round at Bristol City on Sept. 29, 2004.

Harald Schumacher, former Germany goalkeeper, was sacked as Fortuna Koln coach when they were two down at half-time against Waldhof Mannheim (Dec. 15, 1999). They lost 5-1.

MOST GAMES BY 'KEEPER FOR ONE CLUB

Alan Knight made 683 League appearances for Portsmouth, over 23 seasons (1978-2000), a record for a goalkeeper at one club. The previous holder was Peter Bonetti with 600 League games for Chelsea (20 seasons, 1960-79).

PLAYED TWO GAMES ON SAME DAY

Jack Kelsey played full-length matches for both club and country on Wed., November 26, 1958. In the afternoon he kept goal for Wales in a 2-2 draw against England at Villa Park, and he then drove to Highbury to help Arsenal win 3-1 in a prestigious floodlit friendly against Juventus.

On the same day, winger **Danny Clapton** played for England (against Wales and Kelsey) and then in part of Arsenal's match against Juventus.

On November 11, 1987, **Mark Hughes** played for Wales against Czechoslovakia (European Championship) in Prague, then flew to Munich and went on as substitute that night in a winning Bayern Munich team, to whom he was on loan from Barcelona.

On February 16, 1993 goalkeeper **Scott Howie** played in Scotland's 3-0 U-21 win v Malta at Tannadice Park, Dundee (k.o. 1.30pm) and the same evening played in Clyde's 2-1 home win v Queen of South (Div. 2).

Ryman League **Hornchurch**, faced by end-of-season fixture congestion, played **two matches on the same night** (May 1, 2001). They lost 2-1 at home to Ware and drew 2-2 at Clapton.

RECORD CLUB LOSSES

Fulham, brokered by Harrods owner Mohamed Al Fayed, made British football's then record loss of £23.3m. in the year to June 30, 2001 (in which they won promotion to the Premiership as Div. 1 Champions). The club's debts rose to £61.7m. Previous highest loss was £18.7m. by Newcastle Utd. in 2000. In September 2002, **Leeds Utd.** reported a loss of £33.9m. for the year ending June 30. It took their debts to £77m. A year later, in October 2003, **Leeds** declared a loss of £49.5m. (debts £78m). **Chelsea** made losses of £87.8m. in seasons 2003-4 (their first under the ownership of Roman Abramovich) and £140m. in 2004-5.

FIRST 'MATCH OF THE DAY'

BBC TV (recorded highlights): Liverpool 3, Arsenal 2 on August 22, 1964. **First complete match to be televised:** Arsenal 3, Everton 2 on August 29, 1936. **First League match televised in colour:** Liverpool 2, West Ham Utd. 0 on November 15, 1969.

'MATCH OF THE DAY' – BIGGEST SCORES

Football League: Tottenham 9, Bristol Rov. 0 (Div. 2, 1977-8). **Premier League:** Nott'm Forest 1, Manchester Utd. 8 (1998-9).

FIRST COMMENTARY ON RADIO

Arsenal 1, **Sheffield Utd.** 1 (Div. 1) broadcast on BBC, January 22, 1927.

OLYMPIC SOCCER WINNERS

1908 Great Britain (in London); **1912** Great Britain (Stockholm); **1920** Belgium (Antwerp); **1924** Uruguay (Paris); **1928** Uruguay (Amsterdam); **1932** No soccer in Los Angeles Olympics.
1936 Italy (Berlin); **1948** Sweden (London); **1952** Hungary (Helsinki); **1956** USSR (Melbourne); **1960** Yugoslavia (Rome); **1964** Hungary (Tokyo); **1968** Hungary (Mexico); **1972** Poland (Munich); **1976** E. Germany (Montreal); **1980** Czechoslovakia (Moscow); **1984** France (Los Angeles); **1988** USSR (Seoul); **1992** Spain (Barcelona); **1996** Nigeria (Atlanta); **2000** Cameroon (Sydney); **2004** Argentina (Athens).
Highest scorer in Final tournament: Ferenc Bene (Hungary) 12 goals, 1964.
Record crowd for Olympic Soccer Final: 108,800 (France v Brazil, Los Angeles 1984).

MOST AMATEUR CUP WINS

Bishop Auckland set the F.A. Amateur Cup record with 10 wins, and in 1957 became the only club to carry off the trophy in three successive seasons. The competition was discontinued after the Final on April 20, 1974. (Bishop's Stortford 4, Ilford 1, at Wembley).

FOOTBALL FOUNDATION

This was formed (May 2000) to replace the **Football Trust**, which had been in existence since 1975 as an initiative of the Pools companies to provide financial support at all levels, from schools football to safety and ground improvement work throughout the game.

SEVEN-FIGURE TESTIMONIALS

The first was **Sir Alex Ferguson's** at Old Trafford on October 11, 1999, when a full-house of 54,842 saw a Rest of the World team beat Manchester Utd 4-2. United's manager pledged that a large percentage of the estimated £1m. receipts would go to charity.

Estimated receipts of £1m. and over came from testimonials for **Denis Irwin** (Manchester Utd.) against Manchester City at Old Trafford on August 16, 2000 (45,158); **Tom Boyd** (Celtic) against Manchester Utd. at Celtic Park on May 15, 2001 (57,000) and **Ryan Giggs** (Manchester Utd.) against Celtic on August 1, 2001 (66,967).

Tony Adams' second testimonial (1-1 v Celtic on May 13, 2002) two nights after Arsenal completed the Double, was watched by 38,021 spectators at Highbury. Of £1m. receipts, he donated a substantial percentage to Sporting Chance, the charity that helps sportsmen/women with drink, drug, gambling problems.

Sunderland and a Republic of Ireland XI drew 0-0 in front of 35,702 at the Stadium of Light on May 14, 2002. The beneficiary, **Niall Quinn**, donated his testimonial proceeds, estimated at £1m., to children's hospitals in Sunderland and Dublin, and to homeless children in Africa and Asia.

A record testimonial crowd of 69,591 for **Roy Keane** at Old Trafford on May 9, 2006 netted more than £2m. for charities in Dublin, Cork and Manchester. Manchester United beat Celtic 1-0, with Keane playing for both teams.

Alan Shearer's testimonial on May 11, 2006, watched by a crowd of 52,275 at St James' Park, raised more than £1m. for charities. The clubs record scorer, in his farewell match, came off the bench in stoppage time to score the penalty that gave Newcastle a 3-2 win over Celtic.

WHAT IT USED TO COST

Minimum admission to League football was one shilling in 1939. After the war, it was increased to 1s. 3d. in 1946; 1s. 6d. in 1951; 1s. 9d. in 1952; 2s. in 1955; 2s. 6d. in 1960; 4s. in 1965; 5s. in 1968; 6s. in 1970; and 8s. (40p) in 1972. After that, the fixed minimum charge was dropped.

Wembley's first Cup Final programme in 1923 cost three pence (1¼p in today's money). The programme for the 'farewell' F.A. Cup Final in May, 2000 was priced £10.

WHAT THEY USED TO EARN

In the 1930s, First Division players were on £8 a week (£6 in close season) plus bonuses of £2 win, £1 draw. The maximum wage went up to £12 when football resumed post-war in 1946 and had reached £20 by the time the limit was abolished in 1961.

European Cup: 9 Real Madrid; **6** AC Milan; **5** Liverpool; **4** Ajax; Bayern Munich; **2** Benfica, Inter Milan, Juventus, Manchester Utd., Nott'm. Forest, FC Porto; **1** Aston Villa, Borussia Dortmund, Celtic, Feyenoord, Hamburg, Marseille, PSV Eindhoven, Red Star Belgrade, Steaua Bucharest.

Cup-Winners' Cup: 4 Barcelona; **2** Anderlecht, Chelsea, Dynamo Kiev, AC Milan; **1** Aberdeen, Ajax Amsterdam, Arsenal, Atletico Madrid, Bayern Munich, Borussia Dortmund, Dynamo Tbilisi, Everton, Fiorentina, Hamburg SV, Juventus, Lazio, Magdeburg, Manchester City, Manchester Utd., Mechelen, Paris St. Germain, Parma, Rangers, Real Zaragoza, Sampdoria, Slovan Bratislava, Sporting Lisbon, Tottenham, Valencia, Werder Bremen, West Ham Utd.

UEFA Cup: 3 Barcelona, Inter Milan, Juventus, Liverpool, Valencia; **2** Borussia Moenchengladbach, Feyenoord, Gothenburg, Leeds Utd., Parma, Real Madrid, Tottenham; **1** Ajax, Anderlecht, Arsenal, Bayer Leverkusen, Bayern Munich, Dynamo Zagreb, Eintracht Frankfurt, PSV Eindhoven, Ferencvaros, Ipswich Town, Napoli, Newcastle Utd., Real Zaragoza, Roma, Sevilla, Schalke, Galatasaray, FC Porto, CSKA Moscow.

● The Champions League was introduced into the European Cup in 1992-3 to counter the threat of a European Super League.

BRITAIN'S 31 TROPHIES IN EUROPE

Liverpool's success in the 2004-05 Champions League/European Cup took the number of **British** club triumphs in European Football to 31:

European Cup (11)	Cup-Winners' Cup (10)	Fairs/UEFA Cup (10)
1967 Celtic	1963 Tottenham	1968 Leeds Utd.
1968 Manchester Utd.	1965 West Ham Utd.	1969 Newcastle Utd.
1977 Liverpool	1970 Manchester City	1970 Arsenal
1978 Liverpool	1971 Chelsea	1971 Leeds Utd.
1979 Nott'm. Forest	1972 Rangers	1972 Tottenham
1980 Nott'm. Forest	1983 Aberdeen	1973 Liverpool
1981 Liverpool	1985 Everton	1976 Liverpool
1982 Aston Villa	1991 Manchester Utd.	1981 Ipswich Town
1984 Liverpool	1994 Arsenal	1984 Tottenham
1999 Manchester Utd.	1998 Chelsea	2001 Liverpool
2005 Liverpool		

END OF CUP-WINNERS' CUP

The **European Cup-Winners' Cup**, inaugurated in 1960-61, terminated with the 1999 final. The competition merged into a revamped, 121-club **UEFA Cup**.

From its inception in 1955, the **European Cup** comprised only championship-winning clubs until 1998-9, when selected runners-up were introduced. Further expansion came in 1999-2000 with the inclusion of clubs finishing third in certain leagues and fourth in 2002.

EUROPEAN CLUB COMPETITIONS – SCORING RECORDS

European Cup – Record aggregate: 18-0 by Benfica v Dudelange (Lux) (8-0a, 10-0h), prelim. round, 1965-6.
  Record single-match score: 12-0 by Feyenoord v KR Reykjavik (Ice), 1st. round, 1st. leg, 1969-70 (aggregate was 16-0).
Champions League – highest match aggregates: 11 goals – Monaco 8, Deportivo La Coruna 3 (Nov. 5, 2003); 9 goals – Paris St. Germain 7, Rosenborg 2 (Oct. 24, 2000).
Cup-Winners' Cup – *Record aggregate: 21-0 by Chelsea v Jeunesse Hautcharage (Lux) (8-0a, 13-0h), 1st. round, 1971-2.
  Record single-match score: 16-1 by Sporting Lisbon v Apoel Nicosia, 2nd. round, 1st. leg, 1963-4 (aggregate was 18-1).
UEFA Cup (prev. Fairs Cup) – *Record aggregate: 21-0 by Feyenoord v US Rumelange (Lux) (9-0h, 12-0a), 1st. round, 1972-3.
  Record single-match score: 14-0 by Ajax Amsterdam v Red Boys (Lux) 1st. round, 2nd leg, 1984-5 (aggregate also 14-0).
Record British score in Europe: 13-0 by **Chelsea** at home to Jeunesse Hautcharage (Lux) in Cup-Winners' Cup 1st. round, 2nd. leg, 1971-2. Chelsea's overall 21-0 win in that tie is highest aggregate by British club in Europe.
Individual scoring record for European tie (over two legs): **10 goals** (6 home, 4 away) by **Kiril Milanov** for Levski Spartak in 19-3 agg. win CWC 1st round v Lahden Reipas, 1976-7. Next highest: **8 goals** by **Jose Altafini** for AC Milan v US Luxembourg (European Cup, prelim. round, 1962-3, agg. 14-0) and by **Peter Osgood** for Chelsea v Jeunesse Hautcharage (Cup-Winners' Cup, 1st. round 1971-2, agg. 21-0). Altafini and Osgood each scored 5 goals at home, 3 away.

Individual single-match scoring record in European competition: **6** goals by **Mascarenhas** for Sporting Lisbon in 16-1 Cup-Winner's Cup 2nd. round, 1st. leg win v Apoel, 1963-4; **6** by **Lothar Emmerich** for Borussia Dortmund in 8-0 CWC 1st. round, 2nd. leg win v Floriana 1965-6; **6** by **Kiril Milanov** for Levski Spartak in 12-2 CWC 1st. round, 1st. leg win v Lahden Reipas, 1976-7.

Most goals in single European campaign: 15 by Jurgen Klinsmann for Bayern Munich (UEFA Cup 1995-6).

Most goals by British player in European competition: 30 by **Peter Lorimer** (Leeds Utd., in 9 campaigns).

Most European Cup goals by individual player: 49 by **Alfredo di Stefano** in 58 apps. for Real Madrid (1955-64).

(*Joint record European aggregate)

First European 'Treble': Clarence Seedorf is the only player to win the European Cup with three clubs: Ajax in 1995, Real Madrid in 1998 and AC Milan in 2003.

EUROPEAN FOOTBALL – BIG RECOVERIES

In the most astonishing Final in the 51-year history of the **European Cup, Liverpool** became the first club to win it from a 3-0 deficit when they beat AC Milan 3-2 on penalties after a 3-3 draw in Istanbul on May 25, 2005. Liverpool's fifth triumph in the competition meant that they would keep the trophy.

The following season, **Middlesbrough** twice recovered from three-goal aggregate deficits in the **UEFA Cup**, beating Basle 4-3 in the quarter finals and Steaua Bucharest by the same scoreline in the semi-finals.

Only four clubs have survived a **4-goal** deficit in any of the European club competitions after the first leg has been completed:

1961-2 (Cup-Winners' Cup 1st. Rd.): Leixoes (Portugal) beat Chaux de Fonds (Luxembourg) 7-6 on agg. (lost 2-6a, won 5-0h).

1962-3 (Fairs Cup 2nd. Rd.): Valencia (Spain) beat **Dunfermline** 1-0 in play-off in Lisbon after 6-6 agg. (Valencia won 4-0h, lost 2-6a).

1984-5 (UEFA Cup 2nd. Rd.): Partizan Belgrade beat **Q.P.R.** on away goals (lost 2-6 away, at Highbury, won 4-0 home).

1985-6 (UEFA Cup 3rd. Rd.): Real Madrid beat Borussia Moenchengladbach on away goals (lost 1-5a, won 4-0h) and went on to win competition.

In the **Champions League** quarter-final, 2003-04, Deportivo La Coruna lost the first leg 4-1 away to Inter Milan, then won the return match 4-0 to go through 5-4 on agg. This was the first instance in the Champions League of a team over-turning a 3-goal deficit.

In the **European Cup**, there are eight instances of clubs reaching the next round after **arrears of three goals** in the first leg:

1958-9 (Prel. Rd.) Schalke beat KB Copenhagen (0-3, 5-2, 3-1).

1965-6 (Q-final) Partizan Belgrade beat Sparta Prague (1-4, 5-0).

1970-1 (S-final) Panathinaikos beat Red Star Belgrade on away goal (1-4, 3-0).

1975-6 (2nd. Rd.) Real Madrid beat **Derby Co.** (1-4, 5-1).

1985-6 (S-final) Barcelona beat IFK Gothenburg on pens. (0-3, 3-0).

1988-9 (1st. Rd.) Werder Bremen beat Dynamo Berlin (0-3, 5-0).

1988-9 (2nd. Rd.) Galatasaray (Turkey) beat Neuchatel Xamax (Switz.) (0-3, 5-0).

1992-3 (1st. Rd.) **Leeds Utd.** beat VfB Stuttgart 2-1 in play-off in Barcelona. Over two legs, VfB won on away goal (3-0h, 1-4 away) but a third match was ordered because they broke 'foreigners' rule in team selection.

In the **Cup-Winners' Cup**, six clubs survived a **3-goal** deficit:

1963-4 (Q-final) Sporting Lisbon beat **Manchester Utd.** (1-4, 5-0).

1963-4 (S-final) MTK Budapest beat **Celtic** (0-3, 4-0).

1978-9 (2nd. Rd.) Barcelona beat Anderlecht on pens. (0-3, 3-0).

1980-1 (1st. Rd.) Carl Zeiss Jena beat AS Roma (0-3, 4-0).

1984-5 (Q-final) Rapid Vienna beat Dynamo Dresden (0-3, 5-0).

1989-90 (1st. Rd.) Grasshoppers (Switz.) beat Slovan Bratislava (0-3, 4-0).

In the **Fairs Cup/UEFA Cup**, there have been more than 20 occasions when clubs have survived a deficit of **3 goals**, the most notable example being the 1988 UEFA Cup Final, which Bayer Leverkusen won 3-2 on pens., having lost the first leg 0-3 away to Espanol and won the return 3-0 to level the aggregate.

Two Scottish clubs have won a European tie from a 3-goal, first leg deficit: **Kilmarnock** 0-3, 5-1 v Eintracht Frankfurt (Fairs Cup 1st. Round, 1964-5); **Hibernian** 1-4, 5-0 v Napoli (Fairs Cup 2nd. Round, 1967-8).

English clubs have three times gone out of the **UEFA Cup** after leading 3-0 from the first leg: 1975-6 (2nd. Rd.) **Ipswich Town** lost 3-4 on agg. to Bruges; 1976-7 (Q-final) **Q.P.R.** lost on pens. to AEK Athens after 3-3 agg; 1977-8 (3rd. Rd.) **Ipswich Town** lost on pens. to Barcelona after 3-3 agg.

HEAVIEST ENGLISH-CLUB DEFEATS IN EUROPE

(Single-leg scores)

European Cup: Artmedia Bratislava 5, Celtic 0 (2nd. Q. Rd.), July 2005 (agg. 5-4); Ajax 5, Liverpool 1 (2nd. Rd.), Dec. 1966 (agg. 7-3); Real Madrid 5, Derby Co. 1 (2nd. Rd.), Nov. 1975 (agg. 6-5).

Cup-Winners' Cup: Sporting Lisbon 5, Manchester Utd. 0 (Q-final), Mar. 1964 (agg. 6-4).

Fairs/UEFA Cup: Bayern Munich 6, Coventry City 1 (2nd. Rd.), Oct. 1970 (agg. 7-3). Combined London team lost 6-0 (agg. 8-2) in first Fairs Cup Final in 1958. Barcelona 5, Chelsea 0 in Fairs Cup Semi-final play-off, 1966, in Barcelona (after 2-2 agg.).

SHOCK ENGLISH-CLUB DEFEATS

1968-69 (E. Cup, 1st. Rd.): Manchester City beaten by Fenerbahce, 1-2 agg.
1971-72 (CWC, 2nd. Rd.): Chelsea beaten by Atvidaberg on away goals.
1993-94 (E. Cup, 2nd. Rd.): Manchester Utd. beaten by Galatasaray on away goals.
1994-95 (UEFA Cup, 1st. Rd.): Blackburn Rov. beaten by Trelleborgs, 2-3 agg.
2000-01 (UEFA Cup, 1st. Rd.): Chelsea beaten by St. Gallen, Swit. 1-2 agg.

FIFA'S HALL OF CHAMPIONS

Ten retired players, honoured for 'sporting success that contributed to the positive image of the game' – Sir Stanley Matthews, Sir Bobby Charlton (England), Pele (Brazil), Franz Beckenbauer (W. Germany), Johan Cruyff (Holland), Alfredo di Stefano (Argentina), Eusebio (Portugal), Michel Platini (France), Ferenc Puskas (Hungary), Lev Yashin (Soviet Union). Managers: Sir Matt Busby (Manchester Utd.), Rinus Michels (Ajax Amsterdam).

The names were announced in January 1998.

P.F.A. FAIR PLAY AWARD (Bobby Moore Trophy from 1993)

1988	Liverpool		1998	Cambridge Utd.
1989	Liverpool		1999	Grimsby Town
1990	Liverpool		2000	Crewe Alexandra
1991	Nott'm. Forest		2001	Crewe Alexandra
1992	Portsmouth		2002	Crewe Alexandra
1993	Norwich City		2003	Crewe Alexandra
1994	Crewe Alexandra		2004	Crewe Alexandra
1995	Crewe Alexandra		2005	Crewe Alexandra
1996	Crewe Alexandra		2006	Crewe Alexandra
1997	Crewe Alexandra			

RECORD MEDAL SALES

West Ham Utd. bought (June 2000) the late **Bobby Moore's** collection of medals and trophies for £1.8m. at Christie's auction in London. It was put up for sale by his first wife Tina and included his World Cup winner's medal.

A No. 6 duplicate red shirt made for England captain **Bobby Moore** for the 1966 World Cup Final fetched £44,000 at an auction at Wolves' ground in Sept. 1999. Moore kept the shirt he wore in that Final and gave the replica to England physio Harold Shepherdson.

Sir Geoff Hurst's 1966 World Cup-winning shirt fetched a record £91,750 at Christie's on September 28, 2000. His World Cup Final cap fetched £37,600 and his Man of the

Match trophy £18,800. Proceeds totalling £274,410 from the 129 lots went to Hurst's three daughters and charities of his choice, including the Bobby Moore Imperial Cancer Research Fund.

In August 2001, Sir Geoff sold his World Cup-winner's medal to his former club West Ham Utd. (for their museum) at a reported £150,000.

'The **Billy Wright Collection**' – caps, medals and other memorabilia from his illustrious career – fetched over £100,000 at Christie's in Glasgow on Nov. 21, 1996.

At the sale in Oct. 1993, trophies, caps and medals earned by **Ray Kennedy**, former England, Arsenal and Liverpool player, fetched a then record total of £88,407. Kennedy, suffering from Parkinson's Disease, received £73,000 after commission.

The P.F.A. paid £31,080 for a total of 60 lots – including a record £16,000 for his 1977 European Cup winner's medal – to be exhibited at their Manchester museum. An anonymous English collector paid £17,000 for the medal and plaque commemorating Kennedy's part in the Arsenal Double in 1971.

Previous record for one player's medals, shirts etc. collection: £30,000 (**Bill Foulkes**, Manchester Utd. in 1992). The sale of **Dixie Dean**'s medals etc. in 1991 realised £28,000.

In March 2001, **Gordon Banks**' 1966 World Cup-winner's medal fetched a new record £124,750, and at auctions in season 2001-02: TV's Nick Hancock, a Stoke City fan, paid £23,500 for **Sir Stanley Matthews**' 1953 F.A. Cup-winner's medal. He also bought one of Matthews' England caps for £3,525 and paid £2,350 for a Stoke Div. 2 Championship medal (1963).

Dave Mackay's 1961 League Championship and F.A. Cup winner's medals sold for £18,000 at Sotherby's. Tottenham bought them for their museum.

A selection of England World Cup-winning manager **Sir Alf Ramsey**'s memorabilia – England caps, championship medals with Ipswich Town etc. – fetched more than £80,000 at Christie's. They were offered for sale by his family, and his former clubs Tottenham and Ipswich Town were among the buyers.

Ray Wilson's 1966 England World Cup-winning shirt fetched £80,750. Also in March 2002, the No. 10 shirt worn by **Pele** in Brazil's World Cup triumph in 1970 was sold for a record £157,750 at Christies. It went to an anonymous telephone bidder.

In October 2003, **George Best's** European Footballer of the Year (1968) trophy was sold to an anonymous British bidder for £167,250 at Bonham's, Chester. It was the most expensive item of sporting memorabilia ever auctioned in Britain.

England captain **Bobby Moore's** 1970 World Cup shirt, which he swapped with Pele after Brazil's 1-0 win in Mexico, was sold for £60,000 at Christie's in London in March 2004.

September 2004: England shirt worn by tearful **Paul Gascoigne** in 1990 World Cup semi-final v Germany sold at Christie's for £28,680. At same auction, shirt worn by Brazil's **Pele** in 1958 World Cup Final in Sweden sold for £70,505.

May 2005: The **second F.A. Cup** (which was presented to winning teams from 1896 to 1909) was bought for £420,000 at Christie's by Birmingham City chairman David Gold, a world record for an item of football memorabilia. It was presented to the National Football Museum, Preston. At the same aution, the World Cup-winner's medal earned by England's **Alan Ball** in 1966 was sold for £140,000.

October 2005: At auction at Bonham's (London) the medals and other memorabilia of Hungary and Real Madrid legend Ferenc Puskas were sold for £85,000 to help pay for hospital treatment.

LONGEST UNBEATEN CUP RUN

Liverpool established the longest unbeaten Cup sequence by a Football League club: 25 successive rounds in the League/Milk Cup between semi-final defeat by Nott'm. Forest (1-2 agg.) in 1980 and defeat at Tottenham (0-1) in the third round on October 31, 1984. During this period Liverpool won the tournament in four successive seasons, a feat no other Football League club has achieved in any competition.

NEAR £1M. RECORD DAMAGES

A High Court judge in Newcastle (May 7, 1999) awarded Bradford City's 28-year-old striker **Gordon Watson** record damages for a football injury: £909,143. He had had his right leg fractured in two places by Huddersfield Town's Kevin Gray on Feb. 1, 1997.

Huddersfield Town were 'proven negligent for allowing their player to make a rushed tackle'. The award was calculated at £202,643 for loss of earnings, £730,500 for 'potential career earnings' if he had joined a Premiership club, plus £26,000 to cover medical treatment and care.

Watson, awarded £50,000 in an earlier legal action, had a 6-inch plate inserted in the leg. He resumed playing for City in season 1998-9.

BIG HALF-TIME SCORES

Tottenham 10, Crewe Alexandra 1 (F.A. Cup 4th. Rd. replay, Feb. 3, 1960; result 13-2); Tranmere Rov. 8, Oldham Athletic 1 (Div. 3N., Dec. 26, 1935; result 13-4); Chester City 8, York City 0 (Div. 3N., Feb. 1, 1936; result 12-0; believed to be record half-time scores in League football).

Nine goals were scored in the first half – Burnley 4, Watford 5 in Div. 1 on April 5, 2003. Result: 4–7.

Stirling Albion led Selkirk 15-0 at half-time (result 20-0) in the Scottish Cup 1st. Rd., Dec. 8, 1984.

World record half-time score: 16-0 when Australia beat American Samoa 31-0 (another world record) in the World Cup Oceania qualifying group at Coff's Harbour, New South Wales, on April 11, 2001.

● On March 4, 1933 Coventry City beat Q.P.R. (Div. 3 South) 7-0, having led by that score at half-time. This repeated the half-time situation in Bristol City's 7-0 win over Grimsby Town on Dec. 26, 1914.

● Only instance of club failing to win League match after leading 5-0 at half-time: Sheffield Wed. 5, Everton 5 (Div. 1, Nov. 12, 1904; Wed. scored 5 in first half, Everton 5 in second).

TOP SECOND-HALF TEAM

Most goals scored by a team in one half of a League match is eleven. Stockport Co. led Halifax Town 2-0 at half-time in Div. 3 North on Jan. 6, 1934 and won 13-0.

FIVE NOT ENOUGH

Last team to score 5 in League match and lose: Reading, beaten 7-5 at Doncaster Rov. (Div. 3, Sept. 25, 1982).

LONG SERVICE WITH ONE CLUB

Bill Nicholson, OBE, was associated with Tottenham for 67 years – as a wing-half (1938-55), then the club's most successful manager (1958-74) with 8 major prizes, subsequently chief advisor and scout. He became club president, and an honorary freeman of the borough, had an executive suite named after him at the club, and the stretch of roadway from Tottenham High Road to the main gates has the nameplate Bill Nicholson Way. He died, aged 85, in October 2004.

Ted Bates, the Grand Old Man of Southampton with 66 years of unbroken service to the club, was awarded the Freedom of the City in April, 2001. He joined Saints as an inside-forward from Norwich City in 1937, made 260 peace-time appearances for the club, became reserve-team trainer in 1953 and manager at The Dell for 18 years (1955-73), taking Southampton into the top division in 1966. He was subsequently chief executive, director and club president. He died in October 2003, aged 85.

Dario Gradi, MBE, 64, is the longest-serving manager in British football, having completed 23 seasons and more than 1,000 matches in charge of Crewe Alexandra (appointed June 1983). Never a League player, he previously managed Wimbledon and Crystal Palace. At Crewe, his policy of finding and grooming young talent has earned the club nearly £20m. in transfer fees.

Bob Paisley was associated with Liverpool for 57 years from 1939, when he joined them from Bishop Auckland, until he died in February 1996. He served them as player, trainer, coach, assistant-manager, manager, director and vice-president. He was Liverpool's most successful manager, winning 13 major trophies for the club (1974-83).

Ronnie Moran, who joined Liverpool in as a player 1952, retired from the Anfield coaching staff in season 1998-9.

Ernie Gregory served West Ham Utd. for 52 years as goalkeeper and coach. He joined them as boy of 14 from school in 1935, retired in May 1987.

Ted Sagar, Everton goalkeeper, 23 years at Goodison Park (1929-52, but only 16 League seasons because of War).

Alan Knight, goalkeeper, played 23 seasons (1977-2000) for his only club, Portsmouth.

Roy Sproson, defender, played 21 League seasons for his only club, Port Vale (1950-71).

Allan Ball, goalkeeper, 20 seasons with Queen of the South (1963-83).

Pat Bonner, goalkeeper, 19 seasons with Celtic (1978-97).

Danny McGrain, defender, 17 years with Celtic (1970-87).

TIGHT AT HOME

Fewest home goals conceded in League season (modern times): 4 by **Liverpool** (Div. 1, 1978-9); 4 by **Manchester Utd.** (Premier League, 1994-5) – both in 21 matches.

FOOTBALL POOLS

Littlewoods launched them in 1923 with a capital of £100. Coupons were first issued (4,000 of them) outside Manchester Utd.'s ground, the original 35 investors staking a total of £4-7s.-6d (pay-out £2-12s).

Vernons joined Littlewoods as the leading promoters. The Treble Chance, leading to bonanza dividends, was introduced in 1946 and the Pools Panel began in January 1963, to counter mass fixture postponements caused by the Big Freeze winter.

But business was hard hit by the launch of the National Lottery in 1994. Dividends slumped, the work-force was drastically cut and in June 2000 the Liverpool-based Moores family sold Littlewoods Pools in a £161m. deal.

The record prize remains the £2,924,622 paid to a Worsley, Manchester, syndicate in November 1994.

Fixed odds football – record pay-out: **£654,375** by Ladbrokes (May 1993) to Jim Wright, of Teignmouth, Devon. He placed a £1,000 each-way pre-season bet on the champions of the three Football League divisions – Newcastle Utd. (8-1), Stoke City (6-1) and Cardiff City (9-1).

Record for match accumulator: **£164,776** to £4 stake on 18 correct results, October 5, 6, 7, 2002. The bet, with Ladbrokes in Colchester, was made by Army chef Mark Simmons.

TRANSFER DEADLINE

This was introduced by the Football League in 1911, to prevent clubs in contention for honours or fighting relegation gaining an unfair advantage in the closing weeks.

The original deadline was March 16. It is now 5 p.m. on the fourth Thursday in March, after which only in exceptional circumstances (e.g. if a side has no fit goalkeeper) can a transferred player appear for his new club that season.

After the last war, frantic spending was the norm on deadline day, but in recent years last-day business has dwindled to a comparative trickle.

TRANSFER WINDOW

This was introduced to Britain in September 2002 via FIFA regulations to bring uniformity across Europe (the rule previously applied in a number of other countries). The transfer of contracted players is restricted to two periods: June 1–August 31 and January 1–31).

On appeal, Football League clubs continued to sign/sell players through seasons 2002-03, 2003-04, 2004-05, 2005-06 (excluding deals with Premiership clubs).

PROGRAMME PIONEERS

Chelsea pioneered football's magazine-style programme when they introduced a 16-page issue for their First Division match against Portsmouth on Christmas Day 1948. It cost sixpence (2½p).

TRIBUNAL-FEE RECORDS

Top tribunal fee: £2.5m for **Chris Bart-Williams** (Sheffield Wed. to Nott'm. Forest, June 1995).

Biggest discrepancy: Andy Walker, striker, Bolton Wand. to Celtic, June 1994: Bolton Wand. asked £2.2m, Celtic offered £250,000. Tribunal decided £550,000.

LONGEST THROW-IN?

That by Notts Co.'s **Andy Legg** was measured (season 1994-5) at 41 metres (45 yards) and claimed as the longest throw by any footballer in the world, until 1997-8, when **Dave Challinor** (Tranmere Rov.) reached 46.3 metres (50½ yards).

BALL JUGGLING: WORLD RECORD CLAIMS

Sam Ik (South Korea) juggled a ball non-stop for 18 hours, 11 minutes, 4 seconds in March 1995. Thai footballer **Sam-Ang Sowanski** juggled a ball for 15 hours without letting it touch the ground in Bangkok in April 2000.

Milene Domingues, wife of Brazilian star Ronaldo and a player for Italian women's team Fiammamonza, Milan, became the 'Queen of Keepy Uppy' when for 9 hours, 6 minutes she juggled a ball 55,187 times.

SUBS' SCORING RECORD

Barnet's 5-4 home win v Torquay Utd. (Div. 3, Dec. 28, 1993) provided the first instance of **all four substitutes** scoring in a major League match in England.

FOOTBALL'S OLDEST ANNUAL

Now in its 120th edition, this publication began as the 16-page *Athletic News Football Supplement & Club Directory* in 1887. From the long-established *Athletic News*, it became the *Sunday Chronicle Annual* in 1946, the *Empire News* in 1956, the *News of the World & Empire News* in 1961 and, since 1965, the *News of the World Annual*.

QUOTE-UNQUOTE

'If I have a Bentley and an Aston Martin in the garage, it would be foolish to drive to work in the Bentley every day' – **Jose Mourinho**, Chelsea manager, on his team rotation system.

'I had a good time in Madrid, both on and off the pitch, but I missed the UK, I missed the food, the Premiership and being around English people' – **Michael Owen** on his return to English football with Newcastle.

'I was shouting 'get back, get back' at him, then he decides to hit a shot like that' – **Stuart Pearce**, Manchester City manager, on Danny Mills's spectacular goal struck from 30 yards against Everton.

'Nobody should be criticising TV. It is the rocket fuel that has sent this league into the stratosphere, domestically and around the world' – **Richard Scudamore**, Premier League chief executive, on falling attendances.

'From what fans are saying to us, there are fewer complaints about the absolute level of ticket prices and more about the timing of games' – **Prof. Derek Fraser**, chairman of the Independent Football Commission, in a warning to the Premier League about the growing number of fixtures being moved from the traditional Saturday afternoon slot.

'When Manchester United dominate the Premiership it is not boring. When Arsenal dominate the Premiership it is not boring. But Chelsea win seven matches and it is boring' – **Jose Mourinho**, Chelsea manager.

'They'd need to lose a lot of players and Mr Abramovich would need to go skint' – **David O'Leary**, former Aston Villa manager, on how Chelsea could be stopped from retaining the title.

F. A. BARCLAYS PREMIERSHIP CLUB DETAILS AND PLAYING STAFFS 2006-07

(At time of going to press)

ARSENAL

Ground: Emirates Stadium, Highbury, London, N5 1BU.
Telephone: 0207 704 4000. **Club nickname:** Gunners.
First-choice colours: Red and white shirts; white shorts; white socks.
Record transfer fee: £17,400,000 to Seville for Jose Antonio Reyes, January 2004.
Record fee received: £25,000,000 from Barcelona for Marc Overmars, July 2000.
Record attendance: At Highbury: 73,295 v Sunderland (Div.1) 9 March, 1935. At Wembley: 73,707 v Lens (Champions League) November 1998.
Capacity for 2006-07: 60,000. **Sponsors:** O2.
League Championship: Winners 1930-31, 1932-33, 1933-34, 1934-35, 1937-38, 1947-48, 1952-53, 1970-71, 1988-89, 1990-91, 1997-98, 2001-02, 2003-04.
F.A. Cup: Winners 1930, 1936, 1950, 1971, 1979, 1993, 1998, 2002, 2003, 2005.
League Cup: Winners 1987, 1993.
European Competitions: Winners Fairs Cup 1969-70, Cup-Winners' Cup 1993-94.
Finishing positions in Premiership: 1992-93 10th, 1993-94 4th, 1994-95 12th, 1995-96 5th, 1996-97 3rd, 1997-98 1st, 1998-99 2nd, 1999-2000 2nd, 2000-01 2nd, 2001-02 1st, 2002-03 2nd, 2003-04 1st, 2004-05 2nd, 2005-6 4th.
Biggest win: 12-0 v Loughborough Town, Div. 2, 12.3.1900.
Biggest defeat: 0-8 v Loughborough Town, Div. 2, 12.12.1896.
Highest League scorer in a season: Ted Drake, 42, 1934-35.
Most League goals in aggregate: Thierry Henry, 164, 1999-2006.
Most capped player: Patrick Vieira (France) 79.
Longest unbeaten League sequence: 49 matches (October 2004).
Longest sequence without a League win: 23 matches (March 1913).

Name	Height ft. in.	Previous club	Birthplace	Birthdate
Goalkeepers				
Almunia, Manuel	6. 3	Celta Vigo	Pamplona	19.05.77
Lehmann, Jens	6. 3	Borussia Dortmund	Essen	11.10.69
Poom, Mart	6. 4	Sunderland	Tallinn	3.02.072
Defenders				
Clichy, Gael	5.11	Cannes	Paris	26.07.85
Cole, Ashley	5. 8	–	Stepney	20.12.80
Connolly, Matthew		–	Barnet	24.09.87
Cygan, Pascal	6. 5	Lille	Lens	29.04.74
Djourou, Johan	6. 3	Etoile Carouge	Ivory Coast	18.01.87
Eboue, Emmanuel	5.10	Beveren	Abidjan, Iv. Coast	4.06.83
Gilbert, Kerrea		–	Hammersmith	28.02.87
Hoyte, Justin	5.11	–	Waltham Forest	20.11.84
Lauren	5.11	Real Mallorca	Londi Kribi, Cam.	19.01.77
Senderos, Philippe	6. 3	Servette	Geneva	14.02.85
Toure, Kolo	5.11	Mimosa	Abidjan, Iv. Coast	19.03.81
Midfielders				
Diaby, Abou	6. 2	Auxerre	Paris	11.05.86
Fabregas, Francesc	5.10	Barcelona	Vilessoc, Sp.	4.05.87
Flamini, Mathieu	5.10	Marseille	Marseilles	7.03.84
Gilberto Silva	6. 3	Atletico Mineiro	Lagoa Prata, Bra.	7.10.76
Hleb, Alexandr	5.10	Stuttgart	Minsk	1.05.81
Larsson, Sebastian	5.10	Eskilstuna	Eskilstuna, Swe.	6.06.85
Ljungberg, Freddie	5.11	Halmstad	Halmstad	16.04.77

Name		Previous club	Birthplace	Birthdate
Muamba, Fabrice	5.11	–	DR Congo	6.04.88
Rosicky, Tomas	5.10	Borussia Dortmund	Prague	4.10.80
Song, Alexandre	6. 1	Bastia	Douala, Cam.	9.09.87
Walcott, Theo	5. 8	Southampton	Middlesex	16.03.89
Forwards				
Adebayor, Emmanuel	6. 3	Monaco	Lome, Togo	26.02.85
Aliadiere, Jeremie	6. 0	–	Rambouillet, Fr.	30.03.83
Bendtner, Nicklas	6. 3	–	Copenhagen	16.01.88
Henry, Thierry	6. 2	Juventus	Paris	17.08.77
Lupoli, Arturo	5. 9	Parma	Brescia	24.06.87
Reyes, Jose Antonio	5. 9	Sevilla	Seville	1.09.83
Stokes, Anthony	5.11	–	Dublin	25.07.88
Van Persie, Robin	6. 0	Feyenoord	Rotterdam	6.08.83

ASTON VILLA

Ground: Villa Park, Trinity Road, Birmingham, B6 6HE.
Telephone: 0871 423 8100. **Club nickname:** Villans.
First-choice colours: Claret and blue shirts; white shorts; blue and claret socks.
Record transfer fee: £9,500,000 to River Plate for Juan Pablo Angel, January 2001.
Record fee received: £12,600,000 for Dwight Yorke from Manchester Utd., August 1998.
Record attendance: 76,588 v Derby Co. (F.A. Cup 6) 2 March, 1946.
Capacity for 2006-07: 42,573. **Sponsors:** 32 Red.com.
League Championship: Winners 1893-94, 1895-96, 1896-97, 1898-99, 1899-1900, 1909-10, 1980-81.
F.A. Cup: Winners 1887, 1895, 1897, 1905, 1913, 1920, 1957.
League Cup: Winners 1961, 1975, 1977, 1994, 1996.
European Competitions: Winners European Cup 1981-82, European Super Cup 1982-83.
Finishing positions in Premiership: 1992-93 2nd, 1993-94 10th, 1994-95 18th, 1995-96 4th, 1996-97 5th, 1997-98 7th, 1998-99 6th, 1999-2000 6th, 2000-01 8th, 2001-02 8th, 2002-03 16th, 2003-04 6th, 2004-05 10th, 2005-06 16th.
Biggest win: 12-2 v Accrington, Div. 1, 12.3.1892; 11-1 v Charlton Athletic, Div. 2, 24.11.1959; 10-0 v Sheffield Wed., Div. 1, 5.10.1912, v Burnley, Div. 1, 29.8.1925.
Biggest defeat: 0-7 in five League matches from Blackburn Rov., Div. 1, 19.10.1889 to Manchester Utd., Div. 1, 24.10.1964.
Highest League scorer in a season: 'Pongo' Waring, 49, 1930-31.
Most League goals in aggregate: Harry Hampton, 215, 1904-1915.
Most capped player: Steve Staunton (Rep. of Ireland) 64.
Longest unbeaten League sequence: 15 matches (January 1897, December 1909 and March 1949).
Longest sequence without a League win: 12 matches (November 1973 and December 1986).

Name	Height ft. in.	Previous club	Birthplace	Birthdate
Goalkeepers				
Sorensen, Thomas	6. 4	Sunderland	Odense	12.06.76
Taylor, Stuart	6. 4	Aston Villa	Romford	28.11.81
Defenders				
Bouma, Wilfred	6. 0	PSV Eindhoven	Helmond, Hol.	15.06.78
Cahill, Gary	6. 2	–	Dronfield	19.12.85
Delaney, Mark	6. 1	Cardiff City	Haverfordwest	13.05.76
Hughes, Aaron	6. 1	Newcastle Utd.	Cookstown	8.11.79
Laursen, Martin	6. 2	AC Milan	Farvoug, Den.	26.07.77
Mellberg, Olof	6. 1	Racing Santander	Stockholm	9.03.77
Ridgwell, Liam	5.10	–	Bexley	21.07.84
Samuel, Jlloyd	5.11	–	Trinidad	24.05.79
Midfielders				
Barry, Gareth	6. 0	–	Hastings	23.02.81

Berger, Patrik	6. 1	Portsmouth	Prague	10.11.73
Davis, Steven	5. 7	–	Ballymena	1.01.85
Djemba-Djemba, Eric	5. 9	Manchester Utd.	Douala, Cam.	4.05.81
Gardner, Craig	5.10	–		25.11.86
Hendrie, Lee	5.10	–	Birmingham	18.05.77
McCann, Gavin	5.11	Sunderland	Blackpool	10.01.78
Whittingham, Peter	5.10	–	Nuneaton	8.09.84
Forwards				
Agbonlahor, Gabriel	5.11	–	–	13.10.86
Angel, Juan Pablo	5.11	River Plate	Medellin, Col.	21.10.75
Baros, Milan	6. 0	Liverpool	Valasske, Cz.	28.10.81
Moore, Luke	5.10	–	Birmingham	13.02.86
Phillips, Kevin	5. 7	Southampton	Hitchin	25.07.73

BLACKBURN ROVERS

Ground: Ewood Park, Blackburn BB2 4JF.
Telephone: 08701 113232. **Club nickname:** Rovers.
First-choice colours: Blue and white shirts; white shorts; white socks.
Record transfer fee: £8,000,000 to Manchester Utd. for Andy Cole, December 2001.
Record fee received: £17,000,000 from Chelsea for Damien Duff, July 2003.
Record attendance: 62,522 v Bolton Wand., (F.A. Cup 6) 2 March, 1929.
Capacity for 2006-07: 31,367. **Sponsors:** Bet24.com.
League Championship: Winners 1911-12, 1913-14, 1994-95.
F.A. Cup: Winners 1884, 1885, 1886, 1890, 1891, 1928.
League Cup: Winners 2002.
European Competitions: Champions League 1st group stage 1995-96.
Finishing positions in Premiership: 1992-93 4th, 1993-94 2nd, 1994-95 1st, 1995-96 7th, 1996-97 13th, 1997-98 6th, 1998-99 19th, 2001-02 10th, 2002-03 6th, 2003-04 15th, 2004-05 15th, 2005-06 6th.
Biggest win: 9-0 v Middlesbrough, Div. 2, 6.11.1954. Also 11-0 v Rossendale, F.A. Cup 1st Rd, 13.10.1884.
Biggest defeat: 0-8 v Arsenal, Div. 1, 25.2.1933.
Highest League scorer in a season: Ted Harper, 43, 1925-26.
Most League goals in aggregate: Simon Garner, 168, 1978-92.
Most capped player: Henning Berg (Norway) 58.
Longest unbeaten League sequence: 23 matches (September 1987).
Longest sequence without a League win: 16 matches (November 1978).

Name	Height ft. in.	Previous club	Birthplace	Birthdate
Goalkeepers				
Brown, Jason	6. 0	Gillingham	Bermondsey	18.05.82
Enckelman, Peter	6. 2	Aston Villa	Turku, Fin.	10.03.77
Friedel, Brad	6. 3	Liverpool	Lakewood, USA	18.05.71
Defenders				
Gray, Michael	5. 7	Sunderland	Sunderland	3.08.74
Khishanishvili, Zurab	6. 1	Rangers	Tblisi	6.10.81
Kane, Tony	5. 8	–	Belfast	29.08.87
Matteo, Dominic	6. 1	Leeds Utd.	Dumfries	24.04.74
McEveley, James	5.10	–	Liverpool	2.11.85
Mokoena, Aaron	6. 1	Genk	Johannesburg	25.11.80
Neill, Lucas	6. 1	Millwall	Sydney	9.03.78
Nelsen, Ryan	6. 0	DC Utd.	Christchurch, NZ	18.10.77
Nolan, Eddie	6. 0	–	Republic of Ireland	5.08.88
Taylor, Andy	5.11	–	Blackburn	14.03.86
Todd, Andy	5.10	Charlton Athletic	Derby	21.09.74
Midfielders				
Bentley, David	5.10	Arsenal	Peterborough	27.08.84
Douglas, Jonathan	5.11	–	Monaghan	22.11.81

	Height			
	ft. in.			
Emerton, Brett	6. 1	Feyenoord	Bankstown, Aus.	22.02.79
Pedersen, Morten Gamst	5.11	Tromso	Vadso, Nor.	8.09.81
Peter, Sergio	5. 8		Ludwigshafen, Ger.	12.10.86
Reid, Steven	6. 1	Millwall	Kingston	10.03.81
Savage, Robbie	5.11	Birmingham City	Wrexham	18.10.74
Tugay, Kerimoglu	5. 9	Rangers	Istanbul	24.08.70
Forwards				
Derbyshire, Matt	5.10	Great Harwood	Blackburn	14.04.86
Gallagher, Paul	6. 0		Blackburn	9.08.84
Jeffers, Francis	5. 9	Charlton Athletic	Liverpool	25.01.81
Johnson, Jemal	6. 0	–	New Jersey	3.05.85
Kuqi, Shefki	6. 2	Ipswich Town	Kosovo	10.11.76
Roberts, Jason	5.11	Wigan Athletic	Park Royal	25.01.78

BOLTON WANDERERS

Ground: Reebok Stadium, Burnden Way, Lostock, Bolton BL6 6JW.
Telephone: 01204 673673. **Club nickname:** Trotters.
First-choice colours: White shirts; white shorts; white socks.
Record transfer fee: £3,500,000 to Wimbledon for Dean Holdsworth, October 1997.
Record fee received: £4,500,000 from Liverpool for Jason McAteer, September 1995.
Record attendance: At Reebok Stadium: 28,353 v Leicester City (Premier League) 28 December, 2003. At Burnden Park: 69,912 v Manchester City, (F.A. Cup 5) 18 February, 1933.
Capacity for 2006-07: 28,101. **Sponsors:** Reebok.
League Championship: 3rd 1891-92, 1920-21, 1924-25.
F.A. Cup: Winners 1923, 1926, 1929, 1958.
League Cup: Runners-up 1995, 2004.
European Competitions: UEFA Cup rd. of 32 2005-06.
Finishing positions in Premiership: 1995-96 20th, 1997-98 18th, 2001-02 16th, 2002-03 17th, 2003-04 8th, 2004-05 6th, 2005-06 8th.
Biggest win: 8-0 v Barnsley, Div. 2, 6.10.1934. Also 13-0 v Sheffield Utd., F.A. Cup 2nd Rd, 1.1.1890.
Biggest defeat: 1-9 v Preston N.E., F.A. Cup 2nd Rd, 10.12.1887.
Highest League scorer in a season: Joe Smith, 38, 1920-21.
Most League goals in aggregate: Nat Lofthouse, 255, 1946-61.
Most capped player: Mark Fish (South Africa) 34.
Longest unbeaten League sequence: 23 matches (October 1990).
Longest sequence without a League win: 26 matches (April 1902).

Name	Height ft. in.	Previous club	Birthplace	Birthdate
Goalkeepers				
Al Habsi, Ali	6. 5	Lyn Oslo	Oman	30.12.81
Ashton, Sam	5.11	–	Bolton	9.10.86
Howarth, Chris	6. 1	–	Bolton	23.05.86
Jaaskelainen, Jussi	6. 4	VPS	Vaasa, Fin	17.04.75
Walker, Ian	6. 2	Leicester City	Watford	31.10.71
Defenders				
Fojut, Jaroslaw	6. 2	Darzboru Szczecinek	Legionowo. Pol	17.10.87
Gardner, Ricardo	5. 9	Harbour View	St Andrews, Jam.	25.09.78
Haim, Tal Ben	5.11	Maccabi Tel Aviv	Rishon Letzion, Isr.	31.03.82
Hunt, Nicky	6. 1	–	Bolton Wand.	3.09.83
Jaidi, Radhi	6. 3	Esperance	Tunis	30.08.75
Meite, Abdoulaye	6. 1	Marseille	Paris	6.10.80
Midfielders				
Campo, Ivan	6. 1	Real Madrid	San Sebastian	21.02.74
Faye, Abdoulaye	6. 3	Lens	Dakar	26.02.78
Giannakopoulos, Stelios	5.10	Olympiakos	Greece	12.07.74
Nolan, Kevin	6. 1	–	Liverpool	24.06.82
O'Brien Joey	6. 2	–	Dublin	17.02.86

Sissons, Robert	5. 8	–	Stockport	29.09.88
Speed, Gary	5.10	Newcastle Utd.	Deeside	8.09.69
Tal, Idan	5.11	Rayo Vallecano	Petah Tikva, Isr.	12.12.75
Forwards				
Borgetti, Jared	6. 2	Pachuca	Mexico	14.08.73
Davies, Kevin	6. 0	Southampton	Sheffield	26.03.77
Diouf, El-Hadji	5.11	Liverpool	Dakar	15.01.81
Pedersen, Henrik	6. 1	Silkeborg	Jutland	10.06.75
Sinclair, James	5. 6	–	Newcastle	22.10.87
Smith, Johann	5.11	–	Harford, USA	25.04.87
Vaz Te, Ricardo	6. 2	Farense	Lisbon	1.10.86

CHARLTON ATHLETIC

Ground: The Valley, Floyd Road, Charlton, London, SE7 8BL.
Telephone: 0208 333 4000. **Club nickname:** Addicks.
First-choice colours: Red shirts; white shorts; red socks.
Record transfer fee: £4,750,000 to Wimbledon for Jason Euell, July 2001.
Record fee received: £10,000,000 from Chelsea for Scott Parker, January 2004.
Record attendance: 75,031 v Aston Villa (F.A. Cup 5) 12 February, 1938.
Capacity for 2006-07: 27,111. **Sponsors:** Llanera.
League Championship: 2nd. 1936-37.
F.A. Cup: Winners 1947.
League Cup: 4th rd 1963, 1966, 1979, 2001.
Finishing positions in Premiership: 1998-99 18th, 2000-01 9th, 2001-02 14th, 2002-03 12th, 2003-04 12th, 2004-05 11th, 2005-06 13th.
Biggest win: 8-1 v Middlesbrough, Div. 1, 12.9.1953.
Biggest defeat: 1-11 v Aston Villa, Div. 2, 14.11.1959.
Highest League scorer in a season: Ralph Allen, 32, Div. 3 (south), 1934-35.
Most League goals in aggregate: Stuart Leary, 153, 1953-62.
Most capped player: Mark Kinsella (Rep. of Ireland) 33.
Longest unbeaten League sequence: 15 matches (December 1980).
Longest sequence without a League win: 16 matches (August 1955).

Name	Height ft. in.	Previous club	Birthplace	Birthdate
Goalkeepers				
Andersen, Stephan	6. 2	AB Copenhagen	Denmark	26.11.81
Myhre, Thomas	6. 4	Sunderland	Sarpsborg,Nor.	16.10.73
Defenders				
Ashton, Nathan	5. 9	–	Stratford	30.01.87
Brandao, Goncalo	6. 0	Belenenses	Lisbon	9.10.88
El Karkouri, Talal	6. 1	Paris St-Germain	Casablanca	8.07.76
Fortune, Jonathan	6. 2	–	Islington	28.08.80
Hreidarsson, Hermann	6. 1	Ipswich Town	Iceland	11.07.74
Kishishev, Radostin	5.11	Liteks Lovech	Burgas, Bul.	30.07.74
Sankofa, Osei	6. 0	–	Streatham	19.03.85
Sorondo, Gonzalo	6. 3	Inter Milan	Montevideo	9.10.79
Youga, Kelly	6. 1	Lyon	Bangui, CAF Rep	22.09.85
Young, Luke	6. 0	Tottenham	Harlow	19.07.79
Midfielders				
Ambrose, Darren	5.11	Newcastle Utd.	Harlow	29.02.84
Gislason, Rurik	5. 9	Anderlecht	Reykjavik	25.02.86
Holland, Matt	5. 9	Ipswich Town	Bury	11.04.74
Hughes, Bryan	5. 9	Birmingham City	Liverpool	19.06.76
Sam, Lloyd	5. 8	–	Leeds	27.09.84
Thomas, Jerome	6. 1	Arsenal	Brent	23.03.83
Walton, Simon	6. 1	Leeds Utd.	Sherburn	13.09.87
Forwards				
Bent, Darren	5.11	Ipswich Town	Wandsworth	6.02.84
Bent, Marcus	6. 2	Everton	Hammersmith	19.05.78

Euell, Jason	5.11	Wimbledon	Lambeth	6.02.77
Hasselbaink, Jimmy-Floyd	6. 2	Middlesbrough	Surinam	27.03.72
Lisbie, Kevin	5.10	–	Hackney	17.10.78
Rommedahl, Dennis	5.10	PSV Eindhoven	Copenhagen	22.07.79

CHELSEA

Ground: Stamford Bridge Stadium, London SW6 1HS.
Telephone: 0870 300 1212. **Club nickname:** Blues.
First-choice colours: Blue shirts; blue shorts; white socks.
Record transfer fee: £30,800,000 to AC Milan for Andriy Shevchenko, May 2006.
Record fee received: £12,000,000 from Rangers for Tore Andre Flo, November 2000.
Record attendance: 82,905 v Arsenal (Div. 1) 12 October, 1935.
Capacity for 2006-07: 42,449. **Sponsors:** Emirates.
League Championship: Winners 1954-55, 2004-05, 2005-06.
F.A. Cup: Winners 1970, 1997, 2000.
League Cup: Winners 1965, 1998, 2005.
European Competitions: Winners Cup-Winners' Cup 1970-71, 1997-98.
Finishing positions in Premiership: 1992-93 11th, 1993-94 14th, 1994-95 11th,
  1995-96 11th, 1996-97 6th, 1997-98 4th, 1998-99 3rd; 1999-2000 5th,
  2000-01 6th, 2001-02 6th, 2002-03 4th, 2003-04 2nd, 2004-05 1st, 2005-06
  1st.
Biggest win: 7-0 in four League matches from Lincoln City, Div. 2, 29.10.1910 to
  Walsall, Div. 2, 4.2.1989. Also 9-2 v Glossop N.E. Div. 2, 1.9.1906. Europe: 13-0 v
  Jeunesse Hautcharage, Cup-Winners' Cup 1st rd, 29.9.1971.
Biggest defeat: 1-8 v Wolves, Div. 1, 26.9.1923. Also 0-7 v Leeds Utd., Div. 1,
  7.10.1967 and v Nott'm. Forest Div. 1, 20.4.1991.
Highest League scorer in a season: Jimmy Greaves, 41, 1960-61.
Most League goals in aggregate: Bobby Tambling, 164, 1958-70.
Most capped player: Marcel Desailly (France) 67.
Longest unbeaten League sequence: 27 matches (October 1988).
Longest sequence without a League win: 21 matches (November 1987).

Name	Height ft. in.	Previous club	Birthplace	Birthdate
Goalkeepers				
Cech, Petr	6. 5	Rennes	Plzen, Cz.	20.05.82
Cudicini, Carlo	6. 1	Castel di Sangro	Milan	6.09.73
Defenders				
Bridge, Wayne	5.10	Southampton	Southampton	5.08.80
Carvalho, Ricardo	6. 0	FC Porto	Amarante, Por.	18.05.78
Del Horno, Asier	5. 9	Athletic Bilbao	Barakaldo, Sp.	19.01.81
Ferreira, Paulo	6. 0	FC Porto	Lisbon	18.01.79
Gallas, William	6. 1	Marseille	Asnieres, Fr.	17.08.77
Huth, Robert	6. 2	–	Berlin	18.08.84
Johnson, Glen	6. 0	West Ham Utd.	Greenwich	23.08.84
Terry, John	6. 1	–	Barking	7.12.80
Midfielders				
Ballack, Michael	6. 2	Bayern Munich	Gorlitz, Ger.	26.09.76
Cole, Joe	5. 9	West Ham Utd.	Islington	8.11.81
Diarra, Lassana	5. 8	Le Havre	Paris	10.03.85
Duff, Damien	5.10	Blackburn Rov.	Dublin	2.03.79
Essien, Michael	6. 0	Lyon	Accra	3.12.82
Geremi	5.11	Real Madrid	Batousam, Cam.	20.12.78
Lampard, Frank	6. 0	West Ham Utd.	Romford	20.06.78
Makelele, Claude	5. 7	Real Madrid	Kinshasa	18.02.73
Mikel, John Obi	6. 2	Lyn Oslo	Plato State, Nig.	22.04.87
Robben, Arjen	5.11	PSV Eindhoven	Bedum, Hol.	23.01.84
Wright-Phillips, Shaun	5. 6	Manchester City	Greenwich	25.10.81
Forwards				
Crespo, Hernan	6. 1	Inter Milan	Florida, Arg.	5.07.75

Drogba, Didier	6. 2	Marseille	Abidjan, Iv. Coast	11.03.78
Kalou, Salomon	5.10	Feyenoord	Oume, Iv. Coast	5.08.85
Shevchenko, Andriy	6. 0	AC Milan	Dvirkivshchyna, Ukr.	29.09.76

EVERTON

Ground: Goodison Park, Liverpool L4 4EL.
Telephone: 0870 442 1878. **Club nickname:** Toffees.
First-choice colours: Royal blue shirts; white shorts; white socks.
Record transfer fee: £6,000,000 to Southampton for James Beattie, January 2005.
Record fee received: £27,000,000 from Manchester Utd. for Wayne Rooney, August 2004.
Record attendance: 78,299 v Liverpool (Div. 1) 18 September, 1948.
Capacity for 2006-07: 40,565. **Sponsors:** Chang.
League Championship: Winners 1890-91, 1914-15, 1927-28, 1931-31, 1938-39, 1962-63, 1969-70, 1984-85, 1986-87.
F.A. Cup: Winners 1906, 1933, 1966, 1984, 1995.
League Cup: Runners up 1977, 1984.
European Competitions: Winners Cup-Winners' Cup 1984-85.
Finishing positions in Premiership: 1992-93 13th, 1993-94 17th, 1994-95 15th 1995-96 6th 1996-97 15th 1997-98 17th 1998-99 14th, 1999-2000 13th, 2000-01 16th, 2001-02 15th, 2002-03 7th, 2003-04 17th, 2004-05 4th, 2005-06 11th.
Biggest win: 9-1 v Manchester City, Div. 1, 3.9.1906, v Plymouth Argyle, Div. 2, 27.12.1930. Also 11-2 v Derby Co., F.A. Cup 1st rd, 18.1.1890.
Biggest defeat: 0-7 v Portsmouth, Div. 1, 10.9.1949 and v Arsenal, Prem., 11.5.2005.
Highest League scorer in a season: Ralph 'Dixie' Dean, 60, 1927-28.
Most League goals in aggregate: Ralph 'Dixie' Dean, 349, 1925-37.
Most capped player: Neville Southall (Wales) 92.
Longest unbeaten League sequence: 20 matches (April 1978).
Longest sequence without a League win: 14 matches (March 1937).

Name	Height ft. in.	Previous club	Birthplace	Birthdate
Goalkeepers				
Ruddy, John	6. 4	Cambridge Utd.	St Ives, Cambs.	24.10.86
Turner, Iain	6. 4	Stirling Albion	Stirling	26.01.84
Wright, Richard	6. 2	Arsenal	Ipswich	5.11.77
Defenders				
Boyle, Patrick	5.10	–	Glasgow	20.03.87
Hibbert, Tony	5.10	–	Liverpool	20.02.81
Hughes, Mark	6. 1	–	Kirby	9.12.86
Lescott, Joleon	6. 2	Wolves	Birmingham	16.08.82
Naysmith, Gary	5.11	Hearts	Edinburgh	16.11.78
Pistone, Alessandro	5.11	Newcastle Utd.	Milan	27.07.75
Stubbs, Alan	6. 2	Sunderland	Liverpool	6.10.71
Valente, Nuno	6. 0	FC Porto	Lisbon	12.09.74
Weir, David	6. 2	Hearts	Falkirk	10.05.70
Yobo, Joseph	6. 2	Marseille	Kano, Nig.	6.09.80
Midfielders				
Arteta, Mikel	5. 9	Real Sociedad	San Sebastian	28.03.82
Cahill, Tim	5.10	Millwall	Sydney	6.12.79
Carsley, Lee	5. 9	Coventry City	Birmingham	28.02.74
Davies, Simon	5.11	Tottenham	Haverfordwest	23.10.79
Kilbane, Kevin	6. 0	Sunderland	Preston	1.02.77
Neville, Phil	5.11	Manchester Utd.	Bury	21.01.77
Osman, Leon	5. 8	–	Billinge	17.05.81
Van der Meyde, Andy	5.10	Inter Milan	Arnhem	30.09.79
Vidarsson, Bjarni	6. 1	–	Iceland	5.03.88
Forwards				
Anichebe, Victor	6. 1	–	Lagos	23.04.88

Beattie, James	6. 1	Southampton	Lancaster	27.02.78
Johnson, Andy	5. 9	Crystal Palace	Bedford	10.02.81
McFadden, James	5.10	Motherwell	Glasgow	14.04.83
Vaughan, James	5.11	–	Birmingham	14.07.88

FULHAM

Ground: Craven Cottage, Stevenage Road, London SW6 6HH.
Telephone: 0870 442 1222. **Club nickname:** Cottagers.
First-choice colours: White shirts; black shorts; white socks.
Record transfer fee: £11,500,000 to Lyon for Steve Marlet, August 2001.
Record fee received: £12,825,000 from Manchester Utd. for Louis Saha, January 2004.
Record attendance: 49,335 v Millwall (Div. 2) 8 October, 1938.
Capacity for 2006-07: 22,000. **Sponsors:** Pipex.
League Championship: 9th 2003-04.
F.A. Cup: Runners-up 1975.
League Cup: 5th rd. 1968, 1971, 2000.
Finishing positions in Premiership: 2001-02 13th, 2002-03 14th, 2003-04 9th, 2004-05 13th, 2005-06 12th.
Biggest win: 10-1 v Ipswich Town, Div. 1, 26.12.1963.
Biggest defeat: 0-10 v Liverpool, League Cup 2nd Rd 1st leg, 23.9.1986.
Highest League scorer in a season: Frank Newton, 43, 1931-32.
Most League goals in aggregate: Gordon Davies, 159, 1978-84 and 1986-91.
Most capped player: Johnny Haynes (England) 56.
Longest unbeaten League sequence: 15 matches (January 1999).
Longest sequence without a League win: 15 matches (February 1950).

Name	Height ft. in.	Previous club	Birthplace	Birthdate
Goalkeepers				
Batista, Ricardo	6. 3	Vitoria Setubal	Portugal	19.11.86
Crossley, Mark	6. 0	Middlesbrough	Barnsley	16.06.69
Drobny, Jaroslav	6. 4	Panionios	Pocatky. Czech	18.10.79
Niemi, Antti	6. 1	Southampton	Oulu, Fin.	31.05.72
Warner, Tony	6. 4	Millwall	Liverpool	11.05.74
Defenders				
Bocanegra, Carlos	6. 0	Chicago Fire	Alta Loma, USA	25.05.79
Christanval, Philippe	6. 1	Marseille	Paris	31.08.78
Collins, Matty		Swindon Town	Merthyr Tydfil	31.03.86
Elliott, Simon	6. 0	Columbus Crew	Wellington, NZ	10.06.74
James, Chris	5. 8	–	New Zealand	4.08.87
Jensen, Niclas	6. 0	FC Copenhagen	Copenhagen	17.08.74
Knight, Zat	6. 6	–	Solihull	2.05.80
Pearce, Ian	6. 3	West Ham Utd.	Bury St Edmunds	7.05.74
Rosenior, Leroy	5. 9	Bristol City	Wandsworth	9.07.84
Volz, Moritz	5.11	Arsenal	Siegen, Ger.	21.01.83
Zakuani, Gabriel	6. 1	Leyton Orient	Congo	31.05.86
Midfielders				
Bullard, Jimmy	5.10	Wigan Athletic	Newham	23.10.78
Brown, Michael	5. 9	Tottenham	Hartlepool	25.01.77
Diop, Papa Bouba	6. 4	Lens	Dakar	28.01.78
Elrich, Ahmad	5.11	Buscan Icons	Sydney	30.05.81
Jensen, Claus	5.11	Charlton Athletic	Nykobing, Den.	29.04.77
Legwinski, Sylvain	6. 1	Bordeaux	Clermont-Ferrand	10.06.73
Malbranque, Steed	5. 8	Lyon	Mouscron, Bel.	6.01.80
McKinlay, Billy	5. 8	Leicester City	Glasgow	22.04.69
Pembridge, Mark	5. 8	Everton	Merthyr Tydfil	29.11.70
Timlin, Michael	5. 9	–	Lambeth	19.03.85
Forwards				
Boa Morte, Luis	5. 9	Southampton	Lisbon	4.08.77
Ehui, Ismael	5. 7	–	Lille	10.12.86

Helguson, Heidar	6.0	Watford	Akureyri, Ice.	22.08.77
John, Collins	6.0	FC Twente	Zwandru, Liber.	7.10.85
McBride, Brian	6.1	Columbus	Arlington Hgts, USA	19.06.72
Radzinski, Tomasz	5.9	Everton	Poznan, Pol.	14.12.73

LIVERPOOL

Ground: Anfield Road, Liverpool L4 OTH.
Telephone: 0151 263 2361. **Club nickname:** Reds or Pool.
First-choice colours: Red shirts; red shorts; red socks.
Record transfer fee: £14,000,000 to Auxerre for Djibril Cisse, July 2004.
Record fee received: £11,000,000 from Leeds Utd. for Robbie Fowler, November 2001.
Record attendance: 61,905 v Wolves, (F.A. Cup 4), 2 February, 1952.
Capacity for 2006-07: 45,360. **Sponsors:** Carlsberg.
League Championship: Winners 1900-01, 1905-06, 1921-22, 1922-23, 1946-47, 1963-64, 1965-66, 1972-73, 1975-76, 1976-77, 1978-79, 1979-80, 1981-82, 1982-83, 1983-84, 1985-86, 1987-88, 1989-90.
F.A. Cup: Winners 1965, 1974, 1986, 1989, 1992, 2001, 2006.
League Cup: Winners 1981, 1982, 1983, 1984, 1995, 2001, 2003.
European Competitions: Winners European Cup 1976-77, 1977-78, 1980-81, 1983-84, 2004-05; UEFA Cup 1972-73, 1975-76, 2000-01; European Super Cup 1977, 2005.
Finishing positions in Premiership: 1992-93 6th, 1993-94 8th, 1994-95 4th, 1995-96 3rd, 1996-97 4th, 1997-98 3rd, 1998-99 7th, 1999-2000 4th, 2000-01 3rd, 2001-02 2nd, 2002-03 5th, 2003-04 4th, 2004-05 5th, 2005-06 3rd.
Biggest win: 10-1 v Rotherham Utd., Div. 2, 18.2.1896. Europe: 11-0 v Stromsgodset, CWC, 17.9.1974.
Biggest defeat: 1-9 v Birmingham City, Div. 2, 11.12.1954.
Highest League scorer in a season: Roger Hunt, 41, 1961-62.
Most League goals in aggregate: Roger Hunt, 245, 1959-69.
Most capped player: Ian Rush (Wales) 67.
Longest unbeaten League sequence: 31 matches (May 1987).
Longest sequence without a League win: 14 (December 1953).

Name	Height ft. in.	Previous club	Birthplace	Birthdate
Goalkeepers				
Carson, Scott	6. 3	Leeds Utd.	Whitehaven	3.09.85
Dudek, Jerzy	6. 1	Feyenoord	Rybnik, Pol.	23.03.73
Kirkland, Chris	6. 3	Coventry City	Leicester	2.05.81
Martin, David	6. 1	MK Dons	Romford	22.01.86
Reina, Jose	6. 2	Villarreal	Madrid	31.08.82
Defenders				
Agger, Daniel	6. 3	Brondby	Denmark	12.12.84
Aurelio, Fabio	5.10	Valencia	Brazil	24.09.79
Barragan, Antonio	6. 0	Sevilla	Seville	12.06.87
Finnan, Steve	5.10	Fulham	Limerick	20.04.76
Carragher, Jamie	6. 1	–	Liverpool	28.01.78
Hyypia, Sami	6. 4	Willem II	Porvoo, Fin.	7.10.73
Hobbs, Jack	5.11	Lincoln City	Portsmouth	18.08.88
Kronkamp, Jan	6. 2	Villarreal	Makkinga, Hol.	17.08.80
Medjani,Carl	6. 0	St Etienne	France	15.05.85
Paletta, Gabriel	6. 1	Banfield	Argentina	15.02.86
Traore, Djimi	6. 1	Laval	Saint-Ouen, Fr.	1.03.80
Midfielders				
Alonso, Xabi	6. 0	Real Sociedad	Tolosa, Spa.	25.11.81
Anderson, Paul	5. 9	Hull City	Leicester	23.07.88
Diao, Salif	6. 1	Sedan	Kedougou, Sen.	10.02.77
Garcia, Luis	5. 6	Barcelona	Barcelona	24.06.78
Gerrard, Steven	6. 1	–	Whiston	30.05.80
Hammill, Adam	5. 9	–	Liverpool	25.01.88

Kewell, Harry	6. 0	Leeds Utd.	Sydney	22.09.78
Le Tallec, Anthony	6. 0	Le Havre	Hennebont, Fr.	3.10.84
Potter, Darren	5. 10	–	Liverpool	21.12.84
Riise, John Arne	6. 1	Monaco	Molde, Nor.	24.09.80
Sissoko, Mohamed	6. 2	Valencia	Mont St Agnain, Fr.	22.01.85
Warnock, Stephen	5. 10	–	Ormskirk	12.12.81
Zenden, Boudewijn	5. 10	Middlesbrough	Maastricht	15.08.76
Forwards				
Bellamy, Craig	5.9	Blackburn Rov.	Cardiff	13.07.79
Cisse, Djibril	6. 0	Auxerre	Arles, Fra.	12.08.81
Crouch, Peter	6. 7	Southampton	Macclesfield	30.01.81
Fowler, Robbie	5. 11	Manchester City	Liverpool	9.04.75
Gonzalez, Mark	5. 9	Albacete	Durban	10.07.84
Mellor, Neil	6. 0	–	Liverpool	4.11.82
Sinama Pongolle, Florent	5. 10	Le Havre	Saint Pierre	20.10.84

MANCHESTER CITY

Ground: City of Manchester Stadium, Sportcity, Manchester M11 3FF.
Telephone: 0870 062 1894. **Club nickname:** City.
First-choice colours: Sky blue and white shirts; sky blue shorts; sky blue socks.
Record transfer fee: £10,000,000 to Paris St Germain for Nicolas Anelka, June 2002.
Record fee received: £21,000,000 from Chelsea for Shaun Wright-Phillips, July 2005.
Record attendance: At City of Manchester Stadium: 47,304 v Chelsea (Premier League) 28 February, 2004. At Maine Road: 84,569 v Stoke City (F.A. Cup 6) 3 March, 1934 (British record for any game outside London or Glasgow).
Capacity for 2006-07: 47,500. **Sponsors:** Thomas Cook.
League Championship: Winners 1936-37, 1967-68.
F.A. Cup: Winners 1904, 1934, 1956, 1969.
League Cup: Winners 1970, 1976.
European Competitions: Winners Cup-Winners' Cup 1969-70.
Finishing positions in Premiership: 1992-93 9th, 1993-94 16th, 1994-95 17th, 1995-96 18th, 2000-01: 18th, 2002-03 9th, 2003-04 16th, 2004-05 8th, 2005-06 15th.
Biggest win: 10-1 Huddersfield Town, Div. 2, 7.11.1987. Also 10-1 v Swindon Town, F.A. Cup 4th rd. 29.1.1930.
Biggest defeat: 1-9 v Everton, Div. 1, 3,9,1906.
Highest League scorer in a season: Tommy Johnson, 38, 1928-29.
Most League goals in aggregate: Tommy Johnson, 158, 1919-30.
Most capped player: Colin Bell (England) 48.
Longest unbeaten League sequence: 22 matches (April 1947).
Longest sequence without a League win: 17 matches (April 1980).

Name	Height ft. in.	Previous club	Birthplace	Birthdate
Goalkeepers				
Hart, Joe	6. 3	Shrewsbury Town	Shrewsbury	19.04.87
James, David	6. 5	West Ham Utd.	Welwyn Garden City	1.08.70
Schmeichel, Kasper	6. 0	–	Denmark	5.11.86
Weaver, Nicky	6. 3	Mansfield Town	Sheffield	2.03.79
Defenders				
Distin, Sylvain	6. 4	Paris St-Germain	France	6.12.77
Dunne, Richard	6. 2	Everton	Dublin	21.09.79
Jordan, Stephen	6. 1	–	Warrington	6.03.82
Mills, Danny	6. 0	Leeds Utd.	Norwich	18.05.77
Mills, Matthew	6. 3	Southampton	Swindon	14.07.86
Onuoha, Nedum	6. 2	–	Nigeria	12.11.86
Richards, Micah	5.11	–	Birmingham	24.06.88
Sun Jihai	5.10	Dalian Wanda	Dalian, Chi.	30.09.77
Thatcher, Ben	5.10	Leicester City	Swindon	30.11.75

Midfielders

Name	Height ft. in.	Previous club	Birthplace	Birthdate
Barton, Joey	5. 9	–	Huyton	2.09.82
Croft, Lee	5. 9	–	Wigan	21.06.85
Dabo, Ousmane	6. 1	Lazio	France	8.02.77
Flood, Willo	5. 6	–	Dublin	10.04.85
Hamann, Dietmar	6. 3	Bolton Wand.	Waldsasson, Ger.	27.08.73
Ireland, Stephen	5. 8	–	Cork	22.08.86
Reyna, Claudio	5. 9	Sunderland	New Jersey	20.07.73
Sibierski, Antoine	6. 2	Lens	Lille	5.08.74
Sinclair, Trevor	5.10	West Ham Utd.	Dulwich	2.03.73

Forwards

Name	Height ft. in.	Previous club	Birthplace	Birthdate
Cole, Andrew	5.11	Fulham	Nottingham	15.10.71
Dickov, Paul	5. 6	Blackburn Rov.	Livingston	1.11.72
Miller, Ishmael	6. 3	–	Manchester	5.03.87
Samaras, Georgios	6. 4	Heerenveen	Heraklion, Gre.	21.02.85
Vassell, Darius	5. 7	Aston Villa	Birmingham	13.06.80

MANCHESTER UNITED

Ground: Old Trafford Stadium, Sir Matt Busby Way, Manchester, M16 0RA.
Telephone: 0161 868 8000. **Club nickname:** Red Devils.
First-choice colours: Red shirts; white shorts; black socks.
Record transfer fee: £28,250,000 to Leeds Utd. for Rio Ferdinand, July 2002.
Record fee received: £25,000,000 from Real Madrid for David Beckham, July 2003.
Record attendance: Club: 73,006 v Charlton Athletic (Premier League), 7 May, 2006, F.A. Cup (semi-final): 76,962, Wolves v Grimsby Town, 25 March, 1939. Note: 83,260 saw Manchester Utd. v Arsenal, Div. 1, 17 January, 1948 at Maine Road. Old Trafford was out of action through bomb damage.
Capacity for 2006-07: 76,000. **Sponsors:** AIG.
League Championship: Winners 1907-08, 1910-11, 1951-52, 1955-56, 1956-7, 1964-65, 1966-67, 1992-93, 1993-94, 1995-96, 1996-97, 1998-99, 1999-2000, 2000-01, 2002-03.
F.A. Cup: Winners 1909, 1948, 1963, 1977, 1983, 1985, 1990, 1994, 1996, 1999, 2004.
League Cup: Winners 1992, 2006.
European Competitions: Winners European Cup 1967-68, 1998-99; Cup-Winners' Cup 1990-91; European Super Cup 1991.
Finishing positions in Premiership: 1992-93 1st, 1993-94 1st, 1994-95 2nd, 1995-96 1st, 1996-97 1st, 1997-98 2nd, 1998-99 1st, 1999-2000 1st, 2000-01 1st, 2001-02 3rd, 2002-03 1st, 2003-04 3rd, 2004-05 3rd, 2005-06 2nd.
Biggest win: (while Newton Heath) 10-1 v Wolves, Div.1, 15.10.1892, (as Manchester Utd.) 9-0 v Ipswich Town, Premier League, 4.3.1995. Europe: 10-0 v Anderlecht, European Cup prelim. round, 26.9.1956.
Biggest defeat: 0-7 v Wolves Div 2, 26.12.1931, v Aston Villa, Div. 1, 27.12.1930 and v Blackburn Rov. Div. 1, 10.4.1926.
Highest League scorer in a season: Dennis Viollet, 32, 1959-60.
Most League goals in aggregate: Bobby Charlton, 199, 1956-73.
Most capped player: Bobby Charlton (England) 106.
Longest unbeaten League sequence: 26 matches (February 1956).
Longest sequence without a League win: 16 matches (November 1928 and April 1930).

Name	Height ft. in.	Previous club	Birthplace	Birthdate
Goalkeepers				
Foster, Ben	6. 2	Stoke City	Leamington Sp.	3.04.83
Howard, Tim	6. 3	NY MetroStars	New Jersey	3.06.79
Van der Sar, Edwin	6. 6	Fulham	Voorhout, Hol.	29.10.70
Defenders				
Bardsley, Phillip	5.10	–	Salford	28.06.85
Brown, Wes	6. 1	–	Manchester	13.10.79
Eckersley, Adam		–	Manchester	7.09.85

Evra, Patrice	5. 8	Monaco	Dakar	15.05.81
Ferdinand, Rio	6. 2	Leeds Utd.	Peckham	8.11.78
Heinze, Gabriel	5.11	Paris SG	Crespo, Arg.	19.04.78
McShane, Paul	5.11	–	Wicklow	6.01.86
Neville, Gary	5.11	–	Bury	18.02.75
O'Shea, John	6. 3	Waterford	Waterford	30.04.81
Pique, Gerard	6. 2	Barcelona	Barcelona	2.02.87
Silvestre, Mikael	6. 0	Inter Milan	Chambray, Fr.	9.08.77
Vidic, Nemanja	6. 3	Spartak Moscow	Serbia	21.10.81
Midfielders				
Eagles, Chris	5.11	–	Hemel Hempstead	19.11.85
Fletcher, Darren	6. 0	–	Edinburgh	1.02.84
Gibson, Darron	5.10	–	Derry	25.10.87
Giggs, Ryan	5.11	–	Cardiff	29.11.73
Ji-Sung Park	5. 9	PSV Eindhoven	Seoul	25.02.81
Jones, David	5.10	–	Southport	4.11.84
Miller, Liam	5. 7	Celtic	Cork	13.02.81
Richardson, Kieran	5.10	–	Greenwich	21.10.84
Ronaldo, Cristiano	6. 1	Sporting Lisbon	Madeira	5.02.85
Rossi, Giuseppe	5. 9	Parma	New Jersey	1.02.87
Scholes, Paul	5. 7	–	Salford	16.11.74
Forwards				
Campbell, Fraizer	5. 9	–	Huddersfield	13.09.87
Rooney, Wayne	5.10	Everton	Liverpool	24.10.85
Saha, Louis	5.11	Fulham	Paris	8.08.78
Smith, Alan	5. 9	Leeds Utd.	Leeds Utd.	28.10.80
Solskjaer, Ole Gunnar	5.10	Molde	Kristiansund, Nor.	26.02.73
Van Nistelrooy, Ruud	6. 2	PSV Eindhoven	Oss, Hol.	1.07.76

MIDDLESBROUGH

Ground: Cellnet Riverside Stadium, Middlesbrough, TS3 6RS.
Telephone: 0870 421 1986. **Club nickname:** Boro.
First-choice colours: Red and white shirts; red shorts; red socks.
Record transfer fee: £8,150,000 to Empoli for Massimo Maccarone, July 2002.
Record fee received: £12,000,000 from Atletico Madrid for Juninho, July 1997.
Record attendance: At Riverside Stadium: 34,836 v Norwich City (Premier League) 28 December, 2004. 35,000 England v Slovakia 11 June, 2003. At Ayresome Park: 53,596 v Newcastle Utd. (Div.1) 27 December, 1949.
Capacity for 2006-07: 35,120. **Sponsors:** 888.com.
League Championship: 3rd 1913-14.
F.A. Cup: Runners-up 1997.
League Cup: Winners 2004.
European Competitions: UEFA Cup Final 2005-06.
Finishing positions in Premiership: 1992-93 21th 1995-96 12th, 1996-97 19th 1998-99 9th, 1999-2000 12th, 2000-01 14th, 2001-02 12th, 2002-03 11th, 2003-04 11th, 2004-05 7th, 2005-06 14th.
Biggest win: 9-0 v Brighton & H.A., Div 2, 23.8.1958.
Biggest defeat: 0-9 v Blackburn Rov., Div 2, 6.11.1954.
Highest League scorer in a season: George Camsell, 59, 1926-27.
Most League goals in aggregate: George Camsell, 326, 1925-39.
Most capped player: Wilf Mannion (England) 26.
Longest unbeaten League sequence: 24 matches (September 1973).
Longest sequence without a League win: 19 matches (October 1981).

Name	Height ft. in.	Previous club	Birthplace	Birthdate
Goalkeepers				
Jones, Bradley	6.3	–	Armadale, Aus.	19.03.82
Knight, David	6.0	–	Houghton	15.01.87
Schwarzer, Mark	6.4	Bradford City	Sydney	6.10.72

Turnbull, Ross	6. 1	–	Bishop Auckland	4.01.85
Defenders				
Bates, Matthew	5.10	–	Stockton	10.12.86
Cooper, Colin	5.11	Nott'm. Forest	Sedgefield	28.02.67
Davies, Andrew	5.11	–	Stockton	17.12.84
Ehiogu, Ugo	6. 2	Aston Villa	Hackney	3.11.72
Hines, Seb	6. 2	–		29.05.88
McMahon, Tony	5.10	–	Bishop Auckland	24.03.86
Parnaby, Stuart	5.11	–	Durham	19.07.82
Pogatetz, Emanuel	6. 4	Bayer Leverkusen	Steinbock, Aut.	16.01.83
Queudrue, Franck	5.10	Lens	Paris	27.08.78
Riggott, Chris	6. 2	Derby Co.	Derby	1.09.80
Taylor, Andrew	5.10	–	Hartlepool	1.08.86
Wheater, David	6. 4	–	Redcar	14.02.87
Midfielders				
Boateng, George	5. 9	Aston Villa	Nkawka, Gh.	5.09.75
Cattermole, Lee	5.10	–	Stockton	21.03.88
Downing, Stewart	6. 0	–	Middlesbrough	22.07.84
Johnson, Adam	5. 9	–	Sunderland	14.07.87
Kennedy, Jason	6. 1	–	Stockton	11.09.86
Liddle, Gary	6. 1	–	Middlesbrough	15.06.86
Mendieta, Gaizka	5. 8	Lazio	Bilbao	27.03.74
Morrison, James	5.10	–	Darlington	25.05.86
Parlour, Ray	5.10	Arsenal	Romford	7.03.73
Rochemback, Fabio	6. 1	Barcelona	Soledade, Br.	10.12.81
Walker, Josh	5.11	–	Newcastle	21.02.89
Forwards				
Christie, Malcolm	6. 0	Derby Co.	Peterborough	11.04.79
Graham, Danny	5.11	–	Gateshead	12.08.85
Job, Joseph-Desire	5.11	Lens	Venissieux, Fr.	1.12.77
Maccarone, Massimo	5.11	Empoli	Galliate, It.	6.09.79
Viduka, Mark	6. 2	Leeds Utd.	Melbourne	9.10.75
Yakubu, Aiyegbeni	6. 0	Portsmouth	Benin, Nig.	22.11.82

NEWCASTLE UNITED

Ground: St James' Park, Newcastle-upon-Tyne, NE1 4ST.
Telephone: 0191 201 8400. **Club nickname:** Magpies.
First-choice colours: Black and white shirts; black shorts; black socks.
Record transfer fee: £16,500,000 to Real Madrid for Michael Owen, August 2005.
Record fee received: £13,400,000 from Real Madrid for Jonathan Woodgate, August 2004.
Record attendance: 68,386 v Chelsea (Div. 1) 3 September, 1930.
Capacity for 2006-07: 52,387. **Sponsors:** Northern Rock.
League Championship: Winners 1904-05, 1906-07, 1908-09, 1926-27.
F.A. Cup: Winners 1910, 1924, 1932, 1951, 1952, 1955.
League Cup: Runners-up 1976.
European Competitions: Winners Fairs Cup 1968-69, Anglo-Italian Cup 1972-73.
Finishing positions in Premiership: 1993-94 3rd 1994-95 6th 1995-96 2nd 1996-97 2nd 1997-98 13th 1998-99 13th, 1999-2000 11th, 2000-01 11th, 2001-02 4th, 2002-03 3rd, 2003-04 5th, 2004-05 14th, 2005-06 7th.
Biggest win: 13-0 v Newport County, Div. 2, 5.10.1946.
Biggest defeat: 0-9 v Burton Wanderers, Div. 2, 15.4.1895.
Highest League scorer in a season: Hughie Gallacher, 36, 1926-27.
Most League goals in aggregate: Jackie Milburn, 177, 1946-57.
Most capped player: Shay Given (Rep. of Ireland) 67.
Longest unbeaten League sequence: 14 matches (April 1950).
Longest sequence without a League win: 21 matches (January 1978).

Name	Height ft. in.	Previous club	Birthplace	Birthdate
Goalkeepers				
Given, Shay	6. 1	Blackburn Rov.	Lifford	20.04.76
Harper, Steve	6. 2	–	Easington	14.03.75
Defenders				
Babayaro, Celestine	5. 9	Newcastle Utd.	Kaduna, Nig.	29.08.78
Boumsong, Jean-Alain	6. 3	Rangers	Douala, Cam.	14.12.79
Bramble, Titus	6. 1	Ipswich Town	Ipswich	31.07.81
Carr, Stephen	5. 8	Tottenham	Dublin	29.08.76
Elliott, Robbie	5.10	Bolton Wand.	Newcastle	25.12.73
Huntington, Paul	6. 3	–	Carlisle	17.09.87
Gate, Kris	5. 7	–	Newcastle	1.01.85
Moore, Craig	6. 1	Rangers	Canterbury, Aus.	12.12.75
Ramage, Peter	6. 1	–	Newcastle	22.11.83
Taylor, Steven	6. 2	–	Greenwich	23.01.86
Midfielders				
Brittain, Martin	5. 8	–	Newcastle	29.12.84
Butt, Nicky	5.10	Manchester Utd.	Manchester	21.01.75
Clark, Lee	5. 8	Fulham	Wallsend	27.10.72
Dyer, Kieron	5. 7	Ipswich Town	Ipswich	29.12.78
Emre	5.10	Inter Milan	Istanbul	7.09.80
Faye, Amdy	6. 0	Portsmouth	Dakar	12.03.77
Milner, James	5.11	Leeds Utd.	Leeds	4.01.86
N'Zogbia, Charles	5. 7	–	France	28.05.86
O'Brien, Alan	5.10	–	Republic of Ireland	20.02.85
Parker, Scott	5. 7	Chelsea	Lambeth	13.10.80
Pattison, Matthew	5. 8	–	Johannesburg	27.10.86
Solano, Nolberto	5. 8	Aston Villa	Lima	12.12.74
Forwards				
Ameobi, Shola	6. 3	–	Zaria, Nig.	12.10.81
Luque, Albert	6. 0	Deportivo Coruna	Barcelona	11.03.78
Owen, Michael	5. 8	Real Madrid	Chester	14.12.79
Smylie, Daryl		–	Portadown	10.09.85

PORTSMOUTH

Ground: Fratton Park, Frogmore Road, Portsmouth, PO4 8RA.
Telephone: 0239 273 1204. **Club nickname:** Pompey.
First choice colours: Royal blue shirts; white shorts; red socks.
Record transfer fee: £4,100,000 to Auxerre for Benjani Mwaruwari, January 2006.
Record fee received: £7,500,000 from Middlesbrough for Aiyegbeni Yakubu, June 2005.
Record attendance: 51,385 v Derby Co. (F.A. Cup 6) 26 February, 1949.
Capacity for 2006-07: 20,388. **Sponsors:** OKI Printing Solutions.
League Championships: winners 1948-49, 1949-50.
FA Cup: Winners 1939.
League Cup: 5th rd. 1961, 1986.
Finishing positions in Premiership: 2003-04 13th, 2004-05 16th, 2005-06 17th.
Biggest win: 9-1 v Notts Co., Div. 1, 09.04.1927.
Biggest defeat: 0-10 v Leicester City, Div. 1, 20.10.1928.
Highest League scorer in a season: Guy Whittingham, 42, Div. 1, 1992-93.
Most League goals in aggregate: Peter Harris, 194, 1946-60.
Most capped player: Jimmy Dickinson (England) 48.
Longest unbeaten League sequence: 15 matches (October 1924).
Longest sequence without a League win: 25 matches (August 1959).

Name	Height ft. in.	Previous club	Birthplace	Birthdate
Goalkeepers				
Ashdown, Jamie	6.3	Reading	Reading	30.11.80

Kiely, Dean	6. 0	Charlton Athletic	Salford	10.10.70
Defenders				
Duffy, Richard	5.10	Swansea City	Swansea	30.08.85
Griffin, Andy	5. 9	Newcastle Utd.	Billinge	7.03.79
O'Brien, Andy	5.10	Newcastle Utd.	Harrogate	29.06.79
Pamarot, Noe	6. 2	Tottenham	Paris	14.04.79
Pearce, Jason	5.10	–		6.12.87
Primus, Linvoy	5.11	Reading	Forest Gate	14.07.73
Priske, Brian	6. 3	Genk	Horsens, Bel.	14.05.77
Stefanovic, Dejan	5.11	Vitesse Arnhem	Belgrade	28.10.74
Taylor, Matthew	5.11	Luton Town	Oxford	27.11.81
Midfielders				
Davis, Sean	5.11	Tottenham	Clapham	20.09.79
Harris, Scott	5.10	–	Worthing	24.07.85
Hughes, Richard	5. 9	Bournemouth	Glasgow	25.06.79
Mendes, Pedro	5.10	Tottenham	Guimaraes, Por.	26.02.79
O'Neil, Gary	5. 9	–	Beckenham	18.05.83
Songo'o, Franck	5.11	Barcelona	Yaounde, Cam.	14.05.87
Viafara, John	6. 1	Caldas	Robles, Col.	27.10.78
Forwards				
Keene, James	5.11	–	Wells	26.12.85
LuaLua, Lomana	5. 8	Newcastle Utd.	Zaire	28.12.80
Mornar, Ivica	6. 0	Anderlecht	Split	12.01.74
Mbesuma, Collins	5.11	Kaiser Chiefs	Zambia	3.03.84
Mwaruwari, Benjani	6. 2	Auxerre	Bulawayo	13.08.78
Todorov, Svetoslav	6. 0	West Ham Utd.	Dobrich, Bul.	30.08.78

READING

Ground: Madejski Stadium, Junction 11 M4, Reading RG2 OFL.
Telephone: 0118 968 1100. **Club nickname:** Royals.
First-choice colours: Blue and white shirts; blue shorts; blue socks.
Record transfer fee: £1,000,000 to Bristol City for Leroy Lita, July 2005.
Record fee received: £1,750,000 from Newcastle Utd. for Shaka Hislop, August 1995.
Record attendance: At Elm Park: 33,042 v Brentford (F.A. Cup 5) 19 February, 1927. At Madejski Stadium: 24,107 v Chelsea (League Cup 4) 3 December, 2003.
Capacity for 2006-07: 24,200. **Sponsors:** Kyocera.
F.A. Cup: Semi-finals 1927.
League Cup: 5th rd. 1996.
Biggest win: 10-2 v Crystal Palace, Div. 3 (South), 04.09.1946.
Biggest defeat: 0-18 v Preston N.E., F.A. Cup 1st rd., 1893-94.
Highest League scorer in a season: Ronnie Blackman, 39, 1951-52.
Most League goals in aggregate: Ronnie Blackman, 158, 1947-54.
Most capped player: Jimmy Quinn (Northern Ireland) 17.
Longest unbeaten League sequence: 19 matches (October 1973).
Longest sequence without a League win: 14 matches (October 1927).

	Height			
Name	**ft. in.**	**Previous club**	**Birthplace**	**Birthdate**
Goalkeepers				
Federici, Adam		Sardenga	Nowra, Australia	31.01.85
Hahnemann, Marcus	6. 3	Fulham	Seattle	15.06.72
Stack, Graham	6. 2	Arsenal	Hampstead	26.09.81
Defenders				
Golbourne, Scott	5. 8	Bristol City	Bristol	29.02.88
Halls, John	6. 0	Stoke City	Islington	14.02.82
Ingimarsson, Ivar	6. 0	Wolves	Iceland	20.08.77
Makin, Chris	5.10	Leicester City	Manchester	8.05.73
Murty, Graeme	5.10	York City	Saltburn	13.11.74
Shorey, Nicky	5. 9	Leyton Orient	Romford	19.02.81
Sodje, Sam	6. 1	Brentford	Greenwich	29.05.79

Sonko, Ibrahima	5.10	Brentford	Bignaolo, Sen.	22.01.81
Midfielders				
Brown, Aaron		Tamworth	Birmingham	23.06.83
Convey, Bobby	5. 8	DC Utd.	Philadelphia	27.05.83
Cox, Simon	5.10	–		28.04.87
Gunnarsson, Brynjar	6. 1	Watford	Reykjavik	16.10.75
Harper, James	5.11	Arsenal	Chelmsford	9.11.80
Hayes, Jonathan	5.11	–	Dublin	9.07.87
Hunt, Stephen	5. 8	Brentford	Port Laoise	1.08.80
Ki-Hyeon Seol	6. 0	Wolves	South Korea	8.01.79
Little, Glen	6. 3	Burnley	Wimbledon	15.10.75
Oster, John	5. 9	Burnley	Boston	8.12.78
Sidwell, Steve	5.10	Arsenal	Wandsworth	14.12.82
Forwards				
Doyle, Kevin	5.11	Cork City	Ireland	18.09.83
Kitson, Dave	6. 3	Cambridge Utd.	Hitchin	21.01.80
Lita, Leroy	5. 9	Bristol City	DR Congo	28.12.84
Long, Shane	5.10	Cork City	Ireland	22.01.87

SHEFFIELD UNITED

Ground: Bramall Lane, Sheffield S2 4SU.
Telephone: 0870 787 1960. **Club nickname:** Blades.
First-choice colours: Red and white shirts; black and red shorts; black and red socks.
Record transfer fee: £1,750,000 to Burnley for Ade Akinbiyi, January 2006.
Record fee received: £3,00,000 from Derby Co. for Lee Morris, October 1999.
Record attendance: 68,287 v Leeds Utd., F.A. Cup 5th rd., 15 February, 1936
Capacity for 2006-07: 32,500. **Sponsors:** Capital One.
League Championship: Winners 1897-98.
F.A. Cup: Winners 1899, 1902, 1915, 1925.
League Cup: Semi-finals 2003.
Biggest win: 10-0 v Burslem Port Vale, Div.2, 10.12.1892.
Biggest defeat: 0-13 v Bolton Wand., F.A. 2nd rd., 01.02.1890.
Highest League scorer in a season: Jimmy Dunne, 41, 1930-31.
Most League goals in aggregate: Harry Johnson, 205, 1919-30.
Most capped player: Billy Gillespie (Northern Ireland) 25.
Longest unbeaten League sequence: 22 matches (January 1900).
Longest sequence without a League win: 19 matches (February 1976).

Name	Height ft. in.	Previous club	Birthplace	Birthdate
Goalkeepers				
Kenny, Paddy	6. 1	Sheffield Utd.	Halifax	17.05.78
Defenders				
Armstrong, Chris	5. 9	Oldham Athletic	Newcastle	5.08.82
Bromby, Leigh	6. 0	Sheffield Wed.	Dewsbury	2.06.80
Davis, Claude	6. 3	Preston N.E. N. E.	Jamaica	6.03.79
Geary, Derek	5. 6	Stockport Co.	Dublin	19.06.80
Kozluk, Robert	5. 7	Derby Co.	Sutton-in-Ashfield	5.08.77
Lucketti, Chris	6. 0	Preston N.E.	Rochdale	28.09.71
Morgan, Chris	6. 1	Barnsley	Barnsley	9.11.77
Sommeil, David	5.11	Manchester City	Point-a-Pitre, Guad.	10.08.74
Unsworth, David	6. 1	Portsmouth	Chorley	16.10.73
Midfielders				
Ashmore, James	5. 8	–	Sheffield	2.03.86
Flitcroft, Garry	6. 0	Blackburn Rov.	Bolton	6.11.72
Gillespie, Keith	5.10	Leicester City	Bangor, N.I.	18.02.75
Hurst, Kevan	6. 0	–	Chesterfield	27.08.85
Ifill, Paul	6. 0	Millwall	Brighton	20.10.79
Jagielka, Phil	5.11	–	Manchester	17.08.82
Leigertwood, Mikele	6. 1	Crystal Palace	Enfield	12.11.82

Montgomery, Nick	5. 9	–	Leeds	28.10.81
Quinn, Alan	5. 9	Sheffield Wed.	Dublin	13.06.79
Quinn, Stephen	5. 6	St Patrick's	Rep of Ireland	4.04.86
Tonge, Michael	5.11	–	Manchester	7.04.83
Forwards				
Akinbiyi, Ade	6. 1	Burnley	Hackney	10.10.74
Forte, Jonathan	6. 0	–	Sheffield	25.07.86
Horsfield, Geoff	5.10	W.B.A.	Barnsley	1.11.73
Kabba, Steve	5. 8	Crystal Palace	Lambeth	7.03.81
Shipperley, Neil	6. 1	Crystal Palace	Chatham	30.10.74
Webber, Danny	5. 9	Watford	Manchester	28.12.81

TOTTENHAM HOTSPUR

Ground: White Hart Lane, Tottenham, London N17 OAP.
Telephone: 0208 365 5000. **Club nickname:** Spurs.
First-choice colours: White shirts; navy shorts; white socks.
Record transfer fee: £11,000,000 to Dynamo Kiev for Sergei Rebrov, May 2000.
Record fee received: £5,500,000 from Lazio for Paul Gascoigne, May 1992.
Record attendance: 75,038 v Sunderland (F.A. Cup 6) 5 March 1938.
Capacity for 2006-07: 36,252. **Sponsors:** Mansion.
League Championship: Winners 1950-51, 1960-61.
F.A. Cup: Winners 1901, 1921, 1961, 1962, 1967, 1981, 1982, 1991.
League Cup: Winners 1971, 1973, 1999.
European Competitions: Winners Cup-Winners' Cup 1962-63, UEFA Cup 1971-72, 1983-84.
Finishing positions in Premiership: 1992-93 8th, 1993-94 15th, 1994-95 7th, 1995-96 8th, 1996-97 10th, 1997-98 14th, 1998-99 11th, 1999-2000 10th, 2000-01 12th, 2001-02 9th, 2002-03 10th, 2003-04 14th, 2004-05 9th, 2005-06 5th.
Biggest win: 9-0 v Bristol Rov., Div.2, 22.10.1977, F.A. Cup 13-2 v Crewe Alexandra, round four replay, 3.2.1960, Europe 9-0 v Keflavik, UEFA Cup, round one, 28.9.1971.
Biggest defeat: 0-7 v Liverpool, Div.1, 2.9.1979.
Highest League scorer in a season: Jimmy Greaves, 37, 1962-63.
Most League goals in aggregate: Jimmy Greaves, 220, 1961-70.
Most capped player: Pat Jennings (Northern Ireland) 74.
Longest unbeaten League sequence: 22 matches (August 1949).
Longest sequence without a League win: 16 matches (December 1934).

Name	Height ft. in.	Previous club	Birthplace	Birthdate
Goalkeepers				
Burch, Rob	6. 0	–	Yeovil	8.02.84
Cerny, Radek	6. 4	Slavia Prague	Czech Rep.	18.02.74
Fulop, Marton	6. 6	MTK Hungaria	Budapest	3.05.83
Robinson, Paul	6. 2	Leeds Utd.	Beverley	15.10.79
Defenders				
Assou-Ekotto, Benoit	5.10	Lens	Arras. Fr	24.03.84
Davenport, Calum	6. 4	Coventry City	Bedford	1.01.83
Dawson, Michael	6. 2	Nott'm. Forest	Northallerton	18.11.83
Gardner, Anthony	6. 5	Port Vale	Stafford	19.09.80
Huddlestone, Tom	6. 1	Derby Co.	Nottingham	28.12.86
King, Ledley	6. 2	–	Bow	12.10.80
Stalteri, Paul	5.11	Werder Bremen	Etobicoke,Can.	18.10.77
Young-Pyo Lee	5. 9	PSV Eindhoven	Hong Chung, S. Kor.	23.04.77
Midfielders				
Carrick, Michael	6. 0	West Ham Utd.	Wallsend	28.07.81
Davids, Edgar	5. 7	Inter Milan	Paramaribo, Sur.	13.03.73
Ghaly, Hossam	6. 0	Feyenoord	Kafrelshikh, Egy.	
Jenas, Jermaine	6. 0	Newcastle Utd.	Nottingham	18.02.83

Name	Height ft. in.	Previous club	Birthplace	Birthdate
Lennon, Aaron	5. 5	Leeds Utd.	Leeds	16.04.87
Murphy, Danny	5.10	Charlton Athletic	Chester	18.03.77
Reid, Andy	5. 7	Nott'm. Forest	Dublin	29.07.82
Routledge, Wayne	5. 6	Crystal Palace	Sidcup	7.01.85
Tainio, Teemu	5. 8	Auxerre	Tornio, Fin.	27.11.79
Ziegler, Reto	6. 0	Grasshoppers	Servette	16.01.86
Zokora, Didier	5.11	St Etienne	Abidjan, Iv. Coast	14.12.80
Forwards				
Barnard, Lee	5.10	–	Romford	18.07.84
Berbatov, Dimitar	6. 2	Bayer Leverkusen	Bulgaria	30.01.81
Defoe, Jermain	5. 7	West Ham Utd.	Beckton	7.10.82
Keane, Robbie	5. 9	Leeds Utd.	Dublin	8.07.80
Yeates, Mark	5. 9	–	Dublin	11.01.85

WATFORD

Ground: Vicarage Road Stadium, Vicarage Road, Watford WD18 OER.
Telephone: 0870 111 1881. **Club nickname:** Hornets
First-choice colours: Yellow shirts; red shorts; red socks.
Record transfer fee: £2,250,000 to Watford for Allan Nielsen, August, 2000.
Record fee received: £2,300,000 from Chelsea for Paul Furlong, May 1994.
Record attendance: 34,099 v Manchester Utd., F.A. Cup 4th rd., 3 February, 1969.
Capacity for 2006-07: 19,900. **Sponsors:** Loans.co.uk.
League Championship: Runners-up 1982-83.
F.A. Cup: Runners-up, 1984.
League Cup: Semi-finals,1979.
Finishing position in Premiership: 1999-2000 20th.
Biggest win: 10-1 v Lowestoft, F.A. Cup 1st rd., 27.11.1926. League: 8-0 v Sunderland, Div. 1, 25.09.82.
Biggest defeat: 0-10 v Wolves, F.A. Cup 1st rd., 24.01.1912.
Highest League scorer in a season: Cliff Holton, 42, 1959-60.
Most League goals in aggregate: Luther Blissett, 148, 1976-83,1984-88, 1991-92.
Most capped player: John Barnes (England) 31, Kenny Jackett (Wales) 31.
Longest unbeaten League sequence: 22 matches (March 1997).
Longest sequence without a League win: 19 matches (April 1972).

Name	Height ft. in.	Previous club	Birthplace	Birthdate
Goalkeepers				
Chamberlain, Alec	6. 2	Sunderland	March	20.06.64
Lee, Richard	5.11	–	Oxford	5.10.82
Loach, Scott	6. 2	Lincoln City	Nottingham	• 27.05.88
Defenders				
Carlisle, Clarke	6. 2	Leeds Utd.	Preston N.E.	14.10.79
Chambers, James	5.10	W.B.A.	West Bromwich	20.11.80
DeMerit, Jay	5.11	Chicago Fire	Green Bay, USA	4.12.79
Doyley, Lloyd	5.10	–	Whitechapel	1.12.82
Mackay, Malky	6. 1	West Ham Utd.	Bellshill	19.02.72
Mariappa, Adrian	5.11	–	Harrow	3.10.86
Powell, Chris	5.10	Charlton Athletic	Lambeth	8.09.69
Stewart, Jordan	5.11	Leicester City	Birmingham	3.03.82
Midfielders				
Bangura, Alhassan	6. 2	–	Freestown, SL	24.01.88
Blizzard, Dominic	6. 2	–	High Wycombe	2.09.83
Diagouraga, Toumani	5.11	–	Paris	9.06.87
Francis, Damien	6. 1	Wigan Athletic	Wandsworth	27.02.79
Gill, Ben	5. 9	Arsenal	Harrow	9.10.87
Mahon, Gavin	6. 0	Brentford	Birmingham	2.01.77
McNamee, Anthony	5. 6	–	Kensington	13.07.84
Spring, Matthew	5.11	Leeds Utd.	Harlow	17.11.79
Young, Ashley	5.10		Stevenage	9.07.85

Forwards

Bouazza, Hameur	5.11	–	Evry, Fr.	22.02.85
Grant, Joel	5.11	–	Hammersmith	26.08.87
Henderson, Darius	6. 0	Gillingham	Sutton	7.09.81
King, Marlon	6. 1	Nott'm. Forest	Dulwich	26.04.80

WEST HAM UNITED

Ground: Boleyn Ground, Green Street, Upton Park, London E13 9AZ.
Telephone: 0208 548 2748. **Club nickname:** Hammers.
First-choice colours: Claret and blue shirts; white shorts; white socks.
Record transfer fee: £7,250,000 to Norwich City for Dean Ashton, January 2006.
Record fee received: £18,000,000 from Leeds Utd. for Rio Ferdinand, November 2000.
Record attendance: 43,322 v Tottenham (Div. 1) 17 October, 1970.
Capacity for 2006-07: 35,056. **Sponsors:** Jobserve.
League Championship: 3rd 1985-86.
F.A. Cup: Winners 1964, 1975, 1980.
League Cup: Runners-up 1966, 1981.
European Competitions: Winners Cup-Winners' Cup 1964-65.
Finishing positions in Premiership: 1993-94 13th, 1994-95 14th, 1995-96 10th, 1996-97 14th, 1997-98 8th, 1998-99 5th, 1999-2000 9th, 2000-01 15th, 2001-02 7th, 2002-03 18th, 2005-06 9th.
Biggest win: 8-0 v Rothham Utd., Div. 2, 8.3.1958 and v Sunderland, Div. 1, 19.10.1968. League Cup 10-0 v Bury, round 2, 25.10.83.
Biggest defeat: 0-7 v Sheffield Wed., Div. 1, 28.11.1959, v Everton, Div. 1, 22.10.1927, v Barnsley, Div. 2, 1.9.1919.
Highest League scorer in a season: Vic Watson, 42, 1929-30.
Most League goals in aggregate: Vic Watson, 298, 1920-35.
Most capped player: Bobby Moore (England) 108.
Longest unbeaten League sequence: 27 matches (October 1981).
Longest sequence without a League win: 17 matches (August 1976).

Name	Height ft. in.	Previous club	Birthplace	Birthdate
Goalkeepers				
Bywater, Stephen	6. 3	Rochdale	Manchester	7.06.81
Carroll, Roy	6. 2	Manchester Utd.	Enniskillen	30.09.77
Walker, James	5.11	Walsall	Sutton-in-Ashfield	9.07.73
Defenders				
Clarke, Clive	6. 1	Stoke City	Dublin	14.01.80
Collins, James	6. 2	Cardiff City	Newport	23.08.83
Dailly, Christian	6. 0	Blackburn Rov.	Dundee	23.10.73
Ferdinand, Anton	6. 0	–	Peckham	18.02.85
Gabbidon, Danny	6. 1	Cardiff City	Cwmbran	8.08.79
Konchesky, Paul	5.10	Charlton Athletic	Barking	15.05.81
Spector, Jonathan	6. 1	Manchester Utd.	Arlington Hts., USA	3.01.86
Midfielders				
Benayoun, Yossi	5.10	Racing Santander	Dimona, Isr.	5.05.80
Bowyer, Lee	5. 9	Newcastle Utd.	Canning Town	3.01.77
Etherington, Matthew	5.10	Tottenham	Truro	14.08.81
Fletcher, Carl	5.10	Bournemouth	Camberley	7.04.80
Mears, Tyrone	5.11	Preston N.E.	Stockport	18.02.83
Mullins, Hayden	6. 0	Crystal Palace	Reading	27.03.79
Newton, Shaun	5. 8	Wolves	Camberwell	20.08.75
Noble, Mark	5.11	–	West Ham	8.05.87
Reid, Kyel	5. 8	–	London	26.11.87
Reo-Coker, Nigel	5. 8	Wimbledon	Thornton Heath	14.05.84
Stokes, Tony	5.10	–	London	
Forwards				
Ashton, Dean	6. 1	Norwich City	Crewe	24.11.83
Cole, Carlton	6. 3	Chelsea	Croydon	12.10.83

Ephraim, Hogan	5.9	–	Islington	31.03.88
Harewood, Marlon	6.1	Nott'm. Forest	Hampstead	25.08.79
Sheringham, Teddy	6.0	Portsmouth	Highams Park	2.04.66
Zamora, Bobby	6.0	Tottenham	Barking	16.01.81

WIGAN ATHLETIC

Ground: JJB Stadium, Robin Park, Wigan WN5 0UZ.
Telephone: 01942 774000. Club nickname: Latics.
First-choice colours: Blue and white shirts; blue shorts; white socks.
Record transfer fee: £2,000,000 to Brann Bergen for Paul Scharner, January 2006.
Record fee received: £3,000,000 from W.B.A. for Nathan Ellington, August 2005.
Record attendance: At Springfield Park: 27,526 v Hereford Utd. (F.A. Cup 2) 12 December, 1953. At JJB Stadium: 25,023 v Liverpool (Premier League) 11 February, 2006.
Capacity for 2006-07: 25,000. Sponsors: JJB.
F.A. Cup: 6th Rd. 1987.
League Cup: Final, 2006.
Finishing positions in Premiership: 2005-06 10th.
Biggest win: 7-1 v Scarborough, Div. 3, 11.3.1997, 6-0 v Carlisle Utd., F.A. Cup2 nd Rd., 24.11.1934.
Biggest defeat: 1-6 v Bristol Rov., Div. 3, 3.3.1990.
Highest League scorer in a season: Graeme Jones, 31, 1996-97.
Most League goals in aggregate: Andy Liddell, 70, 1998-2004.
Most capped player: Roy Carroll (Northern Ireland) 9.
Longest unbeaten League sequence: 25 matches (January 2000).
Longest sequence without a League win: 14 (October 1989).

Name	Height ft. in.	Previous club	Birthplace	Birthdate
Goalkeepers				
Filan, John	5.11	Blackburn Rov.	Sydney	8.02.70
Pollitt, Mike	6. 4	Rotherham Utd.	Farnworth	29.02.72
Walsh, Gary	6. 3	Bradford City	Wigan	21.03.68
Defenders				
Baines, Leighton	5. 7	–	Liverpool	11.12.84
Chimbonda, Pascal	5.11	Bastia	Les Abymes, Fr.	21.02.79
De Zeeuw, Arjan	6. 1	Portsmouth	Castricum, Hom.	16.04.70
Hall, Fitz	6. 1	Crystal Palace	Leytonstone	20.12.80
Jackson, Matt	6. 0	Norwich City	Leeds	19.10.71
McMillan, Steve	5. 8	Motherwell	Edinburgh	19.01.76
Scharner, Paul	6. 3	SK Brann	Scheibbs, Aut.	11.03.80
Taylor, Ryan	5. 8	Tranmere Rov.	Liverpool	19.08.84
Wright, David	5.11	Crewe Alexandra	Warrington	1.05.80
Midfielders				
Cywka, Tomasz	5.10	Gwarek Zabrze	Gliwce, Pol	27.06.88
Johansson, Andreas	5.10	Djurgardens	Sweden	5.07.78
Kavanagh, Graham	5.10	Cardiff City	Dublin	2.12.73
Landzaat, Denny	5.10	AZ Alkmaar	Amsterdam	28.12.81
Skoko, Josip	5.10	Genclerbiriglii	Mount Gambier, Aus.	10.12.75
Teale, Gary	5.11	Ayr Utd.	Glasgow	21.07.78
Forwards				
Camara, Henri	5.10	Wolves	Dakar	10.05.77
Connolly, David	5. 8	Leicester City	Willesden	6.06.77
Heskey, Emile	6. 2	Birmingham City	Leicester	11.01.78
McCulloch, Lee	6. 1	Motherwell	Bellshill	14.05.78

COCA-COLA LEAGUE PLAYING STAFFS
2006-07 – CHAMPIONSHIP

BARNSLEY

Ground: Oakwell Stadium, Barnsley S71 1ET.
Telephone: 01226 211211. **Club nickname:** Tykes.
First-choice colours: Red shirts; white shorts; red socks.
Main Sponsor: Barnsley Building Society. **Capacity for 2006-07:** 23,186.
Record attendance: 40,255 v Stoke City (F.A. Cup 5) 15 February, 1936.

Name	Height ft. in.	Previous club	Birthplace	Birthdate
Goalkeepers				
Colgan, Nick	6. 1	Hibernian	Drogheda	19.09.73
Defenders				
Atkinson, Robert	6. 1	–	Beverley	29.04.87
Austin, Neil	5.10	–	Barnsley	26.04.83
Hassell, Bobby	5. 9	Mansfield Town	Derby	4.06.80
Heckingbottom, Paul	6. 0	Sheffield Wed.	Barnsley	17.07.77
Laight, Ryan	6. 0	–	Barnsley	16.11.85
Reid, Paul	6. 2	Northampton Town	Carlisle	18.02.82
Togwell, Sam	5.11	Crystal Palace	Beaconsfield	14.10.84
Williams, Robbie	5.10	–	Pontefract	2.10.84
Midfielders				
Devaney, Martin	5.10	Cheltenham Town	Cheltenham	1.06.80
Heslop, Simon	5.11	–	York	1.05.87
Howard, Brian	5. 8	Swindon Town	Winchester	23.01.83
Kell, Richard	6. 1	Scunthorpe Utd.	Bishop Auckland	15.09.79
Kay, Antony	5.11	–	Barnsley	21.10.82
McIndoe, Michael	5. 8	Doncaster Rov.	Edinburgh	2.12.79
McParland, Anthony	5. 7	Celtic	Rotherglen	20.09.82
Tonge, Dale	5.10	–	Doncaster	7.05.85
Wroe, Nicky	5.11	–	Sheffield	28.09.85
Forwards				
Coulson, Michael	5.10	Scarborough	Scarborough	4.04.88
Hayes, Paul	6. 0	Scunthorpe Utd.	Dagenham	20.09.83
Jarman, Nathan	5.11	–	Scunthorpe	19.09.86
Joynes, Nathan	6. 1	–	Barnsley	7.08.85
Nardiello, Danny	5.11	Manchester Utd.	Coventry	22.10.82
Richards, Marc	5.11	Northampton Town	Wolves	8.07.82
Wright, Tommy	6. 0	Leicester City	Kirby Muxloe	28.09.84

BIRMINGHAM CITY

Ground: St Andrews, Birmingham City B9 4NH.
Telephone: 07091 112 5837. **Club nickname:** Blues.
First-choice colours: Blue shits; white shorts; blue socks.
Main sponsor: Phones 4U. **Capacity for 2006-07:** 30,007.
Record attendance: 66,844 v Everton (F.A. Cup 5) 11 February, 1939.

Name	Height ft. in.	Previous club	Birthplace	Birthdate
Goalkeepers				
Taylor, Maik	6. 4	Fulham	Hildeshein, Ger.	4.09.71
Doyle, Colin	6. 5	–	Cork	12.08.85
Defenders				
Bruce, Alex	5.11	Blackburn Rov.	Norwich	28.09.84
Kelly, Stephen	5.11	Tottenham	Dublin	6.09.83

Name	Height ft. in.	Previous club	Birthplace	Birthdate
N'Gotty, Bruno	6. 1	Bolton Wand.	Lyon	10.06.71
Oji, Samuel	6. 0	Arsenal	Westminster	9.10.85
Painter, Marcos	6. 0	–	Birmingham	17.08.86
Sadler, Mathew	5.11	–	Solihull	26.02.85
Taylor, Martin	6. 4	Blackburn Rov.	Ashington	9.11.79
Tebily, Olivier	6. 0	Celtic	Abidjan, Iv. Coast	19.12.75
Upson, Matthew	6. 1	Arsenal	Eye	18.04.79
Midfielders				
Birley, Matthew	5.10	–	Birmingham	26.07.86
Clemence, Stephen	5.11	Tottenham	Liverpool	31.03.78
Danns, Neil	5. 9	Colchester Utd.	Liverpool	23.11.82
Dunn, David	5.10	Blackburn Rov.	Blackburn	27.12.79
Gray, Julian	6. 1	Crystal Palace	Lewisham	21.09.79
Hall, Asa	6. 2	–	Sandwell	29.11.86
Howland, David	5.11	–	Ballynahinch	17.09.86
Johnson, Damien	5.10	Blackburn Rov.	Lisburn	18.11.78
Kilkenny, Neil	5. 8	–	Middlesex	19.12.85
Nafti, Medhi	5. 9	Racing Santander	Toulouse	28.11.78
Pennant, Jermaine	5. 9	Arsenal	Nottingham	5.01.83
Forwards				
Campbell, Dudley	5.11	Brentford	London	12.11.81
Forssell, Mikael	6. 0	Chelsea	Steinfurt, Ger.	15.03.81
Jerome, Cameron	6. 1	Cardiff City	Huddersfield Town	14.08.86
McPike, James	5.10	–	Birmingham	19.04.88

BURNLEY

Ground: Turf Moor, Harry Potts Way, Burnley BB10 4BX.
Telephone: 0870 443 1882. **Club nickname:** Clarets.
First-choice colours: Claret shirts; claret shorts; claret socks.
Main sponsor: Hunters Estate Agents. **Capacity for 2006-07:** 22,619.
Record attendance: 54,775 v Huddersfield Town (F.A. Cup 4) 23 February, 1924.

Name	Height ft. in.	Previous club	Birthplace	Birthdate
Goalkeepers				
Coyne, Danny	6. 1	Leicester City	Prestatyn	27.08.73
Jensen, Brian	6. 1	W.B.A.	Copenhagen	8.06.75
Defenders				
Courtney, Duane	5.11	Telford	Birmingham	7.01.85
Duff, Mike	6. 1	Cheltenham Town	Belfast	11.01.78
Foster, Steve	6. 0	Crewe Alexandra	Warrington	10.09.80
Harley, Jon	5. 8	Sheffield Utd.	Maidstone	26.09.79
Karbassiyoon, Daniel	5. 8	Arsenal	Virginia	10.08.84
McGreal, John	5.11	Ipswich Town	Birkenhead	2.06.72
Sinclair, Frank	5.10	Leicester City	Lambeth	3.12.71
Thomas, Wayne	6. 2	Stoke City	Gloucester	17.05.79
Midfielders				
Branch, Graham	6. 2	Stockport Co.	Liverpool	12.02.72
Elliott, Wade	5.10	Bournemouth	Eastleigh	14.12.78
Hyde, Micah	5.11	Watford	Newham	10.11.74
Mahon, Alan	5.10	Wigan Athletic	Dublin	4.04.78
McCann, Chris	6. 1	–	Dublin	21.07.87
O'Connor, Garreth	5. 7	Bournemouth	Dublin	10.11.78
O'Connor, James	5. 8	W.B.A.	Dublin	1.09.79
Spicer, John	5.11	Bournemouth	Romford	13.09.83
Forwards				
Gray, Andy	6. 1	Sunderland	Harrogate	15.11.77
Jones, Steve	5. 4	Crewe Alexandra	Londonderry	25.10.76
Lafferty, Kyle	6. 4	–	Enniskillen	16.09.87
Noel-Williams, Gifton	6. 1	Watford	Islington	21.01.80

CARDIFF CITY

Ground: Ninian Park, Sloper Road, Cardiff CF11 8SX.
Telephone: 02920 221001. **Club nickname:** Bluebirds.
First-choice colours: Blue shirts; blue shorts; blue socks.
Main sponsor: Redrow Homes. **Capacity for 2006-07:** 21,432.
Record attendance: 61,566 Wales v England, 14 October, 1961. Club: 57,800 v Arsenal
(Div. 1) 22 April, 1953.

Name	Height ft. in.	Previous club	Birthplace	Birthdate
Goalkeepers				
Alexander, Neil	6. 1	Livingston	Edinburgh	10.03.78
Margetson, Martyn	6. 0	Huddersfield Town	West Neath	8.09.71
Worgan, Lee	6. 1	Rushden & Diamonds	Eastbourne	1.12.83
Defenders				
Barker, Chris	6. 0	Barnsley	Sheffield	2.03.80
Johnson, Roger	6. 3	Wycombe	Ashford	28.04.83
Kamara, Malvin	6. 0	MK Dons	Southwark	17.11.83
Parslow, Daniel	5.11	–	Rhymney Valley	11.09.85
Purse, Darren	6. 2	W.B.A.	Stepney	14.02.77
Scimeca, Riccardo	6. 1	W.B.A.	Leamington Spa	13.06.75
Weston Rhys	6. 1	Arsenal	Kingston	27.10.80
Midfielders				
Ardley, Neal	5.11	Watford	Epsom	1.09.72
Cooper, Kevin	5. 8	Wolves	Derby Co.	8.02.75
Fish, Nicholas	5.10	–	Cardiff	15.09.84
Ledley, Joe	6. 0	–	Cardiff	23.01.87
McKoy, Nick	6. 0	MK Dons	Newham	3.09.86
McPhail, Stephen	5.10	Barnsley	Westminster	9.12.79
Parry, Paul	5.10	Hereford Utd.	Chepstow	19.08.80
Whitley, Jeff	5. 9	Sunderland	Zambia	28.01.79
Forwards				
Chopra, Michael	5.10	Newcastle Utd.	Newcastle	23.12.83
Ferretti, Andrea	5.10	Parma	Italy	18.09.86
Thompson, Steven	6. 2	Rangers	Paisley	14.10.78

COLCHESTER UNITED

Ground: Layer Road, Colchester CO2 7JJ.
Telephone: 0871 226 2161. **Club nickname:** U's.
First-choice-colours: Blue and white shirts; white shorts; white and blue socks.
Capacity for 2006-07: 6,143.
Record attendance: 19,072 v Reading (F.A. Cup 1) 27 November, 1948.

Name	Height ft. in.	Previous club	Birthplace	Birthdate
Goalkeepers				
Davison, Aidan	6. 1	Grimsby Town	Sedgefield	11.05.68
Gerken, Dean	6. 2	–	Southend	4.08.85
Defenders				
Baldwin, Pat	6. 0	Chelsea	London	12.11.82
Brown, Wayne	6. 0	Watford	Banbury	20.08.77
Elokobi, George	6. 1	Dulwich Hamlet	Cameroon	31.01.86
Halford, Greg	5.11	–	Chelmsford	8.12.84
Richards, Garry	6. 3	–		11.06.86
White, John	6. 0	–	Colchester	25.07.86
Midfielders				
Duguid, Karl	5.11	–	Hitchin	21.03.78
Izzet, Kemal	5. 8	Charlton Athetic	Whitechapel	29.09.80
Jackson, Johnnie	6. 1	Tottenham	Camden	15.08.82

Watson, Kevin	6. 0	Reading	Hackney	3.01.74
Forwards				
Cureton, Jamie	5. 8	Swindon Town	Bristol	28.08.75
Garcia, Richard	5.11	West Ham Utd.	Perth, Aus.	9.04.81
Guy, Jamie	6. 1	–	Barking	1.08.87
Iwelumo, Chris	6. 4	Alemania Aachen	Coatbridge	1.08.78
Keith, Marino	5.10	Plymouth Argyle	Peterhead	16.12.74

COVENTRY CITY

Ground: Ricoh Arena, Foleshill, Coventry CV6 6GE.
Telephone: 0870 421 1987. **Club nickname:** Sky Blues.
First-choice colours: Sky blue shirts; sky blue and navy shorts; sky blue socks.
Main sponsor: Cassidy Group. **Capacity for 2006-07:** 32,000.
Record attendance: (Highfield Road) 51,455 v Wolves (Div. 2) 29 April, 1967. (Ricoh Arena) 26,851 v Wolves (Championship) 2 January, 2006.

Name	Height ft. in.	Previous club	Birthplace	Birthdate
Goalkeepers				
Marshall, Andy	6. 2	Millwall	Bury St Edmunds	14.04.75
Tuffey, Jonathan	6. 0	–	Belfast	20.01.87
Defenders				
Bischoff, Mikkel	6. 4	Manchester City	Denmark	3.02.82
Giddings, Stuart	6. 0	–	Coventry	27.03.86
Hall, Marcus	6. 1	Stoke City	Coventry	24.03.76
Heath, Matt	6. 4	Leicester City	Leicester	1.11.81
Lynch, Ryan	5.11	–	Solihull	13.03.87
McNamee, David	5.11	Livingston	Glasgow	10.10.80
Page, Robert	6. 0	Cardiff City	Llwynpia	3.09.74
Ward, Elliott	6. 1	West Ham Utd.	Harrow	19.01.85
Whing, Andrew	6. 0	–	Birmingham	20.09.84
Midfielders				
Cameron, Colin	5. 8	Wolves	Kircaldy	23.10.72
Davis, Liam	5. 8	–	Wandsworth	23.11.86
Doyle, Michael	5.10	Celtic	Dublin	8.07.81
Hughes, Stephen	6. 0	Charlton Athletic	Wokingham	18.09.76
Hutchison, Don	6. 1	Millwall	Gateshead	9.05.71
Jorgensen, Claus	5.11	Bradford City	Holstebro, Den.	27.04.76
Osbourne, Isaac	5.10	–	Birmingham	22.06.86
Tabb, Jay	5. 6	Brentford	Tooting	21.02.84
Thornton, Kevin	5. 7	–	Drogheda	9.07.86
Webb, Luke	6. 0	–	Nottingham	12.09.86
Forwards				
Adebola, Dele	6. 3	Crystal Palace	Lagos	23.06.75
Andrews, Wayne	5.10	Crystal Palace	Paddington	25.11.77
John, Stern	6. 1	Birmingham City	Canefarm, Trin.	30.10.76
McSheffrey, Gary	5. 8	–	Coventry	13.08.72
Morrell, Andy	5.11	Wrexham	Doncaster	28.09.74
Scowcroft, James	6. 1	Leicester City	Bury St Edmunds	15.11.75

CRYSTAL PALACE

Ground: Selhurst Park, London SE25, 6PU.
Telephone: 0208 768 6000. **Club nickname:** Eagles.
First-choice colours: Red and blue shirts; blue shorts; blue socks.
Main sponsor: GAC Logistics. **Capacity for 2006-07:** 26,309.
Record attendance: 51,482 v Burnley (Div. 2), 11 May, 1979.

Name	Height ft. in.	Previous club	Birthplace	Birthdate
Goalkeepers				
Flinders, Scott	6. 4	Barnsley	Rotherham	12.06.86
Kiralry, Gabor	6. 4	Hertha Berlin	Hungary	1.04.76
Speroni, Julian	6. 1	Dundee	Federal, Arg.	18.05.79
Defenders				
Boyce, Emmerson	5.11	Luton Town	Aylesbury	24.09.79
Butterfield, Danny	5.10	Grimsby Town	Boston Utd.	21.11.79
Cort, Leon	6. 3	Hull City	Bermondsey	11.07.79
Fray, Arron	5.11	–	Bromley	1.05.87
Granville, Danny	5.11	Manchester City	Islington	19.01.75
Hudson, Mark	6. 3	Fulham	Guildford	30.03.82
Ward, Darren	5.11	Millwall	Harrow	13.09.78
Midfielders				
Black, Tommy	5. 7	Arsenal	Chigwell	26.11.79
Borrowdale, Gary	6. 0	–	Sutton	16.07.85
Hall, Ryan	5.10	–	Dulwich	4.01.88
Hughes, Michael	5. 7	Birmingham City	Larne	2.08.71
Kennedy, Mark	5.11	Wolves	Dublin	15.05.76
McAnuff, Jobi	5.11	Cardiff City	Edmonton	9.11.81
Reich, Marco	6. 0	Derby Co.	Meisenhaim, Ger.	30.12.77
Soares, Tom	6. 0	–	Reading	10.07.86
Watson, Ben	5.10	–	Camberwell	9.07.85
Forwards				
Freedman, Dougie	5. 9	Nott'm. Forest	Glasgow	21.01.74
Grabban, Lewis	6. 0	–	Croydon	12.01.88
Macken, Jon	5.10	Manchester City	Manchester	7.09.77
Morrison, Clinton	6. 1	Birmingham City	Wandsworth	14.05.79
Torghelle, Sandor	6. 1	MTK Hungaria	Budapest	5.05.82

DERBY COUNTY

Ground: Pride Park Stadium, Pride Park, Derby DE24 8XL.
Telephone: 0870 444 1884. **Club nickname:** Rams.
First-choice colours: White and black shirts; black and white shorts; black and white socks.
Main sponsor: Derbyshire Building Society. **Capacity for 2006-07:** 33,597.
Record attendance: (Baseball Ground) 41,826 v Tottenham (Div. 1) 20 September, 1969. (Pride Park) 33,597 England v Mexico, 25 May, 2001. Club: 33,475 v Rangers (testimonial), 1 May, 2006.

Name	Height ft. in.	Previous club	Birthplace	Birthdate
Goalkeepers				
Camp, Lee	5.11	–	Derby	22.08.84
Grant, Lee	6. 2	–	Hemel Hempstead	27.01.83
Defenders				
Addison, Miles	5.11	–	London	7.01.89
Boertien, Paul	5.10	Carlisle Utd.	Carlisle	21.01.79
Hanson, Mitchell	5.11	–	Derby	2.09.88
Edworthy, Marc	5. 9	Norwich City	Barnstaple	24.12.72
Jackson, Richard	5. 7	Scarborough	Whitby	18.04.80
Johnson, Michael	5.11	Birmingham City	Nottingham	4.07.73
Moore, Darren	6. 2	W.B.A.	Birmingham	22.04.74
Nyatanga, Lewin	6. 2	–	Burton	18.08.88
Midfielders				
Barnes, Giles	6. 0	–	Barking	5.08.88
Bisgaard, Morten	5.10	FC Copenhagen	Randers, Den.	25.06.75
Bolder, Adam	5. 8	Hull City	Hull City	25.10.80
Doyle, Nathan	5.11	–	Derby Co.	12.01.87

Holmes, Lee	5. 8	–	Mansfield	2.04.87
Johnson, Seth	5.10	Leeds Utd.	Birmingham	12.03.79
Idiakez, Inigo	6. 0	Rayo Vallecano	Spain	8.11.73
Thirlwell, Paul	5.11	Sheffield Utd.	Washington, Co Dur.	13.02.79
Forwards				
Ainsworth, Lionel	5. 9	–	Nottingham	1.10.87
Ashton, Karl	6. 0	–	Derby	26.01.89
Peschisolido, Paul	5. 7	Sheffield Utd.	Scarborough, Can.	25.05.71
Smith, Tommy	5.10	Sunderland	Hemel Hempstead	22.05.80

HULL CITY

Ground: Kingston Communications Stadium, The Circle, Walton Street, Anlaby Road, Hull, HU3 6HU.
Telephone: 0870 837 0004. **Club nickname:** Tigers.
First-choice colours: Black and amber shirts; black shorts; black and amber socks.
Main Sponsor: Bonus Electrical. **Capacity for 2006-07:** 25,414.
Record attendance: (Boothferry Park) 55,019 v Manchester Utd. (F.A. Cup 6) 28 February, 1949. (Kingston Communications Stadium) 24,277 v Sheffield Wed. (League 1) 30 April, 2005. 25,280 England U-21 v Holland, 17 February, 2004.

Name	Height ft. in.	Previous club	Birthplace	Birthdate
Goalkeepers				
Aspden, Curtis	6. 0	–	Blackburn	16.11.87
Duke, Matt	6. 5	Burton Albion	Sheffield	16.07.77
Myhill, Boaz	6. 3	Aston Villa	Modesto, Calif.	9.11.82
Defenders				
Coles, Danny	6. 1	Bristol City	Bristol	31.10.81
Collins, Sam	6. 2	–	Pontefract	5.06.77
Dawson, Andy	5. 9	Scunthorpe Utd.	Northallerton	20.10.78
Delaney, Damien	6. 3	Leicester City	Cork	20.07.81
Lynch, Mark	5.11	Manchester Utd.	Manchester	2.09.81
Ricketts, Sam	6. 1	Swansea City	Aylesbury	11.10.81
Thelwell, Alton	5.11	Tottenham	Holloway	5.09.80
Turner, Michael	6. 4	Brentford	Lewisham	9.11.83
Wiseman, Scott	6. 0	–	Hull	9.10.85
Midfielders				
Andrews, Keith	6. 0	Wolves	Dublin	13.09.80
Ashbee, Ian	6. 1	Cambridge Utd.	Birmingham	6.09.76
Barmby, Nick	5. 7	Leeds Utd.	Hull	11.02.74
Elliott, Stuart	5.10	Motherwell	Belfast	23.07.78
France, Ryan	5.11	Alfreton Town	Sheffield	13.12.80
Fry, Russell	6. 0	–	Hull	4.12.85
Green, Stuart	5.10	Newcastle Utd.	Whitehaven	15.06.81
Marney, Dean	5.11	Tottenham	Barking	31.01.84
Welsh, John	6. 0	Liverpool	Liverpool	10.01.84
Forwards				
Burgess, Ben	6. 3	Stockport Co.	Buxton	9.11.81
Duffy, Darryl	5.11	Falkirk	Glasgow	16.04.84
Fagan, Craig	5.11	Colchester Utd.	Birmingham	11.12.82
McPhee, Stephen	5. 7	Port Vale	Glasgow	5.06.81
Parkin, Jon	6. 4	Macclesfield Town	Barnsley	30.12.81
Paynter, Billy	6. 0	Port Vale	Liverpool	13.07.84

IPSWICH TOWN

Ground: Portman Road, Ipswich IP1 2DA.
Telephone: 01473 400500. **Club nickname:** Blues/Town.
First-choice colours: Blue shirts; white shorts; blue socks.
Main sponsor: Eon. **Capacity for 2006-07:** 30,305.
Record attendance: 38,010 v Leeds Utd. (F.A. Cup 6) 8 March, 1975.

Name	Height ft. in.	Previous club	Birthplace	Birthdate
Goalkeepers				
Price, Lewis	6. 3	Southampton	Bournemouth	19.07.84
Supple, Shane	6. 0	–	Dublin	4.05.87
Defenders				
Barron, Scott	5. 9	–	Preston	2.09.85
Casement, Chris	6. 0	–	Northern Ireland	12.01.88
De Vos, Jason	6. 4	Wigan Athletic	Ontario	2.01.74
Nash, Gerard	6. 1	–	Dublin	11.07.86
Naylor, Richard	6. 1	–	Leeds	28.02.77
Richards, Matthew	5. 8	–	Harlow	26.12.84
Sito, Luis Castro	5. 9	Racing Ferrol	La Coruna	21.05.80
Wilnis, Fabian	5.10	De Graafschap	Surinam	23.08.70
Midfielders				
Bowditch, Dean	5.11	–	Bishop's Stortford	15.06.86
Brekke-Skard, Vemund	5. 9	–	Norway	11.09.81
Currie, Darren	5.10	Brighton & H.A.	Hampstead	29.11.74
Garvan, Owen	6. 0	–	Dublin	29.01.88
Haynes, Danny	5.11	–	London	19.01.88
Mitchell, Scott	5.11	–	Ely	2.09.85
Peters, Jaime	5. 7	–	Ontario	4.05.87
Trotter, Liam	6. 2	–	Ipswich	24.08.88
Westlake, Ian	5.10	–	Clacton	10.07.83
Williams, Gavin	5.10	West Ham Utd.	Pontypridd	20.07.80
Forwards				
Clarke, Billy	5. 7	–	Cork	13.12.87
Forster, Nicky	5. 9	Reading	Caterham	8.09.73
Knights, Darryl	5. 7	–	Ipswich	1.05.88
Lee, Alan	6. 2	Cardiff City	Galway	21.08.78
Parkin, Sam	6. 2	Swindon Town	Roehampton	14.03.81

LEEDS UNITED

Ground: Elland Road, Leeds LS11 OES.
Telephone: 0113 367 6000. **Club nickname:** Whites.
First-choice colours: White shirts; white shorts; white socks.
Main sponsor: Bet24. **Capacity for 2006-07:** 39,460.
Record attendance: 57,892 v Sunderland, 15 March, 1967.

Name	Height ft. in.	Previous club	Birthplace	Birthdate
Goalkeepers				
Bennett, Ian	6. 0	Birmingham City	Worksop	10.10.71
Sullivan, Neil	6. 2	Chelsea	Sutton	24.02.70
Defenders				
Butler, Paul	6. 0	Wolves	Manchester	2.11.72
Crainey, Stephen	5. 9	Southampton	Glasgow	22.06.81
Gregan, Sean	6. 0	W.B.A.	Guisborough	29.03.74
Harding, Daniel	6. 0	Brighton & H.A.	Gloucester	23.12.83
Kelly, Gary	5. 8	Home Farm	Drogheda	9.07.74
Kilgallon, Matthew	6. 1	–	York	8.01.84
Rui Marques, Manuel	5.11	Maritimo	Luanda, Ang.	3.09.77
Midfielders				
Bakke, Eirik	6. 1	Sogndal	Sogndal, Nor.	13.09.77
Carole, Sebastien	5. 7	Brighton & H.A.	France	8.09.82
Derry, Shaun	5.10	Crystal Palace	Nottingham	6.12.77
Einarsson, Gylfi	6. 1	Lillestrom	Iceland	27.10.78
Griffiths, Joel		Neuchatal Xamax	Australia	21.08.79
Lewis, Eddie	5. 9	Preston N.E.	Cerritos, US	17.05.74
Miller, Liam	5. 8	Manchester Utd.	Cork	13.02.81

Richardson, Frazer	5.10	–	Portsmouth	Rotherham	29.10.82
Stone, Steve	5. 8			Gateshead	20.08.71
Forwards					
Beckford, Jermaine	6. 2		Wealdstone		9.12.83
Blake, Robbie	5. 9		Birmingham City	Middlesbrough	4.03.76
Cresswell, Richard	6. 0		Preston N.E.	Bridlington	20.09.77
Healy, David	5. 8		Preston N.E.	Downpatrick	5.08.79
Hulse, Rob	6. 1		W.B.A.	Crewe	25.10.79
Moore, Ian	5.11		Burnley	Birkenhead	26.08.76

LEICESTER CITY

Ground: Walkers Stadium, Filbert Way, Leicester, LE2 7FL.
Telephone: 0870 040 6000. **Club nickname:** Foxes.
First choice colours: Blue shirts; white shorts; blue socks.
Main sponsor: Alliance and Leicester. **Capacity for 2006-07:** 32,500.
Record attendance: (Filbert Street) 47,298 v. Tottenham (F.A. Cup 5) 18 February 1928.
  (Walkers Stadium) 32,148 v Newcastle Utd. (Premier League) 26 December, 2003.

Name	Height ft. in.	Previous club	Birthplace	Birthdate
Goalkeepers				
Douglas, Rob	6. 3	Celtic	Lanark	24.04.72
Henderson, Paul	6. 1	Bradford City	Sydney	22.04.76
Logan, Conrad	6. 2	–	Letterkenny	18.04.86
Defenders				
Gerrbrand, Patrick	6. 2	Hammarby	Sweden	27.04.81
Heath, Matt	5.11	–	Leicester	1.11.81
Johansson, Nils-Eric	6. 1	Blackburn Rov.	Stockholm	13.01.80
Kenton, Darren	5.10	Southampton	Wandsworth	13.09.78
Kisnorbo, Patrick	6. 2	Hearts	Melbourne	24.03.81
Maybury, Alan	5.11	Hearts	Dublin	8.08.78
McAuley, Gareth	6. 3	Lincoln City	Larne	5.12.79
McCarthy, Patrick	6. 1	Manchester City	Dublin	31.05.83
Sheehan, Alan	5.11	–	Athlone	14.09.86
Smedley, Jay	6. 0	Nott'm. Forest	Nottingham	18.02.87
Stearman, Richard	6. 2	–	Wolverhampton	19.08.87
Midfielders				
Gudjonsson, Joey	5. 8	Real Betis	Akranes, Ice.	25.05.80
Hamill, Joe	5. 9	Hearts	Bellshill	25.02.84
Hughes, Stephen	5.11	Rangers	Motherwell	14.11.82
Johnson, Andy	6. 1	W.B.A.	Bristol	2.05.74
Porter, Levi	5. 3	–	Leicester	6.04.87
Low, Josh	6. 1	Northampton Town	Bristol	15.02.79
Sylla, Mohammed	5.11	Celtic	Ivory Coast	13.03.77
Tiatto, Danny	5. 8	Manchester City	Melbourne	22.05.73
Wesolowski, James	5.10	Northern Spirit	Sydney	25.08.87
Williams, Gareth	5.11	Nott'm. Forest	Glasgow	16.12.81
Forwards				
De Vries, Mark	6. 3	Hearts	Surinam	24.08.75
Dodds, Louis	5.11	–	Sheffield	8.10.86
Fryatt, Matty	5.10	Walsall	Nuneaton	5.03.86
Hammond, Elvis	5.10	Fulham	Accra	6.10.80
Hume, Iain	5. 7	Tranmere Rov.	Brampton, Can.	31.10.83
O'Grady, Chris	6. 0	–	Nottingham	25.01.86

LUTON TOWN

Ground: Kenilworth Stadium, Maple Road, Luton LU4 8AW.
Telephone: 01582 411622. **Club nickname:** Hatters.
First-choice colours: White shirts; black shorts; black socks.
Main Sponsor: Electrolux. **Capacity for 2006-07:** 10,248.

Record attendance: 30,069 v Blackpool (F.A. Cup 6) 4 March, 1959.

Name	Height ft. in.	Previous club	Birthplace	Birthdate
Goalkeepers				
Beckwith, Rob	6. 2	–	London	12.09.84
Beresford, Marlon	6. 1	Barnsley	Lincoln	2.09.69
Brill, Dean	6. 2	–	Luton	2.12.85
Seremet, Dino	6. 4	Maribor	Slovenia	16.08.80
Defenders				
Barnett, Leon	6. 1	–	Stevenage	30.11.85
Coyne, Chris	6. 3	Dundee	Brisbane	28.12.78
Davis, Sol	5. 8	Swindon Town	Cheltenham	4.09.79
Foley, Kevin	5. 9	–	Luton	1.11.84
Heikkinen, Markus	6. 1	Aberdeen	Sweden	13.10.78
Perrett, Russell	6. 3	Cardiff City	Barton-on-Sea	18.06.73
Underwood, Paul	5.11	Rushden & Diamonds	Wimbledon	16.08.73
Midfielders				
Bell, David	5.10	Rushden & Diamonds	Kettering	21.01.84
Brkovic, Ahmet	5. 7	Leyton Orient	Dubrovnic	23.09.74
Edwards, Carlos	5.11	Wrexham	Port of Spain, Trin.	24.10.78
Holmes, Peter	5.10	Sheffield Wed.	Bishop Auckland	18.11.80
Hughes, Paul	6. 0	Southampton	Hammersmith	19.04.76
Keane, Keith	5. 9	–	Luton	20.11.86
Langley, Richard	5.10	Q.P.R.	Harlesden	27.12.79
Leary, Michael	5.11	–	Ealing	17.04.83
Morgan, Dean	6. 0	Reading	Enfield	3.10.83
Nicholls, Kevin	5.11	Wigan Athletic	Newham	2.01.79
O'Leary, Stephen	5.10	–	London	12.02.85
Robinson, Steve	5. 9	Preston N.E.	Lisburn	10.12.74
Stevens, Danny	5.10	Tottenham	Enfield	26.11.86
Forwards				
Andrew, Calvin	6. 0	–	Luton	19.12.86
Feeney, Warren	5.10	Bournemouth	Belfast	17.01.81
Howard, Steve	6. 2	Northampton Town	Durham	10.05.76
Vine, Rowan	6. 1	Portsmouth	Basingstoke	21.09.82

NORWICH CITY

Ground: Carrow Road, Norwich City NR1 1JE.
Telephone: 01603 760760. **Club nickname:** Canaries.
First-choice colours: Yellow shirts; green shorts; yellow socks.
Main sponsor: Proton and Lotus Cars. **Capacity for 2006-07:** 26,034.
Record attendance: 43,984 v Leicester City (F.A. Cup 6), 30 March, 1963.

Name	Height ft. in.	Previous club	Birthplace	Birthdate
Goalkeepers				
Gallacher, Paul	6. 0	Dundee Utd.	Glasgow	16.08.79
Green, Robert	6. 3	–	Chertsey	18.01.80
Lewis, Joe	6. 5	–	Bury St Edmunds	7.07.85
Defenders				
Colin, Jurgen	5.10	PSV Eindhoven	Holland	20.01.81
Doherty, Gary	6. 1	Tottenham	Carndonagh	31.01.80
Drury, Adam	5.10	Peterborough Utd.	Cambridge	29.08.78
Etuhu, Dickson	6. 2	Preston N.E.	Kano, Nig.	8.06.82
Fleming, Craig	5.11	Oldham Athletic	Halifax	6.10.71
Jarvis, Rossi	5.11	–	Fakenham	11.03.88
Louis-Jean, Matthieu	5. 9	Nott'm. Forest	Mont St Aignan, Fr.	22.02.76
Shackell, Jason	5.11	–	Stevenage	27.09.83
Midfielders				
Cave-Brown, Andrew	5.10	–	Gravesend	5.08.88

Name		Previous club	Birthplace	Birthdate
Hughes, Andy	5.11	Reading	Manchester	2.01.78
Robinson, Carl	5.10	Sunderland	Llandrindod Wells	13.10.76
Safri, Youssef	6. 2	Coventry City	Morocco	1.03.77
Spillane, Michael	5. 9	–	Cambridge	23.03.89
Forwards				
Earnshaw, Rob	5. 8	W.B.A.	Zambia	6.04.81
Henderson, Ian	5.11	–	Thetford	24.01.85
Huckerby, Darren	5.10	Manchester City	Nottingham	23.04.76
Jarvis, Ryan	5.11	–	Fakenham	11.07.86
McKenzie, Leon	5.11	Peterborough Utd.	Croydon	17.05.78
McVeigh, Paul	5. 6	Tottenham	Belfast	6.12.77
Thorne, Peter	6. 0	Cardiff City	Manchester	21.06.73

PLYMOUTH ARGYLE

Ground: Home Park, Plymouth PL2 3DQ.
Telephone: 01752 562561. **Club nickname:** Pilgrims.
First-choice colours: Green shirts; white shorts; green socks.
Main sponsor: Ginsters. **Capacity for 2006-07:** 21,118.
Record attendance: 42,684 v Aston Villa (Div. 2) 10 October, 1936.

Name	Height ft. in.	Previous club	Birthplace	Birthdate
Goalkeepers				
Larrieu, Romain	6. 2	Valence	Mont de Marsan, Fra.	31.08.76
McCormick, Luke	6. 0	–	Coventry	15.08.83
Defenders				
Adams, Steve	6. 0	–	Plymouth	25.09.80
Aljofree, Hasney	6. 0	Dundee Utd.	Manchester	11.07.78
Barness, Anthony	5.10	Bolton Wand.	Lewisham	25.03.73
Connolly, Paul	6. 0	–	Liverpool	29.09.83
Doumbe, Mathias	6. 0	Hibernian	Drancy, Fr.	28.20.79
Wotton, Paul	5.11	–	Plymouth	17.08.77
Midfielders				
Buzsaky, Akos	5.11	FC Porto	Hungary	7.05.82
Capaldi, Tony	6. 0	Birmingham City	Porsgrunn, Nor.	12.08.81
Djordjic, Bojan	5.10	Manchester Utd.	Belgrade	6.02.82
Dickson, Ryan	5.10	–	Saltash	14.12.86
Hodges, Lee	6. 0	Reading	Epping	4.09.73
Nalis, Lilian	6. 1	Leicester City	Paris	29.09.71
Norris, David	5. 7	Bolton Wand.	Stamford	22.02.81
Summerfield, Luke	6. 0	–	Ivybridge	6.12.87
Forwards				
Chadwick, Nick	5.11	Everton	Market Drayton	26.10.82
Ebanks-Blake, Sylvain	5.10	Manchester Utd.	Cambridge	29.03.86
Zebroski, Chris	6. 1	–	Swindon	29.10.86

PRESTON NORTH END

Ground: Deepdale, Sir Tom Finney Way, Preston PR1 6RU.
Telephone: 0870 442 1964. **Club nickname:** Lilywhites.
First-choice colours: White shirts; blue shorts; white socks.
Main sponsor: Enterprise. **Capacity for 2006-07:** 20,861.
Record attendance: 42,684 v Arsenal (Div. 1) 23 April, 1938.

Name	Height ft. in.	Previous club	Birthplace	Birthdate
Goalkeepers				
Lonergan, Andy	6.4	–	Preston	19.10.83
Nash, Carlo	6.5	Middlesbrough	Bolton	13.09.73
Neal, Chris	6.1	–	St Albans	23.10.85

Defenders

Name	Height	Previous club	Birthplace	Birthdate
Alexander, Graham	5.11	Luton Town	Coventry	10.10.71
Chivers, Liam	6. 2	Colchester Utd.	Chelmsford	6.11.81
Davidson, Callum	5.10	Leicester City	Stirling	25.06.76
Hill, Matt	5. 8	Bristol City	Bristol	26.03.81
Mawene, Youl	6. 1	Derby Co.	Caen	16.07.79
St Ledger, Sean	6. 0	Peterborough Utd.	Birmingham	28.12.84
Wilson, Kelvin	6. 2	Notts Co.	Nottingham	3.09.85

Midfielders

Name	Height	Previous club	Birthplace	Birthdate
Anyinsah, Joe	5. 8	Bristol City	Bristol	8.10.84
Jarrett, Jason	6. 0	Norwich City	Bury	14.09.79
McCormack, Alan	5. 8	–	Dublin	10.01.84
McKenna, Paul	5. 8	–	Chorley	20.10.77
Neal, Lewis	6. 0	Stoke City	Leicester	14.07.81
O'Neil, Brian	6. 1	Derby Co.	Paisley	6.09.72
Sedgwick, Chris	5.11	Rotherham Utd.	Sheffield	28.04.80
Stock, Brian	5.11	Bournemouth	Winchester	24.12.81

Forwards

Name	Height	Previous club	Birthplace	Birthdate
Agyemang, Patrick	6. 1	Gillingham	Walthamstow	29.09.80
Dichio, Danny	6. 3	Millwall	Hammersmith	19.10.74
Hibbert, Dave	6. 2	Port Vale	Eccleshall	28.01.86
Nugent, David	5.11	Bury	Liverpool	2.05.85
Ormerod, Brett	5.11	Southampton	Blackburn	18.10.76
Smith, Andy	5.11	Glentoran	Lisburn	25.09.80
Whaley, Simon	5.11	Bury	Bolton	7.06.85

QUEENS PARK RANGERS

Ground: Loftus Road Stadium, South Africa Road, London W12 7PA.
Telephone: 0208 743 0262. **Club nickname:** Hoops.
First-choice colours: Blue and white shirts; white shorts; white socks.
Main sponsor: Car Giant.co.uk. **Capacity for 2006-07:** 19,100.
Record attendance: 35,353 v Leeds Utd. (Div. 1) 27 April, 1974.

Name	Height ft. in.	Previous club	Birthplace	Birthdate
Goalkeepers				
Cole, Jake	6. 2	–	Hammersmith	11.09.85
Jones, Paul	6. 3	Wolves	Chirk	18.04.67
Royce, Simon	6. 2	Charlton Athletic	Forest Gate	9.09.71
Thomas, Sean	6. 1	–		5.09.86
Defenders				
Bignot, Marcus	5.10	Rushden & Diamonds	Birmingham	22.08.74
Evatt, Ian	6. 3	Chesterfield	Coventry	19.11.81
Hislop, Matthew	5.11	Arsenal	Wolves	31.01.87
Kanyuka, Patrick	6. 0	–	Kinshasa	19.07.87
Milanese, Mauro	6. 1	Perugia	Italy	17.09.71
Rose, Matthew	5.11	Arsenal	Dartford	24.09.75
Shimmin, Dominic	6. 0	–	Bermondsey	13.10.87
Shittu, Danny	6. 3	Charlton Athletic	Lagos	2.09.80
Midfielders				
Ainsworth, Gareth	5. 9	Cardiff City	Blackburn	10.05.73
Baidoo, Shabazz	5. 8	–	Hackney	13.04.88
Bailey, Stefan	5.11	–	London	10.11.87
Bircham, Marc	5.10	Millwall	Wembley	11.05.78
Cook, Lee	5. 9	Watford	Hammersmith	3.08.82
Doherty, Tommy	5. 8	Bristol City	Bristol	17.03.79
Lomas, Steve	6. 0	West Ham Utd.	Hanover	18.01.74
Rowlands, Martin	5. 9	Brentford	Hammersmith	8.02.79
Forwards				
Donnelly, Scott	5. 8	–	Hammersmith	25.12.87
Furlong, Paul	6. 0	Birmingham City	Wood Green	27.01.69

Gallen, Kevin	5.11	Barnsley	Hammersmith	21.09.75
Moore, Stefan	5.10	Aston Villa	Birmingham	28.09.83
Nygaard, Marc	6. 5	Brescia	Denmark	1.09.76
Townsend, Luke	6. 0	–	Guildford	28.09.86

SHEFFIELD WEDNESDAY

Ground: Hillsborough, Sheffield, S6 1SW.
Telephone: 0870 999 1867. **Club nickname:** Owls.
First-choice colours: Blue and white shirts; black shorts; black socks.
Main Sponsor: Plusnet. **Capacity for 2006-07:** 39,812.
Record attendance: 72,841 v Manchester City (F.A. Cup 5) 17 February, 1934.

Name	Height ft. in.	Previous club	Birthplace	Birthdate
Goalkeepers				
Adamson, Chris	5.11	St Patricks	Ashington	4.11.78
Defenders				
Adams, Steve	6. 0	Plymouth Argyle	Plymouth	25.09.80
Bougherra, Madjid	6. 2	Gueugnon	Longvic, Fr.	7.10.82
Bullen, Lee	6. 1	Dumfermline Ath.	Edinburgh	29.03.71
Collins, Patrick	6. 2	Sunderland	Newcastle	4.02.85
Coughlan, Graham	6. 2	Plymouth Argyle	Dublin	18.11.74
Gilbert, Peter	5. 9	Plymouth Argyle	Newcastle	31.07.83
Hills, John	5. 9	Gillingham	Blackpool	21.04.78
Simek, Frankie	6. 0	Arsenal	St Louis	13.10.84
Spurr, Tommy	6. 1	–	Leeds	13.09.87
Wood, Richard	6. 3	–	Wakefield	5.07.85
Midfielders				
Brunt, Chris	6. 1	Middlesbrough	Belfast	14.12.84
Folly, Yoann	5.11	Southampton	Togo	6.06.85
Lunt, Kenny	5.10	Crewe Alexandra	Runcorn	20.11.79
McAllister, Sean	5. 8	Bolton Wand.	Bolton	15.08.87
O'Brien, Burton	5.11	Livingston	Johannesburg	10.06.81
Small, Wade	5.10	MK Dons	Croydon	23.02.84
Whelan, Glenn	5.11	Manchester City	Dublin	13.01.84
Forwards				
Burton, Deon	5. 9	Rotherham Utd.	Ashford	25.10.76
Corr, Barry	6. 3	Leeds Utd.	Co.Wicklow	2.04.85
Graham, David	5.10	Wigan Athletic	Edinburgh	6.10.78
MacLean, Steven	6. 0	Rangers	Edinburgh	23.08.82
Talbot, Drew	5.10	Barnsley	Barnsley	19.07.86
Tudgay, Marcus	5.10	Derby Co.	Worthing	3.02.83

SOUTHAMPTON

Ground: The Friends Provident St Mary's Stadium, Britannia Road, Southampton, SO14 5FP.
Telephone: 0870 220 0000. **Club nickname:** Saints.
First-choice colours: Red and white shirts; black shorts; white socks.
Main sponsor: Flybe. **Capacity for 2006-07:** 32,000.
Record attendance: At St Mary's: 32,151 v Arsenal (Premier League) 29 December, 2003. At The Dell: 31,044 v Manchester Utd. (Div. 1) 8 October 1969.

Name	Height ft. in.	Previous club	Birthplace	Birthdate
Goalkeepers				
Bialkowski, Bartosz	6. 0	Gornik Zabrze	Poland	6.07.87
Poke, Michael	6. 1	–	Spelthorne	21.11.85
Defenders				
Baird, Chris	5.10	–	Ballymoney	25.02.82
Cranie, Martin	6. 0	–	Yeovil	26.09.86

Name	Height ft. in.	Previous club	Birthplace	Birthdate
Critchell, Kyle	6. 0	Weymouth	Weymouth	18.01.87
Higginbotham, Danny	6. 1	Derby Co.	Manchester	29.12.78
Lundekvam, Claus	6. 4	Brann	Austevoll, Nor.	22.02.73
Ostlund, Alexander	5.11	Feyenoord	Sweden	2.11.78
Pele	5.11	Belenenses	Albufeira, Port.	2.05.78
Powell, Darren	6. 3	Crystal Palace	Hammersmith	10.03.76
Svensson, Michael	6. 2	Troyes	Sweden	25.11.75
Midfielders				
Belmadi, Djamel	5. 8	Al Ittihad	Chamigny-sur-Marne, Fra.	25.03.76
Prutton, David	6. 1	Nott'm. Forest	Hull City	12.09.81
Surman, Andrew	5.11	–	Johannsburg	20.08.86
Wright, Jermaine	5. 9	Leeds Utd.	Greenwich	21.10.75
Wright-Phillips, Bradley	5. 8	Manchester City	Lewisham	12.03.85
Forwards				
Blackstock, Dexter	6. 2	Oxford Utd.	Oxford Utd.	20.05.86
Fuller, Ricardo	6. 3	Portsmouth	Kingston, Jam.	31.10.79
Jones, Kenwyne	6. 2	W-Connection	Trinidad	5.10.84
McGoldrick, David	6. 1	Notts Co.	Nottingham	29.11.87
Rasiak, Grzegorz	6. 3	Derby Co.	Szczecin, Pol.	12.01.79

SOUTHEND UNITED

Ground: Roots Hall, Victoria Avenue, Southend SS2 6NQ.
Telephone: 01702 304050. **Club nickname:** Shrimpers.
First-choice colours: Navy shirts; navy shorts; navy socks.
Main sponsor: Insure and Go. **Capacity for 2006-07:** 12,392.
Record attendance: 31,033 v Liverpool (F.A. Cup 3) 10 January, 1979.

Name	Height ft. in.	Previous club	Birthplace	Birthdate
Goalkeepers				
Collis, Steve	6. 2	Yeovil Town	Harrow	18.03.81
Flahavan, Darryl	5.10	Southampton	Southampton	28.11.78
Defenders				
Barrett, Adam	5.10	Bristol Rov.	Dagenham	29.11.79
Edwards, Andy	6. 3	Rushden & D'mnds.	Epping	17.09.71
Francis, Simon	6. 0	Sheffield Utd.	Nottingham	16.02.85
Hunt, Lewis	5.11	Derby Co.	Birmingham	25.08.82
Prior, Spencer	6. 3	Cardiff City	Southend	22.04.71
Sodje, Efetobore	6. 1	Yeovil Town	Greenwich	5.10.72
Wilson, Che	5.11	Cambridge Utd. City	Ely	17.01.79
Midfielders				
Campbell-Ryce, Jamal	5. 7	Rotherham Utd.	Lambeth	6.04.83
Cole, Mitchell	5.11	Grays	London	6.10.85
Gower, Mark	5.11	Barnet	Edmonton	5.10.78
Guttridge, Luke	5. 6	Cambridge Utd.	Barnstaple	27.03.82
Maher, Kevin	5.11	Tottenham	Ilford	17.10.76
Smith, Jay	5. 7	Aston Villa	London	24.09.81
Forwards				
Bradbury, Lee	6. 2	Oxford Utd.	Isle of Wight	3.07.75
Eastwood, Freddy	6. 0	Grays Athletic	Epsom	29.10.83
Lawson, James	5.10	–	Basildon	21.01.87
Ricketts, Michael	6. 2	Leeds Utd.	Birmingham	4.12.78

STOKE CITY

Ground: Britannia Stadium, Stanley Matthews Way, Stoke-on-Trent ST4 7EG.
Telephone: 01782 592222. **Club nickname:** Potters.
First-choice colours: Red and white shirts; white and red shorts; white and red socks.
Main sponsor: Britannia Building Society. **Capacity for 2006-07:** 28,218.
Record attendance: (Victoria Ground) 51,380 v Arsenal (Div. 1) 29 March, 1937.
(Britannia Stadium) 27,109 v Liverpool (League Cup 4) 29 November, 2000.

Name	Height ft. in.	Previous club	Birthplace	Birthdate
Goalkeepers				
Simonsen, Steve	6. 3	Everton	South Shields	3.04.79
Defenders				
Broomes, Marlon	6. 0	Preston N.E.	Birmingham	28.11.77
Buxton, Lewis	6. 1	Portsmouth	Newport, IOW	10.12.83
Dickinson, Carl	6. 0	–	Swadlincote	31.03.87
Duberry, Michael	6. 1	Leeds Utd.	Enfield	14.10.75
Hill, Clint	6. 0	Oldham Athletic	Liverpool	19.10.78
Hoefkens, Carl	6. 1	Germinal	Lier, Bel.	6.10.78
Wilkinson, Andy	5.11	–	Stone	6.08.84
Midfielders				
Brammer, Dave	5.10	Crewe Alexandra	Bromborough	28.02.75
Chadwick, Luke	5.11	West Ham Utd.	Cambridge	18.11.80
Eustace, John	5.11	Coventry City	Solihull	3.11.79
Harper, Kevin	5. 6	Portsmouth	Oldham	15.01.76
Hazley, Matthew	5. 7	–	Banbridge	30.12.87
Henry, Karl	6. 1	–	Wolves	26.11.82
Russell, Darel	6. 0	Norwich City	Stepney	22.10.80
Sweeney, Peter	6. 0	Millwall	Glasgow	25.09.84
Forwards				
Bangoura, Sambegou	6. 1	Standard Liege	Guinea	3.04.82
Paterson, Martin	5.10	–	Tunstall	13.05.87
Pericard, Vincent	6. 1	Portsmouth	Efok, Cam.	3.10.82
Rooney, Adam	5.10	–	Dublin	21.04.87
Sidibe, Mamady	6. 4	Gillingham	Mali	18.12.79
Sigurdsson, Hannes	6. 2	Viking	Reykjavik	10.04.83

SUNDERLAND

Ground: Stadium of Light, Sunderland SR5 1SU.
Telephone: 0191 551 5000. **Club nickname:** Black Cats.
First-choice colours: Red and white shirts; black shorts; black socks.
Main sponsor: Reg Vardy. **Capacity for 2006-07:** 49,000.
Record attendance: (Roker Park) 75,118 v Derby Co. (F.A. Cup 6) 8 March, 1933.
(Stadium of Light): 48,353 v Liverpool (Premier League) 13 April, 2002

Name	Height ft. in.	Previous club	Birthplace	Birthdate
Goalkeepers				
Alnwick, Ben	6. 0	–	Gateshead	1.01.87
Davis, Kelvin	6. 1	Ipswich Town	Bedford	29.09.76
Defenders				
Arca, Julio	5. 9	Argentinos Jnrs.	Quilmes Bernal, Arg.	31.01.81
Caldwell, Steven	6. 3	Newcastle Utd.	Stirling	12.09.80
Collins, Danny	5.11	Chester City	Chester	6.08.80
Collins, Neil	5.11	Dumbarton	Troon	2.09.83
Cunningham, Kenny	6. 0	Birmingham City	Dublin	28.06.71
McCartney, George	5.11	–	Belfast	28.04.81
Nosworthy, Nyron	6. 0	Gillingham	Brixton	11.10.80
Smith, Dan	5. 9	–	Sunderland	5.10.86
Wright, Stephen	6. 0	Liverpool	Liverpool	8.02.80
Midfielders				
Bassila, Christian	6. 3	Strasbourg	Paris	10.05.77
Delap, Rory	6. 1	Southampton	Sutton Coldfield	6.07.76
Lawrence, Liam	5. 9	Mansfield Town	Retford	14.12.81
Leadbitter, Grant	5. 9	–	Sunderland	7.01.86
Miller, Tommy	6. 1	Ipswich Town	Easington	8.01.79
Welsh, Andrew	5.10	Stockport Co.	Manchester	24.01.83
Whitehead, Dean	5.11	Oxford Utd.	Abingdon	12.01.82

Forwards

Name	Height ft. in.	Previous club	Birthplace	Birthdate
Brown, Chris	6. 1	–	Doncaster	11.12.84
Elliott, Stephen	5.11	Manchester City	Dublin	6.01.84
Kyle, Kevin	6. 3	Ayr Boswell	Stranraer	7.06.81
Murphy, Daryl	6. 2	Waterford	Waterford	15.03.83
Stead, Jon	6. 3	Blackburn Rov.	Huddersfield	7.04.83

WEST BROMWICH ALBION

Ground: The Hawthorns, Halford Lane, W.B.A.wich B71 4LF.
Telephone: 08700 668888. **Club nickname:** Baggies.
First-choice colours: Navy and white shirts; white shorts; white socks.
Main sponsor: T-mobile. **Capacity for 2006-07:** 27,880.
Record attendance: 64,815 v Arsenal (F.A. Cup 6) 6 March, 1937.

Name	Height ft. in.	Previous club	Birthplace	Birthdate
Goalkeepers				
Hoult, Russell	6. 4	Portsmouth	Ashby de la Zouch	22.11.72
Kuszczak, Tomasz	6. 3	Hertha Berlin	Krosno, Pol.	23.03.82
Zuberbuhler, Pascal	6. 6	Basle	Frauenfeld, Swi.	8.01.71
Defenders				
Albrechtsen, Martin	6. 2	FC Copenhagen	Denmark	31.03.80
Clement, Neil	6. 0	Chelsea	Reading	3.10.78
Davies, Curtis	6. 1	Luton Town	Waltham Forest	15.03.85
Gaardsoe, Thomas	6. 2	Ipswich Town	Randers, Den.	23.11.79
Perry, Chris	5. 9	Charlton Athletic	Carshalton	26.04.73
Robinson, Paul	5. 9	Watford	Watford	14.12.78
Watson, Steve	6. 0	Everton	North Shields	1.04.74
Midfielders				
Carter, Darren	6. 2	Birmingham City	Solihull	18.12.83
Chaplow, Richard	5. 9	Burnley	Accrington	2.02.85
Gera, Zoltan	6. 0	Ferencvaros	Pecs, Hun.	22.04.79
Greening, Jonathan	6. 0	Middlesbrough	Scarborough	2.01.79
Inamoto, Junichi	6. 0	Gamba Osaka	Osaka	18.09.79
Koumas, Jason	5.10	Tranmere	Wrexham	25.09.79
Quashie, Nigel	6. 0	Southampton	Peckham	20.07.78
Wallwork, Ronnie	5.10	Manchester Utd.	Manchester	10.09.77
Forwards				
Campbell, Kevin	6. 1	Everton	Lambeth	4.02.70
Ellington, Nathan	5.10	Wigan Athletic	Bradford	2.07.81
Hartson, John	6. 1	Celtic	Swansea	5.04.75
Kamara, Diomansy	6. 0	Portsmouth	Paris	8.11.80

WOLVERHAMPTON WANDERERS

Ground: Molineux Stadium, Wolverhampton, WV1 4QR.
Telephone: 0870 442 0123. **Club nickname:** Wolves.
First choice colours: Gold and black shirts; black and gold shorts; black and gold socks.
Main sponsor: Chaucer. **Capacity for 2006-07:** 28,428.
Record attendance: 61,315 v Liverpool (F.A. Cup 5) 11 February 1939.

Name	Height ft. in.	Previous club	Birthplace	Birthdate
Goalkeepers				
Ikeme, Carl	6.2	–	Sutton Coldfield	8.06.86
Murray, Matt	6.4	–	Solihull	2.05.81
Oakes, Michael	6.1	Aston Villa	Northwich	30.10.73
Defenders				
Breen, Gary	6.1	Sunderland	Hendon	12.12.73
Clyde, Mark	6.1	–	Limavady	27.12.82
Craddock, Jody	6.2	Sunderland	Redditch	25.07.75

Name	Height ft. in.	Previous club	Birthplace	Birthdate
Edwards, Rob	6. 1	Aston Villa	Telford	25.12.82
Little, Mark		–	Worcester	20.08.88
McNamara, Jackie	5. 9	Celtic	Glasgow	24.10.73
Naylor, Lee	5. 8	–	Walsall	19.03.80
Midfielders				
Andrews, Keith	6. 0	–	Dublin	18.09.80
Davies, Mark	5.11	–	Wolves	18.12.88
Ince, Paul	5.11	Middlesbrough	Ilford	21.10.67
Olofinjana, Seyi	6. 4	Brann Bergen	Lagos	30.06.800
Ricketts, Rohan	5. 9	Tottenham	Clapham	22.12.82
Rosa, Denes	5. 9	Ferencvaros	Hungary	7.04.77
Forwards				
Clarke, Leon	6. 2	–	Birmingham	10.02.85
Cort, Carl	6. 4	Newcastle Utd.	Southwark	1.11.77
Frankowski, Tomasz	5. 9	Elche	Poland	16.08.74

LEAGUE ONE

AFC BOURNEMOUTH

Ground: Fitness First Stadium, Dean Court, Bournemouth BH7 7AF.
Telephone: 01202 726300. **Club nickname:** Cherries.
First-choice colours: Red and black shirts; black and red shorts; black and red socks.
Main sponsor: Seward. **Capacity for 2006-07:** 9,287.
Record attendance: 28,799 v Manchester Utd. (F.A. Cup 6) 2 March, 1957.

Name	Height ft. in.	Previous club	Birthplace	Birthdate
Goalkeepers				
Moss, Neil	6. 3	Southampton	New Milton	10.05.75
Stewart, Gareth	6. 0	Blackburn Rov.	Preston	3.02.80
Defenders				
Broadhurst, Karl	6. 1	–	Portsmouth	18.03.80
Cummings, Warren	5. 9	Chelsea	Aberdeen	15.10.80
Gowling, Joshua	6. 3	Herfolge		29.11.83
Hart, Callum	6. 0	Bristol City	Cardiff	21.12.85
Howe, Eddie	5.11	Portsmouth	Amersham	29.11.77
Maher, Shaun	6. 2	Fulham	Dublin	20.06.78
Purches, Steve	5.11	West Ham Utd.	Ilford	14.01.80
Young, Neil	5. 9	Tottenham	Harlow	31.08.73
Midfielders				
Browning, Marcus	6. 0	Gillingham	Bristol	22.04.71
Cooke, Stephen	5. 8	Aston Villa	Walsall	15.02.83
Cooper, Shaun	5.10	Portsmouth	Isle of Wight	5.10.83
Coutts, James	5. 8	–	Weymouth	15.04.87
Foley, Steve	5. 4	Aston Villa	Dublin	10.02.86
Hollands, Danny	5.11	Chelsea	Ashford	6.11.85
Khalil, Tareq	5. 8	Cardiff City	Cardiff	18.12.85
Taylor, Daryl	5.10	Walsall	Birmingham	14.11.84
Tindall, Jason	6. 1	Charlton Athletic	Stepney	15.11.77
Forwards				
Fletcher, Steve	6. 2	Hartlepool Utd.	Hartlepool	26.06.72
Hayter, James	5. 9	–	Newport, IOW	9.04.79
Pitman, Brett	6. 0	St. Paul's	Jersey	31.01.88
Platt, Conal	5. 8	Liverpool	Preston	14.10.86

BLACKPOOL

Ground: Bloomfield Road, Blackpool FY1 6JJ.
Telephone: 0870 443 1953. **Club nickname:** Seasiders.
First-choice colours: Tangerine shirts; white shorts; tangerine socks.
Main sponsor: —. **Capacity for 2006-07:** 9,491.
Record attendance: 38,098 v Wolves (Div. 1) 17 September, 1955

Name	Height ft. in.	Previous club	Birthplace	Birthdate
Goalkeepers				
Edge, Lewis	6. 1	–	Lancaster	12.01.87
Evans, Rhys	6. 1	Swindon Town	Swindon	27.01.82
Jones, Lee	6. 3	Stockport Co.	Pontypridd	9.08.70
Defenders				
Clarke, Peter	5.11	Everton	Southport	3.01.82
Doughty, Phil	6. 2	–	Blackpool	6.09.86
Grayson, Simon	6. 0	Blackburn Rov.	Ripon	16.12.69
Jackson, Michael	6. 0	Tranmere Rov.	Runcorn	4.12.73
Joseph, Marc	6. 0	Hull City	Leicester	10.11.76
Midfielders				
Bean, Marcus	5.11	Q.P.R.	Hammersmith	2.11.84
Burns, Jamie	5. 9	–	Blackpool	6.03.84
Coid, Danny	5.11	–	Liverpool	3.10.81
Donnelly, Ciaran	5. 8	–	Blackpool	2.04.84
Fox, David	5. 9	Manchester Utd.	Leek	13.12.83
Prendergast, Rory	5. 9	Accrington	Pontefract	6.04.78
Southern, Keith	5.10	Everton	Gateshead	21.04.84
Wiles, Simon	5.11	–	Preston	22.04.85
Wood, Neil	5.10	Coventry City	Manchester	4.01.83
Forwards				
Blinkhorn, Matthew	6. 0	–	Blackpool	2.03.85
Murphy, John	6. 2	Chester City	Whiston	18.10.76
Parker, Keigan	5. 7	St Johnstone	Livingston	8.06.82
Shaw, Matthew	6. 2	Sheffield Wed.	Blackpool	17.05.84
Vernon, Scott	6. 1	Oldham Athletic	Manchester	13.12.83
Forbes, Adrian	5. 8	Swansea City	Ealing	23.01.79

BRADFORD CITY

Ground: Bradford and Bingley Stadium, Valley Parade, Bradford BD8 7DY.
Telephone: 0870 822 0000. **Club nickname:** Bantams.
First-choice colours: Claret and amber shirts; claret and amber shorts; claret and amber socks.
Main Sponsor: Bradford and Bingley. **Capacity for 2006-07:** 25,136.
Record attendance: 39,146 v Burnley (F.A. Cup 4) 11 March, 1911.

Name	Height ft. in.	Previous club	Birthplace	Birthdate
Goalkeepers				
Howarth, Russell	6. 2	Tranmere Rov.	York City	27.03.82
Ricketts, Donovan	6. 3	Bolton Wand.	Kingston, Jam.	7.06.77
Defenders				
Ainge, Simon	6. 1	–	Bradford	18.02.88
Bentham, Craig	5. 9	–	Bradford	7.03.85
Bower, Mark	5.10	–	Bradford	23.01.80
Edghill, Richard	5. 9	Q.P.R.	Oldham	23.09.74
Emanuel, Lewis	5. 8	–	Bradford	4.10.83
Holloway, Darren	6. 0	MK Dons	Crook	3.10.77
O'Brien, Luke	5. 9	–		11.09.88
Swift, John	5. 7	–	Leeds	20.09.84
Wetherall, David	6. 3	Leeds Utd.	Sheffield	14.03.71

Midfielders

Name	Height ft. in.	Previous club	Birthplace	Birthdate
Bridge-Wilkinson, Marc	5. 6	Stockport Co.	Nuneaton	16.03.79
Brown, Joe	5.10	–	Bradford	3.04.88
Colbeck, Joe	5.11	–	Bradford	29.11.86
Johnson, Jermaine	6. 1	Tivoli Gardens	Jamaica	25.06.80
McGuire, Patrick	5.10	–	Bradford	29.07.87
Penford, Tom	5.10	–	Leeds	5.01.85
Petta, Bobby	5. 7	Darlington	Rotterdam	6.08.74
Schumacher, Steven	6. 0	Everton	Liverpool	30.04.84

Forwards

Name	Height ft. in.	Previous club	Birthplace	Birthdate
Clarke, Matt	6. 3	Darlington	Leeds	18.12.80
McEvilly, Lee	6. 1	Wrexham	Liverpool	15.04.82
Muirhead, Ben	5.10	Manchester Utd.	Doncaster	5.01.83
Symes, Michael	6. 3	Everton	Great Yarmouth	31.10.83
Windass, Dean	5. 9	Sheffield Utd.	Hull	1.04.69

BRENTFORD

Ground: Griffin Park, Braemar Road, Brentford TW8 0NT.
Telephone: 0845 345 6442. **Club nickname:** Bees.
First-choice colours: Red and white shirts; black shorts; red stockings.
Main sponsor: Samvo.com. **Capacity for 2006-07:** 12,400.
Record attendance: 39,626 v Preston N.E. (F.A. Cup 6) 5 March, 1938.

Name	Height ft. in.	Previous club	Birthplace	Birthdate
Goalkeepers				
Nelson, Stuart	6. 1	Hucknall Town	Stroud	17.09.81
Defenders				
Charles, Darius	6. 1	–	Ealing	10.12.87
Fitzgerald, Scott	6. 0	Colchester Utd.	Westminster	13.08.69
Griffiths, Adam	6. 2	Bournemouth	Sydney, Aust.	21.08.79
Osborne, Karleigh	6. 2	–	Southall	19.03.88
Tillen, Sam	5.10	Chelsea	Reading	16.04.85
Midfielders				
Brooker, Paul	5.10	Reading	Hammersmith	25.11.76
Frampton, Andrew	5.11	Crystal Palace	Wimbledon	3.09.79
Pinault, Thomas	5.10	Grimsby Town	Grasse, Fr.	4.12.81
Skulason, Oli	6. 0	Arsenal	Reykjavik	1.04.83
Forwards				
Ide, Charlie	5. 8	–	Sunbury	10.05.88
Kuffour, Jo	5. 6	Torquay Utd.	Edmonton	17.11.81
Moore, Chris	6. 0	Dagenham & Red.	Blackburn	13.01.80
O'Connor, Kevin	5.11	–	Blackburn	24.02.82
Owusu, Lloyd	6. 0	Reading	Slough	12.12.76
Peters, Ryan	5.11	–	Wandsworth	21.08.87
Rhodes, Alex	5.11	Newmarket Town	Cambridge	23.01.82
Willock, Calum	6. 1	Peterborough Utd.	Lambeth	29.10.81

BRIGHTON AND HOVE ALBION

Ground: Withdean Stadium, Tongdean Lane, Brighton BN1 5JD.
Telephone: 01273 695400. **Club nickname:** Seagulls.
First-choice colours: Blue and white shirts; white shorts; white socks.
Main sponsor: Skint. **Capacity for 2006-07:** 8,850.
Record attendance: (Goldstone Ground) 36,747 v Fulham (Div. 2) 27 December, 1958; (Withdean Stadium) 7,999 v Southampton (Championship) 8 April, 2006.

Name	Height ft. in.	Previous club	Birthplace	Birthdate
Goalkeepers				
Henderson, Wayne	5.11	Aston Villa	Dublin	16.09.83

Kuipers, Michel	6. 2	Bristol Rov.	Amsterdam	26.06.74
Martin, Richard	6. 2	–	Brighton	1.09.87
Sullivan, John	5.10	–	Brighton	8.03.88
Defenders				
Butters, Guy	6. 3	Gillingham	Hillingdon	30.10.69
El-Abd, Adam	6. 0	–	Brighton	11.09.84
Elphick, Tommy		–	Brighton	7.09.87
Hinshelwood, Adam	5.10	–	Oxford Utd.	8.01.84
Lynch, Joel		–	Eastbourne	3.10.87
Mayo, Kerry	5. 9	–	Cuckfield	21.09.77
Reid, Paul	5.10	Bradford City	Sydney	6.07.79
Midfielders				
Carpenter, Richard	6. 0	Cardiff City	Sheppey	30.09.72
Frutos, Alexandre	5. 9	Metz	France	23.04.82
Gatting, Joe	5.11	–	Brighton	25.11.87
Hammond, Dean	5.11	–	Hastings	7.03.83
Hart, Gary	5. 9	Stansted	Harlow	21.09.76
Loft, Doug	6. 0	Hastings	Maidstone	25.12.86
Oatway, Charlie	5. 7	Brentford	Hammersmith	28.11.73
Forwards				
Kazim-Richards, Colin	6. 1	Bury	Leyton	26.08.86
Molango, Maheta	6. 1	Burghaussen	St Imier, Swi.	24.07.82
Revell, Alex	6. 3	Cambridge Utd.	Cambridge	7.07.83
Robinson, Jake	5. 7	–	Brighton	23.10.86

BRISTOL CITY

Ground: Ashton Gate, Bristol BS3 2EJ.
Telephone: 0870 112 1897. **Club nickname:** Robins.
First-choice colours: Red shirts; white shorts; red socks.
Main sponsor: Bristol Trade Centre. **Capacity for 2006-07:** 21,497.
Record attendance: 43,335 v Preston N.E. (F.A. Cup 5) 16 February 1935.

	Height			
Name	**ft. in.**	**Previous club**	**Birthplace**	**Birthdate**
Goalkeepers				
Basso, Adriano	6. 1	Woking	Brazil	18.04.75
Phillips, Steve	6. 1	Paulton Rov.	Bath	6.05.78
Weale, Chris	6. 2	Yeovil Town	Chard	9.02.82
Defenders				
Carey, Louis	5.10	Coventry City	Bristol	22.01.77
Fontaine, Liam	6. 3	Fulham	Beckenham	7.01.83
Fortune, Clayton	6. 3	–	Forest Gate	10.11.82
Heywood, Matt	6. 3	Swindon Town	Chatham	26.08.79
Keogh, Richard	6. 2	Stoke City	Harlow	11.08.86
Partridge, David		Motherwell	Westminster	26.11.78
Woodman, Craig	5. 9	–	Tiverton	22.12.82
Midfielders				
Brown, Scott	5. 9	Everton	Liverpool	8.05.85
Murray, Scott	5. 8	Reading	Aberdeen	26.05.74
Noble, David	6. 0	Boston Utd.	Hitchin	2.02.82
Orr, Bradley	6. 0	Newcastle Utd.	Liverpool	1.11.82
Russell, Alex	5.10	Torquay Utd.	Crosby	17.03.73
Skuse, Cole	5. 9	–	Bristol	29.03.86
Smith, Grant	6. 1	Swindon Town	Irvine	5.05.80
Wilkshire, Luke	5. 8	Middlesbrough	Wollongong, Aus.	2.10.81
Forwards				
Brooker, Stephen	5.10	Port Vale	Newport Pagnell	21.05.81
Cotterill, David	5.10	–	Cardiff	4.12.87
Jevons, Phil	5.11	Yeovil Town	Liverpool	1.08.79
Showunmi, Enoch	6. 4	Luton Town	London	21,04,82
Stewart, Marcus	5.10	Sunderland	Bristol	7.11.72

CARLISLE UNITED

Ground: Brunton Park, Warwick Road, Carlisle Utd. CA1 1LL.
Telephone: 01228 526237. **Club nickname:** Cumbrians.
First-choice colours: Blue shirts; white shorts; blue socks.
Main sponsor: Stobarts. **Capacity for 2006-07:** 16,981.
Record attendance: 27,500 v Birmingham City (F.A. Cup 3) 5 January, 1957, and v
   Middlesbrough (F.A. Cup 5) 7 January, 1970.

Name	Height ft. in.	Previous club	Birthplace	Birthdate
Goalkeepers				
Bradley, Adam	6. 0	–	Carlisle	25.08.88
Westwood, Kieren	6. 1	Manchester City	Manchester	23.10.84
Williams, Anthony	6. 2	Grimsby Town	Manchester	20.09.77
Defenders				
Aranalde, Zigor	6. 1	Walsall	Guipuzcoa, Sp.	28.02.73
Arnison, Paul	5.10	Hartlepool Utd.	Hartlepool	18.09.77
Grand, Simon	6. 0	Rochdale	Chorley	23.02.84
Gray, Kevin	6. 0	Tranmere Rov.	Sheffield	7.01.72
Kirkup, Dan	6. 3	–	Hexham	19.05.88
Livesey, Danny	6. 3	Bolton Wand.	Salford	31.12.84
Raven, David	6. 0	Liverpool	Wirral	10.03.85
Midfielders				
Billy, Chris	5.11	Bury	Huddersfield	2.01.73
Earl, James		–	Carlisle	29.11.87
Hackney, Simon	5.10	Woodley Sports	Manchester	5.02.84
Joyce, Luke	5.11	Wigan Athletic		9.07.87
Lumsdon, Chris	5.11	Barnsley	Newcastle	15.12.79
Murphy, Peter	5.11	Blackburn Rov.	Dublin	27.10.80
Murray, Adam	5. 8	Mansfield Town	Birmingham	30.09.81
Murray, Paul	5. 9	Oldham Athletic	Carlisle	31.08.76
Forwards				
Bridges, Michael	6. 1	Bristol City	North Shields	5.08.78
Ferris, Pete	5.11	–	Carlisle	4.12.86
Gall, Kevin	5. 9	Yeovil Town	Merthyr Tydfil	4.02.82
Hawley, Karl	5. 8	Walsall	Walsall	6.12.81
Holmes, Derek	6. 2	Bournemouth	Lanark	18.10.78
Murray, Glenn	6. 0	–	Workington	25.09.83
Nade, Raphael	6. 0	Woking	France	18.10.80

CHELTENHAM TOWN

Ground: Whaddon Road, Cheltenham GL52 5NA.
Telephone: 01242 573558. **Club nickname:** Town.
First-choice colours: Red and white shirts; white shorts; red socks.
Main Sponsor: George Bence Builders Merchants. **Capacity for 2006-07:** 7,022.
Record attendance: 8,326 v Reading (F.A. Cup 1) 17 November, 1956.

Name	Height ft. in.	Previous club	Birthplace	Birthdate
Goalkeepers				
Brown, Scott	6. 0	Bristol City	Wolves	26.04.85
Higgs, Shane	6. 2	Worcester City	Oxford	13.05.77
Puddy, Will	5.11	Bristol City	Salisbury	4.10.87
Defenders				
Caines, Gavin	6. 1	Walsall	Birmingham	20.09.83
Duff, Shane	6. 1	–	Wroughton	2.04.82
Gallinagh, Andy	5.10	–	Sutton Coldfield	16.03.85
Gill, Jerry	5. 7	Northampton Town	Clevedon	8.09.70
Townsend, Michael	6. 2	Wolves	Walsall	17.05.86
Victory, Jamie	5. 8	Bournemouth	London	14.11.75

Wilson, Brian	5.10	Stoke City	Manchester	9.05.83
Wylde, Michael	6. 2	–	Birmingham	6.01.87
Midfielders				
Armstrong, Craig	5.11	Bradford City	South Shields	23.05.75
Bell, Mickey	5.10	Port Vale	Newcastle	15.11.71
Bird, David	5. 8	Cinderford Town	Gloucester	26.12.84
Connolly, Adam	5. 9	–	Manchester	10.04.86
Devaney, Martin	5.11	Coventry City	Cheltenham	1.06.80
Finnigan, John	5. 8	Lincoln City	Wakefield	20.03.76
McCann, Grant	5.10	West Ham Utd.	Belfast	14.04.80
Melligan, John	5. 9	Wolves	Dublin	11.02.82
Taylor, Michael	5.10	Blackburn Rov.	Liverpool	21.11.82
Yao, Sosthene	5. 4	West Ham Utd.	Ivory Coast	7.08.87
Forwards				
Bradshaw, Gary	5. 6	North Ferriby	Hull	30.12.82
Gillespie, Steven	5. 9	–	Liverpool	4.06.84
Guinan, Steve	6. 1	Hereford Utd.	Birmingham	24.12.75
Odejayi, Kayode	6. 2	Bristol City	Nigeria	21.02.82
Spencer, Damian	6. 1	Bristol City	Ascot	19.09.81
Vincent, Ashley	6. 0	Wolves	Birmingham	26.05.85

CHESTERFIELD

Ground: Recreation Ground, Chesterfield S40 4SX.
Telephone: 01246 209765. **Club nickname:** Spireites.
First-choice colours: Blue shirts; white shorts; blue socks.
Main Sponsor: Autoworld. **Capacity for 2006-07:** 8,502.
Record attendance: 30,698 v Newcastle Utd. (Div. 2) 7 April, 1939.

Name	Height ft. in.	**Previous club**	**Birthplace**	**Birthdate**
Goalkeepers				
Roche, Barry	6. 4	Nott'm. Forest	Dublin	6.04.82
Defenders				
Bailey, Alex	5.11	Arsenal	Newham	21.09.83
Blatherwick, Steve	6. 1	Burnley	Nottingham	20.09.73
Downes, Aaron	6. 1	Frickley	Mudgee, Aus.	15.05.85
Hazell, Reuben	5.11	Kidderminster Harr.	Birmingham	24.04.79
Kovacs, Janos	6. 4		Hungary	11.09.85
Nicholson, Shane	5.10	Tranmere Rov.	Newark	3.06.70
O'Hare, Alan	6. 2	Bolton Wand.	Drogheda	31.07.82
Picken, Phil	5. 9	Manchester Utd.	Manchester	12.11.85
Midfielders				
Davies, Gareth	6. 1	–	Chesterfield	4.02.83
Hall, Paul	5. 9	Tranmere Rov.	Manchester	3.07.72
Niven, Derek	5.10	Raith Rov.	Falkirk	12.12.83
Forwards				
Allison, Wayne	6. 1	Sheffield Utd.	Huddersfield	16.10.68
Allott, Mark	5.11	Oldham Athletic	Middleton	3.10.77
Folan, Caleb	6. 1	Leeds Utd.	Leeds	26.10.82
Larkin, Colin	5. 9	Mansfield Town	Dundalk	27.04.82
Shaw, Paul	5.11	Sheffield Utd.	Burnham	4.09.73
Smith, Adam	5.10	–	Huddersfield	20.02.85

CREWE ALEXANDRA

Ground: Alexandra Stadium, Gresty Road, Crewe CW2 6EB.
Telephone: 01270 213014. **Club nickname:** Railwaymen.
First-choice colours: Red shirts; white shorts; red socks.
Main sponsor: Mornflake Oates. **Capacity for 2006-07:** 10,107.
Record attendance: 20,000 v Tottenham (F.A. Cup 4) 30 January, 1960.

Name	Height ft. in.	Previous club	Birthplace	Birthdate
Goalkeepers				
Tomlinson, Stuart	6. 0	–	Chester	10.05.85
Williams, Ben	6. 0	Manchester Utd.	Manchester	27.08.82
Williams, Owain fon	6. 4	–	Gwynedd	17.03.87
Defenders				
Baudet, Julien	6. 3	Notts Co.	Grenoble	13.01.79
Bignot, Paul	6. 1	–	Birmingham	14.02.86
Coo, Cavell	5. 9	–	Manchester	7.08.87
Cox, Neil	6. 0	Cardiff City	Scunthorpe	8.10.71
Dugdale, Adam	6. 3	–	Liverpool	12.09.87
Lloyd, Robert	6. 0	–	Chester	13.08.86
Otsemobor, Jon	5.10	Liverpool	Liverpool	23.03.83
Moss, Darren	5.10	Shrewsbury Town	Wrexham	24.05.81
Sutton, Ritchie	6. 0	–	Stoke	29.04.86
Midfielders				
Bell, Lee	5.10	–	Crewe	20.11.83
Dillon, John	5.10	–	Liverpool	2.08.88
Flynn, Christopher	5.11	–	Market Drayton	5.11.87
Grant, Tony	5.10	Bristol City	Liverpool	14.11.74
Jones, Billy	5.11	–	Shrewsbury	24.03.87
Lowe, Ryan	5.11	Chester City	Liverpool	18.09.78
O'Connor, Michael	6. 1	–	Belfast	6.10.87
Rix, Ben	5.10	–	Wolves	11.12.83
Roberts, Gary	5. 9	–	Chester	4.02.87
Vaughan, David	5. 6	–	St Asaph	18.02.83
Forwards				
Bailey, Matthew	6. 4	Northwich Victoria	Crewe	12.03.86
Higdon, Michael	6. 0	–	Liverpool	3.09.83
Maynard, Nicky	5.11	–	Winsford	11.12.86
Miller, Shaun	5.10	–	Alsager	25.09.87
Pope, Tom	6. 3	Biddulph	Stoke	27.08.85
Rodgers, Luke	5. 7	Shrewsbury Town	Birmingham	1.01.82
Suhaj, Pavol	6. 4	AS Trencia	Lipany, Slovak.	16.04.81
Varney, Luke	5.10	Quorn	Leicester	28.09.82
Warlow, Adam	6. 2	–	Southport	3.02.87

DONCASTER ROVERS

Ground: Belle Vue, Bawtry Road, Doncaster, DN4 5HT.
Telephone: 01302 539441. **Club nickname:** Rovers.
First-choice colours: Red and white shirts; red shorts; red socks.
Main sponsor: Streetwise Sports. **Capacity for 2006-07:** 10,594.
Record attendance: 37,149 v Hull City (Div.3N) 2 October, 1948.

Name	Height ft. in.	Previous club	Birthplace	Birthdate
Goalkeepers				
Blayney, Alan	6. 2	Southampton	Belfast	9.10.81
Budz, Jan	6. 1	Nordsjaelland	Denmark	20.04.79
Nielsen, Tommy	6. 9	Fremad Amager	Denmark	10.02.84
Warrington, Andy	6. 3	York City	Sheffield	10.06.76
Defenders				
Fenton, Nick	6. 1	Notts Co.	Preston	23.11.79
Lee, Graeme	6. 2	Sheffield Wed.	Middlesbrough	31.05.78
Lockwood, Adam	6. 0	Yeovil Town	Wakefield	26.10.81
McDaid, Sean	5. 6	Leeds Utd.	Harrogate	6.03.86
McGuire, Phil	6. 4	Aberdeen	Glasgow	3.02.82
O'Connor, James	5.10	Bournemouth	Birmingham	20.11.84

Midfielders

Name	Height ft. in.	Previous club	Birthplace	Birthdate
Brown, Adam	5.10	–	Sunderland	17.12.87
Green, Paul	5.10	Sheffield Wed.	Sheffield	10.04.83
Horlock, Kevin	6. 0	Ipswich Town	Erith	1.11.72
Nelthorpe, Craig	5.10	–	Doncaster	10.06.87
Price, Jason	6. 2	Hull City	Pontypridd	12.04.77
Thornton, Sean	5.10	Sunderland	Drogheda	18.05.83

Forwards

Name	Height ft. in.	Previous club	Birthplace	Birthdate
Coppinger, James	5. 7	Exeter City	Middlesbrough	10.01.81
Dyer, Bruce	6. 0	Sheffield Utd.	Ilford	13.04.75
Guy, Lewis	5.10	Newcastle Utd.	Penrith	27.08.85
Heffernan, Paul	5.10	Notts Co.	Dublin	29.12.81
Roberts, Neil	5.10	Wigan Athletic	Wrexham	7.04.78

GILLINGHAM

Ground: Priestfield Stadium, Redfern Avenue, Gillingham ME7 4DD.
Telephone: 01634 300000. **Club nickname:** Gills.
First-choice colours: Blue shirts; blue shorts; blue socks.
Main sponsor: MHS Commercial. **Capacity for 2006-07:** 11,500.
Record attendance: 23,002 v Q.P.R. (F.A. Cup 3) 10 January, 1948.

Name	Height ft. in.	Previous club	Birthplace	Birthdate
Goalkeepers				
Jack, Kelvin	6. 4	Dundee	Trinidad	29.04.76
Knowles, Danny	6. 0	Hastings Utd.	Sidcup	7.01.86
Defenders				
Clohessy, Sean	6. 0	Arsenal	Croydon	12.12.86
Cox, Ian	6. 0	Burnley	Croydon	25.03.71
Easton, Clint	5.11	Wycombe Wand.	Barking	1.11.77
Jackman, Danny	5. 6	Stockport Co.	Worcester	3.01.83
Jupp, Duncan	6. 0	Southend Utd.	Guildford	25.01.75
Sancho, Brent	6. 1	Dundee	Trinidad & Tobago	13.03.77
Midfielders				
Bentley, Mark	6. 2	Southend Utd.	Hertford	7.01.78
Crofts, Andrew	5.11	–	Chatham	29.05.84
Flynn, Michael	5.10	Wigan Athletic	Newport	17.10.80
Jarvis, Matthew	5. 8	–	Middlesbrough	22.05.86
Johnson, Leon	6. 0	Southend Utd.	Shoreditch	10.05.81
Pouton, Alan	6. 0	Grimsby Town	Newcastle	1.02.77
Spiller, Daniel	5.10	–	Maidstone	10.01.81
Stone, Craig	6. 0	–	Gravesend	29.12.88
Forwards				
Collin, Frannie	5.11	–	Gillingham	20.04.87
McDonald, Dean	5. 7	Ipswich Town	Lambeth	19.02.86
Mulligan, Gary	6. 1	Sheffield Utd.	Dublin	23.04.85
N'Dumbu-Nsungu, Guylain	6. 1	Cardiff City	Kinshasa	26.12.82

HUDDERSFIELD TOWN

Ground: Galpharm Stadium, Huddersfield HD1 6PX.
Telephone: 01484 484100. **Club nickname:** Terriers.
First-choice colours: Blue and white shirts; white and blue shorts; white and blue socks.
Main Sponsor: Yorkshire Building Society. **Capacity for 2006-07:** 24,554.
Record attendance: (Leeds Road) 67,037 v Arsenal (F.A. Cup 6) 27 February, 1932; (McAlpine Stadium) 23,678 v Liverpool (F.A. Cup 3) 12 December, 1999.

Name	Height ft. in.	Previous club	Birthplace	Birthdate
Goalkeepers				
Glennan, Matt	6.2	Falkirk		8.10.78

Rachubka, Paul	6. 2	Charlton Athletic	San Luis, Calif.	21.05.81
Defenders				
Adams, Danny	5. 8	Stockport Co.	Manchester	3.01.76
Clarke, Nathan	6. 2	–	Halifax	30.11.83
Clarke, Tom	5.11	–	Halifax	21.12.87
Hudson, Mark	5.10	Chesterfield	Bishop Auckland	24.10.80
McIntosh, Martin	6. 3	Rotherham Utd.	East Kilbride	19.03.71
McCombe, John	6. 2	–	Pontefract	7.05.85
Mirfin, David	6. 2	–	Sheffield	18.04.85
Midfielders				
Ahmed, Adnan	5.10	–	Burnley	7.06.84
Brandon, Chris	5. 7	Chesterfield	Bradford	7.04.76
Collins, Michael	6. 0	–	Halifax	30.04.86
Hand, James	5. 9	–	Ireland	22.10.86
Hardy, Aaron	5. 8	–	Pontefdract	26.05.86
Holdsworth, Andy	5. 9	–	Pontefract	29.01.84
Schofield, Danny	5.10	Brodsworth	Doncaster	10.04.80
Worthington, Jon	5. 9	–	Dewsbury	16.04.83
Young, Matthew	5. 9	–	Leeds	25.10.85
Forwards				
Abbott, Pawel	6. 1	Preston N.E.	York	2.12.81
Beckett, Luke	5.11	Sheffield Utd.	Sheffield	25.11.76
Booth, Andy	6. 1	Sheffield Wed.	Huddersfield	6.12.73
McAliskey, John	6. 4	–	Huddersfield	2.09.84
Taylor-Fletcher, Gary	6. 0	Lincoln City	Liverpool	4.06.81

LEYTON ORIENT

Ground: Matchroom Stadium, Brisbane Road, London E10 5NE.
Telephone: 0871 310 1881. **Club nickname:** O's.
First-choice colours: Red shirts; red shorts; red socks.
Main Sponsor: Poker Million.com. **Capacity for 2006-07:** 7,900.
Record attendance: 34,345 v West Ham Utd. (F.A. Cup 4) 25 January 1964.

Name	Height ft. in.	Previous club	Birthplace	Birthdate
Goalkeepers				
Garner, Glyn	6. 3	Bury	Pontypool	9.12.76
Morris, Glenn	6. 0	–	Woolwich	20.12.83
Defenders				
Barnard, Donny	6. 0	–	Forest Gate	1.07.84
Demetriou, Jason	5.11	–	Newham	18.11.87
Lockwood, Matthew	5. 9	Bristol Rov.	Rochford	17.10.76
Mackie, John	6. 1	Reading	Enfield	5.07.76
Miller, Justin	6. 0	Ipswich Town	Johannesburg	16.12.80
Palmer, Aiden	5. 8	–	Enfield	2.01.87
Tann, Adam	6. 0	Cambridge Utd.	Fakenham	12.05.82
Midfielders				
Corden, Wayne	5. 9	Scunthorpe Utd.	Leek	1.11.75
Duncan, Derek	5. 8	–	Newham	23.04.87
Easton, Craig	5.10	Livingston	Bellshill	26.02.79
Keith, Joe	5. 7	Colchester Utd.	Plaistow	1.10.78
McMahon, Daryl	5.11	West Ham Utd.	Dublin	10.10.82
Saah, Brian	6. 1	–	Rush Green	16.12.86
Simpson, Michael	5. 8	Wycombe Wand.	Nottingham	28.02.74
Tudor, Shane	5. 8	Cambridge Utd.	Wolves	10.02.82
Forwards				
Alexander, Gary	6. 0	Hull City	Peckham	15.08.79
Connor, Paul	6. 1	Swansea City	Bishop Auckland	12.01.79
Echanomi, Efe	6. 1	–	Nigeria	27.09.86
Ibehre, Jabo	6. 2	–	Islington	28.01.83
Steele, Lee	5. 8	Oxford Utd.	Liverpool	7.12.73

MILLWALL

Ground: The New Den, Zampa Road, London SE16 3LN.
Telephone: 0207 232 1222. **Club nickname:** Lions.
First-choice colours: Blue and white shirts; white and blue shorts; blue socks.
Main sponsor: Beko. **Capacity for 2006-07:** 20,146.
Record attendance: (The Den) 48,672 v Derby Co. (F.A. Cup 5) 20 February, 1937.
(New Den) 20,093 v Arsenal (F.A. Cup 3) 10 January, 1994.

Name	Height ft. in.		Previous club	Birthplace	Birthdate
Goalkeepers					
Day, Chris	6.	2	Oldham Athletic	Walthamstow	28.07.75
Pidgeley, Lenny	6.	4	Chelsea	Twickenham	7.02.84
Defenders					
Craig, Tony	6.	0	–	Greenwich	20.04.85
Dunne, Alan	5.10		–	Dublin	23.08.82
Lawrence, Matt	6.	1	Wycombe Wand.	Northampton	19.06.74
Robinson, Paul	6.	1	–	Barnet	7.01.82
Phillips, Mark	6.	2	–	Lambeth	27.01.82
Shaw, Richard	5.	9	Coventry City	Brentford	11.09.68
Whitbread, Zak	6.	2	Liverpool	Houston	4.03.84
Midfielders					
Cogan, Barry	5.	9	–	Sligo	4.11.84
Elliott, Marvin	6.	0	–	Wandsworth	15.09.84
Hendry, Will	5.11		–	Slough	10.11.86
Livermore, David	6.	0	Arsenal	Edmonton	20.05.80
McInnes, Derek	5.	7	Dundee Utd.		5.07.71
Morais, Filipe	5.	9	Chelsea	Lisbon	21.11.85
Morris, Jody	5.	5	Leeds Utd.	Hammersmith	22.12.78
Williams, Marvin	5.11		–		12.08.87
Forwards					
Braniff, Kevin	5.11		–	Belfast	4.03.83
Brighton, Tom	5.11		Clyde		28.03.84
Byfield, Darren	5.11		Gillingham	Sutton Coldfield	29.09.76
Grant, Gavin	5.11		Gillingham	Finchley	27.03.84
May, Ben	6.	1	–	Gravesend	10.03.84

NORTHAMPTON TOWN

Ground: Sixfields Stadium, Upton Way, Northampton NN5 5QA.
Telephone: 01604 757773. **Club nickname:** Cobblers.
First-choice colours: Claret and white shirts; white shorts; claret and white socks.
Main sponsor: Nationwide. **Capacity for 2006-07:** 7,300.
Record attendance: (County Ground) 24,523 v Fulham (Div. 1) 23 April, 1966.
(Sixfields Stadium) 7,557 v Manchester City (Div. 2) 26 September, 1998.

Name	Height ft. in.		Previous club	Birthplace	Birthdate
Goalkeepers					
Bunn, Mark	6.	0	–	Camden	16.11.84
Harper, Lee	6.	1	Walsall	Chelsea	30.10.71
Defenders					
Bojic, Pedj	5.11		Sydney Olympic	Sydney	9.04.84
Chambers, Luke	5.11		–	Kettering	29.08.85
Crowe, Jason	5.	9	Grimsby Town	Sidcup	30.09.78
Doig, Chris	6.	2	Nott'm. Forest	Dumfries	13.02.81
Dyche, Sean	6.	2	Watford	Kettering	28.06.71
Holt, Andy	6.	1	Wrexham	Stockport	21.05.78
Johnson, Brett	6.	1	Aldershot	Hammersmith	15.08.85
Murray, Fred	5.10		Cambridge Utd.	Clonmel	22.05.82

Midfielders

Name	Height ft. in.	Previous club	Birthplace	Birthdate
Aiston, Sam	6. 1	Tranmere Rov.	Newcastle	21.11.76
Burnell, Joe	5.10	Wycombe Wand.	Bristol	10.10.80
Gilligan, Ryan	5.10	Watford	Swindon	18.01.87
Hunt, David	5.11	Leyton Orient	Dulwich	10.09.82
Johnson, Bradley	5.10	Cambridge Utd.	Hackney	28.04.87
Taylor, Ian	6. 2	Derby Co.	Birmingham	4.06.68

Forwards

Name	Height ft. in.	Previous club	Birthplace	Birthdate
Cross, Scott	5.10	–	Northampton	30.10.87
Jess, Eoin	5.10	Nott'm. Forest	Aberdeen	13.12.70
Kirk, Andy	5.10	Boston Utd.	Belfast	29.05.79
McGleish, Scott	5.10	Colchester Utd.	Barnet	10.02.74
Smith, Martin	5.11	Huddersfield Town T	Sunderland	13.11.74

NOTTINGHAM FOREST

Ground: City Ground, Pavilion Road, Nottingham NG2 5FJ.
Telephone: 0115 982 4444. **Club nickname:** Forest.
First-choice colours: Red shirts; white shorts; red socks.
Main sponsor: Capital One. **Capacity for 2006-07:** 30,576.
Record attendance: 49,945 v Manchester Utd. (Div. 1) 28 October, 1967.

Name	Height ft. in.	Previous club	Birthplace	Birthdate
Goalkeepers				
Gerrard, Paul	6. 2	Everton	Heywood	22.01.73
Pedersen, Rune	6. 3	Aarhus	Denmark	9.10.79
Roberts, Dale		Middlesbrough	Horden	22.10.86
Smith, Paul	6. 4	Southampton	Epsom	17.12.79
Defenders				
Breckin, Ian	5.11	Wigan Athletic	Rotherham	24.02.75
Cullip, Danny	6. 0	Sheffield Utd.	Bracknell	17.09.76
Eaden, Nicky	5. 9	Wigan Athletic	Sheffield	12.12.72
Curtis, John	5.10	Portsmouth	Nuneaton	3.09.78
Morgan, Wes	5.11	–	Nottingham	21.01.84
Padula, Gino	5. 9	Q.P.R.	Buenos Aires	11.07.76
Perch, James	6. 0	–	Mansfield	28.09.85
Roberts, Justyn	6. 0	–	Lewisham	12.02.86
Thompson, John	6. 1	–	Dublin	12.10.82
Midfielders				B
Bastians, Felix	6. 2	Borussia Dortmund	Bochum	9.05.88
Clingan, Sammy	5.11	Wolves	Belfast	13.01.84
Commons, Kris	5. 6	Stoke City	Mansfield	30.08.83
Friio, David	6. 0	Plymouth Argyle	Thionville, Fra.	17.02.73
Gardner, Ross	5. 8	Newcastle Utd.	South Shields	15.02.85
Holt, Gary	6. 0	Norwich City	Irvine	9.03.73
Nowland, Adam	5.11	West Ham Utd.	Preston	6.07.81
Southall, Nicky	5.10	Gillingham	Stockton	28.01.72
Forwards				
Dobie, Scott	6. 1	Millwall	Workington	10.10.78
Harris, Neil	5.11	Millwall	Orsett	12.07.77
Holt, Grant	6. 1	Rochdale	Carlisle	12.04.81
James, Kevin	5. 9	Gillingham	Southwark	3.01.80
Johnson, David	5. 6	Ipswich Town	Kingston, Jam.	15.08.76
Lester, Jack	5.10	Sheffield Utd.	Sheffield	8.10.75
Pittman, Jon-Paul	5.10	Aston Villa	Oklahoma City	24.10.86
Tyson, Nathan	5.11	Wycombe Wand.	Reading	4.05.82

OLDHAM ATHLETIC

Ground: Boundary Park, Oldham OL1 2PA.
Telephone: 0871 226 2235. **Club nickname:** Latics.

First-choice colours: Blue shirts; blue shorts; white socks.
Main sponsor: Hillstone Developments. Capacity for 2006-07: 13,624.
Record attendance: 47,761 v Sheffield Wed. (F.A. Cup 4) 25 January, 1930.

Name	Height ft. in.	Previous club	Birthplace	Birthdate
Goalkeepers				
Pogliacomi, Les	6. 5	Parramatta	Perth, Aus.	3.05.76
Smith, Terry	6. 0	Preston N.E.		16.09.87
Defenders				
Branston, Guy	6. 1	Sheffield Wed.	Leicester	9.01.79
Haining, Will	5.11	–	Glasgow	2.10.82
Owen, Gareth	6. 1	Stoke City	Pontypridd	21.09.82
Scott, Rob	6. 1	Rotherham Utd.	Epsom	15.08.73
Stam, Stefan	6. 2	Huizen	Amersfoot, Hol.	14.09.79
Swailes, Chris	6. 2	Rotherham Utd.	Gateshead	19.10.70
Tierney, Marc	6. 0	–	Prestwich	23.08.85
Midfielders				
Bonner, Mark	5.10	Cardiff City	Ormskirk	7.06.74
Edwards, Paul	5.11	Blackpool	Manchester	1.01.80
Hughes, Mark	5.10	Tottenham	Dungannon	16.09.83
Lomax, Kelvin	5.11	–	Bury	12.11.86
McDonald, Gary	6. 1	Kilmarnock	Irvine	10.04.82
Rocastle, Craig	6. 2	Sheffield Wed.	Lewisham	17.08.81
Wellens, Richard	5. 9	Blackpool	Manchester	26.03.80
Forwards				
Hall, Chris	6. 2	–	Manchester	27.11.86
Liddell, Andy	5. 8	Sheffield Utd.	Leeds	28.06.73
Porter, Chris	6. 1	Bury	Wigan	12.12.83
Warne, Paul	5. 9	Rotherham Utd.	Norwich	8.05.73
Wolfenden, Matthew	5. 9	–	Oldham	23.07.87

PORT VALE

Ground: Vale Park, Hamil Road, Burslem, Stoke-on-Trent ST6 1AW.
Telephone: 01782 655800. Club nickname: Valiants.
First-choice colours: White, black and gold shirts; black, white and gold shorts; white, black and gold socks.
Main sponsor: . Capacity for 2006-07: 18,982.
Record attendance: 50,000 v Aston Villa (F.A. Cup 5) 20 February, 1960.

Name	Height ft. in.	Previous club	Birthplace	Birthdate
Goalkeepers				
Anyon, Joe	6. 2	—	Blackpool	29.12.86
Goodlad, Mark	6. 0	Nott'm Forest	Barnsley	9.09.80
Defenders				
McGregor, Mark	5.11	Blackpool	Chester	16.02.77
Miles, Colin	6. 0	Yeovil Town	Boreham Wood	6.09.78
Pilkington, George	6. 0	Everton	Rugeley	1.11.81
Talbot, Jason	5. 8	Mansfield Town	Irlam	30.09.75
Walker, Richard	6. 2	Crewe Alexandra	Stafford	17.09.80
Walsh, Michael	6. 0	Scunthorpe Utd.	Rotherham	5.08.77
Midfielders				
Abbey, George	5. 9	Macclesfield Town	Port Harcourt, Nig.	20.10.78
Birchall, Chris	5. 9	–	Stafford	5.05.84
Harsley, Paul	5. 8	Macclesfield Town	Scunthorpe	29.05.78
Hulbert, Robin	5. 9	Telford Utd.	Plymouth	14.03.80
Smith, Jeff	5.10	Bolton Wand.	Middlesbrough	28.06.80
Sonner, Danny	5.11	Peterborough Utd.	Wigan	9.01.72
Whitaker, Dan	5.10	Macclesfield Town	Manchester	14.11.80

472

Forwards

Name	Height ft. in.	Previous club	Birthplace	Birthdate
Constantine, Leon	6. 2	Torquay Utd.	Hackney	24.02.78
Husbands, Michael	5. 9	Southend Utd.	Birmingham	13.11.83
Lowndes, Nathan	5.10	Plymouth Argyle	Salford	2.06.77
Sodje, Akpo	6. 2	Darlington	Greenwich	31.01.81

ROTHERHAM UNITED

Ground: Millmoor, Rotherham S60 1HR.
Telephone: 01709 512434. **Club nickname:** Millers.
First-choice colours: Red and white shirts; white shorts; red socks.
Main sponsor: Rosehill Press. **Capacity for 2006-07:** 8,287.
Record attendance: 25,000 v Sheffield Wed. (Div. 2) 26 January, 1952 and v Sheffield Wed. (Div. 2) 13 December, 1952.

Name	Height ft. in.	Previous club	Birthplace	Birthdate
Goalkeepers				
Cutler, Neil	6. 4	Stockport Co.	Cannock	3.09.76
Montgomery, Gary	6. 2	Coventry City	Leamington Spa	8.10.82
Defenders				
Brogan, Stephen	5. 7	–		12.04.88
Hurst, Paul	5. 4	–	Sheffield	25.09.74
King, Liam				31.12.87
Mills, Pablo	6. 0	Derby Co.	Birmingham	27.05.84
Murdock, Colin	6. 2	Crewe Alexandra	Ballymena	2.07.75
Robertson, Gregor	6. 0	Nott'm. Forest	Edinburgh	19.01.84
Worrell, David	5.11	Plymouth Argyle	Dublin	12.01.78
Midfielders				
Barker, Shaun	6. 2	–	Nottingham	19.09.82
Cochrane Justin	6. 0	Crewe Alexandra	Hackney	26.01.82
Duncum, Sam	5. 9	–	Sheffield	18.02.87
Keane, Michael	5. 6	Hull City	Dublin	29.12.82
Newsham, Marc	5.10	–	Hatfield,Yorks.	24.03.87
Williamson, Lee	5.10	Northampton Town	Derby	7.06.82
Forwards				
Facey, Delroy	6. 0	Tranmere Rov.	Huddersfield	22.04.80
Hoskins, Will	5.10	–	Nottingham	6.05.86
Taylor, Ryan	6. 2	–		4.05.88

SCUNTHORPE UNITED

Ground: Glanford Park, Doncaster Road, Scunthorpe DN15 8TD.
Telephone: 01724 747670. **Club nickname:** Iron.
First-choice colours: Claret and blue shirts; claret and blue shorts; claret and blue socks.
Main sponsor: Hatfields Jeep. **Capacity for 2006-07:** 9,088.
Record attendance: (Old Show Ground) 23,935 v Portsmouth (F.A. Cup 4) 30 January, 1954. (Glanford Park) 8,775 v Rotherham Utd. (Div. 4) 1, May 1989.

Name	Height ft. in.	Previous club	Birthplace	Birthdate
Goalkeepers				
Capp, Adam	6.2	–	Scunthorpe	17.09.84
Lillis, Josh	6.0	–	Derby	24.06.87
Murphy, Joe	6.2	Sunderland	Dublin	21.08.81
Defenders				
Butler, Andy	6.0	–	Doncaster	4.11.83
Byrne, Cliff	6.0	Sunderland	Dublin	26.04.82
Crosby, Andy	6.2	Oxford Utd.	Rotherham	3.03.73
Foster, Steve	6.1	Doncaster Rov.	Mansfield	3.12.74
Hinds, Richard	6.2	Hull City	Sheffield	22.08.80
Mulligan, Dave	5.8	Doncaster Rov.	Bootle	24.03.82

Ridley, Lee	5.10	–	Scunthorpe	5.12.81
Williams, Marcus	5. 8	–	Doncaster	8.04.86
Midfielders				
Baraclough, Ian	6. 1	Notts Co.	Leicester	4.12.70
Goodwin, Jim	5. 9	Stockport Co.	Waterford	20.11.81
Mackenzie, Neil	6. 2	Macclesfield Town	Birmingham	15.04.76
Sparrow, Matthew	5.10	–	Wembley	3.10.81
Taylor, Cleveland	5. 8	Bolton Wand.	Leicester	9.09.83
Forwards				
Calliste, Ramon		Liverpool	Cardiff	16.12.85
Keogh, Andrew	6. 0	Leeds Utd.	Dublin	16.05.86
Sharp, Billy	5. 8	Sheffield Utd.	Sheffield	5.02.86
Torpey, Steve	6. 3	Bristol City	Islington	8.12.70

SWANSEA CITY

Ground: Liberty Stadium, Morfa, Swansea SA1 2FA.
Telephone: 01792 616600. **Club nickname:** Swans.
First-choice colours: White and black shirts; white and black shorts; white and black socks.
Main sponsor: Travel House. **Capacity for 2006-07:** 20,500.
Record attendance: (Vetch Field) 32,786 v Arsenal (F.A. Cup 4) 17 February, 1968. (Liberty Stadium) 19,288 v Yeovil Town (Lg.1) 18 November, 2005.

Name	Height ft. in.	Previous club	Birthplace	Birthdate
Goalkeepers				
Gueret, Willy	6. 1	Millwall	Guadaloupe	3.08.73
Defenders				
Austin, Kevin	6. 0	Bristol Rov.	Hackney	12.02.73
Iriekpen, Izzy	6. 1	West Ham Utd.	London	10.04.82
Leacock, Dean	6. 2	Fulham	Croydon	10.06.84
Monk, Garry	6. 0	Barnsley	Bedford	6.03.79
O'Leary, Kristian	5.11	–	Neath	30.08.77
Tate, Alan	6. 1	Manchester Utd.	Easington	2.09.82
Watt, Steven	6. 2	Chelsea	Aberdeen	1.05.85
Williams, Tom	6. 0	Barnsley	Carshalton	8.07.80
Midfielders				
Britton, Leon	5. 5	West Ham Utd.	London	16.09.82
McLeod, Kevin	5.11	Q.P.R.	Liverpool	12.09.80
Tudur-Jones, Owain	6. 2	–	Bangor	15.10.84
Way, Darren	5. 7	Yeovil Town	Plymouth	21.11.79
Forwards				
Akinfenwa, Adebayo	5.11	Torquay Utd.	Nigeria	10.05.82
Bond, Chad	6. 0	–	Neath	20.04.87
Fallon, Rory	6. 2	Swindon Town	Gisborne, NZ	20.03.82
Knight, Leon	5. 5	Brighton & H.A.	Hackney	16.09.82
MacDonald, Shaun	6. 1	–	Swansea	17.06.88
Nugent, Kevin	6. 1	Leyton Orient	Edmonton	10.04.69
Pratley, Darren	6. 0	Fulham	Barking	22.04.85
Pritchard, Mark	5.10	–	Tredegar	23.11.85
Robinson, Andy	5. 8	Cammell Laird	Birkenhead	3.11.79
Thomas, James	6. 0	Blackburn Rov.	Swansea	16.01.79
Trundle, Lee	5.11	Wrexham	Liverpool	10.10.76

TRANMERE ROVERS

Ground: Prenton Park, Prenton Road West, Birkenhead CH42 9PY.
Telephone: 0870 460 3333. **Club nickname:** Rovers.
First-choice colours: White and blue shirts; white and blue shorts; white and blue socks.
Mian Sponsor: Metropolitan Borough of Wirral. **Capacity for 2006-07:** 16,587.
Record attendance: 24,424 v Stoke City (F.A. Cup 4) 5 February, 1972.

Name	Height ft. in.	Previous club	Birthplace	Birthdate
Goalkeepers				
Achterberg, John	6. 1	PSV Eindhoven	Utrecht	8.07.71
Palethorpe, Philip	6. 2	–	Wallasey	17.09.86
Ward, Gavin	6. 3	Preston N.E.	Sutton Coldfield	30.06.70
Defenders				
Goodison, Ian	6. 3	Hull City	Kingston, Jam.	21.11.72
McCready, Chris	6. 0	Crewe Alexandra	Chester	5.07.81
Roberts, Gareth	5. 8	Panionios, Gre.	Wrexham	6.02.78
Stockdale, Robbie	6. 0	Hull City	Middlesbrough	30.11.79
Tremarco, Carl	5.11	–	Liverpool	11.10.85
Midfielders				
Brown, Paul	5.10	–	Liverpool	10.09.84
Ellison, Kevin	6. 1	Hull City	Liverpool	23.02.79
Harrison, Danny	5.11	–	Liverpool	4.11.82
Henry, Paul		–	Liverpool	28.01.88
James, Oliver	5.11	–	Birkenhead	13.01.87
Jennings, Steven	5. 7	–	Liverpool	28.10.84
Jones, Mike		–	Birkenhead	15.08.87
McAteer, Jason	5.11	Sunderland	Birkenhead	18.06.71
McLaren, Paul	6. 1	Rotherham Utd.	High Wycombe	17.11.76
Sharps, Ian	6. 3	–	Warrington	23.10.80
Shuker, Chris	5. 5	Barnsley	Liverpool	9.05.82
Forwards				
Davies, Steve	6. 1	–	Liverpool	29.12.87
Greenacre, Chris	5.11	Stoke City	Halifax Town	23.12.77
Mullin, John	6. 0	Rotherham Utd.	Bury	11.08.75
Zola, Calvin	6. 2	Newcastle Utd.	Kinshasa	31.12.84

YEOVIL TOWN

Ground: Huish Park, Lufton Way, Yeovil BA22 8YF.
Telephone: 01935 423662. **Club nickname:** Glovers.
First-choice colours: Green and white shirts; white shorts; white socks.
Main sponsor: Bradfords Building Supplies. **Capacity for 2006-07:** 9,662.
Record attendance: 9,348 v Liverpool (F.A. Cup 3) 4 January, 2004.

Name	Height ft. in.	Previous club	Birthplace	Birthdate
Goalkeepers				
Behcet, Darren	6. 1	West Ham Utd.		8.10.86
Mildenhall, Steve	6. 4	Grimsby Town	Swindon	13.05.78
Defenders				
Amankwaah, Kevin	6. 1	Bristol City	Harrow	19.05.82
Cohen, Chris	5.11	West Ham Utd.	Norwich	5.03.87
Forbes, Terrell	6. 0	Oldham Athletic	Southwark	17.08.81
Guyett, Scott	6. 2	Chester City	Ascot	20.01.76
Kamudimba, Jean-Paul	5.10	Grimsby Town	DR Congo	16.02.82
Skiverton, Terry	6. 1	Welling	Mile End	20.06.75
Midfielders				
Davies, Arron	5. 9	Southampton	Cardiff	22.06.84
Jones, Nathan	5. 7	Brighton & H.A.	Rhondda	28.05.73
Lindegaard, Andy	6. 0	–	Yeovil	10.09.80
Poole, David	5. 8	Manchester Utd.	Manchester	12.11.84
Terry, Paul	6. 0	Dag & Redbridge	London	3.04.79
Forwards				
Gray, Kevin	5.10	Southend Utd.	Camberwell	7.11.80
Harrold, Matt	6. 1	Brentford	Leyton	25.07.84
Williams, Dale	6. 1	–	Swindon	25.02.87

LEAGUE TWO

ACCRINGTON STANLEY

Ground: Fraser Eagle Stadium, Livingstone Road, Accrington BB5 5BX.
Telephone: 01254 356950. **Club nickname:** Stanley.
First-choice colours: Red shirts, white shorts, red socks.
Main sponsor: Fraser Eagle. **Capacity for 2006-07:** 5,057.
Record attendance: 4,368 v Colchester Utd. (F.A. Cup 3) 3 January, 2003.

Name	Height ft. in.	Previous club	Birthplace	Birthdate
Goalkeepers				
Dibble, Andy	6. 3	Wrexham	Cwmbran	8.05.65
Elliott, Robert	6. 1	Charlton Athletic	Chatham	3.04.86
Fearon, Martin	–			30.10.88
Defenders				
Cavanagh, Peter	5.10	Liverpool	Liverpool	14.10.81
N'da, Julian	5.10	Rouen	Niort, Fra.	15.08.85
Richardson, Leam	5. 7	Blackpool	Leeds	19.11.79
Tretton, Andrew	6. 1	Hereford Utd.	Derby	9.10.76
Ventre, Daniel	5.11	Chester City	Liverpool	23.01.86
Welch, Michael	6. 3	Macclesfield	Crewe	11.01.84
Williams, Robbie	5.10	St Dominics	Liverpool	12.04.79
Midfielders				
Cook, Paul	5.11	Burnley	Liverpool	22.06.67
Craney, Ian	5. 9	Altrincham	liverpool	21.07.82
Doherty, Sean	5. 8	Port Vale	Basingstoke	10.05.85
Edwards, Philip	5.10	Wigan Athletic		8.11.85
Procter, Andrew	5.11	Great Harwood	Lancashire	13.03.83
Roberts, Gary	5. 8	Crewe	Chester	18.03.84
Todd, Andy	6. 0	Burton Albion	Nottingham	22.02.79
Forwards				
Boco, Romuald	5.11	Niort	France	8.07.85
Brown, David	5.10	Hereford	Bolton	2.10.78
Mangan, Andrew	5. 9	Blackpool	Liverpool	30.08.86
Mullin, Paul	6. 0	Radcliffe Boro	Radcliffe	16.03.74

BARNET

Ground: Underhill Stadium, Barnet EN5 2DN.
Telephone: 0208 441 6932. **Club nickname:** Bees.
First-choice colours: Black and amber shirts, black and amber shorts, black and amber socks.
Main sponsor: Capacity for 2006-07: 5,189.
Record attendance: 11,026 v Wycombe Wand. (F.A. Amateur Cup 4), January 1954.

Name	Height ft. in.	Previous club	Birthplace	Birthdate
Goalkeepers				
Flitney, Ross	6. 3	Fulham	Hitchin	1.06.84
Tynan, Scott	6. 1	Nott'm. Forest	Knowsley	27.11.83
Defenders				
Batt, Damian	5.11	Dag.and Redbridge	Hoddesdon	16.09.84
Charles, Anthony	6. 2	Farnborough	Isleworth	11.03.81
Gross, Adam		Charlton Athletic		16.02.86
Hendon, Ian	6. 0	Peterborough Utd.	Ilford	5.12.71
King, Simon	6. 0	Oxford Utd.	Oxford	11.04.83
Warhurst, Paul	6. 1	Wrexham	Stockport	26.09.69
Yakubu, Ismail	5.11	–	London	8.04.85

Midfielders

Bailey, Nicky	5.10	Sutton Utd.	Hammersmith	
Graham, Richard	5. 8	Kettering Town	Newry	5.08.79
Soares, Louie	5. 9	Reading	Reading	8.01.85
Strevens, Ben	6. 1	Wingate & Finchley	Edgware	24.05.80
Bowditch, Ben	5.10	Colchester Utd.	Bishop's Stortford	19.02.84
Hickie, Luke		Crystal Palace	Croydon	18.08.84

Forwards

Grazioli, Giuliano	5.11	Bristol Rov.	Marylebone	23.03.75
Hatch, Liam	6. 3	Gravesend	Kent	3.04.84
Norville, Jason	6. 0	Watford	Trinidad	9.09.83
Roache, Lee	5.10	–	London	30.04.84

BOSTON UNITED

Ground: Staffsmart Stadium, Boston, PE21 6HN.
Telephone: 0870 757 9266. **Club nickname:** Pilgrims.
First-choice colours: Amber and black shirts; black shorts; black socks.
Main sponsor: Chestnut Homes. **Capacity for 2006-07:** 6,643.
Record attendance: 10,086 v Corby Town (Friendly) 1955. League: 6,445 v Lincoln City (League 2) 16 February, 2005.

Name	Height ft. in.	Previous club	Birthplace	Birthdate
Goalkeepers				
Abbey, Nathan	6. 1	Burnley	Islington	11.07.78
Defenders				
Albrighton, Mark	6. 1	Doncaster Rov.	Nuneaton	6.03.76
Canoville, Lee	6. 1	Torquay Utd.	Ealing	14.03.81
Ellender, Paul	6. 1	Scarborough	Scunthorpe	21.10.74
Futcher, Ben	6. 7	Lincoln City	Bradford	20.02.81
Greaves, Mark	6. 1	Hull City	Hull	22.01.75
McCann, Austin	5. 9	Hearts	Clydebank	21.01.80
Ryan, Tim	5.10	Peterbrough Utd.	Stockport	10.12.74
Midfielders				
Holland, Chris	5. 9	Huddersfield Town	Clitheroe	11.09.75
Johnson, Gavin	5.11	Colchester Utd.	Stowmarket	10.10.70
Maylett, Bradley	5. 8	Swansea City	Manchester	24.12.80
Melton, Steve	5.11	Hull City	Lincoln	3.10.78
Noble, David	6. 0	West Ham Utd.	Hitchin	2.02.82
Rusk, Simon	6. 0	Peterborough Utd.	Peterborough	17.12.81
Ryan, Richie	5.10	Scunthorpe Utd.	Kilkenny	6.01.85
Thomas, Danny	5. 7	Bournemouth	Leamington	1.05.81
Forwards				
Clare, Daryl	5. 9	Chester City	Jersey	1.08.78
Galbraith, David	5. 9	Northampton T.	Luton	20.12.83
Green, Francis	5. 9	Lincoln City.	Nottingham	25.04.80
Lee, Jason	6. 0	Falkirk	Forest Gate	9.05.71
Whelan, Noel	6. 2	Aberdeen	Leeds	30.12.74

BRISTOL ROVERS

Ground: Memorial Ground, Filton Avenue, Horfield, Bristol BS7 0BF.
Telephone: 0117 909 6648. **Club nickname:** Pirates.
First-choice colours: Blue and white shirts; white shorts; blue and white socks.
Main sponsor: Cowlin Construction. **Capacity for 2006-07:** 11,679.
Record attendance: (Eastville) 38,472 v Preston N.E. (F.A. Cup 4) 30 January, 1960. (Memorial Ground) 11,433 v Sunderland (League Cup 3) 31 October, 2000.

Name	Height ft. in.	Previous club	Birthplace	Birthdate
Goalkeepers				
Book, Steve	5.11	Swindon Town	Bournemouth	7.07.69

Clarke, Ryan	6. 3	–	Bristol	30.04.82
Shearer, Scott	6. 3	Coventry City	Glasgow	15.02.81
Defenders				
Carruthers, Chris	6. 1	Northampton Town	Kettering	19.08.83
Elliott, Steve	6. 1	Blackpool	Derby	29.10.78
Hinton, Craig	5.11	Kidderminster Harr.	Wolves	26.11.77
Ryan, Robbie	5.10	Millwall	Dublin	16.05.77
Midfielders				
Campbell, Stuart	5.10	Grimsby Town	Corby	9.12.77
Disley, Craig	5. 1	Mansfield Town	Worksop	24.08.81
Gibb, Alistair	5. 9	Stockport Co.	Salisbury	12.02.76
Green, Ryan	5. 8	Hereford Utd.	Cardiff	20.10.80
Hunt, James	5. 8	Oxford Utd.	Derby	17.12.76
Lescott, Aaron	5. 8	Stockport Co.	Birmingham	2.12.77
Lines, Chris	6. 2	–		30.11.85
Mullings, Darren	6. 1	–	Bristol	3.03.87
Trollope, Paul	6. 0	Northampton Town	Swindon	3.06.72
Williams, Ryan	5. 5	Hull City	Sutton-in-Ashfield	31.08.78
Forwards				
Agogo, Junior	5.10	Barnet	Accra	8.01.79
Haldane, Lewis	6. 0	–	Trowbridge	13.03.85
Walker, Richard	6. 0	Oxford Utd.	Birmingham	8.11.77

BURY

Ground: Gigg Lane, Bury BL9 9HR.
Telephone: 0161 764 4881. **Club nickname:** Shakers.
First-choice colours: White shirts; royal blue shorts; royal blue socks.
Main Sponsor: Bury Metro. **Capacity for 2006-07:** 11,640.
Record attendance: 35,000 v Bolton Wand. (F.A. Cup 3) 9 January, 1960.

Name	Height ft. in.	Previous club	Birthplace	Birthdate
Goalkeepers				
Fettis, Alan	6. 2	Macclesfield Town	Belfast	1.02.71
Grundy, Aaron	–		Bolton	21.01.88
Defenders				
Barry-Murphy, Brian	6. 0	Sheffield Wed.	Cork	27.07.78
Challinor, Dave	6. 1	Stockport Co.	Chester	2.10.75
Fitzgerald, John	6. 2	Blackburn Rov.	Dublin	10.02.84
Kennedy, Thomas	5.11	–	Bury	24.06.85
Parrish, Andy			Bolton	22.06.88
Woodthorpe, Colin	6. 1	Stockport Co.	Ellesmere Port	13.01.69
Midfielders				
Buchanan, David	5. 8	–	Rochdale	6.05.86
Flitcroft, David	5.11	Macclesfield Town	Bolton	14.01.74
Mattis, Dwayne	6. 1	Huddersfield Town	Huddersfield	31.07.81
Pugh, Marc	5.11	–	Bacup	2.04.87
Scott, Paul	5.11	Huddersfield Town	Wakefield	5.11.79
Forwards				
Bishop, Andy	6. 0	York City	Stone	19.10.82
Goodfellow, Marc	5. 8	Grimsby Town	Swadlincote	20.09.81
Speight, Jake	5. 7	Scarborough	Sheffield	28.09.85
Tipton, Matthew	5.10	Macclesfield Town	Conwy	29.06.80
Youngs, Tom	5. 9	Leyton Orient	Bury St Edmunds	31.08.79

CHESTER CITY

Ground: Saunders Honda Stadium, Bumpers Lane, Chester CH1 4LT.
Telephone: 01244 371376. **Club nickname:** Blues.
First-choice colours: Blue and white shirts; blue shorts; blue socks.
Main sponsor: UK Sameday. **Capacity for 2006-07:** 6,000.

Record attendance: (Sealand Road): 20,500 v Chelsea (F.A. Cup 3) 16 January, 1952.
(Deva Stadium): 5,987 v Scarborough (Conference) 17 April, 2004.

Name	Height ft. in.	Previous club	Birthplace	Birthdate
Goalkeepers				
Danby, John	6. 2	Kidderminster	Stoke	20.09.81
Defenders				
Allen, Graham	6. 0	Tranmere Rov.	Bolton	8.04.77
Artell, David	6. 3	Mansfield Town	Rotherham	22.11.80
Bolland, Phil	6. 2	Peterborough Utd.	Liverpool	26.08.76
Hessey, Sean	5.10	Blackpool	Whiston	19.09.78
Linwood, Paul	6. 2	Tranmere Rov.	Birkenhead	24.10.83
Marples, Simon	5.10	Doncaster Rov.	Sheffield	30.07.75
Sandwith, Kevin	5.11	Macclesfield Town	Workington	30.04.78
Vaughan, Stephen	5. 6	–	Liverpool	22.01.85
Westwood, Ashley	5.11	Northampton Town	Bridgnorth	31.08.76
Midfielders				
Bennett, Dean	5.10	Wrexham	Wolverhampton	13.12.77
Cronin, Glenn	5. 9	Exeter	Dublin	14.09.81
Hand, Jamie	5.11	Watford	Uxbridge	7.02.84
McSporran, Jermaine	5. 8	Doncaster Rov.	Manchester	1.01.77
Wilson, Laurence	5.10	Everton	Liverpool	10.10.86
Forwards				
Blundell, Gregg	5.11	Doncaster Rov.	Liverpool	1.01.76
Branch, Michael	5.10	Bradford City	Liverpool	18.10.78
Broughton, Drewe	6. 3	Rushden & Diamonds	Hitchin	25.10.78
Walters, Jonathan	6. 1	Wrexham	Birkenhead	20.09.83

DARLINGTON

Ground: The Arena, Hurworth Moor, Neasham Road, Darlington, DL2 1GR.
Telephone: 01325 387000. **Club nickname:** Quakers.
First-choice colours: Black and white shirts; black shorts; black and white socks.
Main sponsor: Darlington Building Society. **Capacity for 2006-07:** 25,000.
Record attendance: (Feethams) 21,023 v Bolton Wand. (League Cup 3) 14 November,
1960. (The Arena), 11,600 v Kidderminstre Harr. (Div. 3) 16, August 2003.

Name	Height ft. in.	Previous club	Birthplace	Birthdate
Goalkeepers				
Russell, Sam	6. 0	Scunthorpe Utd.	Middlesbrough	4.10.82
Defenders				
Close, Brian	5.10	Middlesbrough	Belfast	27.01.82
Hutchinson, Joey	6. 2	Birmingham City	Middlesbrough	2.04.82
Martis, Shelton	6. 1	Excelsior	Holland	29.11.82
Midfielders				
Cummins, Micky	6. 0	Port Vale	Dublin	1.06.78
Duke, David	5.10	Swindon Town	Inverness	7.11.78
Keltie, Clark	6. 1	–	Newcastle	31.08.83
Logan, Carlos	5. 8	Manchester City	Wythenshawe	7.11.85
Maddison, Neil	5.10	Middlesbrough	Darlington	2.10.69
Peacock, Anthony	5. 9	Middlesbrough	Middlesbrough	6.09.85
Stamp, Phil	5.11	Hearts	Middlesbrough	12.12.75
Wainwright, Neil	6. 0	Sunderland	Warrington	4.11.77
Forwards				
Conlon, Barry	6. 3	Barnsley	Drogheda	1.10.78
Johnson, Simon	5. 9	Leeds Utd.	West Bromwich	9.03.83
Logan, Richard	6. 0	Peterborough Utd.	Bury St Edmunds	4.01.82

GRIMSBY TOWN

Ground: Blundell Park, Cleethorpes, DN35 7PY.
Telephone: 01472 605050. **Club nickname:** Mariners.

First-choice colours: Black and white shirts; black shorts; white and black socks.
Main sponsor: Young's. **Capacity for 2006-07:** 9,134.
Record attendance: 31,651 v Wolves (F.A. Cup 5) 20 February, 1937.

Name	Height ft. in.	Previous club	Birthplace	Birthdate
Goalkeepers				
Barnes, Phil	6. 1	Sheffield Utd.	Sheffield	2.03.79
Lukic, John	6. 2	Nott'm. Forest	Enfield	25.04.86
Defenders				
Croft, Gary	5. 9	Cardiff City	Burton-on-Trent	17.02.74
Downey, Glen	6. 1	Scarborough	Newcastle	20.09.78
Futcher, Ben	6. 4	Lincoln City	Manchester	20.02.81
McDermott, John	5. 7	—	Middlesbrough	3.02.69
Newey, Tom	5.10	Leyton Orient	Huddersfield	31.10.82
Whittle, Justin	6. 1	Hull City	Derby	18.03.71
Midfielders				
Ashton, Paul		Leicester City		25.10.86
Barwick, Terry	5.11	Scunthorpe Utd.	Doncaster	11.01.83
Beagrie, Peter	5. 9	Scunthorpe Utd.	Middlesbrough	28.11.65
Bolland, Paul	5.11	Notts Co.	Bradford	23.12.79
Harkins, Gary	6. 2	Blackburn Rov.	Greenock	2.01.85
Hegarty, Nick	5.10	Sheffield Wed.	Hemsworth	25.06.86
Jones, Gary	6. 3	Tranmere Rov.	Chester	10.05.75
Toner, Ciaran	6. 1	Lincoln City	Craigavon	30.06.81
Forwards				
North, Danny	5.11		Grimsby	7.09.87
Palmer, Jermaine	6. 1	Stoke City	Nottingham	28.08.86
Rankin, Isaiah	5.10	Brentford	Edmonton	22.05.78
Reddy, Michael	6. 1	Sunderland	Kilkenny	24.03.80

HARTLEPOOL UNITED

Ground: Victoria Park, Clarence Road, Hartlepool TS24 8BZ.
Telephone: 01429 272584. **Club nickname:** Pool.
First-choice colours: Blue and white shirts; blue shorts; white socks.
Main Sponsor: Dove Energy, DNO. **Capacity for 2006-07:** 7,630.
Record attendance: 17,426 v Manchester Utd. (F.A. Cup 3) 5 January, 1957.

Name	Height ft. in.	Previous club	Birthplace	Birthdate
Goalkeepers				
Konstantopoulos, Dimirios	6. 4	Farense	Greece	29.11.78
Provett, Jim	5.11	—	Trimdon	22.12.82
Defenders				
Barron, Michael	5.11	Middlesbrough	Lumley	22.12.74
Brackstone, John	5.11	—	Hartlepool	9.02.85
Butler, Thomas	5. 7	Sunderland	Dublin	25.04.81
Clark, Ben	6. 2	Sunderland	Shotley Bridge	24.01.83
Jones, Carl	6. 1	Chester-le-Street		3.09.86
Nelson, Michael	5. 9	Bury	Gateshead	15.03.82
Midfielders				
Clarke, Darrell	5.10	Mansfield Town	Mansfield	16.12.77
Maidens, Michael	5.11	—	Middlesbrough	7.05.87
Robson, Matty	5.10	—	Durham	23.01.85
Strachan, Gavin	5.11	Southend Utd.	Aberdeen	23.12.78
Sweeney, Anthony	6. 0	—	Stockton	5.09.83
Tinkler, Mark	5.11	Southend Utd.	Bishop Auckland	24.10.74
Turnbull, Stephen	5.10	—	South Shields	7.01.87
Williams, Darren	5.10	Cardiff City	Middlesbrough	28.04.77
Forwards				
Boyd, Adam	5. 9		Hartlepool	25.05.82

Brown, James	5.11	–	Cramlington	3.01.87
Bullock, Lee	6. 1	Cardiff City	Stockton	22.05.81
Daly, Jon	6. 3	Stockport Co.	Dublin	8.01.83
Foley, David	5. 6	–	South Shields	12.07.87
Humphreys, Richie	5.11	Cambridge Utd.	Sheffield	30.11.77
Porter, Joel	5. 9	West Adelaide	Sydney	25.12.78
Proctor, Michael	6. 0	Rotherham Utd.	Sunderland	3.10.80
Williams, Eifion	5.11	Torquay Utd.	Bangor	15.11.75

HEREFORD UNITED

Ground: Edgar Street Ground, Edgar Street, Hereford HR4 9JU.
Telephone: 01432 276666. **Club nickname:** Bulls.
First-choice colours: White and black shirts, black shorts, white socks.
Main sponsor: Sun Valley. **Capacity for 2006-07:** 8,843.
Record attendance: 18,114 v Sheffield Wed. (F.A. Cup 3) 4 January, 1958.

Name	Height ft. in.	Previous club	Birthplace	Birthdate
Goalkeepers				
Brown, Wayne	6. 1	Chester City	Southampton	14.01.77
Thompson, Glyn	6. 3	Shrewsbury	Shrewsbury	24.02.81
Defenders				
Beckwith, Dean	6. 3	Gillingham	Southwark	19.09.83
Gulliver, Phil	6. 2	Rushden	Bishop Auckland	12.09.82
Jeannin, Alex	6. 0	Bristol Rov.	Troyes, Fr.	30.12.77
Mkandawire, Tamika	5.11	W.B.A.	Malawi	28.05.83
Rose, Richard	6. 0	Gillingham	Pembury	8.09.82
Travis, Simon	5.10	Stevenage	Preston	22.03.77
Midfielders				
Ferrell, Andy	5.10	Watford	Newcastle	9.01.84
Gwynne, Sam	5.10	–	Hereford	17.12.87
Purdie, Rob	5. 9	Leicester City	Leicester	28.09.82
Wallis, Jon	5. 7	Gillingham	Gravesend	4.04.86
Forwards				
Fleetwood, Stuart	5.10	Cardiff City	Gloucester	23.04.86
Sheldon, Gareth	5.11	Kidderminster	Birmingham	31.01.80
Sills, Tim	5.11	Oxford Utd.	Romsey	10.09.79
Williams, Andy	5.11	–	Hereford	14.08.86

LINCOLN CITY

Ground: Sincil Bank, Lincoln LN5 8LD.
Telephone: 0870 899 2005. **Club nickname:** Imps.
First-choice colours: Red and white shirts; black shorts; red socks.
Main sponsor: Siemens. **Capacity for 2006-07:** 10,279.
Record attendance: 23,196 v Derby Co. (League Cup 4) 15 November, 1967.

Name	Height ft. in.	Previous club	Birthplace	Birthdate
Goalkeepers				
Marriott, Alan	6. 0	Tottenham	Bedford	3.09.78
Rayner, Simon	6. 5	Port Talbot	Langley, Can.	8.07.83
Defenders				
Beevers, Lee	6. 3	Boston Utd.	Doncaster	4.12.83
Foster, Luke	6. 2	Sheffield Wed.	Mexborough	8.09.85
Mayo, Paul	5.11	Watford	Lincoln	13.10.81
Morgan, Paul	5.11	Preston N.E.	Belfast	23.10.78
Robinson, Steve	5. 9	Swindon Town	Nottingham	17.01.75
Midfielders				
Frecklington, Lee	5. 8	–	Lincoln	8.09.85
Gain, Peter	6. 1	Tottenham	Hammersmith	2.11.76
Kerr, Scott	5. 9	Scarborough	Leeds	11.12.81

Forwards

Name	ft. in.	Previous club	Birthplace	Birthdate
Bacon, Danny	5.10	Mansfield Town	Mansfield	20.09.80
Birch, Gary	6. 0	Walsall	Birmingham	8.10.81
Forrester, Jamie	5. 6	Bristol Rov.	Bradford	1.11.74
Gritton, Martin	6. 1	Grimsby Town	Glasgow	1.06.78
Mettam, Leon	5.11	–	Lincoln	9.12.86
Ryan, Oliver	5.11	–	Boston	26.09.85
Stallard, Mark	6. 0	Shrewsbury Town	Derby	24.10.74

MACCLESFIELD TOWN

Ground: Moss Rose, London Road, Macclesfield SK11 7SP.
Telephone: 01625 264686. **Club nickname:** Silkmen.
First-choice colours: Royal blue shirts; white shorts; royal blue and white socks.
Main sponsor: Cheshire Building Society. **Capacity for 2006-07:** 6,141.
Record attendance: 9,003 v Winsford Town (Cheshire Senior Cup 2) 14 February, 1948.

Name	Height ft. in.	Previous club	Birthplace	Birthdate
Goalkeepers				
Brain, Jonny	6. 4	Port Vale	Carlisle	11.02.83
Lee, Tommy	6. 2	Manchester Utd.	Keighley	3.01.86
Defenders				
Brightwell, Ian	5.10	Port Vale	Lutterworth	9.04.68
Morley, David	6. 1	Doncaster Rov.	St Helens	25.09.77
Regan, Carl	6. 0	Chester City	Liverpool	14.01.80
Swailes, Danny	6. 3	Bury	Bolton	1.04.79
Teague, Andrew	6. 2	–	Preston	5.02.86
Midfielders				
Bullock, Martin	5. 5	Blackpool	Derby	5.03.75
McIntyre, Kevin	6. 0	Chester City	Liverpool	23.12.77
Navarro, Alan	5.11	Tranmere Rov.	Liverpool	31.05.81
Smart, Andrew	6. 1	–	Wythenshawe	17.03.86
Forwards				
Heath, Colin	6. 0	Chesterfield	Matlock	31.12.83
McNeil, Matty	6. 5	Hyde Utd.	Manchester	14.07.76
Miles, John	5.10	Crewe Alexandra	Fazackerley	28.09.81
Robinson, Marvin	6. 0	Lincoln City	Crewe	11.04.80

MANSFIELD TOWN

Ground: Field Mill, Quarry Lane, Mansfield NG18 5DA.
Telephone: 0870 756 3160 **Club nickname:** Stags.
First-choice colours: Amber, white and blue shirts; blue shorts; yellow socks.
Main sponsor: Perry Electrical. **Capacity for 2006-07:** 8,442.
Record attendance: 24,467 v Nott'm. Forest (F.A. Cup 3) 10 January, 1953.

Name	Height ft. in.	Previous club	Birthplace	Birthdate
Goalkeepers				
Muggleton, Carl	6. 2	Chesterfield	Leicester	13.09.68
White, Jason	6. 2	–	Mansfield	28.01.86
Defenders				
Baptiste, Alex	5.11	–	Sutton-in-Ashfield	31.01.86
Buxton, Jake	6. 0	–	Sutton-in-Ashfield	4.03.85
Eaton, Adam	5. 9	Preston N.E.	Liverpool	2.05.80
Hjelde, Jon Olav	6. 1	Nott'm. Forest	Levanger, Nor.	30.07.72
Jelleyman, Gareth	5.10	Peterborough Utd.	Holywell	14.11.80
Mullins, John	5.11	Reading	Hampstead	6.11.85
Midfielders				
Birchall, Adam	5. 7	Arsenal	Maidstone	2.12.84
Brown, Simon	5. 7	Kidderminster Harr.	West Bromwich	18.09.83
Dawson, Stephen	5. 6	–	Ireland	4.12.85

Hamshaw, Matt	5.9	Stockport Co.	Rotherham	1.01.82
Forwards				
Barker, Richie	6.0	Rotherham Utd.	Sheffield	30.05.75

MILTON KEYNES DONS

Ground: National Hockey Stadium, Silbury Boulevard, Milton Keynes MK9 1FA.
Telephone: 01908 607090. **Club nickname:** Dons.
First-choice colours: White shirts; white shorts; white socks.
Main sponsor: Marshalls Amps. **Capacity for 2006-07:** 8,786.
Record attendance: (Milton Keynes): 7,620 v Luton Town (League 1) 20 November, 2004. (Wimbledon): 8,118 v West Ham Utd. (Div. 1), 25 November, 2003.

Name	Height ft. in.	Previous club	Birthplace	Birthdate
Goalkeepers				
Bankole, Ademole	6. 3	Brentford	Lagos	9.09.69
Barker, Matthew	6. 0	Wrexhamn	Harrogate	18.12.79
Defenders				
Chorley, Ben	6. 3	Arsenal	Sidcup	9.09.82
Crooks, Leon	6. 1	–	Greenwich	21.11.85
Diallo, Drissa	6. 1	Sheffield Wed.	Nouadhibou, Maurt.	4.01.73
Edds, Gareth	5.11	Bradford City	Sydney	3.02.81
Lewington, Dean	5.11	–	London	18.05.84
Mitchell, Paul	5. 9	Wigan Athletic	Manchester	26.08.81
Morgan, Craig	6. 0	Wrexham	St Asaph	18.06.85
O'Hanlon, Sean	6. 1	Swindon Town	Liverpool	2.01.83
Oyedele, Shola	5.11		Kano	14.09.84
Midfielders				
Harding, Ben	5.10	–	Carshalton	6.09.84
McGovern, John-Paul	5. 7	Sheffield Wed.	Glasgow	3.10.80
Rizzo, Nicky	5.10	Prato	Sydney	9.06.79
Smith, Gary	5. 8	Middlesbrough	Middlesbrough	30.01.84
Tapp, Alex	5. 9	–	Redhill	7.06.82
Forwards				
McLeod, Izale	6. 1	Derby Co.	Birmingham	15.10.84
Platt, Clive	6. 4	Peterborough Utd.	Wolves	27.10.77
Taylor, Scott	5.10	Plymouth	Chertsey	5.05.76
Wilbraham, Aaron	6. 3	Hull City	Knutsford	21.10.79

NOTTS COUNTY

Ground: Meadow Lane, Nottingham NG2 3HJ.
Telephone: 0115 952 9000. **Club nickname:** Magpies.
First-choice colours: Black and white shirts; black shorts; white socks.
Main sponsor: Medoc. **Capacity for 2006-07:** 20,300.
Record attendance: 47,310 v York City (F.A. Cup 6) 12 March, 1955.

Name	Height ft. in.	Previous club	Birthplace	Birthdate
Goalkeepers				
Deeney, Saul	6. 1	Burton Albion	Londonderry	23.03.83
Pilkington, Kevin	6. 2	Mansfield Town	Hitchin	8.03.74
Defenders				
Edwards, Mike	6. 1	Grimsby Town	Hessle	25.04.80
Hunt, Stephen	6. 1	Colchester Utd.	Southampton	11.11.84
Silk, Gary	5.10	Portsmouth	Newport, IOW	13.07.84
White, Alan	6. 1	Boston Utd.	Darlington	22.03.76
Whitlow, Mike	6. 0	Sheffield Utd.	Northwich	13.01.68
Midfielders				
Curtis, Tom	5. 9	Chester City	Exeter	1.03.73
Parkinson, Andy	5. 8	Grimsby Town	Liverpool	27.05.79
Pipe, David	5. 9	Coventry City	Caerphilly	5.11.83

| Somner, Matt | 6. 0 | Aldershot | Isleworth | 8.12.82 |

Forwards

Dudfield, Lawrie	6. 1	Southend Utd.	Southwark	7.05.80
Lee, Jason,	6. 3	Northampton Town	Forest Gate	9.05.71
Mendes, Junior	5.10	Huddersfield	London	15.09.76
Scoffham, Steve	5.11	Gedling Town	Germany	12.07.83

PETERBOROUGH UNITED

Ground: London Road Stadium, Peterborough PE2 8AL.
Telephone: 01733 563947. **Club nickname:** Posh.
First-choice colours: Blue shirts; blue shorts; blue socks.
Main sponsor: Capacity for 2006-07: 14,655.
Record attendance: 30,096 v Swansea City (F.A. Cup 5) 20 February, 1965.

Name	Height ft. in.	Previous club	Birthplace	Birthdate
Goalkeepers				
McShane, Luke	6. 1	–	Peterborough	6.11.85
Tyler, Mark	5.11	–	Norwich	2.04.77
Defenders				
Arber, Mark	6. 1	Oldham Athletic	Johannesburg	9.10.77
Holden, Dean	6. 0	Oldham Athletic	Salford	15.09.79
Plummer, Chris	6. 2	Barnet	Isleworth	12.10.76
Midfielders				
Boucard, Andre	5.10	Reading	Enfield	10.10.84
Butcher, Richard	6. 0	Oldham Athletic	Peterborough	22.01.81
Carden, Paul	5. 9	Chester City	Liverpool	29.03.79
Day, Jamie	5. 9	–	High Wycombe	7.05.86
Fry, Adam	5. 8	–	Luton	9.02.85
Gain, Peter	6. 1	Lincoln City	Hammersmith	2.11.76
Huke, Shane	5.10	Hornchurch	Reading	2.10.85
Newton, Adam	5.10	West Ham Utd.	Ascot	4.12.80
Semple, Ryan	5.11	–	Belfast	14.07.85
Forwards				
Benjamin, Trevor	6. 2	Coventry City	Kettering	8.02.79
Crow, Danny	5.10	Norwich City	Great Yarmouth	26.01.86
Opara, Lloyd	6. 1	Swindon Town	Enfield	6.01.84
Quinn, James	6. 1	Sheffield Wed.	Coventry	15.12.74

ROCHDALE

Ground: Spotland, Wilbutts Lane, Rochdale OL11 5DS.
Telephone: 01706 644648. **Club nickname:** Dale.
First-choice colours: Royal blue and white shirts; royal blue and white shorts; royal blue and white socks.
Main Sponsor: Keytech. **Capacity for 2006-07:** 10,199.
Record attendance: 24,231 v Notts Co. (F.A. Cup 2) 10 December, 1949.

Name	Height ft. in.	Previous club	Birthplace	Birthdate
Goalkeepers				
Gilks, Matthew	6. 1	–	Rochdale	4.06.82
Woodhall, Danny	6. 1	–	West Bromwich	10.12.87
Defenders				
Boardman, Jonathan	6. 2	Woking	Reading	27.01.81
Brown, Gary	5. 6	–	Darwen	29.10.85
Goodall, Alan	6. 0	Bangor City	Liverpool	2.12.81
Jackson, Mark	6. 0	Kidderminster Harr.	Barnsley	30.09.77
Ramsden, Simon	6. 0	Grimsby Town	Bishop Auckland	17.12.81
Midfielders				
Cooksey, Ernie	5. 9	Oldham Athletic	Bishop's Stortford	11.06.80
Doolan, John	6. 1	Doncaster Rov.	Liverpool	7.05.74
Jones, Gary	5.10	Barnsley	Birkenhead	3.06.77

Forwards

Name	ft. in.	Previous club	Birthplace	Birthdate
Christie, Iyseden	6. 0	Kidderminster Harr.	Coventry	14.11.76
Dagnall, Chris	5. 8	Tranmere Rov.	Liverpool	15.04.86
Lambert, Rickie	6. 1	Stockport Co.	Liverpool	16.02.82
Moyo-Modise, Clive	6. 4	–		20.09.87
Rundle, Adam	5.10	Mansfield Town	Durham	8.07.84

SHREWSBURY TOWN

Ground: Gay Meadow, Shrewsbury SY2 6AB.
Telephone: 01743 360111. **Club nickname:** Shrews.
First-choice colours: Blue and amber shirts; blue and amber shorts; blue and amber socks.
Main sponsor: Morris Lubricants. **Capacity for 2006-07:** 8,000.
Record attendance: 18,917 v Walsall (Div. 3) 26 April, 1961.

Name	Height ft. in.	Previous club	Birthplace	Birthdate
Esson, Ryan	6. 2	Aberdeen	Aberdeen	19.03.80
MacKenzie, Chris	6. 0	Chester City	Birmingham	14.05.72
Defenders				
Ashton, Neil	5.10	Tranmere Rov.	Liverpool	15.01.85
Burton, Sagi	6. 2	Peterborough Utd.	Birmingham	25.11.77
Cadwallader, Gavin	6. 2	–	Shrewsbury	18.04.86
Cowan, Gavin	6. 4	Canvey Island		24.05.81
Hall, Danny	6. 2	Oldham Athletic	Ashton-under-Lyne	14.11.83
Herd, Ben	5. 9	Watford	Welwyn	21.06.85
Hope, Richard	6. 2	Chester City	Stockton	22.06.78
Midfielders				
Davies, Ben	5. 6	Chester City	Walsall	27.05.81
Drummond, Stewart	6. 2	Chester City	Preston	11.12.75
Edwards, David	5.11	–	Pontesbury	3.02.86
Hogg, Steven	6. 3	Manchester Utd.	Bury	1.10.85
Leslie, Steven				5.11.87
Sorvel, Neil	5.10	Crewe Alexandra	Whiston	2.03.73
Tolley, Jamie	6. 1	–	Shrewsbury	12.05.83
Williams, Dale	6. 1	Yeovil Town	Swindon	25.02.87
Forwards				
Adaggio, Marco	5. 8	–	Malaga	6.10.87
Hurst, Glynn	5.10	Notts Co.	Barnsley	17.01.76
Langmead, Kelvin	6. 1	–	Coventry	23.03.85
McMenamin, Colin	5.10	Livingston	–	12.02.81

STOCKPORT COUNTY

Ground: Edgeley Park, Hardcastle Road, Edgeley, Stockport SK3 9DD.
Telephone: 0161 286 8888. **Club nickname:** County.
First-choice colours: Blue and white shirts; blue shorts; white socks.
Main Sponsor: Parfetts. **Capacity for 2006-07:** 10,250.
Record attendance: 27,833 v Liverpool (F.A. Cup 5) 11 February, 1950.

Name	Height ft. in.	Previous club	Birthplace	Birthdate
Goalkeepers				
Spencer, James	6. 3	–	Stockport	11.04.85
Defenders				
Beharall, David	6. 2	Oldham Athletic	Jarrow	8.03.79
Briggs, Keith	6. 0	Norwich City	Glossop	11.12.81
Clare, Rob	6. 2	–	Belper	28.02.83
Kay, Jamie	5.10	Liverpool		12.12.86
Raynes, Michael	6. 4	–	Wythenshawe	15.10.87
Robinson, Mark	5. 9	Hartlepool Utd.	Guisborough	24.07.81
Rose, Michael	5.10	Yeovil Town	Salford	28.07.82
Tunnicliffe, James	6. 4	–	Manchester	17.01.89

Name	Height ft. in.	Previous club	Birthplace	Birthdate
Williams, Ashley	6. 0	Hednesford Town	Wolves	23.08.84
Midfielders				
Allen, Damien	5.10	–	Cheadle	1.08.86
Ellis, Danny	5.10	–	Stockport	18.11.88
Forwards				
Bramble, Tes	6. 2	Southend Utd.	Ipswich	20.07.80
Dickinson, Liam	6. 4	–	Salford	4.10.85
Le Fondre, Adam	5.11	–	Stockport	2.12.86
Malcolm, Michael	5.10	Tottenham	Harrow	13.10.85

SWINDON TOWN

Ground: County Ground, County Road, Swindon SN1 2ED.
Telephone: 0870 443 1969. **Club nickname:** Robins.
First-choice colours: Red shirts; white shorts; red socks.
Main sponsor: Nationwide. **Capacity for 2006-07:** 14,983.
Record attendance: 32,000 v Arsenal (F.A. Cup 3) 15 January, 1972.

Name	Height ft. in.	Previous club	Birthplace	Birthdate
Defenders				
Angus, Stevland	6. 0	Barnet	Westminster	16.09.80
Comyn-Platt, Charlie	6. 2	Bolton Wand.	Manchester	2.10.85
Gurney, Andy	5.10	Swansea City	Bristol	25.01.74
Ifil, Jerel	6. 1	Watford	London	27.06.82
Nicholas, Andrew	6. 2	Liverpool	Liverpool	10.10.83
Smith, Jack	5.11	Watford	Hemel Hempstead	14.10.83
Midfielders				
Brown, Aaron	5.10	Tamworth	Bristol	14.03.80
Monkhouse, Andy	6. 1	Rotherham Utd.	Leeds	23.10.80
Pook, Michael	5.11	–	Swindon	24.06.86
Whalley, Gareth	5.10	Wigan Athletic	Manchester	19.12.73
Wells, Ben	5. 9	–	Basingstoke	26.03.88
Forwards				
Cureton, Jamie	5. 8	Q.P.R.	Bristol	28.08.75
Holgate, Ashan	6. 2	–	Swindon	9.11.86
Jutkiewicz, Lucas	6. 1			
Peacock, Lee	6. 0	Sheffield Wed.	Paisley	9.10.76
Roberts, Christian	5.11	Bristol City	Cardiff	22.10.79
Shakes, Ricky	5.10	Bolton Wand.	Brixton	26.01.85

TORQUAY UNITED

Ground: Plainmoor, Torquay TQ1 3PS.
Telephone: 01803 328666. **Club nickname:** Gulls.
First-choice colours: Yellow and blue shirts; yellow shorts; yellow socks.
Main sponsor: Sparkworld. **Capacity for 2006-07:** 6,279.
Record attendance: 21,908 v Huddersfield Town (F.A. Cup 4) 29 January, 1955.

Name	Height ft. in.	Previous club	Birthplace	Birthdate
Goalkeepers				
Defenders				
Andrews, Lee	5.11	Carlisle Utd.	Carlisle	30.10.82
Hockley, Matthew	5.11	–	Paignton	5.06.82
Taylor, Craig	6. 1	Plymouth Argyle	Plymouth	24.01.74
Villis, Matthew	6. 3	Plymouth Argyle	Bridgwater	13.04.84
Midfielders.				
Garner, Darren	5.10	Rotherham Utd.	Plymouth	10.12.71
Hewlett, Matt	6. 1	Swindon Town	Bristol	25.02.76
Hill, Kevin	5. 8	Torrington	Exeter	6.03.76
Mansell, Lee	5. 9	Oxford Utd.	Gloucester	23.09.82
Phillips, Martin	5. 9	Plymouth Argyle	Exeter	13.03.76
Woods, Steve	5.11	Chesterfield	Davenham	5.12.76

Forwards

Name	ft. in.	Previous club	Birthplace	Birthdate
Evans, Micky	6.1	Plymouth Argyle	Plymouth	1.01.73
Thorpe, Lee	6.1	Swansea City	Wolves	14.12.75
Ward, Jamie	5.5	Aston Villa	Birmingham	12.05.86

WALSALL

Ground: Bescot Stadium, Bescot Crescent, Walsall WS1 4SA.
Telephone: 01922 651410. **Club nickname:** Saddlers.
First-choice colours: Red shirts; white shorts; white and red socks.
Main Sponsor: Banks's. **Capacity for 2006-07:** 11,230.
Record attendance: (Fellows Park) 25,433 v Newcastle Utd. (Div. 2) 29 August, 1961.
(Bescot Stadium) 11,307 v Wolves (Div. 1) 11 January, 2003.

Name	Height ft. in.	Previous club	Birthplace	Birthdate
Goalkeepers				
Gilmartin, Rene	6. 5	–	Ireland	31.05.87
Ince, Clayton	6. 3	Coventry City	Trinidad	13.07.72
Mckeown, James	6. 1	–	Birmingham	24.07.89
Defenders				
Bradley, Mark	6. 0	–	Wordsley	14.01.88
Dann, Scott	6. 2	–	Liverpool	14.02.87
Dobson, Michael	5.11	Brentford	Isleworth	9.04.81
Fox, Daniel	6. 0	Everton	Liverpool	29.05.86
Gerrard, Anthony	6. 2	Everton	Liverpool	6.02.86
Roper, Ian	6. 3	–	Nuneaton	20.06.77
Westwood, Chris	5.11	Hartlepool Utd.	Dudley	13.02.77
Midfielders				
Demontagnac, Ishmel	5.10	Charlton Athletic	London	15.06.88
Keates, Dean	5. 6	Lincoln City	Walsall	30.06.78
Kinsella, Mark	5. 9	W.B.A.	Dublin	12.08.72
Pead, Craig	5. 9	Coventry City	Bromsgrove	15.09.81
Standing, Michael	5.10	Bradford City	Shoreham	20.03.81
Taylor, Kris	5. 9	Manchester Utd.	Stafford	12.01.84
Wrack, Darren	5. 9	Grimsby Town	Cleethorpes	5.05.76
Wright, Mark	5.11	–	Wolves	24.02.83
Forwards				
Barrowman, Andrew	6. 0	Birmingham City	Wishaw	27.11.84
Bedeau, Tony	5.10	Torquay Utd.	Hammersmith	24.03.79
Butler, Martin	5.11	Rotherham Utd.	Wordsley	15.09.74
Constable, James	6. 2	Chippenham	Cirencester	4.10.84
McDermott, David	5. 5	–	Stourbridge	6.02.88
Nicholls, Alex	5.10	–	Stourbridge	9.12.87

WREXHAM

Ground: Racecourse Ground, Mold Road, Wrexham LL11 2AH.
Telephone: 01978 262129. **Club nickname:** Robins.
First-choice-colours: Red shirts; white shorts; red socks.
Main sponsor: Capacity for 2006-07: 15,500.
Record attendance: 34,445 v Manchester Utd. (F.A. Cup 4) 26 January, 1957.

Name	Height ft. in.	Previous club	Birthplace	Birthdate Goal-keepers
Ingham, Michael	6. 4	Sunderland	Belfast	9.07.80
Jones, Michael	6. 3	–	Liverpool	3.12.87
Defenders				
Bayliss, David	6. 0	Luton Town	Liverpool	8.06.76
Evans, Gareth		New Cefn Druids	Wrexham	10.01.87
Harris, Mark	5.10	–	Liverpool	5.12.86
Lawrence, Dennis	6. 7	Defence Force	Trinidad	18.01.74
Pejic, Shaun	6. 1	–	Hereford	16.11.82

Name	Height ft. in.	Previous club	Birthplace	Birthdate
Roche, Lee	5.10	Burnley	Bolton	28.10.80
Smith, Alex	5. 8	Chester City	Liverpool	15.02.76
Spender, Simon	5.11	–	Mold	15.11.85
Midfielders				
Crowell, Matt	5. 9	Southampton	Bridgend	3.07.84
Done, Matt	5.10	–		22.07.88
Ferguson, Darren	5.10	Wolves	Glasgow	9.02.72
Jones, Mark	5.11	–	Wrexham	15.08.83
Mackin, Levi	6. 0	–	Chester	4.04.86
Whitley, Jim	5. 9	Manchester City	Zambia	14.04.75
Williams, Danny	6. 1	Bristol Rov.	Wrexham	12.07.79
Forwards				
Llewellyn, Chris	5.11	Hartlepool Utd.	Swansea	29.08.79
Williams, Marc	5.10	–	Conwy	27.07.88
Williams, Sam	6. 0	Aston Villa	London	9.06.87

WYCOMBE WANDERERS

Ground: Causeway Stadium, Hillbottom Road, High Wycombe HP12 4HJ.
Telephone: 01494 472100. **Club nickname:** Chairboys.
First-choice colours: Light and dark blue shirts; light blue shorts; light blue socks.
Main sponsor: Loans.co.uk. **Capacity for 2006-07:** 10,000.
Record attendance: 9,921 v Fulham (F.A. Cup 3) 8 January, 2002.

Name	Height ft. in.	Previous club	Birthplace	Birthdate
Goalkeepers				
Talia, Frank	6. 1	Reading	Melbourne	20.07.72
Williams, Steve	6. 0	–	Oxford	21.04.83
Defenders				
Antwi, Will	6. 3	Aldershot	Ashford	19.10.82
Palmer, Chris	5. 7	Notts Co.	Derby	16.10.83
Senda, Danny	5.10	Southampton	Harrow	17.04.81
Stockley, Sam	6. 0	Colchester Utd.	Tiverton	5.09.77
Williamson, Mike	6. 3	Southampton	Stoke	8.11.83
Midfielders				
Anya, Ikechi	5. 7	–	Glasgow	3.01.88
Bloomfield, Matt	5. 8	Ipswich Town	Felixstowe	8.02.84
Lee Rob	5.11	West Ham Utd.	West Ham	1.02.66
Martin, Russell	5.10	–	Brighton	4.01.86
Oakes, Stefan	5.11	Notts Co.	Leicester	6.09.78
Torres, Sergio	6. 2	Basingstoke Town	Mar Del Plata, Arg.	11.07.81
Forwards				
Betsy, Kevin	6. 1	Barnsley	Seychelles	20.03.78
Dixon, Jonny	5. 9	–	Mercia, Spa.	16.01.84
Easter, Jermaine	5. 8	Boston Utd.	Cardiff	15.01.82
Griffin, Charlie	6. 0	Forest Green	Bath	25.06.79
Mooney, Tommy	5.11	Oxford Utd.	Billingham	11.08.71
Stonebridge, Ian	6. 0	Plymouth Argyle	London	30.08.81

BANK OF SCOTLAND PREMIER LEAGUE SQUADS 2006-07

ABERDEEN

Goalkeepers: Jamie Langfield, David Preece.
Defenders: Russell Anderson, Andrew Considine, Zander Diamond, David Donald, Michael Hart, Kevin McNaughton.

Midfielders: Derek Adams, Gary Dempsey, Richard Foster, Kyle Macaulay, Scott Muirhead, Barry Nicholson, Scott Severin, Jamie Smith, Ferne Snoyl.
Forwards: Chris Clark, Steven Craig, Stevie Crawford, Steve Lovell, Darren Mackie, Chris Maguire, Gary Shields, John Stewart, Jamie Winter.

CELTIC

Goalkeepers: Artur Boruc, David Marshall, Michael McGovern.
Defenders: Bobo Balde, Gary Caldwell, Mo Camara, Scott Cuthbert, John Kennedy, Stephen McManus, Charlie Mulgrew, Darren O'Dea, Paul Telfer, Stanislav Varga, Adam Virgo, Mark Wilson.
Midfielders: Simon Ferry, Jiri Jarosik, Paul Lawson, Neil Lennon, Shunsuke Nakamura, Stephen Pearson, Stilian Petrov, Evander Sno, Alan Thompson.
Forwards: Craig Beattie, Shaun Maloney, Aiden McGeady, Michael McGlinchey, Kenny Miller, Rocco Quinn, Nicholas Riley, Derek Riordan, Ross Wallace, Maciej Zurawski.

DUNDEE UNITED

Goalkeepers: Derek Stillie.
Defenders: Alan Archibald, Gary Kenneth, Lee Mair, David McCracken, Paul Ritchie.
Midfielders: Craig Conway, Stuart Duff, David Fernandez, Mark Kerr, Steven Robb, Barry Robson.
Forwards: Craig Brewster, Noel Hunt, Lee Miller, Colin Samuel,

DUNFERMLINE ATHLETIC

Goalkeepers: Bryn Halliwell, Allan McGregor, Sean Murdoch.
Defenders: Iain Campbell, Aaron Labonte, Scott Morrison, Greg Ross, Greg Shields, Andy Tod, Scott Wilson.
Midfielders: Frederic Daquin, Gary Mason, Jamie McCunnie, Scott Muirhead, Darren Young, Stephen Simmons, Scott Thomson.
Forwards: Mark Burchill, Craig Wilson.

FALKIRK

Goalkeepers: Allan Ferguson, Darren Hill, Mark Howard.
Defenders: Craig Ireland, Tiago Rodrigues, Andy Lawrie, Jean Francois Lecsinel, Kenny Milne, Craig McPherson, Marc Twaddle.
Midfielders: Darren Barr, Patrick Cregg, Liam Craig, Russell Latapy, Ryan McStay, Stephen O'Donnell, Jack Ross, Densill Theobald, Steven Thomson, Lima Santos.
Forwards: Alan Gow, Ian MacSween, Stephen Manson, Daniel McBreen, Pedro Moutinho, Marc Ramsay.

HEARTS

Goalkeepers: Steve Banks, Craig Gordon, Jamie MacDonald.
Defenders: Nerijus Barasa, Christophe Berra, Takis Fyssas, Jose Goncalves, Jamie McAllister, John Neill, Robbie Neilson, Martin Petras, Steven Pressley, Craig Sives, Ibrahim Tall, Jason Thompson, Andy Webster.
Midfielders: Bruno Aguiar, Mirsad Beslija, Julien Brellier, Samuel Camazzola, Deividas Cesnauskis, Andrew Driver, Chris Hackett, Lee Johnson, Neil McCann, Gary Tierney, Lee Wallace.
Forwards: Roman Bednar, Calum Elliot, Paul Hartley, Hjalmar, Edgar Jankauskas, Juho Makela, Saulius Mikoliunas, Jamie Mole, Michael Pospisil, Ludek Straceny, Graham Weir.

HIBERNIAN

Goalkeepers: Simon Brown, Zbigniew Malkowski.
Defenders: Jonathan Baillie, Chris Hogg, Rob Jones, Oumar Konde, David Murphy, Jay Shields, Lewis Stevenson, Steven Whittaker.
Midfielders: Guillaume Beuzelin, Paul Dalglish, Antonio Murray, Stephen Glass, Jamie McCluskey, Kevin McDonald, Michael Stewart, Kevin Thomson.
Forwards: Abdessalam Benjelloun, Scott Brown, Ross Campbell, Steven Fletcher, Chris Killen, Amadou Konte, Sean Lynch, Sam Morrow, Dean Shiels, Ivan Sproule.

INVERNESS CALEDONIAN THISTLE

Goalkeepers: Mark Brown, Michael Fraser.
Defenders: Darren Dods, Stuart Golabek, Richard Hastings, Stuart McCaffrey, Grant Munro, Ross Tokely.
Midfielders: Ian Black, Russell Duncan, Liam Fox, Richard Hart, Roy McBain, Alan Morgan, David Proctor, John Rankin, Alexander Sutherland, Barry Wilson.
Forwards: Graham Bayne, Craig Dargo, Carricondo Perez Juanjo, Steve Hislop, Liam Keogh.

KILMARNOCK

Goalkeepers: Cameron Bell, Alan Combe, Graeme Smith.
Defenders: Simon Ford, James Fowler, Gordon Greer, Garry Hay, David Lilley, Grant Murray, Lindsay Wilson, Frazer Wright
Midfielders: Rhian Dodds, Jamie Hamill, Danny Invincibile, Allan Johnston, Gary Locke, Stephen Murray, Steven Naismith, Peter Leven, Eric Skora.
Forwards: Robert Campbell, Paul Di Giacomo, Colin Nish, Gary Wales, Gary Wild.

MOTHERWELL

Goalkeepers: Dougie Calder, Colin Meldrum, Graeme Smith.
Defenders: Martyn Corrigan, Stephen Craigan, Marc Fitzpatrick, William Kinniburgh, Brian McLean, Paul Quinn.
Midfielders: Shaun Fagan, Brian Kerr, Kevin McBride, Phil O'Donnell, Jim Paterson.
Forwards: David Clarkson, Richie Foran, Jim Hamilton, Ross McCormack, Scott McDonald, Steven McGarry.

RANGERS

Goalkeepers: Scott Gallacher, Stefan Klos, Lionel Letizi, Allan McGregor, Lee Robinson.
Defenders: Marvin Andrews, Olivier Bernard, Steven Campbell, Jose Pierre-Fanfan, Brian Gilmour, Brahim Hemdani, Alan Hutton, Alan Lowing, Robert Malcolm, Antoine Ponroy, Fernando Ricksen, Julien Rodriguez, Karl Svensson.
Midfielders: Charlie Adam, Thomas Buffel, Chris Burke, Barry Ferguson, Ian Murray, Makhtar N'Diaye, Hamed Namouchi, Dany N'Guessan, Gavin Rae, Libor Sionko.
Forwards: Moses Ashikodi, Kris Boyd, Derek Carcary, Robert Davidson, Nacho Novo, Dado Prso, Steven Smith.

ST MIRREN

Goalkeepers: Craig Hinchcliffe, Chris Smith.
Defenders: Kirk Broadfoot, Tony Bullock, Ian Maxwell, Kevin McGowne, Andy Millen, John Potter, David Van Zanten.
Midfielders: Iain Anderson, Garry Brady, Marc Corcoran, Simon Lappin, Hugh Murray, Alan Reid, Mark Reill.
Forwards: John Baird, Alex Burke, Stewart Kean, Brian McGinty, Billy Mehmet, John Sutton.

ENGLISH LEAGUE FIXTURES 2006-07

Saturday, 5 August
Coca-Cola League Championship
Barnsley v Cardiff City
Birmingham City v Colchester Utd.
Burnley v Q.P.R.
Ipswich Town v Crystal Palace
Leeds Utd. v Norwich City
Luton Town v Leicester City
Plymouth Argyle v Wolves
Preston N.E. v Sheffield Wed.
Southend Utd. v Stoke City
W.B.A. v Hull City

Coca-Cola League One
Bournemouth v Chesterfield
Brentford v Blackpool
Bristol City v Scunthorpe Utd.
Carlisle Utd. v Doncaster Rov.
Crewe Alexandra v Northampton Town
Gillingham v Huddersfield Town
Millwall v Yeovil
Nott'm. Forest v Bradford City
Port Vale v Leyton Orient
Rotherham Utd. v Brighton & H.A.
Swansea City v Cheltenham Town
Tranmere Rov. v Oldham Athletic

Coca-Cola League Two
Barnet v Torquay Utd.
Chester City v Accrington Stanley
Darlington v Macclesfield Town
Grimsby Town v Boston Utd.
Hartlepool Utd. v Swindon Town
Lincoln City v Notts Co.
Milton Keynes Dons v Bury
Peterborough Utd. v Bristol Rov.
Rochdale v Walsall
Shrewsbury Town v Mansfield Town
Stockport Co. v Hereford
Wycombe Wand. v Wrexham

Sunday, 6 August
Coca-Cola League Championship
Coventry City v Sunderland
Derby Co. v Southampton

Tuesday, 8 August
Coca-Cola League Championship
Cardiff City v W.B.A.
Colchester Utd. v Plymouth Argyle
Crystal Palace v Southend Utd.
Hull City v Barnsley

Leicester City v Burnley
Norwich City v Preston N.E.
Q.P.R. v Leeds Utd.
Sheffield Wed. v Luton Town
Stoke City v Derby Co.
Sunderland v Birmingham City
Wolves v Ipswich Town

Coca-Cola League One
Blackpool v Nott'm. Forest
Bradford City v Bristol City
Brighton & H.A. v Gillingham
Cheltenham Town v Tranmere Rov.
Doncaster Rov. v Crewe Alexandra
Huddersfield Town v Rotherham Utd.
Leyton Orient v Millwall
Northampton Town v Brentford
Oldham Athletic v Port Vale
Scunthorpe Utd. v Swansea City
Yeovil v Bournemouth

Coca-Cola League Two
Accrington Stanley v Darlington
Bristol Rov. v Wycombe Wand.
Bury v Chester City
Hereford v Lincoln City
Macclesfield Town v Hartlepool Utd.
Mansfield Town v Milton Keynes Dons
Notts Co. v Shrewsbury Town
Swindon Town v Barnet
Torquay Utd. v Rochdale
Walsall v Stockport Co.
Wrexham v Grimsby Town

Wednesday, 9 August
Coca-Cola League Championship
Southampton v Coventry City

Coca-Cola League One
Chesterfield v Carlisle Utd.

Coca-Cola League Two
Boston Utd. v Peterborough Utd.

Friday, 11 August
Coca-Cola League Championship
Wolves v Preston N.E.

Saturday, 12 August
Coca-Cola League Championship
Cardiff City v Coventry City
Colchester Utd. v Barnsley

Hull City v Derby Co.
Leicester City v Ipswich Town
Norwich City v Luton Town
Q.P.R. v Southend Utd.
Sheffield Wed. v Burnley
Southampton v W.B.A.
Stoke City v Birmingham City
Sunderland v Plymouth Argyle

Coca-Cola League One
Blackpool v Rotherham Utd.
Bradford City v Gillingham
Brighton & H.A. v Brentford
Cheltenham Town v Port Vale
Chesterfield v Millwall
Doncaster Rov. v Tranmere Rov.
Huddersfield Town v Bristol City
Leyton Orient v Bournemouth
Northampton Town v Nott'm. Forest
Oldham Athletic v Swansea City
Scunthorpe Utd. v Crewe Alexandra
Yeovil v Carlisle Utd.

Coca-Cola League Two
Accrington Stanley v Barnet
Boston Utd. v Darlington
Bristol Rov. v Grimsby Town
Bury v Shrewsbury Town
Hereford v Chester City
Macclesfield Town v Milton Keynes Dons
Mansfield Town v Stockport Co.
Notts Co. v Wycombe Wand.
Swindon Town v Rochdale
Torquay Utd. v Lincoln City
Walsall v Hartlepool Utd.
Wrexham v Peterborough Utd.

Sunday, 13 August
Coca-Cola League Championship
Crystal Palace v Leeds Utd.

Friday, 18 August
Coca-Cola League Championship
Coventry City v Leicester City

Saturday, 19 August
Barclays Premiership
Arsenal v Aston Villa
Bolton Wand. v Tottenham
Everton v Watford
Newcastle Utd. v Wigan Athletic
Portsmouth v Blackburn Rov.
Reading v Middlesbrough
Sheffield Utd. v Liverpool
West Ham Utd. v Charlton Athletic

Coca-Cola League Championship
Barnsley v Southampton
Birmingham City v Crystal Palace

Burnley v Wolves
Derby Co. v Norwich City
Ipswich Town v Hull City
Leeds Utd. v Cardiff City
Luton Town v Stoke City
Plymouth Argyle v Sheffield Wed.
Preston N.E. v Q.P.R.
Southend Utd. v Sunderland
W.B.A. v Colchester Utd.

Coca-Cola League One
Bournemouth v Cheltenham Town
Brentford v Huddersfield Town
Bristol City v Blackpool
Carlisle Utd. v Leyton Orient
Crewe Alexandra v Bradford City
Gillingham v Northampton Town
Millwall v Oldham Athletic
Nott'm. Forest v Brighton & H.A.
Port Vale v Chesterfield
Rotherham Utd. v Scunthorpe Utd.
Swansea City v Doncaster Rov.
Tranmere Rov. v Yeovil

Coca-Cola League Two
Barnet v Hereford
Chester City v Wrexham
Darlington v Swindon Town
Grimsby Town v Mansfield Town
Hartlepool Utd. v Torquay Utd.
Lincoln City v Walsall
Milton Keynes Dons v Bristol Rov.
Peterborough Utd. v Macclesfield Town
Rochdale v Notts Co.
Shrewsbury Town v Boston Utd.
Stockport Co. v Accrington Stanley
Wycombe Wand. v Bury

Sunday, 20 August
Barclays Premiership
Chelsea v Manchester City
Manchester Utd. v Fulham

Tuesday, 22 August
Barclays Premiership
Tottenham v Sheffield Utd.
Watford v West Ham Utd.

Wednesday, 23 August
Barclays Premiership
Aston Villa v Reading
Blackburn Rov. v Everton
Charlton Athletic v Manchester Utd.
Fulham v Bolton Wand.
Manchester City v Portsmouth
Middlesbrough v Chelsea

Saturday, 26 August
Barclays Premiership
Aston Villa v Newcastle Utd.
Charlton Athletic v Bolton Wand.
Fulham v Sheffield Utd.
Liverpool v West Ham Utd.
Manchester City v Arsenal
Tottenham v Everton
Watford v Manchester Utd.
Wigan Athletic v Reading

Coca-Cola League Championship
Cardiff City v Birmingham City
Colchester Utd. v Derby Co.
Crystal Palace v Burnley
Hull City v Coventry City
Leicester City v Southend Utd.
Norwich City v Barnsley
Q.P.R. v Ipswich Town
Southampton v Preston N.E.
Stoke City v Plymouth Argyle
Wolves v Luton Town

Coca-Cola League One
Blackpool v Gillingham
Bradford City v Rotherham Utd.
Brighton & H.A. v Crewe Alexandra
Cheltenham Town v Millwall
Chesterfield v Tranmere Rov.
Doncaster Rov. v Bournemouth
Huddersfield Town v Nott'm. Forest
Leyton Orient v Swansea City
Oldham Athletic v Carlisle Utd.
Scunthorpe Utd. v Brentford
Yeovil v Port Vale

Coca-Cola League Two
Accrington Stanley v Rochdale
Boston Utd. v Milton Keynes Dons
Bristol Rov. v Shrewsbury Town
Bury v Grimsby Town
Hereford v Hartlepool Utd.
Macclesfield Town v Wycombe Wand.
Mansfield Town v Lincoln City
Notts Co. v Peterborough Utd.
Swindon Town v Stockport Co.
Torquay Utd. v Chester City
Walsall v Darlington
Wrexham v Barnet

Sunday, 27 August
Barclays Premiership
Blackburn Rov. v Chelsea

Coca-Cola League Championship
Sheffield Wed. v Leeds Utd.

Monday, 28 August
Barclays Premiership
Middlesbrough v Portsmouth

Coca-Cola League Championship
Sunderland v W.B.A.

Tuesday, 29 August
Coca-Cola League One
Northampton Town v Bristol City

Friday, 1 September
Coca-Cola League Two
Darlington v Torquay Utd.

Saturday, 2 September
Coca-Cola League One
Bournemouth v Oldham Athletic
Brentford v Bradford City
Bristol City v Brighton & H.A.
Carlisle Utd. v Cheltenham Town
Crewe Alexandra v Huddersfield Town
Gillingham v Scunthorpe Utd.
Millwall v Blackpool
Nott'm. Forest v Chesterfield
Rotherham Utd. v Northampton Town
Swansea City v Yeovil
Tranmere Rov. v Leyton Orient

Coca-Cola League Two
Barnet v Walsall
Chester City v Swindon Town
Grimsby Town v Macclesfield Town
Hartlepool Utd. v Boston Utd.
Lincoln City v Accrington Stanley
Milton Keynes Dons v Notts Co.
Peterborough Utd. v Bury
Rochdale v Hereford
Shrewsbury Town v Wrexham
Stockport Co. v Bristol Rov.
Wycombe Wand. v Mansfield Town

Sunday, 3 September
Coca-Cola League One
Port Vale v Doncaster Rov.

Saturday, 9 September
Barclays Premiership
Arsenal v Middlesbrough
Bolton Wand. v Watford
Chelsea v Charlton Athletic
Everton v Liverpool
Manchester Utd. v Tottenham
Newcastle Utd. v Fulham
Portsmouth v Wigan Athletic
Sheffield Utd. v Blackburn Rov.

Coca-Cola League Championship
Barnsley v Stoke City
Birmingham City v Hull City
Burnley v Colchester Utd.
Coventry City v Norwich City
Derby Co. v Sunderland
Ipswich Town v Southampton
Leeds Utd. v Wolves
Luton Town v Crystal Palace
Plymouth Argyle v Q.P.R.
Preston N.E. v Cardiff City
Southend Utd. v Sheffield Wed.
W.B.A. v Leicester City

Coca-Cola League One
Bournemouth v Crewe Alexandra
Carlisle Utd. v Northampton Town
Cheltenham Town v Huddersfield Town
Chesterfield v Rotherham Utd.
Doncaster Rov. v Gillingham
Leyton Orient v Brentford
Millwall v Brighton & H.A.
Oldham Athletic v Scunthorpe Utd.
Port Vale v Blackpool
Swansea City v Bradford City
Tranmere Rov. v Bristol City
Yeovil v Nott'm. Forest

Coca-Cola League Two
Boston Utd. v Stockport Co.
Bristol Rov. v Rochdale
Bury v Torquay Utd.
Grimsby Town v Walsall
Macclesfield Town v Barnet
Mansfield Town v Hereford
Milton Keynes Dons v Hartlepool Utd.
Notts Co. v Accrington Stanley
Peterborough Utd. v Darlington
Shrewsbury Town v Lincoln City
Wrexham v Swindon Town
Wycombe Wand. v Chester City

Sunday, 10 September
Barclays Premiership
West Ham Utd. v Aston Villa

Monday, 11 September
Barclays Premiership
Reading v Manchester City

Tuesday, 12 September
Coca-Cola League Championship
Burnley v Barnsley
Crystal Palace v Southampton
Ipswich Town v Coventry City
Leeds Utd. v Sunderland
Leicester City v Hull City
Luton Town v Colchester Utd.
Plymouth Argyle v Cardiff City

Preston N.E. v W.B.A.
Q.P.R. v Birmingham City
Sheffield Wed. v Stoke City
Southend Utd. v Norwich City
Wolves v Derby Co.

Coca-Cola League One
Blackpool v Chesterfield
Bradford City v Carlisle Utd.
Brentford v Swansea City
Brighton & H.A. v Bournemouth
Bristol City v Leyton Orient
Crewe Alexandra v Cheltenham Town
Gillingham v Millwall
Huddersfield Town v Doncaster Rov.
Northampton Town v Yeovil
Nott'm. Forest v Oldham Athletic
Rotherham Utd. v Tranmere Rov.
Scunthorpe Utd. v Port Vale

Coca-Cola League Two
Accrington Stanley v Wrexham
Barnet v Boston Utd.
Chester City v Notts Co.
Darlington v Bury
Hartlepool Utd. v Mansfield Town
Hereford v Wycombe Wand.
Lincoln City v Macclesfield Town
Rochdale v Grimsby Town
Stockport Co. v Shrewsbury Town
Swindon Town v Milton Keynes Dons
Torquay Utd. v Bristol Rov.
Walsall v Peterborough Utd.

Friday, 15 September
Coca-Cola League Championship
Hull City v Sheffield Wed.

Saturday, 16 September
Barclays Premiership
Bolton Wand. v Middlesbrough
Charlton Athletic v Portsmouth
Everton v Wigan Athletic
Sheffield Utd. v Reading
Tottenham v Fulham
Watford v Aston Villa

Coca-Cola League Championship
Barnsley v Wolves
Birmingham City v Ipswich Town
Cardiff City v Luton Town
Colchester Utd. v Q.P.R.
Coventry City v Leeds Utd.
Derby Co. v Preston N.E.
Norwich City v Crystal Palace
Southampton v Plymouth Argyle
Stoke City v Burnley
Sunderland v Leicester City
W.B.A. v Southend Utd.

Coca-Cola League One
Blackpool v Oldham Athletic
Bradford City v Port Vale
Brentford v Bournemouth
Brighton & H.A. v Leyton Orient
Bristol City v Chesterfield
Crewe Alexandra v Millwall
Gillingham v Swansea City
Huddersfield Town v Yeovil
Northampton Town v Tranmere Rov.
Nott'm. Forest v Carlisle Utd.
Rotherham Utd. v Doncaster Rov.
Scunthorpe Utd. v Cheltenham Town

Coca-Cola League Two
Accrington Stanley v Boston Utd.
Barnet v Notts Co.
Chester City v Grimsby Town
Darlington v Bristol Rov.
Hartlepool Utd. v Shrewsbury Town
Hereford v Bury
Lincoln City v Milton Keynes Dons
Rochdale v Wycombe Wand.
Stockport Co. v Wrexham
Swindon Town v Peterborough Utd.
Torquay Utd. v Mansfield Town
Walsall v Macclesfield Town

Sunday, 17 September
Barclays Premiership
Blackburn Rov. v Manchester City
Chelsea v Liverpool
Manchester Utd. v Arsenal
West Ham Utd. v Newcastle Utd.

Wednesday, 20 September
Coca-Cola League Championship
Liverpool v Newcastle Utd.

Friday, 22 September
Coca-Cola League Championship
Preston N.E. v Barnsley

Saturday, 23 September
Barclays Premiership
Arsenal v Sheffield Utd.
Aston Villa v Charlton Athletic
Fulham v Chelsea
Liverpool v Tottenham
Manchester City v West Ham Utd.
Middlesbrough v Blackburn Rov.
Reading v Manchester Utd.
Wigan Athletic v Watford

Coca-Cola League Championship
Burnley v Southampton
Crystal Palace v Coventry City
Ipswich Town v Sunderland
Leeds Utd. v Birmingham City

Leicester City v Colchester Utd.
Luton Town v W.B.A.
Plymouth Argyle v Norwich City
Q.P.R. v Hull City
Sheffield Wed. v Derby Co.
Wolves v Stoke City

Coca-Cola League One
Bournemouth v Scunthorpe Utd.
Carlisle Utd. v Brighton & H.A.
Cheltenham Town v Bradford City
Chesterfield v Brentford
Doncaster Rov. v Blackpool
Leyton Orient v Rotherham Utd.
Millwall v Northampton Town
Oldham Athletic v Gillingham
Port Vale v Bristol City
Swansea City v Huddersfield Town
Tranmere Rov. v Nott'm. Forest
Yeovil v Crewe Alexandra

Coca-Cola League Two
Boston Utd. v Rochdale
Bristol Rov. v Walsall
Bury v Barnet
Grimsby Town v Stockport Co.
Macclesfield Town v Torquay Utd.
Mansfield Town v Accrington Stanley
Milton Keynes Dons v Chester City
Notts Co. v Swindon Town
Peterborough Utd. v Hartlepool Utd.
Shrewsbury Town v Darlington
Wrexham v Hereford
Wycombe Wand. v Lincoln City

Sunday, 24 September
Barclays Premiership
Newcastle Utd. v Everton

Coca-Cola League Championship
Southend Utd. v Cardiff City

Monday, 25 September
Barclays Premiership
Portsmouth v Bolton Wand.

Tuesday, 26 September
Coca-Cola League One
Bournemouth v Bristol City
Carlisle Utd. v Blackpool
Cheltenham Town v Northampton Town
Doncaster Rov. v Bradford City
Leyton Orient v Gillingham
Millwall v Brentford
Oldham Athletic v Rotherham Utd.
Port Vale v Nott'm. Forest
Swansea City v Crewe Alexandra
Tranmere Rov. v Huddersfield Town
Yeovil v Brighton & H.A.

Coca-Cola League Two
Bristol Rov. v Hereford
Bury v Accrington Stanley
Grimsby Town v Hartlepool Utd.
Macclesfield Town v Chester City
Mansfield Town v Darlington
Milton Keynes Dons v Torquay Utd.
Notts Co. v Stockport Co.
Peterborough Utd. v Barnet
Shrewsbury Town v Walsall
Wrexham v Rochdale
Wycombe Wand. v Swindon Town

Wednesday, 27 September
Coca-Cola League One
Chesterfield v Scunthorpe Utd.

Coca-Cola League Two
Boston Utd. v Lincoln City

Friday, 29 September
Coca-Cola League Championship
Colchester Utd. v Ipswich Town

Coca-Cola League Two
Darlington v Grimsby Town

Saturday, 30 September
Barclays Premiership
Bolton Wand. v Liverpool
Charlton Athletic v Arsenal
Chelsea v Aston Villa
Everton v Manchester City
Manchester Utd. v Newcastle Utd.
Sheffield Utd. v Middlesbrough

Coca-Cola League Championship
Barnsley v Luton Town
Birmingham City v Leicester City
Cardiff City v Wolves
Coventry City v Plymouth Argyle
Derby Co. v Southend Utd.
Hull City v Crystal Palace
Southampton v Q.P.R.
Stoke City v Preston N.E.
Sunderland v Sheffield Wed.
W.B.A. v Leeds Utd.

Coca-Cola League One
Blackpool v Leyton Orient
Bradford City v Tranmere Rov.
Brentford v Yeovil
Brighton & H.A. v Chesterfield
Bristol City v Oldham Athletic
Crewe Alexandra v Carlisle Utd.
Gillingham v Cheltenham Town
Huddersfield Town v Bournemouth
Northampton Town v Port Vale
Nott'm. Forest v Swansea City

Rotherham Utd. v Millwall
Scunthorpe Utd. v Doncaster Rov.

Coca-Cola League Two
Accrington Stanley v Wycombe Wand.
Barnet v Milton Keynes Dons
Chester City v Bristol Rov.
Hartlepool Utd. v Wrexham
Hereford v Macclesfield Town
Lincoln City v Bury
Rochdale v Shrewsbury Town
Stockport Co. v Peterborough Utd.
Swindon Town v Boston Utd.
Torquay Utd. v Notts Co.
Walsall v Mansfield Town

Sunday, 1 October
Barclays Premiership
Blackburn Rov. v Wigan Athletic
Tottenham v Portsmouth
West Ham Utd. v Reading

Coca-Cola League Championship
Norwich City v Burnley

Monday, 2 October
Barclays Premiership
Watford v Fulham

Friday, 6 October
Coca-Cola League Two
Darlington v Rochdale

Saturday, 7 October
Coca-Cola League One
Bournemouth v Northampton Town
Bradford City v Huddersfield Town
Brentford v Bristol City
Carlisle Utd. v Millwall
Crewe Alexandra v Gillingham
Doncaster Rov. v Oldham Athletic
Leyton Orient v Chesterfield
Nott'm. Forest v Scunthorpe Utd.
Port Vale v Rotherham Utd.
Swansea City v Tranmere Rov.
Yeovil v Cheltenham Town

Coca-Cola League Two
Accrington Stanley v Swindon Town
Bristol Rov. v Boston Utd.
Bury v Wrexham
Chester City v Walsall
Lincoln City v Hartlepool Utd.
Mansfield Town v Notts Co.
Milton Keynes Dons v Peterborough Utd.
Shrewsbury Town v Macclesfield Town
Stockport Co. v Barnet
Wycombe Wand. v Torquay Utd.

Sunday, 8 October
Coca-Cola League One
Brighton & H.A. v Blackpool

Coca-Cola League Two
Grimsby Town v Hereford

Saturday, 14 October
Barclays Premiership
Arsenal v Watford
Aston Villa v Tottenham
Liverpool v Blackburn Rov.
Manchester City v Sheffield Utd.
Middlesbrough v Everton
Portsmouth v West Ham Utd.
Reading v Chelsea
Wigan Athletic v Manchester Utd.

Coca-Cola League Championship
Burnley v Hull City
Crystal Palace v Cardiff City
Ipswich Town v W.B.A.
Leeds Utd. v Stoke City
Leicester City v Southampton
Luton Town v Birmingham City
Preston N.E. v Sunderland
Q.P.R. v Norwich City
Sheffield Wed. v Barnsley
Southend Utd. v Coventry City
Wolves v Colchester Utd.

Coca-Cola League One
Blackpool v Yeovil
Bristol City v Crewe Alexandra
Cheltenham Town v Doncaster Rov.
Chesterfield v Swansea City
Gillingham v Nott'm. Forest
Huddersfield Town v Carlisle Utd.
Millwall v Bournemouth
Northampton Town v Bradford City
Oldham Athletic v Leyton Orient
Rotherham Utd. v Brentford
Scunthorpe Utd. v Brighton & H.A.
Tranmere Rov. v Port Vale

Coca-Cola League Two
Barnet v Lincoln City
Boston Utd. v Mansfield Town
Hartlepool Utd. v Stockport Co.
Hereford v Darlington
Macclesfield Town v Bury
Notts Co. v Bristol Rov.
Peterborough Utd. v Shrewsbury Town
Rochdale v Chester City
Swindon Town v Grimsby Town
Torquay Utd. v Accrington Stanley
Walsall v Wycombe Wand.
Wrexham v Milton Keynes Dons

Sunday, 15 October
Barclays Premiership
Newcastle Utd. v Bolton Wand.

Coca-Cola League Championship
Plymouth Argyle v Derby Co.

Monday, 16 October
Barclays Premiership
Fulham v Charlton Athletic

Tuesday, 17 October
Coca-Cola League Championship
Barnsley v Plymouth Argyle
Birmingham City v Norwich City
Burnley v Southend Utd.
Cardiff City v Southampton
Colchester Utd. v Sheffield Wed.
Crystal Palace v W.B.A.
Hull City v Luton Town
Ipswich Town v Preston N.E.
Leeds Utd. v Leicester City
Q.P.R. v Derby Co.
Stoke City v Sunderland
Wolves v Coventry City

Saturday, 21 October
Barclays Premiership
Aston Villa v Fulham
Blackburn Rov. v Bolton Wand.
Charlton Athletic v Watford
Chelsea v Portsmouth
Everton v Sheffield Utd.
Middlesbrough v Newcastle Utd.
Tottenham v West Ham Utd.
Wigan Athletic v Manchester City

Coca-Cola League Championship
Coventry City v Colchester Utd.
Derby Co. v Birmingham City
Leicester City v Crystal Palace
Luton Town v Leeds Utd.
Norwich City v Cardiff City
Plymouth Argyle v Burnley
Preston N.E. v Hull City
Sheffield Wed. v Q.P.R.
Southampton v Stoke City
Southend Utd. v Ipswich Town
Sunderland v Barnsley
W.B.A. v Wolves

Coca-Cola League One
Bournemouth v Rotherham Utd.
Bradford City v Scunthorpe Utd.
Brentford v Gillingham
Brighton & H.A. v Northampton Town
Carlisle Utd. v Tranmere Rov.
Crewe Alexandra v Blackpool
Doncaster Rov. v Chesterfield

Leyton Orient v Cheltenham Town
Nott'm. Forest v Bristol City
Port Vale v Huddersfield Town
Swansea City v Millwall
Yeovil v Oldham Athletic

Coca-Cola League Two
Accrington Stanley v Walsall
Bristol Rov. v Macclesfield Town
Bury v Boston Utd.
Chester City v Hartlepool Utd.
Darlington v Barnet
Grimsby Town v Notts Co.
Lincoln City v Rochdale
Mansfield Town v Wrexham
Milton Keynes Dons v Hereford
Shrewsbury Town v Swindon Town
Stockport Co. v Torquay Utd.
Wycombe Wand. v Peterborough Utd.

Sunday, 22 October
Barclays Premiership
Manchester Utd. v Liverpool
Reading v Arsenal

Friday, 27 October
Coca-Cola League Championship
Burnley v Preston N.E.

Saturday, 28 October
Barclays Premiership
Arsenal v Everton
Bolton Wand. v Manchester Utd.
Fulham v Wigan Athletic
Liverpool v Aston Villa
Newcastle Utd. v Charlton Athletic
Portsmouth v Reading
Sheffield Utd. v Chelsea
Watford v Tottenham

Coca-Cola League Championship
Barnsley v Coventry City
Birmingham City v W.B.A.
Cardiff City v Derby Co.
Colchester Utd. v Southampton
Crystal Palace v Plymouth Argyle
Hull City v Sunderland
Ipswich Town v Luton Town
Leeds Utd. v Southend Utd.
Q.P.R. v Leicester City
Stoke City v Norwich City
Wolves v Sheffield Wed.

Coca-Cola League One
Blackpool v Bradford City
Bristol City v Doncaster Rov.
Cheltenham Town v Nott'm. Forest
Chesterfield v Yeovil
Gillingham v Carlisle Utd.

Huddersfield Town v Brighton & H.A.
Millwall v Port Vale
Northampton Town v Swansea City
Oldham Athletic v Brentford
Rotherham Utd. v Crewe Alexandra
Scunthorpe Utd. v Leyton Orient
Tranmere Rov. v Bournemouth

Coca-Cola League Two
Barnet v Chester City
Boston Utd. v Wycombe Wand.
Hartlepool Utd. v Darlington
Hereford v Accrington Stanley
Macclesfield Town v Mansfield Town
Notts Co. v Bury
Peterborough Utd. v Grimsby Town
Rochdale v Stockport Co.
Swindon Town v Lincoln City
Torquay Utd. v Shrewsbury Town
Walsall v Milton Keynes Dons
Wrexham v Bristol Rov.

Sunday, 29 October
Barclays Premiership
West Ham Utd. v Blackburn Rov.

Monday, 30 October
Barclays Premiership
Manchester City v Middlesbrough

Tuesday, 31 October
Coca-Cola League Championship
Coventry City v Birmingham City
Leicester City v Stoke City
Luton Town v Burnley
Norwich City v Colchester Utd.
Plymouth Argyle v Ipswich Town
Preston N.E. v Leeds Utd.
Sheffield Wed. v Crystal Palace
Southend Utd. v Hull City
Sunderland v Cardiff City
W.B.A. v Q.P.R.

Wednesday, 1 November
Coca-Cola League Championship
Derby Co. v Barnsley
Southampton v Wolves

Friday, 3 November
Coca-Cola League Two
Darlington v Chester City

Saturday, 4 November
Barclays Premiership
Aston Villa v Blackburn Rov.
Bolton Wand. v Wigan Athletic
Charlton Athletic v Manchester City
Fulham v Everton
Liverpool v Reading

Manchester Utd. v Portsmouth
Newcastle Utd. v Sheffield Utd.
Watford v Middlesbrough

Coca-Cola League Championship
Barnsley v Leeds Utd.
Burnley v Ipswich Town
Colchester Utd. v Cardiff City
Derby Co. v W.B.A.
Norwich City v Sunderland
Plymouth Argyle v Birmingham City
Preston N.E. v Luton Town
Q.P.R. v Crystal Palace
Sheffield Wed. v Leicester City
Southampton v Hull City
Stoke City v Coventry City
Wolves v Southend Utd.

Coca-Cola League One
Bradford City v Brighton & H.A.
Carlisle Utd. v Rotherham Utd.
Cheltenham Town v Oldham Athletic
Crewe Alexandra v Port Vale
Doncaster Rov. v Leyton Orient
Gillingham v Chesterfield
Huddersfield Town v Scunthorpe Utd.
Northampton Town v Blackpool
Nott'm. Forest v Brentford
Swansea City v Bournemouth
Tranmere Rov. v Millwall
Yeovil v Bristol City

Coca-Cola League Two
Boston Utd. v Notts Co.
Bristol Rov. v Mansfield Town
Grimsby Town v Milton Keynes Dons
Hartlepool Utd. v Barnet
Peterborough Utd. v Accrington Stanley
Rochdale v Bury
Shrewsbury Town v Wycombe Wand.
Stockport Co. v Lincoln City
Swindon Town v Hereford
Walsall v Torquay Utd.
Wrexham v Macclesfield Town

Sunday, 5 November
Barclays Premiership
Tottenham v Chelsea
West Ham Utd. v Arsenal

Saturday, 11 November
Barclays Premiership
Blackburn Rov. v Manchester Utd.
Chelsea v Watford
Everton v Aston Villa
Manchester City v Newcastle Utd.
Middlesbrough v West Ham Utd.
Portsmouth v Fulham
Sheffield Utd. v Bolton Wand.

Wigan Athletic v Charlton Athletic

Coca-Cola League Championship
Birmingham City v Barnsley
Cardiff City v Burnley
Coventry City v Derby Co.
Crystal Palace v Stoke City
Hull City v Wolves
Ipswich Town v Sheffield Wed.
Leeds Utd. v Colchester Utd.
Leicester City v Plymouth Argyle
Luton Town v Q.P.R.
Southend Utd. v Preston N.E.
Sunderland v Southampton
W.B.A. v Norwich City

Sunday, 12 November
Barclays Premiership
Arsenal v Liverpool
Reading v Tottenham

Saturday, 18 November
Barclays Premiership
Arsenal v Newcastle Utd.
Chelsea v West Ham Utd.
Everton v Bolton Wand.
Manchester City v Fulham
Middlesbrough v Liverpool
Portsmouth v Watford
Reading v Charlton Athletic
Sheffield Utd. v Manchester Utd.

Coca-Cola League Championship
Birmingham City v Wolves
Cardiff City v Q.P.R.
Coventry City v Sheffield Wed.
Crystal Palace v Barnsley
Hull City v Stoke City
Ipswich Town v Norwich City
Leeds Utd. v Southampton
Leicester City v Preston N.E.
Luton Town v Derby Co.
Southend Utd. v Plymouth Argyle
Sunderland v Colchester Utd.
W.B.A. v Burnley

Coca-Cola League One
Blackpool v Huddersfield Town
Bournemouth v Carlisle Utd.
Brentford v Crewe Alexandra
Brighton & H.A. v Tranmere Rov.
Bristol City v Gillingham
Chesterfield v Cheltenham Town
Leyton Orient v Yeovil
Millwall v Doncaster Rov.
Oldham Athletic v Bradford City
Port Vale v Swansea City
Rotherham Utd. v Nott'm. Forest
Scunthorpe Utd. v Northampton Town

Coca-Cola League Two
Accrington Stanley v Hartlepool Utd.
Barnet v Rochdale
Bury v Bristol Rov.
Chester City v Stockport Co.
Hereford v Walsall
Lincoln City v Darlington
Macclesfield Town v Boston Utd.
Mansfield Town v Peterborough Utd.
Milton Keynes Dons v Shrewsbury Town
Notts Co. v Wrexham
Torquay Utd. v Swindon Town
Wycombe Wand. v Grimsby Town

Sunday, 19 November
Barclays Premiership
Blackburn Rov. v Tottenham
Wigan Athletic v Aston Villa

Saturday, 25 November
Barclays Premiership
Aston Villa v Middlesbrough
Bolton Wand. v Arsenal
Charlton Athletic v Everton
Fulham v Reading
Liverpool v Manchester City
Tottenham v Wigan Athletic
Watford v Blackburn Rov.
West Ham Utd. v Sheffield Utd.

Coca-Cola League Championship
Barnsley v Ipswich Town
Burnley v Birmingham City
Colchester Utd. v Southend Utd.
Derby Co. v Leicester City
Norwich City v Hull City
Plymouth Argyle v Leeds Utd.
Preston N.E. v Crystal Palace
Q.P.R. v Coventry City
Sheffield Wed. v Cardiff City
Southampton v Luton Town
Stoke City v W.B.A.
Wolves v Sunderland

Coca-Cola League One
Bradford City v Bournemouth
Carlisle Utd. v Port Vale
Cheltenham Town v Brentford
Crewe Alexandra v Chesterfield
Doncaster Rov. v Brighton & H.A.
Gillingham v Rotherham Utd.
Huddersfield Town v Oldham Athletic
Northampton Town v Leyton Orient
Nott'm. Forest v Millwall
Swansea City v Bristol City
Tranmere Rov. v Blackpool
Yeovil v Scunthorpe Utd.

Coca-Cola League Two
Boston Utd. v Hereford
Bristol Rov. v Barnet
Darlington v Milton Keynes Dons
Grimsby Town v Accrington Stanley
Hartlepool Utd. v Wycombe Wand.
Peterborough Utd. v Torquay Utd.
Rochdale v Mansfield Town
Shrewsbury Town v Chester City
Stockport Co. v Macclesfield Town
Swindon Town v Bury
Walsall v Notts Co.
Wrexham v Lincoln City

Sunday, 26 November
Barclays Premiership
Manchester Utd. v Chelsea
Newcastle Utd. v Portsmouth

Tuesday, 28 November
Barclays Premiership
Watford v Sheffield Utd.

Coca-Cola League Championship
Barnsley v Southend Utd.
Burnley v Leeds Utd.
Colchester Utd. v Hull City
Norwich City v Leicester City
Plymouth Argyle v Luton Town
Preston N.E. v Coventry City
Q.P.R. v Sunderland
Sheffield Wed. v W.B.A.
Stoke City v Cardiff City
Wolves v Crystal Palace

Wednesday, 29 November
Barclays Premiership
Aston Villa v Manchester City
Bolton Wand. v Chelsea
Fulham v Arsenal
Liverpool v Portsmouth
Manchester Utd. v Everton

Coca-Cola League Championship
Derby Co. v Ipswich Town
Southampton v Birmingham City

Saturday, 2 December
Barclays Premiership
Arsenal v Tottenham
Blackburn Rov. v Fulham
Chelsea v Newcastle Utd.
Middlesbrough v Manchester Utd.
Portsmouth v Aston Villa
Reading v Bolton Wand.
Sheffield Utd. v Charlton Athletic
Wigan Athletic v Liverpool

Coca-Cola League Championship
Birmingham City v Plymouth Argyle
Cardiff City v Colchester Utd.
Coventry City v Stoke City
Crystal Palace v Q.P.R.
Hull City v Southampton
Ipswich Town v Burnley
Leeds Utd. v Barnsley
Leicester City v Sheffield Wed.
Luton Town v Preston N.E.
Southend Utd. v Wolves
Sunderland v Norwich City
W.B.A. v Derby Co.

Sunday, 3 December
Barclays Premiership
Everton v West Ham Utd.

Monday, 4 December
Barclays Premiership
Manchester City v Watford

Tuesday, 5 December
Barclays Premiership
Charlton Athletic v Blackburn Rov.
Tottenham v Middlesbrough

Coca-Cola League One
Blackpool v Cheltenham Town
Bournemouth v Nott'm. Forest
Brentford v Doncaster Rov.
Brighton & H.A. v Swansea City
Bristol City v Carlisle Utd.
Leyton Orient v Bradford City
Millwall v Huddersfield Town
Oldham Athletic v Crewe Alexandra
Port Vale v Gillingham
Rotherham Utd. v Yeovil
Scunthorpe Utd. v Tranmere Rov.

Coca-Cola League Two
Accrington Stanley v Shrewsbury Town
Barnet v Grimsby Town
Bury v Walsall
Chester City v Boston Utd.
Hereford v Peterborough Utd.
Lincoln City v Bristol Rov.
Macclesfield Town v Rochdale
Mansfield Town v Swindon Town
Milton Keynes Dons v Stockport Co.
Notts Co. v Hartlepool Utd.
Torquay Utd. v Wrexham
Wycombe Wand. v Darlington

Wednesday, 6 December
Barclays Premiership
Newcastle Utd. v Reading
West Ham Utd. v Wigan Athletic

Coca-Cola League One
Chesterfield v Northampton Town

Saturday, 9 December
Barclays Premiership
Blackburn Rov. v Newcastle Utd.
Bolton Wand. v West Ham Utd.
Liverpool v Fulham
Manchester Utd. v Manchester City
Middlesbrough v Wigan Athletic
Portsmouth v Everton
Tottenham v Charlton Athletic
Watford v Reading

Coca-Cola League Championship
Barnsley v W.B.A.
Birmingham City v Preston N.E.
Cardiff City v Ipswich Town
Coventry City v Burnley
Crystal Palace v Colchester Utd.
Leeds Utd. v Derby Co.
Norwich City v Sheffield Wed.
Plymouth Argyle v Hull City
Southend Utd. v Southampton
Stoke City v Q.P.R.
Sunderland v Luton Town
Wolves v Leicester City

Coca-Cola League One
Blackpool v Swansea City
Bournemouth v Port Vale
Brentford v Tranmere Rov.
Brighton & H.A. v Cheltenham Town
Carlisle Utd. v Scunthorpe Utd.
Chesterfield v Oldham Athletic
Crewe Alexandra v Nott'm. Forest
Leyton Orient v Huddersfield Town
Millwall v Bradford City
Northampton Town v Doncaster Rov.
Rotherham Utd. v Bristol City
Yeovil v Gillingham

Coca-Cola League Two
Accrington Stanley v Milton Keynes
    Dons
Boston Utd. v Wrexham
Bristol Rov. v Hartlepool Utd.
Chester City v Lincoln City
Grimsby Town v Shrewsbury Town
Hereford v Torquay Utd.
Mansfield Town v Bury
Notts Co. v Macclesfield Town
Rochdale v Peterborough Utd.
Stockport Co. v Darlington
Walsall v Swindon Town
Wycombe Wand. v Barnet

Sunday, 10 December
Barclays Premiership
Chelsea v Arsenal

Monday, 11 December
Barclays Premiership
Sheffield Utd. v Aston Villa

Wednesday, 13 December
Barclays Premiership
Wigan Athletic v Arsenal

Saturday, 16 December
Barclays Premiership
Arsenal v Portsmouth
Aston Villa v Bolton Wand.
Charlton Athletic v Liverpool
Fulham v Middlesbrough
Manchester City v Tottenham
Newcastle Utd. v Watford
Reading v Blackburn Rov.
Wigan Athletic v Sheffield Utd.

Coca-Cola League Championship
Burnley v Sunderland
Colchester Utd. v Stoke City
Derby Co. v Crystal Palace
Hull City v Cardiff City
Ipswich Town v Leeds Utd.
Leicester City v Barnsley
Luton Town v Southend Utd.
Preston N.E. v Plymouth Argyle
Q.P.R. v Wolves
Sheffield Wed. v Birmingham City
Southampton v Norwich City
W.B.A. v Coventry City

Coca-Cola League One
Bradford City v Chesterfield
Bristol City v Millwall
Cheltenham Town v Rotherham Utd.
Doncaster Rov. v Yeovil
Gillingham v Bournemouth
Huddersfield Town v Northampton Town
Nott'm. Forest v Leyton Orient
Oldham Athletic v Brighton & H.A.
Port Vale v Brentford
Scunthorpe Utd. v Blackpool
Swansea City v Carlisle Utd.
Tranmere Rov. v Crewe Alexandra

Coca-Cola League Two
Barnet v Mansfield Town
Bury v Stockport Co.
Darlington v Notts Co.
Hartlepool Utd. v Rochdale
Lincoln City v Grimsby Town
Macclesfield Town v Accrington Stanley
Milton Keynes Dons v Wycombe Wand.

Peterborough Utd. v Chester City
Shrewsbury Town v Hereford
Swindon Town v Bristol Rov.
Torquay Utd. v Boston Utd.
Wrexham v Walsall

Sunday, 17 December
Barclays Premiership
Everton v Chelsea
West Ham Utd. v Manchester Utd.

Saturday, 23 December
Barclays Premiership
Arsenal v Blackburn Rov.
Aston Villa v Manchester Utd.
Fulham v West Ham Utd.
Liverpool v Watford
Manchester City v Bolton Wand.
Middlesbrough v Charlton Athletic
Newcastle Utd. v Tottenham
Portsmouth v Sheffield Utd.
Reading v Everton
Wigan Athletic v Chelsea

Coca-Cola League Championship
Burnley v Derby Co.
Crystal Palace v Sunderland
Ipswich Town v Stoke City
Leeds Utd. v Hull City
Leicester City v Cardiff City
Luton Town v Coventry City
Plymouth Argyle v W.B.A.
Preston N.E. v Colchester Utd.
Q.P.R. v Barnsley
Sheffield Wed. v Southampton
Southend Utd. v Birmingham City
Wolves v Norwich City

Coca-Cola League One
Bournemouth v Blackpool
Carlisle Utd. v Brentford
Cheltenham Town v Bristol City
Chesterfield v Huddersfield Town
Doncaster Rov. v Nott'm. Forest
Leyton Orient v Crewe Alexandra
Millwall v Scunthorpe Utd.
Oldham Athletic v Northampton Town
Port Vale v Brighton & H.A.
Swansea City v Rotherham Utd.
Tranmere Rov. v Gillingham
Yeovil v Bradford City

Coca-Cola League Two
Boston Utd. v Walsall
Bristol Rov. v Accrington Stanley
Bury v Hartlepool Utd.
Grimsby Town v Torquay Utd.
Macclesfield Town v Swindon Town
Mansfield Town v Chester City

Milton Keynes Dons v Rochdale
Notts Co. v Hereford
Peterborough Utd. v Lincoln City
Shrewsbury Town v Barnet
Wrexham v Darlington
Wycombe Wand. v Stockport Co.

Tuesday, 26 December
Barclays Premiership
Blackburn Rov. v Liverpool
Bolton Wand. v Newcastle Utd.
Chelsea v Reading
Everton v Middlesbrough
Manchester Utd. v Wigan Athletic
Sheffield Utd. v Manchester City
Tottenham v Aston Villa
Watford v Arsenal
West Ham Utd. v Portsmouth

Coca-Cola League Championship
Barnsley v Burnley
Birmingham City v Q.P.R.
Cardiff City v Plymouth Argyle
Colchester Utd. v Luton Town
Coventry City v Ipswich Town
Derby Co. v Wolves
Hull City v Leicester City
Norwich City v Southend Utd.
Southampton v Crystal Palace
Stoke City v Sheffield Wed.
Sunderland v Leeds Utd.
W.B.A. v Preston N.E.

Coca-Cola League One
Blackpool v Carlisle Utd.
Bradford City v Doncaster Rov.
Brentford v Millwall
Brighton & H.A. v Yeovil
Bristol City v Bournemouth
Crewe Alexandra v Swansea City
Gillingham v Leyton Orient
Huddersfield Town v Tranmere Rov.
Northampton Town v Cheltenham Town
Nott'm. Forest v Port Vale
Rotherham Utd. v Oldham Athletic
Scunthorpe Utd. v Chesterfield

Coca-Cola League Two
Accrington Stanley v Bury
Barnet v Peterborough Utd.
Chester City v Macclesfield Town
Darlington v Mansfield Town
Hartlepool Utd. v Grimsby Town
Hereford v Bristol Rov.
Lincoln City v Boston Utd.
Rochdale v Wrexham
Stockport Co. v Notts Co.
Swindon Town v Wycombe Wand.
Torquay Utd. v Milton Keynes Dons

Walsall v Shrewsbury Town

Wednesday, 27 December
Barclays Premiership
Charlton Athletic v Fulham

Saturday, 30 December
Barclays Premiership
Blackburn Rov. v Middlesbrough
Bolton Wand. v Portsmouth
Charlton Athletic v Aston Villa
Chelsea v Fulham
Everton v Newcastle Utd.
Manchester Utd. v Reading
Sheffield Utd. v Arsenal
Tottenham v Liverpool
Watford v Wigan Athletic
West Ham Utd. v Manchester City

Coca-Cola League Championship
Barnsley v Sheffield Wed.
Birmingham City v Luton Town
Cardiff City v Crystal Palace
Colchester Utd. v Wolves
Coventry City v Southend Utd.
Derby Co. v Plymouth Argyle
Hull City v Burnley
Norwich City v Q.P.R.
Southampton v Leicester City
Stoke City v Leeds Utd.
Sunderland v Preston N.E.
W.B.A. v Ipswich Town

Coca-Cola League One
Blackpool v Doncaster Rov.
Bradford City v Cheltenham Town
Brentford v Chesterfield
Brighton & H.A. v Carlisle Utd.
Bristol City v Port Vale
Crewe Alexandra v Yeovil
Gillingham v Oldham Athletic
Huddersfield Town v Swansea City
Northampton Town v Millwall
Nott'm. Forest v Tranmere Rov.
Rotherham Utd. v Leyton Orient
Scunthorpe Utd. v Bournemouth

Coca-Cola League Two
Accrington Stanley v Mansfield Town
Barnet v Bury
Chester City v Milton Keynes Dons
Darlington v Shrewsbury Town
Hartlepool Utd. v Peterborough Utd.
Hereford v Wrexham
Lincoln City v Wycombe Wand.
Rochdale v Boston Utd.
Stockport Co. v Grimsby Town
Swindon Town v Notts Co.
Torquay Utd. v Macclesfield Town

Walsall v Bristol Rov.

Monday, 1 January
Barclays Premiership
Arsenal v Charlton Athletic
Aston Villa v Chelsea
Fulham v Watford
Liverpool v Bolton Wand.
Manchester City v Everton
Middlesbrough v Sheffield Utd.
Newcastle Utd. v Manchester Utd.
Portsmouth v Tottenham
Reading v West Ham Utd.
Wigan Athletic v Blackburn Rov.

Coca-Cola League Championship
Burnley v Stoke City
Crystal Palace v Norwich City
Ipswich Town v Birmingham City
Leeds Utd. v Coventry City
Leicester City v Sunderland
Luton Town v Cardiff City
Plymouth Argyle v Southampton
Preston N.E. v Derby Co.
Q.P.R. v Colchester Utd.
Sheffield Wed. v Hull City
Southend Utd. v W.B.A.
Wolves v Barnsley

Coca-Cola League One
Bournemouth v Brighton & H.A.
Carlisle Utd. v Bradford City
Cheltenham Town v Crewe Alexandra
Chesterfield v Blackpool
Doncaster Rov. v Huddersfield Town
Leyton Orient v Bristol City
Millwall v Gillingham
Oldham Athletic v Nott'm. Forest
Port Vale v Scunthorpe Utd.
Swansea City v Brentford
Tranmere Rov. v Rotherham Utd.
Yeovil v Northampton Town

Coca-Cola League Two
Boston Utd. v Barnet
Bristol Rov. v Torquay Utd.
Bury v Darlington
Grimsby Town v Rochdale
Macclesfield Town v Lincoln City
Mansfield Town v Hartlepool Utd.
Milton Keynes Dons v Swindon Town
Notts Co. v Chester City
Peterborough Utd. v Walsall
Shrewsbury Town v Stockport Co.
Wrexham v Accrington Stanley
Wycombe Wand. v Hereford

Saturday, 6 January
Coca-Cola League One
Bournemouth v Brentford
Carlisle Utd. v Nott'm. Forest
Cheltenham Town v Scunthorpe Utd.
Chesterfield v Bristol City
Doncaster Rov. v Rotherham Utd.
Leyton Orient v Brighton & H.A.
Millwall v Crewe Alexandra
Oldham Athletic v Blackpool
Port Vale v Bradford City
Swansea City v Gillingham
Tranmere Rov. v Northampton Town
Yeovil v Huddersfield Town

Coca-Cola League Two
Boston Utd. v Accrington Stanley
Bristol Rov. v Darlington
Bury v Hereford
Grimsby Town v Chester City
Macclesfield Town v Walsall
Mansfield Town v Torquay Utd.
Milton Keynes Dons v Lincoln City
Notts Co. v Barnet
Peterborough Utd. v Swindon Town
Shrewsbury Town v Hartlepool Utd.
Wrexham v Stockport Co.
Wycombe Wand. v Rochdale

Saturday, 13 January
Barclays Premiership
Blackburn Rov. v Arsenal
Bolton Wand. v Manchester City
Charlton Athletic v Middlesbrough
Chelsea v Wigan Athletic
Everton v Reading
Manchester Utd. v Aston Villa
Sheffield Utd. v Portsmouth
Tottenham v Newcastle Utd.
Watford v Liverpool
West Ham Utd. v Fulham

Coca-Cola League Championship
Barnsley v Preston N.E.
Birmingham City v Leeds Utd.
Cardiff City v Southend Utd.
Colchester Utd. v Leicester City
Coventry City v Crystal Palace
Derby Co. v Sheffield Wed.
Hull City v Q.P.R.
Norwich City v Plymouth Argyle
Southampton v Burnley
Stoke City v Wolves
Sunderland v Ipswich Town
W.B.A. v Luton Town

Coca-Cola League One
Blackpool v Port Vale
Bradford City v Swansea City

Brentford v Leyton Orient
Brighton & H.A. v Millwall
Bristol City v Tranmere Rov.
Crewe Alexandra v Bournemouth
Gillingham v Doncaster Rov.
Huddersfield Town v Cheltenham Town
Northampton Town v Carlisle Utd.
Nott'm. Forest v Yeovil
Rotherham Utd. v Chesterfield
Scunthorpe Utd. v Oldham Athletic

Coca-Cola League Two
Accrington Stanley v Notts Co.
Barnet v Macclesfield Town
Chester City v Wycombe Wand.
Darlington v Peterborough Utd.
Hartlepool Utd. v Milton Keynes Dons
Hereford v Mansfield Town
Lincoln City v Shrewsbury Town
Rochdale v Bristol Rov.
Stockport Co. v Boston Utd.
Swindon Town v Wrexham
Torquay Utd. v Bury
Walsall v Grimsby Town

Saturday, 20 January
Barclays Premiership
Arsenal v Manchester Utd.
Aston Villa v Watford
Fulham v Tottenham
Liverpool v Chelsea
Manchester City v Blackburn Rov.
Middlesbrough v Bolton Wand.
Newcastle Utd. v West Ham Utd.
Portsmouth v Charlton Athletic
Reading v Sheffield Utd.
Wigan Athletic v Everton

Coca-Cola League Championship
Burnley v Norwich City
Crystal Palace v Hull City
Ipswich Town v Colchester Utd.
Leeds Utd. v W.B.A.
Leicester City v Birmingham City
Luton Town v Barnsley
Plymouth Argyle v Coventry City
Preston N.E. v Stoke City
Q.P.R. v Southampton
Sheffield Wed. v Sunderland
Southend Utd. v Derby Co.
Wolves v Cardiff City

Coca-Cola League One
Bournemouth v Huddersfield Town
Carlisle Utd. v Crewe Alexandra
Cheltenham Town v Gillingham
Chesterfield v Brighton & H.A.
Doncaster Rov. v Scunthorpe Utd.
Leyton Orient v Blackpool

Millwall v Rotherham Utd.
Oldham Athletic v Bristol City
Port Vale v Northampton Town
Swansea City v Nott'm. Forest
Tranmere Rov. v Bradford City
Yeovil v Brentford

Coca-Cola League Two
Boston Utd. v Swindon Town
Bristol Rov. v Chester City
Bury v Lincoln City
Grimsby Town v Darlington
Macclesfield Town v Hereford
Mansfield Town v Walsall
Milton Keynes Dons v Barnet
Notts Co. v Torquay Utd.
Peterborough Utd. v Stockport Co.
Shrewsbury Town v Rochdale
Wrexham v Hartlepool Utd.
Wycombe Wand. v Accrington Stanley

Saturday, 27 January
Coca-Cola League One
Blackpool v Bournemouth
Bradford City v Yeovil
Brentford v Carlisle Utd.
Brighton & H.A. v Port Vale
Bristol City v Cheltenham Town
Crewe Alexandra v Leyton Orient
Gillingham v Tranmere Rov.
Huddersfield Town v Chesterfield
Northampton Town v Oldham Athletic
Nott'm. Forest v Doncaster Rov.
Rotherham Utd. v Swansea City
Scunthorpe Utd. v Millwall

Coca-Cola League Two
Accrington Stanley v Bristol Rov.
Barnet v Shrewsbury Town
Chester City v Mansfield Town
Darlington v Wrexham
Hartlepool Utd. v Bury
Hereford v Notts Co.
Lincoln City v Peterborough Utd.
Rochdale v Milton Keynes Dons
Stockport Co. v Wycombe Wand.
Swindon Town v Macclesfield Town
Torquay Utd. v Grimsby Town
Walsall v Boston Utd.

Tuesday, 30 January
Barclays Premiership
Arsenal v Manchester City
Bolton Wand. v Charlton Athletic
Portsmouth v Middlesbrough
Reading v Wigan Athletic
Sheffield Utd. v Fulham
West Ham Utd. v Liverpool

Coca-Cola League Championship
Barnsley v Q.P.R.
Birmingham City v Southend Utd.
Cardiff City v Leicester City
Colchester Utd. v Preston N.E.
Coventry City v Luton Town
Hull City v Leeds Utd.
Norwich City v Wolves
Stoke City v Ipswich Town
Sunderland v Crystal Palace
W.B.A. v Plymouth Argyle

Wednesday, 31 January
Barclays Premiership
Chelsea v Blackburn Rov.
Everton v Tottenham
Manchester Utd. v Watford
Newcastle Utd. v Aston Villa

Coca-Cola League Championship
Derby Co. v Burnley
Southampton v Sheffield Wed.

Saturday, 3 February
Barclays Premiership
Aston Villa v West Ham Utd.
Blackburn Rov. v Sheffield Utd.
Charlton Athletic v Chelsea
Fulham v Newcastle Utd.
Liverpool v Everton
Manchester City v Reading
Middlesbrough v Arsenal
Tottenham v Manchester Utd.
Watford v Bolton Wand.
Wigan Athletic v Portsmouth

Coca-Cola League Championship
Cardiff City v Barnsley
Colchester Utd. v Birmingham City
Crystal Palace v Ipswich Town
Hull City v W.B.A.
Leicester City v Luton Town
Norwich City v Leeds Utd.
Q.P.R. v Burnley
Sheffield Wed. v Preston N.E.
Southampton v Derby Co.
Stoke City v Southend Utd.
Sunderland v Coventry City
Wolves v Plymouth Argyle

Coca-Cola League One
Blackpool v Brentford
Bradford City v Nott'm. Forest
Brighton & H.A. v Rotherham Utd.
Cheltenham Town v Swansea City
Chesterfield v Bournemouth
Doncaster Rov. v Carlisle Utd.
Huddersfield Town v Gillingham
Leyton Orient v Port Vale

Northampton Town v Crewe Alexandra
Oldham Athletic v Tranmere Rov.
Scunthorpe Utd. v Bristol City
Yeovil v Millwall

Coca-Cola League Two
Accrington Stanley v Chester City
Boston Utd. v Grimsby Town
Bristol Rov. v Peterborough Utd.
Bury v Milton Keynes Dons
Hereford v Stockport Co.
Macclesfield Town v Darlington
Mansfield Town v Shrewsbury Town
Notts Co. v Lincoln City
Swindon Town v Hartlepool Utd.
Torquay Utd. v Barnet
Walsall v Rochdale
Wrexham v Wycombe Wand.

Saturday, 10 February
Barclays Premiership
Arsenal v Wigan Athletic
Bolton Wand. v Fulham
Chelsea v Middlesbrough
Everton v Blackburn Rov.
Manchester Utd. v Charlton Athletic
Newcastle Utd. v Liverpool
Portsmouth v Manchester City
Reading v Aston Villa
Sheffield Utd. v Tottenham
West Ham Utd. v Watford

Coca-Cola League Championship
Barnsley v Colchester Utd.
Birmingham City v Stoke City
Burnley v Sheffield Wed.
Coventry City v Cardiff City
Derby Co. v Hull City
Ipswich Town v Leicester City
Leeds Utd. v Crystal Palace
Luton Town v Norwich City
Plymouth Argyle v Sunderland
Preston N.E. v Wolves
Southend Utd. v Q.P.R.
W.B.A. v Southampton

Coca-Cola League One
Bournemouth v Leyton Orient
Brentford v Brighton & H.A.
Bristol City v Huddersfield Town
Carlisle Utd. v Yeovil
Crewe Alexandra v Scunthorpe Utd.
Gillingham v Bradford City
Millwall v Chesterfield
Nott'm. Forest v Northampton Town
Port Vale v Cheltenham Town
Rotherham Utd. v Blackpool
Swansea City v Oldham Athletic
Tranmere Rov. v Doncaster Rov.

Coca-Cola League Two
Barnet v Accrington Stanley
Chester City v Hereford
Darlington v Boston Utd.
Grimsby Town v Bristol Rov.
Hartlepool Utd. v Walsall
Lincoln City v Torquay Utd.
Milton Keynes Dons v Macclesfield Town
Peterborough Utd. v Wrexham
Rochdale v Swindon Town
Shrewsbury Town v Bury
Stockport Co. v Mansfield Town
Wycombe Wand. v Notts Co.

Saturday, 17 February
Coca-Cola League Championship
Cardiff City v Leeds Utd.
Colchester Utd. v W.B.A.
Crystal Palace v Birmingham City
Hull City v Ipswich Town
Leicester City v Coventry City
Norwich City v Derby Co.
Q.P.R. v Preston N.E.
Sheffield Wed. v Plymouth Argyle
Southampton v Barnsley
Stoke City v Luton Town
Sunderland v Southend Utd.
Wolves v Burnley

Coca-Cola League One
Blackpool v Bristol City
Bradford City v Crewe Alexandra
Brighton & H.A. v Nott'm. Forest
Cheltenham Town v Bournemouth
Chesterfield v Port Vale
Doncaster Rov. v Swansea City
Huddersfield Town v Brentford
Leyton Orient v Carlisle Utd.
Northampton Town v Gillingham
Oldham Athletic v Millwall
Scunthorpe Utd. v Rotherham Utd.
Yeovil v Tranmere Rov.

Coca-Cola League Two
Accrington Stanley v Stockport Co.
Boston Utd. v Shrewsbury Town
Bristol Rov. v Milton Keynes Dons
Bury v Wycombe Wand.
Hereford v Barnet
Macclesfield Town v Peterborough Utd.
Mansfield Town v Grimsby Town
Notts Co. v Rochdale
Swindon Town v Darlington
Torquay Utd. v Hartlepool Utd.
Walsall v Lincoln City
Wrexham v Chester City

Tuesday, 20 February
Coca-Cola League Championship
Barnsley v Hull City
Birmingham City v Sunderland

Burnley v Leicester City
Coventry City v Southampton
Ipswich Town v Wolves
Leeds Utd. v Q.P.R.
Luton Town v Sheffield Wed.
Plymouth Argyle v Colchester Utd.
Preston N.E. v Norwich City
Southend Utd. v Crystal Palace
W.B.A. v Cardiff City

Coca-Cola League One
Bournemouth v Yeovil
Brentford v Northampton Town
Bristol City v Bradford City
Carlisle Utd. v Chesterfield
Crewe Alexandra v Doncaster Rov.
Gillingham v Brighton & H.A.
Millwall v Leyton Orient
Nott'm. Forest v Blackpool
Port Vale v Oldham Athletic
Rotherham Utd. v Huddersfield Town
Swansea City v Scunthorpe Utd.
Tranmere Rov. v Cheltenham Town

Coca-Cola League Two
Barnet v Swindon Town
Chester City v Bury
Darlington v Accrington Stanley
Grimsby Town v Wrexham
Hartlepool Utd. v Macclesfield Town
Lincoln City v Hereford
Milton Keynes Dons v Mansfield Town
Peterborough Utd. v Boston Utd.
Rochdale v Torquay Utd.
Shrewsbury Town v Notts Co.
Stockport Co. v Walsall
Wycombe Wand. v Bristol Rov.

Wednesday, 21 February
Coca-Cola League Championship
Derby Co. v Stoke City

Saturday, 24 February
Barclays Premiership
Aston Villa v Arsenal
Blackburn Rov. v Portsmouth
Charlton Athletic v West Ham Utd.
Fulham v Manchester Utd.
Liverpool v Sheffield Utd.
Manchester City v Chelsea
Middlesbrough v Reading
Tottenham v Bolton Wand.
Watford v Everton
Wigan Athletic v Newcastle Utd.

Coca-Cola League Championship
Cardiff City v Preston N.E.
Colchester Utd. v Burnley
Crystal Palace v Luton Town

Hull City v Birmingham City
Leicester City v W.B.A.
Norwich City v Coventry City
Q.P.R. v Plymouth Argyle
Sheffield Wed. v Southend Utd.
Southampton v Ipswich Town
Stoke City v Barnsley
Sunderland v Derby Co.
Wolves v Leeds Utd.

Coca-Cola League One
Blackpool v Millwall
Bradford City v Brentford
Brighton & H.A. v Bristol City
Cheltenham Town v Carlisle Utd.
Chesterfield v Nott'm. Forest
Doncaster Rov. v Port Vale
Huddersfield Town v Crewe Alexandra
Leyton Orient v Tranmere Rov.
Northampton Town v Rotherham Utd.
Oldham Athletic v Bournemouth
Scunthorpe Utd. v Gillingham
Yeovil v Swansea City

Coca-Cola League Two
Accrington Stanley v Lincoln City
Boston Utd. v Hartlepool Utd.
Bristol Rov. v Stockport Co.
Bury v Peterborough Utd.
Hereford v Rochdale
Macclesfield Town v Grimsby Town
Mansfield Town v Wycombe Wand.
Notts Co. v Milton Keynes Dons
Swindon Town v Chester City
Torquay Utd. v Darlington
Walsall v Barnet
Wrexham v Shrewsbury Town

Saturday, 3 March
Barclays Premiership
Arsenal v Reading
Bolton Wand. v Blackburn Rov.
Fulham v Aston Villa
Liverpool v Manchester Utd.
Manchester City v Wigan Athletic
Newcastle Utd. v Middlesbrough
Portsmouth v Chelsea
Sheffield Utd. v Everton
Watford v Charlton Athletic
West Ham Utd. v Tottenham

Coca-Cola League Championship
Barnsley v Norwich City
Birmingham City v Cardiff City
Burnley v Crystal Palace
Coventry City v Hull City
Derby Co. v Colchester Utd.
Ipswich Town v Q.P.R.
Leeds Utd. v Sheffield Wed.

Luton Town v Wolves
Plymouth Argyle v Stoke City
Preston N.E. v Southampton
Southend Utd. v Leicester City
W.B.A. v Sunderland

Coca-Cola League One
Bournemouth v Doncaster Rov.
Brentford v Scunthorpe Utd.
Bristol City v Northampton Town
Carlisle Utd. v Oldham Athletic
Crewe Alexandra v Brighton & H.A.
Gillingham v Blackpool
Millwall v Cheltenham Town
Nott'm. Forest v Huddersfield Town
Port Vale v Yeovil
Rotherham Utd. v Bradford City
Swansea City v Leyton Orient
Tranmere Rov. v Chesterfield

Coca-Cola League Two
Barnet v Wrexham
Chester City v Torquay Utd.
Darlington v Walsall
Grimsby Town v Bury
Hartlepool Utd. v Hereford
Lincoln City v Mansfield Town
Milton Keynes Dons v Boston Utd.
Peterborough Utd. v Notts Co.
Rochdale v Accrington Stanley
Shrewsbury Town v Bristol Rov.
Stockport Co. v Swindon Town
Wycombe Wand. v Macclesfield Town

Saturday, 10 March
Coca-Cola League Championship
Barnsley v Sunderland
Birmingham City v Derby Co.
Burnley v Plymouth Argyle
Cardiff City v Norwich City
Colchester Utd. v Coventry City
Crystal Palace v Leicester City
Hull City v Preston N.E.
Ipswich Town v Southend Utd.
Leeds Utd. v Luton Town
Q.P.R. v Sheffield Wed.
Stoke City v Southampton
Wolves v W.B.A.

Coca-Cola League One
Blackpool v Brighton & H.A.
Bristol City v Brentford
Cheltenham Town v Yeovil
Chesterfield v Leyton Orient
Gillingham v Crewe Alexandra
Huddersfield Town v Bradford City
Millwall v Carlisle Utd.
Northampton Town v Bournemouth
Oldham Athletic v Doncaster Rov.

Rotherham Utd. v Port Vale
Scunthorpe Utd. v Nott'm. Forest
Tranmere Rov. v Swansea City

Coca-Cola League Two
Barnet v Stockport Co.
Boston Utd. v Bristol Rov.
Hartlepool Utd. v Lincoln City
Hereford v Grimsby Town
Macclesfield Town v Shrewsbury Town
Notts Co. v Mansfield Town
Peterborough Utd. v Milton Keynes Dons
Rochdale v Darlington
Swindon Town v Accrington Stanley
Torquay Utd. v Wycombe Wand.
Walsall v Chester City
Wrexham v Bury

Tuesday, 13 March
Coca-Cola League Championship
Coventry City v Wolves
Leicester City v Leeds Utd.
Luton Town v Hull City
Norwich City v Birmingham City
Plymouth Argyle v Barnsley
Preston N.E. v Ipswich Town
Sheffield Wed. v Colchester Utd.
Southend Utd. v Burnley
Sunderland v Stoke City
W.B.A. v Crystal Palace

Wednesday, 14 March
Coca-Cola League Championship
Derby Co. v Q.P.R.
Southampton v Cardiff City

Saturday, 17 March
Barclays Premiership
Aston Villa v Liverpool
Blackburn Rov. v West Ham Utd.
Charlton Athletic v Newcastle Utd.
Chelsea v Sheffield Utd.
Everton v Arsenal
Manchester Utd. v Bolton Wand.
Middlesbrough v Manchester City
Reading v Portsmouth
Tottenham v Watford
Wigan Athletic v Fulham

Coca-Cola League Championship
Coventry City v Barnsley
Derby Co. v Cardiff City
Leicester City v Q.P.R.
Luton Town v Ipswich Town
Norwich City v Stoke City
Plymouth Argyle v Crystal Palace
Preston N.E. v Burnley
Sheffield Wed. v Wolves
Southampton v Colchester Utd.

Southend Utd. v Leeds Utd.
Sunderland v Hull City
W.B.A. v Birmingham City

Coca-Cola League One
Bournemouth v Millwall
Bradford City v Northampton Town
Brentford v Rotherham Utd.
Brighton & H.A. v Scunthorpe Utd.
Carlisle Utd. v Huddersfield Town
Crewe Alexandra v Bristol City
Doncaster Rov. v Cheltenham Town
Leyton Orient v Oldham Athletic
Nott'm. Forest v Gillingham
Port Vale v Tranmere Rov.
Swansea City v Chesterfield
Yeovil v Blackpool

Coca-Cola League Two
Accrington Stanley v Torquay Utd.
Bristol Rov. v Notts Co.
Bury v Macclesfield Town
Chester City v Rochdale
Darlington v Hereford
Grimsby Town v Swindon Town
Lincoln City v Barnet
Mansfield Town v Boston Utd.
Milton Keynes Dons v Wrexham
Shrewsbury Town v Peterborough Utd.
Stockport Co. v Hartlepool Utd.
Wycombe Wand. v Walsall

Saturday, 24 March
Coca-Cola League One
Bournemouth v Tranmere Rov.
Bradford City v Blackpool
Brentford v Oldham Athletic
Brighton & H.A. v Huddersfield Town
Carlisle Utd. v Gillingham
Crewe Alexandra v Rotherham Utd.
Doncaster Rov. v Bristol City
Leyton Orient v Scunthorpe Utd.
Nott'm. Forest v Cheltenham Town
Port Vale v Millwall
Swansea City v Northampton Town
Yeovil v Chesterfield

Coca-Cola League Two
Accrington Stanley v Hereford
Bristol Rov. v Wrexham
Bury v Notts Co.
Chester City v Barnet
Darlington v Hartlepool Utd.
Grimsby Town v Peterborough Utd.
Lincoln City v Swindon Town
Mansfield Town v Macclesfield Town
Milton Keynes Dons v Walsall
Shrewsbury Town v Torquay Utd.
Stockport Co. v Rochdale

Wycombe Wand. v Boston Utd.

Saturday, 31 March
Barclays Premiership
Aston Villa v Everton
Bolton Wand. v Sheffield Utd.
Charlton Athletic v Wigan Athletic
Fulham v Portsmouth
Liverpool v Arsenal
Manchester Utd. v Blackburn Rov.
Newcastle Utd. v Manchester City
Tottenham v Reading
Watford v Chelsea
West Ham Utd. v Middlesbrough

Coca-Cola League Championship
Barnsley v Derby Co.
Birmingham City v Coventry City
Burnley v Luton Town
Cardiff City v Sunderland
Colchester Utd. v Norwich City
Crystal Palace v Sheffield Wed.
Hull City v Southend Utd.
Ipswich Town v Plymouth Argyle
Leeds Utd. v Preston N.E.
Q.P.R. v W.B.A.
Stoke City v Leicester City
Wolves v Southampton

Coca-Cola League One
Blackpool v Crewe Alexandra
Bristol City v Nott'm. Forest
Cheltenham Town v Leyton Orient
Chesterfield v Doncaster Rov.
Gillingham v Brentford
Huddersfield Town v Port Vale
Millwall v Swansea City
Northampton Town v Brighton & H.A.
Oldham Athletic v Yeovil
Rotherham Utd. v Bournemouth
Scunthorpe Utd. v Bradford City
Tranmere Rov. v Carlisle Utd.

Coca-Cola League Two
Barnet v Darlington
Boston Utd. v Bury
Hartlepool Utd. v Chester City
Hereford v Milton Keynes Dons
Macclesfield Town v Bristol Rov.
Notts Co. v Grimsby Town
Peterborough Utd. v Wycombe Wand.
Rochdale v Lincoln City
Swindon Town v Shrewsbury Town
Torquay Utd. v Stockport Co.
Walsall v Accrington Stanley
Wrexham v Mansfield Town

Friday, 6 April
Barclays Premiership
Manchester City v Charlton Athletic

Saturday, 7 April
Barclays Premiership
Arsenal v West Ham Utd.
Blackburn Rov. v Aston Villa
Chelsea v Tottenham
Everton v Fulham
Middlesbrough v Watford
Portsmouth v Manchester Utd.
Reading v Liverpool
Sheffield Utd. v Newcastle Utd.
Wigan Athletic v Bolton Wand.

Coca-Cola League Championship
Birmingham City v Burnley
Cardiff City v Sheffield Wed.
Coventry City v Q.P.R.
Crystal Palace v Preston N.E.
Hull City v Norwich City
Ipswich Town v Barnsley
Leeds Utd. v Plymouth Argyle
Leicester City v Derby Co.
Luton Town v Southampton
Southend Utd. v Colchester Utd.
Sunderland v Wolves
W.B.A. v Stoke City

Coca-Cola League One
Blackpool v Tranmere Rov.
Bournemouth v Bradford City
Brentford v Cheltenham Town
Brighton & H.A. v Doncaster Rov.
Bristol City v Swansea City
Chesterfield v Crewe Alexandra
Leyton Orient v Northampton Town
Millwall v Nott'm. Forest
Oldham Athletic v Huddersfield Town
Port Vale v Carlisle Utd.
Rotherham Utd. v Gillingham
Scunthorpe Utd. v Yeovil

Coca-Cola League Two
Accrington Stanley v Peterborough Utd.
Barnet v Hartlepool Utd.
Bury v Rochdale
Chester City v Darlington
Hereford v Swindon Town
Lincoln City v Stockport Co.
Macclesfield Town v Wrexham
Mansfield Town v Bristol Rov.
Milton Keynes Dons v Grimsby Town
Notts Co. v Boston Utd.
Torquay Utd. v Walsall
Wycombe Wand. v Shrewsbury Town

Monday, 9 April
Barclays Premiership
Aston Villa v Wigan Athletic
Bolton Wand. v Everton
Charlton Athletic v Reading
Fulham v Manchester City
Liverpool v Middlesbrough
Newcastle Utd. v Arsenal
Tottenham v Blackburn Rov.
Watford v Portsmouth
West Ham Utd. v Chelsea

Coca-Cola League Championship
Barnsley v Birmingham City
Burnley v Cardiff City
Colchester Utd. v Leeds Utd.
Derby Co. v Coventry City
Norwich City v W.B.A.
Plymouth Argyle v Leicester City
Preston N.E. v Southend Utd.
Q.P.R. v Luton Town
Sheffield Wed. v Ipswich Town
Southampton v Sunderland
Stoke City v Crystal Palace
Wolves v Hull City

Coca-Cola League One
Bradford City v Oldham Athletic
Carlisle Utd. v Bournemouth
Cheltenham Town v Chesterfield
Crewe Alexandra v Brentford
Doncaster Rov. v Millwall
Gillingham v Bristol City
Huddersfield Town v Blackpool
Northampton Town v Scunthorpe Utd.
Nott'm. Forest v Rotherham Utd.
Swansea City v Port Vale
Tranmere Rov. v Brighton & H.A.
Yeovil v Leyton Orient

Coca-Cola League Two
Boston Utd. v Macclesfield Town
Bristol Rov. v Bury
Darlington v Lincoln City
Grimsby Town v Wycombe Wand.
Hartlepool Utd. v Accrington Stanley
Peterborough Utd. v Mansfield Town
Rochdale v Barnet
Shrewsbury Town v Milton Keynes Dons
Stockport Co. v Chester City
Swindon Town v Torquay Utd.
Walsall v Hereford
Wrexham v Notts Co.

Tuesday, 10 April
Barclays Premiership
Manchester Utd. v Sheffield Utd.

Saturday, 14 April
Barclays Premiership
Arsenal v Bolton Wand.
Blackburn Rov. v Watford
Chelsea v Manchester Utd.
Manchester City v Liverpool
Middlesbrough v Aston Villa
Portsmouth v Newcastle Utd.
Reading v Fulham
Sheffield Utd. v West Ham Utd.
Wigan Athletic v Tottenham

Coca-Cola League Championship
Birmingham City v Southampton
Cardiff City v Stoke City
Coventry City v Preston N.E.
Crystal Palace v Wolves
Hull City v Colchester Utd.
Ipswich Town v Derby Co.
Leeds Utd. v Burnley
Leicester City v Norwich City
Luton Town v Plymouth Argyle
Southend Utd. v Barnsley
Sunderland v Q.P.R.
W.B.A. v Sheffield Wed.

Coca-Cola League One
Blackpool v Northampton Town
Bournemouth v Swansea City
Brentford v Nott'm. Forest
Brighton & H.A. v Bradford City
Bristol City v Yeovil
Chesterfield v Gillingham
Leyton Orient v Doncaster Rov.
Millwall v Tranmere Rov.
Oldham Athletic v Cheltenham Town
Port Vale v Crewe Alexandra
Rotherham Utd. v Carlisle Utd.
Scunthorpe Utd. v Huddersfield Town

Coca-Cola League Two
Accrington Stanley v Grimsby Town
Barnet v Bristol Rov.
Bury v Swindon Town
Chester City v Shrewsbury Town
Hereford v Boston Utd.
Lincoln City v Wrexham
Macclesfield Town v Stockport Co.
Mansfield Town v Rochdale
Milton Keynes Dons v Darlington
Notts Co. v Walsall
Torquay Utd. v Peterborough Utd.
Wycombe Wand. v Hartlepool Utd.

Sunday, 15 April
Barclays Premiership
Everton v Charlton Athletic

Saturday, 21 April
Barclays Premiership
Aston Villa v Portsmouth
Bolton Wand. v Reading
Charlton Athletic v Sheffield Utd.
Fulham v Blackburn Rov.
Liverpool v Wigan Athletic
Manchester Utd. v Middlesbrough
Newcastle Utd. v Chelsea
Tottenham v Arsenal
Watford v Manchester City
West Ham Utd. v Everton

Coca-Cola League Championship
Barnsley v Crystal Palace
Burnley v W.B.A.
Colchester Utd. v Sunderland
Derby Co. v Luton Town
Norwich City v Ipswich Town
Plymouth Argyle v Southend Utd.
Preston N.E. v Leicester City
Q.P.R. v Cardiff City
Sheffield Wed. v Coventry City
Southampton v Leeds Utd.
Stoke City v Hull City
Wolves v Birmingham City

Coca-Cola League One
Bradford City v Leyton Orient
Carlisle Utd. v Bristol City
Cheltenham Town v Blackpool
Crewe Alexandra v Oldham Athletic
Doncaster Rov. v Brentford
Gillingham v Port Vale
Huddersfield Town v Millwall
Northampton Town v Chesterfield
Nott'm. Forest v Bournemouth
Swansea City v Brighton & H.A.
Tranmere Rov. v Scunthorpe Utd.
Yeovil v Rotherham Utd.

Coca-Cola League Two
Boston Utd. v Chester City
Bristol Rov. v Lincoln City
Darlington v Wycombe Wand.
Grimsby Town v Barnet
Hartlepool Utd. v Notts Co.
Peterborough Utd. v Hereford
Rochdale v Macclesfield Town
Shrewsbury Town v Accrington Stanley
Stockport Co. v Milton Keynes Dons
Swindon Town v Mansfield Town
Walsall v Bury
Wrexham v Torquay Utd.

Saturday, 28 April
Barclays Premiership
Arsenal v Fulham
Blackburn Rov. v Charlton Athletic
Chelsea v Bolton Wand.
Everton v Manchester Utd.
Manchester City v Aston Villa
Middlesbrough v Tottenham
Portsmouth v Liverpool
Reading v Newcastle Utd.
Sheffield Utd. v Watford
Wigan Athletic v West Ham Utd.

Coca-Cola League Championship
Barnsley v Leicester City
Birmingham City v Sheffield Wed.
Cardiff City v Hull City
Coventry City v W.B.A.
Crystal Palace v Derby Co.
Leeds Utd. v Ipswich Town
Norwich City v Southampton
Plymouth Argyle v Preston N.E.
Southend Utd. v Luton Town
Stoke City v Colchester Utd.
Sunderland v Burnley
Wolves v Q.P.R.

Coca-Cola League One
Blackpool v Scunthorpe Utd.
Bournemouth v Gillingham
Brentford v Port Vale
Brighton & H.A. v Oldham Athletic
Carlisle Utd. v Swansea City
Chesterfield v Bradford City
Crewe Alexandra v Tranmere Rov.
Leyton Orient v Nott'm. Forest
Millwall v Bristol City
Northampton Town v Huddersfield Town
Rotherham Utd. v Cheltenham Town
Yeovil v Doncaster Rov.

Coca-Cola League Two
Accrington Stanley v Macclesfield Town
Boston Utd. v Torquay Utd.
Bristol Rov. v Swindon Town
Chester City v Peterborough Utd.
Grimsby Town v Lincoln City
Hereford v Shrewsbury Town
Mansfield Town v Barnet
Notts Co. v Darlington
Rochdale v Hartlepool Utd.
Stockport Co. v Bury
Walsall v Wrexham
Wycombe Wand. v Milton Keynes Dons

Saturday, 5 May
Barclays Premiership
Arsenal v Chelsea
Aston Villa v Sheffield Utd.
Charlton Athletic v Tottenham
Everton v Portsmouth
Fulham v Liverpool
Manchester City v Manchester Utd.

Newcastle Utd. v Blackburn Rov.
Reading v Watford
West Ham Utd. v Bolton Wand.
Wigan Athletic v Middlesbrough

Coca-Cola League One
Bradford City v Millwall
Bristol City v Rotherham Utd.
Cheltenham Town v Brighton & H.A.
Doncaster Rov. v Northampton Town
Gillingham v Yeovil
Huddersfield Town v Leyton Orient
Nott'm. Forest v Crewe Alexandra
Oldham Athletic v Chesterfield
Port Vale v Bournemouth
Scunthorpe Utd. v Carlisle Utd.
Swansea City v Blackpool
Tranmere Rov. v Brentford

Coca-Cola League Two
Barnet v Wycombe Wand.
Bury v Mansfield Town
Darlington v Stockport Co.
Hartlepool Utd. v Bristol Rov.
Lincoln City v Chester City
Macclesfield Town v Notts Co.
MK Dons v Accrington Stanley
Peterborough Utd. v Rochdale
Shrewsbury Town v Grimsby Town
Swindon Town v Walsall

Torquay Utd. v Hereford
Wrexham v Boston Utd.

Sunday, 6 May
Coca-Cola League Championship
Burnley v Coventry City
Colchester Utd. v Crystal Palace
Derby Co. v Leeds Utd.
Hull City v Plymouth Argyle
Ipswich Town v Cardiff City
Leicester City v Wolves
Luton Town v Sunderland
Preston N.E. v Birmingham City
Q.P.R. v Stoke City
Sheffield Wed. v Norwich City
Southampton v Southend Utd.
W.B.A. v Barnsley

Sunday, 13 May
Barclays Premiership
Blackburn Rov. v Reading
Bolton Wand. v Aston Villa
Chelsea v Everton
Liverpool v Charlton Athletic
Manchester Utd. v West Ham Utd.
Middlesbrough v Fulham
Portsmouth v Arsenal
Sheffield Utd. v Wigan Athletic
Tottenham v Manchester City
Watford v Newcastle Utd.

SCOTTISH LEAGUE FIXTURES 2006-07

Saturday, 29 July
Bank of Scotland Premier League
Celtic v Kilmarnock
Dundee Utd. v Falkirk
Dunfermline v Hearts
Hibernian v Aberdeen
Inverness CT v St Mirren

Sunday, 30 July
Bank of Scotland Premier League
Motherwell v Rangers

Saturday, 5 August
Bank of Scotland Premier League
Aberdeen v Inverness CT
Falkirk v Dunfermline
Kilmarnock v Hibernian
Rangers v Dundee Utd.
St Mirren v Motherwell

Bell's First Division
Airdrie Utd. v Ross Co.
Dundee v Partick
Gretna v Hamilton
Livingston v Queen of South
St Johnstone v Clyde

Bell's Second Division
Cowdenbeath v Alloa
Forfar v Stranraer
Morton v Raith
Peterhead v Brechin
Stirling v Ayr

Bell's Third Division
Berwick v Albion
East Fife v Stenhousemuir
East Stirling v Elgin
Montrose v Dumbarton
Queens Park v Arbroath

Sunday, 6 August
Bank of Scotland Premier League
Hearts v Celtic

Saturday, 12 August
Bank of Scotland Premier League
Celtic v St Mirren
Hearts v Falkirk
Inverness CT v Hibernian
Kilmarnock v Dundee Utd.
Motherwell v Aberdeen

Bell's First Division
Clyde v Gretna
Hamilton v Dundee
Partick v Airdrie Utd.
Queen of South v St Johnstone
Ross Co. v Livingston

Bell's Second Division
Alloa v Peterhead
Ayr v Cowdenbeath
Brechin v Stirling
Raith v Forfar
Stranraer v Morton

Bell's Third Division
Albion v East Fife
Arbroath v Berwick
Dumbarton v East Stirling
Elgin v Queens Park
Stenhousemuir v Montrose

Sunday, 13 August
Bank of Scotland Premier League
Dunfermline v Rangers

Saturday, 19 August
Bank of Scotland Premier League
Dundee Utd. v Dunfermline
Falkirk v Kilmarnock
Hibernian v Motherwell
Rangers v Hearts
St Mirren v Aberdeen

Bell's First Division
Airdrie Utd. v Queen of South
Dundee v Clyde
Gretna v Ross Co.
Livingston v Partick
St Johnstone v Hamilton

Bell's Second Division
Cowdenbeath v Brechin
Forfar v Alloa
Morton v Ayr
Peterhead v Raith
Stirling v Stranraer

Bell's Third Division
Berwick v Stenhousemuir
East Fife v Arbroath
East Stirling v Albion
Montrose v Elgin
Queens Park v Dumbarton

Sunday, 20 August
Bank of Scotland Premier League
Inverness CT v Celtic

Saturday, 26 August
Bank of Scotland Premier League
Aberdeen v Dunfermline
Celtic v Hibernian
Falkirk v Motherwell
Hearts v Inverness CT
St Mirren v Dundee Utd.

Bell's First Division
Airdrie Utd. v Hamilton
Clyde v Partick
Dundee v Livingston
Queen of South v Gretna
St Johnstone v Ross Co.

Bell's Second Division
Alloa v Stirling
Ayr v Stranraer
Brechin v Forfar
Peterhead v Morton
Raith v Cowdenbeath

Bell's Third Division
Albion v Queens Park
Arbroath v Montrose
Berwick v Dumbarton
East Stirling v Stenhousemuir
Elgin v East Fife

Sunday, 27 August
Bank of Scotland Premier League
Kilmarnock v Rangers

Sunday, 3 September
Bell's Second Division
Cowdenbeath v Peterhead
Forfar v Ayr
Morton v Alloa
Stirling v Raith
Stranraer v Brechin

Bell's Third Division
Dumbarton v Arbroath
East Fife v East Stirling
Montrose v Albion
Queens Park v Berwick
Stenhousemuir v Elgin

Saturday, 9 September
Bank of Scotland Premier League
Aberdeen v Celtic
Dundee Utd. v Hibernian
Dunfermline v Kilmarnock
Hearts v St Mirren
Motherwell v Inverness CT
Rangers v Falkirk

Bell's First Division
Gretna v Dundee
Hamilton v Clyde
Livingston v Airdrie Utd.
Partick v St Johnstone
Ross Co. v Queen of South

Bell's Second Division
Ayr v Peterhead
Brechin v Alloa
Cowdenbeath v Morton
Stirling v Forfar
Stranraer v Raith

Bell's Third Division
Arbroath v Albion
Berwick v East Stirling
Elgin v Dumbarton
Montrose v East Fife
Stenhousemuir v Queens Park

Saturday, 16 September
Bank of Scotland Premier League
Celtic v Dunfermline
Falkirk v Aberdeen
Inverness CT v Dundee Utd.
Motherwell v Hearts
St Mirren v Kilmarnock

Bell's First Division
Clyde v Ross Co.
Dundee v Queen of South
Gretna v Livingston
Hamilton v Partick
St Johnstone v Airdrie Utd.

Bell's Second Division
Alloa v Ayr
Forfar v Cowdenbeath
Morton v Stirling
Peterhead v Stranraer
Raith v Brechin

Bell's Third Division
Albion v Elgin
Dumbarton v Stenhousemuir
East Fife v Berwick
East Stirling v Arbroath
Queens Park v Montrose

Sunday, 17 September
Bank of Scotland Premier League
Hibernian v Rangers

Saturday, 23 September
Bank of Scotland Premier League
Aberdeen v Hearts
Celtic v Rangers
Dundee Utd. v Motherwell
Dunfermline v St Mirren
Hibernian v Falkirk
Kilmarnock v Inverness CT

Bell's First Division
Airdrie Utd. v Dundee
Livingston v St Johnstone
Partick v Gretna
Queen of South v Clyde
Ross Co. v Hamilton

Bell's Second Division
Brechin v Ayr
Forfar v Morton
Raith v Alloa
Stirling v Peterhead
Stranraer v Cowdenbeath

Bell's Third Division
Dumbarton v Albion
Elgin v Berwick
Montrose v East Stirling
Queens Park v East Fife
Stenhousemuir v Arbroath

Saturday, 30 September
Bank of Scotland Premier League
Hearts v Dundee Utd.
Inverness CT v Dunfermline
Motherwell v Kilmarnock
Rangers v Aberdeen
St Mirren v Hibernian

Bell's First Division
Clyde v Livingston
Dundee v St Johnstone
Gretna v Airdrie Utd.
Hamilton v Queen of South
Partick v Ross Co.

Bell's Second Division
Alloa v Stranraer
Ayr v Raith
Cowdenbeath v Stirling
Morton v Brechin
Peterhead v Forfar

Bell's Third Division
Albion v Stenhousemuir
Arbroath v Elgin

Berwick v Montrose
East Fife v Dumbarton
East Stirling v Queens Park

Sunday, 1 October
Bank of Scotland Premier League
Falkirk v Celtic

Saturday, 14 October
Bank of Scotland Premier League
Dundee Utd. v Celtic
Falkirk v St Mirren
Hibernian v Hearts
Kilmarnock v Aberdeen
Motherwell v Dunfermline
Rangers v Inverness CT

Bell's First Division
Airdrie Utd. v Clyde
Livingston v Hamilton
Queen of South v Partick
Ross Co. v Dundee
St Johnstone v Gretna

Bell's Second Division
Alloa v Cowdenbeath
Ayr v Stirling
Brechin v Peterhead
Raith v Morton
Stranraer v Forfar

Bell's Third Division
Albion v Berwick
Arbroath v Queens Park
Dumbarton v Montrose
Elgin v East Stirling
Stenhousemuir v East Fife

Saturday, 21 October
Bank of Scotland Premier League
Aberdeen v Dundee Utd.
Celtic v Motherwell
Dunfermline v Hibernian
Hearts v Kilmarnock
Inverness CT v Falkirk

Bell's First Division
Airdrie Utd. v Partick
Dundee v Hamilton
Gretna v Clyde
Livingston v Ross Co.
St Johnstone v Queen of South

Bell's Second Division
Cowdenbeath v Ayr
Forfar v Raith
Morton v Stranraer
Peterhead v Alloa
Stirling v Brechin

Bell's Third Division
Berwick v Arbroath
East Fife v Albion
East Stirling v Dumbarton
Montrose v Stenhousemuir
Queens Park v Elgin

Sunday, 22 October
Bank of Scotland Premier League
St Mirren v Rangers

Saturday, 28 October
Bank of Scotland Premier League
Aberdeen v Hibernian
Falkirk v Dundee Utd.
Hearts v Dunfermline
Kilmarnock v Celtic
Rangers v Motherwell
St Mirren v Inverness CT

Bell's First Division
Clyde v St Johnstone
Hamilton v Gretna
Partick v Dundee
Queen of South v Livingston
Ross Co. v Airdrie Utd.

Bell's Second Division
Alloa v Morton
Ayr v Forfar
Brechin v Stranraer
Peterhead v Cowdenbeath
Raith v Stirling

Bell's Third Division
Albion v Montrose
Arbroath v Dumbarton
Berwick v Queens Park
East Stirling v East Fife
Elgin v Stenhousemuir

Saturday, 4 November
Bank of Scotland Premier League
Celtic v Hearts
Dunfermline v Falkirk
Hibernian v Kilmarnock
Inverness CT v Aberdeen
Motherwell v St Mirren

Bell's First Division
Airdrie Utd. v Livingston
Clyde v Hamilton
Dundee v Gretna
Queen of South v Ross Co.
St Johnstone v Partick

Bell's Second Division
Cowdenbeath v Raith
Forfar v Brechin

Morton v Peterhead
Stirling v Alloa
Stranraer v Ayr

Bell's Third Division
Dumbarton v Berwick
East Fife v Elgin
Montrose v Arbroath
Queens Park v Albion
Stenhousemuir v East Stirling

Sunday, 5 November
Bank of Scotland Premier League
Dundee Utd. v Rangers

Saturday, 11 November
Bank of Scotland Premier League
Aberdeen v Motherwell
Dundee Utd. v Kilmarnock
Falkirk v Hearts
Hibernian v Inverness CT
Rangers v Dunfermline

Bell's First Division
Gretna v Queen of South
Hamilton v Airdrie Utd.
Livingston v Dundee
Partick v Clyde
Ross Co. v St Johnstone

Bell's Second Division
Ayr v Alloa
Brechin v Raith
Cowdenbeath v Forfar
Stirling v Morton
Stranraer v Peterhead

Bell's Third Division
Arbroath v East Stirling
Berwick v East Fife
Elgin v Albion
Montrose v Queens Park
Stenhousemuir v Dumbarton

Sunday, 12 November
Bank of Scotland Premier League
St Mirren v Celtic

Saturday, 18 November
Bank of Scotland Premier League
Aberdeen v St Mirren
Celtic v Inverness CT
Dunfermline v Dundee Utd.
Hearts v Rangers
Kilmarnock v Falkirk
Motherwell v Hibernian

Bell's First Division
Airdrie Utd. v St Johnstone
Livingston v Gretna
Partick v Hamilton
Queen of South v Dundee
Ross Co. v Clyde

Saturday, 25 November
Bank of Scotland Premier League
Dundee Utd. v St Mirren
Dunfermline v Aberdeen
Inverness CT v Hearts
Motherwell v Falkirk
Rangers v Kilmarnock

Bell's First Division
Clyde v Queen of South
Dundee v Airdrie Utd.
Gretna v Partick
Hamilton v Ross Co.
St Johnstone v Livingston

Bell's Second Division
Alloa v Brechin
Forfar v Stirling
Morton v Cowdenbeath
Peterhead v Ayr
Raith v Stranraer

Bell's Third Division
Albion v Arbroath
Dumbarton v Elgin
East Fife v Montrose
East Stirling v Berwick
Queens Park v Stenhousemuir

Sunday, 26 November
Bank of Scotland Premier League
Hibernian v Celtic

Saturday, 2 December
Bank of Scotland Premier League
Celtic v Aberdeen
Hibernian v Dundee Utd.
Inverness CT v Motherwell
Kilmarnock v Dunfermline
St Mirren v Hearts

Bell's First Division
Clyde v Airdrie Utd.
Dundee v Ross Co.
Gretna v St Johnstone
Hamilton v Livingston
Partick v Queen of South

Bell's Second Division
Alloa v Raith
Ayr v Brechin
Cowdenbeath v Stranraer

Morton v Forfar
Peterhead v Stirling

Bell's Third Division
Albion v Dumbarton
Arbroath v Stenhousemuir
Berwick v Elgin
East Fife v Queens Park
East Stirling v Montrose

Sunday, 3 December
Bank of Scotland Premier League
Falkirk v Rangers

Saturday, 9 December
Bank of Scotland Premier League
Aberdeen v Falkirk
Dundee Utd. v Inverness CT
Hearts v Motherwell
Kilmarnock v St Mirren
Rangers v Hibernian

Bell's First Division
Airdrie Utd. v Gretna
Livingston v Clyde
Queen of South v Hamilton
Ross Co. v Partick
St Johnstone v Dundee

Sunday, 10 December
Bank of Scotland Premier League
Dunfermline v Celtic

Saturday, 16 December
Bank of Scotland Premier League
Falkirk v Hibernian
Hearts v Aberdeen
Inverness CT v Kilmarnock
Motherwell v Dundee Utd.
Rangers v Celtic
St Mirren v Dunfermline

Bell's First Division
Clyde v Dundee
Hamilton v St Johnstone
Partick v Livingston
Queen of South v Airdrie Utd.
Ross Co. v Gretna

Bell's Second Division
Brechin v Morton
Forfar v Peterhead
Raith v Ayr
Stirling v Cowdenbeath
Stranraer v Alloa

Bell's Third Division
Dumbarton v East Fife
Elgin v Arbroath

Montrose v Berwick
Queens Park v East Stirling
Stenhousemuir v Albion

Saturday, 23 December
Bank of Scotland Premier League
Aberdeen v Rangers
Celtic v Falkirk
Dundee Utd. v Hearts
Dunfermline v Inverness CT
Hibernian v St Mirren
Kilmarnock v Motherwell

Tuesday, 26 December
Bank of Scotland Premier League
Aberdeen v Kilmarnock
Celtic v Dundee Utd.
Dunfermline v Motherwell
Hearts v Hibernian
St Mirren v Falkirk

Bell's First Division
Airdrie Utd. v Ross Co.
Dundee v Partick
Gretna v Hamilton
Livingston v Queen of South
St Johnstone v Clyde

Bell's Second Division
Cowdenbeath v Alloa
Forfar v Stranraer
Morton v Raith
Peterhead v Brechin
Stirling v Ayr

Bell's Third Division
Berwick v Albion
East Fife v Stenhousemuir
East Stirling v Elgin
Montrose v Dumbarton
Queens Park v Arbroath

Wednesday, 27 December
Bank of Scotland Premier League
Inverness CT v Rangers

Saturday, 30 December
Bank of Scotland Premier League
Dundee Utd. v Aberdeen
Falkirk v Inverness CT
Hibernian v Dunfermline
Kilmarnock v Hearts
Motherwell v Celtic
Rangers v St Mirren

Bell's First Division
Gretna v Dundee
Hamilton v Clyde
Livingston v Airdrie Utd.

Partick v St Johnstone
Ross Co. v Queen of South

Bell's Second Division
Alloa v Forfar
Ayr v Morton
Brechin v Cowdenbeath
Raith v Peterhead
Stranraer v Stirling

Bell's Third Division
Albion v East Stirling
Arbroath v East Fife
Dumbarton v Queens Park
Elgin v Montrose
Stenhousemuir v Berwick

Monday, 1 January
Bank of Scotland Premier League
Celtic v Kilmarnock
Dundee Utd. v Falkirk
Dunfermline v Hearts
Hibernian v Aberdeen
Inverness CT v St Mirren
Motherwell v Rangers

Tuesday, 2 January
Bell's First Division
Airdrie Utd. v Hamilton
Clyde v Partick
Dundee v Livingston
Queen of South v Gretna
St Johnstone v Ross Co.

Bell's Second Division
Alloa v Stirling
Ayr v Stranraer
Brechin v Forfar
Peterhead v Morton
Raith v Cowdenbeath

Bell's Third Division
Albion v Queens Park
Arbroath v Montrose
Berwick v Dumbarton
East Stirling v Stenhousemuir
Elgin v East Fife

Saturday, 13 January
Bank of Scotland Premier League
Aberdeen v Inverness CT
Falkirk v Dunfermline
Kilmarnock v Hibernian
Rangers v Dundee Utd.
St Mirren v Motherwell

Bell's First Division
Airdrie Utd. v Dundee
Livingston v St Johnstone

Partick v Gretna
Queen of South v Clyde
Ross Co. v Hamilton

Bell's Second Division
Cowdenbeath v Peterhead
Forfar v Ayr
Morton v Alloa
Stirling v Raith
Stranraer v Brechin

Bell's Third Division
Dumbarton v Arbroath
East Fife v East Stirling
Montrose v Albion
Queens Park v Berwick
Stenhousemuir v Elgin

Sunday, 14 January
Bank of Scotland Premier League
Hearts v Celtic

Saturday, 20 January
Bank of Scotland Premier League
Celtic v St Mirren
Hearts v Falkirk
Inverness CT v Hibernian
Kilmarnock v Dundee Utd.
Motherwell v Aberdeen

Bell's First Division
Clyde v Ross Co.
Dundee v Queen of South
Gretna v Livingston
Hamilton v Partick
St Johnstone v Airdrie Utd.

Bell's Second Division
Alloa v Ayr
Forfar v Cowdenbeath
Morton v Stirling
Peterhead v Stranraer
Raith v Brechin

Bell's Third Division
Albion v Elgin
Dumbarton v Stenhousemuir
East Fife v Berwick
East Stirling v Arbroath
Queens Park v Montrose

Sunday, 21 January
Bank of Scotland Premier League
Dunfermline v Rangers

Saturday, 27 January
Bank of Scotland Premier League
Dundee Utd. v Dunfermline
Falkirk v Kilmarnock

Hibernian v Motherwell
Rangers v Hearts
St Mirren v Aberdeen

Bell's First Division
Airdrie Utd. v Clyde
Livingston v Hamilton
Queen of South v Partick
Ross Co. v Dundee
St Johnstone v Gretna

Bell's Second Division
Ayr v Peterhead
Brechin v Alloa
Cowdenbeath v Morton
Stirling v Forfar
Stranraer v Raith

Bell's Third Division
Arbroath v Albion
Berwick v East Stirling
Elgin v Dumbarton
Montrose v East Fife
Stenhousemuir v Queens Park

Sunday, 28 January
Bank of Scotland Premier League
Inverness CT v Celtic

Saturday, 3 February
Bell's Second Division
Brechin v Ayr
Forfar v Morton
Raith v Alloa
Stirling v Peterhead
Stranraer v Cowdenbeath

Bell's Third Division
Dumbarton v Albion
Elgin v Berwick
Montrose v East Stirling
Queens Park v East Fife
Stenhousemuir v Arbroath

Saturday, 10 February
Bank of Scotland Premier League
Aberdeen v Dunfermline
Celtic v Hibernian
Falkirk v Motherwell
Hearts v Inverness CT
St Mirren v Dundee Utd.

Bell's First Division
Clyde v Livingston
Dundee v St Johnstone
Gretna v Airdrie Utd.
Hamilton v Queen of South
Partick v Ross Co.

Bell's Second Division
Alloa v Stranraer
Ayr v Raith
Cowdenbeath v Stirling
Morton v Brechin
Peterhead v Forfar

Bell's Third Division
Albion v Stenhousemuir
Arbroath v Elgin
Berwick v Montrose
East Fife v Dumbarton
East Stirling v Queens Park

Sunday, 11 February
Bank of Scotland Premier League
Kilmarnock v Rangers

Saturday, 17 February
Bank of Scotland Premier League
Aberdeen v Celtic
Dundee Utd. v Hibernian
Dunfermline v Kilmarnock
Hearts v St Mirren
Motherwell v Inverness CT
Rangers v Falkirk

Bell's First Division
Airdrie Utd. v Queen of South
Dundee v Clyde
Gretna v Ross Co.
Livingston v Partick
St Johnstone v Hamilton

Bell's Second Division
Cowdenbeath v Brechin
Forfar v Alloa
Morton v Ayr
Peterhead v Raith
Stirling v Stranraer

Bell's Third Division
Berwick v Stenhousemuir
East Fife v Arbroath
East Stirling v Albion
Montrose v Elgin
Queens Park v Dumbarton

Saturday, 24 February
Bell's First Division
Clyde v Gretna
Hamilton v Dundee
Partick v Airdrie Utd.
Queen of South v St Johnstone
Ross Co. v Livingston

Bell's Second Division
Alloa v Peterhead
Ayr v Cowdenbeath

520

Brechin v Stirling
Raith v Forfar
Stranraer v Morton

Bell's Third Division
Albion v East Fife
Arbroath v Berwick
Dumbarton v East Stirling
Elgin v Queens Park
Stenhousemuir v Montrose

Saturday, 3 March
Bank of Scotland Premier League
Celtic v Dunfermline
Falkirk v Aberdeen
Inverness CT v Dundee Utd.
Motherwell v Hearts
St Mirren v Kilmarnock

Bell's First Division
Gretna v Queen of South
Hamilton v Airdrie Utd.
Livingston v Dundee
Partick v Clyde
Ross Co. v St Johnstone

Bell's Second Division
Cowdenbeath v Raith
Forfar v Brechin
Morton v Peterhead
Stirling v Alloa
Stranraer v Ayr

Bell's Third Division
Dumbarton v Berwick
East Fife v Elgin
Montrose v Arbroath
Queens Park v Albion
Stenhousemuir v East Stirling

Sunday, 4 March
Bank of Scotland Premier League
Hibernian v Rangers

Saturday, 10 March
Bank of Scotland Premier League
Aberdeen v Hearts
Celtic v Rangers
Dundee Utd. v Motherwell
Dunfermline v St Mirren
Hibernian v Falkirk
Kilmarnock v Inverness CT

Bell's First Division
Airdrie Utd. v Livingston
Clyde v Hamilton
Dundee v Gretna
Queen of South v Ross Co.
St Johnstone v Partick

Bell's Second Division
Alloa v Morton
Ayr v Forfar
Brechin v Stranraer
Peterhead v Cowdenbeath
Raith v Stirling

Bell's Third Division
Albion v Montrose
Arbroath v Dumbarton
Berwick v Queens Park
East Stirling v East Fife
Elgin v Stenhousemuir

Saturday, 17 March
Bank of Scotland Premier League
Falkirk v Celtic
Hearts v Dundee Utd.
Inverness CT v Dunfermline
Motherwell v Kilmarnock
Rangers v Aberdeen
St Mirren v Hibernian

Bell's First Division
Clyde v Queen of South
Dundee v Airdrie Utd.
Gretna v Partick
Hamilton v Ross Co.
St Johnstone v Livingston

Bell's Second Division
Ayr v Alloa
Brechin v Raith
Cowdenbeath v Forfar
Stirling v Morton
Stranraer v Peterhead

Bell's Third Division
Arbroath v East Stirling
Berwick v East Fife
Elgin v Albion
Montrose v Queens Park
Stenhousemuir v Dumbarton

Saturday, 31 March
Bank of Scotland Premier League
Dundee Utd. v Celtic
Falkirk v St Mirren
Hibernian v Hearts
Kilmarnock v Aberdeen
Motherwell v Dunfermline
Rangers v Inverness CT

Bell's First Division
Clyde v Queen of South
Dundee v Airdrie Utd.
Gretna v Partick
Hamilton v Ross Co.
St Johnstone v Livingston

Bell's Second Division
Alloa v Brechin
Forfar v Stirling
Morton v Cowdenbeath
Peterhead v Ayr
Raith v Stranraer

Bell's Third Division
Albion v Arbroath
Dumbarton v Elgin
East Fife v Montrose
East Stirling v Berwick
Queens Park v Stenhousemuir

Tuesday, 3 April
Bell's First Division
Airdrie Utd. v Gretna
Queen of South v Hamilton
Ross Co. v Partick
St Johnstone v Dundee

Bell's Second Division
Brechin v Morton
Forfar v Peterhead
Raith v Ayr
Stranraer v Alloa

Bell's Third Division
Dumbarton v East Fife
Elgin v Arbroath
Queens Park v East Stirling
Stenhousemuir v Albion

Wednesday, 4 April
Bell's First Division
Livingston v Clyde

Bell's Second Division
Stirling v Cowdenbeath

Bell's Third Division
Montrose v Berwick

Saturday, 7 April
Bank of Scotland Premier League
Aberdeen v Dundee Utd.
Celtic v Motherwell
Dunfermline v Hibernian
Hearts v Kilmarnock
Inverness CT v Falkirk

Bell's First Division
Clyde v Airdrie Utd.
Dundee v Ross Co.
Gretna v St Johnstone
Hamilton v Livingston
Partick v Queen of South

Bell's Second Division
Alloa v Raith
Ayr v Brechin
Cowdenbeath v Stranraer
Morton v Forfar
Peterhead v Stirling

Bell's Third Division
Albion v Dumbarton
Arbroath v Stenhousemuir
Berwick v Elgin
East Fife v Queens Park
East Stirling v Montrose

Sunday, 8 April
Bank of Scotland Premier League
St Mirren v Rangers

Saturday, 14 April
Bell's First Division
Clyde v St Johnstone
Hamilton v Gretna
Partick v Dundee
Queen of South v Livingston
Ross Co. v Airdrie Utd.

Bell's Second Division
Alloa v Cowdenbeath
Ayr v Stirling
Brechin v Peterhead
Raith v Morton
Stranraer v Forfar

Bell's Third Division
Albion v Berwick
Arbroath v Queens Park
Dumbarton v Montrose
Elgin v East Stirling
Stenhousemuir v East Fife

Saturday, 21 April
Bell's First Division
Airdrie Utd. v Partick
Dundee v Hamilton
Gretna v Clyde
Livingston v Ross Co.
St Johnstone v Queen of South

Bell's Second Division
Cowdenbeath v Ayr
Forfar v Raith
Morton v Stranraer
Peterhead v Alloa
Stirling v Brechin

Bell's Third Division
Berwick v Arbroath
East Fife v Albion
East Stirling v Dumbarton

Montrose v Stenhousemuir
Queens Park v Elgin

Saturday, 28 April
Bell's First Division
Clyde v Dundee
Hamilton v St Johnstone
Partick v Livingston
Queen of South v Airdrie Utd.
Ross Co. v Gretna

Bell's Second Division
Alloa v Forfar
Ayr v Morton

Brechin v Cowdenbeath
Raith v Peterhead
Stranraer v Stirling

Bell's Third Division
Albion v East Stirling
Arbroath v East Fife
Dumbarton v Queens Park
Elgin v Montrose
Stenhousemuir v Berwick

NATIONWIDE CONFERENCE FIXTURES
2006-07

Saturday, 12 August
Aldershot v Gravesend
Altrincham v Stevenage
Cambridge v Northwich
Crawley v Rushden & Diamonds
Forest Green v Dagenham & Redbridge
Grays v Stafford
Kidderminster v St Albans
Morecambe v Burton
Oxford v Halifax
Southport v Woking
Tamworth v Weymouth
York v Exeter

Tuesday, 15 August
Burton v Kidderminster
Dagenham & Redbridge v Oxford
Exeter v Forest Green
Gravesend v Tamworth
Halifax v Southport
Northwich v Morecambe
Rushden & Diamonds v Grays
St Albans v Cambridge
Stafford v Altrincham
Stevenage v York
Weymouth v Aldershot
Woking v Crawley

Saturday, 19 August
Burton v Oxford
Dagenham & Redbridge v Tamworth
Exeter v Altrincham
Gravesend v York
Halifax v Grays
Northwich v Kidderminster
Rushden & Diamonds v Forest Gren
St Albans v Aldershot
Stafford v Southport

Stevenage v Crawley
Weymouth v Cambridge
Woking v Morecambe

Saturday, 26 August
Aldershot v Dagenham & Redbridge
Altrincham v St Albans
Cambridge v Halifax
Crawley v Stafford
Forest Green v Gravesend
Grays v Woking
Kidderminster v Weymouth
Morecambe v Stevenage
Oxford v Northwich
Southport v Rushden & Diamonds
Tamworth v Exeter
York v Burton

Monday, 28 August
Burton v Southport
Dagenham & Redbridge v Cambridge
Exeter v Crawley
Gravesend v Altrincham
Halifax v Morecambe
Northwich v Grays
Rushden & Diamonds v York
St Albans v Tamworth
Stafford v Aldershot
Stevenage v Forest Green
Weymouth v Oxford
Woking v Kidderminster

Saturday, 2 September
Tamworth v Stevenage

Sunday, 3 September
Aldershot v Halifax
Altrincham v Dagenham & Redbridge

Cambridge v Exeter
Crawley v Northwich
Forest Green v Woking
Grays v Burton
Kidderminster v Rushden & Diamonds
Morecambe v Weymouth
Oxford v St Albans
Southport v Gravesend
York v Stafford

Saturday, 9 September
Burton v Weymouth
Crawley v York
Exeter v Aldershot
Forest Green v Cambridge
Grays v Southport
Halifax v Gravesend
Kidderminster v Tamworth
Morecambe v Oxford
Northwich v St Albans
Rushden & Diamonds v Altrincham
Stevenage v Stafford
Woking v Dagenham & Redbridge

Tuesday, 12 September
Aldershot v Stevenage
Altrincham v Halifax
Cambridge v Kidderminster
Dagenham & Redbridge v Crawley
Gravesend v Grays
Oxford v Exeter
Southport v Northwich
St Albans v Woking
Stafford v Burton
Tamworth v Rushden & Diamonds
Weymouth v Forest Green
York v Morecambe

Saturday, 16 September
Aldershot v Northwich
Altrincham v Woking
Cambridge v Stevenage
Dagenham & Redbridge v Morecambe
Gravesend v Exeter
Oxford v Grays
Southport v Crawley
St Albans v Burton
Stafford v Rushden & Diamonds
Tamworth v Forest Green
Weymouth v Halifax
York v Kidderminster

Tuesday, 19 September
Burton v Cambridge
Crawley v Oxford
Exeter v St Albans
Forest Green v Altrincham
Grays v Aldershot
Halifax v Dagenham & Redbridge

Kidderminster v Southport
Morecambe v Tamworth
Northwich v Stafford
Rushden & Diamonds v Gravesend
Stevenage v Weymouth
Woking v York

Saturday, 23 September
Altrincham v Tamworth
Burton v Northwich
Cambridge v Aldershot
Crawley v Grays
Dagenham & Redbridge v Weymouth
Exeter v Stevenage
Halifax v Forest Green
Morecambe v Kidderminster
St Albans v Gravesend
Stafford v Oxford
Woking v Rushden & Diamonds
York v Southport

Saturday, 30 September
Aldershot v Altrincham
Forest Green v Stafford
Gravesend v Dagenham & Redbridge
Grays v Morecambe
Kidderminster v Crawley
Northwich v Woking
Oxford v York
Rushden & Diamonds v Burton
Southport v Exeter
Stevenage v Halifax
Tamworth v Cambridge
Weymouth v St Albans

Tuesday, 3 October
Aldershot v Tamworth
Burton v Crawley
Cambridge v Altrincham
Grays v Exeter
Halifax v Kidderminster
Morecambe v Rushden & Diamonds
Northwich v York
Oxford v Southport
St Albans v Forest Green
Stafford v Dagenham & Redbridge
Stevenage v Woking
Weymouth v Gravesend

Saturday, 7 October
Tamworth v Stafford

Sunday, 8 October
Altrincham v Weymouth
Crawley v Morecambe
Dagenham & Redbridge v Northwich
Exeter v Halifax
Forest Green v Oxford
Gravesend v Cambridge

Kidderminster v Grays
Rushden & Diamonds v Stevenage
Southport v St Albans
Woking v Burton
York v Aldershot

Tuesday, 10 October
Altrincham v Morecambe
Crawley v Weymouth
Dagenham & Redbridge v St Albans
Exeter v Northwich
Forest Green v Burton
Gravesend v Stafford
Kidderminster v Oxford
Rushden & Diamonds v Halifax
Southport v Stevenage
Tamworth v Grays
Woking v Aldershot
York v Cambridge

Saturday, 14 October
Aldershot v Kidderminster
Burton v Gravesend
Cambridge v Crawley
Grays v Forest Green
Halifax v Tamworth
Morecambe v Exeter
Northwich v Rushden & Diamonds
Oxford v Altrincham
St Albans v York
Stafford v Woking
Stevenage v Dagenham & Redbridge
Weymouth v Southport

Saturday, 21 October
Aldershot v Morecambe
Altrincham v Southport
Cambridge v Oxford
Dagenham & Redbridge v Kidderminster
Exeter v Stafford
Forest Green v Crawley
Gravesend v Woking
Halifax v Burton
St Albans v Grays
Stevenage v Northwich
Tamworth v York
Weymouth v Rushden & Diamonds

Friday, 3 November
Burton v Stevenage

Saturday, 4 November
Crawley v St Albans
Grays v Cambridge
Kidderminster v Forest Green
Morecambe v Gravesend
Northwich v Halifax
Oxford v Aldershot

Rushden & Diamonds v Dagenham & Redbridge
Southport v Tamworth
Stafford v Weymouth
Woking v Exeter
York v Altrincham

Saturday, 18 November
Aldershot v Southport
Altrincham v Crawley
Cambridge v Morecambe
Dagenham & Redbridge v Burton
Exeter v Kidderminster
Forest Green v Northwich
Gravesend v Oxford
Halifax v Stafford
St Albans v Rushden & Diamonds
Stevenage v Grays
Tamworth v Woking
Weymouth v York

Saturday, 25 November
Burton v Exeter
Crawley v Halifax
Grays v Altrincham
Kidderminster v Stevenage
Morecambe v Forest Green
Northwich v Gravesend
Oxford v Tamworth
Rushden & Diamonds v Aldershot
Southport v Cambridge
Stafford v St Albans
Woking v Weymouth
York v Dagenham & Redbridge

Saturday, 2 December
Aldershot v Crawley
Altrincham v Burton
Cambridge v Stafford
Dagenham & Redbridge v Southport
Exeter v Rushden & Diamonds
Forest Green v York
Gravesend v Kidderminster
Halifax v Woking
St Albans v Morecambe
Stevenage v Oxford
Tamworth v Northwich
Weymouth v Grays

Saturday, 9 December
Burton v Aldershot
Crawley v Tamworth
Exeter v Dagenham & Redbridge
Forest Green v Southport
Grays v York
Halifax v St Albans
Kidderminster v Altrincham
Morecambe v Stafford
Northwich v Weymouth

Rushden & Diamonds v Oxford
Stevenage v Gravesend
Woking v Cambridge

Tuesday, 26 December
Aldershot v Forest Green
Altrincham v Northwich
Cambridge v Rushden & Diamonds
Dagenham & Redbridge v Grays
Gravesend v Crawley
Oxford v Woking
Southport v Morecambe
St Albans v Stevenage
Stafford v Kidderminster
Tamworth v Burton
Weymouth v Exeter
York v Halifax

Saturday, 30 December
Aldershot v Grays
Altrincham v Forest Green
Cambridge v Burton
Dagenham & Redbridge v Halifax
Gravesend v Rushden & Diamonds
Oxford v Crawley
Southport v Kidderminster
St Albans v Exeter
Stafford v Northwich
Tamworth v Morecambe
Weymouth v Stevenage
York v Woking

Monday, 1 January
Burton v Stafford
Crawley v Dagenham & Redbridge
Exeter v Oxford
Forest Green v Weymouth
Grays v Gravesend
Halifax v Altrincham
Kidderminster v Cambridge
Morecambe v York
Northwich v Southport
Rushden & Diamonds v Tamworth
Stevenage v Aldershot
Woking v St Albans

Saturday, 6 January
Aldershot v Exeter
Altrincham v Rushden & Diamonds
Cambridge v Forest Green
Dagenham & Redbridge v Woking
Gravesend v Halifax
Oxford v Morecambe
Southport v Grays
St Albans v Northwich
Stafford v Stevenage
Tamworth v Kidderminster
Weymouth v Burton
York v Crawley

Saturday, 20 January
Burton v St Albans
Crawley v Southport
Exeter v Gravesend
Forest Green v Tamworth
Grays v Oxford
Halifax v Weymouth
Kidderminster v York
Morecambe v Dagenham & Redbridge
Northwich v Aldershot
Rushden & Diamonds v Stafford
Stevenage v Cambridge
Woking v Altrincham

Tuesday, 23 January
Burton v Tamworth
Crawley v Gravesend
Exeter v Weymouth
Forest Green v Aldershot
Grays v Dagenham & Redbridge
Halifax v York
Kidderminster v Stafford
Morecambe v Southport
Northwich v Altrincham
Ruashden & Diamonds v Cambridge
Stevenage v St Albans
Woking v Oxford

Saturday, 27 January
Aldershot v Burton
Altrincham v Kidderminster
Cambridge v Woking
Dagenham & Redbridge v Exeter
Gravesend v Stevenage
Oxford v Rushden & Diamonds
Southport v Forest Green
St Albans v Halifax
Stafford v Morecambe
Tamworth v Crawley
Weymouth v Northwich
York v Grays

Saturday, 3 February
Burton v Halifax Town
Crawley v Forest Green
Grays v St Albans
Kidderminster v Dagenham & Redbridge
Morecambe v Aldershot
Northwich v Stevenage
Oxford v Cambridge
Rushden & Diamonds v Weymouth
Southport v Altrincham
Stafford v Exeter
Woking v Gravesend
York v Tamworth

Saturday, 10 February
Aldershot v Oxford
Altrincham v York

Cambridge v Grays
Dagenham & Redbridge v Rushden &
  Diamonds
Exeter v Woking
Forest Green v Kidderminster
Gravesend v Morecambe
Halifax v Northwich
St Albans v Crawley
Stevenage v Burton
Tamworth v Southport
Weymouth v Stafford

Saturday, 17 February
Burton v Dagenham & Redbridge
Crawley v Altrincham
Grays v Stevenage
Kidderminster v Exeter
Morecambe v Cambridge
Northwich v Forest Green
Oxford v Gravesend
Rushden & Diamonds v St Albans
Southport v Aldershot
Stafford v Halifax
Woking v Tamworth
York v Weymouth

Saturday, 24 February
Aldershot v Rushden & Diamonds
Altrincham v Grays
Cambridge v Southport
Dagenham & Redbridge v York
Exeter v Burton
Forest Green v Morecambe
Gravesend v Northwich
Halifax v Crawley
St Albans v Stafford
Stevenage v Kidderminster
Tamworth v Oxford
Weymouth v Woking

Saturday, 3 March
Burton v Altrincham
Crawley v Aldershot
Grays v Weymouth
Kidderminster v Gravesend
Morecambe v St Albans
Northwich v Tamworth
Oxford v Stevenage
Rushden & Diamonds v Exeter
Southport v Dagenham & Redbridge
Stafford v Cambridge
Woking v Halifax
York v Forest Green

Tuesday, 6 March
Altrincham v Cambridge
Crawley v Burton
Dagenham & Redbridge v Stafford
Exeter v Grays

Forest Green v St Albans
Gravesend v Weymouth
Kidderminster v Halifax
Rushden & Diamonds v Morecambe
Southport v Oxford
Tamworth v Aldershot
Woking v Stevenage
York v Northwich

Saturday, 10 March
Aldershot v York
Burton v Woking
Cambridge v Gravesend
Grays v Kidderminster
Halifax v Exeter
Morecambe v Crawley
Northwich v Dagenham & Redbridge
Oxford v Forest Green
St Albans v Southport
Stafford v Tamworth
Stevenage v Rushden & Diamonds
Weymouth v Altrincham

Tuesday, 13 March
Aldershot v Woking
Burton v Forest Green
Cambridge v York
Grays v Tamworth
Halifax v Rushden & Diamonds
Morecambe v Altrincham
Northwich v Exeter
Oxford v Kidderminster
St Albans v Dagenham & Redbridge
Stafford v Gravesend
Stevenage v Southport
Weymouth v Crawley

Saturday, 17 March
Altrincham v Oxford
Crawley v Cambridge
Dagenham & Redbridge v Stevenage
Exeter v Morecambe
Forest Green v Grays
Gravesend v Burton
Kidderminster v Aldershot
Rushden & Diamonds v Northwich
Southport v Weymouth
Tamworth v Halifax
Woking v Stafford
York v St Albans

Sunday, 25 March
Burton v Morecambe
Dagenham & Redbridge v Forest Green
Exeter v York
Gravesend v Aldershot
Halifax v Oxford
Northwich v Cambridge
Rushden & Diamonds v Crawley

St Albans v Kidderminster
Stafford v Grays
Stevenage v Altrincham
Weymouth v Tamworth
Woking v Southport

Tuesday, 27 March
Aldershot v Weymouth
Altrincham v Stafford
Cambridge v St Albans
Crawley v Woking
Forest Green v Exeter
Grays v Rushden & Diamonds
Kidderminster v Burton
Morecambe v Northwich
Oxford v Dagenham & Redbridge
Southport v Halifax
Tamworth v Gravesend
York v Stevenage

Saturday, 31 March
Aldershot v St Albans
Altrincham v Exeter
Cambridge v Weymouth
Crawley v Stevenage
Forest Green v Rushden & Diamonds
Grays v Halifax
Kidderminster v Northwich
Morecambe v Woking
Oxford v Burton
Southport v Stafford
Tamworth v Dagenham & Redbridge
York v Gravesend

Saturday, 7 April
Burton v York
Dagenham & Redbridge v Aldershot
Exeter v Tamworth
Gravesend v Forest Green
Halifax v Cambridge
Northwich v Oxford
Rushden & Diamonds v Southport
St Albans v Altrincham
Stafford v Crawley
Stevenage v Morecambe
Weymouth v Kidderminster
Woking v Grays

Monday, 9 April
Aldershot v Stafford
Altrincham v Gravesend

Cambridge v Dagenham v Redbridge
Crawley v Exeter
Forest Green v Stevenage
Grays v Northwich
Kidderminster v Woking
Morecambe v Halifax
Oxford v Weymouth
Southport v Burton
Tamworth v St Albans
York v Rushden & Diamonds

Saturday, 14 April
Burton v Grays
Dagenham & Redbridge v Altrincham
Exeter v Cambridge
Gravesend v Southport
Halifax v Aldershot
Northwich v Crawley
Rushden & Diamonds v Kidderminster
St Albans v Oxford
Stafford v York
Stevenage v Tamworth
Weymouth v Morecambe
Woking v Forest Green

Saturday, 21 April
Aldershot v Cambridge
Forest Green v Halifax
Gravesend v St Albans
Grays v Crawley
Kidderminster v Morecambe
Northwich v Burton
Oxford v Stafford
Rushden & Diamonds v Woking
Southport v York
Stevenage v Exeter
Tamworth v Altrincham
Weymouth v Dagenham & Redbridge

Saturday, 28 April
Altrincham v Aldershot
Burton v Rushden & Diamonds
Cambridge v Tamworth
Crawley v Kidderminster
Dagenham & Redbridge v Gravesend
Exeter v Southport
Halifax v Stevenage
Morecambe v Grays
St Albans v Weymouth
Stafford v Forest Green
Woking v Northwich
York v Oxford

528